Last section : 16, 17, 18
                19, 20, 23, 24

PSYCHOLOGY: AN INTRODUCTION

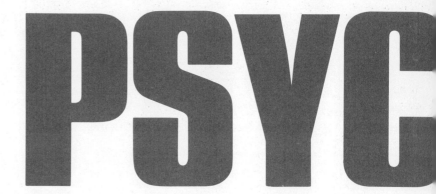

D. C. HEATH AND COMPANY   Lexington, Massachusetts • Toronto

Paul Mussen
Mark R. Rosenzweig

UNIVERSITY OF CALIFORNIA, BERKELEY

Elliot Aronson

University of California, Santa Cruz

David Elkind

University of Rochester

Seymour Feshbach

University of California, Los Angeles

James Geiwitz

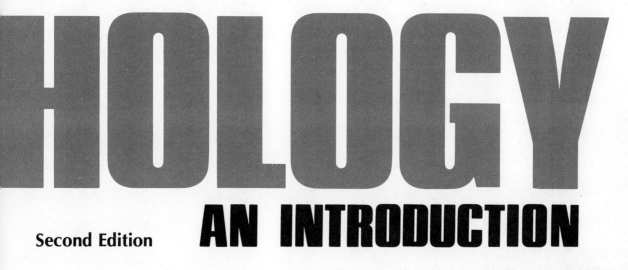

HOLOGY
AN INTRODUCTION

Second Edition

Stephen E. Glickman

University of California, Berkeley

Bennet B. Murdock, Jr.

University of Toronto

Michael Wertheimer
Lewis O. Harvey, Jr.

University of Colorado

Preface FOR STUDENTS AND INSTRUCTORS

Most students in an introductory psychology course expect to study facts and theories related to their own lives and to critical social issues. Instructors and textbook writers want to respond to the students' needs and interests and also to reach three additional goals: (1) to present a well-rounded account of the most significant concepts and findings of contemporary psychology; (2) to give students a basic understanding of how psychologists go about studying behavior—how they conduct research and evaluate their findings; and (3) to provide a firm foundation for students who will take other courses in psychology or who would like to study further on their own. Our attempt to reach these goals has led us to plan and write a book that differs in significant respects from others in the field. The first edition, published in 1973, was well received and used in many colleges and universities in the United States and abroad. This acceptance demonstrated that the basic concept and special features of the book were valuable, and we have built on them in preparing this second edition.

How does this book differ from other introductory textbooks of psychology? One difference is that each of the eight main parts of the book was written by an expert in a basic area of psychology. The expert is best qualified to select, from the vast amount of information available, the subject matter that is most significant, most relevant for understanding personal and social problems, most essential in preparing students for further study in this speciality. Together, the eight main parts of the book present a broad overview of the field of psychology, spanning the range from complex human social interaction to species-characteristic animal behavior. Psychology is defined operationally in terms of the problems with which specialists in psychology are concerned and their methods of working on these problems. The objective scientific approach to psychological problems is stressed, but the contributions of the humanities and philosophy to our understanding of these problems are acknowledged. The field of psychology is viewed as active and changing; many age-old problems are unsolved and many new problems are being formulated. The focus of the book is on how psychologists are trying to solve these problems through research.

To keep the book from being a series of isolated treatises and to achieve integration within the text, the authors collaborated from the very start, meeting together in several sessions, and they continued to exchange ideas, outlines, and drafts. Together they made judgments about what materials should be included and emphasized, and they decided on the order of presentation of topics. A psychologist-writer, James Geiwitz, worked with the authors throughout the project, integrating contributions from the individual authors, editing to achieve some consistency of style and presentation, and moving materials from one part to another to improve the presentation.

The order of presentation of the areas in this book is the reverse of the usual one. We begin with those specialties within psychology that are closest to students' own experiences and interests and are thus intrinsically meaningful to them—the areas of social psychology, personality, and development. The early chapters introduce some of the major problems of psychology, but they require very little technical or specialized background. They help develop interest in the later more technical parts—those dealing with the areas of learning, perception, biological, and comparative psychology.

The design of the book has been carefully thought out to make it highly readable. The type is large, and many headings are used to make the topics clear. When new terms are introduced, they are defined simply and the definitions are clarified by examples. An extensive glossary is given at the end of the book; words included in the glossary are indicated in the text by the use of boldface type. Numerous photographs and drawings illustrate points when words would be inadequate. Color is employed to emphasize headings and to clarify figures. Each chapter contains a number of Spotlights, special short sections that highlight particular points or give examples of research or clinical observations to illustrate topics discussed in the text. There are many cross references, and a detailed index is provided. General sources are briefly annotated at the end of each part; to help the reader follow up on subjects of interest, complete bibliographic data for the many specific studies cited are given in the back matter.

The second edition has been improved in several ways. First, it has been rewritten to incorporate the most recent research and theory in each area of psychology. For example, there is new material on information processing, new approaches to psychotherapy, early infant attachments, gender role, prosocial behavior, adult personality development, biofeedback, sociobiology, and meditation. In addition, the entire text has been rewritten for greater readability. We have also worked hard to eliminate language that might be interpreted as racist, sexist or age-ist. If you find any remaining examples, please let us know.

The second edition contains all the information of lasting importance that appeared in the first edition and adds many new concepts and facts; but careful selection has resulted in a somewhat shorter volume. Finally, we have tried to provide more integration in the second edition, relating the different parts of the book to each other with more cross references and with general schema such as the six key concepts introduced in the first chapter. These six key concepts are used again in a new integrative-summary chapter at the end of the book to link the various fields of psychology and to show that—in many ways— psychology is a unified science.

In planning the introductory psychology course, instructors must consider the needs, interests, and abilities of their students as well as the time available for the course. Some instructors may wish to omit parts of the book or present topics in a different order. The book can be used flexibly; there are many possible alternative arrangements. Here we present three such possibilities: one for

Section	Personal-Social Emphasis	Experimental-Biological Emphasis	Shorter General Course
	Chapters		
Introduction	1	1	1
Social	2	2	2
	3	3	3
	4		4
	5		
Personality	6	6	6
	7		7
	8		8
Developmental	9	9	9
	10	10	10
	11		11
Cognitive	12	12	12
	13	13	13
Learning and Memory		14	14
		15	
Perception	16	16	16
		17	17
		18	
Biological	20	19	19
		20	20
		21	
		22	
Comparative	24	23	
		24	24

a course with a personal-social emphasis; one for a course with an experimental-biological emphasis; and one for a broadly based, but shorter, general course. These are only three of many possible combinations and/or orders. Some instructors may prefer an entirely different order of chapters or parts.

ACKNOWLEDGMENTS

The authors gratefully acknowledge the help of many people in the preparation of this book: our fellow psychologists on whose research we have drawn; our colleagues who made constructive suggestions on the manuscript; our students in a variety of courses who have responded to successive versions of the ideas in this text; and the secretaries, particularly Vivien March, who worked on the many manuscripts involved.

We would also like to thank the following instructors, whose informed comments and criticisms of the first edition have been invaluable to us in preparing the revision:

M. Allen, California State University, Bakersfield
Richard S. Andrulus, Villanova University
Irwin Badin, Montclair State College
B. A. Balogh, Mary College
J. E. Bixler, Francis Marion College
D. I. Blom, University of Tennessee, Martin
Dorothy Booth, Dallas County Community College
Frederick M. Brown, Centre College of Kentucky
Robert C. Cass, Arizona State University
John Cegalu, Syracuse University
Carol Christensen, Vassar College
Ronald L. Classon, University of Tennessee, Martin
David Cooper, University of Tennessee, Martin
Thomas F. Cunningham, St. Lawrence University
T. M. Dembroski, Eckerd College
Dean Diggins, Brookyln College
Tom Dukich, Gonzaga University
Melvin Enns, St. Lawrence University
J. Fabricatore, Occidental College
Daniel A. Gawronski, Calumet College
Barry E. Golinko, Wayne State University
Albert Gorman, Suffolk Community College
Edward M. Gurowitz, Queens College, CUNY
Ralph W. Hansen, Augustana College
Alice F. Healy, Yale University
W. A. Kayson, Iona College
Roger L. Kelley, San Bernardino Valley College
M. B. King, SUNY, Cortland
H. Klatt, Gonzaga University
Anne M. Kleinginna, Georgia Southern College
Sam J. Korn, Hunter College, CUNY
Kathy Kowal, University of North Carolina at Wilmington
Sara Lieberman, Loyola Marymount University
Thomas A. Marshall, Fresno City College

Henry G. Masters, Juniata College
Mickay Miller, Bethany College
Steve Milliser, Gonzaga University
J. A. Moody, St. Anselm's College
Dale Nielsen, Western State College of Colorado
Martin Obler, Brookyln College
Miriam Lewin Papanek, Manhattanville College
J. Trevor Peirce, Bethany College
Nancy Perkins, Kansas State University
E. J. Posavac, Loyola University
Marilyn Rall, Brooklyn College
R. Resnick, Hunter College, CUNY
Samuel Roll, University of New Mexico
John Ross, St. Lawrence University
John Sabrini, Hunter College, CUNY
Paul J. Schafer, St. Bonaventure University
M. A. Schulman, Essex County College
Richard Schweichert, University of Michigan
Robert B. Shilkret, Mount Holyoke College
David Smillie, New College
Murry A. Snyder, John Jay College of Criminal Justice
Dorothy Strauss, Kean College of N.J.
Anne Sutherland, Meredith College
George W. Swope, Westchester Community College
Jerome Thayer, Atlantic Union College
Robert B. Thomas, Northwest Bible College
Timothy Thomas, Alma College
D. P. A. Tyler, Indiana University, Northwest
Ralph Underwager, St. Olaf College
Wayne Van Zomeren, Northwest Missouri State University
Brent C. White, Centre College of Kentucky
D. Louis Wood, University of Arkansas, Little Rock
Dorothy D. Wollin, St. Cloud State College
Murray Work, California State University, Sacramento

About the Authors

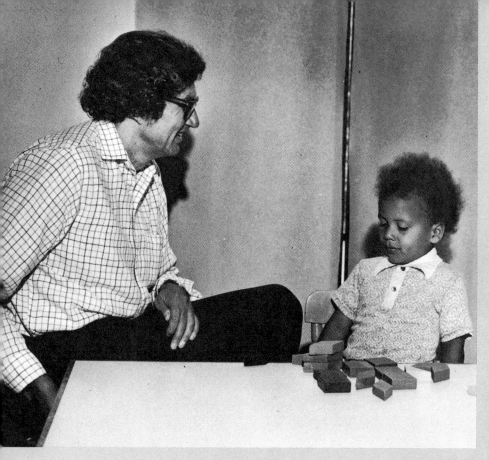

Paul Mussen
Director, Institute of Human Development, University of California, Berkeley
The author of Part Four, Developmental Psychology, specializes in research on socialization and personality and social development. He has served as president of the Division of Developmental Psychology of the American Psychological Association. He is co-author of *Child Development and Personality* (Harper & Row), author of *The Psychological Development of the Child* (Prentice-Hall), and editor of *Carmichael's Manual of Child Psychology* (Wiley).

James Geiwitz
The general editor is a professional writer, particularly in the area of personality. He is author of *Non-Freudian Theories of Personality* (Brooks-Cole), *Looking at Ourselves* (Little, Brown), and co-author of *Psychological Development: A Life-Span Approach* (Harper & Row).

Mark R. Rosenzweig
University of California,
Berkeley
The author of Part Eight, Biological Psychology, is active in research on brain functions in behavior. He is a member of the Executive Committee, International Union of Psychological Science, co-editor of *Annual Review of Psychology*, author of *Biologie de la Mémoire* (Presses universitaires de France), co-editor of *Neural Mechanisms of Learning and Memory* (M.I.T. Press), and a member of the National Academy of Science.

Elliot Aronson
University of California,
Santa Cruz
The author of Part Two, Social
Psychology, is active in
research on interpersonal
attraction and winner of the
American Association for the
Advancement of Science prize
in social psychology (1970). He
is author of *The Social Animal*
(Viking) and *The Jigsaw
Classroom* (Sage Publications),
and co-editor of *Handbook of
Social Psychology* (Addison-
Wesley).

Seymour Feshbach
**Chairman, Department of Psychology, University of
California, Los Angeles**
The author of Part Three, Personality, is active in research
on violence and aggression. He is involved in analyses of
children's rights with his wife, Dr. Norma Feshbach, and in
intervention programs designed to reduce children's
aggression in the schools. He is author of *Television and
Aggression* (Jossey-Bass).

David Elkind
**Chairman, Department of Child Study, Tufts
University**
The author of Part Five, Cognitive Psychology, does
research in cognitive development. He spent a year
studying with Piaget at the University of Geneva.
He is author of *Children and Adolescents* (Oxford),
The Child and Society (Oxford), and *The Child's
Reality: Three Developmental Themes* (Lawrence
Erlbaum Associates); co-author of *Child
Development: A Core Approach* (Wiley); and co-
editor of *Studies in Cognitive Development*
(Oxford).

Bennet B. Murdock, Jr.
University of Toronto
The author of Part Six, Learning and
Memory, has contributed many studies of
human learning and memory. He now
concentrates his research on human short-term
memory. He is author of *Human Memory:
Theory and Data* (Lawrence Erlbaum
Associates).

Stephen E. Glickman
Chairman, Department of Psychology
University of California, Berkeley
The author of Part Nine, Comparative Psychology,
does research on behavior of animals in the
laboratory, in zoos, and in natural settings. He has
studied animals of many species, including
anteaters, hawks, gerbils, skunks, opossums, lions,
and owls.

Michael Wertheimer
University of Colorado,
Boulder
The co-author of Part Seven (left, in
photograph), Perception, has done much
research in perception. He has served as
president of the Divisions of General
Psychology, Philosophical Psychology, and the
History of Psychology of the American
Psychological Association. He is author
of *A Brief History of Psychology* (Holt,
Rinehart and Winston) and co-author of
Psychology: A Brief Introduction (Scott,
Foresman).
Lewis O. Harvey, Jr.
University of Colorado,
Boulder
The co-author of Part Seven conducts research
in pattern and form perception and visual
processes. He is a member of the Executive
Committee of the National Academy of
Science–National Research Council Committee
on Vision and a consulting editor for the journal
Perception and Psychophysics.

Contents

"Where do we come from . . . What are we . . . Where are we going?" by Paul Gauguin.
Courtesy, Museum of Fine Arts, Boston, Tompkins Collection.

PSYCHOLOGY: AN INTRODUCTION

"Where do we come from . . . What are we . . . Where are we going?" (detail) by Paul Gauguin. Museum of Fine Arts, Boston, Tompkins Collection.

PART ONE

Psychology: The Study of Behavior

By Paul Mussen, Mark R. Rosenzweig, James Geiwitz

Chapter 1   The Science of Psychology

1 The Science of Psychology

What is psychology?
How do psychologists study behavior?
Are there genuine psychological laws?
What are the ethical problems in psychological research?
Where do we begin the study of psychology?
What are the key concepts in psychology?

What is psychology? We can begin by defining psychology as "the scientific study of behavior." This is necessarily a very broad definition, for psychologists study many kinds of actions and responses they can observe directly. From their observations, they then draw various inferences about internal processes—such as learning, memory, and thinking—and about fundamental psychological attributes—such as intelligence, motivation, and emotion. Given such an encompassing and sweeping area for study, it is not surprising that the field has expanded continuously and rapidly since its beginning only a century ago. New areas of psychological research are continually opening up—often stimulated by questions raised by earlier research. Psychological principles are being applied in more and more situations; in fact, there seems no limit to the number of problems and issues to which psychology can contribute. It is easy, therefore, to understand why psychology has become the most popular major in many colleges and universities (see Spotlight 1-1).

As a brief introduction to the work of psychologists, we will present in this chapter a small sample from the vast array of problems with which they are concerned. Questions that have interested philosophers and writers since long before the existence of a science of psychology are still topics of extensive research today. How do we learn? To what extent are our personalities shaped by biological factors and to what extent by environmental ones? What is "mental illness" and how can it be treated? The concern of early psychologists with problems of adjustment has stimulated research into the origins of maladjustment; and the findings of this research are used to alleviate emotional problems as well as to develop various explanations of personality that can be applied to adjusted as well as maladjusted people.

In the social arena too, full understanding of many critical problems require psychological investigation. For example, psychologists study the development and reduction of antisocial activities and attitudes, such as violence and prejudice, and investigate ways to encourage altruism, cooperativeness, and other prosocial behaviors.

In educational institutions, some psychologists investigate and evaluate teaching techniques and learning environments. Others, in industrial settings, study workers' reactions and efficiency as they relate to different arrangements of working materials; they also seek to improve labor-management communications. As part of a search for self-fulfillment and self-improvement, many people have recently been attracted to humanistic psychology, as well as to various forms of group encounter and do-it-yourself methods.

The vast scope of these interests and the numerous problems that psychology can help to solve make it very difficult to define the field precisely. To complicate matters further, the subject matter of psychology interests almost everyone. Serious scholars, writers, educators, philosophers, and theologians, as well as lay people—and even some charlatans—have learned important psychological truths through their own experiences and observations. These people differ from professional psychologists in that they do not share scientific psychologists' twin commitment to the *scientific investigation* of psychological phenomena and the *application of scientifically discovered principles*. Later in this chapter we will discuss how scientific investigation is carried out in psychology.

THE FIELDS OF
PSYCHOLOGICAL
RESEARCH

The real substance of the definition of psychology is what psychologists actually *do*, both as scientific investigators and as practitioners. As researchers have tackled new areas and problems, the broad definition of psychology inevitably has expanded and been enriched. This book represents our attempt

areas of investigation

The increasing popularity of psychology among college students has been noted in a number of magazines and newspapers. An article by Larry Van Dyne, which appeared in *The New York Times,* is representative. Its title is the title of this Spotlight. Here are some excerpts.

A combination of traditional and untraditional reasons has made psychology a college campus favorite.

A decade ago 17,000 students earned bachelor's degrees with psychology as their major discipline; next June the number will be about 57,000. Master's degrees and doctorates have gone up proportionately during the same period. And students majoring in other fields are taking a wide variety of psychology courses. . . .

One reason for the enrollment growth, experts believe, is the increased interest among young people in behavioral and consciousness experiences. This interest is reflected in their attraction to quasi-religious cults, astrology, extrasensory perception, meditation and mysticism. . . .

The bulk of the discipline's new recruits, however, seems to have more conventional motives.

"The popularity is in part due to the importance of the problems dealt with by psychology," says Professor Donald Campbell of Northwestern University. . . . Introspective students, for instance, apparently find in psychology the promise of help with their personal problems; others, who look outside themselves, believe psychology will lead them toward helping relieve social injustice. . . .

Another factor, some observers say, is that, despite the crowded job market for psychologists, the discipline offers more career possibilities than, for example, history. It can serve as preparation for law school or medical school; and it is useful for students aiming at pure science or social service. . . .

What career use psychology majors eventually find for their studies is not entirely clear, because few departments keep close track of their graduates. Undoubtedly some go into careers that have nothing much to do with psychology. Others plunge deeper into the field in graduate school. In-between, the job market offers a variety of applied jobs in health institutions, and in school counseling offices. Some graduates are also finding jobs teaching newly introduced psychology courses in the high schools.

Still, there is considerable worry that the job market is already unable to absorb fully a major share of the students who major in psychology. And last year graduate schools received 130,000 applications for 13,700 openings in psychology. "That," says an official of the American Psychological Association, "is a little frightening."

From Larry Van Dyne, "For Some Reason, Psychology Is Popular," *New York Times,* November 9, 1975, p. 16E.

to amplify the fundamental definition, adding, in each new part, more information about what psychologists do and the results of their activities.

We can begin by pointing out that there are many different areas of psychology today, each with specialized research interests. Eight main kinds are reflected in the eight principal parts of this textbook: social psychology, personality, developmental psychology, cognitive psychology, learning psychology, perception, biological psychology, and comparative (or animal) psychology. Each specialty has a particular view of the factors that are critical in determining human behavior. The following paragraphs capsulize these views.

Social Psychology

The text begins from the perspective of *social psychology,* in which human behavior is linked intimately and in complex ways with the society and culture in which the individual lives. Thus social psychologists investigate such topics

The scientific study of behavior—human and animal—takes place both in natural settings and in the laboratory.

as the influence of interpersonal and intergroup relationships on conformity, attitude change, prejudice, attraction, and other social behaviors and attitudes.

Personality - how people differ from one another and why? ingrained or subjective.

We then move from a consideration of human social behavior to a focus on the individual. The psychology of *personality* is concerned with the uniqueness of the individual, and how and why people differ from each other. Much of the research in the field is specifically directed to the assessment of individual differences. Personality psychologists are also interested in the general "structure" of personality—an issue of some controversy. Are the most important aspects of personality deeply ingrained traits such as introversion, dominance, and aggressiveness? Or do expectancies and subjective values, determined largely by the situation in which people find themselves, play a pre-eminent role in behavior?

Developmental Psychology - studies social and intellectual development to understand adult behaviour.

From the viewpoint of *developmental psychology*, understanding adult human behavior is difficult without knowledge of the social and cognitive ("intellectual") development of the child and adolescent. Recently, developmental investigations of age changes, and the processes underlying these changes, have been extended to the adult years and old age, so that this field now covers the entire life-span.

Cognitive Psychology

Handwritten note: knowledge acquisition processing + utilization

Cognitive psychology regards the "higher mental processes"—the acquisition, processing, and utilization of knowledge—as of utmost importance in human behavior. Language, intelligence (and its measurement), thinking, reasoning, concept formation, problem-solving, and creativity are the chief topics of the research of cognitive psychologists.

Learning and Memory *—stimulus and response*

Handwritten note: formation of associations, losses " ", retention " "

Much behavior, particularly distinctively human behavior, is learned. *Learning psychology* studies the formation of associations where they did not exist before. These include simple associations between a stimulus and a response—such as that between a green light (stimulus) and "go" (response)—as well as complex relationships among "ideas." Memory (the retention of associations) and forgetting (the loss of associations) have become increasingly important topics in this area. Because learning and memory are such fundamental psychological processes, the theories and findings of learning psychologists have a strong impact on research in other specialties.

Perception *—what we acquire*

Handwritten note: through receptors and how creative constructive processes intervene in our perception

How are the bits of information acquired through our *receptors*—eyes, ears, nose, mouth, and skin—translated into *percepts*—loosely, what we *think* we see, hear, smell, taste, or touch? What active, creative, constructive processes intervene between objects or events in the external world and our organized, meaningful perceptions of them? These are the questions that specialists in *perception* try to answer.

Biological Psychology *— neural and hormonal factors that underlie behaviour.*

Biological psychology seeks to uncover the neural and hormonal factors that underlie behavior. A biological psychologist's investigation of aggression or memory, for example, focuses on the roles played by different brain structures and hormones. In studying perception, the biological psychologist investigates chemical changes in the eye and the neural processes in specialized areas of the brain.

Comparative Psychology *— uniqueness of humans compared to other animals.*

Handwritten note: - roles of heredity and learning in the development of responses for adjustment and survival.

Comparative psychology views behavior from the broadest perspective, one that encompasses all species of animals. By comparing different kinds of responses—such as aggression and cooperation—as they occur in various species, comparative psychologists can determine the ways in which humans resemble all other animals and those in which they are unique. At the same time, the significance of particular responses for adjustment and survival, and the roles of heredity and learning in the development of these responses, become clarified through comparative studies.

BASIC AND APPLIED PSYCHOLOGY

Handwritten note: research areas give rise to fundamental facts and principles of psyche.

Handwritten note: ↳ principles of basic research used to accomplish practical goals

The fields or specialities reviewed in the preceding paragraphs are considered *basic:* they are the research areas from which the fundamental facts and principles of psychology are derived. These fields are stressed in this text. In *applied* psychology, on the other hand, facts and principles discovered in basic research are used to accomplish some practical goals. For example, some psychologists help people to adjust better to their social environment (clinical psychology); some work at educating children more effectively (educational psychology); and others try to improve relations between two

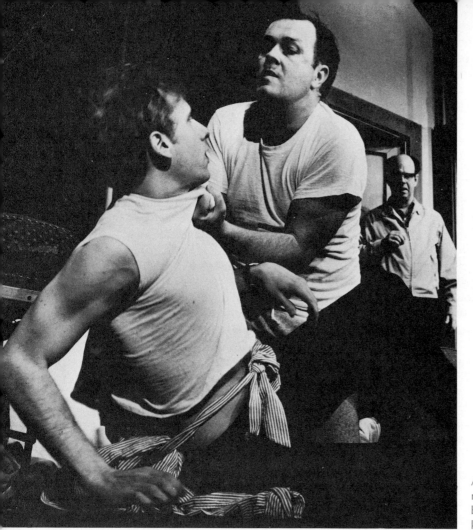

A thorough understanding of the roots of aggressive behavior combines the research of many different kinds of psychologists.

groups in conflict or introduce new hiring procedures to lessen unintentional discrimination (industrial psychology).

Of course, the distinction between basic and applied psychology is not always clear-cut. A clinical psychologist who diagnoses and treats adjustment problems—an applied activity—may in the process gather "case histories" that can be used in the scientific investigation of factors underlying mental disorders—a basic activity. Moreover, what is "basic" to one psychologist may be "applied" in the view of another. A study of classroom learning may uncover principles of learning that seem basic to a school psychologist; but to a learning psychologist, who is interested in more general principles, a study in school is an applied one. Nonetheless, if we do not push it too far, the distinction between basic and applied psychology can be useful.

Applied Psychologists

As Spotlight 1-2 shows, the most common type of psychologist—the *clinical psychologist*—is an applied psychologist. The two primary activities of the clinical psychologist are diagnosis and treatment of behavioral problems. A problem may be as specific as a "reading deficiency" or as general as a "neurosis." By using information from tests, interviews, and observations, the clinical psychologist attempts to diagnose the exact nature of a patient's difficulty. The method of treatment (therapy) used in attempting to eliminate or reduce the difficulty depends largely on the theory of personality the clinician holds. For example, some therapists would attempt to alleviate a phobia (an extreme, irrational fear) by using techniques derived from learning theory, while others would employ intensive interviews to discover the underlying causes of the phobia.

People often confuse the various types of *clinical psychologists, psychiatrists,* and *psychoanalysts,* all of whom are psychotherapists. The clinical psychologist has an academic degree (Ph.D.) rather than a medical one (M.D.) and more extensive training in psychology than the psychiatrist. The psychiatrist, a medical specialist, can prescribe drugs whereas a clinical psychologist cannot. The psychologist treats difficulties by "talking them out" or by using scientifically based principles of behavior modification (*see* pp. 207–09). The psychiatrist usually knows more about bodily functions, while the psychologist typically has more specific knowledge of psychological processes and the diagnosis of personality difficulties through personality tests and questionnaires. Quite often, especially in hospitals, the clinical psychologist and the psychiatrist work as a team.

A psychoanalyst treats patients according to the personality theory initially formulated by Sigmund Freud (psychoanalytic theory; *see* pp. 158–65). Psychoanalysts have extensive training at psychoanalytic institutes and most have medical degrees as well.

Of course, not everyone who seeks help from a psychologist has a severe emotional problem. Some *guidance counselors* work in educational settings, helping students choose careers, *family counselors* help parents and children resolve family problems. The *industrial psychologist* may counsel labor and management on effective techniques for conflict resolution, while the *management psychologist* focuses on the human factors involved in executive decisions. The *personnel psychologist* is an expert in placing people in the right jobs.

Psychologists are experts in behavior and for this reason their knowledge is of use to a wide variety of people, groups, and organizations. Applied activities range from training animals in a zoo, advising advertising agencies on the effects of different kinds of messages, to directing national polls on presidential preferences. These are just a few of the many activities and work settings in which you might find an applied psychologist.

It is important to understand that some of the most interesting social problems and psychological issues may be investigated by several different kinds of psychologists. In many cases, a thorough comprehension of complex problems—and their solution—depends on a multi-dimensional approach, an integration of knowledge obtained from several specialists, both basic and applied. Each works on a different facet of the problem and brings to the investigation his or her own perspectives and research techniques.

Consider as an example the striking increase in violence in contemporary society and the urgent need to promote altruism and cooperation. Biological and comparative psychologists contribute data about neural and hormonal factors associated with violence and altruism and about the functions of such behaviors in various species. The effects of social class and exposure to violent or altruistic behavior in the mass media (television, newspapers, films) are investigated by social and personality psychologists. The impact of early parent-child interactions and specific learning experiences — including imitation — are researched by developmental and learning psychologists. Cognitive psychologists explore the nature of children's and adults' thinking and reasoning about violence and altruism; they also explore the methods people use to solve problems involving these behaviors. Applied psychologists make use of all these findings from basic fields in efforts to reduce tendencies toward violence or to increase positive feelings between groups in conflict. They may use psychotherapy, educational programs in schools, communication in the mass media, or the resources of a government bureau or community service organization.

Whether basic or applied, all scientific psychologists abide by the canons of objective investigation and interpretation. It is to these principles that we now turn.

Guidance and counselling, an important applied activity, occupies about 12 percent of the members of the American Psychological Association.

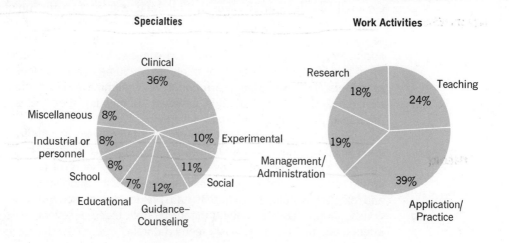

Specialties

Clinical 36%

Miscellaneous 8%

Industrial or personnel 8%

School 8%

Educational 7%

Guidance–Counseling 12%

Social 11%

Experimental 10%

Work Activities

Research 18%

Teaching 24%

Management/Administration 19%

Application/Practice 39%

In 1972, the American Psychological Association (APA) mailed a questionnaire to its 35,361 members. From the responses to the questionnaire, the following picture of American psychology emerges (Boneau and Cuca, 1974).

1. Designations of specialties show clinical psychology as the most common (36 percent). "Experimental," which includes specialties in learning, perception, biological, and comparative psychology, accounts for 10 percent, and "Social," which includes personality and developmental psychology as well as social, accounts for 11 percent. Obviously there is some overlap among the categories in the diagram; clinical psychologists could, for example, designate their specialties as "clinical," "personality," or even "educational" or "industrial," depending on where they work and what they do—and, no doubt, on how they would prefer to see themselves.

2. The most common work activity is "Application/Practice" (39 percent). This category includes psychotherapy, counseling, industrial applications, and many other activities. "Research" and "Teaching"—the "basic" activities of discovering and communicating knowledge—together account for 42 percent. A surprising 19 percent of psychologists list their main activity as "Management/Administration." Supervision of research programs, clinical treatment programs, and community-health programs are some of the activities included in the latter category.

3. Some other statistics not shown on the diagrams are worth noting. About 50 percent of APA psychologists work at colleges and universities. About 25 percent of all psychologists are women. Of every four APA members, about three have a doctor's degree (usually Ph.D.); almost all of the others have master's degrees.

Almost everyone has his or her own "theory" of human behavior based on personal experience and observations. In this sense, almost everyone is a psychologist. Many people believe that "war is inevitable because aggression is an innate characteristic of human beings." How do they know this is true? Usually the evidence for personal theories of behavior is based on such casual, unsystematic, and often biased observations as "well, there are always wars someplace, aren't there?" But the psychologist uses more formal, systematic

formal, systematic procedures—collectively called the [scientific method]—in gathering evidence and formulating theories.

One of the first steps in the scientific method is formulating a **hypothesis.** Generally this hypothesis takes the form of a tentative explanation of relationships among characteristics, conditions, or events (variables). For example, some psychologists have hypothesized that permissive childrearing fosters adolescent rebelliousness; others have suggested that a stimulating environment in early life promotes later intelligence. Some hypotheses reflect current or popular beliefs; others are founded on preliminary observations or pilot research. Still others are creative, new ways of thinking about behavior, which often lead to the most important advances.

HYPOTHESIS

A coherent, integrated set of interrelated hypotheses is called a **theory.** A good scientific theory is useful in summarizing, bringing together, integrating, and explaining different kinds of data. Einstein's theory of relativity, for example, encompassed explanations for two kinds of phenomena—gravitation and electromagnetic forces—that had previously seemed unrelated. Analogously, Freud's psychoanalytic theory brought together several psychological phenomena that had previously seemed unrelated: dreams, slips of the tongue, humor, and personality disorders.

THEORY

But a good theory does more than integrate; it is also a source of suggestions and hypotheses for further research. With a good theory we can make predictions that can be tested scientifically. In this sense, hypotheses or theories *guide* research; they point to the next steps that must be taken in research.

Unlike lay people, scientists systematically test their hypotheses and theories to determine whether or not they are valid. They accept or reject hypotheses on the basis of empirical evidence derived from careful and objective observation. Quantitative, precise measurements are used wherever possible. Experiments are conducted and observations made very carefully, so that they can be repeated, and thus verified, by others.

Psychologists vs. casual observation.

Hypotheses must be stated in testable form. Suppose we want to know if children are affected by watching adults engage in some altruistic activity. We could hypothesize that "setting a good example" will have a positive effect. In order to gather data relevant to this hypothesis, we must define our terms. What do we mean by "having a positive effect"? What do we mean by "altruistic activity"? So that everyone knows exactly what is meant, scientists define each term in the hypothesis objectively—as an observable response or measurement. These are called **operational definitions.** In our example, we could define one kind of *altruistic behavior* as "donating to a fund for orphans"; a *positive effect* could be operationally defined as "producing similar behavior by the children who have watched an altruistic adult."

Once the terms have been defined operationally, the researcher can proceed with the investigation. The preferred method of research in many areas of psychology, as in most scientific fields, is the laboratory experiment. We will therefore take this up first and will later consider nonexperimental, but objective research methods.

EXPERIMENTAL METHOD

The experimental method has two distinctive characteristics. First, the experimenter manipulates something—the **independent variable**—creating, changing, or controlling it. Second, he or she systematically observes or measures the effects of the manipulation on some other behavior or condition — the **dependent variable.** For example, to investigate the hypothesis that children will imitate the altruistic behavior of adults, the experimenter could first arrange a situation in which *some children* — the **experimental group** — observed adults giving to charity. Other children would have no such experience; they would be the **control group,** which is used for comparison purposes. "Observation of a charitable adult" would be the independent variable controlled by the experimenter.

In the second phase of the experiment, both groups of children would be observed in situations in which they have an opportunity to donate to a charity. For example, they might play a game in which prizes were awarded for successful performances. Near the game area there would be a box clearly marked for orphans' fund donations — the same box used by the charitable adults observed by children in the experimental group. The dependent variable could be either whether or not the children donate or how much they give. To test the hypothesis the behavior of the experimental group would be compared to that of the control group. We would expect more children in the experimental group to give or their average donation to be greater — *if* the hypothesis is valid. Note that the control group is necessary to determine whether the experimental group is more charitable than it would have been without the experience of observing an adult acting charitably. In fact, this experiment has been conducted, and the results supported the hypothesis (*see* p. 225).

Creating Experimental and Control Groups

In a similar experiment, the effects of observing an *aggressive* adult were studied (Bandura, Ross, & Ross, 1963). Children in the experimental group witnessed an adult hammering a large plastic doll (a "punching-bag" toy). Later, given an opportunity to play with the toy, these children hammered

A classical experiment showed that children who observed an aggressive model themselves behaved aggressively in the same situation.

the doll much as the adults had done. Control-group children, who had not previously observed an aggressive adult, showed much less aggression toward the doll.

The investigators interpreted these results as supporting their hypothesis, which was that children will imitate aggression they observe in adults. But suppose we objected, saying perhaps that the children in the experimental group were more aggressive to begin with; in that case, their greater aggression, rather than their observations of aggressive adults, would have accounted for the results. This alternative interpretation is always possible, but it is quite unlikely if the children are *randomly* assigned to one group or the other—as they would be in a good experiment.

Random assignment of children to groups is a procedure something like putting all their names in a hat, mixing them thoroughly, then drawing blindly an equal number for each group or subgroup. This means essentially that *no characteristic of the subject is used to determine which group a child will join.* So when a large group is subdivided at random into subgroups, we assume that these subgroups are essentially equal in all respects—in characteristics that

Figure 1-1
Outline of Steps in an Experiment

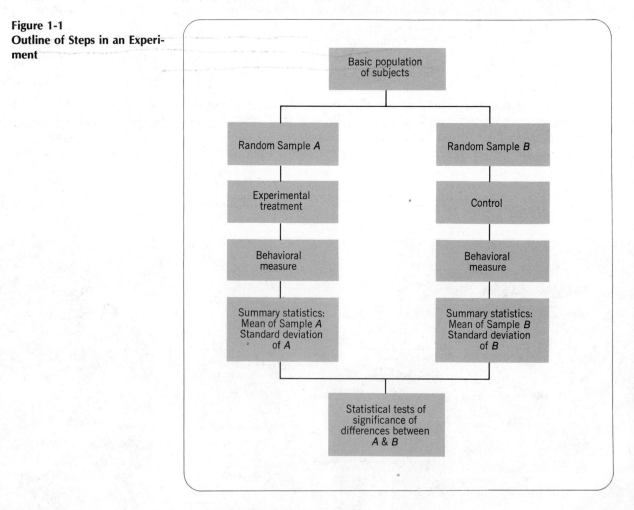

might affect aggressive behavior, such as sex, health, intelligence, excitability, and neurotic trends, and even in nonessential characteristics, such as hair or eye color.

If children are assigned randomly to the groups, the two groups are closely similar at the beginning of the experiment. *Then* the independent variable is applied—that is, one group is treated differently from the other. Any difference between them *after* the experiment must be due to the effect of the independent variable—in this case, exposure to aggressive models—since there were originally no other differences between the groups. The dependent variable was the amount of aggression expressed toward a doll; and the children who observed the aggressive model were more aggressive than those who had not. We can conclude that this difference was the result of watching the models because the groups differed from each other *only* in that one way—their exposure to aggressive models. Thus the unique and critical advantage of the experimental method is that it makes possible a clear interpretation of the changes that occur in dependent variables. The logic of the experiment is simple and straightforward. Groups are matched at the outset; the subjects in one group are given an experimental intervention, but those in the other do not receive this treatment. A response measure, the dependent variable, is then recorded. Any significant differences between the experimental and control groups are attributable to the experimental intervention. (*See* Figure 1-1.)

Deciding When a Difference Is Significant

When we compare the performances of experimental and control groups in any task, we will almost always find *some* difference between them. Suppose, for illustration, we want to test the hypothesis that a particular vitamin will increase students' mental abilities. We could use two randomly formed groups of students from a psychology class as subjects. One group, the experimental group, would be given the vitamin pills; those in the other, or control, group would be given a pill that looked and tasted like the vitamin pill but which contained no vitamins or other active substance (a placebo). At the end of the experiment, a test of problem-solving ability would be given to both groups. The average test score for the experimental group might be 83.4 and that for the control group 80.7. Is it reasonable to attribute this difference to the independent variable; that is, can we conclude that the vitamin had an effect? More specifically, we want to know the probability that the difference we found could have occurred by chance alone and not because of the independent variable—the vitamin.

There are mathematical ways of deciding when a difference between groups in the dependent variable is large enough to be considered trustworthy, that is, related to the independent variable rather than attributable to chance factors alone. These *statistical tests of significance* (described in the Appendix) are used to determine the probability that the difference observed could be obtained by *chance* alone, when there is, in truth, no relationship between the independent and dependent variables. If the probability that the difference could have occurred by chance alone is very *small,* we can be confident that a real relationship exists. Typically, if the probability that the difference could be obtained by chance is less than 5 in 100 (indicated by the symbol $p < .05$), it is considered statistically significant. A difference with a chance probability of less than 1 in 100 (indicated by the symbol $p < .01$) leads to even more confidence.

SYSTEMATIC OBSERVATION AND NATURE'S EXPERIMENTS

Despite its obvious advantages, many problems of human behavior cannot be investigated by the experimental method. Consider the hypothesis that permissive childrearing (allowing children a great deal of freedom) produces rebelliousness against authority. In this case, permissiveness would be considered the independent variable; the child's tendency to rebel or not would be the dependent one. Obviously researchers cannot control or manipulate parents' ways of raising children simply for experimental purposes. But they can go into the "field" (that is, people's homes), and carefully and systematically observe parents' interactions with their children. On the basis of these **naturalistic observations,** the psychologists can select a group of children raised permissively and a group raised nonpermissively. Permissiveness might be defined operationally in terms of such variables as strictness or laxity of rules of the home and children's participation in making their own, and family, decisions. Rebelliousness could be measured operationally by teachers' ratings of children's tractability in the classroom, as revealed by their willingness to comply with rules and instructions. The amount of rebellion in the permissively and nonpermissively reared groups would then be compared. If the permissively reared children actually manifest more rebelliousness than those raised by nonpermissive parents, the hypothesis would be supported: permissiveness would, in fact, be shown to be related to rebellion against authority. The study cannot be considered an experiment in the usual sense, however, for the experimenters did not intervene in any way. They did not actively manipulate the independent variable, permissiveness. Instead, the hypothesis was tested by observing naturally occurring events and determining relationships between these—in essence, by observing an "experiment" in which nature manipulated the independent variable.

Naturalistic observations are of special value in the early phases of the study of a phenomenon. They provide valuable information about behavior as it occurs in life situations, information that often forms the basis for more analytical laboratory experiments. Field studies of smokers, for example, showed them to be particularly susceptible to lung cancer. By itself, this finding was not conclusive evidence that smoking caused cancer; but it did provide the impetus for controlled laboratory experiments on animals. The combination of findings from observational studies and laboratory experiments leaves little doubt now of the health hazards of cigarette smoking.

CORRELATIONAL STUDIES

Sometimes the question under investigation is how closely two variables are related. In such cases psychologists often use a direct measure of the relationship between two variables; it is called the **coefficient of correlation,** generally referred to simply as the correlation. For example, how closely are the I.Q. scores of children related to those of their parents? Table 1-1 presents representative data for sixty-three families, with one parent and one child taken from each family. Looking over the figures, you get the impression that if the parent has a relatively high score, so does the child, and that low parental scores tend to be associated with low children's scores. But the relationship is not

TABLE 1-1	I.Q. scores of 63 real parent-child pairs							

Parent	Child		Parent	Child		Parent	Child		Parent	Child
136	131		117	113		112	96		114	105
98	125		92	107		116	95		112	109
114	126		94	106		118	99		124	106
113	129		93	100		120	98		121	108
102	122		96	108		83	91		83	100
111	121		103	104		94	90		87	104
115	123		105	100		95	92		89	101
127	124		108	103		104	94		121	91
93	116		107	111		107	93		83	85
97	119		114	102		118	94		88	89
118	117		132	118		107	78		86	86
126	118		80	95		76	82		120	88
127	119		84	99		99	84		124	87
125	117		79	99		87	80		107	81
129	115		76	97		63	67		102	79
112	111		104	98		107	107			

perfect. Some parents with relatively high scores have children with relatively low scores. We can get a better idea of the relationship if we plot the scores in what is called a **scatterplot,** as shown in Figure 1-2. Here each parent-child pair is represented by one point on the graph. To place the point, you find the parent's score on the horizontal axis and then go over to the position of

Figure 1-2
Scatterplot Showing Relationship Between Child's and Parent's I.Q.'s
This scatterplot is constructed from the data given in Table 1-1 to show the relationship between the I.Q. scores of parents and their children. The point for Parent 136–child 131 is shown in black to illustrate how points are plotted on the graph.

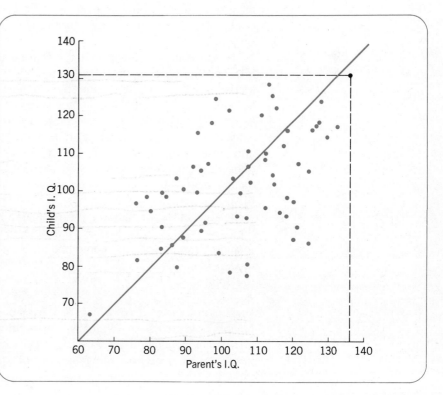

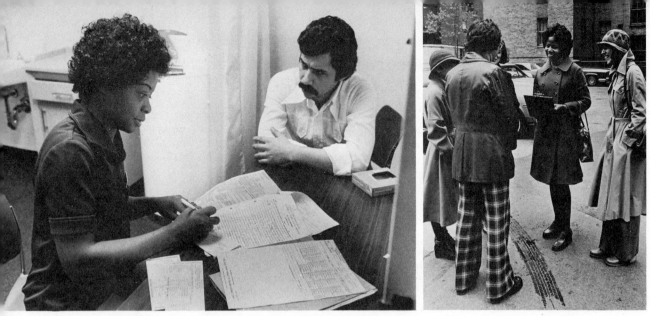

There are numerous techniques of gathering scientific information about behavior. Two of the most frequently used are the case-history approach and the questionnaire.

the child's score on the vertical axis. The first pair in the table—parent, 136, child, 131—is represented by a black point; broken lines show the two scores on the axes.

The correlation coefficient is the statistic used to express numerically the relationship. Correlation values range from 0.00 (no relationship) to 1.00 (perfect relationship); the higher the coefficient, the stronger the relationship. In Figure 1-2 the correlation (abbreviated r in statistical work) is 0.52 ($r = .52$). In general, in psychological research, a correlation of 0.50 or more is considered relatively strong; correlations between 0.30 and 0.50 are moderate; and those below 0.30 are considered low. Correlations can be positive (+ or, often, no sign) or negative (always indicated by −). A positive correlation indicates that if the score on one variable is high, the other is also likely to be high. For example, if the parent's I.Q. is high, the child's is also likely to be high. A negative correlation indicates that if the score on one variable is high, the other is likely to be low. For example, many studies show a negative correlation between I.Q. and conformity; the *higher* the individual's intelligence, the *less* often he or she will yield, in experimental situations, to group pressures to conform.

SURVEYS

Psychologists use surveys to gather valuable data on the attitudes and behaviors of large groups. Typically, a scientifically selected portion (or sample) of a larger population (of voters, Catholics, nuclear physicists, etc.) is questioned by interview, questionnaire, or both. The results may be generalized, within a slight margin of error, from the sample to the larger group. Thus, in the famous Kinsey surveys of sexual behavior (1948, 1953), the interview answers of a few thousand people were used to estimate the sexual activities and attitudes of Americans in general. National opinion polls and television rating systems also generalize the opinions of a sample of the population on a wide range of topics from voting preferences, prejudice, childrearing practices, to favorite situation-comedies.

CASE HISTORIES

The intensive investigation of a single individual—a single case—results in a large body of data called a case history. Included may be information on personality structure, social relationships, and significant life events, as well as scholastic and vocational data and the judgments of clinical psychologists who have examined the person. Similar information on the individual's parents and grandparents may also be collected. From this scientific biography, psychologists try to piece together the jigsaw puzzle of a single life and personality. In addition to their use in understanding the individual, case histories can be used for more general purposes. Since many such studies are made of people with emotional problems who have been receiving therapy, case histories are especially valuable in exploring the nature and causes of such problems. By examining a number of histories, psychologists can distinguish general factors from those that may be unique to particular individuals.

Are there genuine psychological laws?

Are there genuine psychological laws that always predict relationships between psychological variables? Can findings from experiments be practically applied to life situations? People are so different and variable, their reactions are so complex and influenced by such a multiplicity of factors that it sometimes seems as if real scientific understanding of human behavior is impossible. Adages such as "one man's meat is another man's poison" and "there's no accounting for tastes" emphasize the difficulties of making generalizations about human behavior.

On the other hand, some regularities in behavior clearly exist, and we rely on these regularities in our everyday lives. For example, in North America we expect everyone to drive on the right side of the road, while in Great Britain everyone is expected to drive on the left. We drive in accordance with these regularities, operating with well-learned habits; furthermore, we assume that everyone in our culture has learned these same habits.

While some aspects of behavior are generally predictable, it is impossible to be accurate in every case; individual exceptions do occur. In a way, psychology may be compared to meteorology. Even though meteorologists have learned a great deal about the physical processes that cause variations in the weather, prediction is far from perfect. It would be wonderful to be able to predict exactly when the weather will be favorable for harvesting crops, for launching a satellite, or for picnicking. Nonetheless, the fact that meteorologists make mistakes does not lead us to doubt that it is worthwhile to try to predict the weather.

GENERALIZATION AND INTERACTION

Discovering the broad and most general principles of behavior—the ways in which all people (or even all mammals) are alike (**generalizations**)—is of course a major goal of psychological research. Recently, however, many psychologists have suggested that, in many areas, the search for broad generalizations may *not* be the most effective strategy (Bem & Allen, 1974; Cronbach, 1975). In many cases, especially those involving human social behavior, one principle may apply for people with certain characteristics and another, different principle to those with other characteristics. For example, some students like to discover things for themselves; they do well in a relatively loosely structured class in which the instructor permits freedom of inquiry and encourages "learning by discovery." Other students flounder in such courses; they prefer a more structured class in which the "facts" are laid out in detail and examinations cover clearly specified material. There is no broad principle—such as, students should be allowed to discover things for themselves—that works best for all students.

When the same situation affects different people in different ways, we say there is an **interaction.** When there is an interaction, one cannot predict the results from just a knowledge of the situation, nor from only knowing who the people are; one must know both. For example, in one recent study (Schacter & Rodin, 1974), students were given the task of proofreading some printed material; they were to find as many errors as possible in ten minutes. Some of the participants worked in quiet surroundings; some heard a voice reciting random numbers; some heard a tape describing seashells; and still others heard a vivid description of the psychological effects of dying from leukemia. What do you suppose was the effect of the different types of tape recording on the students' performances? Did increasingly engrossing tapes result in greater distraction and worse performance? Or did subjects try harder in the presence of more interesting tapes and therefore actually perform better?

The results of the experiment showed that two types of subjects responded differently. One kind performed better, on the average, as the tapes became more interesting (note the solid line in Figure 1-3). The other type tended to do worse while hearing more interesting tapes (as shown by the broken line in Figure 1-3). The subjects had not been divided into these two groups on the basis of distractability but on the basis of being overweight or of normal weight! Previous research had led the investigators to hypothesize that overweight people are more sensitive to external stimuli and therefore more distractable than those of normal weight; the results of the experiment supported their hypothesis. (*See* Spotlight 20-2, p. 557.)

What is the answer then? Does a distracting stimulus impair performance? You can't give a yes-or-no answer that is true for everyone, but you can conclude that different individuals respond in characteristic ways to such stimulation. Furthermore, you may be able to predict how a person will respond if you know other facts about him or her (for example, overweight or not). So

Figure 1-3
Accuracy of Proofreading Under Different Types of Distraction
Fifteen subjects are represented by each point on the graph. Sixty subjects were of normal weight (within 10 percent of the norms) and 60 were overweight (at least 15 percent above the norms). (After Schachter & Rodin, 1974)

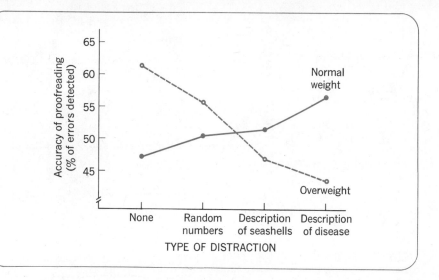

to predict behavior when there is an interaction, you need to know *both* the situation *and* the particular type of individual.

Interactions place limits on how far psychologists can generalize. Although there are broad generalizations in psychology—especially in biological, learning, and perception psychology—it is also important to investigate the ways in which people differ. Knowledge of such differences is essential in selecting the most effective treatment for each individual in psychotherapy, the most effective means of instruction for each student, and the fairest way of testing each job applicant.

It is also important to recognize that many of the "general" principles of psychology are based on a limited number of observations and on a limited range of subjects; children, rats, and college sophomores are popular subject populations. A conclusion derived from observations in a highly specialized situation, such as a laboratory, may prove on later testing to have rather broad applicability; on the other hand, it may not. Or a conclusion based on a particular sample, such as nursery-school children, may or may not prove to have generality. The important caution is this: conclusions from such studies can be generalized only *after* they have been tested more widely. The investigator studying learning processes in rats cannot be sure that the principles derived apply to humans unless they are actually tested on humans. In the same way, we cannot be sure, without further testing, that a program of instruction that helps students of average intelligence will also benefit mentally retarded children or gifted ones.

We must also be careful about generalizing from one experimental situation to other, different situations. In the study cited earlier, exposure to aggressive models produced increased aggression among children—in this specific laboratory situation. Does this mean that seeing violent television programs at home leads to more aggressive behavior? We cannot be sure without more direct tests, since this situation is different in many respects from the laboratory.

"I DON'T KNOW WHERE HE LEARNED THAT. WE DON'T EVEN HAVE A TELEVISION SET."

In spite of strong feelings on both sides of the issue, the role of television in influencing a child or adult toward violent behavior has not yet been scientifically established.

In fact, more direct tests have been made, and they indicate that a number of factors must be considered; we cannot make simple and direct generalizations about children and violence. (See p. 144.)

What are the ethical problems in psychological research?

As psychology grows in scope and effectiveness, psychologists are increasingly concerned that their scientific knowledge be used to promote human welfare. Many achieve that goal directly in their professional activities: clinical psychologists strive to relieve anxiety and enhance personal adjustment; counseling psychologists seek to help people make rational decisions that will be in their best interests; educational psychologists are pleased if their work and advice facilitate effective learning and greater creativity among school children.

In other circumstances, however, the desire to promote human welfare can sometimes place a psychologist on the horns of an ethical dilemma. Suppose a researcher discovers something that could potentially benefit humanity —perhaps a technique to reduce prejudice or intergroup tension. But this same technique could be used in unfair or inhumane ways—for example, to control votes or political behavior. Should the psychologist communicate this finding, which could benefit millions of people, but which, if misused, could have harmful or immoral effects? What are the actions appropriate to the "moral" scientist as a knowledgable citizen? What role should professional associations such as the American Psychological Association play? Should they actively lobby in Congress for sound and humane governmental programs and regulation of the use of research findings?

With the extensive scope of topics that it covers, psychology has become a worldwide activity. All the advanced nations and many of the developing countries have large numbers of psychologists engaged in teaching, research, and application. An international congress is held every four years to encourage direct communication among psychologists of different nations; and many psychological journals and books are read around the world.

Illustrated here are scenes from the 21st International Congress of Psychology held in Paris in 1976, and the 20th Congress in Tokyo, 1972. The next Congress is scheduled for Leipzig in 1980, to celebrate the centennial of psychology as a separate discipline. The present Executive Committee of the International Union of Psychological Science includes members from Australia, Belgium, Cuba, France, Great Britain, Japan, Mexico, Nigeria, Poland, Sweden, the U.S., and the U.S.S.R.

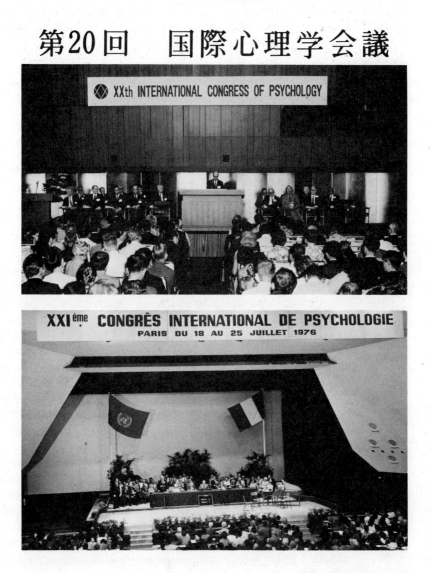

Two concrete incidents will indicate the nature of the ethical dilemmas faced by psychological researchers. These are two actual accounts taken from a report of the American Psychological Association. (APA *Monitor*, 1971, p. 28.)

> One investigator describes a study involving behavioral measures of the effect of chemical substances and notes that among the uses intended for the substances was the lowering of the will to resist and fight during war and riots. While he hesitated to become involved, he pointed out that the chemical substances were to be substituted for more lethal weapons. He wondered, nevertheless, whether the substances might not be used in military and police actions to which he would be opposed.

What should he have done? If he discovered that a chemical affects the "will to resist," how should that discovery be made public? If you were the scientist, would you publish at all?

> A psychologist contributed to a pool of survey research data the data from his study of determinants of opinion on key social and political issues. Among his variables were religious and ethnic affiliation. Later he discovered that another investigator was using his data . . . [to advise] a candidate for political office who hoped to use the results to guide his political campaign. The psychologist in question believed the election of this candidate would be a serious blow to the welfare of the people whom the candidate would govern. . . . Should he do everything possible to withdraw his data or should he take the position that to conduct the proposed analysis . . . , however much he disliked it, is the right of the other investigator?

How would you answer these ethical questions?

Another ethical problem with which researchers must come to grips is the treatment of people who participate in research—the research subjects. Respect for subjects and their rights is of paramount importance. Of course, no ethical psychologist would investigate the sources of mental illness by subjecting babies to cruel and harsh treatment or by depriving them of psychological care and attention. Such experiments are unthinkable, however great their potential benefit to others. Unfortunately, ethical decisions are rarely so clear-cut. Should psychologists do experiments involving mental or physical stress or drugs use? Should subjects be asked to reveal embarrassing or possibly incriminating information? These are not easy questions to answer. Psychologists generally agree that the researchers are, first and foremost, responsible for the welfare of subjects. They must take all necessary steps to guarantee privacy and are ethically bound to protect confidences. (*See also* pp. 58–59.)

Because of concern about ethical problems, the American Psychological Association has enacted a code of ethics dealing with these and other issues. The psychological associations of most other countries have similar codes. In addition, many research institutions have their own ethics committees that must approve experiments *before* they can be conducted. There was a time when scientists believed that their sole responsibility was the "search for the truth." Today most scientists do not hold that view. In a technological age, the scientist is often the only one with enough information and understanding to anticipate the possible harmful effects on subjects of an experimental treatment or to evaluate the societal consequences of applying the results of his or her research. Moreover, if someone does plan improper use, it is the scientist who can best design effective countermeasures.

Where do we begin the study of psychology?

This textbook begins with parts on social psychology, personality, and human development. Our introduction to the major areas of theory and research ends with the psychological specialities most closely related to the natural sciences —learning, perception, biological psychology, and comparative psychology. This order is the reverse of that found in most introductory textbooks; we believe it has two great advantages.

First, the social-personal areas require little in the way of specialized or technical background. The issues discussed are immediately recognizable and intrinsically interesting from the reader's own experience, although many of the findings go far beyond common sense or general knowledge. Second, the earlier parts will help develop an interest in later, more technical chapters. As you read the chapters on social psychology, personality, and development, you will find that many topics that will be explored in later parts are being introduced. Learning, for example, is a key concept in the early parts; it is discussed in detail in Part Six. Then, in Part Eight, Biological Psychology, the biological processes that underlie motivation and learning are described. The subject matter of Comparative Psychology, Part Nine, includes information on the learning of animals in the laboratory and in their natural environments. Thus the later portions of the book are made more interesting by the meaningful foundation laid for them in earlier parts.

Another unusual feature of this book is that it has many authors, rather than the usual one or two. All eight major parts were written by experts in the area — experts who are in the best position to know which facts and principles are the most important, both for increasing an understanding of the particular specialty and for preparing for further study. As an introductory survey can do no more than present some of the major findings and trends, selectivity is necessary. Recognized authorities in a field can make the soundest and most knowledgable selections.

What are the key concepts in psychology?

Before we turn to the first of the major substantive parts, let us briefly consider six basic concepts that are important throughout the text. These concepts will provide some background for studying the various specialties covered by the text. They will also be useful as bridges, relating the parts to each other and becoming richer and more meaningful as they are used in different contexts throughout the book.

[handwritten margin note: MOTIVATION – individual's desires and wishes, and biological drives like hunger.]

[handwritten margin note: primary drives – unlearned secondary drives – learned]

The first concept, **motivation,** is used to refer to an individual's desires and wishes, as well as to biological drives such as hunger. Motivations are *inferred* internal states or processes that may help us to understand why human beings and animals behave as they do. Some motives or drives are called **primary drives,** by which we mean that their occurrence does not depend on learning (although learning may affect the social expression of these drives). An example is hunger, a primary drive to obtain food, which is based on unlearned biological needs. Other motives, sometimes called **secondary drives,** are learned or acquired desires for particular goals such as attention, affection, approval, power, money, acceptance, or achievement. For purposes of this brief discussion, the important point is that motives, needs, or desires impel (drive) the individual to action. We are not, of course, always consciously aware of our motivation; all of us, at some time or another, do things for reasons that we do not understand and cannot state. So we say that we are sometimes driven by *unconscious* motives.

Remember that all motives are inferred; they are theoretical explanations of behavior rather than directly observable facts or relationships. Therefore, when a given behavior is attributed to the influence of a particular motive, it is always worthwhile to inquire carefully into the evidence. If an acquired need for higher social status is presumed to explain an executive's competitive behavior, then facts (other than competitive behavior!) must indicate the existence of that motive.

INFORMATION PROCESSING

In analyzing complex behaviors, many psychologists are finding it useful to devise **information-processing theories.** This is especially true of behaviors related to thought and language, the recognition of perceived patterns, and learning and memory. The information-processing approach involves the fundamental assumption that complex behaviors can fruitfully be broken down into more basic stages. For example, tests of memory have at least two stages, a memory stage and a decision stage (*see* p. 408). If people are shown a word and asked if it was in a list they were shown yesterday, they first compare the word with their memory of yesterday's list. Then, on the basis of this comparison and other factors (for example, whether the experimenter might punish subjects for incorrect responses), they *decide* to say yes or no.

Information-processing theorists often use computers as a metaphor or model for human intellectual processes (cognitive behavior). Computers have two types of memory—a large semipermanent storehouse for any information that might ever be useful and a smaller storage for information that is currently being processed. It has been proposed that the human information processor has two analogous types of memory: a large, permanent long-term store and a smaller, impermanent short-term store for data presently in use. Experiments, both psychological (Chapter 15) and biological (Chapter 21), provide evidence in support of the idea of multiple kinds of memory storage.

LEARNING

Learning—the profit from experience—is clearly a vital aspect of human behavior. Many, many years of research have made it clear that much of human behavior is learned, that is, is a result of training and practice. "Precisely that behavior which is widely felt to characterize man as a rational being or as

The rat learns to press the lever to get a food reward. By studying rats and other animals, psychologists have begun to gain an understanding of learning behavior in humans.

a member of a particular nation or social class is learned rather than innate" (Dollard & Miller, 1950, p. 25).

Acquisition of language and culture are obvious examples of learning. Learning is also involved in personal mannerisms and motor skills. Recent research has shown that it is even involved in internal bodily functions; as we shall see, digestion and blood circulation—and hence emotional reactions—can be modified through learning. Detailed discussions of learning and memory are presented in Part Six of this book, Chapters 14 and 15.

REINFORCEMENT - *changes in behaviour because of favourable or unfavourable outcomes.*

A person's behavior often changes depending upon the consequences of that behavior in the past. When an act leads to a favorable outcome, it is more likely to occur again in the same setting. For example, a two-year-old girl, in the process of learning to say words, is being coaxed by her father to say "cookie." He holds a cookie before her; after several attempts she makes a sound somewhat like "cookie." The delighted father hugs the child affectionately and gives her the cookie as a reward. The next time the child sees a cookie, she is likely to repeat the word. We say that a particular speech behavior has been *reinforced*. With older children, an unfavorable outcome, such as a punishment, may be used to suppress words that parents deem undesirable.

Changes in behavior because of favorable—or unfavorable—outcomes are basic to the psychology of learning. The delivery of a reward for a response is called **positive reinforcement;** and giving punishment for an act is referred to as **negative reinforcement.** Either type can be used in training situations. For example, a rat will learn a maze if the experimenter provides food at the end of it (positive reinforcement) or if it receives a shock (negative reinforcement) whenever it enters a blind alley.

The more often the rat is rewarded for taking the correct path through the maze (or the child for saying cookie), the greater the likelihood that these responses will be made again. On the other hand, if the response is not followed by reinforcement, the probability of repetition decreases; this is called **extinction.** If the rat running the maze does not find a reward (food) at the end of the maze, it is less likely to run the next time. After many experiences of nonreinforcement, it may not run at all. In technical terms, the response has been extinguished.

Clearly much of our learning involves reward, but does *all* learning occur through reinforcement? Some theorists suggest that the answer to this question is "yes," that reinforcement is involved even in cases where no experimenter, parent, or other person delivers rewards. For example, without receiving any external rewards, the infant learns how the shape of an object changes as it moves or as it is seen from different angles; he or she also learns that objects persist even when they are lost from sight. It has been suggested that in these cases of early perceptual learning, the reinforcement is *internal*—that an increase in knowledge *in itself* is reinforcing to the child. This is a plausible argument, although it is difficult to test, even though, as we shall see, external manipulation of rewards does not seem to be important in many cases of human and animal learning (see p. 384).

FEEDBACK

Feedback is another key concept that applies to the behavior of human beings and animals as well as to complex mechanisms. People or animals are constantly active, even during sleep. They continually monitor and adjust activity in accordance with their intentions and with changing circumstances. In the restricted sense, feedback means "the return of part of the output of a system to the input for purposes of regulation and control." For example, when you reach to pick up a pencil, you use visual information (input) to reduce steadily the distance between your hand and the pencil (output) (see Figure 1-4). At the same time important information, internal feedback, is also coming from the sense organs in your muscles, tendons, and joints. While you are not aware of most of this internal feedback, unconscious processes of coordina-

Food, praise, and monetary rewards can all function as reinforcements in learning new behavior.

Figure 1-4
Feedback Involved in Visually Guided Reaching

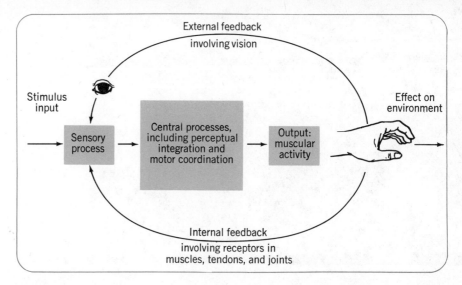

tion regulate the activities of many muscles to achieve the intended goal.

Feedback occurs in social behavior too. Suppose, for example, that you join a new group where you hope to make friends. You make several statements about current social issues that elicit expressions of opinion from other members of the group. You then examine your opinions in relation to theirs; and, very possibly, you attempt to reduce the differences among the various opinions. You may do so by changing your own position or restating it in a more acceptable form, or you may try to persuade others to change theirs. Feedback in social situations is complex, but in order to understand social behavior, we must be attentive to the continual interactions between the individual and the social environment.

HEREDITY-ENVIRONMENT INTERACTIONS

While we have concentrated primarily on the role of learning in shaping and changing an individual's interactions with the environment, we cannot ignore the critical hereditary determinants of behavior. Since ancient times scholars have been asking: "which contributes more to human behavior—heredity or environment?" The question is the core of the long-lasting controversy between the proponents of **nativism** and **empiricism.** Historically, the extreme nativist position held that most behavioral tendencies are innate, inborn—in effect, that they are "wired into" the organism as part of its biological makeup. In contrast, empiricists viewed behavior as resulting almost entirely from training, learning, and past experience; they minimized the constraints imposed by heredity.

Few contemporary psychologists adhere to either of these extreme positions. Instead, most accept the view that an individual's behavior is the outcome of *complex interactions* between his or her hereditary potentials (nature) and experiential and environmental factors (nurture).

We can of course ask whether heredity or environment contributes more to specific characteristics or *traits,* such as height, intelligence, or activity level. But in most cases the interactions between heredity-environment forces are so complex that it is virtually impossible to disentangle their separate con-

Identical twins are often used as subjects in studies of the relative influences of heredity and environment on behavior.

tributions. Certainly individual differences in height and in activity level are attributable in large part to heredity. But an individual's height is also influenced by nutritional, as well as genetic, factors. Similarly, a person's activity level is strongly influenced by the environment in which he or she grows up. In more complex, psychological phenomena, such as intelligence, it is even more difficult to separate the influences of heredity and environment (*see* pp. 310–14).

SUMMARY

The field of psychology is continually expanding and undergoing redefinition. To give substance to the general definition—"Psychology is the scientific study of behavior"—each part of the book depicts one part of the range of psychologists' activities and the results of these activities.

A useful but admittedly arbitrary distinction may be drawn between *basic* and *applied* psychology. The discovery of fundamental facts and principles is considered basic. Applied psychologists use these facts and principles to accomplish practical goals, such as educating children or helping people to adjust more effectively.

The research psychologist often begins by posing significant questions about behavior, which are then formulated as specific **hypotheses**. Each term in the hypothesis must be **operationally defined** as an observable response or measurement. In an experimental test of the hypothesis, the psychologist manipulates the **independent variable** and systematically measures its effect on another, **dependent variable.** Subjects (participants) in an experiment are typically assigned randomly to an **experimental group** or a **control** (comparison) **group.** Differences between groups are then tested to ascertain whether they are *statistically significant*.

In addition to the experiment, other systematic studies add to our knowledge of behavior. These include observations of naturally occuring behavior, correlational studies, surveys, and case histories. The **coefficient of correlation** expresses the degree of relationship between two variables; it ranges from 0.00 (no relationship) to 1.00 (perfect relationship) and can be positive or negative.

Caution must be used in generalizing psychological research findings from one group of subjects to another (for example, from rats to humans or from members of one human group to members of another) or from one situation to another (from a labotory to a school). Where **interaction** exists, the same situation affects different people in different ways; so to predict behavior, you need information about both the situation and the individual.

The ethical psychologist is concerned with the welfare and rights of the research subject. Moreover, he or she must always be alert to the possibility that research findings may be improperly used and take precautions against such misuse.

We begin our study of the content of psychology with six key concepts: **motivation, information processing, learning, reinforcement, feedback,** and **heredity-environment interactions.** Each of these concepts is important in many areas of psychology; you will encounter them frequently in subsequent parts of the text.

RECOMMENDED READING

SELECTED BOOKS

American Psychological Association. *A Career in Psychology*. Washington: American Psychological Association, 1970.
Descriptions of the major basic and applied fields of psychology, together with information about the training required to become a professional psychologist.

HARDYCK, C. D., & PETRINOVICH, L. F. *Introduction to Statistics for the Behavioral Sciences*. Text edition. Philadelphia: Saunders, 1975.
A sound, easy-to-understand presentation of the basic concepts and methods of statistics, as applied to psychological research.

MILLER, G. A., & BUCKHOUT, R. *Psychology: The Science of Mental Life*. 2nd ed. New York: Harper & Row, 1973.
A short, readable book that presents some of the main currents of psychology in terms of the work of such pioneers as William James, Sigmund Freud, Francis Galton, Alfred Binet, and Ivan Pavlov.

NORDBY, V. J., & HALL, C. S. *A Guide to Psychologists and Their Concepts*. San Francisco: W. H. Freeman & Co., 1974. Paperback.
Brief biographies of forty-two influential psychologists and succinct statements about their main concepts and contributions.

Psychology in Progress: Readings from Scientific American. San Francisco: W. H. Freeman and Company, 1975.
A panorama of recent research in psychology in the form of thirty-nine articles reprinted from *Scientific American*. Each of the five sections has an introduction by psychologist Richard C. Atkinson. The book also contains a study guide.

WERTHEIMER, MICHAEL. *A Brief History of Psychology*. New York: Holt, Rinehart & Winston, 1970. Paperback.
A quick overview of the history of psychology—its main currents and contributors.

PERIODIC PUBLICATIONS.

These regularly appearing sources provide information about current research and theory.

Annual Review of Psychology. Palo Alto, Calif.: Annual Reviews, Inc.
Chapters by experts survey and evaluate research in all the main areas of psychology. Some subjects are reviewed annually; others appear every few years. There are also special chapters devoted to timely topics that are not included in the *Review*'s master subject list.

Psychological Abstracts. Washington, D.C.: American Psychological Association.
Every book or article published in psychology is described in a paragraph. Issues appear monthly, with an index every six months. Using the index, you can locate research on almost any topic in psychology.

Dance, 1909, by Henri Matisse. Collection, The Museum of Modern Art, New York.

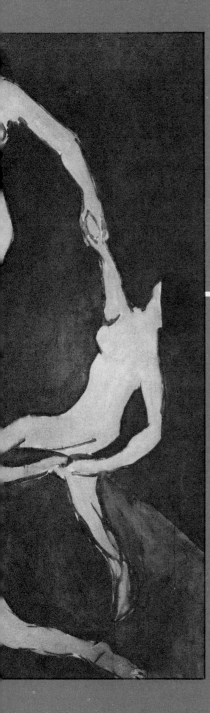

PART TWO

Social Psychology

By Elliot Aronson

A few years ago the United States was engaged in a tragic war in Vietnam, a war that divided the nation. Sometime during that period, I hired a young man to help me repaint my house. He was a Vietnam veteran who had recently returned to civilian life and taken up the craft of housepainting. I enjoyed working with him; he was friendly, honest, industrious, and proud of his work. One day, during a coffee break, we were chatting about the war. I made the point that a great number of innocent people—men, women, and children, in South Vietnam as well as in North Vietnam—were being slaughtered. His answer was given without apparent anger or vindictiveness. Indeed, it was stated in a mild and matter-of-fact tone, and it chilled me to the bone. He said, "Hell, Doc, those aren't people, those are Vietnamese." Further probing convinced me that this was no mere figure of speech; the house painter firmly believed that the Vietnamese were less human than he or I.

How did the young veteran acquire such an attitude? What is it based on? What function does it serve for him? How basic or permanent is it? How does it affect and how is it affected by his behavior? Can such an attitude be changed? How?

These questions—and their tentative answers—constitute much of the subject matter of *social psychology*. Along with related ones—Is a systematic attempt to change attitudes desirable? Is it ethical?—they are among the most important issues facing society today. In this part we will review some of the research data that have a bearing on the answers we give to these crucial questions. But—because the specialty of social psychology is a young and rapidly growing science—we have not yet found definitive answers to these questions. In part, it is the quest for these answers that makes the field so exciting.

There are many ways of defining social psychology. On a very general level, it has been described as the study of a person's relationship with the rest of humanity. This definition makes sense and has a touch of poetry in it. But a moment's reflection reveals that as a definition it is at once too broad and too narrow. It is too broad in the sense that the word "relationship" covers a multitude of qualitatively different associations, from the love between a husband and wife to the obedience of an army recruit to a sergeant's commands. It is too narrow in the sense that social psychological phenomena are not limited to *Homo sapiens;* for, while human beings are decidedly social animals, many other species are not less so.

Therefore, to provide a more systematic and functional definition of social psychology, it might be useful to mention the kinds of problems social psychologists commonly investigate. These include such diverse topics as conformity, communication, aggression, prejudice, human attraction, opinion change, leadership, group dynamics, and propaganda. The topics are diverse, but they have one common factor: they all involve *social influence*—one

individual influencing the perception, opinions, or behavior of another. For humans, the simple fact that other people exist is profoundly important, for no one is immune to the influence of others.

On an obvious level we see that a devoted husband is influenced by the wishes of his wife, that an obedient young child is influenced by a mother's demands, and a timid bureaucrat is influenced by specific orders from his or her superior. On a more subtle level, however, we would point out that the mother is also influenced by her young child and that even such apparently "antisocial" people as revolutionaries are influenced by the system they are attempting to overturn. Even a hermit living in a secluded cave is influenced by prior associations with people.

It is clear that none of us escapes the effects of social influence, and images of revolutionaries and hermits do not dominate the thinking of social psychologists as they study the influence process. We are more frequently concerned with the individual yielding to the explicit pressure of the mass media or to the implicit or explicit pressure of a culture or subgroup. In short, social psychologists think about social influence in the form of communication, persuasion and conformity. It is to these topics that we now turn.

37

Social Influence: Communication, Persuasion, and Conformity

Are people aware of communications?
What is the difference between attitudes and opinions?
Is it possible to change attitudes through communication?
What is conformity?
Mob violence—Is it conformity or deindividuation?

Are people aware of communications?

We live in an age characterized by a communication barrage in which serious and almost continuous attempts are made to influence our opinions, attitudes, and behavior. Political candidates make speeches in an effort to win our votes; manufacturers of consumer goods spend vast amounts of money on television commercials and magazine layouts in an attempt to induce us to buy their products; films are shown in public schools warning us of the dangers of drug abuse. We may watch a television message sponsored by the American Cancer Society telling us why we should "kick the habit" while glancing at a two-page, full-color magazine ad implying that smoking is debonair, exciting, "springtime fresh," even manly.

The efforts of the communication media can also be more subtle and less direct. A news report may focus on the violent behavior of individuals—college students, antibusing protestors, or policemen. "Action," makes after all, more exciting viewing than a verbal description of people behaving in an orderly manner. A preponderance of such news items might influence viewers to believe that almost everyone is behaving violently these days; people may, accordingly, be unduly depressed about the temper of the times or the state of the nation. Their voting behavior, their willingness to contribute money to an alma mater, even their desire to visit major cities may be affected. In the aftermath of the Watergate scandal, a similar affect was evident when the media focused a great deal of attention on illegal actions by such government agencies as the CIA and the FBI. These revelations seemed to produce a sense of helplessness and apathy among vast numbers of people. Thus, because it has become such an ubiquitous and powerful influence, television has raised serious political and moral problems. For example, the days have long since passed when a candidate for a major political office could wage a winning campaign on a shoestring, relying on whistlestops and personal appearances. To be effective, he or she must buy television time—an expensive commodity. In the past, substantial political advantages were enjoyed by candidates with great personal wealth or rich supporters. Recently, the abuses of the system have led to corrective legislation, although it is not yet clear how effective it will be.

The above problems are indeed provocative, but, unfortunately, they extend beyond the scope of this chapter. We mention them only to suggest some of the important practical ramifications of the communication process. In these next four chapters we will confine ourselves to a discussion of the major factors involved in attitude formation, attitude change, and resistance to attitude change.

What is the difference between attitudes and opinions?

What do we mean by an *attitude?* Most people use the terms "attitude" and "opinion" interchangeably. There are, in fact, real and important differences between them. In the simplest sense, an *opinion* is what the individual believes to be a fact. For example, it is my opinion that Mexico City is about a mile-and-a-half above sea level and that the summer temperatures are higher in Austin, Texas, than in Santa Cruz, California. Opinions are transient and cognitive—"transient" meaning that they can be changed in the face of evidence to the contrary, and "cognitive" meaning that they are a product of mental rather than emotional processes.

An **attitude** is more enduring and complex. It consists of three components: a cognitive component, an emotional component, and a disposition toward action. An attitude is usually judgmental or evaluative. If we say that a woman has a positive attitude toward sensitive men, we usually mean that she has some opinions (cognitive component) about them that are favorable, that she is happy in their presence (emotional component), and that she is likely to associate with them whenever possible (action component). If a man has a negative attitude toward Jews, chances are that his description of them will be less than complimentary. He will be sullen, uncomfortable or angry in their presence, and probably he will not vote for a political candidate who is Jewish. An attitude, thus, is more complex than an opinion; but sometimes the distinction is not easy to draw. A person may believe, for example, that blacks tend to be taller than Caucasians. The belief may or may not be accurate, but that does not concern us here. The question is whether or not it has an emotional or evaluative component and whether it implies action. In the above example, it seems unlikely—thus the belief is a simple opinion. However, if he or she made the statement in the midst of a discussion of why blacks excel as basketball players, it could be part of a negative attitude toward blacks. Going one step further, if a person holds that blacks are shiftless, or that Jews are money-grubbers, or that Orientals are sneaky, it is reasonable to assume that implicit in these opinions is a negative attitude toward the group in question.

As mentioned earlier, simple opinions are relatively easy to change. If some people believe American blacks are taller than Caucasians and someone presents scientific evidence to the contrary, they will probably change their opinion. An opinion that represents the cognitive aspect of an attitude, however, is much more resistant to change, even though the specific opinion *can* be changed by absolutely irrefutable evidence. For example, a person might have a negative attitude toward Native Americans that is bolstered, in part, by the belief that they are inherently stupid and uncivilized. If shown documentary evidence that Native Americans who grow up under favorable environmental conditions are as intelligent and refined as other people, he or she may change this specific opinion (although not easily). At the same time, it is important to note that opinion change may have very little effect on a person's overall negative attitude. Attitudes—because of their emotional component—are not easy to change.

Initial opinions and attitudes are probably learned much as other behaviors and habits are. (Learning is discussed in Ch. 14.) A young child may develop a negative attitude toward excessive drinking after being exposed to an alcoholic father whose behavior within the family is destructive and abusive. Less directly, a child may learn that crime does not pay by seeing television programs that depict criminals as unsavory characters who come to a bad end.

Who is persuading whom?

How do social psychologists measure attitudes on a specific question? Basically, it is a matter of inducing a person to reveal his or her feelings about an issue; but it is not quite that simple. The question must be unambiguously phrased and presented in such a way that the answers can be quantified. Suppose, for example, that we ask someone: "How do you feel about drugs?" This is an example of poor phrasing for several reasons. First, what are "drugs"? Marijuana? Heroin? Aspirin? Penicillin? Second, "feel" is ambiguous. Does it mean "Do I enjoy them?" "Do I think they're dangerous?" "Do I think they're useful?" Finally, if one person answers with the word "enthusiastic" and another person with the words "awfully good," which person has the stronger attitude?

The question could be improved by the following rendering: "Do you agree or disagree with the following statement: Marijuana should be legalized?" This would give us a fairly accurate idea of attitudes toward the legalization of marijuana. A more precise technique, developed by Likert (1932), is designed to provide finer gradations. For example:

Q. *Circle a number which best represents your agreement with the following statement: Marijuana should be legalized.*

1) *strongly agree*
2) *agree*
3) *undecided*
4) *disagree*
5) *strongly disagree*

One could pose a number of assertions about marijuana on the same questionnaire (such as, "marijuana is injurious to the health," "this would be a better place if marijuana were freely available"). By summing up an individual's responses to these items, the investigator could derive a fairly precise index of that person's general views on marijuana and compare them to those of other people.

The type of scale developed by Likert is only one way of measuring attitudes. We will mention one more scale —"the social distance scale" invented by Bogardus (1925). It measures people's attitudes toward ethnic, racial, or religious groups by asking them to indicate how close they would permit people of a particular group to come. The degrees are as follows:

1) To close kinship by marriage
2) To my club as personal chums
3) To my street as neighbors
4) To employment in my occupation in my country
5) To citizenship in my country
6) As visitors only to my country
7) Would exclude from my country

Thus, if a person rated Chinese as 5, he would be considered to have a more "distant" attitude toward them than a person who rated them 3. Looking at it a different way, if a large group of people rated Chinese at an average of 4.3 and Germans at 1.9, one could conclude that this group prefers Germans to Chinese.

Guttman (1944) generalized this scale so that it can be used to measure other factors. For example, one could use this kind of scale to measure sexual behavior by presenting a list of sexual practices—from hand holding at one end, through kissing and petting, and intercourse, anchoring the other end with some esoteric sexual practice. The key attribute of this type of scale is that, for the most part, if a person agrees to item 4 (for example), you can determine how he or she feels on all preceding items. A person who would not want to allow Chinese to be employed in this country would obviously not admit them to close kinship by marriage; a person who did not go along with passionate petting would probably also steer clear of sexual intercourse.

It should be noted that one limitation with all these rating scales is that the intervals are *not equal;* that is, we have no way of knowing whether the attitude of a person whose score is 4 is the same distance from 3 as the person whose attitude is 2. Thus, we cannot accept the statement that Person A is so much higher than Person B in any absolute sense. We are limited to an analysis of the *relative* strengths of attitudes. For most research purposes, however, this is an adequate measure.

But what of the child of the slums who sees on the streets impressive, cool characters with big cars and beautiful clothes who make book or push drugs? For this child, the pushers are living documentation that crime not only pays, it pays well. Of course, as we shall see, the process of attitude formation and change is more complicated than this. Not all of the information we are exposed to is consistent; thus, on mother's knee, a child may learn negative attitudes toward black people but end up cheering the incredible athletic exploits of Rod Carew or O. J. Simpson.

Is it possible to change attitudes through communication?

Let us look at the relationship between attitudes and communication in more detail. What is the best way to influence attitudes through communication? Suppose social psychologists were concocting a communication to convince the veteran-house painter that Vietnamese people are human and should be treated with the same respect and dignity as Americans. How would they do it? First, they would consider the three classes of communication variables that are of utmost importance in attitude change. They are—(1) the source of the communication (who says it); (2) the nature of the communication (how it is said); and (3) the characteristics of the audience (to whom it is said).

THE SOURCE OF THE COMMUNICATION

One of the most pervasive advertising ploys involves the endorsement of a product by a famous person, an individual with prestige. Indeed, it is difficult to turn on the television set without finding an athlete endorsing a shaving cream, a movie starlet raving about a soap, or, alas, an aging actor discussing some tonic guaranteed to revive "tired blood." One can conclude that advertisers have an implicit theory: the source of a communication plays an important role in attitude change.

A "Trustworthy" Communicator

This is, of course, not a recent theory. Some two thousand years ago Aristotle, in his classic work on communication, *Rhetoric,* indicated that "we believe good men more fully and more readily than others." Aristotle's conjecture was systematized and subjected to scientific scrutiny in a series of experiments by Carl Hovland, perhaps psychology's most innovative investigator in the area of communication and persuasion. In one experiment (Hovland & Weiss, 1951), people were exposed to identical communications on a variety of topics. For example, one of the messages used in this experiment argued that nuclear-powered submarines were feasible. (The study was done in 1951, when there was still great doubt about the practicality of such submarines.) Some members of the audience were told that the message came from a source having high prestige, J. Robert Oppenheimer, the renowned physicist. To others, it was attributed to a source having relatively low prestige, the Soviet newspaper *Pravda*—a publication of dubious credibility. The important fact to bear in mind is that, in this experiment, the *content* of the communication was the same for all subjects: only the identification of the source of the communication was changed. The opinions of the audience were measured both

TABLE 2-1 Net changes of opinion as a function of the trustworthiness of the source of the communication

Topic	Net Change (percentage)	
	Trustworthy source	Untrustworthy source
1. Are atomic-powered submarines feasible?	36.0	0
2. Should antihistamines be sold without a prescription?	25.5	11.1

Adapted from C. I. Hovland & W. Weiss, "The Influence of Source Credibility on Communication Effectiveness." *Public Opinion Quarterly,* 1951, *15,* 635–50.

before and after they were exposed to the communication. The results were clear-cut. Far more opinion change was produced by Oppenheimer than by *Pravda.* The same basic results were obtained for other topics and different "trustworthy" or "untrustworthy" communicators, as shown in Table 2-1.

Before concluding that high-prestige communicators *always* have a great effect on attitudes, let us take a closer look at the situation. What is meant by "prestige"? Most researchers in this area have defined it as a combination of expertise and trustworthiness. Clearly, J. Robert Oppenheimer fits into this classification; he was an expert physicist and generally regarded as an honest and decent man. He seemed to fit perfectly Aristotle's term a "good" man. But what does a linebacker know about shaving cream that qualifies him as an expert? Not very much. Moreover, in television commercials, the trustworthiness of a communicator may be called into question. Most people, if they thought about it, would probably conclude that a person endorses a product for personal financial gain. The key phrase in the last sentence may be *"if they thought about it."* Commercial endorsements may have an effect on people because they do not always think about the intentions of the communicator. In most situations, they probably attribute good intentions to other people unless there is some evidence to the contrary.

Communicators as Subtle Persuaders

So we have raised two serious questions: First, must a person be an expert on an issue in order to have a great effect on people's opinions? What does a linebacker know about shaving cream? Perhaps any attractive person—such as a movie star or a talented athlete—can influence us. Second, are the intentions of the communicator important? If the selfish intentions of an otherwise attractive figure are made clear, does this decrease his or her effectiveness? On the other hand, if an unattractive communicator is shown to have no ulterior motive for endorsing a given position, does this increase that person's effectiveness?

Let us look at the second question first. How important to the audience are the apparent intentions of the communicator? In one experiment (Walster, Aronson, & Abrahams, 1966) it was dramatically demonstrated that a "bad" man (a convicted criminal) could be at least as persuasive as a respected public official if the criminal had nothing to gain by convincing his audience. Half the members of an audience were presented with a newspaper clipping that included a strong argument that the police and courts should be given more

Which of the two speakers would be more effective in persuading you? Why?

power. The other half of the audience received a clipping arguing the reverse —that police and courts had too much power and that the rights of the accused needed more protection. Half of those who received each clipping were led to believe that the source of the argument was G. William Stephens. Stephens was described as a prosecuting attorney who had sent more criminals to prison than any other public prosecutor in the country. Half the people who received each clipping were led to believe that the communicator was Joe "The Shoulder" Napolitano, a convicted dope peddler.

Imagine yourself in the situation. Suppose you had read a communication by Joe "The Shoulder" saying that the laws were too tough. How would you react? Chances are you would say, "Big deal, he's only trying to protect his own interests." Accordingly, his argument would not be very convincing. Similarly, if the prosecutor were arguing for *more* court power, you might conclude that he was out to further his own personal achievement; again, you might be skeptical. But suppose Joe "The Shoulder" called for more court power, arguing against what would appear to be his own best interests? Might his effectiveness be expected to increase because he has no ulterior motives?

The results of this experiment showed that the greatest opinion change occurred when the criminal argued for *more* court power and the prosecutor argued for *less* court power. Indeed, they showed that a convicted criminal who argued for more court power even had slightly more impact than a respected public figure delivering exactly the same argument. This is a particularly striking result, which has added flavor because it calls into question Aristotle's dictum that we are more likely to believe good men than men of dubious character.

We can now turn to the first question raised above. Is it necessary for a communicator to be an expert in order to have an effect on people's opinions? Remember that most investigators in this area have indicated that expertise is a major aspect of the effectiveness of a communicator. But many advertising agencies clearly believe that expertise is unnecessary and employ athletes to endorse such products as shaving cream, razor blades, and hair tonics. While it may be argued that athletes, by dint of their profession, know more than the average person about physical conditioning, proper diet, and

A celebrity does not need to be an "expert" to be a good communicator.

perhaps even treatment of athlete's foot, it is hard to believe that they are more expert than most other men about razor blades.

The experimental evidence indicates that advertising men are not wasting their money: people do tend to be influenced by people they like, admire, or consider attractive, even if the communicators are not experts. One experiment (Mills & Aronson, 1965) demonstrated that a beautiful young woman who spoke to an audience of male undergraduates was more effective in changing their opinions about the topic—specialized education—than the same woman made up to appear physically unattractive. It should be clear that beautiful women are generally not more expert on education than unattractive ones. Why, then, were more young men influenced by her when she looked pretty? They were not trying to please her, for they knew that the speaker would never see the questionnaires they filled out after her speech. There is strong evidence to suggest that they were more influenced by the attractive person simply because she was attractive. They liked her and therefore wanted to be in agreement with her on an issue she considered important.

It should be noted that this phenomenon may be limited to issues that are not of earthshaking importance. That is, if a man needs a shaving cream, it really does not matter whether he buys brand "X" or brand "Y"—so he may go along with Joe Namath or Hank Aaron! But, if the athletes were endorsing a particular political policy in the Middle East, they would probably be less effective. Similarly, a young woman—no matter how beautiful—would probably find it impossible to convince young male members of the campus conservative club to actively support her liberal candidate for president.

THE NATURE OF THE COMMUNICATION

We have discussed the importance of the source of a communication to its effectiveness. We will now turn to the communication itself. There are several ways in which communications can differ from each other. Consider these three important questions:

1. Is it preferable to present *both sides* of an argument or only the one being championed?

2. When two sides are presented, as in a debate or courtroom summation, does the *order of presentation* have an effect?

3. Finally, how does the *discrepancy* between the audience's original opinion and the opinion advocated by the communication affect opinion change?

One-Sided vs. Two-Sided Presentations

one-sided

two-sided

Suppose you are attempting to convince an individual or group that your beliefs on an issue are the right ones. All other things being equal, would it be more effective to present only the one side of the issue you favor, or both sides of the argument? This is a simple question, but it does not have a simple answer. Whether or not a two-sided argument is more effective depends on some important characteristics of the audience—specifically, their intelligence and initial opinion. Several experiments have shown that a one-sided argument is most effective when delivered to relatively unintelligent or poorly informed people—or to people who already agree with your position. For example, at a political fund-raising dinner, the listeners—all of them allied with the party giving the dinner—seem deeply moved by and appreciative of the "give 'em hell," one-sided approach associated with such politicians as Harry Truman. On the other hand, if people are on the fence and generally well-informed, and intelligent, they are often aware that there is more than one side to the issue; such people tend to resist one-sided presentations. To convince them, a two-sided argument has been shown to be more effective.

The Order of Presentation

Suppose you are engaged in a public debate: would it be to your advantage to state your case first or last? This is a vital question with important ramifications throughout society. For example, in a court of law, the defense summarizes its case first, followed by the attorney for the plaintiff. Does either

If you were the speaker, would you use a one-sided or a two-sided presentation with this audience?

Spotlight 2-2   Attitude Change

To determine attitude change, social psychologists frequently measure the attitudes of their subjects just *before* the experimental treatment and then, once again, immediately *after* treatment. Any change in attitude can then be safely attributed to the treatment—to the nature of the communication, the prestige of the communicator, or whatever.

This technique has the virtue of immediacy. Suppose a researcher measures a person's attitude on September 27, 1976, at 3:00 P.M. At 3:05 P.M. the subject is exposed to a fifteen-minute communication that attempts to change his or her attitude. At 3:20 P.M. the attitude is measured again. Under these circumstances, the researcher can be reasonably certain that any attitude change is due to the communication, since few, if any, other pertinent events had intervened between the two measures.

There are problems, however. The initial measurement *itself* may have some effect on the subject, and the influence might show up in the second measurement—after the communication. In addition, many people value consistency so highly that they may be reluctant to let the experimenter know their attitudes have changed. Even

though the communication has influenced them, they may respond as if it has not.

There are many ways to avoid this problem. The simplest is to test subjects' attitudes several weeks prior to the experiment; this is most effective when attitude measures are embedded in a much longer questionnaire on a variety of topics. By the time subjects' attitudes on the crucial issue are measured again—after being exposed to the communication—initial attitudes will be less salient and may even be forgotten.

Of course, if several weeks elapse between the pre- and post-experimental measures, other events may have modified the subjects' attitudes. The researcher cannot know if change is due to experimental manipulation on to these outside events. Appropriate control conditions can be used to avoid this problem, however. For example, in an experiment in which a researcher is interested in a particular effect—such as the influence of the communicator's prestige—two groups are used. If one group is exposed to a high-prestige source and another to a low-prestige source, an outside event might affect both groups; but the *relative* difference would still reflect the impact of the experimental variable.

---

lawyer have the advantage merely as a result of the order of presentation? One of the country's most successful trial lawyers, Louis Nizer (1961), contends that lawyers for the plaintiff have a decided advantage; by summing up last they get a chance to criticize their opponents' arguments.

The situation, however, is more complex than Nizer's observation would suggest. While appearing last does give the speaker a chance to criticize an opponent's argument, speaking first may have the advantage if a person's first impression is the dominant one. Social psychologists refer to this as the **primacy effect.** It can also be argued that, under some circumstances, the last speaker has a greater effect. This is not only because, as Nizer believes, the opportunity to criticize the opponent's argument is crucial but also because the last piece of information heard by the listener remains more vivid and is therefore more effective than earlier communications. This phenomenon has been labeled the **recency effect.**

What evidence has research into the subject compiled? One of the crucial determinants of whether a primacy effect (first argument more effective) or a recency effect is more powerful is *time:* specifically, (1) the length of time that elapses between the first and second communication; or (2) the time between the end of the second communication and the assessment of opinion. Suppose that the first argument is stated and is immediately followed by the second argument. Suppose further that the opinion of the audience is measured immediately after the second one. Will there be much difference in the memory the listener has of the first and second arguments? Probably not, for the time factor is minimized. There should be no advantage to giving either the first or second argument. Similarly, there should be no advantage to either primacy or recency if both communications were given fairly long ago, so that both are approximately equally forgotten by the time the opinion is measured. About one week qualifies as "fairly long ago" in this case; but there must be a week, not only following the second communication, but also *between* the first and second communications. Otherwise the results will be different, as we shall see.

What if a person hears the first argument, a week passes before the second argument is heard, and his or her attitude is measured immediately afterward? We would expect to find a substantial recency effect because the second argument would be much more vivid. The research evidence supports the expectation. In one representative study, subjects (the "audience") were presented with condensed versions of the transcript of an actual jury trial (Miller & Campbell, 1959). Each side of the argument consisted of both witness testimony and speeches by an attorney. In the experiment, all the pro-plaintiff material was presented in one block and all the pro-defendant material in another. In a real trial, of course, information is not so conveniently arranged, especially not the testimony of witnesses.

There is one set of conditions included in this experiment that remains to be discussed; and this arrangement is perhaps the most interesting of all because it includes the most common circumstances in an actual jury trial. In this situation, the first argument is presented, followed immediately by the second argument. A week is then allowed to elapse, and then the "jury's" attitude is measured. This condition produced a significant primacy effect — that is, the first argument swayed more people than the second. Thus, when little or no time elapses between the first and second arguments, the first has an advantage. Why? Probably because the first argument people hear is the one they tend to believe more. Moreover, although the effect does not show up immediately, as memory begins to decline, the tendency becomes more and more prominent. This is particularly interesting, not only because it is a typical situation but also because it places the plaintiff at a disadvantage — contrary to the belief of Mr. Nizer, an experienced trial lawyer.

The Size of the Discrepancy Suppose a counselor at a boys camp sees that all the kids in camp are hooked on a new soft drink called "Super-cola." They each consume eight bottles of the vile stuff a day. Suppose further that the counselor is convinced that the drink is injurious to their health. Ideally, he would like them to abstain completely, but he would feel somewhat better if they cut back to four or five bottles a day. Would he have a greater chance of influencing their attitude and behavior if he argued that Super-cola is poisonous and that people shouldn't drink any of it, or would it be more effective to argue that too much Super-cola can be harmful and that one should not drink more than four or five bottles per day? This is an issue every communicator must come to terms with. In attempting to change attitudes, is there an optimal level of discrepancy

In the 1950s, Senator Joseph McCarthy frequently derogated his opponents by questioning their loyalty.

between the attitudes of the audience and the position advocated by the communicator?

Why do people change their attitudes anyway? We have suggested several reasons, and we will be discussing this issue in even greater detail in the next chapter. For now, let us make the general statement that when a person discovers that someone else feels differently from the way he or she feels, it produces a feeling of discomfort—which produces, in turn, a strain directed toward change. It would seem to follow, then, that the greater the discrepancy, the more intense this strain; and the more intense the strain, the greater the tendency to change attitudes. Indeed, several studies show a simple positive relationship between discrepancy and attitude change (Hovland & Pritzker, 1957). Other studies, however, show a more complex trend; attitude change increased as discrepancy increased, but only up to a point. As the discrepancy became very large, there was less attitude change than with a moderate degree of discrepancy (Hovland, Harvey, & Sherif, 1957).

What accounts for these conflicting results? When results of different studies conflict, it is usually an indication that not all the important variables are being taken into account. With this in mind, a group of psychologists (Aronson, Turner, & Carlsmith, 1963) formulated the following speculation: When people learn that their position is in disagreement with a communicator's, they do experience discomfort; but changing the attitude is only one of several possible ways to relieve the discomfort. An interesting alternative might be to derogate the communicator—that is, to convince oneself that the communicator is stupid, misinformed, or dishonest. Moreover, the more discrepant the communicator's position, the more likely it is that the recipient would derogate him. For example, if I drank eight Super-colas a day and you advised me that more than five was unhealthful, this might not seem too unreasonable. But if you told me that even one bottle a day was bad for my health, this view would be so different from my own that I would probably dismiss the warning as that of a health nut. Accordingly, I might not change my attitude at all. Why should I let myself be persuaded by a health nut?

This sounds like a fairly reasonable speculation, but how can we be certain it is correct? The psychologists carried their speculation further. They hypothesized that, instead of changing their attitudes, in high-discrepancy situations people have a tendency to derogate the communicator. One way to prevent this outcome would be to use a communicator whose wisdom, expertise, and trustworthiness is beyond refute. It would be very difficult to belittle such a person; and therefore, even when the discrepancy is large, such a communicator would produce a high degree of attitude change. Indeed, when these psychologists looked again at the conflicting research in the area, they made an interesting discovery: <u>experiments that had demonstrated a simple and direct correlation between discrepancy and attitude change had invariably used communicators with higher prestige than those in experiments in which attitude change *decreased* when discrepancy became very high.</u>

In an effort to pin down their speculation, the psychologists investigated both degree of discrepancy and the prestige of the communicator (Aronson, Turner, & Carlsmith, 1963). Subjects (college students) read a statement in which a person expressed opinions about a poem—opinions that were slightly discrepant, moderately discrepant, or extremely discrepant from their own previously measured opinions. When the discrepant opinion was attributed to T. S. Eliot (high prestige), maximum opinion change occurred where the discrepancy was greatest. When the discrepant opinion was attributed to a fellow college student (moderate prestige), maximum change occurred when the discrepancy was moderate and decreased when the discrepancy was greater. Figure 2-1 presents these results in graphic form, along with the theoretical results that could be predicted with a *perfectly* credible or incredible communicator.

[handwritten margin note: high and low prestige vs. discrepancy]

Figure 2-1
Opinion Change as a Function of Credibility and Extent of Discrepancy
Both theoretical and observed curves are indicated. (From Aronson, Turner, & Carlsmith, 1963)

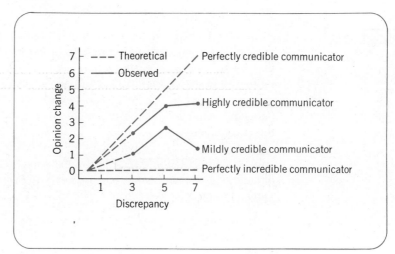

The Effects of Familiarity

There is an old adage that "familiarity breeds contempt." And yet, manufacturers of toothpaste, detergent, and headache remedies continue to bombard us with repetitious commercials in an obvious attempt to make *Colgate, Tide,* and *Bayer* household words. Can the old adage be false? Apparently it is. In a series of well-controlled experiments (Zajonc, 1968), individuals repeatedly exposed to stimuli formed increasingly positive attitudes toward them. This conclusion applies to such stimuli as nonsense syllables, unfamiliar music, unusual color combinations, pictures of faces and — by implication — *Colgate, Tide,* and *Bayer.*

CHARACTERISTICS OF THE AUDIENCE

The third variable of importance in attitude change is the fact that not all listeners or readers or viewers are alike. Some people are easier to persuade than others. Moreover, the kind of communication that appeals to one person may not appeal to another. We have already seen, for example, that the intelligence of members of the audience, as well as their prior opinion, will determine whether a two-sided communication or a one-sided communication will be more effective.

There are a few other factors that play a role. For example, in experimental situations women change their attitudes more readily than men. This parallels the finding that women are more prone than men to conform to group pressure. Both results may be due to the fact that most women in our society have been encouraged to be more submissive and less skeptical than men. If this is the case, we should soon witness a change in the data as women move increasingly away from traditional passive roles.

Amount of Self-Esteem

The most thoroughly investigated personality variable relating to attitude change is **self-esteem.** An individual who feels inadequate as a person is more easily influenced by a persuasive communication than one with high self-esteem (Janis & Field, 1959). This makes good sense. After all, if people do not think very highly of themselves, it follows that they don't have a high premium on their own ideas. Consequently, if these ideas are challenged, even by someone whose prestige is not terribly high, they may not be reluctant to give them up. For individuals with low self-esteem, a communicator's prestige will appear high relative to their own.

The Inoculation Effect

People's past experiences, what they have heard in the past, influence how they will respond to new experiences or communications. It has been shown that by making a mild attack upon certain established beliefs and then refuting the points of the attack, the beliefs seem to become able to withstand stronger attacks (McGuire & Papageorgis, 1961). When exposed to a full-fledged threat, the tendency of people to resist changing their attitudes parallels the reaction that occurs when a small amount of a virus has immunized a patient against a full-blown attack by that virus. This phenomenon has been called the **inoculation effect.** In this experiment a group of people stated their attitudes on several health issues. They were asked to rate the extent of their agreement or disagreement with the following statements (p. 330):

1) *Everyone should get a chest X-ray each year in order to detect any possible tuberculosis symptoms at an early stage.*
2) *The effects of penicillin have been, almost without exception, of great benefit to mankind.*

3) *Most forms of mental illness are not contagious.*
4) *Everyone should brush his teeth after every meal if at all possible.*

Their attitudes were then subjected to mild arguments which were then refuted. The same people were then subjected to a powerful attack on their initial attitudes. Members of this group showed a much smaller tendency to change their attitudes than members of a control group whose attitudes had not been previously subjected to the mild attack. In effect, they had been inoculated against attitude change. Not only is it more effective as a propaganda technique to use a two-sided refutational presentation, but—if used skillfully—such a presentation tends to increase the audience's resistance to subsequent propaganda.

STUART LEEDS

Commitment

The degree of commitment an individual feels toward a position also affects how readily he or she can be persuaded to comply with a request. If you want to persuade a person to undertake a difficult or unpleasant job, therefore, you would be wise to begin by getting a commitment to a small aspect of that job. This technique is referred to as "the foot in the door" (Freedman & Fraser, 1966). Obtaining someone's compliance with a small request substantially increases the likelihood that he or she will agree to a subsequent, larger request. In their research, Freedman and Fraser (1966) first tried to convince people to allow them to place a huge unsightly sign—reading "DRIVE CAREFULLY,"—in front of their house. Only 17 percent of the people complied with the request. But, using the "foot in the door" technique, 55 percent of a comparable sample of homeowners were persuaded to agree to the request to put up the ugly sign. The latter group was first induced to agree to a small request—to support a safe-driving campaign by simply signing a petition. A few weeks later, the same homeowners were asked if they would allow the sign to be put on their lawn, and many agreed. Apparently, they found it difficult to refuse, since they had already complied with a smaller request and thus made a commitment to safe driving.

Reciprocal Concessions

Another effective technique to persuade someone to do a difficult job or comply with a request is just the opposite of the "foot-in-the-door" method. Compliance is induced by first making an extreme request, which is sure to be rejected, then following it with a more moderate request—the one desired from the outset (Cialdini et al., 1975). The technique has been labelled reciprocal concessions (or "door-in-the-face" technique) because both the requester and the "target person" make concessions before the latter agrees to grant the favor.

In an experimental demonstration of this technique, students at a college were approached on the campus by a student-experimenter; the young man claimed to be recruiting volunteer, nonpaid chaperones to accompany a group of children from the County Juvenile Detention Center to the zoo. Only 25 percent of those approached in this way (the control group) agreed. Another group of students were treated differently. They were first asked to serve as volunteer nonpaid counselors to work two hours a week for two years at the County Juvenile Detention Center. All of them refused. The student-experimenter then asked them if they would be interested in another program—simply chaperoning a group of boys and girls from the detention center on a trip to the zoo. It was the same as the request made to the control group. Under these circumstances, 50 percent of the students agreed to go on the trip. Clearly "making an extreme request which is sure to be rejected and then moving to a smaller request, significantly increases the probability of a target person's agreement to the second request" (Cialdini, p. 209).

Feeling Good

All other things being equal, the effectiveness of a communication is increased if the audience is in a receptive mood when you deliver it. There is a great deal of folk wisdom that makes this very point. Sales people wine and dine a prospective client before trying to sell their product or services. Traditionally, a romantically inclined male attempted to ply his young lady (the "target") with flowers or poetry before "popping the question" or "making his move." While these specific behaviors may miss the mark (especially if the "target" is unhappy with being treated like an object), research has demonstrated that the general notion is a sound one. For example, in one study (Janis et al., 1965) two groups of people were asked to read persuasive arguments on a variety of issues (such as the feasibility of reducing the size of the armed forces). The only difference between the experimental conditions was that one group was provided with a snack to eat while reading. It worked. Those who were given something to eat were more thoroughly persuaded by the arguments than those in the snackless group. Similar effects were found when pleasant music was used instead of food (Galizio and Henrick, 1972).

Application of These Findings

How do social psychologists apply these various techniques? Could they use some of them to induce the house painter who believes Vietnamese are not really people to change his mind? Why not simply construct a two-sided message that is widely discrepant from his own position, attribute it to a high-prestige source, then sit back and wait for the transformation? Alas, it is not that simple. As mentioned previously, attitudes are not easy to change, for human beings are not totally objective or predictable in their manner of receiving and processing information. This fact will be elaborated upon, and some of its exciting ramifications will be discussed, in the next chapter.

What is conformity?

Thus far we have been discussing direct attempts to change attitudes and behaviors through communication. There are other forms of pressure that are often more subtle than direct, overt attempts at influence. In our society, people adapt their behavior or attitudes to fit the demands, behavior or attitudes of those around them. This is called **conformity** — a change in a person's opinions or behavior as a result of real or imagined pressure from another person or a group. In common parlance, conformity usually has some negative connotations; to be called a conformist is to be called weak, a follower, a person who cannot or will not think independently. This connotation is bolstered by the mass media. Films and television consistently make heroes of nonconformists — dashing figures who go their own way in spite of tremendous group pressure. And yet, a moment's reflection should make it clear that, if there is to be a society at all, there must be a significant degree of conformity to the laws and customs of that society. A society of nonconformists is a contradiction in terms. Conformity in certain cases may be weakness, but without a basic, underlying, and willing conformity to sensible laws and values, there would be chaos. There would not be enough policemen to protect us from the looters and the rapists. Yet, even in a society with a high degree of conformity, many people complain of the lack of law and order. But there is an interesting question on the other side too. Why is it possible to have any law and order in the first place?

must be conformity to have a society

CAUSES OF CONFORMITY

overt pressure

implicit pressure

What causes people to conform? In some instances, the answer is simple. If I held a gun to your head and told you I would blow your brains out if you did not wear a tie to dinner tonight, chances are you would conform to my wishes—even if you are a woman! Similarly, if I were to offer you $1,000 to wear a tie for one evening, you would probably conform. These punishments and rewards are unsubtle pressures. They are direct, overt, explicit, and very powerful. And various segments of our society extract conformity from us by applying just such pressures. If the garbage collector sleeps in for a few days, the garbage collector will not get paid for that time. Sleeping late for a few weeks will almost certainly mean the end of the job. Presumably, this implicit threat is what induces sanitation workers to leap out of bed at 4:00 A.M. to pick up your garbage. It is likely that they are not delighted to collect garbage but are delighted to collect a steady salary. Similarly, if a student decides not to take any exams and simply does not show up at exam time, he or she would eventually be ushered out of the university. Again, the punishment is real and severe. And, for those who want a college degree, it works—doesn't it?

But a great deal of conformity occurs as a result of much more subtle pressures that may not even be apparent. Imagine the following scene: you have volunteered to participate in an experiment on perceptual judgment. You enter a room with four other students. The experimenter shows all of you a straight line, labeled X. Simultaneously, he shows you three comparison lines, labeled A, B, and C. Your job is to judge which of the three lines is closest in length to line X (see Figure 2-2). The judgment is an incredibly easy one. It is perfectly clear to you that line B is the correct answer, but it is not your turn to respond. The man whose turn it is first looks carefully at the lines and chooses A. You sit there in disbelief. "How can he believe it's A when it's clearly B?" you say to yourself. "He must be either blind or crazy." Now it's the second person's turn to respond. This student also indicates that it's A. You are inclined to conclude that both these people are blind. But then the next person responds, and she also points to line A. You take another look at those lines—"Maybe *I'm* the one who's blind," you murmur inaudibly. Now it's the fourth person's turn and this student too judges the correct line to be line A. Finally it's your turn. "Why, it's A, of course," you murmur. "Any fool can see that!"

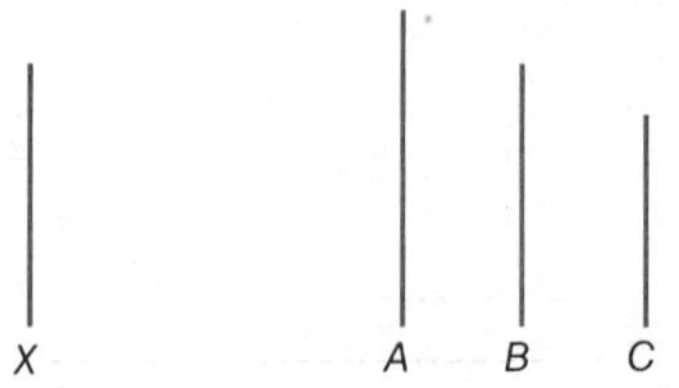

Figure 2-2
Asch Comparison "Test"
Subjects were asked to state which of the three comparison lines (A, B, or C) is equal in length to X.

X   A   B   C

You will probably disagree with my guess about what you would do, and you may be right. You might actually stand up and state your initial judgment, even in the face of unanimous opinion to the contrary. Social psychologists have no way of knowing what any specific individual would do. But we do know how *most* people would behave because the situation described above

In the Asch line-judging conformity experiment, the naive subject is puzzled by the judgments of others, but he finally decides to "call them the way I see them."

is not a nightmarish fantasy; it is very similar to a classic experimental situation designed by Solomon Asch (1951). But, you ask, how could the experimenter be so lucky as to have all those people making the wrong guess? Of course, he wasn't lucky, he was diabolical. (For a discussion of ethical constraints, see Spotlight 2-3.) In this, as in many social psychological experiments, the experimenter employed the technique of the accomplice, the confederate or "stooge." The first four people who responded were the experimenter's accomplices, who had been instructed to answer incorrectly. The purpose of the experiment was not to investigate perceptual judgment but the effects of group pressure on conformity.

When the real subjects in Asch's experiment (male college students) were not under group pressure, they always answered correctly; so it is clear that as a perceptual task the line-judging test was easy. However, when faced with several fellow students who all gave the same incorrect answers, many subjects conformed to what they perceived as implicit pressure from the group.

In reading the details of the Asch line-judging experiment, the reader may have felt a twinge of pain and empathized with the experimental subject who was being put through this procedure. Or perhaps you felt a rush of anger at the apparent callousness of the researcher. Experiments in social psychology do raise some serious ethical questions, which often hinge on the fact that individuals are deliberately manipulated, often without prior consent. Basically, there are two problems: deception and discomfort. We will illustrate these problems by using Asch's line-judging experiment as an example.

Deception. In the line-judging study the experimenter lied to the participants, telling them he was interested in testing perceptual judgment. The experimenter also implied that the other people involved were behaving honestly; they were not—they were stooges who had been instructed to behave dishonestly.

Discomfort. The experimental subjects were put into a state of conflict that was almost certain to cause them some uneasiness. If an individual succumbed to group pressure, he might feel like a coward afterward; if he resisted pressure, he might worry that he had embarrassed the other participants.

Some readers may feel that no research employing deception or causing subjects psychological discomfort should ever be done. Others may feel that the ends are so important that they justify any means. Most social psychologists take a position somewhere between these extremes and wrestle with the ethical question while perched on the horns of this dilemma.

Why *do* social psychologists lie to people and cause discomfort? Are they sadists? Probably not. The major reason is that it is frequently the best way to find the answers to important questions. For example, how does one find out about conformity? One might, of course, simply ask people if they would conform in such a situation. That has been tried, and it is easy to guess what happened. Lo and behold, few people stated that they would have yielded if placed in a situation similar to the one in Asch's experiment. Why? People have a desire to look good, and conformity is generally regarded as unattractive behavior. Few people would admit to it—perhaps not even to themselves. By the same token, if participants had been informed in advance that the experiment involved conformity, they would have been on their guard. Consequently, the results would not be generalizable to a real social situation—one in which people are faced with pressure to conform and react naturally, without being scrutinized by psychologists. By the same token, if the subjects had been told the truth

---

The term "perceived as implicit pressure" is used to refer to the subtle nature of this pressure. No one told students they had to conform. And yet, they *did* indeed conform: approximately three out of four subjects conformed on at least one trial; of the entire series of trials, 35 percent of the responses conformed to the incorrect judgment of the stooges. Thus, although it is not known how any specific person would have responded, we do know that relatively few male college students were able to resist completely the pressures to conform, at least part of the time.

CHARACTERISTICS OF CONFORMERS

Are there certain kinds of people who conform and those who do not in a situation like the line-judging experiment? Yes. The most consistent findings are that unintelligent people conform more than intelligent people, and that subjects with low self-esteem conform to a greater extent than do those with high self-esteem. In addition, data from early research indicated a strong sex difference: women conform to a greater extent than men (Allen and Crutchfield, 1963; Iscol and Williams, 1963). More recent data suggest a more complicated picture: women do tend to conform to a greater extent than men, but primarily on issues and tasks that are unfamiliar or of little interest to them

about the other people—that is, that they were stooges—the results would not have been very interesting.

Even if they decide that some questions cannot be answered without the use of experiments involving deception or discomfort, experimenters should obey certain rules. First and foremost, they should not take lightly the consequences of deception or causing discomfort. This means two things: (1) researchers should not conduct an experiment unless they are convinced of its importance; and (2) they should try to design the experiment so that a minimum of discomfort and deception is employed—consistent with a reasonable test of the hypothesis. The importance of an experiment can be evaluated by asking whether the results are worth the results of lying to people (and possibly harming one's own scientific reputation) and the price participants must pay in terms of discomfort. Since these prices are occasionally steep, experimenters should not conduct a piece of research out of idle curiosity to see what would happen.

The most important overall concern, therefore, should be the welfare of the subjects. If a particular procedure seems to be causing a great deal of discomfort, a moral experimenter will curtail the experiment. In addition, at the end of the session experimenters should spend some time with each subject, explaining the true purpose of the study, why they are interested in the problem, and why the deception was necessary. If this is done in a gentle and considerate manner, experimenters can provide participants with an educational experience as well as some insight into their own behavior. Most important, by taking the time and effort to describe the experimental situation, experimenters can relieve somewhat the discomfort that may have been caused by the procedure.

It should be noted that in most cases judgment of the acceptable degree of discomfort and deception is not left to a single experimenter. Most universities have committees of respected scholars who monitor the ethics of experiments at those schools; most of the research supported by funds of the U.S. Government must satisfy certain minimal ethical requirements; and, if all else fails, the American Psychological Association will "excommunicate" members who practice in violation of clearly stated ethical standards. (For a more complete discussion of ethical issues in social psychology, see Aronson and Carlsmith, 1969.)

(Sistrunk and McDavid, 1971). The picture that emerges is a coherent one and makes sense. People who have been encouraged to assert themselves and are successful learn to think well of themselves; consequently, they have greater resistance to group pressure. In our culture, men have been encouraged to assert themselves far more than women—at least in most endeavors. If they are intelligent, the chances are good that their judgment will be correct more often than not. People who are often correct and whose judgment is respected do tend to develop high self-esteem, which—again—helps them resist pressure to conform.

CONFORMITY AS
GROUP PRESSURE

The ramifications of the Asch experiment are not, of course, confined to the social psychological laboratory. The situation devised illustrates a subtle conformity situation—that is common in our society—one in which *explicit* group pressure is nonexistent. No one told the subjects to behave in a particular way; no one offered them bribes for responding against their initial visual judgment; nor did anyone overtly threaten to punish them if they did not comply. Each accomplice was apparently acting on his own—and collectively they created the illusion of unanimous agreement. It was this unanimity that apparently induced subjects to behave as if they were being pressured to conform to the group's judgment.

Experimental investigations of conformity to group pressure have not been limited to unimportant phenomena such as judgments of the size of a line; they have involved opinion situations and matters of fact as well. The important situational determinant of conformity in all these studies was the unanimous agreement of the majority. If everyone in the vicinity is making the same erroneous judgment (whether of the length of a line, the life expectancy of a baby born in America, or the distance between San Francisco and New York), there is a strong tendency for people to conform—even when the correct choice is obvious and unambiguous. Once the unanimity is broken, however, conformity decreases sharply.

REASONS FOR CONFORMITY

Let us take a closer look. If in the Asch situation there was no explicit punishment offered for nonconformity and no explicit reward offered for conformity, why did so many people yield to the unanimous group pressure? There are

It seems "natural" for children to copy the behavior of adults and to learn to behave in identical ways under certain circumstances. Is this behavior functional or dysfunctional?

several reasons, and these can be stated as two broad possibilities: (1) the unanimous majority managed to convince lone subjects that their perceptions were inaccurate; and (2) the rewards and punishments were implicit in the situation—that is, the lone subjects, even though they knew they were correct, changed their minds and went along with the majority in order to please them or avoid antagonizing them. In other words, they were trying to live up to the group's expectations in order to be liked or to avoid being ridiculed and disliked. One of the students in Asch's experiment subsequently expressed it this way: "I felt disturbed, puzzled, separated, like an outcast from the rest. Every time I disagreed I was beginning to wonder if I wasn't beginning to look funny" (Asch, 1952, p. 465).

Conformity Is Sensible

When we look at the "why" of conformity, the complexity of the phenomenon begins to emerge. There may be some real and important differences in the nature of the group pressures involved in various types of conformity. In some cases it seems reasonable to assume that conventions or customs develop and people conform to them because the conventions are adaptive and make sense. Driving on the right-hand side of the road makes sense—people do it not *simply* because everyone else does; but because when everyone else is driving on the right side, conformity is a good way to avoid accidents. Conformity in this example is highly adaptive. Similarly, people visiting England without knowing anything about the driving behavior of the natives, very soon begin driving on the left side. Seeing other people driving on the left convinces them that this is the custom in England and that it would be a senseless and dangerous display of individuality to do otherwise.

One can, therefore, also argue that under certain conditions it makes sense to rely on other people's judgments as a way of finding out what reality is. In an unfamiliar physical or social situation, people might look at the behaviors of others to help them determine what is going on. Suppose, for example, that you are suddenly thrust into an exotic culture you know nothing about, and you are accompanied by three anthropologists who are experts on that culture. You notice that when encountering natives wearing green turbans, all the anthropologists invariably bow deeply. It would seem reasonable for you to emulate their behavior because the anthropologists are experts in the customs of these people. You can reasonably assume that people with green turbans are nobles and that bowing to them constitutes good and reasonable behavior in that culture.

What is the difference between the group pressures in the examples of the exotic culture and England and those operating in the line-judging situation? In the former, the conformist relies on the behavior of other people as a frame of reference in an ambiguous situation; he or she receives information from reliable sources and uses it to decide what kind of behavior is right, reasonable, polite, or safe. In the line-judging situation, on the other hand, it is more likely that conformists are *knowingly* making errors but are going along in order to live up to the expectations of others and to avoid ridicule.

Conformity and Status

This distinction is pointed up by a very simple experiment by psychologists (Lefkowitz, Blake, and Mouton, 1955) who instructed an accomplice, a 31-year-old male, to walk across a busy thoroughfare against the light. Half of the time he was dressed like a bum: he wore dirty patched trousers, old scuffed shoes, and a wrinkled shirt. (This experiment was performed over 20 years ago, when such attire was more clearly a sign of low status!) The other half of the time he wore a high quality suit, shirt, tie, and shiny shoes. How many people followed the accomplice in violation of the law? When he was poorly dressed, only 4 percent of the pedestrians followed him across the street against the light. When he was well-dressed, however, more than three times as many (14 percent) broke the law in response to his lead. In this situation, there was no possibility of being rewarded or punished by the individual in question. Being thought "queer" or strange would hardly be a factor either since the people involved were in a wide-open area and were not interacting with one another; indeed, they barely paid any attention to one another. Instead, the fact that far more people conformed to the lead of the high-status person than the "bum" strongly suggests that high status implies knowledge — that is, implies that the accomplice knew what he was doing, knew that it was safe to cross there, and knew that one was unlikely to get hit by either a car or a citation. In effect, he was a high-status communicator.

Compliance and Internalization

How can we be certain that the situation was different in the Asch experiment? How do we know that Asch's subjects did not actually become convinced that the unanimous majority was correct in its judgment of the lines? How might psychologists find out? They could ask the subjects who participated in Asch's experiment. Indeed, Asch did just that, and several conformists insisted that they had actually become convinced. This is probably not, however, the best way to find out; people do not like to admit they have conformed to group pressure; several might even insist that their influenced judgment was correct, although secretly they know it is not. Perhaps a better way to discover the truth would be to duplicate the Asch experiment, except that subjects would be allowed to indicate their judgments in private. If the subjects' actual perceptions of physical reality were influenced by the unanimous majority, the influence should show up even when they answer privately. If, however, their actual perceptions were not influenced by the other people and if their responses had originally coincided with the majority response only to please or avoid displeasing the group, the private answers should reveal less conformity. Psychologists who have compared private and public responses have found very little evidence of conformity when subjects are allowed to remain anonymous (Deutsch and Gerard, 1955).

So it appears that conformity to group pressure in the Asch situation is temporary behavior, behavior that is greatly reduced when subjects are allowed to cloak their identity from those applying the pressure. In short, it is clear that the subjects would not continue to see lines incorrectly after leaving the experiment. The kind of conformity produced in the Asch situation, which does not last beyond the presence of the group that caused it, is referred to as compliance. Compliance is conformity in order to achieve a reward or avoid punishment. If the reward or punishment is removed, the behavior does not persist.

But of course *all* conformity is not transient. Recall the example of the three anthropologists bowing to people in green turbans. If you made a subsequent visit to that country alone and you met a native in a green turban, wouldn't

Compliance - temporary behaviour in response to reward or punishment.

Compliance can almost always be achieved if the threat is powerful enough. But this is a poor way to change attitudes.

you bow? You would do so not because you fear to displease the people who influenced you (the anthropologists) but because they had provided you with a model you could regard as right, reasonable, or appropriate. This kind of relatively permanent conformity is referred to as **internalization.** Thus, conformity—a kind of persuasion—can be either temporary or relatively permanent.

Mob violence—Is it conformity or deindividuation?

We have all read accounts of mobs performing violent acts. For example, mobs have lynched blacks in the South, rioted in the streets of Detroit and Pittsburgh, and smashed windows and overturned cars after something as innocuous as a World Series or Super Bowl victory. From time to time in Latin America, a referee is mobbed and killed because of an unpopular decision during a soccer match. The striking thing about mob behavior is that many of the individuals who comprise a mob are rather mild-mannered people who at other times seem incapable of violence.

Even though few people have any firsthand experience of mobs, these phenomena seem familiar because of exposure to second-rate Hollywood westerns. Picture the scene. The hero has been arrested (for a crime he did not, of course, commit) and placed in a small jail cell behind the sheriff's office. Several people gather outside, and there is a low murmur of conversation. Then someone says loudly that anybody who would do a thing like that deserves to be dead. A few people shout their agreement. Several others join the group, lured by the excitement. Another person yells "What are we waiting for?" "I say, get a rope." "Yeah," is the reply . . . and the next thing you know this group of people—which includes the mild-mannered barber and the naive kid who works in the livery stable—has become a bloodthirsty mob that storms the jail, trampling over their "friend" the sheriff on the way to the cell.

Is this, in fact, the way a mob is formed? Unfortunately, most accounts of mob behavior are based on observation or interviews conducted after the fact, and it is frequently difficult to know how valid the data are. And it is also hard to imagine, it would be quite impossible to design and perform an experiment involving full-scale mob violence.

Writing at the turn of the century, the French sociologist, Gustave Le Bon (1895) suggested three factors in mob behavior. One of these is *suggestibility*. According to Le Bon, because of the size and power of the crowd, the individual is lulled into a state of blind conformity—similar to the popular conception of the suggestibility imposed by a stage hypnotist. In this state, the individual sees the mob as invincible and right and is swept along by its power and force. Another mechanism is *contagion*: the emotions of a mob spread rapidly from person to person in a manner analogous to the spread of disease. The third mechanism is quite different in its implications from the other two. Le Bon called it *anonymity*. In a violent mob, an individual becomes anonymous—one bears no individual responsibility for one's actions. "The mob did it, I didn't." The headlines read: "Mob Riots Downtown Kansas City," not "Sam Reynolds, Harry Jones and their friends from Steele Street smashed some windows, overturned cars, and raped a woman." Being a member of a crowd produces feelings of **deindividuation**, which apparently allow people to express some of the violence they may have been longing to express for a long time. The processes involved in deindividuation are virtually the opposite of those involved in conformity in that going along with the crowd allows people to do things they want to do but would not otherwise dare to.

Reconsider the Hollywood western, and suppose you are the sheriff. How

Uniforms and the facelessness of similar training can induce feelings of deindividuation.

Handwritten margin note:
mob behaviour
① suggestibility
② contagion
③ anonymity

might you quell the riot? One possibility, not missed by screenwriters, would be to re-individuate the individual members of the mob. "Is that you, Sam? Sam, I think your wife has dinner ready for you. Would you really rather murder the man in this here jail? And you, Harry; why don't you go back to the shop and shave old man Smith. He's been waiting in the chair with lather on his face for half an hour." In the movies, at least, the individuals go shuffling back to their wives and customers.

As mentioned earlier, these hypotheses are difficult to test in the real world. But analogous situations have been investigated. In one experiment (Zimbardo, 1969), groups of four female college students were instructed to deliver apparently painful electric shocks to a fellow woman student. (The "victim" never actually received the shocks.) In one experimental condition, the subjects wore large name tags and were pointedly introduced to one another prior to the experiment. In another condition, they were deindividuated, but not by being placed in a mob. Instead, (1) they wore large, oversized lab coats and hoods to cover their clothes and faces; (2) they were not referred to by name; and (3) the lights were turned down very low. The deindividuated group went wild, delivering almost twice as many shocks as the group of recognizable individuals.

Thus, while we are not sure of the role that conformity plays in mob violence, we can be reasonably certain that it is not an essential part of mob violence. Even when people are alone, _if they are deindividuated, the lack of individual responsibility seems to release behaviors that are usually kept under control_. The focus of this experiment was, of course, on the effects of deindividuation. It should be mentioned, however, that a great many people in this study behaved humanely—even when deindividuated. The study does show that deindividuation increases violent tendencies in most people.

SUMMARY

Communications are often designed to change the opinions or attitudes of the listener or reader. Opinions, or simple beliefs, can often be changed easily by simply presenting contrary facts. **Attitudes** too have "belief" or cognitive components, but they also involve emotions and dispositions toward certain behaviors and thus are altered less easily than opinions.

In the persuasion process, the prestige of the communicator is among the most influential factors. In general, the greater the prestige, the more the influence. Even a low-prestige communicator, however, can be effective if it is clear that his or her motives are decent and not self-serving.

The nature of the communication is also important. A one-sided argument is more effective with a poorly informed audience or with people who already agree with the position advocated, but presenting both sides is better for undecided but intelligent people. The first of two arguments presented is sometimes more effective (the **primacy effect**)—as when both are presented and a week elapses before changes are measured. But if the week elapses between the first and second arguments and attitudes are then immediately assessed, the second has more influence (the **recency effect**) A message that is moderately discrepant from the initial opinion of the subject is more effective than one that is highly discrepant, unless the source of the message is very prestigious. Repetitious commercials may be effective because stimuli do become more attractive as they become more familiar.

Attitudes, opinions

communicator

one-sided, two-sided
primacy effect, recency effect
discrepancy.
repetition

audience characteristics
innoculation
good-mood factor

compliance
internalization

deindividuation

The characteristics of the audience must also be considered. Some people are more susceptible to influence—those with low **self-esteem**, for example. People can sometimes be "inoculated" against a powerful argument by first exposing them to a mild form of the argument and then refuting it. Persuading someone in a good mood is easier than persuading someone who is not.

Social influences need not involve explicit communications. Studies of **conformity** experiments indicate that people sense subtle, unspoken pressures to "go along" with the majority. Many subjects do not want to appear ridiculous by differing from the group *in its presence,* whereas, when allowed to make their judgments in private, few people conformed. This type of temporary conformity is called **compliance.** More permanent conformity (**internalization**) occurs in situations in which, by watching other people, we learn valuable information about appropriate behavior in novel circumstances.

In mob violence, many individuals conform to the behavior of the majority. While such factors as suggestibility, contagion, and conformity may be important, some research indicates that the **deindividuation** or anonymity produced in mobs is a prominent factor.

In the next chapter we shall investigate a different form of persuasion—one in which people come to believe in the reasonableness or goodness of a particular action, not because others have convinced them of its merit, but because they succeed in convincing themselves that it is reasonable.

Attitude Change by Self-Persuasion

Do you see what I see?
What is cognitive dissonance?
What changes attitudes?
How are attitudes formed?

In the previous chapter we saw how people can be influenced by others either through the presentation of a communication or through conformity. In this chapter we will discuss a more subtle and more powerful determinant of attitude change and behavior change—self-persuasion. We can begin with an example.

About 25 years ago, when athletic contests were taken very seriously in the Ivy League, there was a celebrated football game played between Dartmouth and Princeton. It was famous—or rather, infamous—not for its outcome or any particularly spectacular plays, but because it was one of the roughest and dirtiest games in the history of college football. Several fights erupted on the field that day; there were obvious infractions of rules and much unsportsman-like conduct. Many players were injured as a result of roughness far beyond the usual requirements. In the second quarter, Princeton's star player, who had just been named to the all-American team, left the game with a broken nose. A short time later a Dartmouth player was carried off the field with a broken leg. Tempers flared, and fights broke out both during and after the game—involving both players and spectators.

Do you see what I see?

In the aftermath of the contest, an interesting study was conducted (Hastorf & Cantril, 1954). An impartial film of the game was shown to about fifty students from each of the two colleges. Students were asked to write down all infrac-tions of the rules that they noticed as they watched the film, noting which team had committed the infraction. The results showed that people do not view the same material in exactly the same way; but they do view it in predictable ways. On the average, Princeton students saw twice as many Dartmouth violations as the Dartmouth students saw.

This study demonstrates graphically one of the weaknesses inherent in a direct approach to attitude change; namely, that, to change a deeply in-grained, important attitude, a direct or "factual" approach might not be ef-fective. A person's interpretation of the facts may be very different from their objective content. An example of this phenomenon occurred in 1974, when Nixon was being criticized for his role in the Watergate conspiracy. Many citizens interpreted the criticisms as biased, vicious attacks on the presidency itself. In short, where important attitudes are involved, people are not passive and objective receivers of information; they have a tendency to *distort* a message to bring it more in line with their existing attitudes. Why? In order to understand this phenomenon, it is useful to posit the existence of a motive that we will call the *need for consistency*.

Watch Number 80 (at the right of the picture). He is about to run into the kicker—or is he? If you were rooting for the kicking team which way would you see it?

What is cognitive dissonance?

In recent years several **theories of consistency** have evolved. In this chapter we will restrict our discussion to one of these theories—Leon Festinger's theory of **cognitive dissonance** (Festinger, 1957). We have chosen this theory because it has generated a great deal of research and because it has been applied to a very wide range of social situations.

The core notion is extremely simple: whenever an individual simultaneously holds two **cognitions** (ideas, attitudes, beliefs, opinions) that are psychologically inconsistent, dissonance occurs. We can say that two cognitions are dissonant when the opposite of one is the logical conclusion of the other. For example, a person who smokes and, simultaneously, believes that cigarette smoking causes cancer almost certainly experiences dissonance. Specifically, the cognition "I smoke cigarettes" is psychologically inconsistent with the cognition "cigarette smoking produces cancer." When there is a discrepancy between attitude and behavior, dissonance results.

REDUCING DISSONANCE

Since dissonance is presumed to be unpleasant, the theory predicts that people will strive to reduce it. Typically this is done in one of two ways: (1) by adding new cognitions that are "consonant" with one of the dissonant elements, thus reducing dissonance by strengthening one element vis-à-vis the other; (2) more directly, by changing one of the dissonant cognitions. Since the cognition "I smoke cigarettes" is obviously related to behavior, the most efficient ways to reduce dissonance is to stop smoking. But, as many people have discovered, quitting is by no means easy, and they usually work on the other cognition. There are several ways in which people can make cigarette smoking seem less threatening. They might belittle the evidence linking cigarette smoking to cancer ("Most of the data are clinical rather than experimental"). They might associate with other cigarette smokers ("If Sam, Jack, and Harry smoke, then it can't be very dangerous"). Or, they might smoke filter-tipped cigarettes and delude themselves that the filter traps cancer-producing materials. They will often convince themselves that smoking is a highly pleasurable activity that is essential to the enjoyment of life. ("You don't live longer, it just seems longer! Ha, ha.") At the furthest extreme, they may even make a virtue out of smoking, developing romantic, devil-may-care images of themselves flouting danger by smoking. All these techniques reduce dissonance by diminishing the absurdity of going out of one's way to contract cancer. In effect, individuals form or change their attitudes by a process of *self-persuasion*.

DISTORTING REALITY

What the theory of cognitive dissonance implies, then, is that people attempt to justify their own behavior, attitudes, commitments, and associations through self-persuasion. This process frequently involves a distortion of objective reality. Consider the typical Dartmouth student watching the game film. The chances are good that his general opinion of Dartmouth players is that they are skillful, fair, and decent people because they represent his school. While watching the film, every unfair, dirty, and indecent act committed by a Dartmouth player is dissonant with this cognition. In order to reduce dissonance he must, therefore, either not notice many of these actions, or distort their meaning by viewing them as reasonable retaliations for the dirty deeds committed by the Princeton team.

It should be obvious from the foregoing that this tendency toward self-justification frequently runs counter to the need to be correct. You will recall that in Chapter 2 we asked why people conform and concluded that, in most situations, it feels good or makes sense to do so. First there is a reward that comes from being liked, accepted, praised; second, there are benefits stemming from being correct—from making wise decisions. To these we can now add a third reward: the good feeling that comes from having a high self-image—that is, from believing that you are a wise, decent, and clever human being. Dissonance theory focuses on this last benefit and a person's desire to maintain it.

Although all three of these motives are directed to the same end—achieving rewards—they are frequently tugging in opposite directions. A person acts differently, depending upon his or her motive in a particular situation. Accordingly, before one can predict how most people will behave in a given situation, it is necessary to understand the situation thoroughly; by doing so, we can get a clearer idea of which of the above motives will predominate.

Let us look first at the last two motives—the "need to *be* right" and the "need to *appear* right." The need to be right is a very rational and functional motivational force. It is what drives people to seek impartial information, to observe what is going on around them, and to make careful, rational judgments based on the facts. Thus, to return to an example used in the last chapter, the need to be right is what motivates a person to pay close attention to the behavior of the anthropologists when in a strange culture—and to imitate them when they bow to natives in green turbans.

The theory of cognitive dissonance also implies the existence of a need to convince oneself that one is right—that is, to appear right in one's own eyes. Far from seeking *impartial* information, therefore, the individual is said to be motivated to seek supportive and reject critical information. The two needs to *be* right and to *appear* right are thus in constant tension. This duality is nicely illustrated by observing the behavior of people before and after making an important decision—for example, purchasing a new car. Before buying a car, people are motivated to make a wise purchase. They may read *Consumer Reports,* seek information from friends who own various makes of cars, and test-drive several cars. In short, they seek to expose themselves to as much information as possible about as many cars as possible. But what happens after they make a purchase? One investigator (Ehrlich *et al.,* 1957) found that individuals who had recently purchased a new car read many advertisements about the brand of car they had purchased but few ads about brands they had considered but not purchased. This selectivity was not present among people who had not recently bought new cars. What does it mean? It would seem that after buying a car, people want to justify themselves, reassure themselves that they have made the right choice. To justify the wisdom of their choice, people seek out information favorable to their action and avoid information unfavorable to it.

The ad looks better *after* you have bought the product.

So the data suggest still another reason why a direct information campaign is often an ineffective means of changing a person's mind. Not only do people tend to distort information presented to make it consonant with their attitudes, values, and beliefs, but frequently they simply choose not to expose themselves to information they suspect is dissonant with these. A left-wing radical, for example, would probably not go out of the way to hear a speech by William F. Buckley, Jr. or George Wallace, and this is an important problem for the would-be persuader. In the case of the veteran-housepainter, for example, direct communication would probably not succeed in changing his attitude that the Vietnamese are "unpeople." In the first place, if he were informed in advance about the nature of the communication, he would probably choose not to listen, just as the people who had recently bought a new car chose not to read advertisements about other makes of cars. Second, even if he allowed himself to be exposed to the information, he would tend to distort it, change it, and bring it into line with his previous ideas, much as the students watching the film of the Princeton-Dartmouth football game did.

Dissonance-reducing behavior is defensive behavior; that is, people reduce dissonance as a way of maintaining positive self-images that makes them feel smart or good or worthwhile. Dissonance-reducing behavior can also be considered irrational or malfunctional, however; for while it is good for the self-image, it often prevents people from solving very real problems in their environment. Thus, in the case of the automobile buyer, if, after purchasing a new car, a man continues to convince himself that it is the best car ever made and exposes himself only to positive information about the car, he might fail to learn facts about it that, although negative and unpleasant, might be very useful. What if the car has brakes that tend to fail in wet, slippery weather, and this information had been published? If he had failed to expose himself to this information or minimized its importance (to protect his self-image), it could conceivably lead to his death.

The conflict between the needs to be right and to appear right is well illustrated by an experiment involving racial attitudes (Jones & Kohler, 1958). The subjects were people who were either in favor of racial segregation or opposed to it. They were presented with sets of statements that either supported or opposed segregation. Some of the statements were very plausible, while others were totally implausible. Specifically, the plausible pro-segregation statement read: "Southerners will have to pay the price of lowered scholastic standards if they yield to the pressures to integrate their schools." The implausible pro-segregation statement read: "If Negroes and whites were meant to live together, they never would have been separated at the beginning of history." The plausible anti-segregation statement read: "The present inferior condition of the Negro is the result of long and effective suppression by the Southern whites." And the implausible anti-segregation statement read: "The real reason why most Southern whites oppose integration is their realization that the Negro is more capable than they are." (Jones & Kohler, 1958, pp. 316–317.)

PREDICTING ATTITUDE
FORMATION

Which statements would the subjects learn and remember best? From a perfectly rational point of view, one would guess that people would learn all the plausible statements better than all the implausible ones. After all, what sense is there in filling one's head with implausible statements? Surely it is more important to learn statements that make some degree of sense—whether one happens to agree with them or not. According to dissonance theory, however, people dislike hearing ridiculous arguments in favor of their own view because the ease with which they can be discounted casts doubt on the view in general. More important, a plausible statement opposed to one's own position creates dissonance because it suggests that there are good arguments on the other side. In fact, the results of the Jones & Kohler experiment were consistent with predictions that would be made by the theory of cognitive dissonance. People learned the plausible statements that supported their own position better than the implausible statements supporting those views. But for the opposing view, the results were just the opposite. They were more likely to remember the implausible support of the opposition than the plausible. It is in this case, of course, that the need to *appear* right and the need to *be* right are in direct conflict. In most of the subjects, the need to appear right controlled the learning and memory processes.

What changes attitudes?

INSUFFICIENT REWARDS
AND BEHAVIORAL
CHANGE

The tendency to reduce dissonance is a powerful one. We have seen how it can be used by an individual to maintain established attitudes and thwart attempts to change them. But the same process that generally prevents attitude change, can also be utilized to produce attitude change. This can be accomplished by placing a person experiencing dissonance in a situation in which the path of least resistance in reducing dissonance involves a change in attitude.

One way to do this is to induce a person to take a course of action that is dissonant with his or her own attitudes, values, and beliefs. Suppose Sam Schlunk is running for mayor of your town. Suppose further that you believe that he is a complete idiot and would make an awful mayor. What if someone induced you to stand up in a public place in the presence of hundreds of people and make an impassioned speech telling the voters that Sam Schlunk is, in actuality, a very wise and upright person who would make an absolutely perfect mayor. After having done this, you would experience dissonance: your cognition "I believe Schlunk is an idiot who would make an awful mayor" is dissonant with the cognition "I told a bunch of people Schlunk is a wise man who would make a perfect mayor." How would you reduce this dissonance?

Perhaps the best way would be by convincing yourself that the things you said were not completely wrong; in other words, the dissonance motivates you to try to justify your behavior. The world is so constructed that reality is very rarely a matter of good and bad; there are many in-between areas. You might go back over some of Sam Schlunk's previous political speeches and extract from these some small pearls of wisdom you had previously missed. Or you might convince yourself that some of the things he said actually meant something other than what you previously thought. The astute reader may begin to notice some similarities to the behavior of the Dartmouth students watching the Dartmouth-Princeton game film. This kind of distortion could help you justify your support of Schlunk's candidacy. Note what the dissonance does: it induces you to change your attitudes, opinions, and beliefs about Sam Schlunk. The very fact that you made a speech supporting him is now causing you to change your attitudes.

This example, of course, intentionally leaves out some relevant information; to fill it in we need to turn the clock back a day. The day before your speech you are standing in the city square, and a man approaches you; he attempts to persuade you to make a speech favoring Sam Schlunk for mayor. He says: "Hey, how would you like to make a speech favoring Sam Schlunk?" You refuse. Suppose then that he pulls out $50,000, hands it to you, and says: "If you make a speech favoring Sam Schlunk, you can keep this $50,000." So you take the $50,000 and you stand up and say, "Sam Schlunk is a wise man and would be a perfect mayor." Would you experience much dissonance? Probably not. The cognition "I believe Schlunk is an idiot" is, indeed, dissonant with the cognition "I have said Schlunk is a wise man." But added to that is another cognition: "I said those things to get $50,000." In short, the $50,000 is consonant enough with the statement that you made. There is no further need to justify your behavior by actually changing your attitudes. Similarly, if he held a gun to your head and said, "Either you make positive statements about Sam Schlunk or I'm going to blow your brains out," you would comply. And you would experience no dissonance and no attitude change. The cognition that "my head will be blown off if I don't make these statements" is very consonant with making those statements.

The thrust of the argument is this: In trying to produce momentary conformity, the greater the reward, the greater the probability that a person will

TABLE 3-1 The effect of reward on attitude change

Condition	"Enjoyed Task"	"Willing to Participate in Similar Experiments"
$1 reward	+1.35[a]	+1.20
$20 reward	− .05	− .25
Control[b]	− .45	− .62

[a] The more positive the number, the greater the attitude change in the direction of the oral statement.
[b] Subjects who participated in the boring task but were not asked to "lie."

Adapted from L. Festinger & J. M. Carlsmith, "Cognitive Consequences of Forced Compliance." *Journal of Abnormal and Social Psychology, 58*(1959):203–11.

conform. But to produce a more enduring change in attitude in situations such as the one outlined above, the greater the reward, the *less likely* it is that any attitude change will occur. If all the man wants you to do is to make a speech for Schlunk, the best inducement is the largest possible reward or the worst possible punishment. Either would increase the probability that you would comply. But if he desires to change your attitudes and beliefs, just the reverse is true. Some minimal reward is, of course, necessary to induce you initially to perform the behavior. Beyond that minimal amount, however, the less you are given, the more likely it is you will seek additional justification to convince yourself that the things you said were actually true. This process of self-persuasion would result in true attitude change rather than mere compliance.

These speculations were put to the test in a classic experiment (Festinger & Carlsmith, 1959) that parallels the Sam Schlunk example. The subjects were first asked to perform a very boring and laborious set of tasks. The experimenter then asked them to lie about the task; specifically, he induced them to tell another person (who was waiting to perform the task) that it was interesting and enjoyable. Some of the subjects were offered $20 for telling the lie; others were offered only $1. After the experiment, an interviewer asked the "lie-tellers" how much they had enjoyed the tasks they had performed earlier in the experiment. The results are shown in Table 3-1. Subjects who had been offered $20 for lying—that is, for saying that the tasks had been enjoyable—found them dull, as did the control subjects who were not asked to lie. Subjects who had been paid only $1 for lying, however, rated the task an enjoyable one. In other words, people who had a lot of justification for telling a lie told the lie, but didn't believe it. But people who told the lie with very little justification did, indeed, come to believe that what they said was true.

INCENTIVES AND ATTITUDE CHANGE

Of course, the drive to reduce dissonance is not the only motivational force operating in human beings. People are also motivated to secure more tangible rewards—such as food or money—and there are circumstances in which these incentives *can* and *do* result in changes in attitude. Social psychologists try to understand the difference between circumstances in which high incentives produce attitude change and those in which dissonance effects (low incentives) do so.

What they have discovered is this: Dissonance is greatest when commitment is greatest _and_ the person's self-esteem is on the line. (See Spotlight 3-1 for additional qualifications of dissonance theory.) Thus, all other things being equal, a person would experience more dissonance from telling a lie directly to someone's face than from writing it in an anonymous letter. Moreover, a lie that concerned an issue important to the hearer would produce more dissonance than one about an unimportant matter. In the high-dissonance situation, one would be most likely to convince oneself that the lie is, in fact, true.

When might high incentives produce high attitude change then? Suppose a confirmed smoker were asked to compile a list of reasons why smoking is bad for one's health. If the smoker were paid a quarter to do this job, he or she would probably not think up many arguments—after all, why work hard for such a pittance? But a person who was paid $50 might do more research into the matter. Indeed, for that much money one might even look up the facts in medical journals, and the resulting list would inevitably be richer and more thoroughly documented. Consequently, the smoker would be exposed to a better set of arguments in the high-reward condition than in the low-reward condition and might be more convinced that cigarette smoking is unhealthful. Indeed, one researcher (Rosenberg, 1965) has demonstrated that when dissonance is low—that is, when the individual is not committed and when his or her self-concept is not involved—high incentives produce richer information and, consequently, greater attitude change. (See also Aronson, 1968, 1969.)

This reasoning has been supported by a number of experiments. In one (Carlsmith, Collins, and Helmreich, 1966) face-to-face lying about an issue produced more attitude change for low incentives (50 cents) than for high incentives ($5); writing an anonymous essay on the same issue produced more attitude change for higher incentives ($5) than for low incentives (50 cents).

PUNISHMENT AND ATTITUDE CHANGE

Suppose you have a young son who likes to beat up his little brother and you want him to stop. Probably the best way to stop him is to threaten to hit him and hit him hard. The more severe the threat, the greater the likelihood that he will stop, at that moment, _while you're watching him._ That is compliance. However, he may very well hit his brother again as soon as you turn your back.

But suppose that, instead you threaten him with a very mild punishment, such as turning off his favorite television program—a punishment that is just barely severe enough to get him to stop misbehaving at the time. In either case—under threat of severe punishment or of mild—the child experiences dissonance. He is aware that he is not beating up his little brother, and he is aware that he wants to. When the little brother is present, the child has the urge to beat him up; and, when he refrains, he asks himself in effect: "Why aren't I beating up my little brother?" Under severe threat, he has a ready answer: "I know why I'm not beating up my little brother. I'm not beating him up because, if I do, that giant over there (my father) will knock the hell out of me if I do." In effect, the severe threat of punishment has provided the child with strong justifications for not beating up his brother, at that moment, while he is being watched.

Now consider the child in the mild threat situation; he experiences dissonance too, asking himself, in effect, "Why aren't I beating up my little

A severe punishment will stop aggression while the punisher is present, but a mild threat tends to produce a more lasting change in behavior.

brother?" But he does not have a good answer; the threat is so mild that by itself it does not provide an adequate reason. He continues to experience dissonance because there is no simple way to reduce it by blaming his inaction on a severe threat. He must, therefore, find other reasons for not hitting his little brother. He can, for instance, convince himself that he really does not like to beat up his brother, that he did not want to do it in the first place. In sum, one way to cause a person to refrain from an activity is to get him or her to devalue it; and one way to make the person devalue it is to stop the behavior in the first place with a mild rather than a severe threat.

To test this notion, two experimenters (Aronson & Carlsmith, 1963) tried to influence a rather mundane value—children's toy preferences. Children were first asked to rate the attractiveness of several toys. The experimenter then told them they were not allowed to play with one of the toys—one that had been rated as attractive. One experimental group was threatened with a mild punishment for transgression: "I would be a little annoyed." The other experimental group was threatened with severe punishment: "I would be very angry. I would have to take all of my toys and go home and never come back again. I would think you were just a baby." The experimenter then left the room and allowed the children to play with the other toys, and to resist the temptation to play with the forbidden one. On returning to the room, the experimenters found that children who were forbidden to play with a toy under a threat of mild punishment now found the toy much less attractive, while children under a severe threat did not devalue it. As Table 3-2 shows, eight of twelve children under mild threat gave the toy a lower rating; of fourteen children under strong threat, none lowered their ratings. The prediction of dissonance theory was supported: "I like this toy" and "I am not playing with this toy" are dissonant in both cases. In the severe-punishment group, how-

TABLE 3-2 Change in attractiveness of forbidden toy

	Rating	
Strength of Threat	Increase	Decrease
Mild	4	8
Severe	14	0

Adapted from E. Aronson & J. M. Carlsmith, "Effect of the Severity of Threat on the Devaluation of Forbidden Behavior." *Journal of Abnormal and Social Psychology* 66(1963):584–88.

ever, the calamitous consequences of playing with the toy resolve the dissonance. In the mild-punishment group, the relative absence of such external justification makes the children change the cognition "I like . . ." into "I don't really like . . ." in order to reduce the dissonance.

Subsequent research has shown that this effect is long-lasting. Once devalued, the toy remained unattractive to the children, even when they were retested some sixty-four days later (Freedman, 1965).

The effects demonstrated in these experiments may well apply to more basic and important values. For example, parents might have more overall success in controlling a child's aggressiveness by using threats of mild rather than severe punishment. By doing so, they might help the child become convinced that aggression is undesirable and so bring about a lasting change in behavior. Studies in child development suggest clearly that parents who use severe punishment to stop a child's aggression do not succeed in curtailing it in any permanent sense. Such children, although not aggressive at home, tend to display a great deal of aggression at school and at play (Sears, Whiting, Nowlis, & Sears, 1953).

THE NEED TO JUSTIFY CRUELTY

Suppose you performed an action that caused physical harm to an innocent person. You think of yourself as a basically decent, fair, and careful person, and your cognition "I am a decent, fair, and careful person" is dissonant with the cognition "I have harmed an innocent person." How might you reduce dissonance? The three most feasible directions are (1) to minimize the harm done; (2) to attempt to compensate the victim; or (3) to maximize the culpability of the victim, that is, to convince yourself that the "innocent" bystander wasn't so innocent after all. You might protest that the victim brought on the situation through carelessness or that he or she is a reprehensible person and deserved to be hurt. To reduce dissonance, a person could apply any of these lines of thought. However, to the extent that the damage done to the victim is unambiguously severe (such as a serious injury or death), the one who causes the injury will be unable to either minimize the damage cognitively or provide adequate compensation. Therefore, he or she will rely heavily on the third technique—convincing oneself that the victim was responsible.

I am reminded of an article I read on the sports page of a local newspaper. A defensive tackle for a professional football team had succeeded in cracking a few ribs belonging to an opposing quarterback by intentionally belting him

While dissonance theory has generated a great many hypotheses and led to scores of interesting experiments, the theory *as a theory* has at least two important weaknesses. First, its basic statement is rather vague, making it difficult to determine whether or not dissonance exists in a given situation. The reason for the difficulty is that the theory does not limit itself to *logical inconsistency*, but also deals with *psychological inconsistency*. For example, if I learn that my favorite novelist beats his wife, does this arouse dissonance? It is difficult to be certain. Strictly speaking, being a wife-beater is not incompatible with being a great novelist, and there is no logical inconsistency in continuing to admire his work. However, there may be a sense in which the term "great novelist" implies great wisdom, sensitivity, empathy, and compassion—and wise, sensitive, empathic, and compassionate people do not beat their wives. This is not a logical but a psychological inconsistency.

This problem has led to several revisions that have limited the scope of the theory; but they have also made it more precise. For example, Jack Brehm and A. R. Cohen (1962) limited the theory's application to situations in which the individual voluntarily committed himself or herself to a particular action. The present writer (Aronson, 1968, 1969) limited the theory to situations in which the individual's self-concept is involved. It should be noted that the data reported in this chapter are based on the clearest predictions from the theory—predictions that fit most neatly into the confines of the revisions mentioned above.

Another problem with the theory is that in most situations, there are many ways to reduce dissonance. For example, suppose that a woman, a college senior with a high self-concept, applies to graduate school at Harvard University and fails to be admitted. Her cognition "I am an extremely good student" is dissonant with the cognition "I was passed over by the Harvard professors." How does she reduce dissonance?

1. She could lower her self-concept: "Perhaps I'm not as good as I thought I was."

2. She could derogate the Harvard professors who turned

---

hard *after* the quarterback had thrown a pass. When interviewed afterward, the tackle maintained that it was all part of the game; he claimed the quarterback was out to "humiliate me in front of my friends" by completing passes, and that, accordingly, he deserved whatever injuries he sustained.

In an experimental test of this technique (Davis & Jones, 1960) male students were cajoled into "helping" the experimenter. They were to watch another

Reducing dissonance by vilifying the victim.

STUART LEEDS

her down: "If those people can't recognize the talent of a genius like me, they must be stupid, senile, or male chauvinist. I'm glad I'm not going to such a backward institution."

3. Finally, she might *increase* her esteem for Harvard and its professors: "If they turn down a genius like me, Harvard must have astronomical standards. Surely everyone connected with the place must be out-of-sight."

In a laboratory experiment aimed at testing whether or not a phenomenon exists, it is good experimental practice to create a situation in which all possibilities but one are systematically controlled or eliminated. But in the real world it is of practical importance to know *which* of the alternatives people will use (*see* Tedeschi et al., 1971). Thus (to extend our example), if Harvard's goal is to build its prestige, this aim would backfire if a sizable number of rejected applicants reduced their dissonance by derogating the university.

It is encouraging to note that experimenters are be-ginning to focus their efforts on this kind of problem. A recently formulated hypothesis exemplifying this trend suggests that individuals will choose the means of dissonance reduction least likely to be challenged by future events (Walster, Berscheid, & Barclay, 1967). In the experiment, children were asked to choose between two toys. Half of the children were then led to expect that they would subsequently hear objective information about the toy they chose; the other half were led to expect that they would be told all about the rejected toy. They were then asked to rate the attractiveness of the two toys again. In a situation such as this, dissonance could be reduced in two ways: by cognitively *increasing* the attractiveness of the chosen alternative and/or by cognitively *decreasing* the attractiveness of the unchosen alternative. The investigators found, as predicted, that the children reduced dissonance by downgrading the attractiveness of the toy they were *not* going to hear about. That is, they chose to reduce dissonance in a manner that was less likely to run up against the objective reality of the information they were to receive.

student being interviewed and then to tell the student their impressions of him; but, as a helper, they were instructed to give negative impressions such as: "You are shallow, untrustworthy, not very interesting, and not very attractive." The major finding in this experiment was that the subjects succeeded in convincing themselves that they really did not like the person they evaluated negatively. After saying things that almost certainly hurt the other student, they convinced themselves that that person deserved it; they liked the "victim" less than they had before they hurt him. Similar results were obtained when "helpers" used electric shocks rather than verbal statements to hurt the other person (Glass, 1964).

How are attitudes formed?

We can now go back once more to the house painter we discussed at the very beginning of this part. How did his attitude that the Vietnamese are not quite human develop? Here are a few of the numerous possible ways. (1) He might have had some unpleasant encounters with a few Vietnamese people, disliked them, and generalized his dislike to all of them. (2) Other people he respected and liked—his lieutenant or his buddies—may have had a similar, negative attitude, which he may have adopted through conformity. (3) Still a third possibility is that he came to dislike the Vietnamese as a way of justifying his own oppressive behavior. Like the tackle who broke the quarterback's ribs and the college students who said uncomplimentary things to their peers, the house painter may have performed acts in Vietnam that caused him to experience dissonance. To reduce dissonance, he might have attempted to justify these activities by derogating those whom he had caused to suffer. By stoutly maintaining, "Hell, Doc, those aren't people, those are Vietnamese," he conveniently gets off the hook. He can maintain his self-image as a decent and fair person while justifying behavior that would otherwise threaten it. It should be noted too that once he reduces dissonance by this process of self-persuasion, he not only justifies past negative behavior, but also—for as long as he remains in the situation—justifies (and virtually guarantees) future negative behavior.

One way to reduce dissonance.

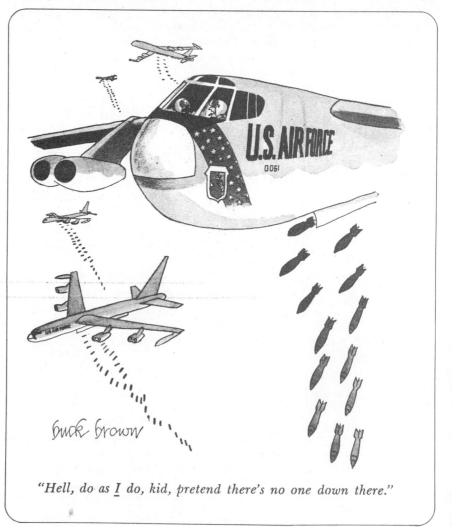

"Hell, do as *I* do, kid, pretend there's no one down there."

Let us broaden the base of this question of attitude formation slightly. Suppose you live in a culture in which whites treat blacks unfairly. The whites prevent blacks from attending first-rate public schools, providing them instead with a second-rate and stultifying education. As a consequence, after twelve years of schooling, the average black is less well-educated than the average white and does poorly on achievement tests. Such a situation provides a marvelous opportunity for white leaders to justify their discriminatory behavior and hence reduce dissonance. "You see," they say, "Black people are stupid (because they perform poorly on the achievement test). Therefore it would have been foolish for us to waste our resources by providing them with high-quality education." This **self-fulfilling prophecy** provides an airtight justification for all kinds of racial and economic injustice. So, almost without realizing it, we have entered the area of prejudice—an area as important as it is complex, which deserves a chapter all to itself.

SUMMARY

People do not digest information exactly as it is given. They have a tendency to alter it to fit their needs. One such need is self-justification—the attempt to justify their behavior and attitudes. For example, an individual who has recently invested a great deal of money in the purchase of a new automobile will tend not to notice its deficiencies. Noticing them, after all, might suggest that his or her choice of a car was stupid. By the same token, most people are not inclined to accept—or even listen to—negative information about their own team or university, or any person, object, or opinion to which they have committed themselves.

This phenomenon has been described and explained in terms of the theory of **cognitive dissonance.** A person experiences cognitive dissonance when he holds two inconsistent ideas or attitudes; this state is unpleasant and leads to efforts to reduce the dissonance. This theory has led to a great deal of research with important ramifications for individual attitude development and social change. For example, if an individual hurts someone, he or she will try to justify the action by becoming convinced that the victim deserved to be hurt. This results in an interesting phenomenon in which the harmdoer thinks less of the victim *after* hurting him or her than *before.*

There are other nonobvious findings from dissonance theory. If, for example, your goal is permanent attitude change, the *smallest* reward or the *mildest* punishment (low incentive) necessary to alter the behavior related to the attitude often has the greatest effect. This is true because people cannot justify their actions (reduce dissonance) by pointing to the severity of threats or the size of the reward. Instead they will tend to alter the original attitude. If, however, a large reward (high incentive) or the threat of a severe punishment results in greater effort to obtain information that is contrary to one's initial attitude, the dissonance effect might not be obtained.

Berlin, 1938

Prejudice

What causes prejudice?
How can prejudice be reduced?

Karl Pearson, a prominent British scientist, concluded a long-range study of ethnic differences by writing: "Taken on the average, and regarding both sexes, ———— population is somewhat inferior physically and mentally to the native population." It might be interesting for the reader to guess which ethnic minority the writer was referring to. Was he talking about an immigrant Polish population? A Mexican-American population? A Puerto Rican population? No. He was describing an immigrant Jewish population that had come to England around 1900.

The example is instructive. Although anti-Semitism has not been eliminated, few people in the third quarter of the twentieth century would attribute intel-

82

lectual inferiority to the ethnic group that produced Freud, Marx, and Einstein. Of course, targets of prejudice change from generation to generation, just as the characterizations do. Thus, in contemporary America, it might be blacks or Chicanos who would be pictured as stupid, while Jews would more likely be seen as shrewd and powerful. Recently, a high-ranking military officer charged that Jews own most of the banks in the United States—a statement as false as Pearson's allegation of their stupidity.

Prejudice has been defined in a number of different ways. As the term has been used by social psychologists, it denotes a set of hostile attitudes directed toward a distinguishable group and based on generalizations derived from faulty or incomplete information. Thus, when we say that Sam is prejudiced against Italians, we mean that he behaves with hostility toward Italians and that his information about them is either totally inaccurate or contains a germ of truth that is overzealously applied to the group as a whole.

What causes prejudice?

At the close of the previous chapter we presented a brief explanation of one possible reason behind prejudice—namely, a need to justify one's actions and beliefs. Admittedly, it was an oversimplified version of how prejudice develops and is maintained, and there are many others. In fact, social scientists have proposed several explanations for the etiology (causation) of prejudice. It seems reasonably certain that there is no *one* cause of prejudice that holds true for all people; and there are undoubtedly multiple causes even in a single case. Presumed "causes" of prejudice range from broad societal factors to the narrow mind of a single individual.

On a broad social level, prejudice can be viewed as the result of economic and political forces. One version of this theory is the Marxist argument that intergroup hostility has been fostered by the ruling classes to justify and perpetuate the economic exploitation of minority groups. But one need not subscribe to an exploitation theory to be aware that prejudiced attitudes develop between groups in conflict—whether they be blacks and whites competing for scarce jobs, Arabs and Israelis fighting over territory, or Northerners versus Southerners disputing the extension of slavery. The linkage between prejudice and job discrimination is particularly well documented. For example, as late as 1966, only 2.7 percent of union-controlled apprenticeships in the United States were filled by blacks—an increase of only 1 percent over the previous ten years. A few years later, a four-city survey conducted by the U.S. Department of Labor failed to turn up a *single* black apprentice among union plumbers, steamfitters, sheet-metal workers, stonemasons, lathers, painters, glaziers, and operating engineers. The finding prompted one commentator to observe that it is apparently easier for a black to enter an Ivy League college than to join a craft union (Levitas, 1969).

STEREOTYPING

Economic and political conflict also results in the formation of unfavorable **stereotypes**—that is, attributions of identical characteristics to all members of one group or race. For example, in the middle of the nineteenth century, when jobs were plentiful, Chinese immigrants were performing back-breaking labor building the western sections of the transcontinental railroad. At that time, there was little negative feeling toward them; indeed, they were generally regarded as sober, industrious, and lawabiding. But after the completion of the railroad and the end of the Civil War, employment opportunities grew scarce, and the Chinese were competing with whites for more desirable jobs. There was a sharp increase in negative attitudes toward them during this period, and the stereotype changed from "hardworking" to "criminal," "conniving," "crafty," and "stupid." The stereotype of Japanese people (both Japanese nationals and Japanese-Americans) also changed negatively during World War II, then changed again — this time positively — when Japan became one of our staunchest and most reliable allies in the fifties and sixties.

While stereotyping often results from economic or political conflicts, such factors are not the only causes. Indeed, stereotyping seems to be the product of a general human tendency to go beyond the information given. The positive value of this tendency is that it enables us, to some extent, to predict the unknown; at the same time, it is likely to produce misconceptions. For example, suppose a visitor from Mars walks into the backyard of an American nursery school. The Martian sees two kinds of people: big ones and little ones. All of the little ones (kids) seem to be running around a lot. Some of them fall down; others drop things or knock things over. The big people (adults) are usually standing, sitting, or walking slowly. They almost never fall, drop things, or knock things over. A good observer and a reasonable analyst, the Martian might conclude that on this planet little people are active and clumsy, and big people are inactive and competent. Chances are, however, that the Martian would go beyond the information given and, leaving the nursery school and wandering into a first-grade classroom, would expect the little people there to be active

A young American awaits relocation in a government internment camp. Her crime? Having Japanese ancestry. Such internments were a matter of national policy during World War II.

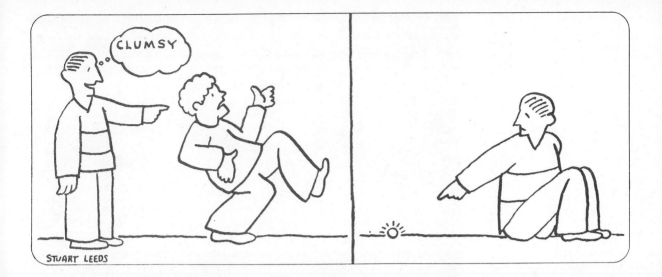

STUART LEEDS

and clumsy too. The alien visitor would be shocked to see them pursuing their studies fairly quietly, often sitting at tables.

As the above example indicates there are two problems with the tendency to go beyond the information given. One is that it frequently leads one to make *dispositional attributions* — that is, to make inferences about a people's characteristics from what they do. Research has shown (Jones & Nisbett, 1971) that if I were to trip and fall I would tend to explain the act in terms of the situation. ("The sun got in my eyes, the sidewalk is uneven. I feel sick today.") If *you* were to trip and fall, however, I would be more likely to attribute it to a more permanent trait. ("You are clumsy.") This tendency to attribute a situational cause to one's own behavior but a dispositional cause to the same behavior in others is one of the reasons the visitor from Mars failed to predict accurately — the alien made a typically human dispositional attribution!

The other problem with going beyond the information given is that it frequently results in faulty overgeneralization. Viewing all fat people as jolly because you have a couple of fat, jolly friends decreases your ability to understand the feelings of other fat people. Moreover, faulty generalizations pigeonhole individuals and thus rob them of their uniqueness — even when the stereotype is not particularly negative. ("All blacks are good athletes.")

Furthermore, stereotypes tend to be faulty because for most people the majority of these generalizations are not the result of direct experience but of the popular media. For example, many people who have never been to New York City think they know what a New York City cab driver looks and talks like. Similarly, in the thirties and forties many people from rural areas of the North and Midwest, who had hardly ever seen a black person, developed — from films or from the "Amos 'n Andy" radio program (in which the black characters were played by white actors!) — an image of the black man as stupid, uneducated, shiftless, cowardly, and fawning. They imagined the black woman as a fat, nurturant "mammy" like the person pictured on the box of Aunt Jemima pancake mix.

The media communicates and thereby perpetuates racial and ethnic stereotypes. This is a scene from the 1941 film "Among the Living."

AN EXPERIMENT IN PREJUDICE—A SOCIAL APPROACH

In the complexity of the world at large, a great many factors interact to establish stereotypes and produce prejudice. In order for researchers to examine prejudice more closely, a less complex situation is needed. Such an environment was produced by Muzafer Sherif and his colleagues (1961), who performed an experiment on the effects of conflict and cooperation at a summer camp for boys.

Establishing Internal Cohesiveness

The researchers divided the campers into two separate groups—the "Bulldogs" and the "Red Devils"—and attempted to knit each group into a cohesive unit by making the members interdependent in most of their daily activities. In order to eat, for example, a good deal of cooperation was required within each group to secure the food, gather wood, prepare a cooking fire, and dish out the food.

Introducing Competition

Once a feeling of "we-ness" was established within the groups, the researchers began to foster competitive situations between them; they wanted to determine whether animosities would develop and, if so, whether they could be reduced later. The competitions took the form of games; in order to increase tension, prizes were awarded to the winning team.

While the games began in a rather friendly manner, unpleasantness gradually began to develop. At one point the Red Devils accused the Bulldogs of not playing fair and subjected them to much verbal abuse. The investigators set up a number of situations aimed at enhancing these tendencies. In one of them, they arranged a joint party and contrived to have the Red Devils arrive before the Bulldogs. By the time of the party, resentment between the two groups was so high that the Red Devils cornered the most appetizing-looking refreshments for themselves, leaving mostly squashed and unappetizing-looking refreshments for the Bulldogs. When the Bulldogs arrived and saw what was going on, they were understandably miffed. Hostilities increased, and namecalling soon escalated into the throwing of food, cups, tableware, and other objects.

Reducing Hostility

After the psychologists had succeeded in building within-group attraction and between-group animosity, they explored the possibilities of reducing animosity. First, they eliminated competitive, conflict-ridden situations and tried to increase simple, noncompetitive contact between the groups. The two groups

Competitiveness tends to produce animosity among opponents . . .

While cooperation tends to reduce animosity.

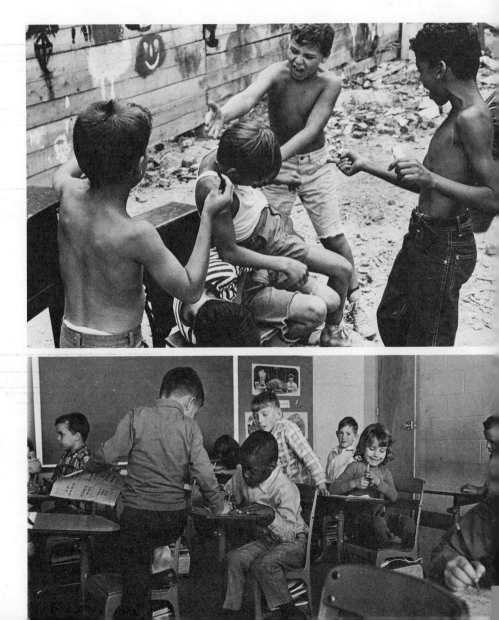

watched movies together, ate in the same dining room, and played in the same area. But, once hostility had been aroused, simple contact did nothing to reduce it. Indeed, close proximity served to *increase* hostility between the groups.

Since cooperativeness within each group had built strong attraction among group members, the researchers attempted to create one large, cooperative group to see if this would reduce hostility. They formed an all-star softball team in which the best players from each group participated in a game against boys from a nearby town. They also created a crisis, surreptitiously damaging the water supply system so that all the boys had to cooperate to repair the damage. These cooperative ventures reversed the trend of out-group animosity and increased the attractiveness of the boys for each other, regardless of group affiliation.

An Individual Approach — The Scapegoat Theory

A totally different explanation for prejudiced behavior focuses on what goes on inside the individual, rather than on the external situation. Suppose a person is angry or frustrated. These feelings result in a tendency to lash out at the source of frustration. But frequently the cause is either unidentifiable or too powerful to strike at without risk of serious retaliation. If a person is insulted by the boss or a boy is pushed around by a bigger, stronger bully, a counterattack would almost certainly be dangerous. According to the **scapegoat theory** of prejudice, the individual in this instance might *displace aggression by taking out his or her anger on an innocent but safer target*. The scapegoat might be a person, an object, or an entire group. Thus, a person who is insulted by the boss might yell at the kids or kick over a wastebasket; the boy who was pushed around by a bully might slug his kid sister or pull his dog's tail. Alternatively, either might blame the trouble on some relatively powerless minority group. The latter tendency is particularly common when the source of the frustration is vague or unknown. For example, if an individual is unemployed or if serious inflation is eating into one's savings, who is there to lash out at? In Nazi Germany it was safe to blame the Jews; in the rural South it used to be safe to take it out on the blacks.

Individual Differences in Scapegoating

Some people become frustrated or angry more easily than others, and some tend to displace aggression (choose another target) more readily. In short, there are people whose personalities predispose them toward being prejudiced. It has been argued that, because of overly strict parental upbringing, some individuals develop deep-seated personality characteristics that increase the likelihood of certain clusters of beliefs and attitudes being formed. Such people have been said to have *authoritarian personalities* (Adorno et al., 1950).

In this major study of the authoritarian personality, psychologists used a questionnaire called the F-scale (*F* for fascism). It consisted of items with which the individual was to indicate agreement or disagreement—"Sex crimes such as rape and attacks on children deserve more than mere imprisonment; such criminals ought to be publicly whipped, or worse." "Most people don't realize how much our lives are controlled by plots hatched in secret places." "Obedience and respect for authority are the most important virtues children should learn."—The psychologists found that people who agreed with these statements tended to show a great deal of distrust and dislike for minority groups and an inordinate degree of ethnic and national pride.

Some other interesting experiments provide support for the scapegoat theory of prejudice. In one (Weatherley, 1961), individuals who scored either high or low on measures of anti-Semitism were subjected to a procedure designed to make them angry at the experimenter. The experimenter aroused their ire by simply assuming a nasty demeanor, putting them down, and insulting their intelligence in the course of administering a brief paper and pencil test. The subjects were angry but, as mentioned earlier, it is often dangerous to express anger directly to a high-status person. The subjects were then allowed to interact with a fellow student, actually an accomplice of the experimenter. This accomplice was introduced by a name that was either Jewish or non-Jewish. Predictably, subjects who had scored high in anti-Semitism demonstrated more hostility toward the "Jewish" student than toward the non-Jewish one; low-prejudice subjects were more or less equally angry toward both students or simply did not take out their anger on anyone. Angry at the experimenter, the prejudiced group displaced its aggression, but only to what they considered a safe target—a Jew.

<table>
<tr><td>PREJUDICE VIA
CONFORMITY</td><td>

It should be clear to the reader that the two major explanations for prejudice discussed above—namely, the social and the individual—are not mutually exclusive. In most situations, the two can and do support and strengthen each other. Yet a third explanation involves conformity. It is likely that many individuals adopt prejudiced attitudes and behaviors as a result of implicit or explicit social pressure. Attitude tests of white college students in South Africa show they are more prejudiced against blacks than white American students are (Pettigrew, 1958). These data are not terribly surprising; if there is a country with manifestly more anti-black prejudice than the United States, it is certainly South Africa. Its attitudes of segregation and discrimination are explicitly written into its legal code as the policy of apartheid. What *is* interesting is that white South Africans showed no more evidence of authoritarianism than white Americans. In other words, their negative feelings against blacks were probably not a result of personality structure. Moreover, South Africans who were generally strong conformists—as tested by conformity to other social customs unrelated to prejudice—also showed the most prejudice against blacks.

</td></tr>
</table>

If prejudiced attitudes are affected by a tendency to conform to group norms and pressures, one might expect that, as children get older, they would become more uniform in their attitudes toward minority groups. It takes time to learn the rules, regulations, expectations, and prejudices of one's society. (As the Rodgers and Hammerstein song goes, "You've got to be carefully taught.") And, indeed, researchers have found more uniformity of anti-Semitic and anti-black attitudes among 17–18-year-olds than among 13–14-year-olds (Wilson, 1963).

What happens to prejudice then when people change their place of residence? If conformity is a factor, one would expect individuals to show dramatic increases in prejudice when they move into areas where the norm is greater prejudice. This sort of increase did, in fact, occur among some people who had recently moved to New York City; those who came into direct and frequent contact with anti-Semitic people became more anti-Semitic (Watson, 1950).

Conformity with the prejudices of those around you might be the result of the kind of implicit group pressure we described in Chapter 2 in discussing Asch's line-judging experiment. Recall that Asch's data indicated that conformity occurs most frequently when one's judgment is different from that of a *unanimous* majority. Applying this finding to the facts of Southern prejudice against blacks, one psychologist observed that "many Southerners, faced with what appears to be solid unanimity, submit to the distortion [that is, anti-black attitudes]. But when even one respected source—a minister, a newspaper editor, even a college professor—conspicuously breaks the unanimity, *perhaps* a dramatic modification is achieved in the private opinions of many conforming Southerners" (Pettigrew, 1961, pp. 109–10).

Nonetheless, it would be simplistic to imply that bigoted attitudes develop only through contact with bigoted people. They are sometimes intentionally or unintentionally fostered by a bigoted society. We have already seen how negative stereotypes can be fostered and spread by the mass media. Moreover, if economic and educational discrimination is based on ethnic background, a disproportionate number of people from ethnic minorities will be employed in menial jobs. This can result in the faulty impression that "that's all they're good for." Another variation on this theme was brought out in interviews with white South Africans designed to discover the reasons for their negative attitudes toward blacks (MacCrone, 1957). Among other things, respondents were convinced that most crimes were committed by blacks. Why? Because they saw a great many black convicts working in public places and *no* white convicts. What the respondents either did not realize or did not think about was that white convicts were not allowed to work in public! In short, a society can create prejudiced beliefs by law or by custom. In our own society—until very recently—newspapers almost always identified a nonwhite criminal or suspect by race but very rarely did so when a white was involved. Naive readers could easily have developed a distorted picture of the proportion of crime attributable to nonwhites.

It is undoubtedly true that some people are prejudiced because they are conforming to group pressures or simply because they have not been exposed to accurate or true information about the group in question. These people have been referred to as "latent liberals," meaning that liberalizing them is simply a matter of freeing them from these pressures and misconceptions. But for others, prejudice does seem to fill an important personal or social need; accordingly, it would be a mistake to assume (as many people in the 1930s and 1940s did) that overcoming prejudice is simply a matter of exposing people to the truth. We have already seen that people tend not to listen or read material that is dissonant with their beliefs. During World War II, for example, a series of radio broadcasts were aimed at reducing ethnic prejudice by presenting sympathetic informational programs about various ethnic groups. One week there was a program on people of Italian origin; the next week a program on people of Polish origin, and so forth. Who was listening? Well, the Poles listened to the program about Poles; the Italians listened to the program about Italians; and each of the other ethnic groups followed suit (Lazarfeld, 1944).

What happens if you *force* people to listen? There is some evidence that, if the need to maintain a prejudiced attitude is strong enough, such a procedure may actually boomerang; people may misinterpret the information to fit their prejudice. Even in the seventies, after two decades of communication and persuasion by courts, civil rights groups, scholars, the government, and the media, many white Americans still cling to their anti-black prejudices. If some people believe that blacks are stupid, and you show them a film of a highly intelligent, articulate black man, they are apt to conclude that the fellow is a "smart-ass, uppity nigger" (see Cooper & Dinerman, 1951).

How can prejudice be reduced?

If simple information campaigns do not work, how then do we reduce or eliminate prejudice? It should be clear from reading this chapter that there are no simple solutions to the problem of prejudice. There are, however, some intriguing possibilities based upon social-psychological theory. Our belief in the feasibility of these approaches has been strengthened by some well-designed laboratory experiments. Admittedly, evidence from laboratory experiments is far from conclusive when dealing with a complex and highly emotional phenomenon like prejudice; it is encouraging to note, however, that preliminary reports from the "real world" seem to confirm the laboratory data.

INCREASING
FAMILIARITY

—*See that man over there?*
—*Yes.*
—*Well, I hate him.*
—*But you don't know him.*
—*That's why I hate him.*

(Allport, 1954)

Being different or unfamiliar arouses hostility. As one woman put it, commenting on the fatal shooting, in 1970, of four students at Kent State University: "Anyone who appears on the streets of a city like Kent with long hair, dirty clothes or barefooted deserves to be shot" (Michener, 1971). While this is obviously an extreme reaction, it is not qualitatively different from the initial reaction of the students at Oregon State University to the mysterious student in the black bag.

The what? Several years ago a person arrived every Monday, Wednesday, and Friday at a speech class at Oregon State University. The student was dressed in a big black bag that covered her/his entire body—except for the feet (bare), which protruded from the bottom (Zajonc, 1968). The bag came to class every week for about two months. The initial reaction of the other students was somewhat hostile; but gradually they began to approach out of curiosity, and eventually they became quite friendly. As social psychologist Robert Zajonc puts it, "Familiarity breeds content" (*see* p. 52).

Nonetheless, the relationship between unfamiliarity and prejudice is not a simple one. In the thirties, forties, and fifties, while prejudice against blacks was higher among whites in the South than those in the North, exposure to blacks was also greater. Clearly, the nature of the contact and familiarity play

Shared coping produces a feeling of camaraderie that can break through artificially imposed ethnic or racial barriers.

an important role—as do historical and economic factors and the norms of the community. What can be said is that, all *things being equal, people tend to experience less hostility and less prejudice as they become increasingly familiar to one another.* Increasing familiarity, in and of itself, is not a cure for prejudice; but it is an opening wedge. Something else must follow.

SHARED COPING

One factor that can follow familiarity and has been shown to reduce hostility is **shared coping.** Recall that in our discussion of conflict as a cause of prejudice, we described the experiment in which two groups of boys at a summer camp were intentionally placed in conflict situations until intergroup hostility developed. The hostilities were relieved only when the boys found themselves in situations in which it was essential for them to join with each other in coping with a universal problem. For example, on a camping trip the truck broke down. To get it going again, it was necessary to pull it up a hill; and to pull it up the hill it was essential that both groups cooperate. After a number of these cooperative ventures, a sharp reversal of hostile feelings and negative stereotyping was observed among members of the two rival groups. Friendships developed between members of the different groups, they began to cooperate spontaneously even in noncrisis situations, and a relaxed atmosphere was eventually established.

The data from this experiment seem to square with common experience. It has long been recognized that there are fewer racial incidents among military personnel in combat areas—where cooperation is vital—than in areas free of crisis. Clearly, it is difficult to maintain hostile feelings about people with whom you are engaged in fighting a war and preserving your lives.

In shared-coping situations, individuals become partners aiming for a common goal. An interesting example of the partnership aspect comes from a recent experiment performed in elementary-school classrooms (Aronson et al., 1975). Instead of competing with each other for high grades and teacher approval (as in traditional classrooms), fifth-graders were divided into six-person cooperative groups. Each of the six children received a small piece of the assignment; in order to master the entire assignment, they had to teach and learn from each other. One lesson involved the life of Joseph Pulitzer. The experimenters wrote a six-paragraph biography of the man; each paragraph covered a major aspect of Pulitzer's life—how his family came to the U.S., his childhood, his education, first jobs, and his later success. They cut up the biography into sections and gave each child in the learning group one paragraph. Thus, every learning group possessed the entire life story of Joseph Pulitzer, but each child had no more than one-sixth of the story and was dependent on the others to complete the big picture.

The results were striking. Children who worked together came to like each other better—even across ethnic and racial lines—as compared to children in traditional classrooms. They also liked school better and learned the material somewhat better than children in traditional classrooms.

A DISSONANCE APPROACH   One of the difficulties of utilizing shared-coping situations to break down prejudices is that they do not often occur naturally. Investigators can sometimes engineer situations carefully so that cooperation between groups becomes essential. But it is unlikely that enough of these crises will occur by accident or that a major change will take place in our still essentially competitive educational system or in other social and economic institutions.

In recent years, some progress has been made by government in the direction of decreasing the segregation of racial groups. A notable example was the landmark 1954 decision of the Supreme Court, which decreed that so-called "separate-but-equal" educational facilities were, in fact, unequal and therefore unconstitutional. Theoretically, it could be argued that this decision has had a profound effect on reducing prejudice. Opponents of integration have argued, however, that it has failed because you cannot legislate morality; people will not like and respect each other simply because a law is passed. In the simplest sense, of course, they are right. As we have suggested, simply increasing the opportunities for contact does not in and of itself reduce prejudice, although it can set the stage for other processes that might have some effect on people's attitudes. One of these processes might be contact between groups of equal status, as in schools; such contact increases the possibility of shared coping and the understanding that can stem from it.

Another possibility is that such contact, or even the anticipation of it, will produce a change in attitude through the operation of a process known as the *psychology of inevitability.* Basically, this means that if an individual holds the cognition that a particular event is almost certain to be unpleasant and at the same time knows that it is inevitable, he or she experiences dissonance. One way to reduce dissonance is to convince oneself that the upcoming event is not as unpleasant as previously imagined. In short, people tend to change their attitudes toward events, objects, or people they must inevitably encounter. In a laboratory experiment (Darley and Berscheid, 1967), college women volunteers were asked to discuss their sexual behavior and standards in a small group, along with another woman they did not know — a situation in which they might well feel uncomfortable. Before the group met, they were given two folders; each contained a personality description of a woman — a mixture of pleasant and unpleasant characteristics. Half the subjects were led to believe they were going to interact in the intimate discussion group with the person described in folder A, while the woman described in folder B would be assigned to a different group. The other half of the subjects were told they were going to interact with the woman described in folder B. Before actually meeting the women, all the subjects were asked to evaluate them on the basis of the personality descriptions they had read. Subjects who felt that they would inevitably have to interact with the woman described in folder A found *her* much more appealing than the woman described in folder B. Those who believed they were going to participate in the discussion with the woman described in folder B found *her* much more appealing. The knowledge that they would be spending some time with a particular person — the feeling of inevitability — increased her attractive qualities or at least decreased the negative ones. In short, people tend to reduce dissonance by making the best of something they know is bound to occur.

In many communities, attempts to implement the landmark 1954 Supreme Court decision by means of school busing have met with vocal and physical opposition.

Admittedly, a laboratory experiment involving attitudes toward hypothetical college women is a far cry from an attempt to change imbedded attitudes between blacks and whites. Few people are so naive as to believe that deep-seated racial intolerance can be eliminated either by shared coping or by the reduction of dissonance that stems from coming to terms with inevitable events. What I would suggest is that such events *can* provide the opening wedge toward producing a diminution of hostile feelings in many individuals.

OBSERVATIONS FROM THE FIELD

The data from the real world lend some support to these speculations. In addition to the recent elementary-school research already cited, there are some earlier results from an investigation of the attitudes of whites toward blacks who lived in the same public-housing projects (Deutsch and Collins, 1951). In one project, black and white families were segregated; they were assigned to separate buildings in the same project. In another project, the races were integrated; black and white families of reasonably similar status were assigned to apartments in the same building. Whites in the integrated project reported a greater positive change in their attitudes toward blacks (compared to their attitudes before moving into the project) than residents of the segregated project.

It should be emphasized that psychologists were observing a public-housing project, in which the residents shared a low economic status. When blacks move into private housing in formerly all-white neighborhoods, the situation may be very different. White residents frequently feel that their social status and economic well-being are being threatened, and consequently there is a tendency for their attitudes to become more unfavorable (Kramer, 1949). On the other hand, there are in the United States—North and South—residential neighborhoods that have been successfully and peacefully integrated. Putting all these findings together, I would conclude that people try to adjust their attitudes to make inevitability as pleasant as possible; but if conflict, frustration, and rancor already exist in a situation, the psychology of inevitability will not, of itself, produce a positive change in attitudes. In such situations, additional work must be done to overcome the hostility that is frequently generated by desegregation. The major point is that—to begin to combat prejudice and to bring the races together—conditions of equal status must exist. Under these conditions, unless it is done in a manner that generates hostility and suspicion, the mere fact of desegregation can lead people to accommodate their attitudes to this accomplished fact. If shared coping becomes a part of the situation, the probability of harmony and understanding is increased still further.

PREJUDICE AGAINST WOMEN

Thus far, we have limited our discussion of prejudice to ethnic and racial conflicts. In recent years, however, our society has become increasingly aware of the discrimination and stereotyping that occurs as a result of differential sex roles. The notion of *sex roles* is quite useful in understanding the pressures to conform that society places on both men and women (*see* pp. 134, 178). The most striking feature differentiating male and female sex roles is the great diversity of acceptable role behaviors available to men and the lack of such choice and diversity for women. Traditionally, femininity has been correlated consistently with high anxiety, low self-esteem, and low social acceptance (Gall, 1969; Gray, 1957; Sears, 1970). The female role has been centered around the home, children, and marriage, with concomitant limited access to high-status occupations and to more differentiated jobs. The popular image of the "housewife" and mother remains dominant, even though many women do work outside the home.

Sex role researchers (e.g., Bem, 1975) and members of the feminist movement point out that our current system of sex-role differentiation has long since outlived its usefulness, and that it now serves only to prevent both men and women from developing their full potential as human beings. Feminists believe that people need no longer be socialized to conform strictly to outdated standards of masculinity and feminity. Instead, both sexes should be encouraged to exhibit "masculine" behaviors—instrumental and assertive—or "feminine" behaviors—warm and expressive—depending upon the situational appropriateness. The degree to which sex roles have become less rigid in recent years is still a subject for debate. It seems safe to say, however, that there is at least an increased recognition that redefinition is necessary.

Sexism—the idea that women are inherently inferior to men—shares many attitudes and behaviors with racist thinking and activity. Thus we can look to the social-psychological literature on prejudice covered in this chapter to shed light on possible causes and possible alternatives to sexism.

The study of white South Africans mentioned earlier in this chapter can help to explain how some of society's sexist attitudes are formed. The investigator (MacCrone, 1957) argues that a society can create prejudiced beliefs by law or by custom; and indeed we know that women have often been denied easy access to certain educational opportunities, occupations, and political positions. Consequently, when the media portray women in news reports, documentaries, or situation comedies, they are not—for the most part—seen as authority figures, intellectuals, or adventurers. They are much more likely to be portrayed as exactly the opposites—as powerless, stupid, or cowardly. And, because people tend to absorb without examination what they frequently see or are continually told, they rarely ask _why_ women are usually seen in inconsequential roles. For example, in 1975, the National Organization of Women (N.O.W.) monitored 114 hours of local news broadcasting by the major San Francisco television stations. They found that only 8 percent of all people on camera were women in career roles, compared with 52 percent of men depicted in career roles (San Francisco N.O.W., April 1976). In San Francisco, 43 percent of all workers are women.

On the individual level, women, like many minorities, have often been reinforced for behaviors that support the notion that they are inferior, overly emotional, passive, dependent, indecisive, and even neurotic. Consequently, a self-fulfilling prophecy is initiated; cognitive dissonance is likely to be aroused in a woman who attempts to view herself as different from the socially accepted feminine norm. If a male truck driver and a female homemaker were to change roles, for example, it is clear that much dissonance would occur, especially when they interacted with their peers. Because people can foresee the dissonance, they would probably avoid the situation, and a socially conditioned stereotype would thus be perpetuated.

Restrictive sex roles for women have been promoted, surreptitiously, by the media of communication.

People tend to like individuals whose values and beliefs seem similar to their own. Thus, especially in the past, if women deviate from the traditional sex role by being assertive or seeking jobs usually reserved to men, they risk losing friendships and incurring prejudices of a different, more overt type—those directed against so-called "masculine" women. Moreover, since people need to compare themselves to others they perceive as similar, they are less likely to step out of an accepted position without a role model. This is especially true of members of groups that are insecure and low in self-esteem. As long as society defines the sex roles rigidly, only the very secure, independent person will venture into unconventional roles.

Prejudice against women is not limited to males; several studies show that some women have a lower opinion of women in general than they do of men. In one experiment (Goldberg, 1968), female college students were asked to read several scholarly articles and evaluate them in terms of competence, style, and so on. To some students, specific articles were attributed to male authors (for example, John T. McKay); to others, the same articles were attributed to female authors (for example, Joan T. McKay). On the average, the women students rated the articles much higher when they were attributed to a male author. This was true even when the articles dealt with topics regarded as the especial province of women. In other words, most of the women tested had "learned their place"; they regarded female output as necessarily inferior to male output.

From studies reviewed earlier in this chapter, it seems clear that if men and women work cooperatively—and as equals—on important tasks, a greater mutual respect could be cultivated, and social and economic equality may eventually result. But some women are still isolated in their households; and, until recently, they have been unable to share and compare feelings and ideas with other women, to identify with "women," or to unite in common cause. They often lacked the group cohesiveness and sense of shared coping needed to overcome an oppressive situation. The feminist movement has now given some women a rallying point and provided a source of support, information, and increased self-respect.

The problem of generalized hostility is broader than what has typically been defined as prejudice. It extends to the feelings any person has for any other person. That is, when one looks over the hill of racial, ethnic, and sexist prejudice, one sees the vast valley of interpersonal relations. Moving beyond the problem of reducing prejudice, one encounters the fundamental problem of determining what makes people like and trust each other. How do we move from mere tolerance to important relationships involving mutual responsibility? What happens *after* schools are integrated? What happens after dissonance has been reduced and shared coping has taken place? In our day-to-day life, why do we like some people more than others? It is to this question that we turn in the following chapter.

SUMMARY

Prejudice is defined as a set of hostile attitudes based on and supported by generalizations derived from faulty or incomplete information. Among the many causes of prejudice is conflict between groups—for example, competition for scarce jobs or, on a national scale, territory or influence. If conflict decreases—if jobs become plentiful or enemies become allies—the **stereotype** (general image) of all individuals in a group may change from negative to positive. But prejudging an individual, even positively, ignores his or her unique traits.

Another cause of prejudice is the displacement of aggression aroused by high-status individuals or abstract forces to safe, identifiable targets, who function as **scapegoats.** Angered by one's powerful boss, a person may strike out against his or her children. Frustrated by "the economy," people may choose relatively powerless and less abstract targets for retaliation—such as the Jews in Nazi Germany.

Conformity to existing norms of a group or society can also produce prejudice. In South Africa, discrimination is written into the legal system; it is thus no surprise to find that whites in that country are strongly prejudiced against blacks. In the United States, conformity to traditional social and class norms has resulted in a similar prejudice.

While some individuals, because of early childhood experience, show a greater propensity toward being prejudiced than others, it is overly pessimistic to assert that prejudiced attitudes cannot be changed short of intensive psychotherapy. At the same time, it is clear that prejudice cannot be substantially reduced simply by exposing individuals to favorable information about the "out-group"; such efforts founder on people's tendency to ignore or distort information that is contrary to their attitudes. Moreover, once established, prejudice is not greatly affected by simply increasing contact between individuals or groups.

Frequent contact with someone leads to familiarity, and familiarity does usually decrease hostility, *if* the contact does not directly reinforce prejudice. **Shared coping,** in which people must cooperate to gain some mutually desirable goal, reduces prejudice markedly. Another promising technique involves placing people in inevitable situations that run directly counter to their prejudices. Since the situation is unavoidable, the person may reduce dissonance (and prejudice) by changing his or her attitudes.

Both men and women have become increasingly aware of prejudice against women in recent years. Because of societal sex-role stereotypes, women may find it difficult to assert themselves, while men may be embarrassed to show sensitivity and warmth. The stereotypes are hardest on women, however, who suffer economic and social discrimination by conforming and possible loss of friends and personal conflict if they try to "play a man's role." Feminist organizations can provide information and support and help both sexes adjust to changing times.

Attraction: Who Likes Whom and Why

Why do we like certain people?
Is a reward theory an adequate explanation of attraction?
How might the gain-loss theory explain interpersonal attraction?

"And that's the wonder, the wonder of this country, that a man can end with diamonds here on the basis of being liked!" So says Willy Loman, the pathetic hero of Arthur Miller's modern classic *Death of a Salesman*. Even if it brings no diamonds, people do believe that it is important to be liked. Polls conducted among high-school students, over and over again, have shown that their most common concern and desire is to be liked by others.

Moreover, the idea that it is important to be liked is not limited to adolescents. It pervades our society, reaching even into its most hallowed institutions, including the legal system. Clarence Darrow, perhaps the most famous American trial lawyer ever, once said, "Jurymen seldom convict a person they like or acquit one they dislike. The main work of a trial lawyer is to make a jury like his client or at least to feel sympathy for him; facts regarding the crime are relatively unimportant." Several laboratory experiments, in which people have played the roles of jurors, have confirmed Darrow's observations. For example in one such study (Landy and Aronson, 1969), psychologists presented "jurors" with a case of negligent homicide. A pedestrian was struck down and killed on Christmas Eve by a driver who had been drinking heavily. To one set of "jurors," the driver was presented in a positive light (as an insurance ad-juster, a widower, who was on his way to spend Christmas Eve with his son, daughter-in-law, and grandchildren). To another "jury," he was presented in a less positive light (as a janitor, twice divorced, who was on his way to visit his new girlfriend in her apartment). The difference resulted in significantly longer jail sentences for the janitor than for the insurance adjuster—although the crimes were identical. Moreover, the characteristics of the *victim* also affected the decisions of the jurors: other things being equal, when the victim was an attractive person, the defendant was punished far more severely than when he or she was unattractive.

Why do we like certain people?

It is clear that personal attractiveness is one important factor in liking or dis-liking a person in our society. The overall question of what causes us to like some people better than others is one that almost everyone has considered. In that sense, all people are social psychologists, although only a few of us get paid for it. We live in the world; consequently, we interact with other people. Through our experiences we develop social-psychological theories. Nowhere is this more prevalent than in the area of interpersonal attraction. I have, on occasion, asked the undergraduates in my classes what makes them like their

best friend more than they like other people. I usually get a multitude of responses, including: (1) similarity of values, attitudes, beliefs, and/or interests; (2) skills, abilities, or competencies; (3) pleasant or "admirable" qualities such as loyalty, pleasantness, reasonableness, honesty, and kindness.

These reasons sound like good common sense. They also square with the results of a great deal of systematic research in the areas. The data show that people like people who cooperate rather than compete, who have pleasant characteristics, who agree with them, who praise rather than criticize them, and who help rather than obstruct them.

One can include all of these aspects of attractiveness under one simple and sweeping generalization: We like people whose behavior brings us maximal reward. This proposition has been stressed by a number of theorists (for example, Homans, 1961), and, as generalizations go, it is a useful one. We can begin by looking at the wide array of situations in which it make sense, saving the problems with this general statement for later.

REWARDS THROUGH DOING FAVORS

If you were starving and I provided you with a nourishing meal, *that* would be rewarding and the chances are good that you would like me for it. Similarly, if you were drowning and I plunged into the water and rescued you, you would like me better than if I had walked by and left you to struggle on your own.

This phenomenon can be illustrated by any number of experiments. Of course, experimenters in the field of social psychology usually stop short of setting up situations in which human subjects are actually starving or drowning. But, as we have seen, they do attempt to set up situations that are reasonably analogous to extreme situations. In one study (Lott & Lott, 1960), children were put into three-person groups to play a game that involved choosing various pathways on a game board. Choosing the right pathways led to safety; choosing the wrong pathways led to disaster. The children were, in effect,

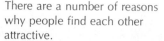

There are a number of reasons why people find each other attractive.

There are many ways to measure a person's liking for another. Since, in one sense, attraction can be considered an attitude, we can measure liking for a person much as we measure attitudes. For example, in many experiments liking is measured by two simple scales: the first asks the person to indicate how much he or she would like or dislike another person by circling a number on a seven-point scale (7 being most positive and 1 being most negative); the second scale might ask a related question, such as whether the subject would enjoy working with the other person (7 indicating the person would enjoy it very much and 1 meaning he or she would dislike it very much).

Rating scales are easy to administer; for this reason they are the most commonly used measure of attraction. They have one major flaw, however: precisely because they are so easy to fill out they may not be totally accurate. Since it costs nothing to indicate feelings on a piece of paper, they may be inclined to treat the ratings rather casually. They may not think very deeply about their own feelings, or they may be inclined to write that they like someone even when they don't—just to be a nice guy.

Because of this factor, social psychologists have recently begun to employ indices of attraction that require a heavier commitment. Such indices are called behavioral measures. For example, consider the experiment in which the college students liked the supervisor who punished their enemy. In this study, investigators were interested in how much subjects liked the experimenter's supervisor, who was a psychology professor. After the experiment was over, the departmental secretary told each subject that the professor desperately needed volunteers to make a number of phone calls right away. She asked each subject to volunteer to do the professor this favor. If the subject agreed, she asked him how many phone calls he or she was willing to make. The number of phone calls was used as an index of liking; that is, subjects who volunteered to make fifteen phone calls were considered to like the professor more than those who agreed to make eight phone calls; and eight phone calls expressed ''more liking'' than four calls, or none. The underlying assumption of the measure is that if we like someone, it pleases us to see that person happy. If we do him or her a favor, we increase this happiness. Therefore, the more we like a person, the more favors we will volunteer—all other things being equal.

But all other things are not always equal. Perhaps one of the students in the above experiment really liked the professor a great deal and would have liked to do him or her a favor but was extremely busy. Accordingly, that person could volunteer to make only one or two phone

walking single file through a mine field, except that the mine remained active even after it had exploded. The leader who chose the wrong path was "blown up" (and put out of the game), and the child next in line would, of course, choose a different path. If the leader chose correctly, he or she led the others to a successful completion of the game. The researchers found that children who were rewarded (that is, who arrived safely at the goal) showed a greater liking for their teammates—who were instrumental in helping them achieve the reward—than did children who never reached the final goal. In short, we like people who contribute to our victory better than people who do not.

There are all kinds of favors people can do for each other; one class of them involves punishing our enemies. In an experiment (Aronson & Cope, 1968), college students were placed in a situation in which they were treated either kindly or cruelly by a graduate research assistant. They then chanced to overhear that assistant being chastised harshly by the supervisor on a totally unrelated matter. Those who had been cruelly treated by the assistant ended up with great liking for the supervisor who treated their enemy harshly. (Although

calls. So, although the student liked the professor a lot, it would not show up in the score.

There are, of course, simpler behavioral measures than favor-doing. One of these is eye contact. It has been shown that when two people talk to each other they look into each other's eyes off and on for short periods, ranging from 30 to 60 percent of their interaction. The frequency of eye contact has been shown to correlate with subjects' expressed liking for each other (Argyle, 1967).

Still another measure of attraction, the *sociometric scale*, combines the simplicity of a rating scale with the commitment of a behavioral measure. Individuals are asked to indicate (on a rating scale) whether they are willing to have another person as a roommate, as a work partner on an actual project they are about to begin, as a seat-partner on an upcoming bus excursion, and so forth. While such a measure is easy to obtain, it also includes a real commitment to spend some time with the person. Therefore, it is much less likely that individuals would answer the question casually or haphazardly.

A sociogram—an illustration of data from rating scales—can show the structure of a social situation. Shown here are several elementary-school students' choices of classmates they liked best, along with their second and third choices.

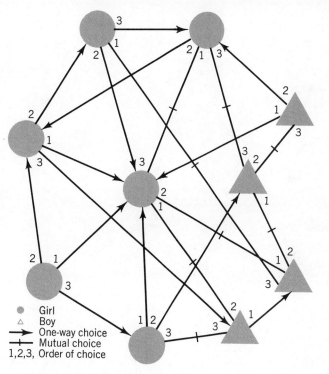

- ● Girl
- △ Boy
- → One-way choice
- —+— Mutual choice
- 1,2,3, Order of choice

we have described these experimental situations in very simple terms, measurement of such a complex concept as attraction is not easy, as you can see from Spotlight 5-1.)

REWARDS THROUGH SIMILARITY

Another way people provide rewards for each other is to agree on some issue. If all we know about a person are his or her opinions on some issues, the closer those opinions are to our own, the more we like the person (Byrne, 1969). Similarly, experiments have shown that the person who deviates from the opinions and attitudes of a group is rejected by that group (Schachter, 1951). You will recall that in Chapter 2 we asked why people conform. One of the reasons was found to be the desire to be liked or to avoid being rejected. If that is their goal, people who conform are in fact behaving rationally, for—although in the abstract people tend to admire and respect individualists—in most personal situations they dislike those who disagree with them and like those who agree. In effect, we seem to be telling other people: "It's fine if you are in disagreement—as long as it's not with me!"

We tend to like people with whom we share values, attitudes, and experiences, as illustrated by the obvious affection displayed by these Israeli soldiers.

Why *do* we like people who agree with us? There are three important possibilities. One is that people who share our opinion on an issue provide us with a kind of social validation for our beliefs—that is, they give us the feeling that we are right. This is rewarding and, hence, we like those who agree with us. If a person disagrees with us, this suggests that we may be wrong. This is punishing; hence, we don't like people who disagree with us.

A second reason for the relationship between similarity and liking is more subtle. People tend to make certain negative attributions about the motives or character of a person who disagrees with us on a substantive issue. It is not simply that his or her disagreement indicates that we may be wrong, but rather that we suspect the opinion indicates that he or she is the kind of person we have found to be unpleasant, immoral, or stupid. As we saw in the preceding chapter, humans have a tendency to go beyond the information given and to make dispositional—rather than situational—attributions for the behavior of others. **Attribution theory** deals with (1) the rules most people use in attempting to infer the causes of the behavior they observe; and (2) the different situations that produce different kinds of attributions. For example, if a prejudiced woman saw a Chicano man asleep in the park, she would be likely to attribute this behavior to laziness; a relatively unprejudiced person might simply see a hard-working person taking a well-deserved rest.

As the reader may gather, attributions flow in vicious circles. That is, if we do not like people of a particular racial or ethnic background, we attribute negative motives and dispositions to them. Once we have made these negative attributions, we have supportive "evidence" for our dislike. Therefore, the woman can say she does not dislike the Chicano man because he is resting in the park, but because he is lazy!

There is a third reason why we like people who agree with us. We have learned that people who agree with us generally like us, and a person's liking for us is an extraordinarily powerful reward in itself. People like to be liked. A professional businessman and amateur psychologist named Dale Carnegie made a fortune by selling this idea. In 1937 he wrote a book called *How to Win Friends and Influence People,* which continues to be a best seller and has been translated into thirty-five languages. Essentially, Carnegie advised his readers to be pleasant, to pretend that they liked the people they talk to, to seem interested in the things their companions are interested in, and to "dole out praise lavishly." As we shall see, pretense has only limited value. But the assumption behind the advice *is* sound: people like to be liked, and they like those who like them. This fact has been demonstrated in numerous experiments.

The reader, may well be yawning by this time. More likely, he or she is wondering, with some impatience, whether social psychologists spend their time performing experiments that prove conclusively what every one already knows. On one level, I am inclined to agree. As an experimentalist, I admit I get more satisfaction from doing research to test a somewhat surprising and innovative hypothesis than in trying to prove something my grandmother already knows is true. And yet, I have come to realize that we never really know for sure that something is true unless it has been demonstrated under controlled conditions. My grandmother is a pretty good social psychologist; but many phenomena that she "knows" to be true turn out *not* to be true when we put them to the test.

With this in mind, let us look at the phenomenon of liking someone who likes us. The reciprocation of sentiment is a common phenomenon — but which causes which? It could be that Sam likes Harry because Harry has shown that he likes Sam. Since being liked feels good to Sam and since Harry is the cause of this good feeling, Sam comes to like Harry. On the other hand, the causal sequence could be reversed. Sam could come to like Harry; then, as a consequence of this liking, he may have convinced himself that Harry likes him. In the complexity of an interpersonal relationship, it is often difficult for participants to unravel which of these causal sequences is operating. Accordingly, it makes sense for an experimenter to attempt to arrive at a definitive answer by constructing a controlled situation and observing the relationship in a dispassionate manner.

Such an experiment was constructed by two psychologists (Backman & Secord, 1959), who formed groups of people who were strangers to each other. Before the first meeting, each person was given a personality test and informed that — based on the results of this test — designated people in the group would almost surely like him or her a great deal. Actually, the designations were made at random. The information they were given had a very large *initial* effect on the feelings of the subjects; there was a strong early attraction to people the subjects were told would probably like them. The effects of this deceptive information did not, however, last for long. After the first few meetings, the designated people were not liked better than the others. With actual contact, the subjects received much more realistic information about each other, and, as a consequence, their feelings changed. The experiment demonstrated that, in the absence of information to the contrary, the suspicion that someone likes us increases our tendency to like that person. But it also showed that the phenomenon is ephemeral; no matter how much people expect or want to be liked, they will not usually continue to believe that they *are* liked in the face of the continued absence of concrete evidence.

Self-Esteem and Being Liked

One way of looking at these data is to suggest that people need to be liked because of feelings such as insecurity, anxiety, and low self-esteem. If someone reduces these unpleasant feelings by liking us, we like that person. An unusually "realistic" experiment provided graphic evidence to support this interpretation by showing that as the feeling of insecurity grows more intense, so too does our tendency to like someone who demonstrates liking for us. The experiment (Walster, 1965) was performed with female university students. Each woman arrived at a general reception room, where she was greeted and asked to wait for the experimenter. While she was waiting, a good-looking, well-dressed male student came in. Through his conversation with a receptionist, it was established that he was waiting to participate in a totally different experiment. The young man, who was actually an accomplice, then struck up a conversation with the subject, indicated that he found her attractive, and, after a while, asked her to go out with him.

At this point the experimenter entered and led the young woman into the experimental room. She was told that the purpose of the study was to examine the results of various personality tests she had taken previously. The student was then given a contrived evaluation of her personality. Half of the women were led to believe that the tests indicated that they were sensitive, original, and interesting people possessing great integrity. This information was designed to raise their self-esteem temporarily. The other women were informed that they were immature, inflexible, and had a weak personality. This information was designed to lower their self-esteem and thus increase their feelings of insecurity. Finally, as part of the experiment, all the subjects were asked to rate how much they liked a wide variety of people—a teacher, a friend, others. "And since we have one space left, why don't you also rate that fellow whom you were waiting with?" The results indicated that the students who received unfavorable information about themselves showed far more liking for the young man than those who had received favorable information about themselves. In short, we like to be liked—and the more insecure we feel, the more we appreciate being liked and, consequently, the more we like someone who likes us.

THE RELATIONSHIP BETWEEN SIMILARITY AND BEING LIKED

As we have suggested, these two causes of attraction—similarity and being liked—are not independent of each other. One reason we like a person with similar beliefs may be precisely because we infer that a person who shares our opinion on several issues, would—after getting to know us—probably like us. If this is true, we would expect being liked to be a stronger force than similarity of opinion. And it is. When both variables are present in the same experiment, being liked appears to be a more powerful determinant of attraction than similarity—although both have an effect (Aronson & Worchel, 1966).

Birds of a feather often flock together.

But the sociopsychological world is not always simple. Attraction is not the sum of the two factors but the result of an interaction between them that is discernible but not immediately obvious. For example, it has been shown (Jones, Bell, & Aronson, 1971) that there is something especially exciting about being liked by someone who does not share your opinions on various issues. In one experiment, women college students were first allowed to discover that another woman had opinions that were either similar or dissimilar to their own. After having a conversation with that person, they then eavesdropped on her while she was describing them favorably to a third party. The results showed that the students indicated the greatest liking for a person with dissimilar attitudes who liked them. Thus, although we generally like people who have attitudes similar to our own, if we encounter someone who likes us *in spite of the fact that our opinions differ,* we are inclined to infer that there must be something special and unique about us that he or she finds attractive. In effect we think, "Sue likes me for myself—not for my opinions." Since this realization is especially gratifying, we tend to like Sue very much.

The relationship between similarity and attraction becomes even more complicated when we move from opinion similarity to similarity of personality characteristics. Is it true that "birds of a feather flock together," as the old adage goes? Or do you believe that other old adage, "opposites attract"? Interestingly, investigators who have studied the needs and values of engaged and married couples have found support for both these possibilities (Banta & Hetherington, 1963; Winch, 1958). One explanation for these differences is that whether opposite personalities attract or repell each other depends on what characteristics are being considered. A person who valued neatness and tidiness to the point of obsession would almost surely find it difficult to live with a slob. And, of course, the slob would not be too happy with an overly neat person either. It seems reasonable to assume that neat people would flock to neat people and slobs would flock to slobs. Similarly, an extrovert, a person who needs to socialize with others frequently, might not get along too well with an introverted person whose idea of a good time was to sit home with a good book—and vice versa. It seems reasonable to assume that introverts would seek out introverts and extroverts would seek out extroverts. But what of a different set of characteristics, such as nurturance and dependency? A person who is very nurturant (likes to take care of others) and a person who has high dependency needs (likes to be taken care of) probably would get along swimmingly. In actuality, of course, many sets of characteristics are involved in any one relationship; some of these demand similarity to achieve compatability, while others demand complementarity.

PHYSICAL ATTRACTIVENESS AS A REWARD

One of the most powerful determinants of interpersonal attraction, especially in women, is physical attractiveness. This characteristic is so important that it tends to have an even greater impact on men than such powerful determinants of attraction as similarity of attitudes. In a recent study (Kleck and Rubenstein, 1975), male subjects and a female confederate interviewed each other. The confederate was made to appear very attractive when interviewing half of the subjects and rather ugly when meeting with the others. Before the encounter with the confederate, each subject filled out a questionnaire measuring his attitudes. During the interview, the confederate expressed attitudes that were either similar or dissimilar to the subject's. At the end of the interview, another experimenter asked the subject a number of questions about the encounter and the confederate. Between two and four weeks later, the subject was contacted again and completed another questionnaire about the situation and his impression of the confederate.

The results were striking. According to the ratings given immediately after the encounter, the subjects who saw her as a physically attractive woman liked the confederate far more than those who saw her as an unattractive one. Similarity or dissimilarity of attitudes did not affect their feelings about her at all. Two to four weeks later, those who had interacted with the woman when she was attractively made up and well dressed indicated that they thought about her more, continued to like her, and remembered more details about her appearance than those who had interacted with her when she looked frumpy. Again, similarity of attitudes had no impact on these measures.

The effect of physical attractiveness, like other factors related to attraction, depends on the individual's level of self-esteem. In one study (Kiesler and Baral, 1970) Yale men were led to believe that they had performed either exceptionally poorly or exceptionally well on an intelligence test. Each young man was then "accidentally" allowed to meet a young woman who was an experimental accomplice. Again, in half the cases, the woman's makeup and clothing made her look extremely attractive; in the other half, she was made to appear rather homely. The men who had been led to feel good about themselves tended to show more romantic interest in her as an attractive woman; those who had been made to feel discouraged about themselves tended to show more romantic interest in her as a less-attractive woman. People do regard physical attractiveness as important; and if they are feeling good about themselves they are more apt to reach out for it (and brave possible rejection) than if they are not.

Is a reward theory an adequate explanation of attraction?

All of the above situations support a reward theory of attraction. We do in fact seem to like people whose behavior is rewarding and dislike those whose behavior is punishing. But, although this generalization covers a wide array of human behavior, we often find that in more complex social situations, it is difficult to predict the conditions under which a person will be liked, disliked, or yawned at as a consequence of performing a specific action. One reason for this difficulty is that, in these situations, the meaning of the term *reward* is not always clear. We have already seen some indication of this complexity in the finding that, while both attitude similarity and being liked are rewarding, being liked by a similar person is apparently *less* rewarding than being liked by a dissimilar person. There are other conditions, too, in which we like someone better if he or she disagrees with us. For example, we like disagreers more than agreers if we can convert the disagreers to our point of view (Sigall,

1970). Of course, it can also be argued that the feeling of effectiveness gained by converting someone is also a reward. But, if agreers are rewarding and if converting a disagreer is also rewarding, the concept of reward may be extended too broadly to be of much practical use.

THE ROLE OF COMPETENCY

Moreover, the social context in which the "reward" is provided can change the meaning of the reward. Some behaviors that might appear rewarding in one context are anything but rewarding in a slightly different setting. For example, let us look at the *competence* of another person. Being around able, competent people is usually more rewarding than being around incompetent people. People like to be right, and one way to increase the probability of being right is to be in the vicinity of people who know what they are talking about — people available for consultation. Thus, if we assume that able, competent people are more rewarding to us than incompetent people, does it not follow that we like people of extremely high ability and competence to a greater extent than people who are moderately or poorly endowed? This seems like a truism; yet, as obvious as this relationship may seem to be, there is some disquieting evidence that it does not always hold. Experiments on group interactions, for example, have demonstrated that group members considered the most able are not necessarily the best liked. Other studies have shown that people generally acknowledged as the initiators of most of the best ideas in a group are most often *not* among the best-liked members (Hollander & Webb, 1955; Bales, 1953).

Why should this be true? Perhaps for most people a great deal of ability in another person makes that person appear too good, too unapproachable, too distant, too nonhuman. If this is the case, some manifestation of fallibility (humanness) on the part of highly effective people might actually increase their attractiveness.

Test of a Hypothesis

This proposition was tested experimentally (Aronson, Willerman, & Floyd, 1966), using the disguise of an investigation of social perception. Male subjects listened to a tape recording of one of four stimulus persons: (1) a near-perfect person; (2) a near-perfect person who commits a clumsy blunder; (3) a mediocre person; and (4) a mediocre person who commits a clumsy blunder. The subjects were told that they were to listen to a candidate for the college quiz bowl and that they should rate him in terms of what kind of an impression he made and how much they liked him. The tape itself was an interview between the candidate (stimulus person) and an interviewer. It consisted primarily of a set of extremely difficult questions posed by the interviewer — the kind generally asked on the college quiz bowl. On one tape the stimulus person was of very high intellectual ability and seemed to be virtually perfect. He answered 92 percent of the questions correctly. On another tape (which used the same voice) the stimulus person was presented as one of average ability; he answered only 30 percent of the questions correctly. In two additional conditions (one involving the superior person, one involving the average person), the stimulus person committed an embarrassing blunder. Near the end of the interview, he clumsily spilled a cup of coffee all over him-

TABLE 5-1 Mean attraction scores		
	Blunder	*No Blunder*
Superior Ability	30.2	20.8
Average Ability	−2.5	17.8

From E. Aronson, B. Willerman, & Joanne Floyd, "The Effect of a Pratfall on Increasing Interpersonal Attractiveness." *Psychonomic Science*, 1966, 4, 227–28.

self. Thus there were four conditions: a person of superior ability, who either blundered or did not blunder; and a person of average ability, who either blundered or did not blunder. The results were clear-cut, as shown in Table 5-1. The stimulus person who was rated most attractive was the superior person who committed a blunder; while the least attractive was the person of average ability who also committed a blunder.

Several years later, another experiment (Deaux, 1972) replicated the basic results, but found them more limited than had been expected. A blunder did increase the attractiveness of competent males in the eyes of other males, but not in the eyes of females. Nor did it increase the attractiveness of females in the eyes of males or females. Thus, the blunder phenomenon may be limited to situations in which the male subject's sense of competitiveness is aroused.

The major finding in these experiments would seem to conflict with a simple reward theory. Again, after the fact, an ingenious psychologist could explain these data in terms of a general reward theory: If a person who is perfect poses a threat, then a blundering (but competent) person is less threatening (less punishing); hence, overall he or she is more rewarding. This is a sensible explanation. But the purpose of a theory is not merely to explain results after they occur, but also—and far more important—to predict relationships. After the fact, a general reward theory can be invoked to explain any and all behavior. For example, suppose I were to state that when offered a choice between two alternatives, an individual will always choose the more pleasant. Unless I have, in advance, a clear idea of which events are pleasant and which are unpleasant in the eyes of the subject, the statement is in danger of being circular. So, suppose you said to me, "Aha! So people always choose the more pleasant alternative, eh? Then how do you explain the fact that some Christian martyrs chose to be thrown to the lions rather than recant their faith?" "That's easy," I reply, "for those people a painful death was more rewarding than renouncing their faith." The circularity occurs because I have defined reward in terms of the behavior I was supposed to be predicting.

THE EFFECTS OF PRAISE   Let us now look at *praise*, which at first glance might seem always to be rewarding. Suppose a person does a fine piece of work and the boss says, "Nice work, Jane." That phrase would almost certainly function as a reward, and Jane's liking for her boss would probably increase. Suppose, however, that Jane did a very poor job—and knows it. Along comes the boss and delivers the exact same phrase in exactly the same tone of voice. Will the phrase function as a reward in this new situation? We cannot be sure. Jane *may* interpret this statement as the boss's attempt to be encouraging, even in the face of a poor performance. Because of this display of considerateness, she may come to like the boss even *more* than when she *had*, in fact, done a good job. On the other hand, Jane might feel that the boss, in praising her, has some ulterior motive. In that case, she might view her boss's behavior as sarcastic, manipulative, dishonest, or patronizing. Would this interpretation diminish Jane's liking for the boss or would the praise feel good anyway?

A good deal of research has been done on this question. Perhaps the best way to summarize their findings is by borrowing the title of an article written by Edward Jones (1965), an expert on the psychology of ingratiation and flattery. The article is entitled "Flattery Will Get You Somewhere." In short, people do like to hear positive things about themselves, even when they have some reason to suspect the speaker of insincerity. We should also note that, on the one hand, they like a person most if they share his or her positive evaluation; but, at the other extreme, they do not like a blatant flatterer, at all. Nonetheless, people do tend to give the subtle flatterer the benefit of the doubt. These findings can best be illustrated by two experiments. In one (Deutsch & Solomon, 1959) subjects were presented with one of four situations: (1) a positive evaluation for a very good performance; (2) a negative evaluation for a poor performance; (3) a positive evaluation for a poor performance; and (4) a negative evaluation for a very good performance. As one might expect, subjects liked the evaluator best when they were given a positive evaluation for a very good performance and liked the evaluator least when they were given a negative evaluation for a very good performance. But the subjects also liked him or her a great deal when their poor performances were positively evaluated; in fact, they liked the evaluator almost as much then as when they had actually performed well—*even though they knew* the evaluator should have known the performance was, indeed, a poor one. In the second experiment (Dickoff, 1961), however, when the evaluator was clearly trying to obtain a favor, subjects saw the behavior as blatant, self-motivated dishonesty. In this setting, they disliked the flatterer.

Let us reexamine Dale Carnegie's advice in the light of these experiments. It is clear that people do like people who say positive things about them—especially when they believe that the statements are sincere. But if they have good reasons to suspect that the compliments are insincere, they dislike the complimenter. One could also generalize this beyond compliments; specifically, one might make the same case in regard to doing *any* favor for another person. Generally people like favors. But sometimes they feel their freedom is being restricted—especially when the favor-doer could benefit from the favor. For example, if you were a teacher, you would almost surely react negatively toward a student who presented you with an expensive gift just before you were to grade his or her term paper. These speculations are supported by the results of an experiment in which college students were asked to participate in a study (which was labeled as important) involving their first impressions of another person (Brehm & Cole, 1966). While the subject was waiting for the experiment to begin, the "other person" (actually a stooge) asked to leave the room to get a soft drink. When he returned, he brought a drink for the subject as well. The question that must have arisen in the minds of the subject was, "Why is he doing this? Is he trying to buy a better rating from

Spotlight 5-2 Benjamin Franklin Anticipates the Theory of Cognitive Dissonance

Doubts have been raised whether phenomena of cognitive dissonance can be observed outside the laboratory (e.g., Tedeschi *et al.*, 1971). It is therefore interesting to note the following example, which occurred well before the hypothesis of cognitive dissonance was stated.[1]

Benjamin Franklin in 1736, at the age of 30, owned a printing shop in Philadelphia and was in that year chosen to be clerk of the General Assembly of Pennsylvania. The next year he was again nominated as clerk and reappointed, but over the opposition of a new member of the House who favored another candidate. Franklin was disturbed by the opposition of this man who was wealthy, educated and talented and seemed likely to become influential in the House. What should he do about it?

"... I did not ... aim at gaining his favour by paying any servile respect to him but, after some time, took this other method. Having heard that he had in his library a certain very scarce and curious book I wrote a note to him expressing my desire of perusing that book and requesting he would do me the favour of lending it to me for a few days. He sent it immediately and I return'd it in about a week with another note expressing strongly my sense of the favour. When we next met in the House he spoke to me (which he had never done before), and with great civility; and he ever after manifested a readiness to serve me on all occasions, so that we became great friends and our friendship continued to his death. This is another instance of the truth of an old maxim I had learned, which says, *'He that has once done you a kindness will be more ready to do you another than he whom you yourself have obliged.'*"

[1] Quoted from *The Autobiography of Benjamin Franklin.* J. Bigelow (Ed.) New York: G. P. Putnam's Sons, 1916. Pp. 216–17.

me?" The actual measure of liking, however, was *not* the paper and pencil ratings but a behavioral measure. The subjects were later asked to help the stooge perform a dull task supposedly unrelated to the impression-formation experiment. The students who had *not* been given the soft drink by the stooge were more likely to help him than those who had.

Clearly, then, doing someone a favor is not a surefire way of getting his or her liking. Indeed, as we have seen, under some conditions it may even backfire. A more certain way of using favors to increase your own attractiveness is to get someone to do *you* a favor. In our discussion of the theory of cognitive dissonance we described "the justification of cruelty," in which a person who caused harm to another attempted to justify the behavior by devaluing the victim (*see* p. 17). By the same token, we would argue that a person who does someone a favor tends to justify this action by increasing the value of the recipient. In other words, the individual asks, in effect: "Why in the world did I go to all of this effort (spend all of this money, help him, or whatever) for Joe so and so? Because he's a hell of a nice guy, that's why!" (*See* Spotlight 5-2 for an illustrative example by Benjamin Franklin.)

This proposition was tested in an experiment (Jecker & Landy, 1969) in which students participated in a concept-formation task that enabled them to win a substantial sum of money. After the experiment, a third of the subjects were approached by the experimenter, who explained that he was using his own funds for the experiment and was running short. He might even be forced to stop the experiment. He asked: "As a special favor to me, would you mind returning the money you won?" All of these subjects complied with the request. Another third of the subjects were approached, not by the experimenter, but by the departmental secretary; she asked subjects to return the money as a special favor to the psychology department's research fund, which was running low. These subjects also complied with the request. The remaining third of the subjects were not asked to return their winnings. Finally, all subjects were asked to fill out a questionnaire in which they got a chance to rate the experimenter. The students who had been cajoled into doing a special favor for the experimenter himself liked him better than the other subjects did.

How might the gain-loss theory explain interpersonal attraction?

If one considers the overall mass of research on interpersonal attraction, the generalization emerges: While it is true that people like to be liked, they also like to believe that they have earned it. On the basis of this generalization (and some systematic research), a somewhat different theory of interpersonal attraction has been proposed (Aronson, 1969). Like the more general reward theory, the **gain-loss theory of attraction** deals with the rewarding behaviors of others and the resulting effects on liking. But, unlike reward theory, it focuses on the gain or loss of rewards, rather than on the rewards themselves. More specifically, gain-loss theory holds that *increases* in reward will have more impact than constant and invariant reward. Thus, if we consider esteem as a reward, a person whose esteem for us increases over time will be liked better than one who has always liked us. This would be true even if the latter were the source of a greater overall number of rewards. Similarly, *decreases* in rewarding behavior have more impact than constant punitive behavior. Thus, a person whose esteem for us decreases over time will be disliked more than someone who has always disliked us—even if the total number of punishments are greater in the latter situation.

Imagine that you are at a cocktail party having a conversation with a man whom you have never met before. After several minutes he excuses himself and drifts into a different conversational group. Later that evening, while standing out of sight behind a potted palm, you happen to overhear this person in conversation—talking about a person he met earlier in the evening. Lo and behold, it's you that he is talking about! Suppose further that you attend seven consecutive cocktail parties, have a conversation with the same person at each of these parties and, as luck would have it, overhear him talking about you each time.

There are four outcomes that are particularly interesting: (1) You overhear the person saying exclusively positive things about you on all seven occasions; (2) you overhear him saying exclusively negative things about you on all seven occasions; (3) his first couple of evaluations are exclusively negative, but they gradually become increasingly positive; (4) his first couple of evaluations are exclusively positive, but they gradually become more negative. These four possibilities are presented graphically in Figure 5-1. Which situation would render the person most attractive to you? The gain-loss theory would predict that you would like him best in the "gain" condition (3), and least in the "loss" condition (4).

To test this theory, two psychologists set up an experiment quite similar to the cocktail party situation (Aronson & Linder, 1965). Women college students interacted during seven sessions with another student, who was actually a paid confederate. After each session the subject was cleverly "allowed" to overhear the confederate evaluate her to the experimenter. The results, shown in Table 5-2, confirmed the predictions of the gain-loss theory. A person who began with negative comments and gradually became more positive was liked more by the subject than a person who made only positive comments. Also, a person who began with positive comments that gradually became negative

Figure 5-1

Graphic Representation of Experimental Conditions (From Aronson, 1969)

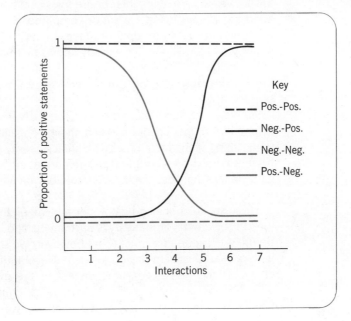

TABLE 5-2 Means and standard deviations for liking of the confederate

Experimental Condition	Mean[a]	S.D.
Gain	7.67	1.51
Positive	6.42	1.42
Negative	2.52	3.16
Loss	0.87	3.32

[a] The higher the number, the greater the attraction.

Adapted from E. Aronson and D. Linder, "Gain and Loss of Esteem as Determinants of Interpersonal Attractiveness." *Journal of Experimental Social Psychology*, 1965, *1*, 156–71.

was liked less than a person who made only negative comments. These results have been extended and elaborated in several recent experiments (Sigall, 1970; Mettee, 1971; Mettee et al., 1973).

One of the implications of gain-loss theory is that once we have grown used to the goodwill (rewarding behavior) of a person (a mother, a spouse, a close friend), that person may become less useful as a source of reward than a stranger. Since a gain in esteem is a more potent reward than the absolute level of the esteem, a close friend (by definition) is operating near ceiling level and, therefore, cannot provide us with a gain. On the other hand, the constant friend and rewarder has great potential as a punisher. The greater the past history of invariant esteem and reward, the more devastating is its withdrawal. Such withdrawal, by definition, constitutes a loss of esteem. In effect, then, one has power to hurt loved ones, but very little power to reward them.

An example may help clarify this point. A couple who had been married for ten years are leaving their house for a cocktail party one evening. The husband has always made a point of complimenting the wife on her appearance, and this time is no exception: "Gee, honey, you look great!" Her response might well be a yawn. She already knows he thinks she is attractive. But if the attentive husband were suddenly to tell her she was becoming quite ugly, this would cause a great deal of pain, since it would represent a distinct loss of esteem.

Suppose that, soon after arriving at the party, the woman is approached by a distinguished, intelligent-looking man who engages her in interesting conversation. After a while he tells her with great sincerity that he thinks her very lovely. Chances are she will not find this remark at all boring. It represents a distinct gain, makes her feel good, and probably increases the attractiveness of the stranger.

These speculations and data offer a bleak picture of the human condition — forever seeking favor in the eyes of strangers and being hurt by familiar people. Before we leap to this conclusion, however, we should discuss the impact that gain or loss of esteem has on the *behavior* of individuals — quite aside from its effect on the perceived attractiveness of the evaluator. In one experiment (Floyd, 1964) a psychologist paired young children who were either close friends or strangers. The first child of each pair was then allowed to earn several trinkets and was instructed to share these with the second child. The real object of the study was the perceived stinginess or generosity of the sharer. Some subjects were led to believe that the friend (or stranger) was treating them generously; others were led to believe that the friend (or stranger) was treating them in a stingy manner. The second children of the pairs were then allowed to earn several trinkets on their own, and they too were instructed to share them with their partners. As predicted, subjects showed the most generosity in the gain and loss conditions—that is, toward the generous stranger and the stingy friend. They were relatively stingy to the stingy stranger (why not, the stranger had behaved as they might have expected) and to the generous friend ("Ho-hum, so my friend likes me—what else is new?"). But when it looked as if they might be gaining a friend (the generous stranger), they reacted with generosity; likewise, when it looked as if they might be losing a friend (the stingy friend), they also responded with generosity.

The last finding is a rather touching aspect of the human condition. It suggests that individuals do indeed have some motivation toward the maintenance of stability in their relationships. Let us return to the married couple at the cocktail party. While either partner in an important relationship has the power to hurt the other, the hurt partner will be motivated to regain what was lost by trying to become more attractive to the other person.

The two adversaries seem to be anything but friendly. But suppose that the person on the left began to soften his attitude toward his opponent? What effect would this have on the latter's liking for him? (See the discussion of the gain-loss model.)

Carrying this speculation a step farther, we would add that a relationship tends to stagnate when people sit on minor annoyances and keep their negative feelings to themselves. This results in the *appearance* of unambiguous esteem, which can be devastated by a sudden shift in sentiment. In an open, authentic relationship, in which people are more able to share their feelings and impressions—even their negative ones—no plateau is reached. Rather, there is a continuous zigzagging of sentiment around a line of generally increasing esteem, leaving the partners in a situation that is reasonably close to the "gain" condition of the gain-loss theory. In this sense, Dale Carnegie's advice can be seen as inadequate in the long run. If two people are genuinely fond of each other, the ability and opportunity to express both positive and negative feelings—openly, honestly—will probably result in a much more deeply satisfying relationship.

SUMMARY

Generally, we like people who are attractive and who are useful or rewarding to us, as the **reward theory** suggests. Another person may gain our liking by doing us a favor, either by providing something of value or by punishing our enemies. He or she might have similar attitudes and opinions, which is also rewarding because: (1) agreeing with us "validates" our opinions; (2) from these similar opinions, we attribute to the person many desirable character traits; and (3) similar opinions probably mean a person likes us, and it is rewarding to be liked.

A person with divergent opinions who likes you, however, may be more attractive than one with similar beliefs who also likes you. A disagreer whom we can convert to our point of view is liked more than one who has always held similar opinions. These and other findings are hard to fit neatly into a reward theory of attraction and may be indicative of its limited value. Competent people, for example, should be rewarding to be around, but on this point the research evidence is mixed. In fact, clumsiness in an extremely competent male makes him more, not less, likable, at least in the eyes of other males. Praise or favors are generally rewarding and generally lead to increased liking. But if the praise—or the favor-giver—is obviously self-serving, the rewards may backfire. The **gain-loss theory** of interpersonal attraction, which holds that increases and decreases in rewards will have more impact than constant levels, can incorporate many of these discrepant findings.

The theory of cognitive dissonance (introduced in Chapter 3) also explains some findings in attraction research. One way to get someone to like you, for example, is to induce him or her to do *you* a favor. He or she will then be inclined to justify the favor—reduce dissonance—by liking you more than before doing the favor.

RECOMMENDED READING

ALLPORT, G. *The Nature of Prejudice.* Garden City, N.Y.: Doubleday & Co., Inc., 1958. A classic piece of work in which one of the pioneers of social psychology takes a long, hard look at the causes and cures of ethnic prejudice.

ARONSON, E. *The Social Animal.* San Francisco: W. H. Freeman Co., 2nd ed. 1976. A provocative introduction to the field of social psychology, designed to acquaint students with basic research in social psychology and to make them aware of the relevance of the field to everyday life.

BERSCHEID, E., and WALSTER, E. *Interpersonal Attraction*. Reading, Mass.: Addison-Wesley Publishing Co., 1969; 2nd ed. forthcoming.

A scholarly and up-to-date attempt to conceptualize the research on why people like one another.

FESTINGER, L. A. *A Theory of Cognitive Dissonance*. Stanford: Stanford University Press, 1957.

In this volume one of the foremost theorists and researchers in the field presents a theory that has revolutionized the way scientists approach the area of social psychology.

LINDZEY, G. and ARONSON, E. *Handbook of Social Psychology*, vols. 1–5. Reading, Mass.: Addison-Wesley Publishing Co., 2nd ed. 1968.

Just about everything we know about social psychology is summarized in these five volumes. It does not read like a novel, but it is the most complete and most up-to-date compendium of theory and research available.

MIDDLEBROOK, P., *Social Psychology and Modern Life*. New York: Alfred A. Knopf, 1974.

A thorough compendium of research and theory in social psychology, written in clear, understandable prose.

SHAVER, K. G. *An Introduction to Attribution Processes*. Cambridge: Winthrop Publishers, Inc., 1975.

A lively introduction to an important new social-psychological theory.

ZIMBARDO, P. and EBBESEN, E. B. *Influencing Attitudes and Changing Behavior*. Reading, Mass.: Addison-Wesley Publishing Co., 1969; 2nd ed., forthcoming.

A highly readable look at persuasion, attitude change, and behavior change, with an eye toward their relevance for society.

The Cry by Edvard Munch. Courtesy, Museum of Fine Arts, Boston.

PART THREE

Personality

By Seymour Feshbach

Personality study is the area of psychology that coincides most closely with most people's impressions of the content of psychology. It concerns what each of us is like—really like. To see how psychologists study this question we will examine an individual biography or case study. This will introduce the kinds of questions we need to ask in order to understand something about an individual and the kinds of conclusions we can draw from the answers about his or her personality. Throughout Chapter 6, we will refer back to and enlarge on the case history as we introduce the various issues in personality study.

In presenting this summary of the case of Richard Paulder, we have disguised his name and other possible sources of identification but have left intact the essential factors of his life and character. The author first met Richard when he was a college sophomore. Unsure about his goals, he sought the assistance of the counseling service to help him define and resolve his career conflicts. He was somewhat depressed at the time—upset by a drop in his grades, a lack of interest in his courses, and recent arguments with his girl friend. It was also the first time he had sought outside help, and he felt uncomfortable with the idea. With Richard's permission, we sent out questionnaires to his parents to obtain additional biographical data as part of a research study. We also interviewed several of his classmates. From these sources, and from our personal interviews with Richard, we began to put together the following case history.

> Richard, a tall, reserved person, was the younger of two children. His sister Ellen was an attractive, very able student who was completing her senior year at another college. Richard's early life was uneventful, marked only by continual spats with his sister. His mother notes that as a child, her daughter was well-behaved and responsible, much as she is now as an adult. Richard, although not a "problem" child, tended to be more buoyant and difficult. He often struck his sister and once, when he was six, he hit her in the leg with a rock. He was severely punished by his parents; and, although he had many subsequent arguments with Ellen, it was the last time he ever hit her.
>
> Richard states that both he and Ellen felt closer to his mother than to his father. His father had been disappointed that his firstborn was a girl, and he had especially high demands for Richard; Richard felt that his father liked him but that he was overly critical. His father's activities as a business executive kept him very busy, although he did find time to take Richard camping and fishing on occasional weekends. Richard's father was a reserved man who, except for his critical comments, revealed very little about his feelings or his work experiences. Richard reciprocated, finding it difficult to communicate with his father, although he could talk easily with his sister and mother. Richard's mother was an outgoing, fairly assertive woman who saw her principal role as that of homemaker, although she also occasionally did magazine editorial work.
>
> The marital relations between Richard's parents, on the whole positive, went through a crisis when Richard was about twelve; and the parents were briefly

separated. Ellen was extremely upset and angry; she got into a number of minor difficulties at school, experimented with marijuana, and stayed away from home several nights without permission. By the time she entered high school, however, her behavior had returned to normal. In contrast to his sister, Richard displayed little reaction—other than some sadness—to the separation. He seemed to spend more time on his studies and somewhat less time with the school "crowd."

Richard was never a popular boy, and during high school he struck some people as taciturn, isolated, and quarrelsome. His mother reports, however, that he seemed to get along well with other members of a photography club in which he was quite active, and Richard himself speaks enthusiastically about his activities in this club. During his senior year in high school, he had his first experience of sexual intercourse with a girl he had known for several years. Although their relationship changed when they went off to separate colleges, they remained good friends.

During his senior year in high school and, especially, his first year at college, Richard seemed much more open and involved with other people. He did, however, occasionally get into serious quarrels with people—usually men—in positions of immediate authority—a graduate student instructor, a parking attendant, a dormitory proctor. He had several close male friends and a girl friend to whom he was quite attached when he entered counseling.

The major problems in the description and study of personality can be discerned in our efforts to describe and understand Richard Paulder. How can we take into account individual differences in behavior as well as universal human tendencies? Does a person show relatively stable traits or is behavior consistent only within specific situations? How do psychologists define, measure, and assess the major aspects of personality? Many psychologists have formulated theories of personality—efforts to explain the organization of a person's characteristics and ways of behaving. Which of these various theories —and what theoretical constructs—have proven most helpful in understanding the individual and his or her unique motivations, goals, and lifestyles? What is known about human motivation—the forces that incite, sustain, and direct behavior? When is behavior considered abnormal? How is abnormality diagnosed and treated? These are the questions we will discuss in the next three chapters.

6 Personality and Assessment

Personality study deals with what major issues?
What is the focus of personality dynamics?
How does an analysis of aggression help us understand motivation and personality?
What is involved in assessing the human personality?

Personality study deals with what major issues?

INDIVIDUAL DIFFERENCES

Recall how differently Richard and Ellen Paulder reacted to their parents' separation; their reactions revealed essential personality differences. In contrast to his sister's anger and distress, Richard seemed to have responded calmly and constructively. Although Richard and Ellen shared similar aspirations for achievement and both were hardworking students, Richard's striving persisted during the family crisis, while his sister's ambitions seemed to diminish. There are, of course, many other points of similarity and difference between Richard and his sister; the ones noted are simply those made most evident

That each person is unique does not mean that individual behavior is governed by individual laws. General principles can account for individuality in two ways. First, each person can be described in terms of a unique combination of traits. For example, let us consider measures of ten personality traits, such as anxiety, introversion, generosity, aggression. Assume that each measure is independent of the others and the scores on each trait range from 1 to 10. Ten independent tests, with ten possible scores on each, yield 10^{10} or 10 billion combinations, enough for a unique description of every individual on this planet, plus some allowance for the population explosion. It is through the application of a similar kind of classificatory principle that it is possible to locate and identify fingerprints that are also unique to each individual.

The second approach to the understanding of the unique and the unusual is through the application of general psychological principles and theory to a particular set of circumstances. Suppose, for example, we were to find a child who had been raised in the jungle by a band of apes. Such a child would certainly be a unique and rare individual. Nevertheless, we could apply the theories and principles of personality development derived from a more conventional population to these unusual child-rearing conditions; and we would be able to predict much of his or her behavior and would have some understanding of the child's personality.

by the family crisis. One of the principal objectives of the study of personality is the determination of the most relevant dimensions of behavior along which individuals differ and the development of measurement procedures, such as tests, to assess these individual differences. These dimensions of behavior— relatively stable characteristics of a person—are typically referred to as **traits.** The study of traits provides a basis for the comparison of individuals and, in addition, helps account for the uniqueness of each individual (see Spotlight 6-1).

GENERALITY AND SPECIFICITY

One striking aspect of Richard's life pattern is the inconsistency of his behavior. One can well ask what is his real personality? Is he shy or open, warm or distant, aggressive or friendly, direct or devious? Richard's behavior is consistent within a specific situation: he was unfriendly and withdrawn in his high school classes, but cheerful and open when involved in his photography interests. In college, he has good relationships with his peers but is very aggressive with older males. Some psychologists feel that personality traits are quite specific to particular situations and that behavior changes as situations are altered. According to this view, it is fruitless to seek for broad, general behavior patterns that are descriptive of individuals (Mischel, 1968). Other psychologists, however, argue that fundamental, underlying individualistic consistencies can be discerned if we analyze situations and behavior appropriately (Allport, 1961; Bem & Allen, 1974; Cattell, 1965). (See Spotlight 6-2.) Probably the majority of personality psychologists consider personality traits to be moderately general, although they might differ in which characteristics they view as most useful in predicting behavior.

KEY DIMENSIONS OF PERSONALITY

"Body Language"

The history of the study of personality is the history of a search for key dimensions of personality with wide generality. One area of early interest that continues to intrigue psychologists is bodily postures and movements. Both theory and experience suggest that the way in which we walk, stand, talk, and write may express our personalities, constituting a kind of "body language." In a pioneer experiment, men and women who scored at the extreme end of a questionnaire measure of social dominance were asked to carry out a series of motor tasks including walking, drawing geometrical figures, handwriting, and gripping a pencil as strongly as possible (Allport & Vernon, 1933). Although only slight differences were obtained between low and high dominant women, the men high in dominance wrote and drew more rapidly, covered larger areas of a page, and exerted more pressure on a pencil than those low in dominance. Even though the suggestion that aspects of handwriting may reflect personality traits is especially intriguing, there is little evidence to support graphologists' claim that specific handwriting signs are associated with particular personality characteristics. However, expressive styles—as reflected in handwriting, in the vigor of one's stride, or in the rigidity of bodily movements—do appear to be broadly related to other features of the personality.

Motivation

Another key personality dimension in which important individual differences can be found is motivation. People differ in the goals they seek, the values they believe to be most important, and in the stimulus events they find most reinforcing. Returning to Richard Paulder, one can point to certain motivational tendencies that appear to be consistent over a wide range of situations

A person without strong achievement motivation would probably not spend the long and sometimes uninteresting hours needed to collect data in biochemical research. Personality psychologists are interested in the bases of such motivation and in how it may be measured and predicted.

The Search for Cross-Situational Consistencies in Behavior

The degree of generality or consistency of a personality trait depends not only on the trait in question but also on the particular individual. Recent research (Bem and Allen, 1974) has shown that the same trait can be quite general for some people and quite specific for others—that is, some people almost always display a certain characteristic, while others show it only in very specific situations. Moreover, one may be able to determine whether a trait is general or specific for a particular person simply by asking that person how much he or she varies from one situation to another with respect to that trait. In one experiment, college students were administered a questionnaire measure of friendliness. Reports about their friendliness were also obtained from peers and from parents. Finally, observations were made of the degree of friendly behavior manifested by the students in a waiting room and in a group discussion. Analysis of the correlations among the three measures of friendliness indicated that degree of friendliness was indeed a general trait among students who had rated themselves as consistently friendly or unfriendly in different situations. The correlations were quite high, averaging close to 0.60. Friendliness/unfriendliness was a quite specific trait, however, for students who saw themselves as very variable in friendly behavior. For these students, the average correlation among the measures of friendliness was 0.27. These data indicate that personality traits may be useful theoretical constructs for predicting the behavior of at least "some of the people some of the time."

and lend a unity and common dimension to his personality. One such tendency is his *need for achievement*. It is important to Richard that he excel, and he is willing to work hard for success. When he is not achieving well—for example, when his grades drop—he becomes depressed and willing to accept help. He would not have sought help solely because he was unhappy or had interpersonal conflicts. For Richard, achievement motivation is a general trait that is reflected in much of his behavior. At a later point in this chapter, we will consider the measurement of achievement motivation and some evidence of its generality across very different situations (*see* p. 153).

It is evident in examining Richard's behavior that there are emotions and other motivations besides achievement that are significant components of his personality. Richard displays marked anger and aggression, particularly in his interactions with intermediate authority figures such as proctors and parking-lot attendants. At the same time, he seeks the approval of "real" authority figures such as his college professors. This conflict is manifested in his ambivalence (mixed feeling) toward authority. Richard chafes—most often covertly, but sometimes overtly—when he is required to conform to the demands and regulations imposed by individuals in authority, as if he were trapped by his own ambivalence. It is noteworthy that this ambivalence is not manifested in some other important situations—for example, in his relationships with women, which appear to be socially and sexually satisfying.

Sex, aggression, need for social approval, and conflict are some of the major motivational dimensions that have been investigated by psychologists. Among other important human motivations that contribute to personality differences

The different personality and cognitive styles of two conductors—how they think about and conceptualize the music, themselves, and the world—may be reflected in their facial expressions and body language.

are the needs for independence, affection, power, and nurturance and some negative ones—fear and anxiety, guilt and shame. It is instructive to attempt to discern in ourselves and in others which motivations—including some that have not been enumerated—are central and broad in their consequences and which are peripheral and restricted to very specific situations.

People differ in their responses to similar motivations. Richard and Ellen, it is clear, deal with anger and aggression very differently. Richard suppresses his anger, seething inside; or he explodes irrationally, directing his feeling toward an essentially innocent target. Ellen, on the other hand, attempts to escape from situations that evoke intense anger and aggression; in less severe circumstances, she is likely to communicate her feelings openly to the person who has provoked her. Moreover, Richard tends to be taciturn and something of an introvert (attentive to and interested in one's inner thoughts and feelings) while Ellen is more communicative and extroverted (attention and interest directed toward other people and the outside world).

Introversion-Extroversion

The dimension of **introversion-extroversion,** first discussed by the eminent personality theorist, Carl Jung, seems to interact with many motivations; it is one factor that influences how people respond to their own motives. According to researchers, artists and scientific researchers tend to be introverted, while engineers and others in mechanically oriented occupations are likely to be extroverts (Cattell, 1965). In anxiety-provoking situations, extroverts are much more likely than introverts to choose to be with other people than to be alone (Shapiro & Alexander, 1969). Other temperamental traits and interaction styles have also been found helpful in explaining and describing personality; examples are activity level, emotionality, and impulsivity.

Cognitive Styles

In recent years, personality psychologists have become interested in individual differences in cognitive functions. **Cognitive styles** describe differences in the ways individuals characteristically perceive events and draw inferences from them (*see also* pp. 341–42). They can be viewed as *information-processing traits*. An example is the dimension that runs from "field independent" to "field dependent." A field-independent individual makes perceptual judgments analytically and tends to disregard environmental information that may distort the judgment; a field-dependent person tends to make global judgments and is markedly influenced by the field or immediate environment of the stimulus being judged. On one of the measures of **field independence-dependence,** the rod-and-frame test, the subject is shown a rod contained within a square frame and is required to adjust the rod to the vertical position as the frame tilts. The extent to which the tilt of the frame influences the person's judgment determines the degree of field dependence of the individual. Field dependence, as assessed by these and other measures, is often related to social dependency and conformity (Linton, 1955; Witkin et al., 1962) (*see also* pp. 343–44).

Locus of Control

A related personality dimension, but one that taps more complex cognitive functions, has been described as perceived "internal" versus "external" control of reinforcement (Rotter, 1966). This dimension refers to an individual's tendency to perceive himself or herself as able to influence events (internal control) or as largely controlled by outside forces (external control). It is a trait that operates at both the cognitive level (how one thinks about one's world) and at the decisionmaking level (how one decides to act). A useful measure of this dimension is a twenty-three item, forced-choice inventory referred to as the I-E (for internal-external) scale. The following sample of items is illustrative. The subject is asked to choose the alternative in each pair with which he or she agrees.

a) Without the right breaks, one cannot be an effective leader.
b) Capable people who fail to become leaders have not taken advantage of their opportunities.

a) I have often found that what is going to happen will happen.
b) Trusting to fate has never turned out as well for me as making a decision to take a definite course of action.

a) Sometimes I can't understand how teachers arrive at the grades they give.
b) There is a direct connection between how hard I study and the grades I get.

In each instance, alternative a) is the "external" response. You may find it difficult to choose between alternatives, but keep in mind that it is the total score rather than the choice on any one item that is important. As one might expect, Richard Paulder chose a preponderance of "internal" alternatives.

The utility of the I-E scale has been demonstrated in many different kinds of situations. For example, black students who were willing to participate in such civil actions as a march on the state capitol or a "Freedom Ride" scored significantly more "internal" on the I-E scale than students who were uninterested in participation (Gore & Rotter, 1963). Also, nonsmokers were found to be more "internal" than smokers (Straits & Sechrest, 1963). In addition, among male smokers who had quit smoking, fewer "internal" people resumed smoking compared to those who felt less control of their own destiny (James, Woodruff, & Werner, 1965). In a quite different study concerned with persuasion, "externals" were much more likely than "internals" to yield to others' arguments (Sherman, 1973). A wide range of behaviors would thus appear to be influenced by differences in the expectancy of internal versus external control of reinforcement.

Of course, perceived locus of control, whether internal or external, is related to situational factors as well as to personality. For example, the perceived difficulty of a task is an important determinant of whether we attribute our success or failure to internal or external factors. When we are successful

Some individuals feel that they can chart their own course through the mountains or through life. Others see themselves as victims of "fate" and circumstance—like riders on a crowded subway.

at difficult tasks, we are more likely to attribute our success to internal factors. By contrast, we tend to blame failures in easy tasks on external factors (Weiner & Kukla, 1970).

George Kelly (1955) proposed that much of personality can be understood if we consider each person a sort of scientist who is continually observing the world, formulating his or her own personal theory of personality, and acting on the basis of predictions made from the theory. According to this view, each individual has a set of theoretical ideas—called "personal constructs"—that are like the traits used by personality psychologists; they may, however, be adopted after far less systematic "testing" than a scientist would accept. For example, another person might be labeled good or bad, happy or sad, masculine or feminine. If labeled good and sad, you may be disposed to give help or sympathy; whereas if you see the person as bad and sad, you might do nothing. People vary in the number and kind of personal constructs they employ. Those with fewer constructs are less "cognitively complex" and tend to see most of the world and its problems in simple black-and-white terms. Richard Paulder might be said to use one particular kind of construct in relation to figures of authority—"critical or accepting"—and resent those he sees as critical. Quite different behaviors could be expected from people who view authority figures as primarily "just or unjust."

ORGANIZATION AND STRUCTURE

We have described Richard's personality as if it consisted of a number of behavior patterns that existed in isolation from each other. In delineating individual differences, one almost inevitably adopts a kind of cataloging approach, enumerating a series of distinctive behaviors. Thus, Richard is described as introverted, ambitious, ambivalent toward authority, given to sporadic conflict and hostile outbursts, open with women but reserved with men, disposed to perceive himself as responsible for his successes and failures (internal), and to perceive authority figures in a constant judgmental critical role. The listing of traits, however, while often useful, does an injustice to the unity and organization of personality. Richard's ambition is related to his feelings toward authority. These in turn are related to his hostile outbreaks. Richard's hard work and striving is in part based on his desire to impress authorities and obtain their approval. He is unduly sensitive to any implied criticism and resents it, while blaming himself and feeling inadequate. This resentment sometimes finds expression in inappropriate angry behavior. Richard's relationship to authority thus has the quality of a self-fulfilling prophecy: his readiness to resent authority brings about the very disapproval he anticipates.

You can see evidence of organization and structure in Richard's behavior. And in others too, the meaning and implication of any particular personality trait depends to a considerable extent upon this overall organization—upon the context in which the trait occurs. We saw that Richard's need to succeed has a different quality and connotation than ambition in his sister. On the theoretical level too, students of personality are very interested in understanding the interrelations and interactions among traits. In one study of the relationship between introversion-extroversion and handwriting, for example, it was found that extroverts wrote larger or smaller than introverts, depending on their level of anxiety or neuroticism. Extroverts high in anxiety wrote smallest, while extroverts who were less anxious had the largest handwriting (Taft, 1967). These data serve to emphasize the point that personality traits do not operate in isolation but are organized in meaningful patterns.

What is the focus of personality dynamics?

Although there is an intimate relationship between the organization and dynamics of personality, the terms refer to different aspects of personality. *Organization* refers to structure or "anatomy" of personality—how the different elements of personality are linked or go together. *Dynamics,* on the other hand, is concerned with the meaning and function of behavior. In considering personality dynamics, you look for the purpose or objective of an act and ask why the individual behaved as he or she did. Questions of dynamics are also typically addressed to the immediate situation in which action is taking place, while questions of organization generally deal with relatively enduring and stable aspects of behavior.

The response of Richard's sister, Ellen, to her parents' separation provides an excellent example of motivational dynamics. Her usual behavior patterns were conformity and acceptance of parental standards. They were responses to her need for her parents' love—in effect, attempts to obtain that love. Her parents' separation elicited feelings of rejection, anger, and betrayal—including betrayal of the social conventions to which she so conscientiously adhered. All these feelings were expressed in her defiant and deviant behaviors, which were superficially, but not dynamically, inconsistent with her personality structure. To understand Ellen's behavior one must also consider the effects of her feelings of rejection and anger on her ability to process information. Psychologists have found that under conditions of strong emotional arousal, the ability to make discriminations declines, and people often fail to notice relevant changes in a stimulus situation. Thus, according to Richard, when Ellen was very upset by her father's departure from the home, she was unable to recognize his very genuine expression of affection toward her.

Studies of motivational dynamics also show that a person's feelings and desires may color his or her thoughts and perceptions. If an individual is sexually aroused, ambiguous stimuli are more frequently seen as having a sexual significance (Gaibraith, 1968). After being frightened or angered, one is more likely to perceive others as malicious and threatening (Feshbach & Feshbach, 1963). Thus, under strong drive, a *feedback* situation is produced, in which one's feelings facilitate judgments and perceptions that tend to strengthen and justify these very feelings.

The relationship between motivation and information processing is reciprocal. Just as motives can affect thoughts and perceptions, the way we perceive a situation often strongly influences our motivated behavior. An unfamiliar airplane noise which we have attributed to a malfunction may induce anxiety, but our fears are lessened when the pilot explains that the landing gear has just been lowered. A more subtle example is provided by a study of the effects of information—the reason for failure—on the behavior of students high and low in need for achievement (Weiner & Sierad, 1975). Prior to participation in a task requiring the coding of numbers into geometric symbols, subjects were given a placebo (non-active) pill and were told that it would interfere temporarily with their eye-hand coordination. They then received four trials on the coding task. Compared to subjects who had not taken the pill, the opportunity to attribute failure to an external cause—in this instance, a pill—actually improved the performance of subjects low in achievement motivation. An opposite effect was found for subjects high in achievement motivation; their performance declined when they believed their failure was due to an external cause.

Structure and dynamics are two important areas of inquiry in the study of personality. The origins or antecedents of personality provide a third set of issues. While we have a fairly clear picture of the personality of Richard Paulder and, to a lesser extent, of Ellen Paulder, we can only speculate on the determinants of their personalities. These factors may be grouped into the following four categories: cultural context, social role, biological factors, and developmental history.

<table>
<tr><td>CULTURAL CONTEXT AND
SOCIAL ROLES</td><td>Richard and Ellen Paulder are products of the times and culture in which they live. Their values and attitudes are different in a number of respects from their parents' and from those held in other cultures. Expectations, norms, values, and prescribed modes of behavior vary *between* cultures and also *within* a particular culture. Every society is structured by a pattern of social positions and corresponding *social roles;* which position you occupy and which role you are playing at any given time determines your behavior in many situations. A mature man is not supposed to behave like a child; the behavioral demands made of a political leader are not the same as those made of the average individual; and in most societies the expectancies for women are different from those for men. Social roles shape behavior in the sense that people ordinarily conform to role expectations. The male business executive generally wears a suit to work. The schoolteacher follows appropriate "rules" in relationships with students. But social roles not only affect behavior; they also influence the way in which people perceive events. A general has a very different perception of war than a private. We all occupy simultaneously a number of social positions and roles. Thus, Richard acts out the roles of a male, a son, and a student.</td></tr>
</table>

The differences in aggressiveness between Richard and Ellen must be understood partly in the light of differences in sex roles—the differences in the social behaviors expected of males and females in this society. Males are generally expected to be more combative than females. A further question is whether these culturally determined sex-role behaviors have any biological basis. This issue, applied to many behaviors that differ between sexes in our culture, is one of considerable importance in contemporary personality study. And it is an issue that has direct relevance to current controversies, stimulated by the feminist movement, concerning the behaviors and social roles of men and women. Much of the rationale for the traditional role of women has been based on the assumption that women are constitutionally (biologically) more emotional, more dependent, more passive, and less assertive and aggressive than men.

What is considered proper and normal conduct and attire depends to a great extent on the cultural context and society's role expectations.

Sex Differences

Before trying to determine the cause of sex differences in personality, we should first establish what these differences are. It is surprising how few of our stereotypes and preconceived beliefs about sex differences are supported by empirical evidence. A careful and thorough review of the research indicates that females are *not* more "social" than males, *not* more suggestible, and *not* less motivated to achieve (Maccoby & Jacklin, 1974). Still, there are some sex differences that are fairly well established. Girls have greater verbal ability than boys, but they tend to do less well on tasks requiring mathematical skill or visual-spatial ability. These differences are more evident during adolescence and adulthood.

Consistent sex differences have also been found in aggressive behavior. By nursery-school age, boys already behave more aggressively than females, a pattern that extends into adulthood (Feshbach, 1970; Maccoby & Jacklin,

1974). However, even the universality of greater aggressiveness in males has been questioned. In her famous monograph "Sex and Temperament in Three Primitive Societies," Margaret Mead (1935) described striking variations among societies in the aggressive behavior displayed by the two sexes. In a relatively small geographical area in New Guinea, she found one tribe in which both males and females were violent and aggressive; a second in which both sexes were mild and unaggressive; and a third in which there was a real reversal of the pattern of our own culture—the women being more aggressive and the men milder and more dependent. Several experiments conducted with American middle-class boys and girls have reported data indicating that girls express aggression more indirectly than boys (Feshbach, 1969; Feshbach & Sones, 1971). While girls made less use of physical aggression, they were more likely than boys to reject another child or to act unfriendly. Under some circumstances girls will behave in an overtly aggressive manner, conveying an unmistakably hostile message. In one experiment, college students were placed in an apparently competitive situation and given an opportunity to retaliate against their competitor with electric shock (Taylor & Epstein, 1967). The use of strong shocks was greatest among female students who were led to believe their opponents were males.

There are many unresolved issues about sex differences in personality, and some questions have only begun to be explored. One must therefore be cautious in making generalizations. Even in traits in which the sexes clearly differ, there are marked *individual* differences within each sex and great overlap between boys and girls. Perhaps the culture exaggerates sex differences that are rooted in biologically based tendencies, providing yet another instance of heredity-environment interaction.

In any case, the results of psychological and anthropological research indicate that both males and females are capable of a great variety of behaviors. Individual differences and cultural definitions and prescriptions probably play a greater role than biological differences in determining men's and women's ways of expressing emotions and in their occupational and professional choices. The processes involved in the establishment of sex identity and the development of distinctive sex interests will be discussed at greater length in Chapter 11.

BIOLOGICAL DETERMINANTS OF PERSONALITY

Although the influence of biological factors on personality differences may be less evident and less direct than the impact of culture, there have been a number of investigations demonstrating the influence of biological factors on behavior. There is some support for the conjecture that ectomorphs—lean, linear individuals—tend to be introverted and highly sensitive; mesomorphs (muscular people) tend to be assertive and competitive; and endomorphs (stout, rounded people) tend to be easygoing and sociable (Sheldon, 1942). In other words, there is some slight basis in reality for Shakespeare having made his jolly characters fat (Falstaff) and his scheming characters lean (Iago).

Differential use of the right and left halves of the brain is another biological factor of interest to personality theorists. Sperry and his associates (Sperry, 1968; Sperry, Gazzaniga & Bogen, 1968) were able to delineate the independent functions of each half of the brain by severing the fibers connecting

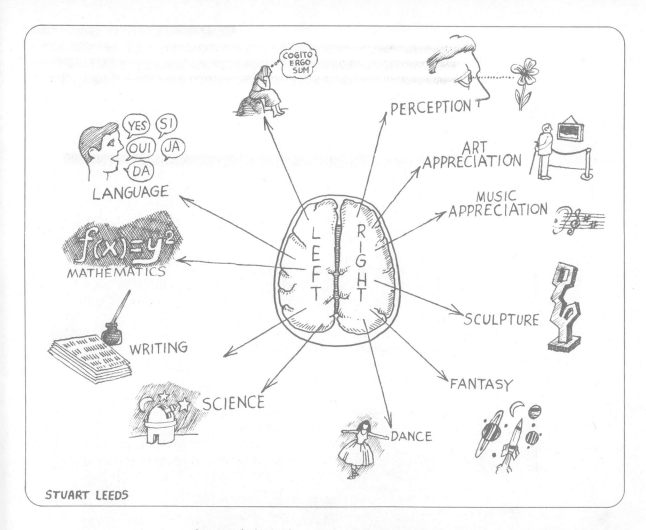

COGITO ERGO SUM

PERCEPTION

ART APPRECIATION

MUSIC APPRECIATION

YES SI OUI JA DA
LANGUAGE

$f(x)=y^2$
MATHEMATICS

LEFT RIGHT

SCULPTURE

WRITING

FANTASY

SCIENCE

DANCE

STUART LEEDS

the two halves (the corpus callosum) in animals. They also had the opportunity to study human patients on whom split-brain surgery had been performed to alleviate epilepsy (*see* pp. 588–89). It is also possible to study the functions of the two halves of the brain in normal individuals by recording brain waves and by the ingenious use of the relationships between movements in the left and right side of the body and the left and right brain halves or hemispheres. In general, movements on one side of the body are primarily controlled by the brain hemisphere on the opposite side. For example, in the case of vision, looking to the right of a fixed point is controlled by the left hemisphere; looking to the left is controlled by the right hemisphere.

On the basis of an extensive series of studies carried out by different investigators, it appears that the left hemisphere is primarily involved in analytic thinking and verbal behavior—including writing, speech, and verbally encoded thoughts. The right hemisphere is implicated in spatial relations: recognition of auditory patterns (for example, a musical melody) and faces—in general, more global kinds of functions. (These findings apply to right-handed individuals; left-handers show the opposite or less differentiated results.) In popularized extensions of these studies, left-hemisphere "types" are assumed to be logical and analytical, while right-hemisphere "types" are assumed to be intuitive and imaginative. The possibilities of relating personality traits and cognitive skills to individual differences in hemispheric activity are promising (Bakan, 1969; Day, 1967; Weiten & Etaugh, 1973). The research, however, is very much in its early stages and caution is necessary in making generalizations.

Heredity Factors

The question of the influence of inherited differences upon personality is another important biological issue. The study of twins provides much of the evidence in the search for genetic factors. Twins are of two types: identical and fraternal. Identical twins develop from one fertilized ovum (egg) and have identical heredities; but fraternal twins develop from two ova and have different genetic makeups. In one carefully executed study, Gottesman (1963) compared pairs of identical and fraternal twins — high school students — on scores on the Minnesota Multiphasic Personality Inventory (MMPI) (see p. 149), another personality questionnaire, and I.Q. Identical twins resemble each other much more than fraternal twins in I.Q., introversion-extroversion, aggressiveness, moodiness, dependency, and shyness. Other twin studies indicate that genetic factors also influence degree of sociability, activity level, and emotionality (Buss & Plomin, 1975).

DEFINITION OF PERSONALITY

We have discussed a number of questions to which the study of personality is addressed, but we have as yet offered no definition of the term "personality," except by implication. Personality is not a precise concept or area, and psychologists are not in complete agreement about all of its connotations. We can, however, propose a more formal and explicit definition of personality, which you may find helpful. **Personality** refers to (1) relatively enduring behavior

There is some evidence that certain cognitive abilities are associated with dominance by one or the other side of the brain. According to these preliminary findings, aesthetic imaginativeness may be a right-brain activity and mathematical problem-solving a left-brain ability.

patterns and traits that distinguish people, groups, and cultures; (2) the organization and structure of these enduring behavior patterns and characteristics; and (3) the interaction between these patterns—and fluctuations in an individual's internal state—and the external stimulus situation.

The reader will recognize most of the elements of this definition from previous discussions. A key phrase is "relatively enduring behavior patterns and characteristics"—that is, distinctive patterns of response that occur frequently. Unusual responses are not always disregarded or thought to be insignificant, however. They often represent interactions between prominent characteristics and response tendencies and an unusual "external stimulus situation." Ellen's response to her parents' separation is an example of an important, although unusual, response. An unusual way of tying shoelaces, on the other hand, is hardly likely to interest a personality theorist.

Enduring behavior patterns have been conceptualized in different ways in different theories of personality. The analysis of aggressive behavior provides an excellent example of the interaction between dynamic and structural factors in an important human motivation. It illustrates the various issues that have been raised in describing and explaining personality and also serves as an introduction to the discussion of theories of personality presented in the next chapter.

How does an analysis of aggression help us understand motivation and personality?

Aggression can take many forms—fighting, torture, burning, a nasty remark, or an angry grimace. Why do people engage in such destructive activity? One possible answer is that aggressive behavior is a manifestation of an *aggressive drive;* according to this idea, people, like other animals, have a need to aggress.

Instances of instrumental aggression — using force to obtain a valued toy — are common among nursery-school children.

This was the view of Freud, the originator of psychoanalysis, and is also the view of some students of animal behavior (*see* p. 695). The particular form in which aggression is expressed is dependent upon prior learning. Another contrasting answer is that aggressive behavior is a habit (rather than a drive) that has been reinforced. A preschool child finds that by pushing or hitting peers, he or she gets a bicycle to ride. The child is displaying instrumental aggressive behavior — aggressive behavior that wins him or her a desired object. Later in life, aggression may be instrumental in the attainment of money, sex, food, safety, and other goals.

Both answers are partially correct, for aggression has both *instrumental* and *drive* components. The thief who assaults victims in order to rob them of their money is carrying out instrumental aggressive acts. The mugger who assaults victims simply to hurt them is expressing an aggressive drive; we call this kind of behavior hostile aggression.

FRUSTRATION AND AGGRESSION

Freud maintained that the aggressive drive is innate, a vestige of our animal inheritance, and, like sex and hunger, due to internally generated biochemical changes. Systematic observations of animals — discussed more extensively in Chapter 24 — provide evidence of innate aggressive tendencies but do not support the notion that there is a generalized drive to attack. Instead, studies of animal aggression indicate that only certain situations and stimuli — "invasion of territory," threatening gestures, competition for food — have a high probability of eliciting anger and attack reactions. Thus, in contrast to the Freudian position of innate aggressive drives, the animal observations suggest that aggression is linked to external stimulus events that act as provokers or releasers.

The frustration-aggression hypothesis is an important modification of the innate aggressive drive theory. The hypothesis (Dollard *et al.*, 1939) states that every frustrating event produces an instigation to aggression and that the strength of the individual's aggressive drive is a function of the number and type of frustrating events he or she has encountered. This simple formulation provides a quantitative basis for accounting for individual and group differences in the strength of aggressive drive. It also helps provide a uniform theoretical way of thinking about aggressive phenomena as diverse as lynchings and violent fantasies. In addition, it offers a more optimistic outlook on the possibility of reducing violence in human affairs.

Subsequent research and analysis revealed deficiencies in the original frustration-aggression formulation, however, and the initial hypothesis has been revised. The revision reflects the increasing importance that psychologists give to *cognitive* factors in explaining human motivation. How we *perceive* and *think* about events are powerful determinants of feelings and actions. In reviewing the following factors—which need to be taken into account in relating frustration to aggression—the student may think about how some of these same factors affect motives other than aggression.

1. Type of Motivation. First we must define **frustration.** A frustrating event is any obstacle that blocks or interferes with an organism's striving toward a goal. However, not all goals are of equal importance, and physical pain usually elicits even more aggression than the blocking of goal attainment (Buss, 1963, 1966). Frustration of self-esteem motives through insult and humiliation is often a much more powerful provocation than the frustration of the primary drives (Feshbach, 1970; Maslow, 1941; White & Lippitt, 1960; Worchel, 1960). A prisoner of war may experience far more anger and frustration because of the false accusation that he is an informer than to the physical frustrations of inadequate food and shelter—and even torture.

2. Intentionality. We respond differently when we believe that someone has deliberately frustrated us than when we believe the frustration was unintentional. Think of your reaction when you feel you have been deliberately tripped; compare it with your reaction to being tripped accidentally. Intentional frustration elicits much more aggression than unintentional frustration

How people respond to the frustration of being unemployed—with aggressiveness, passivity, or constructive activity—depends on their individual personality structure and whether they believe they are being intentionally thwarted.

(Nickel, 1974). One reason for Richard Paulder's aggressiveness was his tendency to interpret any frustration at the hands of authority as having been deliberate and intended.

Closely related to intentionality is the degree of arbitrariness or unfairness of an action (Cohen, 1955; Pastore, 1952). A failure on an examination will seem less frustrating and produce less anger toward the instructor if you feel that the grade was fair than if you feel it was arbitrary and unrelated to your actual performance. We can state this relationship in terms of internal versus external locus of control (*see* p. 130): if you attribute the failure to internal factors—such as your own lack of ability, preparation or effort—you will be much less frustrated than if you attribute it to external factors such as the grader's carelessness or malice. (Of course, you may also be angry with yourself for failing to study hard enough or frustrated by your own inability to learn a subject.)

3. Relativity of Frustration. Frustration and its effects are a function of the difference between what one wants and what one can get—not simply of the absolute level of deprivation. Frustration is relative to one's expectations. Two students may both be disappointed in a C grade. However, one who aspired to an A is likely to feel more frustrated than one who had hoped only for a B. Although two families may have the same level of income, one may experience much more frustration than the other if its members feel a need to "keep up with the Jones" or simply have higher economic aspirations. Moreover, an increase in material gains and privileges can be accompanied by increased dissatisfaction. Thus it may be true that blacks in American society have a higher standard of living and enjoy more civil rights than they did thirty years ago. However, their economic position, *relative* to the white majority, has changed much less and, for certain subgroups, has even worsened. With the greater articulation of black consciousness and greater recognition of and unwillingness to accept subordinate socioeconomic status, frustrations may have been heightened, even though the absolute level of tangible benefits may have increased.

A similar process arises from the relationship between intensity of motivation and proximity to a goal. Motivation to attain a goal increases as one gets closer to it; this is called the **goal gradient.** In these terms, an obstacle close to the goal is much more frustrating than the same obstacle encountered some distance from the goal. Compare the frustration of a runner who trips and falls at the beginning of a race with the level of frustration he or she experiences in tripping and falling five yards from the finish line, with victory almost within grasp. Frustration occurring close to a goal produces more aggression than frustration occurring at a distance from the goal.

4. Alternative Responses to Frustration. Aggression is only one of many responses to frustration (McClelland & Apicella, 1945). Frustration can also be the impetus for problem solving and creativity. Demosthenes, working to overcome his speech impediment, became a great orator. Other possible responses are the adoption of a substitute goal or simply giving up.

Responses to frustration can be markedly influenced by learning. In one experiment, seven- to nine-year-old children were given a series of training

It is more frustrating to "almost win" than to lose by a mile.

sessions in which half the children were praised for aggressive behavior and the other half for cooperative, task-oriented responses (Davitz, 1952). After seven sessions, the children were placed in a frustrating situation: a movie they were seeing was interrupted just as it approached the climax. In addition, they had to return a candy bar they had just been given. After the frustration, the children had a free-play session. Those who had been previously trained to respond constructively displayed cooperative reactions, while the group that had been rewarded for being aggressive displayed much more aggression.

This study is one of a number of investigations that indicate that the rewards and punishments society metes out for aggressive behavior have profound influence on responses to frustration. People raised in families in which their aggression is reinforced are more likely to behave aggressively than people raised in situations in which aggression is discouraged. So, in predicting an individual's level of aggressiveness, we must consider the history of both past frustration and the encouragement received for aggressive behavior. "Encouragement," of course, can take more subtle forms than praise or the material rewards that result from successful aggressive actions. The father who beats his son because the boy has gotten into a fight is delivering a conflicting message. While ostensibly punishing aggression, the father is acting aggressively himself. Thus, he serves as an aggressive model his son may imitate. Children who have been exposed to an aggressive model are much more likely to behave aggressively than those who have not (see p. 15).

Social and situational variables can also markedly influence whether or not we feel angry and how we behave when we are frustrated and angry. In a classic experiment (Schachter & Singer, 1962), college students were initially injected with either epinephrine (adrenalin) or a placebo—a salt solution with no medical value or side effects. Epinephrine increases blood pressure and heart rate, resulting in palpitation (rapid heart beat), tremors, and sometimes accelerated breathing. Some subjects given epinephrine were informed about epinephrine and its effects; others were kept ignorant or misinformed of its side effects. Following the injection, the experimenter introduced the subject to a stooge who presumably had received the same injection. The subject and stooge were then given a series of questionnaires to complete, during which time the stooge behaved either in a euphoric, happy, and somewhat silly manner or in an angry, irritated, hostile way. In answering questions about their reactions, subjects in the epinephrine-informed condition were uninfluenced by the stooge's responses. Because of the information given them, they did not need to rely on the behavior of someone else to "interpret" their own feelings. However, the behavior of the uninformed subjects and the feelings they reported were markedly affected by the stooge's emotional reactions. The degree of these subjects' feelings of happiness or anger directly related to the euphoria or anger displayed by the stooge. The effect was particularly pronounced in subjects who showed a clear-cut physiological response to the drug; clearly, anger and euphoria were in part influenced by *cognitive* interpretations of the aroused physiological states. Anger and aggression thus are not simple manifestations of an internal-drive state; they are strongly influenced by external, environmental stimulus factors.

THE REDUCTION OF
AGGRESSION

According to psychoanalysts, aggressive impulses will be expressed in a socially destructive form unless the ego (sense of self) "defends" against them. However, the expression of angry impulses should be distinguished from instrumental aggressive acts. There is no evidence that instrumental aggression—such as war or robbery-murder—is either a psychological or a biological necessity.

The reduction of an impulse by expressing it directly or indirectly, particularly in verbal ways or in fantasy, is called **catharsis.** Can thought and fantasy reduce anger and overt aggression? This question has been the topic of considerable research and controversy. For example, what are the effects of the aggressive fantasies children may engage in when they are exposed to violence on television and in other mass media? Does the portrayal of violence on television act as a catharsis for aggression or does it, as many contend, stimulate aggressive behavior and serve as an aggressive model? The most frequent research finding has been that aggression is increased rather than reduced by exposure to aggressive actions on films (Bandura, Ross, & Ross, 1963; Berkowitz & Alioto, 1973; Hartmann, 1969; Lovaas, 1961; Mussen & Rutherford, 1961; Walters & Thomas, 1963). In all these studies, brief film sequences of aggressive behavior were employed in laboratory settings. In two studies that used lengthier motion pictures, there was little evidence of either enhancement or reduction of aggression (Albert, 1957; Emery, 1959).

Investigations in which participants watched regular network television programs in natural viewing situations produced mixed results. Some find evidence that viewing violence influences the viewer to behave more aggressively (Lefkowitz et al., 1972). Other studies show little or no effect of any kind (Hallaron et al., 1970); still others find evidence for a reduction of aggression in some personality groups (Feshbach & Singer, 1971). These diverse results are probably indicative of the number and complexity of variables operating in the natural viewing situation.

The best way to handle frustration varies with the situation. By expressing his anger verbally this man may reduce his frustration through catharsis. Attempting to solve the problem that causes the frustration is even more constructive. Both ways of dealing are undoubtedly preferable to just giving up.

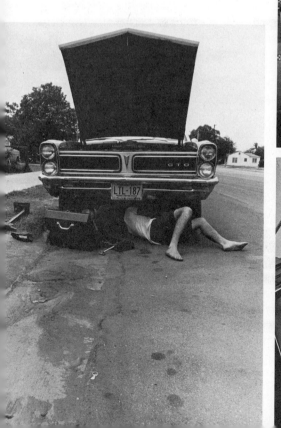

What is involved in assessing the human personality?

How do we know if a person is prone to anxiety? How can we determine whether males or females are higher in the need for achievement? How can we test a hypothesis about, say, the relationship between a certain trait or need and overt behavior? To answer these questions, we must have some way of assessing individual differences in traits or characteristics. If we hypothesize, for example, that "high anxiety" will lead to poor performance on an exam, we must be able to distinguish between students who are anxious and those who are less so. We can do this with personality tests. Personality measures also have important practical applications. They are often used to diagnose emotional instability or mental illness or to aid in personnel selection.

For a measure to be useful, it must have certain properties. First of all, it must have **reliability;** that is, it must give approximately the same answer each time the measure is used. A bathroom scale that fluctuated wildly by as much as 75 pounds on different readings would not be very helpful if someone was attempting to keep track of his or her weight. The scale lacks the property of reliability. In the same manner, personality scales need to have adequate reliability in order to be useful. Suppose you want to measure anxiety by a questionnaire containing such questions as "Do your hands frequently tremble?" "Do you often feel afraid without knowing why?" "Do you feel upset when you have to talk to a group?" If the questions were ambiguously written or subjects answered at random, someone who obtained a high-anxiety score at one time might just as easily obtain a low score on a retest. You could not discover any systematic relationships between anxiety and performance on examinations if you had to depend upon such an unreliable measure.

Reliability is necessary, but it is not sufficient, to ensure the usefulness of a measure. It must also have **validity,** that is, it must measure what it was designed to measure. Our bathroom scale would not be of much help if it gave reliable readings of some attribute other than weight (such as the size of one's feet). Thus, our measure of anxiety could yield highly consistent scores, but nevertheless be measuring something other than anxiety—such as sensitivity to one's own feeling, or self-honesty (Jackson & Messick, 1958; Couch & Kenniston, 1960). Whether the personality measure is a questionnaire, an electronic lie detector, a projective test, or our own judgment, its reliability and validity must be demonstrated.

Establishing the validity of a personality measure is a painstaking and often complex task. There are several types of validity research, each of which deals with a different aspect of the question, "To what extent does this test measure what it is supposed to measure?" A major type of validity is **criterion validity**— the demonstration that a test can successfully predict the behavior or performance it is intended to predict. For example, to evaluate the criterion validity of a measure of psychological adjustment designed to screen out recruits who are unable to cope with the demands of military service, psychologists would determine the *actual* military adjustment of a sample of recruits to whom the test had been administered. A valid test would have to discriminate between recruits who adjusted satisfactorily and those who were emotionally upset by the service.

Most measures of personality dimensions that relate to personality theory require the evaluation of their **construct validity,** which is a rather complex process. No *single* behavior or assessment is used as a definitive criterion. Rather, the investigator begins with a theory or hunch about the properties of a particular trait or construct and some hypotheses about how this trait is manifested in behavior. The hypotheses are then tested, using the measure of the trait we are interested in evaluating. For example, the test-maker's hypotheses about anxiety might include the following: anxiety increases when subjects are threatened; alcoholics are high in anxiety; anxiety is lowered by certain drugs; anxious people perform poorly in complex learning tasks. Each of these hypotheses would then be investigated, using the test-maker's operational measure of anxiety. Confirmation of the hypotheses would be evidence of construct validity. In validating a test in this way, we also learn more about the construct being measured.

TECHNIQUES OF
MEASUREMENT

There are many different types of techniques used to assess personality constructs. These range from paper-and-pencil tests to physiological recordings. Often the psychologist functions as a measuring instrument, observing, judging, and recording. In each instance, a sample of behavior is recorded and used as an indicator of a broader category of behavior. The samples of behavior might be responses to test items, changes in heartbeat, answers to questions, emotional reactions in an interview, or play activities in the schoolyard. From these samples, estimates are made of the level, degree, or intensity of traits such as anxiety, dependency, or emotional stability.

All of us act as personality "testers" at times. Whenever we size up — "psych out" — another person, we are assessing aspects of personality. The *interview* is a more structured method of sizing up people. The behaviors evaluated in an interview are largely the verbal responses of the interviewee, but psychologists are also attuned to body movements, gestures, changes in skin color (blushing, turning pale), and other indirect ways in which individuals may reveal personality traits (Fast, 1970; Mehrabian, 1969).

Types of Rating Scales

A **rating scale** is a very helpful instrument for quantifying the impressions obtained in an interview or in observing behavior in a natural setting. Assume, for example, that the observer is asked to rate the trait of hostility. A scale is provided that consists simply of the trait name and a sequence of numbers — 1 indicating a low degree and 7 a very high degree of hostility. To increase the reliability and validity of the scale, the observers usually discuss in advance the definition and scoring of the trait and are given behavioral examples of the varying degrees of hostility. Thus, indicators of "very high" hostility might be "makes angry remarks, gets into fights frequently"; indicators of "very little" hostility could be "acts friendly, rarely gets into arguments."

One of the problems with rating scales is the *halo effect:* the rater may judge a person high on one trait simply because he or she is high on another trait. Thus, a person rated as "very friendly" might also be rated as "highly intelligent," even though there is no objective reason for the latter rating. There are negative halos as well; if the subject is unfriendly, she or he might be rated as unintelligent. In general, great care should be taken to avoid halo effects—both in the construction of the rating scale and in the training of raters.

Another widely used technique similar to the rating scale is the *adjective checklist*. The rater is given a long list of adjectives—for example, active, ambitious, intelligent, friendly—and checks off those that are characteristic of the person being rated. Each item (adjective) on an adjective checklist is really

Figure 6-1
A Simple Rating Scale
Prior to using the scale, raters are usually given behavioral examples of the various degrees of hostility.

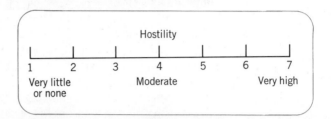

a rating scale with two points—1 and 0 (characteristic or not characteristic)—and permits the rater to attend to the behaviors that are most descriptive of the individual. In one study, the assessment staff of a research institute rated forty graduate students in various fields; half of them had been previously characterized by their instructors as outstandingly original and half as low in originality (Gough, 1960). Among the adjectives used to describe the highly original students were "adventurous," "alert," "curious," "quiet," "imaginative," and "fair-minded." Among those characterizing the less original subjects were "confused," "conventional," "defensive," "polished," "prejudiced," and "suggestible."

While the adjective checklist reduces the rating scale to two points, the *Q-sort technique* is a more elaborate rating procedure (Stephenson, 1953). The rater is given a set of adjectives or statements, which are sorted into piles—usually 7 or 9—according to the degree to which they are descriptive of the subject. Statements very characteristic of the subject are placed in pile 9, while the least descriptive items are placed in pile 1. The rater is required to place a certain number in each pile, more in the middle piles and fewer at the extremes. This procedure forces the rater to discriminate carefully and to decide which descriptive items are really the most characteristic.

These examples of Q-sort statements are taken from the California Q sort (Block, 1961):

> Has a wide range of interests.
> Is productive; gets things done.
> Is self-dramatizing; histrionic.
> Overreactive to minor frustrations; irritable.
> Seeks reassurance from others.
> Appears to have a high degree of intellectual capacity.
> Is basically anxious.

Q sorts, rating scales, and adjective checklists can also be used to assess a person's self-concept. For example, we had Richard Paulder do a Q-sort rating of himself. Two of the statements he placed in piles 8–9 (very descriptive) were "Overreactive to minor frustrations; irritable," and "Is basically anxious." In pile 2 (not descriptive) appeared the statement, "Appears to have a high degree of intellectual capacity."

Personality Inventories

To be accurate, rating scales require that the rater have an adequate opportunity to observe the subject under varied conditions. Other personality measures, simpler to administer, are based on *self*-descriptions. The first of these *personality inventories*, the Personal Data Sheet, was developed during World War I, as a rapid-screening device for detecting individuals who could not stand the stress of military life (Woodworth, 1919). The inventory consisted of 116 yes-no questions, such as "Do you daydream a great deal?" and "Do you feel like jumping off when you are on high places?" This scale became the prototype of subsequent, further refined personality inventories.

TABLE 6-1 Personality traits measured by the MMPI	
Trait	*Symptoms*
1. Hypochondriasis	Exaggerated complaints about bodily health.
2. Depression	Self-disparaging and despondent tendencies.
3. Hysteria	Exaggerated emotional displays vying with inappropriate emotional blandness, physical impairment without an organic basis.
4. Psychopathic deviate	Impulsive, antisocial, amoral tendencies.
5. Masculinity-Femininity	Heterosexual and homosexual tendencies (applicable to males); masculine and feminine interests.
6. Paranoia	Suspicious hostile tendencies.
7. Psychasthenia	Indecision, overconscientiousness, obsessive (uncontrolled thoughts) and compulsive (ritualistic acting out) tendencies.
8. Schizophrenia	Withdrawal from other people, disturbed thinking, odd behavior.
9. Hypomania	Exaggerated feelings of excitement and elation, overactivity.
10. Social introversion	Interest in inner events.

Personality inventories can be scored easily and objectively. The questions are unambiguous and the subject's responses are straightforward, yes or no answers or numerical ratings. Among the best known of the instruments in current use is the Minnesota Multiphasic Personality Inventory (MMPI), which assesses a number of personality traits described in Table 6-1. The 550 items in the MMPI, answered true, false, or "can't say," include the following:

> I work under a great deal of tension.
> I like to read newspaper articles on crime.
> No one seems to understand me.

The MMPI was initially developed as a test of particular psychiatric disturbances (Hathaway & McKinley, 1943). Nonetheless, the items in each of the subscales of the MMPI—such as depression and schizophrenia—discriminate between psychiatric patients and normal subjects. For example, depressed patients obtain higher scores on the depression scale than normal people. Since many psychiatric symptoms are extreme forms of tendencies that can also be observed in normal individuals, MMPI scales are generally useful in assessing the personality characteristics. However, the personality labels for the subscales do have an unfortunate and distinctly psychiatric connotation and may erroneously suggest emotional disturbance rather than a normal degree of a particular personality dimension.

The MMPI is widely used, but many psychologists have reservations about its utility as a personality measure (Goldberg, 1974; Norman, 1972). Most of its subscales are complex, and scores can have several different meanings. For example, the overall masculinity-femininity score obscures the important distinction between a person's *identity* as a male or female and his or her *interests,* which may be socially defined as masculine or feminine. A well-adjusted female may be interested in math and sports, and a male with no problems with his sexual identity may have interests in cooking and art. In fact, one study has shown that well-adjusted college students of both sexes have strong interests in both traditionally feminine and traditionally masculine activities (Bem, 1975).

The complexity of the MMPI scales has led to a search for more basic factors common to several of the scales and underlying these presumably separate measures. The statistical technique of *factor analysis* is especially designed to discover these factors. The method is somewhat analogous to chemical analyses that discover that hundreds of compounds are combinations of only a few basic elements. Psychological "compounds," such as test behaviors, are mathematically analyzed. When factor analysis is applied to the MMPI, two general factors or traits are found (Block, 1965; Tyler, 1951; Welsh, 1956). The first and most important is *general adjustment or psychological health.* The second, more difficult to label, is the degree of *control over feelings and actions* the individual exercises. General factors found in other personality measures are presented in Table 6-2.

Projective Tests

In contrast to the personality inventories, **projective tests** deliberately use vague and ambiguous stimuli such as inkblots and pictures. These stimuli permit a wide array of responses that are sometimes difficult to standardize

Leading exponents of factor analysis (Cattell, 1946; Eysenck, 1947) have used this procedure to analyze many types of inventories, rating scales, physiological measures, and other tests. Listed are the most important of twelve fundamental personality traits, according to Cattell.

TABLE 6-2 Personality dimensions found through factor analysis		
Cyclothymia (emotionally expressive, outgoing)	vs.	Schizothymia (withdrawn, emotionally restrained)
Intellectually efficient (high in general intelligence)	vs.	Intellectually deficient (low in general intelligence)
Emotionally stable (calm, emotionally appropriate)	vs.	Emotionally unstable (impulsive, unrealistic)
Dominance (assertive, aggressive)	vs.	Submissiveness (mild, compliant)

Administering a Rorschach Inkblot Test.

and quantify. Scoring and interpretation of projective tests usually requires considerable skill and training. Advocates of projective techniques believe that these disadvantages are more than compensated for by the richness of the data yielded.

There are certain similarities between projective tests and psychoanalytic procedures, which will be described in Chapter 8. The subject is presented with a stimulus—an inkblot, a picture, a word—and is encouraged to respond with whatever association comes to mind. There are no clearly correct or socially desirable answers, so true reactions are more difficult to disguise. Unconscious factors have a much greater opportunity of influencing the response to a projective stimulus than to a questionnaire item. Confronted with an ambiguous stimulus and attempting to give it meaning and order, the individual can be said to "project" onto the stimulus some part of his- or herself. For these reasons some feel that projective tests reveal more about the individuality of people than personality inventories do.

Of the many different kinds of projective measures, the Rorschach inkblot test is perhaps the best known. Designed by a Swiss psychiatrist, Hermann Rorschach (1942), this test consists of ten cards, each with an inkblot similar to the one depicted in Figure 6-2. The blots vary in shape, shading, and color, half of them being black and white. The subject is shown one card at a time, and usually gives several associations to each card. The responses given by college students to the blot in Figure 6-2 include a butterfly pattern, a discus thrower, an octopus, a juggler, a tumbling team, the head of a bear, an animal skin, a man caught in a trap, a nose, a human profile, and the island of Crete. Subject's responses may be based on the whole card or on parts of the card, and associations may be determined by the shape of the blot, its color, or its shading. Some responses are quite common, frequent associations, while

Figure 6-2
Inkblot Similar to Those Used
in Projective Tests

others are quite rare. All of these factors enter into the scoring and interpretation of the test.

Trained clinical psychologists use the Rorschach test for the diagnosis of
psychopathology and for the assessment of such variables as self-concept, self-
control, ego strength, relationship to others, creativity, and style of coping
with stress and conflict. Because the Rorschach is so flexible an instrument
and demands sensitive interpretation, it has been very difficult to validate.
Many psychologists question its utility, and currently it is less widely used
than it was ten or twenty years ago. Nevertheless, there is substantial research
supporting the use of the Rorschach to assess certain dimensions, such as
self-control and ego strength (Klopfer, 1954; Zubin, Eron, & Schumer, 1965).

The Thematic Apperception Test (TAT), designed by Henry A. Murray
(1943), is another commonly used projective test. It consists of twenty picture
cards (one of which is blank); the subject is asked to make up a story about
each picture. Most of the pictures show one or several people engaged in
some ambiguous action. Thus, one picture depicts a kneeling figure with its
head resting on a bench. The figure is sometimes seen as male and sometimes
as female; he or she is perceived as crying, tired, or guilty, as remorseful over
a shooting, as discouraged over a school failure, and so on. A second picture
depicts a girl lying semi-nude on a couch, with a man in a distressed posture
standing nearby. This stimulus elicits stories of illness, sexual seduction, impotence, rape, murder, and other such themes. The range of stories given

to any card is great, but there are recurring themes for certain pictures. Stories with sexual themes are more likely to be given to particular pictures; aggressive themes are usually given to others.

The individual's responses are analyzed to determine if there are predominant themes running through many of the stories. The key assumption is that the descriptions of the characters in the stories reflect the subject's own needs, conflicts, and feelings. For example, the following themes were salient in the stories Richard Paulder told in response to the Thematic Apperception Test: intense hostility to father figures; feelings of rejection by older males; fear of punishment for aggressive behavior; strong needs for achievement and superiority; positive feelings coupled with the denial of hostility toward women. The story he gave to a picture of a young man apparently conversing with an older man was particularly revealing:

> This fellow is a college student. He wants very much to go to medical school but is worried about his poor grades. He's working about thirty hours a week on a job in addition to going to school and feels that if he could quit the job, his grades would improve. The other guy is his father. He tells his father about his situation, hoping that he will offer to pay his college expenses for at least one year. But the old man won't budge. He tells his son that he has to be responsible for his grades at college and maybe medical school is not for him.
> [Question of psychologist to Paulder: "How does the son feel?"] He's as mad as hell at his father but can't tell him off.

The TAT can be interpreted in a clinical, subjective manner, or the content can be quantitatively analyzed to yield reliable scores on specified personality dimensions. For example, a quantitative measure of the "achievement motive"—the need to accomplish, to compete with a standard of excellence—has been developed (McClelland et al., 1953); it has been found to be related to a number of behaviors. In risk-taking situations, people high in achievement motivation prefer the 50/50 chance—neither too easy nor too

What people see in pictures of ambiguous situations are projections of their own personalities.

difficult. This general tendency applies to the occupational choices of students, too. Those with a high need to achieve, choose careers that will require hard work but not occupations that are unrealistically beyond their capabilities (Atkinson, 1964).

Sexual and aggressive motives are also inferred from TAT stories, although in these cases there is a question about whether the TAT themes are *representational* or *compensational*. For example, does a high degree in the TAT aggressive content indicate that the individual is overtly aggressive (representation)? Or does it reflect an outlet (compensation) for inhibited aggressive tendencies? This issue becomes especially important when psychologists are trying to predict whether an individual with high TAT aggression is a good risk for release from a mental hospital or prison. Research indicates that high TAT aggression scores are not reliable indicators of overt aggressive behavior (Murstein, 1963; Zubin et al., 1965). However, prediction of overt aggression from the TAT is considerably enhanced if one also measures the amount of inhibition of and anxiety about aggression that is reflected in responses to the TAT. Strong aggression on the TAT is associated with aggressive "acting out" behavior when inhibitory tendencies are weak (Feshbach, 1970).

Objective Measures

In an effort to achieve greater objectivity, psychologists have developed a number of procedures with primary emphasis on **behavioral samples** that can be readily quantified. In some of these, an observer notes and records the actual behavior of the subject, making no inferences such as those usually involved in a rating scale. In assessing a child's aggression, for example, an observer might count the number of fistfights, arguments, destruction of objects, and similar behaviors in which a child participated over a particular time period (Feshbach, 1970; Lovaas et al., 1965).

Ideally, a subject would be observed under many different conditions for periods of time sufficient to obtain reliable samples of behavior. Psychological tests are, of course, shortcuts to lengthy and costly observational procedures, and one can reduce the time and cost of observation by eliciting the behavior under more controlled conditions. For example, candidates for positions in the Office of Strategic Services during World War II found themselves placed in "crisis situations" (Murray, 1948). A group of candidates, armed with weapons and other military equipment, might be approaching a wide stream; one of the group would be placed in charge and given the task of bringing the men and equipment across the stream as quickly and as efficiently as possible. His performance in this situation was carefully observed, and personality assessments were made on the basis of this behavior.

A related method is the "stress" interview, in which an individual is deliberately subjected to verbal pressure. The examiner may alternate between a friendly and critical attitude, pop embarrassing questions at the interviewee, and shout and demand immediate answers. All of this untoward behavior is designed to appraise the interviewee's reaction to stress (and to penetrate deception).

Another type of objective measure commonly used to assess personality is the *physiological recording*. While verbal statements and even actions can be altered to disguise true feelings, it is extremely difficult to control physiologi-

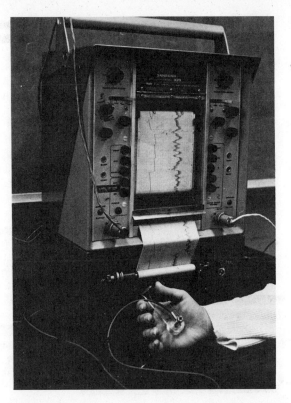

One means of assessing certain physiological reactions is a machine that measures a person's galvanic skin response (GSR).

cal responses. Try as you might to hide the fact you are embarrassed, blushing gives you away. The lie detector (polygraph) uses a number of physiological recordings and is based on the assumption that a "lie" will produce a marked emotional reaction.

Perhaps the most commonly used physiological measure in personality assessment is the *galvanic skin response*, or *GSR*. It reflects relatively minute changes in the electrical characteristics of the skin related to sweating and, therefore, is frequently used as an indication of emotional arousal or anxiety. The electromyograph (EMG) records muscle tension and has been used in a fashion similar to the GSR, especially when muscle tension can be assumed to reflect psychological tension or stress. The electroencephalograph (EEG) records certain electrical characteristics of brain activity and has been used in the study of dreams (Dement, 1960; *see* pp. 558–59).

SUMMARY

The study of personality is concerned with the individual's characteristic behaviors and with the basic tendencies that direct these behaviors. One important question is the degree of consistency or generality in behavior. In their search for *basic* dimensions of personality—the most central dimensions of the widest generality—psychologists have focused on temperament and expressive movements, on thinking and perceiving, and, most importantly, on motivational dynamics and feelings. **Introversion-extroversion,** generalized expectancies of **locus of control** (internal or external) of reinforcement, and achievement motivation are examples of important personality **traits** that psychologists have investigated.

Personality differences arise from diverse causes including culture and social roles, biological and genetic factors, and developmental experiences and learning history. The study of aggression provides an example of the interaction of the multiplicity of influences that affect personality. Cognitive factors, such as the intentionality and arbitrariness of frustration and the individual's prior expectancy, have been shown to be important determinants of the degree of aggressive drive elicited by a frustrating situation. A person's aggressive behavior, in addition to being influenced by aggressive drive, is markedly affected by the history of rewards and punishments for aggressive actions, by social norms, and by the models the person has encountered. Aggressive drive may be reduced through direct or indirect aggressive acts (catharsis) or through modification or elimination of stimuli that elicit hostile behavior.

Tests and other measures of personality are needed for testing theoretical propositions about personality and, for practical purposes, as aids in diagnosis and guidance. For personality measures to be useful, they must be reliable and valid. **Validity** can be assessed by testing the relationship between the personality measure and a specific standard or criterion **(criterion validity)** or to a variety of behaviors that are theoretically related to the construct the measure is designed to assess **(construct validity).**

Many different types of procedures have been used to measure personality. Some, such as the **rating scale** and the adjective checklist, are based on the judgments of an observer. Personality inventories, such as the MMPI, make use of the individual's self-report in response to a questionnaire. In contrast to the "yes-no" format of the personality inventories, the vague, ambiguous stimuli used in **projective tests** such as the Rorschach inkblot test and the Thematic Apperception Test elicit responses that are presumably more reflective of individual style and unconscious motivations. Readily quantified behavioral samples used as personality measures range from "stress" interviews to physiological responses.

In 1909 Sigmund Freud (left) lectured on psychoanalysis at Clark University. To his right (front row) are University President G. Stanley Hall and Carl Jung; standing are A. A. Brill, Ernest Jones (Freud's biographer), and Sandor Ferenczi.

Theories of Personality

What did Freud mean by "psychoanalysis"?
What elements of psychoanalysis led to dissent?
What do actualization theories stress?
How do learning theories explain personality?
What is the Oriental approach to personality?

In very broad terms, a theory of personality is an attempt to explain personality structure and functioning. It provides a set of relevant personality dimensions, an explanation of the origins of these dimensions, and principles to account for the effects of personality factors on behavior. A theory can help integrate a wide array of behavioral observations and experimental data. In formulating a theory of personality, the theorist attempts (1) to define meaningful fundamental concepts; (2) to indicate how these concepts are related to one another; and (3) to show how the theoretical constructs are reflected in observable behavior. There are many personality theories. Some focus on unconscious mental forces (Freudian psychoanalysis), some on the person's potential—and motivation—for psychological growth (self-actualization theories), and some on the ability of individuals to change with experience (learning theories). In this chapter we will consider each of these approaches and a few more, including an Oriental approach quite different from Western theories.

What did Freud mean by "psychoanalysis"?

The greatest single figure among personality theorists is still Sigmund Freud, the originator of **psychoanalysis.** The impact of psychoanalysis extends far beyond psychology, influencing much of twentieth-century intellectual history. Although psychoanalysis plays a less central role in current psychological and psychiatric thinking than it did twenty years ago, it remains a major theory of personality.

Freud's initial interests were in the nervous system, and he appeared destined for a brilliant research career in neurology (Jones, 1957). His medical practice, however, forced him to confront the more pragmatic problems of treating patients who suffered from such "nervous" disorders as extreme anxiety, excessive fatigue, and loss of memory. When conventional physical treatments failed to help these patients, Freud turned to hypnosis, in collaboration with his older colleague and good friend, Josef Breuer.

Freud soon became disenchanted with hypnosis as a therapeutic method too, for many patients were incapable of entering a trance state; moreover the patient's memories of the past, which seemed related to present difficulties, were often "lost" again upon reawakening. Gradually Freud developed the method of **free association,** instructing the patient simply to focus on a symptom or an event in the past and to "associate freely" to it—that is to say anything that came to mind, no matter how trivial or embarrassing it might seem. The method of free association became the cornerstone of psychoanalytic technique. It remains so today.

By listening carefully to the patient's associations, Freud detected consistent themes, which on further analysis were shown to be manifestations of the patient's unconscious wishes and fears. The idea that much of behavior appears to be a compromise between wishes and fears assumed a central role in Freud's understanding of neurotic symptoms, dreams, slips of the tongue, humor, sexual behavior, and even occupational interests. In his analyses of these phenomena, he found evidence of unresolved childhood conflicts, unconscious incestuous wishes, and hostile impulses. From observations such as these, Freud formulated the psychoanalytic theory. We turn now to some of the findings and interpretations that form the core of this theory.

LIBIDO

Freud used the concept of **libido** to describe what he believed to be a fundamental pleasure-seeking drive that motivates us from birth. The distinctive feature of libidinal behavior is its erotic (sexual) quality, a quality that remains even though the pattern of libidinal expression changes radically as the child matures. Freud proposed that in childhood—long before mature, adult sexuality develops—the libidinal impulses undergo three **psychosexual**

stages of development—oral, anal, and phallic. During the first year of life, the baby is in the *oral* stage; the libidinal impulses are gratified through stimulation of the membranes of the mouth. During the child's second and third year—the *anal* stage—pleasures stemming from excretion and retention of feces dominate the child's erotic life. Sometime at the end of the third or beginning of the fourth year, the child enters the *phallic* stage of development in which excitation and stimulation of the genital areas provide the primary source of erotic pleasure. Following the phallic stage, libidinal impulses enter a period of quiescence or "latency," from which they are reawakened at the onset of puberty. Many adult emotional problems were traced by Freud back to specific disturbances that had occurred during the oral, anal, and phallic periods of early childhood.

Freud postulated that there was a fixed amount of libidinal energy or libido. In his view, if libidinal impulses are not directly expressed because of fear or guilt, tension and pressure in the energy-system increase, compelling some release in the form of neurotic symptoms or antisocial behavior. Thus, from a psychoanalytic point of view, it is essential that society provide a safety valve for the indirect expression of libidinal and other impulses (such as aggression) whose direct expression is prohibited. Such notions are difficult,

REPRESSION

Is smoking a carryover from the oral stage of psychosexual development?

if not impossible, to test; and the concept of a fixed amount of libidinal theory is considered by many to be the least satisfactory aspect of psychoanalytic theory.

ID, EGO, AND SUPEREGO

Sigmund Freud

Aggressive impulses are another basic energy source; and, like the libido, they are biologically rooted and present at birth. Freud used the concept of the **id** to denote both the primordial libidinal and aggressive drives. The id consists of unconscious impulses that seek *immediate* expression and gratification. The pressure for rapid discharge of these drives—without regard to consequences—is referred to in psychoanalytic theory as the "**pleasure principle**."

The process of learning to delay impulse expression and to take into account the immediate and future consequences of behavior is referred to as the "**reality principle**." The reality principle governs the actions of the **ego**, which is responsible for coordinating and directing the organism's behavior. The ego mediates between the unreasoning id and the constraints of reality. Its function is to select patterns of action that will permit the maximum achievement of id impulse gratification under the limiting circumstances imposed by the world.

A number of important human motives can be traced to the ego's function as mediator between id impulses and reality. Ego motives involve self-enhancement and are most clearly reflected in strivings for status, achievement, and power. Whereas id motives are governed by biological pleasures, ego motives are based on the broader calculus of self-interest.

Human behavior is also governed by a third system of motives, the **superego,** which has an "I ought or should" rather than an "I want" (id) or an "I can" (ego) quality. The superego is made up of internalized social and moral prohibitions that act to suppress id and ego satisfaction, even when there is no possibility of punishment by an external agent. Largely unconscious, the superego can be discerned in the feelings of guilt and pricks of conscience almost everyone experiences at times. The superego is frequently in conflict with id and ego motives. Since superego demands are so often based on the child's unconscious internalization of arbitrary and excessively strict standards, they may prevent the enjoyment, as an adult, of simple, socially acceptable pleasures (for example, sexual intercourse with one's spouse).

Other important psychodynamic processes are related to the child's development of the superego. For example, in the case of the boy, it is suggested that about age five or six his libidinal impulses are directed toward his mother. He resents his father, whom he sees as a rival for the affections of the mother. Freud labeled this classic rivalry the **Oedipal conflict** (or Oedipus complex) after a character in a Greek legend who unknowingly killed his father and married his mother. The young boy also fears that his father will retaliate by castrating him. Freud labeled this fear **castration anxiety** and considered it the prototype of all subsequent anxiety. The fear of castration normally leads to repression of the boy's erotic feelings toward the mother and to identification with the father as a powerful figure. Any disturbances in the resolution of this central developmental conflict, in Freud's view, would have serious and lasting effects on future personality development.

The **identification** process permits the boy to express his love toward his

Being a winner in the eyes of the world and oneself is a powerful ego motive for any athlete.

In Freud's time, the privileged social and cultural position accorded to men often left women to run along behind without hope of catching up.

mother indirectly, with minimal anxiety. According to psychoanalytic theory, it also provides the basis for the formation of the superego. The male child internalizes his father's values—which tend to be idealized—as if the father were perfect or godlike. Neither the son nor the father can completely live up to these standards, a fact that underlies many later conflicts. Psychoanalysts direct their efforts to trying to modify the superego of patients who can neither live by, nor reject, the idealized moral demands internalized as very young children.

The young girl also is presumed to undergo a transformation at about the same age of five or six, although the situation is more complex and takes longer to resolve. Psychoanalytic theory, in fact, is much less "worked out" for females. It is believed, however, that the girl at this time begins to internalize a sense of weakness and inferiority; the concept of **penis envy** was developed to indicate this sense of being "incomplete." The identification with the mother is seen to be a result of a kind of "shared misfortune." Only by getting a man (a husband) and bearing a male child can a woman fulfill herself.

Freud's psychology of women has been criticized as pure male chauvinism, and the criticism is neither new nor without some basis. Psychoanalytic theory was certainly influenced by traditional views of the female role in European, Victorian society. Many later psychoanalytic scholars (such as Thompson, 1964) prefer the concept of "privilege envy"—a social and changeable state—to "penis envy"—a biological and hence irreversible state. Most psychologists would agree that Freud's view of the nature and origins of femininity and of conflict in women is in serious error.

REPRESSION AND THE UNCONSCIOUS

One of the more provocative aspects of psychoanalytic theory is the assertion that a significant part of our behavior is governed by forces of which we are unaware—the **unconscious.** Our choice of a marital partner or vocation, our hobbies, quarrels with friends, careless acts, and incompetent performances may reflect the influence of impulses and fears that remain unconscious—that is, inaccessible to our conscious mind. Impulses and feelings such as shame, guilt, or fear—and the memories associated with these unacceptable feelings—may also be excluded from awareness. When Freud encouraged his patients to recall painful memories and to confront unacceptable feelings, they appeared to resist his efforts. Freud hypothesized that this resistance was a function of an active, although unconscious, attempt to exclude unpleasant events and feelings from memory. He called this **repression** (see Spotlight 7-1).

The concepts of repression and the unconscious have long been sources of contention. The use of the term "the unconscious" may be somewhat misleading. The unconscious is not a *place* situated deep in the recesses of the brain, but rather a *property of behavior*—a description of the degree of awareness of the factors that affect our behavior. Many argue that while behavior *can* be influenced by stimuli of which the individual is not aware, it is illogical and unnecessary to hypothesize unconscious feelings and motives. Moreover, say the critics, since unconscious factors cannot be observed directly, it is difficult to refute or confirm their influence.

The evidence for unconscious motivation stems primarily from the study of clinical cases. Richard Paulder, for example, did not know why he got into arguments with certain adults. He was not aware that he was reacting to a particular type of person; sometimes he was even unaware that he was behaving aggressively. Similar behavior can be produced with hypnosis. A hypnotist can instruct a good hypnotic subject to do something after awakening and to have no memory of the instruction; this is called "posthypnotic suggestion." The subject will be unconscious of the reason for the action. Interestingly, if a subject of posthypnotic suggestion is asked to explain the odd behavior—such as—say, combing his or her hair, the person will usually give a plausible, although incorrect answer: "I thought my hair might be messy from lying on the couch."

Several experimental findings also indicate that behavior can be modified without the person's being aware of the source of influence. For example, in studies of verbal conditioning, experimenters have reinforced, by a nod of the head or by simply saying "uh-huh," a subject's use of a particular word category such as plural nouns. Subjects will then utter the reinforced words with increased frequency, without awareness of either the change in behavior or the experimenter's pattern of reinforcement (Greenspoon, 1955; Krasner, 1958).

It seems likely that choices more complex than a simple verbal response—such as the selection of a husband or wife—will be affected, at least in part, by feelings and associations of which we have little or no awareness. For Freud, a principal goal of maturity is to bring these unconscious feelings, insofar as possible, into consciousness. Although personality theorists differ in the importance they attribute to conscious and unconscious forces in behavior,

One of my patients in therapy could not acknowledge any feeling of anger. He would sometimes wake up in a panic with his hands clasped around his wife's throat. Yet he stoutly maintained that his wife neither irritated nor angered him and that he had no hostile feelings toward her. As therapy progressed, he became aware of his anger toward his wife and of the source of this anger in his own feelings of inadequacy. It took many months before he could recall any situation in which his mother had behaved unfairly or irrationally. These memories had been repressed because they elicited angry feelings which he could not tolerate. At the termination of the therapy, his irrational fears and obsessive thoughts had disappeared and he felt much more relaxed. Nevertheless, he still had difficulty in acknowledging ever having experienced hostile feelings toward his mother, even after he was able to recall "forgotten" memories of his mother having unfairly and hysterically beaten him. Repression was a key defense he unconsciously employed to preserve his self-image and his image of his mother.

almost all of them have incorporated Freud's concept of the unconscious in one form or another.

RECENT TRENDS IN PSYCHOANALYTIC THEORY

A number of different theories of human personality are called psychoanalytic. Some only loosely warrant this classification, while others are closely related to Freud's thought and may be considered extensions or "descendants" of his basic discoveries. The extensions have come primarily in two areas. Since Freud spent most of his time working out the dynamics of the id and the conflicts between the id and superego, later developments focused directly on the ego and ways of dealing with conflict.

Defense Mechanisms

Much of our understanding of the means of coping with prohibited impulses (for example, a conflict between sex and guilt or anxiety) is derived from the works of Freud himself and that of his daughter, Anna Freud (A. Freud, 1946). She expanded her father's notion of defense mechanisms, while other psychoanalytic theorists (Hartmann, 1958) examined more closely the adaptive cognitive functions of the ego.

Defense mechanisms are conflict-resolving mechanisms, which may be used in dealing with many kinds of motives including sex, aggression, envy, or pride. We all use these mechanisms to some extent to deal with our conflicts and anxieties. For Freud, the key defense employed by the ego is *repression,* which we have already mentioned as the unconscious exclusion from awareness of unacceptable impulses and ideas. Other common defense mechanisms are defined below.

In **denial,** unacceptable impulses and associated ideas are simply denied; that is, the individual refuses to believe that he or she has such impulses. For example, one patient could not express any feelings of anger toward his mother and would deny or make light of actions toward her that others would construe as arbitrary and selfish. Unwillingness to check up on physical or mental symptoms that might be indicative of serious illness is another example of denial, as is the tendency of combat veterans to engage in banter and jest as they go into battle (denial of fear).

Reaction formation is the manifestation of behavior that is directly opposite to unconscious feelings and attitudes. For example, a parent may defend against unconscious feelings of resentment toward an unwanted child by reacting with overly solicitous affection toward the child. Extreme hostility to homosexuals can be a reaction formation against latent homosexual impulses. A literary prototype of this defense is seen in Charles Dickens' character Uriah Heep, whose unctuous politeness and humility were barely concealed reactions against strong feelings of arrogance and envy.

How then can one distinguish among genuine expressions of feeling, deceptions, and reaction formations? Clinically, behavior arising from reaction formation is exaggerated, inflexible, and often inappropriate. In addition, the reaction formation may permit partial gratification of the repressed impulse against which the individual is defending. The overly solicitous parent is also harassing the unwanted child; and the antihomosexual, in the course of efforts to censor homosexual literature and movies, can become intimately acquainted with these materials.

In **projection,** the individual attributes to others his or her own unacceptable, repressed feelings and ideas. For example, people who are unable to accept their own hostile impulses, frequently see others as hostile. This mechanism is often manifested in social prejudice—for example, hostile whites say blacks are aggressive. When frightened, children are more likely to see other children as frightened and adults as threatening (Murray, 1933; Feshbach & Feshbach, 1963). Projective tests (pp. 150–54) were developed largely on the assumption that people will project their own feelings onto an ambiguous picture or inkblot.

Displacement is the expression of repressed feelings toward an innocent target. (See p. 88 for a discussion of the relationship between displacement and prejudice.) Richard Paulder displaced his hostility toward his father onto other authority figures. In this instance, there was displacement from one *object* or person to another. Displacement may involve the response as well as the object. For example, hostile dreams may be a displacement for the direct expression of hostility.

Sublimation is a form of displacement in which an unacceptable or unsatisfied impulse is expressed in a socially acceptable form. Ungratified sexual impulses may be expressed in highly approved ways in lyrical poetry or in painting. Meat cutting may be a socially acceptable means by which hostile, sadistic impulses can be partially gratified. It would be absurd, however, to suggest that being a meat cutter is *necessarily* a form of sublimated hostility. The point here is that *some* people may utilize the constructive behavior of meat cutting to satisfy ordinarily destructive impulses.

There are many other defenses against painful, anxiety-producing feelings and thoughts. We are all certainly familiar with and use **rationalization** of shortcomings we are reluctant to admit; we justify our behavior to make it appear rational, giving a "good" rather than a "true" reason for our actions. We blame circumstances rather than ourselves for failures. ("I missed the ball because the sun was in my eyes.") Anxiety-arousing impulses may also un-

Some observers would say that the painter is *sublimating* certain needs by his choice of subject. Probably few artists would agree.

dergo **intellectualization,** so that they can be discussed in an elaborate, detailed manner, avoiding the feelings involved in the conflict. In **isolation,** the individual is defended from anxiety-arousing ideas, keeping them in psychological "compartments," separate from related thoughts and attitudes.

Defenses vary in their psychopathological consequences. **Regression,** in which the individual adopts an earlier, immature model of functioning when confronted with a difficult conflict, can result in seriously inappropriate behavior. In contrast, sublimation is a much more adaptive defense.

Defenses can be highly specific reactions to particular conflict situations, or they may become generalized traits, central to the individual's personality structure. Thus projection is a key mechanism employed by the paranoid individual, who is overly suspicious and sensitive (*see* p. 199). Within the normal population, "repressors" tend to avoid a conflict or painful stimuli; and "sensitizers" are unduly sensitive and excessively preoccupied with conflict (Byrne, 1964).

Another recent trend in psychoanalytic thinking is a more detailed examination of the social and cultural influences on personality. Thus Freud's view of the development of the female personality has been criticized as being too biological and not taking into account the powerful influence of the social milieu.

environmental influences

Erik Erikson

Both trends—more emphasis on the ego and on cultural influences—are exemplified in the writings of Erik Erikson (1950). Erikson's views on the early stages of development are similar to Freud's, but he examines these stages from the perspective of ego functions and the particular social or interpersonal

Erik Erikson

problems posed by each stage. Moreover, the pattern of personality is not seen as essentially completed and unchangeable by the time the child enters school. Instead, Erikson extends his analysis of development to embrace the full life span from infancy to maturity (see also pp. 283–85).

Erikson proposes eight **psychosocial stages** in personality formation. Each stage is critical in the development of certain fundamental personality characteristics (see Spotlight 7-2). For example, in the earliest stage—the oral-sensory stage—the infant interacts primarily with its mother, and the "goal" of the interaction is food. It is the infant's first interaction with the social world. Are basic needs fulfilled generously and with affection, or is the world harsh and unpredictable, giving supplies grudgingly without love? According to Erikson, the infant develops during this period a basic sense of trust or mistrust toward the world. It is not that later events cannot alter the basic dispositions, but that the infant's first experience of expectations fulfilled or unfulfilled is of critical importance. (See also pp. 267–68.)

Erikson's thoughtful analysis is especially appealing to contemporary readers because of his emphasis on factors determining a sense of identity and relationships with other people. If sexual problems can be said to have been the dominant preoccupation in the Victorian era, then confusion of identity, sense of self, and feelings of isolation from other human beings are the preeminent problems in modern, technologically advanced Western societies. Erikson's writings speak directly to these problems.

What elements of psychoanalysis led to dissent?

There are a number of personality theories that appear to be psychoanalytic and obviously owe a great debt to Freud's original thinking. Each of them, however, deviates in certain fundamental respects from the classical psychoanalytic model. The clearest examples of such theories are those of Alfred Adler, Carl Jung, and Otto Rank—all early associates of Freud who eventually decided that some of Freud's basic concepts had to be revised. Because of their dissent on basic issues, they separated (or were separated) from Freud with the request, "Do not call your theory psychoanalytic."

In one form or another, both early and later dissent from Freud took the form of rejection of his postulate concerning human motivation: that it is sexual in nature (libido). The alternatives to libido theory proposed by Adler (1930), Jung (1959), Rank (1945), and later dissidents such as Fromm (1941), Horney (1937), and Sullivan (1953) are diverse; Spotlight 7-3 provides a brief description, reflecting only part of the original thinking and contribution of these theorists.

Still, among the dissenters from Freud, certain general themes emerge. The need for relating to others—for loving and being loved—as developed in the writings of Horney, Fromm, and Sullivan, has quite a different connotation than Freud's needs for libidinal gratification. These theorists emphasize interpersonal relationships; the erotic aspects are seen as only one component of these relationships.

Another dimension of interpersonal relationships, which sometimes con-

Psychosocial Stages	Personality Dimensions
1. Oral-Sensory (first year)	Basic trust vs. Mistrust
2. Muscular-Anal (ages 2–3)	Autonomy vs. Shame and doubt
3. Locomotor-Genital (ages 3–5)	Initiative vs. Guilt
4. Latency (ages 5–12)	Industry vs. Inferiority
5. Puberty and Adolescence	Identity vs. Role confusion
6. Young Adulthood	Intimacy vs. Isolation
7. Adulthood	Generativity vs. Stagnation
8. Maturity	Ego integrity vs. Despair

Erikson observed that young adults often experience simultaneous feelings of isolation and desires for social relatedness.

flicts with the need for relatedness, is the need for separateness, for independence. This basic human motivation, a critical aspect of human striving, was first emphasized by Rank (1929; 1945). It also appears in different forms in the writings of the psychologists listed in Spotlight 7-3. Fromm, in particular, but also Adler, Jung, and Rank, suggested that needs for relatedness and independence can function in harmony in the mature individual and can be satisfied by appropriate interpersonal relationships.

Alfred Adler

Will to power, feelings of inferiority, and striving toward superiority or perfection.

Erich Fromm

The expression of one's human nature, as contrasted to animal nature; and identity and a stable frame of reference for perceiving and comprehending the world, as reflected in the needs for relatedness to and transcendence from other people and physical nature.

Karen Horney

Basic anxiety, as reflected in exaggerated needs for love (moving toward people); independence (moving away from people); and destruction (moving against people).

Carl Jung

Striving for self-actualization, as reflected in integrating the "wisdom" of the personal and collective unconscious with the products of conscious experience.

Otto Rank

The struggle for independence, with separation anxiety being the primary source of conflict.

Harry Stack Sullivan

The need for security in conjunction with the need for biological satisfactions; postulation of a self-dynamism as a major motivational outgrowth of the need for security.

The concept of a need for independence requires a **self** that is asserting its independence. The self and the self-concept have many other motivational attributes, expressed, for example, in the needs for self-esteem, for power, or for approval and reassurance. The concept of self as a fundamental source of human motivation is reflected in Adler's concept of the individual's striving toward perfection and in Jung's postulation of a striving for self-actualization.

Carl Jung made the concept of self-actualization one of the cornerstones of contemporary personality theory.

CARL JUNG

self-actualization

Carl Gustav Jung's distinctive theory has had a significant impact on modern thought. Jung placed much greater stress on the role of a person's aims and aspirations in determining behavior than Freud did. In Jung's writings, the ultimate goal toward which each individual is striving is **self-actualization**—the realization of his or her aims and potentials. This goal directs the person's development and destiny.

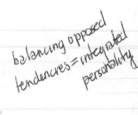

balancing opposed tendencies = integrated personality

In the actualized personality, according to Jung, there is an acceptance and integration of opposing forces and tendencies. There are many opposing forces to be balanced. Each of us, for example, has both masculine and feminine tendencies; and the integrated personality balances aggressiveness with sensitivity. A similar integration must be maintained between opposing tendencies toward introversion and extroversion, personality orientations first discussed in detail by Jung (*see* p. 129). An integrated personality, in his view, is one in which the need for social contact and the need for privacy and reflection are both satisfied. He further proposes that if one tendency is exaggerated, the other will somehow manage to express itself—in dreams, in psychopathological symptoms, or in overt action (acting out). This view is similar to Freud's notion concerning the individual's need for some sort of discharge of repressed impulses.

collective unconscious

One of Jung's most original and intriguing concepts is that of the **collective unconscious.** The collective unconscious is conceived of as containing all the psychological "residue" of our ancestral past. It consists of certain innate ideas, feelings, and attitudes called **archetypes.** For example, all of our ancestors had experience with males and females. According to Jung, some of this experience is passed on to us. In a woman, there is an archetype of a male called the "animus"; in a man, the idea of the archetypical female is the "anima."

The suggestion of a racial inheritance based on the acquired experiences of the species is not acceptable to modern geneticists. However, the notion of innate emotional and behavioral dispositions to particular stimuli—such as fear of the dark, fear of strangers, and attachment to warm objects—is not incompatible with biological theory. The collective unconscious may be viewed as innate predispositions to particular feelings and beliefs resulting from repeated experiences by the human species over many generations.

What do actualization theories stress?

Just as there are many different views of personality that are considered psychoanalytic—in basis if not in name—so there are varied conceptions of human behavior that can be grouped together under the label **actualization theories.** These theories, also described as humanistic approaches, share a number of broad characteristics, of which the following are the most important.

Common Emphases

1. They assume that human beings have a *self-actualizing tendency*—similar to that proposed by Jung—that guides their behavior. Activities that are self-actualizing, that help one realize one's aims and potentials, are fulfilling, satisfying, and self-enhancing. Activities incompatible with self-actualizing strivings are frustrating.

2. There is an emphasis on *present experiences* as determinants of behavior, in contrast to psychoanalysts' preoccupation with the critical influence of the past. This focus on the present has several roots. One is the philosophical theory of existentialism, which is concerned with the *now* as compared to the distant future. Another is the personality theory of the late Kurt Lewin, one of the seminal thinkers in the recent history of psychology. In Lewin's formulation, all the variables determining behavior are in the present situation (Lewin, 1935). Both the future and the past are to be understood in terms of their present psychological representation. Lewin emphasized the forces

Increasingly, self-disclosure is seen as a necessary attribute of the healthy personality.

Carl Rogers

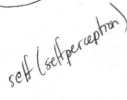

Psychoanalyst vs self-actualizationist

behaviour result of coping with the tensions of repressed conflict

behaviour a result of a search for identity

and constraints induced by *situations,* an emphasis reflected in the writings of a number of actualization theorists (Goldstein, 1939; Rogers, 1959).

3. *Cognition* is emphasized. Actualization theorists begin with the premise that understanding the individual's thoughts and perceptions is essential to understanding his or her behavior. In the case of Richard Paulder, for example, what matters is not the objective situation but how he perceives himself, his opportunities, and the attitudes of his girl friend and authority figures. The effects of early experiences, such as the anger and resentment generated by his father's punishment, are important only insofar as they influence his current thinking and perceptions.

4. Actualization theorists stress the *positive forces* in personality. Psychoanalysts working with Richard Paulder would focus on his unconscious resentments, his fears, and the maladaptive defenses he uses to cope with unacceptable feelings. Actualization theorists would see Paulder in the light of his struggle to assert his independence, his strong aspirations for achievement, his willingness to work hard for his goals, and his need for affection and acceptance—especially from an older man. The psychoanalyst tends to perceive the individual as beset by socially unacceptable impulses and preoccupied with the problems of reducing the tensions generated by these impulses. In contrast, the actualization theorist sees people as engaged in a valiant effort to achieve understanding of themselves and of others, and searching for novel, creative modes of expression.

5. The *love relationship* is seen as a positive force with a very special role. For the psychoanalyst, love is a direct or derivative manifestation of the libido. For the actualization theorist, erotic feelings are either ancillary to or a consequence of love; they are not a necessary component. The primary qualities of the love relationship are intimacy and mutual acceptance. The feelings of closeness and warmth that are expressive of intimacy can be manifested in many types of human relationships, even in essentially religious experiences. Mutual acceptance is reflected in shared high regard, in openness, trust, spontaneity, and noncritical attitudes.

CARL ROGERS

self (self perception)

influence of others.

One of the most influential of the actualization theorists is Carl Rogers, whose conception of personality emerged from his work in psychotherapy. Rogers, in contrast to the psychoanalysts, communicates a fundamental faith and trust in human nature. This faith is expressed in the concept of the *actualizing tendency*—"the inherent tendency of the organism to develop all its capacities in ways which serve to maintain or enhance the organism" (Rogers, 1959, p. 196). Of particular importance is *self*-actualization, the maintenance and enhancement of the self. The **self,** a central construct in Roger's theory, consists of one's perceptions of oneself—attractiveness, abilities, achievements, relationships with other people—and of the values attached to these perceptions (for example, good-bad, worthy-unworthy). It will be recalled that Richard Paulder generally placed a low evaluation on himself; he perceived Richard Paulder as irritable, anxious, and not very intelligent.

A critical factor in the formation of the self-concept is the way in which one is accepted and valued by others. According to Rogers, human beings have a basic need for positive regard from others in the form of warmth, love, and acceptance. This regard and acceptance, however, is usually offered on a

In expressing strong approval and affection for their children, many parents unconsciously apply Rogers' principle of unconditional positive regard.

conditional basis. Typically, the individual receives love or recognition as a result of some particular actions. Consequently, one's perception of oneself as a valuable human being often depends on these actions and the evaluations of other people. In contrast, the truly healthy personality perceives his or her whole self in a positive manner; specific actions can be regarded as good or bad, but the self is always valuable—unconditionally.

In order to attain this level of adjustment, the individual needs the experience of **unconditional positive regard,** of being valued for oneself regardless of the degree to which specific behaviors are approved or disapproved. The love of a parent for a child often has such an unconditional quality. A mother may disapprove of her four-year-old's hitting a younger sibling or of the child's sloppy table manners, but she nevertheless will communicate her fundamental love and acceptance of the child. According to Rogers, one should criticize the action, not the person. He developed a psychotherapeutic approach, **client-centered therapy,** in which a key element is the therapist's manifestation of unconditional positive regard for the client. The Rogerian therapist is understanding, accepting, friendly, and empathic, and, consequently, the client acquires greater self-acceptance. Experiences and feelings that have been denied because they conflicted with self-perceptions based on the _conditional_ regard of others can now be accepted by the client and integrated into the self-concept. The client's "ideal" self—the qualities that are most highly valued, become more realistic—closer to, more congruent with, the "real" self. The consequence of these changes is an individual open to experience, spontaneous, and capable of exercising the judgments that will foster self-actualization.

[handwritten annotation:] healthy, basically good, though individual actions can be bad requires!

For Rogers, the attitudes of the therapist toward the client is the prototype of all productive interpersonal relationships—between husband and wife, parent and child, teacher and student. Rogers himself has extended his ideas to education (Rogers, 1969), and a number of educational innovations and parent training programs reflect his influence. In more recent years, Rogers' exploration of the interpersonal implications of his theory has led to study of the therapeutic "growth" possibilities of sensitivity and encounter groups (*see* p. 211).

ABRAHAM MASLOW

Abraham H. Maslow

Abraham H. Maslow, another eminent actualization theorist, contrasted two broad categories of human motives—**growth motives** and **deprivation motives** (Maslow, 1954). The first is characterized by a push toward actualization of inherent potentialities, while the second is oriented toward the simple maintenance of life, not its enhancement. Deprivation motives are arranged in a developmental hierarchy. The first are physiological needs—for water, food, sleep. These are followed by safety needs—characterized by the avoidance of pain and discomfort (for example, the child needs shelter or is uncomfortable until the diaper is changed). When these needs are satisfied, the needs for belongingness (for love and intimacy) become significant; and these, in turn, are superseded by needs for esteem (approval of others and of self). Satisfaction of needs lower in the hierarchy makes possible the pursuit of needs higher in the hierarchy.

Only when the individual's survival needs are satisfied—when he or she is not "hung up" in their pursuit—can actualization tendencies, or growth motives, be expressed strongly. One of the manifestations of self-actualization is a **peak experience**—variously described as a moment of pure happiness, rapture or ecstasy, a sense of oneness with the world, and a feeling of having perceived an ultimate truth. Peak experiences occur in a wide variety of

Probably most people live through moments of pure joy and ecstasy that are similar to Maslow's "peak experiences."

contexts—religious worship, moments of love, aesthetic appreciation, a creative effort, childbirth, as a response to nature, and even, simply, from recognition of a job well done. According to Maslow (1962), everyone has peak experiences now and then—they might be termed "psychologically healthy moments." Truly healthy, self-actualizing people have them much more frequently.

On the basis of his study of several self-actualized people, Maslow (1963) developed a list of qualities such people have in common, including:

1) Efficient perception of reality.
2) Spontaneity and unconventionality of thought (rather than unconventionality of behavior).
3) Acceptance of themselves, of others, and of nature.
4) Independence from their environment and an affinity for solitude and privacy.
5) Concern for basic philosophical and ethical issues.
6) Continued freshness of appreciation for ordinary events such as sunsets and even the moment-to-moment business of living; the ability to enjoy means as well as ends.
7) Experiences of "the oceanic feeling," which has elements of ecstasy, awe, and both power and helplessness.
8) A genuine desire to help others, in conjunction with deep ties with relatively few people.
9) A truly democratic orientation, a philosophical sense of humor, and creativeness.

You may well question whether these characteristics are a consequence of a psychological process called actualization or the reflections of Maslow's particular value system. Operational definitions of these qualities are difficult to construct, and testing Maslow's assumptions is not easy. Nevertheless, Maslow's descriptions have called attention to significant dimensions of experience and behavior that many other personality theorists have neglected.

How do learning theories explain personality?

There are many theories of personality that emphasize the learning process, and differences among these theories are as great as differences among the various psychoanalytic theories. Still, they have certain common properties. The strategy of learning theorists is to begin with empirically established, basic principles of learning and then to build a model of personality and of complex behavior made up of these simple elements. (*See* Chapter 14 for a detailed description of learning processes.)

B. F. SKINNER

B. F. Skinner's theory of operant conditioning (Skinner, 1953) has had a profound influence on both personality theories, and psychotherapy. (Behavior modification, the application of Skinnerian principles to psychotherapy, is discussed on pp. 207–09.) The theories of Skinner and his adherents deal with the establishment of links between a stimulus situation and the individual's response. These links are formed or strengthened whenever the response is rewarded or reinforced. The process of reinforcement increases the probability

STUART LEEDS

B. F. Skinner

of a response's being emitted when a particular stimulus is present. The response, called an operant or instrumental response, is then said to be under stimulus control. To train a dog to shake hands, the trainer holds out his or her hand and feeds the dog a biscuit whenever it raises its paw and places it in the trainer's hand. Raising the paw is the operant response; it is instrumental in gaining a reward in situations marked by the stimulus of an outstretched hand. This stimulus can be said to "control" the dog's response. After the response is established, it can be maintained through occasional reinforcement by a dog biscuit. In the case of humans, one of the principal tasks of the psychologist is to determine the stimuli that control, and the reinforcers that maintain a pattern of behavior.

A Skinnerian examining Richard Paulder's behavior would select a particular pattern of behavior—say his tendency to quarrel with authority figures—and look for the elements that reinforce his verbal aggressive responses. Perhaps when Richard is quarrelsome, authority figures pay him more attention or are more likely to satisfy his complaints. The reinforcement for Richard's behavior may be either subtle or obvious. The quarrels may eventually result in some type of punishment to Richard. However, the closer a reward or punishment occurs in time to a response, the stronger are its effects. Consequently, the positive reinforcement, which is more immediate in this situation, will prove more powerful than the punishment that may come later.

Skinnerian analyses tend to focus on basic, narrow units of behavior that can then be *shaped* into more complex segments. To improve a student's study habits, for example, one might initially get the student to read at the desk for only a five-minute period. The reinforcement might be food, money, or attention. Gradually the complexity of study activities would be increased, step by step, to include longer study periods, efficient notetaking, and systematic review—with systematic reinforcement occurring at each step in the process.

Skinner's emphasis on behavior change has led to significant modifications in educational practices through the use of programmed learning, teaching machines, and innovations in classroom management procedures. Methods of child rearing and the treatment of behavior disorders were also affected. An additional appeal of Skinnerian personality theories is their focus on *observable* stimuli and responses. There is no need to hypothesize and investigate the complex mental apparatus and motivational systems that psychoanalytic and actualization theories have postulated.

Many psychologists have objected that the Skinnerian approach greatly oversimplifies the processes determining human behavior, neglecting causes such as emotions, judgments, and desires. The humanistic psychologists, in particular, maintain that the individual has more freedom of choice and self-direction than they see expressed by Skinner's strict deterministic framework. Skinner has responded that the freedom we perceive is illusory and that humans—no less than other biological species—are subject to the rule of natural laws.

MILLER AND DOLLARD

Skinner's model makes minimal assumptions about any processes occurring *within* the individual. The learning approach of Miller and Dollard (1941), in contrast, makes heavy use of the concept of internal motivational states or drives. Most human drives, through the processes of learning and association, can be aroused by a variety of internal and external cues or signals. In Richard's case, a male authority figure and criticism have become cues or signals that elicit feelings of anger and hostility (aggressive drive). What Richard, or anyone, else learns to do when angry depends on which responses are most effective in relieving the feelings of anger—in other words, in reducing the aroused drive. As in the Skinnerian model, the individual learns behaviors that are rewarded or reinforced; Richard has learned quarreling, and, to a lesser extent, avoidance and withdrawal.

The critical concepts in the Miller-Dollard analysis are *cue, drive, response,* and *reinforcement*. Note that the response that results in a reduction of drive and is thus rewarded is more likely to occur again when the same or similar situation reoccurs. In this theoretical analysis there are also internal, mediating responses, usually elicited by external stimuli (cues), that may also have drive functions. Thus, external cues may elicit internal responses—such as anger, fear, or sexual feelings. These mediating responses can motivate or drive the organism and, at the same time, provide internal cues to learned behavior. For example, during Richard's high school years, members of his family often elicited his anger—a mediating response—which in turn evoked another mediating response—fear. He apparently resolved these conflicting tensions by avoiding people who were "reminders" (re-evokers) of the disturbing conflict and concentrated on his studies.

Through the ingenious application of these concepts, Miller and Dollard showed how many psychoanalytic propositions can be reconciled with a more rigorous learning orientation (Dollard & Miller, 1950). For example, one study of unconscious motivational influences on behavior centered on the reinforcing effects of being able to inflict pain (Feshbach, Stiles & Bitter, 1967). The subject was initially angered by another "subject,"—in reality a confederate of the experimenter who was deliberately insulting. The subject was then asked to observe the confederate carrying out a complex task under the stress of periodic electric shock and to make repeated ratings of the person's emotional reactions. Between ratings the subject was asked to make up a sentence using any one of the following pronouns: I, we, they, he she, you. He or she would then return to the main task of judging the confederate's emotional reactions.

The confederate was supposedly being administered electric shock on a random basis. Actually, every time the subject used the pronouns *we* or *they*, the confederate would receive a shock. Subjects who had been angered by the confederate significantly increased their use of the pronouns *we* and *they*; a control group of nonangered subjects did not. Yet detailed interviews of the subjects after the experiment showed they had *no awareness* that their use of the particular words was related to the shocks. Thus subjects demonstrated a classic psychoanalytic phenomenon—motivated behavior without awareness. From the perspective of Miller and Dollard, a drive state (anger) was elicited by an external cue (insult), leading to an increasingly frequent response (using plural pronouns) because of reinforcement of this response (seeing the confederate in pain).

SOCIAL LEARNING THEORY

One of the major contributions of Miller and Dollard was their application of learning principles to complex social behavior. However, other personality theorists who stress social learning processes have criticized Miller and Dollard's emphasis on drives and drive reduction as the primary basis for reinforcement. In addition, they feel that Miller and Dollard have overgeneralized from studies of animal learning to human learning situations—a criticism that is also made of Skinner. These critiques have resulted in several related personality approaches that, as a group, are commonly referred to as **social learning theory.**

Expectancy

The theory of Julian Rotter (1954, 1972) emphasizes the construct of *expectancy*, the individual's belief in the probability of a specific behavior leading to satisfactions or valued goals. For example, on the basis of prior experiences, a student may have, simultaneously, a high expectancy that diligent study will bring the approval and affection of one parent and low expectancy that it will be reinforced by the other parent. To predict how hard the student will study, one has to know the *value* of the goals provided by the parents. Of special importance are the values assigned to different goals. Each of us has our own hierarchy of values for such common human goals as money, affection, status, entertainment, sex, and power.

The likelihood that a particular behavior will occur—its *behavior potential*—is a joint function of the person's expectancy that the behavior will lead to satisfactions or goals *and* the value attached to the goals that would be thus achieved. In other words, people will generally choose actions that, on the basis of previous experience, they expect will lead to highly valued goals. Thus, children are likely to say "please" in requesting something if previous experience has shown that there is a high probability (expectancy) of getting what they want (highly valued goals) when they do so. Behaviors with low expectancies of satisfaction are not likely to be used at all *unless,* under some circumstances, they are associated with high reward. For example, 12-year-olds are not likely to cry when trying to convince their parents to do something; they have found that, at this age, such behavior has low expectancy of bringing satisfaction. But they may cry if their crying might result in obtaining some very great satisfaction, such as permission to stay overnight at a friend's house. Characteristics of the specific situation also play a central role in Rotter's theory, since expectancy and reinforcement value vary with circumstances. The personality dimension of *internal* versus *external* control of reinforcement (*see* pp. 130–32) can be conceptualized as a generalized expectancy about the results of one's efforts. Internal control means the individual believes that he or she can significantly determine whether or not a goal is reached. External control means the person believes that fate and not personal effort is most important.

Modeling Behavior

One need only watch young children for a short time to realize that they learn much of their behavior by imitating adult models.

Another prominent social learning theory was first proposed by Bandura and Walters in 1963 and subsequently developed by Bandura and his students. Like Skinner, Bandura and Walters place great emphasis on the importance of the consequences of a response—the *feedback* provided by rewards and punishments of the behavior. However, the Bandura-Walters model also incorporates internal mediating processes, such as attention, covert rehearsal (silently reviewing) of externally provided information, self-criticism, and self-reinforcement. A number of different learning mechanisms are used to account for the social development of the child; in particular, the importance of *imitation* or *modeling* is stressed. Many social responses and personality characteristics are acquired simply by imitating (copying) the behavior of models.

The mechanism of **modeling** has three properties that give it special significance for the understanding of personality development. First, modeling typically entails a social situation (the model and the imitator) and a social relationship. The model can be an actual person or a film or cartoon representation. Second, modeling is a means by which complex behaviors can be readily acquired. The reinforcement methods proposed by Skinner require painstaking, time-consuming efforts to shape a complex social behavior. In contrast, imitation can produce very rapid acquisition of social behaviors. Third, direct reinforcement of imitated behavior is not required for learning to take place.

Bandura and his students have shown that a wide variety of behaviors—from self-control and altruistic behavior to aggressive responses—can be acquired through modeling. Modeling procedures can also be utilized in reducing irrational fears and inhibitions. This application was effectively demonstrated in an experiment in which children with extreme fears (phobias) of dogs became less fearful after watching another child happily interacting with a dog (Bandura, Grusec, & Menlove, 1967; *see* p. 281). The use of modeling in the reduction of fears is a form of *desensitization,* a therapeutic procedure we will discuss in the next chapter.

Through Hathayoga, the Hare Krishna movement, and various forms of meditation, the Oriental approach to consciousness and the self is becoming better known in Western countries.

What is the Oriental approach to personality?

While psychoanalytic, actualization, and learning theorists use different terms and deal with different phenomena of personality, they all share a Western framework that stresses an "action" orientation. This can be contrasted to the approaches to personality associated with important Eastern religious and philosophical traditions. Of the theorists cited, Jung, and perhaps Maslow, can be considered as intermediaries, although they are still more Western than Eastern in outlook. Eastern conceptions of behavior are no less varied and complex than Western, and an adequate description of Oriental psychologies goes well beyond the scope of this chapter. We will only briefly comment on that aspect of Eastern psychology offering a conception of personality that differs greatly from the Western theories we have considered.

One striking feature of Eastern theologies is their concern with consciousness and the liberation of consciousness (Murphy & Murphy, 1968), a concern, however, that westerners have begun to share. In that very important sense, they are much more psychologically oriented than traditional Western religious thought. As in the Western tradition, the activities of the mind are more highly valued than activities of the body. However, the "higher" level of man is itself arranged in a hierarchical manner. Above the body are the senses; while the mind is even greater than the senses. And above the mind is the intellect, with the self being greater than the intellect. The "true self" is perceived as imperishable and unchanging.

The qualities of the self are complex and paradoxical. Of particular psychological interest is the notion of the self as a witness rather than an actor. The notion of the ego or individual *causing* events is thought to be illusory. People are not seen as agents of action. True mastery of the self can only be achieved when one acts *without* being involved in action. The following stanzas from the Bhagavad-Gita may help convey something of these ideas:

> But who takes delight in the self alone,
>   The man who finds contentment in the self,
> And satisfaction only in the self,
>   For him there is found (in effect) no action to perform.
>
> He has no interest whatever in action done,
>   Nor any in action not done in this world,
> Nor has he in reference to all beings
>   Any dependence of interest.
>
> Therefore, unattached ever,
>   Perform action that must be done;
> For performing action without attachment
>   Man attains the highest.

From a Western perspective, this conception of human personality has the effect of diminishing interest in achievement, encouraging a fatalistic and passive attitude toward experience, and turning the individual's energies inward. While effective action (in the Western sense) in the real world is not discouraged, self-actualization is achieved internally rather than through externally directed efforts. According to this Oriental view, the highest level of personal fulfillment is the achievement of a state of consciousness in which — through meditation and concentration — the individual becomes aware of the "true self." This state is difficult to describe and has been characterized as having the qualities of empty space, a lack of consciousness of individuality, of body, and of specific thoughts. Feelings of serenity, well-being, and sometimes ecstasy appear to accompany the achievement of this state.

The student may have noted certain similarities, as well as differences, between Eastern and Western psychologies — for example, the resemblance of Maslow's peak experience to the state of awareness of the "true self." Jung's conception of universal archetypes also has its origins in Eastern thinking. Perhaps the most immediate and important current influence of Eastern, Oriental psychology on Western psychology is the widespread utilization of meditation exercises — in personal-growth programs, for purposes of relaxation, and also as a component of psychotherapy.

SUMMARY

Of the many theories that attempt to explain personality structure and dynamics, one of the most influential has been the **psychoanalytic theory** formulated and elaborated by Sigmund Freud. Freud proposed that human beings were motivated from birth by a fundamental, biologically rooted sexual energy, which he called **libido.** The primary modes of expression of libidinal impulses change as the child progresses through the oral, anal, and phallic periods during the first five years of life. Toward the end of this developmental period, libidinal impulses are typically directed toward the parent of the opposite sex. Freud maintained that the personality of the adult was basically determined by the pattern of resolution of these conflicts and the child's experiences during the early **stages** of **psychosexual** development. Freud also maintained that the child repressed the painful aspects of these conflicts and that much of human motivation occurred at an unconscious level.

Other psychoanalytic theorists, such as Carl Jung, Erik Erikson, Alfred Adler, and Erich Fromm, have differed from Freud in placing greater emphasis on cultural determinants of behavior and in proposing alternative motives to the libido as basic to human striving. These psychoanalysts also tend to place greater stress on the positive forces in personality—a theme that is particularly central to the writings of the **actualization theorists.** The latter assume that human beings have a self-actualizing tendency, which guides behavior; they also emphasize the importance of present experience and cognitive factors—as contrasted to the role of early childhood and unconscious emotional influences—in determining behavior. Among the most prominent actualization theorists are Carl Rogers and the late Abraham Maslow. Rogers' many contributions include an alternative therapeutic approach to psychoanalysis, called **client-centered therapy.** Maslow focused his attention on the hierarchy of human motivations and the characteristics of the truly healthy, self-actualized person.

In contrast to the psychoanalytic and actualization theorists, the learning theorists attempt to use simpler, empirically established principles of behavior in their explanations of human personality. B. F. Skinner and his adherents see behavior as largely a function of the specific reinforcements or rewards received for making particular responses in the presence of specific stimuli. Miller and Dollard emphasize the role of drives and drive reduction in personality and behavior. Their work has provided a bridge between psychoanalytic theory and learning-theory interpretations of personality. **Social learning** theorists such as Rotter and Bandura emphasize the importance of reinforcement in personality development; they also acknowledge the relevance of cognitive variables. Learning mechanisms other than direct reinforcement—notably **modeling**—are also considered important.

A very different conception of personality is provided by Oriental religious and philosophical traditions, which have addressed themselves to states of consciousness and the procedures through which higher levels of consciousness can be achieved.

Psychopathology and Therapy

How have conceptions of mental illness changed?
What do we mean by "abnormality"?
How many kinds of mental disorders are there?
What are the goals of therapy?

In our discussion of normal personality, we made frequent references to abnormal behavior. Some theories of personality, such as psychoanalysis, can be applied to both the psychologically disturbed and the psychologically adjusted individual.

The study, assessment, and treatment of individuals whose behavior is irrational, inappropriate, bizarre, or uncontrolled is called **psychopathology,** an important specialty within psychology. Although all areas of psychology have a bearing on the study of psychological disturbances, clinical psychologists are most immediately concerned with these problems. The clinical psychologist is a specialist in psychological methods of treatment for the emotionally disturbed, in the use of psychological tests in diagnosis, and in methods of research and evaluation.

Mental patients occupy more hospital beds than any other patient group in the United States; the number of seriously disturbed patients is between 1 and 2 percent of the total population. It is estimated that about one in ten individuals will develop a severe mental disorder sometime during life, not including the senility problems that sometimes occur in old age.

How have conceptions of mental illness changed?

Mental disturbances are by no means a phenomenon of recent history. It does not appear that the stresses of contemporary life have produced an increase in mental illness—at least in those types severe enough to require hospital admission. Rates of hospital admission for 1840 and 1940 are surprisingly similar (Dunham, 1966; Goldhamer & Marshall, 1949). Moreover, primitive societies seem to be no less vulnerable to severe forms of psychopathology than more developed societies (Dohrenwend & Dohrenwend, 1967). The basic nature of psychopathology appears to be similar in different cultures, although the symptoms may assume different, more or less exotic, forms. In the syndrome called "running amok," the Malaysian native is suddenly seized with a fit of rage and runs madly about slashing at people with a dagger. An Ojibwa Indian brave with the disorder called "windigo" believes he is possessed by a cannibalistic monster. He sees his family and friends taking on the characteristics of edible animals; he may commit suicide or ask others to kill him in order to avoid destroying others. (I once saw a patient who believed that an unwanted child to which she had given birth resembled a wolf. The patient was hospitalized in order to prevent her from harming the child.)

HISTORICAL VIEWS
OF MENTAL ILLNESS

Of course, conceptions of mental illness and its treatment have changed tremendously in the course of Western history. In ancient Egypt, Israel, and Greece, it was generally believed that madness was due to possession by evil spirits; yet as early as approximately 400 B.C., Hippocrates, the Greek physician, proposed that mental illness was due to disease of the brain and should be treated like other diseases. While this notion was accepted for many centuries in the Arab world, the prevailing view of psychological derangement in Europe during the Middle Ages was that of possession by demons. Between the fourteenth and sixteenth centuries, thousands of the mentally ill—especially women—were accused of witchcraft. Church and state combined in a joint effort to pursue and punish these presumed agents of the devil, and many were burned at the stake (Lea, 1939).

Even after the belief in witchcraft declined, the mentally ill were still treated with scorn and abuse. They were often isolated, locked in cellars and attics, or, if seen as dangerous, confined in lunatic asylums; there they were kept in chains and controlled with whips. Among the more ignominious aspects of the treatment of the mentally ill (in a history filled with ignominy) was the public display of the mentally ill for a fee. As late as the eighteenth century, Londoners could amuse themselves by watching the lunatics at the Bethlehem asylum. The term "bedlam" is derived from the popular pronunciation of

At Bedlam Hospital, visitors amused themselves by watching psychotic patients. Notice the chains on the patient in the foreground.

Bethlehem and refers to wild, disorganized activities such as those that took place there. By the end of the eighteenth century, several enlightened leaders in Western Europe were demanding more humane treatment for the insane. The Salpêtrière hospital in Paris was reorganized by Philippe Pinel (1745–1826), who trained attendants to regard the insane as patients who needed treatment rather than brutes who needed coercion.

Early in the nineteenth century, American Quakers established several hospitals for the mentally ill; but the great majority of disturbed people in the United States were still confined in almshouses, jails, and cellars. They were "chained, naked, beaten with rods, and lashed into obedience" (Dix, 1843, p. 4). Dorothea Dix, a Massachusetts schoolteacher, became a prime mover in the founding or enlarging of over thirty state hospitals, even extending her activities to Europe. Nevertheless, as the twentieth century opened, primitive practices persisted in the treatment of the mentally ill. In 1908, Clifford Beers, a former mental patient, published a book, *A Mind That Found Itself,* describing his illness and recovery. Beers hoped to eliminate the stigma associated with mental disorders and to modify the widespread belief that mental disorders were incurable. To further these aims, he established the National Committee for Mental Hygiene, which encouraged the early recognition and prevention of mental illness and stimulated the development of child guidance clinics. He also continued to work for the improvement of conditions in mental hospitals.

MENTAL HEALTH

The mental health movement is still very active in the United States; and, although there have been significant changes in most mental hospitals, there is a continued need to improve treatment of the mentally ill. Recent anthropological and social-psychological studies of the mental hospital as a community, indicate that the hospital itself—and the practices employed there—often prolongs and exacerbates emotional disturbances. Efforts must be made—and in some places they are being made—to restructure mental hospitals so that patients have freer choices and take greater responsibility for themselves. In **milieu therapy,** the hospital patient is encouraged to establish relationships with other patients and to relate to the staff on a more informal, human level— rather than as "patient" and "caretaker" (Sanders et al., 1967). In some hospitals there are wards in which efforts are made to modify the behavior of chronic hospitalized patients by reinforcing desirable responses directly—for example, by granting extra privileges and various material benefits when a patient tries to help another patient (Ayllon & Azrin, 1968).

A number of programs have also been initiated to maintain the patient in the regular community. Special "halfway houses" have been established where discharged patients can live or visit while becoming adjusted to life outside the hospital. One group of chronically ill patients were moved to a halfway house, which they actually successfully administered by themselves (Fairweather et al., 1969). Outpatient clinics, the use of medications, sheltered workshops, and home visits provide additional support to the newly discharged patient. Ironically, these programs are reversing the earlier trend toward removing patients from the community to place them in a hospital. Begun by people like Dorothea Dix, whose motivations were of the most humane sort, this practice was appropriate to a period when the community had little understanding of mental illness. Increasing knowledge and a more sympathetic attitude have removed some of the stigma of psychological maladjustment, and it is now possible to treat some cases of mental illness within the community.

Even in well-run, humane settings, the problem of combatting loneliness and boredom remains. Contemporary opinion favors shorter hospital stays and an active treatment program in which patients play responsible roles.

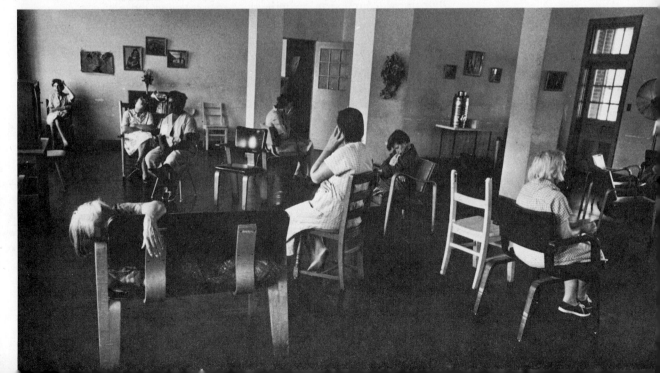

Until Freud's time, most psychiatrists believed that mental illness was the result of a malfunction of some bodily process—particularly in the brain. The idea that mental illness has an organic basis was bolstered by the discovery—late in the nineteenth century—that the disease of general paresis was caused by syphilis. The symptoms of paresis include defective speech, disturbances in memory, lack of insight, grandiose and unrealistic self-descriptions, and deterioration of motor functions. The finding of a biological cause for one mental illness excited the hope that similar infectious agents could be found for other forms of mental illness. The first task was to identify other collections or complexes of symptoms, and a fundamental step in this direction was made by the German psychiatrist Kraepelin (1855–1926). He identified and defined two major mental diseases: **manic-depressive psychosis** and **dementia praecox**—now more generally called **schizophrenia.** The manic-depressive symptom complex was primarily characterized by abrupt changes in mood; patients display either extreme euphoria and excitement (mania) or deep melancholy (depression). The dementia praecox (schizophrenia) classification consisted of the grouping of a variety of symptom patterns that displayed two common threads: early onset, often in adolescence (praecox), and a marked deterioration and disturbance in thinking (dementia).

The consensus among psychologists today is that while these disorders may be associated with abnormal biochemical or neural processes, there are no clear physical causes—at least none as clear as in the case of paresis. Probably there is an interaction between biological (including genetic) and environmental factors; it may be that people with a biologically "weak constitution" require less disturbed environments to become severely mentally ill.

The distinction between "biological" and "psychological" is not so absolute in human functioning as it seems in some theoretical accounts. There are **psychosomatic reactions**—physical problems "caused" by mental conflicts (e.g., many ulcers)—as well as *somatopsychic illnesses*, in which mental conflicts are "caused" by physical problems (e.g., paresis). Sometimes it is difficult to determine in an individual case whether the physical or mental disorder is primary. (*See* Spotlight 8-1.)

What do we mean by "abnormality"?

When we speak of "abnormal" behavior, we often speak as if the concept of **abnormality** were easily defined. But in fact there are many definitions of abnormality; each has some merit, none are without some shortcomings. How we define it, of course, is a matter of no small importance, for the definition of abnormality has implications for therapeutic treatment, legal proceedings, and social acceptability.

The word itself—*ab-normal*—implies a deviation from a norm. Using a statistical criterion, the norm could be considered the average; thus "abnormal" would describe the infrequent or rare instance. If we accept this definition, we can easily apply quantitative measures—such as test scores—in making diagnoses. For example, we have discussed the MMPI, which yields ten scores; exceptionally high scores are considered indicative of pathol-

The curious character of the Mad Hatter in *Alice in Wonderland* was not a pure invention. Like many of Lewis Carroll's characters, this one was based on shrewd observation. Hatmakers in Carroll's time did tend to show eccentric and irrational behavior. Later it was found that their abnormal behavior was caused by damage to the nervous system because of a mercury compound used in treating felt for hats. Once this was clear, use of the mercury compound was discontinued in hatmaking. Neural damage due to mercury still causes behavioral problems and is a serious ecological concern. For example, newspapers recently reported the case of a woman whose failing memory and difficulties of concentration were treated unsuccessfully by psychiatrists for several years. Finally it was found that she had a toxic concentration of mercury in her body, apparently due to a diet high in swordfish from contaminated waters. The cooperative investigations of several specialists are often necessary to reveal the true nature of a particular case.

ogy. The disadvantage of the statistical criterion, taken literally, is that it does not differentiate between the exceptionally gifted and the exceptionally lacking in talent. A moron and a genius are both "abnormal." In the MMPI, where a score of 50 on any scale is average or normal, a score of 70 or above is indicative of pathology; a score of 30 or below, however, is equally abnormal by a statistical criterion. Yet we rarely interpret the "low" exceptions, for these point to the abnormally cheerful, exceptionally trusting, or extremely considerate individuals.

For these reasons, social criteria are often added to the statistical criterion in diagnosing abnormality and in formulating plans for care and treatment. Geniuses are statistically abnormal, but they are socially valuable. Imbeciles are considered pathologically abnormal—they contribute little and may require expensive care. Social maladjustment is certainly an important aspect of abnormality, but nonconformity is not in itself a sign of mental illness, and conformity cannot be equated with mental health. The use of social criteria makes the concept of normality culturally relative; for example, an anti-Hitler intellectual might have been considered pathologically abnormal in Germany in the late 1930s or early 1940s. And only within the past few years, changes in social standards and attitudes have permitted homosexuality to be deleted from the official psychiatric classification of "mental disorders."

To avoid cultural relativism, many have sought to define abnormality in terms of certain basic characteristics and deficiencies, which are presented in Spotlight 8-2. Consistent inability to cope with one's environment is the

1. *Inadequate Reality Testing*   Impaired cognitive functioning—that is, disturbances in thinking, in perception, in memory, in judgment, and in the ability to communicate in a coherent manner.

2. *Inappropriate Affect or Feelings*   Emotional expression not reasonably related to eliciting stimuli. Includes irrational fears, anger without provocation, and persistent feelings of depression that are only remotely related to current experiences.

3. *Inability to Exercise Voluntary Control over Behavior* Tendency to act on impulse. The most serious manifestations of lack of control are aggressive outbursts. But more subtle manifestations are found in conflicts between conformity and nonconformity to such social norms as those about dress, language, marriage, and so on. What matters is not the *specific* behavior—whether the individual conforms or does not conform—but rather the degree of voluntary control exercised over this behavior. A person can also suffer from *overcontrol*, from rigidity and inhibition, and a lack of spontaneity.

4. *Deficient Social Functioning*   High degrees of egocentricism, lack of interest in other people, incapability in forming stable, close emotional ties. Absence of social awareness. Excessive distrust of, and negativism toward, other people. Inability to assume a socially responsible role.

---

overriding criterion, with the emphasis on *inability*. All of us at times may *choose* to behave in an extraordinary manner—to reject a Hitler, to refuse to conform, to express an impulse. But those who have no choice, who *cannot control* their inappropriate emotions or actions, are considered pathologically abnormal.

From the individual's own perspective, a critical indicator of mental disorder is *psychological distress*. It is when one feels persistently anxious and tormented, at odds with oneself and others that a psychological difficulty is recognized and help is sought. For milder disturbances, self-reports of psychological distress may be the only evidence of psychopathology.

The legal definition of abnormality differs from the psychological definition; its purpose is not to describe behavior disorders but to excuse certain individuals from the punitive sanctions in criminal law. The term *insanity* is a legal rather than a medical concept. The legally insane are not considered responsible for their actions, as responsibility is defined as the capacity to exercise a free and rational choice.

How many kinds of mental disorders are there?

The label "mental illness" has been applied to a wide variety of behavior deviations. Spotlight 8-3 shows the ten major classifications or diagnostic categories used by the American Psychiatric Association. It should be noted, however, that the categories are more easily distinguished in theory than in practice, and diagnoses are often difficult and tentative.

A major distinction is made between psychoses and neuroses. A **psychosis** is a profound behavior disturbance characterized by personality disintegration and loss of contact with reality. A **neurosis** is not so severe. The neurotic can

Classification

General Description

1. *Mental Retardation*

Subnormal intellectual function, originating at birth or early childhood. Learning ability and social maturation are impaired.

2. *Organic Brain Syndrome*
   a) Nonpsychotic
   b) Frequent psychotic syndromes: senile dementia (disease of aging), alcoholic psychosis, general paresis (due to syphilitic infection), cerebral arteriosclerosis

Disorders related to impairment of brain tissue function; impaired orientation, memory, comprehension, etc. Unstable and shallow affect.

3. *Psychoses*
   Schizophrenia (major thinking disturbance. Social withdrawal; regressive and bizarre behavior)
   Affective disorders (extreme depression or elation dominates mental life)
   Paranoid states (delusions, persecutory or grandiose, dominate mental life)

Impairment in mental functioning sufficient to grossly interfere with meeting demands of daily life; deficits in perception, language, or memory; profound alterations of mood; hallucinations and delusions.

4. *Neuroses*
   Anxiety neurosis
   Hysteria
   Phobias
   Obsessive-compulsive neurosis
   Depressive neurosis
   Neurasthenia
   Depersonalization syndrome
   Hypochondria

Anxiety is primary symptom; it may be experienced or controlled through unconscious mechanisms. No gross breaks with reality or gross personality disorganization appear.

5. *Personality Disorders*
   Some subtypes include:
   Paranoid personality
   Schizoid personality
   Antisocial personality
   Fetishism
   Voyeurism
   Alcoholism
   Drug dependence

Deeply ingrained, usually life-long maladaptive behavior patterns; includes generalized personality and character disturbances; also, more focused symptomatology as in alcoholism and drug addiction.

(Continued next page)

usually function fairly adequately in society, in spite of being distressed by morbid fears and anxieties, unusual compulsions, or other severe hang-ups. In some cases, the neurotic disturbance is not an isolated symptom but a deep-seated personality trait; the individual is then said to have a neurotic character structure or a personality disorder. In other cases, the emotional disturbances produce physical symptoms ranging from a minor rash to serious heart dysfunction; such cases are classified as psychophysiological disorders or, as they are

Classification	General Description
6. *Psychophysiological Disorders* Subcategories are the various bodily areas and functions that can be affected by psychological factors; e.g., skin disorders as in neurodermatitis; respiratory disorders as in asthma; cardiovascular disorders as in hypertension and migraine	Physical disorders of presumably psychogenic origin; physical symptoms caused by emotional factors and usually involving a single organ system.
7. *Special Symptoms*	Patients manifesting single specific symptoms that are not part of a broader mental disorder; e.g., tics, speech disturbances, sleep disorders, learning disorders; can be very specific.
8. *Transient Situational Disturbances*	Transient disorders occurring in individuals without an underlying mental disorder, and representing an acute reaction to extreme environmental stress.
9. *Behavior Disorders of Childhood and Adolescence* Examples of subcategories are: Hyperkinetic reaction Withdrawing reaction Runaway reaction	Behavior disorders, occurring in childhood and adolescence, that are more resistant to treatment than transient situational disturbances but more transient than psychoses, neuroses, and personality disorders.
10. *Conditions Without Manifest Psychiatric Disorder and Nonspecific Condition*	Individuals who are psychiatrically normal but have problems sufficiently severe to warrant examination and treatment.

Adapted from Official Manual of American Psychiatric Association, 1968.

more commonly known, psychosomatic illnesses. We will now consider several of the major diagnostic categories in greater detail.

SCHIZOPHRENIA

The diagnosis of schizophrenia covers a broad array of puzzling and profound symptoms, such as bizarre speech and ideas, a split between emotional and intellectual processes, and strange behaviors. There are schizophrenics in every culture; they make up about 1 percent of the general population (Slater, 1968). The disorder strikes males and females with equal frequency, and the peak incidence occurs between the ages of 25 and 35.

There are several major types of schizophrenia, distinguished by different symptom clusters. While we will focus our attention on these symptoms, the reader should realize that each patient is a whole person, and, although seriously disturbed, he or she has resources as well as psychological difficulties. Most schizophrenics are *not* raving maniacs or bizarre comics as some Hollywood films suggest. Only some ideas are delusional, only some language is unintelligible. Hallucinations do not necessarily occur every day, nor even every week.

The simple schizophrenic's withdrawal from social and family contacts may be so gradual as to go unnoticed for some time.

I am reminded of a relevant personal experience. After a day consulting at a state mental hospital, I was invited to join one of the staff in an indoor tennis game. There were several players already on the court; but since I was a guest, they courteously invited me to play in the next doubles match. During the course of the match, the players were very solicitous and encouraging. (I was unaccustomed to the court and only a modest player.) I was quite surprised when, at the conclusion of the game, I learned that my companions, whom I had believed to be staff members, were actually patients, and two of them were schizophrenics.

The primary symptoms of *simple* schizophrenia are social withdrawal, loss of interest, and emotional apathy. The onset and development of the simple schizophrenic reaction is gradual and insidious. The disorder may begin, as in the case of one adolescent boy, with quitting school and lounging around the house, doing nothing. He began to spend more and more time alone in his room, and he rarely spoke to members of his family. When hospitalized, he lay in bed most of the day, did not shave or bathe for several months, and responded to questions only with anger or monosyllables. Many simple schizophrenics who work in solitary occupations or become vagrants are able to maintain marginal adjustments without hospitalization.

The *hebephrenic* schizophrenic's reactions resemble the common stereotype of the psychotic patient: they include silly mannerisms, inappropriate emotional reactions, hallucinations, bizarre delusions, giggling at unpredictable times, and talking to themselves or to fantasy companions. One such patient, when asked how she felt, stated: "My heart is rock-a-bye; he wants me to grow high." Perhaps relevant to this remark is the fact that several years previously, the patient had reluctantly undergone an abortion.

In contrast to the hebephrenic, the *catatonic* schizophrenic is either in a stupor or displays extreme excitement. The patient's speech — often repetitive — is difficult to comprehend. Peculiar postures or rigid stance may be assumed for hours on end. Catatonic schizophrenics are unresponsive and uncommunicative; in some cases they remain mute for several years, often seeming resistant and negativistic. During outbreaks of excitement, they may become dangerous to themselves and others.

The distinguishing characteristic of *paranoid* schizophrenics is delusions of persecution or grandeur; they also tend to be overly sensitive, egocentric, and suspicious. One paranoid patient believed that he was marked for destruction by the Martians and accused several acquaintances of being in league with the alien beings. Another patient thought that people were resentful because of his secret ability to dominate other people's minds and bodies. In both cases, these delusions were supported by hallucinations. The first patient heard "messages" being sent over the radio, while the second heard God speaking to him.

Related to paranoid schizophrenic reactions are the psychotic reactions labeled the "paranoid states," which are described in Spotlight 8-4.

Theories of Schizophrenia

While our knowledge of schizophrenia is substantially greater than it was when Kraepelin first described it, the disorder still remains very much of an

Common to both paranoid schizophrenics and paranoid states are persecutory and grandiose delusions and the notion that others are talking about them (ideas of reference). However, in the paranoid state, the delusional system is well organized, the patient's feelings of distress or anger are more closely related to his or her distorted judgments and beliefs, and thought processes outside the delusional area are relatively intact. Of course, many people misinterpret events because of their suspicion and egocentricity; they are characterized as having paranoid personalities, but they are not psychotic. The paranoid state, in contrast, entails a serious break with reality.

Individuals who suffer from a paranoid-state psychosis sometimes assume leadership roles in society because of their single-minded, inflexible, and emotional attachment to a delusional system that has partial cultural support. It has been proposed that Adolf Hitler was such a case, and clinical studies of the other top Nazi leaders suggest serious psychopathology in many of them. It must be emphasized that adherence to a particular belief system or ideology is not *in itself* a manifestation of psychopathology. However, some ideologies — especially those emphasizing real or unreal conspiratorial threats — may attract paranoid personalities and paranoid psychotics.

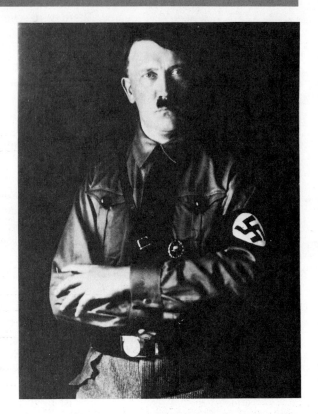

enigma. Research on schizophrenia has been concerned with two principal questions:

(1) What are the psychological and physiological processes underlying the schizophrenic symptoms?
(2) What are the origins of the schizophrenic reaction?

Studies reveal many cognitive and affective differences between schizophrenic and normal people. Schizophrenics have difficulty in distinguishing relevant from irrelevant stimuli. Sometimes they respond to too many stimuli — they are distracted — and sometimes they seem to focus on a few aspects of a situation to the exclusion of other important stimuli. In Skinnerian terms, their behavior appears to be primarily controlled by stimuli in the *immediate* environment (Salzinger, 1971). The impaired thought processes of the schizophrenic and the characteristic social withdrawal have also been interpreted as reflections of a high level of physiological *arousal* (excitation) and as reactions to the stress of chronic anxiety (Mednick, 1958; Rodnick & Garmezy, 1957; Venables, 1966).

There are several important distinctions among schizophrenics that must be taken into account in making generalizations about the disorder. The patient's premorbid history—his or her development prior to the illness—is an important variable. Differences between poor or good premorbid adjustment overlap with the distinction between *chronic* (slow, gradual onset) and *acute* (rapid onset) schizophrenia. The chronic patient with a poor premorbid history is likely to profit from drug therapy, while the recovery of acute patients with a good adjustment prior to illness is hindered by drug treatment (Goldstein et al., 1969). Moreover, there is more evidence of genetic transmission of schizophrenia among chronic, poor premorbids than among acute, good premorbid patients (Kety et al., 1968).

Increasingly, there is evidence that some forms of schizophrenia have a biological basis. Studies of twins suggest that genetic factors may be involved (Gottesman & Shields, 1966). The percentage of cases in which *both* members of a pair suffer from schizophrenia is significantly higher among identical twins (with the same heredity) than among fraternal twins (developing from two fertilized eggs). Drug studies give further indications of the role of biological factors in this psychosis. Many schizophrenics, for example, improve when treated with *chlorpromazine,* a drug that blocks the actions of *dopamine*—an important chemical agent in the brain (Snyder et al., 1974). While such findings are intriguing, they do not yet fully explain the genetically transmitted neural or chemical deficits associated with schizophrenias.

Schizophrenia can probably be best understood in terms of **heredity-environment interactions** (Meehl, 1962)—that is, as a consequence of *both* a genetic predisposition and an unfavorable family environment. The families of schizophrenics tend to be characterized by marked discord (Lidz, 1967).

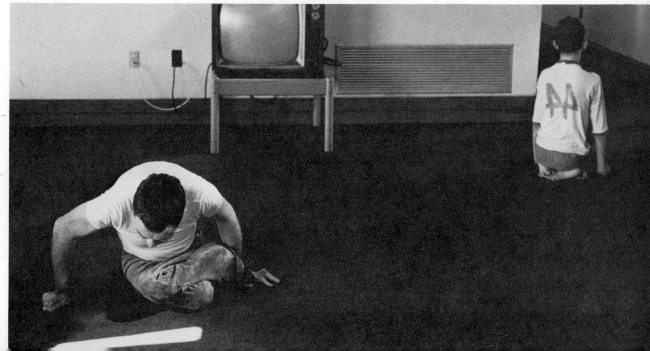

Rigid, unresponsive, and uncommunicative, catatonic schizophrenics may in fact be quite aware of what is going on around them.

According to the *double-bind hypothesis,* the schizophrenic as a child is exposed to contradictory messages from the mother. For example, she might *say* "I love you" but couple the statement with "cold" kisses and other signs of rejection. Since there is no rational way the child can cope with these conflicting communications, the response is one of confusion and withdrawal, precursors of a subsequent schizophrenic reaction.

R. D. Laing, a British existential psychiatrist, maintains that the social interactions that take place in most families and elsewhere in society are so irrational that most of us are half-mad and suffer from a split between our false outer selves and true inner selves (Laing, 1967). A psychotic breakdown, according to Laing, represents an effort to regain wholeness as a human being when the split has become intolerable. These views led to the establishment of a therapeutic community that provided a sympathetic environment in which patients could work through their "schizophrenic" adjustment efforts. Although striking clinical changes in some patients have been reported, the numbers involved are small and evaluation has so far been unsystematic.

Treatment of Schizophrenia

The cure for schizophrenia is as elusive as its causes. Chemotherapy—the use of drugs such as chlorpromazine—has produced striking changes in the behavior of many schizophrenics and in the length of time patients spend in mental hospitals. These drugs can relax tensions and dissipate anxiety without interfering with attention, memory, and other cognitive functions. The patient can be entrusted with more responsibility and privileges. Many patients who had been incoherent become capable of discussing their problems; hence they are more accessible to psychotherapy and to out-patient management. Because of chemotherapy, the number of patients residing in mental hospitals has decreased since 1955, although the number of admissions has not changed.

In contrast to the changes in patient behavior produced by chemotherapy, the various psychotherapeutic approaches have proved to be relatively ineffective in treating schizophrenics. But certain techniques based on research in learning, particularly **operant conditioning** (see Chapter 14), have shown considerable promise for the reduction of many schizophrenic symptoms and the modification of behavior on hospital wards. The therapist begins by delineating clearly the specific symptoms that need to be modified and the specific behaviors that should be encouraged. The desired behaviors are then systematically reinforced by therapist and hospital staff, while the symptoms are ignored or mildly punished. These techniques have limited effectiveness and they lay no claim to curing schizophrenia. However, as Spotlight 8-5 indicates, they sometimes produce impressive improvements in patient behavior.

AFFECTIVE DISORDERS

The distinguishing characteristic of the affective psychoses is an extreme and persistent disturbance in mood so serious that it interferes with rational judgment. The depressed patient feels personally unworthy and sees the future as hopeless. The elated psychotic, in contrast, denies any evidence of mistakes or misfortune; his or her optimism and feelings of grandiosity are boundless and unrelated to the real world. Most patients hospitalized for an **affective**

In a study designed to reduce apathy, the patient was reinforced whenever he or she made a positive social interaction (helped another patient) or made a desirable personal hygienic response (brushed hair). Among the reinforcements used were verbal praise and tokens that could later be exchanged for various amenities. Patients placed on this experimental program displayed a marked improvement in behavior over the two months of the program, compared to a control group that showed little change (Schaefer & Martin, 1966).

Quite striking improvements in behavior were also found following the initiation of a "token economy" in a psychiatric hospital ward. The tokens served as a kind of substitute for money. Performance of a desired behavior—cleaning floors, grooming oneself, serving meals—was reinforced with tokens that could then be exchanged for such privileges as a more comfortable bed, desired foods, cigarettes, a pass, or an opportunity to see a physician or psychologist (Ayllon & Azrin, 1965).

disorder are depressed. About one-fifth of them suffer from alternating periods of euphoria and depression.

The **manic-depressive** reaction, which usually begins in early adulthood, is characterized by severe mood swings. Some mood changes—ups and downs—are, of course, a quite normal occurrence. But patients in manic states are more than simply elated; they are overly excited and distractible, as if under extreme pressure. The excessive activity is often accompanied by weight loss and insomnia. The gaiety has a thin veneer; it is rapidly transformed into anger and arrogance when the patient is frustrated.

Sudden and extreme changes in mood are most characteristic of people suffering from manic-depressive psychosis.

There are many possible reasons for committing suicide: hopelessness, guilt, depression, shame, hostility, and attempts to punish others. Suicide is not necessarily a manifestation of psychopathology. It can be heroic, as in the case of a captured spy who takes lethal poison rather than endanger his or her nation's safety. Or it may be an expression of conformity to social norms; traditionally, many Japanese who had disgraced their family or social group committed hara-kiri (ritual suicide).

In the United States suicide is the tenth-ranking cause of death, with an annual rate of 11 per 100,000. Although the rate of suicide tends to increase with age, it is the fifth most important cause of death among the 15- to 24-year-old age group; it is more common among college students than among others of this age. Suicide rates are markedly influenced by social factors such as nationality and religious affiliations. Catholics, for whom suicide is a mortal sin, have lower rates than Jews or Protestants. Three times more males than females commit suicide, although women make many more suicide attempts than men.

A hopeful aspect of the suicide problem is that, whatever the underlying reason, people who commit suicide usually reveal their intention before the suicide act (Shneidman & Farberow, 1961). Centers have been established in many cities throughout the United States to provide emergency help via twenty-four-hour telephone service to those contemplating suicide. Anyone with suicidal thoughts is encouraged to call one of these centers and speak to someone about his or her problems and fears.

In the depressive phase of the manic-depressive psychosis, the patient manifests a completely opposite pattern of behavior, feeling sad, worthless, guilty, and sometimes suicidal. (See Spotlight 8-6.) Motor reactions are significantly retarded; the patient appears lethargic and apathetic. Depressed patients can also become quite agitated, displaying excessive worry and anxiety. Reduced sexual interest, indecisiveness, and inability to concentrate also accompany depression, and there may be delusions and preoccupations with somatic complaints.

Before becoming psychotic, victims of affective disorders are characteristically conforming, conscientious, and socially responsible people. When they fall short of the high standards they set for themselves—or feel they have disappointed parents or others they love—they react with discouragement, self-criticism, and guilt. All of these behavioral tendencies become exaggerated in the psychotic episode. The manic reaction can also be seen as an overcompensation for the underlying despair.

Genetic predispositions may also play a role in the manic-depressive reaction patterns (Rosenthal, 1970). If one of a pair of identical twins is a manic-depressive, the chances that the co-twin will also be a manic depressive are seven out of ten; the rate is two out of ten for fraternal twins.

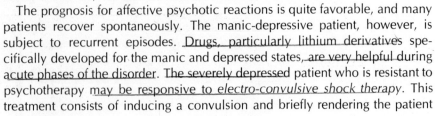

The prognosis for affective psychotic reactions is quite favorable, and many patients recover spontaneously. The manic-depressive patient, however, is subject to recurrent episodes. Drugs, particularly lithium derivatives specifically developed for the manic and depressed states, are very helpful during acute phases of the disorder. The severely depressed patient who is resistant to psychotherapy may be responsive to electro-convulsive shock therapy. This treatment consists of inducing a convulsion and briefly rendering the patient

Lady Macbeth's hand-washing compulsion was an outward sign of her feelings of guilt.

unconscious, through the administration of electric shock to the brain. We do not yet have a clear understanding of why the procedure is often effective in alleviating depression.

THE NEUROSES

All of us fall short of achieving a fully efficient and adaptive level of psychological functioning. We may get angry without apparent reason, need assurance that we are loved, conceal from ourselves and others the motives for our behavior, and, occasionally, feel intense anxiety. In the neurotic person, these needs and feelings become so exaggerated and persistent that they interfere with social adaptation and produce personal misery. Neurotics, unlike psychotics, are aware of their unhappiness, even if unaware of underlying reasons. They usually recognize their "symptoms" and would like to get rid of them. And, most importantly, the neurotic's thought processes and grasp of reality are more intact than the psychotic's.

Intense anxiety appears to be a common element of all neuroses. Neurotic reactions are interpreted as either direct manifestations of anxiety or as behaviors that help avoid the pain of anxiety. Thus impaired concentration, insomnia, inability to make a decision, and sexual impotence may be manifestations or direct consequences of anxiety. In contrast, compulsive rituals (such as hand washing), amnesias, and exaggerated social conformity may be ways of reducing anxiety. (*See* discussion of defense mechanisms in Chapter 7.)

role of anxiety

symptoms: manifesting anxiety or reducing anxiety

Hysteria

A young woman was referred for psychological study by a throat specialist who could find no physical basis for her extreme hoarseness. The woman was very upset by her symptom, for she hoped to obtain a lead part as a singer in a musical comedy. After several sessions with a psychologist, it became apparent that she had been extremely anxious about the possibility of being rejected for the part. The development of the laryngitis enabled her to avoid the anxiety and the threat to her self-image that rejection would have entailed. She recovered her voice after five weeks of treatment—unfortunately, after the part had been given to someone else.

This young woman was suffering from a symptom of **hysteria** (often referred to as a "conversion reaction")—the impairment of a bodily function for psychological, as contrasted to organic, reasons. Included in this category are cases of hysterical blindness, deafness, paralysis of the limbs, anesthesia, and the well-known writer's cramp. Hysterics do not deliberately put on or fake their symptoms; the conversion process is an unconscious one.

Another extreme type of hysterical disturbance is "dissociative reactions," in which components of the individual's personality are excluded from conscious functioning. Amnesia for past events and dual personalities are two examples of dissociative reactions. In dramatic cases of dual or multiple personalities, one personality assumes the moral, superego, "Dr. Jekyll" role while the other takes on the more negative, id-dominated, "Mr. Hyde" aspects (Thigpen & Cleckly, 1957).

Phobias

Phobias are irrational, intense fears of specific objects and situations that persist despite the individual's recognition that the fears are groundless—at least from a rational point of view. Some phobias can be extremely disabling. *Acrophobia* (fear of high places) and *claustrophobia* (fear of closed places), for example, greatly limit the individual's freedom of movement.

According to psychoanalytic theory, phobias are displaced reactions, substitutes for the fear of repressed impulses. For example, "Little Hans," a classic case of Freud's, was a five-year-old boy who would not go into the street because of a persistent fear that he would be bitten by a horse. After detailed investigation of the case, Freud concluded that the phobia was a symbolic expression of his fear of castration by his father.

Learning theories would suggest a conditioning explanation of phobias. In the case of Little Hans, a clinical psychologist using a learning approach would look for a previous association between a horse and a frightening event; such an association would explain how the sight or thought of a horse would evoke fear. In fact, Little Hans was involved in a traumatic incident in which he was almost run over by a horse.

Obsessive-Compulsive Neuroses

Obsessions are recurrent thoughts, words, or impulses that a person cannot control. One patient was obsessed with exaggerated doubts as to whether he had locked the door of his house whenever he left it. On one occasion, he returned six times to see if the door was "really" locked.

This same patient also had many **compulsions** (repetitive motor acts that the individual feels impelled to carry out). For example, he had a compulsion to wash his hands repeatedly "to get rid of the germs"—much like Lady Macbeth

1. The *paranoid personality* is an individual who is suspicious of others, hypersensitive to slights, egocentric, hostile, and very self-righteous.

2. The *schizoid personality* is shy, aloof, emotionally cold, and frequently asocial, avoiding social interactions that are fear-arousing.

3. The *hysterical personality* is self-dramatizing and given to role-playing, with superficial and often misleading emotional accompaniment. For example, he or she may be an outrageous flirt but basically sexually repressed.

4. The *obsessive-compulsive personality* is typically rigid, orderly, and strict in adherence to social convention, preoccupied with schedules and regularity, over-controlled and overintellectualized. The disturbance becomes apparent when the situation calls for a change in behavior and the person is utterly inflexible and responds with irritation.

trying to cleanse her hands of the bloodstains of the murdered king. The patient, like most obsessive-compulsive neurotics, was a rigid, guilt-ridden individual, trying to control impulses that he could not consciously accept.

PERSONALITY DISORDERS

Many individuals who do not display clear-cut, isolated symptoms have **personality disorders** — styles and character structures that reflect emotional disturbance. These individuals, unlike neurotics, do not perceive themselves as being disturbed. They may seek psychological help because others recommend it or because of problems such as inability to keep a job or a spouse. Because their problems and ways of adjusting are so ingrained, they do not respond readily to therapy and may require years of treatment. Therapists must first help such patients to see that they have personality problems; only then can they begin to help the patients change their behavior. Many personality disorders appear to be counterparts of neurotic and psychotic disturbances, as the list in Spotlight 8-7 shows.

The Antisocial Personality

Antisocial (or sociopathic) personalities are people who lack a sense of responsibility and morality and are unable to develop attachments to other people or feel empathy for them. They are concerned with their own immediate satisfactions and unrestrained by remorse; they exhibit no regard for the consequences of their actions for others. Moreover, they seem unable to profit from the "lessons" of experience. Some can be quite charming and adroit in their exploitation, appealing to the sympathy of their victims, lying unhesitatingly, and acting contrite — then promptly pursuing their errant ways. Other sociopaths are less charming and can, in fact, be openly hostile and cruel. Many become juvenile delinquents and criminals. (On the other hand, many professional criminals are not antisocial personalities and are capable of loyalty, warmth, and responsible behavior toward their family or cultural group.) Sociopaths are very difficult to treat because they lack insight and a desire to change. They are unable to establish the kind of trusting relationship that is required for effective psychotherapy.

The use of alcohol is widely approved and even encouraged by broad segments of Western society. In some individuals, it leads to addiction and a disabling personality and social disorder.

Drug Addiction

ALCOHOLISM Alcohol is the most widely used and the most socially acceptable of the psychoactive drugs. When taken in moderate amounts, it can produce relaxation and a "high." When taken in large doses, it can be extremely toxic. Heavy drinking also results in defective cognitive and motor functioning; driving while drunk is the leading cause of auto accidents. Alcoholism can disrupt family relationships, lead to occupational difficulties, produce irreversible liver and brain damage, and even result in psychosis.

The term *alcoholism* is restricted to heavy, regular drinking by people who are unable to control their alcoholic intake. Four percent of American adult males and about 1 percent of females are alcoholics. An additional 7 percent of adults are classified as "problem drinkers" (Cahalan, 1970). Typically, alcoholism starts with increased social drinking, followed by surreptitious private drinking and increasing signs of emotional dependence on alcohol. The final phases of alcoholism are usually marked by solitary drinking, long drinking bouts, and physiological dependence. At this point, the alcoholic may suffer *delirium tremens, a state marked by confusion, tremors, and disturbing hallucinations.* Also, because the alcoholic generally eats poorly, there may exist a vitamin deficiency that produces degeneration of brain tissue.

Alcoholism is the complex result of a number of interacting factors. Social variables determine the extent to which alcohol is available and is approved.

Among the personality traits related to the abuse of alcohol as an escape from anxiety and the pressures of daily living are dependency, exaggerated emphasis on masculinity (in males), repressed hostile tendencies, and inadequate impulse control. But the correlations between personality traits and alcoholism are small; there is little evidence on which to postulate an "alcoholic personality."

Alcoholism has proved very resistant to psychological treatment. In a therapeutic-conditioning procedure called aversive conditioning—which has had some success—alcohol is paired with nausea-inducing drugs or a painful electric shock (Frank, 1967; McBrearty et al., 1968). In group therapy, a group of alcoholics meets several times a month to discuss their drinking and emotional problems. This form of therapy is employed by Alcoholics Anonymous (AA), an organization run by alcoholics who have stopped drinking. Members also are encouraged to seek each other's support when they have an urge to drink. While no precise statistics on the effectiveness of AA are available, it appears to work for many alcoholics.

NONALCOHOLIC DRUG USE, ABUSE, AND DEPENDENCE   Nonalcoholic drugs have been used for centuries in many cultures to relieve tension and pain, to achieve heightened sensations and feelings of pleasure and well-being (euphoria), to produce mystical experiences, and to expand consciousness. Then in the mid-sixties came the psychedelic revolution, and the use of drugs—many kinds of drugs—became very widespread, especially in the 18 to 30 age group. Many parents were concerned and threatened by their children's use of drugs, not only because of possible damaging physical effects but also because drug use was regarded as a mark of membership in a counterculture that rejected traditional values and goals such as the accumulation of wealth and the pursuit of occupational success. Many parents felt guilty, believing that their child's use of drugs was reflective of personal maladjustment or basic feelings of insecurity—for which they, as parents, were to blame.

While it is true that people who belong to groups in which drug use is prevalent are likely to experiment with drugs, this does not necessarily lead to drug dependency. What drugs mean to the individual depends on his or her personality and personal history. Some people become heavily dependent upon the use of drugs because of their own neurotic needs, but most who try drugs and use them occasionally do not become dependent. From the social and psychological points of view—which may be quite different from the legal point of view—the use of drugs becomes a problem only when it is damaging to the user or to society. The criteria of drug abuse include impairment of the individual's functioning, inability to mobilize energy, the undermining of moral restraints, and criminal and violent behavior.

We can better understand the problem of drug abuse if we know something about the characteristics of the most widely used drugs and their effects, both positive and negative. There are four major types, each with its own properties, characteristics, and effects.

1) _Hallucinogens_   These include a varied group of drugs, such as marijuana and LSD, that can alter visual experience—producing hallucinations and

other perceptual changes—and typically induce a euphoric state. Some can bring about unpleasant mood changes as well. Users may become *psychologically* dependent on the drug; that is, they may feel that they must continue to use the drug to ease tensions or to feel good. But the drugs do *not* produce *physiological* dependence or addiction; the body does not become dependent on chemical effects of the drugs—as it does, for example, with heroin.

Marijuana, the dried flowers and leaves of the hemp plant, is undoubtedly the most frequently used illegal drug; it was estimated in 1972 that between 15 to 20 million Americans had tried it, and that number has certainly increased since then. The effects of the drug are those of a mild intoxicant; it induces a mild euphoria, increased awareness, greater openness to other people and to colors, tastes, smells, and sounds. The feelings produced are typically relaxation, peacefulness, and freedom from anxiety; hostility is rare, although "bad trips" can occur and produce great anxiety. Time perception may be altered so that the individual focuses clearly only on the present, responding in immediate, natural ways. A 21-year-old artist who frequently used marijuana described it this way:

> You notice many things, you become very interested in the little details. For instance, you may have noticed things like handles, or bottles, or pebbles, and children's attitudes, and you'd find that children aren't so young as you think and that you aren't as old as you think and that you don't become an adult if you don't understand that you aren't going to become any greater than a child. (Carey, 1968, p. 54)

The hazards of marijuana have probably been exaggerated. In one experimental test of the effects of small amounts of the drug, first-time users showed slight impairments in motor and cognitive functioning; habitual users, however, showed no such impairment (Weil, 1968). Marijuana consumption over an extended period of time may result in decreased productivity (Canadian Commission, 1972) and work efficiency (Schaeffer, 1973), although it is difficult to attribute such effects solely to the drug. The "stoned" driver may suffer from perceptual distortion, loss of sense of direction, poor judgment, and poor reflexes; thus he or she may become as much of a traffic hazard as the drunk driver. But there is no evidence that the use of marijuana leads to criminal behavior, delinquency, sexual excitement, or addiction. Nor is there any scientific basis for the popular belief that using marijuana leads to using heroin.

LSD (lysergic acid diethylamide) is a potent—and, under some circumstances, dangerous—drug. First used in psychiatric research and treatment, it was originally called a "psychotomimetic" because it produced a variety of psychosislike experiences. It is still sometimes used by psychiatrists in treating alcoholism and neuroses; it may aid in establishing rapport with chronically withdrawn patients, and it may help them to verbalize memories and feelings they could not otherwise express.

The drug is now called **psychedelic,** meaning "mind manifesting," opening the mind to new experiences and sensations. About thirty minutes after a small quantity of LSD is ingested, the "trip" begins, and the drug's influence generally lasts approximately eight to twelve hours. Effects are highly individual and unpredictable, depending on the social setting as well as the age and

" YOU SHOULD START GETTING A REACTION
TO THE L.S.D. ABOUT NOW "

personality of the user. Mood changes and heightened emotionality are the first obvious effects; intense happiness or unhappiness can be stimulated by the most casual remarks of others, and sensitivity to all kinds of stimuli is tremendously enhanced. Tactile and visual distortions, including vivid hallucinatory experiences, occur; the distinction between self and the environment may become blurred. Later the user is likely to become introspective, extremely suggestible and, in some cases, paranoid. Many LSD users are convinced that they have achieved greater self-understanding and that creativity is enhanced by the drug, but there is little evidence to support this view.

Bad trips may occur among habitual LSD users or among those trying the drug for the first time. These may be characterized by confusion, paranoia, or feelings of omnipotence or invulnerability. Some may experience panic reactions, a sense of helplessness, overwhelming intense anxiety, fear of losing control and going crazy. There may be recurrent reactions after the trip is over; sometimes there is a spontaneous return of perceptual distortions or feelings of unreality, often accompanied by panic and anxiety. Heavy users of LSD have sometimes become so preoccupied with subjective experiences and sensations that they withdraw from normal social activities, lose their critical judgment, and seem unable to mobilize themselves or to make plans. Essentially they "drop out" of the culture.

2) Stimulants Amphetamines or pep pills—including dexedrine sulfate (dexies) and methamphetamine (speed or meth)—have an energizing and psychologically stimulating effect. They are used for weight control (through reduction of appetite) and for counteracting fatigue and depressive moods.

Occasionally, they are employed by athletes to try to enhance their performance in contests and by students staying up late to study. These drugs produce feelings of euphoria, increased alertness, restlessness, motor and verbal activity, irritability, and wakefulness. These effects may be accompanied by irrationality, paranoia, and anxiety.

Prolonged and heavy use of amphetamines can be very dangerous and highly addictive. Tolerance for the drug builds up rapidly; the pill-popper has to take more pills at shorter intervals to reach the same high and to combat depression and fatigue. "Speed freaks" ingest or inject large quantities of these drugs several times a day. These people keep on the go all the time, not eating or sleeping for several days and frequently manifesting paranoid symptoms. Sometimes they have to take sedatives, barbiturates, or tranquilizers to calm their nerves. Finally, exhaustion sets in, and they may sleep for a day or more. Afterwards they are likely to be quite depressed. To escape the miserable "down" the user takes amphetamines again. A cycle is begun and psychological dependence on the drug develops.

Cocaine, the drug that Sherlock Holmes frequently self-administered, has increased in recent years in its usage in the United States. Although cocaine has anesthetic properties, it is a cortical stimulant like the amphetamines. Cocaine produces a euphoric state characterized by reported feelings of peace and contentment (although the onset of this state is frequently preceded by headache and general discomfort). Chronic use of cocaine can result in frightening hallucinatory experiences and related acute psychotic symptoms.

3) *Sedatives* This group includes habit-forming barbiturates such as Seconal (reds), Nembutal (yellow jackets), and Amytal (blue heavens). They all have relaxing and, in larger doses, sleep-inducing effects. The chronic user becomes too dulled to cope with life adequately; hence the drugs serve as an escape. In taking barbiturates, the user risks the dangers of a lethal overdose. In addition, the physiological effects of withdrawal from the drugs are extremely debilitating—they can, in fact, be fatal.

4) *Opiates* This category of drugs includes opium—the parent drug—morphine, heroin, and codeine—opium derivatives. The most widespread of these is heroin; no drug is more potent in producing euphoric effects and relief from pain, tension, and anxiety. Initially, the major effect is only a pleasant high that lasts about four hours. But the drug is dangerously and severely addicting. In the United States the vast majority of drug addicts use heroin. Heroin addiction is of the classic type; there is a compulsion to use the drug and a tendency to increase the dose as one gets more "hooked." Psychological and physical dependence on the drug have enormous detrimental effects on the user and on society. The habit becomes the dominant motif in the addict's life, and in order to support this expensive habit, he or she may be forced to resort to theft, prostitution, or other illegal activities. Social contacts, conversations, and thoughts revolve around drugs, especially the next "fix." Even sexual activity diminishes. Contrary to popular belief, heroin inhibits the sex impulse.

After taking heroin steadily for a period of several weeks, the user is hooked and requires the drug in order to feel normal. If deprived of it, he or she experiences intensely uncomfortable withdrawal symptoms, beginning with feelings of tension, restlessness, and nervousness. These become progressively worse as time goes by; within twenty-four hours of withdrawal, most habitual users are acutely miserable, shivering and experiencing intense cramps and pain in the back and extremities. Arms, legs, and feet twitch almost constantly. The symptoms are most intense in the second or third day after withdrawal, then decline for the next week. The remaining complaints are likely to be nervousness, insomnia, and weakness, which may not disappear for a period of weeks or even months. A single dose of the drug during the withdrawal period will produce a prompt and pronounced — albeit temporary — reduction of these disturbances.

The heroin addict is extremely resistant to treatment. About 90 percent of hospital-treated users who kick the habit become addicted again within about six months of discharge (Hunt & Odoroff, 1963). The Synanon movement, founded in 1958 by a former alcoholic, Charles E. Dederich (who had been helped by Alcoholics Anonymous), has provided a promising treatment approach. The addict becomes part of an autocratic structure of former addicts who provide guidance until he or she develops sufficient resources to control the habit without their aid. A special group-therapy technique is employed in which addicts are given direct and sometimes harsh feedback about the consequences and meaning of their behavior.

More recently a number of drugs, particularly methadone, have been developed which substitute for or block the action of heroin. While methadone is also habit-forming, it is much less expensive than heroin. It can be prescribed by a physician (under appropriate conditions) and is generally considered less damaging to the individual and to society. Methadone programs are by far the most common treatment method employed in the United States for heroin addicts. Nevertheless, there are some authorities who object to its use because of its addictive properties and the possible physiological harmfulness of excessive use and rapid withdrawal.

What are the goals of therapy?

Various treatments of mental disorders have been mentioned at various points in this chapter: chemotherapy, milieu therapy, shock therapy, operant-conditioning procedures, and group therapies have all been touched on. While there are many kinds of psychotherapy, most of them are variants of one or another of four approaches: (1) psychoanalysis; (2) client-centered therapy; (3) behavior modification; and (4) group therapy.

PSYCHOANALYSIS

The goal of **psychoanalysis** as a therapy is to uncover and resolve the emotional problems — usually these stem from the patient's childhood — that are the causes of a patient's symptoms. The process is a long and costly one. Standard psychoanalytic treatment involves seeing an analyst an hour a day, four or five times a week, for from two to five years — sometimes more. The psychoanalyst uses the technique of free association (see p. 158), and the patient's resistance (silences and blocks in associations and discussion) provides clues to areas of conflict, which the patient finds painful and attempts to avoid. Psychoanalysts interpret these resistances, as well as the content of the patient's associations and dreams.

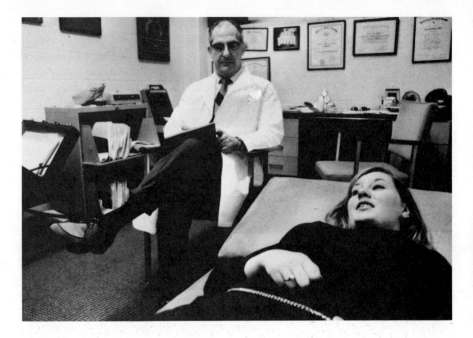

The keystone of classical psychoanalytic therapy is an intense doctor-patient relationship.

As treatment progresses, patients develop an intense emotional relationship with the analyst called the _transference neurosis_. They transfer to the therapist characteristics of significant figures in their childhood (for example, their father); they re-enact with the therapist major childhood conflicts that remain unresolved. The transference neurosis has a paradoxical effect. It temporarily interferes with the patients' progress, but it is the key to the eventual successful resolution of the conflicts. Through the analyst's interpretation of the transference neurosis, the patients acquire insight into their emotional reactions and into the nature of their psychological defenses. Thus, in working out feelings toward the analyst, the patient may be able to resolve some basic conflicts.

It is very difficult to obtain convincing evidence of the effectiveness of psychoanalytic treatment. There is little doubt that it has proved helpful to many people, but questions have been raised as to its utility in a great many cases. It is very costly and is therefore inaccessible to the great majority of the psychologically disturbed who are in need of treatment.

CLIENT-CENTERED THERAPY The **client-centered therapist** attempts to help clients accept their feelings and open up to experiences that have been distorted or shut out (Rogers, 1951). Therapists using this approach are nondirective; they do not provide advice to the client or offer interpretations of the client's verbalizations and behavior. Rather, _unconditional positive regard_ is demonstrated for the client (see p. 172). Through recognition and clarification of the client's feelings, the therapist conveys to the client a sense of empathy, understanding, and acceptance (see pp. 172–73).

The client is seen as the central agent in client-centered therapy; the therapist essentially provides a warm, accepting environment in which positive growth can take place. From the very first therapeutic hour, clients are informed that the hour is theirs to talk about whatever they please. A client may at first find it difficult to take all the initiative, but he or she soon adapts and begins to express feelings that, at first, are predominantly negative ones of inferiority, guilt, anxiety, and anger. When these feelings are accepted and clarified, positive feelings of love and self-respect begin to emerge, along with the achievement of insight. As clients feel better about themselves and become aware of alternatives other than those they have been pursuing, they relinquish their neurotic behavior patterns and engage in more positive modes of action.

Client-centered therapy is much less time-consuming than psychoanalysis; it is frequently completed with only six to fifteen contacts (Rogers, 1942). While several studies indicate that client-centered therapy has a positive effect, there are many clients who are not helped by this type of treatment and who might benefit from other types of intervention.

BEHAVIOR MODIFICATION In recent years there has been a rapid increase in the use of therapeutic techniques based on learning principles. In contrast to more traditional therapies that focus on childhood antecedents, internal psychological processes, and insight, behavior modification procedures are designed simply to reduce or eliminate undesirable behavioral symptoms and to increase the probability of productive activities. The use of these procedures is known as **behavior therapy.**

There are many instances in which **operant conditioning** can be used effectively in modifying behavior problems. For example, in a case of a socially withdrawn nursery-school child, teachers were advised by a clinical psychologist to make a concerted effort to watch the girl and to reward her with maximum attention whenever she approached, or played with, another child. At the same time, they did not reward withdrawal behavior; they tried to extinguish these responses by paying no attention to the child when they occured. (Under ordinary circumstances, sympathetic teachers would probably do the opposite—that is, notice her and give her particular attention when she was withdrawn.) Almost as soon as the treatment began, the child's behavior changed drastically. She began to interact with other children actively and spent relatively little time in isolated activities. Even after the reinforcements were discontinued, she continued to spend most of her time interacting with other children. In general, she became a happier, more confident, and more sociable child.

Operant techniques have also been used with considerable success in work with *autistic* children who are extremely withdrawn and so unresponsive to social stimuli that in many cases they have not learned to speak. Many are self-destructive; they may bang their heads on a table so hard that they have to be fitted with gloves, football helmets, or even straightjackets for protection against themselves. Behavior therapists working with these children have used systematic and carefully controlled programs of rewards—food, attention, and affection—to increase the incidence of meaningful speech and social responsiveness. Punishment is sometimes used to reduce aggressive and self-destructive behavior, while friendly and responsive acts are reinforced.

In **systematic desensitization,** the therapist attempts to teach a patient how to relax in situations that typically produce anxiety. First, the patient is taught how to relax physically and emotionally. Then the anxiety-provoking situation is introduced, but only gradually, never exceeding the patient's capacity to deal with it. For example, if the problem is an extreme fear of heights, the person might be asked to *imagine* looking out of a second-story window—while relaxing. Gradually the imagined height is increased to the third story, the fourth story, until finally the person can visualize himself or herself on top of the Empire State Building—while relaxing. Often this imagined activity is

Trying to break into the emotional fortress of an autistic child, the behavior-modification therapist rewards her with a bit of food for establishing eye contact.

enough. In some cases, however, the therapist may actually take the patient to a high building, having the patient actually look out of a first-story window, then a second-story window, and so on to the top. The procedure was effectively applied to a nine-year-old girl who suffered night terrors, severe abdominal pain, and fear of separation from her mother (Lazarus, 1960). Immediately prior to the appearance of the girl's symptoms, a school friend had drowned, a playmate had died of meningitis, and she witnessed an accident in which a man was killed. But these factors are not critical to the process of behavior modification. The behavior therapist first trained the girl to relax, and then had her imagine increasingly long periods of separation from her mother. Each new step was introduced only after she could manage the previous step without anxiety. The girl's symptoms were eliminated after only five sessions.

Often desensitization procedures are combined with modeling (*see* p. 178) and also operant techniques. A nine-year-old boy's extreme fear of school was reduced by desensitization—by taking him to school for a short visit, accompanied by his therapist who tried to allay his anxiety by talking with him, trying to make him feel relaxed, telling him jokes, and distracting him. In the second stage of the treatment, the boy was rewarded with tokens—which could be exchanged for prizes—for remaining in school on his own; the longer he remained the more tokens he received. The treatment proved to be very effective in overcoming the boy's school phobia.

Behavior therapies appear to be quite effective for eliminating specific neurotic symptoms, such as phobias and nervous mannerisms. Similarly, they have been found to be useful in alleviating a variety of sexual problems such as frigidity, impotence, and premature ejaculation. They are less easily applied to personality disorders and to the modification of neurotic symptoms that are manifestations of deep-rooted conflicts.

Within recent years, **biofeedback** methods have been developed to provide the patient with information regarding changes in significant biological processes. Feedback information enables the patient to monitor and modify biological processes—heart rate, blood pressure, stomach contractions—that had hitherto been believed to be automatic and outside his or her control (Miller, 1969; Dicara, 1970). In one study designed to teach male subjects to lower blood pressure, a monitoring device provided a sound signalling increasing or decreasing blood pressure. In addition, a red flashing light indicated lowered blood pressure (Shapiro et al., 1970). Each drop in blood pressure was reinforced with money and other rewards. Almost all subjects learned to lower their blood pressure by themselves.

The ability to lower blood pressure may prove to be helpful to patients suffering from hypertension (high blood pressure). Similar procedures have been successfully applied in training heart rate and galvanic skin responses, autonomic reactions that are associated with heightened tension (Engel & Chism, 1967; Greene, 1966). By training individuals to control these responses, a therapist may help them to learn to relax. Related relaxation methods have been developed by training individuals through feedback from an electroencephalograph recorder (EEG). The subject learns to increase alpha wave activity in the brain; such patterns are associated with relaxation and pleasant states of feeling (Brown, 1971). (*See* pp. 558–61.)

Biofeedback, one of the newer methods of analyzing and treating certain emotional and medical problems, stresses the complex interactions of mind and body.

GROUP THERAPIES

Within the last two decades, **group therapy** — usually in groups of five to fifteen people — has become increasingly common. Since many psychological problems exhibit themselves in interpersonal relations, activity in a group setting allows the therapist to observe directly such behaviors as hostility, nurturance, and anxiety and the means by which the individual copes with threats and frustrations.

A group setting may also be highly effective in modifying or eliminating maladaptive behaviors. Group members, interacting under a qualified therapist's leadership, may help each other to gain insights into their problems and conflicts and to achieve new perspectives. The group is also like the real world in many ways; it is a social situation in which one can "try out" new behaviors and new means of adjustment. It can also be a kind of laboratory where new skills can be tested and refined in an understanding environment before they are applied in everyday life. And along with the changed behaviors, the perception of oneself often becomes more positive as the individual interacts with others in the group and begins to feel more competent. At best, then, group therapy can help produce a self-assured individual with confidence in his or her ability to cope with a world that had been confusing and anxiety-producing.

There are also potential disadvantages to group therapy. Many psychologists feel that the interactions in groups are too superficial to be of much use — especially if the patient's conflicts are deep-seated. For some individuals, the group's focus on their defensive tactics can be highly threatening and could be more harmful than helpful. Today more and more groups are probing complex personality dynamics, in many cases without anyone in the group who is qualified to recognize or treat serious psychological crises. Attacks on a person's defenses may produce breakdowns, and many psychologists worry about the apparent disregard for such potentially devastating events.

Therapeutic groups today can be categorized on the basis of their goals and the characteristics of group members. On the one hand, there are what might be termed "traditional" groups; their members experience some degree of emotional maladjustment or neurosis. The goal of these groups is to promote adequate or normal adjustment. Included in this category are groups organized to combat a specific problem such as alcoholism or drug addiction. On the other hand, there is an increasing number of groups with the goal of self-improvement for its members, members who may not be emotionally disturbed. These groups include sensitivity groups and encounter groups. A _sensitivity group_ is one in which the goal of the participants is to recognize and become sensitive to the emotional response their actions produce in others. An _encounter group_ gets its name from the belief that if people really communicate with each other, are open and honest, and "encounter" one another, the natural human "growth" forces will become operative. It is believed that the encounter will result in self-actualization and enrichment of the personality. The philosophies of many of these groups are based on the writings of Carl Rogers and Abraham Maslow.

Role-playing groups are designed to produce insight by having the individual improvise a scene or drama about personally disturbing situations. J. L. Moreno's technique of **psychodrama** (1946) is the most commonly known form of role-playing. For example, an adolescent girl might be asked to "play" herself in a scene portraying her and her overprotective mother arguing about the time she must be home after a date. (Another member of the group would play her mother.) Presumably, the psychodrama promotes open expression of feelings and conflicts. The girl might also be asked to play the role of mother in the same scene, promoting empathy and understanding; this technique is called "role reversal."

A sort of microcosm of the real world, the therapy group can provide a setting in which patients learn to see themselves and others more clearly.

In psychodrama, people act out disturbing situations, sometimes playing the parts of other people in their lives and seeing their own actions from a different point of view.

In family groups, the therapist may meet with all members of the family at the same time. Very often, the problems of an individual in a family—a child, for example—cannot be clearly understood unless the therapist sees the interactions within the family. A child's emotional problems may stem from interactions with his or her parents. They may be overly dominating or overly critical, or they may have too high standards for the child. These parental characteristics might be extremely difficult to detect ordinarily, but they may become apparent in family group therapy sessions. They then can be discussed, and, with the resulting increased insights of the family members, the child's problems may be alleviated.

SOME WORDS OF CAUTION

You should be aware that it is, unfortunately, extremely difficult to evaluate the general effectiveness of any of the foregoing kinds of therapy. Therefore, some words of caution seem appropriate in closing this section. Many people feel they can benefit from psychotherapy and many can. But one must be careful to select the kind of therapy that is most likely to be of benefit. There are many fads in therapy, and any new approach is likely to be greeted with enthusiasm and to gain many adherents. Often case reports of therapeutic success sound convincing, but a hard second look usually leads to a less optimistic appraisal. Because of the complexity of emotional problems there has been relatively little controlled research on the effectiveness of particular kinds of psychotherapy. Generally research findings indicate that the therapy technique has less success than its adherents think. By the time a proper evaluation is completed, the technique is likely to have lost popularity, only to be replaced by another therapy approach—also of unknown value. The moral of this is simple: If you seek psychotherapy or guidance, choose your therapist with great care; check on his or her record and credentials (Meltzoff & Kornreich, 1970).

SUMMARY

Mental illness is a very significant contemporary problem, but it is not a new one. The ancients wrote about it, and it is common in both simple societies and sophisticated urban cultures. Attitudes toward mental problems have changed slowly over the centuries: beginning with a belief in possession by the devil we have moved slowly to the view that they reflect underlying illness and should be treated as such. Conceptions of mental disorders are still in flux. Some theorists regard **psychopathology** as a reflection of the problems of living we face or our maladaptive habits rather than as an illness.

Mental disturbances vary in degree and in types of symptoms manifested. The most severe are the **psychoses,** the most common of which is **schizophrenia.** That diagnosis embraces a wide range of diverse behaviors, including profound thought disorder and social withdrawal. The causes of schizophrenia are not yet established. There is evidence of genetic determinants and unfavorable family environment; related social and experiential factors also have a significant role in the development of the disorder. Chemotherapy has reduced markedly the time schizophrenic patients spend in mental hospitals, and the application of **operant-conditioning** principles in hospital wards has produced some dramatic modifications in patient behavior and schizophrenic symptoms.

The affective disorders, such as **manic-depressive psychosis,** are characterized by severe disturbances in mood. Extreme elation or—more typically—extreme depression dominate the patient's attitudes and thoughts. Judgment and motivation are seriously disrupted. Genetic predispositions appear to contribute to manic-depressive reactions, and people with certain kinds of personality characteristics seem to be especially vulnerable to this disorder. Many patients suffering from affective psychoses recover spontaneously, while others are responsive to drugs or to shock therapy.

The **neuroses** are characterized by intense emotional discomfort and by symptoms the individual recognizes as maladaptive. Examples of the many types of neurotic symptoms are amnesia, loss of sensory or motor function (without organic basis), phobias, and obsessive recurrent thoughts and compulsive repetitive actions. People who do not have neurotic symptoms may have personality disorders—that is, a personality style and character structure that reflect emotional disturbance. Included are antisocial personalities, who lack a sense of responsibility or morality, drug addicts, and alcoholics.

The therapeutic approaches used in the treatment of the neuroses and the personality disorders are closely linked to the personality theories described in the first chapter of this section. The first, **psychoanalytic therapy,** is directed toward uncovering early childhood conflicts; the therapist helps the patient interpret his or her resistances and achieve insight into the unconscious motivations responsible for the symptoms. In **client-centered therapy,** by contrast, the *patient* is the active participant, and the therapist offers little or no interpretation. Instead, the therapist is accepting and empathic as he or she tries to clarify the client's feelings. The techniques of **behavior therapy** are based on learning theory and rely on various types of conditioning procedures. They appear to be quite effective in eliminating specific neurotic symptoms and maladaptive behavior. Traditional **group therapy** provides a facilitating social setting that enables patients to gain insight into their problems. More recently, a number of group therapy approaches—such as sensitivity and encounter groups—have become popular. These are intended to enhance self-actualization among normal participants by encouraging the recognition and open expression of feeling.

RECOMMENDED READING

American Psychological Association. Special Issue: Testing and Public Policy. *American Psychologist* 20(1965):857–93.

This publication provides a thought-provoking discussion of the issues involved in the practical application of tests and provides a guide to their proper use.

BYRNE, D. *An Introduction to Personality.* (2nd ed.) Englewood Cliffs: Prentice-Hall, 1974.

This revised edition of a personality text, written from an experimental-theoretical framework, reviews an extensive range of investigations on many different issues and can be used as a source book.

CRONBACH, L. J. *Essentials of Psychological Testing.* (3rd ed.) New York: Harper & Row, 1970.

This excellent text reviews the principles underlying psychological testing and also the major psychological tests.

FESHBACH, S. "Dynamics and Morality of Violence and Aggression: Some Psychological Considerations." *American Psychologist* 26(1971):281–92.

This paper provides a theoretical analysis of aggressive behavior, summarizes some pertinent experimental data, and—on the basis of theory and data—draws some inferences regarding the evaluation of various manifestations of violence in contemporary life.

FREUD, A. *The Ego and the Mechanisms of Defense.* New York: International Universities Press, 1946.

This volume by Anna Freud extends psychoanalytic theory and offers a detailed and interesting account of the sundry psychological mechanisms people use to avoid shame, fear, guilt, and conflict.

GEIWITZ, P. J. *Non-Freudian Personality Theories.* Monterey, Calif.: Brooks/Cole, 1969. This brief text offers an excellent summary of the more significant personality theories, other than psychoanalytic. A particularly useful attribute of the book is the attention given to the empirical consequences of the different theories.

HALL, C. S., & LINDSEY, G. *Theories of Personality.* New York: Wiley & Sons, 1970.

This standard text provides excellent summaries of the views of the leading personality theorists.

KLINE, P. *Fact and Fantasy in Freudian Theory.* London: Methuen, 1972.

This volume provides an excellent summary of the empirical evidence bearing on a great range of psychoanalytic hypotheses.

MASLOW, A. H. *The Farther Reaches of Human Nature.* New York: Viking Press, 1972. This collection of papers by Dr. Maslow, written from a humanistic perspective, provides interesting insights into several aspects of self-actualization.

MUNROE, RUTH. *Schools of Psychoanalytic Thought.* New York: Holt, 1955. Offers a detailed, comprehensive summary of psychoanalytic concepts and theories; it also traces the changes and developments in psychoanalytic theories.

ROGERS, C. R. *Client-Centered Therapy.* Boston: Houghton Mifflin, 1951.

A readable presentation of the nondirective psychotherapeutic approach initiated by Rogers.

ORNSTEIM, R. E. *The Psychology of Consciousness.* San Francisco: W. H. Freeman & Co. 1972.

This interesting and original analysis of consciousness is the outcome of an effort to integrate the experimental psychology of experience with insights into consciousness offered through meditation and related practices associated with "Eastern" religions.

SKINNER, B. F. *Beyond Freedom and Dignity*. New York: Knopf, 1971.

In this readable, provocative volume, Professor Skinner considers some of the implications of a scientific psychology based on reinforcement control principles, conceptions of human freedom, responsibility, and social management.

SARASON, S. B. *The Psychological Sense of Community*. San Francisco: Jossey-Bass, 1974.

This thoughtful, stimulating volume provides a contemporary perspective on the relevance of a community-psychology approach to problems of mental health and psychological growth and satisfaction.

ZILBOORG, G., & HENRY, G. W. *A History of Medical Psychology*. New York: Norton, 1941.

The authors present a thorough and well-written overview of the history of conceptions of mental illness and the changes that have taken place in the treatment of mental illness.

ZUBIN, J., ERON, L. D., & SCHUMER, F. *An Experimental Approach to Projective Techniques*. New York: Wiley, 1965.

An excellent reference for the student who wants to find out more about the validity of various projective techniques.

9, 10, 11

PART FOUR

Developmental Psychology

By Paul Mussen

A couple of very simple exercises can help you to understand the goals and objectives of the field of developmental psychology. The first requires spending only an hour or so observing, and listening to, children of various ages—of say three or four to twelve—playing in your neighborhood or on a playground. You will soon be struck by the vast differences among them. What are the major differences—other than size—between the younger and older children? Compare and contrast the behavior and activities, skills and attributes, and patterns of social interactions of different age groups.

Then concentrate for a few minutes on two or three preschool children playing together; on the basis of your observations, describe each of them. Even at this age, each individual is unique and manifests his or her own distinctive patterns of personality traits, interests, and abilities. One youngster may be energetic, joyful, vigorous, outgoing, carefree, self-confident, explorative and "getting into everything." Another child of the same age may be slow-moving and deliberate in action, serious, sober looking, and withdrawn from others. To describe other children accurately, you will need to use many different adjectives.

The second exercise is a purely mental one. Think about what you were like when you were a junior-high-school student. What were your outstanding qualities, interests, motives, goals and ambitions? Who were your best friends? In what ways were they similar to you and in what ways were they different? Who were the school leaders, the followers, the loners? What were their significant personal characteristics and patterns of reaction? What interested and motivated them?

Of course, these exercises do not teach you anything new. Their purpose is simply to focus your attention on two obvious facts: (1) behavior, thought, personality, and interests change with age; and (2) within any age group, from infancy to old age, there is an enormous range of individual differences along many dimensions. When you think about such vast differences, you cannot help wondering about their sources or origins. To what extent are they attributable to hereditary (genetic) or constitutional factors—to "nature"? Or are people primarily the products of their environments—or "nurture," as it is called—that is, their experiences, learning, and training?

These are the fundamental issues that define the field of developmental psychology. The central question is—*How do people become who they are?* How do they acquire their personality, styles, motives, goals, and social behaviors? There are many other questions related to this basic one. For example, do early established characteristics remain stable and enduring, or are they likely to be modified? Is the very aggressive four-year-old boy likely to become a highly aggressive young man? Is the offbeat, independent, highly creative ten-year-old girl who lives next door likely to become a highly creative young woman? How and why do "problem" behaviors develop; that is, what factors produce mental illness, delinquency, or addiction? What accounts for the lack of academic motivation and the high percentage of school dropouts among children and adolescents from poverty-stricken families? Why are some young people intolerant and prejudiced against foreigners or people of other races, while others are egalitarian in their attitudes and behavior?

To understand people and their behavior, we must investigate their development and the forces that shape their behavior. If we understand what these forces are and how they operate, we may be able to use our knowledge for the improvement of society and the enhancement of human welfare.

What is Developmental Psychology?

How has developmental psychology developed?
What research methods are used?
What has research yielded?

The central concerns of the science of developmental psychology are the origins of behavior and psychological functions—thought, personality, abilities, feelings, motives, emotions, and attitudes—and how and why these change during the course of our lives. The major objectives or goals of the field may be defined simply as (1) *description* of age changes in behavior and psychological functions and (2) *explanation* of the underlying processes, that is, the biological and environmental factors that produce these changes. Another goal, clearly related to the explanation of age changes, is *understanding* the emergence and development of individual differences in behavior and psychological functioning.

221

How has developmental psychology developed?

Although many fundamental questions about development are still unsolved, people have been concerned with them for many centuries. In the fourth century B.C., Plato wrote that individual differences in abilities and aptitudes are, to some degree, inborn; but he also believed that later motivations and vocational adjustment are influenced by early childhood training.

The writings of early philosophers, like the studies made by developmental psychologists today, reveal a variety of theories of the nature of the child and of human development. For example, in the seventeenth century, British philosopher John Locke maintained that the mind at birth was a **tabula rasa** or a blank slate. As he viewed it, the child's development was completely shaped and molded by teaching, learning, and experience. In contrast, Jean-Jacques Rousseau, the French philosopher writing about a century later considered the young child to be a "noble savage" with an innate sense of justice and morality. In his view, the restrictions imposed by society and its representatives—parents and teachers—"mar and distort" the child's development. "The child that man raises is almost certain to be inferior to the child that nature raises."

Each of these philosophers was convinced that his conception of human development was valid, and each of them gave advice about how to raise children. Thus from its earliest days theory and practical action have often been very closely linked in the area of developmental psychology. Locke, for example, told parents to begin training their children in self-denial and rational behavior from the very earliest infancy.

The early philosophers did not test their theories scientifically. They speculated and observed, but they did not conduct research. Beginning late in the eighteenth century, however, a few educators, philosophers, and biologists began to make observations and records of early growth and changes. In the next century, a number of "baby biographies" were published, each of them an account of the development of one child, generally the author's son or daughter, niece or nephew. One of these was by Charles Darwin, who made careful observations of his son's development, using the observations to support his theory of human evolution.

While these baby biographies were interesting and provocative, they were not scientific works. The writers were biased in their observations, lacking in objectivity, and probably selective in their perceptions—seeing what they wanted to see in the child's behavior. Furthermore, since each biographer observed only one child, it is difficult to determine whether his conclusions are applicable to others.

The systematic study of developmental psychology began with the work of the American psychologist G. Stanley Hall at the beginning of this century. He attempted to study "the contents of children's minds" by administering questionnaires to large groups of children of different ages, asking them about their beliefs, attitudes, and emotions. From their responses, he traced the changes in children's feelings and thoughts as they grew older; that is, he was able to describe *age trends* in these functions.

With the establishment of developmental psychology as a scientific disci-

G. Stanley Hall

pline, investigators turned their attention to many phenomena of growth and change, and they devised more precise and objective methods for their studies. A major advance came in 1903 when the French psychologist Alfred Binet was asked by Paris school authorities to help identify mentally retarded children at an early age. To accomplish his goal, Binet constructed the first useful intelligence test. It consisted of a series of tasks or items that measured what Binet thought were the essential components of intelligence—judgment, comprehension, and reasoning. To establish age norms for the test (average performance at different ages), the tests were administered to large samples of children between the ages of three and eleven. Subsequently, any child's relative intellectual status—advanced, average, or retarded—could be assessed by comparing his or her performance with the established norms. (For a more complete account of intelligence testing *see* Chapter 12.)

In constructing a useful intelligence test, Binet demonstrated that objective measurement (or quantification) could be applied in the investigation of all kinds of complex psychological functions. This finding opened the door for scientific research on many other aspects of development: perception, motor abilities, language, thinking, reasoning, and, finally, motives, emotions, conflicts, and mechanisms of adjustment.

For example, by means of careful and objective studies, the exact nature and step-by-step development of motor activities—such as grasping, sitting, and walking—have been established. Psycholinguists (psychologists interested in language) have traced language development with a great deal of precision from the earliest utterances of crude infantile sounds to communication in complex grammatical sentences. Cognitive psychologists have successfully traced intellectual development from the infant's earliest reflexes and perceptions to adult thinking and reasoning (*see* pp. 245–52). And, in the area of emotional and social development, while our present-day understanding

Much of children's growth and learning follows a fixed sequence of development. Before babies begin trying to copy adult speech, for example, they invariably go through a period of non-imitative babbling.

is far from complete, many important facts have been discovered and valuable insights have been achieved. These are a few of the areas that have been systematically explored. In the next two chapters we will discuss some of the major research findings and the issues they have raised.

Even though there has been enormous and rapid progress in the field of developmental psychology, especially in the last 30 years, there are some basic issues that remain the subjects of controversy. One of these pertains to the child's *role* in his or her own development. Are children primarily *active* or *passive* in these processes; are they *shaped by* external forces or in *control* of their development? Some psychologists, like Locke, regard the child's role as a primarily passive one; they believe that development is determined by external events—that is, by training or experience. This is essentially the view of modern learning theorists, who regard the child's development as a product of the rewards and punishments encountered in the course of growing up. In Freudian or psychoanalytic theory, which is very different from learning theory, the child is also seen as passive; development is shaped by strong biological forces or instincts and by parental relationships and treatment.

By contrast, Jean Piaget, the brilliant Swiss psychologist whose interests are centered on cognitive, intellectual development (*see* pp. 244–52), maintains that children are highly active and, to a significant degree, in control of their development. Even neonates (newborns) and very young babies, in Piaget's view, continually seek to make sense of the world about them, select the experiences they will react to, and impose organization and structure on what they perceive.

Clearly there is a diversity of points of view about how the child develops. At present, there is no single theory that can explain all the facts of human development. Rather, as we shall see, some explanatory principles and concepts seem most appropriate for certain aspects of development—such as emotional development—while others are more useful in explaining the phenomena of cognitive development.

What research methods are used?

Just as there are differences among developmental psychologists in conceptions and theories about the nature of development, there are diverse approaches to research. Furthermore, some researchers study one aspect of behavior and development, such as cognition, while others investigate others. Each researcher chooses the methods that in his or her opinion are most valid and will yield the most accurate and significant information about the problems being investigated.

Observation is the fundamental method. Some **naturalistic observations** are made in "real life" settings, such as the child's home, nursery school, or playground. For example, in exploring the development of sympathy or altruism, a researcher might observe children as they interact "naturally" during a free-play period, recording all acts of helping, sharing, or expressing concern or sympathy.

Often, more detailed and precise observations can be made under *standard-*

The window of the observation room is a one-way mirror. It enables developmental psychologists to observe the behavior of an individual child as well as to study groups of children in various situations.

ized, controlled conditions. To study the early development of altruism, the researcher might observe thirty young children—ten (five boys and five girls) at each of three ages—perhaps three, four, and five years old. Each child might be observed first while playing at a table on which there is a standard set of attractive toys. After the child plays awhile, another child, a stranger, is sent into the room and approaches the table. The episodes can be video-taped to provide permanent, objective records of children's reactions to a new child. The tapes can be analyzed carefully and the frequency of various responses noted. Does the child smile, approach the new child, offer toys, attempt to prevent him or her from using toys, explain the use of some of the materials? Comparing records of children of different ages would reveal age trends in the development of generosity and altruism, as well as in other variables such as sociability.

Much developmental research involves *experiments*—manipulation by the investigator of relevant variables to discover mechanisms underlying changes in behavior. An experiment is simply a special type of standardized observation, one which is made under controlled conditions. Suppose, for example, that a psychologist hypothesizes that children will become more altruistic if they have an opportunity to observe others—models—behaving generously. The hypothesis can then be checked by conducting an experiment. A pair of researchers interested in the development of altruistic behavior did just that (Rosenhan & White, 1967). Their subjects were two groups of children between ten and twelve years of age—an experimental and a control group. Each child in the experimental group played a bowling game with an adult model; they alternated turns, and each of them had ten turns. On a table in the room was a pile of 5¢ gift certificates, which were redeemable at a nearby toy store known to all the subjects. In introducing the game to the child, the model explained that a player would win two of the gift certificates each time he or she reached a score of 20. Also prominently displayed was a container labelled "Trenton Orphans Fund," clearly a charity collection box.

The game was programmed so that the model won twice; each time he or she took two gift certificates and deposited one of them in the charity box. While the subject played the model looked away so that the child's behavior would not be influenced by attention from the adult. At the end of the game the model pretended to have to do something somewhere else and allowed the child to play the game some more alone. The model then departed, and the child took twenty more trials, obtaining (programmed) winning scores on four of them. Each of the control subjects went through the same procedures, except that the models did not put any of their winnings into the charity box.

This experiment permits the researcher to make unambiguous and precise evaluations of the effects of the independent variable—observation of a model behaving generously—manipulated by the experimenter. The original hypothesis was confirmed: many of the children who had observed altruistic models imitated their charitable behavior, even when the model was not present. None of the controls, who had not observed a model's altruism, contributed to the charity.

You can see that variations in this experimental procedure could be used to examine other important issues in the development of altruism. For example, another investigator (Bryan, 1970) was interested in the *relative* effectiveness of preaching and practice in increasing a child's altruism. He used the same basic procedure described above, except that the model behaved greedily with some subjects and charitably when with others. At the same time, he or

Studies of family structures and childrearing practices in various areas of the world can provide a cross-cultural perspective and a clearer understanding of the critical elements of parent-child relations.

she did some talking. For example, in one variation, the model behaved greedily but preached the virtue of charity, saying things like "It is better to share than to keep everything for yourself." In another, the model gave generously but preached greed ("We have to be sure we have enough for ourselves before we give to others"). A number of variations were tried, but there was one consistent outcome. Practice—what the model does—influences behavior more than preaching. If the model behaved charitably, so did the children—even when the model preached greed. And, conversely, if the model preached charity, but practiced greed, the child followed the model's behavior and did not contribute to charity. There is a moral in those experiments!

LONGITUDINAL STUDIES

There are two basic contrasting approaches to the study of human development. In a **longitudinal study** the same children are followed and studied over an extended period of time. They may be observed, tested, and interviewed repeatedly at specified intervals, for example, every year between the ages of four and sixteen. A broad range of behaviors may be assessed: intellectual functions, personality characteristics, and social attitudes and opinions. Analysis of the results would reveal age trends in the development of these functions. But much more can be done with the longitudinal data. With such data we could evaluate the effects of early experiences such as rejection during infancy on later behavior and emotional adjustment during childhood and adolescence. Unless the same individuals are observed and tested repeatedly at different ages, it is not possible to determine whether characteristics such as high intelligence or neurotic traits are stable, enduring, consistent, and predictable from earlier to later age periods. Obviously the longitudinal method is a very useful one, but it is expensive, time consuming, and difficult to use.

CROSS-SECTIONAL STUDIES — Using the more common research method, the **cross-sectional study,** the investigator selects groups of children of different ages and collects all the data at one time. Thus, to trace the growth of reasoning ability, he or she might select a group of twenty children at each of six ages—four, six, eight, ten, twelve, and fourteen—and administer reasoning tests to all of them. Then, by comparing the average test performances of the different age groups, the investigator could define age trends in this ability. Using the longitudinal method, a researcher works with the *same* group of children, testing them first at age four and again at ages six, eight, ten, twelve, and fourteen. Since the cross-sectional method is less expensive and less complicated, it is more likely to be used in this kind of study and, in fact, in most developmental research.

What has research yielded?

COMPLEXITY OF DEVELOPMENT — As you search for the explanations for the processes underlying growth and change, you become aware of the enormous complexity of all developmental phenomena. Every aspect of development is influenced by many factors that are interrelated in intricate ways. Consider a relatively simple characteristic like height, which is largely determined by genetic, constitutional factors. If a girl's parents are tall, she is likely to be tall. But state of health and nutrition may also have marked effects on physical growth. Early in this century, it was discovered that Japanese-Americans born and raised in the United States were taller and heavier than their Japanese-born parents and their brothers and sisters reared in Japan. This difference was undoubtedly due to better nutrition and health in America. Other physical attributes—such as weight, physiological reactivity (tendency to sweat and change of heart rate in response to emotional situations), and longevity—are also partially determined by genetic factors; but nutrition, health, and psychological adjustment may also exert significant influences over them. Obesity may be affected by genes or brain malfunction (*see* pp. 553–57), but it can also be a result of overeating that stems from feelings of anxiety or strong dependency needs.

The development of psychological functions is even more complicated and affected by many more factors. Intelligence, as measured by standard intelligence tests, is to some extent determined by hereditary factors—although the precise contribution of heredity to intelligence is not known (*see* pp. 310–14). But a person's performance on intelligence tests can also be very substantially influenced by motivations, by the amount of stimulation received in infancy, and by the quality of early mother-child interactions.

Because aspects of development are interrelated—that is, they interact—they affect one another; changes in one function feed back on others. For example, as the child grows in height and weight and as intellectual capacities increase, perceptions of the self and of the world are modified. These changes may be reflected in personality characteristics—such as increased self-confidence—and in improved interactions with others. Greater self-confidence and better social relationships, in turn, may affect later intellectual functioning and personal adjustment. Analogously, in the course of cognitive development, the child's ability to take or share someone else's view improves markedly. This has implications for social behavior, logical thinking, and moral judgments. As they become less egocentric, children become more tolerant of others, engage in more open, reciprocal, equalitarian social interactions, interpret rules of games more flexibly, and take more variables into account in solving problems.

Because of the enormous complexities of developmental processes, we must be very cautious in making generalizations from research findings, especially if we want to apply these findings to particular individuals. Consider, for example, the evidence that, in American culture, democracy in the home, warmth, and understanding generally have positive effects on the child's personal development (Baldwin, 1949). Parents with these characteristics foster the growth of their children's self-confidence, independence, leadership, creativity, good social adjustment, and happiness. But these home variables would have significantly different effects in other cultures or in different social situations. What would happen, for example, if a boy brought up in a democratic home and encouraged to think independently, found himself in an authoritarian culture that stressed conformity, obedience, and suppression of individuality rather than self-expression and independence? The child's excellent adjustment, established early, might be undermined. In brief, in applying generalizations to individuals, you must consider additional factors that may alter outcomes of good or poor early family interactions.

SOME GENERAL PRINCIPLES

In spite of the enormous complexity of developmental phenomena, and the difficulty of understanding these, some broad principles of human development have been established.

1. Development is, to a very great extent, orderly and predictable, proceeding in an unvarying sequence. The head, eyes, trunk, arms, legs, heart, lungs, genitals, and other organs of all fetuses emerge and develop in the same order and at approximately the same prenatal ages. All fetuses can turn their heads before they can extend their hands. After birth too, motor and cognitive abilities develop in regular patterns, and all children go through the same successive stages of speech development. Babbling precedes talking, and certain sounds are invariably uttered before others; for example, the aspirate *h* (as in house) always occurs before the consonants *n, l,* and *b.*

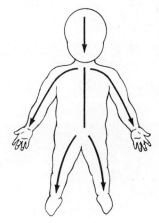

The pattern of early physical and motor development is clearly seen in a number of so-called *directional* trends. Growth and development proceed in a **cephalocaudal** (or head-to-foot) **direction.** Beginnings of arms appear in the fetus before the beginnings of legs; the head is well-developed before the legs. Eye-hand coordination is achieved before the infant's arms and hands can be used effectively in reaching and grasping. The **proximodistal** (or center-to-periphery) **direction** of development is manifested in the relatively early voluntary control of the upper arm and upper leg, which precedes control of the forearm, foreleg, hands, and feet. *Mass activity* develops before *specific activity.* The infant's earliest movements are gross, diffuse and undifferentiated, involving large segments of the body; these are gradually replaced by more refined and differentiated actions. The baby's initial attempts to grab an object are clumsy, but within a few months he or she can move thumb and fingers precisely in an accurate grasping motion.

2. *Although development is continuous, it is not always smooth or gradual.* There are spurts in physical growth and in some psychological functions. Height and weight increase extremely rapidly during the first year and again during adolescence. The growth of the genital organs is very slow during childhood but accelerates tremendously during adolescence. Size of vocabulary rises sharply during the preschool years, and many motor skills improve markedly at the same time. Certain adult-like processes of reasoning and thought seem to emerge spontaneously and develop rapidly between the ages of five and seven. And, in adolescence, the child rather suddenly becomes capable of thinking logically (that is, in accordance with the rules of formal logic), of formulating scientific hypotheses, and of solving complex problems (*see pp. 245–52*).

Some major theorists such as Freud and Piaget describe progress toward psychological maturity in terms of a series of rather abrupt shifts or *stages*. Each new, more advanced stage is qualitatively distinct and different from the preceding stages; each encompasses new abilities and new ways of interpreting the world, of thinking and reacting. Furthermore, according to the theorists, every child goes through the same series of stages in the same invariant order, as he or she matures.

3. *The child's experiences at early stages may significantly affect his or her later development.* The infant who lives in a dull, unstimulating environment is likely to perform poorly in tests of intellectual functions later on. "Inadequate mothering" (too little warmth, love, and attention) in the first year may lead to an emotional instability and maladjustment during adolescence.

4. *There appear to be critical or sensitive periods in the development of body organs, physical attributes, cognitive functions, and personality and*

"When I was ready to read, they taught me to tie my shoes—when I was ready to tie my shoes, they taught me to read."

Most psychologists concur in Erikson's conclusion that mother-child relations in the first year are important in the child's later development.

social characteristics. A **critical period** is one during which certain developments of organs or functions typically occur. At these periods, the organism is most ready for these developments, and interruption or interference with the course of normal development is likely to result in permanent impairment or malfunction. For example, a severe virus infection or German measles (rubella) at a certain point in pregnancy—a critical period in the fetus's development— may produce mental defects in the infant or irremediable damage to the baby's heart, eyes, or lungs. A **sensitive period** is one in which the development of a function ordinarily proceeds more readily than it does at other times. However, interference with development at this point does not necessarily entail permanent damage; that is, deficiencies or impairments due to interferences at sensitive periods may be overcome by later developments. The first year of life is a sensitive period for the development of trust in others, according to Erik Erikson (Erikson, 1950). If the infant does not receive sufficient gratification and love from his or her mother at this time—does not learn to trust and depend on her—the child may not ever acquire a sense of trust in others.

Consequently, even as an older child or adult, such a person may have persistent difficulties in relationships with others, although it is at least possible that later positive experiences with others will help overcome these difficulties.

5. *Two basic though complex processes are involved in all developmental changes:* **experience** (learning or practice) and **maturation** (the physical, neural, physiological, and biochemical changes that take place within the organism as it grows older). These two processes almost always interact; hence it is difficult to determine the precise contributions of each of them to development. Clearly, changes in body proportions and in the structure of the nervous system in early infancy depend on maturational processes rather than on the child's experiences. But the development of motor skills and cognitive functions depends on *both* maturation and experience—and on the interaction between them. For example, the age at which the child first sits or walks is largely determined by maturation rather than by experience or practice. Restrictions on practice do not ordinarily retard the development of these skills, except in extreme cases. Thus, Hopi Indian infants, who are kept bound to cradleboards for most of the first three months of life and for part of each day thereafter, begin to walk at the same age as children who are not restricted in moving. Furthermore, you cannot teach a baby to sit or stand or walk unless he or she is sufficiently mature—that is, until the muscular apparatus has ripened to a certain point. Of course, once acquired, these basic motor skills improve with experience and practice. Walking becomes better coordinated, waste movements are eliminated, and steps become longer, straighter, and more rapid.

Babies also do not talk until they attain a certain level of maturity—until they are "ready" to talk—regardless of how much coaching they may be given. But the language the child acquires and the degree of verbal facility attained are strongly dependent on experience—on what language he or she hears others speaking and on the encouragement and rewards received for talking.

6. *Development continues throughout the life cycle; it does not cease with the attainment of physical or cognitive maturity.* Although the bulk of the systematic study of human growth and change deals with childhood and adolescence, it is obvious that the course of the individual's life is not "fixed" or static from the end of adolescence to death. Rather, at each period of life we encounter challenging new circumstances, problems, or crises; and in seeking to handle them appropriately and successfully, we modify our ways of thinking and reacting. Thus, the entire life-span is characterized by a continuous process of change, adaptation, and development.

In adult life, some abilities may decline while others increase, and the total structure and organization of intellectual functions may be altered substantially. The young adult's personality is not identical with the same person's in adolescence, although there may be some striking continuities; many basic attitudes and traits may be retained. At the same time, young adulthood is a period marked by the need for making many vital decisions—about vocation, marriage, parenthood—and these decisions may bring many modifications—some radical, some minor—in personality and lifestyle. For many people early adulthood is likely to be a period of great productivity and happiness. Later maturity or old age presents other "life crises"—retirement, widowhood,

Developmental psychologists are increasingly interested in describing and understanding the changes that occur at *all* stages of the life-span.

children leaving home. Cognitive abilities generally decline, and activities are likely to be restricted. New kinds of adjustments and modified lifestyles may be called for, although many people remain physically and intellectually active—as well as independent—all their lives. Erikson maintains that the individual becomes more profound and richer in personality as each successive "life crisis" or "developmental task" is successfully resolved (*see* pages 165–67).

SUMMARY

The major goals of the scientific study of developmental psychology are the *description* of age changes in behavior and psychological functions and the *explanation* of the processes underlying these changes. In contemporary psychology, as in ancient philosophy, there are diverse theories about the fundamental nature of development and the child's active or passive role in it. There are many research methods in this field, observation being a basic one that is used both in *naturalistic* (real-life) settings (e.g., school, playground, or home) and under standardized, controlled conditions. Experiments are employed wherever possible, but many critical problems in developmental psychology—for example, investigation of the effects of parental rejection on personality development—cannot be studied experimentally. Such problems must be studied in other ways, for example, by means of interviews and home visits.

In **longitudinal studies,** the same children are studied repeatedly—observed and tested—over an extended period; in **cross-sectional studies,** children of different ages are studied at one time. Either method can be used effectively to study age trends in psychological functioning and behavior. Longitudinal data, however, are required to study the relations between early experiences and later behavior.

Almost all aspects of development are interrelated and influenced by many factors — genetic, constitutional, social, and familial. Changes in one function are likely to have repercussions on others. Thus, a child's growth in height may lead to an increase in self-confidence that enhances intellectual performance and social relationships. All psychological changes involve both **experience** (learning or practice) and **maturation** (physical neural and biochemical changes within the organism).

Many aspects of development are regular and predictable, proceeding in orderly sequences. There are "directional trends" in early physical and motor growth (for example, head-to-foot (**cephalocaudal**) and central-to-periphery (**proximodistal**)). Moreover, all children go through the same stages in cognitive and speech development. Progress is not always smooth and gradual, however; physical growth sometimes proceeds in spurts, and language skills advance more rapidly at certain periods than at others. There are **critical** or **sensitive** periods in many phases of development, and experiences at early ages may significantly affect later behavior. Development is not restricted to the periods of childhood and adolescence; rather there is continuous change and adaptation throughout the life-span.

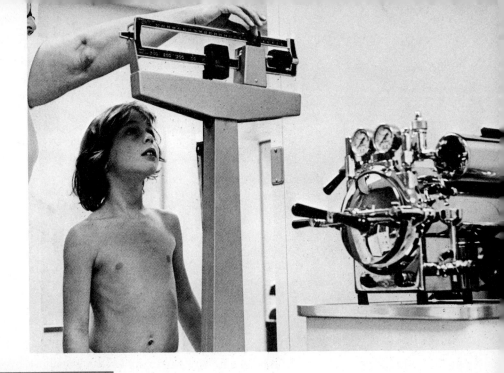

10 Growth and Cognitive Development

What are the beginnings of development?
Is there a pattern of intellectual development?
How do moral judgments develop?
Is language learned?

The expression "the miracle of growth" is a cliché. Yet early growth is so swift and dramatic and the underlying processes are so poorly understood that perhaps "miracle" is the proper word after all.

To a very great extent, the infant's early growth and development are dependent on biological, maturational forces. Prenatal development ordinarily proceeds according to a biological "program," although this program may be adversely affected by the mother's illness or malnutrition. The newborn's needs, sensory capacities, and motor abilities are not learned, nor are most of the sensory, motor, and cognitive abilities that emerge shortly after birth. In considering the critical importance of biological forces, however, we must not lose sight of the fact that—from very early days onward—experience and learning interact with growth and maturation in shaping behavior. As we shall see,

235

the very young infant's contacts with the environment and the people in it, particularly the mother, profoundly influence later development. Even newborns can be conditioned and can learn. Moreover, the baby is not simply a passive organism that is molded and shaped by environmental forces. Infants are *active* participants in their learning, in processing and filtering environmental stimuli, and in adapting to the world. This is made particularly clear by Piaget's observations of intellectual development, which we will discuss later in this chapter.

What are the beginnings of development?

In order to understand how children develop and progress, we need to know what they start with. What is the neonate (newborn) like and what can he or she do? From the start, the baby changes very rapidly. What are the most significant changes occurring during early infancy and in the first year?

PHYSICAL DEVELOPMENT

Babies are about twenty inches long, on the average, at birth; boys weigh about seven pounds, girls slightly less. During the first year, the body grows in size and weight at a faster rate than at any other time. Weight is approximately doubled during the first six months and almost tripled during the first year. Body length increases to about twenty-eight or twenty-nine inches.

The proportions of the infant's body also change rapidly, becoming more like the adult's. The neonate appears to be "top-heavy"; the head is disproportionately large—it is already about 60 percent of its adult size—but it grows less than other parts of the body. Brain size, however, doubles during the first two years of life. The neonate's legs, which are relatively short—only about a third of the length of the body—grow rapidly, until, at maturity, they are about half the individual's height.

The dramatic physical growth that occurs during the first year of life is accompanied by equally rapid developments in cognitive, motor, and sensory abilities.

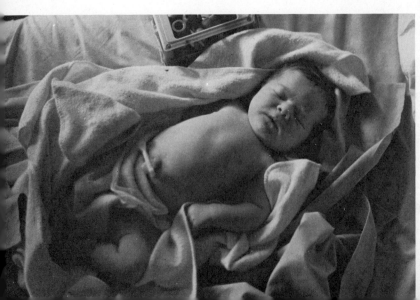

Figure 10-1
Body Changes in Form and Proportion
(After Jackson, 1929)

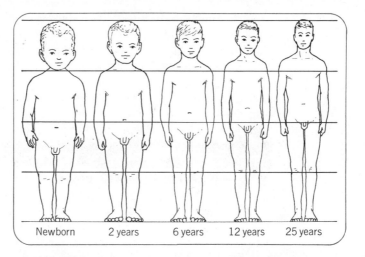

Newborn   2 years   6 years   12 years   25 years

Neonatal Behavior: Needs and Reflexes

Certain reflexes—such as grasping—are characteristic of all babies in the first few months of life.

Biological needs present at birth—needs for oxygen, for elimination, for food and drink, for temperature regulation—must be satisfied if the infant is to survive. Fortunately, the neonate's reflexes gratify most of these needs in a self-regulatory way, that is, without learning, voluntary control, or active participation by the infant or by others. The neonate can suck to get milk; reflex breathing responses provide oxygen; reflexes also take care of needs for elimination. Automatic physiological reactions generally keep the body at a relatively constant temperature, and chemical and physiological balances are maintained through sleep.

Other reflexes, present at birth or developed very shortly thereafter, also assist in the neonate's survival and adjustment. The pupils of the eyes constrict as a protection against bright lights, and they dilate in the dark. The newborn

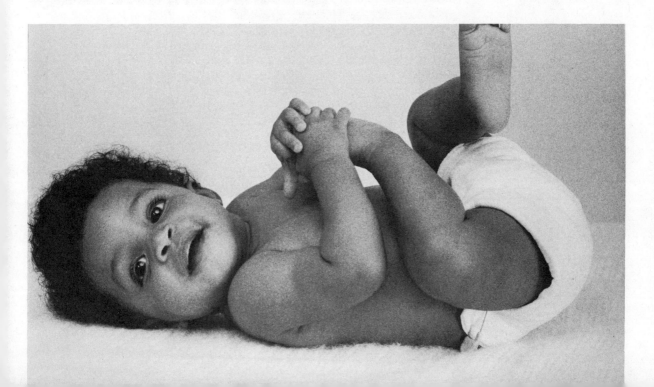

can cry, cough, turn away, vomit, lift his chin, flex his muscles, extend his limbs, smack his lips, and chew. Sudden stimulation by loud noises or other kinds of strong stimuli is likely to elicit a "startle response"—throwing the arms wide apart, throwing the head back, and extending the legs.

The Infant's Motor and Sensory Abilities

Although there is variation in the age at which they occur in different children, the sequence of locomotion is universal.

Sitting, crawling and creeping, walking, and voluntary grasping are not behaviors present at birth, but they are manifested in early infancy. By and large, they develop independently of learning, without training or practice. Maturational forces—growth of bone, muscle, and neural tissues and increased complexity of the nervous system—determine when the child is ready to sit up, to walk, and to manipulate objects. Early restrictions on practice do not ordinarily delay the emergence of these activities (see p. 232); nonetheless, practice makes them better coordinated, smoother, and more precise. Waste motions are eliminated from walking and balance improves. In reaching and grasping, responses become quicker and less awkward; useless movements are eliminated, and reaching becomes direct and precise. Detailed analyses show that each of these motor activities progresses through a fixed sequence of stages. Practically all infants go through the same series of developmental steps.

You can get some idea of the vast range of the young child's motor abilities by looking at the items on a motor development scale for young children. One such scale was devised by Dr. Nancy Bayley of the Institute of Human Development at the University of California. She made extensive and detailed studies of young children's motor abilities and then constructed a scale of eighty-one items (Bayley, 1969). The scale was administered to a very large, representative sample of children between one and twenty-one months of age. Then, for each item, Bayley determined the *norm* or age placement—the average age at which children could perform the task. Some of the first-year items are presented in Table 10-1, together with the norms. The scale provides the basis for evaluating whether a particular child's progress in motor development is average, accelerated, or retarded (Bayley, 1969).

TABLE 10-1 Some items from motor scale of the Bayley scales of infant development

Item	Age Placement (months)
Crawling movements	0.4
Holds head erect: vertical	0.8
Sits with support	2.3
Turns from back to side	4.4
Pulls to sitting position	5.3
Sits alone 30 seconds or more	6.0
Early stepping movements	7.4
Raises self to sitting position	8.3
Fine prehension of pellet (pincer-like movement)	8.9
Walks with help	9.6
Walks alone	11.7
Throws ball	13.3

N. Bayley. Bayley Scales of Infant Development. New York: Psychological Corporation, 1969.

Figure 10-2
Development of Posture and Locomotion in Infants
(After Shirley, 1933)

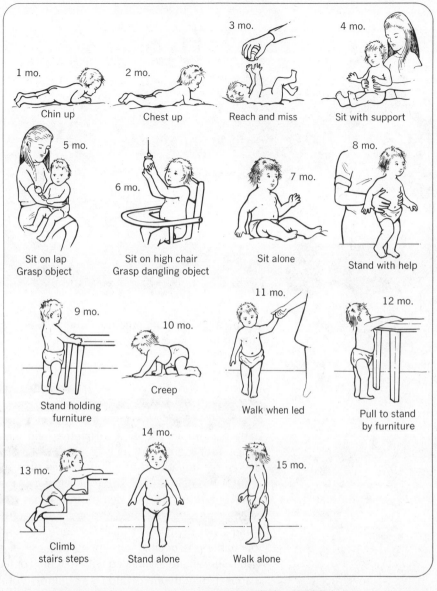

1 mo. Chin up

2 mo. Chest up

3 mo. Reach and miss

4 mo. Sit with support

5 mo. Sit on lap Grasp object

6 mo. Sit on high chair Grasp dangling object

7 mo. Sit alone

8 mo. Stand with help

9 mo. Stand holding furniture

10 mo. Creep

11 mo. Walk when led

12 mo. Pull to stand by furniture

13 mo. Climb stairs steps

14 mo. Stand alone

15 mo. Walk alone

The sensory system functions reasonably well at birth, and it improves rapidly within the first weeks of postnatal life. Newborns can see, hear, and smell; they are sensitive to pain, touch, and change of position; and they have some sense of taste, sucking in response to sweet substances and grimacing in response to sour ones.

Infants as young as fifteen days old can discriminate differences in brightness and color. Coordination and convergence of the eyes, which are necessary for visual fixation and for depth perception, begin to develop immediately after birth and are fairly well established by seven or eight weeks. From the age of sixteen weeks onward, the infant is capable of adjusting his or her eyes in order to focus on objects that are near or far, just as an adult does.

"Making a playful response" to his reflection, as this baby is doing, is a six-month item of the Bayley Scale of Infant Development.

Not all visual stimuli are equally likely to attract the infant's attention. Stimuli that move or have a great deal of contour (black edge on white background) are noticed and looked at for the longest periods. Even a five-day-old baby sucking on a nipple is likely to stop sucking momentarily if a light moves to his or her visual field. Apparently, attention to movement and contrast is unlearned. Within a very few months, however, the infant's experience begins to affect these responses. Attention becomes more selective, and the baby pays more attention to familiar and meaningful stimuli than to others. When four-month-old infants are shown schematic diagrams that vary in degree of similarity to the human face, they pay most attention to those that are like the human face and thus are most familiar (Kagan, 1970).

Recent research also demonstrates that some rather complex perceptual abilities are "wired" into the organism, rather than learned. For example, some have maintained that we *learn* to identify objects as being solid and touchable—as having substance—because of repeated experiences in which visual stimuli are associated with touching or feeling an object. Now, however, it appears that the perception is "built in," not the product of experience; even babies as young as two weeks react to an object as though it were solid and touchable. This was demonstrated in a recent experiment in which researchers created an optical illusion—an intangible but solid-appearing, real-looking cube. All of the neonates in the experiment reached out for the illusory object and showed surprise (crying and startle responses) when they touched and felt nothing. The investigator interpreted this as evidence that there is a "built-in" association between visual objects and the "expectation" that they are solid and tangible (Bower, 1974).

Depth perception, another complex perceptual ability, is also achieved early. (*See* p. 459.) In one experiment, babies just a few months old were placed, individually, in the center of a table covered by a heavy, solid glass sheet. Extending from the center of a table on one side was a checkerboard pattern placed directly beneath the glass; on the other side, the same kind of pattern was placed several feet below the glass, giving the illusion of a drop-off or visual cliff. If the infant's mother called from the shallow end of the table, the infant crawled over to her. But if she called from the deep side, the child would not cross the cliff, even though he or she could pat the glass and discover that the surface was firm. From this, it was concluded that the ability to perceive depth is innate, or at least developed very early in life (Gibson & Walk, 1960).

INDIVIDUAL DIFFERENCES AMONG INFANTS

Although there are many "universal" characteristics of neonatal behavior and development, marked and clear-cut individual differences in temperament, activity level, irritability, and speed and strength of response are apparent from birth onward. Some infants are extremely active and restless, thrashing their arms continually, crying loudly, kicking their legs with vigor, and sucking with great energy. Others are more placid and quiet, move about less, nurse less vigorously, and sleep more peacefully. Some infants show a startle reaction to rather weak stimuli—such as gentle stroking or sounds or light flashes of low intensity—while others show this reaction only in response to strong stimulation. Pain sensitivity also varies from child to child, girls generally responding more readily to mild pain stimulation than boys. These differences, manifested so early in life, may be attributable to genetic and/or constitutional factors.

These neonatal or infantile characteristics may affect the child's future learning and development in a number of ways. Certainly the lively, energetic infant's approaches to the world and reactions to experience are very different from those of the calm, relaxed, slow-moving infant. And parents' attitudes toward their baby and their ways of handling the child may be strongly affected by the infant's personality and temperamental characteristics. For example, quiet, placid, low-keyed parents may find it very difficult—or even frightening and irritating—to deal with a vigorous, noisy baby girl. They may reject the child or try very hard to "train" her to be quieter and less active. More exuberant, accepting parents, on the other hand, would be delighted with such a highly active offspring, rewarding and encouraging her liveliness and energetic reactions. Thus, directly and indirectly, the personal qualities of neonates can influence how and what they learn.

LEARNING

As we have seen, many perceptual and motor abilities seem to be "wired into" the organism, emerging as a consequence of biological maturational processes. Once these basic skills appear, they improve rapidly with practice and experience.

Indeed, learning and experience play major roles in development from birth on. Newborns can be conditioned, and they learn from experience. For example, three-day-old infants have been trained to turn their heads to the right whenever they heard the sound of a bell coming from that direction (Papousek, 1967). This response was conditioned by repeatedly ringing a bell to the right of the neonate's head and presenting a nipple from which to suck milk every time he or she turned in that direction. If the infant did not respond during the first few trials, the experimenter touched the right corner of the

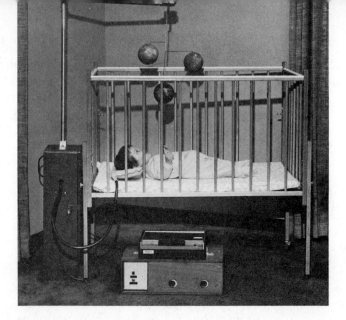

The infant learns to turn the mobile by moving her head back and forth on the pressure-sensitive pillow, which is connected to an electronic device.

child's mouth lightly with the nipple, a stimulus that elicits head-turning to the right.

In each experimental session, the sound of the bell was paired ten times with receiving milk. During the first sessions the infants sometimes turned their heads to the right when the bell sounded; sometimes they did not. However, after seventeen or eighteen such experimental sessions—a total of about 177 trials on the average—three-day-olds learned to turn their heads in the right direction every time the bell sounded. In other words, the neonates' head-turning response had been conditioned to the sound of the bell; an association had been formed between the external stimulus (bell) and a specific response (head-turning).

Thus infants respond very early to a variety of reinforcements or rewards. In one ingenious experiment (Ramey & Watson, 1972), infants eight weeks old readily learned to move their heads frequently when their movements produced an interesting "show"—the turning of a brightly painted mobile hanging over the crib. The infants' heads rested on a "pressure sensing" pillow; they could control the rotation of the mobile simply by moving their heads slightly. A control group of infants the same age also saw a mobile turning, but it was not regulated by their head movements.

The number of head movements made by the infants who controlled the rotation of the mobile increased continuously for the entire fourteen days of the experiment. There was no change in the number of head movements made by the controls during the same period. The investigators concluded that "the rise in pillow activation . . . by the experimental infants was due to the fact that their turning displays were contingent on their head movements on their pillows. They reacted to this response-contingent stimulation by learning to control it" (Watson & Ramey, 1972, p. 221).

Incidentally, the babies in the experimental group seemed to enjoy the experience of controlling the mobiles; they watched with rapt attention, often smiling vigorously and cooing. Control infants showed no such response to the rotation of their mobiles.

Social stimulation by adults can also be very effective in changing behavior of infants—even very young ones. The frequency of vocalization by three-month-olds has been found to increase greatly in response to the experimenter's smiling, saying "tsk-tsk," and patting the baby's stomach (Rheingold, Gewirtz, & Ross, 1959; Weisberg, 1963; Bloom & Esposito, 1975). When the social stimulation was removed—in extinction periods—the frequency of the infant's vocalizations decreased to the baseline level (their frequency before experimental treatment). These findings have generally been interpreted as showing that adults' social responses were rewarding or reinforcing—and thus served to increase the infant's vocalization. Recently, however, this interpretation has been questioned. One experiment (Bloom & Esposito, 1975) showed that social stimulation by adults led to increased levels of infant vocalization "whether or not the stimulation was contingent upon responding"; that is, the increase occurred both when vocalizations were immediately followed by an adult's responses and when adult stimulation was given independently of the infant's vocalization. It is possible, therefore, that the adult stimulation served primarily to *elicit* rather than to reward the infant's vocalizations.

Four-month-old infants' smiles—in a sense their first real social responses—also became more frequent in an experimental setting when they were followed immediately by adult stimulation (picking up, smiling at, and talking to the infant). When the experimenter discontinued her reactions to the smiles, the frequency of the infant's smiling response diminished significantly (were extinguished), and protest responses (crying, kicking) increased. Clearly adults

Young babies whose mothers offer frequent affection and stimulation are generally high in social responsiveness.

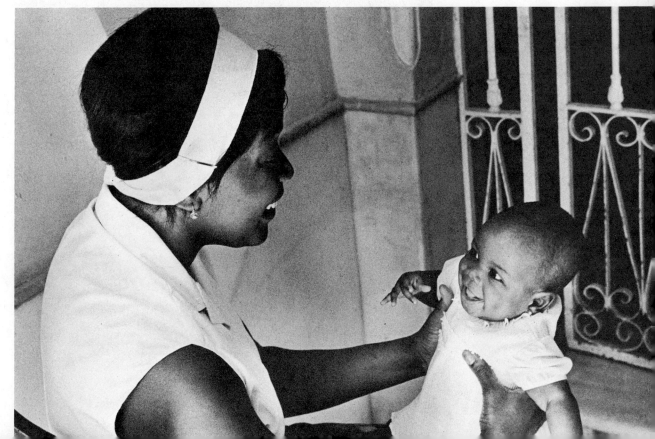

have a significant degree of control over the behavior of infants—both by giving and withholding social stimulation and rewards (Brackbill, 1958).

Confirmation of these experimental findings comes from a naturalistic study of five-month-old black infants who were observed alone and in interactions with their mothers in their homes. Mothers who responded to their infant's babbling by talking to them, stimulated vocalization. Their infants vocalized more, and for longer periods, when playing alone than those who received less reinforcement for vocalization from their mothers. Furthermore, the babies' level of social responsiveness—"talking" to people, adjusting the body to being lifted, enjoying play, and approaching and smiling at their own reflection in a mirror—was directly related to the amount of the mother's reinforcement of the infant's social behavior. Mothers of highly socially responsive babies tended to remain close to their children and to talk with them, touch them, hold them, and play with them; they were demonstrative and encouraged motor responses (Hess and Shipman, 1965).

Is there a pattern of intellectual development?

No name looms larger in contemporary developmental psychology than that of Jean Piaget, the Swiss psychologist. Piaget's many years of research in the area of intellectual development have yielded a brilliant and influential theory. The theory is derived largely from his own carefully detailed and extensive observations. He began by studying his own children during infancy—using both naturalistic and informal experimental techniques. Later he observed and interviewed older children, to whom he presented problems to solve.

Piaget views intelligence as the ability to adapt to the environment and to new situations, to think and act in adaptive ways. His demonstrations make clear the *active and creative nature of children's thinking*. From the very

Swiss psychologist Jean Piaget.

beginning, children are curious about their environment; they do not simply wait for events to happen; rather, they actively seek out stimulation and excitement. Curiosity and intellectual activity are characteristic throughout early childhood development.

PIAGET'S COGNITIVE STAGES

Intellectual development from infancy to adolescence is divided into four major periods or stages: (1) sensorimotor (birth to two years); (2) preoperational (two years to seven years); (3) concrete operational (seven years to eleven years); and (4) formal operational (eleven years and over). New, qualitatively different cognitive abilities emerge at each successive stage. The age ranges for these stages are only approximate, and there are wide individual differences. What is important is the *regular, invariant order of succession of the stages*. There are no reversals, no "skipping" of stages. A child does not, for example, reach the stage of concrete operations without first going through the preoperational stage.

While Piaget believes that the sequence of cognitive stages is universal, he does not maintain that the child's abilities at each stage evolve simply as a consequence of maturation. Rather, cognitive development is regarded as the result of the **interaction** between the structure of the organism and the environment. That is, at each stage, the individual has certain organizing and structuring tendencies; and these determine how the child interacts with— "operates on" or organizes—his or her environment and experiences. Clearly, experience is a necessary element in cognitive development, but it does not direct or shape the development. The individual *actively* selects, organizes, integrates, and interprets experiences, and gives them significance. *Feedback* from experience results in qualitative changes in the child's cognitive structures (rules for processing information), advancing the child to the next, more highly developed stage. Unfortunately, the processes underlying the transitions from one stage to the next are not yet completely understood.

Sensorimotor Period

During the **sensorimotor period**—approximately the first eighteen months of life—the infant adapts to the environment through the senses and by means of motor activities. Patterns of behavior called *schema*, which have both sensory and motor components, become increasingly complex. Beginning with vague awareness and simple, often gross, reflexes, schema are gradually refined into more distinct and accurate perceptions of the environment, accompanied by well-coordinated motor responses. The infant during this stage is not yet capable of mental images, nor of thought processes that depend on symbols or language.

The neonate's perceptions and reflexes are altered, elaborated, and made more effective through experience. For example, the sucking "instinct" or "reflex" is soon modified or adapted so that the infant can suck the mother's breast or a bottle more efficiently. Simple reflexes and responses—such as hand and eye movements—become coordinated: the infant reaches for objects, grasps them, and sucks them. Soon, finding that certain actions produce pleasant results, the child attempts to repeat them. Thus, to many infants sucking the hands is enjoyable, and they actively try to put their hands in their mouths.

Sometime between the fourth and the eighth month, infants begin to crawl and to manipulate objects, and to show real interest in the surroundings. They begin to *anticipate* that their actions will have specific effects on objects in the environment, and they begin to act *intentionally* to produce interesting results. If the child can shake a rattle hanging over the crib by kicking it, he or she will kick intentionally.

The very young infant does not really have any sense of objects as distinct from itself; when an object disappears—when it drops for example—it no longer exists. But, at about eight or ten months of age, the child will follow the movements of a desirable object and, when it disappears from view, will search for it. This demonstrates that the infant has achieved the important concept of **object permanence:** the idea that objects continue to exist even though they are out of view or out of reach (Piaget, 1952).

As the baby progresses further in the sensorimotor period, at eleven or twelve months of age, he or she experiments more actively, explores, seeks novelty, varies and modifies behavior more. Real curiosity is manifested, and actions become more deliberate, constructive, and original. Objects are dropped just to watch them fall, toys are pulled around on strings, and sticks are used to push things around.

At the end of the sensorimotor period, somewhere between eighteen and twenty-four months of age, the beginnings of real thought emerge, and infants become capable of thinking about objects or events that are not immediately observable. They construct "mental images" and begin to "think out" problems before attempting to solve them, using ideas and images to invent new ways of accomplishing goals. They practice what Piaget calls "internal experimentation." Piaget observed his sixteen-month-old son use a stick to push an object so that he could reach it with his hands; he had never used a stick in this way previously. The sensorimotor period thus ends with the development of *imagery,* a primitive kind of mental representation (Piaget, 1952).

In brief, gradual and continuous developments take place during the sensorimotor period—not sudden transformations. The infant advances from an initial undifferentiated state to a level characterized by possession of cognitive structures that make possible a variety of adaptive reactions and anticipation of the consequences of behavior. By the end of this period the child understands means-ends relationships, invents new ways of doing things, represents objects mentally (imagery), and solves simple problems.

Preoperational Period

With the beginning of imagery and language, at about two years of age, the child enters the next major stage of intellectual development—the **preoperational period.** Thinking and actions are no longer tied, as in the sensorimotor period, to real objects and events that are immediately present and directly perceived. Rather, the preoperational child can manipulate objects and events symbolically, representing them by images and words. The child can imitate models that are no longer present (Piaget calls this *deferred imitation*). A little boy, for example, may shout like someone he saw at the playground yesterday or "read" a book as he had seen his mother do. Symbolic play becomes very important; a stick becomes an airplane, an orange crate is a ship. The ability

The preoperational child may imagine that a box is a train, a spaceship, or a witch's castle.

to treat objects as symbolic of other objects is an essential characteristic of this stage.

Preoperational thought is superficial, primitive, and confused. It is generally egocentric—that is, children in this period are unable to take the role or point of view of others. In their speech, they hardly take into account the needs of the listener. They often seem to be involved in monologues or "collective monologues," rather than communication; a child may say things to another child, apparently without intending that the other should reply or

WALL STREET JOURNAL

"...No, he can't really fly ... no, the bad guys don't really have a ray gun ... no, this cereal really isn't the best food in the whole world ... no, it won't make you as strong as a giant ..."

Piaget's experiments show that the preoperational child does not understand the notion of conservation (*see* Spotlight 10-1).

even hear. As preoperational children see it, the sun and moon follow them around. They are unable to imagine what things would look like from someone else's perspective. This point was neatly demonstrated in an experiment by Inhelder and Piaget (1958), in which three "mountains" are set on a table and one chair is placed at each side of the table. The child sits in one of the chairs and a doll is placed sequentially in each of the other three. The child's task is to identify what the doll is seeing from each of the three positions, either by constructing the doll's view from cardboard cutouts or by choosing from a set of drawings. Children in the preoperational stage cannot perform this task.

In solving problems, the preoperational child primarily focuses on, and responds to, the aspects of the immediate environment that are perceived directly. Only a limited amount of the available information is used; for example, a child will concentrate on a single feature of a problem and fail to take into account other equally important dimensions. Piaget's famous conservation experiments nicely illustrate this preoperational trait. A four-year-old girl is shown two identical glasses filled equally high with grape juice. Then the liquid from one glass is poured into a taller and thinner glass, reaching a higher level than it did in its original container. When asked to compare the amount of drink in the two glasses, the child is likely to say that the tall, narrow container contains more than the other one. The amount of drink is seen as equal to its level in the container. Clearly, the child has concentrated solely on the height of the liquid in the glass. She does not consider height and width in relation to each other. A child at this stage does not realize that the increase in height is compensated for by the decrease in width. Thought is dominated by the perception of only one dimension or aspect of the stimulus — its height (Inhelder & Piaget, 1958, 1959).

Period of Concrete Operations

Two or three years later the same child, now in the **period of concrete operations,** will respond differently to the conservation problem. The seven-year-old is able to focus on several dimensions of a problem at the same time and to understand the relationships among these dimensions. Thus the girl explains immediately that the amount of liquid in a tall narrow glass is exactly the same as the amount in the shorter wider glass because "nothing was added or taken away" or because "what is gained in height is lost in width." By this time she has achieved the concept of conservation, the realization that the quantity of the liquid remains unchanged in spite of changes in its appearance.

Related to this recognition is the understanding of *reversibility*—the idea that, *in thinking,* steps can be retraced, actions can be cancelled, and an original situation can be restored. This realization renders the child's thought much more flexible and less egocentric. He or she becomes capable of logical processes or what Piaget calls *operations*—adaptive actions performed on objects. In mental operations, these actions are carried out internally, that is, in thought.

Preoperational children are able to classify, that is, to group objects according to characteristics they share in common; for example, they can sort red and blue blocks into separate piles. But—according to Piaget—they do not think of them as "classes" in an abstract sense. In the concrete operational stage, however, children have a more advanced notion of classes, particularly when real objects are involved. They sort things according to the common characteristics and understand the hierarchical order or relationships in which classes (or groups) include subclasses (subgroups); they recognize that an object can belong simultaneously to both a class and a subclass. If a four-year-old boy is shown ten brown beads and four white beads and asked, "Are there more brown beads or more beads?" he is likely to say, "More brown beads." The boy in the stage of concrete operations, on the other hand, understands that brown beads are a subclass of beads; and he will answer— as adults do—that there are more beads than brown beads (Inhelder & Piaget, 1959).

Whereas the preoperational child tends to think in terms of absolutes, during the period of concrete operations, the child becomes capable of handling relational terms. If a preoperational child is given ten sticks varying in length and asked to arrange them in order, he or she is likely to arrange them incorrectly, or manages to order a few of the sticks but not all of them. If the child at this stage does succeed in ordering the ten sticks, it is done with great difficulty—by frequently rearranging the order, shifting them from one position to another. The child is proceeding in a trial-and-error way; there is no evidence of overall plans, guiding principles, or systematic comparisons among the lengths of the sticks. In the concrete operational period, however, combinatorial skills—the ability to manipulate numbers, to add, subtract, and multiply—appear and develop. The abilities to see relationships, order things, and apply combinatorial operations are all necessary for learning and understanding arithmetic.

The achievements of the operational period reflect the child's increased ability to perceive regularities in the physical world, to understand relationships among objects and events, and to reason in a systematic and logical way from premise to conclusion. As a result, the child can create and follow rules. But keep in mind that these abilities are still limited. Logical operations are applied only to *concrete* objects, events, and perceptions—or to representations of them. The child still does not think in abstract terms or reason about hypothetical propositions.

Period of Formal Operations

Abstract thought is the hallmark of the most advanced stage of intellectual development, the **stage of formal operations,** which begins at approximately twelve years old and lasts through adulthood. The thought of adolescent children involves abstractions, reasoning by hypothesis, and adult logic. They can *think about thinking* and evaluate their own and others' ideas and thoughts. They are concerned with beliefs, values, and abstractions such as liberty and freedom—in short, with the world of thoughts and ideas, with hypotheses as well as real situations. These concerns complement the world of rules, symbols, and objects with which the operational child is preoccupied. In addition, the feedback adolescents give each other is extremely important in the development of their capacities for abstract thought.

According to Piaget, thinking in terms of logical propositions and applying logical rules and reasoning to abstract problems are the essences of mature intellectual ability. Adolescents in the period of formal operations can clearly follow the form of an argument, regardless of its content. They understand that if $A = B$ and $B = C$, then $A = C$. They can readily solve abstract problems such as "Ruth is taller than Mary, and Mary is taller than Jane; who is the tallest of the three?" In other words, formal operational thinking does not depend on immediate perceptions, experiences, and manipulation of concrete objects—as concrete operational thinking does. Instead, reasoning is logical and deductive. Furthermore, adolescents who have attained the stage of formal operations consider the full set of possible outcomes and many hypotheses about what might occur; they take into account possible combinations of factors and mentally manipulate several factors simultaneously. They then proceed to test their hypotheses, either in reality or mentally, by experiments that can support some and disprove others. In brief, in comparison with the concrete operational child, the thinking of the adolescent at the formal reasoning level is more flexible and abstract; it involves hypothesis testing and takes into account the many possibilities in a situation. The differences in thinking are illustrated in Spotlight 10-1, which describes an experiment of Inhelder and Piaget that used children at both levels.

In a sense, adolescents are *capable* of thinking very much as scientists do, but that doesn't mean they necessarily do so. For many reasons—cultural, educational, and intellectual—not all adolescents, or adults, are capable of formal operations and flexible problem solving. It is important to note, however, that without the abilities associated with the period of formal operations, there can be no real scientific thinking or logical deductive reasoning.

Cognitive development has customarily been investigated by asking children questions, posing problems for them to solve, or observing them while

During the period of concrete operations, the child enjoys manipulating things and is beginning to perceive the relationships between objects and events.

Spotlight 10-1   An Experiment in Formal Operational Thinking

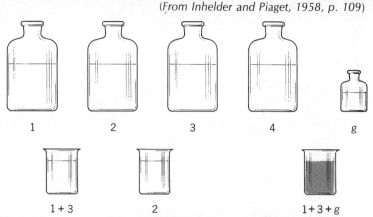

(From Inhelder and Piaget, 1958, p. 109)

The diagram illustrates Piaget's problem of the colored and colorless chemicals. Bottles 1 through 4 contain colorless, odorless liquids: (1) dilute sulphuric acid; (2) water; (3) oxygenated water; (4) thiosulphate. While the child watches, the experimenter adds several drops of g—potassium iodide—to each of two glasses: one contains 1 + 3, the other 2 only. The liquid in the first glass turns yellow. The child is then instructed to reproduce the color, using all or any of the five bottles.

Here are two protocols that illustrate the behavior of two children attempting to solve this problem. Ren is in the stage of concrete operations, while Cha has achieved the formal operational level.

R<small>EN</small> *(7;1)* [7 years, 1 month] tries 4 × g, then 2 × g, and 3 × g: "I think I did everything. . . . I tried them all."—"*What else could you have done?*"—"I don't know." *We give him the glasses again: he repeats 1 × g, etc.*—"*You took each bottle separately. What else could you have done?*"—"Take two bottles at the same time" [*he tries 1 × 4 × g, then 2 × 3 × g, thus failing to cross over between the two sets (of bottles), for example 1 × 2, 1 × 3, 2 × 4, and 3 × 4*].—*When we suggest that he add others, he puts 1 × g in the glass already containing 2 × 3 which results in the appearance of the color:* "Try to make the color again."—"Do I put in two or three? [*he tries with 2 × 4 × g, then adds 3, then tries it with 1 × 4 × 2 × g*]. No, I don't remember any more" (p. 111).

C<small>HA</small> *(13;0):* "You have to try with all the bottles. I'll begin with the one at the end [*from 1 to 4 with g*]. It doesn't work any more. Maybe you have to mix them [*he tries 1 × 2 × g, then 1 × 3 × g*]. It turned yellow. But are there other solutions? I'll try [*1 × 4 × g; 2 × 3 × g; 2 × 4 × g; 3 × 4 × g; with the two preceding combinations this gives the six two-by-two combinations systematically*]. It doesn't work. It only works with" [*1 × 3 × g*].—"*Yes, and what about 2 and 4?*" —"2 and 4 don't make any color together. They

are negative. Perhaps you could add 4 in 1 × 3 × g to see if it would cancel out the color [*he does this*]. Liquid 4 cancels it all. You'd have to see if 2 has the same influence [*he tries it*]. No, so 2 and 4 are not alike, for 4 acts on 1 × 3 and 2 does not."—"*What is there in 2 and 4?*"—"In 4 certainly water. No, the opposite, in 2 certainly water since it doesn't act on the liquids; that makes things clearer."—"*And if I were to tell you that 4 is water?*"—"If this liquid 4 is water, when you put it with 1 × 3 it wouldn't completely prevent the yellow from forming. It isn't water; it's something harmful" (p. 117).

Notice that Ren, the preoperational child, actually tried only a limited number of the total possible combinations, combining only one chemical at a time with another, or combining all four with g. Cha, on the other hand, *began* by testing many of the possible combinations, and he did this in very systematic and orderly ways. He also reasons in a logical, hypothetical or deductive way, while Ren does not. Cha's formal operational thinking is evidenced in a number of "if . . . then" sentences and in statements about the *possible* rather than real. "What if" statements are not characteristic of the thought of the younger child.

"Of greater developmental significance is the fact [he is able to make] a statement about these statements, a proposition about propositions: namely, the assertion that one statement (liquid 4 is water) logically implies another (liquid 4 will not prevent the yellow from forming)" (Flavell, 1963, p. 108).

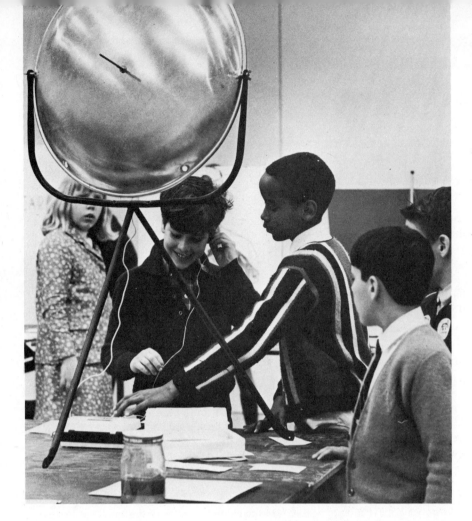

To carry out a meaningful scientific experiment, children must have attained the ability to think abstractly and to hypothesize about the relationship among variables.

they work on various kinds of problems. But cognitive abilities are also reflected in other kinds of activities. Consequently, some researchers have approached the problem of cognitive development in other ways—for example, by interviewing subjects about moral issues and social institutions. The roles of cognition and cognitive development in response to humor—specifically to jokes and riddles—have also been investigated (*see* Spotlight 10-2).

How do moral judgments develop?

Studies in American and other cultures (Swiss, Belgian, Chinese, Mexican, Israeli, Hopi, Zuñi, Sioux, Papago) conducted by Lawrence Kohlberg of Harvard University and his colleagues (Kohlberg, 1963, 1969; Turiel, 1966, 1974) demonstrate that the development of moral judgments—the cognitive aspects of morality—advances through a sequence of universal, regular stages. (The development of moral behavior will be discussed further in Chapter 11,

Children's understanding of humor and their reactions to jokes are related to their level of cognitive development. Freud suggested that young children notice and react to incongruities, while older children prefer more meaningful jokes in which the incongruity is resolved or explained.

This notion was studied experimentally by two investigators who presented a series of jokes—each of them involving an interaction between two people—to subjects between six and twelve years of age (Schultz & Horibe, 1974). There were three forms of each joke. In the original joke, someone makes an ambiguous statement which is subsequently resolved. Here are two of the jokes used in the study in their original forms:

"Call me a cab."
"You're a cab."

"Waiter, what's this?"
"That's bean soup, ma'am."
"I'm not interested in what it's been,
I'm asking what it is now."
(Schultz & Horibe, 1974, p. 14)

In the second form of the joke, labelled "resolution removed," an incongruity or ambiguity remains, but it is of a nonsensical kind for which there is no obvious explanation. To illustrate, the resolution-removed forms of the two jokes given above are:

"Call a cab for me."
"You're a cab."

"Waiter, what's this?"
"That's tomato soup, ma'am."
"I'm not interested in what it's been,
I'm asking what it is now."

The third form contained no incongruities:

"Call me a cab."
"Yes, ma'am."

"Waiter, what's this?"
"That's bean soup, ma'am."
"That's what I thought, but I wasn't sure."

Each subject heard the recorded jokes and had a typed version of each one. Appreciation and comprehension of the jokes were assessed by the experimenter's rating of each child's reactions (no reaction, smile, or laugh) and by the child's rating of the "funniness" of each joke on a five-point scale. Then the experimenter asked the child to explain what, if anything, was funny about the joke.

Six-year-olds' overt reactions and ratings of the jokes showed that they found the original form and the "resolution removed" form—which still contained an incongruity, although of a nonsensical type—equally funny. They appreciated both of these forms more than the "jokes" in which there were no incongruities. In other words, for them, stories with incongruities are funnier than stories without incongruities; but they do not yet appreciate the humor of the resolution—that is, the original form. However, eight- to twelve-year-olds found the original jokes funnier than the second, "resolution-removed" form; and the latter were regarded as funnier than the forms without incongruities. Apparently, "children can appreciate pure incongruity (or nonsense) before they are able to resolve or explain this incongruity. The finding is perhaps related to the more general principle that much of cognitive development proceeds by the child's first noticing an incongruity (an initial nonsense) and then resolving it by moving to a more advanced level of thinking (resolution)" (Ginsburg & Koslowski, 1976, p. 43).

The findings of this study suggest that the transition between the stage of appreciating pure incongruity and the stage of comprehending resolvable incongruity in humor occurs between the ages of six and eight—that is, just at the onset of the period of concrete operational thought (Shultz & Horibe, 1974).

pp. 279–80). Kohlberg devised a series of stories that present moral dilemmas and asked subjects to react to these. Here is an example.

In Europe, a woman was near death from a special kind of cancer. There was one drug that the doctors thought might save her. It was a form of radium that a druggist in the same town had recently discovered. The drug was expensive *to make, but the druggist was charging ten times what the drug cost him to make. He paid $200 for the radium and charged $2,000 for a small dose of the drug. The sick woman's husband, Heinz, went to everyone he knew to borrow the money, but he could only get together about $1,000 which is half of what it cost. He told the druggist that his wife was dying and asked him to sell it cheaper or let him pay later. But the druggist said: "No, I discovered the drug and I'm going to make money from it." So Heinz got desperate and broke into the man's store to steal the drug for his wife. Should the husband have done that?*

It is not the content of the subject's reponses but the thinking and reasoning underlying the responses that is evaluated. Careful analysis indicates that there are six developmental stages of moral judgments, grouped into three broad levels, each containing two stages. At the *preconventional level,* the child is guided by an orientation toward obedience and punishment (Stage 1) or simply selfish satisfaction of needs (Stage 2). At the second level, the morality of *conventional order,* judgments are based on the approval of others—what Kohlberg called "good boy" or "good girl" morality (Stage 3) or reliance on authority and doing one's duty (Stage 4). At the highest level, *principled morality,* conformity to shared standards of rights or duties is the basis of moral judgments. Thus, in Stage 5, morality is viewed in terms of laws that are arrived at and generally accepted. There is an acceptance of a social contract between the individual and his or her group, and the individual is therefore obliged to comply with the rule or law. In Stage 6, the highest stage, the individual's judgments are regulated by his or her own conscience and ethical principles, which are applied universally. Spotlight 10-3 describes the levels and stages briefly and gives examples of responses to the above story that illustrate each stage.

The *sequence* of development through these stages appears to be universal and invariant, although there are individual and cultural differences in the ages at which the stages are attained. In most cultures studied, ten-year-olds typically give Stage 1 moral judgments; Stage 2 responses are the next most frequent. At age thirteen, the "good-boy," "good-girl" Stage 3 responses predominate. Stage 4 responses are the ones most commonly given by sixteen-year-olds, although a large percentage of adolescents give Stage 5 responses. Very few subjects give Stage 6 responses.

The development of conceptions of justice and the functions of laws and the legal system parallels the trends in moral development (Tapp, 1976; Tapp & Kohlberg, 1971). In one intensive interview study, children in the United States and six other countries were asked questions such as—"What is the law?" "What if there were no rules?" "Are there times when it might be right to break a rule?" (Tapp & Kohlberg, 1971). The responses of children in kindergarten through second grade indicated that they were at the preconventional level: they were oriented toward obedience, deference to authority, and avoidance of punishment. These children "neither conceptualized a generalized legal system or underlying moral order, nor recognized a difference between legality and morality. They accepted rules or laws as fixed and immutable acts made and enforced by authority to restrain 'bad' behaviors and prevent physical harm. As such, they demand obedience" (Tapp & Kohlberg, 1971, p. 84).

Children between the ages of nine and fourteen were predominantly at the

Levels and Stages　　　　　　　　　　　　　　**Responses to Story of Heinz Stealing the Drug**

Level I　*Moral value resides in external happenings, in bad acts, or in needs rather than in persons and standards*

Stage 1　Obedience and punishment orientation. Egocentric deference to superior power or prestige, or a trouble-avoiding set.

It isn't really bad to take it—he did ask to pay for it first. He wouldn't do any other damage or take anything else, and the drug he'd take is only worth $200; he's not really taking a $2,000 drug.

Stage 2　Naïvely egoistic orientation. Right action instrumentally satisfies the self's needs and occasionally the other's. Orientation to exchange and reciprocity.

Heinz isn't really doing any harm to the druggist, and he can always pay him back. If he doesn't want to lose his wife, he should take the drug because it's the only thing that will work.

Level II　*Moral value resides in performing good or right roles, in maintaining the conventional order*

Stage 3　Good-boy orientation. Orientation to approval and to pleasing and helping others. Conformity to stereotyped images of natural role behavior, and judgment by intentions.

Stealing is bad, but this is a bad situation. Heinz isn't doing wrong in trying to save his wife; he has no choice but to take the drug. He is only doing something that is natural for a good husband to do. You can't blame him for doing something out of love for his wife. You'd blame him if he didn't love his wife enough to save her.

Stage 4　Orientation toward authority and maintaining social order. Orientation to ''doing duty'' and to showing respect for authority.

The druggist is leading a wrong kind of life if he just lets somebody die. You can't let somebody die like that, so it's Heinz's duty to save her. But Heinz can't just go around breaking laws and let it go at that—he must pay the druggist back and he must take his punishment for stealing.

Level III　*Moral value resides in conformity by the self to shared or sharable standards, rights, or duties*

Stage 5　Contractual legalistic orientation. Recognition of an arbitrary element in rules or expectations. Duty defined in terms of contract, general avoidance of violation of the will or rights and welfare of others.

Before you say stealing is wrong, you've got to really think about this whole situation. Of course, the laws are quite clear about breaking into a store. And, even worse, Heinz would know there were no legal grounds for his actions. Yet, I can see why it would be reasonable for anybody in this kind of situation to steal the drug.

Stage 6　Conscience or principled orientation. Orientation to principles of choice, involving appeal to logical universality and consistency, to conscience as a directing agent, and to mutual respect and trust.

Where the choice must be made between disobeying a law and saving a human life, the higher principle of preserving life makes it morally right—not just understandable—to steal the drug.

Adapted from L. Kohlberg. ''Moral and Religious Education and the Public Schools: A Developmental View,'' in T. Sizer (ed.), *Religion and Public Education*. Boston: Houghton Mifflin, 1967; and J. Rest. ''Level of Moral Development as a Determinant of Preference and Comprehension of Moral Judgments Made by Others,'' Symposium: Recent Research in Moral Development. Society for Research in Child Development, March 1969, Santa Monica, Calif.

conventional level characterized by a "rule-maintaining perspective"—a prevalent concern with law and order. The child at this level respects rules and laws as guides for "good" behavior that prevent social disorganization and chaos. While rules or laws may be changed or broken under extreme circumstances or in emergencies, obeying the law is said to be of critical importance in maintaining the social order and moral values.

At the post-conventional or *principled* level, achieved by many college students, an orientation to principles of morality and justice prevails. At this level, rules and laws are perceived as norms or standards that are generally accepted in order to maximize personal and social welfare. Noncompliance with the law should be based on rational considerations and universal principles of justice. "This perspective offered a coherent, responsive guide to social change and the creation of new norms: Those that served no purpose or were unjust should be changed; those that violated fundamental individual rights and universal moral principles could be legitimately broken" (Tapp & Kohlberg, 1971, p. 85).

In summary, then, moral judgments and conceptions of the law, like other cognitive functions, evolve in a regular, predictable order. Although the processes underlying transition from one moral stage to the next have not been adequately investigated and consequently are not fully understood, Kohlberg maintains that the stages "emerge from the interaction of the child with his social environment rather than directly reflecting external structures given by the child's culture. . . . While these . . . spring from the child's awareness of the external social world, they also represent active processes of organizing or ordering this world" (Kohlberg, 1969, p. 386).

Turiel has hypothesized that "increased conflict or disequilibrium is a condition for [moral] development" (Turiel, 1974, p. 15). That is, certain experiences may make people aware that their present ways of thinking about moral issues involve inconsistencies or contradictions and are therefore inadequate. For example, contact with others from different backgrounds may convince an adolescent oriented toward showing respect for authority and the social order (Stage 4) that other cultures have perfectly legitimate standards, rules, and laws—standards that are quite different from those of his or her own society. This may create a state of *disequilibrium*—manifested in conflict and confusion—and a period of self-questioning and re-evaluation of present ways of thinking may ensue. Feedback from self-appraisal may lead to a new mode of thinking that "is a more adequate way of understanding moral problems and resolving the conflicts encountered" (Turiel, 1974, p. 15). "Every transition involves a modification of the preceding state [which] is integrated, in transformed fashion, into the next stage" (p. 17).

Is language learned?

It would be difficult to overestimate the importance of language in cognitive development. The child's intellectual abilities take great strides forward as language is acquired. Abstraction, concept formation, thinking, planning, reasoning, remembering, judging and solving problems—all are greatly facilitated by the use of language. (A fuller discussion of the relationship between language and cognition appears in Chapter 13). In addition, a major part of a child's learning—at home, in the neighborhood, in the schools, and from the mass media—depends on language, as does practically all social communication.

The process of language acquisition is not yet fully understood, although there has been considerable research progress recently. Environmental conditions and learning have strong impacts—babies can only learn to speak a language that they hear around them. But biological and maturational factors also loom large. The neurological basis of speech for most people is in the left side of the cortex of the brain, and injury or disease to this area can result in language deficiencies. (*See also* p. 576–77 Chapter 21.) A number of interesting facts attest to the critical role of maturation in language development. For example, totally deaf babies who hear no sounds utter the same elementary speech sounds (phonemes) at about the same time as children who hear normally. Babies are not taught to coo and babble (repeat the same sound over again like "ma-ma-ma"). They do so from about the third month until about the end of the first year, apparently for their own amusement. Imitation of adult speech does not generally begin until after approximately nine months; but, even then, new sounds are not learned by imitation. The baby imitates only those sounds he or she has already uttered spontaneously.

The development of real language—understanding and using words in sentences—obviously depends on environmental input (the child must hear the language) and learning. Yet most psycholinguists (psychologists who investigate the psychological aspects of language and its development) are convinced that the laws of learning by reinforcement and observation of others cannot fully explain the amazingly rapid development of the child's comprehension and use of language. Their arguments are based on several facts that will be clarified in the following discussion. One is the fact that even babies generate (invent) *new* and reasonably well-constructed sentences (or phrases that serve as sentences)—sentences they have not heard previously and could not have learned by imitation. In addition, young children three

Although young children cannot state the complex grammatical principles that govern speech, by about four years old they can apply them with considerable skill.

or four years old speak in ways that reveal a "knowledge" or understanding of complex grammatical rules that have not been directly taught or learned.

At about ten months of age, the average baby will respond to simple commands; and he or she will speak a first word — generally a single or duplicated syllable (for example, ma-ma) — sometime around the end of the first year. At this age, a single "word" may function as a whole sentence; "ma-ma" may mean "where is mamma" or "I want mamma."

At approximately 18 months, babies begin putting two words together in simple sentences such as "see doggie," "mamma walk," "allgone candy," and "Bobbie eat." The child *generates* (creates) these two-word sequences; he or she has not heard the exact sentences before. Yet even these early sentences express basic grammatical relations such as those among the subject of the sentence, the predicate, and/or the object of the verb.

As the baby's vocabulary grows, longer sentences are spoken, which use primarily nouns, verbs, and a few adjectives. The speech of children between the ages of two and three is "telegraphic"; small words such as prepositions, conjunctions, articles, and auxiliary verbs are left out. This telegraphic quality is seen in both imitative and spontaneous speech. If you tell a two- or three-year-old to say "We are now going to drink some milk," he or she is likely to respond "Drink milk" or "We drink milk." The child preserves the word order of the model and clearly regards the sentence as "some kind of construction and not simply as a list of words" (Brown, 1973).

The rules of grammar are almost completely acquired by children by about four years of age — an enormous intellectual achievement. Word order is generally correct, plurals are formed properly, and past, present, and future tenses are expressed accurately. Of course, the child may make some errors, but even these show comprehension of the basic rules of grammar. For example, a nursery-school girl may tell her mother that "the teacher *bringed* some white *mouses* to school today." The words "bringed" and "mouses" are not correct forms, so we can be sure that she is not imitating adult speech. But, in using these words and in constructing the sentence, the child shows that she knows the rules of sentence construction and of forming the past tense and plural. She has simply overgeneralized the rules, treating irregular words as though they were regular (Brown, 1965; Chomsky, 1967).

Children do not, of course, have explicit knowledge of grammatical rules and cannot state them; but they do extract — and then apply — construction rules, many of them abstract, from the speech they hear all around them. This system of rules makes it possible to speak, understand, and invent an infinite variety of sentences.

Until recently, psycholinguists paid less attention to the meaning (semantics) than to the grammar and syntax of the young child's speech, but this situation is changing. Clearly, a child's two-word phrase has different meanings in different contexts. For example, "Mamma milk" may mean "mamma is getting some milk for me" or "mamma is drinking milk." Semantic development appears to be closely linked with general cognitive development; the children's earliest two-word constructions reflect their sensorimotor cognitive level — that is, their motor activities and immediate perceptions. For example, many of a baby's simple utterances name or label objects immediately present

Typical meanings expressed in two-word utterances of children in many cultures (Slobin, 1972).

Identification:	*See doggie*
Location:	*Book there*
Repetition:	*More milk*
Nonexistence:	*Allgone thing*
Negation:	*Not wolf*
Possession:	*My candy*
Attribution:	*Big car*
Agent-Action:	*Mama walk*
Action-Object:	*Hit you*
Agent-Object:	*Mama book*
Action-Location:	*Sit chair*
Action-Recipient:	*Give papa*
Action-Instrument:	*Cut knife*
Question:	*Where ball?*

("that ball"), describe them ("red hat"), note presence or absence ("allgone doggie"), or indicate an action ("baby eat").

A foremost psycholinguist, Dan Slobin, has studied the earliest utterances of children speaking a wide variety of languages, including English, German, Russian, Finnish, Turkish, and Samoan. He found "a striking uniformity across children and across languages in the kinds of meanings expressed in two-word utterances" (Slobin, 1972, p. 199). In fact, all these simple utterances could be classified semantically into fourteen basic relationships or propositions, which are listed in Spotlight 10-4. As Slobin notes, "the universality of the list is impressive" (p. 199).

SUMMARY

Early growth and development are to a large extent regulated by biological, maturational forces. The newborn's sensory system functions well, and many of his needs, motor abilities, and even some very complex perceptual abilities—such as depth perception and the perception of objects as solid and graspable—are biologically programmed or "prewired" into the organism. Reflexes present at birth or very shortly afterward gratify many needs in self-regulatory ways, helping the infant to adjust and survive. Sensory and motor abilities improve very rapidly—and in fixed, invariant sequences or stages—during the first few months.

From the very earliest days, infants are capable of learning and conditioning. Three-day-olds can be conditioned to turn their heads in the direction of the sound of a bell. By eight weeks of age, they can learn to move their heads in response to the reinforcement of an interesting visual "show" under their own control. By twelve weeks, they will smile and vocalize more frequently if they are rewarded for making these responses.

As Piaget has demonstrated, children's thinking is active and creative from the beginning. According to his theory, intellectual ability develops in a sequence of four major periods. In the first, or **sensorimotor, period** (the first eighteen months, approximately), the baby perceives and performs motor actions, but operates without symbolic language. In the **preoperational period**—approximately two to seven years—symbols, images, and words are used, but thought is superficial, primitive, and egocentric. The child's thought in the **stage of concrete operations** is much more flexible and involves some logical operations—ordering things, classifying objects, and understanding the relationships between classes and subclasses. The final stage, **formal operational** (from approximately age 12 through adulthood), is characterized by abstract thought, reasoning by hypothesis, and consideration of all possible outcomes in solving problems. Adolescents "think about thinking" and evaluate their own thought processes.

Moral judgments—the cognitive aspects of morality—also progress through a universal and invariant series of stages. Maturation plays a critical role in language development, which proceeds extremely rapidly in the early years. The laws of learning by reinforcement or imitation hardly seem adequate to explain the amazingly rapid development of the child's comprehension and use of language, particularly the ability to generate new sentences and to understand complex grammatical constructions. Semantic (meaning) development is closely linked to general cognitive development. In fact, children in all cultures express the same meanings in their earliest sentences.

11

The Development of Personality and Social Behavior

What is the content of socialization?
How does socialization proceed in the second year?
What effects do parental practices have on the nursery-school child's personality?
What influence do peers have on personality development?
Does personality development continue throughout life?
Is there stability in personality?

A child's personal and social characteristics are to a very large extent molded by social experiences, although biological and cognitive factors are also influential. Comparisons of identical and fraternal twins indicate that some traits are, at least in part, genetically determined. Among these are inhibition and introversion (and their opposites), tendencies to smile at or to show fear of strangers, aggressiveness, moodiness, dependency, and shyness. From the earliest days, such temperamental characteristics—shaped by genetic and constitutional factors—may influence how the child reacts to the environment and how parents treat the child. Active, responsive infants generally expose themselves to a greater variety of learning experiences than quiet, passive children. Some parents respond best to energetic, attentive infants, giving them a great deal of love and attention, while others prefer children who are quiet and placid (Thomas *et al.*, 1963).

What is the content of socialization?

Socialization, a concept of central importance in this discussion, refers to the acquisition of personality attributes, motives, values, attitudes, opinions, and patterns of social behavior as consequences of social experiences. Included in the broad range of significant social experience are (1) cultural pressures to develop certain types of behavior and characteristics; (2) interactions within the family, particularly with parents; (3) training in school, imitation of peers, and religious teaching; (4) communication through the mass media; and (5) major social events such as war, depression, and social unrest. The **agents of socialization** are the people and institutions participating in the socialization process—parents, teachers, neighbors, ministers, friends, "culture heroes," and characters in fiction, movies, and on television. Socialization is a lifelong process. After childhood, we are socialized for age roles—for example, "young adult" and later "mature adult"—as well as for occupational and family roles such as "mother," "uncle," "doctor," "mechanic," and "teacher."

To make the concept of socialization more concrete, think about the people and events that have shaped your own development and contributed to making you who you are today. What are the lasting outcomes of growing up as a member of your own particular social class and/or ethnic group? How would you characterize your early interactions with your parents? Were your parents warm, supportive, permissive; were they strict or authoritarian? What effects did their treatment have on your behavior? Your brothers and sisters, friends, teachers you liked or disliked, people you read about—how have they influenced you?

CULTURAL FACTORS

Children live and develop within society, growing up in the company of an interacting group of people. Every society or culture has its own distinctive ways of thinking and behaving, its own norms and standards regarding how children should be raised, and its own definitions of acceptable or desirable behavior. There are innumerable cultural variations in personality traits, motives, attitudes, and values. Yet somehow each culture manages to train its children to adopt behavior that is approved or expected in *that* culture. The traits, motives, and values acquired by a Mexican-Indian peasant girl are appropriate for her way of life, but they are vastly different from those of a middle-class American girl. As a result of the way she is brought up, the Mexican girl is likely to be less competitive, less interested in personal achievement, less influenced by her peers, more sharing and more cooperative than her American counterpart. Even as a young child, she participates more than the

American girl in the work of her community, helping with the household tasks, shopping, and taking care of younger brothers and sisters.

Within pluralistic societies each of the many socioeconomic and ethnic groups impresses upon its members its own definitions of appropriate behavior and values. Compared with middle-class children, children of the lower classes are generally more aggressive and more expressive sexually. They may be less concerned with achievement and educational accomplishments and relatively lower in self-esteem and self-assurance.

Most of what we know about socialization and the development of personality and social behavior comes from studies of different types of parent-child relationships and their effects on children. Investigations of this sort are of both theoretical and practical importance. They serve to test hypotheses—derived from theory—about the roles of social and environmental influences in shaping personality. At the same time, the systematic findings may be useful in guiding parents; they may help them to promote in their children such positive characteristics as good emotional adjustment, independence, and competence and to prevent the development of maladaptive behavior and attitudes.

There are, of course, innumerable dimensions of parent-child relationships and children's personality and social traits that could be studied. The investigator must select only one or a few to focus on, and the researcher's decision will depend on many factors. Among the most important are his or her own theoretical orientation and the age or developmental status of the children involved. For example, an investigator who is psychoanalytically oriented might be concerned with the effects of early maternal attachment or of feeding practices on infants' present and future adjustments. A social-learning theorist, on the other hand (see pp. 177–78), is more likely to center attention on global

This Mexican-Indian girl assumes her family and community responsibilities as a matter of course. Her counterparts in the United States and Canada are subject to quite a different set of cultural expectations.

familial variables such as democracy in the home, parental control, and how parental standards relate to the personality development and social behavior of preschool children. The differences will be seen clearly in the following sections, which sample a number of important studies of socialization in children of different ages, derived from various theoretical perspectives.

Attachment and Dependency

Almost all infants in all cultures show attachment to—and dependence on—the caretaking parent, usually the mother. They seek to be close to their mothers (or others who fill the "mother role") and seem most comfortable when they are. At a very early age, the infant clearly differentiates between mother and other people; he or she turns toward her, smiles and vocalizes at her, seeks her out and follows her, tries to make physical contact, clings to her, and embraces her. **Separation anxiety,** the child's marked distress when the mother leaves, and fear of strangers, a temporary reaction related to the child's disappointment at seeing a stranger when the mother was expected, are also signs of attachment and dependency.

Social-learning theorists view attachment and dependency as learned or conditioned responses, the result of repeated associations between the mother's presence and gratifications such as food, warmth, and security. For the infant, the mother's presence signifies satisfaction, pleasure, comfort, and contentment. Consequently, the baby seeks her out, approaches her, and stays close to her.

ANIMAL STUDIES OF ATTACHMENT   Other theorists consider attachment and dependency to be instinctual rather than learned. In a classic series of studies, Professor Harry Harlow and his colleagues at the University of Wisconsin placed infant monkeys in cages with "mothers" constructed of wire mesh (Harlow & Zimmerman, 1959; Harlow & Harlow, 1966). Some of the infants were nursed from a bottle attached to the chest of a wire-mesh "mother"; others were fed from a bottle attached to a "mother" who was covered with terry cloth, which is easy to cling to. When both "mothers" were accessible

The infant monkey prefers the terry-cloth "mother," even though it nurses from the wire "mother."

and the infant monkeys were free to go to either one, most of them—including those fed by the wire-mesh mothers—ran to the terry-cloth mother spontaneously and clung, especially when frightened. Perhaps this means that the clinging response—a component of attachment—is instinctive rather than a product of association and learning.

What happens to infant monkeys who are deprived of opportunities to form attachments to mothers? Harlow and his colleagues (Suomi & Harlow, 1971) reared some experimental animals from birth in total isolation. They lived in stainless steel chambers; food and drink were supplied by remote controls, and they saw no living creatures. The length of the periods of isolation was varied in different experimental groups. After they were taken out of isolation, the animals were extensively observed in interactions with others and in experimental settings. If the isolation lasted only three months, there was no lasting damage to social behavior. But six months of isolation had dramatic effects. Monkeys isolated for this period showed a great deal of agitation, withdrawal, and strange patterns of behavior—for example, rocking, huddling, and biting themselves. Those who experienced a full year of social isolation became "little more than semi-animated vegetables" (Suomi & Harlow, 1971, p. 507). They were fearful, withdrawn and inactive, indulging in very little play or exploration. Years later, the isolated animals—especially those isolated for a full year—were still more fearful and less playful than monkeys reared with mothers and peers, and they proved to be sexually inadequate.

Another fascinating study shows that the damaging effects of six months of isolation could be overcome by "therapy" (Suomi & Harlow, 1971). Monkeys who had served a six-months isolation period and showed little exploration and considerable abnormal behavior (the patients) spent two hours a day in contact with "therapists"—young, immature, female monkeys who would not attack them. Gradually the "patients" began to approach the youngsters and to interact with them; after six months of therapy, they had recovered completely—even their sexual behavior was normal. Clearly, some abnormal patterns of behavior, even though established very early, can be modified by treatment.

ATTACHMENT IN HUMANS   Among humans, clear indications of attachment to the mother generally emerge by the middle of the first year, at six, seven, or eight months of age; they become more intense during the next three or four months (Ainsworth, 1967; Schaffer & Emerson, 1964). The upper limit of the *sensitive period* for developing attachment appears to be eighteen to twenty-four months. If infants do not have adequate opportunity to become attached to a single figure by this time—if, for example, they are reared in overcrowded orphanages—they are not likely to form strong attachments later in life.

Variations in the intensity of attachments are largely attributable to the infants' experiences in their interactions with their mothers or caretakers. A baby will become strongly and securely attached to a mother if the mother devotes a good deal of time to the baby and if "she is accessible enough to receive the [baby's] signals, if . . . she can interpret them accurately, and if her response to them is prompt and appropriate . . ." (Ainsworth, 1973, p. 49). Mothers who are less attentive and responsive, less sensitive to their infants'

"The repeated experience of being hungry, seeking food, and feeling relieved and comforted assures the baby that the world is a dependable place." (Erikson)

needs, who give only routine, impersonal care, evoke only weak attachments from their infants (Schaffer & Emerson, 1964).

The most systematic studies of attachment behavior have been conducted by Mary Ainsworth, who observed babies of approximately one year old in a controlled "strange situation" (Ainsworth, Bell, & Stayton, 1971). Mother and baby were first observed in a room in which there was an array of attractive toys. In this situation, the baby who is securely attached to the mother regarded her as a secure base. The baby explored the environment without anxiety, but looked back or returned to the mother from time to time. After three minutes, a stranger entered and approached the baby; then the mother left, leaving the baby with the stranger; then the mother returned, and the stranger departed. Particular attention was given to the episodes of mother-child reunion. Among children securely attached to their mothers, attachment behavior increased after separation; when the mother returned, the infants made particularly strong attempts to be near her and to contact her. Less securely attached babies showed different reactions to the mother's return. Some avoided or ignored her. Other infants seemed in conflict, showing tendencies both to approach and to get away from her by crawling, turning, or looking away. Another group of babies showed heightened attachment at the reunion, but they also showed anger; infant-mother interactions were clearly ambivalent.

At home, the mothers of the securely attached group were generally sensitive, accepting, cooperative, and accessible in their interactions with their babies. In contrast, the mothers of the proximity-avoiding babies were ordinarily rejecting and insensitive. They disliked physical contact and showed little facial expressiveness (Main, 1975). Some of them were also inaccessible, and others frequently interfered with their babies' activities (Ainsworth et al., 1972).

The quality of early attachment and the mother's reactions to her child's dependency are critical determinants of the child's future adjustment. Erik Erikson theorizes that the individual's basic sense of trust—and its opposite, mistrust—has its roots in these early mother-child interactions (see also p. 166). Secure and healthy attachment to the mother in infancy is "a prime source for the development of trust. . . . The repeated experience of being hungry, seeking food, receiving food and feeling relieved and comforted assures the baby that the world is a dependable place" (Erikson, 1953, p. 219). Trusting

Figure 11-1
Schematic Drawing of Mother, Stranger, and Child in the "Strange Situation"
The reactions of all three principals are videotaped. (*Drawing after schematic by Jolly Roberts, Institute of Child Development, University of Minnesota.*)

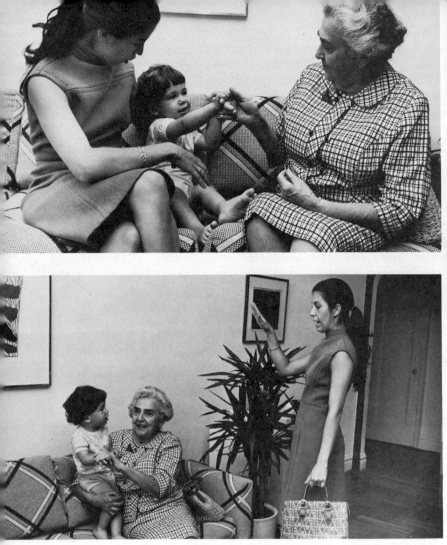

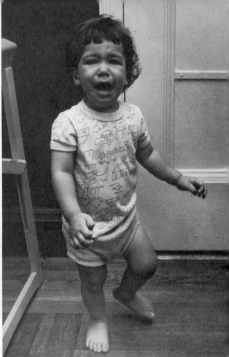

Normal Attachment Behavior

As long as Mother is there, the baby will play games with the stranger. He watches as Mother prepares to leave. Sure of his loss, he breaks into heartrending sobs. The stranger tries to comfort him without success. Mother returns, and there is a joyous reunion. Once more serene, he can even smile at the stranger.

the mother generalizes to a basic sense of trust of others. But if there is little nurturance from the mother, the infant does not form secure attachments to her and begins to mistrust her. Mistrust may generalize to others, laying the groundwork for subsequent difficulties in social relationships.

There is considerable empirical support for Erikson's hypotheses. There are indeed some striking adverse, enduring effects of failure to establish secure attachments in the first year. Much of the evidence stems from research on infants and young children reared in emotionally cold environments, such as orphanages and other institutions where they have little opportunity to form secure attachments to a mother figure.

One relevant study compared two groups of orphans with markedly different early experiences. Those in one group were adopted in early infancy by foster parents who stimulated them and gave them individualized, loving, nurturant care; these children formed healthy attachments to their parents. The orphans

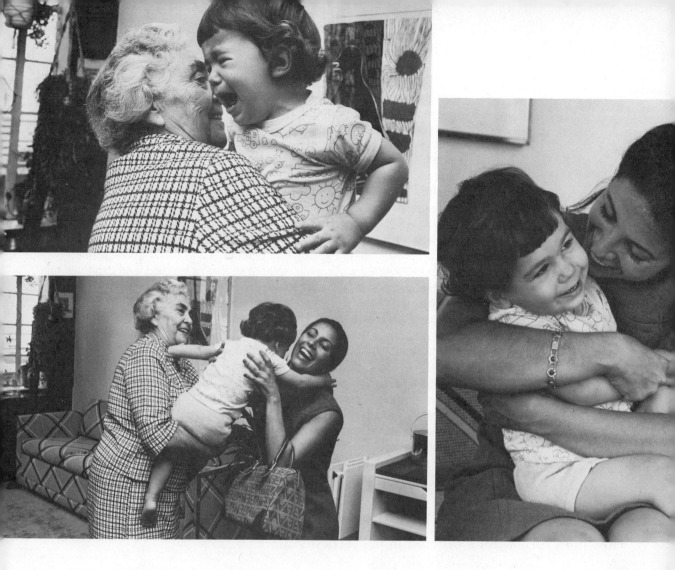

in the other group lived in an unstimulating institution for their first three years. They were handled impersonally, without sensitive mothering and, thus, they failed to become attached to any adult during the sensitive period. Most of the children in the second group were later adopted. In later childhood and adolescence, those who had been reared in foster homes and had been strongly attached to foster parents were intellectually superior and better adjusted socially and emotionally than those who spent their first three years in an orphanage (Goldfarb, 1943). The children who had been adopted as infants performed better on all intelligence tests—especially those involving concept formation, reasoning, and abstract thinking. They were more mature, independent, and self-controlled, less aggressive and distractible. In contrast, the institution-reared children were aloof, emotionally detached, unresponsive, dependent on adults, easily angered, and demanding of attention.

These adverse consequences of prolonged and severe maternal deprivation during infancy may be avoided if unsatisfactory conditions last for less than a year or 18 months—that is, if they do not extend beyond the sensitive period for the development of attachment. An infant who is adopted from an institution at the age of 13 months may become securely attached to the foster mother and develop normally and happily.

Secure early attachments may have enduring beneficial results while early mother-avoidance may be associated with later maladjustment. Using the "strange situation" described above, Main (1973) was able to classify one-year-old subjects as (1) *securely attached* to their mothers, (2) *lacking secure attachments,* or (3) *mother-avoiding* (looking or turning away from the mother). Nine months later, when the children were twenty-one months old, the same babies were given an infant test and were observed with an adult playmate who was a stranger to them. The babies who were mother-avoiding at twelve months old behaved in ways indicative of emotional and social maladjustment. They tended to avoid the playmate, seldom smiled or laughed, and exhibited many strange behaviors (inexplicable fears, inappropriate laughter and repetitive movements). Moreover, they frequently behaved aggressively—for example, hitting and banging toys. In contrast, babies who were securely attached to their mothers at twelve months seemed happy and well-adjusted; they reacted positively to the adult playmate, approaching her readily and playing with her. They were also more advanced than the insecure or mother-avoiding babies in cognitive performance. They had larger vocabularies, spoke more, and used more different words.

These studies of attachment have many significant implications for the various practitioners who work with children and mothers—pediatric nurses, family counselors, the staffs of day-care centers and orphanages. Ainsworth (1973) has pointed out some of them, and they are summarized in Spotlight 11–1.

How does socialization proceed in the second year?

During the second year, as we have seen, children make enormous gains in cognitive functions—thinking and problem solving—and in language learning. At the same time, their motor skills improve, expand, and become more refined; they can exercise greater and more precise control over muscles. Except for those who are anxious and insecure, children in the second year seem eager to test out these new skills and abilities. They explore the territory, investigating objects and events, walking, running, climbing, jumping, carrying, picking things up, and throwing things down. The quest for *autonomy*—independence and self-reliance—seems to be dominant.

At the same time, children begin to encounter some pressures from their parents to accept the demands of reality and to learn that there are definite limitations on freedom. Toilet-training is generally begun, and may be completed, during this period. And the child must learn that some objects—such as expensive lamps and dangerous tools—must be avoided; some activities are prohibited, even though the child feels capable of performing them.

Spotlight 11-1　Ten Conclusions about Attachment

On the basis of theories and research on attachment, Professor Mary Ainsworth has drawn a number of conclusions for practitioners working with children and mothers:

1. *Interaction with a mother figure, with resulting attachment, is essential for healthy development.* It has been demonstrated beyond doubt that infants reared under conditions in which they have insufficient opportunity to interact with a mother figure (i.e., are maternally deprived) may show anomalies of development. It is both difficult and expensive to provide adequate interpersonal interaction in a "motherless" environment, . . . [or] to arrange enough individual care and continuity for an infant to be able to establish the basic infant-mother attachment that is one of the foundation stones of healthy social development.

2. *Although there is a "sensitive period" for the development of infant-mother attachment, under appropriate conditions an attachment may develop beyond this phase.* So strong is an infant's bias to become attached to a specific mother figure, however, that attachments may be formed when opportunity is finally provided for a one-to-one relationship, even though this opportunity may be delayed beyond the usual "sensitive phase"—a finding attested by studies of adoptions which take place when the infant is a year old or somewhat older. If, on the other hand, adoption or fostering is delayed so long that the child cannot become attached to his foster parents, anomalies of social development are a conspicuous outcome. . . . It is not enough to provide food, warmth, and protection to infants reared apart from their parents; they should also be given plenty of stimulation, including kinesthetic modalities stimulated in physical contact.

3. *There is at present no known substitute for a family environment for child-rearing.* Although the basic requirements for child development during the first few weeks and months of life may be met in an institutional environment, no institution can provide a further requirement—the opportunity for enough continuity of interaction with one or a few specific figures for the infant to become attached. Therefore, at this time no acceptable substitute for family-based child-rearing can be specified. . . .

4. *Major, prolonged maternal separations cause distress to the child.* There is no reason to doubt that, once an infant-mother attachment has been formed, separation causes distress and tends to set in train processes which, if not arrested, can lead to pathological outcomes. . . . "Major" separations are clearly to be avoided, especially during the age range of about six months to about three years. Optional hospitalizations should be avoided during this period. If hospitalization of the child is unavoidable, every effort should be made for the mother to stay with the child, or if this is not feasible, to spend extended periods of time with the child in the hospital. . . .

5. *Upon reunion after a major separation, attachment behavior is likely to be heightened.* If, . . . a child within the vulnerable age has suffered a separation, the parents' behavior in the reunion period may either exacerbate or reduce the adverse behavioral effects attributable to the separation. If the child displays heightened attachment behavior (as is very likely), parental compliance will tend to reduce its duration and intensity, whereas resistance to it, perhaps for fear that this may "spoil" the child, will tend to prolong it. If, on the other hand, the child has been separated long enough for detachment processes to have become truly consolidated, the optimum parental behavior is to offer contact and intimacy, patiently and despite rebuff, over long periods in the hope that the child may gradually be able to regain confidence and lower his defenses. . . .

6. *Minor, everyday separations may also produce effects.* Not only are these very difficult to avoid, but very few mothers in our society are willing to keep their babies constantly close to them as, in all likelihood, mothers did in the dawn of the human species. Many infants reared in our present-day society adapt well to minor everyday separations. Such an infant becomes used to his mother's going in and out of the room. . . . Most young children can adapt to being left with baby-sitters for a few hours now and then. Although initial separation distress is common, children three years old or older usually adjust to half-day nursery school.

7. *Exploratory behavior is dependent upon a secure infant-mother attachment.* . . . If the attachment relationship is reasonably secure, the baby can leave his mother for increasingly long periods to explore his environment, to acquaint himself with the physical objects in it, to manipulate these and to learn their properties, and thus gradually to develop both his general cognitive capacities

and specific ways of dealing with the specificities of his environment. It is not only the physical world which the mother's presence makes it safe to explore, but also the social world of other adults and other children. . . . When the mother is present, the relatively strange may be interesting and explorable; when she is absent, it may be merely frightening. When his mother is present a baby may not only tolerate the presence of strangers but also interact with them and learn something about them and extend his range of knowledge of people. But when his mother is absent, an infant or young child may be afraid of the strange or of strangers and inhibited in any explorations of the strange that might eventually make it familiar. . . .

8. *Attachments are formed to more than one person.* It is usual for an infant to form more than one attachment even in the first year of life. Although it is possible that two attachment relationships may be equivalent in significance, it is probably more usual for one to be primary and the other secondary to it, not only in sequence of development but in significance. In any event, it seems certain that too many potential attachment figures may militate against the formation of any attachment to any one. . . .

9. *Fostering attachment behavior does not spoil a child.* . . . Crying is a behavior that promotes proximity and contact, but the outcome depends on the response of the adult to it. . . . A baby cries because he is uncomfortable, hungry, in pain, or alone and out of contact.

It is only toward the end of the first year that he begins to use crying as a mode of communication intended to influence the behavior of others. Although there is little doubt that some young children may have learned to control other people through crying, babies during the first year tend to cry expressively when something is "wrong." Maternal interventions that result in terminating an infant's crying during the early part of the first year have been found to be associated with minimal crying in the latter part, whereas failure to intervene appropriately is associated with a relatively large incidence of crying later. Similarly, it does not spoil a baby to pick him up. Physical contact in response to crying is both the most frequent and the most effective intervention, and seems likely to be provided for in the basic ground plan of both infant and maternal behavior. . . . To give a tiny baby much contact, particularly tender and affectionate holding, does not make him into a clinging and overdependent child. On the contrary, contact given when and for as long as an infant seems to wish it results . . . in his being content to be put down and to move off independently to explore the world. . . .

10. *A highly desirable maternal trait is sensitivity to an infant's signals.* . . . Probably the fundamental ability underlying sensitivity is the ability to see things from the baby's point of view. . . . Perhaps the soundest pronouncement one could make as a guide to mothers is for them to gear their interventions to the infant's signals (Ainsworth, 1973, pp. 77–82).

Erikson regards this period as the second *critical period* of the child's life, following the establishment of trust. The central problem at this time, as he sees it, is

the child's sense of autonomy, the sense that he is an independent human being and yet one who is able to use the help and guidance of others in important matters. This stage of development becomes decisive for the ratio between love and hate, between cooperation and willfulness, for freedom of self-expression and its renunciation in the make-up of the individual. The favorable outcome is self-control without loss of self-esteem. The unfavorable outcome is doubt and shame (*Midcentury White House Conference, 1951, p. 222*).

PARENTAL REACTIONS
TO AUTONOMY

Some parents welcome and encourage the child's emerging striving for autonomy and increasing maturity, while others discourage attempts to be independent. Parental permissiveness or support of the child's exploratory "testing out" activities—or their restrictiveness—are critical dimensions of socialization at this period. To develop a sense of self-reliance and adequacy —the major components of autonomy—the child must, according to Erikson,

> experience over and over again that he is a person who is permitted to make choices. He has to have the right to choose, for example, whether to sit or whether to stand, whether to approach a visitor or to lean against his mother's knee, whether to accept offered food or whether to reject it, whether to use the toilet or to wet his pants. At the same time he must learn some of the boundaries of self-determination. He inevitably finds that there are walls he cannot climb, that there are objects out of reach, that, above all, there are innumerable commands enforced by powerful adults. (Midcentury White House Conference, 1951, p. 223).

Overprotective mothers are affectionate, warm, and nurturant when their babies are very young, but counter children's striving for independence and try to keep them dependent. By restricting exploration and experimentation, such mothers "infantilize" their children—"tying them to the mother's apron strings." Overprotected children who are dominated and strictly controlled by their mothers are likely to become submissive, shy, compliant, and inhibited, afraid to initiate activities or to act independently (Levy, 1943).

Fortunately, most parents are pleased about their child's developmental progress and growing independence. They reward initiative, exploration, experimentation, and attempts at mastery. Consequently, their children are

If children's explorative behavior is encouraged and rewarded, they will show initiative and a sense of adventure.

motivated to investigate new places and new things, to test out their skills, and to attempt to solve challenging problems.

Parental stimulation of such motives as curiosity, autonomy, independence, achievement, and mastery during the second year may also have long-lasting positive effects. In one study, nursery-school children were observed in interaction with their mothers and in spontaneous play at home and at school. Some of the mothers characteristically praised and rewarded their children when they acted independently, accomplished a goal, or tried out new activities. In free play, the children of these mothers showed a lively interest in mastery, achievement, and competence; they spent a great deal of time and energy in challenging activities such as painting, making clay models, and reading books. Children whose mothers did not encourage or reward independence and initiative were much less interested in these kinds of activities (Crandall, Preston, & Rabson, 1960).

Another investigation dealt with the backgrounds of two groups of boys between eight and ten years of age. One group scored high in a test of achievement motivation and were strongly oriented toward academic success. Interviews with their mothers indicated that the women had expected, and rewarded, their sons' early manifestations of initiative, self-reliance, and independence. This was not true of the mothers of boys who scored low in a test of achievement motivation and were unconcerned about academic success. Apparently early training and reward for independence are effective in stimulating strong motives for achievement that last at least until the elementary school years (Winterbottom, 1958). And, as we shall see, achievement motivation is a highly stable characteristic; those who are highly motivated during childhood are also likely to strive for achievement in adolescence and adulthood (see p. 286).

What effects do parental practices have on the nursery-school child's personality?

As a child advances intellectually, socially, and emotionally, his or her relationships with others become more extensive and intensive, more complex and subtle. Parental reactions to specific needs—such as hunger or striving for autonomy—probably have less impact on the child's development than general, global qualities of home atmosphere—warmth, nurturance, affectionateness, permissiveness (or restrictiveness), democracy (or authoritarian control), and firmness of discipline.

DEMOCRACY VERSUS CONTROL

In one study, conducted at the Fels Institute in Ohio, a home visitor observed a few hours of interaction between nursery-school children and their parents. She assessed many qualities of the home atmosphere—affectionateness, acceptance, control, and severity of punishment—using carefully defined scales. Many of these ratings were interrelated; that is, they formed clusters or constellations that measured some common features of parent-child relationships. Two of the most significant clusters—democracy and control—represented opposite kinds of childrearing practices. Democratic parents were

Interesting studies of peer influences and the effects of communal childrearing have been carried out among children of the kibbutzim of Israel.

characteristically permissive; they encouraged their children's curiosity and self-expression and frequently interacted with them verbally. Family rules were not arbitrary; instead, decisions were formulated on the basis of family discussions. At the other end of this scale were parents who rated high in control and were restrictive of the child's freedom. They formulated rules of behavior and disciplinary procedures unilaterally—and demanded obedience and conformity—without discussion with their children.

At school, both nursery-school teachers and trained observers rated the children on many dimensions such as aggression, dependency, creativity, competition, originality, and leadership (Baldwin, 1949; Baldwin, Kalhorn, & Breese, 1945). Using the two sets of data—the home visitor's assessments and the nursery-school behavior ratings—the investigators could systematically examine the differing impacts of democratic and controlling home environments on children's personalities. Not surprisingly, children from the two kinds of home had markedly different personality structures. The children of democratic parents were active, outgoing, expressive and competitive; they were high in leadership qualities, original, playful, curious, planful, self-assertive, aggressive, and, frequently, nonconforming. In contrast, the children from homes high in control were conforming, obedient, socially unaggressive, well-behaved, quiet, lacking in curiosity and originality, and inhibited.

Thus, it is apparent that responses stimulated and rewarded—and therefore learned—at home do generalize to the school situation. The children of democratic parents are rewarded for curiosity and spontaneity, and they manifest these characteristics in school as well as at home. Controlling parents reward their children's conformity and acquiescence to demands, at the same time suppressing curiosity and self-expression. The outcomes of this learning are generalized to the nursery-school situation.

In another series of studies (Baumrind, 1967), nursery-school pupils were rated on a number of components of competence and maturity, including self-control, curiosity about new and exciting stimuli, affiliation with peers, self-reliance, and enthusiasm. Two contrasting groups of children were selected for further study: one group consisted of the most mature, competent, independent, and content youngsters in the school; and the other was made up of the most immature, dependent children, who were lacking in self-control and self-reliance. The parent-child interactions of both groups were observed in the home and in structured situations, and parents were interviewed. These data were the bases for assessments of parental control, demands for maturity (pressures on the child to perform at his level of ability), clarity of communications, and nurturance (warmth and involvement with the child).

The pattern of parental practices that proved most likely to facilitate the development of maturity and competence was labelled *authoritative* (not authoritarian) parental control. It consisted of an effective balance of nurturance, warmth, love, support, and encouragement of the child's strivings for autonomy. At the same time, there were firm parental control and discipline, demands for mature behavior, and explanations of the reasons for their decisions. The childrearing practices of the parents of the least mature and competent children differed considerably from this pattern. Although warm and nurturant, these parents were overprotective and lax in discipline. They exercised very little control over their children, and made few demands for maturity, self-reliance, and independence.

Both the Baldwin and the Baumrind studies—conducted at different times and places and using different research techniques—demonstrate that the development of competence and maturity, interest in others, affiliation, self-control, and self-reliance is fostered by parental warmth, support, and nurturance, together with encouragement of independence and responsibility. These parental characteristics and practices are most effective if they are accompanied by control and firmness about decisions and high maturity demands—*not* authoritarian discipline, punitiveness, or overprotection.

While our focus has been on the role of parent-child relations in shaping behavior during early childhood, the family has a powerful and persisting—often lifelong—impact on development. For example, among children of school age, the preconditions of high self-esteem or self-confidence—an essential component of happiness and effective social interaction—are close ties to parents, siblings, and peers. Parents of children high in self-confidence are likely to be emotionally stable, self-reliant, and effective. Their childrearing practices are close to the *authoritative* pattern described above: they are consistently supportive, accepting, and affectionate; their children participate fully in making family decisions; and, at the same time, they maintain clearly defined and consistently enforced rules. In contrast, parents of children of low self-esteem tend to be emotionally distant, inattentive, and neglectful; and their children are indifferent or hostile to them (Coopersmith, 1967).

The enduring effects of parents' treatment of their children are also apparent in the remarkably consistent findings from investigations of the backgrounds of juvenile delinquents. Their parents have been found to be hostile, rejecting, indifferent, or apathetic. In their disciplinary techniques, they are characteristically lax, erratic, or overly strict.

As we have seen, many personal and social characteristics are learned because they are rewarded or reinforced (*see,* for example, pp. 274–75); others may be acquired by *observation* and *imitation* (*see* pp. 225–27 for examples). But these processes cannot account for all of the child's characteristics and responses. Some complex personal traits, motives, and attitudes—some *patterns* of behavior—seem to emerge spontaneously, that is, without direct training or reward, and without the child's intending to learn. A more subtle process, **identification,** is involved (Mussen, 1967).

Let me illustrate this concept by telling of a recent experience. I was visiting a nursery school attended by the three-year-old daughter of an old friend. Although I had not seen the girl since she was an infant and she did not look like her mother, it was very easy to pick her out from among the twenty pupils. Her ways of moving were clear duplicates of her mother's: the same erect posture; the same quick, deliberate steps in walking; swinging her arms in the same somewhat loose manner. She also used her mother's expressive gestures and inflections when she spoke, pausing frequently between words just as her mother did. My friend had not trained her daughter to walk, move, and speak as she did. Nor is it likely that she rewarded the child directly for emulating her behavior and mannerisms. Nevertheless, the child adopted these responses, through identification with her mother.

Identification may be regarded as a desire or motive to be like another individual. When the girl identifies with her mother, she begins to think, behave, and feel as though her mother's characteristics are her own. In identifying with a parent, Freud said, the child "attempts to duplicate in his own life the ideals,

The boy's desire to "be like Dad" is a fundamental mechanism of his personality development.

attitudes, and behavior of that parent'' (Freud, 1921, p. 62). The person with whom the child identifies is referred to as the *model* or **identificand.**

Identification is a fundamental mechanism of personality development. Through identification, the child acquires many of the parents' characteristic reactions, attitudes, emotions, feelings, and ways of thinking. And, since parents are representatives of their culture, identification provides the child with the personal qualities and skills that are culturally typical and approved. The American middle-class child becomes competitive and achievement-oriented; the Hopi becomes cooperative and democratic; the Mundugumor boy in New Guinea, harsh and aggressive.

Learning theorists maintain that the motivation to identify is rooted in satisfying interactions with the identificand; that is, a model who is nurturant and gratifying to a child becomes associated with feelings of satisfaction, pleasure, and comfort. The model's personal qualities and actions also acquire reward value for the child. By identifying with the model—by manifesting the model's characteristics and behaving as he or she does—the child can experience feelings of gratification that were originally associated with the model. Through identification, children become their own source of rewards that originally came from a model.

In an investigation of this theory, mothers of kindergarten girls were categorized, on the basis of interviews, as nurturant (warm, attentive, gratifying to the child) or nonnurturant. Each mother was then observed instructing her daughter on solving maze problems. During the teaching sessions, the mothers performed some acts that had nothing to do with solving the problems. For example, they drew very slowly, hesitating at each choice point and making unnecessary loops in their tracings. The daughters of the nurturant women identified with their mothers; they copied many of these irrelevant behaviors. The daughters of the nonnurturant mothers did not do this (Mussen & Parker, 1965).

Freud theorized that two consequences of identification with parents are particularly significant for later development. One is **sex-typing,** the adoption of personality traits, social and emotional behavior, values, interests, and attitudes culturally defined as appropriate for one's sex. The other is the development of the *superego,* or conscience—the organization of moral standards, judgments, ideals, attitudes, and values (*see* p. 160).

SEX-TYPING

Almost all cultures have traditionally assigned different roles to men and women and expect the two sexes to manifest different behaviors, interests, and personality characteristics. The definitions of masculine and feminine are arbitrary, however; they vary from culture to culture and from time to time within one culture. Consider the differences between the notions of feminine roles in the 1970s and in Victorian times. In the latter half of the nineteenth century, women were supposed to be dependent, submissive, and noncompetitive—and most of them were. Sex differences in most characteristics—for example, dependency and occupational choice—are regulated by cultural prescriptions and hence are modifiable. They are not inherent in the biological structure of the two sexes, not innate or immutable (*see* p. 136).

Many widely held beliefs about sex differences are myths entirely without

Traditionally there has been an emphasis on separate role behaviors and functions for boys and girls. More recent thinking is moving toward acceptance of a broader range of behaviors for both sexes.

empirical support. Girls are *not* more sociable or suggestible, *not* less achievement-oriented, or lower in self-esteem, than boys. Nor has it been clearly established that boys are naturally more active, competitive, and dominant — or less compliant — than girls. In fact, only a few sex differences have been fairly well established in systematic research. Males are consistently — at all ages and in all cultures studied — more aggressive and superior in visual-spatial and mathematical abilities. Girls excel boys in verbal abilities. These last three sex differences, however are only apparent in adolescence and adulthood, not in early childhood (Maccoby & Jacklin, 1974; *see* also pp. 135–36).

How, then, are sex-typed behaviors acquired? There is clear evidence that parents encourage their children to develop sex-typed interests, in part through providing sex-typed toys for them and by rewarding and reinforcing their participation in sex-typed activities. "Even more strongly [parents] *discourage* their children — particularly their sons — from engaging in activities they consider appropriate only for the opposite sex" (Maccoby & Jacklin, 1974, p. 339). Observational learning — imitating the characteristics and behaviors of others of the same sex — probably contributes to the development of sex-typing, especially in later childhood. However, experimental evidence on the role of imitation in young children's sex-typing is not clear-cut. In several studies, preschool children have been found to copy from male and female models equally.

Identification with the same-sex parent also fosters the development of sex-typing. Kindergarten boys who are highly masculine in interests perceive their fathers as highly nurturant and rewarding, and their fathers actually are affectionate and show great interest in their sons. Boys who are not very masculine do not view their fathers in this way; and their fathers are in fact less affectionate and less interested in their sons (Mussen & Distler, 1959, 1960). These findings are consistent with the hypothesis that sex-typing in boys is related to their identifications with their fathers.

OTHER PRODUCTS OF IDENTIFICATION

There is also some support for the psychoanalytic conception of conscience as a product of identification with parents. Among kindergarten children, those with a strong conscience — those who confess, feel guilty, apologize, or make reparations after wrongdoing — are children of warm mothers. Children who are more likely to lie or deny wrongdoing characteristically have mothers who are less warm and less close to their children. Boys with accepting fathers also manifest more guilt following wrongdoing and higher levels of conscience development than boys with rejecting fathers (Sears, Maccoby, & Levin, 1957). And boys with warm, giving, and loving fathers—fathers who induce identification—are more generous. They more readily share with other children than boys whose fathers reject them (Rutherford & Mussen, 1968).

Failure to establish strong identifications with parents, often as a result of insufficient parental warmth and affection, may have some persistent damaging effects on adjustment. The child who does not acquire the characteristics, motives, and attitudes essential to adjustment may suffer long-lasting social and emotional insecurity. Delinquency or criminal behavior may be one consequence of inadequate parental identification—because of the resulting failure to incorporate parental and cultural moral and ethical standards.

Parents are generally the child's first and most significant models. But as the child's social world expands, he or she finds other models to identify with—peers, teachers, ministers, and characters from fiction, movies, and television. As a result of these new identifications, established behavior patterns may be altered and new patterns of thought and behavior may develop. Adult personality structure is the product of a long series of such identifications. In some respects, people are like their parents; in other respects they are like admired peers, teachers, and fictional heroes.

What influence do peers have on personality development?

As children become more independent, they begin to spend progressively more time away from home and in the company of **peers** (equals) in the school, neighborhood, and playground. Most youngsters are eager to associate with others their own age and to become members of a group, and peer interactions increase in scope and complexity as the child grows older. Inevitably, peers become powerful agents of socialization: they reward certain behaviors and punish others, and they serve as models for imitation and identification. The extent to which a child's behavior is affected by peers varies according to many factors—outgoingness, dependence or independence, and willingness to try new activities. Popular children are the most *influential;* at the same time, they are also most likely to be *influenced by* their peers (Hartup, 1970).

From the adult's point of view, some of the changes resulting from interaction with peers are desirable; others are not. Some behaviors acquired at home—selfishness or overdependency, for example—will be punished by peers. They may therefore be weakened or extinguished by peer-group associations. Play with preschool peers who are socially more mature may lead to increased cooperation, better ability to work for a common purpose, and more frequent use of requests and suggestions (rather than force) in dealing with others (Hartup, 1970). Among elementary-school children, observing peers behaving generously is likely to raise the level of a child's own generosity (Rosenhan & White, 1967). Peer models may also help children to overcome some of their maladaptive responses. In a controlled experiment, three- to five-year-olds who were excessively fearful of dogs observed another child petting and playing with a dog on eight occasions ("treatment" sessions). After these experiences, the children lost their fears and approached a dog readily. Tested one month later, they showed no fears of either familiar or unfamiliar dogs (Bandura, Grusec, & Menlove, 1967).

Much to the annoyance of many parents, however, aggressive behavior is frequently rewarded by peers. Children, much more than adults, are likely to yield to the wishes of an aggressive peer and thus permit the aggressor to attain his or her goals. Consequently, children who are already aggressive may even increase their aggressive tendencies. Moreover, relatively unaggressive children are often the targets of aggression when they enter school, and many eventually counterattack. If they achieve some success by being aggressive, their assertive and aggressive behaviors become more frequent (Patterson, Littman, & Bricker, 1967).

Interactions with peers in middle childhood offer excellent opportunities for learning and practicing new social responses such as team cooperation, relating to leaders, and leading others. Children teach each other about society's expectations, and assist each other in adapting to the larger community.

Peers exert a more powerful influence in contemporary American culture than in many other societies. For example, compared with Americans, Mexican

Given the opportunity to see that her friends have not been harmed, the girl gradually overcomes her fear of the dog. A similar clinical procedure utilizes peer models to overcome extreme responses to many kinds of stimuli.

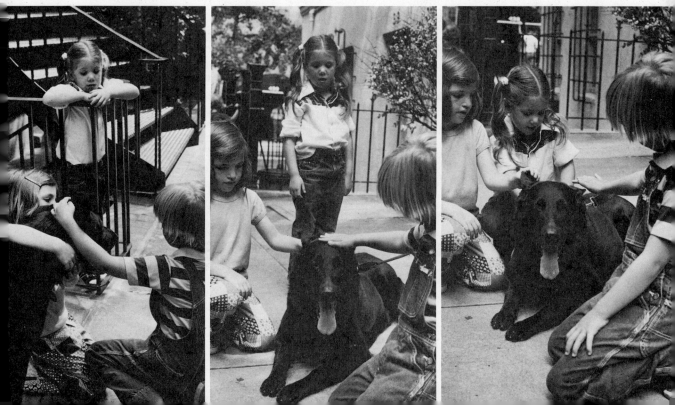

Parents often worry that peer pressures will be the dominant influence on their teenagers' behavior. In most cases, however, parental influences will continue to be felt, even when the opinion of the peer group is also sought.

children are much more oriented toward their families and much less concerned with their peer group's attitudes, judgments, and behavior. However, in some societies, such as Israeli *kibbutzim* (communal settlements) and the Soviet Union, peer approval may be valued more highly than parental approval.

At adolescence, peer influence, particularly the influence of close friends, is at its height. Conflicts with parents and contradictory emotions toward them are intensified. Children yearn to be independent but feel dependent in many respects; they may respect parental standards but also accept their peers' values. Often parents fail to understand these conflicts, and, inevitably, the adolescent turns to others his own age for support, advice, approval, and security. Under these circumstances, peers act as models, teachers, "therapists," and critics.

ADOLESCENT DEVELOPMENT AND ADJUSTMENT

Adolescence is often a period of stress and conflict, particularly in Western society. The adolescent confronts a host of new, varied, and difficult problems of adjustment within a brief period of time. Physiological changes—rapid body growth, sexual maturity, increases in sex hormones—often precipitate special conflicts and self-doubts. Almost simultaneously, the adolescent is expected to achieve independence from the family, establish satisfying relationships with peers of both sexes, decide on—and prepare for—a meaningful vocation, and develop a philosophy of life—a set of consistent moral principles to guide decisions and actions.

According to Erik Erikson, the **identity crisis** is the major psychosocial problem of adolescence:

> The identity the adolescent seeks to clarify is who he is, what his role in society is to be. Is he a child or is he an adult? Does he have it in him to be someday a husband and father? What is he to be as a worker and an earner of money? Can he feel self-confident in spite of the fact that his race or religious or national background makes him a person some people look down upon? Overall, will he be a success or a failure? By reason of these questions adolescents are sometimes morbidly preoccupied with how they appear in the eyes of others as compared with their own conception of themselves (Erikson, 1953, p. 215).

Adolescents, having identified with many models, have incorporated many different characteristics. Now they must integrate, synthesize, and reorganize these, dropping some characteristics and strengthening others. A new, unique, and coherent identity emerges, one in which "the whole has a different quality than the sum of its parts" (Erikson, 1959, p. 90). Achievement of an adequate sense of identity is reflected, subjectively, in "accrued confidence in one's ability to maintain inner sameness and continuity"; "a feeling of comfort with one's own body, a sense of knowing where one is going"; and "an inner assuredness of anticipated recognition from those who count." The individual who fails to acquire a sense of identity suffers **ego diffusion**—uncertainty about oneself and where one is going. Even in the best of circumstances, most adolescents experience some ego diffusion.

Because of the complexity and rapid social change in contemporary American culture, the adolescent must make choices from a tremendous range of values, lifestyles, goals, and models. To make matters worse, many parents do not understand their adolescent children's needs and cannot serve as effective models or guides; consequently, as we have seen, young people are highly peer-oriented. Nevertheless, for most adolescents, parental influences are still the most powerful ones, especially if their parents continue to show support and affection. Overly strong orientations toward peers may be "more a product of parental disregard than of the attractiveness of the peer group . . . [the adolescent] turns to his agemates less by choice than by default. The vacuum left by the withdrawal of parents and adults from the lives of children is filled with an undesired—and possible undesirable—substitute of an age-segregated peer group" (Condry, Simon, & Bronfenbrenner, 1968).

In searching for ego identity and a place in society, some adolescents become scornful and hostile toward the "establishment" and its obvious faults. Others become preoccupied with self-doubts and uncertainties, with what they perceive as their own inadequacies. Still others react more extremely, withdrawing into their own subjective world of drugs or schizophrenia—or both.

Happily, the vast majority of adolescents respond in less extreme ways. Probably those who will have the greatest ultimate impact neither blindly accept yesterday's customs and morals nor reject totally both the good and the bad in contemporary society. They will be somewhat uncertain about themselves and somewhat doubtful about society's "wisdoms," but they will be responsibly independent (Conger, 1974). If they use drugs, including alcohol, they will do so judiciously, not in a way that severely damages their problem-solving capacities. The individual who has achieved ego identity has a sense of personal worthiness, and operates on the basis of reality, rather than "pipe dreams." He or she has confidence in his or her ability to differentiate between desirable and undesirable attitudes and goals, together with a generally optimistic view of the future.

Does personality development continue throughout life?

While events and experiences of early life may have very significant long-lasting effects, personality continues to develop and change throughout the individual's life-span, as he or she copes with changing situations and crises, new demands, relationships, and roles (lover, husband or wife, parent, worker, voter).

Erikson describes three major psychosocial crises of adulthood—crises that occur *after* the identity crisis and achievement of a sense of identity (*see* p. 283). As each successive crisis is resolved, he says, personality becomes richer, more fully developed, and mature. If a particular crisis is not resolved adequately, the person acquires a negative quality, just as unresolved childhood crises may result in mistrust or shame and doubt (*see* p. 268).

In considering these possible outcomes, Erikson is explicit that the negative potentials "not only remain the dynamic counterpart of the positive potentials throughout life but are equally necessary to psychosocial life. A person devoid of the capacity to mistrust would be as unable to live as one without trust. . . . What the child acquires at [each] given stage is a certain *ratio* between the positive and the negative which, if the balance is toward the positive will help him to meet later crises with a predisposition toward the sources of vitality" (Erikson, 1968, p. 325).

The fundamental crisis of young adulthood, as Erikson sees it, revolves about *intimacy versus isolation*. Intimacy means sharing with, and caring about,

Erikson sees the resolution of conflicts between intimacy and isolation as the major developmental task of the young adult.

someone else, giving and receiving love and pleasure with that person—without sacrificing ego identity. Intimacy does not always involve sexuality; the relationship between friends is included. Failure to develop a sense of intimacy produces feelings of isolation, of being alone and alienated from others.

In middle adulthood, the psychosocial crisis involves *generativity versus stagnation*. The positive outcome of the crisis—a sense of generativity—is productive concern for one's family and children, as well as for future generations and for society at large. The negative outcome is a sense of stagnation, excessive concern with the self and with personal needs and self-aggrandizement.

Finally, in late adulthood, in the final psychosocial crisis, the individual reflects on the course of life. A person who is generally satisfied, accepts the circumstances of life without distortion, feels life has had meaning, and is able to face death without great fear, has achieved a sense of *integrity*. The opposite outcome of this crisis is a sense of *despair*—a view of life as a series of missed opportunities and regrets.

The resolutions of these successive psychosocial crises are not independent of each other. On the contrary, the individual's ability to deal with each new crisis depends in large part on how well previous crises have been resolved, on the personality he or she has developed, and on well-established patterns of reactions. And, of course, the environmental influences and external circumstances encountered—fortunate or unfortunate, beneficial or handicapping—also help shape the outcomes of the crises.

Is there stability in personality?

Granted that throughout life we encounter crises and events that alter personality, we must still face a fundamental question about continuity or stability. Specifically, can we predict the adult's personality from knowledge of the child's? At least a few early-established characteristics persist into adolescence or adulthood. Adult maladjustment often seems to be an extension of maladjustment in childhood; children who have intense conflicts, feelings of rejection, and inadequacy are more likely than others to become emotionally disturbed adults.

The most definitive information about the stability of personality comes from longitudinal studies of normal subjects. In one, seventy subjects were interviewed and observed on many occasions—and in many situations—between birth and early adulthood. They were rated on characteristics such as dependency, aggression, social withdrawal, mastery, and achievement. A substantial number of fundamental personality characteristics on which the subjects were rated proved to be relatively stable. This was particularly true of traditionally sex-typed traits—for example, aggression in boys and dependency in girls. Boys who had many temper tantrums at early ages became easily angered adolescents and, later, adults who became highly verbally aggressive when frustrated. Girls who were highly dependent on others during the nursery-school years were also closely tied to their families—especially their mothers—and they remained reliant on others to help solve problems during adolescence and young adulthood. Adolescent girls who were relatively independent of their families were also self-sufficient as young adults.

Level of achievement motivation was one of the most stable aspects of personality. Preschool children interested in solving cognitive problems were likely to be strongly oriented toward academic success when they went to school, and as adolescents and young adults they were still likely to be concerned with intellectual competence (Kagan & Moss, 1962).

Two other more recent studies of the stability of personality were based on longitudinal data at the Institute of Human Development at the University of California. The subjects of one of these — 45 boys and 40 girls — had been rated repeatedly on a wide variety of behaviors between the ages of five and sixteen. These ratings were grouped into several dimensions that describe general behavior styles and orientations to the environment. Two of these dimensions, *emotional expressiveness–reserve* and *placidity–explosiveness,* were found to be generally stable throughout the period studied. Children who scored high on emotional expressiveness at five or six — youngsters who were spontaneous in expressing their feelings, at ease in social situations and usually lively — were also likely to be high in these characteristics in middle childhood, preadolescence, and adolescence. Children rated high in placidity — who were generally calm and docile, infrequently and only mildly angry — were also relatively calm and placid later on. And there were even longer-lasting outcomes: expressive boys turned out to be warm, likable, expressive, and gregarious men (assessed at age 30), while expressive girls, as adults, were likely to be rebellious and self-dramatizing. Boys who were placid and stolid as youngsters were, in adulthood, dependable, consistent, and calm (Bronson, 1968).

Block (in collaboration with Haan, 1971), using another set of longitudinal data, found many continuities in personality between early adolescence and young adulthood (early thirties). He focussed on aggressive reactivity in males and anxiety about social interactions, introspectiveness, impulsivity, and achievement motivations in both sexes. Block was also interested in changes in personality. As subjects reached adulthood, the men progressed toward greater integration and self-assurance; they generally became "more dependable, more productive, more satisfied with self, more clearcut and consistent in their personality; . . . less rebellious . . . less seeking of reassurance, less self-defeating, less withdrawing and frustrated" (Block, 1971, p. 69). The women changed in similar, although not identical, ways between adolescence and early adulthood. They became more dependable, had higher aspirations, and were less self-indulgent and rebellious. At the same time, they moved toward more conventional feminine roles — "more arousing of nurturance, more sympathetic, more giving, more productive, more submissive, more warm, more cheerful; less intellectual capacity, less negativistic, less power oriented" (Block, 1971, p. 73). By their mid-thirties, the women subjects had consolidated and clarified their sense of ego-identity, and they had become more psychological-minded, committed, and tender in their attachments.

AGE AND PERSONALITY

No discussion of personality development through the life-span would be complete without some attention to the "senior" period. Advances in medicine and technology have increased life expectancy in the last several decades.

An important future area of research in developmental psychology will deal with the issues of adulthood and the personality changes that come with increasing age.

Among people born in the United States in 1900, average life expectancy was 47.3 years, while for those born in 1971 it is 71. Women, on the average, out-live men by seven years. In 1900 only 4 percent of the U.S. population was over sixty-five years of age; in 1975 over 10 percent was in this age group. Projected percentages for 1980 and thereafter are even higher. As a society, we are tilting more and more toward the older ages.

In view of these facts, it is unfortunate that we know so little about personality changes in old age. There are fairly consistent research reports demonstrating that older people have poorer self-concepts and less self-confidence than younger people. Achievement motivation declines in the later years, as do power-seeking and efforts at self-actualization. The elderly tend to be more introverted, more cautious, less impulsive, and more rigid than younger people. But there are such great individual differences in these attributes and in social and personal adjustment that it is difficult to apply any generalizations to individuals.

Moreover, there is little reason to believe that old age generally brings radical changes in lifestyle. According to one recent longitudinal study, subjects who were anxious and worrisome, with low activity levels and low self-esteem at age thirty revealed these same characteristics at seventy. Analogously, those who were exuberant, enjoyed life, and were busy socially and in their work at thirty derived a great deal of satisfaction from these same patterns at seventy (Maas & Kuypers, 1974).

As the proportion of older people in the population continues to increase, there will be stronger pressures from the public—and from governmental and social agencies—for more information about the changes associated with aging. So we may expect that in the future, research and theory in developmental psychology will focus more sharply on the later years.

SUMMARY

Socialization is a concept that refers to the vast range of social experiences that influence the development of personality, motives, values, attitudes, opinions, and beliefs. People and institutions that participate in socialization—parents, teachers, neighbors, peers—are the **agents of socialization.**

Infants ordinarily show attachment to their caretakers (usually mothers) beginning at about eight months of age, and the caretaker's reactions may have lasting effects on the child's adjustment. Sensitivity to the baby's needs and warm, intimate "mothering" foster sociability, alertness, and a basic sense of trust, while impersonal care produces only weak attachments and less interest in others. Prolonged and severe maternal deprivation—lasting for longer than the first year or eighteen months—may result in profound emotional maladjustment.

In the second year, the baby's striving for autonomy and independence seems to be dominant. At the same time, adults begin to pressure the child to accept the demands of reality and limitations on freedom. Parental rewards for independent activity and initiative stimulate the development of motives such as curiosity, autonomy, achievement, and competence.

As the child becomes more mature and his or her relationships with others become more complex, the characteristics of home atmosphere and childrearing practices—for example, democracy, control, demands for maturity—play a critical role in shaping behavior. For example, nursery-school children from democratic homes are outgoing, active, competitive, original, and self-assertive. Those from highly controlled restrictive homes tend to be conforming, well-behaved, quiet, and lacking in curiosity and originality. Parents who are supportive, warm, loving, and secure—as well as firm and reasonable about discipline—are more likely to have mature and competent children.

Identification, the desire to be like another person, is a fundamental mechanism of personality development and socialization, and children are motivated to identify with models who are nurturant and gratifying. Through identification, the child acquires many of the parents' characteristics, reactions, attitudes, and ways of thinking. **Sex-typing** (the adoption of personality traits, behavior, and attitudes appropriate to the individual's own sex, as these are defined in his culture) and conscience or superego are two major products of identification.

Peers are also important agents of socialization, teaching through reward and punishment and serving as models for imitation and identification. Both desirable responses, such as generosity, and undesirable behavior, such as aggression, may be acquired or strengthened by imitating peers.

Personality develops and changes throughout the life-span as the individual copes with changing conditions and psychosocial crises, social demands, and new relationships and roles. The principal problem of adolescence in Western culture revolves about the **identity crisis,** the individual's attempt to acquire a sense of identity, a sense of who one is and where one is going. Later there are crises about establishing intimate relationships with others without sacrificing ego identity, and about commitment to future generations, one's family, and children. In the last years, people deal with the critical conflict of whether or not life has been satisfying and meaningful.

Some early-established personality characteristics persist into adolescence and adulthood: achievement motivation, emotional expressiveness, placidity, anxiety about social interactions, introspectiveness, impulsivity, aggression (in boys), and dependency (in girls). However, in adulthood, most people become more highly integrated and self-assured, more dependable, and more productive. In old age, people generally have poorer self-concepts, less self-confidence, and lower achievement motivation; but there are vast individual differences in social and personal adjustment.

RECOMMENDED READING

CONGER, J. *Adolescence and Youth: Psychological Development in a Changing World.* (2nd ed.) New York: Harper & Row, 1977. A discussion of the major facts and theories regarding adolescence, emphasizing the problems of this period of life and the personal and social factors related to adjustment.

ERIKSON, E. *Identity: Youth and Crisis.* New York: Norton, 1968. A stimulating group of essays on the social and psychological problems of adolescence and the search for identity.

FLAVELL, J. *The Developmental Psychology of Jean Piaget.* New York: Van Nostrand, 1963.
A comprehensive, definitive account of Piaget's theory and research.

GINZBURG, H., & OPPER, S. *Piaget's Theory of Intellectual Development.* Englewood Cliffs, N. J.: Prentice-Hall, 1969.
A brief introduction to Piaget's major concepts of cognitive development, with rich illustrative material taken from Piaget's observations.

GOSLIN, D. (ed.). *Handbook of Socialization Theory and Research.* Chicago: Rand McNally, 1969.
In-depth discussions of theories and approaches to socialization, together with summaries of research on the development of personality and social behavior.

KESSEN, W. *The Child.* New York: Wiley, 1965.
The history of the field of child development presented in a series of excerpts from the writings of major contributors to this field.

KIMMEL, D. C. *Adulthood and Aging.* New York: Wiley, 1974.
A thorough survey of empirical research on development after adolescence, including cognitive functioning, personality, and social adjustment.

LANGER, J. *Theories of Development.* New York: Holt, Rinehart and Winston, 1969.
A short authoritative survey of the major theories of child development.

MUSSEN, P. (ed.). *Carmichael's Manual of Child Psychology* (3rd ed.). New York: Wiley, 1970.
A comprehensive, advanced treatment of the major theories and research areas of child psychology, each chapter written by a recognized authority in his field.

MUSSEN, P. H., CONGER, J. J., & KAGAN, J. *Child Development and Personality* (4th ed.). New York: Harper & Row, 1974.
A comprehensive textbook on child development that stresses learning, cognition, and socialization.

ROHWER, W. D., JR., AMMON, P. R., & CRAMER, P. *Understanding Intellectual Development.* Hinsdale, Ill.: The Dryden Press, 1974.
Lucid Discussions of intellectual development, viewed from several different theoretical perspectives, including S-R, Piagetian, psychoanalytic.

WOODRUFF, D. S., & BIRREN, J. E. (eds.). *Aging.* New York: Van Nostrand, 1975.
An interesting series of papers on physiological, psychological, cognitive, and emotional aspects of development in the later years.

PART FIVE

Cognitive Psychology

By David Elkind

Eugene is a nine-year-old boy who was brought to the Child Guidance Clinic because of his bad temper and his poor school work. He is a slender, nice-looking child who is rather small for his age. According to a report from the school, Eugene is inattentive in class, frequently disturbs other children by talking and annoying them, and shouts at any teacher who criticizes his behavior or his work. On the playground he is basically a loner, seldom communicating or playing with other children, but he frequently teases younger children, and he has been in many fights. He generally does poorly, or fails tests in arithmetic, reading, or spelling.

On the intelligence test he performed with some reluctance and disinterest; his overall I.Q. was 105. On a test of creativity, however, he did extremely well; his answers were original and ingenious. A more extensive evaluation was carried out by placing him in an experimental classroom for a few weeks. He was sensitive, distractable, and sometimes hostile toward other children, but he worked well, especially in one-to-one situations with the teacher. Here is a bit of his poetry:

> Orange is a Cheeta racing with the wind
> Orange is a flaming race car, racing down the street
> Orange is the sun shining between the clouds and a bright color.

This brief description of a problem child illustrates two different related approaches to the study and assessment of human intellectual ability—namely, the quantitative and the qualitative. The *quantitative* approach, reflected in the I.Q. score, is useful because it tells immediately where the individual ranks in brightness in comparison to others his own age. In this case, the score tells us the boy is of average intelligence, which means that retardation can be ruled out as a factor in his behavior. It also suggests that he should be able to do most schoolwork without difficulty.

Many people have special talents, however, that are not tapped by a general measure of intellectual ability. The *qualitative* statements about particular mental abilities give us a richer picture of intellectual strengths and weaknesses, as demonstrated by the revelation of Eugene's creative gifts. It was suggested to his teacher that he be given praise and recognition for creative expression in writing and art. The teacher followed this prescription, and Eugene became more interested in school work and less disruptive in the classroom.

In the first chapter of this section, we will discuss the quantitative approach—the origin and development of intelligence testing, one of the great achievements of modern psychology. We will review several controversial issues that have stimulated a great deal of research, including questions about the best way to measure general intelligence, the basic nature and structure of intelligence, the stability of I.Q., the hereditary and environmental determinants of intelligence, and the nature of intellectual functioning in later life.

Researchers and theorists interested in the qualitative aspects of cognition and intelligence have been concerned with the essential components of intellectual activity such as thinking, reasoning, abstraction, concept formation, comprehension, problem solving, and creativity. They have explored development and age changes in these abilities as well as their verbal, social, and personality determinants. And, because language plays a significant part in intellectual activity, many researchers and theorists have been studying the acquisition of language and its relationships to intelligence and intellectual functioning. These topics are the subject matter of Chapter 13. Of course, you have already been introduced to an outstanding example of the qualitative approach to intelligence in an account of Piaget's view of mental growth and the stages through which new, qualitatively different mental abilities emerge in the course of development (*see* pp. 245–52).

12

Human Intelligence and Its Measurement

What were the beginnings of human ability measurement?
What issues have been raised by intelligence testing?
How do psychologists conceptualize intelligence?

What were the beginnings of human ability measurement?

The measurement of human abilities has a relatively short history. It began with the work of Sir Francis Galton in the latter part of the nineteenth century. Galton, strongly influenced by the theory of evolution proposed by his cousin, Charles Darwin, was convinced that human abilities were inherited and variable and that they could be assessed by scientific methods. Furthermore, Galton and others who followed his lead believed that the higher order mental abilities, such as reasoning and problem solving, could be inferred from such measures as rate of tapping, strength of handgrip, estimation of the length of a line, and other simple motor and perceptual tasks. This approach grew out of Galton's not unusual belief that complex ideas and mental skills depended on simple perceptual or motor abilities. An idea comes from a sensation, does it not? Therefore, superior perceptual abilities mean, ultimately, superior reasoning. In his anthropometric laboratory individuals were measured on a variety of simple tests of perception, motor skill, and memory. Some of Galton's tests, or variations of them, are still in use today.

BINET-SIMON SCALES

Alfred Binet

Another early worker, probably the most prominent in the field of the assessment of intellectual ability, was a French psychologist, Alfred Binet. Binet was asked by the school authorities to devise a test that would help in the early detection of mentally retarded children, especially in distinguishing between retarded children and those with sufficient ability but low motivation. Unlike Galton, Binet believed that to evaluate intelligence, you must devise *direct* measures of complex processes such as reasoning and problem solving, the ability to use past experience to solve present problems, and the ability to adapt to new situations. One cannot simply infer complex processes from simple skills. So, in 1905, Binet and his colleague Theodore Simon published the first Binet-Simon scale, measuring *not* perceptual-motor skills but "reasoning, judgment, and imagination" (Binet & Simon, 1908).

This version was the first of three scales published by Binet and Simon; the last was in 1911, shortly before Binet's death. In developing their tests, they were interested in two major criteria. First, because mental ability improves with age during the school years, a good mental-test item should be *age-graded*, that is, easier for older than for younger children. Thus, an item that 15 percent of six-year-olds can pass, 60 percent of seven-year-olds can pass, and 100 percent of eight-year-olds can pass would be useful; such an item would be used as part of the subtest for age level seven. Second, performance on a test should be *related to school achievement;* that is, children who were considered bright by their teachers should perform better on these tests than children regarded as dull.

STANFORD-BINET SCALES

Lewis Terman

Because the Binet-Simon scales were very good measures, judging by the second criterion (while Galton's and similar scales were poor), they were quickly adopted in other countries. In America, Lewis Terman of Stanford University was largely responsible for the translation and revision of what came to be the most widely used intelligence test in the United States. The Stanford-Binet was first published in 1916, revised in 1937, and revised again in 1960 (Terman & Merrill, 1960). It samples a wide variety of cognitive functions such as memory, verbal and mathematical reasoning, comprehension, vocabulary, and the ability to pick out important ideas.

Binet repeatedly emphasized the importance of expressing the measurement of mental ability in psychological rather than in physical units. In the second version of the Binet-Simon Intelligence scale (1908), Binet introduced a purely psychological dimension for describing a subject's level of intellectual functioning. This psychological measure, also adopted for scoring the Stanford-Binet, was the *mental age* (M.A.), derived in the following way. In the tests, items are grouped according to the age at which a substantial proportion (60 to

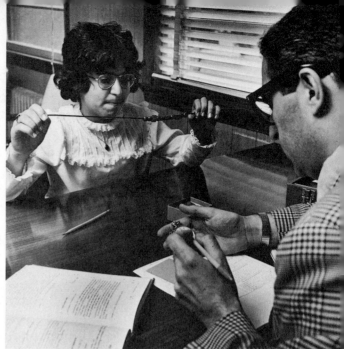

The Bead-Stringing Test, an item of the Stanford-Binet Scales, requires the subject to duplicate the pattern of beads shown by the tester.

90 percent) of children pass them. The 1960 Stanford-Binet has six items, tapping a variety of functions, at each age level. Thus the eight-year-old level consists of the following items: (1) defining eight words, such as orange, gown, eyelash; (2) answering from memory questions about a short story read to the child; (3) telling what is foolish about some absurd statements (for example, "A man had flu twice. The first time it killed him, but the second time, he got well quickly."); (4) naming similarities and differences in pairs of objects such as an airplane and a kite; (5) answering questions involving comprehension ("What makes a sailboat move?"); and (6) naming the days of the week.

In administering the tests, the examiner first presents easy tasks—usually those for an age level lower than that expected for the child—to build rapport, motivation, and confidence. This determines the child's **basal age,** the mental age level at which all tests are passed. Tests for higher age levels are then given in order; and the child is credited two months for each additional test item passed. This is added to the basal age. The total number of items passed by the child could thus be expressed in years and months; a test score expressed in this way is the **mental age.**

Suppose, for example, an eight-year-old boy passes all the tests for age level eight; his basal age then is eight. He is next given the items of age level nine and he passes two of these, thus earning an additional four months of mental age (two months for each item). At the ten-year-old level he passes one item and thus earns two more months of mental age credit. He fails all the tests at the age eleven level. His mental age therefore would be eight years and six months.

Intelligence Quotient

To express the test results in a way that would indicate immediately how bright a child was—whether accelerated or retarded relative to agemates—Terman adopted a concept from the German psychologist William Stern. This was the **intelligence quotient** or I.Q., expressed as the ratio of the mental age to the chronological age (C.A.) of the child

$$I.Q. = \frac{M.A.}{C.A.} \times 100.$$

The ratio is multiplied by 100 simply to remove the decimal point. Thus, if a child 8 years old has a mental age of 8, his or her I.Q. is 100 (average). A child with a mental age of 7 has an I.Q. of 88. And if the mental age is 10, the I.Q. is $\frac{10}{8} \times 100$ or 125.

The I.Q. scores of all children in a given population fall into a normal distribution with a mean (average) of 100 (*see* p. 19). The percentage of children in the standardization sample of the 1960 Stanford-Binet falling at various I.Q. levels is given in Table 12-1. As that table shows, 47 percent of the population falls into the I.Q. range between 90 and 109. Approximately 1 percent have I.Q.'s of 140 or over and only 3 percent fall below 70, into the mental deficient range (Terman & Merrill, 1960).

TABLE 12-1   Percentage distribution of I.Q.'s and classifications

I.Q.	Classification	Approximate Percentage in Standardization Sample
140 and above	Very superior	1
120–139	Superior	11
110–119	High average	18
90–109	Average	47
80– 89	Low average	15
70– 79	Borderline	6
69 and below	Mental defective	3

Since its popularization by Terman, the I.Q. has been one of the most used and abused concepts within psychology. Test-makers such as Binet and Terman were careful to emphasize that the M.A. and the I.Q. were psychological measures, different in many respects from physical measurements. A person with an I.Q. of 120, for example, does not have "twice as much" intelligence as a person with an I.Q. of 60. Despite the fact that an I.Q. is expressed in numerical terms, it is no different, in principle, from the rank positions accorded in a creative-writing contest. Although everyone might agree on the best short story, it would be nearly impossible to quantify how much better it was than any other. An I.Q. test can tell us who are the brightest people but not how much brighter, in unit terms, they are than the rest.

THE WECHSLER SCALES

Though the Stanford-Binet remains the standard instrument for intelligence testing with young children, it is less frequently used today with older children and adults. In 1939 the Wechsler-Bellevue intelligence scale was introduced, which is much easier to administer and score than the Binet (Wechsler, 1939).

The Wechsler scale, which gives a picture of a subject's *overall* strengths and weaknesses, is frequently used to measure intelligence in older children and adults. Shown here are two of the subtests of the performance scale— Object Assembly and Block Design.

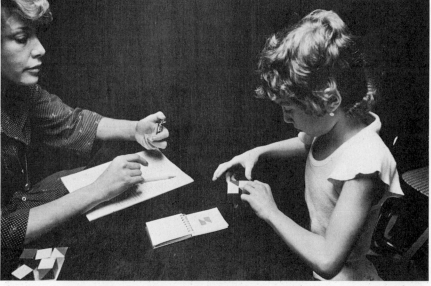

It has the added virtue of providing a picture of the subject's *pattern* of performance—his or her intellectual strengths and weaknesses. The Wechsler scale is divided into two subscales, a verbal scale and a performance scale. Though the items in the Stanford-Binet tests are grouped according to difficulty level, with each level containing a sampling of cognitive functions, the items in the Wechsler are grouped into eleven subtests of various types. The *verbal scale* includes tests of Information (such as "How many weeks are there in a year?"), Comprehension ("Why should we keep away from bad company?"), Digit Span (repeating digits forward and backward), Similarities ("In what way are air and water alike?"), Arithmetic (simple numbers problems), and Vocabulary. The *performance scale* includes five subtests. In the Picture Arrangement test the story is told in three or more cartoon panels presented in random order; the subject must piece them together in a way that tells the story. Each picture presented in the Picture Completion test has something missing from it; the subject tells what is lacking. In the Block Design subtest, the subject uses small blocks to copy a design presented by the examiner. In Object Assembly, the subject is given parts and required to discover how they go together to form such objects as a profile, hand, or elephant. The Digit Symbol test requires the subject to learn a code symbol for each number and to fill in the code symbol in a series of blank spaces under the numbers.

A subject's score on these subtests gives an immediate picture of intellectual strengths and weaknesses. In standardizing the scales, the average score (scaled score) for each subtest was set at 10. The subject's scores in the eleven subtests make up a **test profile** that indicates the evenness of performance, as well as the level of functioning in different kinds of cognitive tasks.

There are now three Wechsler scales, the WAIS (Wechsler Adult Intelligence Scale), WISC (Wechsler Intelligence Scale for Children—ages 7 to 16), and most recently the WPPIS (Wechsler Preschool-Primary Intelligence Scale) for children ages 4 to 6½ (Wechsler, 1939, 1949, 1963). These scales are currently the most widely used individual tests of intelligence in America.

Although the Stanford-Binet and the Wechsler scales differ greatly, scores from the two tests are highly correlated. Stanford-Binet I.Q. correlates about +.80 with the verbal scale of the Wechsler Intelligence Scale for Children (WISC), +.65 with the performance scale, and +.80 with the full scale.

GROUP TESTS

The success of individual tests of intelligence, particularly the Stanford-Binet, led many workers to design tests that could be given to large groups of subjects at the same time. Such group tests were needed because individual testing was expensive and time-consuming, and because the detailed information derived from an individual test was unnecessary when only rough screening of many people was required. In 1914 when America prepared to enter World War I, Arthur S. Otis was working on a group test of intelligence. He turned his work over to a group of psychologists appointed to construct a mental test for rapid screening of Army recruits. With the Otis tests as a basis, the psychologists created the famous Army Alpha tests of mental ability (Yerkes, 1921). The Alpha proved extremely useful in screening recruits. For example, about eight thousand men were discharged because of limited ability; others were assigned to special battalions because of either very low or very high test scores. The value of the Alpha test was demonstrated by the fact that it was highly correlated with such measures as officers' ratings and rank eventually attained.

One finding was a surprise to many Americans—almost a third of all men tested were illiterate. Because they could not read or write, they obviously could not be tested with the Alpha. A second test that did not use language and did not require reading ability, the Beta, was created for use with illiterates and foreigners who could not read English (Yerkes, 1921). Scores from the Beta also proved useful and demonstrated once again the difference between ignorance (lack of knowledge) and lack of intelligence. Many illiterate people were highly intelligent; they simply had not had the opportunity to learn to read.

In World War II, improved versions of Alpha and Beta were used. The new Alpha was called the Army General Classification Test, and recruits scored much higher, on the average, than the soldiers in World War I. This change was not caused by the new test items—a representative sample of World War II soldiers tested on the *old* version of the Alpha scored much higher than World War I soldiers had. Moreover, the difference was sizable: only one sixth (16 percent) of the soldiers in World War I scored as high as the median score of World War II soldiers. Better education probably accounts for much of the difference, but factors such as better nutrition, health, facility in English most likely, and more "test experience" probably also played their part.

INFANT TESTS

With the rapid growth of the testing movement in America, particularly during the 1920s, interest in assessing the I.Q. of young infants (below age two, the youngest age test in the Stanford-Binet), mounted rapidly. In part this interest grew out of the natural curiosity of parents anxious to be assured their children were "normal." There were practical considerations as well. If mental retardation could be detected early, parents could be better prepared for the fact that their offspring might not talk or walk at the usual ages and that they might require special education. If any treatment or intervention techniques might be helpful for problems the tests revealed, early application of such techniques would have a higher probability of success. Infant tests were also useful to adoption agencies in their efforts to match infants as closely as possible to adoptive parents. Such matching usually involves matching coloration (giving brown-haired infants to brown-haired parents) and racial, socioeconomic, and educational background of real and adoptive parents. Using infant tests, the intelligence of parents and adoptive children could, it was hoped, be matched as well.

Bayley Scales

Among the most notable of the currently used infant tests is the Bayley Scale of Infant Development, which was developed after many years of research. The latest version was published in 1969 (Bayley, 1969). Sample mental-scale items, together with their age placements (norms), are given in Table 12-2. (A description of the *motor items* in the Bayley scale is included in Chapter 10.)

TABLE 12-2   Examples of infant intelligence test items from Bayley Scales of Infant Development

Item	Age Placement (*months*)
Responds to voice	0.7
Visually recognizes mother	2.0
Turns head to sound of rattle	3.9
Lifts cup with handle	5.8
Responds to verbal request (e.g., to wave bye-bye)	9.1
Turns pages of book	12.0
Points to shoes (or other clothing) on request	15.3
Imitates crayon stroke	17.8
Uses 2-word sentence	20.6
Names 3 objects shown	24.0

N. Bayley. *Bayley Scales of Infant Development.* New York: Psychological Corporation, 1969.

The infant tests differ in many important respects from intelligence tests devised for children and adults. Tests for older subjects inevitably involve a great deal of language; tests for infants do not. Indeed, many of the infant subtests, such as following an object with both eyes, have no parallel in the tests designed for adults. In brief, the abilities measured by the infant tests are vastly different from those measured by the Binet or Wechsler scales. Not surprisingly, therefore, test scores earned in the first year or two do not correlate highly with later tests of intelligence and are not good predictors of later intellectual ability. Infant tests are most useful in detecting the extremes of mental ability and neurological deficit.

What issues have been raised by intelligence testing?

THE INTELLIGENCE QUOTIENT AND ACADEMIC AND , VOCATIONAL SUCCESS

Since the introduction of intelligence tests, I.Q. scores have proved to be important and useful in clinical work and educational guidance. Certain types of learning appear to be directly related to intelligence, while others are not. Specifically, learning performance in complex tasks, such as those involving understanding rules or solving problems, is directly related to I.Q., while learning rote associations is not (Harter, 1965). In general, tests administered during middle childhood or adolescence predict academic success with a reasonable degree of accuracy. For example, Stanford-Binet I.Q. scores of ninth-graders correlate highly (between 0.50 and 0.70) with achievement tests in reading, English, history, biology, and geometry a year later. Correlations between Wechsler-Bellevue I.Q. scores and school grades are approximately the same. Predicting grades from I.Q. scores is hardly infallible, but it is much better than a guess.

Predictions of academic success are not equally good at all levels of I.Q., however. Although people who do poorly on intelligence tests rarely do well in

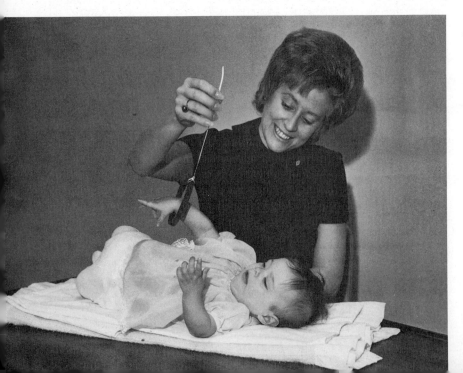

"Reaching for the ring" is a three-month item on the Bayley Scale of Infant Development.

Although a high I.Q. is generally an asset for academic achievement, many other emotional and motivational factors contribute to success or failure in school. Children who have been encouraged to be independent tend to do well in school, while those with inadequate self-concepts and low motivation for achievement are likely to do poorly and to be maladjusted.

Not surprisingly, the child's past experiences of success or failure in school influence his or her achievement goals. Children who have been generally successful in school set realistic goals for themselves. In contrast, many with histories of failure set unreasonable, unrealistically high goals, while others set their goals very cautiously, much below the levels they can achieve. In the case of the latter children, failure has led to demoralization and fear of further failure; they consequently aspire to very little.

Many children have acquired unusually intense fears of failure. They doubt their ability to learn their schoolwork and to pass tests; they are easily discouraged and cannot concentrate. Excessive anxiety, a common symp-tom of maladjustment in both adults and children, may interfere with learning and thinking, leading to withdrawal of interest in school and, consequently, to school failure.

Underachievers are students—generally in junior or senior high school—of average or better than average intelligence, as measured by standard tests, who are doing poorly or failing in school. Specific causes of under-achievement must be determined on an individual basis. Emotional instability is a frequent source of under-achievement, particularly in boys with poor identification with their fathers. Such boys may develop poor self-concepts, have low self-esteem, doubt their own ability to achieve success in school, and lack the security necessary to accomplish as much as they could. One case referred to a school psychologist was a boy with an I.Q. of 142 who was failing school. Inquiry revealed that his father was dead; his mother was an alcoholic who was entertaining strange men in their home. The boy was so preoccupied with his personal problems that schoolwork had little interest for him.

school, people with high I.Q.'s do not always excel. A high I.Q. may be a pre-requisite to high academic achievement, but it is not enough in itself. Among students with high I.Q.'s, those with good work habits who are highly motivated and emotionally stable are the most successful in school (see Spotlight 12-1).

Although many believe that mental ability as measured by intelligence tests is also related to occupational level and vocational success, this issue is more controversial. Generally, people in high-prestige, demanding occupations—involving decision making and high salaries—have higher average intelligence-test scores than people in lower-status occupations. Again, the predictions for people of low I.Q. are more accurate than for those with high I.Q.'s. Some high-prestige occupations (such as medicine or law) are essentially closed to people of low intelligence. And, not surprisingly, among those who enter executive and professional occupations, the higher the I.Q. the more successful and proficient the person (Ghiselli, 1966). But people with high I.Q.'s do not *necessarily* enter high-status jobs; in fact, they are distributed across the entire range of occupations.

Recently, some social scientists have become skeptical of the assumed relation of intelligence-test scores to job success (for example, McClelland, 1973). Several studies show no consistent relationship between intelligence-tests scores in college and subsequent accomplishment in social leadership, the arts, and science (Holland & Richards, 1965; Elton & Shevel, 1969). The correlations between intelligence and job proficiency found in other investigations, it is argued, may be attributable to social-class status. That is, members of the middle or upper class are more likely than those of the lower class to get high test scores. High ratings in job proficiency also may depend heavily on such variables as habits, values, ways of expressing oneself, speech accent, and interests—variables also associated with social-class membership. Therefore, according to this reasoning, the relationship between job proficiency and intelligence-test score may be attributed to factors of social-class background. There is no hard evidence to indicate that high intelligence has a direct effect on vocational success. "Instead of accepting the myth that test scores are so much synonymous with 'intelligence' and that 'intelligence' is the key to economic [vocational] success, we would do better to recognize that economic success depends largely on other factors" (Jencks, 1972).

LIMITATIONS IN THE USEFULNESS OF STANDARD INTELLIGENCE TESTS

Clearly, there are limitations to the utility of intelligence tests. Tests are important and useful in many cases, but we must be aware of problems in their use and exercise caution in interpreting intelligence-test data. Too often the I.Q. is taken as a fixed, unchangeable value—a dependable measure of inborn, underlying capacity—to be gloated over or bemoaned. In fact, I.Q. is neither fixed nor inexorable; the test measures the individual's *present* ability to perform certain kinds of tasks. It is not a sure predictor of success or failure in life.

It is undoubtedly possible to design a test that would be biased against the white middle class—the population toward which intelligence tests are ordinarily oriented—and in favor of lower-class blacks. Such a test would be made up of items that use the vocabulary and concepts known to people in the ghetto but not to the white middle class. Adrian Dove, a black sociologist, has attempted to do this, half humorously, in the Dove Counterbalance General Intelligence Test (the "Chitling Test"). Some items from the test are given in Spotlight 12-2.

There have also been some serious attempts to construct **culture-fair tests,**

Spotlight 12-2 The Chitling Test

Adrian Dove, a black sociologist, was struck by the differences in the vocabularies of the "street people" and the corporation executives he worked with after the Watts riots. A primary obstacle to understanding and constructive progress that he noted was the lack of a common language. Dove often found himself in the role of translator. He wondered how the executives would like taking an intelligence test written by black ghetto residents. Perhaps they would get a sense of what black children feel when they take a test written by white, middle-class educators. So Dove constructed, only half in jest, the Dove Counterbalance General Intelligence Test or, more popularly, The Chitling Test. Here are a few of the items:

1. A "handkerchief head" is: (a) a cool cat, (b) a porter, (c) an Uncle Tom, (d) a hoddi, (e) a preacher.

2. Which word is most out of place here? (a) splib, (b) blood, (c) gray, (d) spook, (e) black.

3. A "gas head" is a person who has a: (a) fast moving car, (b) stable of "lace," (c) "process," (d) habit of stealing cars, (e) long jail record for arson.

4. "Hully Gully" came from: (a) East Oakland, (b) Fillmore, (c) Watts, (d) Harlem, (e) Motor City.

5. If you throw the dice and seven is showing on the top, what is facing down? (a) seven, (b) snake eyes, (c) boxcars, (d) little Joes, (e) 11.

6. T-Bone Walker got famous for playing what? (a) a trombone, (b) piano, (c) "T-flute," (d) guitar, (e) "Hambone."

[The correct answers are 1,c; 2,c; 3,c; 4,c; 5,a; 6,d.]

Source: Dove, A. "The Chitling Test." In "Taking the Chitling Test," *Newsweek*, July 15, 1968.
© Copyright Newsweek, Inc., 1968, reprinted by permission.

---

that is, tests less culturally biased than those already available. Many such tests, including the Leiter International Performance Scale (Leiter, 1950) and the Peabody Picture Vocabulary Test (Dunn, 1965), use pictures in the belief that these reduce some of the difficulties present in existing tests. Such culture-fair tests, however, on the whole, have been unsuccessful. Perhaps they cannot be successful in principle. A test cannot really be culture fair because every individual is, in part at least, a product of his or her culture, and intelligence is, in part, knowledge of that culture. A person's performance will always be affected by his or her background and experience, no matter what the nature of the test. Perhaps more important than culture-fair tests, therefore, are culture-fair *interpretations,* which take into account a subject's background and experience in evaluating the meaning and significance of test scores.

The problem of fairness in the interpretation of tests is very complex. The fundamental question is: Are predictions made from the scores on the test accurate for all groups? "What the test constructor or test user must do . . . is to try the test out on different groups of people who may eventually be asked to take it, and find out not only whether some groups obtain lower average scores than others but also how their scores are related to a relevant criterion" (Tyler, 1971, p. 35). If, for example, most members of a minority group tend to score low on a scholastic aptitude test that predicts success in college and these same people also tend to do poorly in college, the test may be fair even though it seems to work against this minority group. But such a test would be considered unfair or biased against that group if it consistently predicted their performance in school or on a job *lower* than it actually was (Cleary, 1968).

Suppose, for example, that a liberal arts college uses an aptitude test standardized primarily on white, middle-class students in selecting applicants for admission. On the average, students who score 87 on the test achieve a grade-point average of 2.05 (a C in a 4-point system) their freshman year. Among native American (Indian) students admitted to the college, however, the grade-point average for those scoring 87 on the same test was 2.95 (about a B level)—much higher than would be predicted by the usual standards. The test would be considered unfair or biased because it *underpredicted* the performance of individuals of native American background. Moreover, if the test were used to select Indian students, many members of this group would be rejected even though they were capable of adequate or good performance. (*See* Schmidt & Hunter, 1974, for a more complete discussion.)

The use of intelligence tests has raised many questions about I.Q. constancy, possible genetic determinants of I.Q. differences, mental growth after maturity, mental development in exceptional children, and the relevance of I.Q. testing to personal and social success. These questions have been the starting points of extensive research projects.

STABILITY OF THE I.Q.

Because the I.Q. is essentially a rank, there are no true units of intellectual ability. It is, however, important to know whether the measure is relatively stable—in other words, whether individuals tend to maintain their relative intellectual standing over time. If I.Q. is relatively stable, we can fairly confidently make long-range predictions about an individual's future intellectual status that can be used in educational and vocational planning.

Many studies indicate that for most people, relative intellectual standing is in fact stable. It does not change radically from test to retest, even over a fairly long time. This has come to be known as **stability of I.Q.** Though infant tests are not good predictors of later intelligence, tests given during preschool and after, when language functions are well established, are highly correlated with later tests. For example, Stanford-Binet scores at age four correlate 0.70 with mental-test scores at age sixteen. In general the child who is superior in intelligence at age six remains so; the child whose score is inferior at this age generally scores low at later ages (Honzik, Macfarlane, & Allen, 1948).

This does not mean that every individual's standing is fixed; some do change markedly from one time to another. The correlations between a test given between the ages of six and nine and a second test given later depends on the interval between tests. The correlation between tests given a few days apart is 0.91; with an interval of three years, the correlation is 0.84. Significant changes in I.Q. are more likely when there are even longer intervals between tests. At least 10 percent of children change at least fifteen points in an interval of six to eight years.

The most relevant data on individual changes in I.Q. come from longitudinal studies in which the same subjects are tested repeatedly over a long time. Figure 12-1 shows the results of repeated tests of three subjects of a longitudinal guidance study at the Institute of Human Development at the University of California at Berkeley. The three children had very similar I.Q.'s at age four, but two of them changed markedly over the years (Honzik, Macfarlane, & Allen, 1948).

Identical twins, when reared apart, can have I.Q. scores that differ by as much as twenty points.

The histories of the three children whose I.Q. test scores are shown in the figure suggest causes of change but at the same time show that simple causal hypotheses may be inadequate. Case 783 changed very little in I.Q. through the years, although he had poor health, was insecure, did poorly in school, and had a number of symptoms of emotional disturbance. Case 946 scored as low as 87 and as high as 142. She was the daughter of unhappily married immigrant parents who were divorced when the girl was seven. When she was nine her mother remarried but the girl was very insecure and unhappy at home. When she became better adjusted in her family, her I.Q. scores rose. Case 567 showed consistent improvement. In her early years she was sickly and shy, but after age ten her social life expanded, and she became intensively involved in music and sports. These changes were reflected in her improved test scores.

Gains or declines in I.Q. also appear to be correlated with personality and emotional factors. Among children with the same I.Q. at an early period, those who gain are likely to be vigorous, emotionally independent, aggressive, non-conforming, curious children actively engaged in exploring their world and are interested in intellectual pursuits (Sontag, Baker, & Nelson, 1958).

Changes in a child's intellectual standing may occur if there is a major change in environment—and in opportunities for learning—either from good to bad or vice versa. One study provides a dramatic illustration. A small group of children were removed from a foundling home where they were given physical care but little else. The babies were placed in a home for mentally retarded girls who "adopted" the infants and raised them with much love and care. At the time the children were removed from the foundling home their I.Q.'s were in the sixties (in the mentally defective range). Retested after years with their surrogate mothers, these youngsters attained close to normal or average I.Q. scores; thirty years later the majority of them were leading normal productive

Figure 12-1

A Longitudinal Study of I.Q.
The graph shows I.Q. scores of three children on successive tests (plotted in standard scores, with the mean for children in this study indicated as 0). (From Honzik, Macfarlane, & Allen, 1948)

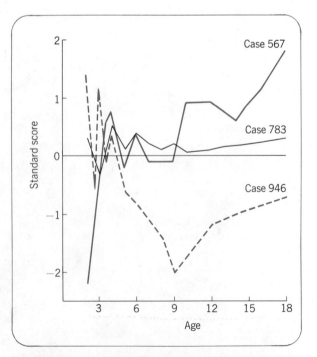

Many studies have demonstrated the crucial effects of environment on the growth of intelligence. There are, nonetheless, different kinds of stimulation from those to which middle-class children are usually exposed.

lives. Here is a rather remarkable demonstration of change in I.Q. associated with a dramatic change in environment. A control group who had not been adopted but remained in the foundling home presented a much different picture as adults. Most of them were living in institutions of one sort or another (Skeels, 1966).

A change in the other direction is often observed among minority children such as native Americans and blacks. Although these children may score close to average intelligence when they are young, they score increasingly poorly as they grow older; in fact, they seem to undergo a kind of progressive retardation. The reasons for this are not entirely obvious, but one possible factor is motivation. As minority children grow older, they become increasingly aware of their low status in the larger society (a situation that, we hope, is changing today); they see the lack of opportunity available to minorities, even when they have an education. As a result, they lose interest in academic matters. Exposure to societal prejudice may thus have a retarding effect on intellectual growth.

In general, people tend to retain their relative intellectual standing when they grow up in an environment that provides opportunities and nourishment to maximize mental growth. When, however, a child growing up in an optimal environment moves to a less favorable one, or vice versa, then there may well be large shifts in intellectual performance. In short, nothing is fixed or immutable about the I.Q. score.

**MENTAL GROWTH
AFTER MATURITY**

Most investigators agree that intelligence grows very rapidly in the early years, but more slowly with increasing age. Intelligence-test performance ordinarily reaches its peak in late adolescence or early adulthood; at this period, people

Figure 12-2
Curve of the Growth of Intelligence
This curve is based on data from a longitudinal study. The scores are units of growth derived from a method of absolute scaling. (From N. Bayley, "Development of Mental Abilities," in P. H. Mussen, ed., *Carmichael's Manual of Child Psychology*, Vol. 1, 1970, p. 1176)

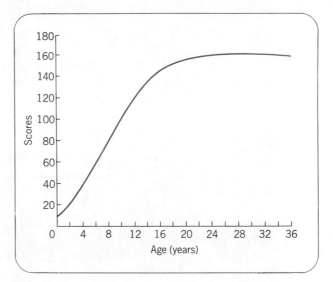

seem to stop acquiring new intellectual powers. For example, immediate memory span grows until the age of fifteen but not after that. The average fifteen-year-old can repeat seven digits immediately after they are presented, but so can the average fifty-year-old. Other items of the Binet scale level off at about the same age. Early studies indicated rather sharp decreases in mental abilities, especially after the age of forty (see Figure 12-2); but more recent data suggest that whether a particular kind of mental ability is maintained or declines in later years depends on *both* the intellectual function *and* the person. One cannot really generalize about the course of mental growth. Tests that require speed, close attention, and concentration seem to show decreasing scores earliest (in the mid-twenties or even earlier). Abilities such as deductive reasoning, language, and vocabulary show little decline with age. The rate of decline of specific abilities is also known to be influenced by an individual's occupation. On the average, bright people and those in more intellectually demanding occupations do not decline in mental ability as early as others do. Teachers, writers, artists, and scientists maintain their productivity—if not their creativity—into their later years with little apparent loss. Persons of lesser ability are likely to lose some of their mental alacrity earlier. Physical health is also a factor; elderly people in optimal health show relatively little deterioration in intellectual-test scores, while those with chronic ailments decline significantly.

Motivation must also be taken into account in considering the course of mental growth after maturity. Every college teacher has encountered highly motivated students of middle age or older whose motivation to learn more than compensated for somewhat lessened mental acuity. Because of their maturity and desire to get the most out of their courses, these students are often a delight to teach and are exuberant witnesses to the fact that intellectual prowess and achievement are not solely the province of the young.

GENETIC DETERMINANTS OF I.Q.

We still have no definite answer to the question: "Is intelligence determined by heredity or environment?" Most psychologists agree that heredity contributes to intellectual ability, but they do *not* believe that intelligence is somehow established at conception and is therefore unchangeable. Heredity probably sets limits, but they are flexible—or even elastic—so that they can be stretched considerably under special circumstances.

The evidence for the role of heredity in intelligence is of several sorts. One kind comes from studies of the I.Q. scores of parents and children. On the average, the correlation between the I.Q.'s of parents and their natural children is on the order of 0.50; but between parents and their adopted children, it is about 0.25. Even more impressive are the data from identical and fraternal twins. The I.Q.'s of fraternal twins correlate about 0.55, while the I.Q.'s of identical twins (who have the same genetic makeup) correlate about 0.90. Even if reared apart in different environments, the I.Q.'s of identical twins correlate 0.75. A summary of studies of this kind is presented in Figure 12-3.

Although such evidence clearly suggests that intelligence is significantly influenced by genetic factors, it is also clear that environmental factors—including everything from diet to education—play a role. Partly because of environmental determinants, children's I.Q.'s tend to be closer to the average than their parents' are. Extremely intelligent parents will have intelligent children, to be sure, but the children on the average will be slightly less intelligent, closer to the mean for the general population. Children of parents with extremely low intelligence will tend to be brighter than their parents—again, closer to the population mean. This phenomenon is called **regression to the mean.** An extremely intelligent person, for example, probably represents an unusually fortunate coincidence of many genetic factors related to high I.Q. *and* a highly favorable environment; it is unlikely that his or her child will be as fortunate.

One of the most consistent findings with regard to intelligence testing of black and white Americans is that blacks on the average score ten to fifteen points below whites on most standard measures of ability. Obviously, this

Figure 12-3
Correlation Coefficients of Intelligence Test Scores

Test scores from 52 studies are of pairs of people of different degrees of genetic similarity. Median coefficients are shown by large dots on the horizontal lines, which represent the ranges. (From Erlenmeyer-Kimling & Jarvik, 1963)

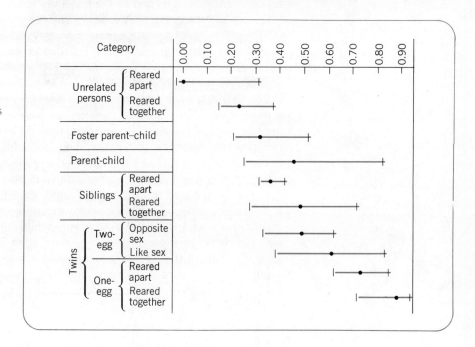

does not mean that every black is less bright than every white. Rather, it means that 33 percent of blacks are brighter than 50 percent of whites. Put differently, intelligence is randomly distributed in a normal curve for both blacks and whites, and the differences *within* each group are much larger than the differences *between* the two groups.

What factors could account for the finding that blacks score lower on the average? It has been suggested that the difference may be attributable to genetic differences; but most psychologists believe that black-white differences in I.Q. cannot readily be explained by genetic factors alone. For one thing, whites and blacks live in vastly different environments and have different experiences, on the average. They react differently to the content of the tests and to being tested. In addition, social prejudices against blacks—and blacks' awareness of their status in society—stifle intellectual motivation. Furthermore, in the past black children have had few role models who have used intellectual skills and education to get ahead in the world.

A few examples may help to make concrete how environmental factors can affect intellectual growth. Recent studies suggest that protein deficiency during a mother's pregnancy can have lasting negative effects upon her offspring's intellectual ability. Blacks are on the average poorer than whites and are more likely to have diets high in fat, starch, and carbohydrates and low in protein— the reverse of what is required for optimum prenatal intellectual growth. The diet of the infant after birth is also important for later intellectual development, and at least some of the differences between black and white children in test performance could be caused by these nutritional differences. In addition, family size among those of low income tends to be larger than that among those of middle income. Some investigators (Zajonc, 1976) contend that I.Q. is inversely correlated with family size.

Perhaps the most important factor contributing to black-white differences in test performance is related to the generally low socioeconomic level of most blacks. Many lower-class families can provide only restricted experiences and little intellectual or cultural stimulation for their children. Those factors are consistently related to intellectual retardation. Finally, despite recent positive changes in racial attitude, prejudice against blacks is still a fact. It is difficult to motivate the black child to learn and to get an education if he or she is not convinced that academic success will lead to greater rewards—a better job, a more prestigious position, or greater self-esteem. The possible effects of any genetic differences cannot be separated from the effects of differential nutrition, differing environmental stimulation, and inequality of opportunity.

Nonetheless, in the past the observed I.Q. differences between races have frequently been interpreted as *genetic* differences. The issue is highly emotional for obvious reasons, and it is complicated. *Race* itself is defined socially, not genetically; someone with all white ancestors except for one black great-grandfather—who is, genetically, mostly white—is still labeled black. So the term "race" is ambiguous from a genetic point of view. And *intelligence*— what it is, how it should be measured, and whether present tests are fair to all groups—also remains a somewhat indefinite theoretical construct. Nevertheless, the relationship between race and intelligence remains controversial, as may be seen in Spotlight 12-3.

Spotlight 12-3 Race and Intelligence

Recently, sophisticated statistical techniques for estimating the *relative* contribution of heredity and environment—which is *more* important?—have permitted a number of scientific publications that are highly controversial. The most heated arguments develop when the findings are used to suggest that blacks are genetically inferior in intelligence compared to whites. Many in our imperfect society are eager to discover and publicize any "scientific" conclusions that support their bigotry and justify their discriminatory behaviors. So the question—and the answers—have profound social implications.

Writing in the prestigious *Harvard Educational Review*, Arthur R. Jensen (1969) raised the possibility of genetic inferiority of blacks. In essence, he cited these facts to support his suggestions: (1) Analysis of numerous studies of blood relatives, especially those of identical twins raised in different environments (same heredity, different environments), leads to the estimate that approximately 80 percent of the variation in I.Q. can be accounted for by genetic factors. In other words, heredity is *far more important* than environment in determining I.Q. scores. (2) Blacks, on the average, score lower than whites in I.Q. If intelligence is largely inherited, this fact alone could lead to the conclusion of black genetic inferiority. But Jensen mentioned a third fact as well: (3) Special remedial programs designed to increase the I.Q.'s of disadvantaged children—mostly blacks—have not been generally effective. This evidence, he suggested, supports the notion of high heritability of I.Q. scores because it shows how little impact results from changing the environment and educational program.

Many psychologists have reacted to Jensen's findings by saying that his analyses are overinterpreted and misleading. For example, even if one concedes that intelligence is 80 percent heritable in the white middle class—the group from which almost all of the subjects in important twin studies were drawn—one cannot assume that the same estimate holds for blacks or for lower social classes. Indeed, recent evidence indicates that I.Q. scores are determined much more by environment in these cases (Scarr-Salapatek, 1971a). In other words, a white middle-class child is much less likely to be "held back" by the lack of opportunity or by overt discrimination (environmental factors); thus his or her I.Q. score might more directly reflect genetic endowment.

An outstanding researcher in genetics and intelligence says: "The finding of average differences between populations does not favor either a genetic or environmental explanation. Even if the heritabilities of intellectual performance *within* each group of two populations have

been shown to be high, there is practically no connection between within-group heritability and between-group heritability. . . . Intelligence score differences within two populations can be related primarily to genetic differences among individuals while average differences between groups can be related primarily to environmental differences" (Scarr-Salapatek, 1975, p. 36). To clarify this point consider this relevant analogy to a population of corn seeds and their height and productivity. Suppose a farmer took 100 seeds of varying genetic characteristics and randomly assigned them to two groups. There would then be two subgroups of equal genetic potential, on the average. Now the farmer plants one group in rich soil, the other in poor sandy soil. *Within* each plot, corn plants will vary in height and productivity, and the variations will be almost entirely a result of genetic differences in the seeds (almost 100 percent heritability). Plants in poor soil, however, will be — on the average — shorter and less productive than those in rich soil. The average differences *between* the two plots will be almost entirely a function of environmental (soil) differences. It would be nonsense to assert that the seeds planted in poor soil were genetically inferior. Now consider the average differences between the living conditions of whites and blacks and the pervasive nature of prejudice and discrimination in the United States. The analogy between poor and rich soil and the usual environmental conditions in which black and white children are raised becomes very meaningful.

Jensen's thesis has also been criticized on the grounds that his estimate of the heritability of intelligence (80 percent) is extremely high; other investigators find heritability coefficients to be as low as 30 or 40 percent. If hereditary factors were as powerful in determining I.Q. as Jensen maintained — and environmental factors as of little importance — it would be virtually impossible to raise or lower I.Q. through any kind of environmental manipulation or intervention. Yet several studies show that children adopted into intellectually stimulating environments score as much as 20 points higher than their natural parents (Skeels, 1966; Skodak & Skeels, 1949). In a recent study directly related to Jensen's argument, Sandra Scarr-Salapatek examined the I.Q.'s of a large number of black children who had been adopted, at an average age of twenty-two months, by upper middle-class, white families who were highly educated and above average in occupational status and income. The average I.Q. of the adoptees was 106, over 16 points

above the average usually achieved by black children reared by their natural parents in that part of the country. Those who were adopted before their first birthday scored even higher — 110 on the average. In addition, statistical analysis showed that "placement and adoptive family characteristics account for a major portion of the I.Q. differences among the [adopted] Black children" (Scarr-Salapatek & Weinberg, 1975, p. 18). Those who were adopted early, spent more years in the adopted homes, and were placed in more stimulating intellectual environments had higher I.Q. scores. In general, the data "strongly suggest that the I.Q. scores of Black children are environmentally malleable" (Scarr-Salapatek & Weinberg, 1975, p. 18), and that environmental changes can indeed have significant impacts on intelligence-test scores.

The question of *how* heredity and environment interact is perhaps more meaningful than the question of which is more influential. No doubt, genetic factors affect general intelligence; but without environmental support or stimulation, they could not produce their effects. Consider another appropriate analogy. By the standards used to estimate the inheritance of intelligence, tuberculosis would be judged highly heritable. If one identical twin has tuberculosis, the other is very likely to have it; this situation has been found in 87 percent of identical twins with tuberculosis. However, the figure drops to 26 percent for fraternal twins, who may share the same — or very similar — environments but do not have the same heredity (Hebb, 1966). We cannot conclude, however, that tuberculosis is inherited, for in this case we know that the direct cause of the illness is environmental — a bacillus. At most, we can conclude that some form of susceptibility to tuberculosis is inherited. The environment and the genetic factors interact to produce the disease.

The same is very likely true of intelligence. An individual's potential intelligence may be inherited, but certainly the environment determines whether or not that potential is realized — and to what degree. In the environment the average black encounters, he or she is less likely to actualize his or her full potential; hence it cannot be asserted that measures of "functional intelligence" (I.Q. scores) reflect genetic differences between races. (For a more complete discussion, see the outstanding review by J. C. Loehlin, G. Lindzey, & J. N. Spuhler, *Race Differences in Intelligence*, 1975.)

So far we have discussed mainly individuals in the broad middle ranges of intellectual ability. What about the intellectual futures of those at the extremes, the mentally retarded and the gifted? Recent research has laid to rest some long-standing myths about both groups of individuals.

The diagnosis of **mental retardation** commonly involves some statement about the determinants of the retardation. The usual distinction is between the endogenous (genetically determined) retarded and exogenous (environmentally determined) retardation. In many cases, the endogenously retarded have poor coordination, physical problems, and sensory deficits as well as low intelligence; the mental deficit is part of a larger picture of total organismic deficit. (See Spotlight 12-4.)

Among the exogenously retarded, such physical and physiological correlates of retardation are generally absent. Retardation can be produced by a variety of environmental traumas that affect the delicate tissues of the brain, including insufficient oxygen during the birth process, prolonged high fever, injury, or a disease such as encephalitis. In recent years it has been recognized that many children suffer from "minimal brain damage," which can be quite selective in its effects. Premature babies, for example, may later show perceptual problems and reading difficulties although they show no other signs of retardation or defect.

A different sort of exogenous retardation is **pseudoretardation.** Such retardation is present in individuals who perform at the retarded level because of severe emotional or social deprivation or both. One disturbed young man's I.Q. was 60 when he first came for psychiatric treatment, but it was 125 after some of his problems were relieved. Pseudoretardation is a frequent phenomenon among ghetto children and others who have been deprived of all but the most minimal forms of intellectual stimulation.

The intellectually gifted person is usually not weak physically, with poor health and limited eyesight, as the bookworm myth supposes; rather, he or she is usually gifted physically as well as intellectually. The gifted are, on the average, taller, better coordinated, and less subject to illness than those of lesser ability. Moreover, gifted people tend, on the average, to realize their ability and to attain high positions in their vocations. There are, of course, many exceptions to this rule but the general trend is quite clear and consistent.

How do psychologists conceptualize intelligence?

When Binet and Simon began work on their intelligence scale, they started from a fairly broad conception of what **intelligence** was, namely: "To judge well, to comprehend well, to reason well, these are the essentials of intelligence." As new and different tests came into existence and as new statistical procedures were devised, different conceptions of intelligence began to prevail. Each investigator constructed his test to assess intelligence as he conceptualized it. The situation became so ambiguous that Edwin G. Boring seriously proposed in 1923 that intelligence be defined as "what intelligence tests measure."

Some varieties of mental retardation are produced by genetic abnormalities that occur in the process of cell division during the embryonic period of fetal growth. It is believed today that in some cases of incomplete separation, the new cells may have one too many or too few chromosomes. Cells with too few chromosomes tend to die but those with too many may continue to thrive and produce a viable individual with an abnormal number of chromosomes in all of his or her body cells. Individuals with an extra chromosome in their cells manifest a form of mental retardation known as **Down's Syndrome** or "mongolism." The syndrome includes the following features: thick tongue with many fissures, flattened face, extra eyelid folds, physical deficits, and defective intelligence (I.Q. between 20 and 60). Such children sometimes grow up to be semi-independent individuals who can do certain types of menial work. This tends to be the exception, however, and most such individuals tend to die in adolescence because of such congenital defects as heart disease.

Spearman was among the first of the mental testers to propose a general theory of intellectual development, a two-factor theory of intelligence (Spearman, 1927). He argued that all individuals have a **general intelligence factor, g,** but in differing amounts. This **g factor**—which is genetically determined, according to Spearman—played a part in all intelligence-test performance. In addition to g, however, there were also *specific* or *s* factors for particular abilities or forms of tests (arithmetic and vocabulary tests, for example). A person's intelligence could thus be described in terms of the magnitude of the g and s factors.

Spearman's theory has been called a theory of general intelligence because it assumes that there is some common factor in all intelligence functioning. Other investigators, however, disputed the general theory and suggested that intelligence-test performance is a product of many different and separate factors. Such theories, called **multifactor theories,** have been proposed by men such as Thurstone and Guilford.

Thurstone (1938) is perhaps best known for his test of Primary Mental Abilities (PMA), which is still in widespread use in schools (last revision, 1962). Thurstone argued that there was no underlying general intelligence but rather a system of interrelated **primary mental abilities.** Although it is difficult to say precisely how many primary mental abilities there are—the numbers appear to be different for children and adults, for example—the following seven factors (primary abilities) have been found in many studies:

1. *Verbal comprehension* (V) The ability to understand words.

2. *Space* (S) A visualizing ability such as that exhibited in the accurate reproduction of a design from memory.

3. *Perception* (P) The ability to see quickly similarities and differences between pictures of objects.

4. *Number* (N) The ability to work with numbers and to compute.

5. *Memory* (M) The ability to recall verbal stimuli such as words.

6. *Word fluency* (W) The ability to think of words quickly—for example, in public speaking or in doing crossword puzzles.

7. *Reasoning* (R) The ability to find an underlying rule or structure in a series, for example, a sequence of numbers; in some studies, inductive and deductive reasoning were distinguished.

Spotlight 12-5 gives two items from a test for young children, one for word meaning (V) and the other for perceptual speed (P).

The work of Thurstone and other investigators formed the basis of *hierarchical theories of intelligence* (Burt, 1949; Vernon, 1950). According to these theories, an almost infinite number of very specific abilities can be grouped into a few "primary mental abilities." These few abilities, in turn, are all influenced by a general factor—g, in Spearman's terms. People high in the general factor can be expected to be slightly above average on all intellectual tasks, but a better picture of their strengths and weaknesses can be obtained by measuring specific primary mental abilities. These theories also suggest that if a specific ability is needed for a particular job, such as the ability to spot discoloration of eggs before marketing, it is preferable to test this ability directly—rather than rely on a less specific predictor such as a score on a general intelligence test.

One notable investigator (Guilford, 1967) denies that there is a single general factor in intelligence, and suggests that there are at least 120 unique intellectual abilities! Guilford distinguished among four kinds of content: (1) *semantic* (verbal material where meanings are critical); (2) *figural* (the traditional nonverbal material, mostly pictures, but also including auditory content); (3) *symbolic* (mostly letters and numbers); and (4) *behavioral* (interpretations of human behavior). "Operations" refer to what you can do with content, and there are five categories: (1) *cognition* (essentially knowing, as one knows the meaning of a word); (2) *memory* (retaining information); (3) *convergent production* (producing one correct answer); (4) *divergent production* (like creativity; producing many possible answers to questions, such as "How many uses can you think of for a brick?"); and (5) *evaluation* (judging wisely).

Intellectual abilities can also be distinguished in terms of the *products* resulting from the particular operation on the specific content. In other words, the final outcome (answer or answers) can be one of six types: (1) *a unit* (such as a word); (2) *a class of units* (a noun); (3) *a relationship between units* (similar); (4) *a system of information* (a plan); (5) *a transformation* (a change); or (6) *an implication* (a prediction).

Each unique ability is a combination of a type of content, an operation, and a certain product. For example, a vocabulary test has *semantic* content, calls

The following two items are from the Test of Primary Mental Abilities for ages five and six (Gwynn & Thurstone, 1938).

The first row of pictures is from the test of word meaning. The instructions are: "Mark the picture that answers this question: Which one do you look at if you want to know how cold it is? Mark it."

The second row is from the test of perceptual speed. The instructions are: "In every row of pictures you are to do two things. First mark the picture all by itself in the little box. Then find the picture in the big box which is exactly like the picture in the little box and mark it too. Work fast. Do as many as you can on these two pages before I tell you to stop. Are you ready? Begin!"

for *cognition,* and the product is a discrete chunk or *unit:* "What is an albatross?"—"It's a bird." With four contents, five operations, and six products, therefore, there are a total of 120 abilities (4 × 5 × 6); this theory is shown graphically in Figure 12-4.

Guilford's theory of intelligence is respected but by no means universally accepted; it is still controversial. But multifactor theories, in general, raise some interesting questions, not the least of which has to do with the hereditary basis of intelligence. If there are 120 (or more) unique intellectual abilities, it makes little sense to ask if global "intelligence" is inherited. Each individual ability must be investigated; some abilities appear to be highly dependent on genetic factors, while others apparently are not.

Figure 12-4
Representation of Guilford's Multifactor Theory
Each cell of the cube represents a unique intellectual ability. (From J. P. Guilford, 1967, p. 63)

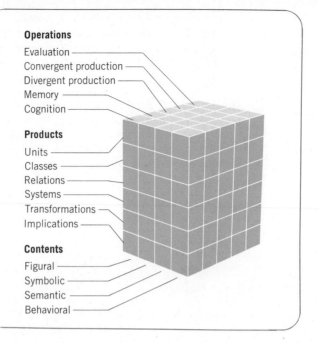

Operations
Evaluation
Convergent production
Divergent production
Memory
Cognition

Products
Units
Classes
Relations
Systems
Transformations
Implications

Contents
Figural
Symbolic
Semantic
Behavioral

SUMMARY

The measurement of human intelligence began in the latter part of the nineteenth century with the work of Galton and Binet. The tests devised by the French psychologist Alfred Binet, in which he stressed reasoning and problem-solving abilities, were found useful in diagnosing mental retardation and in predicting scholastic achievement. The Binet tests became widely used and revisions such as the Stanford-Binet are still used today. The concept of **intelligence quotient** (I.Q.) was developed to describe an individual's **mental age** as a ratio of his or her chronological age. An I.Q. of 100 indicates average mental ability.

The Wechsler scale is a second important intelligence test. Because it is made up of several verbal and performance subtests, it can give a clearer picture of specific strengths and weaknesses. Group tests such as the Army Alpha enable the investigator to test many people at the same time. Intelligence tests for infants have been devised, but assessments before the age of two have not been successful in predicting later achievements, except at the extremes of mental ability.

Intelligence-test scores can be used to predict academic success with reasonable accuracy, but the relationship between I.Q. and vocational success is controversial. Although those in high-status jobs generally have higher test scores, such social-class factors as proper manners and the right connections may be more important. Intelligence tests seem to be unfair to disadvantaged minority children because their experiences are different from those of the standardization group and they have not had parallel experience in taking tests. Available tests work best with white, middle-class children or adults. Scores from other populations must be interpreted cautiously. Attempts to create a **culture-fair test** have been unsuccessful but culture-fair interpretations are even more important.

The stability of the I.Q. is frequently questioned. Generally, the I.Q. is fairly constant over the years, but major environmental changes can produce significant increases in test scores; and, in at least some components, older people (over age forty) show decreases. General intelligence is clearly determined by both genetic and environmental factors, although the relative contribution of each class of factors remains controversial. One of the most controversial issues has been the suggestion that differences between races in mean I.Q. result from genetic differences.

There are various theories of intelligence, depending upon the theorist's definition of what intelligence is. Some theories focus on a general factor, such as Spearman's g, presumably common to all intellectual performance. Others have described a set of between five and ten **primary mental abilities.** Still others posit even more distinct components of intelligence, up to 120. The popular hierarchical theory of intelligence suggests that a few primary abilities influence performance in a large number of specific tasks. These primary abilities, in turn, share a general common factor that could be called general intelligence.

13

Thought and Language

How has human thought been studied?
How do individuals differ in cognitive processes?
What is the relationship between language and thought?

Thought and language are the most prominent capacities that mark the distinction between humans and other animals. The ability to think about the consequences of an action before acting and to use insight to make changes are evolutionary advances of such magnitude that philosophers for centuries refused to consider humans as part of the animal world. Thought and language permit abstractions that can lead to intelligent decisions in new situations. We can consider the past and conceptualize the future in ways no other animal can. We can also "make a mountain out of a molehill" or see a "tempest in a teapot." For better or for worse, human thought and language are among the most significant features of human behavior. And yet, as we shall see, recent research on the symbolic skills of chimpanzees suggests that these animals may not be as far behind humans in symbolic ability as was once believed.

Thought, as it has typically been studied by psychologists, could be defined as the construction, manipulation, and acquisition of symbols and ideas—"The achievement of a new representation through . . . mental operations" (Posner, 1973, p. 147). The construction of new symbols and ideas to overcome barriers to desired ends is the focus of studies of problem solving. Studies of *reasoning,* in contrast, deal with the manipulation of symbols and ideas according to logical rules. And the acquisition of new symbols and ideas is the concern of studies of *concept identification.* People go about solving problems in different ways. There are striking variations in *cognitive styles*—in individuals' characteristic, stable ways of approaching problems. For example, some people seem to arrive intuitively at a solution to a problem, regardless of its content, while others use a more analytic approach.

The processes of symbolization known as *language* are closely related to thinking; language and thought affect each other in many ways. Presumably, frequent or necessary thoughts eventually become identified verbally as words in a language system. On the other hand, a language system might facilitate certain kinds of thought and inhibit others. One investigator (Whorf, 1956) noted that Eskimos have in their language several different words for different kinds of snow. He suggests that they therefore think differently about snow than people with only one word, "snow."

Still, the relationship of thought and language is not simple. People may use a word accurately with little or no conceptual understanding, as young children may use the word "brother" for their but no one else's brother. And one may have a concept with no verbal label, as children seem to understand "pressure" (push hard to open a door that sticks) even though they do not know or understand the concept. Philosophers, linguists, and psychologists have debated the issue of the thought-language relationship for centuries, but the controversy continues. We will examine research on several aspects of cognition, specifically the nature of thinking and problem solving, individual differences in cognitive styles and creativity, and some facts and theories about the relationship between language and thought.

How has human thought been studied?

PROBLEM SOLVING

Problem solving occurs when an individual seeks to attain a desired goal but is prevented from doing so by some barrier. The variety of problems faced by human beings is almost infinite, as this definition makes clear. To give some order to this multitude, problems have been classified in various ways. Some problems are simple, some complex. For example, sharpening a pencil without a pencil sharpener is easier than designing a machine to package lettuce. Problems can also be classified as *tool* or *symbol* problems. Putting objects together to get an object out of reach is a tool problem, whereas solving an anagram (for example, making a word from the letters *HTO*) is a symbol

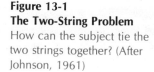

problem. There are social and emotional problems as well (how to win a loved one) that are dealt with extensively by novelists. Most fictional narratives are accounts of problem solving on the part of the hero or heroine.

In their research, psychologists generally have constructed relatively simple tasks that permit them to observe the processes of problem solving. A classic task is the two-string tool problem (Maier, 1931). The subject is presented with two strings hanging from the ceiling, which are to be tied together. The strings, however, are too far apart to grasp both at the same time (*see* Figure 13-1). One solution is to tie a weight to one string and set it swinging like a pendulum. Once the string is swinging, the subject can move to the other string, catch the weighted string on the move, and tie the two together.

In one study with college students, the investigator sought to facilitate the solution by leaving a pair of pliers (usable as a weight) on a table in clear view. Even so, only 39 percent of the subjects solved the problem within 10 minutes. Another 38 percent were able to come up with the solution when the experimenter provided another clue; one string was set into a pendulum motion by brushing a finger against it. Solving the problem requires the use of two common objects (string, pliers) in uncommon ways (as pendulum, as weight); most people are unable to overcome their tendency to see only the common uses of the objects, at least without help.

The two-string problem highlights many of the abiding issues in the study of problem solving. For example, why do some subjects succeed? Explanations of successful problem solving have postulated such processes as *trial and error, insight,* and, more recently, *information seeking* and *hypothesis testing.*

And why do some subjects fail? Failures have been explained as caused by *functional fixedness* and *set*. We will look briefly at each of these factors.

One dimension of the debate over how individuals solve problems has to do with the extent to which their behavior is directed by (a) clear and insightful understanding of the problem, (b) systematic analysis and planning, or (c) random, trial-and-error efforts. The first studies, using animals as subjects, strongly favored the trial-and-error hypothesis. Early researchers, such as Thorndike (1898), found little evidence of understanding, planning, or goal direction in the problem-solving behavior of hungry cats and dogs. In one problem, the animals had to learn to push a lever to open their cage door and gain access to food outside. At first, the hungry animals made many random responses, such as thrashing about and running around the cage. During these random behaviors, some movement or action would accidentally trip the lever. Gradually, this effective response became more immediate, more direct, and more frequent, while other, ineffective responses decreased. Thorndike proposed that the correct response was only gradually stamped in or strengthened, automatically and mechanically, as the animal was rewarded.

Insightful Behavior

The behavior of Thorndike's cats and dogs gave little indication of planned, organized problem-solving behavior or of **insight**—the sudden recognition of the nature of the problem and its correct solution. Later studies, however, have indicated that higher animals like apes do use insight in solving problems. Wolfgang Köhler (1925) worked with a very intelligent chimpanzee named Sultan. One day Sultan had a short stick with him in his cage, and Köhler placed some fruit outside the cage—too far away to be reached by hand or with the short stick. He also placed outside the cage a long stick, too far to be reached by hand but close enough to be pulled in by the short stick. Sultan first tried to reach the fruit with his hand and then with the short stick. Failing, he paused and looked about, saw the long stick, then suddenly took his short

Tool use among wild chimpanzees has been observed many times. This chimp's insightful behavior may also depend on his past experience with trial and error.

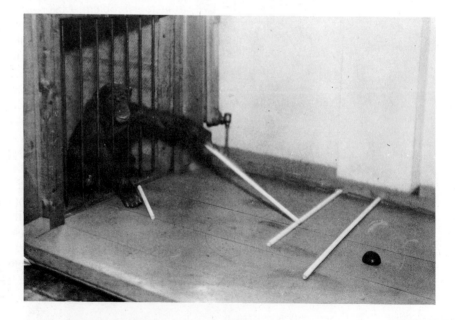

stick and used it to scrape the longer one toward the cage; then he used the long stick to get the fruit.

Köhler concluded that Sultan's use of the stick to solve a new problem was clear evidence of insightful behavior. By insight Köhler meant a sudden, more or less unpredictable reorganization of experiences, something that happens to a person and is more or less outside his or her direct control. It is the kind of insight suggested by cartoons in which a bulb suddenly lights above someone's head, as if a new idea had come from out of the blue.

> The criteria for insight are both subjective and objective. Köhler stresses the importance of the feeling of comprehension or understanding which accompanies insight. This is sometimes called the "Eureka" experience, and involves a feeling of satisfaction that the problem is understood completely (Posner, 1973, p. 178).

Hypothesis Testing

Contemporary theorists believe that the problem solver is much more actively involved than either the trial-and-error or passive-insight theories suggest. In their research, the subjects appear to seek information, to organize their thoughts and plan solutions, and to test hypotheses. The tasks typically used in this research are rather complex problem-solving situations involving, for example, medical diagnosis, finding the trouble with malfunctioning equipment, or the game of twenty questions. The experimenters' conception of their subjects' capacities, however, is reflected in the complexity of the problem-solving tasks. In fact, many psychologists now believe that the early findings supporting trial-and-error conceptions were the result of setting tasks that did not allow or require active thinking, planning, and hypothesis testing; the researchers got "silly" answers because they asked "silly" questions.

An example of the **hypothesis-testing** approach to problem solving is provided in a study in which the task was to discover a hidden pattern (Neimark & Lewis, 1967). Subjects were given several potentially correct patterns and a problem board that concealed the hidden pattern (see Figure 13-2). The problem board contained four shutters, one over each of the concealed elements of the pattern. The subjects were told to predict the pattern by opening as few shutters as possible.

College students became quite adept at finding the pattern. They were able to verbally formulate their problem-solving strategies — the manner in which they went about acquiring information and testing hypotheses. Generally, they used one of two strategies. The *safe* strategy prescribes moving a shutter to provide information that will definitely eliminate some of the possible patterns, but it requires additional shutter moves to arrive at the correct pattern. Using a *gambling* strategy, the student chooses a shutter that, if it provides the right information, could solve the problem at once. If the opened shutter does not provide the right information, however, more moves would be required than in following the safe strategy. Consider the problem in Figure 13-2. Moving shutters A or D first would be safe; either will eliminate two possibilities and the correct answer will be apparent in one additional move. Moving shutters B or C first would be a gamble; if the circle is black, the answer is pattern 4, but if the circle is white, two additional moves will be required.

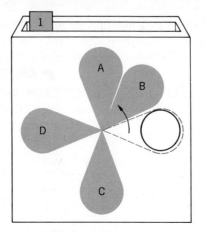 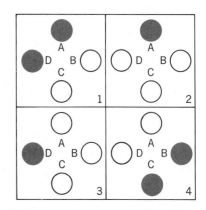

Figure 13-2
Hypothesis Testing with a Problem Board
A problem board with four shutters and an answer array containing four patterns. Shutter *B* has been opened, revealing a white circle beneath; thus patterns 1, 2, or 3 might be the answer, but pattern 4 could not be. In this instance, gambling is not rewarded. (From Neimark & Lewis, 1967)

The strategies employed on this and other types of problem-solving tasks may vary with the situation. In the hidden-pattern study, for example, the students were able to change their strategies in response to changing incentives; they used safe strategies more often when these were rewarded and gambling strategies more often when these were rewarded (Neimark, 1967). In addition, young children are more likely to gamble, whereas older children prefer a safe strategy. Preschool children may be unable to formulate safe strategies that require consideration of more than one move at a time.

The analysis of X-rays is one method of hypothesis-testing as applied to problem solving in medical diagnosis.

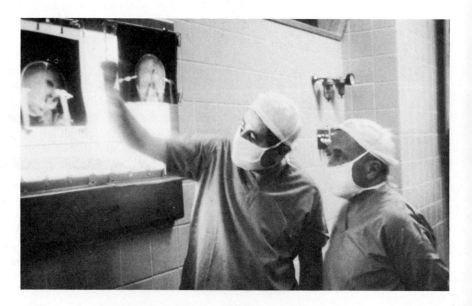

It now appears that trial and error, insight, and hypothesis testing are not mutually exclusive. (Indeed, trial and error and insight might even be regarded as certain kinds of strategies.) Rather, it seems that the type of approach is determined partly by the nature of the problem (simple or complex, tool or symbolic) and partly by the nature of the subject (level of mental development, I.Q., personality, and preference for safe or gambling strategies). Subjects can also shift from one approach to another in the same problem-solving task. Sometimes trial and error is the only way to get sufficient information to formulate hypotheses and strategies. Sometimes, too, trial and error may be necessary to acquire a sufficient backlog of experience to achieve insight.

In an ingenious set of experiments, psychologist Harry Harlow demonstrated one of the ways that insightful behavior depends on previous trial-and-error experience. Monkeys were presented with several discrimination problems. For each problem, the animal was shown two objects that differed in size, shape, and color—a green square and a red circle, for example. If he chose the correct object, he was immediately reinforced, because he found some raisins or peanuts under it. The pair was presented over and over, in different positions, but the reward was always under the same object. When it was clear that the monkey had learned the correct object—when he chose this one on every trial—a new pair of objects was presented. The animal was given another series of trials in which the correct choice was immediately rewarded and trials were continued until this problem was mastered. Animals were presented with a long series of discrimination problems, 344 in one experiment. The animals' problem-solving behavior changed dramatically as they acquired more experience. The first problems presented were solved with a great deal of trial and error, and the solutions were arrived at gradually. After more experience, however, the animals showed a kind of insight; toward the end of a long series, they would reach a correct solution after one, or very few, trials. They had "learned to learn," they knew how to deal with this type of problem; in Harlow's terms, they had developed a "learning set" (Harlow, 1949).

Analogously, in his or her first attempt to set up a chemistry laboratory experiment, the student ordinarily exhibits a great deal of inefficient, trial-and-error activity. After some experience, however, the student can set up experiments quickly and efficiently, even when using different apparatus and chemicals. He or she has learned something of general applicability: how to handle laboratory equipment and chemical substances.

Set and Functional Fixedness

The Harlow experiments nicely illustrate the importance of past experience to problem-solving behavior. Viewed experimentally, past history includes the instruction and training given to subjects before they engage in the problem-solving task. Such past experiences can both facilitate and hinder problem solving. When past experience is regarded as *facilitative*, as in the Harlow experiments, it is usually spoken of as "training." But when past experience is inhibiting, it is usually spoken of as "set" or "functional fixedness." Some examples of these inhibiting effects of past experiences are given below.

A study that measured eye movements demonstrates the effects of **set** (what the subject is "set" or expects to perceive, based on past experience) on problem-solving behavior. The investigators used spatial anagrams (arranged in a square with a single letter in the center) that could be solved by reading the letters in a particular order (Kaplan & Schoenfeld, 1966). For example, the solution to the anagram below is to read the letters in the order of positions, 3 4 5 2 1 ("brick").

The subjects in these investigations were shown several series of anagrams. In the series the first twenty anagrams were unraveled by following one order, the next ten by a different order, and the following ten by still another order. The subjects' progress in anagram solution was measured in two ways: the time it took to attain a solution and the number of visual fixations per anagram.

Results for three subjects are shown in Figures 13-3 and 13-4. The effects of set can be observed in all subjects on the twenty-first and thirty-first trials when there was, in effect, a "failure" of expectancy—that is, when the anagram could not be solved by applying the previously learned rule or order. On these trials both the time necessary for solution and the number of fixations rose significantly above the times and fixations immediately preceding. The increase in time and number of fixations reflected the need to change the set established by the previous pattern of exploring. The data also reveal another facet of problem solving—individuals differ greatly in the rapidity with which they solve problems.

Another negative consequence of past experience for human problem solving has been called **functional fixedness,** the idea that if an object has a customary, usual use, it is difficult to see many other potential uses. A person who needs a screwdriver and is holding a dime shows functional fixedness if he or she does not recognize that the dime could be used as a screwdriver as well as a coin. Past experience with dimes led to seeing dimes as having only a single function and to being blind to its alternative uses.

Functional fixedness was decidedly not demonstrated by a man who, according to newspaper accounts, was taken from his car, robbed, and locked in the trunk. When breathing became difficult he recognized his spare tire as a source of air and by slowly releasing the spare air he managed to survive until help came.

In an early experiment on functional fixedness, the investigator (Duncker, 1945) seated subjects at a table that held a candle, three matches, and a small box of tacks. Control subjects were also shown the same items, but the tacks were not in the box; the box was empty. The subject's task was to attach the candle to a door at about eye level, using the objects on the table. The solution was to tack the box on the door as a holder for the candle. The investigator's hypothesis was that the subjects who first perceived the box as a container (of other objects) would be less likely to see it as a candleholder than subjects who had seen the empty box. His hypothesis was confirmed. All the control subjects (who saw the boxes empty) solved the problem, whereas only

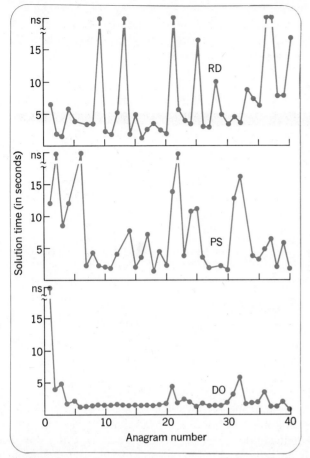

Figure 13-3
Solution Times in Measuring Set

Solution times on successive anagrams are given for three subjects; *ns* indicates no solution. The first 20 anagrams were solvable by the rule 34521; the next 10 by the rule 31245; and the last 10 by the rule 52143. (From Kaplan & Schoenfeld, 1966)

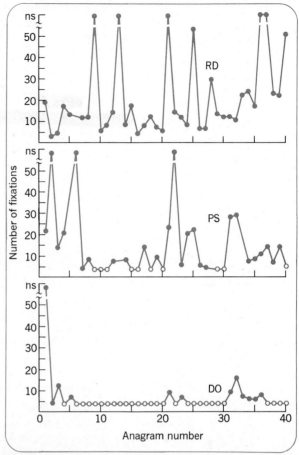

Figure 13-4
Fixations in Measuring Set

Shown are the number of fixations per anagram for subjects of Figure 13-3. The open circles indicate solutions reached after only five fixations in the order of the rule. (From Kaplan & Schoenfeld, 1966)

a few of the experimental subjects (who saw the box as a container) were successful.

Functional fixedness can be diminished by demonstrating to people some uncommon functions of objects. If subjects are trained to use things in unusual ways—for example, rolling newspapers to make a tube—most will spontaneously employ these objects in these ways to solve other, similar problems (Sangstad & Roaheim, 1960). In another experiment, subjects who had used familiar objects such as electric switches or relays in their customary ways were likely to manifest functional fixedness in the two-string problem (*see* p. 323); they were unlikely to use the objects as weights. Other subjects had used the objects in uncommon ways—as a straight edge for drawing lines, or as a container for pins. These subjects were less likely to show functional fixedness and many of them used these objects as weights in solving the two-string problem (Flavell, Cooper, & Joiselle, 1958).

REASONING

Studies of reasoning in adults have been primarily concerned with formal logical **reasoning.** In particular, psychologists have been interested in the errors subjects make in assessing and drawing valid (logical) conclusions. One line of research investigates errors in logical thinking as a function of *task difficulty.* For example, an early study probed the relative difficulty of reasoning with abstract or concrete content (Wilkins, 1928). The investigator asked college students to choose the valid conclusions from syllogisms that were logically identical, but phrased in terms of either familiar words, letters, or unfamiliar (made-up) words (the most abstract content). Try to find the logical conclusion for each of these examples (Wilkins):

A. All the people living on this farm are related to the Joneses; these old men live on this farm; therefore,

　1) these old men are related to the Joneses.
　2) all the people related to the Joneses are these old men.
　3) some people related to the Joneses are not these old men.

B. All X's are Y's; all Z's are X's; therefore,
　1) all Z's are Y's.
　2) all Y's are Z's.
　3) some Y's are not Z's.

C. All lysimachion is epilobium; all adenocaulon is lysimachion; therefore,
　1) all adenocaulon is epilobium.
　2) all epilobium is adenocaulon.
　3) some epilobium is not adenocaulon.

In each example (1) is the valid conclusion.

You probably discovered, as most subjects do, that syllogisms using familiar words, as example *A* above, were the easiest to solve logically; those using symbols or letters were significantly more difficult, and those with unfamiliar, abstract terms (example C) were the most difficult.

When a syllogism has a constant predicate, it is *linear;* when the form of the predicate is altered in one or more of the premises, it is *nonlinear* (Desoto, London & Handel, 1965). Linear syllogisms are easier than nonlinear ones. For example, the syllogism posed by DeSoto et al. (1965):

1) Mantle is better than Mays.

2) Mays is better than Moskowitz.

3) Mantle is better than Moskowitz.

is easier to evaluate than the following, which is equally valid:

1) Mays is better than Moskowitz.

2) Mays is worse than Mantle.

3) Moskowitz is worse than Mantle.

Apparently subjects have to transform the nonlinear syllogisms into their linear equivalents before judging their validity, and this extra step increases the chances of error. The problem is comparable to that faced by a child who can solve the problem $3 + \square = 10$, but not the problem

$$
\begin{array}{r}
3 \\
+\,\square \\
\hline
10.
\end{array}
$$

In the latter case, the child has not only to subtract the 3 from the 10 to get the answer, he or she must also translate the line under "$+\,\square$" into the equal sign and understand that the linear arrangement, $a + b$, and the nonlinear form,

$$
\begin{array}{ccc}
a & & a \\
+b & \text{or} & b,
\end{array}
$$

are equivalent. The more translations and transformations required, the more difficult the problem.

Probabilistic Inference and Personal Convictions

In addition to the structural dimensions of abstractness and nonlinearity, other "content" characteristics of syllogisms can induce errors of reasoning. When persons who are untrained in applying the rules of formal logic are confronted with nonlinear problems, they often rely upon nonlogical, verbal cues in trying to choose a correct solution. For example, consider the following syllogism: "Some redheads are lucky at cards. Some card sharks are redheads. Therefore, we can conclude that some card sharks are lucky at cards." In this premise, the term "some" might lead the untrained reader to assume that the conclusion was correct because it also included the term "some." If a subject forms a global impression of affirmation or negation based on terms like "all" or "none," he or she is more likely to draw false conclusions. Presumably, an "atmosphere effect," created by the presence of the universal term "all" or "none," leads the subject to accept an *invalid* conclusion in which the same universal appears—for example, considering this syllogism valid: No *A*'s are *B*'s; all *B*'s are *C*'s; therefore, no *A*'s are *C*'s.

More recent investigations (Chapman & Chapman, 1959), challenging the concept of atmosphere effects, presented subjects with many different arrangements of syllogisms and provided them with multiple-choice solutions. Here is an example:

Some *L*'s are *K*'s.

Some *K*'s are *M*'s. Therefore,

1) No *M*'s are *L*'s.   *4) None of these.

2) Some *M*'s are *L*'s.   5) All *M*'s are *L*'s.

3) Some *M*'s are not *L*'s.   (*Correct answer.)

After testing several hundred college students the investigators concluded that many of the predictions made by the atmosphere effect theory did not hold up. What they did observe was that the students often showed two types of *para reasoning*, "behaving as fairly reasonable but incautious people" (Chapman & Chapman, 1959, p. 91). In some cases they reasoned as if propositions were reversible, as if "all A's are B's" meant "all B's are A's." In other cases the students reasoned on the basis of *probability* rather than logic. For example, a psychologist might argue: Some hooded rats bite their caretakers; some of the rats in these cages are hooded; therefore, some of the rats in these cages will bite their caretakers. The probability of a bite is high enough to lead the psychologist to exercise caution, but logically one cannot conclude that a caretaker *will* be bitten. The tendency to reason on the basis of probability rather than on formal rules of logic has been called **probabilistic inference.** Such inferences together with the assumption of the reversibility of logical premises appear to account for all the errors of logic that were once attributed to atmosphere effect.

Personal convictions may also affect an individual's response to syllogistic reasoning, especially to propositions involving controversial issues. A syllogism can be constructed, for example, in which the logically correct (valid) answer is factually false. "All men are immortal. I am a man—therefore I am immortal." Another possible response to this syllogism is "I am mortal," which is true but not logically valid. When the topic of the syllogism is controversial and deals with strong personal beliefs, logic is less likely to determine the choice of conclusions. For the premises, "Abortion is a right of women" and "The rights of women should be protected by law," the logical conclusion is that abortion should be legalized. But people with strong attitudes against abortion are likely to see this conclusion as invalid. For the premises, "Abortion is murder" and "Murder should be prohibited by law," the logical conclusion is that abortion should be prohibited. People strongly favorable to abortion would be more likely to see this conclusion as invalid.

Errors in reasoning do not necessarily reflect an *inability* to reason logically. Sometimes errors result from a failure to apply rules of argument to statements that do not appear in a syllogistic format. Consider the following: "We spend so much time in the kitchen that of course household problems are on our minds. So it is important to talk about them." When students were asked whether the conclusion, "So it is important to talk about them," was valid, they avoided the formal, logical aspects of the task and responded in terms of content. One student wrote: "Yes, . . . by talking about household problems a problem can be solved or worked through" (Henle, 1962).

Other errors in logical reasoning are attributable to the subject's supplying an additional premise that is not part of the syllogism. In responding to an argument about comic books, for example, one subject concluded: "If comic books are an evil influence, they should be got rid of." What the subject added was an implicit premise that "evil influences should be eliminated." Such added premises—often based on the subject's personal convictions, moral and emotional commitments, and the assumption that they are universal—may lead to conclusions that are not *logically* valid (Henle, 1962).

Reasoning in Children

Studies of reasoning in children have been more varied than those with adults and reflect more concern with the development of **mediating processes,** internal processes that enable children to reason and solve problems "in their heads." In research on adult reasoning, it is taken for granted that the subjects have the *ability* to reason logically, so factors that produce errors in reasoning

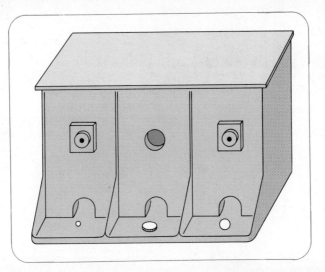

Figure 13-5
Apparatus to Study Reasoning
By pressing the button on the left, the subject can get a steel ball that, when placed in the center hole, will produce a charm. Preschool children have difficulty solving the problem of how to get a charm.

are examined. But in children the abilities that make reasoning possible are in question. What is the nature of the mediating processes and when do they appear during development? Piaget has addressed much of his work to this question, and his theory of the development of *mental operations* (his term for mediating processes) is discussed elsewhere (p. 249). Here we will look at experimental studies of reasoning in children.

Several investigators (Kendler & Kendler, 1962, for example) have used a basic experimental design that requires the child to combine two different experiences to reach a desired goal. For example, in learning to use the apparatus shown in Figure 13-5, the child is first taught that if he or she presses a button on the left, a steel ball will be delivered; pressing the button on the right brings a marble. After this is learned, the center section is opened and the side sections closed; the child then learns that if he or she puts a steel ball into the center hole, an attractive charm drops out of the slot at the bottom; if a glass marble is inserted, nothing happens. Finally, all three sections are opened and the child is instructed to get the charm. All he or she has to do is press the left button (which the child knows will yield a steel ball), and then put the steel ball in the center hole to get the charm. Can the child combine these two bits of learning to solve the problem? Preschool children have difficulty. For some reason they do not associate the steel ball that comes from pushing the button on the left with the steel ball that gets the charm. Children over seven or eight and adults solve this two-part problem easily.

Perhaps the younger children fail to solve the two-stage reasoning problems because they lack verbal labels that might function as mediators. Perhaps if the child was taught to say "ball" when the steel ball was delivered after a button was pressed and "ball" again when the steel ball was inserted in the center section to get the charm, this verbal label would mediate the necessary association between these two actions. Such labeling was done in one study. Although performance did improve, the increase in number of correct solutions was much less than expected—at least for nursery-school children. These data led to the hypothesis that there are three stages in verbal

Without the ability to manipulate verbal mediators such as "more" or "less," "thicker," or "thinner," the child is unable to solve many quantity problems.

mediation. In the *preverbal stage*, the child does not have or understand the words necessary for solution. In the *verbal deficiency stage*, the child seems to know the appropriate words, but the verbal labels do not mediate behaviors to similar stimuli. In our example, the child might spontaneously say "ball" when the steel ball comes out after a button press, and "ball" when he or she inserts the steel ball in the top hole to get a charm. But the use of these verbal mediators does not help to put the two actions together and solve the problem. The third stage could be called the *verbal mediation stage*, in which words are both available *and* effective in mediating responses. The last stage is characteristic of most school children and, of course, adults.

A more cognitive approach to children's reasoning is seen in Donaldson's work (1963). She used a variety of tasks or problems, for example, the following:

> Five boys, Jack, Dick, James, Bob, and Tom, go to five different schools in the same town. The schools are called North School, South School, East School, West School, and Central School.

> Jack does not go to North, South or Central School.
> Dick goes to West School.
> Bob does not go to North or Central School.
> Tom has never been inside Central School.

> 1) What school does Jack go to?　　3) What school does James go to?
> 2) What school does Bob go to?　　4) What school does Tom go to?

Children's errors fell within a few more or less circumscribed categories. Some were *structural* and really reflected the child's failure to grasp the problem and what was required for a solution. Other errors were *arbitrary* in the sense that the child did not sufficiently attend to the data that was provided. Last but not least were *executive* errors; the child understood the problem and the manipulations required for its solution but for one reason or another failed to execute the required operation. Such executive errors may be attributed to "some defect of concentration, of attention, or of immediate memory" (Donaldson, 1963).

A third approach to understanding reasoning in children derives from a developmental, educational, and pedagogical perspective. In one study (Suppes & Hull, 1961) children between six and eight were presented with simple problems in logic. They were given two or three premises after which they were required to judge whether or not a particular conclusion followed from them. One item read: "If that boy is John's brother, then he is ten years old. That boy is not ten years old. Is he John's brother?" The six-year-olds got 71 percent of the items correct, the seven-year-olds 80 percent, and the eight-year-olds 86 percent. A control group solved the same problems but did not have the first premises of the arguments; these subjects provide an estimate of how many items will be correct by guessing. For example, the control group's version of the illustrated item was "If that boy is not ten years old, is he John's brother?" Not surprisingly, the control group averaged only 52 percent correct, just about what would be expected by chance. Clearly, even "six-year-old children performed at quite a high level, in contradiction to the view of Piaget and his followers that such children are limited to concrete operations" (Suppes, 1970, p. 526) and that the ability to draw correct logical inferences from hypothetical premises increases steadily with age. Logical reasoning may be useful even in teaching young children!

CONCEPT FORMATION

Concepts are indispensable tools of mental activity and make up the content of human thought. When you think, you generally use concepts. What is a **concept?** As it is used by psychologists today, a concept is either: (1) a symbol or representation of a class of objects that have a common characteristic (or characteristics)—even though they differ in other ways; or (2) a rule (or set of rules) designating how objects are to be grouped. For example, a child who calls both a dachshund and a Great Dane "dog" would be said to understand the concept "dog." Similarly a child who calls twelve M&M's a "dozen" would be said to have grasped the rule that any group of twelve things can be called a dozen. Early studies of **concept formation** examined the processes by which subjects discovered the characteristics common to diverse objects. More recent investigations have studied how rules for grouping diverse objects are learned and applied.

Studies of the discrimination of common stimulus characteristics have often been based on a classic investigation by Hull (1920). Hull presented subjects with packs of cards containing Chinese symbols (called characters). The characters were given a label, like "oo" or "na," assigned on the basis of their sharing a common embedded element. Somewhere embedded in the following "oo's" is the symbol shown last:

The subject was instructed to give the proper label when each character was presented. If he or she did not respond within a certain time, or if the response was incorrect, the experimenter indicated the correct answer. The first time through a set of characters, of course, no correct replies were possible, but the subjects quickly learned the concepts. Learning was greatly facilitated by making the embedded element stand out (by outlining it in a different color, for example). This procedure proved to be much more effective in facilitating concept learning than presenting the critical elements in isolation.

In a similar experiment, subjects had to learn to associate arbitrary labels such as "relf" and "fard" to different kinds of pictorial stimuli (Heidbreder, 1946). The subjects learned the nonsense words associated with concrete objects (faces, buildings, articles of clothing) more quickly than they learned the labels associated with such abstract stimuli as geometric forms or numbers. In brief, concepts were more easily attained if they had realistic qualities, and perceptually prominent features—those which stood out—were more easily learned as concepts.

Learning Rules for Concepts

Recent research in this field has been centered on more complex concepts and rules for identifying the critical stimulus attributes that define a concept. For example, in one well-known series of investigations (Bruner, Goodnow, & Austin, 1956) subjects were presented with a display of eighty-one cards with figures and borders. The figures varied in color, shape, and number, and the cards had single or double borders (see Figure 13-6). The subjects' task was to identify which cards were "positive" and which were "negative"— that is, which exemplified, and which did not exemplify, a concept that the experimenter had in mind. Suppose that the experimenter's concept was *red circles*. If the subject pointed to a card with two crosses, he or she would be informed that this choice was incorrect (negative). If the next card chosen had three red circles, he or she would be told that this answer was positive. If the next card designated had any red circles, the subject would again learn that this selection was positive. The procedure continued until the correct concept was stated. Subjects were also given one other important piece of information: they were told whether the concept the experimenter had in mind was conjunctive or disjunctive. A **conjunctive concept** is defined by the joint presence of several attributes, and all members of the class share all the designated attributes, such as two red circles. "WASP" is a conjunctive concept, referring to an individual who is white, Anglo-Saxon, and Protestant. A **disjunctive concept** is defined by the presence of one attribute (or set of attributes) or another, in either/or fashion. A disjunctive concept is illustrated by all figures that are red *or* circles, but not both. The concept "child" refers to *either* boys *or* girls; *either* three-year olds *or* ten-year olds.

The ease or difficulty of acquiring a concept is partially a function of its complexity (for example, the number of dimensions it employs—color, shape, number of figures) and also of its logical structure. Conjunctive concepts are much easier to learn than disjunctive ones.

There is a hierarchy of levels of difficulty in learning the rules for combining attributes to form concepts (Neisser & Weene, 1962). A rule (Level I) dealing with a single dimension ("all red figures") is the easiest to acquire. Next (Level II) in difficulty are simple conjunctive ("and") and disjunctive ("or") rules, such as "figures that are small *and* red," or "figures that are small *or* red." Finally, the most difficult rules to acquire (Level III) are those that demand either more than one conjunction or disjunction or a combination of conjunction and disjunction (for example, "all the red figures except the red figures on cards that have two borders").

While subjects are learning attributes or acquiring rules, they often test or try out various hypotheses one after another. If the subject uses a hypothesis-testing approach to concept attainment, he or she will not make any more errors after arriving at the correct hypothesis; it is as though concept learning were an all-or-none process. Bower and Trabasso (1964) analyzed the pattern of errors made by subjects as they were working on a concept-attainment task. Before the subjects achieved the correct solution and identified the concepts—that is, before their last error—there was no evidence of learning. Instead, subjects performed at a chance level and were correct only about as often as they would be blind guessing. During the guessing period, subjects were not attempting to solve the problem through trial and error; rather, they were testing various hypotheses until they arrived at the correct solution. Once this occurred, the correct response was completely established and there were no further errors.

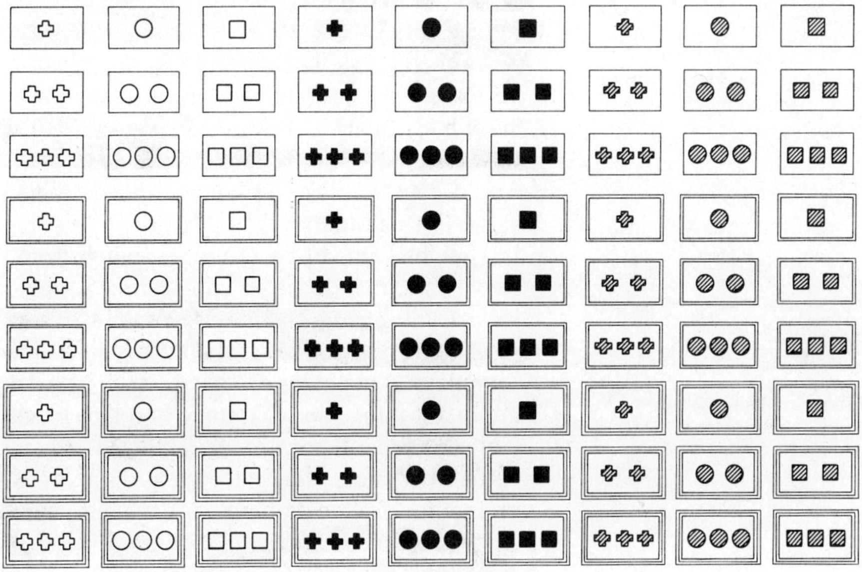

Figure 13-6
Cards Used in Studying Conjunctive and Disjunctive Concepts

Cards vary in four attributes: color, shape, number of figures, and number of borders. Outlined figures are in green, solid figures in black, striped figures in red. (From Bruner, Goodnow, & Austin, 1956)

The assumption of all-or-nothing concept learning has been challenged. For one thing, the hypothesis itself may be constructed from the subject's history of successes and failures; a gradual reduction of errors could have been going on in the subject's mind even though it was not manifest in his or her behavior (Dodd & Bourne, 1969). In some ways the issue of all-or-nothing versus gradual learning (hypothesis testing versus discrimination of relevant attributes) is like the issue of insight versus trial-and-error learning in problem solving. In both cases, it is probable that both types of strategy are applied and that these complement rather than contradict one another.

Rule Learning Among Children

Research on rule learning among children has a somewhat different emphasis than the research on adults. This difference is easier to understand if you will recall the three levels of rules described by Neisser & Weene (1962). What level of rules can children employ? Piaget's work (p. 245) demonstrates that young children operate at Level I, elementary school children at Level II, and adolescents at Level III in the Neisser scheme. In the experimental literature, Level I behavior is often described as "unmediated," whereas Levels II and III behavior is described as "mediated."

An excellent experimental paradigm for demonstrating the role of mediating processes (high-level rules) in concept formation is the **reversal shift** problem (Kendler & Kendler, 1967, 1975). In a typical task, the subject is presented with two squares at a time and has to learn to choose one of them (*see* Figure 13-7). The squares vary in size (large and small) and color (black and white). The subject is consistently reinforced or rewarded (given a marble) for choosing *either* color *or* size. If color is the relevant dimension, the subject would be rewarded every time he or she chose the black square regardless of its size. The size dimension would be irrelevant in this instance; that is, it is not used in making the correct discrimination. In a reversal shift, the subject must learn to reverse responses. Previously positive stimuli become negative; to obtain the reward, the child must do exactly the opposite of what he or she has done previously in the same situation. After learning to choose the black square, for example, the child is confronted with a new problem in which choosing the white square is rewarded. In a **nonreversal** (extradimensional) **shift,** the previously irrelevant dimension becomes relevant; in our example, the child would have to make a choice—and be rewarded for it—on the basis of size (large or small) rather than of color.

It might seem to be easier to switch from black to white choices, the reversal shift, than to begin considering a previously irrelevant dimension. And, in fact, the reversal shift is easier than the nonreversal shift for children over seven and for adults, probably because they can use verbal mediators or formulate a hypothesis. That is, they can tell themselves that "color is the important thing" so when they find that black is no longer rewarded, they try white. However, because younger children and animals lack the ability to use verbal mediators, they have great difficulty with reversal shifts and do better on nonreversal, extradimensional shifts. Apparently, to do the opposite of what you have been trained to do is easier if you use verbal mediators like color to identify the critical dimension.

In the reversal-shift studies, one interpretation is that as the child grows older

Figure 13-7
Examples of a Reversal and a Nonreversal Shift

In a reversal shift, the subject first learns to select the large stimuli; then, on the second discrimination, he or she is reinforced for selecting the small stimuli. In a nonreversal shift, the subject must respond to another dimension (color or brightness) in the second discrimination. (From Kendler & Kendler, 1962)

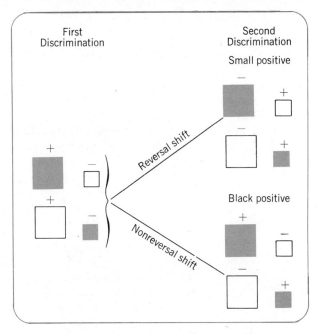

he or she moves from Level I to Level II behavior as a result of acquiring verbal mediators that make possible the formulation of higher order rules. This is essentially the position of Jerome Bruner (1964), who suggests that cognitive development is essentially an improvement in the child's representational skills, from motor to truly symbolic representation. Piaget, in contrast, argues that the development from Level I to Level II behavior (from the preoperational to the concrete operational level; see p. 249) is a matter of the development of qualitatively new mental abilities that are quite different from those possessed earlier. This whole matter involves the relationship between language and thought, which will be dealt with in more detail later in this chapter (see p. 349).

Schema Approach to Concept Formation

A recent development in concept-formation research (which nonetheless has roots at least as far back as Bartlett, 1932) assumes that a concept is a **schema** or a composite photograph of the many instances of a class of objects. Advocates of this approach argue that a concept can be defined in terms of this composite or prototype, rather than in terms of particular stimulus elements.

Although the schema approach to concept assessment has been used with a variety of perceptual stimuli (Franks & Bransford, 1971; Lasky, 1974), it is perhaps best illustrated with verbal materials (Bransford & Franks, 1971). In one study the investigators constructed prototype sentences that contained all the ideas in an imaginary scene (see Figure 13-8). Subjects were then read simpler sentences that contained one or more but not all of the ideas in the prototype sentence. Then they were read additional "recognition sentences" that also contained some but not all of the prototypic ideas. When the subjects were asked to identify which recognition sentences were read to them first, subjects were more likely to say that they had heard the prototype sentence

Figure 13-8

PROTOTYPE SENTENCE AND THREE IDEAS

Prototype The ants in the kitchen ate the sweet jelly which was on the table.
(On Recognition Only)

Three Ideas The ants ate the sweet jelly which was on the table.
(On Acquisition Only)
The ants in the kitchen ate the jelly which was on the table.
(On Acquisition Only)
The ants in the kitchen ate the sweet jelly.
(On Recognition Only)

Two Ideas The ants in the kitchen ate the jelly.
(On Acquisition Only)
The ants ate the sweet jelly.
(On Both Acquisition and Recognition)
The sweet jelly was on the table.
(On Recognition Only)
The ants ate the jelly which was on the table.
(On Recognition Only)

One Idea The ants were in the kitchen.
(On Acquisition Only)
The jelly was on the table.
(On Acquisition Only)
The jelly was sweet.
(On Recognition Only)
The ants ate the jelly.
(On Recognition Only)

The top sentence is the prototype sentence. The remaining sentences present one or more ideas from the prototype. Each sentence is presented either during learning or during recognition.

Reprinted from Bransford, J. D., & Franks, J. J. Abstraction of linguistic ideas. *Cognitive Psychology*, 1971, 2, 331–50.

than the sentences which had actually been read to them. These results are explained, according to schema theory, by saying that in memory, information was lost about individual instances while a general representation was stored that captured the overall idea.

This prototype approach to concept attainment has not gone unchallenged. One investigator (Neumann, 1974) has carried out several experiments that support an alternative explanation of the prototype data. Neumann argues that even though the subject does not see or hear the prototype, the elements contained within it are presented more frequently than in the transformation which the subject does experience. From this standpoint, the frequency with which particular elements are presented determines concept attainment, rather than the abstraction of some overall whole.

At this point it is not clear which position will prove to be correct. Possibly, concepts are attained in more than one way; and some may be formed by the abstraction of general prototypes, while others are formed by attention to specific attributes. Darwin once said that people could be grouped as "lumpers" and "splitters." Perhaps prototypic and specific attribute approaches to concept attainment reflect these two basic ways in which humans go about conceptualizing their world.

How do individuals differ in cognitive processes?

COGNITIVE STYLES

The individual's performance in tasks involving problem solving, reasoning, and concept learning often reflects his or her motivations and personality. Stable, characteristic ways of approaching and handling cognitive tasks are called **cognitive styles.** In a way, the strategies described earlier can be regarded as cognitive styles; it is easy to imagine the kind of person who might consistently adopt a gambling strategy and the kind who usually adopts a safe one (see p. 325). The cognitive styles described below are related to other personality traits and to such variables as sex and childrearing.

Reflectivity-Impulsivity

Some people are *impulsive* in solving problems; they act on the basis of the first solution that comes to mind with little consideration for its adequacy. Others are *reflective,* thinking about many possible solutions, evaluating alternatives, censoring their ideas, and weighing the products of their thinking. Individual differences in **reflective-impulsivity** are evidenced as early as age two and seem to be consistent and stable over time (Kagan, 1966).

In a test for reflectivity-impulsivity, the Matching Familiar Figures test, the child is asked to select one stimulus from six variants that is identical with a standard (Kagan, 1966). (See Figure 13-9.) The time it takes the subject to make his or her first choice (response time) and the number of errors made before choosing the correct response are the two variables scored. At every age between five and eleven there is a negative correlation between response time and errors; those who are fastest in responding tend to make the most errors—they are the impulsive ones. Reflective children respond more slowly and make fewer errors. Impulsive children make more errors than reflective children in several tasks, including reading aloud. In tests of inductive reasoning they respond more quickly and make more errors. Reflective children tend to use orderly, systematic strategies, trying to solve problems by asking the experimenter yes or no questions; few impulsive children work this way. In general, reflective subjects generate more efficient hypotheses and systematically consider more alternatives than impulsive children. The latter seldom formulate abstract hypotheses and characteristically use information in random, trial-and-error ways (McKinney, 1973).

Leveling-Sharpening

In a classic study on remembering, Sir Frederick Bartlett (1932) observed that when a story was passed around from person to person it underwent certain transformations. Some of the unusual elements of the story became more

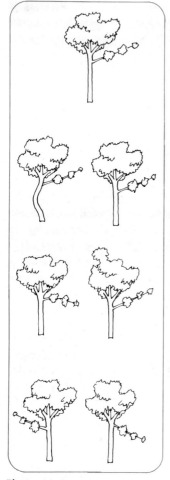

Figure 13-9
Matching Familiar Figures
Response time and errors in matching figures indicate degree of impulsivity or reflectivity.

common or usual ("leveled"), while other unusual aspects were increasingly accentuated ("sharpened"). It has been noted that some individuals tend to level (see similarities among things and make them alike), and others are more likely to sharpen (to accentuate differences) in handling cognitive problems.

For example, when making judgments about the sizes of a series of squares of progressively increasing size, some subjects (levelers) tend to see new stimuli as very similar to those previously presented, often missing an actual change. Others (sharpeners) notice changes quickly and accurately (Holzman & Klein, 1954). The tendency to level or to sharpen seems to be generalized, applicable to many cognitive performances. Sharpeners are superior to levelers in recalling stories they heard years earlier (Holzman & Gardner, 1960); and levelers are more likely to simplify the grammatical structure of verbal materials they are asked to recall (Levant, 1962).

Field Independence and Dependence

Perhaps the best-known of individual differences in cognitive styles is **field independence** or **dependence.** Field-dependent people rely on external stimuli (stimuli in their environment) for their judgments; field-independent people rely more on internal cues. An illustrative situation—one in which the distinction was first observed—is a pilot flying in a cloud or fog. Some pilots in such a situation (without instruments) emerge from the cloud upside down (and thoroughly surprised). Such pilots would be called field dependent. Without external cues, they literally could not tell up from down. Field-independent pilots did not rely so heavily on the view (or lack of it) and estimated their position in relation to the ground by using cues from their own bodies.

In a similar laboratory test, subjects sat in complete darkness facing a luminous rod that was surrounded by a luminous frame. Both the rod and the frame could be tilted independently, and the subject saw them first in a tilted position. Then, while the frame remained tilted, he or she was told to direct the experimenter to move the rod until it appeared vertical. Some subjects adjusted the rod so that it appeared vertical in the context of the visual frame (field) that surrounded it. Other subjects ignored the orientation of the frame and directed the experimenter to align the rod so that it was vertical with respect to their own body position. The first solution was called field dependent, the second field independent (Witkin et al., 1962).

Field dependence or independence, as measured by the rod-and-frame test, turned out to be related to a number of other variables. Women tend to be more field dependent than men, and young children are, on the average, more field dependent than are older ones. Field-dependent people are more likely to change their opinions when they learn that these are different from

The subject taking the rod-and-frame test indicates when the adjustable rod is straight up and down.

the opinions of an authority. Furthermore, field-dependent people tend to be socially oriented; they are good at remembering people and faces and often choose occupations involving contact with people.

The cognitive-style approach to human thinking brings us closer to the unique individual. It is important to remember, however, that no one is consistently impulsive or reflective, field dependent or field independent in all situations. The notion of cognitive styles is useful if we remember that it is basically a typology that never fits any one individual perfectly.

CREATIVITY

Some people say intelligence and creativity are synonymous because both involve cognition or thought; others say the two are completely different. What is the relationship between the two, if any? What distinguishes the creative person from the ordinary?

Consider the relevant distinction between convergent and divergent thinking. **Convergent thinking** applies to questions that have one correct answer, such as, "What is the capital of Nebraska?" or "What is the best way to milk a cow?" **Divergent thinking** is reflected in answering such questions as, "How many uses can you think of for a kitchen knife?" or "How are these two objects—a potato and a carrot—alike? List as many ways as you can" (Guilford, 1964).

Many psychologists believe this distinction is necessary to the understanding of **creativity.** Traditional intelligence tests do not assess creativity because they are designed to measure only convergent thinking, the extent to which the individual follows accepted patterns of thought. On the vocabulary test of most intelligence scales, for example, the subjects' score reflects how closely their definitions of particular terms correspond to the dictionary definition. Tests of creativity assess divergent thinking, the extent to which the individual's thinking is innovative or unique and diverges from customary thought patterns.

Many different measures of divergent thinking have been devised. In one, subjects are told to create as many words as they can from the letters of a word like "generation." The originality score is the number of *uncommon* responses (not occurring more than once in a hundred responses) (Barron, 1957). A similar test, called "Unusual Uses," requires the subject to think of uses other than the common one for particular objects such as a brick. Responses are then scored on a five-point scale of originality by a team of raters (Guilford, 1964).

In one study, a large sample of entering freshmen at Duke University was asked to list as many uses they could think of for common objects such as a shoe, as many meanings they could imagine for abstract drawings, and as many similarities they could see in pairs of common objects such as "potato-carrot" (Wallach & Wing, 1969). The number and uniqueness of their responses were unrelated to their scores on standard intelligence tests; apparently this kind of creativity is quite different from general intellectual ability—at least among college students. But divergent thinking was found to be correlated with creative achievement (winning prizes and awards) in the fields of art and writing.

Furthermore, highly creative college freshmen—those scoring high in tests of divergent thinking—approach problem-solving tasks in ways that are quite different from those used by less creative students (Goor & Sommerfield, 1975). The subjects talked aloud while they solved three problems, and their verbalizations were recorded and analyzed. The two groups of freshmen began to work on the problems in similar ways, but their thought patterns gradually became more discrepant as they continued to work. The highly creative subjects spent significantly more time than the low-creatives in "generating new information," "in developing or working on a hypothesis," — the categories most representative of the creative process—and in "self-reference or self-criticism."

Not all psychologists consider creativity and general intelligence as independent concepts, however. Some, like Guilford, consider divergent thinking as a neglected aspect of intelligence (see p. 317), while others consider it a very limited aspect of creativity.

Characteristics of Creative Persons

Another way to approach the question of creativity is to investigate the characteristics of people who are generally recognized as very creative. What are famous creative writers such as Truman Capote, Norman Mailer, MacKinlay Kantor, Frank O'Connor, and Kenneth Rexroth really like? One psychologist (Barron, 1957) convinced a number of writers to spend three days in a research center taking tests and undergoing extensive interviews. Some of them were rated (by other writers) as highly creative; others were less creative. Mathematicians and architects of varying degrees of creativity were also studied.

After the interviews and tests were completed, staff members of the research center rated the subjects on a large number of personality dimensions. Table 13-1 gives the correlations between some of the personality items (rated by Q sort; see p. 148) and degree of creativity. In general, the highly creative subjects were judged to be independent, nonconforming, unconventional in

TABLE 13-1 Q-sort items correlated with creativity

Q-Sort Item	Correlation with Creativity Rating
Thinks and associates to ideas in unusual ways: has unconventional thought processes.	+.64
Is an interesting, arresting person.	+.55
Tends to be rebellious and nonconforming.	+.51
Genuinely values intellectual and cognitive matters.	+.49
Appears to have a high degree of intellectual capacity.	+.46
Is self-dramatizing; histrionic.	+.42
Has fluctuating moods.	+.40
Judges self and others in conventional terms like "popularity," "the correct thing to do," "social pressures," and so forth.	−.62
Is a genuinely dependable and responsible person.	−.45
Behaves in a sympathetic or considerate manner.	−.43
Favors conservative values in a variety of areas.	−.40
Is moralistic.	−.40

Certain aspects of creativity can be measured by scientific means. But wouldn't there be some disagreement among these three groups as to what constitutes musical creativity?

thought and action, rebellious, moody, flexible, self-accepting, and relatively lacking in self-control, responsibility, and dependability. They reported less of a sense of well-being than the less creative subjects and were less concerned with "making good impressions." Creative writers and creative research scientists were remarkably similar in personality, despite the differences in their professional work. It must be remembered that these findings represent only trends and that they do not characterize any one creative person completely. Indeed, one of the predominant characteristics of creative people is that they are original and do not fit into general types, categories, or pigeon-holes.

Creativity, Intelligence, and Personality

As we have seen, creativity as measured by the number and uniqueness of ideas is not highly correlated with intelligence, at least not in people who are above average in I.Q. The independence of these two traits makes it possible to identify people who are high in one but not the other, people who are high in both, and others who are low in both. In one extensive study, the personalities and social behavior of these four types were thoroughly investigated (Wallach & Kogan, 1965).

The subjects were 151 fifth-grade pupils who were average or above average in intelligence and generally from middle-class families. In general, high

creativity was associated with self-awareness, openness to experience, and stimulation from both internal and external sources. Children who were highly intelligent *and* creative were successful in school and in their relationships with peers. They were self-confident and popular with their friends, free of anxiety about having unconventional ideas. Highly creative children of average intelligence had little self-confidence and tended to be cautious and hesitant in social situations. Those who were highly intelligent but low in creativity were sought out by their peers but seemed to be a bit aloof and cautious with others. Spotlight 13-1 summarizes the evaluations of the children in the various groups.

Stages in the Creative Process

When creative people tell about how they arrive at their ideas, a common pattern emerges that seems to be constant for most intellectual endeavors. It must be remembered, however, that our ability to reconstruct our own mental processes is subject to error. Although the phases of the creative process outlined below do occur, they probably do not invariably occur in the sequence described here. To illustrate these stages we will use material provided by Watson in his book *The Double Helix* (1968), in which he describes how he and his colleague Crick finally solved the mystery of the secret of the genetic code.

In the first **preparation stage,** a person acquires all possible information about a problem. Watson has described his preoccupation with the problem of

High Creativity

High Intelligence
These children exercise both control and freedom, exhibit both adultlike and childlike behavior.

Average Intelligence
These children are in angry conflict with themselves and with their school environment and are beset by feelings of unworthiness and inadequacy. In a stress-free context, however, they can blossom cognitively.

Low Creativity

High Intelligence
These children can be described as "addicted" to school achievement. Academic failure is perceived as catastrophic, so they continually strive for academic excellence, to avoid the possibility of pain.

Average Intelligence
Basically bewildered, these children engage in various defensive maneuvers, ranging from useful adaptations—such as intensive social activity—to regressions—such as passivity or psychosomatic symptoms.

Abstracted from M. A. Wallach & N. Kogan, *Modes of Thinking in Young Children.* New York: Holt, Rinehart and Winston, 1965.

finding the structure of the DNA molecule. The first step toward a solution was immersing himself in all the available information about the structure of molecules gleaned from laboratory and library research. This period of intensive preparation set the stage for the next phase.

In one period during the search for the answer, work seemed to be going nowhere; there were many blind alleys. During this time Watson and Crick went on ski trips and engaged in other relaxing activities. This was the **incubation stage** during which the material they had acquired could be absorbed and assimilated. To the creative person, the incubation period often appears to be barren and unproductive, but it is in fact very important. Creative people often "sleep" on a problem and awaken with a solution. Undoubtedly there is a great deal of unconscious mental activity during this stage.

After the period of incubation there is a rather sudden **illumination stage,** in which new ideas arrive quite unexpectedly. In the case of Watson and Crick, the idea of a double helix came suddenly after Watson had attended an old movie in which there was a spiral staircase. Of course, such sudden insights can turn out to be quite misleading, although in the first glow of illumination, the idea seems perfect. Many people get so infatuated with new ideas that they act on them immediately without going through the final all-important **verification stage.**

The notion that the DNA molecule was a double helix had to be tested. Watson and Crick constructed a physical model of the molecule and then did the experimental tests that supported the predictions based upon the double helix hypothesis. Their results were confirmed by other investigators, and both men won the Nobel prize in chemistry. Although the actual process of discovery is more complex than the one just described, the phases of preparation, incubation, illumination, and verification have been noted in the histories of many creative productions.

What is the relationship between language and thought?

Recently a young preschool child, absent from nursery school for several days due to illness, was asked about the nature of her illness. "I had dia-perrhea," she replied. This creative reply reflects a very important facet of human intelligence—the ability to manufacture symbols to express our inner thoughts, feelings, and experiences. **Language** is the primary symbolic system created to communicate and to codify meaning.

The relationship between language and thinking are complex and entail varied and difficult problems. All theories of thinking are concerned with language. Can animals, which are less intelligent than humans, be taught to communicate with symbols? This issue is examined in Spotlight 13-2. A second question has to do with the origins of thought and language. Which comes first? Does language induce thought or does thought induce language? Still another issue has to do with the relationship among culture, language, and thought. To what extent do different languages contribute to different ways of thinking about and experiencing the world?

ORIGINS OF THOUGHT AND LANGUAGE

Is the ability to think dependent on the possession of words, a language, to think with? Psychologists have given different answers to this important question. Some of the early investigators believed that language was the essence of thought. According to John B. Watson (1913), "thought processes are really motor habits in the larynx." In his view, the child, under pressure not to talk out loud, internalizes speech; speech becomes subvocal, and thus the equivalent of thought (Slobin, 1971). Thought, in this view, is nothing more than responses associated with speech.

Skinner's Approach

Basically, B. F. Skinner's position (1957) is consistent with Watson's: language and speech, no less than thought, are **behaviors** and can be understood in terms of behavioral principles, particularly reinforcement. Words are first and foremost responses; and the speech that occurs in a particular situation will depend on the stimulus conditions and the reinforcement history of the speaker. For Skinner, language, although more complex than other forms of behavior, is as predictable and modifiable, in principle, as the pattern of bar-pressing by a rat that receives direct reinforcement (a pellet of food) every time it presses a bar.

At the same time, however, Skinner acknowledges that verbal behavior is unique in one respect: it brings reinforcements indirectly rather than directly. The rat that presses the bar is rewarded *directly* for its act by a food pellet; when the young child says "water" (or something that sounds like it), the

That animals communicate with members of their own species and even with animals of other species is clear. But can a subhuman animal learn the highly complex language systems of humans? Possibly because the high phylogenetic status of humans is often ascribed in large part to language capacities, psychologists have long been interested in attempts to teach language to other animals. Most of the attempts have involved the highly intelligent primate, the chimpanzee, and at first they were notably unsuccessful. In one study, a female chimp was raised as a member of the family (Kellogg & Kellogg, 1933). The chimp learned to follow directions to some extent, but she never learned to speak. In another attempt, the chimp was given special speech training but managed, finally, to produce only three recognizable human words—"Mama," "Papa," and "cup" (Hayes & Hayes, 1952). The studies were often stated as evidence that only humans could learn a true language.

More recent research shows this conclusion to be at least misleading. One pair of researchers (Gardner & Gardner, 1969) suggested that chimps should not be expected to learn *vocal* language because they lack the physiological apparatus necessary for such speech. But they are capable of fine motor coordination and can use their hands and arms in intricate motions. Therefore, the Gardners reasoned, if one tried to teach a chimp to use the language of human mutes—sign language—the results might be quite different. They obtained a female chimp whom they named Washoe and made a home for her in a house trailer with a yard enclosed by a fence. Washoe lived a pleasant life with one unusual feature: no human spoke in her presence; all human-to-human, human-to-chimp, and (eventually) chimp-to-human communication was carried out using sign language.

Washoe was actively trained to use sign language. She was deliberately watched and rewarded for the proper motions, which of course occurred infrequently at first. The proper signs were usually taught directly, either by the method of **shaping**—using successive approximations (*see* p. 377)—or by actively moving her hands into the proper position. She also learned by observation. Washoe learned "language" more rapidly than previous research had suggested was possible. In three years, Washoe learned close to a hundred word-phrases, quite an increase over "Mama, Papa, cup."

One of the most interesting features of subhuman language learning that Washoe demonstrated was the ability to generalize words learned in a specific context.

Washoe first sees the picture of a cat.

She then learns sign language for "cat."

Washoe makes the sign for "cat," using two hands.

Signs for "more," "please," and "come" or "give me," originally learned in conjunction with a particular desired object, food, or activity were soon used in conjunction with other desirables. "More" tickling was generalized to "more" food, for example, without training. Washoe was also able to combine words into simple sentences. After committing some action that she perceived as offensive to her keepers, she would signal, "Come—hug—love—sorry."

Sarah is another chimp trained by a psychologist interested in language learning (Premack, 1970). Like Washoe, Sarah was not asked to speak in human tongue and, like Washoe, she was asked to learn a language in signs. In Sarah's case, however, the "words" were pieces of colored, metal-backed plastic in different shapes. Each different piece, she was taught, referred to a different object; for example, a blue triangle meant "apple." Sarah quickly learned a vocabulary of close to a hundred words. This means that she was able to put a blue triangle on a magnetized "language board" when shown an apple; if she did so, she got the apple.

Now, suppose Sarah has a blue triangle and a red square (banana) before her, and an apple is presented. Can she match the correct word with the object? Will she place the blue triangle on the language board? Yes, most of the time. Her errors were not so much mistakes, the experimenters perceived, as requests for a more preferred food. Thus, if shown apple and banana and given the blue triangle and red square, she would almost invariably place the red square on the language board; she much preferred bananas.

Another phase of training was more complex: Could Sarah understand sentences? For example, if given the instruction (in signs on the language board) "Sarah—insert—banana—pail—apple—dish," would she put the banana in the pail and the apple in the dish, as requested? She did.

Sarah also learned to answer questions, the meaning of relational terms (such as "same" and "different"), and quite complicated linguistic categories. A good general illustration is this question: "What is the relation between 'red' and 'apple'?" Her answer was a choice of four possibilities: red is the "color of" apple, the "size of" apple, the "name of" apple, or the "shape of" apple. Sarah said that red is the "color of" apple over 80 percent of the time.

Perhaps the most intriguing bit of language behavior Sarah exhibited was in response to the blue plastic sign for apple. Shown this, she was asked if this *blue triangle* was a match for a round or a square object. She chose the round one. Similarly, her choices showed that she understood the apple symbol to be red and to have a stem!

Duane Rumbaugh and his colleagues (Gill & Rumbaugh, 1973) engineered a computerized communication system to teach chimpanzees a specially constructed language called Yerkish, consisting of a number of symbols for various parts of speech—nouns, prepositions, adjectives. The symbols are mounted on lighted keys connected to a computer console. Pressing the appropriate key will produce a particular event—for example, when the symbol for M&M is pressed, several M&M's are dispensed into a cup. Similarly, when the key embossed with the symbol for milk is pushed, milk can be obtained by sucking at a bottle.

Rumbaugh's chimpanzee, Lana, was trained by an **operant procedure;** whenever she pressed an appropriate button, she was rewarded. Because all her nourishment was obtained from the machine she learned the basic symbols for food quite quickly. By withholding rewards, Lana was trained to combine words to ask for things; she can press the key for the name of an object held up by the experimenter.

I had the opportunity recently to visit Lana and see her in action. Lana was in a plastic-walled cubicle with the computer console at one end. It was morning when we saw her, and she had not yet had breakfast. When she saw Tim, the graduate student who was responsible for most of her training, she went to the keyboard and pressed several buttons. The symbols were translated into English by the computer; the printout read, "Tim, give Lana milk." Tim filled the dispenser. Lana repeated her request several times until she satisfied her desire for milk.

Then an event occurred that suggested Lana really understood how to use a symbol system. While looking at the group of visitors she became particularly interested in one of the women in our group. The two looked at and gestured at one another. Then Lana went to the keyboard and punched "Open window"; a shade on the far side of Lana's cage opened. Lana then came back to our side, looked at her friend, and punched "Go outside" on the keyboard. The visitor went to the uncovered window, and she and Lana spent a little time making faces at each other.

Although these chimps certainly show more ability to communicate than had previously been thought possible, some psycholinguists feel that their accomplishment still falls short of genuine language behavior. These psycholinguists hold that the free use of syntactic structure is the basic characteristic of human language and that this use is yet to be demonstrated in a nonhuman organism. In addition, the artificial systems were devised by human beings and taught by human tutors to the chimpanzees. Chimpanzees' language in their natural habitat is very different indeed. But at the very least, the current research and debate over "chimp language" is helping to sharpen our thinking about what should and what should not be included in the concept of language.

Although these studies were undertaken as basic research on relations between human and animal communication, some of the techniques recently have been applied to help people suffering from aphasia (loss of speech because of damage to the brain). If adults sustain severe damage to their cortical speech areas, which in most individuals are located in the left cerebral hemisphere, they usually cannot regain speech even though the other hemisphere is intact. But Premack and other psychologists (Gazzaniga, 1972) have reported encouraging progress in teaching aphasic patients to communicate again; they use the colored symbols that were designed for the research on communication with chimpanzees.

parent gets water and brings it to him or her. The reinforcement for verbal behavior is produced through the intervention of another person.

In describing verbal behavior, Skinner introduces the concepts of *mands* and *tacts*. Verbal behavior often develops when the child wants to ask for something. Any verbal response that directs some other person to action — a request, demand, or command — is a **mand.** Mands are usually elicited in the presence of an audience that has reinforced such behavior in the past. A child, for example, easily discriminates between two uncles — the one who always responds to a request for ice cream and the one who does not. After a while, the child will make the request in the presence of the reinforcing uncle but not in the presence of the nonreinforcing uncle. If saying "please" when stating a mand ("Please give me some ice cream") has produced reinforcement, the child is more likely to include this word in future mands.

Skinner defines **tacts** as comments that are elicited by nonhuman stimuli the speaker has contact with. Naming responses — "This is a hat" — are tacting responses. In informing his or her mother that "the spaghetti water is boiling over," a child is responding to physical events. The statement is likely to be reinforced by the parent's expression of thanks. The physical environment partly determines the tact; that is, the child learns to match words and external events as closely as possible. By and large, mands benefit the speaker, whereas tacts benefit the listener. By rewarding the tacts, however, the listener helps strengthen the speaker's information giving (tacting) and increases the frequency of occurrences of tacts.

According to Skinner, the meaning of language resides in what it does or accomplishes. If a child says "get me water" and the parent does so, the parent's behavior provides the behavioral meaning of the verbal response.

For Skinner, therefore, the problem of meaning is not "What do words represent?" but rather "What do words do?"

Vygotsky's Hypothesis

A more developmental approach to the origins of language and thought was taken by the Soviet psychologist L. S. Vygotsky. Although Vygotsky died in 1934, his major opus, *Thought and Language,* remains a seminal work today. Vygotsky argued that the behavior of the infant and young child gives evidence of thought without language (tool use and problem solving) and language without thought (facial expression and gestures).

He maintained that all speech is social in origin but that, in the course of development, egocentric (nonsocial) speech becomes progressively "more abbreviated and idiosyncratic, eventually becoming inner speech, or verbal thought, qualitatively different from outer speech" (Slobin, 1971, p. 118). One step in this internalization of speech is whispering; children begin to whisper about the same time that overt egocentric speech begins to decline. The child's egocentric speech does not merely accompany activity; it has practical functions (Vygotsky, 1962, p. 133):

> it serves mental orientation, conscious understanding; it helps in overcoming difficulties; it is speech for oneself, intimately and usefully connected with the child's thinking. . . .

Piaget's View

According to Piaget, true language depends on the emergence of the **symbolic function** during the second year of life. This function is evidenced by the child's newfound ability to create symbols—for example, he or she might cross two sticks and say "Look, Mommy, an airplane"—and by dreams and "deferred" imitation, the mimicking of an action observed hours before (*see* pp. 246–47). Piaget's theory holds that cognitive development and thinking are not dependent on the acquisition of language. To the contrary, the child's cognitive development, progressing through a series of stages (*see* pp. 245–52), is *followed* by language development and is reflected in the child's speech. "Rather than language being the determining influence on what and how the child learns, what the child learns about language is determined by what the child already knows of the world" (Bloom, 1975, p. 289). And, according to another researcher (Flavell, 1963, p. 155):

> the symbolic function is a very general and basic acquisition which makes possible the acquisition of both private symbols and social signs [language]. . . . thought is . . . far from being a purely verbal affair, neither in its fully formed state nor . . . in its developmental origins. . . . what happens is that language, first acquired through the auspices of a symbolic function which has arisen earlier, will . . . lend tremendous assistance to the subsequent development of [thought].

The first words reflect the young child's cognitions of the world of objects, events, and relations. Thus, first words are highly idiosyncratic and closely related to the child's particular perceptual and motor experiences and to ever-changing actions rather than to "fixed and stable classes of objective realities" (Flavell, 1963, p. 155). An early word like "Mommy" can signify not a person or class of objects but simply that the child wants something.

Chomsky's Theory

A distinguished linguist, Noam Chomsky (1957) developed a linguistic theory to explain how proficient speakers of a language are able to do what they do. For example, the average speaker of English is able to distinguish between these two sentences:

John is easy to please.   John is eager to please.

Although the structure of the two sentences is similar, in the first sentence something is done to John while in the second sentence John is the actor. In Chomsky's terms the two sentences have similar **surface structures,** but their **deep structures** reveal quite different meanings.

The distinction between surface and deep structure can be illustrated with ambiguous sentences—sentences with more than one possible interpretation. The following example is given by Slobin (1971, p. 6):

15) Visiting relatives can be a nuisance.
One way to "disambiguate" such a sentence is to relate it to different proposi-tions which, in some sense, may be thought of as underlying sentence (15). We can explain the ambiguity by showing that the sentence can be related to two other sentences in which the ambiguity can be is realized in two different ways:
16) Visiting relatives are a nuisance.
17) Visiting relatives is a nuisance.
Again, we can say that there is a difference between surface and deep struc-ture: This sentence (15) has one surface structure, but two different deep, or underlying structures.

Chomsky also distinguishes between linguistic *competence* and linguistic *performance*. People do not always speak in grammatically correct ways even if they know the requisite grammatical rules. How people actually speak constitutes their linguistic performance. How they might speak ideally—if they took full advantage of their abstract, underlying knowledge of the rules of the language—is regarded as their linguistic competence. Lower class ghetto children may ordinarily use grammatically simple, restricted, tough language when they are with peers in their own neighborhood, but much more elaborate speech—showing greater linguistic competence—in school (Robinson, 1965).

How can the speakers of a language—even very young children—discrimi-nate between surface and deep structure? How is linguistic competence ac-quired so early in life (see p. 257)? Chomsky believes that a very strong, innate component in language acquisition, some uniquely human linguistic structure—perhaps a "language acquisition device"—receives the input of spoken language and somehow enables the listener (a child) to process this language and derive the rules required for understanding and using that lan-guage. According to Chomsky (1965, p. 59):

it seems reasonable to suppose that a child cannot help constructing a particular kind of . . . grammar to account for the data presented to him, any more than he can control his perception of solid objects or his attention to line and angle. Thus it may well be that the general features of language structure reflect, not so much the course of one's experience, but rather the general character of one's capacity to acquire knowledge—in the traditional sense, one's innate ideas and innate principles.

It is difficult to gather evidence that supports these different theories of the origins of language. What research does demonstrate, however, is the close interdependence of language and thought. Some studies demonstrate the effects of thought on language; others give evidence of the effects of language on thought.

Such words as "same" and "different," "more" and "less," and "right" and "left" may be used correctly by children in some instances, but the words may not mean exactly the same things they mean to adults. A little boy once asked me what my "true identity" was. When I asked what he meant, the child replied, "Well, Clark Kent is Superman's true identity." Piaget maintains that to understand a child's language you must understand a child's ways of thinking; the meaning children attach to words is, to a great extent, a function of their level of mental development.

An experimental illustration may help to make this point concrete. Suppose children at different age levels are presented with identical beakers filled to equal heights with colored liquid (as in Piaget's conservation experiments discussed in Chapter 10, p. 251). The liquid from one container is then poured into another, which is much taller and thinner than the first. Young children under the age of five or six typically agree that the amounts of liquid are equal when in identical containers, but say that the two quantities are no longer the same when they are in two differently shaped containers. After the age of six or seven children recognize that even though there is a change in appearance, the amount has not changed.

For young children the terms "more" and "same" do not have the same meaning as they do for older children and adults. For them "same amount" means "same height" or "same width." If the two liquids differ in either or both these dimensions, the young child regards them as unequal. The child's difficulty in understanding "same," "more," and "less" derives from cognitive immaturity—the inability to coordinate height and width mentally to arrive at a concept of quantity that incorporates both. Young children's limited understanding of words thus derives from limitations in their mental operations.

A recent experiment further clarifies the relationship between mental operations and language (Sinclair, 1969). The subjects were three groups of children. One group of preoperational children entirely lacked notions of "conservation"; they did not regard the liquid quantities as the same when poured into different containers, even when they saw the liquids returned to the original containers. The second group, in a transition stage, believed that the quantities would be the same if returned to the original containers but not when poured into taller, thinner containers. The third group had clearly attained conservation; they said the liquid quantities were the same when poured into the containers of different shapes. These children were then given some tasks involving verbal description and comprehension. For example, they were shown two dolls, one holding four large red balls, the other holding only two small red balls; they were asked "Is this fair?" and "Why not?" They were also asked to state the difference between two pencils, a short thick one and a long thin one. Children in the three groups responded to these tasks differently. About 90 percent of the children who were lacking in conservation used *absolute* terms in their descriptions ("one doll has a lot, the other has few," "this one is big, the other is little"); they did not employ comparative terms. Among the children who had attained conservation, however, 80 percent used comparative terms in their descriptions—for example, "one is fatter and smaller and the other is bigger and thinner." The responses of children at the intermediary stage were somewhere in between.

These results suggest that, at least in some domains, thought and conceptual development determine language usage. As further evidence, only when children attain the level of *formal operations,* at age eleven or twelve (*see* p. 250), do they spontaneously begin to use abstract categorical terms such as "belief," "intention," and "nationality." The use of these abstract words and expressions requires the development of high-level mental abilities.

Language, however, also affects thought in important ways. We know that words are not absolutely essential to thinking. Many deaf children who are severely retarded in language can reason and solve cognitive problems very well. But language very frequently does *facilitate* thought. Certainly it would be much more difficult to solve many problems if we had to rely only on direct manipulation of objects and images. Symbolic systems such as language permit us to solve complex problems rapidly, efficiently, and accurately. In some ways, language is to thought as mathematics is to science, an indispensable tool and handmaiden. As most cognitive theorists would agree, "the study of language is a part of the subject of thinking, but not the whole of it" (Posner, 1973, p. 8).

Here is a clear and simple demonstration of the influence of language on cognitive processes. Two groups of subjects viewed the stimulus figures shown in the center column of Figure 13-10. The figures were described to one group by the words on Word List I, while the other group saw the figures paired with Word List II. Later the subjects were asked to reproduce the figures from memory. As the figure shows, they made reproductions much more like the verbal labels from the word list they had seen than the original figures.

Language, of course, has many other obvious influences on thought. Propaganda and advertising of all sorts are attempts to influence thinking by the use of words. Names of cars and of movie stars are often selected with the thought of their appeal to the consumer. A skilled actor or actress can move an audience to tears or to rage, and the religious evangelist can inspire a conversion experience, both through the use of language.

LANGUAGE, CULTURE, AND THOUGHT

To what extent does a particular culture and language system determine the nature of one's modes of thinking? Languages clearly direct our attention to different "cuts" of reality (Whorf, 1956). As we mentioned before, Eskimos, who have many words for it, are obviously much more sensitive to different types of snow than we are. And what is the effect of language in which even inanimate objects are regarded as masculine and feminine? And of languages that have both formal and familiar forms of address? A French-speaking person who addresses another as *tu,* is signifying a more intimate relationship than that conveyed by the pronoun *vous.* This distinction fosters continual discriminations of degrees of friendship—discriminations that are cumbersome

Figure 13-10
Test of Visual and Language Influences

The figures in the outer columns, drawn from memory, are more like the verbal labels than the stimulus figures, which were to be reproduced. (From Carmichael, Hogan, & Walter, 1932)

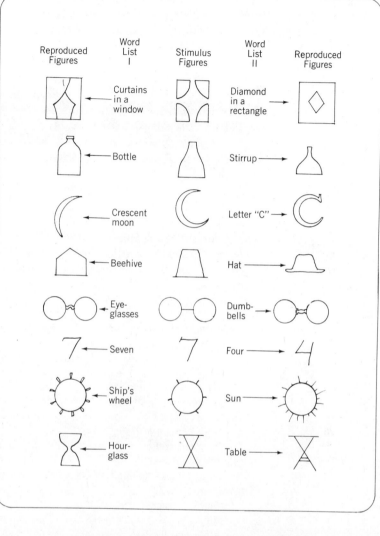

and are less frequently made in English. Thus, differences among languages affect how we think about things and our relationships with others.

The effects of different languages on thinking and cognition was neatly demonstrated in a study of two groups of Navajo children, one group Navajo-speaking, the other English-speaking (Carroll & Casagrande, 1958). The forms of Navajo verbs for actions such as "to pick up," "to drop," and "to hold in the hand" vary depending on the material being handled. If the object of the verb "to pick up" is a round thin thing, Navajos use a verb different from that used if the object is long and flexible. The children were asked to sort a group of objects on the basis of either shape or color. The Navajo-speaking children sorted on the basis of shape, whereas English-speaking children sorted on the basis of color. Presumably the fact that Navajo grammar requires the speaker to pay attention to shapes and forms makes those who speak that language more likely to think and categorize on the basis of these features.

Differences Among Social Classes

A somewhat different approach to the interactions among language, culture, and thought examines differences among social classes in the same culture. For example, the language used by the lower classes in England has been characterized by Basil Bernstein, an English sociologist, as a "restricted" code, while the language code utilized by the upper classes is "elaborated" (Bernstein, 1970). This distinction does not refer to linguistic ability or structure, but to levels of conceptualization. Restricted codes rely heavily on context for their meaning; they involve simple words and only low levels of conceptualization, directing attention to the here-and-now, to the concrete, direct, and immediate. In elaborated codes, meanings are made explicit; language is more individualized, complex, abstract, differentiated, precise, logical, and grammatical. Comparable class differences have been observed in American families. Middle-class mothers use more words than lower-class mothers in communicating with their children, offer more opportunities for considering alternative solutions to the problems and for labeling and identifying objects and feelings (Hess & Shipman, 1965).

These distinctions are illustrated in the following records of mother-child interactions made while mothers were trying to teach their children to sort plastic toys by color. The first is a middle-class mother, the second lower-class (Hess & Shipman, p. 88):

> The first mother outlines the task for the child, gives sufficient help and explanation to permit the child to proceed on her own. She says:
>
> "All right, Susan, this board is the place where we put the little toys; first of all you're supposed to learn how to place them according to color. Can you do that? The things that are all the same color you put in one section; in the second section you put another group of colors, and in the third section you put the last group of colors. Can you do that? Or would you like to see me do it first?"
>
> Child: "I want to do it."
>
> A second mother's style offers less clarity and precision. She says in introducing the same task:
>
> "Now, I'll take them all off the board; now you put them all back on the board. What are these?"
>
> Child: "A truck."
>
> "All right, just put them right here; put the other one right here; all right put the other one there."
>
> This mother must rely more on nonverbal communication in her commands; she does not define the task for the child; the child is not provided with ideas or information that she can grasp in attempting to solve the problem; neither is she told what to expect or what the task is, even in general terms.

Do the language patterns that children acquire in their family settings affect their thought processes? According to Bernstein, lower-class children, using a restricted code, fail to specify their reasoning, logical processes, or abstractions. Consequently, they do more poorly than their middle-class peers in tests dependent on language skills—intelligence tests and tests of cognitive functioning (thinking, reasoning, conceptualization)—and in school. Apparently, the language acquired by children at home strongly affects their cognitive and academic performance.

**A Practical Problem
of Language Learning**

Minority-group children—blacks, Mexican-Americans, and native Americans (Indians)—often suffer major language handicaps. The majority of schools in America are middle-class oriented, and the principals and teachers have middle-class values, attitudes, and behavior. They speak a particular English dialect—standard English—which is characteristic of the middle class. Written English also represents this dialect. American schools, well suited for middle-class children, may be much less appropriate for children from minority or lower socioeconomic groups whose values, attitudes, and language differ significantly from those of the prevailing culture.

Some educators and psychologists have maintained that minority children, especially blacks, use a language that is simpler grammatically, less differentiated, and more concrete than the language used by middle-class whites. Black children appear less willing or able to use language; they are more likely to speak in very short sentences and to reply to questions with one-word answers. Their pronunciation and vocabulary may be so different from standard English that teachers may have difficulty understanding them.

According to some linguists, ghetto children speak an entirely separate and colorful language—one whose structure may be as complex as standard English.

But linguists who have studied the language of black children intensively, observing them in their homes and neighborhoods, find no reason to consider them deficient in language. In fact, with friends and family, black children express themselves with a great deal of richness, ease, and fluency; and they play many language games. Nor is there any evidence that their language is less differentiated or complex than the whites' (Houston, 1970).

The deficiencies of some black children in standard English are hardly evidence that they cannot handle the language. Clearly, they understand standard English, and if this language becomes a major and significant part of their environment, they can master it. It has been suggested that black children have a language of their own and must be taught standard English as a second language or dialect, not as a refinement or superior form of the language they already speak.

Related problems have been met by Mexican and native American children who also must speak a different language in school from the one used at home. In the past, it was always the child who was forced to accommodate to the language of the school, which often worked to his or her educational detriment. Furtunately this situation is changing, and many schools in the southwestern United States now have Spanish and Indian-speaking teachers who teach English as a second language. This approach may help to remove one of the inequalities in the educational opportunities of minority groups.

SUMMARY

Thought, as studied by cognitive psychology, involves the manipulation of symbols and ideas for the purpose of adapting more effectively to the environment. In studies of **problem solving,** both trial-and-error and solution by insight have been demonstrated; indeed, **insight** often depends on earlier trial-and-error learning. Adult humans usually engage in **hypothesis testing;** but their hypotheses may be limited in some instances by past experiences that lead to **set** and **functional fixedness.**

Logical reasoning in adults is impaired by abstract terms and nonlinear structures in syllogisms. Many people also err in assuming that what is probable is true; that is, that if "all A's are B's," then the reverse, "all B's are A's," is also true. Personal convictions may also compete with logic in drawing conclusions. In children, studies of **reasoning** have concentrated on the development of verbal and other mediators.

Concepts are based on shared characteristics of diverse objects or ideas. **Conjunctive concepts** are defined by the presence in all cases of two or more attributes (red + circle = all red circles). The characteristics of **disjunctive concepts** are of the "either-or" variety—*either* boys *or* girls are children.

There are marked individual differences in how people form concepts, reason, and solve problems; that is, their **cognitive styles** differ. Some individuals are reflective and think before acting, whereas others are impulsive and act before thinking. Some are **field independent** and make judgments on the basis of internal cues, whereas others are **field dependent** and make judgments primarily on the basis of external cues.

Because intelligence tests assess mainly **convergent** (conventional) **thinking,** new tests measuring **divergent** (nonconventional) **thinking** have been devised. It has been found that creative people tend to be more independent, unconventional, flexible, and self-accepting than less creative people. The process of creative thinking generally involves the successive stages of **preparation, incubation, illumination,** and **verification.** A particular individual may be gifted with both **creativity** and high intelligence, or with neither, or only one. Different personality configurations are associated with different combinations.

The multifaceted effort to understand the relationship between **language** and thought includes teaching human language to chimpanzees, who seem able to learn at least rudimentary forms of grammar. Theoretical views of the thought-language relationship include those of Skinner—both are behaviors and subject to behavioral laws; Vygotsky—thought is inner speech; Piaget—language depends on cognitive development; and Chomsky—language (and thought) depends on innate linguistic abilities. Different cultures or subcultures have different languages that may result in different ways of thinking. A practical problem is the difficulty minority-group children have in acquiring the standard English spoken and written in most American schools. Linguists suggest that these children do not have a language deficiency but that they are essentially bilingual, and that standard English is their second language.

RECOMMENDED READINGS

ADAMS, P., ed. *Language in Thinking.* Hammondsworth, Middlesex, England: Penguin Books, Ltd., 1972.

An excellent collection of articles dealing with the relations between thought and language—from the biological to the cultural perspective.

BLOOMBERG, M., ed. *Creativity: Theory and Research.* New Haven: College & University Press, 1973.

Many different theoretical and research approaches to the study of human creativity are presented in this well-selected collection of readings.

COLE, M. et al. *The Cultural Context of Learning and Thinking: An Exploration in Experimental Anthropology.* New York: Basic Books, 1971.

Some of the difficulties in doing cross-cultural research on cognition are nicely illustrated by the authors' investigations of African peoples.

ESTES, W. K., ed. *Handbook of Learning and Cognitive Processes.* New York: Erlbaum Associates, 1975.

The seven chapters of this book cover current research in many different areas of cognitive psychology, including such topics as cross-cultural research, individual differences, and motivation.

JENSEN, A. R. *Genetics and Education.* New York: Harper & Row, 1972.

This collection includes Jensen's famous *Harvard Educational Review* paper that heated up the race-and-IQ issue. Jensen also describes, in the introduction, the personal abuse he suffered as a result of publishing his research.

JOHNSON, D. M. *Systematic Introduction to the Psychology of Thinking.* New York: Harper & Row, 1972.

An up-to-date, comprehensive review of the research and theory on human thinking.

LOCHLEM, J. C., LINDZEY, G., & SPUHLER, J. N. *Race Differences in Intelligence.* San Francisco: W. H. Freeman & Co., 1975.

The authors present a well-documented, balanced, and objective account of the race-and-IQ controversy.

MACCOBY, E. E., & JACKLIN, C. N. *The Psychology of Sex Differences.* Stanford, California: Stanford University Press, 1974.

The compilation of research on sex differences in many different domains helps to challenge many well-accepted premises about male-female differences in mental ability.

MISCHEL, T., ed. *Cognitive Development and Epistemology.* New York: Academic Press, 1971.

The authors in this book deal with many of the abiding issues in cognitive development from both philosophical and empirical perspectives.

SCHIEFELBUSCH, R. L., & LLOYD, L. L., eds. *Language Perspectives: Acquisition, Retardation, Intervention.* Baltimore: University Park Press, 1974.

This well-integrated collection of readings covers most of the major contemporary issues in language acquisition.

"Dancers Practicing at the Bar" by Edgar Degas. The Metropolitan Museum of Art,
The H. O. Havemeyer Collection. Bequest of Mrs. H. O. Havemeyer, 1929.

PART SIX

Learning and Memory

By Bennet B. Murdock, Jr.

In the earlier sections of this book, you have seen principles of learning applied in discussing social behavior, the development and functioning of personality, and thinking and problem solving. The processes and principles of learning were largely taken for granted. Now we can deepen your understanding of how learning and memory function; to do so, we will take up the research of specialists in the psychology of learning. These investigators—although they acknowledge the importance of learning in everyday life and in social behavior—study the learning process under controlled laboratory conditions. In this way they can analyze learning and memory and subject their hypotheses and theories to experimental tests.

The investigation of learning and memory is so broad—involving so many different kinds of research and using so many different methods and so many kinds of human and animal subjects—that it is sometimes hard to see its main themes. Several levels of analysis in current research are indicated in Preview Table 1. At the first level, investigators are trying to develop adequate descriptions of learning and memory. Many aspects of work at this level are taken up in chapters 14 and 15, in which the discussion focuses mainly on research conducted in the laboratory—with both human and animal subjects. Other

---

PREVIEW TABLE 1 Levels of analysis in research on learning and memory

A) Behavioral Descriptions of Learning and Memory

In what ways do learning and memory occur? What are adequate descriptions of the conditions under which associations are formed? (*See* Chapter 14.) What are adequate descriptions of the conditions under which memories are formed? (*See* Chapter 15.)

How do learning and memory differ among species? Can analyzing the behavior of a particular species in its ecological niche help us to predict particular features of its learning and memory, including novel or unusual forms of adaptiveness? How have the abilities to learn and remember evolved? (*See* Chapter 23.)

B) Formal Systems

What hypothetical processes could account for the observed features of learning and memory? Work under this heading ranges from rather general descriptions to precise mathematical or network specifications to actual devices that learn and remember. (Some representative systems are considered in Chapter 15, pp. 422–32.)

C) Neural Processes of Learning and Memory

Are there electrophysiological or chemical processes that occur in all neurons, or in wide regions of the brain, that underlie learning and memory? Research in this area ranges from the search for the biological form of the memory trace to investigations of chemicals that might affect the rate of learning or the permanence of memory. (*See* Chapter 21.)

---

research at the descriptive level either is carried out under naturalistic conditions or compares how different species learn. Animal learning in a comparative perspective is considered in Chapter 23 of Part Nine, Comparative Psychology.

At the second level, investigators are trying to draw up formal systems or theories to account for the observed features of learning and memory. Some examples of these theories are taken up in the latter part of Chapter 15. At the third level, researchers are investigating how learning and memory occur in terms of processes in the nervous system. Many different kinds of biological research are being conducted on learning and memory; some of these will be discussed in Chapter 21 in the part on Biological Psychology. Each of these three levels of analysis is interesting and important by itself; taken together, they give a comprehensive view of current knowledge of learning and memory.

Before beginning our behavioral description of learning in Chapter 14, it seems appropriate to review briefly some of the facts and principles about learning that have been presented in earlier chapters.

According to B. F. Skinner, reinforcement is the key factor in shaping and forming responses—that is, in learning. Skinner's theory is simple in structure and, perhaps for this reason, it has been widely applied. Earlier we discussed some dramatic examples of the application of reinforcement in psychotherapy, specifically in the technique of behavior modification (*see* p. 207). In this technique, the therapist (or teacher) attempts to modify a patient's (or child's) maladaptive behavior by rewarding (reinforcing) his or her positive, socially desirable responses, while disregarding (not rewarding) undesirable or neurotic behavior. These techniques have produced some dramatic changes in behavior. A more complete explication of Skinner's theory will be given in Chapter 14.

What follows a response is most important; Skinner is not concerned with the internal forces—motives, drives, and needs—that instigate goal-directed behavior. These motivational variables do loom large in other theories, notably those of Clark Hull and his disciples, who were the leading learning theorists of the 1940s and 50s. In Hull's view, drives and reinforcements are the critical concepts, and the two are intimately related; reinforcement is defined in terms of drive reduction. A hungry (that is, motivated) rat turns right in a T-maze and finds food at the end of the alley. Food is a reinforcement because it reduces hunger, which is a primary, biologically determined drive. The response of turning right has been reinforced; consequently, the rat is more likely to turn right again the next time it is at that point in the maze.

Hull's theory appealed to many psychologists who saw its vast implications for social, personality, and developmental psychology. The theory seemed helpful in explaining the acquisition of important secondary social drives, called "learned" drives. The process of acquiring secondary drives was illustrated by an experiment in which a rat learned to fear a white compartment of a box where it received electric shocks. Subsequently, the rat learned to turn a wheel that opened a door that allowed it to escape from the white compartment (see p. 581). The reinforcement was the reduction of fear, a learned drive. Another learned drive is an infant's love for his or her mother. This drive is not primary according to learning theory; rather it is learned from the association between the mother's presence and the infant's feelings of satisfaction that stem from food, warmth, support, and relief from pain—all supplied by the mother. The mother begins to stand for gratification—that is, she acquires reward value—and, when the baby is hungry or upset, her mere presence is comforting. She becomes a social reinforcer; the child becomes attached to her, and frequently seeks her out even when not hungry or upset.

The Hullian concepts of generalization and mediation are helpful in explaining why some responses are learned relatively easily and why some problems are readily solved. According to the principle of generalization, the behavior learned in response to one stimulus is likely to be transferred to—generalized to—similar stimuli. For example, if a little girl has learned to make friendly outgoing responses to her mother, she is more likely to make such responses to other friendly women. And, after a child has learned a label—a verbal mediator—applying to an object or an event, he or she is likely to respond in the same way to all stimuli having the same label (see p. 335). Thus if a little boy has learned to smile and be polite to someone called "uncle," he is likely to react this way to other men whom he hears called "uncle."

Clearly this kind of learning theory is flexible and useful in explaining how many kinds of behavior are acquired and developed. Yet many phenomena of learning cannot readily be explained in terms of motivation and reinforcement. For example, much of your own current learning is not motivated by primary biological drives nor reinforced by drive reduction. Motivation and reinforcement, traditionally the key concepts of learning, no longer seem adequate to explain all the phenomena of learning. And they are no longer the sole interests of learning psychologists. Of course, motivation remains an important topic in psychology. It is a primary interest to social, personality, and developmental psychologists who study people in the social world and want to investigate the question of why they act as they do. For example, the theory of cognitive dissonance discussed in Part Two is concerned with the motivation or drive that results from holding two incompatible beliefs. And, as we shall see in Part Eight, biological psychologists investigate the physical mechanisms underlying basic drives that control eating and drinking. Reinforcements—social rewards or basic physiological mechanisms—are also being intensively studied in other areas. Social psychologists who espouse dissonance theory see any act that results in dissonance reduction (drive reduction) as likely to be learned, a notion that could account for changing attitudes.

Thus, the concepts of motivation and reinforcement—once the more-or-less exclusive domain of learning theorists—are now major concerns to psychologists in other areas.

We begin with a discussion of some basic principles of reinforcement, formulated in the well-known theories of Pavlov and Skinner, then move to consider contemporary issues in learning and memory. What are the basic mechanisms and processes of learning? This is the question addressed in Chapter 14. Chapter 15 takes up questions about memory. How is information encoded and stored? How is it retrieved when needed? Why do we forget? How can memory be improved? Toward the end of Chapter 15, we will examine some models or theories that try to integrate the findings on learning and memory. We will also summarize some practical suggestions for effective learning and memory that come from research in these fields.

14

Learning

How are single associations learned?
How are sets of associations learned?
How does past learning help or hinder new learning?
What is required to learn a skill?
What are the current issues of learning psychology?

Learning is one of the most characteristic activities of human beings — learning names of people, learning such skills as driving a car or dancing or pronouncing French words, learning such complex bodies of knowledge as organic chemistry or Beethoven's symphonies. We even learn how to learn more efficiently. All these examples are called **learning** because in each case a person's behavior is modified through experience. Everyone accomplishes enormous amounts of learning on the way to becoming an adult (and we usually keep on learning, too). The newborn infant has a very limited set of effective behaviors and is almost totally dependent on parents for survival. Even during the first few years, a complex repertoire of skills develops. Some of these are relatively simple, such as basic discriminations: when faced with a green traffic light, the schoolchild "goes," but if the light is red, "stops." Other changes in behavior are much more complex: the three-year-old has already mastered much of the grammar of language. Still more elaborate are the integrated skills of a professional athlete, a secretary, a singer, a business executive, or an artist.

Despite the obvious importance of learning and memory in human behavior, these topics were not part of the original agenda when psychology became an independent discipline around the 1870s. The reason for this omission was simple: at that time no one had any idea how learning and memory could be investigated. Then the breakthroughs came quickly. In 1885 the German psychologist Hermann Ebbinghaus revealed the first practical methods for doing research on human verbal learning and memory. In 1898 the American psychologist Edward L. Thorndike reported methods for studying learning by animals; and in 1902 the Russian physiologist Ivan Pavlov began his influential publications on conditioning in animals. Once these pioneers opened the way, many other investigators joined in the exploration of this varied and intricate field; it has become one of the most productive areas in all of psychology.

In this chapter and the next, we will describe some of the methods the pioneers invented and some of the improvements made by later investigators. You will see some of the main discoveries that have been made, some of the concepts that help to integrate these facts, and some of the puzzles that yet remain. Simple answers to simple questions inevitably produce a host of more complex questions; we do not realize the extent of our ignorance until we gain a little knowledge. The result is that questions about the learning process are continually increasing—in depth and in breadth. Scientists must dig deeper to find basic principles underlying the "basic" principles already discovered. They must simultaneously expand their observations to related questions (an increase in breadth), for they know that the answers will solve parts of a larger puzzle. In this chapter, therefore, you will find some of the current attempts to understand rather intricate phenomena. For instance, we already know that giving a "reward" (reinforcement) after a response is made is likely to increase the probability of that response. But is it best to give the reinforcement every time the response occurs or only some of the times? Perhaps some optimum spacing or patterning of reinforcements will yield the best learning and the surest memory? At the same time that we are digging deeper into such questions, we are also expanding our study horizontally. For example, moving on from earlier work on simple, single associations, we will examine evidence about the learning of more complex patterns of behavior, including skills.

Ivan Pavlov

How are single associations learned?

Traditionally, theories of learning have been based on the concept of **association.** An association is a basic learning-theory concept much like the concept of the particle in physics, the molecule in chemistry, or the gene in genetics. In the simplest sense, an association is a connection, a link, or a bond between a stimulus (S) and a response (R). Functionally (that is, defined by what it *does* rather than by what it *is*), an association results in a response to a stimulus. For example, we think of a person's name when we see his or her face; we run when we see a bull approach our picnic in his pasture; and we write an answer in response to a quiz question. One of the basic ways in which associations have been studied is by the classical-conditioning procedure.

CLASSICAL CONDITIONING **Classical conditioning** refers to the formation of a single association by means of a procedure developed by Ivan Pavlov in the early 1900s. Pavlov's special field of study was the digestive secretions of the body, for which he received the Nobel Prize in 1904. One of the secretions being studied was salivation. To obtain a precise measure of secreted saliva under varying conditions, Pavlov inserted a small tube into the salivary glands of experimental dogs (*see* Figure 14-1). When the dog salivated, the fluid was routed into Pavlov's measuring cups. By this method, he could determine not only when salivation occurred but also how much and at what rate. For the time—indeed, even for today—it was a remarkably clear and rigorous estimate of response strength.

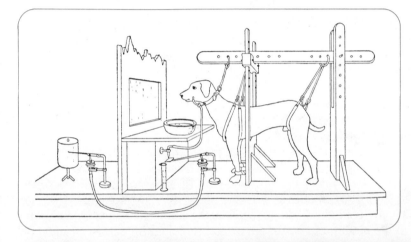

Figure 14-1
The drawing is from the first major English account of Pavlov's experiments in conditioning the salivary response in dogs. An old photograph (below) shows him demonstrating his work at the Russian Military Medical Academy.

During his studies of salivation, Pavlov noted what he called "psychic secretions." If food is placed in the mouth of an animal, it will secrete saliva automatically—this response is innate, not learned. But the dogs in Pavlov's apparatus soon began to salivate to other stimuli as well. For example, the *sight* of food, the sight of the person who fed them, and even the feeder's footsteps in the hall were enough to elicit salivation. These associations had to be learned. They were in effect anticipations of food in the mouth. Because the response (salivation) was not controlled by the simple reflex connections, some higher neural processes had to be involved. It was as if the mind took over control of the reflexive act—hence, "psychic" secretions—as if the thought of food was enough to produce the same response as food itself.

Psychic secretion was hardly a new and unexpected phenomenon; the phrase "the mouth waters" dates back at least to the sixteenth century. That psychic secretions involved associations of a response to a "new" stimulus was similarly common knowledge (Rosenzweig, 1959). In physiological research, these deviant responses were generally considered a nuisance, much like unexpected noises, sights, and smells that could distract the animal from its true purpose, which was to be an experimental subject in the study of automatic body reflexes. Great efforts were made to eliminate or at least to control these secondary influences. Pavlov's genius lay in his decision to study the "nuisance" phenomena directly and in his careful and brilliant experimental programs. That classical conditioning is sometimes called Pavlovian conditioning is testimony to the impact of one scientist's endeavors.

Pavlov called the innate automatic responses (for example, salivation to food) *unconditional responses* because they happened uniformly and without any special requirements. He called responses acquired through training (such as salivation in response to hearing a tone) *conditional responses* because they occurred only under certain conditions. If a particular tone is to elicit salivation in the dog, that tone must be followed by the food in repeated instances. Such "conditions" do not apply to the automatic reflex; food must be placed in the mouth, of course, but a food stimulus will cause salivation on all occasions, including the very first.

All this terminology with the root word "condition" helped the subsequent research. Pavlov set out to discover the exact nature of the *conditions* in which a previously neutral stimulus could elicit a response. Early theorists had known well enough that the sight (or thought) of food was often enough to elicit salivation; they had even speculated that past pairings of the sight of food with food itself was responsible. But they did not take the next step. If the sight of food causes salivation because of its relationship with the actual presentation, then it should be possible to associate an unrelated stimulus to the same response: a bell or buzzer, for example, or a flash of light. Pavlov took the next step.

Because of a somewhat unfortunate early translation of the Russian into English, the terms "conditional" and "unconditional" are usually rendered "conditioned" and "unconditioned." If the stimulus-response (S-R) pair is natural or reflexive (if it does not require learning), the stimulus is called the **unconditioned stimulus** (US) and the response the **unconditioned response** (UR). If the S-R association develops from experience, the stimulus is called

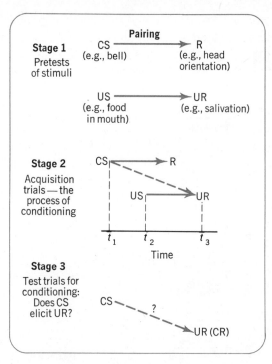

Figure 14-2
Procedures for Classical Conditioning
Stage 1 ensures that CS does not initially evoke UR. Stage 2 is the paired presentations of CS (a bell) and US (food) during which conditioning is gradually established. Stage 3 tests whether CS does evoke the response. If it does, then UR has become CR and learning has occurred. If Stage 3 is continued, extinction will result—that is, CS will no longer elicit CR.

the **conditioned stimulus** (CS) and the response the **conditioned response** (CR). For example, food in the mouth is a US to salivation (UR); the sight of the experimenter might become a CS to the same response, now called CR. The process of classical conditioning was conceived as one in which a new stimulus (CS) is substituted for another (US) in provoking the response (UR, changing to CR).

Stages of Classical Conditioning

According to the procedures developed by Pavlov, as presented in Figure 14-2, classical conditioning includes three stages. The changes in response strength during these three stages are shown in Figure 14-3. The first stage involves choosing two stimuli—one a US to the response of interest, the other clearly not (we hope to make it our CS later). In Stage 1, therefore, we must demonstrate that US does reliably elicit UR and that CS as yet does not. CS may well produce a response, if only an orienting response, but we hope to demonstrate that it does not naturally produce UR.

The US-UR pair used in most of Pavlov's experiments was food and salivation, but other pairs are equally good. Much research has been done with humans, using the eyeblink caused by a puff of air directed at the eye. Other research has studied emotional responses, such as fear, that can be triggered by a US, a loud noise or an electrical shock. The CS in research has typically been a light or a tone; the advantage of these simple stimuli is that their intensity and frequency can be rather precisely described.

Stage 2 in classical conditioning represents the learning process: the **acquisition** pairings (trials). Say that CS is a pure tone and that UR is salivation. Then Stage 2 might consist of the brief presentation of the tone, followed by

Figure 14-3
Three Stages of Conditioning
Response strength of CR is plotted in the various stages. The spontaneous recovery of some strength occurs when CS is presented some time later (say 24 hours), after extinction is seemingly complete.

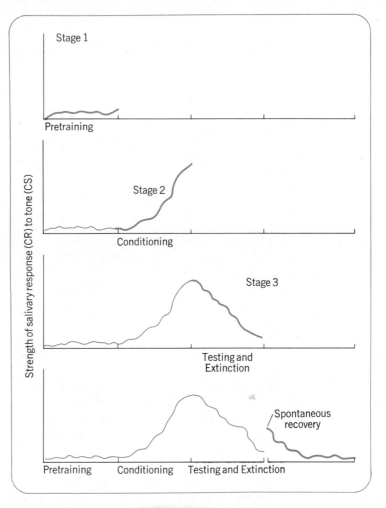

the food stimulus (US), which elicits salivation. This pairing is repeated several times. If CS forms an association with the response, it can be demonstrated in Stage 3; here the CS is presented but the US is not. If UR (CR now) occurs, the CS-CR bond can be said to be in effect. The tone now elicits salivation, whereas it did not before. Conditioning has been accomplished.

The trials of Stage 1 are usually called pretests. Those of Stage 2 are called conditioning trials, acquisition trials, or, simply, trials. Stage 3 trials are called test trials if their purpose is to test the CS alone to see if the association has been formed. But they are also **extinction** trials. If the tone produces salivation but is *repeatedly* presented without the US (food), as in Stage 3, eventually the response will cease following CS—it will be *extinguished*. The response will be elicited if the tone means food is coming, but if several tones sound and no food comes, the anticipatory salivation stops.

The acquisition trials shown in Figure 14-2 represent only the most common and effective sequence of CS and US. Exactly what is the most effective, of course, is a question to be answered by experimental investigation; and the meticulous research of Pavlov was directed to this end. It was found that if

CS precedes US—if the tone precedes food—conditioning occurs; but if the CS follows US, little or no learning results. More precisely, it can be shown that the optimal sequence in this situation is to have CS precede US by a half-second; any longer or shorter interval will produce a weaker conditioned response.

Spontaneous Recovery

The acquisition and extinction phenomena are not the only characteristics of learning that can be studied in classical conditioning. After a response has been extinguished and a period of time has elapsed, the conditioned response may *spontaneously recover*—regain some of its strength (*see* the lower part of Figure 14-3). Why this occurs is not known for certain, but in many cases there appears to be some kind of inhibition effect in the extinction stage. It is as if the organism still has some "association" left but is unable to exhibit it at the end of a set of extinction trials. The next day, however, the refreshed organism demonstrates the remaining strength. Spontaneous recovery is of theoretical importance, of course, because any theory worth considering must somehow explain it. It is also of practical significance. A psychotherapist may try to extinguish a fear of horses by exposing an anxious client to pictures of horses and, eventually, to real horses (*see* pp. 208–09). Spontaneous recovery of the fear reaction later could be very upsetting to the client. Several additional extinction sessions may be necessary.

Generalization

Another feature of conditioning is **generalization.** Once a CR has been established, not only will CS elicit it, but so will a variety of other stimuli. These other stimuli are marked by their *similarity* to the CS. The conditioning has generalized to other similar stimuli. For example, suppose a dog learns to salivate to a tone of a certain frequency, say 500 cycles per second (written 500 Hz or hertz); it will then also salivate to similar tones such as 480 Hz or 520 Hz, even though these tones have never been paired with US-UR in any acquisition trials. The closer the stimulus is to the original CS, the more response strength is demonstrated, as indicated in Figure 14-4. A tone of 2400 Hz would elicit very little, if any, response.

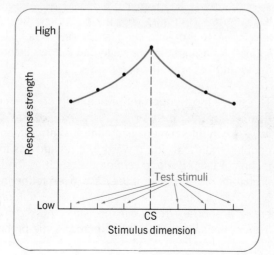

Figure 14-4
Generalization Gradient
The CS denotes the original training stimulus. The test stimuli are similar to CS but at different points along the stimulus dimension. The farther the stimulus is removed from CS, the weaker the resulting response strength.

Generalization is in part a failure of discrimination. Sometimes it is very important, in the laboratory or in real life, that fine discriminations be made. To establish greater discrimination, you first present the CS *with the US* repeatedly; and on other trials you present stimuli that differ somewhat from the CS—*without the US*. Thus, in our example, a tone of 500 Hz would be presented repeatedly *with* food, while tones of 480 and 520 Hz would be repeatedly presented *without* food. Thus the CR to 480 and 520 would disappear but the CR to 500 Hz would remain. A finer discrimination would thus be achieved.

This is another way of saying that the generalization curve in Figure 14-4 will be much sharper, with steeper gradients, after discrimination training. This is an important feature of conditioning. Consider this real-life example: a man with a conditioned-fear response to snakes lives in a region populated by many snakes, some of which are not only harmless but quite useful to the environment. If he does not learn to discriminate among snakes, his life will be one of constant terror, and the environment might well suffer by his fear-induced destruction of harmless reptiles. (The relevance of classical conditioning for real problems is also discussed in Spotlight 14-1.)

OPERANT CONDITIONING

B. F. Skinner

Reinforcement as Key to Association

If Pavlov was the founder of classical conditioning, then the founder of operant conditioning is an American psychologist, B. F. Skinner. The impact of his discovery of a second type of conditioning may well exceed Pavlov's. **Operant conditioning** is defined as conditioning in which the response is determined by what *follows* it (unlike classical conditioning in which the *preceding* stimuli are important). Operant conditioning applies to those cases in which someone *does* something to *get* something. He pulls the knob on the vending machine to get a candy bar; she says nice things to her father in hopes of getting the car this weekend; he studies German in the expectation of a better grade. In other words, he or she *operates* on the environment in some way—hence the term "operant"—to achieve some goal or reward.

To distinguish operant responses from the elicited responses in classical conditioning, Skinner called them "emitted responses." An elicited response is controlled by a stimulus that precedes it; emitted responses are under the control of stimuli that follow it. If the critical factor in learning to answer a telephone is the ring, then answering would be considered an elicited response. If, instead, the message that follows is the reinforcement, then answering would be an emitted response.

The single most important principle in operant conditioning is that **reinforcement** following a response will increase the probability of that response in the future. A reinforcement is a stimulus, an attractive one in some sense; most people would call it a reward (but reward has too much surplus meaning for technical use). *Positive reinforcers,* such as food and water, will increase the probability of response if they are given following the response (assuming the organism is hungry or thirsty). *Negative reinforcers,* like electric shock, increase response strength if they are *removed* following the response; taking aspirin alleviates pain, which increases the probability of taking aspirin when pain strikes.

Experiments on classical conditioning in the psychologist's laboratory may sometimes seem unreal and not very relevant, dealing as they do with dogs with surgical inserts, precisely measured pure tones, and the like. Surely the need for precision and rigor in scientific experiments is clear. But the principles determined at this level are not easily integrated into our understanding of everyday human behavior. As a more homely illustration, we can give an example, a true case history of a young girl's encounter with a large dog.

The girl was six years old at the time. She and her parents had just arrived at a small New England inn and were outside, about to enter the dining room. A dog, a large Saint Bernard, was sitting some forty yards from them. Suddenly, without warning, the dog gave a fierce bark and charged directly at the small girl. Her unconditioned response was naturally one of fear and she ran screaming to her parents. The dog charged by, within a few feet, in fierce pursuit of his real target, a squirrel in the parking lot.

It was several minutes before the parents could quiet the girl's anguish, but the remainder of the day passed without incident. The next day, however, provided ample evidence that the encounter had not been without effect. The neighbor's dog, a collie, appeared. It did not bark or charge; it simply entered the girl's field of vision. The girl broke into tears and ran home. Throughout the week, various neighborhood dogs evoked similar reactions, until

finally the girl was afraid of even leaving the house for fear of seeing a dog—almost any dog, although the bigger, the more terrifying. A psychotherapist would have diagnosed her condition as a **phobia,** an extreme and unnatural fear. Therapy was clearly needed. Luckily the parents were psychologists and had little trouble alleviating this phobia. If you were her parent and knew the principles of classical conditioning, what would you have done? Can you imagine the form of the "therapy"? Consider these questions, too: What do you think, precisely, the unconditioned stimulus was? If you are constructing in your mind a reasonable therapy, have you considered spontaneous recovery?

Most classical conditioning takes several "trials," not one traumatic event as in this case. Moreover, a scientist would not be too happy with the description of the CS as "the sight of a Saint Bernard." But the procedure is fairly well illustrated, and the principle of generalization is also clearly at work.

Many of us have phobias, if only the mild variety. Psychotherapists treat people with severe cases. In any case, there is increasing acceptance of the view that a high proportion of phobias are conditioned responses in the classical-conditioning mold. They can be treated, accordingly, with extinction procedures. A lot of Pavlovian conditioning happens in the normal (and abnormal) world.

So much is perhaps common sense, although the technical details in even the simplest case are more complex than might at first be imagined. But there is a simple prescription: wait for the response you want, reinforce it, and the association will build in strength. Now add a pinch of complexity: Suppose the response you want is *never* "emitted," then what? You could wait for years before your white rat would stand up on its hind legs and press the bar in its cage (which is hooked up to a food-delivery mechanism). Skinner developed a technique for these very situations; it is called **shaping** or the method of successive approximations. Say you want to train a rat to play basketball. You set up a small hoop in its cage and throw in a small ball—you want the rat to pick up the ball and drop it through the hoop. Don't bother to wait for the first natural occurrence; it will never come. But you can train the rat by successive approximations. First, any sign of attention to the ball (looking at it, moving toward it) is reinforced. Then greater "involvement" is reinforced (moving closer and closer). Soon the rat must touch the ball to get its reinforcement; then it must pick the ball up; then it must carry it; then it must

In operant training, food rewards *after* the animal makes the desired response reinforce the behavior and encourage repeat performances.

carry it toward the hoop; then it must carry it to the hoop; and finally, the rat must pick it up, carry it to the hoop, and drop it through. And there you have it. It's surprisingly easy to train an animal once you know how. (*See* Skinner's article, "How to Teach Animals," in *Scientific American,* December 1951.)

Here is another complexity. What happens if you reinforce not every single correct response but only every other one? every tenth response? every twentieth response? It is certainly a rare case, particularly in real life, in which every single response gets reinforced. Take gamblers in Las Vegas, for example, responding furiously to the promised reinforcement from the "one-armed bandit." They do not win every time, but **partial reinforcement** does occur. Is there a difference in behavior with an intermittent schedule of reinforcement? Yes, there is, and most of what we know about the effects of various schedules follows from Skinner's thought and research.

Reinforcement Schedules

The four basic families of **reinforcement schedules** are called fixed-ratio, variable-ratio, fixed-interval, and variable-interval schedules. A *fixed-ratio schedule* delivers a reinforcement once every so many responses; every tenth time the correct response is made, for example, would be a 10:1 fixed-ratio

schedule. A *variable-ratio schedule* delivers one reinforcement every so many responses but only *on the average;* a 10:1 variable-ratio schedule might "pay off" after 8, then 12, then 10 — in the long run, the average ratio is 10:1. A simple slot machine works on a variable-ratio schedule. It can't pay every time; and, if it paid *exactly* every tenth time, the house regulars would make a fortune. The schedule is therefore variable.

Interval schedules are based on time intervals rather than on the number of responses. A reinforcement is delivered for the first response after an interval of elapsed time, say one minute or five minutes or thirty. Again, *fixed-interval* means the interval is always exactly the same and *variable-interval* means the interval varies around some average period. As an example, a writer on religion has suggested that preachers stop using twenty-minute sermons all the time and use five, ten, twenty, thirty, or thirty-five minutes as the topic demands. Churchgoers would always pay more attention because they would never be sure when the point would be made (or when they would have to wake up to sing the next hymn!). The writer was suggesting changing from a fixed-interval schedule to a variable-interval schedule.

This suggestion also implies that behavior is different under different schedules, and research supports this assumption. In laboratory studies of operant conditioning, the most common measure of response strength is the probability of response; more specifically, what is measured is the rate of response. In a typical experiment, a rat presses a bar or a pigeon pecks a key that activates a *cumulative recorder,* a revolving drum type of instrument that makes a horizontal line when no response occurs and "jumps up" vertically a small distance each time a response is made. Figure 14-5*A* shows a picture of such a device and Figure 14-5*B* some of the typical records. A fixed-interval schedule produces a funny kind of record that includes "scalloping" — a slow rate of response immediately following a reinforcement, increasing to a very fast rate immediately preceding the time for the next reinforcement. Variable schedules, both of the ratio family and the interval family, produce records more like a steady state — a more or less constant rate of responding. "You never know when the sermon will end, so you pay attention throughout."

Although operant conditioning deals with emitted responses and therefore with the stimulus *following* the response (the reinforcement), it is also affected by preceding stimuli. Although the prior stimuli may not elicit the response, they often provide information or cues that affect the operant response. For example, if your phone rings, it is a cue: if you pick it up, you will be "reinforced" by hearing someone's voice. Such informative preceding stimuli are called **discriminative stimuli** because they signal the availability (or nonavailability) of reinforcement if the response is made. In the laboratory, one can flash a green light to indicate that the food-delivery mechanism is in operation and a red light to indicate that it is not. Eventually the pigeon or human will respond only when the green light has flashed. In real life many

The operant responses of pigeon, rat, and human are all dependent on the schedule used to reinforce their behavior. A variable-ratio schedule in the slot machine insures that the odds will always be in favor of the house.

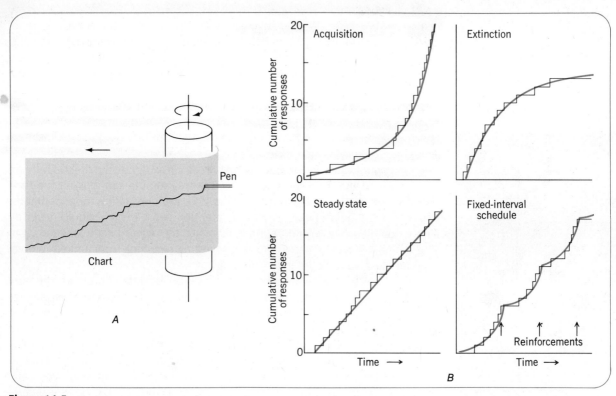

Figure 14-5
Cumulative Recorder and Records

Every response moves the pen up a notch on the recorder, as the paper moves to the left at a constant speed. The tracing steepens as the frequency of response increases. The curves on the right show that rate of response speeds up for acquisition and slows down during extinction. The slope is constant during steady-state responding. The "scalloping" is characteristic of FI schedules; after reinforcement the responses start slowly but gradually pick up speed.

responses will gain a reward only under the proper circumstances; hitting someone is unlikely to gain a reward unless the cues are right—a boxing ring surrounds you, for example.

By using discriminative stimuli properly, scientists can increase their control of a response. They can increase the probability of that response in one situation and decrease it in others. A child-training specialist (a parent, for example) has similar desires for **stimulus control** of a response; romping and playing are encouraged responses on vacation in the woods, but the same behaviors are decidedly discouraged in church. Parents try to teach their children to discriminate between the cues identifying each situation.

Punishment

One procedure is the direct opposite of reinforcement. Suppose you use **punishment** after a response, depriving the subject of something desired or causing him or her pain, discomfort, or injury. Reinforcement, we know, results in the *increased* probability of a response. Does the opposite procedure result in the opposite effect—a *decreased* probability of response? In short, is punishment for error an effective aid in learning? Folklore would seem to indicate that it is, but actually the research issue is complicated and not yet fully resolved.

Experimental data do make it clear, however, that punishment is *not* as effective as experimental extinction in eliminating habits. Often punishment results in temporary suppression of a response, but the response is not really weakened. This finding was demonstrated in an experiment in which two groups of rats learned to press a bar in a Skinner box to get food (the reinforcement). After the bar-pressing response was learned, the rats were given extinction trials in which food was withheld. For the first few extinction trials, one group of rats was shocked (punished) through the bar every time they pressed it. No shock was administered during the rest of the extinction trials. The other group of rats received no shock during the extinction trials; food was simply withheld. The effects of the punishment proved to be short-lived. The animals that had been shocked made fewer bar-pressing responses only during the time that they were being punished and shortly thereafter. In the later part of the extinction trials they pressed the bar at the same rate as they had before the shock; by the end of the experiment they had made as many responses as the unpunished rats. In short, punishment led to temporary suppression of the response but did not weaken it.

Using rather severe intensities of shock in a similar procedure, however, psychologists have been able to demonstrate permanent effects of punishment applied during extinction trials (Boe & Church, 1967). If punishment is used on

Learning studies in the laboratory indicate that punishment is only effective when it induces the subject to find an alternative and acceptable behavior.

behaviors that are also being rewarded—if the rat gets food as well as a shock for a bar press—then the effects are invariably temporary. The animal returns to previous levels of response after punishment ceases. This latter case is probably more like real-life situations than punishment during extinction. (See Hulse, Deese, & Egeth, 1975, for a more complete discussion of this complex issue.)

Punishment may be effective in changing behavior, however, by forcing the individual to find a desirable *alternative response* that may subsequently be rewarded. If behavior is to be modified, this consideration may be very important. For example, a parent can punish a son for throwing rocks at windows; and for a time at least the son will suppress this response. He will stop throwing rocks. In the meantime, the boy may learn other ways of "releasing excess energy" or "attracting attention"; he may learn to play baseball—a more socially acceptable way of breaking windows. If no adequate substitute response is learned, however, the boy may soon revert to his old habits with undiminished intensity. Simply punishing children for undesirable behavior is not enough. They must at the same time be given an opportunity for practicing and being reinforced for more desirable responses. In fact, under some circumstances, punishment may serve to strengthen or "fix" a response rather than to eliminate it—perhaps because of the fear and anxiety attached to the punishment. Punishing a child for stuttering may actually increase the frequency of this behavior.

Furthermore, punishment for some particular behavior, especially if it is repeated, may lead to self-punishment or "guilt feelings." Though guilt is basically a human emotion, many lower animals seem to exhibit "guilty" behavior after performing a response that has been punished in the past. Some psychologists have viewed such behaviors as conditioned responses to the stimuli present *after* the response. For example, a dog leaps up at the window and knocks a vase to the floor. The sight and sounds of shattering glass (CS) have been paired with a sharp painful slap (US) on its nose, leading to flinching and withdrawal (UR). Now if the dog knocks something down, it flinches and slinks away (CR) even before it is slapped. The dog "looks guilty." Guilt and anxiety become associated with the forbidden response even though they were not present until the forbidden behavior had occurred. Because these feelings are unpleasant, the individual may suppress anxiety- or guilt-producing responses. Avoiding these feelings, like avoiding punishment, may be rewarding. But again the fact that the response is suppressed does not mean it is weakened or unlearned. Guilt or anxiety, like punishment, will have little long-range effect on behavior unless the individual has an opportunity to acquire a new response. For example, a woman may be punished or feel guilty about overeating, which is her response to anxiety. However, unless she learns new ways of handling her anxiety, the overeating response will not be suppressed for long. She may continue to feel guilty about overeating but will continue to overeat.

Much human and animal learning occurs with no use of such primary reinforcers as food, drink, sex, and the elimination of pain. Those psychologists who hold to the universality of reinforcement explain such learning in terms of **secondary reinforcement** (see Spotlight 14-2). Other psychologists have

Spotlight 14-2　Secondary Reinforcement

If we had to rely entirely on such primary reinforcers as food, water, avoidance of pain, and even sex, little of everyday learning could be explained. Why does the student study or the secretary type? In some "eventual" sense, perhaps their behaviors could be related to basic necessities, but what bridges the gap between the response and this eventual reward? What are the immediate reinforcements?

Secondary reinforcement is a concept that offers an answer. In laboratory studies, the concept can be most easily demonstrated with operant conditioning, although classical conditioning shows similar effects. If a previously neutral stimulus is consistently associated with a primary reinforcer, the neutral stimulus itself will acquire the power of reinforcement—it will become a secondary reinforcer. For example, an animal in an operant-conditioning situation performs a response, then receives food from a food-delivery mechanism. This mechanism usually makes some noise as it releases the pellet of food—a click. This sound becomes reinforcing; an animal will work just to hear it. (If the click sounds too often without food, of course, gradually the secondary reinforcer will lose its power and return to its previously neutral status.)

In the study of human behavior, thought and language add to the complexity of the issue. But such generally effective techniques as giving praise or money for desired behaviors are typically interpreted in terms of their secondary reinforcing powers. Praise and money have no intrinsic value, but they are commonly associated with the basic satisfactions of life.

Approval from peers is a powerful secondary reinforcement in learning school subjects.

denied the necessity of reinforcement altogether. An illustration of their view is the research on latent learning discussed in Spotlight 14-3. Obviously different views exist in this area of psychology, and only further research will settle the questions.

Generality or Specificity of Principles of Learning?

Pavlov, Skinner, and many other investigators of learning have assumed that the same principles of learning would hold for all organisms. That is, according to Pavlov, any stimulus that a particular organism could perceive could become a conditioned stimulus to evoke any response the organism was capable of making. Skinner stated that any response of an organism could come to be controlled by the use of any reinforcer that is operative for that organism. Recently, however, investigators have been finding that it is much easier to condition certain stimulus-response linkages than others; and certain reinforcers can be used successfully to train certain kinds of behavior but not others. Some theorists have concluded that each species of animal has evolved

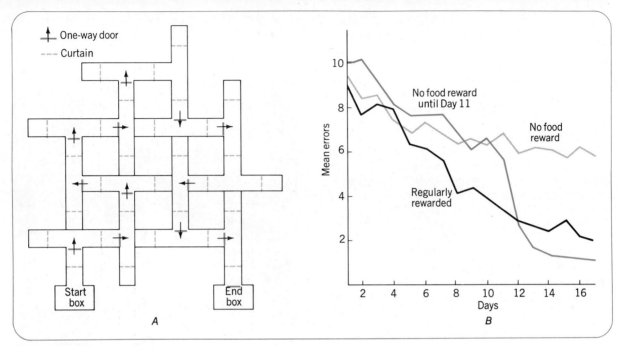

Latent Learning

A. A complex maze is used to study learning in rats.
B. When one group of rats (shown by the dark colored line) found food in the end box of the maze for the first time on Day 11, their performance on Day 12 was just as good as that of the rats that had received food every day. Reward brought to view the latent learning that had occurred on earlier trials.

One prominent theorist who considered reinforcement unnecessary for learning was Edward C. Tolman. In his view, experience with the environment resulted in "cognitive maps" that were formed whether or not reinforcement followed the behaviors. Typically, Tolman said, such learning is latent—that is, it is not reflected in behavior until there is an incentive to act. The concept of **latent learning** came from the following sort of experiment with rats (Tolman & Honzik, 1930). Three randomly selected groups of rats were run in a large maze with twelve T-shaped choice points, as shown in part A of the figure. Each rat in each group was placed in the start box after several hours of food deprivation. As the rat came to a choice point, a door closed behind it, preventing it from retracing its steps; each rat eventually reached the end box. Animals in one group received a food reinforcement in the end box, while rats in the other two groups found the end box empty.

Each entry into a blind alley at a choice point was counted as an error. By the end of ten days (one trial per day) the reinforced rats were making on the average less than half the errors of the first day, while the other rats showed only a slight reduction in errors. On Day 11, one of the two nonreinforced groups suddenly encountered food in the end box. The question was, had they learned something in the past ten days, something *latent* (not exhibited in overt behavior)? If so, we could expect them to perform with only a few errors on Day 12. If not, we would expect a *gradual* improvement in performance until they *eventually* equaled the efficiency of the reinforced rats. As the figure shows, the improvement of the "not-reinforced, then-reinforced" rats is sudden and dramatic. The data support the notion that these rats learned a great deal but did not exhibit their learning until there was incentive to do so. This is latent learning.

to learn specific responses easily while other learning is difficult or even impossible. The easy acquisition of language by babies may be an example (*see* p. 257). Because these considerations are closely related to work on the evolu-

"You can't miss it. Go down to the corner and make a left, then another left, then a right..."

tion of behavior, we take them up in some detail in Chapter 23 (*see* especially pp. 639–45 and pp. 646–57). For the present, you should bear in mind that each species shows important constraints on its learning; so too our general principles have to be limited when they are applied to particular cases.

How are sets of associations learned?

Both classical and operant conditioning describe the formation of single associations. In this section we will be concerned with the learning of many associations in a collection or set. Suppose, for example, you must learn a list of terms or names in a specific order — the alphabet, perhaps, or the presidents of the United States. You would have to learn each term or name of course but also the order, that *b* follows *a* and precedes *c* and that Eisenhower falls between Truman and Kennedy. There is no single association to be made but a collection of them. Such a task is called **serial ordering.** Another task might be to learn **paired associates.** Here the procedure involves the presentation of terms in pairs as in learning a language — "Spanish word–English equivalent" — over a vocabulary of such pairs. A third type of learning is called **free recall,** which is the same as serial ordering except that the order is not important. Suppose you were on a television show and they offered you $10 for each vice-president you could name, in any order. That would be a free-recall task.

SERIAL ORDERING

Serial ordering is a procedure in which a string or list of items is presented one by one, and the subject is asked to reproduce them in the same order. In laboratory studies, such lists are usually words or **nonsense syllables.** A nonsense syllable is a collection of letters that has no obvious meaning, like "CEV" or "GZL." Hermann Ebbinghaus, who began his study of learning and memory in the previous century, was the first to use nonsense syllables; he hoped that they would be meaningless and thus be of value in studying the formation of associations where none existed before. It was a somewhat forlorn hope. Many nonsense syllables have clear meanings: FBI, for example, or LSD, and of course your own initials. The **association value** of an item in a list—roughly defined as the degree of meaning an item has for the subject—quickly became an important variable in research. The reason for its importance is obvious; after all, you are not likely to forget your own initials, no matter where in the list they occur. Any material that is already highly meaningful—that has many associations—is more readily learned than less meaningful material.

The two common methods of testing in serial ordering are the study-test method and the anticipation method. In the study-test method, items are presented to a subject, who then attempts to repeat the items in the same order. In the anticipation procedure, the first item is presented, then time and opportunity is given for the subject to anticipate what the following item will be (which of course would be impossible in the first round); then the second item is presented and the subject is asked about the third, and so on through the list. The advantage of the anticipation method is that there is a cue or prompt

Figure 14-6
Bowed Serial-Position Curves
Curves are for list lengths of 8, 13, and 18. The data points are actual experimental values, and they are fitted by smoothed theoretical curves. In all cases, there are fewest errors for items in the beginning and most for items in the middle of the list. (After Atkinson, 1957)

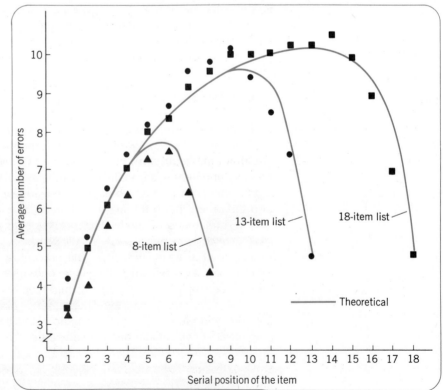

for every single item in the list (*A* is the cue for anticipating *B*, *B* for *C*, and so on). With the study-test method, a subject could fail to recall an item because he or she had forgotten the prompt item. Had the prompt been shown, perhaps the subject could have recalled what followed it. On the other hand, the study-test method is more often used in real life—in classwork, for example—and the subject can recall at his or her own rate.

The single most important finding from research on serial-order learning is that items in the middle of a list are learned more slowly than items either at the beginning or at the end of the list. Graphically, this fact is represented by a bowed or U-shaped curve when a measure of learning (such as number of errors) is plotted against the position in the list (*see* Figure 14-7). The first and last items in the list are learned quickly and most of the errors occur in the middle positions. This finding holds regardless of the length of the list—in Figure 14-6 lists of 8, 13, and 18 items show the same effect.

This **serial-position effect** is very common. Indeed, if an experiment failed to show one, that in itself would be very surprising. Furthermore, it does not much matter whether the list is easy or difficult to learn. Although the absolute number of errors will differ, the proportion of total errors will show the same trend. To give a concrete example, suppose you learn two lists: in one you learn to order the names of twelve of your friends; in the other you learn to order twelve nonsense syllables. The names of your friends (in an order) will be much easier to learn—that is, you will make fewer *total* errors before getting it perfect. But the *proportion* of errors occurring at each serial position would be approximately the same in both cases.

PAIRED ASSOCIATES

In paired-associate learning, items are presented two by two rather than singly. In your next exam in this course, for instance, the instructor might present one item of a pair—such as "the serial-position effect"—and ask you to supply its paired associate, in this case its definition. Or in a German class, you are given *Haus* and asked to supply "house," its English equivalent. In the laboratory the pairs might be arbitrary. I might tell you that whenever I say "inspire" I want you to say "legend." In most cases, a collection of these pairs is presented.

An important principle of paired-associate learning is—rather surprising— the **total-time hypothesis.** In learning a list of paired associates the *total* study time is important; but how this time is *distributed* has little or no importance. For example, suppose you are to learn a list of eighteen pairs of words. If you can learn it in five "go-throughs" (trials) spending four seconds per pair, this requires a total of 20 seconds per pair. The hypothesis states that if you spend only two seconds per pair per trial, you will need ten trials. In other words, you need 20 seconds per pair no matter how you go about it. Five trials at four seconds per pair, ten trials at two seconds per pair, or twenty trials at one second per pair—the result is always the same.

Approximately. The total-time hypothesis is only approximately correct, and one can even find situations in which the approximation is rather poor. But science is a pragmatic endeavor, and one exception is not enough to discredit an assertion. Exceptions add to the puzzle, often pointing to ways in which the original assumption should be revised. But the "approximate laws" of psychology are still useful until they are replaced by more precise formulations.

The total-time hypothesis does encompass a wide range of situations and organizes a considerable amount of research data.

In any case, some implications of the total-time hypothesis are worth discussing. One of them is that there is no quick and easy way to learn paired associates; the more time you spend the more you will learn. You cannot learn without spending the time. Second, there appears to be little advantage to either "distributed" practice or to "massed" practice. The issue of the **distribution of practice** has been controversial. Students have often been advised that distributed practice is preferable to a concentrated effort: "study one hour a day for a week; don't cram for seven hours the night before the exam." Such advice appears sound in certain cases—skill learning, for example (*see* p. 397). But in other cases, such as learning a language, the advice might be less appropriate. One must consider the specific task before applying such generalities.

The motivation to learn is a related issue. It is perhaps universally accepted that a student with higher motivation will learn more than one with little motivation. But the matter is not quite so simple. Clearly students who are motivated to learn French will spend more time at their studies and hence learn more. There is little evidence, however, that highly motivated students will learn more *if* both they and poorly motivated students study for equal amounts of time. (The relationship between motivation and learning is complex; *see* Spotlight 14-4.)

MEDIATION IN LEARNING

Another consideration, **mediation** (both in the laboratory and in more practical situations), means that the association between a stimulus and response is not direct but is accomplished by an interrelating associate. Faced with the task of

STUART LEEDS

One implication of the total-time hypothesis is that motivation does *not* affect paired-associate learning in a direct way. If the time spent on study is held constant, the poorly motivated person will learn as much as the highly motivated one. Great care must be taken, however, before generalizing this finding beyond paired-associate learning. On the other hand, additional evidence can be cited; the area of **incidental learning** shows similar results.

Incidental learning is to be contrasted with "intentional learning." As you read this page, you *intend* to learn the facts and principles of psychology; if the instructor asks you to recall whether a particular experiment was described in a spotlight or in the main text, or to identify the color used in a certain illustration, you would be rightfully upset with such pedagogic techniques. Nonetheless, you might be able to answer correctly. This is incidental learning. In laboratory studies of incidental learning, the general conclusion is that intent to learn leads to better results, as you would expect. But not because of motivation (the intention). Rather, it appears that the intention to learn leads to more frequent rehearsal of the material. If frequency of rehearsal is equal, then incidental learning can be as effective as intentional learning.

No psychologist would suggest that motivation does not affect behavior; and none would assert that it has no effect on learning, at least indirectly. But as the broad concept of motivation is refined by accumulating data and changing theories, more and more of the effects are being defined with precision. So motivation may be translated into an effect on time spent studying, for example, or as an effect on rehearsal frequency. As another illustration, take the hypothesis that a more highly motivated animal will work faster—run faster in a maze, for instance—if it is hungrier than another. That fact is easily demonstrated. But the speed of running can be considered as an aspect of the *conditioned response;* one could just as easily devise an experiment in which highly motivated animals ran very slowly. All that is required is an operant-conditioning procedure whereby the animal is not reinforced unless . . . (can you complete the sentence?).

Nevertheless, it is equally inaccurate to say that no psychologists feel that motivation directly affects learning. Obviously it is a complex issue. The interested reader can consult Cofer and Appley (1964) or Haber (1966).

---

learning the vocabulary of a foreign language, many students report that they make up sets of words or mental images to link the two terms to be learned. For example, in learning the pair UMBRELLA-BOTTLE, you might picture to yourself an umbrella thrust into a bottle or an umbrella smashing a bottle.

To test whether this procedure is really helpful, Bower (1970) performed experiments of the following sort. One set of subjects was instructed to imagine for each pair of words a visual scene or mental image in which the two items interact. Examples were given, and then the subjects were allowed to form their own images for the experimental list of pairs. The control group was simply instructed to learn the list of paired words. The results showed a clear superiority of recall for the group using mental images; in both immediate and delayed recall, the students using imagery recalled about twice as many pairs as the control students. When students in another experiment were instructed to visualize the two terms separately, their performance did not improve; only interactive imagery aided in linking the terms to be associated.

Patients with certain types of brain injuries often perform poorly on learning tests, partly because they do not spontaneously employ associative strategies. In one recent study, patients with damage to the frontal lobes scored poorly on paired-associate learning; but when the items were presented in picture form (like the umbrella in the bottle), the patients recalled almost as well as normal subjects (Signoret & Lhermitte, 1976).

Even normal college students can benefit by having foreign language vocabulary presented to them with "keywords" that link the sound of the foreign word to a visual image (Atkinson, 1975). After favorable results in laboratory tests of foreign-vocabulary learning, the following procedure was used recently in a second-year Russian course. For each Russian word, an English word with a similar sound was chosen. For example, in the case of the Russian word *óseń* (meaning "autumn") the related key word was "ocean." The students were instructed first to associate the spoken foreign word with the sound of the keyword (*óseń-ocean*), then to form an imaginary link, connecting the meaning of the keyword with the translation of the foreign word. For example, the student might visualize *autumn* leaves falling into the *ocean*. Students in the course were free to use the keywords or not. Most did, and the results pleased both the students and their instructors. Further research is going on to apply this work from experimental psychology to a variety of practical learning situations.

FREE RECALL

The word "free" in free-recall tasks refers to the freedom to repeat the items in any order. In serial ordering, the correct order is necessary or required; in free recall, the order is not demanded.

Free-recall experiments allow the investigator to study organizational processes in learning. Suppose a list with items like these is presented: FORD, JANE, DATSUN, PINK, MARY, ORANGE, LOUISE, BLUE, BUICK. . . . If subjects are asked to recall freely (in any order), they typically cluster their responses by categories—automobiles come together, as do girls' names and colors.

In lists with no obvious basis for categorization, subjects still tend to group. That is, they invent or discover some means of forming useful classifications of the items. Subjects who organize the material in some way generally learn more rapidly than those who do not. Learning and organization, in other words, are apparently two highly related processes. The controversy centers on which is cause and which is effect. (Organization in learning is discussed on p. 403.)

Free-recall learning also demonstrates a regular and systematic **learning curve.** Years ago psychologists were interested in finding the "true learning curve"; they wanted to graph a measure of learning against the number of trials (amount of practice) in such a way that would uniquely specify the progress of learning in its true form. Unfortunately, learning curves have been and are quite variable for different tasks. The learning curve for free recall, however, is close to the smooth function the early investigators were seeking (*see* Figure 14-7).

The typical learning curve in Figure 14-7 can be described as an exponential function rising quickly at first and then leveling off. It can be shown that such a curve would result if, on each trial, the subject remembered all previously recalled words plus a constant fraction of the previously unlearned items. In the figure the constant fraction is one-third. Thus, after one trial, the subject remembers one-third of the 30 items—10 items. After the second trial, he retains

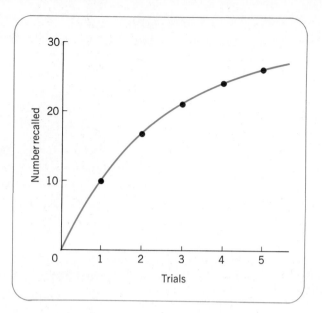

Figure 14-7
Exponential Learning Curve of Single-Trial Free Recall
On each trial the average subject remembers all the items previously recalled, plus a constant fraction of the number of items yet to learn. The learning curve is simply the smooth function drawn through the points representing the number of items recalled on each successive trial.

these 10 and adds a third of the remaining 20 (6.7, on the average over several subjects)—16.7 items, and so on. Obviously there are variations for the individual, but this curve occurs regularly enough to be called the free-recall curve of learning. The value of the constant fraction may vary with experimental conditions; it is the general shape that reappears frequently.

Today, the search for the true learning curve seems unrealistic. Learning curves for serial-order learning and paired-associate learning are quite different from the free-recall curve, and there are other differences too. The serial-position effect in free recall is quite different from that found in serial-ordering experiments. The total-time hypothesis developed in paired-associate experiments does not seem to apply to serial ordering. We are coming to appreciate the many differences among various types of learning, but we do not yet have a good synthesis.

Does past learning help or hinder new learning?

What we have learned in the past can affect our learning in the present. That is the concept described in psychology as **transfer of training.** Learning to drive a car with a standard transmission, for example, probably enables one to learn to drive a car with an automatic transmission more rapidly than someone who has never learned to drive. This is *positive transfer*. The driver with the previous experience might step frequently on an imaginary clutch pedal, a wasteful and ineffective behavior. This is *negative transfer*.

Not too long ago students were required to learn Greek and Latin, under the assumption that such disciplined training would transfer positively to more relevant studies. Although it is difficult to conduct conclusive research on such a problem, most experiments testing this assumption offered little support, even when the transfer was fairly direct—as with Latin to English vocabulary.

Suppose you are faced with a triangle and a circle and are asked to choose one. The experimenter has arbitrarily decided to reward you for one choice only. Perhaps reward lies with a choice of the left or the right, or perhaps with the triangle (or circle) regardless of position. You would experiment a little until you had unearthed the proper clue; in so simple a task, it would not take long. For a monkey, however, or for a very young child, such a task is more difficult.

Harry Harlow, a psychologist, offered this choice to monkeys (1949). After several trials they were able to solve the problem, but Harlow did not stop there. He offered a similar choice to the same monkey, this time involving new geometric shapes or reversing the "correct" choice in the previous task. The monkey solved this problem; then still another task was presented, and so on. Literally hundreds of similar tasks were solved, all of the same general type (using two stimuli, one correct and the other incorrect). After several such tasks, monkeys were solving each new task swiftly, typically taking no more than two trials. (The first choice is always random; if it is correct, you stay with it; if it is not rewarded, you switch.)

Harlow was researching what he called "learning sets," whether subjects could "learn to learn." Apparently they did not learn the specifics of the task, but how to approach it—how to get the necessary information and how to apply it to solve the problem at hand.

These ingenious experiments, which have also been applied to human subjects (children) with similar results, have affected the thinking of psychologists on many issues. To cite just two examples: positive transfer from previous learning (as in school) is now being considered

The monkey is learning not only which object hides the peanut but also how to solve such problems.

more frequently in terms of learning a general approach to problems, than in terms of the specific facts that may have constituted the original learning task. Also, an entire range of topics such as insight and hypothesis testing is illuminated, especially if the subjects are animals. If one of Harlow's monkeys were observed only on the 300th task, the quick solution might be attributed to insight following effective hypothesis testing (even if the surprised observer did not believe animals capable of such "higher" activities). Harlow has given us a glimpse into the events preceding such abilities.

Learning how to learn is a special case of positive transfer that results from repeated practice on the same type of task (see Spotlight 14-5).

Laboratory studies can yield more precise evidence on the question of transfer. We will discuss three common paradigms used in transfer studies. ("Paradigm" is used in the sense of a general pattern or arrangement of experimental conditions.) First, subjects learn a list of paired associates. Then they learn a second list, in which the stimulus words are the same as in the first list, but the "correct" responses are new. This paradigm is labeled *A-B, A-D* to indicate that the stimuli are the same but the proper responses change (see part I of Table 14-1). This arrangement yields negative transfer, as you might well expect. Subjects who have previously learned List 1 have more trouble with List 2 than those with no prior experience because—when a stimulus word is presented—there is conflict between the previously learned associate and the new one.

Another negative-transfer paradigm is labeled $A\text{-}B_r$, and it is illustrated in part II of Table 14-1. The stimulus words are the same in both lists, but here the responses are rearranged (hence the subscript r). Again, those who learn List 1 first have trouble with List 2 because of negative transfer.

An example of a positive-transfer arrangement is the three-stage chaining paradigm $A\text{-}B$, $B\text{-}C$, $A\text{-}C$, illustrated in part III of Table 14-1. Someone who had learned the first two lists would have an easier time learning the third than a subject without that experience. When GALLANT is presented from List 3, the experienced subject presumably thinks of THEREFORE because of the association formed from learning List 1, and this thought triggers (as the next link in a chain) LEGEND from List 2. LEGEND, of course, is the correct response for GALLANT in List 3.

In the $A\text{-}B$, $B\text{-}C$, $A\text{-}C$ paradigm, the second list in a sense mediates the other two. Because of the $B\text{-}C$ associations, $A\text{-}B$ transfers more readily to $A\text{-}C$. Similar mediation effects can be shown from associations already built-in. For example, in one experiment (Russell & Storms, 1955) only two lists were used to obtain

Typical lists for three transfer paradigms. In I and II, learning List 1 impairs learning List 2; but in III, learning List 1 aids learning List 3. Paradigms I and III are quite similar, differing by the inclusion of a mediating list in III. These lists are only illustrative. In an actual experiment, lists would be longer than three pairs, and the order would be varied randomly from trial to trial.

TABLE 14-1 Transfer paradigms

I. A-B, A-D (negative transfer)

List 1	List 2
GALLANT-THEREFORE	GALLANT-LEGEND
INSPIRE-UNTIL	INSPIRE-STANDING
COCKTAIL-PURSUIT	COCKTAIL-BRIEFLY

II. A-B$_r$ (negative transfer)

List 1	List 2
GALLANT-BRIEFLY	GALLANT-LEGEND
INSPIRE-LEGEND	INSPIRE-STANDING
COCKTAIL-STANDING	COCKTAIL-BRIEFLY

III. A-B, B-C, A-C (positive transfer)

List 1	List 2	List 3
GALLANT-THEREFORE	THEREFORE-LEGEND	GALLANT-LEGEND
INSPIRE-UNTIL	UNTIL-STANDING	INSPIRE-STANDING
COCKTAIL-PURSUIT	PURSUIT-BRIEFLY	COCKTAIL-BRIEFLY

the chaining effect described above. In List 1, the stimuli were nonsense syllables and the responses were common words. In List 2, the stimuli were the same nonsense syllables and the responses were different words but associated in our culture with those in List 1. List 1 might have the pair ZIL-OCEAN and then List 2 would have ZIL-DRINK. Both "ocean" and "drink" will elicit the response "water" in a free-association situation; presumably because of this mediating influence, List 2 is learned faster by subjects who have learned List 1 than it is by those who learned similar lists with no such mediating associations. The built-in associations help to produce positive transfer even though the paradigm (*A-B, A-D*) is one that usually produces negative transfer.

Interference is usually discussed in the memory chapter of a textbook, not in the learning chapter. But its close relationship with negative transfer suggests that we would do well to discuss the two concepts together.

The two types of interference designs are shown in parts II and III of Table 14-2. One is for the study of **proactive interference:** subjects learn one list (designated *A-B*) and then learn a second list (*A-D*); proactive interference is indicated by the difficulty they have in *remembering* the second list. ("Proactive" means "acting forward" and suggests that memory for the first list "acts forward" to interfere with the memory for the second.)

In **retroactive interference** (retroactive: acting backward), subjects learn two lists but are tested for their memory of the *first* list—to see if the second has interfered. Note the similarity of this paradigm with that for negative transfer, shown in part I of Table 14-2. In negative transfer, subjects also learn two lists, and the effect is indicated by the difficulty experienced in *learning* the second list.

Let's consider the possibilities logically. Subjects who learn one list (*A-B*),

---

TABLE 14-2 Transfer and interference paradigms

Condition	Task 1	Task 2	Test
I. Negative Transfer	*A-B*	*A-D*	Learning of Task 2
Comparison group	Nothing or an unrelated list: *X-Y*	*A-D*	Same; learning is more rapid
II. Proactive Interference	*A-B*	*A-D*	Later: memory of Task 2
Comparison group	Nothing or an unrelated list: *X-Y*	*A-D*	Same; memory is superior
III. Retroactive Interference	*A-B*	*A-D*	Later: memory of Task 1
Comparison group	*A-B*	Nothing or an unrelated list: *X-Y*	Same; memory is superior

Figure 14-8
Effects of Retroactive Interference
Clearly, the more trials on the second list, the less the recall on List 1. This indicates retroactive interference, even when the chances of response competition are reduced or eliminated. (From Barnes & Underwood, 1959)

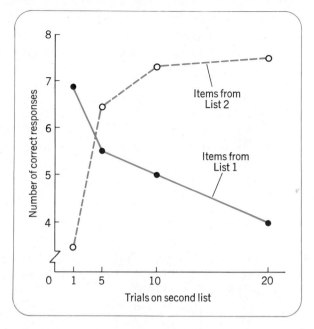

and then learn a second list with the same stimuli but different responses (*A-D*), generally perform poorly on *A-D*, especially compared to a control group without the prior *A-B* learning. This is true whether you test the learning of *A-D* (transfer) or whether you test memory of *A-D* (proactive-interference procedure). Why? Interference theory suggests the following: In learning *A-D*, the *A-B* associations conflict with or *interfere* with the *A-D* associations; hence, slower learning or poorer memory results.

What produces the interference effect? According to interference theory, there are two factors: response competition and unlearning. Response competition means that when you are given the stimulus word, two responses come to mind—one from *A-B* and one from *A-D*. With only a limited time to respond, you might choose the wrong one. The unlearning hypothesis is straightforward: while you are learning the second list (*A-D*) you may be unlearning the first list (*A-B*) associations.

In an experimental attempt to isolate the unlearning component (Barnes & Underwood, 1959), each subject learned the first (*A-B*) list of eight paired associates until he or she could correctly anticipate all eight pairs on a single trial. Then four groups of subjects were randomly formed and given 1, 5, 10, or 20 learning trials on the second (*A-D*) list. Finally, each of the eight *A* terms were shown and the subject was asked to recall *both* the appropriate *B* term from the first list and the appropriate *D* term from the second list. Because the subject could take as long as he or she wanted to respond, and because both responses were to be given, the investigators felt that this method minimized or perhaps even eliminated response competition.

What was left, then, is a relatively pure measure of the unlearning component of retroactive interference. The results of the experiment, pictured in Figure 14-8, provide strong evidence for unlearning as a factor in interference.

The more trials the subjects had on List 2 the fewer items they were able to recall from List 1. (It is interesting to note that the *sum* of the two curves is approximately the same regardless of the number of trials on the second list.)

All this is fine for retroactive interference, but what about proactive interference? As shown in Table 14-2, later memory for *A-D* is worse if an *A-B* list had been learned first. **Spontaneous recovery** is the basic concept used to explain these results. Following the unlearning interpretation of retroactive interference, we could say that, when the subject learns *A-D*, the prior *A-B* associations undergo unlearning. However, over time these unlearned associations show spontaneous recovery. Because the *A-B* associations have recovered (and perhaps some *A-D* associations have been forgotten) the two sets of associations may be in a position to interfere with each other, presumably because of response competition. Thus, one would reasonably expect the group given the interfering list, *A-B*, to recall fewer *A-D* items than the comparison group, which had not learned list *A-B*.

Unfortunately, the findings turn out to be somewhat more complex. First, if response competition were a major factor, proactive interference should be greatly reduced by allowing subjects unlimited time to respond and by asking them for both the *A-B* and the *A-D* items. However, eliminating response competition does *not* eliminate proactive interference. Second, direct evidence for the spontaneous recovery of verbal associations has been difficult to obtain. Correct recall of items from the first list *should* increase as the time after the second list increases; but most of the research evidence shows just the opposite. Thus, although the interpretation of proactive interference in terms of unlearning, spontaneous recovery, and response competition is ingenious and plausible, experimental confirmation of these processes is not yet very convincing.

Where do we stand now? The facts seem clear enough; both retroactive interference and proactive interference occur; and they are surely potent effects in the learning situations of everyday life as well as in controlled laboratory experiments. Only interference theory has made a serious attempt to explain them. The basic notions of unlearning, response competition, and spontaneous recovery are not in themselves adequate to explain all the results, but they are probably parts of the picture. At this time we just do not know. At any rate, half a theory is better than none at all, so psychologists will continue to generate testable hypotheses from interference theory until their research leads to a better theory.

What is required to learn a skill?

Skills are complex patterns of behavior that are gradually acquired over a long period. Hitting a baseball that is traveling at perhaps 100 miles per hour is a skill, and so is playing the cadenza of a Beethoven piano sonata or writing a computer program. Skills may be based on simple associations (until you know some Spanish vocabulary, speaking or writing Spanish is impossible), but they clearly involve much more. Skills involve the synthesis, integration, and coordination of a number of simpler and more basic components; they

After the initial teaching, a certain amount of practice will produce a great improvement in an athletic skill. As the level of skill increases, however, much more practice is required to achieve the same amount of improvement.

also may be based on rules or higher-order principles. The view that skills are simply a collection of habits is no longer very popular.

One of the principles most frequently demonstrated in the direct investigation of skills is that distributed practice is preferable to massed practice. To perfect some athletic skill, for example, practicing one hour a day for five days would yield better results than practicing five hours all at once. This statement contradicts one we made earlier in regard to paired-associate learning,

in which the total-time hypothesis was applied; five hours of practice on paired associates is equally effective with massed or distributed study—it is the total time, and no other factor, that is important. What causes this discrepancy? No one knows for sure, although certainly the answer lies somewhere in the complexity of skills.

Another difference between simple and more complex learning turned out to be less discrepant than at first thought. For many years, textbook descriptions of skill learning talked of a "learning plateau"; that is, ability increased up to a point (the plateau) after which no further improvement could be expected. It was as if some sort of psychological or physiological limit had been reached. Athletes often experience the plateau: they learn rapidly at first and then, as they become more skilled, improvement is less pronounced, less rapid. Finally, they reach a point where more practice seems to have no effect at all for a long period. Numerous experiments in psychology seemed to demonstrate the same phenomenon.

This principle of skill learning was difficult to reconcile with results from the study of simpler examples of learning, which showed no evidence of plateaus. There is so much to be learned in any complex skill that it is hard to accept the notion that one cannot learn more.

We now have good evidence that the so-called plateau in skill learning is nothing more than a statistical phantom. A psychologist named Fitts (1964) studied a number of skills in considerable detail; in one case practice effects were observed over seven years. On the basis of his results, he formulated a law. **Fitts' law** states that the relationship between performance and practice of a skill is what is known in mathematics as a power function. In other words, when one is beginning to learn, performance improves rapidly, but as skill increases, the same amount of improvement takes much more practice; see Figure 14-9 for a hypothetical example of Fitts' law. The plateau is never reached; there is always improvement with practice. It only seems as if improvement stops because it proceeds so slowly, ever more slowly. An assembly-

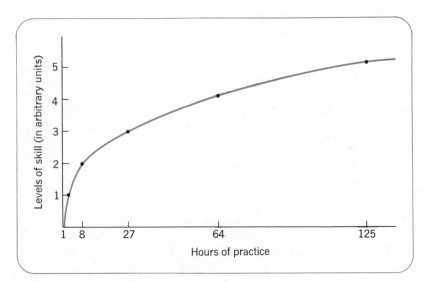

Figure 14-9
How Skill Increases with Practice, According to Fitts' Law

This hypothetical skill develops by the power function, $y = x^{1/3}$ (or $y = \sqrt[3]{x}$), where $x =$ amount of practice and $y =$ level of skill.

line worker may double his output in the first year; to double it again may require ten years; to double it a third time may require a thousand more years. Time runs out, of course, but there is no evidence that skill stops improving with practice.

What are the current issues of learning psychology?

Now that we have discussed specific topics, let us examine two of the most significant general issues in the field of learning. **Pluralism** deals with the question of whether or not all learning is the same. The second issue, **continuity,** asks about the fundamental nature of an association. Is an association formed gradually with practice, continuously increasing in strength, or does each single association either exist or not, in all-or-none fashion?

Obviously, both issues are matters of basic concern for all learning psychologists, whatever their specialized domains. These issues have long been matters of controversy and remain so today.

THE ISSUE OF PLURALISM

Is learning all of one type? (This is called the monistic position.) Or are there several phenomena lumped under the general heading of learning? (This is called the pluralistic position.) One recent classification listed seven different types of learning: classical conditioning, operant conditioning, chaining, multiple-discrimination learning, concept learning, principle learning, and problem solving (Gagné, 1965). At the other extreme from *pluralism* is the argument that the principles of classical conditioning are (or could be) sufficient to account for all known types of learning. This concept is known as **monism.** The monistic position is the "official" Soviet one (Pavlov was Russian).

Because it is impossible to discuss all facets of the pluralism issue, we will restrict our attention to two of the most common questions: (1) Are classical and operant conditioning two distinct processes or only one? (2) Are association principles and organizational principles opposed to each other or complementary?

Classical versus Operant Conditioning

On the surface, classical and operant conditioning appear to be quite different. In classical conditioning, the response is controlled by the stimulus *preceding* it (the US or CS); in operant conditioning, the response is controlled by the stimuli *following* it (reinforcement). Many psychologists have suggested that classical conditioning applies to certain types of responses and operant conditioning to others. Classical conditioning has usually been applied to involuntary bodily responses to certain stimuli; these include the commonly known reflexes that control salivation, eyeblinks, knee jerks, breathing, heart rate, and other such actions typically regulated without conscious thought. In other words, these UR's are elicited by clearly defined US's and generally are subject to classical conditioning. In contrast, the voluntary physical responses, those under conscious control, have no clear US. What is the automatic stimulus to talking or running? These processes are generally subject to operant conditioning. It is a common theoretical position, therefore, to assert that there are at least two types of learning—learning of involuntary responses affected by classical conditioning and learning of voluntary responses affected by operant conditioning.

On the other hand, those who believe that there is really only one type of learning argue that we have little basis for distinguishing between two types, despite their surface differences. Consider the similarities between the US in classical conditioning and the reinforcement in operant conditioning. In each case, presence of these stimuli results in acquisition of an association, and absence results in extinction; operationally, very similar processes seem to be involved. Some situations even seem to combine components of classical conditioning and some components of operant conditioning (see the discussion of autoshaping in Spotlight 14-6).

Let us be more precise. In classical-conditioning paradigms, the CS is presented, and *no matter what the animal does* the US is subsequently presented. In the operant-conditioning paradigms, the experiment delivers the reinforcement (US) *only* if the animal makes a desired response. Consider the following general sequence of events: stimulus 1, then response 1, then stimulus 2, then response 2 (see Table 14-3). In classical conditioning, the first stimulus is the CS but the initial response to it is usually ignored; interest focuses on the association between CS and the second response (UR). In operant conditioning, the first response is all-important, and the second stimulus (the US or reinforcement) is contingent on its presence. The second response (UR) is ignored.

TABLE 14-3   A diagrammatic view of the one-type-of-learning approach

A. Learning in general works in this sequence:
   Stimulus 1 → Response 1 → Stimulus 2 → Response 2

B. Classical conditioning

$$S_1 \longrightarrow R_1 \longrightarrow S_2 \longrightarrow R_2$$
(CS)   ( )   (US)   (UR)
$$CS \longrightarrow CR$$

S_1 (CS) is presented systematically.
R_1 is of no interest.
S_2 (US) is delivered regardless of occurrence of R_1; S_2 is reinforcing in an operational sense.
R_2 becomes the conditioned response (CR).

C. Operant conditioning

$$S_1 \longrightarrow R_1 \longrightarrow S_2 \longrightarrow R_2$$
( )   (operant   (rein-   ( )
         response or CR)   forcement)

S_1 and R_2 are of no interest.
R_1 is the operant response (or CR).
S_2 is the reinforcement and is delivered only when R_1 has occurred.

Part *A* shows the general sequence of stimuli and response.
Part *B* shows the foci of interest in classical conditioning.
Part *C* shows the foci of interest in operant conditioning.

Why does a pigeon peck at a key in a food-reward apparatus? This behavior has long been used as a standard example of the operant-conditioning approach of Skinner. Recent observations and experiments, however, suggest that Pavlovian classical conditioning may also be involved. Research on this question has given rise to the rather curious terms, *superstitious behavior* and *autoshaping*. Let us see what is involved in both of these.

Skinner (1948) called attention to the fact that if a food delivery apparatus is set to operate automatically every twelve seconds—regardless of what the pigeon does—pigeons nevertheless develop regular, stereotyped responses. One bird might flap its wings frequently; another might stretch out its neck. Skinner called these acts "superstitious" because they were performed regularly even though they had no effect on obtaining the reward. He proposed that the particular response had occurred once, by accident, just before a food reward was delivered. This "rewarded" response was then repeated, and the repetitions too seemed to be rewarded. Thus the response was reinforced by instrumental conditioning, even though the experimenter had not chosen which particular response to reward. Later experiments showed that the superstitious response most likely to develop in this situation was pecking at the wall around the food hopper (Staddon and Simmelhag, 1971).

An apparently simple variant of the preceding experiment has now given rise to an influential line of research on **autoshaping** (Brown and Jenkins, 1968). In this study, the pigeons first learned to peck grain from an illuminated food tray. Food was available for four seconds at irregular intervals, so the pigeons learned to peck promptly. When the response was well-established, a disk on the wall of the apparatus was illuminated for eight seconds just prior to each appearance of food. The unexpected result was that after forty to sixty trials, the birds began to peck regularly at the disk when the light went on, even though this behavior was not required for access to food.[1] In fact, the pigeons pecked even when pecking turned off the light and prevented access to food on that trial! (Williams and Williams, 1969) In this case the pigeons maintained the pecking response, even though it was counterproductive. This result seems to run contrary to all of our ideas about reinforcement in instrumental learning. But it has been suggested that the behavior becomes understandable if we notice a classically conditioned component of the supposedly instrumental situation. In essence, the illuminated disk becomes a conditioned stimulus (CS) through frequent pairing with the unconditioned stimulus (US), grain. The unconditioned response to food—pecking—is then made to the CS. Pecking at the disk could then be considered a conditioned response (CR).

This interpretation is strengthened by the observation that when birds peck at a disk and water is the reward, they give a distinctly different kind of peck than they do for food (Moore, 1973). "Water pecks" are soft and prolonged, whereas "food pecks" are forceful and brief. In this respect, pecking at the disk mirrors some of the normal behavior of eating or drinking. Furthermore, even with prolonged training, pigeons cannot learn to give a food-like peck to obtain a water reward.

Taken together, these experiments have several broad implications for our understanding of learning processes. They suggest that components of classical conditioning may occur even in a prototypical operant-learning situation. They indicate that the responses given in a situation will reflect, in part at least, the typical responses of the species to the reinforcing stimulus. And they suggest that the species-specific responses evoked by the situation may limit the learning that can occur there. (These constraints on learning will be considered further in Chapter 23, pp. 646–57.)

[1] The experimenters called this procedure "autoshaping" because there was no need for step-by-step shaping of the key-pecking behavior by successive approximations as described earlier (p. 377). In the autoshaping situation, the pigeons seem to shape their own behavior automatically.

For example, food is commonly used as a US in classical conditioning and as a reinforcement in operant conditioning. When used as reinforcement, food produces salivation just as readily as when used as US, but experimenters are not interested in this. They are interested in the response preceding the US. When food is used in classical conditioning, responses of various types do occur before US, but the experimenters are not interested. They deliver the "reinforcement" (US) regardless of the response. In some cases, the animal salivates after CS and before US, in which case the experimenters are proud to have found a CR; but the response of salivation could be as well termed "instrumental" — an active preparation for the US (food) rather than a passive response to it. In short, the superficial difference between the two types of conditioning seems less pronounced on closer examination, and many of the differences may be credited to the experimenters' interests — and therefore their procedures — instead of different underlying processes.

This singular or "monistic" view of learning raises certain questions. What about the view that classical conditioning applies to involuntary responses and operant to voluntary responses? For many years, the monist's position was suspect because of considerable evidence that involuntary responses could not be conditioned by operant procedures. A person could not control his or her blood pressure to gain a reward, for example.

Dramatic new research by several investigators, however, has shown that operant conditioning of involuntary responses may indeed occur. In one study (Miller & Banuazizi, 1968), rats were trained to modify such involuntary responses as heart rate or intestinal contractions by using careful techniques that included reinforcement by direct electrical stimulation to the brain (see Chapter 20, p. 571).

Although several laboratories reported such effects in the late 1960s, these results have since become difficult to replicate (Miller, 1973). Apparently the situation is more complex than was originally thought. Fortunately, positive results have been obtained reliably with people. They have been trained to control heart rate, blood pressure, body temperature, and brain waves, to name a few involuntary responses (Schwartz, 1975). It has been possible to train some people simultaneously to raise the temperature in one hand and to lower it in the other, presumably by controlling dilation and constriction of blood vessels (Roberts, Kewman, & MacDonald, 1973). In the past, the subjects could not control their involuntary responses because they could not know what was going on inside their body. If subjects can actually see or hear their internal responses by means of electronic recording devices, they can learn to control them for reinforcement. For example, a temperature recording device can be attached to the fingertips of each hand and connected with two large dials — one for each hand — so that the subjects can easily monitor their finger temperatures. When such feedback is made available, some subjects can learn in a few sessions to raise finger temperature in one hand and lower it in another, producing a difference of about 10°F.

Feedback of information about biological processes in the subject's own body has been called **biofeedback,** and this has become an active area of research. Biofeedback experiments have exciting medical implications. Drugless control of high blood pressure, for example, might be highly desirable for patients suffering from hypertension. As is often the case with a new area of research, publicity and optimism have run ahead of solid demonstrations that the findings can be applied.

But in the world of learning theory, the monist's position has been strengthened by fairly clear evidence that at least one of the pluralist's assumptions is in error. There is no simple partitioning by which voluntary responses are conditioned only operantly and involuntary responses are conditioned only classically.

Needless to say, however, the issue is far from resolved. Differences in facts and principles among various surface types of learning—among serial-order, paired-associate, and free-recall learning, for instance—strengthen the pluralist position. In addition, the monist is also typically an associationist, suggesting that all learning can be explained through principles of association. This view is criticized by theorists who see a need for other principles, especially organizational principles. We now turn to this issue.

Association versus Organization

Association is the basic building block for studying learning, as we have seen. In explaining more complex types of learning, psychologists commonly apply the principles of classical or operant conditioning. For example, if you were to ask an associationist the "meaning" of a word, the answer would most likely be given in terms of the word's "association value"; that is, meaning is construed in terms of what the subject associates with the stimulus word—what responses and how many associates. The more associations you make to a word, the greater its meaning and the greater its association value for you.

For many situations, association value is an easy and apt measure. Evidence is clear and abundant that meaningfulness as estimated by association value has a significant effect on learning; the greater the meaningfulness, the faster the learning. However, many feel this definition does not capture the true and essential characteristics of meaning.

There are many possible criticisms of the associationistic view of meaning. Here we will consider an organizational criticism that proposes that much of what we understand of a word derives from (1) the position or context of that word in a greater organization or arrangement and (2) the rules that give meaning to the position regardless of the particular word. (*See* Chapter 13 for a more complete discussion of language and meaning.) For example, the sentence "They are eating apples" is ambiguous because we do not know whether "eating" is supposed to be an adjective or a verb (Neisser, 1967). If we did know, the meaning would be clear—the meaning would come from the rules of grammar, not entirely from the word itself.

The association versus organization debate is clearly evident in the study of language learning. It is at least possible to devise an associationistic interpretation of language development: babbling is selectively reinforced or extinguished by parents so that common usages are strengthened and uncommon usages weakened. More recent data, however, seem to give strong support to organization hypotheses; language appears to be learned by induction of rules rather than by formation of specific associations. Still, the issue is unresolved, perhaps primarily because language learning is complex; one cannot be sure that associations do not in some way account for the so-called organizational principles.

Even in simpler tasks, organizational effects are not easily dismissed. We have seen in the section on free-recall learning that the subjects' organization of the items has a marked impact on their learning rate. Consider, for example, the experiments that involve what is called "part-to-whole transfer." Subjects first learn a list—say of twelve words—and are asked to recall them in any order. The list is designated as "noncategorized," meaning that it has no simple a priori basis for categorization selected by the experimenter. Subjects will still impose their own organization on such a list, even if they do not know precisely what rule is used. The subjects are next presented with a second list of twenty-four words, twelve of which are the same as the first and twelve of which are new. (The list is completely scrambled, of course). An associationist would predict positive transfer because, after all, the twelve words of List 1 are repeated in List 2, so whatever associations are needed have already formed; only the twelve new words need to be learned. Actually, however, the control subjects — who have learned a prior list of twelve words, none of which is repeated in List 2 — learn the second list of twenty-four faster than the experimental group. They start slowly (the experimental group does better on the first trial) but soon overtake their "privileged" competitors, even though — for them — all twenty-four words are completely new.

Such findings may be interpreted as supporting the organizational point of view. The argument here is that the experimental subjects suffer because, when presented with List 2, they try to add the twelve new words to the structure or organization they have already devised for the twelve old words. The new words may not fit very well. The control group, by contrast, starts fresh; therefore these subjects have a better chance of creating an *optimal* organization for the twenty-four items.

Thus, the evidence supports the pluralist in this aspect of the issue: there seem to be two types of learning, associationistic and organizational. The associationist-monist can, of course, broaden the conception of "associations" to include hierarchies — a kind of organization — thus making many of the same predictions as the organization theorist. So the controversy continues. We will meet it again in the chapter on memory (*see* p. 420).

THE ISSUE OF CONTINUITY

Are associations formed in an all-or-none fashion, or is the formation incremental, gradually increasing in strength from very weak to very strong? The obvious and common answers are all on the side of continuity, a gradual increase in strength. The typical learning curve, to the extent that such a curve exists, shows a gradual and continuous increase in response strength plotted against trials. This is true for a wide variety of tasks, simple and complex, and for a wide variety of response measures. Such curves were shown in Figures 14-6 and 14-7.

Nevertheless, several investigators in the 1930s adopted the view that learning is not continuous but sudden and abrupt. These all-or-none theorists held that learning consists of forming, testing, and confirming hypotheses. Their research dealt mainly with rather complex behavior, such as rats' learning of mazes that included many choice points. At each choice point, the rat had to make a hypothesis about whether a right turn or a left turn was correct. Each hypothesis was presumed not to vary in strength; it was either correct or not. Although the overall learning curve for the maze *looked* gradual, the researchers held that it was so only because so many hypotheses were involved.

For a clearer test between the continuity and noncontinuity positions, the situation was simplified to learning which of two stimuli was correct. The rat had to learn to go to one stimulus rather than to the other. For the first few trials, the animals behave at chance level. Their odds of being correct are 50/50. According to the all-or-none theorists, the animal has not yet found the correct hypothesis—it has learned nothing. The continuity theorists, on the other hand, would suggest some strengthening of the correct association over these first few trials, but not enough to be exhibited in behavior yet. Suppose at this point we reverse the stimuli for an experimental group, making the correct stimulus incorrect and the previously unrewarded stimulus the proper choice. Because they believe that "some strengthening" has occurred, the continuity theorists would predict *negative transfer;* that is, slower learning for the animals that got the reversal than for the controls. The all-or-none theorists would predict no difference between experimentals and controls. The results of such experiments usually show that animals with the brief prior experience did learn more slowly than control animals with little or no relevant prior experience. This evidence of negative transfer from the few initial trials to the later reversal trials supported the continuity position.

The controversy reappeared in the late 1950s, when several ingenious experiments seemed to support the all-or-none position. In one study, students learned lists of paired associates; if the second member of any pair could not be recalled on a trial, an entirely new pair replaced it (Rock, 1957). The substitution procedure continued until the entire list was recalled correctly. These subjects were then compared with control subjects who had simply learned a list of the same length, but without substitution. The reasoning was as follows: If learning is all-or-none, then substitution of new items for incorrect (presumably unlearned) ones should have no effect. But if learning is gradual, then the loss of the incorrect (but partially learned) items should make the task more difficult for the experimental subjects. In fact, both groups learned the list in about the same number of total trials—results that appeared to support the all-or-none hypothesis.

Psychologists who favored the continuity position were quick to point out a problem with the substitution procedure. By replacing incorrect items with new ones on each trial, the experimenters almost inevitably created easier lists for the experimental subjects. Subjects were more likely to fail difficult items; these items were replaced on each trial until the subjects got items they could handle. Thus if experimental subjects learning easier lists did no better than the control subjects, the evidence actually supports the continuity position. If the lists were equally difficult, the experimental subjects would presumably require *more* trials to learn them.

Although the continuity theorists could explain away the results of many of the so-called all-or-none experiments, interest in the all-or-none position was revived. Several mathematical models of learning were developed, based on the assumption that an association either exists or does not, at any given moment. These models, it was discovered, could explain most of the so-called continuity experiments (*see* Atkinson, Bower, & Crothers, 1965). Thus the controversy reached a standoff. The all-or-none theories applied well to the simpler tasks—such as those involving a choice between two stimuli—and the continuity theories applied better to more complex learning.

Recently, the issue of continuity has been reformulated as a question about memory rather than learning. Are memory traces all or none, or do they gradually increase in strength? The issue of continuity was not decisively settled one way or the other in the early research on learning, partly because the issue was phrased in broad and uncompromising terms and studied in rather complex situations. Now that the early research has been made more precise in both theory and method by the increased emphasis on memory, the results represent a significant scientific advance.

SUMMARY

Learning is the process by which an organism modifies its behavior as a result of experience. The formation of single **associations** has been studied by both classical-conditioning and operant-conditioning techniques. **Classical conditioning** begins with a natural pairing: US-UR or **unconditioned stimulus–unconditioned response.** By repeatedly pairing a CS **(conditioned stimulus)** with a US, CS eventually evokes UR or some related response, now called the **conditioned response** (CR). Repeated presentations of CS *without* US lead to **extinction;** the CR is no longer elicited.

Unlike classical conditioning, in which the response depends on the *preceding* stimulus, in **operant conditioning** the response is controlled by the stimuli *following* it—the **reinforcement.** Results differ according to the schedule of reinforcement; the schedule can be expressed as a ratio of the number of reinforced responses to total responses or, if the time between reinforcements is the important variable, as a temporal interval.

More complex learning tasks involve a combination of associations and include serial ordering (learning a list in order), paired associates (two-by-two pairings), and free recall (no order requirements). Performance can be tested by either the anticipation method, which uses one item as a cue for the next, or by the more traditional study-test method.

Serial-order learning is characterized by the serial-position curve—middle items in the list are learned more slowly. In **paired-associate** learning, the total-time hypothesis states that learning is a function of the total study time but not of how that time is distributed. **Mediators** such as visual images help in acquiring foreign language vocabulary or other paired items. **Free-recall** learning introduced the notion that organization imposed by the subject aids acquisition.

Sometimes prior learning helps in new learning (positive **transfer of learning**), but at times it may hinder (negative transfer). **Interference** theory seeks to explain transfer effects by means of the notions of **proactive** and **retroactive interference.** Operationally, negative transfer and retroactive interference are clearly related; the explanation of one increases our understanding of the other.

Skill learning is difficult to investigate because of its complexity. It has been discovered that skills do continue to improve with practice, although progress becomes progressively slower (Fitts' law).

Two of the most significant issues in the field are the **pluralism-monism** question and the continuity issue. The plurality issue encompasses the many forms of the question, Is there one kind or many kinds of learning? We considered just two aspects of this issue: first, are classical and operant conditioning in essence the same, or are they different? There are good arguments on both sides of this question. Theory and research are also somewhat equivocal concerning the second aspect of the question: Are principles of association sufficient, or must principles of organization be added to provide a workable account of human learning? It seems clear that associationists, if they are to remain so, must do better in interpreting organization effects within their scheme.

The **continuity** issue asks whether the increase of response strength during learning occurs gradually (continuously) or all at once, from none to all. This issue was studied in the animal-learning field in the 1930s, in the human-learning field around 1960, and is now a basic issue in human memory research.

Memory

What are the processes and stages of memory?
How is memory tested?
What have we discovered about memory?
How have memory theories integrated the data?

How do you remember your own past? This is the question of memory over which philosophers have puzzled for centuries. William James, the great American psychologist-philosopher, explained it in terms of learning; he stated that associations are formed and brought back to re-excitation (1890): James was much more precise in his descriptions of the formation of associations than he was in his discussion of re-excitations. Historically, his approach has been typical. It was believed that if we truly understood the learning process, we would also understand memory. Does not learning involve laying down a memory trace? Is not memory the indication of past learning? Are not the two processes intimately related? The close relationship between learning and memory can hardly be denied, but in recent times research emphasis has shifted from learning to memory. Similarly, the underlying assumption has changed to this form: If we can understand memory, then we will also understand learning.

We begin this chapter by considering some of the basic processes and stages in memory. Next we will describe some techniques for testing memory. The following section examines what research has revealed about six different aspects of memory. The concluding portion of the chapter summarizes some of the recent theories of memory that attempt to systematize the major findings.

What are the processes and stages of memory?

ENCODING, STORAGE, AND RETRIEVAL

It is generally agreed that three processes are involved in memory: encoding, storage, and retrieval. The first process, **encoding,** involves the registration of the basic information, the representation of one thing by another. When you look at a painting, hear a friend's phone number, or try to learn the meaning of a new word, this information is initially registered or encoded through the operation of sensory receptors and internal nervous circuits.

Storage, the second process, reflects the fate of the information encoded. How long does the information stay with us? How does the information change over time? Is storage a *passive* process ("stored" books are passive—they do not lose or gain content) or is it an *active* process (as skin is maintained by replacing cells)?

Retrieval is the third process of memory; it describes the utilization of stored information. If I were to ask the name of your third-grade teacher, it is not enough that it was originally encoded and stored; you must be able to find it and retrieve it from your mental storehouse. Even if it is there, somewhere, it is still possible that you will not come up with it; it may be *inaccessible*. **Inaccessibility** should be distinguished from **unavailability.** If information is "lost," it is unavailable, not simply inaccessible at the moment. If a book is misplaced in a library or if its catalog card is out of order, the book is inaccessible; but if the book is not in the library (discarded or stolen), then it is unavailable.

Because memory depends on these three processes—encoding, storage, and retrieval—the failure to remember something does not tell us much about where the fault lies. Perhaps it was never encoded. Perhaps it was encoded but not kept in a permanent store, and so it is unavailable. Or maybe it was encoded and stored but is currently inaccessible. In everyday situations it is often impossible to pinpoint the precise source of the memory failure, but the psychologist can discriminate these processes in the laboratory.

MEMORY AND DECISION

Although we have discussed three processes involved in memory, memory itself is only one of two stages in the information-processing system. The other is the decision stage. For example, if you are asked for some information that may or may not be in your memory, you first check your memory. On the basis of what you find there, you decide to respond "Yes," "No," or "I'm not sure." Memory might not provide clear information—"My third-grade teacher? Let's

Figure 15-1
The Two Stages of Information Processing

When a probe item is presented, information in the memory stage is activated as a function of what has been encoded, stored, and retrieved. The output from the memory stage is fed into a decision stage, which then produces a response.

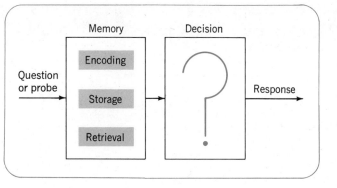

see. Johnson?"—so your actual response is based partly on the amount of information recovered and partly on how valid you feel this information is. The amount of information required to make a definite decision can vary considerably among individuals. You know the different types: some people are "absolutely certain" no matter how foggy their memory and no matter how many times their absolute certainty has been proved absolutely wrong in the past. At the other extreme are those who are unwilling to commit themselves no matter how clear their memory—"I can't be sure." So there are at least two stages in the information-processing system, one involving memory, the other decision, as diagramed in Figure 15-1. Obviously, identical memories could result in different responses because of variations in decisional processes, as we will see more clearly in the following section on recall and recognition memory tasks.

How is memory tested?

RECALL AND RECOGNITION

Recall and recognition are the standard methods of testing memory. "What was her name?" asks for **recall;** "Was her name Alice or Jane?" asks for **recognition.** In school examinations, memory for course content is tested by essay questions or definitions—recall tasks—or by multiple-choice and true-false questions that call for simple recognition of the correct answer. More precisely, recall methods ask you to retrieve a certain item from your memory and direct your search only by the question itself. "What was her name?" identifies what is to be remembered, but you are left to your own resources to dredge up the correct response.

Recognition methods are of three main types, each using a different kind of probe question. The first is a simple yes-no question, in which a possible reply or response is presented and you are to describe it as true (yes) or false (no): "Her name was Jane. True or false?" A second type presents several possible responses and you are asked to choose the correct one; it is called the multiple-alternative forced choice method or, more commonly, multiple choice. The third type is called batch testing, in which a batch or collection of items are randomly mixed and the subject is asked to identify the correct items. For example, you could be presented with a list of city names and asked to identify

The graph on the left shows actual data averaged for a number of subjects and lists of items. The graph on the right shows how the results would appear if the search with positive probes terminated whenever subjects found a match.

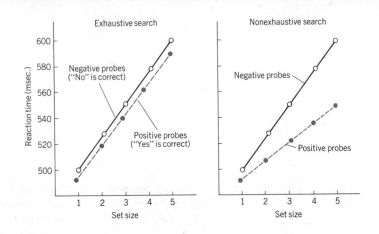

Exhaustive search

Negative probes ("No" is correct)

Positive probes ("Yes" is correct)

Nonexhaustive search

Negative probes

Positive probes

Reaction time (msec.)

Set size

The comparison process presumed to occur in recognition memory tasks is not directly observable, but recent studies have demonstrated some of its characteristics (Sternberg, 1969). Here is an experimental situation used for this purpose: The experimenter presents a short list of items once and then a single test item. For example, he or she gives a list of five digits—8, 3, 7, 4, 9—and then a test or probe item—for example, 3. The subject's task is to respond "yes" ("this is one of the items in the preceding list") or "no" as quickly as possible. Half the test items are correctly designated "yes" (positive probes) and half "no" (negative probes). The dependent variable is reaction time—how long the subject takes to answer. The independent variable, that which is expected to affect the response measure, is set size—the number of items in the list (1, 2, 3, 4, or 5).

The results, as plotted on a graph, show a constant (linear) relationship between set size and reaction time.

Hermann Ebbinghaus, nineteenth century pioneer of memory research, began by testing recall of nonsense syllables.

state capitals. Some would actually be state capitals (targets) while others would not (such false items are called "lures").

When a person is presented with a recognition task, presumably some sort of *comparison process* begins. The item (one of the batch, one of the alternatives in multiple choice, or the single possibility in yes-no tasks) is compared with the information in memory. The results of this comparison process form the input to the "decision system," as indicated in Figure 15-1, and eventually a response is made. A clear "match" of the presented (probe) item and something in memory should result in a positive response, and a clear "no match" in a negative response. Where there is some doubt, the comparison process may be repeated before a response occurs. The comparison process seems to occur at a very fast rate, but with the aid of careful techniques we can learn something about it (see Spotlight 15-1).

In recall no comparison is possible because no potential "matches" are given. Here, presumably, some sort of *search process* begins. With the aid of the pointers provided by the probe question ("What was the name of your third-grade teacher?"), the individual searches his or her memory for relevant information and transmits this information to the decision system. Presumably the decision system seeks to define the acceptability of the proposed response. If acceptable, the response is made; if not, a second search begins. These

The longer lists produce longer reaction times. In the comparison process, subjects compare the probe with each of the list items in a *sequential* (serial) and *exhaustive* fashion.

Now, what does this statement mean? The term "sequential comparison" is used in contrast to simultaneous comparison. We believe that comparison in the experiment is sequential because the longer the list of items, the longer the subjects take to produce a response. Each additional item in the presented list adds a relatively constant amount to the reaction time, as shown in the graph. If subjects compared items simultaneously, they could respond as rapidly with five alternatives as with two. The finding that comparisons are made sequentially is perhaps intuitively plausible. But the data also suggest that the comparison process is *exhaustive,* and this is rather surprising. "Exhaustive" means the comparison process proceeds item by item (sequentially) through the entire list, regardless of whether a "match" is found in one of the first few items. In the example we gave with the items 8, 3, 7, 4, 9, and the positive probe 3, "exhaustive" means the subjects do not stop when they come to the 3 in the list. Instead, they continue to compare the probe with 7, 4, 9, before answering "yes."

How do we know this? Consider the alternative possibility, that comparisons are *not* exhaustive and stop when a match is made. With negative probes (items not in the list, for example, 6), each additional item in the set would add a constant amount of time; all must be scanned because none affords a match. With positive probes, however, we would expect the curve to rise more slowly than for negative probes, as illustrated in the panel on the right. In a set of five items, for example, sometimes the match would come on the first comparison, sometimes on the second, the third, or the fourth, and sometimes on the fifth. On the average over many trials, the positive match would be made on the third comparison. Thus, with positive probes, a list of five items should show the same reaction time that is required for a list of three items with a negative probe—*if* the comparison process stops when a match is made. This is clearly *not* what we observe, and the hypothesis of exhaustive comparison is thereby strengthened.

These data also suggest that the comparison process is very rapid. Because each additional item adds about 35-thousandths of a second to the reaction time, it appears that the comparison process goes on at the rate of about 30 comparisons per second.

search cycles continue until an acceptable alternative is generated or until the decision is made to stop the search and to respond "I don't know."

Recall and recognition can be utilized to distinguish between storage and retrieval processes in memory. Often subjects cannot *recall* information—that is, reproduce it by themselves—but they can *recognize* the "answer" if it is presented to them. In such cases, failure of recall is clearly a retrieval problem; the information was available but inaccessible, for the success of recognition indicates that the information was stored.

Even within recall tasks, the difference between storage and retrieval can be demonstrated. The recall pointers (probes) identify what is to be remembered, and some pointers are better than others. If instead of simply asking you the name of your third-grade teacher, I specify in addition the teacher's appearance, the number of syllables in the name, and the first letter of the last name, I am providing more help. If you could not remember at first but do remember with the enriched clues, the failure before was clearly a retrieval problem, not a storage deficiency.

| SIGNAL-DETECTION THEORY | To distinguish between the memory and decision processes in memory tasks (*see* Figure 15-1), some psychologists have employed **signal-detection theory.** This theory was originally developed by engineers interested in the problem |

of how human observers go about detecting infrequent and relatively weak signals in the visual clutter of a radar display; it is discussed in some detail in the section on perception (*see* pp. 491–94). By employing this theory in experiments on memory, we can discover the extent to which a particular treatment affects a person's memory or decision criterion; telling the subject that there will be penalties for wild guessing chiefly affects the decision criterion. This example is rather obvious, but the methods of signal-detection theory have also been used in more subtle cases to produce information of value to the memory psychologist, the educational psychologist, and the perception psychologist.

EXPERIMENTAL METHODS

In the previous chapter we discussed several experimental methods that are also used in studies of memory (*see* pp. 385–91). Most prominent among these are the study-test method, the anticipation method, and the modified method of free recall which asks for the associates from *both* lists in a two-list sequence and gives more response time. For studies of human short-term memory two additional techniques have been developed recently: the distractor technique and the probe technique.

A memory drum shows the subject one word or syllable at a time. It can be used to study various dimensions of memory.

Distractor Technique

The **distractor technique** was devised to study memory for a single item. Suppose I read you a nonsense syllable, CQF, wait 20 seconds, and ask you to recall that item. During the 20-second wait, you might repeat to yourself over and over CQF, CQF, CQF . . . until it is time to recall. This intervening (uncontrolled) rehearsal makes it difficult for me to study forgetting—you won't forget. Therefore, in the distractor technique, I give you something to do during the wait, something to occupy your attention and thus preclude rehearsal. A very commonly used distractor activity is counting backwards by threes, starting with a number given by the experimenter following the presentation of the target item.

Probe Technique

The **probe technique** was designed to overcome "output interference." If a subject is asked to recall all the items in a long list, he may forget some of them during the process of recall itself—hence the term "output interference." In the probe technique, only one item is requested with a probe (pointer) similar to those we have discussed in previous sections: "What was the third word?" "What word followed RECLUSE?" or the like. By asking for only one randomly selected item, output interference is eliminated. Rehearsal is less of a problem when the original list is long and the probe technique is used. Any item can be the target item, but the subject does not know which one until the probe is given, so rehearsing the target item is unlikely.

What have we discovered about memory?

We have discussed some general assumptions about memory processes and stages and some of the experimental tools used in testing those assumptions. We will now summarize some of the research findings pertaining to six empirical phenomena—six facts in search of a theory. As you read these summaries, try to observe relationships or trends, and notice any apparent inconsistencies. This is the same type of procedure used by those who have tried to integrate the various findings into a general theory of memory. We will examine some of these theories in the following section.

1. MEMORY SPAN

Suppose you were presented with a collection of items to be remembered after a single presentation—say, an unfamiliar telephone number with seven digits. Could you remember it? Suppose we try ten digits, similar to a phone number plus area code; could you remember that after one presentation? What we are trying to determine is the *number* of items you can consistently recall after the one presentation. This value is called your span of immediate memory or, simply, your **memory span.**

Memory span is determined by presenting collections or lists of different lengths; such items are often included on intelligence tests. Most people can recall all members of collections up to five units (size 5); most fail on collections over size 9. Lists of size 7 are recalled perfectly about 50 percent of the time; that percentage is therefore arbitrarily defined as the memory span. The value of memory span varies somewhat with different people but not much. It also varies with different material but not much; in fact, to the surprise of many, the memory span for a collection of zeros and ones (to be recalled in order) is about the same as for a list of unrelated words (to be recalled in order). Because of the amazing regularity of this list size—seven plus or minus two—some have called it a magic number. By this they mean it refers to something in the memory system that is very basic—not that it will bring you good luck!

The seven items that can be stored in the memory span are referred to as **chunks.** A chunk can be a single letter, but it can also be a word, or a familiar phrase (such as "red, white, and blue"), or even a familiar sentence (such as "To be or not to be, that is the question"). When you have become familiar with certain material and have organized it, then you can chunk together a considerable amount of this information and store it efficiently as a unit.

2. FORGETTING CURVES

Forgetting curves represent the amount of material forgotten plotted against some other important variable such as time or serial position in a list. Just as psychologists have historically been interested in the "true" learning curve (*see* p. 390), they have also tried to somehow depict the "true" curve of forgetting. For similar reasons, both quests have been more or less abandoned; curves for different methods and for different tasks produce quite different pictures.

Before the more sophisticated experimental techniques of recent times, forgetting curves were often plotted against a time measure of days since learned. The curves showed that forgetting was most rapid in the first day or two, then leveled off to a less rapid memory decrease over the next month or so. It came as somewhat of a shock, therefore, to read reports of studies using the distractor technique; subjects were forgetting a considerable amount within twenty *seconds!*

The evidence for rapid forgetting in some situations is now very clear. Figure 15-2 presents a family of curves for lists of different lengths presented only once. The lists are made up of familiar items—for example, digits or letters of the alphabet. The distractor technique was used to prevent rehearsal. The probability correct (the vertical axis) is estimated by using the proportion of subjects who recalled the entire list correctly after the number of seconds shown on the horizontal axis. After only a few seconds, practically no one could recall all items in a seven-item list; after 5 seconds, almost all had forgotten at least one member of a six-item collection. Only with the very short lists, one or two items, does perfect recollection extend beyond twenty seconds.

A free-recall forgetting curve is shown in Figure 15-3. In this situation, a subject is given a single trial with a list of items. Each item is presented individually for a second or two. The subject is then asked to recall as many of the items as he can. In this example there are three cases: a list of 20 items, each presented for 1 second (designated 20-1); a list of 40 items, each presented for 1 second (40-1); and a list of 40, each presented for 2 seconds (40-2). The

Figure 15-2
Short-Term Forgetting
The probability that an item will be recalled correctly is plotted as a function of the duration of the retention interval. Each curve is identified by the number of items to be remembered. (After Melton, 1963)

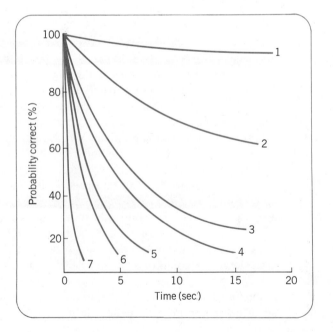

Figure 15-3
**Serial-Position Curves of
Single-Trial Free Recall**

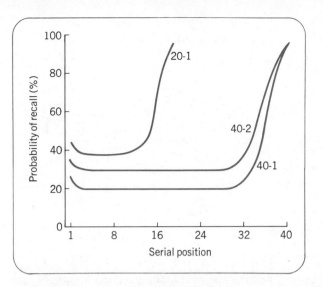

Forgetting curves are for lists of 20 or 40 words with a presentation time of one or two seconds per word. All curves show a primacy effect, a recency effect, and a flat middle section. The longer the list or the shorter the presentation time per item, the lower the curve. (After Murdock, 1962)

probability of recall, expressed as a percentage, is shown on the vertical axis; the horizontal axis shows the serial position, the rank order of the item in the list. The items presented in the first few positions and those presented in the last few positions are favored in recall over those in the middle of the list; this is called the serial-position effect. The **recency effect** (better recall of the items presented last) is more pronounced and extensive than the **primacy effect** (better recall of the first items). The differences between (1) a 20-item list and a 40-item list and (2) a 1-second presentation and a 2-second presentation are clearest in the middle range.

3. INTERFERENCE EFFECTS

We have already discussed the detrimental effects of prior learning (proactive interference) or later learning (retroactive interference) in the learning chapter. Because they are important for any theory of memory, we will consider them again here.

In proactive-interference procedures, subjects learn List 1, then List 2, and then are tested for their memory of the second or more recent list. Generally they show poorer memory than subjects who have not learned the first list (or who had some control procedure). In retroactive-interference procedures, subjects learn both lists but are tested for their memory of List 1. They generally show poorer memory than those who have not learned the second list.

These interference effects also occur in studies of short-term memory in which the probe technique is used. Figure 15-4 illustrates proactive and retroactive interference for a five-word list.

Suppose the probe asks for the first item; then, as you can see from Figure 15-4, you have no proactive interference (no preceding items) and four "units" of retroactive interference. The fifth word has four units of proactive interference and no retroactive interference. The third has two units of each. By manipulating list length and probe target, an investigator can study any combination of interference effects.

Now let's turn to the situation in which the subjects learn several lists of words or numbers successively. First they will learn one list and be tested on

**Figure 15-4
Proactive and Retroactive
Interference**
Each item exerts proactive
effects on items following it
and retroactive effects on the
preceding items. The first item
of the list suffers no proactive
interference from other items
on the list—this explains the
primacy effect. The last item
suffers no retroactive
interference—this explains
the recency effect. Proactive
effects can also extend from
one list to another.

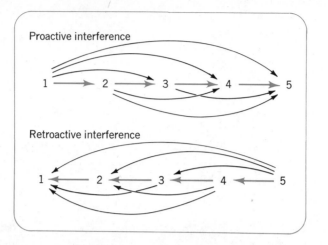

it; then they will learn a second list and be tested on that one; and so on for a series of lists. Under such circumstances the shape of the serial-position curves changes progressively. On the very first list, the subjects remember the first few items much better than they remember the items in the middle part of the list—there is a large primacy effect. They remember the last few items somewhat better than the middle ones—there is a moderate recency effect. On later lists, this relative balance between the primacy and recency effects shifts. The subjects show more of a recency effect but less of a primacy effect.

This change over successive lists is the result of accumulating proactive interference. On the first list there is no prior learning, so proactive interference is negligible for the first few items; hence there is a relatively large primacy effect. On later lists, the associations from earlier lists interfere—proactively—with all items, and so the primacy effect decreases. The last few items of the list being tested, however, suffer no retroactive interference, so these items are remembered relatively well. The serial-position curve for these last lists will therefore show more of a recency than a primacy effect.

Fortunately, even after we have learned a great deal, we are not permanently handicapped because of proactive interference. "Release from proactive interference" can be achieved by several techniques, even within a single experimental session. For example, the experimenter might introduce a long delay between two of the later lists. Or the type of material to be remembered might be changed from polysyllabic words to monosyllabic words, from abstract nouns to concrete nouns, or from nonsense to meaningful stimuli. Or the investigator might shift from auditory presentation of the material to visual presentation. In all cases, some release from proactive interference seems to occur.

4. SIMILARITY EFFECTS

It has long been known that learning two sets of similar materials produces more mutual interference (less memory) than two dissimilar sets. Students studying for final exams in say, French, psychology, and sociology, might well be advised to position their French studies between the other two.

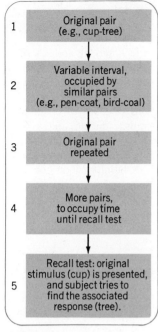

1	Original pair (e.g., cup-tree)
2	Variable interval, occupied by similar pairs (e.g., pen-coat, bird-coal)
3	Original pair repeated
4	More pairs, to occupy time until recall test
5	Recall test: original stimulus (cup) is presented, and subject tries to find the associated response (tree).

Figure 15-5
Steps of Peterson Paradox Studies

In studies of memory, similarity is defined more precisely. The words "happy" and "carefree" are similar in a "meaning" or semantic sense; the words "blink" and "drink" are also similar in their sounds, but not in their meaning—they are acoustically similar. One of the first important discoveries in this field was that long-term memory was affected by semantic confusion but short-term memory seemed to be unaffected by similarity among items.

Additional research soon required some revision in this simple notion that one memory system was affected by similarity and the other was not. More specifically, it was discovered that **acoustic similarity** has a considerable effect on short-term memory, even though **semantic similarity** has relatively little effect. For example, suppose your short-term memory span was tested either with lists such as CUFF, ROUGH, SNUFF, BUFF, and TOUGH or with lists such as SUNNY, HAPPY, CHEERFUL, CAREFREE, and PLEASANT. Lists of the first kind (CUFF, ROUGH, SNUFF . . .) yield rather poor memory spans, which is why we say that they suffer from acoustic confusion. In short-term memory, a semantically similar list (SUNNY, HAPPY, CHEERFUL . . .) would probably give results no different from lists of unrelated words.

A few years ago, therefore, investigators concluded that there were two different memory systems, each affected by similarity of a different type. Short-term memory is affected by acoustic similarity, and long-term memory is affected by semantic similarity. But even this view encounters problems, as research continues. As an example, long-term memories often show the "tip-of-the-tongue" phenomenon—you can almost remember a word, but not quite. Your attempts to retrieve the word—the close guesses—often yield words similar in sound rather than meaning. This would indicate that there are some acoustic-similarity effects in long-term memory, even though the semantic effects are more prominent. (*See* Spotlight 15-2.)

5. REPETITION EFFECTS

Fifth in our series of memory phenomena that require explanation are some puzzling effects of repetition. Repetition affects memory; it helps. No experiment need be cited to document that fact, although careful experimentation has shown us how much and in what way repetition aids memory. One unexpected discovery is called the Peterson paradox (after Lloyd R. Peterson).

The **spacing effect** or the **Peterson paradox** states that spaced repetitions are better for memory than massed repetitions. This has been found in studies in which the same pair of items is presented twice during a trial, separated by a time interval. Then, in subsequent trials using different items, this time interval is varied. Five steps are used, as shown in Figure 15-5. On a given trial (1) the experimenter presents a pair of words to be associated (such as CUP—TREE); (2) then he or she gives a few other pairs of the same general kind (PEN–COAT; BIRD–COAL); (3) then presents the original pair again; (4) then gives more items to occupy the time until the recall test; (5) finally the original stimulus is given as a probe (CUP) to see whether the subject can recall the associated response (TREE). In subsequent trials with different critical pairs the interval between repeated presentations (Step 2) and the interval between the second presentation and recall (Step 3) are varied systematically. Data are collected for many subjects.

In 1890 William James described an experience that you have probably had: "Suppose we try to recall a forgotten name. The state of our consciousness is peculiar. There is a gap therein; but no mere gap. It is a gap that is intensely active. A sort of wraith of the name is in it, beckoning us in a given direction, making us at moments tingle with the sense of our closeness and then letting us sink back without the longed-for term. If wrong names are proposed to us, this singularly definite gap acts immediately so as to negate them. They do not fit into its mould. And the gap of one word does not feel like the gap of another . . ." (1893, p. 251).

To study this elusive phenomenon in greater detail, Brown and McNeill (1966) devised the following method.

They assembled a group of college students and described the state of mind in which you can't think of a word but believe that you know it—the word seems to be on the tip of your tongue. Then the experimenters presented, one at a time, the definitions of a list of uncommon English words, such as ambergris, caduceus, and sampan. Whenever subjects could not state the word but felt that it was on the verge of coming back, they were asked to write down the following kinds of information about the missing word:

The number of syllables in the word
The initial letter
Words of similar sound

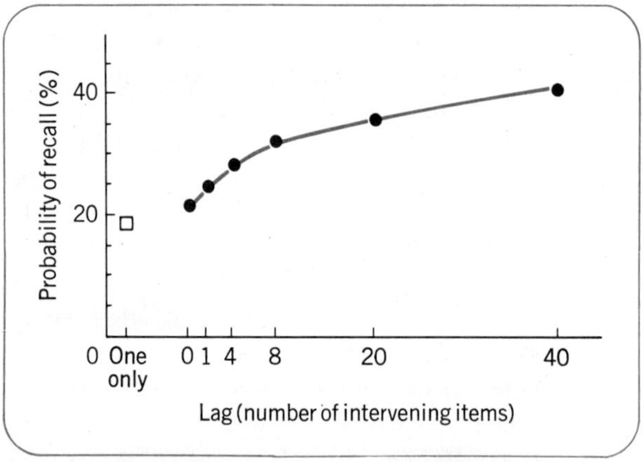

Figure 15-6
Peterson Paradox

The probability of recall for an item increases as a function of the lag or interval between successive presentations of an item. The "one only" point indicates memory for a single presentation; all other points are for repeated items. The steepest increases are at short lags, but even at lag 40 the curve seems to be rising. (After Melton, 1970)

Results show that as the interval between the two presentations (Step 2) is *increased* (up to a point), the subject does better on the recall test. Figure 15-6 shows results from a typical experiment of this sort. The probability of recall increases as the number of items between the two presentations increases.

Why is this a paradox? Well, why should a longer interval between repetitions facilitate memory? If anything, the longer the interval, the more forgetting should occur by the time of the second presentation. The more you forget, the more you remember? That is a paradox!

6. FACTORS INFLUENCING RETRIEVAL

Retrieval is one process of memory, the process of finding and using information from memory storage. As we have seen, when discussing memory failure, we must be careful to distinguish between storage problems and retrieval problems. If the desired information is in storage, it is *available* although

Words of similar meaning
Words that came to mind

Here is an example. When the target word was *sextant*, the subjects heard this definition: "A navigational instrument used in measuring angular distances, especially the altitude of sun, moon, and stars at sea." Nine students out of fifty six reported having a tip-of-the-tongue feeling as they sought for the word. The words that came to mind includes some of similar sound (secant, sextet, and sexton) and some of similar meaning (astrolabe, compass, and protractor).

Subjects tended to be quite accurate in guessing the length of the word in number of syllables. The words that came to mind had the correct initial and final letters in about 50 percent of the cases, but the middle letters were correct only about 25 percent of the time. Thus the gap often had a precise start and end but a vague middle. The words offered by the subjects were similar to the target in sound in 62 percent of the cases and similar in meaning in 24 percent. So even "wrong" responses revealed that the subjects had considerable information about the missing words. And the responses also showed that even in long-term memory acoustic encoding is important.

it may be momentarily *inaccessible*. When we speak of factors influencing retrieval, therefore, we are talking about the determinants of accessibility; availability is assumed, at least until the evidence becomes overwhelming that there is no relevant information in storage.

We can review a few factors influencing retrieval from previous discussions. The method of soliciting information from memory, for example, can be quite important. Recognition tests elicit greater memory than recall tasks. Within different recall tasks, those with the greatest amount of "pointing" information produce the most evidence of remembering—"Your third-grade teacher, whose last name starts with J" is more likely to gain the correct recall than simply "Your third-grade teacher."

Organizational cues seem to function as beneficial retrieval cues, even if the organization is supplied by the subject. Suppose you give subjects fifty words, each written on an index card, and you tell them you are investigating how people categorize things. The subjects are to sort these cards into as many categories as they wish, up to seven, on whatever basis they like. When subjects have completed the task they are asked, without prior warning, to recall as many of the fifty words as they can. The more categories they have formed, the more words they will remember. It seems as if the categories somehow provide retrieval cues to the stored information.

Retrieval cues can also be provided by the experimenter. Thus, one could present the subjects with a list of words, giving them the following instructions: "You will see a list of words in pairs. In each pair, one will be in small letters and the other will be in capital letters. You will be tested later for your memory only of those in capital letters, but look at those in small letters too; they may help you later." The list consists of pairs like leg-MUTTON, dirty-CITY, girl-SHORT, vigor-HEALTH, hurt-STOMACH, and soar-EAGLE. Later, the subjects are given a "cued" recall test in which the retrieval cues (the words in small

How does a conductor working without a score retrieve from the permanent filing cabinet of memory just the right music?

letters) are given. These subjects remember many more of the target items than subjects who go through exactly the same procedure but are asked to recall the target items without being given the cues.

It has also been demonstrated that subjects can use the paired cues more effectively than they can use other cues you might expect to be more effective. One might think that for subjects who could not recall SHORT, the cues "tall" (opposite) or "small" (similar) might jog their memory. They don't. But the cue "girl," which was paired with SHORT in the original list, does. Results such as this suggest that an effective retrieval cue must be stored with the target at the moment of encoding. This fact must also be considered by any potentially satisfactory theory of memory. Special memory strategies employed by professional memory experts are described in Spotlight 15-3.

We have now surveyed many facts and basic principles. Let us turn to the integrative attempts, the "models" of memory that aid our understanding of memory and direct our future investigation.

How have memory theories integrated the data?

A primary consideration in any current theory of memory is the apparent distinction between short-term and long-term memory. The experimental observation of the course of memory in the first few seconds after material is

John Stone is a professional mnemonist, that is, he does memory tricks for money, charity, or the simple amusement of his audience. In his most spectacular tricks he asks his audience to provide four common words such as GEORGE, STOLEN, MARKER, and ARMPIT. Stone then quickly writes on the blackboard:

G N W T E Ǝ ∀I O T Я Ꝑ R O K M G Ɩ E Я E S Ʀ A

Gradually the audience realizes he has interspersed the four words, one directly (**GEORGE**), one backward and upside down (**NƎ1O1S**) one upside down (**W∀ꝚꝀEꝚ**), and the last backward (**TIꝱMЯA**), each word occupying every fourth position. An impressive feat, made more impressive by the fact that while Stone is writing down the proper sequence of letters, he is reciting "The Shooting of Dan McGrew"!

How does he do it? Psychologist Gordon Bower (1973) asked him and received the unsatisfactory reply, "my hand just automatically knows what to do. . . ." His answer is not really surprising, however, because skills like these are not easily described. How would you explain your ability, say, to balance while riding a bicycle or to understand rapid speech?

Mnemonists use what are commonly called **mnemonic devices** — aids to memory. These devices or strategies are usually quite specific — that is, they do not improve memory generally. Bower attended a mnemonists' convention and, although amazed by their tricks, he noted that several participants forgot the time of place of the banquet, where they had parked their car, and his name: "It's been a pleasure meeting you, Dr. Flowers." Among the mnemonic strategies that have been identified by psychologists are the use of mediating images, as described on p. 388. Rhymes are also useful as in "i before e except after c." Rhymes are constricted; one cannot say "e before i except after c." They are therefore more useful than such nonrhyming devices as, "Feed a cold, starve a fever." Or is it "Starve a cold, feed a fever"?

Two common mnemonic strategies are the *method of loci* and the *pegword system*. In the method of loci (locations), you visualize several familiar locations along a familiar route — your typical path to school in the morning, for example, or a common routine in your house, apartment, or dormitory. Suppose you need to remember Pavlov, Skinner, the total-time hypothesis, and Fitts' law to write an essay on a question you expect will be given on the final exam. You might visualize Pavlov ringing the bell of your alarm clock, and Skinner reinforcing you for your morning ablutions. And you could conceptualize the total-time hypothesis as applying to your walk to school (it doesn't matter whether you walk "very fast, then very slow" or "moderately fast throughout"), and apply Fitts' law (there is no limit to your ability!) to your performance on the exam. In the pegword system, common objects are used instead of common locations. One list of pegwords combines common objects and rhymes: *One* is a *bun, two* is a *shoe, three* is a *tree, four* is a *door, five* is a *hive*, and so on. The items to be remembered are hooked onto these pegwords, usually by images. If you have to pick up milk, bread, apples, coffee, and beer at the grocery, you might form images of (1) milk being poured on a *bun*, (2) a *shoe* kicking a loaf of bread, (3) apples on an apple *tree*, (4) coffee beans on a *door*, and (5) a group of drones drinking beer after work in the bee*hive*.

Several gimmicks improve memory, but the most impressive organize information in a way that is relevant to personal experience. Chess players, for example, do not have exceptional memories in general, but their recollection of familiar chess board positions is exceptional. Politicians know the names of senators of each state, not because the politicians have exceptional memories, but because the senators — their names, their histories, their philosophies — are important to the politician's view of what's important. Everyone has a better than average memory for terms associated with his or her occupation. So the study of mnemonists and mnemonic devices and the investigation of the effects of personal relevance lead us to the same conclusion. Information that fits into an organized system developed either artificially — as with memory tricks — or organically, in terms of schema that are personally relevant, is remembered better than unorganized, unimportant materials.

---

presented, made possible by recent methodological advances, has produced data that are not easily integrated into older theories of long-term memory. Long-term memories are more susceptible to interference from confusions between items that have similar meanings; short-term memories are more likely to exhibit detrimental effects with items that sound the same. More generally, memory for presented material shows extremely rapid decline using short-term procedures—a matter of seconds. Somehow a theory of memory must integrate this fact with the retention of material over years—as shown by long-term studies. (Quite a different kind of support for the distinction between short-term and long-term memories is the observation that patients with certain types of brain damage show normal short-term memory but seem to be unable to form long-term memories. *See* pp. 576–77.)

Thus, perhaps the most common theory of memory today is the type that postulates two kinds of memory and suggests the means by which short-term storage can be converted to long-term storage. We will consider this type of theory in two forms: Broadbent's "filter theory" and Atkinson and Shiffrin's "buffer model." Broadbent's was one of the earliest two-memory theories and influenced the direction of subsequent research and theories. The Atkinson and Shiffrin buffer model is representative of current formulations. But, although two-factor theories may dominate the present scene, we should point out that current and respected theories make no distinction between "types" of memory. Some of these theories will be discussed at the end of this chapter.

BROADBENT'S FILTER THEORY

In 1958 British psychologist D. E. Broadbent presented a carefully constructed theory of "information processing"; it had general relevance not only to memory but also to attention, perception, and certain information-processing skills such as vigilance (for example, watching radar screens for significant information). One of the features of this **filter theory** was the distinction between short and long-term storage systems in memory.

We can consider the "information" to be processed as an input from the external world—action on the television screen, material presented by an experimenter, or whatever. The first impact on the organism is on the *sense organs,* as shown in Figure 15-7. According to the theory, this sensory information next goes to a *short-term storage system.* Memory from this store decays very rapidly without further processing. Further processing, however, is not random; it is directed by a *selective filter,* which favors some material over the rest. (Many arrows go into the filter in Figure 15-7 but only one points out.)

[handwritten note: meaningful stuff is processed]

To oversimplify a bit, the filter is included in the theory because the human information-processing system cannot possibly handle *all* the information transmitted to it from the outside world. It has a *limited-channel capacity,* which means its abilities to process information to a useful form are limited. The filter ensures that these limited capacities are not overloaded. It selects the most relevant information for further processing, much as a tuning mechanism on a radio selects a certain signal for amplification. The selected material then goes into *long-term memory storage.*

The two feedback or "backward-going" loops in Figure 15-7 require explanation. One goes back from the "channel" to the short-term store. This loop is meant to represent rehearsal and repetition. If something is relevant, it may be recycled to prevent decay before going into long-term storage. In ordinary language, if some important information is transmitted (the phone number of a new friend), you repeat it over and over to make sure you don't forget it. The second feedback loop goes from long-term storage to the filter; it represents the influence of already-stored information on the selectivity of

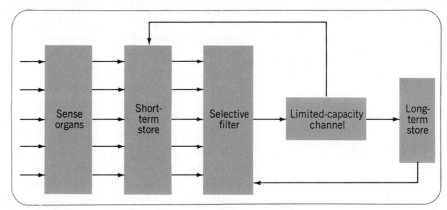

Figure 15-7
Broadbent's Filter Theory
Arrows indicate the flow and amount of information through this system. The information bottleneck is the limited-capacity channel, which attends to only one thing at a time. The filter must select material that will pass into the channel when there is an opening. Information may be either recirculated back through the short-term store for rehearsal or deposited in long-term memory. (After Broadbent, 1958)

provides categories for organization

the filter. In layman's terms it indicates that relevant material (related to previous experience) is to be tuned in.

Many of the empirical data used to formulate the filter theory came from studies of **dichotic listening,** in which a subject hears a different message in each ear. (The term "dichotic" is from the Greek root *dich* meaning different and *otic,* pertaining to the ear.) Using a stereophonic tape recorder, it is possible to present one list of words or numbers to one ear and another collection

In dichotic listening, a person can attend to words in one ear and ignore the different message that reaches the other ear. Such experiments have provided some clues to short-term storage of information.

to the other ear; it is somewhat analogous to listening (or trying to listen) to two separate conversations at a noisy party. (*See* discussion in Chapter 16, p. 452.)

In one type of dichotic listening task, the subject is asked to repeat all items going into one ear and to disregard the material channeled into the other. It is not an easy task, but with practice it is possible. In general, these studies showed that when asked later to recall the "disregarded" items subjects could not do so. In fact, even if one of these to-be-disregarded items is *repeated* several times, subjects cannot even *recognize* it as familiar. Only if the dichotic presentations are *suddenly* stopped and subjects are *immediately* queried can they recall even the last item or two on the unattended channel. Evidence of this kind led Broadbent to postulate a short-term storage system with rapid decay occurring *before* the filter (*see* Figure 15-7). Only material attended to is retained for any length of time—that is, filtered through to long-term storage.

In a second type of dichotic listening task, the subjects are asked to repeat all items from both ears. Suppose we deliver to the left ear the digits 2, 7, 3 and simultaneously to the right ear 4, 1, 8. What will subjects report? It depends on how fast the items are delivered. If the rate of presentation is relatively slow, they will report either *pair by pair* (2, 4; 7, 1; 3, 8—the two first items first, then the two second items, and so forth) or *by ear* (2, 7, 3; 4, 1, 8—all the left-ear items, then all the right-ear items). If the presentation rate is increased, a point is reached where, if subjects can report at all, they report only *by ear;* that is, first the items presented to one ear and then the items presented to the other ear. This effect is attributed to difficulty in switching attention rapidly. What is of interest to us, however, is the implication—in theory terms—that the channel (or ear) reported second must be stored temporarily in the short-term system while the first channel is being fed directly through the filter. If this explanation is reasonable and if the short-term store does show rapid decay, we would expect memory failures for the second channel. The data show that the information given in the channel (or ear) reported first is usually correct; more errors occur on the channel reported second.

Shortly after the Broadbent model was published, some dramatic new data were reported that seemed to provide considerable support for Broadbent's notion of a short-term store with rapid decay. An experimenter (Sperling, 1960) flashed three lines of three letters each on a screen for a brief time. Immediately following the disappearance of these stimuli (just a small fraction of a second later), he gave a probe indicating which line was to be recalled. Under these circumstances memory for letters was two to three times better than "normal" —that is, two to three times better than it would be if memory were tested a second or two after the stimuli disappeared. There appears to be a brief "sensory memory," which has been termed **iconic memory** (*see* Spotlight 15-4).

Although these experiments supported some of Broadbent's hypotheses, they also instigated new controversies. The time period covered was extremely short. Theorists who liked to think in terms of two memory storage systems had pegged short-term memory as applicable to time periods measured in seconds, but a quarter-second was too brief. Some began thinking in terms of three systems and called the first very brief storage the *sensory* (preperceptual) store.

You may have experienced this problem: You see a telephone number given briefly on a television screen and as you write the first digits down, the latter ones fade from memory. If you could have started with the last digits, you would surely have had them correct, but then you might have lost the first digits. The whole number was probably available for a brief moment, but during the time required to write down part of it, the rest of it vanished.

Sperling (1960) found an ingenious way to test memory *immediately* after a visual presentation. He flashed a 3 × 3 block of letters, like the one shown here, on a screen for 50 milliseconds (one-twentieth of a second)—a very brief presentation. After the letters disappeared, memory was rather poor for the brief visual stimulus. The subjects typically recalled about three or four of the nine letters correctly—only about 30 or 40 percent.

Sperling then used a tonal signal to instruct the subjects which row to recall—a high tone meant the top row, a middle tone signaled the second row, and a low tone was for the bottom row. If the tone was simultaneous with the flash, the row was reported with about 75 percent accuracy. If the tone was given 150 msec after the flash, accuracy was about 60 percent; at 300 msec after, about 55 percent. Apparently a fleeting visual memory could be scanned to find the information specified by the tonal signal. (This has been called "iconic memory" from the Greek word *eikon,* meaning likeness or image.)

But the fact that subjects were able to recall, with great accuracy, whichever row was designated *immediately* after the stimulus had disappeared, indicates that they must have had most of the letters in all three rows accessible right at the start. So forgetting can be measured over a one-second duration, as the graph demonstrates.

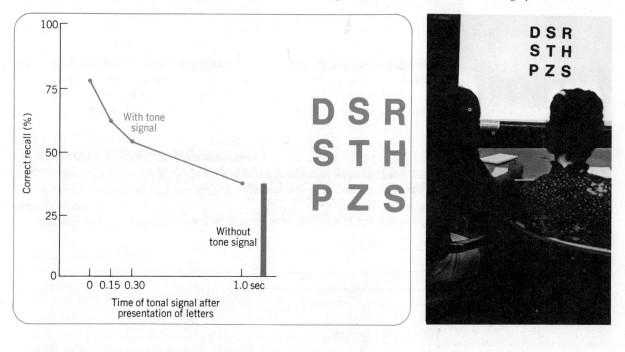

Others argued that this preperceptual store, if it exists, is not a *memory* problem, because information in it (by all reports) is not actually encoded; the material is reported literally, without change, something like a sensory "after-image" you see if you stare at a bright light and then close your eyes. Most investigators of memory ignore these very brief fraction-of-a-second effects and measure only effects occurring in intervals of a second or more. It remains controversial whether information storage in sensory memory is fundamentally different from information storage in short-term and long-term memory.

Simply by positing two kinds of memory storage systems, the Broadbent filter theory was able to integrate and direct much of the research on memory. With separate short-term and long-term stores, the governing principles of each were studied. If the principles were found to be discrepant, why not? They apply to two different systems. We entered a period of scientific investigation that sought in large part to discover discrepancies. As we have seen, many differences were found such as the relative effects of semantic and acoustic similarity (see p. 416). It is only fitting that later theories of memory were devised that not only distinguished between two memory stores but also explained in more detail the relationship between the two. We now turn our attention to one such theory.

THE ATKINSON-SHIFFRIN BUFFER MODEL

A representative current theory of memory is the **buffer model,** formulated and developed by R. C. Atkinson and R. M. Shiffrin and their colleagues (Atkinson & Shiffrin, 1968, 1971). The buffer model diagramed in Figure 15-8 has three storage systems. The sensory registration system or sensory store reflects the evidence for the very short (quarter-second) preperceptual stage discussed above. The other two stores represent short-term and long-term memory—the short-term store (STS) and the long-term store (LTS).

The buffer model theory centers on the control processes in the short-term store. In this model, what happens in STS is most significant in considering memory as a whole. STS accepts the information coming in from the sensory registration system, and STS delivers *some* of that information to LTS. What happens to the information in STS?

The key concept in this system is the rehearsal buffer, from which the model takes its name. Broadly defined, *buffer* means "protector," and here the term is used to signify a process that protects the LTS from incoming information. By rehearsing the incoming material, the buffer maintains information in STS that builds up its strength in LTS. According to the model, the longer an item stays in the rehearsal buffer the greater the buildup of its strength in LTS.

Figure 15-8
The Buffer Model of Memory
Various sensory stores receive input, but attention determines what enters the short-term store. Here material passes through a rehearsal buffer. Rehearsal transfers information to the long-term store. The forgetting mechanism and time values are shown below each store. (After Atkinson & Shiffrin, 1968)

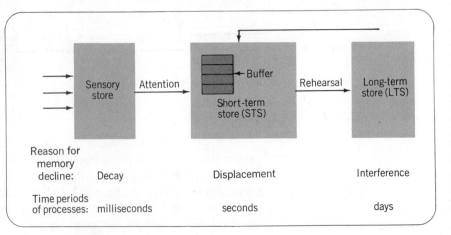

Structurally, one can think of the buffer as a file box with a very limited number of slots with one chunk of information in each slot. It is a situation somewhat analogous to a basketball team. Five starting positions are up for grabs and possibly a hundred candidates show up for the first day of practice. Once the five best players have been chosen, they can add to their advantage because they get the game experience. But a talented new player may displace one of the starters. Someone has to be displaced if the new player wants to make the starting team—you can't simply increase your team size to six. Similarly, much memory information "fights" for a spot in the rehearsal buffer, but only a few items can be chosen.

Information is lost from the three stores in different ways. Loss from the sensory store occurs through decay. This decay occurs rapidly—in a fraction of a second. Information is lost from the rehearsal buffer in STS by displacement. To continue our analogy, if a new player does start, an old player must drop out. In STS, the time period discussed is in terms of several seconds. In LTS, we speak of days, months, and years; and here the main reason for memory loss is believed to be *interference*. We cannot remember because some similar association is interfering—although certainly other reasons can be demonstrated (such as destruction of nerve cells in injuries or the aging process). There is some question whether interference should be called memory loss, which implies loss from storage; many interference effects, as you have learned, might be better explained in terms of retrieval problems.

The arrows in Figure 15-8 deserve some comment. Transfer from the sensory store to STS is seen primarily as *attention,* which is a little more sophisticated way of saying that "importance" determines not only what gets into the buffer but also what gets in STS at all. Rehearsal of course is a prime determinant of transfer from STS to LTS, and this arrow is so represented. But other considerations may also be lumped under the general heading of "coding." Information that can be classified according to the established categories in LTS will be passed more easily. Coding is also significant with new information; it must be classified in some way. LTS has been likened to a permanent filing cabinet of large capacity, and if you have tried to file your own material, you know the problems: Here's a letter with content on the integration of A and B on the basis of some creative new ideas (C); you have an A file and a B file, no C file; where do you put the letter? If it can't be easily filed, it is almost impossible to retrieve later.

Figure 15-8 also has an arrow feeding back from LTS to STS. This represents the constant interaction between the two systems. LTS affects what in STS is deemed important, both for attention and rehearsal. LTS also feeds information into STS—like an activated file—so that the behavioral output of memory is presumed to be coming from STS, even in the ordinary cases in which the information comes from LTS and not from the senses.

To illustrate application of the buffer theory, we can consider an experiment on free-recall memory. A list is presented to be recalled later in any order. Two groups of subjects, however, differ in *when* they are asked to recall; one is asked to do so immediately after presentation; the other only after several seconds. The distractor technique is used to fill the waiting period. Results from such an experiment are shown in Figure 15-9, which plots the percentage

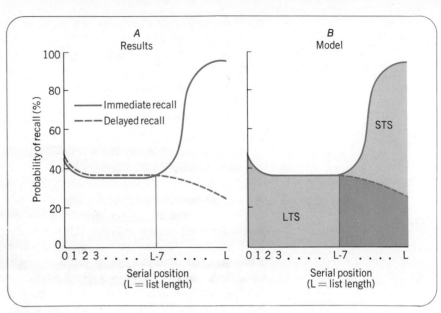

Figure 15-9
Immediate and Delayed Recall Results and Theoretical Model
A shows the effect of the distractor technique upon the serial-position curve of free recall. Recall after the distraction (delayed recall) has no recency effect according to the buffer model. Items can be in either STS (upper right corner), LTS (lower left), or both. The interpolated distraction eliminates the STS effect, but the LTS is unchanged. (After Glanzer, 1972)

of recall against serial position of the item in the presented list. The results are essentially the same for both groups *except* for the items at the end of the list; in delayed recall the recency effect is eliminated.

How does the buffer model account for such results? Figure 15-9 is a graphic representation of the theoretical interpretation. The flat middle portion of the serial-position curve is attributed to information retrieved from LTS; this interpretation holds for both groups. The recency effect, on the other hand, extends over approximately the last seven items, and only the immediate-recall subjects show this effect. This portion of the curve is affected by information in STS but only if the recall is asked for immediately. If recall is delayed for just a few seconds, the buffer "dumps" the list items and presumably gets filled by distractor material; hence no recency effect shows up in the delayed-recall condition.

Now consider how the buffer model handles the other facts and findings presented in this chapter. Memory-span data are interpreted directly; they represent the number of slots in the buffer. The section on forgetting curves considered the distractor technique and the primacy and recency effects in the serial-positions curve. The distractor technique is believed to prevent rehearsal by filling the buffer with the distracting material. It thereby prevents transfer of information to LTS and results in a curve showing very rapid memory decay. The recency effect, as previously discussed, is presumed to result from superior recall of material being actively processed in STS. The primacy effect may be caused by slightly more rehearsal time for the first few items in a list (more time in the buffer). The second item need not displace the first because there is still room in the buffer; similarly, other initial items may also have an advantage. Their greater processing time would result in greater strength in LTS and, therefore, greater recall later.

Interference effects (proactive and retroactive) in LTS can be seen as a sort of competition at the moment of attempted retrieval. In STS, they must be viewed in terms of displacement—knocking out information put in previously (retroactive effects) or leaving no room for material coming later (proactive effects). One has to make a further assumption to account for the similarity effects. Because the file system in STS is based on simple classifications such as sounds, acoustic similarity causes confusion in the buffer. In LTS, semantic coding by "meaningful" linguistic file categories is more prevalent, so semantic similarity causes more problems there.

Everything considered, the buffer model is one possible interpretation of the empirical data we have gathered. Repetition effects, however, remain something of a puzzle. The findings on retrieval processes that might pose problems—for example, the evidence that retrieval cues are stored in STS with their target—represent a vein of research that is still too new to be well integrated into any theory. These phenomena are not so well explained, but they are not incompatible with the buffer model. Future formulations of a buffer model might well be devised to handle these facts.

OTHER VIEWS OF MEMORY

Though filter theory and the buffer model have provided a useful way of looking at human memory, in the last few years some researchers have developed different approaches. One particularly promising view is the "levels-of-processing" approach of Craik and Lockhart (1972). These theorists suggest that the two (or three) distinct stages in other theories (STS, LTS) are better conceptualized as different levels in a *continuous* process of memory storage. More specifically, it is the *type of processing* an item receives when it is encoded into memory that determines its durability and later retrievability. A major distinction is made between Type I and Type II processing. Type I processing can be called "maintenance rehearsal"; an example would be the simple repetition of a telephone number to keep it in active memory before you dial it. This works for the short term, but is not very effective for the long term. Type II processing is a more elaborative encoding, in which the individual tries to develop or elaborate some of the meaningful features of the item.

An experiment by Craik (1973) illustrates the distinction among various types of processing. Individual words were briefly exposed in a small viewing machine (tachistoscope). On any given trial, the subject was instructed to make one of the following decisions: (1) whether the stimulus was a word or a nonword; (2) whether the word was in capital letters or lower case; (3) whether

The research described in chapters 14 and 15 can be applied to your own studies to foster more effective learning and memory. Spotlight 15-3 suggested ways of improving your memory with mnemonic devices. Spotlight 14-5 showed the beneficial effects of repeated experience with the same type of problem: we learn something about the learning process, as well as about specific content, each time we master a problem.

One of the most general principles of effective study is that organization of material promotes learning and memory. Research shows that subjects who organize items on a list learn more rapidly than subjects who do not (p. 390). Moreover, these experiments have demonstrated that the better you package or chunk material, the greater your memory span will be (p. 413). Perhaps the most common way of organizing material is to develop or to elaborate the meaningful features of the material—thus making long-term retention more likely than studying by using simple repetition (p. 389). Therefore, to make it more meaningful, you should attempt to relate the information in this book to your own experience.

Can you think of examples in which positive or negative transfer of training have occurred in your life? We have supplied some common examples, but you will learn the concept better if you actively search for your own as well.

Organization of the material by headings and summaries also helps you learn and remember. In Chapter 1, for example, we described six key concepts that provide a unifying scheme for the different chapters of this text. But again you can aid yourself by supplying additional organization. How does the discussion of operant conditioning in Chapter 14 relate to the behavioral psychotherapies described in Chapter 8 and to the biological explanations of reinforcement in Chapter 21? Learning the special terminology—in this book the words in boldface type—not only will improve quiz scores but provides "hooks" of sorts that can represent large chunks of information in memory. Once you understand the Freudian term "repression," for example, you can use it to organize such related concepts as the unconscious, defense mechanisms, and the goals of psychoanalysis.

In addition to the widespread advantages of meaning-

---

the word presented rhymed with another word; (4) whether the word presented was a member of a particular category; or (5) whether the word presented fit into a particular sentence. Then, unexpectedly, at the end of the experiment the subjects had to recall all the words they could remember. Memory was best for condition 5 and worst for condition 1, as predicted. The five conditions were arranged to reflect five levels of processing, ranging from the simplest—"Is it a word or not?"—to the complicated judgment of whether the word presented was appropriate for a particular sentence, a judgment that required an analysis of the word's meaning. Thus, the more deeply (semantically) the subject had to process the items at the time of initial presentation, the better the subsequent retrieval.

More generally, the levels-of-processing view proposes that recency effects in short-term memory are essentially continued attention to the items. Such continued attention may provide an effective short-term trace but not a very durable long-term trace. For this reason the positive recency effect shows up in immediate free recall but the negative recency effect in final free recall (see Figure 15-9). Moreover, Type I rehearsal, even if carried to extreme lengths, might not be very effective in delayed retention tests. This view is in striking contrast to predictions of the buffer model, and several recent experiments give it good support. In one study (Craik & Watkins, 1973), the researchers induced Type I rehearsal in varying amounts; they instructed subjects to report the last word that began with a given letter in a twenty-one-word

distractor material

ful organization, the research mentioned in these two chapters suggested benefits from a number of other techniques you may find helpful:

1) The use of mediators often aids learning and retrieval. The use of an image as a bridge between a foreign word and its English equivalent was discussed on p. 388, and many mnemonic devices (Spotlight 15-3) are mediational. Don't *waste* time thinking up elaborate mediators, though; often simple and direct learning is better.

2) Although distributed practice is not always preferable to massed practice, spacing your learning sessions will lead to better learning in more complex situations—for example, in skill learning (p. 397).

3) You can reduce interference among your subjects by making sure that you do not study similar subjects one right after the other (p. 416). Study Spanish, math, and then French, not Spanish, French, and math.

For further suggestions for effective learning based on psychological research, see Virginia Voeks, *On Becoming an Educated Person* (1970) or Morgan and Deese, *How To Study* (1969).

The practical applications of memory studies are important to students who must, each day, encode, store, and retrieve many chunks or items of information.

list. The letter might be G, and the list could proceed as follows: DAUGHTER, OIL, RIFLE, GARDEN, GRAIN, TABLE, FOOTBALL, ANCHOR, GIRAFFE. . . . The subject focuses on "garden" only until the next item, "grain"; "grain" is presumably rehearsed through the next three presentations, until "giraffe" comes up. After several such lists, the experimenters found that the amount of such Type I rehearsal was unrelated to recall.

New approaches and the resulting research have led to a more general distinction between episodic and semantic memory (Tulving, 1972). **Episodic memory** is memory for items and events that can be dated by a certain episode in your life: the weather yesterday, what you had for breakfast this morning, or the items that appeared in the list of words the experimenter just showed you—all are episodic memories. In contrast, the capital of Florida, the name of the largest continent, and the meaning of the word "breakfast" are all in **semantic memory.** You cannot remember when you learned them. Episodic memories may last less long, on the average, and be more subject to interference than semantic memories. You may not remember tomorrow whether or not "toad" was in the list just presented to you, but you will remember what "toad" means. Episodic memories may be affected more by rehearsal and semantic memories more by the level of processing.

Semantic memory opens the way to a larger domain—the representation of knowledge in the human mind. The importance of this topic is exceeded only by its complexity, but work in the area is at least beginning (*see* Anderson &

Bower, 1973; Kintsch, 1974). The implications for you and me are significant. As many of us have found informally, long hours spent at rote (nonmeaningful) memorization may result in a good grade, but the material is quickly forgotten. If, however, we learn material in some meaningful way, incorporating the information into a broader organization, we remember it longer.

SUMMARY

Memory involves encoding, storage, and retrieval of information. **Encoding** is the initial registration in memory, **storage** is the persistence of information over time, and **retrieval** refers to utilization of stored material. Forgetting may mean the material was never encoded; it may mean the information was not stored (it is unavailable); or it may reflect retrieval difficulties (it is inaccessible).

One way to distinguish between storage and retrieval is to compare results from different tasks. Recognition tasks provide possible responses for the individual and require a relatively simple comparison process. In **recall,** the subject must search memory for the target information, and performance is usually worse than on a recognition test. Thus, if something cannot be recalled but can be recognized, the recall problem was one of retrieval — recognition shows the material was available, however inaccessible.

Two new techniques have been developed to obtain data on memory. The distractor technique tries to prevent rehearsal by having subjects do something else (such as counting backward by threes) between presentation and recall. The probe technique presents a list of items but asks for only one of them by means of a directed probe. Both techniques give evidence of substantial forgetting within a few seconds after presentation.

Experimental findings cover many aspects of memory, and six examples were discussed: (1) Memory span is about 7 ± 2 chunks of information. (2) Of the two forgetting curves discussed, one shows rapid loss of information using the distractor technique. The second shows the three main parts of a serial-position curve: the **primacy effect,** the less frequently remembered middle items, and the **recency effect.** (3) Interference effects (proactive and retroactive) were briefly reviewed, and the proactive interference effects were seen as a possible explanation of the primacy-to-recency shift that occurs when many lists are presented in one session. (4) Sometimes data indicate apparent contradictions, and these challenge our understanding. The **Peterson paradox** suggests that the further apart in time the repetitions of items, the greater the memory. (5) The two types of similarity effects are acoustic and semantic. Acoustic confusions occur among words that sound alike and are most characteristic of short-term memory. Semantic confusions occur among words with similar meanings, and they are more characteristic of long-term memory. (6) The amount retrieved from memory differs significantly, depending on the method used to solicit information from memory. Retrieval cues must be encoded or stored at the time of presentation to be maximally effective at the time of recall.

Broadbent's **filter theory** was an early attempt to distinguish between a short-term memory store with rapid decay and a long-term memory with more permanent storage. Evidence for the theory from **dichotic listening** tasks included (1) an inability to recall material presented to the ear the subject had been previously instructed to disregard and (2) forgetting of material to the ear that was reported second when the subject was to report both channels. Taken together, these findings support the notion of a short-term store before the filter, a store characterized by rapid memory loss through decay. The Sperling experiment showed that iconic memory decays in less than one second.

The **buffer model** of Atkinson and Shiffrin postulated three stores: a brief sensory store **(iconic memory),** a short-term store with a rehearsal buffer, and a long-term store. Forgetting occurs from these stores by different processes — by decay, displacement, and interference, respectively. The central explanatory concept in buffer theory is the rehearsal buffer itself. It is viewed as a file with a limited number of slots in which material is protected by rehearsal. The number of slots is related to the number of items (or chunks of information) defining the memory span. Explanations of empirical phenomena are assumptions about what material gains access to buffer slots, and when. Displacement (of one chunk by another) in a slot is an important consideration because "time in slot" determines the amount of rehearsal and the eventual storage in the long-term store.

An alternative view to the multistore models of memory stresses *levels* of processing and emphasizes the depth of encoding as a prime factor in storage and retrieval. Type I processing is simple maintenance by repetition; Type II processing involves encoding in more meaningful terms. Type II rehearsal is more effective than Type I in fostering long-term memory. The distinction between **episodic** and **semantic memory** (memory for episodes or dated events versus memory for meaning) has provided a further impetus and support for recent theoretical endeavors, especially since the idea of semantic memory deals with the complex and exciting problem of the representation of human knowledge.

RECOMMENDED READING

ANDERSON, J. R., & BOWER, G. H. *Human Associative Memory*. Washington, D.C.: Winston, 1973.

An account of a major theoretical and experimental study of semantic memory.

BROADBENT, D. E. *Decision and Stress*. London: Academic Press, 1971.

An extensive review of the experimental and theoretical work on human information processing, with an updated version of filter theory.

EBBINGHAUS, H. *Memory: A Contribution to Experimental Psychology*. New York: Dover reprint, 1964.

Still a classic and well worth reading.

KAUSLER, D. H. *Psychology of Verbal Learning and Memory*. New York: Academic Press, 1974.

A detailed and systematic review of the human verbal learning and memory area.

KINTSCH, W. *Learning, Memory, and Conceptual Processes*. New York: Wiley, 1970.

A review of the field which includes higher level conceptual processes as well as learning and memory. Difficult but rewarding.

MURDOCK, B. B., JR. *Human Memory: Theory and Data*. Potomac, Md.: Lawrence Erlbaum Associates, 1974.

A fairly technical review of the recent research on human memory.

NEISSER, U. *Cognitive Psychology*. New York: Appleton-Century-Crofts, 1967.

A serious and scholarly review of the higher mental processes from a cognitive point of view. Particularly good in synthesizing many experimental findings into a coherent theoretical framework.

NORMAN, D. A. *Memory and Attention*. New York: Wiley, 1976 (2nd Ed).

A very readable introduction to the topics of memory and attention from an information-processing viewpoint, with emphasis on broad issues and an overview of how the system might work.

SKINNER, B. F. *Walden Two*. New York: Macmillan, 1948.

A novel applying principles of operant conditioning to a utopian community.

PART SEVEN

The Psychology of Perception

By Michael Wertheimer and
Lewis O. Harvey, Jr.

When an environmental event occurs in the presence of some people or animals, how can we tell if they saw it or heard it? Exactly what did they perceive? Are the perceptions of two people the same or different? If different, why? Does one's culture or motivation affect perception?

In this section we examine questions like these, all encompassed by the topic of *perception*. In other sections of this book, perception is often simply assumed. In most learning and memory studies, for example, the stimuli are presented in such a way that the investigator can be reasonably sure that they are perceived, register on the subject's consciousness, and are encoded. Such assumptions allow the examiner to consider the processing of information *within* the particular learning or memory system under study.

The section on social psychology describes an experiment on conformity in which subjects had to judge the length of lines (p. 56). This experiment was set up so that almost all participants would have reached the same perceptual judgments if no social pressure had been involved. The experimenter had chosen and tested stimuli with large enough differences to be sure that participants would give the correct responses if they were by themselves. The experimenter also made sure that subjects perceived the responses of other participants, who were actually confederates of the experimenter. Social pressure arose when the subjects believed that their own perceptions and those of the others did not agree. We have learned that perceptions of other people usually agree with our own—at least when the stimulus situation appears to be clear and when none of us suffers from an obvious sensory defect (such as color blindness or deafness).

But we also know that perceptions often differ in complex situations. These differences may be related to group membership and allegiance—for example, when students at two colleges watch the same movie of a football game between their teams and see significantly more rule infractions by the opposing team than by their own (p. 68). Some differences in perception are so consistent and stable that they have been labeled "cognitive styles" or even "personality traits" (p. 341). Some people determine whether a target is vertical by referring chiefly to surrounding objects (they are called "field-dependent"); others determine verticality by reference to cues from their own body ("field independent") (*see* p. 343). This difference has been found to be related to many social behaviors such as conformity.

The key concepts introduced in Chapter 1 all play a major role in perception. *Motivation* determines what we are aware of and sometimes even how we perceive a particular stimulus. Perception is the input phase of the *information-processing* activities of the person or animal. *Learning* and *reinforcement* are integral molders of perception; especially in ambiguous stimulus situations, our past experience crucially affects how we form or interpret our perceptions. All sensory and perceptual systems use *feedback;* without feedback from sensory changes caused by our locomotion through the environment, our sensory systems cannot develop normally. And finally, perception has been a major area for the study of the *heredity-environment* question. While some of our perceptual competencies are innate, a complex interaction of hereditary and environmental factors is responsible for normal perception.

Moreover, whether the determinants of perception are clear and reliable or complex and variable, the perceiver is actively engaged in processing environmental stimuli. "Our curiosity does not let us wait for environmental events to happen; rather we search them out and seek levels of stimulation and excitation. When some environmental event occurs, we do not register it passively, but instead interpret it. It is this interpretation, not the event itself, which affects our behavior." This quotation—only slightly paraphrased from the Piagetian description of the active role the infant plays in interpreting its environment (p. 224)—applies to adults too. We are constantly forming perceptual hypotheses and testing them in feedback interactions with the environment.

In Chapter 16, we will consider the creative role of the perceiver and examine some perceptual phenomena that are especially susceptible to personal variables of set, attitude, motivation, and personality. The chapter ends with a discussion of how heredity and environment interact in producing perceptual abilities, some of which are present in early infancy and some of which develop only after prolonged experience.

In Chapter 17 we examine how relations among parts of the stimulus field crucially determine perception—contrasts between parts of the field, pattern and organization of forms, and movement. Why do we perceive parts of a complex field as belonging together coherently? How, on the contrary, can perceptual laws be used to hide or camouflage objects? Which characteristics of forms are good and distinctive, and which are poor?

The rudiments of sensory processes, the raw material out of which perceptions are constructed, are considered in Chapter 18. We shall discuss such topics as the perception of visual brightness, hue, auditory loudness, and pitch. Research on these aspects of perception has progressed to the point where some relations between stimulus conditions and perceptual responses can be stated quantitatively. Vision and hearing are the main topics of Chapter 18, but some features of other senses are also included.

Several phenomena of visual perception are illustrated on the following pages. Each relates to discussions in the chapters of this section. Other examples of interesting perceptual phenomena are included in the color section on perception.

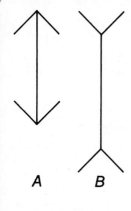

Figure 1
Which vertical line is longer? Line
B seems longer, but they are equal.
The magnitude of the illusion varies
among individuals and among
cultures. (*See* pp. 457–58.)

A *B*

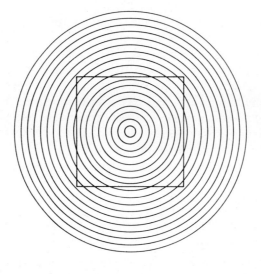

Figure 2
Are the sides of the square
straight? Check for yourself.
The sides appear curved
because of the contrast with
their background. (*See* the
discussion of contrast on
pp. 480–82.)

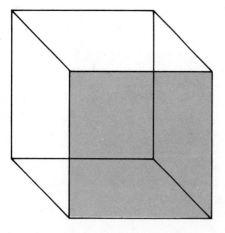

Figure 3
Is the colored face of this cube at
the front or at the rear? Your answer
will change suddenly if you stare at
the cube for several seconds. (*See*
the discussion of hypotheses in
perception on pp. 444–51.)

Figure 4
Do you see a man or a woman here?
Look again for the other face. You
can prepare a friend to see either
of the two faces by using the
pictures on p. 454. If you find it
difficult to see a second face here,
you can check there for the other.

Figure 5

Look at the gray ring. Then place a pencil over the black-white boundary and note that the two halves of the ring no longer seem the same shade. You can "pull" the darker gray into the left half by slowly moving the pencil in that direction. What happens when you move the pencil in the other direction? This is another contrast effect. (*See* pp. 480–82.)

Figure 6

Is the odd line to the left or to the right in the upper and lower sets of lines? The two sets are identical except for the horizontal extensions in the lower set. But the change affects what you see as "going together." (*See* p. 468.)

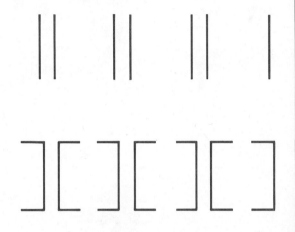

Figure 7

Notice that one pattern appears to recede from you, whereas the other seems to stay in the plane of the page. Depth perception is discussed on pp. 472–76.

The perception of infants (and animals) who cannot tell you what they see can be studied by observation of their behavior in carefully designed situations. Studies of young animals (including infants) tell us much about the contributions of hereditary and environmental factors to perception.

Figure 8
Babies' eye movements can be observed while they look at patterns such as these. Do you think they spend more time looking at one than at the others? (*See* p. 463.)

Figure 9
Can the baby perceive depth? Do you think the baby will crawl onto the transparent surface over the drop? (*See* pp. 459–61.)

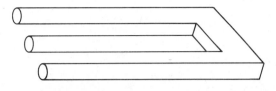

Figure 10

Figure 11

Does Figure 10 have two or three prongs? You get different answers from looking at the different ends. Now look at Figure 11. What is your point of view—upward, downward, or sideways? As with Figure 10, small portions of the engraving allow a clear answer, but there is no single answer for the figure as a whole. Some portions are even "impossible"; look at the stairway near the top of the drawing. One man is walking up while the other, although facing in the same direction, is walking down the stairs. There is no danger of their bumping into one another, however, because they exist in two different worlds! (*See* the discussion of hypotheses in perception on pp. 445–51.)

"Relativity" by M. C. Escher, courtesy Escher Foundation, Haags Gemeentemuseum, The Hague.

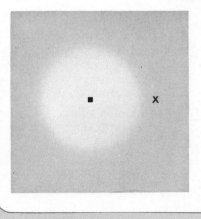

Figure 12

Stare at the small black square in the left box for a minute and the disc will fade away. If you then shift your focus to the *X*, the disc will reappear. In the second box, the disc does not fade as quickly. The eye, like the other sense organs, responds best to sharp differences in stimulation. (*See* pp. 480–82.) (After Cornsweet, 1969)

The Creativity of Perception

Is perception a hypothesis?
How do we recognize patterns?
How do attention and motivation affect perception?
How do hereditary and environmental factors interact to determine perception?

How do we know what we know? Philosophers originally posed this question, which lies at the root of the study of perception; two opposing answers were given. Some philosophers, like René Descartes (1596–1650) and Immanuel Kant (1724–1804), argued that much of our knowledge is innate (the **nativist** position) while others, such as John Locke (1632–1704), asserted that we gain knowledge only through our senses (the **empiricist** position). Experimental investigations stimulated by these two viewpoints began in the nineteenth century. Physiologists wanted to know how the eye converted light into nerve impulses and transmitted the impulses to the brain. Another group of scientists examined the nature of perceptual experience. Current perceptual psychology has developed largely from those two sources.

The next three chapters will examine at different conceptual levels how psychologists have been trying to answer that question: "How do we know what we know?" The study of perception involves descriptions that fall into one of four categories. To avoid confusion, the reader should keep these categories clearly separate:

1) descriptions of the physical world

2) descriptions of the observed behavior of nerve cells

3) descriptions of subjective, internal mental experiences

4) descriptions of the perceiver's observed behavior, both verbal and nonverbal

A complete understanding of a particular visual perception, for example, would involve descriptions of (1) the visual stimulus, in physical terms; (2) the physiological activity in the nerve cells of the eyes and in the visual and other areas of the brain; (3) the mental experiences of the viewer; and (4) what a person says and does about what he or she is seeing. Psychology is a long way from providing such a complete understanding of perception, but it has made substantial progress. Let's see how far we have come.

Is perception a hypothesis?

Perception is an active process, not a mere passive reception of information from the outside world. In the broadest sense, **perception** is the construction of meanings (Neisser, 1967; Pylyshyn, 1973). These meanings are actively constructed from the physical input to the senses, from memory of previous experience, and from motivations and expectations. The net result of the construction is an experience of a three-dimensional world filled with objects and events that we call reality. For example, presented with a pattern of colored dots in Color Figure 10, we form a perception of people in a landscape. It is as if we continually (and unconsciously) form hypotheses about "what is out there" (Gregory, 1972; Solley & Murphy, 1960). What we experience is the hypothesis itself. Some physical stimuli could represent two equally plausible hypotheses about what is out there. As you look at Figure 16-1 you will see one of two "realities": a cube seen from above or a cube seen from below. The very fact that these lines printed on a flat piece of paper can cause you to see a cube at all is a remarkable illustration of how we construct our perceptions. As perceptual processes first construct one cube and then the other from the drawing, the perception changes, and the feeling of "switching" from one to the other is striking. Because neither of these perceptual hypotheses is more plausible than the other, neither one prevails for long.

Thus a given stimulus object can look different at various times even to the same observer. Furthermore, because factors other than the physical stimulus enter into the construction of perception, it is entirely possible for different people to have different perceptions of the same stimulus. For example, each of several witnesses to a crime or an accident often reports different and even conflicting versions of what happened. The Rorschach inkblots (Figure 16-2) and Thematic Apperception Test (TAT) used in clinical psychology (see p. 150)

Figure 16-1
Necker Cube
The lines in *A* can represent one of the three-dimensional cubes shown in *B* and *C*. Our perceptual processes switch back and forth between these two alternatives. This phenomenon was discovered by the Swiss mineralogist L. A. Necker in 1832.

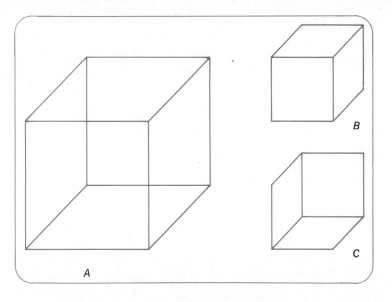

are designed to reveal the individual motivational and emotional factors that enter into the construction of perceptual experience by asking people to describe ambiguous stimuli.

One problem facing psychologists is that perception is an inner, private experience not directly observable by others. We must rely on behavior ordinarily related to the inner experience, such as verbal reports—what people *say* they experience—to infer anything about the perception. But many factors

Figure 16-2
Rorschach Inkblot Test
The perception of ambiguous stimuli—such as this inkblot—is highly dependent on motivational and emotional factors.

enter into verbal reports, and they should not be confused with perception itself. Decision processes, for example, are important: people may see something but report that they have not. Signal detection theory (pp. 411–12) has helped to distinguish between perceptual experience and decision processes in verbal reports. Subjects may decide *not* to report what they perceive, a fact that has been used in experiments on conformity (p. 56). So the psychologist must remember that verbal reports (category 4 above) are not the same as internal perceptions (category 3).

How do we recognize patterns?

Both human beings and animals have a remarkable ability: they are able to recognize different stimulus patterns as the "same." For example, we can recognize the letter *a* in a wide variety of type and handwriting styles; we can recognize a melody regardless of the musical key in which it is played; we recognize a spoken word uttered by people of widely different voice properties and accents; we recognize a cat as a cat even in various sizes, colors, and markings.

Pattern recognition is so much a part of perception that we take it for granted. Yet understanding how we do it is the fundamental mystery in understanding perception (Pitts & McCulloch, 1947). It seems simple, yet the most sophisticated computers available today cannot equal the pattern-recognition abilities of even a seven-year-old child. The processes of pattern recognition are currently receiving considerable research attention, directed by four important hypotheses: (1) template-matching, (2) feature analysis, (3) prototype comparison, and (4) analysis-by-synthesis. These ideas are not mutually exclusive.

Template-matching means comparing the stimulus with a fixed standard form (the template) that presumably is stored in memory (*see also* p. 651).

An explicit form of prototype comparison is utilized in one method of teaching speech to the deaf. The boy first sees the pattern made by the sound he is to learn, then tries to duplicate the visual pattern with his own voice.

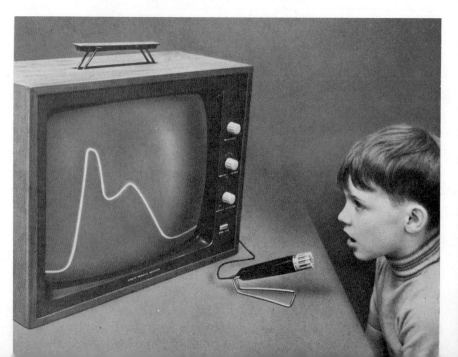

Figure 16-3
The McCollough Effect
How does your perception
of this pattern change as a
result of viewing Color Figure
11?

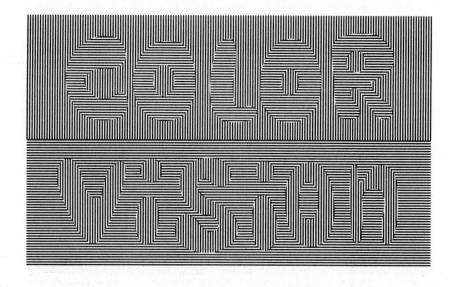

Machines that "read" the curiously shaped magnetic numerals on the bottom of bank checks use a template-matching procedure. The bank machine has no problem reading them because the numerals are of a standard form, size, orientation, and position; but if any of these stimulus aspects were changed from the standard, the machine could no longer function. Template-matching is not, however, an adequate model for human pattern recognition, mainly because we are able to recognize an almost endless number of new versions of a pattern.

Numerous experiments in perception suggest that the visual system analyzes the visual stimulus and "decomposes" it into specific features. Such **feature analyses** include assaying the orientation and size of contours, the stimulus's depth in space, and its color. Specific values of a feature are detected by specific detectors in the nervous system. For example, when you look at a square, two sets of horizontal contour detectors and two sets of vertical detectors are highly active in your brain. The activity of this specific combination of feature detectors means "square." When you look at an isosceles triangle, only one set of horizontal detectors is active (for the horizontal base). They are joined, of course, by one set of oblique left and one set of oblique right contour detectors. This particular combination of feature detectors signals "isosceles triangle."

Experiments that desensitize certain feature detectors show their highly selective nature (Sekuler, 1974). A particularly dramatic example of the selective adaptation of specific feature detectors was discovered in 1965 by Celeste McCollough. To see this effect, first look at Figure 16-3 and assure yourself that it is made up of black and white lines. Now turn to Color Figure 11. While viewing the book in a bright white light, look first at the center of the green vertical lines and then at the center of the red horizontal lines, alternating back and forth every 10 seconds or so. After 3 minutes, look back at Figure 16-3. How does it now appear? Rotate the book 90 degrees; what happens to the color? This *McCollough effect* is caused by the selective adaptation of green vertical detectors and horizontal red detectors.

Prototype comparison is the process of comparing incoming information with "ideal" representations of patterns stored in memory. These ideal patterns are called prototypes. A prototype could be a list of features that members of a particular class of patterns (*A*'s, for example) have in common, or it could be a representation of the neural activity evoked by viewing a perfect example of a particular pattern. In either case, pattern recognition occurs by assigning to an incoming pattern the meaning of the prototype it *most closely* resembles. An exact match is not necessary; a handwritten capital *A* is recognized because it more closely resembles the prototype *A* stored in memory than it does any other prototype. The particular set of prototypes selected for comparison depends heavily on context. A set of three lines might match with the prototype *A* in a reading context; in another context, however, it might match a representation of an artist's easel.

Analysis-by-synthesis is the process by which the outputs of a feature analysis are constructed into a perception. Neisser (1967) compares the process of perception with the job of the paleontologist who sees a mass of bone chips, dirt, and rocks. The paleontologist extracts a few fragments he or she considers important and constructs a dinosaur! Analogously, the perceiver takes sensory information, selects some of it as important and discards the rest as irrelevant; then, using information from memory, the perceiver constructs a percept of the event. The process occurs rapidly and largely unconsciously. What we consciously experience as a **percept** is the result of the construction.

SPEECH PERCEPTION

Listening to speech is an excellent example of the synthesizing nature of perception. When people talk to us in our own language, we clearly perceive that they are uttering a series of words. We can tell where one word ends and where the next word begins; we recognize the pattern. But when we listen to an unfamiliar language, the words seem jumbled together in a hurried flow, and we perceive few distinct separations. These perceptual experiences are not caused by the physical stimuli; analysis of the acoustic patterns of speech has shown that words in English are no more separate and distinct than words in other languages. Indeed, some pauses in the middle of English words are longer than most of the pauses between words. The separation of words in a familiar language thus occurs not in the stimulus but in the perceptual reconstruction of words and phrases. Sometimes, when speaking to foreigners or young children, people try to assist their perception of separate words by introducing artificial pauses within a sentence.

An ingenious experimental procedure supports these indications that we perceive speech in meaningful units rather than in the acoustical properties of the words. In the experiment, a click was superimposed on a tape-recorded sentence, and the subjects were asked to identify exactly where in the sentence it occurred (Ladefoged, 1959; Ladefoged & Broadbent, 1960). Subjects made rather large errors in placing the click, usually locating it at a major grammatical break—even when the break was not signaled by an acoustic gap or pause. As listeners analyzed the sentence by synthesizing it, they processed or constructed it in rather large chunks that were difficult to interrupt with

Figure 16-4
Visible Speech
The *d* sound of the word "dough" is represented as inflections at the beginning, and the *o* sound by the concentrations of frequencies (formants) depicted as horizontal bars. Most of the energy is concentrated in the first two formants, and these are sufficient for recognition of the sound if the higher frequencies are filtered out, as they are in Figure 16-5.

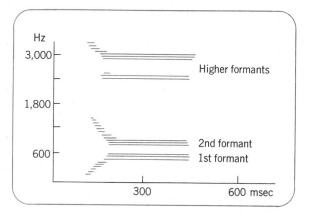

other perceptual processes. To make sure that an acoustic feature in the sentence did not seem to "call for" the click, one group of investigators constructed pairs of sentences with a special property (Garrett, Bever, & Fodor, 1966). The final portions of the sentences were identical—they were actually taken from the same strip of recording tape—but the first parts were different; the last parts of the sentences thus required different grammatical structures. Here is a pair of such sentences, with the identical parts printed in italics:

1) As a direct result of their new invention's *influence the company was given an award.*

2) The retiring chairman whose methods still greatly *influence the company was given an award.*

In sentence 1) the major grammatical break is just after *influence,* whereas in 2) it follows *company.* A click was delivered simultaneously with the first syllable in *company.* It was usually heard much earlier in sentence 1) than in sentence 2); and in each case the sound was reported near the main grammatical break, even though the italic portions of both sentences were *acoustically identical.* Thus, the perceived place of the interruption was largely determined by how the listener mentally constructed the pattern of the sentence.

Research in speech perception, then, has provided a wealth of information about pattern recognition. If you stop to think about it, recognizing spoken messages, with all their acoustic and linguistic intricacy, is a remarkable accomplishment of the sensory system and the brain. The information that is processed, and the meaning that is derived from it, is incredibly complex.

The basic information in a speech stimulus is contained in the frequencies of the component sounds, their intensities, and the changes that occur in frequencies and intensities. If this information is electronically recorded, it looks like the speech spectrogram shown in Figure 16-4. (This kind of "visible speech" contains the main auditory information of speech.) The figure is a visual representation of the sound of a particular speaker saying "dough." The consonant *d* sound is represented by the initial inflections, called the *transition state;* and the vowel sound *o* is represented by the horizontal concentrations of frequencies, called the *steady-state* part of the word. The **frequencies** at which these steady-state concentrations of sound energies occur are called

**Figure 16-5
Simplified Speech
Spectrograms**
The inflections at the left of
each formant bar represent
the *d* sound. In the upper
formant, the slope of this
initial part varies with the
height of the formant; it
seems to start with reference
to the frequency of 1,800 Hz.
We recognize all these
patterns as *d,* whether they
move up or down. (Modified
from Liberman et al., 1967)

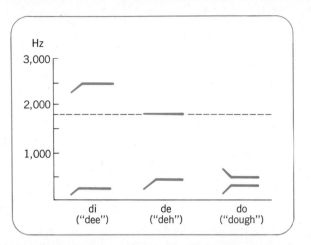

formants. For the word "dough," the frequencies of the first and second formant of the vowel sound *o* are about 530 Hz. and 720 Hz. respectively. Our perception of the vowel sound depends almost entirely on the frequencies of the formants. For example, had the speaker said "dee" instead of "dough" the first and second formant frequencies would have been 300 Hz. and 2500 Hz.—as seen in Figure 16-5.

Do our brains then perceive vowel sounds by analyzing the frequencies at which the formants of the vowel sounds occur? The findings of a remarkable series of experiments by the Dutch psychologist Rainer Plomp (Pols, van der Kamp, & Plomp, 1969; Klein, Plomp, & Pols, 1970) indicate that they do. In one experiment, fifty male speakers pronounced each of the twelve Dutch vowel sounds. The frequency content of each vowel sound was analyzed, and a prototype (or average) was calculated for each vowel. When subjects were asked to identify each vowel sound, it was discovered that the vowel subjects perceived corresponded to the prototype that was closest in frequency content to each vowel. When subjects made mistakes—for example calling an *o* sound *u*—it turned out that the particular *O* mistakenly identified was closer in frequency to the prototype *u* than to the prototype *o.*

Although each vowel sound corresponds to a specific frequency content, there is no such coincidence of frequencies for consonants. As is seen in Figure 16-5, the initial part of the sound spectrum for *di, de* and *do* is physically different—even though we perceive a constant sound, the consonant "d." Thus the physical nature of the "d" part of the word depends upon what vowel sound follows it. The brain circuits that analyze the consonant parts of words are evidently far more complicated than those that analyze the vowel sounds. Research in this area is just beginning to provide clues as to how these mechanisms function.

IMPOSSIBLE FIGURES

We have examined how we perceive by forming and testing hypotheses such as—What word was spoken? Who was the speaker? Was it someone we know —a man, woman, or child? We can next reconsider the two "impossible figures" included in the preview. Figure 10 seems to have three prongs at one end but two prongs at the other, with an inexplicable transition between the two. Figure 11 is the drawing "Relativity" by M. C. Escher. Each part of the scene can be understood, but no single overall perspective holds true for the whole drawing. In both figures we try to see the two-dimensional drawing as an indication of a three-dimensional object or scene. But, since no hypothesis about a three-dimensional object will fit all the information in either figure, in a sense they cannot be perceived. The figures are intriguing because they baffle our attempts to find hypotheses that will fit all the parts together into a self-consistent percept.

How do attention and motivation affect perception?

SELECTIVE ATTENTION
The amount of information in the environment around us is far greater than even our complex brain can handle simultaneously. Perception is highly selective. Are you wearing shoes? Until you read this sentence, you probably were not aware of the pressure of your right shoe on your right foot. Most of the background sounds around you probably were not in your awareness until we mentioned them. By shifting your attention, you can affect what you notice. The limited capacity of perception is well illustrated at large parties. You cannot listen to and fully comprehend more than one conversation at a time. But you can selectively attend to a specific conversation out of the many around you and even switch attention at will among several conversations.

Motivation can also play a role in selective perception. If you are very hungry, you become more likely to notice the smell and sight of food. A hungry person may be quite aware of the restaurant across the street, but not notice the clothing shop next door, while the person looking for a coat might notice the clothing store but not be aware that a restaurant is next to it.

Past experience also structures which aspects of the input will be noticed. Thus the artist, the geologist, the rock climber, and the child from the city will each notice different aspects of a particular cliff in the Rocky Mountains: its aesthetic proportions, its strata, the best route for ascent, or its sheer overwhelming bulk.

Of course, it is not only the characteristics of the perceiver that determine attention. Characteristics of the stimulus also play a major role. Other things being equal, stimuli that are particularly intense, that move, or that are new and unusual are likely to be noticed. Repetition of a stimulus also attracts attention, as long as it does not occur too frequently. All these characteristics come down to the basic principle of contrast: anything that differs markedly from routine input is more likely to be noticed. A colored picture in a black-and-white magazine will stand out, as will a black-and-white figure in a full-color context. Similarly, a few lines of type set at a slant on a page in a newspaper or an ad printed upside down will catch the viewer's eye. So will a PHRASE PRINTED IN CAPITAL LETTERS embedded in a page of regular type.

This knowledge, of course, can be and is imaginatively used in advertising. You can easily cite examples that use motivation to gain attention; for example, sales pitches often use sex to get us to read or hear the company's message—which is usually totally unrelated to sex. Television commercials often employ intense or unusual graphic or auditory stimuli, rapid changes, and other devices based on the principle of contrast. Such stimulus characteristics attract the attention of children even before they have learned to speak. Recently, some of these advertising devices have been used for educational purposes, by such television programs as "Sesame Street."

ATTENDING TO
ONLY ONE EAR

If we put an earphone headset on a subject, we can present one message to one ear and another to the opposite ear; this is called **dichotic stimulation** (from the Greek roots *dich,* meaning in two parts, and *otic,* pertaining to the ear). This apparatus has proved to be valuable in the study of selective attention. For example, one investigator (Treisman, 1960) instructed subjects to "shadow" the message in one ear—that is, to repeat it out loud as it was heard. Usually subjects could perform this task quite well. It was discovered that the material coming into the other ear—to which the subjects were not attending— was rarely retrievable; it was as if this message had been blocked out by conscious intention induced by the instructions. (*See* pp. 423–24) for a discussion of dichotic phenomena and short-term memory.)

Expectation and context also play a role, however. If the two messages were switched from one ear to the other in the middle of a sentence, subjects could not maintain their attention to only one ear. For example, consider the following messages:

Left ear: SITTING AT A MAHOGANY / three POSSIBILITIES. . . .
Right ear: Let us look at these / TABLE with her. . . .

The subject was instructed to shadow the left ear, but when the messages were switched (at the slash), the subject followed the message to the right ear for one word. (The words in capitals were the subject's report.)

Other experiments have provided evidence that some information does get through the "unattended" channel after all (Cherry, 1953). For example, subjects noticed the change when a low-frequency tone replaced prose or when a man's voice was substituted for a woman's in the unshadowed message. Further, if the unshadowed message was identical to the shadowed one, subjects noticed that it was the same, even if one message lagged behind the other by several seconds. Whether or not we will notice a stimulus seems to depend on such factors as familiarity; familiar messages are heard even when the stimulus is coming along a channel that seems to be shut down. Thus subjects who are shadowing prose in one ear will notice their name being mentioned to the other "inactive" ear—a finding that fits well with common sense (Moray, 1959). Even sleeping subjects respond more to their own name—as measured by physiological recordings—than they do to other names (Oswald, Taylor, & Treisman, 1960).

That the message in the unattended ear can be processed in a complex way, even though the subject is intentionally shadowing the input to the other ear, was shown in another ingenious experiment (Korchin, personal communication to authors). The investigator had subjects listen to, repeat, and write down a list of unrelated words presented to the right ear; another list of words was given simultaneously to the left ear. Among the words presented to the right ear were several homonyms such as "see (sea)"; the subjects thus had to decide

PART SEVEN 452 The Psychology of Perception

whether to write "see" or "sea"—even though subjects were usually unaware that a choice was involved. Each homonym was paired with a specially chosen word in the other, unattended ear. For example, when "see (sea)" was delivered to the right ear, half the subjects had the word "wave" in their left earphone, while the other half had "look." These unheard words in the other ear definitely influenced what was written down. Although the effect did not occur in every case, subjects most often chose the homonym that was suggested by the simultaneous word in the other ear. We will see in succeeding pages (p. 457) that personality characteristics help to determine how much the subject is influenced by unconscious stimuli.

EFFECTS OF MOTIVATION

The selectivity of perception can obviously be affected by one's motivation, as we have seen in the ability of subjects to shadow one ear and ignore stimuli reaching the other ear. We have also noted the unintentional deviations that occur when, for example, messages are switched from one ear to the other. Motivation to attend to something is not, of course, in and of itself a guarantee of success. Even well-motivated subjects find it easier to focus their attention on sensory inputs and targets than on such stimulus dimensions as intensity. For example, subjects told to focus on an auditory stimulus (and ignore a visual one) or to listen to the violins (and not the flutes) will find those tasks easier than attending to one degree of intensity (such as loud sounds) while ignoring another degree of the same dimension (not-so-loud sounds) (Treisman, 1969).

EFFECTS OF AMBIGUITY

Many stimuli are ambiguous—that is, our perceptual processes can give them one of several meanings, depending on previous experience. Does Figure 16-6 show the letter *B* or the number 13? It could be either, but which of the two meanings is perceived can be influenced by other stimuli.

Fisher (1967) sought to quantify this kind of effect, using the series of drawings shown in Figure 16-7. He showed each drawing to subjects—starting either with drawing 1 or drawing 15—and asked them to describe the picture. Not surprisingly, drawing 1 was described as a man 100 percent of the time, while drawing 15 was always described as a woman. The drawings in the middle of the series were described as a man by some subjects and as a woman by others. Which description is given for such ambiguous figures can be influenced by previous experience: subjects who saw the man's face first (drawing 1) described the ambiguous drawings as a man; subjects who saw the woman first (drawing 15) described the ambiguous drawings as a woman (Leeper, 1935).

Figure 16-6
An Ambiguous Figure

If this pattern is shown to subjects after they have seen a series of single capital letters—such as *F, R, M*—they tend to report it as the letter *B*. If it follows a presentation of a series of two-digit numbers—such as 24, 36, 87—they tend to report it as the number 13.

Figure 16-7
Ambiguous Figures: A Sequence of Pictures Representing a Man at One End of the Sequence and a Woman at the Other

The stimuli in the middle are ambiguous, and the perceptions they evoke are dependent on previous experience. (From Fisher, 1967)

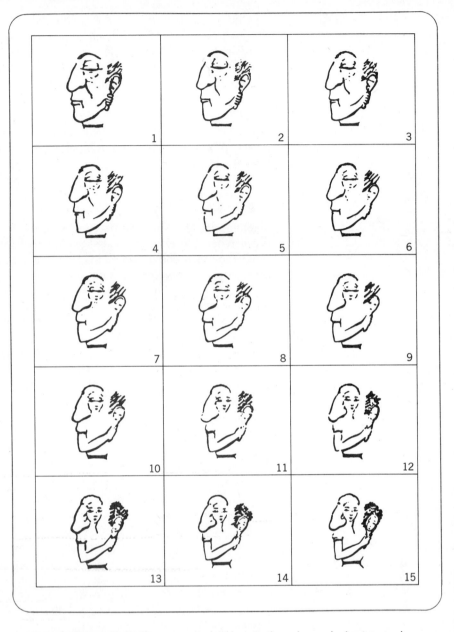

The problem of ambiguous stimuli has induced psychologists to be very careful not to confuse subjects' verbal responses with their perceptual experiences. In a celebrated experiment, children estimated the size of various coins (Bruner & Goodman, 1947). The size of the coins was consistently overestimated—with the degree of overestimation increasing with the value of the coin. Furthermore, children from poorer families tended to overestimate the size of coins more than children who were reasonably well-off (see Figure 16-8). The investigators concluded that poor children *perceived* the coins as larger than did the richer children because they had a greater need for money.

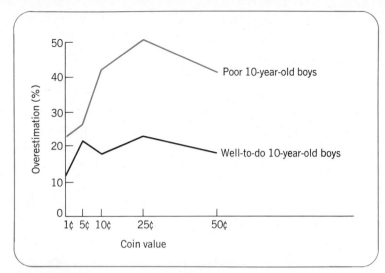

Figure 16-8
The Effect of Coin Value on the Estimation of Coin Size
When asked to judge the sizes of coins, 10-year-old boys tended to overestimate the sizes of coins more when the coin was of greater value. Moreover, boys from poorer families, who presumably had a greater need for money, overestimated the sizes of the coins more than boys from well-to-do families. (After Bruner & Goodman, 1947)

Later experiments, however, strongly suggested that this finding did not reflect the perception of the children but simply their interpretation of what the experimenter wanted to hear (Orne, 1962, 1970). In a complex social interaction such as exists between subjects and researcher, there is always this danger that subjects' responses will be based on what they think the experimenter wants them to say (the **demand characteristics**) or on what they believe to be the "correct" answer rather than on their own perceptions. In designing experiments, psychologists must be extremely careful to ensure that the demand characteristics will produce unbiased results.

PERCEPTUAL DEFENSE

Another example of confusion between response characteristics and perceptual characteristics occurs in experiments on perceptual defense. If there is a stimulus we do not want to see, is it harder to recognize? To answer this question, researchers presented words to subjects for very short durations on a machine called a tachistoscope. First each word was exposed for such a brief time that it could not be recognized. The length of the exposure was gradually increased until the subject correctly reported the word. Under these conditions, common and socially acceptable words are correctly reported at exposures substantially shorter than various taboo words (for example, "whore," "pimp") interspersed within the list (McGinnies, 1949). The results were originally interpreted as evidence of **perceptual defense**—the idea that people refuse to see unwanted stimuli.

Later the results were interpreted in terms of response bias (Goldiamond,

1969); that is, it was claimed that subjects hesitated to say taboo words out loud in the social setting of the psychology laboratory—at least until they were very sure of what they had seen. Still another explanation suggested that the commonness or uncommonness of words was the main determinant. According to this explanation, uncommon words—those used less frequently in magazines and newspapers—take longer to recognize, even if they are not taboo. Printed sources, of course, may not yield a good estimate of the commonness of taboo words in the spoken language. More recent work, using intricate controls for response bias, has suggested that some genuine perceptual defense effect may exist (Erdelyi, 1974); but the issue is still far from settled.

PERSON PERCEPTION

During the last two decades or so, psychologists have begun investigating people's perceptions of others; such research has been labeled "person perception" or "impression formation." How do we come to judge others as kind, generous, cold, beautiful, or intelligent? Such impressions are often quite compelling, and they can be formed very quickly. Because many of these attributions of characteristics are not directly perceivable—they are judgments, sometimes very tenuous ones—many psychologists call this area "person cognition" rather than "person perception."

Experiments have shown that the processes of person cognition are very complex and that interaction plays a major role in these impressions. A particular act performed by the same person in two different contexts may lead to very different impressions of what the act means about the person's personality. In one study (Lambert et al., 1960), residents of Quebec who were fluent in both French and English recorded passages in each language. English-speaking listeners who understood French were asked to rate many of the speakers on such traits as likability, sincerity, and reliability. They were unaware that each person was heard twice, once in English and once in French. The same speaker consistently received more favorable ratings when speaking English than when speaking French, indicating a distinct bias for English-speakers on the part of these listeners. The research demonstrates how our impressions of others depend in an intricate, interactive way on expectations we hold ourselves, on what the other person does, on our social relationships, and on a host of other factors (Beach & Wertheimer, 1961).

How individuals employ unconscious material in forming impressions of others was investigated using the dichotic-perception technique described earlier (Korchin, personal communication to authors). In the right earphone, a subject heard and repeated aloud a story about a young man named Harry. Harry went from his small town to the big city. He took up city ways and began to forget about his home; his hometown girlfriend heard from him less often. Would he remain loyal to her? While the subjects were following this story in the right ear, they were told to ignore sentences in the left. For some subjects, the sentences in the left ear were favorable to Harry: "Harry is good," "Harry is kind," "Harry is thoughtful," and so forth. For other subjects, the sentences were neutral. And for a third group of subjects, the sentences in the left ear were unfavorable: "Harry is bad," "Harry is selfish," "Harry is inconsiderate," and so on.

When the presentation ended, subjects were asked to complete the story and to fill out adjective checklists about Harry. Subjects who received unfavorable or neutral material in the left ear gave similar responses, but subjects who received favorable material had a significantly more favorable impression of Harry—both in the ways they concluded the story and in the adjectives used to describe him. Checks showed that subjects were not aware of the content of the messages to the left ear; nevertheless, their personality judgments were influenced by them.

The subjects' own characteristics were also found to predict how strongly they would be influenced by the unconscious input to the left ear. Subjects who tested out as field dependent—who relied heavily on external rather than internal clues in forming judgments—were apt to be more strongly affected by the unconscious material. The experiment was also carried out with hospitalized mental patients who were well enough to cooperate. The results for most schizophrenic subjects were similar to those of normal subjects, but paranoid schizophrenics were much more influenced by the unattended sentences. Paranoid schizophrenics, you will recall from Chapter 8, are characteristically suspicious of their environment and highly alert to it. Thus, the research indicates that personality variables—both within and outside the normal range—have measurable effects on person perception.

CULTURAL EFFECTS

Experience with specific stimulus material may vary from culture to culture. For example, technologically developed cultures often use two-dimensional line drawings to represent three-dimensional objects. People from cultures with little or no experience with such line drawings may perceive them differently (Miller, 1973). In a now classic study (Segall, Campbell, & Herskovits, 1963, 1966), almost 2,000 people from 17 different cultures were asked to estimate the lengths of lines in the four illusions shown in Figure 16-9. In all

Figure 16-9
Illusions Used with Subjects of Several Different Cultures
Subjects of some cultures tend to make relatively larger errors in judging illusions involving acute and obtuse angles (A and B), whereas subjects of other cultures tend to make larger errors on illusions involving horizontal and vertical lines. (From Segall, Campbell, & Herskovits, Science, 1963)

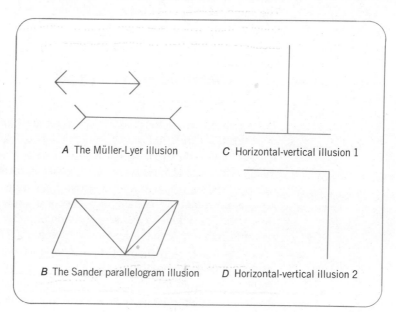

A The Müller-Lyer illusion

C Horizontal-vertical illusion 1

B The Sander parallelogram illusion

D Horizontal-vertical illusion 2

four drawings, the two lines are physically equal in length, but they appear unequal. The magnitude of the **illusion** was recorded for each subject.

The results of most interest and generality can be best described by classifying subjects as either European (including United States subjects and South African whites) or non-European (in this study, mostly black Africans), and by classifying illusions as "horizontal-vertical" (*C, D*) or "involving acute and/or obtuse angles" (*A, B*). On the average, Europeans made larger errors on illusions involving acute and obtuse angles; non-Europeans made larger errors on horizontal-vertical illusions.

The investigators interpreted these results as reflections of cultural demands learned in response to typical visual environments. Most Americans and Europeans are surrounded by many rectangular objects—buildings, books, tables, and television screens. People in such environments tend to see obtuse and acute angles as representing three-dimensional objects in perspective. For example, they may see a parallelogram as a rectangle extending away from them, like a book lying on a table. Accustomed to inferring the "true" lengths of lines that are foreshortened by perspective in such three-dimensional figures as buildings, they make similar but incorrect inferences in two-dimensional figures.

Most non-European groups in this study lived in dwellings that have few regular angles; many also lived in open countryside where the terrain is flat. The investigators reasoned that their exaggeration of the vertical lines might come from experience in such an environment. The vertical line might be interpreted as a road or some natural feature that stretched away into the distance; in that case, the line might be assumed to be longer than it looks. Whether either of these explanations is correct or not, the data do suggest measurable and characteristic differences in perception among people of different cultures. A cautious attitude toward such studies is indicated, however, because cross-cultural research is fraught with methodological problems, including those of communication between experimenters and subjects (Miller, 1973).

How do hereditary and environmental factors interact to determine perception?

The extent to which perceptual processes are built into the organism (the nativist position) and the extent to which they are learned (the empiricist position) has long been debated; recent research has provided some answers. Experiments with people who were born with cataracts (a clouding of the eye that prevents vision) and had them removed as adults show that at first all of them have great difficulty recognizing objects visually. After much practice some people become quite good at perceiving objects; others make very little progress and may even give up attempts to see objects (von Senden, 1960; Gregory & Wallace, 1963). Similar experiments with human beings and with animals reveal a general conclusion. We are born with many of our perceptual abilities, but these can be greatly modified through experience; they remain plastic. Two types of experiments have investigated this plasticity: in one kind, experimenters rearrange the normal visual input of human beings with special glasses; in the other, animals are raised in unusual visual environments.

In 1897 Professor George Stratton of the University of California surprised his students and colleagues by wearing odd eyeglasses that made everything look upside down. He wore these spectacles from morning till night, whenever he had his eyes open; after a few weeks he could walk around easily and perform skilled tasks guided by vision.

More recently, a psychology professor at Innsbruck, Austria, performed a similar experiment. After several weeks of adapting to his glasses, he was able to carry on his usual routines, even riding his bicycle through the steep, twisting streets of the area (Kohler, 1962). These adaptations show that visual orientation and space perception can indeed be modified by experience with rearranged sensory input. It appears likely, however, that adaptation is more proprioceptive—that is, relative to movement—than visual (Harris, 1965; Rock & Harris, 1967). No subject has ever reported that the visual world "looks right" even after weeks of experience with such rearranged input; it just becomes easier to get around in the peculiar-looking world. (See Spotlight 16-1 for a description of the effects of modified visual input on space perception in chicks.)

For more than a decade Richard Held has studied the effects of rearrangement of sensory input on people and other mammals (Held, 1970). In people, adaptation to a visually rearranged environment occurs when subjects can make physical movements and see their perceptual effects. For example, you can adapt comparatively quickly to upside-down glasses when you move around while wearing them; just sitting and looking through them does not help you to adapt. But this finding raises the question of whether active movement is necessary for the *original* development of visual perception and visual-motor coordination? To answer this question, Held and Hein designed an animal experiment (1963).

Pairs of kittens were raised in the dark (with their mothers) until they were about ten weeks old. They then received three hours a day of visual experience in the apparatus shown in the photograph. The active kitten could walk around in its yoke, turning in one direction or the other. The other kitten of the pair was carried passively in its gondola. The mechanical linkages assured that both would get fairly equal visual stimulation. When the active kitten turned toward the wall, the gondola also swiveled toward the wall. Neither animal could see its own body or the other animal, but both saw the stripes on the wall and on the central pillar. When not in the apparatus, the kittens remained in the dark with their mothers. After several days, their space perception was tested.

How do you test visual space perception in animals? One convenient method is by use of a **visual cliff** (Gibson & Walk, 1960); this is illustrated in the photograph on p. 443 and in Preview Figure 9. The animal is placed on a narrow central platform where it can step down an inch or so to a large pane of glass. On the "deep" side the animal can see down through the glass to a patterned surface 30 inches below; on the "shallow" side the pattern is just below the glass. Many species of animals, including young children, have been tested on the visual cliff. They almost invariably go to the shallow side. Babies do

Chicks improve the accuracy of their pecking between the ages of one and four days. Is this improvement a matter of learning?

Eckhard H. Hess performed an ingenious experiment to find out (1956). To measure the accuracy of their pecking, he allowed young chicks to peck at a brass nail embedded in modeling clay; the pecks left little indentations in the clay, providing a convenient record of their behavior. The pattern of pecks made by a one-day-old chick is represented by A, while the pecks of a four-day-old chick are shown in B. Clearly, the older chick did much better than the younger one. One might guess that the older chick had learned to improve its accuracy in the first few days of its life: when the chick was pecking at grains, it got food if it hit, but didn't get food if it missed.

To find out whether this kind of reinforcement was indeed responsible for the improvement, Hess made special hoods that were placed on the heads of some chicks as soon as they were hatched. The hoods were fitted with prisms that were held in front of the chicks' eyes in such a way that visual objects were displaced seven degrees to the right. Compare the pecks of a one-day-old chick (C) and a four-day-old chick (D) wearing the hood. The C records show that the prisms had the intended effect; the pecks are clearly displaced to the right. But look at the record in D. The pecks are indeed more tightly clustered, as in the normal chick's record, but they are still clearly displaced to the right. These

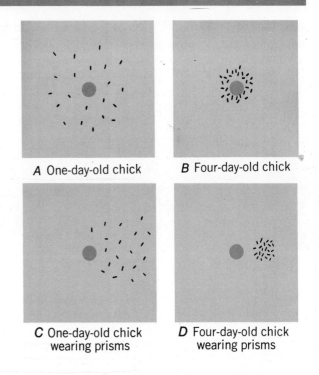

A One-day-old chick   **B** Four-day-old chick

C One-day-old chick wearing prisms   **D** Four-day-old chick wearing prisms

rather surprising results show that the visual space perception of young chicks, and the improvement in their pecking behavior, does not depend on learning; it is a matter of maturation.

---

that as soon as they can crawl, which has led some investigators to think that some aspects of depth perception must be innate (see p. 458). The kittens in the Held and Hein experiment were tested after they had been in the visual exposure apparatus for as little as three sessions or as many as twenty-one sessions (9 to 63 hours). Six tests were given to each kitten on two successive days.

The results were clear-cut. Every kitten that moved actively in the apparatus stepped to the shallow side on every trial. No kitten that moved passively showed any consistent discrimination between the two sides. The passive kittens had normal pupillary responses to light and could follow moving objects with their eyes, but they had not developed depth perception or other responses to visual space.

In a later experiment (Hein, Held, & Gower, 1970), each kitten was given both active and passive experience. In the active condition, one eye was open and the other was covered; in the passive condition, the eye coverings were

PERCEPTION

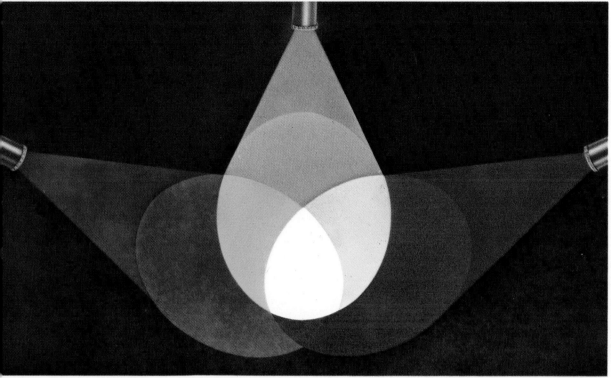

FIGURE 1
ADDITIVE COLOR MIXTURE

Three projectors cast circles of red, green, and blue light, and these are made to overlap on a colorless background. The areas of overlap show what hues result when different wavelengths are added to each other in this way. For example, red light plus green light yields yellow. Where all three circles overlap in the center, the addition of red plus green plus blue yields white.

FIGURE 2
SUBTRACTIVE COLOR MIXTURE

Pigments absorb light, and different pigments absorb different parts of the spectrum. A red pigment absorbs light from most of the spectrum and allows chiefly "red" wavelengths to be reflected back to the observer's eye. When pigments are mixed, the mixture absorbs the wavelengths absorbed by each of the pigments; therefore the more pigments are used, the darker the mixture appears. The combination of red, yellow, and blue pigments (in the center) absorbs almost all the light and therefore appears black. Note that this effect is the opposite from addition of lights above where all three lights together yield white.

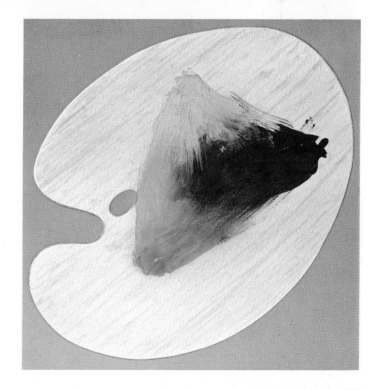

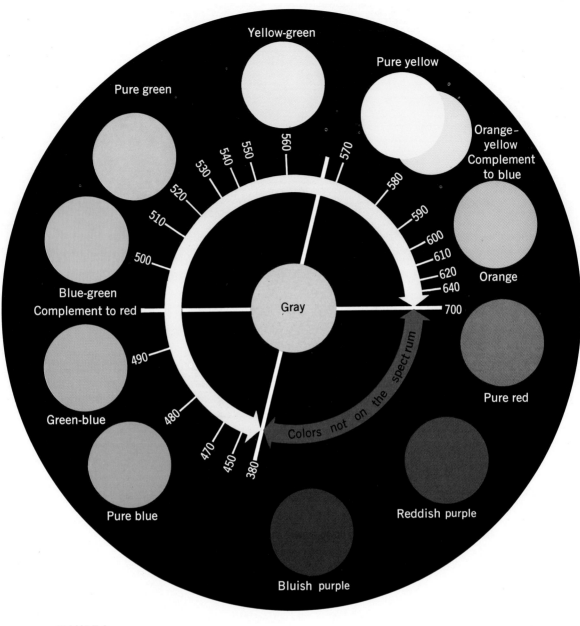

FIGURE 3
THE COLOR CIRCLE

All the hues of the rainbow, and more besides, are placed in order around the color circle. Complementary hues are placed directly opposite each other; thus green-blue (produced by light of wavelength 490 nanometers) is the complement of orange (607 nm). Green has no complementary hue in the spectrum; its complement is purple, which cannot be produced by a single wavelength of light. Two complementary lights, if added together in the proper proportions, will produce neutral gray. If you stare at any of the discs of color for half a minute and then shift your gaze to a neutral background, you will see an afterimage of the complementary hue.

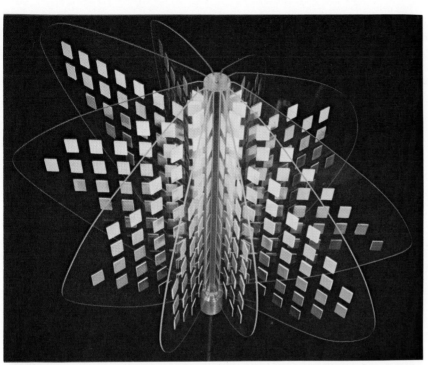

FIGURE 4
THE COLOR SOLID SHOWS THE THREE DIMENSIONS OF COLOR

Hue varies around the perimeter of the color solid, as it does in the color circle on the opposite page. **Saturation** varies from the perimeter to the center; that is, colors are rich and vivid at the outside but become paler as you follow any radius in toward the center. **Brightness** varies along the vertical axis. The color circle is a horizontal section through the color solid.

A vertical section through the color solid is shown below. It has brighter colors toward the top and darker colors toward the bottom, richly saturated colors at the edges and neutral gray in the center, and the yellow hue to the left is the complement of the blue hue to the right.

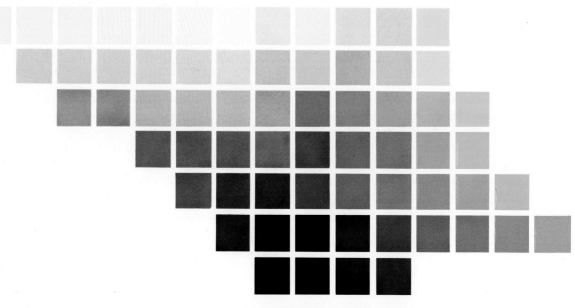

FIGURE 5
SIMULTANEOUS COLOR CONTRAST

The three gray circles are identical physically, but they appear to have slightly different hues because they are on three different backgrounds. The hue induced in each circle is the complement of the hue of the background.

This effect is enhanced if you blur the contour separating circle and background somewhat — by squinting your eyes or by laying a piece of onionskin paper over the figure.

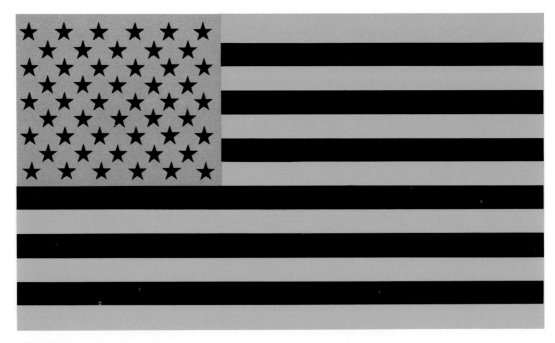

FIGURE 6
AN AFTERIMAGE AMERICAN FLAG

Keep your eyes fixed on the bottom right corner of the orange field for about thirty seconds, then quickly shift your gaze to a point on a neutral (gray or white) surface. The complementary afterimages of the colors will yield a more familiar experience.

FIGURE 7
SIMULTANEOUS COLOR CONTRAST

First look at the gray circle and see whether its left and right halves appear the same or different from each other. Then separate the two halves by laying a pencil along the vertical line between the red and green backgrounds, and compare the two halves of the circle again. Now move the pencil back and forth a little to the right and a little to the left of the midline and observe what happens. It appears that color contrast depends not only on the colors but also on the way in which the figure is divided.

FIGURE 8
THE BLIND SPOT

How many apples do you see? It depends on how you look. This figure allows you to locate the blind spot (the place where nerve fibers leave the eyeball; there are no receptor cells where this "cable" goes through the retina). The figure also shows how a pattern is "filled in" or "completed" across the blind spot. Close your left eye and look at the yellow apple, holding the book about fifteen inches in front of your eyes. Adjust the distance until the red apple disappears. Does this leave a "hole" in the checkered background or does it appear to be continuous? Now repeat the procedure, closing your right eye and looking at the red apple. The fact that the background pattern appears continuous when the apple disappears is an example of the principle of Prägnanz discussed in Chapter 21.

FIGURE 9
DAY VISION AND NIGHT VISION

The eye perceives differently in daylight and at night. At daylight levels of illumination, the cone receptors of the eye function and we see different hues. In dim illumination the rod receptors of the retina take over; they are color-blind and so we see only varying shades of gray.

"Sunday Afternoon on the Island of La Grand Jatte" by Georges Seurat
Helen Birch Bartlett Memorial Collection, Courtesy of the Art Institute of Chicago

FIGURE 10
DOTS ORGANIZED INTO FORMS

When you look at the enlarged detail from this pointillist painting by Seurat, you can see that it is made up of small juxtaposed spots of different colors. But when you look at the painting from a distance, the dots seem to merge together and you see forms clearly. This can be understood in terms of the principles of perceptual organization and of figure formation.

FIGURE 11 (over)
ADAPTATION PATTERNS FOR THE McCOLLOUGH EFFECT

Brightly illuminate the next page. Using a gray piece of paper, cover the red grating at the top and look at the center of the green grating. After about 15 seconds, cover the green grating and look at the center of the red. In this fashion, alternate between the two gratings for about three minutes. Then look back at Figure 16-3 in text.

reversed. These kittens were later tested on the visual cliff, with each eye separately. When a kitten used the eye that had been open during active locomotion, it typically chose the shallow side on each of eight trials. When it used the other eye, it typically chose the shallow side only five out of eight times. Perception of depth developed with the eye used in active locomotion but not with the eye used only during passive movement. Also, learning was not transferred from one eye to the other. In normal cats, as in normal people, a task learned with one eye can be performed with the other eye. These experimental kittens, however, had never used both eyes together—one or the other had always been covered whenever they were in the light—and the kittens had not acquired the normal ability to recognize with one eye what had been seen with the other.

SPECIES RECOGNITION

All seagulls probably look pretty much the same to you, unless you happen to be a birdwatcher or an ethologist—or a seagull. Actually, several species clearly differ in coloration, especially of the head and bill. How do the chicks of different species come to recognize their own kind?

The chicks of various species of gulls get food in the nest by pecking at the bill of the parent; this behavior is called "begging response." In response to the chick's pecking, the parent disgorges food. Different species of gulls have different colored heads and bills. How well can the chick recognize the adult of its own species? Is this discrimination innate or learned? Hailman (1967) worked on these questions with two species of gulls. In the laughing gull the adult has a black head and a red beak; the adult herring gull has a white head and a yellow beak with a red spot at the end of the lower bill.

In controlled tests, chicks pecked from their first day at any long vertical rod. The color was not very important. On their first day, herring gull chicks pecked about as much at a model head of an adult laughing gull as at a model of the head of a herring gull. During the first few days, however, they made an increasing percentage of responses to the model of their own parent (see Figure 16-10). These chicks lived with their parents except for the time spent advancing science; they were fed ordinarily by their parents. The increasing discrimination pictured in Figure 16-10 could result from learning; the chicks were being reinforced for pecking at a herring gull in "real life." But there is also the possibility that an innate response was maturing, like the pecking accuracy of chicks described in Spotlight 16-1. A controlled laboratory experiment was necessary to distinguish between these two possibilities.

Three groups of newly hatched laughing gulls were used. They were fed by hand for a week, using an operant-conditioning procedure. Chicks of one group were shown a laughing gull model and given a piece of food whenever they pecked at the model. The second group was treated similarly but with a herring gull model. The third control group was fed without any model. Occasional nonreinforced tests were made with both models. Each of the first two groups showed an increasing proportion of pecking directed to the model associated with food; the control groups did not develop a preference for either model. Thus, the gull chicks were hatched with sufficient form perception to see the

During the first few days of its life the seagull chick learns to beg for food from whichever gull feeds it.

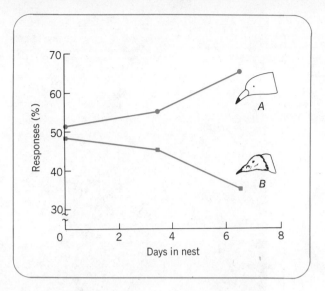

Figure 16-10
Response of Herring Gull Chicks to Model Head of Herring Gull (A) or Laughing Gull (B)
A controlled laboratory experiment demonstrated that a chick's naturally occurring preference for its species is learned through reinforcement.

parents' bill and sufficient motor control to peck at it; but their <u>preference for a particular adult model was *learned* through reinforcement.</u>

The ability to recognize their own species develops quite differently in different kinds of birds. This difference is consistent with the general principle that sensory and motor capacities of species vary in their development according to the requirements of the life of the particular animal. Thus fowl such as ducks, which are hatched by the mother, do not require an inborn capacity to recognize the mother. At the start they have a tendency to follow and become attached to (imprinted on) any moving and sound-emitting object—even if that object happens to be a kindly old ethologist like Konrad Lorenz (*see* p. 647). In nature, this tendency usually results in the ducklings becoming attached to the mother; but in experimental situations they may become imprinted on objects as diverse as a scientist or an electric train. On the other hand, a cuckoo or cowbird requires an innate recognition of its own kind; eggs of these species are laid in the nests of other birds. The cuckoo grows up exclusively with members of another species, yet it manages to recognize another cuckoo when the time comes to mate.

DEVELOPMENT OF PERCEPTION IN CHILDREN

In people, as in other animals, some perceptual abilities are present from birth; others develop through experience. A kind of primitive space perception can be demonstrated with newborn babies. If you snap your fingers to one side of a baby's head, the baby will most likely respond by moving its eyes and even head in the direction of the sound (Wertheimer, 1961). This means that there is coordination between hearing and eye movements at birth, and perhaps also a crude awareness of auditory space.

Other experiments have been done with young babies by suspending stimuli (such as those in Figure 16-11) over the crib and measuring the length of time a child looks at each pattern (Fantz, 1963). It turns out that pattern *A* receives

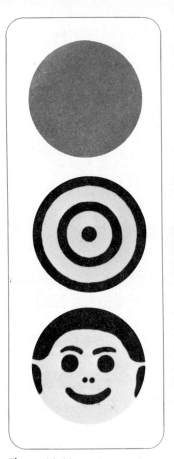

Figure 16-11
Visual Stimuli Used with Neonates
(David Linton; © *Scientific American*, May 1961)

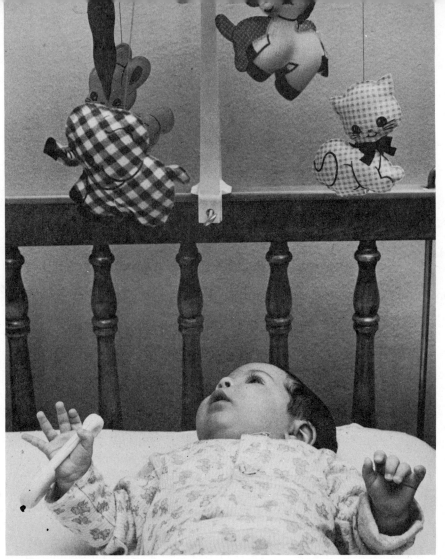

the least attention, *B* somewhat more, and *C* the most. (Responses are consistent whatever the relative positions of the stimuli.) Differences in "complexity" of a stimulus pattern lead to differences in interest, even with very young babies. The more complex patterns seem to be more interesting.

NATIVISM VERSUS EMPIRICISM

It should be clear by now that the old controversy of whether perception is innate or learned is no longer much of an issue in psychology. Some perceptual abilities in some species seem to be innate, and some appear to result from experience. What is innate in one species may be learned in another. Moreover, even innate capacities are significantly influenced by experience, and learning is significantly influenced by genetic capacity. Thus, psychologists have more or less abandoned the old controversy as a pseudo-issue. Instead they concentrate on understanding how innate and experiential factors *interact* to produce the behavior patterns we observe. "Nativism versus empiricism" has become "heredity *in interaction with* environment"—a scientific advance of no small magnitude.

SUMMARY

Perception is a constructive activity; its raw materials are stimulus input, memories, and motivational and emotional states. The creative and fundamentally illusory nature of most normal perception raises this question: How is it that our perceptions allow us to get along so well in the real world within which we move and behave?

Part of the answer lies in hypothesis testing. That is, if perception often involves construction of a *percept* that is a sort of hypothesis about what's really out there, then this hypothesis can usually be tested by acting as if the hypothesis were true. If you reach for an imaginary object, the lack of tactile feedback is a new input; and ordinarily you will revise your percept-hypothesis. In adapting to new or rearranged sensory input, we normally move around and thereby vary the input to test hypotheses about the new environmental conditions.

Recognizing patterns is a complex task. Explanations in terms of **template-matching, feature analysis,** and **prototype comparison** can account for some phenomena. Another current hypothesis is **analysis-by-synthesis;** that is, the perceiver recognizes an object (which may be visual or auditory or in some other sense) by actively synthesizing a percept of it from a portion of the available sensory information plus whatever information is stored in memory. If possible, this provisional percept is then checked further against other sensory information or knowledge of the situation.

Speech perception also involves pattern recognition, and our knowledge of grammatical structure strongly influences how we perceive a spoken sentence. The speech stimulus can be displayed visually on an electronic viewer, from which it can be literally read. Some patterns that look quite different sound quite similar (*d* in different words). Thus, the pattern recognition capacities of the human are quite complex and amazing.

Because we must select from all the various inputs reaching us at any given time, attention is an important feature of perception. Set and expectation, past experience, and motivation are all determinants of attention. Attention can operate both at the level of the sense organs and in stages of processing that occur in the central nervous system.

Forming impressions of people is a perceptual and cognitive activity. Subjects often use information of which they are unaware in forming their judgments of others. Some of the information can be classed as "cultural": for example, people generally give more favorable ratings to persons speaking in their own native tongue—even compared to the same person speaking a foreign language. Cultural differences in the judgment of illusions also suggest that people may organize their percepts partly on the basis of the typical visual experiences encountered in their culture.

The nativism-empiricism controversy arises again within the context of perception. As research evidence shows, much of the controversy now seems irrelevant to understanding human and animal behavior. Normal experience (moving around) is necessary for the development of capacities (such as depth perception) that may be at least partly innate. Some species recognize their own kind through experience and some do so instinctively; the requirements of life for each species can explain into which category a particular animal falls. Most psychologists, therefore, are less interested in taking a strong nativist or empiricist stand than they are in exploring the subtle interactions of heredity and environment in specific behavioral patterns.

The Relativity of Perception

How do we organize what we see?
How does context affect our perception?
How do we perceive movement?

How do we organize what we see?

A fundamental question in perception is how we are able to organize the bewildering jumble of stimulation from the environment so that coherent perceptions result. One goal of our perceptual processes is to create a three-dimensional space and fill that space with meaningful objects. These objects, of course, differ in size, color, location, distance from us, and importance to us. The principles by which the perceptual processes create meaningful objects from the stimulus input were first studied extensively by **Gestalt** psychologists (Wertheimer, 1923; Koffka, 1935). The German word *Gestalt*, roughly translated, means ''configuration.''*

* The currently popular ''Gestalt'' therapy bears essentially no relationship at all to the traditional Gestalt principles, which were formulated primarily in the areas of perception, learning, thinking, and problem solving (Henle, 1975).

466

We usually perceive some parts of the visual field as objects or figures and other parts as background. The parts that we organize as objects seem quite different from the parts that we relegate to the background. For one thing, the figure is always seen as in front of or on top of the ground, and the ground seems to be continuous behind the figure. The figure is more significant—not only perceptually, but also in memory. The contour or line separating figure and ground is seen as belonging to the figure, not to the background. Because the background typically looks as though it continues behind the figure, it does not seem to have an edge or contour of its own where it meets the figure —we are able to perceive it as a separate whole. Some stimulus arrays are ambiguous and can be perceived in one of several figure-ground relationships. Figure 17-1 shows such a stimulus, first described by the Danish psychologist Edgar Rubin (1915). Of the two meanings your perceptual processes are able to construct from this drawing—either a vase, or two faces in profile—you typically experience only one at a time.

An analogous form of processing is found in hearing. When confronted with several conversations, it is only possible to attend to one (see p. 452). That one becomes the "figure" heard against the "ground" of the other conversations.

Figure 17-1
Two Profiles or a Vase?
You see either two black profiles against a white background or a white vase on a black background. At any given moment, you can see only one alternative. The shape of the contour depends on which one you are seeing, and in each case the figure stands out in front of the background.

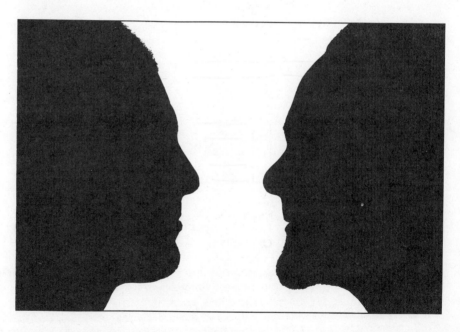

PRINCIPLES OF PERCEPTUAL GROUPING

The Gestalt psychologists discovered certain principles—relationships among stimulus inputs that strongly influence what is perceived as figure and what as ground. They also investigated how and what stimulus elements are grouped together to form a perceptual unit. Our perceptual processes are continually looking for stimulus parts that are consistent with the hypothesis that the parts belong to objects in three-dimensional space.

① **Similarity**

The perceptual processes tend to group parts of the stimulus input that are similar into a coherent whole. For example, in Figure 17-2, we perceive vertical columns of X's and O's rather than horizontal rows alternating X, O, X, O.

Figure 17-2
The Principle of Similarity
You are more likely to perceive columns of X's and O's than rows of alternating X's and O's.

X O X O X O

X O X O X O

X O X O X O

X O X O X O

X O X O X O

X O X O X O

② **Proximity**

Elements near each other tend to be perceptually grouped together—the principle of **proximity.** Part A of Figure 17-3 is perceived as five columns or posts because the lines close together are grouped into figures.

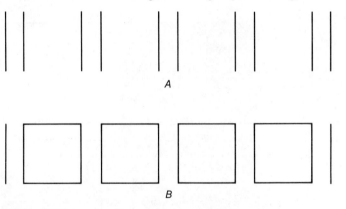

A

B

Figure 17-3
Proximity and Closure as Principles of Perceptual Organization
Following the principle of proximity, pattern A tends to be described as five pairs of vertical lines. The same vertical lines are perceived very differently in B. The second and third lines are now generally described as belonging together, as part of the same rectangle; so are the fourth and fifth, and so on. Even partial horizontal lines—as in Preview Figure 6—are enough to suggest closure.

③ **Closure**

Stimulus elements that form a continuous, closed contour are strongly organized into a figure. In Figure 17-3B we spontaneously perceive four closed squares plus two lines, rather than the five pairs of lines in A. Even if continuous contours are not quite closed, as in Preview Figure 6, the principle of **closure** still groups contours into figures. See also Preview Figure 12B, in which closure actually completes the gap in the line.

Common Fate

Parts of the stimulus array that move together or share other qualities have a **common fate;** they grow brighter at the same time, have an object approach them, and so on. Because of their common fate they tend to be perceived as a group. Marchers in a parade are distinguished from the people watching the parade; the marchers are walking in step while the onlookers are stationary or are moving about aimlessly. The same principle is illustrated abstractly in Figure 17-4, using dots. Pattern A is an undifferentiated row of nine equally spaced dots; proximity and similarity are the same, so the set does not break down into subgroups. Closure plays little role in this pattern. Then, in B, three dots suddenly move up and to the right; they return to their original position in C, so that again there is just an undifferentiated row of nine equally spaced dots (D). But while they are moving the common motion of the three dots yields a strong perceptual bond among them; even after their motion ceases they remain for some time perceptually segregated as a group distinct from the rest. A frog, salamander, or other creature with protective coloration may be quite indistinct in its natural surroundings—until it moves.

Figure 17-4
Common Fate as a Principle of Perceptual Organization
Parts of the field that move together are perceived as belonging to the same group.

Good Continuation

Both the patterns in Figure 17-5 are typically organized spontaneously into *continuous* curves and lines. On the basis of proximity, however, A *could* be seen differently: the two straight lines forming a right angle on the left might be perceived as belonging with the bottom left section of the curved line; the remaining right-hand vertical line could belong with the remaining, upper part of the curve. But such a percept is neither typical nor possible without effort. Similarly, pattern B usually looks like a curve of dots sweeping up to the right

Figure 17-5
Good Continuation as a Principle of Perceptual Organization
The spontaneous grouping in A typically is of three sides of a square and a curved line; in B, of two lines of dots crossing each other.

A   B

from the lower left, crossing another curved line of dots undulating down to the right from the upper left. (Notice that this percept abrogates the principle of proximity for some dots near the crossing point.)

In a complex stimulus, all these principles may operate simultaneously. The perceptual outcome will be partially determined by the relative strengths of the various principles and whether they are able to operate together or in opposition. Figure 17-6 illustrates how several principles combine to form the perception of horizontal and vertical lines.

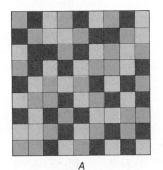
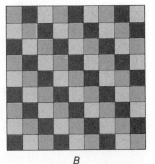

A   B

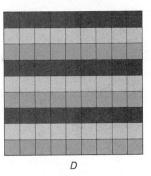

C   D

Figure 17-6
Pattern A yields no clear overall coherence, but B appears to be composed of diagonals running from upper left to lower right. C is seen as vertical columns and D as horizontal rows. In all cases, there are 27 squares of each color. The squares of a given color tend to "go together" in perception, especially when proximity and good continuation favor this view.

LAW OF PRÄGNANZ   Generally, figures look "better" to us—that is, more aesthetically satisfying and regular—if they are construed in one particular way than in any of many other ways that might be consistent with the sensory input. This principle of economy of organization, which we have met several times in this section, has been summarized in the **law of Prägnanz;** it states that any whole will be as "good" as conditions allow. (*Prägnanz* is a German word with no exact equivalent in English; in the sense employed here, it means roughly the tendency to assume a characteristic or distinctive form.) **Goodness,** in this formulation, signifies such qualities as regularity, symmetry, simplicity, and stability. Since the law of Prägnanz was first proposed, various researchers have attempted to state it more precisely and quantitatively. For example, it has been proposed that the less the amount of information needed to define a given organization — as compared to other alternatives — the more likely is it that the input will be perceived according to that organization (Hochberg & McAlister, 1953). Thus Preview Figure 3 can be seen as either a cube in perspective or a complex set of triangles and quadrilaterals lying in the same plane; it requires less information to specify it as a cube. Recent experiments have demonstrated that such assumptions can predict rather effectively how both simple and complex inputs will be perceived (Attneave & Frost, 1969; Garner, 1970). By such methods, the goodness of a figure can be quantified. Good figures are relatively simple, symmetrical, and easy to describe.

Other principles of organization in perception can be seen as special cases of the more general law of Prägnanz. Consider the principle of proximity in hearing in this illustration. If you tap a table with a pencil according to this pattern — .. .. —a rhythm of repeated pairs of taps will be perceived. If you use this pattern — ... ... —a percept of triads occurs. Why? Because of temporal proximity, of course. Moreover, it is not difficult to predict what will follow two taps in the first example (a pause) and what will follow two in the second (another tap). There is little uncertainty — and uncertainty is the opposite of having information. Thus, little uncertainty means much information, and much information means goodness in the sense implied by the law of Prägnanz. In this case, goodness is a function of proximity relations; but any of the other principles — similarity, continuity, or closure — can also provide information about what comes next.

CAMOUFLAGE

By clever use of Gestalt principles, the perception of a specific pattern can become extremely difficult. Such principles are all used in camouflage. What do the drawings of Figure 17-7 look like to you? To most observers, A is a fairly regular collection of sticks or lines; they are somewhat startled when told it contains the name of a month. In the same way, pattern B looks like a mildly interesting arrangement of a few circles, a couple of triangles, and a rectangle. An observer doesn't immediately recognize the digits specifying a particular year.

Figure 17-7
Camouflage
The principles of organization are used to camouflage.

A   B

Figure 17-8 gives away what Figure 17-7 camouflages. Obviously, Figure 17-8 contains more clutter; but camouflage is more than simply cluttering. Successful camouflage is an application of the principles of organization in per-

Figure 17-8
Unsuccessful Camouflage
This figure is a giveaway of
what was hidden in Figure
17-7.

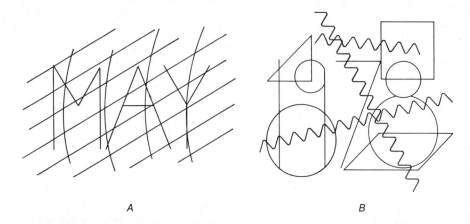

A   B

ception. (Which principles can you identify in Figure 17-7?) Probably you have
never seen the particular patterns in Figure 17-7; you have, however, seen
capital letters, digits, words, and numbers innumerable times in the past. When
pitted against a few simple perceptual principles, you begin to realize that the
effect of past experience is very slight.

SPACE PERCEPTION

Not only does our perceptual processing organize stimuli into meaningful
figures and objects, but it also localizes them in three-dimensional space. Without localization, we would find selecting the appropriate behavior (for example, approaching or fleeing) a difficult task. How do our perceptual processes yield awareness of objects located in three-dimensional space?

Visual Depth Perception

The ability to know that objects we see lie at different distances from us is
called **depth perception.** This ability is created by our perceptual processes in
a variety of ways, using a variety of information.

Examine Figure 17-9 carefully. Because the two eyes see the world from
slightly different positions, each eye has a slightly different image of the scene.
The difference between the two views is called **binocular disparity.** Our visual
systems have developed very sensitive mechanisms for analyzing binocular
disparity to create impressions of relative depths; they do so by means of a
process called **stereopsis.** The effects of stereopsis, typically taken for granted,
can be noticed if, for example, you try playing table tennis with one eye closed.
Spotlight 17-1 provides another demonstration of depth effects produced by
binocular disparity.

The depth achieved with A and B and with B and C in Spotlight 17-1 might
be attributed in part to our experience in looking at simple geometrical objects.
Each eye gets its own view of the object; then, it was formerly believed, these
two slightly different views are put together by the brain to yield a perception
of depth. Now, however, a radical advance has occurred in our understanding
of binocular vision. The development of random-dot stereograms by Julesz
(1964) (D and E of Spotlight 17-1) was a major contribution to this advance. To
construct one of these figures, say D, each little square in a large field is made
either black or white, as determined by a random process, so there is no observable pattern. The paired field, E in this case, is identical to D, except that

Figure 17-9
The Visual Scene as Viewed by Each Eye
The difference between the two views is called binocular disparity.

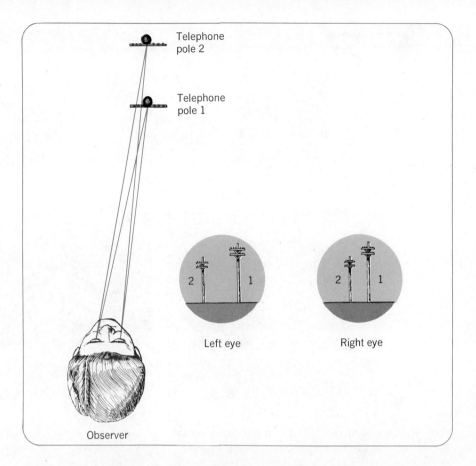

Telephone pole 2

Telephone pole 1

Left eye

Right eye

Observer

certain sections are shifted horizontally from the rest of the figure to provide for binocular disparity. A percept of depth in *D* and *E*, moreover, cannot be attributed to past experience, because we have never seen such patterns before.

Research with such patterns has led to several novel conclusions. Not only is familiarity not essential, but even perception of form is not required for perception of depth. In *D* and *E* you cannot see form until depth perception occurs. Before these studies, it had been thought by many that form must be perceived first; that is, a figure must be perceived before you can locate it in three dimensions. This does not seem to be the case, and some researchers (Bishop & Henry, 1971) conclude that the underlying neural mechanisms for depth perception operate *earlier* in the processing of visual experience than do the mechanisms for form perception.

Depth perception is also achieved by processes other than stereopsis. These processes use information (or cues) available to either eye and thus do not require binocular vision for their use. The most important of these monocular cues is **motion parallax.** As you move your head or walk or ride, objects near you change their position within your visual field more rapidly than distant objects. Furthermore, objects nearer to you than your point of fixation move in the direction opposite to your own, while objects beyond the point of fixation

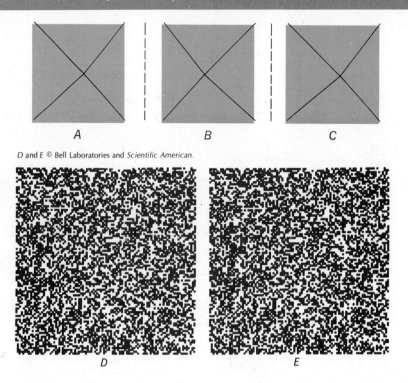

D and *E* © Bell Laboratories and *Scientific American.*

These diagrams illustrate how depth perception results from the fact that our two eyes get slightly different inputs. Try this experiment. Put the book down flat, take a manila folder or a piece of cardboard about twelve inches long and place it vertically between *A* and *B* along the dotted line. Now put your head on the upper end of the cardboard so your left eye sees only *A* and your right eye only *B* (cover *C* with a piece of plain paper). Stare "through" the page, focusing farther away, until the two figures fuse; a solid appearance should result. Is the point of the pyramid directed toward or away from you? Next, cover *A*, move the cardboard between *B* and *C*, and look with

your left eye at *B* and your right at *C*. Fuse, and what do you see? Why do you suppose this occurs?

Figures like *A, B,* and *C* are familiar, so experience might be supposed to play some role in your perceptions of them. Now look at the random-dot patterns of figures *D* and *E* (Julesz, 1964). Does either *D* or *E* show any recognizable pattern? Put the cardboard between them, stare into space and achieve binocular fusion of *D* and *E*. Don't be discouraged if this takes some time. What depth perception occurs as you continue to stare at the center of the merged figure?

move in the same direction. Motion parallax is a powerful cue to depth, and it allows a person with one eye to make depth judgments almost as accurately as a binocular person. Thus a person with one eye has lost stereopsis, but has certainly not lost depth perception.

Most of the other monocular cues to depth were discovered by Renaissance artists like Leonardo da Vinci and were used by them to create startling three-dimensional perceptions on a two-dimensional surface (flat canvas). Most of the cues in Figure 17-10 are used to create the perception of depth; but two of them, motion parallax and stereopsis, tell us that Figure 17-10 is really a flat

Figure 17-10
A Renaissance Perspective
Observe how the artist
conveys the dimension of
depth.

Figure 17-11
Principle of Linear Perspective
This engraving by Brook
Taylor, 1811, is a study in
the eye's perception of
converging lines. It shows
how the solid block at the
left can be projected onto
the flat surface of the window.
(From M. H. Pirenne, *Optics,
Painting and Photography,*
1970)

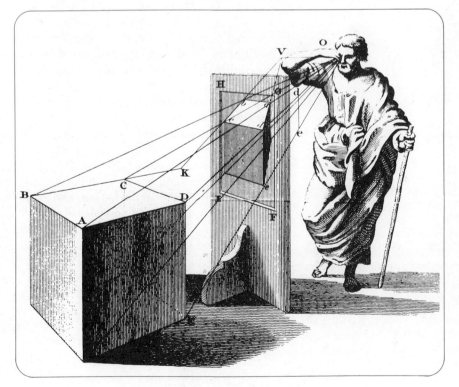

piece of paper. Therefore, if you close one eye (to eliminate stereopsis) and hold your head very still (to eliminate motion parallax) the depth effect in Figure 17-10 can be substantially enhanced.

Some of the monocular cues to depth discovered by Renaissance artists are linear perspective, relative size, aerial perspective, interposition, and location within the visual field. **Linear perspective** is a consequence of geometry and optics (see Figure 17-11). The images of parallel railroad tracks become closer together the farther away they are—that is, they are *not* parallel in the image. Yet we perceive a parallel set extending into three-dimensional space. The cue of relative size again follows from optics: the farther away an object is, the smaller is its image in the eye. Gradients of size can produce a strong perception of depth, as illustrated in Preview Figure 7. We also see more detail in nearby objects than in distant ones (aerial perspective), partly because more air (including dust particles) obscures the farther objects. Scattering of light by the air also makes distant objects appear more bluish than close ones. A close object can block the view of a farther one (interposition), and the farther object tends to be higher in the visual field. Examine Figure 17-10 again. How many cues to depth can you find?

Auditory Localization

Just as there are monocular and binocular cues to visual space, so there are **monaural** (one ear) and **binaural** (two ears) **cues** to auditory space. By stimulating either ear alone, we can get some idea of the distance of a sound source if we know something about the intensity and the sound spectrum at the source. The less intense the sound, the farther away the source must be; and the weaker the high frequencies relative to the low frequencies, the farther away the source must be, since high frequencies are transmitted through space less well than low ones. (Think of the sound of a foghorn nearby as opposed to one far away.) But, just as the differential location of both eyes yields the powerful cue of retinal disparity, so too a significant aspect of our auditory space localization equipment is the fact that our two ears are separated by a few inches. Because of this fact, the pattern of stimulation of the two ears at a given moment is usually slightly different—unless the sound source is directly in front, directly above, or directly behind the hearer (or, for that matter, located anywhere on the surface of a plane that perfectly divides the right from the left half of the body). If the sound comes, say, from the right of the observer, the right ear will receive a slightly more intense stimulus. Some of the frequency components may be a little weaker at the left ear, and the right ear will receive the stimulus a tiny fraction of a second earlier than the left ear. The ears and the brain are organized so that these binaural differences result in a perception of a sound source located in a particular direction from the observer—in this case, to the right. Our brain can detect time differences in the arrival of a sound at the two ears as small as 10-millionths of a second!

The ability to localize sound adds to both our acuity and our enjoyment of sound. In a noisy situation, we can hear voices or other signals better when we can localize them and separate them from the background. In the case of music, sound localization aids us in attending separately to the different instruments in an orchestra; this is why stereophonic records are preferred to monaural ones.

"Excuse me for shouting—I thought you were farther away."

How does context affect our perception?

PERCEPTUAL CONSTANCIES

One consequence of the perceptual goal of creating a stable three-dimensional world filled with objects is that our perception remains fairly constant despite great changes in the physical stimulus presented to our sense organs. We are able to recognize quite different stimulus patterns as representing the same object, a phenomenon known as **perceptual constancy**. Furthermore, our knowledge of certain attributes of objects—size, shape, and brightness—normally remains stable even when the physical stimulation changes greatly.

Size Constancy

The size of an object's image on the retina of the eye changes as a function of viewing distance (Figure 17-12). As people move away from you, their retinal image becomes smaller and smaller, yet your perceptual processes maintain the knowledge that their physical size is remaining constant; it is the distance that changes. The ability to know that the physical size of an object has not changed despite changes in retinal image size is called **size constancy**.

If the available cues indicating the distance of objects are good, an adult's ability to judge the true size of objects is almost perfect for distances up to a

Figure 17-12
How the Size of the Retinal Image Varies

The same size retinal image can be produced by an infinite number of different distal sizes (1, 2, 3, and 4 are examples), as long as they all reach the eye from the same angle. The same size distal object (4 and 5) casts a larger image when it is closer to the eye.

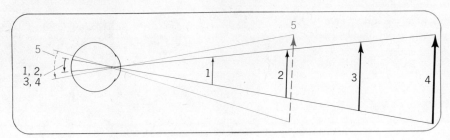

mile. Size constancy at these distances is not as good in children, who are able to judge size accurately only at closer viewing distances (Leibowitz, Pollard, & Dickson, 1967). But even in infants, some degree of size constancy is found for objects quite close (Bower, 1966). We do not yet know what mechanisms recognize the stability in the true size of objects when retinal images change.

Brightness Constancy

Size constancy depends on the integration of at least two types of information: the size of the retinal image of an object and its distance from the observer. **Brightness constancy** depends upon a similar integration; it can be seen to be a perceptual conclusion about the amount of light falling on an object and the percentage of this light that is reflected to the eye.

Brightness is a perceptual experience: it ranges from white to black. The brightness of an object depends not on the absolute intensity of light, but on the relative amount of light compared with other objects in the visual field. Thus a white piece of paper appears white whether viewed in bright sunlight or in a dark cellar, even though 10,000 times more light may be present in the sunlight than in the cellar. The fact that the brightness of an object remains perceptually the same in spite of changes in illumination is called brightness constancy.

It appears that what is crucial for brightness constancy is the *ratios* of the intensities of light in different parts of the stimulus field. Figure 17-13 presents two arrays with identical structures. Both *A* and *B* consist of a small disc within a larger ring; the intensity of white light in both the ring and the disc is independently variable. If the illumination of the ring in *A* is at an intensity of 100 (arbitrary) units and the disc at an intensity of 50 in an otherwise dark field, the ring will look white and the disc light gray. The experimental question is, If the outer ring illumination is set at 40 in *B*, how intense should the inner disc be to look just as bright as the disc in *A*? If perceived brightness simply corresponds to the local intensity, then the illumination of the disc in *B* would have to be 50 units, the same as in *A*. But an intensity of 50 turns out to make the disc in *B* look much brighter than the disc in *A*. Instead, as repeated experiments have shown, the disc in *B* must be illuminated with only about 20 units to look as

Figure 17-13
The Relational Determination of Brightness

How many units of illumination are needed in the inner circle in *B* to make it look just as bright as the inner circle in *A*, which has an illumination of 50 units?

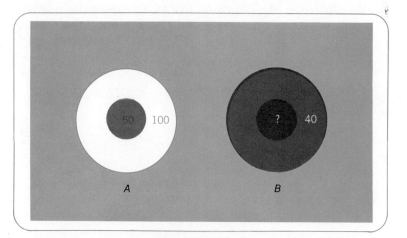

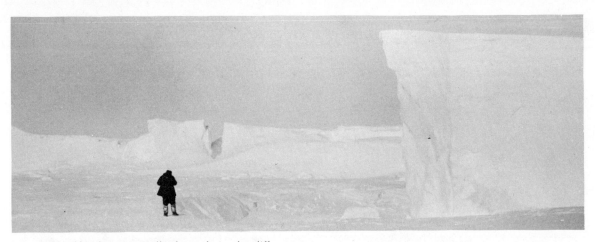

Perception of brightness usually depends on the different reflectances among objects in view.

bright as the disc in *A*. In other words, the *ratio* of the critical intensity to the surrounding intensity seems to determine brightness: 50 is to 100 as 20 is to 40. This generalization holds over a broad range; we can change the intensity of the ring in *B* and predict reasonably well what intensity the disc will have to have for it still to look just as bright as the disc in *A*. For a ring intensity of 50, the disc intensity must be about 25; for a ring intensity of 500, the disc intensity should be about 250, and so on (Hess & Pretori, 1894).

Notice how well relational perception accounts for brightness constancy. If the proportion of the light falling on any surface that is reflected into the eyes remains constant, the apparent brightness of an object *relative to its surrounding* does not change with changes in the absolute amount of illumination. The experiment described in the preceding paragraph provides a fairly good analogue for the everyday situation. You seldom see a single object in isolation, with nothing else in the stimulus field; nearly always there are various objects of different reflectance arranged in a complex spatial relationship. Although the amount of light reflected from any one surface may vary as the illumination changes, the *proportion* of the light falling on it that it reflects — relative to the reflectances of the surrounding objects — does not change. It is possible, however, to fool the perceptual processes into perceiving a black object reflecting a low percentage of light as white (*see* Spotlight 17-2).

Determining Brightness

Shape Constancy

We have described in detail size and brightness constancies, but there are many other constancies as well — for example, shape constancy. A rectangular door or table looks rectangular even though we are rarely in a position in which the sensory input is truly rectangular. The retinal image of an opening door, for example, or of a table below eye level, is really a trapezoid — the edge nearer us casts a longer image than the edge farther away — but the door and table still look rectangular to us. Gibson (1950, 1966) has suggested that relation to other objects in the visual field can explain shape constancy, just as it can explain size and brightness constancies.

(*After* Gelb, 1929, and Wertheimer, 1960)

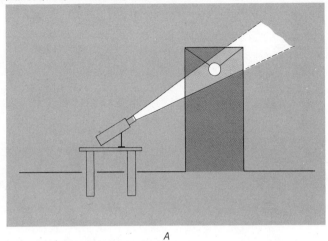

A

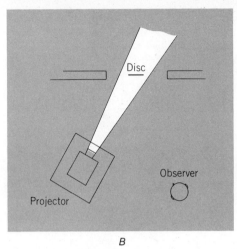

B

You can demonstrate for yourself that your perceptual experience of brightness is not just caused by what you know about the situation. Cut a circle, about 6 to 8 inches in diameter, out of a piece of nonglossy black cardboard. Suspend it, using fine black thread, in an open doorway at eye level. Now set up a projector so that it illuminates the disc but not the door frame or the wall; place the projector somewhat to one side so that the observer cannot see the wall that is lit up in the next room. Part *A* of the diagram shows how the setup looks to the observer, and part *B* shows the arrangement from above.

When the projector is off, there is nothing remarkable about the setup. You see a black disc hanging in a doorway. When the projector is turned on, however, suddenly the disc looks white. If perception of brightness were a matter of taking all relevant factors like illumination into account, your knowledge that the projector is on should result in a percept of a black disc in high illumination. But that is not the way it works. By changing the ratio of the amount of light coming to you from the disc relative to the amount of light coming to you from the background —the wall of the room visible behind the disc—you have changed the apparent brightness of the disc.

If a small piece of white paper is held immediately in front of the disc so that it too is illuminated by the projector, the disc snaps back to its black appearance. Why? Apparent brightnesses depend on stimulus *ratios*. The piece of white paper reflects much more light into your eyes than the disc; what determines the brightness of the disc now is the relation between the amount of light reflected from it and the amount of light reflected from the piece of white paper.

PERCEPTUAL CONTRAST

In **perceptual contrast,** the percept of the same stimulus is substantially altered by its *surround* or *context*. The context can either be other stimulation occurring at the same time (*simultaneous* contrast) or it can be the preceding pattern of stimulation (*successive* contrast). In general, perceptual contrast operates in such a way that a *difference* between a particular area and its surround, background, or context is enhanced. This exaggeration of a difference is not limited to vision. Water of room temperature feels cool to a hand previously held in warm water, but warm to a hand previously held in cold water; a tone can sound loud if preceded by silence but soft if it follows very loud stimulation; a moderate weight may feel heavy if preceded by a series of lightweight stimuli, light if preceded by heavy ones. In the same way, a beagle may look fairly large in a pack of toy poodles and Chihuahuas, but small if socializing with Great Danes and Saint Bernards.

Whenever the stimulus differs from its context, contrast effects are at least possible. The straight lines in Preview Figure 2 look curved in the context of concentric circles. Color Figures 5 and 7 illustrate color contrast effects, where identical gray areas take on the hue complementary to the context. Flagmakers know these effects; thus you will often see flags and pennants in complementary colors. Blue in a context of yellow is bluer than usual because of contrast.

In such phenomena as simultaneous brightness contrast (Preview Figure 5), the strength of the contrast effect depends on the magnitude of the difference between the critical area and its context as well as on the area of contrasting background — other things being equal. These "other things," which we assume to be equal but which rarely are in life, include the configuration of the stimulus. For example, in Figure 17-14 the small gray triangle in *A* looks darker than the same triangle in *B*, despite the fact that the area of the black surround is greater in *A*. We perceive the figure in *B* as a large, dark triangle with a small, lighter one on top of it; we see the figure in *A* as a dark cross with a piece attached. Thus we see the little gray triangle as lying on the black background in *B* and lying on a white background in *A*. In contrast to its white background in *A*, therefore, the triangle looks darker; but in contrast to the black background in *B*, it looks lighter. These atypical contrast effects depend on the complex processes that govern our perception of figures — some of which were discussed earlier in this chapter.

Preview Figure 5 is another illustration of how configurational variables can affect contrast. When the figure is first viewed, it tends to be seen as a reasonably uniform gray ring on a background, with the left half black and the right half white. According to the principle of simultaneous contrast, the left half of the gray ring *should* look lighter than the right half; but the *unity* of the ring seems to be sufficient to overcome this effect. If the perceptual unity of the ring is destroyed by placing a pencil along the contour separating the black and white backgrounds, the left half of the ring does look noticeably lighter than the right. You can even pull along the induced contrast effect to some extent by slowly moving the pencil to the right or left. Even though a bit of white background might begin to become visible as you move the pencil to the right, the

Figure 17-14
Relational Determination of Simultaneous Brightness Contrast

The small gray triangle in *A* is of equal intensity to that in *B*, but it looks darker. Why? Actually, *B* is simply a part of *A*, as diagram *C* shows. (After Benary, 1924)

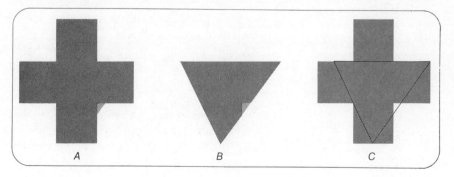

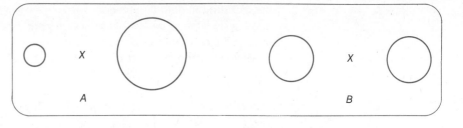

Figure 17-15
Figural Aftereffect Producing a Size Distortion
Stare at the X in figure A for 60 seconds, then stare at the X in figure B. The left-hand circle will look larger than the right-hand circle in B, even though both circles are the same size.

small amount of gray ring on the white background still continues to look light because it continues to be perceptually organized as belonging to the perceptually homogeneous left portion of the ring. Similarly, if you move the pencil to the left, you can pull the apparently darker right half of the ring partly over onto the black background. (For more on simultaneous contrast, *see* Spotlight 17-3.)

Figural Aftereffects

Successive shape and size contrast effects have been studied systematically during the last several decades. Thus, a particular set of distortions of the perception of a figure can be produced by prior stimulation with another figure. Such **figural aftereffects** have been demonstrated to occur in several sensory modalities (vision, hearing, touch, kinesthesis), and they follow certain predictable regularities. Figure 17-15 can be used to demonstrate a figural aftereffect that produces a distortion in perceived size. Stare at the X between the two circles in A (the inspection figure) for about a minute. Then immediately shift your gaze to the X in the center of B (the test figure). Which B circle now looks larger? (To convince yourself that the apparent size difference really isn't just the way the figure is drawn and is caused by the preceding exposure to A, you might repeat the experiment, but quickly turn the book upside down before you look at the X in B.) A circle looks larger if its image falls on a place on the retina previously stimulated by a small circle than if its image falls on a place on the retina previously stimulated by a large circle. Similar phenomena can also be demonstrated for the tactual-kinesthetic senses. If you rub a curved edge like the rim of a cup or the edge of a phonograph record for a minute or so, then rub a straight contour like the edge of a table, the straight edge will seem to be curved in a direction opposite to the curvature of the object you rubbed just before (such effects work better if you keep your eyes closed during the experiment). These results are predictable. Most people, when presented with analogous situations, will respond in the same way. Spotlight 17-4 is a discussion of the effects of prolonged perceptual distortion.

Another quite dramatic aftereffect can be obtained by staring at the center of a rotating spiral for 30 to 60 seconds (*see* Figure 17-16). If the spiral is rotating in one direction, it appears to be contracting; if it is rotating in the other direction, it appears to be expanding. If the spiral is stopped, it will appear to shrink if it was expanding before, but to expand if it was shrinking before. This aftereffect can even be applied to a friend's face, which will appear to shrink after you have looked at an expanding spiral for some time.

A particular simultaneous brightness-contrast effect has been named after a nineteenth-century scientist, Ernst Mach (1838–1916) who first studied it intensively. (Mach's name has also been given to high velocities—*Mach 2* means twice the speed of sound.) The **Mach effect** is a discrepancy between the perceived brightness and the physical luminance in a luminance gradient. Each of the gray rectangles to the right is of uniform reflectance (that is, luminance), yet they do not *appear* uniform, especially in the region between two different rectangles. On the dark side of the edge, the gray appears darker than it should, and on the light side, lighter than it should. This enhancement of the edge is probably caused by lateral interactions in the retina (see Chapter 22, esp. pp. 603–04).

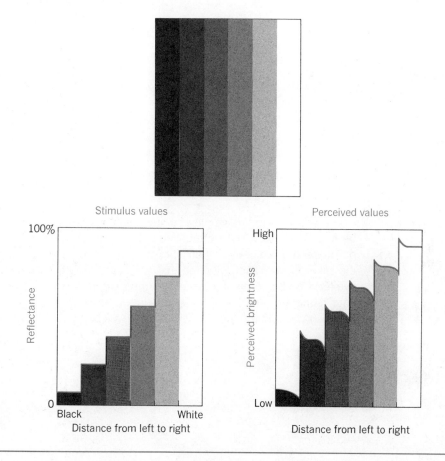

Stimulus values   Perceived values

How do we perceive movement?

By now, the naive view that our eyes passively register the real size or brightness or shape of an object in our visual field should be suspect. How about the naive view of movement? An object moves, and the image on our retina moves and that's all there is to it. Or is it?

Figure 17-16
Aftereffects of Spiral Expansion or Contraction

When the spiral is rotated clockwise, it appears to expand. If, after a minute of observation, the spiral is stopped, it will appear to contract. If you shift your gaze quickly to a friend's face, it will appear to contract too.

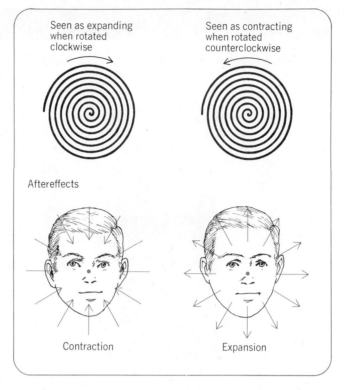

Seen as expanding when rotated clockwise

Seen as contracting when rotated counterclockwise

Aftereffects

Contraction

Expansion

The successive stimulation of different points on the retina induces the perception of movement.

In one sense, the naive view of movement is correct, although *how* it could be true has been a puzzle until quite recently. Consider what happens both out there and at the eye when, for example, a car passes by on the street. For the sake of illustration, assume that your eyes are focused on a point below eye level on the trunk of a tree across the road from you. At first, some cells on your retina are stimulated by the gray of the tree trunk. Then, as the car passes between you and the tree, those same cells are suddenly stimulated by the light

Ivo Kohler at Innsbruck, Austria, has been engaged for years in a series of experiments in which subjects wear goggles that distort the visual field in various ways (Kohler, 1962; *see* p. 459). The course of adaptation to such altered visual input is studied, sometimes over a period of several weeks or longer; during this period the only visual experience the subject has is through the distorting goggles. When the goggles are removed, readaption to normal input can take place. For example, if the lenses produce apparent curvature of vertical lines, successive contrast effects occur. When the goggles are finally removed, vertical lines look curved in the *opposite* direction.

A particularly dramatic finding was obtained in an experiment in which the subject wore spectacles with split-color lenses. Yellow glass made up the right half and blue glass the left half of each lens, so that when subjects looked to the right, the world looked yellow, and when they looked to the left, it looked blue. Soon, as in other experiments, adaptation to the altered visual input occurred and everything looked reasonably normal. But when the spectacles were removed, the world looked blue for a time when the subjects turned their eyes to the right and yellow when they looked to the left. That is, colors *complementary* to those of the spectacles were induced in subsequent vision, depending on which way the eyes were turned. An interesting aspect of this finding is the implication that not only visual input but also some kind of signal indicating eye direction affects the percept.

---

reflected to your eyes from the passing car; after the car passes they are again stimulated by the tree trunk. Any individual retinal cell receives one stimulus at one time (from the tree), a different one at another time (from the car), then the first one again (from the tree). So at one time any nerve cell fires more or less vigorously than at another. How can we, under these circumstances, perceive any movement?

The answer is that the retina receives information from a broad visual field. The car stimulates cells on one side of the retina before it stimulates others; and cells at higher stations in the nervous system receive inputs from different parts of the retina. Therefore, the relative timing of stimulation at different retinal positions provides information about movement. (*See also* p. 613.)

THE RELATIVITY OF PERCEIVED MOTION

Perception of speed, like perception of brightness, size, and other attributes, appears to be mainly relative. We do not see speed in an absolute sense, but always how fast something is moving in relation to something else. Behind each of the two rectangular apertures in Figure 17-17 a continuous strip of paper moves to the right. Every part of the diagram on the right is twice the size of its corresponding part in the left-hand diagram. Assume that the two apertures are physically much farther separated than they are in the figure so that the observer cannot see both at once, but must look first at one and then

Figure 17-17
The Relational Determination of Apparent Speed
Apparent speed varies with the size of the stimulus. (After Brown, 1928)

Figure 17-18
The Relational Determination of Apparent Direction of Motion. (After Wallach, 1935)

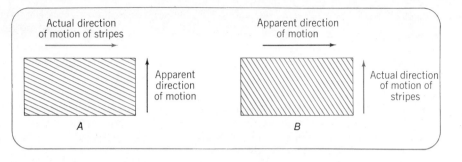

at the other. How fast must the paper move behind the larger opening for it to look as though the dots are moving to the right just as fast as the dots are moving in the smaller diagram? If the same paper speed is used for both, it looks as though the dots in the larger framework are moving much more slowly than the dots in the smaller framework. To make it look as though the speeds of the dots are the same in both frames, the paper speed in the larger one will have to be about twice as fast as the paper speed in the smaller one. The perception of speed, in other words, seems to follow principles very similar to those obtaining in the constancies: it is *relative* displacement that counts.

The apparent *direction* of motion also depends on relational, interactive processes. The framework within which motion occurs plays a substantial role in the perceived direction of motion. If, for example, on a partly cloudy day, you look up at the sky to try to determine in which direction the clouds are moving, the apparent direction will depend greatly on the characteristics of other stationary and moving things visible at the same time. As you look up, if you can see the edge of the roof of a building, the clouds will often seem to be moving in a direction that is at right angles to that contour. The perceived direction of motion also tends to be economical; in ambiguous situations, apparent motion yields the smallest apparent displacement per unit time that is consistent with the physical stimulus conditions.

An experiment that demonstrates this principle is illustrated in Figure 17-18. In both cases, assume that a continuous strip of paper is moving behind the rectangular apertures in the direction indicated by the arrow. Even though the paper is actually moving from left to right in A, it looks as though a series of stripes is slowly moving upward. Similarly, in B, even though the paper is actually moving upward, it looks as though the stripes are moving to the right.

The perception of motion, then, like many other aspects of perception, is economical. We perceive the pattern of motion that entails the least change. If

Figure 17-19
Depth from Motion

Successive views of a changing, flat, two-dimensional pattern can result in the perception of a stable, rotating, three-dimensional object. (After Wallach and O'Connell, 1953)

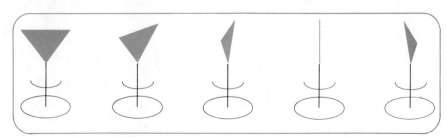

we obtain successive views of a rotating object (Figure 17-19), it would be possible to see a sequence of flat patterns of different shapes; but a percept of a single rotating, three-dimensional object of unchanging shape is simpler—which is the typical output when such incoming information is processed. Shape constancy, then, can play a significant role in the perception of motion.

INDUCED AND APPARENT MOTION

There is not a perfect correspondence between the part of a physical stimulus that is actually moving and the part that is perceived as moving. Generally, the enclosing framework is seen as stationary, and smaller parts contained within it are seen as moving. On a windy, moonlit night, with variable clouds, it can look as though the clouds are standing still while the moon goes scudding across the sky in a direction opposite to that of the actual motion of the clouds. A laboratory analogue of such **induced motion** is shown in Figure 17-20. If a spot of light is projected on a screen, and the screen is slowly moved to the right, the screen appears to be stationary while the spot seems to move to the left (Duncker, 1929). Movement as a perceptual experience does not have to be caused by a physical stimulus moving across the retina.

Apparent movement, that is, perceived motion in the absence of actual physical displacement in the image on the retina, is often indistinguishable from real motion. There are many different kinds of apparent motion. Motion can be perceived in stimulus patterns in which nothing is being displaced. One way to do this is to remove the framework entirely, say by having a stationary pinpoint of light in a completely dark room. When there is no framework to which the pinpoint can maintain a stable relationship, the light appears to move all by itself. This phenomenon has been called **autokinesis** (from Greek roots meaning "self" and "movement").

Whenever you watch a movie, you are, of course, experiencing apparent motion; the film is just a rapidly presented series of still pictures. An apparatus far simpler than a movie projector can be used to study the determinants of this kind of apparent movement, called **stroboscopic motion.** The simplest consists of two lights presented side-by-side. If these two lights are switched on and off on an appropriate schedule, it will appear as though a single light is *moving* back and forth. (Neon display lights often illustrate this motion.) With such an arrangement, the optimal time and space intervals for producing stroboscopic motion can be investigated. If the time interval is too short, the observer reports two simultaneous flashes; if the time interval is too long, the observer reports two successive flashes. Optimal apparent motion is typically obtained with a time interval of 30 to 60 milliseconds between flashes (Wertheimer, 1912).

Figure 17-20
The Relational Determination of Motion

If a spot of light is projected from a fixed point onto a screen that is moved to the right (A), the screen appears stationary, while the spot is perceived to move to the left (B).

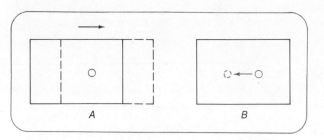

SUMMARY

Perception organizes the sensory input into figures and grounds according to various **Gestalt** principles: **similarity, proximity, closure, common fate,** and good continuation. These principles are special cases of a general tendency toward economy of organization, the **law of Prägnanz,** which states that the organization or structure of any whole will be as good as conditions permit. The **goodness** of a figure can be assessed in several ways, such as how little information is required to describe it. In camouflage, the principles of perceptual organization are applied to break up natural figures.

Binocular disparity produces visual **depth perception** by a process of **stereopsis,** which does not seem to depend on familiarity with the perceived objects. Among monocular cues to depth perception are **motion parallax, linear perspective,** relative size, aerial perspective, interposition, and location in the visual field. The location of objects in auditory space is discovered through such **monaural cues** as intensity and the relative amount of high-frequency components in the sound, and through **binaural cues** such as the differences in intensity and latency at the two ears.

The **perceptual constancies** are relational processes. Our perceptions of objects remain fairly stable, even though the same object may present very different stimulation to the sense organs on different occasions; we tend to perceive objects' characteristics *in relation to* the characteristics of other stimuli in the perceptual field. The apparent size of an object does not change as the size of its retinal image changes **(size constancy)** if the object's distance is understood from other cues. Nor does the apparent brightness of an object change with the illumination it reflects into the observer's eye **(brightness constancy);** rather, apparent brightness is determined by the ratio of the amount of light the object reflects to the amount of light reflected by the object's surroundings.

The opposite of perceptual constancy is **perceptual contrast.** Depending on the context, the same stimulus may appear quite different at different times. In both simultaneous and successive contrast, perception operates to exaggerate the differences between an object and its context. Simultaneous contrast includes the enhancement of brightness differences and the induction of complementary hues, as well as temperature, loudness, and size effects. Among successive contrast phenomena are **figural aftereffects** —systematic distortions in the apparent shape and size of figures perceived after prolonged prior stimulation by other figures—and various motion aftereffects.

Perception of real movement is also determined by relations among stimuli, including both the integration of information from separate sensory elements and the apparent speed and direction of perceived motion. Objects whose image is not actually being displaced on the retina may nevertheless be perceived as moving. Instances of such apparent motion include **induced movement, autokinesis,** and **stroboscopic motion.**

18

Sensory Bases of Perception

How does psychophysics relate the physical world to the psychological world?

How relatively sensitive are we?

How do our sensory systems function?

The processes of perception construct meanings out of sensory stimulation received from the environment, as we have seen. We will now explore how perceptual experience depends on physical stimulation. Using the four conceptual categories we mentioned at the start of Chapter 16, we are now relating level 1—descriptions of the physical world—to level 4—descriptions of the perceiver's behavior, both verbal and nonverbal.

How does psychophysics relate the physical world to the psychological world?

PHYSICAL DIMENSIONS VERSUS PSYCHOLOGICAL DIMENSIONS

Psychophysics is the branch of psychology that tries to express mathematically the relationships between the physical dimensions of the stimulus and the psychological dimensions of perception. Visual brightness is a useful illustration. A light bulb converts electrical energy (measured in joules or joules/sec = watts) into radiant energy, some of which is felt as heat and some of which is seen as visible light. The amount of light emitted by a bulb is also expressed in energy units, such as watts or lumens. A typical 100-watt bulb emits 97 watts of heat and 3 watts of visible light. When light enters the eye it can evoke the psychological experience of brightness. But the magnitude of the brightness sensation is not related to the physical energy of the light in a simple way. For example, a 100-watt bulb does not look twice as bright as a 50-watt bulb; the exact relationship will be taken up later in this chapter.

ABSOLUTE THRESHOLD

Did the telephone just ring next door? Did the baby just cry? Can you see that faint star? Our senses are very sensitive, and under good conditions we can detect amazingly small amounts of stimulus energy. The weakest stimulus that can be detected is called the **absolute threshold,** and it is expressed in physical units. The absolute thresholds for the five senses are given in Table 18-1.

Measuring the Threshold

How do we actually measure a threshold? If we were randomly to present to a person a series of sounds of different intensities, ranging from strong to very weak, and after each presentation ask, "Did you hear the sound?" we would obtain the results shown in Figure 18-1. The person always hears intense sounds. But to weaker sounds, on some trials the response would be "yes" and on other trials "no." Finally, for very weak sounds, the response would be "No, I didn't hear anything" almost every time. Figure 18-1 represents a fundamental finding of psychophysics: there is no single stimulus

TABLE 18-1	The absolute thresholds of some senses
Sense	*Absolute Threshold*
Vision	Candle flame at a distance of 30 miles on a dark clear night (about 10 quanta of light energy)
Hearing	Tick of a watch 20 feet away, in a quiet setting (about 0.0002 dyne/cm²)
Taste	One teaspoon of sugar dissolved in 2 gallons of water (about one part in 2,000); saccharine, about one part in 1,000,000
Smell	A single drop of perfume diffused in the volume of air in an average three-room apartment (about one part in 500,000,000)
Touch	The wing of a bee falling on your cheek from a distance of 1 centimeter

After Galanter, 1962.

Figure 18-1
The Threshold Zone
The absolute threshold is often defined as the intensity at which the stimulus will be detected on 50 percent of the trials. You can also think of the threshold as a zone or region surrounding the 50 percent report intensity.

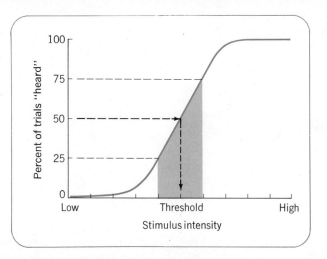

energy above which a person will *always* detect it and below which the person will *never* detect it. Then what is a threshold? It is the amount of stimulus energy that will result in detection on some specified percent of the trials. In Figure 18-1, 50 percent detection is used to define threshold, but other values could be (and often are) used. Thus, to say that a stimulus is below threshold is *not* to say that it is not detectable; it is to say that it will be detected on fewer than, say, 50 percent of the trials.

THEORY OF SIGNAL DETECTION

The experimental procedure just described contains a serious weakness: it does not separate the person's decision to say that the sound was heard from the actual detection. Suppose, for example, that people on each trial said "yes," regardless of whether they thought they heard the tone. Such people would appear to have a fantastically low threshold because no stimulus energy would cause them to say "yes" less than 100 percent of the time. Even honest subjects differ, based on how cautious they are in deciding to say "yes." Some people may be very eager to say that they hear the test sound; such people may say yes whenever they have the slightest hint that they heard it. Others may be more cautious, saying "yes" only when absolutely certain that they hear the sound. When two such hypothetical people are tested on the sound detection task described above, the results might look like those in Figure 18-2. At a sound intensity level to which person *B* says "Yes, I heard it" 50 percent of the time, person *A* says "Yes" 90 percent of the time. It would appear that the cautious person (*B*) has a higher threshold than the less cautious one (*A*). But is this difference caused by a difference in *sensitivity* to the sound or by the different *decision strategies* each used? The theory of **signal detection** has provided psychologists with a powerful theoretical framework and practical methodologies that allow us to separate the willingness to say yes (the **response criterion**) from detectability.

To judge a person's performance adequately we need to know not only the rate at which "yes" is said when the sound is really there (the hit rate) but also the rate at which "yes" is said when the sound is really *not* there (the

Figure 18-2
Psychometric Functions
The graph shows the thresholds for persons *A* and *B*. Although they appear to have different thresholds, they do not necessarily have different detection sensitivities.

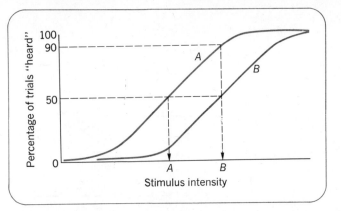

false-alarm rate). Generally, if one's hit rate for detecting a weak signal is greater than the false-alarm rate, it means that one does have some perceptual sensitivity to the signal. People have been carefully studied to see how the hit rate and the false-alarm rate for detecting a fixed weak signal change when they are asked to vary their response criterion. For example, on one day they are instructed "Be extremely cautious; don't say 'yes' unless you are absolutely sure that the sound was present" (high criterion). On another day they are told, "Say 'yes' if there is the slightest possibility that the sound is present" (low criterion). On still other days the instructions are intended to induce intermediate criteria. Two types of experimental trials are presented: those where a faint signal (sound) is actually present and those where no signal is present. As subjects change their criterion, their hit and false-alarm rates vary in the manner shown in Figure 18-3.

When a person exercises great caution (holds a high criterion), the hit rate is low, but so is the false-alarm rate. An example of this is shown by subject 1 in Figure 18-3, who has a hit rate of 50 percent and a false-alarm rate of 8.9 percent. By exercising less caution, one can increase the hit rate, but only at the expense of increasing the false-alarm rate as well. For example, subject 2 has a hit rate of 75 percent, but a false-alarm rate of 25 percent. Throwing caution to the winds, saying yes at the slightest hint of a sound — as the subject 3 in Figure 18-3 might be said to have done — might give a high hit rate (90 percent) but would also result in a high false-alarm rate (47 percent).

The bowed curve in Figure 18-3 is called a "relative (or receiver) operating characteristic (ROC)" (Swets, 1973). The ROC curve is derived mathematically from the **theory of signal detection.** It enables one to predict for a given degree of detection sensitivity all the possible combinations of the hit and false-alarm rates for different response criteria. (If the hit rate on the curve in Figure 18-3 is 70 percent, what is the false-alarm rate?) The degree to which the ROC curve bows away from the diagonal indicates the degree of detection sensitivity: the more bowing, the greater a person's sensitivity to a given stimulus. The amount of bowing is indicated by a statistic called d' (dee prime).

A different statistic, called β (beta), measures the degree of caution exercised by the subject. In Figure 18-3, points 1, 2, and 3 reflect different β values (2.48, 1.00, and 0.44, respectively); but all three points correspond to the same sensitivity ($d' = 1.35$). Point 4 on the other hand indicates greater sensitivity ($d' = 2.12$) while point 5 represents lower sensitivity ($d' = 0.89$).

Now return to the two people represented in Figure 18-2. At the stimulus strength where person B showed a hit rate of 50 percent, person A had a hit rate of 90 percent. Do they have the same sensitivity? To find the answer, we need to know their false-alarm rates for the same stimulus. If we assume that person A had a false-alarm rate of 8.9 percent and B one of 47 percent, then point 1 in Figure 18-3 would represent person A and point 3 would represent person B. Because these points fall on the same ROC curve, we can conclude that persons A and B have the same detection sensitivity ($d' = 1.35$); they differ only in their response criteria. If the false-alarm rate for person B had been only 20 percent, then we can conclude that B is more sensitive than person A ($d' = 2.12$; point 4). If the false-alarm rate for B were 65 percent, then B would be less sensitive than A ($d' = 0.89$; point 5).

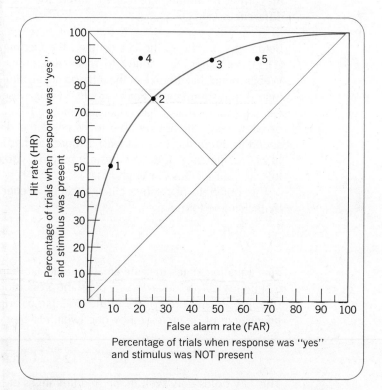

Figure 18-3
A Relative Operating Characteristic (ROC) Curve for an Auditory Detection Experiment
Performance of a subject is described by the combination of hit rate (HR) and false-alarm rate (FAR). Although subjects 1, 2, and 3 have different response criteria (β), they have the same detection sensitivity (d') because their HR-FAR pairs fall on the same ROC curve. Subject 4 has a higher sensitivity (d') because the HR-FAR pair falls farther from the diagonal than 1, 2, and 3; subject 5 has a lower sensitivity.

Signal detection theory has widespread applications in many areas of human performance. Depending on the relative consequences of a hit, a false alarm, or a miss ("no" when a stimulus is present), it is possible to adjust the criterion to best advantage. For example, a physician trying to detect cancer in patients should adopt a very lenient criterion, because the consequences of missing the signs of cancer are far more serious than those of falsely detecting some.

How relatively sensitive are we?

We have gone into some detail to examine the advanced techniques used to measure the least amount of physical energy that is necessary to elicit detection. Of equal importance to psychologists is *how* different two things have to be for the difference to be detected. Such measures, specified in terms of the physical stimuli, are called **difference thresholds,** or **just noticeable differences (jnd's).**

WEBER'S LAW

Before the middle of the last century, the German physiologist E. H. Weber (1834) measured the ability to make discriminations between two events. Weber found that the size of the jnd was not absolute, but relative to the magnitude of the stimulation. For example, Weber observed that even though you *can* just notice that it has gotten brighter if 1 candle is added to 12 burning candles, you will not be able to perceive the difference when 1 candle is added to 24. In this case, at least 2 more candles are required before you can detect a difference. If 60 candles are burning, you must add at least 5 candles to notice an increase in brightness.

This principle of relative change, called **Weber's law,** can be symbolized by the simple formula:

$$\frac{\Delta I}{I} = k$$

This equation states that the smallest detectable increment in the intensity of a stimulus (ΔI or delta I) is a constant proportion (k) of the intensity of the stimulus already present (I). In the example of brightness above, the stimulus intensity must be increased by one-twelfth to be detected:

$$\frac{\Delta I}{I} = k = \frac{1}{12} = \frac{2}{24} = \frac{5}{60}$$

This law holds very well in the middle ranges of intensity, although it breaks down at the extremes; at very low and very high intensities more must be added than the formula indicates to notice a change. The constant k is different for different stimulus dimensions; it can be readily determined by discovering by what proportion a stimulus must be changed to yield a just noticeable difference. This fraction turns out to be about $\frac{1}{20}$ for the intensity of a tone, $\frac{1}{7}$ for pressure on the skin, $\frac{1}{50}$ for lifted weights, $\frac{1}{12}$ for the saltiness of a liquid, and $\frac{1}{333}$ for the frequency of a tone, to list a few (Teghtsoonian, 1971). One could argue that Weber's law was one of the first clear demonstrations of relativity in psychology.

We have discussed the minimum energy required to just detect a stimulus (absolute threshold) and to just detect a difference between two stimuli (jnd). But in everyday life, most stimuli are well above threshold and evoke within us sensations that are related to the amount of physical energy in the stimulus. What then is the relationship between physical energy and psychological sensation?

PSYCHOLOGICAL MAGNITUDE AND THE POWER LAW

To relate the magnitude of the physical stimulus to the magnitude of the perceptual sensation, we need a measure of the sensation magnitude. In 1860 Gustav Theodor Fechner developed methods for measuring the strength of such sensations as loudness and brightness in his landmark book, *Elements of Psychophysics*. Fechner was the first to develop a mathematical relationship between psychological magnitude, Ψ (psi), and physical magnitude, Φ (phi):

$$\Psi = k \log \Phi \qquad \textbf{(Fechner's law)}$$

This relationship makes strong and explicit predictions: two candles will *not* seem twice as bright as one; doubling the intensity of a sound will *not* make it sound twice as loud!

Before we continue, do the following experiment. In Figure 18-4 each row contains a black square, a gray square, and a white square. We have arbitrarily called the brightness of the black square 0.0 and of the white 20.0. Using these two values as anchors, assign a number between 0 and 20 to the gray square in each row; let the number represent the brightness of the gray relative to the black and white; that is, the darker the gray, the closer to 0.0 you will rate it; the lighter the gray, the closer to 20.0 you will judge it. It will help if you prop the book open in such a way that the page is evenly illuminated without glare.

Fill out this table of brightness ratings before reading further:

A _____, B _____, C _____, D _____, E _____, F _____

Figure 18-5 is a graph on which you can plot your own results. On the colored line running up from A, put a dot at the height for your rating of the gray square in row A; then do the same for your judgments of the other squares. Now draw a line connecting your successive ratings from left to right across the graph (D, F, B, A, C, E).

The bowed line in Figure 18-5 presents the means of ratings of the gray squares made by twenty students; each means is represented by a black dot. Each colored line represents the actual reflectance of each of the squares. For example, the black square reflects only about 6.5 percent of the light falling on it, while the white square reflects 80 percent. Probably your ratings do not agree exactly with those printed in Figure 18-5, and they may not make a smooth graph. Some variability is to be expected. But which line do your ratings more closely resemble—the curve connecting the black points or the diagonal line? The diagonal line shows the results that would have occurred if your perception of brightness were a direct, linear function of the amount of light reaching your eye from the page. In that case, then C (which reflects about 40 percent of the light) would have been judged about half as bright as

Figure 18-4
Rating the Brightness of
Various Shades of Gray
Follow the directions on
p. 495 and do these ratings
before proceeding.

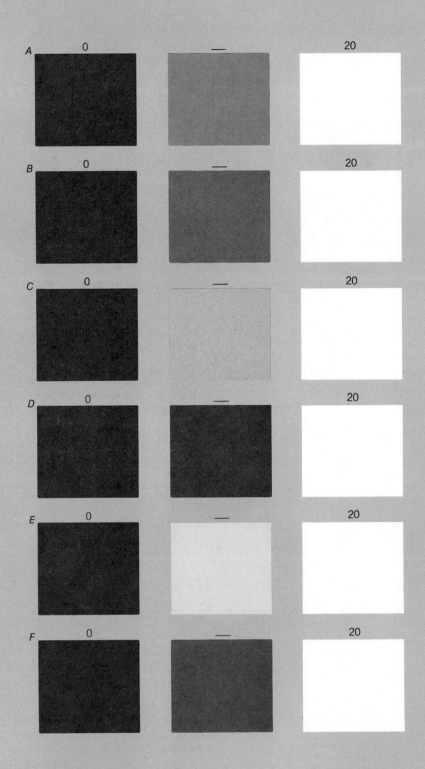

Figure 18-5
Ratings of Grays

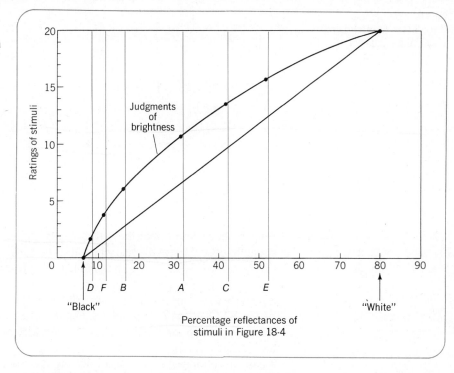

white. But as you see, your perception of brightness is *not* a linear function of the amount of light, but forms a bow-shaped curve.

Your results are rather like (but not exactly like) the predictions made by Fechner's law. The intensities of our sensations are not linear fun~ ns of physical intensities. Even before Fechner's time, astronomers classii. stars' intensities in "magnitudes" of about equal steps of perceived brightness. When their physical intensities were later measured, each magnitude was found to be about one logarithmic unit removed from the next; the astronomers had devised a logarithmic scale of brightness without planning to do so! The physical intensity of sound is measured in **decibels,** another logarithmic unit. Sixty decibels represents *ten times* as much sound power as 50 decibels and is *one hundred times* as powerful as 40 decibels. The Richter scale, used to measure the intensity of earthquakes, is also logarithmic; an earthquake that registers 6.3 is ten times as powerful as one that registers 5.3.

More precise measurements have shown that the relationship between stimulus intensity and perceptual magnitude is not exactly logarithmic, but more closely follows a **power law.** According to this law, perceptual magnitude increases in proportion to the physical intensity raised to some power (n):

$$\Psi = k \, \phi^n$$

The value of the exponent n depends on the particular sense organ. As before, Ψ stands for the psychological magnitude, Φ for the physical intensity, and k is a constant. The power law is also known as **Stevens' law,** named for the American psychologist S. S. Stevens, who first formulated it (Marks, 1974; Stevens, 1975).

Figure 18-6
How Some Psychological Magnitudes (Ψ) Vary With Some Physical Magnitudes (ϕ)
On the left, data are plotted on linear coordinates; on the right, on double logarithmic coordinates. The fact that all the functions become linear in the second graph is a demonstration of Stevens' power law. (After Stevens, 1975)

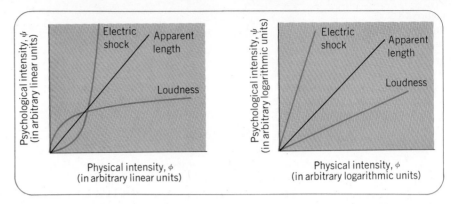

It has been found that the senses differ from each other in how rapidly the strength of experience rises when the intensity of the stimulus is increased (Teghtsoonian, 1971). The exponent *n* reflects this difference. For the judged length of a line in vision, the exponent is 1.0; that is, apparent length increases directly and linearly with physical length. This linear relationship is shown by the black lines in the graphs of Figure 18-6. For many senses, however, the value of the exponent is less than 1.0. For a point source of light presented to the darkness-adapted eye, $n = 0.5$; and for loudness, $n = 0.6$. The slow increase in loudness with sound intensity is shown by the lower curves of the graphs in Figure 18-6. In some cases, sensation increases more rapidly than stimulus intensity; for judgments of weights lifted by the hand, $n = 1.45$. And when electric shock is applied to the fingertips, the sensation increases rapidly with shock strengths: $n = 3.5$!

How do our sensory systems function?

The sensory systems convert physical energy from the environment into nerve impulses to be interpreted by the brain. We will take up vision first and in greater detail; then we will turn to hearing.

VISION

The physical energy to which our visual system responds is electromagnetic radiation. This radiation comes in very small packets of energy called **quanta.** Each quantum can be described by a single number, its **wavelength.** (The wavelength is the distance between two adjacent crests of a vibratory activity.) Quanta with very long wavelengths (several meters long) are radio energy. Gamma rays and X rays have very short wavelengths. Our visual system only responds to quanta whose wavelengths lie within a very narrow range, from about 400 to 700 nanometers (1 **nanometer** = 10^{-9} meters). (See Figure 18-7.) Such quanta of light energy are called **photons** (from the Greek word **photos,** meaning "light"). Each photon is a very small amount of energy; the exact amount depends on its wavelength. A single photon of wavelength 560 nanometers (abbreviated "nm") contains only 3.55×10^{-19} joules of energy! A 100-watt light bulb, which gives off about 3 watts of visible light, is actually

Figure 18-7
The Electromagnetic
Spectrum and the Visible
Spectrum
The lower part, the visible
spectrum, is an expansion of a
small region of the upper
electromagnetic spectrum. It
is only this narrow range—
from about 400 to 700
nanometers—that the visual
system processes as light.
(After Chapanis, Garner, &
Morgan, 1949)

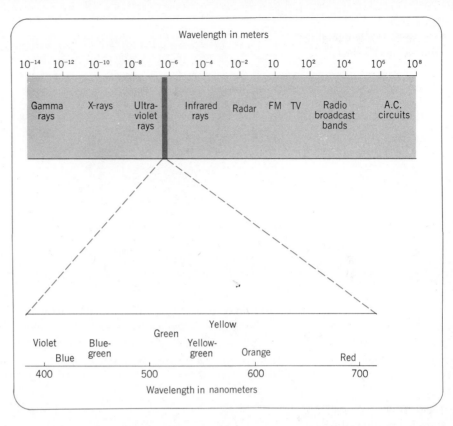

radiating about 8,000,000,000,000,000,000 photons per second! When
quanta enter the eye, they can evoke visual sensations. The exact nature of such
sensations depends both on the wavelengths of the quanta and the number
of quanta per second.

Scotopic Vision

If the number of quanta per second is low—for example at night—the sensations evoked by the light are described as shades of gray. No color is experienced. Such vision is called **scotopic vision** (from the Greek word *skotos,*
meaning "darkness") and is mediated by photoreceptors in the eye called
rods. The eye is not equally sensitive to all wavelengths of light. The solid
line in Figure 18-8 shows the threshold energy in scotopic vision for different
wavelengths of light. The least amount of energy (highest sensitivity, or lowest
threshold) is required of a wavelength of 507 nm. At 400 nm, 108 times more
energy is required; and for 700 nm of light, about 56,000 times more energy is
needed to see the light at all! At scotopic levels of light, our visual system
has no ability to discriminate among wavelengths. Thus the visual sensation
evoked by 1 unit of energy at 507 nm will be *identical* to the sensation evoked
by 108 units of energy at 400 nm—they would both appear gray.

Photopic Vision

If the energy of the 507 nm light is increased (more quanta per second), the
visual experience undergoes a remarkable change. When the energy is about

Figure 18-8
**Relative Energy Required for
Scotopic and Photopic
Vision**

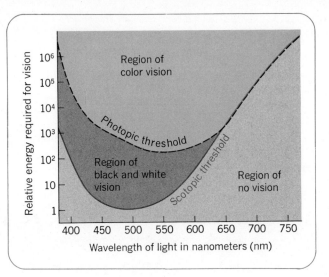

400 times that at threshold, the appearance of the light changes from gray to green. Color experiences are only generated at higher levels of light energy, such as in daylight, and represent a shift to a different kind of retinal receptor called the **cone.** The neural activities of the three different kinds of cones (*see* Chapter 22) are combined by the nervous system in such a way as to create

Figure 18-9
**Eye's Range of Sensitivity
to Light**

The range from the most intense to the weakest visible stimulus is over 10 billion times, or over 10 logarithmic units. At any one time, however, the eye adapts to the prevailing level of luminance and can discriminate over a range of only about 2 log units. (From Riggs, 1965)

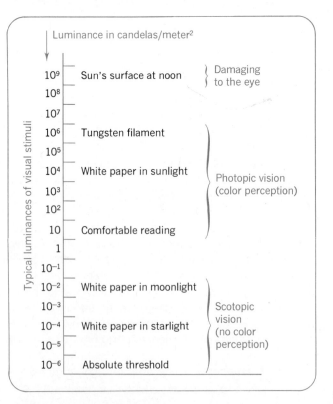

Figure 18-10
The Dark Adaptation Function
The curve shows the threshold intensity (the smallest amount of light energy that can be detected) as a function of length of time in darkness. The rate of increase in sensitivity rather closely parallels the rate at which sunlight fades at dusk. The discontinuity in the curve is caused by, first, adaptation of the cones, and then, of the rods.

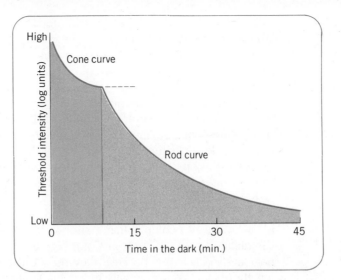

the experience of color. Such vision is called **photopic vision.** Photopic vision occurs at daylight levels of light energy, involves the cone photoreceptors, and is marked by the perceptual experience of color. By contrast, scotopic vision occurs at low levels of light, involves the rod photoreceptors, and gives no experience of color, only shades of gray. (To compare photopic and scotopic vision, *see* Color Figure 9.)

The eye can function over the very wide range of energies shown in Figure 18-9. The most intense light that the eye can view without damage has over 10 billion times the energy as the dimmest light you can see. This total range is over 10 logarithmic units wide. At any one time, however, the effective range of sensitivity is much less (about 2 logarithmic units—that is, the most intense light is about 100 times the energy of the weakest). If the eye is adapted to high photopic levels of light, and then is exposed to the dark, it takes time for it to adjust (or adapt) to the new level. The time course of this process of dark adaptation is shown in Figure 18-10. Almost everyone has entered a movie theater on a sunny afternoon. At first it is so dark that finding a seat is difficult. But after a few minutes, when the eye has adapted to the lower level of light, one can see quite well.

If the sensitivity of the eye shifts from photopic to scotopic vision the relative brightness of colors changes. This effect is called the **Purkinje shift,** after the Czech scientist who discovered it. Look again at Figure 18-8. Photopic vision is most sensitive to light of 560 nm wavelength. Thus if you compared the visual appearance of a 560 nm light with an equal amount of energy of 510 nm light, the 560 nm light would look brighter (the 560 nm light also appears yellowish-green and the 510 nm light appears deep green). When you shift to scotopic vision, however, the relative brightness of equal amounts of 560 nm and 510 nm energy reverses. Now the 510 nm light appears brighter than the 560 nm light (one appears as a lighter shade of gray compared to the other), because the scotopic system is most sensitive to wavelengths around 510 nm.

Color Experience

Wavelength and energy are physical properties of light. Color is a perceptual experience created by the brain. The color experience can vary along three dimensions: hue, saturation, and brightness (see Color Figure 4). **Hue** is the dimension along which the color experience is given different color names. Red, purple, green, orange, yellow, and violet are hues. The dimension of **saturation** describes how rich the hue experience is relative to white light. Pink is a desaturated red, for example. The third dimension of color experience is **brightness,** or how light or dark the color is. Navy blue is a relatively dark blue. The lower half of Color Figure 4 illustrates these three dimensions. The hue yellow is on the left and the hue blue on the right. The horizontal distance to the center represents saturation and the vertical distance represents brightness.

Effect of Wavelength   The perception of a specific color or hue, for people who are not color "blind," strongly depends on the wavelength of the stimulating light, as shown in Color Figure 3. Most objects in our world appear a specific color because they reflect to our eyes the particular wavelengths of light associated with that color. Sunlight and light from incandescent bulbs radiate energy at all visible wavelengths. When our visual system is stimulated by equal energy at each wavelength, we have the perceptual experience of white. A leaf looks green because it absorbs short and long wavelength light and reflects back to our eye those middle wavelengths that evoke the color sensation green. A bluebird's feathers look blue because the pigment in the feather absorbs the long and middle wavelengths and reflects back only the short wavelengths, those that evoke the color experience of blue.

Color Mixing   If you were to shine light of one wavelength from a projector onto a screen and then shine light of different wavelength from a second projector onto the same spot on the screen, a viewer would experience a color that is different from either of the two colors evoked by the lights (*see* Color Figure 1). For example, if light of 700 nm wavelength (which normally appears red) is mixed in this manner with light of 520 nm (which alone appears green), the color experience is neither red nor green, but yellow. This process is called **additive color mixture;** it should be remembered, however, that it is the lights of different wavelengths, not the color experiences, that are being mixed. Color is a perceptual experience. The experience of yellow evoked by the mixture of two wavelengths is identical to and indistinguishable from the experience of yellow evoked by the single wavelength of 575 nm.

Several principles of additive color mixture are efficiently summarized in the **color circle** (Color Figure 3). Any two colors directly opposite each other in the circle (such as orange-yellow and blue) are **complementary;** complementary colors are those which, when added together, produce an experience of white or gray (depending on brightness). If the two colors are not directly opposite, the hue resulting from the combination will be midway between the two on the color circle. (The caption of Color Figure 3 explains some of the laws of color mixture symbolized in the circle.)

The result of mixing lights is quite different from mixing pigments like watercolors. Colored lights *add* their dominant wavelengths to the mixture; colored pigments, on the other hand, *subtract* (that is, they absorb) wavelengths other than those that give the pigment its particular hue. Compare

Color Figures 1 and 2 to see the difference. In an additive mixture, the complementary colors orange-yellow and blue produce white. In a **subtractive color mixture** — as when an artist mixes blue and orange-yellow paints — the result is pigment that looks green.

Color experiences are not produced only by stimulation with particular wavelengths of light. Pressure on the eyeball, the ingestion of various toxic substances, minute electric currents applied to the eye, or a blow on the head can all yield the experience of highly saturated, brilliant colors. Color is in the perception of the observer; it is not in the visual stimulus.

Prolonged exposure to particular stimuli can also lead to the experience of colors after the initial stimulation is terminated. If you stare at a brilliant red patch for 30 seconds and then look at a neutral gray or white section of wall or at a blank sheet of white paper, you will see an eerie green **afterimage** of the red object floating there mysteriously. Comparably, a strong yellow stimulus will produce a blue afterimage. (The color circle in Color Figure 3 helps to predict these effects; a **negative afterimage** is typically complementary in color to the inducing stimulus.)

A rather striking instance of a negative afterimage is the complementary-colored American flag in the color section (Color Figure 6). The size of such negative afterimages, incidentally, varies with the distance of the surface on which they are projected. You can demonstrate this readily for yourself by developing a good afterimage, then projecting it on the page of a book, on a near wall, and on a farther wall. The farther away you look, the larger the afterimage seems to be.

Visual Acuity

The ophthalmologist's or optometrist's eye chart, designed to assess your need for glasses, is really a test of the resolving power of the visual system. If you can distinguish at a viewing distance of 20 feet what a "normal" eye can distinguish at 20 feet, then you are said to have a visual **acuity** of 20/20. If, however, at 20 feet you can resolve what a normal eye can resolve at a viewing distance of 200 feet then you have 20/200 vision, and you need to wear glasses. Figure 18-11 shows typical patterns used to test visual acuity.

Figure 18-11
Patterns for Measuring Visual Acuity
In *A*, the viewer must indicate which way the letter E is pointing; in *B*, where the break in the circle is. In *C*, you report the letters that you can read, and in *D*, you indicate which line is broken. The patterns in *B* are called the Landolt rings and are the international standard acuity test pattern.

Figure 18-12
Grating Patterns Used to Measure the Modulation Sensitivity Function

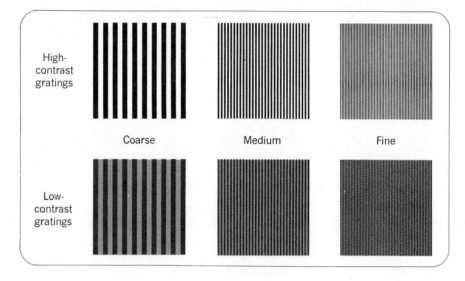

Recently a new, more complete way to specify the resolving power of the visual system has been developed in the laboratory. This technique measures the **modulation sensitivity function** and uses as test patterns gratings like the ones shown in Figure 18-12. These gratings can be varied in fineness (bars to the inch), and in contrast; that is, they can be made to appear as light and dark gray bars (low contrast) or as black and white bars (high contrast). In fact, the contrast can be made so low that one cannot see the bars at all. The technique of measuring the modulation sensitivity function is to measure the threshold contrast required for detection of gratings of different widths. A normal person has a modulation sensitivity function like the one graphed in Figure 18-13. As the grating is made finer and finer, greater and greater contrast is needed to make the lines visible. Finally, at the limit of resolution, the contrast necessary for visibility is at the maximum possible (black and white lines), and the spacing between the lines corresponds to the visual acuity of the individual as measured in the clinic. The modulation sensitivity function is a more complete description of the resolving power of our visual system than the clinical measure of acuity. It measures not only how well we see very small objects but also how well we see objects of all sizes. Some patients who have suffered brain damage complain that "things don't look normal"; but when tested with an acuity chart such as those in Figure 18-11, they are found to have normal acuity. When the modulation sensitivity function is measured, however, some of these patients are found to have a selective loss of sensitivity —only in the middle range of sizes (Bodis-Wollner, 1972).

Visual acuity in photopic vision is highest in the center of the retina, the **fovea,** and drops off rapidly to either side, as shown in Figure 18-14. There is a blind spot on one place of each person's retina. It is located at the point where the optic nerve leaves the eyeball and the blood vessels enter; no receptors are present in this small area in each retina. See Color Figure 8 for a demonstration of the blind spot.

The resolving power of the visual system is very high. Under optimum condi-

Figure 18-13
The Modulation Sensitivity Function
The higher the curve, the more sensitive the eye. Where the curve crosses the horizontal axis corresponds to clinical visual acuity. Under good lighting, normal human observers are most sensitive to stimuli with about 6 cycles per degree. Sensitivity falls off as the test pattern becomes either coarser or finer than this optimum value.

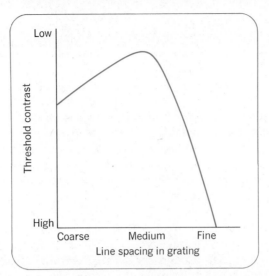

Figure 18-14
How Visual Acuity Varies Across the Eye
In daylight vision, acuity is best in the center of the retina, the fovea. Taking foveal acuity as 100 and then testing acuity at other positions, we find that it drops off rapidly toward the periphery—which is why we use the fovea to look at objects and to read. Acuity is zero at the blind spot, the point at which the optic nerve leaves the eyeball and there are no retinal receptors.

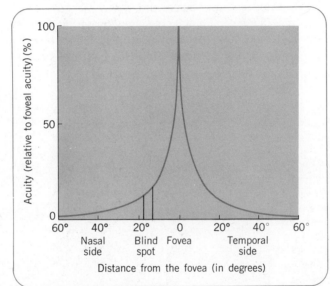

tions, we are able to detect a single black line against a white background when the line occupies less than 0.5 seconds of visual angle. (Each degree of visual space is divided into 60 seconds of arc.) Such performance amounts to detecting a ¼-inch telephone wire at a viewing distance of 1.6 miles! This performance is especially astonishing when it is realized that each cone receptor in the fovea itself occupies a visual angle of about 20 seconds of arc.

HEARING

As we have seen, the human visual system is astoundingly sensitive and can respond to a low level of light. But the auditory system is also remarkably sensitive: under optimal conditions, it can respond to a vibration of the eardrum as minute as the diameter of a hydrogen atom!

We made a careful distinction in vision between the physical properties of light and the psychological properties of the perceptual experience. We must do the same in hearing. The physical stimuli for hearing are pressure waves that travel through the air (usually) or other media, such as water. These waves can be described in physical terms by the **amplitude** of the pressure differences, by the frequency at which the pressure changes, and by the number of different frequencies present in a given wave. A simple wave, a **sine wave,** contains only one frequency of one amplitude. A complex wave contains many frequencies, each frequency having its own amplitude. The sound of a flute contains only three frequencies, while the more complex wave form of a violin may contain eight or more. The intensity of sound waves is measured in decibels (db); the unit, the *bel,* was named in honor of Alexander Graham Bell. Frequency is measured in **hertz** (Hz, or cycles per second, in honor of Heinrich Hertz). Study Figure 18-15 to refresh your memory of these physical concepts.

A complex sound can be analyzed into a pattern of frequencies at various intensities. For example, the rustling sound produced by a six-year-old stomping enthusiastically through a pile of leaves is a noise composed of many different simultaneous frequencies at fairly low intensities. A foghorn has more low-frequency components than high-frequency components, while the sound of a whistling teakettle has more high- than low-frequency components.

Figure 18-15
The Auditory Stimulus

A vibrating body produces pressure waves in the surrounding medium. A pure tone with a single frequency of vibration is shown here. The larger the vibration, the greater the amplitude of the waves. The more frequent the vibration, the more closely spaced are the waves—that is, the shorter is their wavelength.

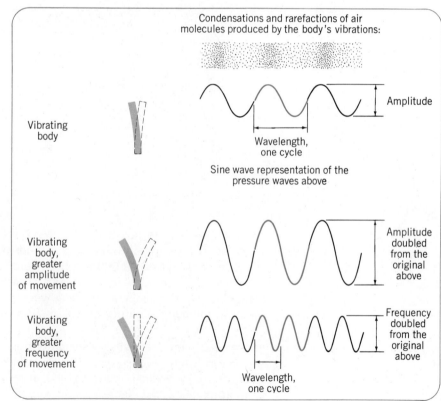

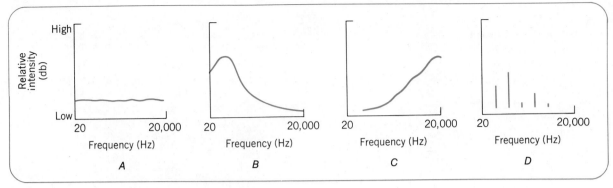

Figure 18-16
Frequency Compositions of Some Common Sounds
Approximate sound spectra represent the amplitude or relative
intensity of various frequencies present in the sound: *A*, a child
rustling leaves; *B*, a nearby foghorn; *C*, a whistling teakettle; and *D*,
a tone played on a musical instrument.

A musical tone, by contrast, has a much more circumscribed sound spectrum; energy is present only at a certain frequency and its multiples (see Figure 18-16). Middle C, for example, has the frequency of 264 Hz. This fundamental frequency is the same whether middle C is played on a piano, on a violin, on a clarinet, or sung by the human voice. There is also energy present at some of the overtones—the frequencies that are multiples of the fundamental tone. For middle C the overtones are 528, 792, 1056, 1320, and so on). The relative intensities of the various overtone frequencies differ among the various instruments, which give them their **timbre** or distinctive sound quality.

When pressure waves strike the ear, they are converted into a pattern of nerve impulses in the acoustic nerve, which evokes a perceptual experience of sound. This perceptual experience can vary along three major dimensions: loudness, pitch, and timbre.

What determines loudness?

A major determinant of **loudness** is, of course, the **intensity** or amplitude of the stimulus. Stimulus intensity is measured in decibels, which is a logarithmic scale; the intensities of several common sounds are shown in Figure 18-17. Some are near or exceed the threshold of pain—the level of intensity most subjects report as painful. Prolonged exposure to high intensities can damage the auditory system, and in laboratory animals prolonged exposure to very high intensities (around 150 db) has resulted in death.

But loudness does not increase linearly with sound intensity, just as brightness does not increase linearly with light intensity. Furthermore, just as brightness varies with the wavelength of light, so loudness varies with the frequency of sound. Figure 18-18 shows how the threshold of hearing varies with the frequency of sound. A sound of 40 db intensity is inaudible if its frequency is much below 100 Hz; it is just about at threshold intensity at a frequency of 100 Hz; and it is about 40 db above threshold and within the range of conversational speech if its frequency is around 2,000 Hz.

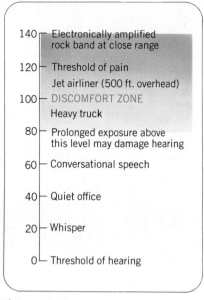

Figure 18-17
Intensities of Some Common Sounds

The stimulus intensity is measured in decibels (db).

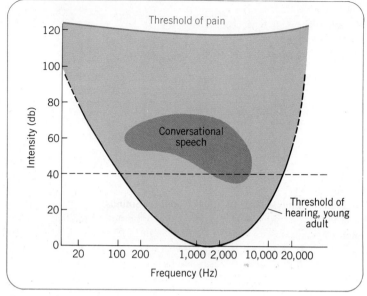

Figure 18-18
Thresholds of Hearing

The black line shows the minimum intensity required at each frequency for the tone to be barely audible. The darker central region shows the range of frequencies and intensities within which most speech sounds occur. If sound is too intense, as shown by the colored line at the top of the diagram, it becomes painful; if prolonged it can damage the inner ear. The dotted line at 40 db shows how loudness varies with frequency of sound: at frequencies below 100 Hz, a 40 db sound is below threshold; at 200 Hz it is about 20 db above threshold; and at 1,000 Hz it is 40 db above threshold.

The way in which loudness varies as a function of intensity is shown by Figure 18-19. To provide a standard for loudness, a sound with a frequency of 1,000 Hz and an intensity of 40 db is defined to have a loudness of 1 *sone*. As intensity is increased above threshold, loudness increases very slowly at first and then (above 70 db) it rises rapidly. Because the decibel scale is useful in telephonic and engineering applications, it is sometimes believed that it accurately represents perceived loudness, but this is clearly not the case. Fechner's law had predicted a logarithmic response such as that shown by the dashed line in Figure 18-19. (*See* the discussion of psychophysical laws on pp. 490–98.) A more accurate representation is given by the power law, with an exponent of 0.6. Loudness = k sound intensity$^{0.6}$, where intensity is expressed in pressure units of dynes / cm^2.

What determines pitch?

Besides loudness, the other main dimension of auditory experience is **pitch**, how low or how high the tone sounds. The frequency of the acoustic stimulus is the primary determinant of pitch, although stimuli of the same frequency sometimes sound higher or lower if intensity is varied. To provide a standard

Figure 18-19
Loudness as a Function of Sound Intensity

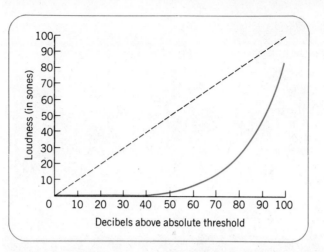

The colored line represents judgments of loudness of a 1,000 Hz tone. A sound of 40 db intensity was taken as the standard; that is, a 1,000 Hz–40 db tone was assigned the loudness value of 1 sone. Loudness does *not* vary linearly with intensity in decibels. If it did, the loudness function would be the linear dashed line.

for pitch, a sound with a frequency of 1,000 Hz and an intensity of 40 db is said to have a pitch of 1,000 **mels** (from "melody"). Pitch is not a linear correlate of frequency, as shown in Figure 18-20. Doubling frequency in the middle range results in a greater change of pitch than doubling it at the lower or higher audible frequencies. It turns out that a tone of 2,200 Hz is judged as about twice as high as one of 1,000 Hz; a tone of 550 Hz sounds about half as high as a 1,000-Hz tone; and one of 300 Hz sounds about a quarter as high as a 1,000 Hz tone, and so on.

Figure 18-20
Pitch as a Function of Frequency

This curve was generated by a magnitude estimation procedure. A tone 40 db above threshold, at 1,000 Hz, was defined as having a pitch of 1,000 mels; corresponding mel values of the other frequencies were determined by magnitude estimation. Although the pitch of a tone increases with its frequency, the relationship is not linear (even when frequency is represented logarithmically, as it is here). (After Stevens, Volkmann, & Newman, 1937)

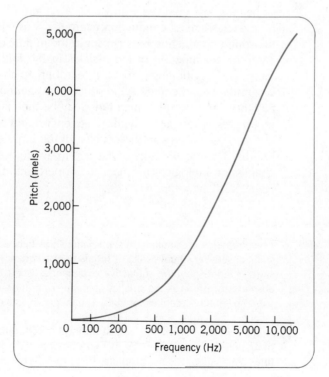

In conduction deafness, the impairment is fairly evenly distributed across all frequencies.

Deafness

All people become somewhat deaf as they get older; the main form of deafness produced by aging is a raised threshold for the higher frequencies. Clinically, two kinds of deafness can be distinguished (see Figure 18-21 for the pattern of hearing loss involved with each). A pattern of fairly uniform loss across all frequencies, called **conduction deafness,** is usually caused by some defect in the sound-conduction mechanism in the middle ear. Such defects as a broken eardrum, malfunction of the ossicles in the middle ear (the tiny bones that transmit the vibrations from the eardrum to the cochlea of the inner ear, where the sound energy is transduced into neural activity), or stoppage of the auditory canal or Eustachian tube may be the cause. **Nerve deafness** involves much greater loss at the higher frequencies and typically results from damage to the receptor cells in the cochlea of the inner ear or to other neural mechanisms. The mechanisms of the inner ear are described and discussed in the chapter on biological mechanisms of perception (Chapter 22; see especially Figure 22-12 and pp. 617–19).

SUMMARY

Psychophysics is the study of the relationships between measurable, physical dimensions of sensory stimuli (such as **intensity** or **frequency**) and the psychological dimensions of corresponding subjective experiences (such as brightness or **loudness**). The **absolute threshold** is the smallest amount of stimulus energy that can be detected on some specified percentage of trials. The **theory of signal detection** can help distinguish response bias from actual detectability.

The difference threshold, or **just noticeable difference (jnd),** is the smallest amount of *change* in stimulus energy that can be detected some specified percentage of the time. This amount is not absolute, but varies systematically in ratio to the magnitude

Figure 18-21
Audiograms of Normal and Hard-of-Hearing Individuals
The figure shows how much each test frequency has to be increased in intensity relative to average, normal hearing for the tone to be heard.

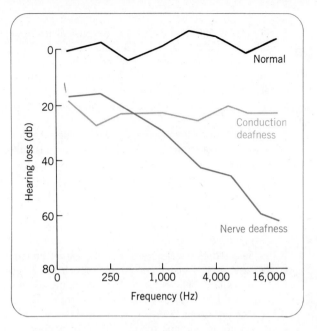

of the initial amount of stimulus energy. This principle is summarized in Weber's law: $\Delta I / I = k$. The constant (k) in the formula is different for different stimulus dimensions.

The relationship between the magnitude of physical stimuli and the magnitude of psychological sensations is not directly linear. More than a century ago, Fechner formulated his famous law: he stated that psychological magnitudes vary as the *logarithm* of physical intensities, or $\Psi = k \log \Phi$. (Ψ represents the psychological magnitude and Φ, the physical magnitude.) More recently, it has been found that a **power law** fits the data even better: the formula $\Psi = k \Phi^n$ is also called **Stevens' law.** The value of the exponent n varies widely across different dimensions of stimulation.

Sensory systems convert the physical energy they receive into nerve impulses that are transmitted to the brain. In vision, the energy is a narrow band of the electromagnetic spectrum, which also contains radio waves and X rays. **Scotopic vision,** mediated by the retinal **rods,** is colorless and most sensitive at about 510 **nanometers** (nm). **Photopic vision,** mediated by the retinal **cones,** provides color experience and is most sensitive at about 560 nm. The eye adapts its range of sensitivity to fit the illumination of its environment, but the relative brightness of various parts of the visible spectrum changes as vision switches from scotopic to photopic (the **Purkinje shift**).

Color experiences vary along the dimensions of hue, saturation, and brightness. **Hue** is largely determined by wavelength, although particular hues can also be produced by mixtures of appropriate wavelengths. The principles of **additive color mixture,** such as adding complementaries to get white or gray, are summarized in the color circle; this also predicts the hue of **negative afterimages.** (The apparent size of afterimages varies with the distance of the surface on which they are projected by the eye.) Several phenomena demonstrate that colors are products of the observer's perception rather than physical dimensions of the visual stimulus itself.

The resolving power of the eye, or visual acuity, can be measured in several ways; the most sensitive is the **modulation sensitivity function,** which assesses the threshold contrast required for detection of gratings of different widths. Photopic visual acuity is best at the **fovea,** dropping steeply toward the periphery; it is zero at the blind spot on the retina.

The physical stimuli for hearing are pressure waves composed of different frequencies at various **amplitudes.** Sounds of musical instruments vary in timbre because of the different patterns of overtones they generate. The primary psychological dimensions of sound are **loudness, pitch,** and **timbre;** the first two are complex functions of both frequency and intensity. Loudness is maximal at about 2,000 Hz and drops off above and below that frequency; it increases in relation to intensity at a rate of the intensity raised to a power of about 0.6. Pitch increases with frequency, but not in a linear fashion.

People normally become somewhat deaf to higher frequencies as they get older. Two kinds of deafness are clinically distinguishable: conduction deafness caused by malfunction of the mechanical transmission system in the ear, and nerve deafness resulting from damage to the receptor cells or to other auditory neural mechanisms.

RECOMMENDED READING

BEARDSLEE, D., & WERTHEIMER, M. (eds.). *Readings in Perception.* New York: Van Nostrand-Reinhold, 1958.
Selected classical papers from the earlier literature on perception.

CORNSWEET, T. N. *Visual Perception.* New York: Academic Press, 1970.
A brilliant, detailed, lucid account of the sensory aspects of perception.

GIBSON, E. J. *Principles of Perceptual Learning and Development.* New York: Appleton-Century-Crofts, 1969.
An award-winning survey of theories of perceptual learning that also reviews what is known about perceptual development.

GIBSON, J. J. *The Senses Considered as Perceptual Systems.* Boston: Houghton Mifflin, 1966.
A detailed account of how the perceptual systems work as information-seeking devices.

GREGORY, R. L. *Eye and Brain* (2nd ed.) New York: McGraw-Hill, 1972. Paperback.
A delightful, authoritative, profusely illustrated popular account of perception.
————. *The Intelligent Eye.* New York: McGraw-Hill, 1970. Paperback.
Another fascinating book by Gregory with many intriguing illustrations.

GULICK, W. L. *Hearing: Physiology and Psychophysics.* New York: Oxford, 1971.
A clear presentation of the basic knowledge in hearing.

HELD, R., & RICHARDS, W. (eds.). *Perception: Mechanisms and Models.* San Francisco: Freeman, 1972. Paperback.
A collection of articles reprinted from *Scientific American.*

JULESZ, B. *Foundations of Cyclopean Perception.* Chicago: University of Chicago Press, 1971.
A spectacular and provocative book illustrated with over fifty random-dot stereograms.

LOWENSTEIN, O. *The Senses.* Baltimore: Penguin, 1966. Paperback.
A brief introduction to the psychology of sensation, written for lay persons, including interesting details about the sensory capacities of animals.

MASSARO, D. W. *Experimental Psychology and Information Processing.* Chicago: Rand McNally, 1975.
A thorough information-processing description of both vision and audition, including the perception of art.

MCCLEARY, R. A. (ed.). *Genetic and Experimental Factors in Perception.* Chicago: Scott, Foresman, 1970. Paperback.
A collection of representative papers on the nativism-empiricism problem in perception.

NEISSER, U. *Cognitive Psychology*. New York: Appleton-Century-Crofts, 1967.

An award-winning presentation of the analysis-by-synthesis theory of information processing, with a wealth of detail and careful surveys of experimental evidence. This book has had a major impact on the field of perception.

PIRENNE, M. H. *Optics, Painting and Photography*. Cambridge, Eng.: The University Press, 1970.

A detailed analysis of linear perspective and space perception, richly illustrated with ingenious experiments and art reproductions.

STEVENS, S. S., & WARSHOFSKY, F. *Sound and Hearing*. Life Science Library. New York: Time Inc., 1965.

A very readable and profusely illustrated account of hearing in people and animals. The first author was one of the leading investigators of psychoacoustics.

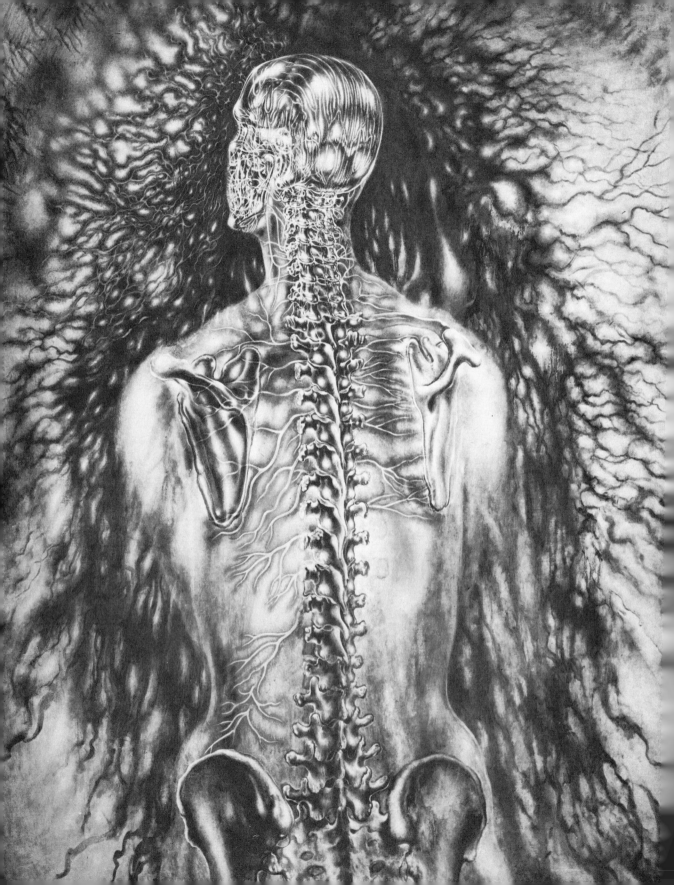

PART EIGHT

Biological Psychology

By Mark R. Rosenzweig

Biological psychology is one of the newest ways to study behavior. People have always had to know a great deal about human behavior to live together, but accurate knowledge of bodily mechanisms of behavior is recent and still incomplete. Writings that are thousands of years old—such as the Old Testament or those of Confucius and Buddha—show many insights into human nature that still strike us as applicable or even sometimes as being surprisingly modern, but discussions of the activity of the nervous system written even fifty years ago are hopelessly outmoded. Psychologists like B. F. Skinner claim that psychologists should study only behavior and not its bodily mechanisms. But from the time psychology became an independent discipline—about a hundred years ago—many psychologists have devoted themselves to studying the biological bases of behavior.

Combining behavioral techniques with those of other biological sciences

Figure 1
What neurological procedure can tame a savage lynx?

Removal of a small area in the base of the temporal lobes on both sides of the brain appears to tame wild animals, but it also produces other changes in behavior. Some neurologists have suggested using a similar brain operation to cure pathological aggressiveness in humans, but this suggestion has evoked much criticism (see pp. 570–71).

is advancing our understanding of many aspects of behavior. The other sections of this book consider many central problems about behavior: how individuals differ in temperament, how behavior changes through learning, how perception reflects the outside world accurately in some cases and how it leads to distortion or illusions in others, and the extent to which nativistic or empiristic interpretations are valid. In this part we will see how biological techniques are helping to solve these and other important behavioral problems.

Let us look at a few specific examples of research in biological psychology before we go farther. Each question is followed by a brief answer, printed upside down, and each of these topics will be taken up in later chapters of this part.

Figure 2

Some young monkeys usually behave like little ladies, while others frequently wrestle like little boys. Is there a biological basis for their difference in temperaments?

Some sex differences occur even in the absence of "culture" (Harlow). These differences in temperament can be modified by early hormonal treatment (see p. 566).

Figure 3

Why does this rat press the lever repeatedly, hundreds of times per hour, for hour after hour?

Each press causes a brief electrical shock to be delivered through the implanted electrode to a "reward" region of the brain (Olds & Milner, 1954). Brain processes involved with reinforcement of behavior are being studied (see p. 571).

517

Figure 4
Why doesn't this man's left hand know what his right hand is doing? When the examiner places one hand in a particular position, the subject cannot copy it with his other hand.

Most people can perform this task easily, but this man has had his corpus callosum—the band of fibers that connects the two cerebral hemispheres—transected in a surgical procedure. Such people seem, in some ways, to have two separate minds. Research with these subjects is helping to reveal the different roles of the two hemispheres and how they interact (see pp. 588–89).

Figure 5
What unexpected facts about obese people have been discovered by extending research on animals that were made obese by physiological techniques?

Obese people are not more inclined to start eating than are people of normal weight, but they do not have an effective shut-off mechanism. Their taste preferences do not change after eating, as do those of normal-weight people. The obese eat fewer meals, but their meals tend to be longer. These and other findings were first suggested by observations with rats made obese by lesions of the brain (see p. 553).

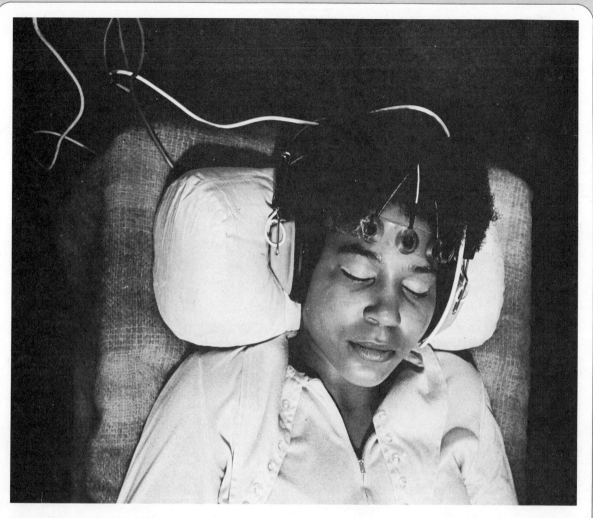

Figure 6

Sleep researchers sometimes want to waken a subject during a dream. How will they know when to awaken her?

The pattern of electrical brain waves changes from dreamless sleep to dreams. By watching the ongoing recordings, researchers can tell how deep sleep is and whether dreams are occurring. Nightmares have been shown in this way to be a different state (see pp. 561–63).

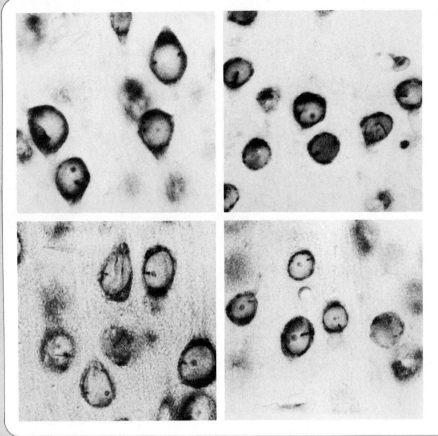

Figure 7
What behavioral treatment made the brain cells shown in the left column larger than those in the right column? The photographs are of rat cerebral cortex stained to show the nuclei of neurons and enlarged 1,000 times. The top pair came from the brains of two brother rats. The bottom photos are from brains of another pair of brothers. Rats whose cells are shown in the outside column were kept in an enriched environment that provided varied opportunities for informal learning. Their brothers—cells shown on the inside—were kept in an impoverished environment. This behavioral treatment causes many changes in the brain (Rosenzweig, Bennett, & Diamond, 1972). (See p. 595.)

Understanding the bodily processes involved in kinds of behavior like those in the illustrations—aggression, social interaction, problem solving, visual perception, and learning—has long been part of the program of psychology. Even before psychology became a formal discipline, some physiologists and philosophers speculated on the neural bases of behavior, but not much progress could be made until the physiology of basic body processes was understood.

The difficulty of trying to cope with a problem when you don't know its basic principles was illustrated in a science-fiction story that I read a few years ago. In the story, scientists were baffled about the function of metal objects from outer space. One scientist said, "These things probably work by some principle that we don't even know. Even a great scientific mind like Aristotle couldn't have discovered the function of a radio, if one could have been placed in his hands." It occurred to me that while Aristotle never examined a radio, he did examine and dissect brains. How successful was he in understanding them? The answer shows the progress since then—Aristotle suggested that the brain acts as a refrigerating unit to cool the hot blood coming from the heart!

Realistic conceptions of how the brain works had to await discoveries of the nineteenth and twentieth centuries. The fact that messages in the nervous system are electrochemical was established around 1860, and detailed knowledge of the nerve impulse was gained only in this century; the fact that nerve cells make functional contacts with each other but do not actually grow into each other was demonstrated around 1890; how messages are transmitted across the functional contacts between nerve cells was definitely established only in the 1950s. Knowledge of the hormonal system is also recent; the term "hormone" was coined in 1906.

As the principles of neural activity were discovered, they were applied first to sensory and motor processes; the organs involved in these processes are peripheral (near the surface of the body) and are therefore relatively accessible. Only recently have improved techniques permitted investigators to observe directly processes occurring deep in the brain and to manipulate them.

Early attempts to treat higher mental processes as neural functions were bound to be largely speculative. They were largely based on a simple model of reflex responses. In the present century, views of body mechanisms have become more flexible and more complex. Pavlov showed that reflexes could be trained or conditioned, and psychologists like Donald O. Hebb showed that it is possible to investigate the neural bases of mental processes. Biological psychology today is fully engaged in the attempt to establish mechanisms of higher mental processes such as learning, perceiving, and thinking.

Chapter 19 outlines some of the most basic aspects of neural and hormonal functions, and provides background necessary for the other chapters of this section. Chapter 20 deals with motivation. It takes up the different brain processes that occur in wakefulness, sleep, and dreaming. It discusses the relations between brain processes and aggressiveness, sex behavior, and reinforcement. Chapter 21 shows how investigators are trying to find out what happens in the brain during learning and how memories are stored in the brain. Then Chapter 22 describes biological methods that are providing answers to some of the questions raised in Chapters 16–18 on perception: How are we able to discriminate form, brightness, and color? How do different parts of the brain participate in different aspects of perception?

19

Neural and Hormonal Integration of Behavior

How do nerve cells transmit information?

How does the hormonal system work with the nervous system?

How does observable behavior depend on activity of muscles and glands?

All behavior depends on integration of processes within the body, and the two chief systems of integration are the nervous system and the endocrine (hormonal) system. Any behavior — perceiving the world around us, making an emotional response, satisfying basic needs — requires such integration. These integrative systems are therefore fundamental to understanding the biological bases of behavior.

To be specific, let us consider what happens when a skier sees a red flag on the slalom course and swerves around it. First, the skier *sees* the flag; in biological terms, the neural impulses from the sense organs are transmitted by a series of relays to brain centers where various features of the stimulus are

extracted and analyzed. Information from memory, structural and chemical changes induced by past experience, are integrated with the incoming information.

The skier swerves; as a result of the processes underlying the seeing of the flag, certain patterns of activity occur in the motor areas of the brain, leading to muscular responses. Parts of the endocrine system are also stimulated, leading to changes in heart rate, blood circulation, and metabolic activity. Before completing the turn, the skier may make finer adjustments. Feedback stimulation from the muscles is integrated with the changing visual information, providing a basis for modification of ongoing behavior.

These processes are complex but, especially in cases of well-practiced behavior, they can occur very rapidly. The person is not consciously aware of most of them, but they can be studied by behavioral and biological methods.

The information used to achieve these complex neural and hormonal integrations is transmitted from place to place in the body by the **nerve cells** or **neurons.** These cells make up the brain and all the other parts of the nervous system. To see how the activity of nerve cells coordinates behavior, we will consider what these cells are like and what kind of signals they transmit. Then we will see how these neural signals encode information about processes and events inside the body and about stimuli that reach us from the outside world. Neural messages make possible the flexibility and variety of our behavior, but they also impose certain limitations and make us susceptible to various disorders, as we shall see.

How do nerve cells transmit information?

BASIC ANATOMY OF
NEURONS

The brain, like other tissues in the body, is made up of millions of individual cells. Although a neuron is like cells of other organs in many respects, its specialized features allow it to convey messages rapidly from one part of the body to another. Like other cells, the neuron has a nucleus and various other parts that manufacture materials and carry on metabolic functions. Also like other cells, the neuron has a thin wall or membrane that separates it from neighboring cells. The membrane contains a variety of specialized channels that regulate the passage of certain substances in and out of the cell; by these exchanges across its membrane the cell is nourished and it communicates with other cells. In keeping with their communication functions, neurons differ from most other cells: neurons have specialized complex shapes with many branches (see Figure 19-1), and many neurons are much longer than any other cells in the body. For example, neurons that carry sensory information from your big toe run up your leg and into the spinal cord in the middle of your back; such neurons are over a meter long (depending on your height). Certain other neurons are much shorter, less than a millimeter long.

Shapes of some of the large variety of neurons are shown in Figure 19-1. Whatever their shapes, most neurons have the same functional parts. There is an input zone in which the cell receives neural signals; in many types of neuron the input region includes the cell body and also branches called **dendrites** (from the Greek for "tree"). Then there is usually a conducting zone over which nerve impulses are conveyed; in most kinds of neurons this is a single long branch called the **axon.** The output zone (the axon terminals) is where neurons deliver signals to other cells—to muscle cells, gland cells, or other neurons.

Figure 19-1
Shapes of Neurons
Each type has a cell body that contains the nucleus. In addition, each neuron has one or more branches. Neurons receive stimulation from other neurons or from sense receptors; the input to some neurons is directly to the cell body as in the olfactory neuron (A in the figure), in some cases to branches called dendrites (C), and in some cases to both cell bodies and dendrites (D-F). Conduction of the nerve impulse takes place along the axon in many types of neurons (A, D-F), but in some types of neurons the dendrites also conduct (B, C). Neurons deliver impulses to other neurons or to muscles or glands; this output always occurs over terminal branches of axons. In many cases, the branches of a neuron are very long so breaks have been indicated in diagrams A-E to allow us to show both ends of the neuron and the cell body without including long stretches of axon.

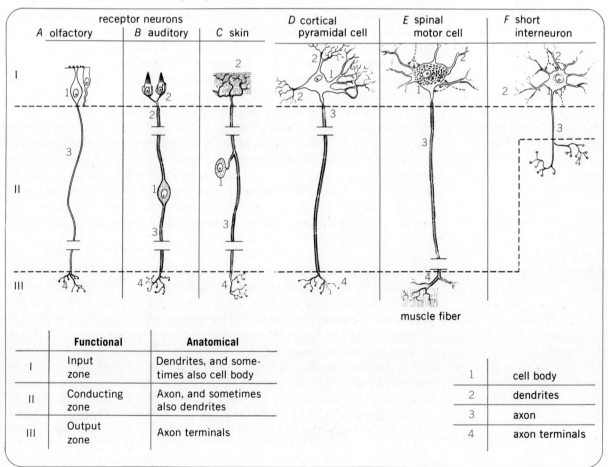

	Functional	Anatomical
I	Input zone	Dendrites, and sometimes also cell body
II	Conducting zone	Axon, and sometimes also dendrites
III	Output zone	Axon terminals

1	cell body
2	dendrites
3	axon
4	axon terminals

NEURAL SIGNALS

Neural signals have been studied by recording and amplifying the tiny electrical charges that occur in neurons and by chemically analyzing the fluids inside and around the neurons. The nerve impulse is an abrupt change of about one-tenth of a volt in the potential that normally exists between the inside and outside of the neural membrane. When one segment of a neuron is stimulated, it responds actively; in turn the next segment is stimulated, so that the impulse sweeps down the length of the neuron. The fastest axons in the human body carry impulses at the speed of about 100 meters per second (roughly 220 miles per hour); in the slowest fibers the speed is less than 0.5 meters per second. At any given point on a large and rapidly conducting axon, the nerve impulse lasts only about one-thousandth of a second (1 millisecond). During this time, special channels in the membrane admit sodium ions into the neuron from the surrounding extracellular fluid, and then potassium ions flow out of the neuron. The movement of these charged particles accounts for the changes in electrical potential across the membrane.

Surprisingly, the neuron restores itself to its resting state in about a millisecond. Thus the neuron can carry several hundred impulses per second or, in some cases, even a thousand per second. All impulses in a given neuron are of the same size and speed, although neurons differ from each other in the sizes of their impulses and rates of conduction. The stimulus that triggers off this activity does not supply the energy for the impulse or affect its size or speed; once the neuron is stimulated it responds in its characteristic total way.

For a model of some aspects of neural activity, you can think of what happens when you ignite a string of small firecrackers. If you don't hold the match close enough, the wick may just turn brown without catching fire; similarly, small subthreshold electrical changes in the neuron are too weak to trigger a full-blown response. But with greater heat, the wick catches fire and then the first firecracker explodes; this explosion ignites the next firecracker in line, and a series of explosions travels quickly down the length of the string. The size of the explosions and their speed of progression are determined by characteristics of the string of firecrackers, not of the match used to ignite the wick. If the firecrackers could then spring back intact from their ashes, ready to be ignited again, they would have the wonderful feature of recovery that neurons show.

SYNAPTIC TRANSMISSION

The place where one neuron makes functional contact with another is called a **synapse** (from the Greek words for "clasp together"). The term synapse includes both the axon end button of the neuron that is sending the signal (the presynaptic neuron) and the facing receptor membrane of the postsynaptic neuron (see Figure 19-2 and Color Figure 7); the membranes of these two neurons are usually separated by a narrow gap or cleft. In a few locations in the mammalian nervous system, the electrical activity in the presynaptic neuron can stimulate the postsynaptic neuron across the gap, the way one string of firecrackers ignites an adjacent string. But in most locations, the synaptic gap is bridged by release of a chemical **transmitter agent;** this chemical is stored inside the end button in tiny globules called **synaptic vesicles** (see Figure 19-2).

Figure 19-2
How Impulses Get from One Neuron to Another
When a neural impulse reaches the end button of an axon, some synaptic vesicles discharge their contents into the synaptic cleft. The transmitter substance combines with a receptor chemical in the receiving cell. This chemical reaction sets up an electrical charge that may excite or inhibit the receiving cell.

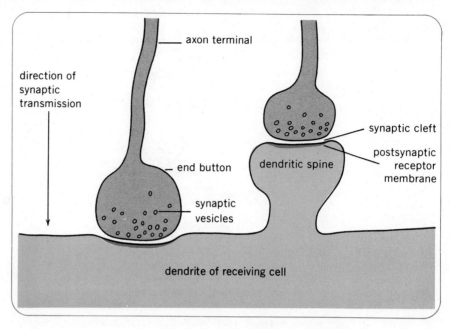

When a nerve impulse reaches the end button of an axon, some vesicles release the chemical transmitter agent into the synaptic gap. The chemical agent diffuses across the gap and combines with another chemical in the receptor membrane. This chemical reaction sets up an electrical change in the receiving cell. At some synapses, this change tends to excite the postsynaptic neuron. At other synapses, the change is inhibitory; that is, it makes the cell harder to excite. These two kinds of changes are of opposite electrical polarity: At excitatory synapses, arriving signals cause a decrease of the normal resting potential of the postsynaptic cell. But at inhibitory synapses, arriving signals cause an increase of the resting potential of the postsynaptic cell. Most neurons are constantly receiving a barrage of input signals from many other cells; only if the excitatory signals predominate over the inhibitory signals does the postsynaptic neuron fire off impulses.

Various transmitter chemicals are employed in the nervous system. Some synapses use a transmitter compound called **acetylcholine** (*see* Figure 19-3). Others use *norepinephrine,* and other synapses use still other agents.

Synaptic transmission accounts for several characteristics of the nervous system. For example, the synaptic junctions allow switching so that messages can be routed into one channel or another, depending on how impulses from different neurons converge. It usually takes many impulses converging on a neuron to fire it. The fact that synaptic action can be either excitatory or inhibitory permits control in both directions, like the use of both the accelerator and the brakes in a car. The chemical nature of most mammalian synapses has the further consequence of making them susceptible to various chemical agents; examples of such chemical effects at the synapse are shown in Figure 19-3.

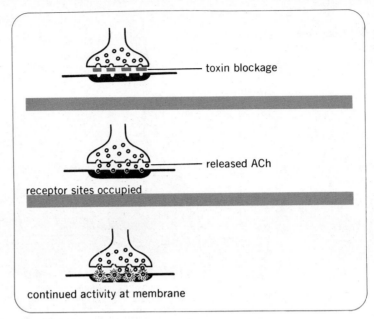

toxin blockage

released ACh

receptor sites occupied

continued activity at membrane

Figure 19-3
Effect of Drugs on Synaptic Activity
The diagram shows synapses where acetylcholine (ACh) is the chemical transmitter. Certain drugs can block release of ACh (1 below), can block its receptor chemical in the receiving cell (2), or can prolong its activity (3). Other drugs affect synapses where different chemical transmitters are active.
1. Botulinus toxin (which can form in improperly canned vegetables) blocks the release of ACh from the end button. The result can be a fatal paralysis.
2. Curare (a South American Indian arrow poison) occupies the receptor sites in the postsynaptic membrane and prevents ACh from acting. It also results in paralysis.
3. Certain nerve gases destroy the enzyme (acetylcholinesterase or AChE) that normally inactivates ACh. This causes a buildup of ACh, which blocks further transmission across the junction. This too causes paralysis.

HOW NEURAL IMPULSES ENCODE INFORMATION

How do nerve cells transmit information? Take a case where you must react rapidly to a stimulus. You pick up a plate, and then feel that it is too hot to hold, so you quickly put it down. Your responses are based on neural messages. The fact that you feel burning heat and not just touch means that different sensory receptors are involved, and the resulting neural impulses are carried along different neural fibers, some for heat and some for touch. You feel the heat in your right hand and not in your left, which also involves different neural fibers running to different parts of the brain. The intensity of the sensation is related to the number of neural impulses conducted per unit of time—a barrage of impulses for a strong sensation but only sparse impulses for a weak one.

Nerve impulses travel from the sensory receptors up special fiber tracts to sensory areas in the brain in 50 to 100 milliseconds. In the brain, the synaptic junctions allow switching so that messages can be routed into one channel or another, depending on the convergence of excitatory and inhibitory effects. This processing of information will probably require at least 100 milliseconds in the simplest cases, and considerably longer times are required for more complicated behavior such as pattern recognition. (If synaptic transmission is impaired by alcohol or other drugs, the reaction will be slower and will probably also be modified.) Then, from motor areas of the brain, volleys of nerve impulses go down the spinal cord, causing messages to go out the motor nerves and activate the muscles. Again coding in terms of routing of impulses is required to determine which muscles contract and which relax, and the rate of neural firing regulates the appropriate strengths of responses of the different muscles.

Natural selection has favored the evolution of animals that can respond quickly and selectively to many aspects of the environment, including other beings. Thus the nervous system has evolved to encode information clearly, to conduct signals rapidly, and to process the information in sophisticated ways.

BASIC GEOGRAPHY OF THE NERVOUS SYSTEM

The neurons that we have been describing run to all parts of the body, but by far the greatest number are concentrated in various functional systems that make up the brain and spinal cord. Some of the basic anatomy of the **nervous system** is introduced in Figures 19-4 to 19-7 and Color Figures 1 to 7. This is just a first overview, and later we will see how the main parts of the nervous system function. Don't worry about mastering the names and locations now; they will become more meaningful as you study them later in connection with their functions.

How to describe and name the parts of the nervous system was a puzzle to early anatomists during the Renaissance, especially because they had little notion of how the brain works. They settled in most cases by naming parts of the brain according to their resemblances to familiar shapes, using Latin or Greek, which were the scientific languages of the time. Here are some examples: When early anatomists opened the skull and examined the brain from above, it looked roughly like a globe divided into two halves; they named these halves the **cerebral hemispheres.** The furrowed outer layer of the hemispheres was named the **cortex,** from the Latin word for the bark of a tree. A band of fibers was seen to unite the two hemispheres across the midline; because this band feels rather tough in contrast to the soft cortex, the band was named the **corpus callosum**—from the Latin words for "body" and "hard" (a callus in the skin is a hard spot). Behind the cerebral hemispheres is a formation that seemed to be another smaller brain, which was named the **cerebellum,** from the Latin for "little brain." Arching forward between the two sides of the cerebellum is a bridge of fibers that is called the **pons,** from the Latin for bridge. Color Figure 5 shows deep in the core of the brain a large structure surrounding a narrow cavity filled with fluid; the cavity was named the **ventricle** (from the Latin for "little belly"), and the surrounding structure was called the **thalamus** (from the Greek for "inner chamber").

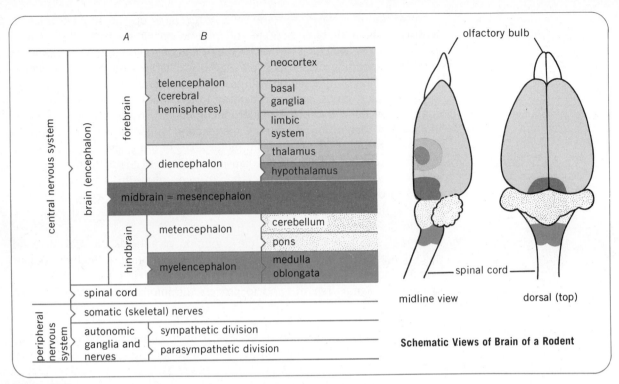

Figure 19-4
Subdivisions of the Nervous System
The table shows increasing specificity of terms from left to right. The subdivisions listed under *A* become apparent early in the embryonic development of the brain; those under *B* are seen later in development, as shown in Figure 19-5.

These anatomical terms range from highly inclusive ones (such as *central nervous system* and *brain*) to rather specific terms (such as *cerebellum, pons,* and *thalamus*). We can use the block diagram in Figure 19-4 to see how some of these terms relate to each other, going from the most inclusive terms at the left of the block to more specific ones at the right. The main divisions of the nervous system appear especially clearly during the embryonic development of the brain, as you can see by examining Figure 19-5 in conjunction with Figure 19-4. Very early in the embryo, the primitive nervous system is a tube whose wall is made of cells. This tube develops three wider portions toward the head end; these are called the forebrain, the midbrain, and the hindbrain. As the embryonic brain becomes more complex, the **forebrain** subdivides into the **telencephalon** and the **diencephalon** (or between brain); the telencephalon grows into the large **cerebral hemispheres,** and the diencephalon includes the **thalamus** and **hypothalamus.** The **midbrain** (or mesencephalon) remains relatively small in the human brain, overshadowed by the large growth of the forebrain and the hindbrain. The **hindbrain** subdivides into the metencephalon and the myelencephalon (or medulla oblongata); the metencephalon includes the large **cerebellum** and the **pons.**

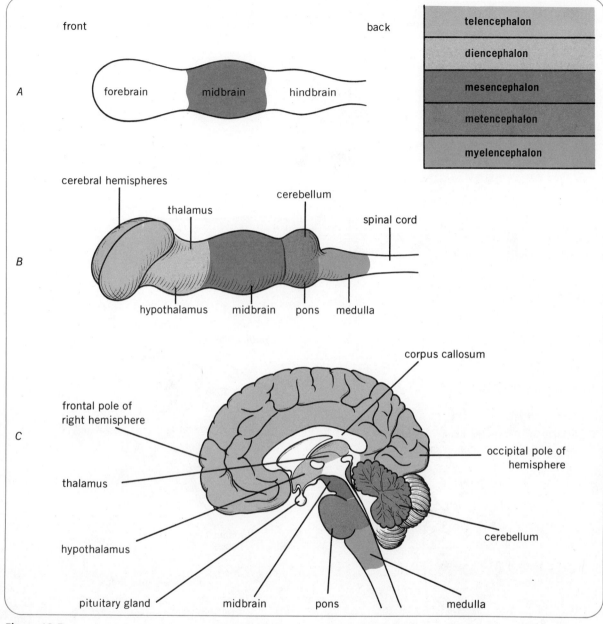

Figure 19-5
Embryonic Development of the Human Brain
A. In a very young embryo, the primitive tubular brain develops three subdivisions—forebrain, midbrain, and hindbrain.
B. As the brain develops, five main subdivisions emerge, and they will persist in the adult brain. "Encephalon" is the Greek word for brain, and the five subdivisions, from front to back, are called respectively the telencephalon, diencephalon, mesencephalon, metencephalon, and myelencephalon.
C. The right hemisphere of the adult human brain is viewed from the midline after the left hemisphere has been removed.

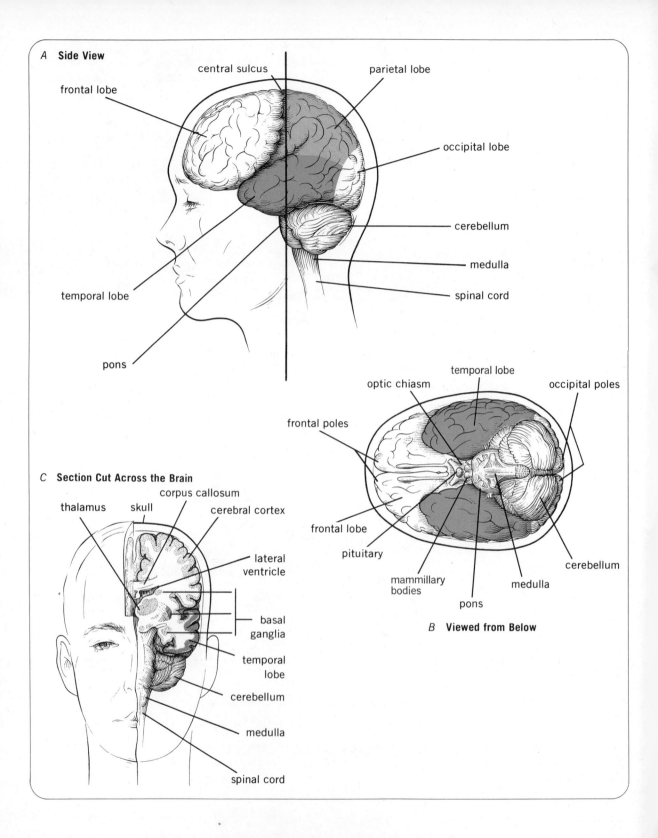

A **Side View**

central sulcus

frontal lobe

parietal lobe

occipital lobe

cerebellum

medulla

spinal cord

temporal lobe

pons

C **Section Cut Across the Brain**

thalamus   skull

corpus callosum

cerebral cortex

lateral ventricle

basal ganglia

temporal lobe

cerebellum

medulla

spinal cord

optic chiasm

temporal lobe

occipital poles

frontal poles

frontal lobe

pituitary

cerebellum

mammillary bodies

medulla

pons

B **Viewed from Below**

The main parts of the brain and their anatomical relations are quite similar in all mammals, which is evident from the paired diagrams of the human and rat brains in Figure 19-7. The human brain is, of course, much larger than the rat brain, but in both cases the brain weighs about 2 percent of the total body. In the human brain, the cerebral hemispheres are relatively large, and the outer bark (the **cerebral cortex** or **gray matter**) has many folds. The rodent cortex, in contrast, is smooth and has no fissures.

Two-thirds of the cortex in the adult human brain lies buried in fissures. If it were spread out flat, the cortex of the average human brain would cover over two square feet. Beneath this surface layer of gray matter millions of nerve fibers run to and from the cortical cells; each fiber is covered with a fatty insulating sheath. When this fibrous part of the brain is exposed, the insulating sheaths give it a white shiny appearance, and it is therefore called **white matter** (*see* Figure 19-6c and Color Figure 5).

How does the hormonal system work with the nervous system?

Integration of behavior is achieved by the **endocrine glands** as well as by the nervous system. These glands secrete **hormones**—special chemical messengers that are carried throughout the body by the bloodstream. Thus the hormonal messages are distributed widely, rather than in the localized manner of neural messages, and hormonal communication is considerably slower than neural communication. But the endocrine glands and the nervous system should not be thought of as completely separate or independent. Secretion of some endocrine glands is controlled by the brain, as we shall see, and several hormones, in turn, modify the excitability of neural cells. A major endocrine gland, the **pituitary,** is partly an outgrowth of the brain and is joined to the base of the brain (*see* Figures 19-7 and 19-8). The location and the principal functions of the main endocrine glands are given in Figure 19-8.

Figure 19-6
Three Views of the Human Brain
View *A* shows some of the main surface features of the human brain as they would be seen if the skin, muscles, and skull were transparent. The cerebral hemispheres are usually divided into four main lobes—frontal, parietal, occipital and temporal. The vertical line shows the cross section of drawing C.
View *B* shows the brain as seen from below. The pituitary gland is in the center of the drawing, attached just below the hypothalamus (refer back to Figure 19-5). Just behind it can be seen the pons, which got its name from the Latin word for "bridge" because many of its fibers bridge between one side of the cerebellum and the other. Just ahead of the pituitary gland, the optic nerves cross, forming the chiasm (named after the Greek letter Chi—χ).
View *C* shows how the brain would appear if the left side of the head were removed back to about the ear. The cerebral cortex, or gray matter, starts at the surface and goes down to a depth of a few millimeters. Inside this is white matter, composed mainly of neural fibers that are insulated with light-colored fatty material. One large band of fibers, the corpus callosum, interconnects the two cerebral hemispheres. Buried deep in the brain are structures such as the basal ganglia and the thalamus, which we will consider later.

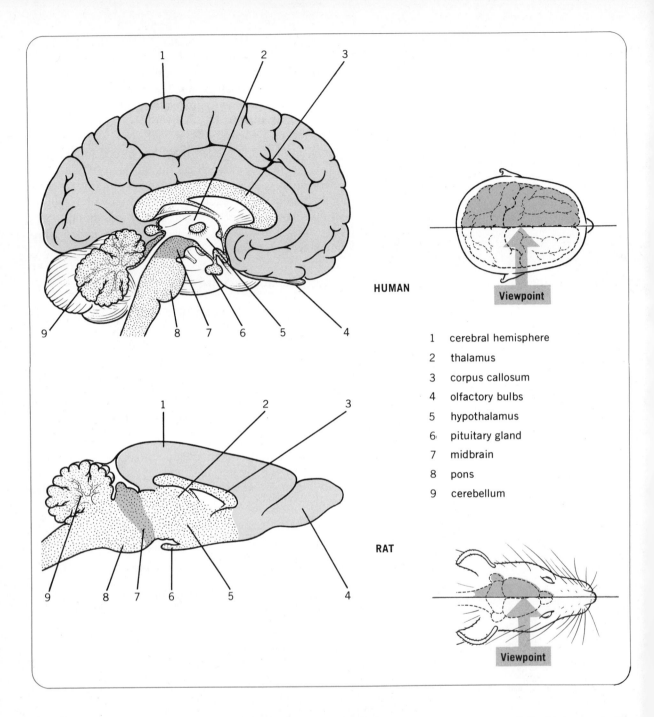

HUMAN

1 cerebral hemisphere
2 thalamus
3 corpus callosum
4 olfactory bulbs
5 hypothalamus
6 pituitary gland
7 midbrain
8 pons
9 cerebellum

RAT

In our case of the skier, both the precise responses and the high metabolic level are facilitated by secretion of the hormone epinephrine (also called adrenalin) from the **adrenal medulla** (the inner core of the *adrenal gland*). Epinephrine helps to distribute the blood supply to the skeletal muscles and away from the internal organs, and it increases heart rate and blood pressure;

Figure 19-7
Comparison of Human and Rat Brain Structures
The brains shown here have been cut along the midline of the body, and one half
has been removed, as shown in the small diagrams. This allows you to see structures
along the midline of the brain. The parts that were cut are shown stippled in the
midline views. The rat brain has been enlarged about six times in relation to the human
brain.

The main parts of the brain are in similar positions in people and rats (and in
all species of mammals). The relative sizes of some parts differ considerably,
however. The cerebral hemispheres occupy a much greater proportion of the human
brain than they do in the rat, whereas the rat has the relatively larger midbrain
and much larger olfactory bulbs.

it releases blood sugar from the liver into the bloodstream, making a ready
supply of energy available; it causes the blood to clot more quickly in case of
injury.

In many of these activities, the hormonal system works in conjunction with
the nervous system, and each system depends in part on the other. The rates
of secretion of certain endocrine glands—the posterior pituitary and the
adrenal medulla—are directly controlled by the neurons that innervate them.
Other endocrines are controlled chemically, several of them by secretions of
the anterior pituitary gland, which is therefore often called the master gland.
For example, the pituitary manufactures some hormones that directly stimulate
the release of sex hormones from the gonads. The anterior pituitary in turn is
controlled in part by the secretions of the endocrine glands it influences
(a *feedback* relationship) and in part by secretions of special cells located in
the base of the brain. These cells are governed by adjacent neurons.

Here is an example of neural-hormonal interaction in the control of mating
behavior: In some female birds, the sight of a courting male does not lead
directly or promptly to mating behavior. As the female perceives this courting

The female peacock (right, at
fence) appears uninterested
in the male's display. Later,
however, the neural
and hormonal activity
induced by his courting will
lead her to display appropriate
mating behavior.

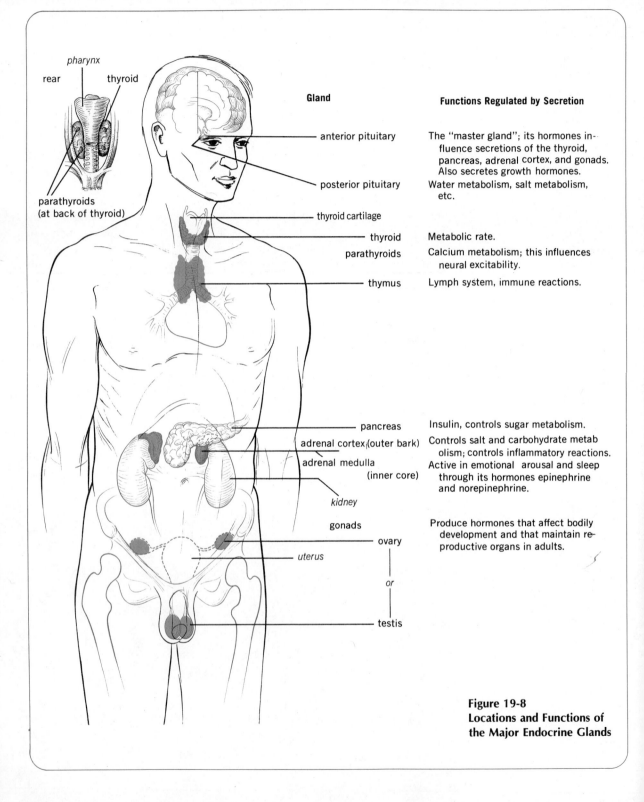

Gland

pharynx
rear
thyroid

parathyroids
(at back of thyroid)

anterior pituitary

posterior pituitary

thyroid cartilage

thyroid
parathyroids

thymus

pancreas

adrenal cortex (outer bark)

adrenal medulla
(inner core)

kidney

gonads

ovary

uterus

or

testis

Functions Regulated by Secretion

The "master gland"; its hormones influence secretions of the thyroid, pancreas, adrenal cortex, and gonads. Also secretes growth hormones.

Water metabolism, salt metabolism, etc.

Metabolic rate.

Calcium metabolism; this influences neural excitability.

Lymph system, immune reactions.

Insulin, controls sugar metabolism.

Controls salt and carbohydrate metabolism; controls inflammatory reactions.

Active in emotional arousal and sleep through its hormones epinephrine and norepinephrine.

Produce hormones that affect bodily development and that maintain reproductive organs in adults.

Figure 19-8
Locations and Functions of the Major Endocrine Glands

over a period of a few days, the resulting neural activity causes the anterior pituitary gland to secrete a specialized hormone. When this hormone reaches the ovaries, it stimulates them to increase the level of sex hormones circulating in the blood. Thus behavior and neural activity have led to a change in hormonal secretion. These hormones, in turn, selectively affect both certain brain cells and cells in the reproductive tract. The hormonal influence on the brain cells makes the female more ready to engage in copulatory activity. Thus a neural-hormonal-hormonal-neural sequence of events underlies the female bird's response to the male's courtship and helps to coordinate the behavior of the pair. We will consider hormonal influences on behavior further in Chapter 20 on biology of motivation (see pp. 564–65). We will also see there how sex hormones determine aspects of body form and how they influence humans' gender roles.

How does observable behavior depend on activity of muscles and glands?

The processes that we will take up in the next three chapters—biological perception, motivation, and learning—are usually inferred from observable behavior of people or animals. The smiles and frowns we see, the voices we hear, the touches we feel, the swerving of the skier around the flag—all these are the products of muscular activities. Other responses are glandular; cold air on the skier's eyes may cause the secretion of tears from the tear glands. Therefore, before going on to the next chapters, it will be helpful to consider briefly motor behavior. ("Motor" is a term used to indicate the behavioral or output functions of the body—muscles and glands and their direct control—as contrasted with the "sensory" input functions or the inner "associative" activities.)

The muscular systems of the body are controlled by the nervous system. A muscle will contract if you stimulate it electrically, but you can use a weaker current if you stimulate the motor nerve that runs to the muscle. The motor neurons form special junctions with muscles; these neuromuscular junctions are similar in many ways to the synaptic junctions between neurons. Impulses in the motor neurons lead to the release of a transmitter chemical at the neuromuscular junction, and this excites the muscle and causes it to contract.

When muscles are mentioned, you probably think first of muscles in your arms and legs that you can move voluntarily. Many other muscles are usually not under voluntary control but nevertheless function in coordination with ongoing bodily activities: the heart, the stomach and intestines, the blood vessels, the iris of the eye, and the little muscles in the skin that raise the hairs, causing "gooseflesh" when they contract.

CENTRAL NERVOUS SYSTEM CONTROL

We will consider first the control of the skeletal muscles that move the arms and legs and other visible parts of the body around the joints. Under microscopic examination, these muscles have a striped appearance, so they are also called *striate muscles*. Most muscles inside the body cavity—in the intestines and blood vessels—have a uniform appearance, so they are called *smooth*

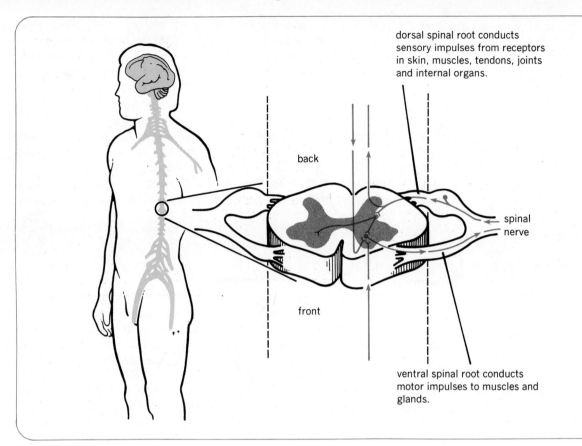

dorsal spinal root conducts
sensory impulses from receptors
in skin, muscles, tendons, joints
and internal organs.

back

front

spinal
nerve

ventral spinal root conducts
motor impulses to muscles and
glands.

Figure 19-9
Neural Connections in a Spinal Reflex
The position of the spinal cord in the body is shown at the left. One of its 22
segments is enlarged at the right to show details. At each segment there is a spinal nerve
on each side of the cord; just before the spinal nerve joins the cord, it divides into
two roots—the dorsal (back) root and the ventral (front) root. Sensory impulses
come in from receptors in the body (in the skin, muscles, joints) through the
dorsal spinal root. Motor neurons have their cell bodies in the gray matter in the
ventral side of the cord, and their axons go out to skeletal muscles through the
ventral spinal root. Insulated sensory and motor fibers run up and down within the
cord in columns of white matter. There are millions of fibers and connections at
each segment.

muscles. The skeletal muscles are controlled by neurons whose cell bodies
are inside the spinal cord. The smooth muscles are controlled by neurons outside the spinal cord—the so-called autonomic nervous system, which we will
discuss a little later.

The motor neurons in the spinal cord that control skeletal muscles are affected by excitatory and inhibitory impulses from many levels. For example,
when a muscle is stretched—when a doctor taps below your knee with a

rubber mallet or when a skier's leg drops a little over a hollow in the snow—a special type of receptor cell within the muscle is stimulated by the stretch. When these receptors are activated, they send impulses along sensory nerves to the spinal cord and up to the brain. Some of these impulses stimulate motor neurons that send impulses to the muscle that was stretched, and these impulses cause a reflex contraction of the muscle. This contraction quickly restores the initial posture of the leg. Such reflex integration occurs within a single level or segment of the spinal cord (see Figure 19-9), but it is also modulated by nerve impulses from other levels of the cord and by impulses from the brain. The exact origin of these impulses has been pinpointed in the brain.

A surprising finding was made in 1870 when two German doctors stimulated exposed brain tissue of a wounded soldier, using weak electrical currents. They found that different sites of stimulation regularly led to different precise muscular responses. Careful mapping was then done on animal brains by many investigators, who found that points along a strip of the cortex would yield restricted motor responses when *weak* stimulation was employed; stronger currents gave only gross convulsive responses.

A map of the human motor cortex is given in the upper part of Figure 19-10. The size of each motor subregion is related to the precision with which we can control that part of the body. Thus the fingers, lips, and tongue have large representations, whereas the trunk, although it is a much larger part of the body, has a rather small representation in the motor cortex. The sensory cortex that receives input from the skin is shown in the middle part of Figure 19-10. The size of subregions of the sensory cortex is related to the precision of sensitivity on the skin, just as the size of representations in the motor cortex is related to the precision of motor control. For example, on the fingertips and on the lips you can accurately distinguish points that are separated by a millimeter or two, but on the back you cannot distinguish points unless they are centimeters apart. The fingertips and lips, compared to the back, have large representations in the sensory cortex.

The motor connections are largely, but not completely, crossed over. Most axons from the left motor cortex cross over to the right and end on or near spinal motor cells that run to muscles on the right side of the body. Similarly, most motor fibers originating in the right side of the brain help to control muscles on the left side of the body—which is why damage to one side of the brain can cause paralysis on the other side of the body. In most individuals, the muscles for speech are controlled by the left hemisphere of the brain, but in a few, speech is controlled by the right hemisphere; and in an occasional person, both hemispheres are used in speech. For this reason, damage to the left hemisphere often impairs a person's speech, but damage to the right hemisphere rarely does so.

Complex circuits in the brain provide for such elaborate coordinated movements as walking, making a turn in skiing, or writing a word. These might be thought of as neural "programs," analogous to computer programs. As these motor programs run off, they are constantly being monitored for accuracy by the sensory systems, and this feedback allows corrections and adjustments to be made. Consider the coordination required to say a word. The tongue alone contains many muscles, and their activities must be coordinated with others in

Figure 19-10
How the Muscles and Skin Are Represented at the Cerebral Cortex

The **primary motor cortex** sends impulses to the muscles. This area is shown in darker color on the lower part of the diagram; it is located just ahead of the central sulcus, which is a major fissure or groove in the cortex. Each muscle is represented in a particular strip of motor cortex, as is indicated by the names of body parts or movements on the upper diagram; this shows a cross section of the brain through the motor cortex. Most motor functions are represented symmetrically in the two cerebral hemispheres, impulses from each hemisphere going to muscles on the opposite side of the body. Control of speech muscles, however, is located only in the left hemisphere of most people.

When the skin is stimulated, some of the resulting neural impulses reach the **primary somatosensory cortex.** This area is located just behind the central sulcus and is shown in light color on the diagram. Each section of skin is represented in a particular strip of sensory cortex, as is shown on the cross section in the middle diagram. Here, too, each side of the body connects with the opposite side of the brain.
(Based on Penfield & Jasper, 1954)

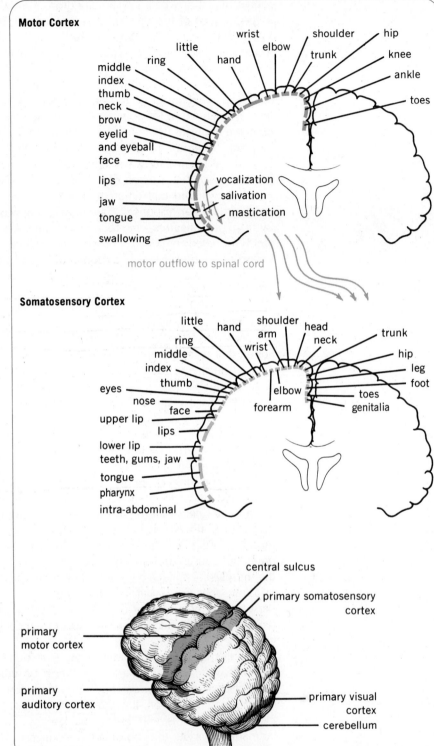

the larynx, throat, lips, chest, and diaphragm to produce speech sounds. For example, the difference between "time" and "dime" depends partly on whether the vocal cords are left relaxed or are tensed during the initial consonant; in both words the cords are tensed during the vowel. The initial consonant lasts less than 100 milliseconds, and the vocal cords must be in the correct position during most of that time, so that the timing must be accurate to about 10 msec (one hundredth of a second). Certain types of damage to the brain may impair such coordination or even make speech impossible. Speech sounds are monitored by hearing, so that normal speech is difficult to attain for a deaf person who lacks auditory feedback.

Sensory feedback from receptors within the muscles and in the tendons and joints helps achieve precise control of movements. This is called "proprioception" (perception of one's self). When you go to pick up a pencil from a desk, you normally use both visual and proprioceptive feedback to steadily reduce the distance between your hand and the pencil. If you eliminate visual feedback by closing your eyes before starting to move your hand, you can still do quite well, although you may sometimes miss the pencil.

Skilled movements of the hand involve not only the musculature of the hand and forearm, but also muscles of the upper arm, shoulder, chest, and neck. For any particular movement of the hand (such as reaching forward, reaching with the palm up), there is a different pattern of activation of these associated muscles (see Spotlight 19-1). Movement at each joint in the body is controlled by at least two muscles, so that motion can be made in both directions. For example, a finger can be raised (extended) or lowered (flexed). The muscles that control these oppositely directed movements are called "antagonists" because they work in opposite directions. In controlled movements, however, both muscles contract and the motion results from delicate shifts in balance of the relative activation of the two; we might think of this as "cooperative antagonism."

AUTONOMIC NERVOUS SYSTEM

The motor neurons that control the heart, smooth muscles, and glands are located in two long chains, one on either side of the spinal cord; see Color Figure 6. To early neuroanatomists these chains of neurons seemed to be almost a separate nervous system, and the processes they controlled seemed to be autonomous and independent of voluntary control, so this motor outflow was named the **autonomic nervous system.** We now know that this is simply a part of the motor system and that it is controlled by neural impulses from the brain and spinal cord. Connections between the spinal cord and autonomic neurons are shown in Figure 19-11.

The autonomic system has two divisions; they work antagonistically for some functions and cooperatively in others, as shown in Table 19-1. The **sympathetic division** generally predominates when the skeletal musculature is active—it routes blood to the skier's skeletal muscles, speeds the heart beat, releases sugar from the liver, and causes secretion of adrenalin. The **parasympathetic division** predominates in restoring body energy—for example, it promotes digestion.

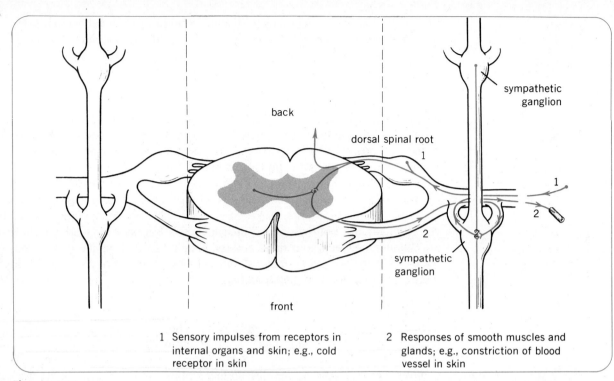

back

dorsal spinal root

sympathetic ganglion

1

front

sympathetic ganglion

1   2

1   Sensory impulses from receptors in internal organs and skin; e.g., cold receptor in skin

2   Responses of smooth muscles and glands; e.g., constriction of blood vessel in skin

Figure 19-11
Autonomic Reflex Connections

Two chains of autonomic neurons run along the two sides of the spinal cord. (These sympathetic chains were omitted for the sake of simplicity from Figure 19-9.) As an example of an autonomic reflex, consider what happens when cold receptors in the skin are stimulated. Impulses run to the spinal cord, where some make connections with cells that send axons out the ventral root to sympathetic ganglia. The sympathetic impulses constrict blood vessels in the skin and thus protect the body from losing too much heat.

TABLE 19-1 Some functions of the two divisions of the autonomic nervous system

Organ or Function	Sympathetic Division	Parasympathetic Division
Pupil of eye	Dilation	Constriction
Tear glands	——	Secretion
Salivary glands	——	Secretion
Sweat glands	Secretion	——
Body hair	Hairs raised (piloerection)	——
Heart rate	Increased	Decreased
Blood vessels		
In skin	Constriction	——
In striate muscles	Dilation and constriction	——
In smooth muscles	Constriction	——
In heart	Dilation	Constriction
Adrenal medulla	Secretion	——
Liver	Sugar liberated	——
Stomach	Mainly inhibition of secretion and peristalsis	Mainly stimulation of secretion and peristalsis
Intestines	Inhibition	Increased tonus and movement
Rectum	Inhibition	Defecation
Bladder	Inhibition	Urination
Genital organs		
Female	——	Tumescence
Male	Ejaculation	Erection

The motor neurons of the sympathetic division are located in the two chains on either side of the spinal cord. Corresponding to each segment of the spinal cord is a cluster of autonomic cell bodies and synapses; such a clump of neural tissue is called a **ganglion** (see Figure 19-11). The motor neurons of the parasympathetic system are located still farther away from the spinal cord and close to the organs they innervate (Color Figure 6). The hypothalamus integrates many of the autonomic responses into patterns. Dr. Walter Hess, the Swiss physiologist and a Nobel Prize winner (1949), found that he could produce sympathetic "fight-or-flight" responses by stimulating one part of a cat's hypothalamus. When he stimulated another part of the hypothalamus, he observed an opposite relaxed response.

Although the actions of the smooth muscles are often thought of as involuntary, control over many of them can be learned—for example, control of urination and defecation. As mentioned in the sections on personality (Part Three) and learning (Part Six), many autonomic functions can be brought under control by operant conditioning. By this means, new relations can be established between internal responses and emotional motivational conditions.

Research in biofeedback conditioning has shown that subjects can learn to regulate such autonomic nervous system responses as finger temperature. In the experiment illustrated here, auditory signals through earphones provide feedback to the subject about her success in lowering finger temperature in one hand and raising it in the other hand.

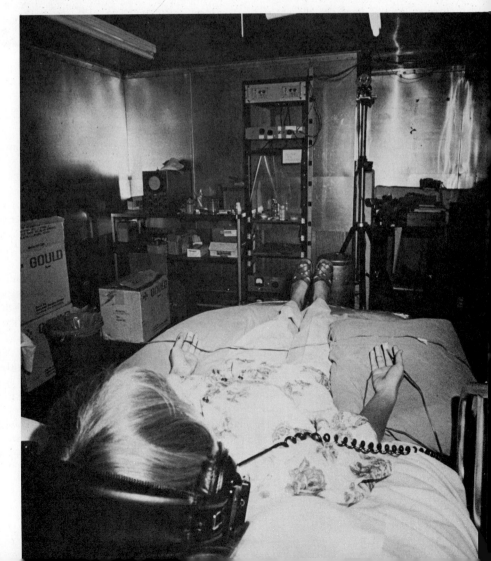

Newspaper stories with titles like this spotlight's appeared a few years ago. They referred to the development of superior artificial limbs that an amputee can use with little or no special training. The artificial arm seems to do whatever the user intends. The operation of motors in the artificial arm is actually controlled by the pattern of activity in the intact muscles of the shoulder, chest, and neck. Electrical signals are recorded from these muscles, and a small electronic circuit decides what pattern is being produced. According to this pattern, the different motors in the artificial arm are then operated with more or less force. Feedback occurs both visually and from the pull of the artificial arm on the rest of the body.

Researchers are now attempting to provide more complete feedback of the movements and stresses within the artificial arm. To do this they are placing various detectors within the arm that produce stimulation in the form of touches or vibrations on adjacent patches of skin. This gives more adequate feedback, but the amputee has to learn how to interpret and use it.

SUMMARY

Complex behavior requires the integration of many simultaneous biological processes, which is accomplished by the neural and endocrine systems. The basic physiology of neurons can be summarized in this way: **Neurons** conduct impulses (bioelectrical potentials) along their membranes. At the synaptic junctions with other neurons, chemical **transmitter agents** are released to bridge the narrow synaptic gap. The chemical activity at some synapses excites the postsynaptic neuron, whereas at others it inhibits. To be activated, a neuron requires a preponderance of excitatory incoming messages over inhibitory messages. Because many neurons receive inputs from hundreds or thousands of other cells these neurons can integrate a great deal of information. The **endocrine glands** affect behavior by secreting **hormones.** Among the effects of various hormones are the facilitation of certain responses (for example, in sex behavior) and modulation of metabolic activity and growth. In many cases the neural and hormonal systems work together, each influencing the other, and sequences of behavior may include both neural and endocrine steps.

Skilled movements require the coordinated activity of many muscles; this means accurate timing of the contractions of certain muscles and of the relaxation of others. The muscles are represented in the primary motor cortex, principally in the contralateral or "opposite-side" **cerebral hemisphere.** The size of the cortical representation of a muscle is related to the precision of control of its motion. Muscular coordination demands the participation of the **motor cortex,** other motor centers within the brain, and peripheral neurons. These motor circuits appear to develop and to store elaborate "programs" of acts. Feedback from sensory receptors within muscles, tendons, and joints allows monitoring and correction of behavior in progress.

The **autonomic division** of the **nervous system** controls the heart, certain glands, and the smooth muscles in internal organs and in blood vessels. The **sympathetic division** of the autonomic system generally predominates when a person is active; many of its functions help the body to expend energy. The **parasympathetic division** predominates during the restoration of bodily energy; for example, it promotes digestion. Thus, the nervous system coordinates the activities of the skeletal muscles with the activities of the heart, smooth muscles, and glands. Many autonomic functions can be conditioned, thereby establishing new relations between these responses and emotional or motivational states.

Biological Processes in Motivation

How do neural circuits regulate drinking and eating?

How does neural activity produce wakefulness, dreamless sleep, and dreaming?

What are the roles of genes, hormones, neural circuits, and experience in sex behavior?

To what extent can biological research help to explain and control aggression?

What is reinforcement in terms of neural activity?

At any given time you could be engaging in any one of a large variety of activities, but you are actually performing only one. Instead of studying, you could be sleeping or swimming or skiing or socializing, drinking or dreaming, feeding or fighting. Selecting among possible behaviors is the key problem of motivation. How can knowledge of biological processes help us understand the transition from one state to another—for example, from alert wakefulness to dreamless sleep to dreaming? How can it help us to understand individual differences in motivation—why some individuals eat voraciously while others shun food, why some are more active sexually than others, why some are more aggressive than others? Most behavior is determined by multiple factors. Although biological processes cannot provide the whole story, information about how they operate is essential to a well-rounded understanding of many aspects of motivation. For example, studying biological processes in sleeping has increased our understanding of dreams and nightmares—subjects that have long intrigued and puzzled both laymen and psychologists.

With the increasing knowledge of biological factors in motivation, the possibilities of "brain control" have been raised; for example, it is possible that electrical stimulation of the brain or surgical removal of diseased brain tissue could cure deviations of personality and could control violent behavior. Although some people view such possibilities with hope, others worry that such techniques could be used to suppress nonconformity or political dissent. Both the proponents and the opponents of brain control may be exaggerating its potential, and a realistic assessment is important both for personal understanding and for participation in the formation of social policy.

During and after extreme physical exertion, several neural and hormonal systems interact to restore normal fluid balance.

Despite much recent progress, the biological approaches to motivation are no more complete or final than the personality approaches described in Chapters 6–8. In fact, our understanding of biological processes in motivation has been changing rapidly during the last thirty years, and further changes will undoubtedly occur. Beginning in the 1940s, more and more specific motivational locations have been found in the brains of experimental animals. It first appeared that each kind of motivated behavior was controlled by a different brain center—a specific region whose activity would initiate and integrate that kind of behavior. More recently, however, some investigators have found evidence that the different functional sites are only parts of complex circuits that integrate behavior. Furthermore, circuits for different behaviors may overlap in part, and stimulation of a particular small brain region may evoke different behaviors depending on the external stimulus situation (for example, whether or not a goal object such as food is available).

In our sampling of research in this area, we will consider several kinds of behavior. Some, like drinking and eating, function primarily to maintain internal body conditions that are necessary to support all other kinds of behavior. (Of course, the ways in which drinking and eating are performed may also serve social functions and may express one's personality.) Sleep has also been thought of as maintaining or restoring readiness for activity, but we will see that there are now serious reasons to doubt this interpretation. Other kinds of motivated behavior do not serve internal needs; instead they regulate an organism's relations with the external world, including relations with other organisms. The kinds of externally oriented motivated behaviors that we will consider are wakefulness, sex, and aggression. Finally, we will consider how we can interpret reinforcement in terms of neural activity.

How do neural circuits regulate drinking and eating?

REGULATION OF
FLUID BALANCES

In the last century it was believed that bodily processes were mainly regulated by sensation; a source of discomfort would promptly evoke appropriate remedial action. Thus the sensation of thirst would lead a person or an animal to drink; hunger would lead to eating; a burning pain in the fingers would lead to withdrawal of the hand from a hot object, and so on. To understand regulation, then, it was necessary to find how the sensation of need or discomfort arose. Many believed that drinking occurred because a deficiency of water in the body caused a decrease in secretion of saliva which in turn led to dryness of the mouth and throat. Other physiologists suggested that the origin of thirst was more general—that the deficiency of water was detected by cells throughout the body. Late in the nineteenth century, a few neurologists noticed cases of excessive thirst and drinking following injury or disease of the brain, and they suggested the existence of a thirst center in the brain.

Actually, the regulation of fluid balance depends on multiple mechanisms and processes, as we will see. So each of the narrow unitary approaches was bound to fall short of providing an overall account. Only in the 1960s and 1970s has a comprehensive picture emerged (Epstein, Kissileff, & Stellar, 1973). The current view is called the **double depletion hypothesis of fluid regulation.**

This hypothesis is based on the fundamental fact that water is divided into two separate compartments within the body: (1) cellular fluid—the fluid within cells; and (2) extracellular fluid, the fluid that is either in the small spaces between the cells or in the blood vessels (see Figure 20-1 A). The hypothesis proposes that separate mechanisms monitor water in these two compartments and initiate responses to a deficit in either one. The amount of water in the body is determined both by intake (in water and food) and by output (through excretion, respiration, perspiration, and hemorrhage). When depletion of fluid is detected in either the intracellular or the extracellular compartment by receptors within the hypothalamus and within the blood vessels, this leads to responses that favor intake of fluid and also reduce the formation of urine. (The control of removal of water from the blood to form urine is an important aspect of regulation of body fluids, even though we are totally unaware of the operation of this mechanism.)

Cellular dehydration is detected because cells in two overlapping regions of the anterior hypothalamus are stimulated when they lose water and shrink (see Figure 20-1 B). In one anterior hypothalamic nucleus, this stimulation facilitates drinking responses. Stimulation at this site through implanted electrodes can lead to impressive increases of water intake. When such stimulation was given to unanesthetized, freely moving rats, they stopped other activities, went to water and promptly began to drink. As the stimulation was continued,

Figure 20-1
System That Responds to Depletion of Intracellular Fluid

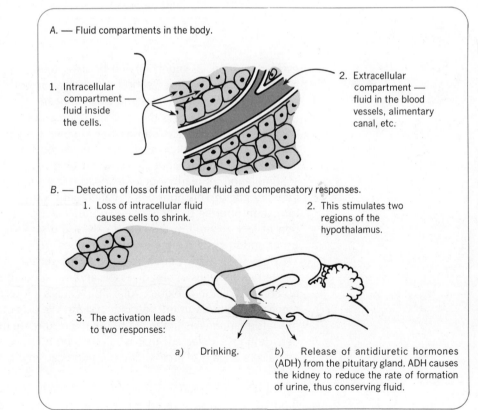

A. — Fluid compartments in the body.

1. Intracellular compartment — fluid inside the cells.

2. Extracellular compartment — fluid in the blood vessels, alimentary canal, etc.

B. — Detection of loss of intracellular fluid and compensatory responses.

1. Loss of intracellular fluid causes cells to shrink.

2. This stimulates two regions of the hypothalamus.

3. The activation leads to two responses:

a) Drinking.

b) Release of antidiuretic hormones (ADH) from the pituitary gland. ADH causes the kidney to reduce the rate of formation of urine, thus conserving fluid.

Figure 20-2
System That Responds to
Depletion of Extracellular
Fluid

Loss of extracellular fluid reduces the volume of blood flow; this is detected in two different ways:

A. — Reduced blood flow causes altered response rate of receptors in blood vessel walls, and this is reported to the brain, activating two regions of the hypothalamus and causing two compensatory responses.

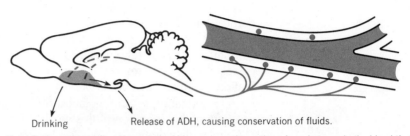

Drinking   Release of ADH, causing conservation of fluids.

B. — Reduced blood flow through the kidney causes formation of a substance in the blood that stimulates two regions of the hypothalamus.

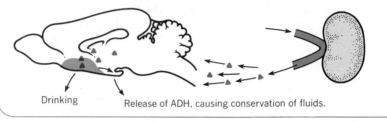

Drinking   Release of ADH, causing conservation of fluids.

some rats drank as much in one hour as they usually drank in twenty-four hours; during a ten-hour period of stimulation some rats drank almost their body weight in water. This stimulation appears to activate motivation to drink rather than just eliciting the motor responses of drinking. We conclude this because the stimulation causes the animal to search out fluid and then to drink. When no fluid was available, the rats did not engage in responses similar to drinking—such as lapping at a water tube.

Stimulation in nearby nuclei leads to release of a special hormone from the pituitary gland. This hormone is called **antidiuretic** because it acts against the formation of urine by the kidney and thus keeps water in the body. So detection of lack of fluid in the cells leads at the same time to attempts to secure water and to conserve the existing supplies.

Extracellular dehydration is detected by receptors of mechanical pressure located in the walls of blood vessels and in the heart (see Figure 20-2). Reduction of the volume of extracellular fluid causes a lowered rate of firing by these **mechanoreceptors** in the vascular system. We do not yet know exactly where this information goes in the brain, but the results are the same as when cellular dehydration is detected; that is, there is both an increased tendency to drink and also a release of antidiuretic hormone causing conservation of fluid by the kidney.

Not only is the kidney affected by the brain, but the kidney itself monitors fluid volume and can send a chemical messenger that affects brain function.

Reduced blood flow through the arterioles of the kidney causes formation of a substance called *angiotensin*. As this substance circulates through the blood-stream, it stimulates some brain cells that lead to increased drinking and others that cause release of antidiuretic hormone. Precise experimental injection of angiotensin into different sites has been used to map the brain regions that facilitate drinking and those that cause release of antidiuretic hormone.

Under most normal conditions, *all* of these mechanisms regulate the re-sponses of drinking and of urine concentration, as shown by Figure 20-3. These mechanisms make up a feedback system to restore losses or to remove excess body fluids. In the case of drinking behaviors, the hypothalamic systems probably facilitate or inhibit motor patterns that are integrated at midbrain or medullar levels.

One further feedback system is required. The system as described so far would not allow for the delay in absorbing water from the gut into the blood-stream and cells. That is, if a person or animal kept on drinking until the deficits of cellular and extracellular water had been made up, there would already be too much water in the body. So intake has to be monitored and shut off before an oversupply is ingested. This process is accomplished largely by kinesthetic receptors in the mouth and throat. In experiments to test this system, the esophagus of a dog was diverted so that water passed through the mouth and throat but did not enter the stomach. The dog would promptly drink an amount of water proportional to its deficit and then stop. A short time later it would be ready to drink again, whereas if the water had entered the stomach the dog would still be satisfied. So a short-term inhibitory feedback from the act of drinking must be included in the system.

Drinking is also intimately related to eating. Because the brain regions con-trolling the two kinds of ingestion overlap, we will refer to some further aspects of fluid regulation when we discuss regulation of eating in the next section of this chapter.

Figure 20-3
Complete System That Responds to Depletion of Both Intracellular and Extracellular Fluid

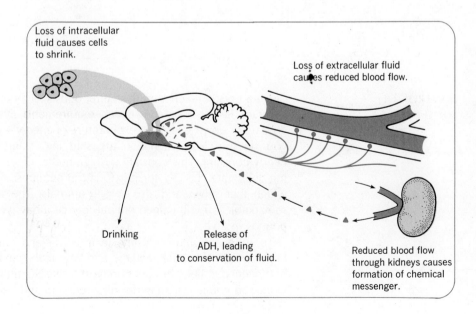

Loss of intracellular fluid causes cells to shrink.

Loss of extracellular fluid causes reduced blood flow.

Drinking

Release of ADH, leading to conservation of fluid.

Reduced blood flow through kidneys causes formation of chemical messenger.

Figure 20-4
Relationship of Food Intake and Activity

When work ranged from light to heavy—as shown to the right of the dashed line— intake was proportionate to energy output, and body weight remained constant. But among sedentary people, food intake was as high as among heavy workers, and body weight was greater than among heavy workers. (Modified from Mayer, 1956)

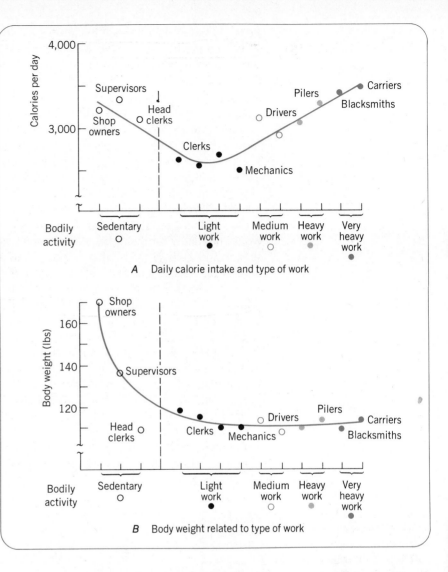

A   Daily calorie intake and type of work

B   Body weight related to type of work

CONTROL OF FOOD INTAKE

Once a person reaches adult stature, body weight usually remains surprisingly constant despite fluctuating energy requirements. Even though your food intake goes up or down with your expenditure of energy—you need more food when you ski and less when you are studying—your weight probably remains nearly constant. This constancy isn't a matter of watching the scales and making deliberate choices, for it is found in human societies where people do not weigh themselves and also among animals. The stability of adult weight is remarkable—if you gained only an ounce a day, you would gain over twenty pounds in a year.

yep!

To study this more closely, Jean Mayer and colleagues (1956) measured body weights, calorie intakes, and physical activity in males of a racially homogeneous Bengali community in India. Starting with clerks who did light work and going to men performing medium and heavy work, the daily calorie intake went up steadily with the energy expenditure, so average body weights were practically identical for all these classes of workers; this is illustrated in Figure 20-4, to the right of the dashed line in *A* and *B*. The data to the left of the dashed line show a very different relation. The sedentary men ate more than necessary for their level of energy expenditure, and the shop owners and supervisors were the heaviest groups of all. Weight control broke down when activity was reduced to a minimum. Programs to control obesity have been found to be more effective when they include exercise than when they consist only of dieting (Buskirk, 1963).

When muscular activity is kept within a normal range, how does intake of food balance the body's need so accurately? At one time this question was answered in terms of appetite and sensations of hunger, but now we know that several mechanisms are at work, including (1) monitoring of food supplies in the body, (2) monitoring of eating behavior, and (3) learned controls.

The picture of brain control of eating has been shifting in the 1970s from an emphasis on brain centers to greater consideration of influence distributed among several brain nuclei. Only a few years ago it was generally agreed that eating behavior was integrated and controlled by two main centers in the hypothalamus—a nucleus in the lateral hypothalamus—the **lateral nucleus**—that integrated feeding behavior and a nucleus in the ventromedial hypothalamus that inhibited eating (*see* Figure 20-5). There seemed to be abundant evidence for control by these centers. For example, experimental lesions (localized destruction of tissue) in the **ventromedial nuclei** (and tumors in this region in human patients) were reported to cause excessive eating and weight gain.

But now experimenters have found that overeating and obesity can be caused not only by lesions in the ventromedial nucleus but also by lesions in a tract that runs just below this nucleus. Furthermore, these two effects are independent: when lesions are made both in the nucleus and in the tract, the effects are additive (Ahlskog, Randall, & Hoebel, 1975). Refusal to eat and

Figure 20-5
Regions in Rat Brain Where Lesions Can Induce Overeating or Starvation

This cross-section of rat brain was cut through the hypothalamus, as shown in the small dorsal view to the left. The hypothalamus is shown in color, and two of its several sets of nuclei are labeled—the *ventromedial nucleus,* close to the base of the brain and near the medial ventricle, and the *lateral nucleus.* The right and left halves of the hypothalamus each contain a ventromedial and a lateral nucleus. Just outside each lateral nucleus is a lateral tract; the dots are used to indicate cross-sections of fibers running lengthwise. Interruption of this lateral tract causes undereating or starvation. Just below each ventromedial nucleus is the ventral hypothalamic tract; either bilateral interruption of this tract or damage to the ventromedial nuclei causes overeating and obesity.

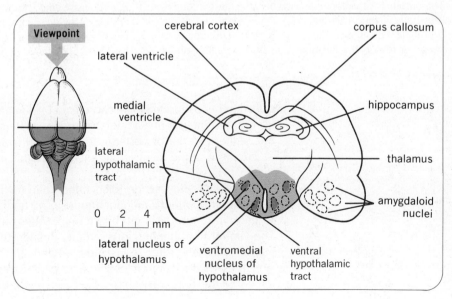

Most of our knowledge of the functions of the hypothalamus comes from animal experimentation. This is because brain damage in humans caused by accidental injury or by disease usually invades several different parts of the small but complex hypothalamus, and it is therefore difficult to assign the various symptoms to particular regions of the hypothalamus. A case involving a small sharply localized tumor in a woman's brain showed that results of the animal experiments could help in interpretation of human motivated behavior; it also reflected the multiple functions of the hypothalamus (Reeves & Plum, 1969).

The patient was a twenty-year-old bookkeeper. She came to the hospital because about a year previously she had developed an abnormal appetite so that she ate and drank large amounts and gained weight rapidly. During the same period she had frequent headaches and her menstrual periods had stopped. She was mentally alert, performed her work well, and did not show any emotional abnormalities.

Another year passed and her family brought her back to the hospital because of changes in her behavior. She was often uncooperative and at times attacked people around her. She was confused and sometimes could not remember correctly. She would not attempt arithmetic calculations. Tests showed reduced endocrine function, involving the gonads, the thyroid gland, and the adrenal cortex. An operation revealed a tumor at the base of the brain, but its position did not permit removal of the tumor. The outbursts of violent behavior became more frequent, especially if food was withheld. Toward the end of her hospitalization, she had to be fed almost continuously to keep her reasonably tractable, and she was eating about

10,000 calories a day. When she died, three years after the onset of her illness, the position of the tumor was determined precisely; it is shown in the figure on the facing page.

The tumor had destroyed a part of the hypothalamus called the "ventromedial nucleus" ("ventro"—on the belly side; "medial"—along the midline). In animal studies that are described in the Figure 20-5 caption, destruction of the ventromedial nucleus or of an adjacent fiber tract frequently causes overeating and obesity. In some species, such as the cat, lesions of the ventromedial nucleus usually make the animal display rage behavior more frequently and more readily than a normal animal does. Hypothalamic areas particularly involved in sexual receptivity and in mating behavior are also found nearby, although in the case of this patient, the reduced gonadal function was probably caused by interruption of pathways by which the hypothalamus regulates the pituitary gland. This would also explain the observed decreases in thyroid and adrenal cortex function, because these endocrine glands are also regulated by the anterior pituitary gland (see Figure 19-8). The causes of the confusion and the disturbances of memory are not clear, although hypothalamic structures have been implicated in learning and memory, as we will see in Chapter 21.

This case shows how a small tumor—about the size of the last joint of the little finger—because of its location in a critical region of the brain could affect a variety of motivated behaviors, eating, aggression, and sex. The neurologists who reported the case conclude, "The findings provide a close functional correlation between the human and homologous lower mammalian ventromedial hypothalamic structures."

---

drink has been reported to be caused not by damage to the lateral hypothalamus itself but to interrupting a tract that runs just lateral to the nucleus. Cutting this tract either anterior or posterior to the lateral hypothalamus is just as effective as cutting it at the level of the lateral hypothalamus (Ungerstedt, 1971; Oltmans & Harvey, 1972).

The recent emphasis on tracts rather than nuclei means more than just the substitution of one location for another. The findings support the current trend to think in terms of circuits and multiple sites rather than in terms of centers. The ventral fiber bundle, for example, includes fibers that come from several nuclei in the brainstem (pons and medulla), and the fibers go to a number of structures in the anterior hypothalamus and elsewhere in the basal central region of the brain. The basal bundle is a strategic spot for interfering with

The Human Hypothalamus and Nearby Structures

The entire hypothalamus is shown in color. The darker oval shows the location of the tumor; it extends somewhat beyond the boundaries of the ventromedial nucleus of the hypothalamus. The position of the region within the brain is indicated on the upper diagram, which presents a medial section of the brain. (Modified from Figure 3, Reeves & Plum, 1969)

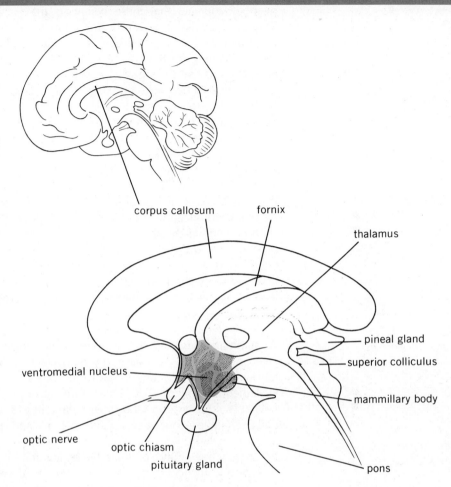

corpus callosum

fornix

thalamus

pineal gland

superior colliculus

ventromedial nucleus

mammillary body

optic nerve

optic chiasm

pituitary gland

pons

regulation because it interconnects so many structures, but it is not a center that organizes the regulation.

Other factors, including peripheral monitoring and learning, also help to determine eating. Monitoring of more peripheral processes includes taste and smell, and the motor acts of ingesting food and loading of the stomach also provide inhibitory feedback to prevent overeating.

Learning also governs eating from the very start. Human babies and other young mammals learn many aspects of nursing behavior. In a laboratory situation young infants can learn to suck on an artificial nipple in different ways to control visual displays (*see* p. 242). Learning also helps to determine the schedule of eating. Under normal circumstances our eating anticipates need — we eat regularly rather than to make up for lack of food.

EATING AND DRINKING AS INSTRUMENTAL BEHAVIORS

It is customary to think of eating and drinking as **primary drives**—activities undertaken for their contributions to basic metabolism—but we should not overlook the fact that these behaviors may also occur for other reasons. Through learning, a person or animal may eat or drink to engage in another more preferred activity. Children can be induced to eat by offering to let them play when they finish dinner. A rat that is not thirsty will lick water from a tube after it learns that licking will activate a mechanism that allows the rat to run in an activity wheel. The drinking in this case is not primarily *consummatory behavior* but rather should be classed as *instrumental behavior*. A dramatic demonstration of this principle is found in a study of anorexia nervosa (nervous loss of appetite), a condition that affects women especially. People suffering from this condition show a distaste for food; they eat little and become emaciated. The cause of the disease is not known. Stunkard (1972) observed women patients with anorexia nervosa in a hospital ward, and he noticed that they walked around a great deal. He then instituted the following program of behavior modification: each patient was allowed to go out of the hospital for six hours only if she showed an increase in weight of at least one-half pound over the previous day. Patients gained weight in this program, and the results were reported to be more favorable than with any of the other kinds of therapy that had been tried. In this case, eating was principally determined by the learned association—eating was necessary to procure the opportunity for the preferred response of walking.

SUMMARY OF DRINKING AND EATING

To summarize, we see that whether or not an individual drinks or eats on a given occasion is determined by many factors. Some of the most important follow: (1) internal monitoring of the body's supplies of fluid and food, and kinesthetic monitoring of recent drinking and eating; (2) the availability of palatable fluid or food (and often palatability is a matter of learning); (3) the daily schedule—one learns when to drink and eat regardless of the state of need; (4) what other behaviors are going on—a more important or more interesting activity may dominate the behavioral hierarchy and prevent drinking or eating from occurring; (5) the instrumental value of drinking or eating—whether or not it may be rewarded by a more highly preferred activity.

How does neural activity produce wakefulness, dreamless sleep, and dreaming?

Wakefulness is of course the state in which we interact directly with others and with our environment, but sleep is now known to be a much more active and varied state than was believed in the 1950s. In fact, during a usual night you alternate between two quite different kinds of sleep, even though you do not remember having done so. One kind of sleep, which occurs in adults about every 90 minutes during the night, is usually accompanied by vivid **dreams.** The other kind of sleep is also accompanied by mental content, but it is more abstract and less striking than what we usually call dreams. By studying the electrical activity of the brain, psychologists have learned more about these different kinds of sleep activity and the differences between sleeping and

The many and varied observations on eating and obesity that have been made with animal subjects since the 1940s have recently inspired psychologists and physiologists to make novel observations on human subjects.

Preview Figure 5 introduced such research with rats. Rats made obese by brain lesions differ in many ways from normal controls: the obese rats eat a somewhat greater amount per day, eat *fewer* meals per day, eat more per meal, eat faster, and are less active. Which of these characteristics do you suppose are also true of fat people as compared with people of normal weight? Psychologists Stanley Schachter and Judith Rodin (1974) surveyed the research literature and found that each of these facts is also true of obese humans. They and their collaborators then ran experiments to see whether other findings on obese rats would also hold for obese humans.

One often-repeated observation has been that fat rats will actually eat less than normals if the taste is made slightly bitter or if it takes effort to obtain the food. To test whether this last characteristic would be observed with humans, the psychologists tested eighty students, one at a time. Each student sat at a desk, ostensibly to fill out a questionnaire. On the desk was a bag of almonds; the experimenter helped herself to a nut, invited the subject to do the same, and then left the room for 15 minutes. For half the subjects the nuts had shells on them; for the other half, the shells had been removed. The presence or absence of shells had no effect on the forty normal-weight students—about half ate nuts in either case—but it was of crucial importance for the obese. Nineteen of twenty obese subjects ate the shelled nuts, but only one of the twenty ate when the shells still had to be cracked!

Other investigators had studied extremely obese persons who were hospitalized to reduce their weights. Given a bland unappealing liquid diet, the obese people readily cut their caloric intake and lost weight. Normal subjects when given the same diet maintained their caloric intake and kept their weight up. When the formerly obese individuals left the hospital and reentered the world of attractive cues to eating, they all became obese again. Thus the obese seem to be stimulus-bound; that is, they are strongly influenced by external stimuli but they are relatively unaffected by cues arising from within their own bodies.

Schachter and his associates found that the greater sensitivity of the obese to external stimuli is not limited to food but is true of a wide variety of situations. Thus,

Obesity is not new. The Venus of Willendorf, a Stone Age figurine, indicates that obesity was recognized and perhaps even revered in very ancient times.

obese subjects recognized words flashed on a screen more quickly than did normals, and they worked harder to avoid a threatened electrical shock than did normals. The greater distractibility of obese students was found in an experiment reported in Chapter 1, p. 23. But the obese are more responsive only to highly noticeable stimuli; they are not more responsive than normal people to stimuli that are inconspicuous. It is intriguing to see many differences of behavior between obese and normal individuals are encompassed under the same generalization, but it is not yet known what neural processes mediate these effects.

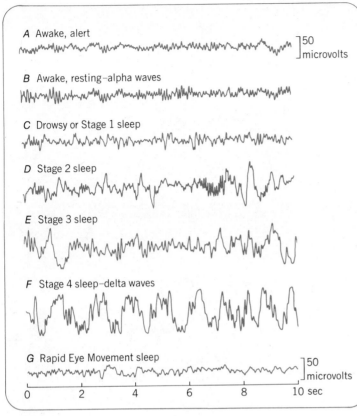

A Awake, alert
50 microvolts

B Awake, resting–alpha waves

C Drowsy or Stage 1 sleep

D Stage 2 sleep

E Stage 3 sleep

F Stage 4 sleep–delta waves

G Rapid Eye Movement sleep
50 microvolts

0   2   4   6   8   10 sec

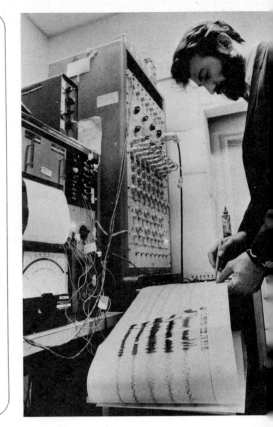

Figure 20-6
Brain-Wave Patterns in Waking, Quiet Sleep, and Dreaming
The EEG records on the left show that the electrical activity of the brain has characteristic patterns that vary with the state of the person. When a person is awake and mentally active, the EEG record shows relatively rapid waves of low amplitude, as in *A*. When a waking person is relaxed, and especially if his eyes are closed, there may be an 8–12 Hz rhythm called alpha waves (*B*). As a person becomes drowsy and falls into deep sleep, the EEG waves become slower in frequency and larger in amplitude (*C–F*). During dreaming, the EEG pattern (*G*) resembles that of wakeful activity (*A*) or of drowsiness (*C*).

waking. Related studies have clarified the nature of nightmares and have shown how to overcome them (*see* Spotlight 20-4).

In 1929 Berger showed that by putting electrodes on the head and amplifying the tiny potentials, he could record fluctuating electrical activity of the brain. These records were called "brain waves" or, more formally, the **electroencephalogram** (abbreviated as **EEG**). When a person is awake and alert, the EEG record usually shows rather rapid irregular waves of low amplitude, as shown in Figure 20-6 by the top trace, *A*. When a person is awake but resting and with the eyes closed, there are often periods of rather regular activity at 10 Hz; this is called the **alpha rhythm** (see trace *B* in Figure 20-6). As a person becomes drowsy and falls asleep, the EEG waves become slower in frequency and larger in amplitude (*see* traces *C* through *F* in the figure)—**slow-wave sleep.** Regular waves of large amplitude mean that millions of brain cells must be acting in synchrony—either firing impulses together or showing shifts in membrane potentials at the same time.

A surprising exception to this regular picture of synchronous activity during sleep was discovered in 1953. After perhaps 90 minutes of sleep, the EEG suddenly resembles the asynchronous waking pattern with high-frequency low-voltage waves (*see* the bottom trace, *G,* in Figure 20-6). Moreover, although the person remains asleep, movement of the eyes can now be detected under the closed lids. If sleepers are awakened during this stage, they usually report a dream—a vivid, detailed experience. This is true even of people who ordinarily do not remember their dreams the next day. This stage of sleep is most often called **rapid-eye-movement sleep** (or **REM** sleep). Because the brain appears to be highly active while the body is relaxed, this stage is also sometimes called **paradoxical sleep;** it is also called **fast-wave sleep** because of the relatively rapid EEG. The cycles of sleep stages are shown in Figure 20-7. Now that investigators can tell when dreams are occurring, they are making far more complete and useful collections of dream reports than were available previously.

Because the cat is a common laboratory animal that sleeps for long periods of time, more research on sleep has been done with the cat than with any other animal, including human beings. Although some reports of research assume that all the findings made with cats also hold true for human beings, there are real differences between the patterns of electrical and motor activities of these two species during sleep; some of these differences are summarized in Table 20-1. Although we often think of sleep in terms of muscular relaxation and a reclining posture, many animals (such as horses and birds) remain upright and their antigravity muscles are active while they sleep.

TABLE 20-1	Differences between cat and human in patterns of rapid eye movement sleep	
	Cat	*Human being*
Eye movements during REM sleep	Very rapid, unlike waking movements	Slower than shifts in fixation during waking but similar in form
Electroencephalographic (EEG) pattern	Extremely fast and activated	Resembles the somewhat slowed and random pattern found at the initial transition from waking to sleep
Muscle tonus	Great drop in tonus	Subtle and irregular changes
Thresholds of arousal	Elevated, so sleep is especially deep during REM periods	Somewhat lower than in other phases of sleep, so REM sleep is not deep

From F. Snyder, 1971.

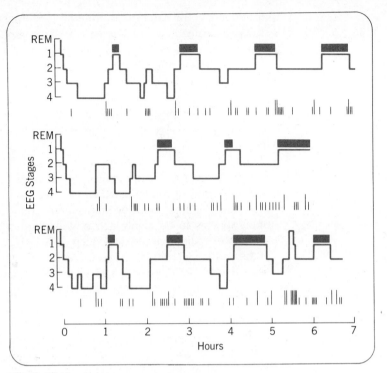

Figure 20-7
Dream Periods During a Normal Night
These graphs are based on electroencephalogram (EEG) records made during a night's sleep for each of three adults. They show fairly regular cycles from EEG Stage 1 through 2 and 3 to Stage 4, and then in reverse order to Stage 1. Rapid eye movement (REM) sleep is marked by colored bars. The deepest sleep, Stage 4, tends to occur only early in the sleep period. REM occurs on emerging from Stage 1. If a person is awakened from REM sleep, he usually reports an active dream; during other stages dreams may occur but they are much less frequent. Body movements are shown by the vertical lines at the bottom of each graph—tall lines for large movements and short lines for minor movements. Body activity tends to be absent during Stage 4 sleep and to occur in lighter stages and at transitions between stages.
(Modified from Dement & Kleitman, 1957)

CIRCADIAN RHYTHMS

We tend to think of sleep as a night-time state, but many animals (such as foxes, bats, and owls) are *nocturnal*—they sleep during the day and are active at night. Other animals have several cycles of sleep during a twenty-four-hour period; rats, for example, fall asleep and then waken frequently, although they are more active during the night than during the day.

Almost all animals show a twenty-four-hour cycle of activity, even though they differ from each other in the distribution of activity within their cycles. Moreover, this rhythm seems to follow a neural clock; when experimenters place people or animals in environments that remain the same at all hours and

Spotlight 20-3 Meditation—A Fourth State of Being?

Various types of meditation—including forms of Yoga, Zen, and Transcendental Meditation—have gained many adherents in recent years. Some advocates have even claimed that meditation is a fourth state of existence, in addition to wakefulness, slow-wave sleep, and fast-wave sleep. Meditation in this sense does not conform to the dictionary definition of "sustained consecutive thought or contemplation"; rather it is an attempt to block thought and to achieve relaxation or altered states of consciousness.

In the 1950s and 1960s, some studies of yogis in India and Zen monks in Japan found that certain highly practiced individuals could significantly lower their oxygen consumption (basal metabolic rate) while meditating. Then in the early 1970s it was reported that oxygen consumption was lowered during Transcendental Meditation (TM). The subjects of these tests were Americans of many occupations, the majority of whom had practiced TM for two or three years (Wallace & Benson, 1972). TM was also accompanied by other physiological changes, including reduced heart rate and increased alpha rhythm.

Dr. Herbert Benson (1975) then surveyed the wide variety of meditational procedures that have been described over the last 3,000 years in many different sects and philosophies. Four practices were shared by many of these forms of meditation:

1) *A quiet environment.*
2) *A comfortable position,* but not one that induces sleep.
3) *A mental device* to encourage relaxation and to block intruding thoughts. A recommended device is to close the eyes, breathe regularly, and to repeat a neutral word (such as "one") silently in time with each expiration.
4) *A passive attitude,* not worrying about how well you are doing or about distracting thoughts, but simply repeating the neutral word.

Use of these techniques has been found to produce as great a drop in metabolic rate and the other physiological effects that accompany Transcendental Meditation as TM itself. Benson suggests that the techniques produce a "relaxation response" that is the opposite of the "fight-or-flight" pattern of the sympathetic division of the autonomic nervous system (see p. 541). The relaxed meditative condition would then be only a variety of the wakeful state and not a separate stage of existence.

Further research is being pursued in several laboratories concerning stress, meditation, and relaxation. For example, individual patterns of stress may differ, so that effective strategies for relaxation may also have to be different for different people (see, for example, Schwartz, 1975).

---

that provide no clues about the time, behavior still shows a periodicity that is about twenty-four hours long. This periodicity of behavior is called the **circadian rhythm** (from the Latin words *circe,* "about" and *dia,* "day"). Not only is there alternation between waking and sleep, but subrhythms during waking affect sensory thresholds and learning ability (Rusak & Zucker, 1975).

BRAIN MECHANISMS OF WAKEFULNESS AND SLEEP

In trying to find what brain mechanisms account for the various states we go through during the twenty-four-hour cycle and what triggers the transitions from one state to another, scientists have used many techniques—recording the EEG, stimulating specific brain regions, making lesions in parts of the brain, and studying people with abnormal sleep. Out of all this research a comprehensive, complex picture is slowly emerging (Williams, Holloway, & Griffiths, 1973). Let us state only five summary points of this research:

1) Each of the three states—wakefulness, slow-wave sleep, and fast-wave sleep—is integrated by different brain areas; that is, stimulation in some sites will cause a waking animal to engage in presleep behavior (relaxing, closing the eyes) and then fall asleep, and stimulation in other areas causes a sleeping animal to awaken.

2) No state is governed by a single brain area, as used to be thought. Rather, different aspects of the state (such as cortical activity and level of muscular contraction) are usually controlled by different brain areas acting in collaboration.

3) The onset of sleep is partly a matter of reducing sensory input (like closing your eyes) and of altered evaluation of sensory messages. The sensory systems continue to process information during sleep, but they classify most of it as unimportant. A novel or important stimulus readily wakes a sleeper—a baby's cry wakes its parents, and the smell of fresh meat wakes a cat.

4) Sleep onset is also caused by specific inhibitory areas whose activity suppresses the brain areas that control wakefulness.

5) Although external and internal stimuli can cause the transition from one state to another to occur somewhat sooner or later, there are basic rhythmic timers in the brain. In addition to the twenty-four-hour circadian sleep-waking rhythm, there is another cycle of about ninety minutes. During sleep this shorter cycle regulates the transition from slow-wave to fast-wave states, and during waking there are some indications of a similar rhythm in alertness.

WHY WE SLEEP

What are the functions of sleep? We still do not know clearly the answer to this basic question, let alone why there are two kinds of sleep. The customary answer that sleep is necessary to help us recover from effort is now seen to be incomplete at best. The brain and thought processes are not resting during sleep, as we have seen; brain cells are as active in sleep as during waking hours. Furthermore, studies of individuals and comparisons among species show that length of wakefulness correlates negatively with length of sleep (Webb, 1971). That is, if you stay awake longer on a particular day, you tend to sleep *less* that night; if you go to bed earlier, you sleep longer. You tend to wake up at about the same time no matter when you went to sleep; your internal circadian alarm awakens you. If sleep occurred primarily to provide rest, its length would correlate positively, instead of negatively, with the hours of preceding wakefulness. Further evidence that sleep is *not* needed to provide rest is that there are people, otherwise normal, who regularly sleep an hour or less per day. Some of these people hold both a daytime and a night-time job.

Quite a different hypothesis is that sleep and its brain mechanisms evolved to keep animals quiet and inconspicuous during the part of the daily cycle when their behavior was least efficient and when they were most likely to fall prey to other animal forms. Thus animals that evolved to be most efficient in the light (such as primates, dogs, and deer) sleep at night. Others, which are very efficient in the dark (like cats, rats, and bats), sleep during much of the daytime.

The specific functions of fast-wave sleep are even more speculative. Here are a few suggestions that have been made:

1) REM sleep provides an internal source of stimulation that aids in the development of the brain of the child. (This hypothesis would explain why REM sleep occupies a much larger part of the sleep of the infant than of the

Spotlight 20-4 Nightmares

Study of the brain activity of people subject to **nightmares** has brought us to a new understanding of this phenomenon (Broughton, 1968). Previously it was commonly assumed that a nightmare was simply a bad dream, one in which a person's mental conflicts, facing less repression than in the waking state, came to consciousness even if only in weird distorted images. If nightmares were dreams, then they would be expected to occur during fast-wave sleep, but they do not. Instead, like certain other disturbances of sleep—sleeptalking, sleepwalking, and bed-wetting—nightmares occur either in the deepest level of nondreaming sleep or, more often, during sudden arousal from deep sleep. They seem to be disorders of arousal before the person has regained waking contact with his environment. There is lack of coordination, confusion, and usually amnesia for the occurrence. If anything is remembered, it is usually only a scene, not a prolonged episode as in the case of a dream.

Because nightmares occur during a particular stage of slow-wave sleep, they can be controlled by the use of drugs that reduce the amount of time spent in this stage. When nightmares are overcome in this way, the person reports a general increase in well-being. This finding is inconsistent with the psychoanalytic hypothesis that nightmares are only a symptom of a deep-seated mental conflict, and therefore removing only the symptom (and not the cause) would result in the appearance of a new symptom.

adult—80 percent versus 20 percent. But it does not explain why REM still is prominent in adult sleep.)

2) REM sleep reorganizes neuronal firing patterns that have become disorganized during slow-wave sleep.

3) REM sleep provides practice of coordinated movements of the eyes during sleep so that accurate binocular vision can occur promptly on waking.

4) REM sleep and dreams provide a "safety valve" for discharge of patterns that otherwise would lead to unacceptable behavior during waking.

5) REM sleep and dreams serve to review activities of the preceding day and aid their consolidation in long-term memory.

Each of these hypotheses is related to a different aspect of REM sleep. Most of these hypotheses are not necessarily incompatible with each other, and each may explain some of the diverse phenomena of REM sleep. Clearly much research must be done before we understand fully why we spend one-third of our lives asleep and one-fifth of that in the peculiar state of fast-wave sleep.

What are the roles of genes, hormones, neural circuits, and experience in sex behavior?

You can usually tell at a glance whether an adult whom you meet is a man or a woman. The outward appearance and behavior of being male or female is called **gender role.** In most cases this role coincides with the person's sex chromosomes; typically there are two X chromosomes in the female, whereas the male has one X and one Y chromosome. But the chromosomal pattern and gender role do not always agree because gender role is determined by interaction between hereditary and environmental factors.

Both female and male potentialities exist in each fetal mammal; originally, a fetus has two systems of ducts—one that could develop into parts of the female reproductive tract and another that could develop into parts of the male reproductive mechanisms. When the chromosomal pattern is male (XY), the fetal gonads develop into testes and begin secreting hormones. The fetal testicular hormones determine the development of the male reproductive system and male genitals, and they cause the female duct system to disappear. When the chromosome pattern is XX, the gonads develop into ovaries, but fetal ovaries do not organize the development of body structures. The *absence* of testicular hormones permits female development—the growth of female genitals and the reproductive tract.

During childhood practically no **sex hormones** are produced; but at puberty, the male and female hormones help to organize the adult secondary sexual characteristics—the differences of skeletal form and distribution of body hair, growth of breasts in the female, deepening of the voice in the male, and so on. As well as organizing these body structures, the sex hormones will also help to activate patterns of behavior, as we will see later.

The differences between the sexes in hormone production are relative, not absolute. That is, the **androgens** (so-called male hormones) are actually secreted by both sexes but in greater amounts by males. The **estrogens** (so-called female hormones) are secreted by both sexes, but in greater amounts by females. The adrenal cortex also secretes both androgens and estrogens, and sometimes abnormal activity of the adrenal cortex can exert a strong masculinizing influence.

Although the chromosomal pattern usually determines the hormonal pattern and subsequent body development, there are cases in which the chromosomal pattern is not reflected in the appearance of the person. For example, there are rare individuals who are genetically male and secrete normal amounts of sex hormones but whose cells are completely insensitive to the androgens. In this case, even though androgens are present, the cells do not respond to the "male" hormones. Because the development of the genitals is governed by action of fetal testicular hormones, these individuals are therefore born with female-appearing genitals. At puberty the body responds to the low level of circulating estrogens and develops normal feminine contours. Because the testes early secreted a substance to prevent growth of the female reproductive tracts, these individuals cannot become pregnant. Nevertheless, in psychological reports, as well as in appearance, they are clearly feminine. Some of these people have married, adopted children, and proved to be good mothers (Money & Ehrhardt, 1972, p. 111).

In other cases the appearance of the genitals at birth is neither completely masculine nor completely feminine, and the parents or physician may err in identifying the baby's sex. For example, an overactive adrenal cortex during the fetal period may cause a girl's genitals to develop a masculine appearance. At birth some of these genetic females are recognized as girls, but some are classified as boys. In the latter case, the child raised as a boy usually acts like a boy and wants to develop into a man. At the age of puberty, masculinization of the body can be induced by means of androgen therapy; and this biological treatment is necessary to provide a body form that corresponds to the learned gender identity. Such a person is a man in gender identity and gender role, although his chromosomal pattern is XX. (We will consider this adrenal-genital syndrome again later in relation to its behavioral effects.)

In some cases a later, more accurate identification of sex causes a reversal of sex assignment; that is, parents decide to shift and rear the child as a boy rather than a girl, or vice versa. When such a change is made before age three or four, it proceeds easily (Hampson, 1965). Beyond this age, personality problems may arise because the child's own gender identity—the identification of one's self as girl or boy—seems to be established by about age three. Sometimes adults have appeared able to switch from living as one sex to the opposite sex with considerable success. Hampson claims that in all such cases of successful sex reversal he has studied, the persons had had long-standing reservations about their "true sex" and had viewed themselves as a kind of role "imposter" prior to the change.

Usually, of course, the genetic pattern and sex behavior agree. Some investigators have suggested that the nervous system, like the reproductive tract, originally has the potentialities of both sexes, but that usually only one of the set of neural circuits is allowed to develop. In support of this hypothesis, they describe the results of secretion or administration of androgen during the first few days after birth in the rat (Levine, 1966). The presence of androgen during this early period, either normally or by injection, increases the probability of male mating behavior in adulthood in the male and, to a somewhat lesser degree, even in the female. The early influence of the male hormone seems to cause the nervous system to become "male." If there is no androgen during the early postnatal period, certain female mating responses will occur in adulthood, such as arching the back and raising the rump **(lordosis)** when the rat is primed with female hormones and stimulated either by another rat mounting it or by the experimenter touching it on the back. The absence of androgen early in life is normal in the female; it can be produced in the male either by castration or by injection of chemical compounds that combat androgens.

Direct evidence of differences in brain anatomy between adult male and female rats has been reported. For example, in one study it was found that the two sexes differed significantly in the size of nuclei of nerve cells in four brain regions (Pfaff, 1966). Furthermore, when male rats were castrated seven days after birth, the adult brain measures were either intermediate between male and female or differed significantly from males but not from females. In these respects, male hormones must normally influence brain development.

Rough-and-tumble play is characteristic of young male monkeys and is seen much less frequently among young females. Females that receive androgen prenatally, however, engage in significantly more rough play than normal females.

SEX-LINKED BEHAVIORS

Many kinds of behavior are **sex-linked** even though they are not involved in mating. For example, women are more sensitive to some tastes than are men; female rats have a significantly greater preference for sweet tastes than do male rats, and injections of estrogen increase the preference for saccharin in both sexes. In their patterns of play, young male monkeys show much more of the following kinds of social behavior than do the females: rough-and-tumble play, threatening acts, pursuit play. (*See also* Preview Figure 2.) This genetic difference can be influenced by early hormonal treatment. Administering androgen prenatally produced female monkeys with malelike genitalia and with relatively malelike behavior (Phoenix, Goy, & Resko, 1968). Some aspects of temperament are therefore strongly conditioned by sex. Here the male hormones acted by organizing neural structures during fetal development.

Can the fact that human males are more aggressive than human females also be attributed to early hormonal influences? A searching examination (Maccoby & Jacklin, 1974) indicates that males are more aggressive than females in all societies for which evidence is available. They found little to support the common argument that sexes are differentially trained or rewarded for aggression. Furthermore, similar sex differences are found in man and in subhuman primates, and aggression can be changed by experimental administration of these hormones: androgens increase aggressive behavior and estrogens decrease it.

Clinical research with people who have hormonal aberrations has taught us a great deal about the effect of prenatal hormones on behavior. In the **adrenogenital syndrome (AGS)** that we referred to briefly above, the adrenal cortex does not produce one of its usual hormones but instead produces a hormone that has prenatal masculinizing effects. At birth the external genitals of AGS girls are modified in varying degrees in the masculine direction. Such modifications can readily be corrected by surgery. The internal reproductive organs are female. The continuing excessive output of adrenal androgen is treated by giving the hormone cortisone throughout life. AGS also occurs in males, and administration of cortisone is needed in them to prevent premature pubertal development.

A recent study compared AGS children with their unaffected siblings of the same sex (Ehrhardt & Baker, 1974). The AGS girls had a high level of energy expenditure in rough outdoor play; they were significantly more often tomboys, and many preferred playing with boys to playing with girls. They showed significantly less interest than their sisters in playing with dolls or taking care of infants, less rehearsal of the adult roles of wife and mother, and less concern about the attractiveness of their clothing, hair, or jewelry. Yet the AGS girls were not seen as outside the normal female range, and they accepted the female role. The AGS boys differed from their unaffected brothers only in showing significantly higher energy expenditure in sports and rough outdoor activities. Ehrhardt and Baker speculate that finer variations in hormonal levels during fetal development may also cause some of the "normal" individual differences we see in behavior.

HORMONES AND ACTIVATION OF SEX BEHAVIOR

Once the body systems for sex behavior have developed under the influence of the sex hormones, are these hormones required to activate mating behavior? The answer depends on both the species and sex being considered and also upon prior experience. In the adult rat of either sex, removal of sex hormones abolishes mating behavior. In dogs and cats, the female promptly becomes unreceptive when the supply of ovarian hormones is removed, but the experienced male may continue to mate for some time or even indefinitely; a male that was not sexually experienced before castration is unlikely, however, to initiate mating afterward. In adult men and women, sexual drive and activity may continue despite a loss of sex hormones through illness or a decrease through age, but individuals react quite differently. Thus, as one goes from rat to dog to human beings the evolutionary trend seems to be toward relative independence from hormonal control.

To what extent can biological research help to explain and control aggression?

Emotions are sometimes considered to be purely subjective states, to be studied only through one's own introspections or through verbal reports of other people. But we are learning about brain processes that affect emotion from studies of both human and animal subjects. Emotional behavior involves changes not only in experienced moods but also in sensory systems and motor

In humans and animals, aggression is accompanied by changes in sensory and motor response patterns and increases in hormonal activity.

response patterns. As an example, we will consider violent or aggressive behavior, on which much research has been done in recent years. Let us start with a case report:

Paul M., a handsome muscular twenty-year-old man, came into Boston City Hospital voluntarily because he was afraid that he was "going wild" and "didn't want to hurt anybody." Shortly before this time he had had an attack of violence in his own apartment. He had ripped plaster off the walls with his bare hands and had smashed a mirror; with pieces of the mirror he had cut deep gashes in his chest and abdomen. Further information pointed to brain damage as the cause of the violent behavior. Just before his rampage, Paul had suffered a spell of unconsciousness from which he awoke dazed and violent. Five months earlier he had had an attack of grand mal epilepsy. (In a grand mal epileptic seizure, the person falls unconscious, his limbs may contract repeatedly; he may salivate, bite his tongue, and urinate or defecate. The electroencephalogram shows a characteristic pattern of very large spikes during this time. A seizure may last from thirty seconds to five minutes; after it is over the person is often confused, tired, and sleepy.) Paul's seizure had occurred after prolonged use of stimulant drugs, although other factors in his history may have contributed to brain damage.

Although his earlier behavior had often been aggressive and antisocial, Paul had always kept within limits. But after his grand mal seizure, the situation changed. He experienced dreamlike states that convinced him that he was losing his mind, and he could no longer restrain his violent impulses toward other people or even toward himself. Neurological tests led to a diagnosis of mild brain damage, and Paul was placed on a type of medication used to prevent seizures. Since being on medication he has had no violent outbursts, and he says he feels once again in control of himself (Mark & Ervin, 1970).

In this case drugs used to prevent epileptic seizures keep the attacks of violence under control. These drugs have little effect on normal excitability of neural tissue; but they do inhibit abnormally large EEG responses, those caused by many cells working in synchrony. Presumably, the attacks of violence involved overactivity of brain regions that integrate such behavior.

Studies with experimental animals have also demonstrated that stimulation in some brain regions elicits well-coordinated attack behavior. Experimenters have selected cats that do not spontaneously attack rats; such a cat will normally remain quiet when placed in a cage with a rat. When permanent electrodes are implanted in the brain, the freely moving cat can be stimulated at various sites. Dramatic full-blown rage responses and attacks are elicited by stimulation in particular hypothalamic sites. The cat shows a Halloween posture with back arched and hair on end, hissing and snarling; it strikes and tears the rat with its claws. This motivational state is apparently unpleasant for the cat, because it seeks to avoid or escape from the place where it has received such stimulation in the past. In contrast, a quiet biting attack is elicited by stimulation at other hypothalamic sites. In this case, the cat stalks the rat quietly and then attacks by biting instead of using its paws. The cat does not avoid but rather seeks to obtain the stimulation that elicits this motivational state (Flynn, 1967). Not only motor behavior but even perception may be affected; recording from sensory cells in the visual cortex demonstrated that some receptive fields are altered by hypothalamic stimulation that induces attack (Flynn, Edwards, & Bandler, 1971). Such studies are telling us how kinds of attack behavior are organized in the brain. But some investigators have questioned their relevance to aggression, claiming that hunting and killing prey is more properly classified as feeding behavior than as aggression. The belligerent rage response does, however, look like the way aggressive cats confront each

Electrical stimulation of certain areas of a cat's brain produces the same aggressive behaviors and postures observable during a cat fight.

other. Perhaps abnormal excitability of such regions can lead to uncontrolled violence in some human beings.

Not all cases of abnormal violence respond to medication. If all other treatments fail, some neurologists have advocated removing small amounts of damaged tissue that may cause unusual excitability and trigger storms of large brain waves. The idea of treating uncontrollable violence by a brain operation came from a series of animal experiments that started in the 1930s. Removal of a little almond-shaped group of cells near the front of each **temporal lobe** appeared to tame irritable or savage animals; this nucleus is called the **amygdala** (from the Greek for "almond"). (The location of the amygdala is shown in Color Figure 3.) The effect of this operation was tested on a lynx, a savage member of the cat family. The lynx was so vicious that the investigators injected it through the bars of the cage with an anesthetic agent; they then surgically destroyed the small amygdaloid nuclei in both hemispheres. As soon as the anesthesia wore off, the lynx was no longer savage. It tolerated small animals in its cage and could even be petted or fed by hand (Schreiner & Kling, 1956).

The animal experiments encouraged some neurosurgeons to try similar operations on humans whose attacks of violence were not controlled by anticonvulsant drugs. One active practitioner is Dr. Hirataro Narabayashi of Japan, who has made it possible since the 1950s for many mentally defective and some "criminally insane" patients to leave the hospital and return home. One patient said after his operation, "Now I can't get mad even if I want to." To destroy the right tissue—and no more than is necessary—some neurosurgeons insert several electrodes and map the responses of the awake patient to electrical stimulation of different points within the brain. Even points that are near each other may elicit quite different emotional experiences. Thus, electrical stimulation at one point in a patient's brain brought a report of a pleasant calm feeling; when stimulated at another point, the patient described a strange detached sensation of "looking on" at the world. With stimulation at another point, only a few millimeters away in the middle of the amygdala, he reported pain in his teeth, then in his face, and he felt that everything was "going wild." Subsequent surgical destruction of this area of the amygdala in both hemispheres was reported to terminate the attacks of violence that had plagued the patient for seven years (Mark & Ervin, 1970, pp. 92–97).

But this kind of "psychosurgery" to alleviate personality problems has been criticized for several reasons. For one thing, it is inadequate to describe the effects of amygdalectomy in animals as simply taming them. Such animals have been described as being less responsive in general and as "emotionally flat." They sometimes seem not to recognize rewarding or punishing situations that they had learned before the operation. Kling, who took part in the experiment with the lynx, later decided to study the effects of removing the amygdala on monkeys living under natural conditions. Rhesus monkeys living on an island were observed and then some were captured. Following the operation, the animals were tested and then released back into their troop. Several unoperated monkeys were used as controls to compare effects of capture, caging, and release. The operation made the monkeys less aggressive toward the experimenters, but back in the troop they showed inappropriate behavior.

Seeming not to understand the significance of gestures by other monkeys, the altered animals sometimes fled from ordinary social contact and sometimes attacked a dominant male. Although the animals that were not operated on rejoined the troop without difficulty, all the amygdalectomized animals became social isolates and either died of starvation or were killed by predators (Kling, Lancaster, & Benitone, 1970). Flynn, whose experiments on eliciting aggression in cats were noted earlier, found that stimulation of the amygdala and certain other brain areas in cats could modulate the attacks but did not initiate them.

Another reason for concern about psychosurgery is that even in the case of well-studied areas of the brain, the maps may not yet be sufficiently accurate. Furthermore, the evidence of multiple representation of eating and other behaviors makes it unlikely that any single brain locus controls aggressive behavior. It is also true that similar brain structures do not always play comparable roles in different species (for example, the much more restricted representation of "reward" areas in the brain of the cat than in the brain of the rat; *see* p. 572).

In a thoughtful and extensive discussion of psychosurgery, Valenstein (1973) has pointed out that almost every development in psychosurgery beginning in the last century has been based on animal research. In each case, the neurosurgeons paid attention to only part of the animal data, stressing effects that might be beneficial and ignoring the rest. Nevertheless, in a poll conducted among brain scientists, most wanted research on psychosurgery to continue under careful scrutiny and with informed consent by all participants (*Society for Neuroscience Bulletin*, 1974). Research for human benefit requires human subjects, at least at the final stages; and so the eventual evaluation of psychosurgical operations will, of course, be their success or failure with human patients. Unfortunately, we will have to wait for the verdict, for the results are still controversial (Chorover, 1973; Mark, 1973; Valenstein, 1973).

What is reinforcement in terms of neural activity?

Reinforcement is a key concept related to both motivation and learning; investigators have sought to understand reinforcement in terms of biological processes as well as in purely behavioral terms. Research on brain functions has suggested some hypotheses about how reinforcement may work.

ELECTRICAL SELF-STIMULATION OF THE BRAIN

Animals will work hard to get electrical shocks to certain parts of the brain (Olds & Milner, 1954); they will work hard to avoid shocks to other parts (Delgado, Roberts, & Miller, 1954). These two effects have led to hundreds of studies that may help to explain the brain mechanisms of reinforcement. In many of these experiments, an electrode is implanted in the brain and an electrical circuit makes it possible for the animal to stimulate its brain by pressing a bar or lever. Each press sends a brief shock to the brain. Some rats press the bar at amazingly high rates—for example, 2,000 presses per hour for 24 hours. (*See* Preview Figure 3.) Other brain points are not reinforcing; the rat presses the bar occasionally but does not seem to do so deliberately. Other

Figure 20-8
Rewarding and Punishing Regions in Rat Brain
This medial section of a rat brain shows areas where electrical stimulation is rewarding (colored) or punishing (striped). Rewarding effects are found in a band of cortex just above the corpus callosum, in the hippocampus, septal area, olfactory bulbs, and hypothalamus. Punishing effects are found in the medial brain stem tracts and nuclei. Neutral or weak effects are found in the unshaded areas. (Modified from Olds, 1958)

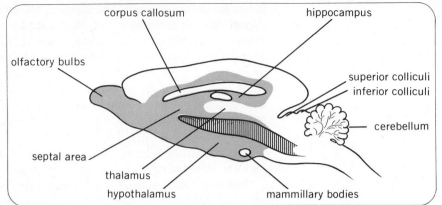

points are aversive or negatively reinforcing; after the rat has pressed the bar once or twice, it carefully avoids pressing it again.

Mapping the locations of such points in many rats showed that a large part of the rat brain gives positively reinforcing effects; a relatively small part yields negative effects (see Figure 20-8). The brains of other species also have been mapped in this way, and they reveal similar basic phenomena but with species differences. The cat, for example, has relatively few positively reinforcing areas, and the effect of the shock is not as strong as it is in rodents. Some observations of this sort have also been made in human psychiatric patients in the attempt to relieve depression (Sem-Jacobsen & Torkildsen, 1960; Bishop, Elder, & Heath, 1963). Some of these patients have reported that stimulation of certain brain regions brings warm or enjoyable feelings, although it does not appear that these feelings are unusually or intensely pleasurable. On the basis of the early animal experiments, some investigators referred to these brain regions as "pleasure centers," but further work suggests a rather different interpretation, as we will see shortly. Because the motivational effectiveness of these centers has been exaggerated in some journalistic accounts and in science fiction, many questions about "brain control" have been raised. But even rats that show high rates of lever-pressing for brain stimulation do not ignore other needs. They drink, groom, sleep, explore the environment, and they eat enough to maintain their weight over weeks in which brain stimulation is available at any time the rat presses to obtain it.

STIMULATION-BOUND BEHAVIOR

How can we put together the facts about animals controlling the stimulation of their own brains and the observations on brain stimulation that evokes behaviors suggestive of motivational states? It will be recalled that stimulation of particular brain sites was reported to evoke eating or drinking or male sex behavior when the appropriate goal object was present; the stimulation also inhibited other behaviors that might compete with the one elicited. **Stimulation-bound behavior** is behavior that is elicited by direct stimulation of the brain and that seems like normal motivated behavior. Often it lasts only as long as the brain stimulation continues. When you find a brain site that yields stimulation-bound behavior, it is likely to show self-stimulation when the animal is allowed to control the stimulation. Because the two sorts of behavior are related, how can stimulation-bound behavior help us to understand more about the brain mechanisms of reinforcement?

Because of their apparent purposiveness and flexibility, stimulation-bound behaviors have been considered by many investigators to be *motivated,* rather than simple elicited motor acts. The behavior will not be shown unless the appropriate goal object is present and, during stimulation, animals will perform a learned task to obtain the goal object. Furthermore, the animal will tolerate painful or unpleasant stimuli to reach the goal object. Therefore many psychologists have concluded that the brain stimulation activates specific neural circuits underlying such motives as hunger or thirst or sex.

Other psychologists have raised doubts about this interpretation (Valenstein, Cox, & Kakolewski, 1970). For one thing, the brain regions for different stimulation-bound behaviors were found to overlap when the same animals were tested with different goal objects. That is, the same electrode site that induced a rat to go to food and eat when food was present would also induce going to water and drinking when water was present. Often two electrodes spaced rather widely apart in the brain would elicit exactly the same behavior. Furthermore, careful examination showed that the behavior was not always as purposive and flexible as normal motivated behavior. For example, animals eating in response to brain stimulation did not readily switch to another familiar food when the first food was removed. Animals showing stimulation-bound drinking sometimes continued to lap at the tube even when the water was removed; something other than satisfaction of an induced need maintained the behavior.

On the other hand, other experimenters have found equally compelling evidence for the motivational interpretation of stimulation-bound behavior. The normal motives for eating and drinking are affected by depriving the animal of food and water, and these normal motives decrease with intake of food and water. Can the same phenomena be demonstrated with the "stimulated motives"? Devor and his colleagues (1970) found brain sites that could evoke either eating or drinking, and they studied how the thresholds for these behaviors varied with deprivation or intake of food or water. They found that depriving the animal of food lowered the electrical threshold for evoking eating but did not alter the threshold for evoking drinking; feeding the animal raised the threshold for stimulation-bound eating but again did not change the threshold for drinking. Similarly, manipulating the water balance altered the brain thresholds for drinking but not for eating. Thus, in these experiments, the eating and drinking elicited by electrical stimulation are affected separately and appropriately by external events, just as are normal eating and drinking.

Our present understanding can be summarized in this way: Some brain sites are specific to one motivational state, but at other sites stimulation may evoke whatever behavior is *prepotent* or ready to be tripped off. The prepotency is based partly on the current state of body need, partly on the goal objects present, and partly on training to respond to one or another type of goal. Because the stimulus electrode touches only a small part of a complex circuit, it is not surprising that in some cases the evoked behavior does not show all the characteristics of normal motivated behavior.

A few experiments show that a combination of self-stimulation and stimulation-bound behavior may be especially reinforcing. Rats that ran a maze to receive brain stimulation performed better when they also received food in the goal area (Mendelson, 1966). In another experiment, rats received a reinforcing brain shock whenever they reached either end of a chamber, so they shuttled back and forth from end to end. When the chamber contained small wooden pellets that the rats could carry in their mouths, they preferred to do this, taking a pellet to one end, dropping it, and carrying another pellet back to the other end (Valenstein, Cox, & Kakolewski, 1970). Such carrying behavior is natural for rats, and it seemed to add to the effectiveness of this reinforcing situation.

A FORMULATION OF REINFORCEMENT

Stimulation or activation of brain regions seems to have reward value when the sites are parts of brain circuits involved in performing positive motivational patterns or in the feedback from such acts. The more completely the pattern is activated, the greater is the reinforcement. The sites may involve sensory, central integrative, or motor components of motivational circuits, and the stimulation need not itself satisfy any biological needs. Thus the sweet taste of saccharine and the salty taste of lithium are rewarding even though neither has any nutritive value. The motor acts of eating lead to satisfaction and cessation of ingestion long before the food is digested and the bodily need is made up by metabolism. The direct electrical activation of circuits involved in eating behavior is reinforcing even if the full response pattern is not acted out. Similarly perhaps, activating certain brain patterns by thinking about desirable activities can be gratifying. Depending on the person, thinking about eating or sex or money or sports or a hobby may be a pleasant way to spend time, and conditions that favor such central representations may themselves become reinforcing. When the feedback of motor response patterns is added to the central patterns of positive motivational state, the strongest reinforcing effects are achieved.

SUMMARY

Research into biological processes in motivation is helping to explain why individuals engage in one or another activity at any given time. This research aids us to understand such diverse phenomena as eating, **dreams** and **nightmares,** sex and gender role, aggression, and **reinforcement.**

Some kinds of motivated behavior primarily maintain internal body conditions that are necessary to support all other kinds of behavior; we considered regulation of body fluids and of food supplies as examples. The **double depletion hypothesis of fluid regulation** refers to separate monitoring of intracellular fluid and extracellular fluid. Depletion of intracellular fluid is detected by shrinkage of cells in the anterior hypothalamus. Depletion of extracellular fluid is detected by **mechanoreceptors** in the heart and blood vessels and also by a chemical liberated when blood flow is reduced through the arterioles of the kidney. In whichever way depletion is detected, it leads to two responses organized by somewhat different brain sites: (1) attempts to find and to ingest fluid, and (2) conservation of fluid by reducing the rate of formation of urine. The act of drinking also provides short-term inhibitory feedback and prevents over-ingestion.

Food supplies in the body are monitored in the brain. Food intake is accurately regulated to conform to changing energy needs, provided an individual is active enough to stimulate weight-control mechanisms in the brain. One widespread circuit integrates feeding behavior, and another circuit inhibits eating. Eating and drinking may also be performed as instrumental behaviors to engage in other more preferred activities.

Body activity usually shows a twenty-four-hour **(circadian)** cycle. The electrical activity of the brain **(electroencephalogram** or **EEG)** differs between waking and sleep; furthermore, one kind of sleep is characterized by slow, synchronous EEG waves, while the other kind shows fast, desynchronized waves and **rapid eye movements (REM)** and is usually accompanied by vivid dreams. Each of these three states—waking, **slow-wave sleep,** and **fast-wave sleep**—is integrated by different brain circuits, and each circuit inhibits the others. Sleep cannot be explained completely by the need to rest; it may have evolved to keep animals quiet and inconspicuous during the part of the daily cycle when their behavior was least efficient. Many hypotheses have been advanced to account for fast-wave sleep, each related to a different aspect of this paradoxical state of sleep.

A person's gender role as a man or woman usually corresponds to his or her chromosomal pattern, but gender role is also determined by **sex hormones,** neural circuits, and experience. The presence of **androgens** in the fetal period determines the development of male reproductive structures; the absence of androgens allows development of female reproductive structures. Some sex differences in behavior, such as the greater amount of rough-and-tumble play and aggressiveness in the male, are determined by action of androgens during the fetal period. Hormonal imbalances or insensitivity to hormones can lead to discrepancies between chromosomal pattern and genital structure. During the first years of life, sex assignment or reassignment can alter a child's gender identity. Certain secondary sex characteristics (such as facial hair or breasts) are determined by the presence of androgens or **estrogens** at puberty. During and after puberty, sex hormones also help to activate patterns of mating behavior. With evolution, the activation of sex behavior has become progressively less dependent on hormones, and sex behavior continues in many human beings who no longer produce sex hormones.

Aggressive behavior can be triggered off by stimulating certain brain sites and can be inhibited by stimulating others. Pathologically violent behavior has been controlled in some patients by drugs that prevent seizure activity in the brain. Where drugs have proved ineffective, intervention by brain surgery has been tried in some cases; and such psychosurgery is a subject of current debate. It appears unlikely that destruction of a small region of brain can suppress violence without having other effects on behavior.

The concept of **reinforcement** has been studied with regard to (1) electrical stimulation of brain sites that seem to bring reward or pleasure, and (2) stimulation of sites that seem to evoke motivational states **(stimulus-bound behavior).** Activating brain regions by natural or artificial means appears to be reinforcing when the sites are parts of brain circuits involved in the performance of positive motivational patterns or in the feedback from such acts.

In several specific cases, it was noted that stimulating a particular motivated behavior also inhibits competing behaviors; this is probably a general phenomenon that helps to explain why only one main motivation is shown at any given time. As the ongoing activity becomes less strong its inhibition of other activities also weakens, until another behavior emerges, which in turn inhibits all the rest. Which behavior dominates at a given time is determined by many factors: (1) internal monitoring of bodily supplies and deficits; (2) monitoring of recent consummatory activities—recent eating or recent mating tends to inhibit further activity of the same sort; (3) the availability of goal objects appropriate to different motivations; (4) the daily schedule of motivational activities—not only are waking and sleeping on a circadian rhythm but other motivated activities acquire regular schedules; and (5) whether the behavior can be instrumental in securing a more preferred activity.

Biological Psychology of Learning and Memory

What conditions affect consolidation of long-term memory?
Are specific brain regions chiefly responsible for learning and memory?
In what forms are memories stored in the brain?

Destruction of a localized region of the brain appears to abolish the ability to form memories, as the following case shows.

> *Mrs. A, a schoolteacher, had a severe case of a virus disease that attacks the brain (herpes encephalitis). When she recovered, her family found her strangely prone to forget. She could hold a conversation normally, but a few minutes later she would not remember anything that had been said or even that there had been a conversation. If she put something on the stove to cook and then went to the next room, she would forget the cooking and the food might burn. Mrs. A could read a short story with pleasure, but she could not read a novel because when she*

picked up the book after a lapse of time, she had forgotten the characters and the situations. Moreover she could read the same short story with equal pleasure day after day—or the same newspaper—it seemed new each time. When Mrs. A went to the hospital for further observations, she never learned that the toilet was close to her room; she always had to ask a nurse where to find it. Though there were some gaps in her memories of the past, Mrs. A's chief handicap was her inability to form new memories that would last more than a few minutes. An X-ray examination of Mrs. A's brain indicated that the encephalitis had destroyed the region called the **hippocampus** *(see Figure 21-1). In a patient with similar behavior who died after a few years of observation, direct examination of the brain after death confirmed destruction of the hippocampus in both cerebral hemispheres (Lhermitte & Signoret, 1975). The neurologists were alerted to look for such damage because operations done on this region of the brain in other patients during the 1950s had been found to impair memory (Scoville & Milner, 1957). One of these patients has been studied many times since then; he is now well known in psychological reports by his initials—H. M. A comment that H. M. sometimes made between tests gives us an indication of what life is like when you can't form new memories: ". . . at this moment, everything looks clear to me, but what happened just before? That's what worries me. It's like waking from a dream; I just don't remember" (Milner, 1966, p. 115).*

Fortunately such cases are rare, because learning and memory are such characteristic parts of our lives that it is not possible to live normally if they are seriously impaired. Study of how brain damage of various sorts affects memory is helping us to understand normal memory and ways in which it can fail. In the cases above old memories are largely intact; for example, Mrs. A and H. M. retain their knowledge of language and can converse normally. The fact that they can converse also means that they can learn and can form short-term memories—they grasp and retain what has just been said to them and they reply meaningfully. It therefore appears that the short-term or working memory (discussed on pp. 420–29 in the section on learning and memory) is normal. Because storage of prior memories is good and short-term memories are formed without difficulty, many investigators have concluded that the specific impairment in these cases concerns the ability to form long-term memories. Some investigators have suggested that the hippocampus is necessary for transforming short-term memories into long-term ones, but, as we will see later in this chapter, there is now considerable reason to doubt this interpretation.

RESEARCH ON NEURAL MECHANISMS OF LEARNING AND MEMORY

Research on memory impairments caused by brain injury is fascinating, but this approach is only one of many currently being followed to try to unlock the mysteries of learning and memory. Specialists from many disciplines—anatomists, chemists, neurologists, physiologists, psychologists—have joined the search. They are observing and experimenting with subjects ranging from normal human learners and laboratory animals to portions of nervous systems in invertebrates (insects and mollusks) and even to cultures of neural cells. Experimental procedures include electrical recording of brain activity and of single cells, use of drugs to impair or improve memory, and anatomical measurements and chemical analyses of neural tissue from trained and control animals. The wide variety of disciplines, experimental subjects or preparations, and procedures reflects the fact that the phenomena of learning and memory

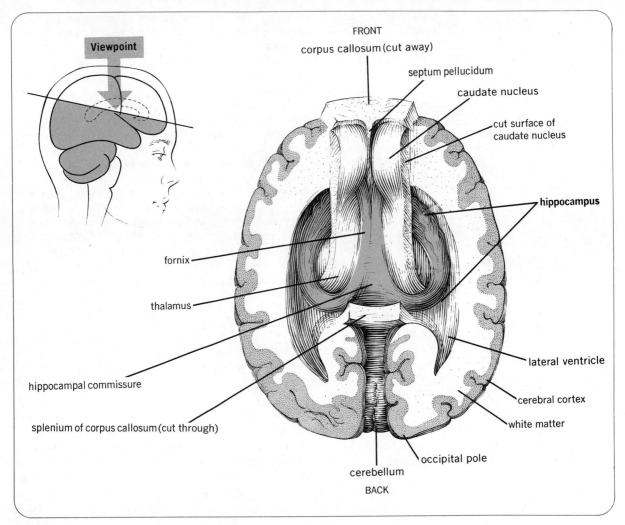

Viewpoint

FRONT

corpus callosum (cut away)

septum pellucidum

caudate nucleus

cut surface of
caudate nucleus

hippocampus

fornix

thalamus

hippocampal commissure

splenium of corpus callosum (cut through)

lateral ventricle

cerebral cortex

white matter

occipital pole

cerebellum

BACK

Figure 21-1
The Hippocampus—Old Cortex Implicated in Memory Storage
The brain is cut to show the position of the hippocampus and other structures. The upper portion of the cerebral hemispheres is removed, as indicated by the small diagram at the left, and the cross section is viewed from above. The corpus callosum has been cut and most of it removed, exposing the lateral ventricles, which normally are filled with cerebrospinal fluid. The hippocampus curves around the floor of the lateral ventricles. Severe impairment of memory has been observed in people who have lost the hippocampus bilaterally because of disease or surgery. (*See* p. 576, the case description, and pp. 589–91.)

can be analyzed at many levels—from purely behavioral analyses, through formal models, to biological phenomena in regions of tissue, to events at the level of single cells. These levels of analysis are stated more fully in Table 21-1 along with typical questions investigated at each level.

A shorter version of this table was presented in the preview of Part Six (on

TABLE 21-1 Levels of analysis in research on learning and memory

A) **Behavioral Descriptions of Learning and Memory**

In what ways do learning and memory occur? What are adequate descriptions of the stimulus conditions under which associations are formed? (*See* Chapter 14.) What are adequate descriptions of the conditions under which memories are formed? (*See* Chapter 15.)

How do learning and memory differ among species? Can analyzing the behavior of a particular species in its ecological niche lead us to predict features of its learning and memory, including novel or unusual forms of adaptiveness? How have the abilities to learn and remember evolved? (*See* Chapter 23.)

B) **Formal System Approaches**

What hypothetical processes could account for the observed features of learning and memory? Work under this heading ranges from rather general descriptions, to precise mathematical or network specifications, to actual devices that learn and remember. (Some model systems are considered in Chapter 15, pp. 422–32.)

C) **Molar or General Neural Processes**

Are there generalized electrophysiological or chemical processes that occur in all neurons or in wide regions of the brain and that underlie learning and memory?

How much time is required for such processes? (This question has been a main focus of research on "consolidation of memory.")

D) **Regional Localization of Neural Processes**

Are certain regions of the brain particularly involved in learning and memory? (The role of the hippocampus is indicated by the case history on p. 576.)

E) **Changes in Synapses and Neural Circuits**

Can memories be stored in terms of changes in existing synapses? Can memories be stored in terms of growth of new synapses (or disappearance of certain old ones), thus forming new or altered neural circuits?

---

learning and memory, p. 364). The two top levels of the table—behavioral analysis and formal models—are treated there in Chapters 14 and 15. Research at each level can increase our understanding of learning and memory; and progress at one level does not render work at other levels superfluous—just as study of behavior of individuals does not lessen the need to study behavior of groups.

In the rest of this chapter we will sample some of the main directions of research into neural mechanisms of learning and memory. We will ask three main sets of questions:

1) What conditions affect the consolidation of long-term memory? That is, what treatments given *after* learning can impair or improve subsequent memory—sleep, electrical stimulation of the brain, various chemical agents? What do these observations tell us about *general* processes of neural tissue in learning and memory?

2) Are specific regions of the nervous system chiefly responsible for learning and memory?

3) In what forms are memories stored in the brain? Can learning cause changes in existing synapses? Do anatomical changes in the nervous system result from training?

What conditions affect the consolidation of long-term memory?

One of the best established facts about memory is also the most intriguing. Newly formed memories are easily disturbed and tend to vanish, but older memories are tenacious and survive all sorts of changes in the individual and even damage to the brain. To explain this and related facts about memory, many investigators have employed the concept of **consolidation of memory;** that is, that the neural basis of memory can be transformed from an unstable, temporary form into a stable, long-lasting form. A useful analogy is what happens when wet concrete is poured into wooden forms to make a bridge. At the beginning, the wood maintains the shape of the structure; remove the wood and the bridge will collapse. But when the concrete has hardened, the wooden, short-term forms can be removed and the long-term, concrete structure remains.

The idea that memories can exist in two forms—an unstable short-term form and a stable long-term form—is related to the multistage models of memory discussed in the latter part of Chapter 15 (see pp. 420–29). Those behavioral models are essentially elaborations of the "perseveration-consolidation" model first proposed in 1900 by the German psychologists Müller and Pilzecker; it has influenced both behavioral and biological ideas about memory ever since.

In some of their verbal learning experiments, Müller and Pilzecker trained subjects in one session and had them come back for tests of recall at later sessions. They requested the subjects not to rehearse the material between sessions, but some subjects reported that they had been unable to keep themselves from rehearsing. This suggested to the experimenters that perhaps all subjects rehearse, whether consciously or not. They then hypothesized that perseverating (that is, rehearsing or keeping up activity) is necessary to consolidate memory (to transform it into a stable, long-lasting form).

The perseveration-consolidation hypothesis was brought back to prominence in a biological form by Hebb (1949) as the "dual trace" hypothesis. Hebb proposed that memory traces may take either of two forms. He hypothesized that the first, active form consists of circulating neural impulses. If this activity continues long enough, it could bring about a structural form of memory, involving new synaptic junctions. The idea that neural activity can lead to the formation of new or more efficient synapses and that memory can be stored in this way was actually first proposed about eighty years ago, but biopsychological research of the 1940s and thereafter gave this theory new meaning and importance. This research studied first the effects of head injuries on memory losses in humans and then the effects of experimental treatments that impair or improve memory in animals.

RETROGRADE AMNESIA

A driver whose head is injured in an automobile accident often cannot remember the actual impact, although he or she can remember approaching the intersection where the accident occurred. An analysis of hundreds of cases of brain concussion that left the patients unconscious for a time showed that the events just before the injury typically were forgotten (Russell & Nathan, 1946). In about three-quarters of these cases, this **amnesia** obscured the period of one to several minutes before the accident. This type of amnesia is usually called **retrograde,** as if the injury worked backward on the previous registration of information. But undoubtedly the injury actually affected succeeding events by disturbing processes that lead to permanent memory storage. Presumably the accident stopped the process of rehearsal and also the physiological events that are necessary for transferring material to the long-term store. The observations on effects of head injuries show that the short-term memory trace is fragile and can be impaired by treatments that leave long-term traces intact. The consolidation hypothesis offers an explanation for the observations.

Posttrial Treatments

Though observations about effects of head injuries have provided valuable information about memory processes, experimentation with animal subjects has yielded more specific findings and permitted more powerful tests of hypotheses. Such animal experiments, begun in the late 1940s, have used various procedures administered shortly after training trials to impair or to improve memory. These treatments include electrical shock to the brain or the use of various drugs.

Yesterday when the mouse stepped from the black starting chamber into the white compartment, it received a shock through the floorbars. What determines whether it will step through today? (Courtesy J. Flood)

One experimental design that is frequently used is called a one-trial, passive avoidance task. "Passive avoidance" means that on the recall test, the animal can avoid punishment if it simply remains passively in the start area and does not venture into the other part of the apparatus. In the single-training trial, the animal (usually a mouse or a rat) is placed in a small chamber that connects through a small doorway to a larger chamber. The time it takes the animal to step into the large chamber is recorded automatically. Once it is in the large chamber, the mouse receives a shock through the floor bars until it runs back to the "safe" start area. It is then returned to its home cage. When the mouse is returned to the apparatus for a test, it shows that it remembers by remaining in the start box and passively avoiding the other chamber. Whether the test occurs a day, a week, or even a month after the training trial, the mouse either refuses to go through the doorway or it waits several minutes before doing so.

But interference with brain processes just after the training trial can prevent the establishment of such long-term memory. An effective type of treatment is to give **electroconvulsive shock (ECS)** to the head. ECS makes the animal unconscious briefly, and during this time it usually shows some convulsive movements of the limbs. A mouse that received ECS shortly after the training trial appears to have forgotten the shock; on a retest it promptly steps through to the area where it received footshock. Furthermore, the closer in time the ECS follows the footshock, the more completely the memory is disrupted (see Figure 21-2). In the experiments, some mice receive ECS immediately after the footshock, and others after delays of minutes or hours. Those that had the longer intervals between footshock and ECS were more likely to show memory for the punishing situation—that is, a larger percentage of these subjects refused to step through the doorway (Kopp, Bohdanecky, & Jarvik, 1966).

These results are consistent with the consolidation hypothesis, but investigators are still cautious about accepting it. First, even if an animal appears to show complete amnesia so far as one measure of response goes, it may still show memory by another measure. Thus, a rat that steps promptly through the

Figure 21-2
Amnesia from a Brain Shock
Data are results of three experiments with 141 mice to test the effect of ECS (electroconvulsive shock) on memory. Mice that received ECS 5 seconds after the training trial showed a high degree of amnesia at the test trial 24 hours later—they stepped into the compartment in an average of 5 seconds. Those mice that received ECS 80 seconds after training showed a mean latency of 50 seconds on test—still considerable amnesia. In fact, even mice that received ECS six hours after training showed some amnesia; their mean latency was 195 seconds, whereas controls that received no ECS waited almost 300 seconds before entering the white compartment. (After Kopp, Bohdanecky, & Jarvik, 1966)

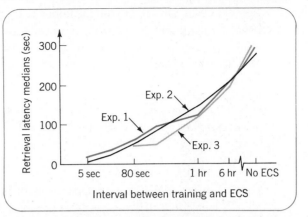

door to be shocked may nevertheless have a higher than normal heart rate, indicating an emotional response. In another experiment, rats could make a choice and step through to either of two different chambers. In whichever one a rat entered, it received footshock and then was given ECS. On retest the rats again left the start chamber and thus appeared to show amnesia for the footshock. But most rats did not step into the chamber they had chosen originally, and thus they revealed memory by avoiding the place in which they had received the footshock (Carew, 1970). Subjects learn many different responses in even an apparently simple situation. Apparently some memories are more easily disrupted than others. Even the more resistant responses are disrupted when the interval between training and footshock is very short.

Many investigators had hoped that these experiments would reveal the time required for consolidation of long-term memory (consolidation being measured by the increasing resistance of memory to interference as the interval between the trial and the ECS was lengthened). But the time courses that were found actually varied greatly among experiments. Some investigators found that if they delayed ECS by more than 10 seconds after the trial, memory was not impaired (such as Chorover & Schiller, 1966). Others found that they could produce impairment with ECS given hours after training (such as Kopp, Bohdanecky, & Tarvik, 1966; McGaugh, 1966). The stronger the disruptive treatment, the longer you can delay giving it after the learning trial and still interfere with the animal's memory. Life and research might be simpler if there were only one fixed time gradient of memory for all behaviors, but the facts show this is not the case.

Localized Stimulation and Retrograde Amnesia

Is a relatively strong shock across the entire brain required to block the formation of memory? Or can stimulating certain small brain regions with relatively weak shocks prevent establishment of long-term memory? In experimental tests, electrodes have been implanted in various sites in the brains of rats, and passive avoidance training has been used. It turns out that weak stimulation, given after a training trial, can cause amnesia if the electrode is located in the hippocampus or in the amygdaloid nucleus (McDonough & Kesner, 1971; McGaugh & Gold, 1975). No convulsion is required in this case. But these results do not mean that these specific regions are vital to memory storage; destruction of the hippocampus or of the amygdala in the rat does not prevent learning and memory of the behavioral test. Apparently, because of their widespread fiber connections, the hippocampus and the amygdala are strategic sites for interfering with consolidation processes going on in other brain regions. Which connections are important is currently under investigation. So, although shock does not have to be delivered to the whole brain to prevent formation of memory, the processes of consolidation are probably fairly widespread in the brain, as we will also see from other evidence.

Drugs and the Formation of Long-Term Memories

Under appropriate doses of some general anesthetics, a person can converse and show short-term memory, but the memory is soon lost. For example, the drug scopalamine is sometimes used during childbirth. Under the effects of this drug the mother can hear the doctor's directions and can help with the birth; but afterward she has no memory of the event. Experimental studies have confirmed that there is only poor memory for items that were learned well during the anesthetic state (Osborn et al., 1967). So intelligent behavior and short-term memories are not enough to guarantee that lasting memories are being laid down.

If long-term memory storage involves structural changes in the nervous system (and we will see evidence that this is true), then synthesis of proteins would be required. For this reason, investigators have studied whether formation of memory can be prevented by using drugs that strongly inhibit the synthesis of protein in the brain. Many such drugs are being produced, largely in the hope of finding anticancer agents, and several have been tested for their effects on memory in animals. Even when a drug has reduced protein synthesis in the brain of a mouse to only 5 percent of the normal rate, mice can learn simple habits. But when retested a week later, most of the mice that learned under the drug show no memory for the training, whereas control mice remember well. The stronger the training, the longer the protein synthesis must be inhibited after training (up to several hours) to prevent memory storage (Flood et al., 1974). The inhibition must start within minutes after training if it is to cause amnesia, so apparently crucial first steps of protein synthesis take place almost immediately (Bennett et al., 1975). Drugs that foster alertness can counteract the effects of inhibitors of protein synthesis; drugs that depress the neuron system enhance the effects of inhibition of protein synthesis in impairing memory.

BRAIN STIMULATION AND IMPROVING MEMORY

Another kind of support for the consolidation hypothesis comes from research on improving retention by the use of mild chemical or electrical stimulation of the brain. Experiments with excitant drugs are shown in Figure 21-3. In these experiments the behavioral task was a maze that required several daily sessions to learn. The animal was given an injection of a stimulant drug shortly *after* each training session, so the injection could affect only the cerebral afteractivity but not behavior during training. Several excitant drugs can speed learning. The drug-injected animals learned the task faster and with fewer errors than did controls. This effect is sometimes called retrograde facilitation of memory, because the posttrial treatment appears to work back on the training session, although it actually works forward on formation of the memory trace. The closer the drug injections follow the daily learning trials, the more they facilitate learning. Some drugs yield positive effects even when the delay between training and drug injections is as long as an hour (see Figure 21-3). Thus chemical facilitation of neural activity appears to aid consolidation, just as disruption by ECS appears to impair it.

As another way of testing effects of alertness on memory storage, some researchers implanted electrodes in the reticular activating system in the brainstem of rats. A weak electric current to such an electrode causes a desynchronized wakeful pattern in the EEG. They gave this stimulus for thirty seconds *after* a training trial. Because the brain stimulation was given after the training, it could not affect the receipt of information but only the later processing. The results showed significantly better retention by rats that received the posttrial reticular stimulation (Denti et al., 1970).

Figure 21-3
Brain Stimulation Improves Learning

Giving small doses of certain stimulant drugs before or after each daily learning session can help rats to learn a maze faster than control animals do.
A. With increasing dosage of the drug, there are progressively fewer errors to reach criterion, until the optimal dosage — for these subjects and for this task. A separate group of subjects was tested with each dosage. (Krivanek & McGaugh, 1968)
B. Improvement can be obtained — for these subjects and for this task — if the drug is given as much as 60 minutes before daily trials or as much as 60 minutes after daily trials. Somewhat different time courses have been reported in other studies. (McGaugh & Krivanek, 1970)

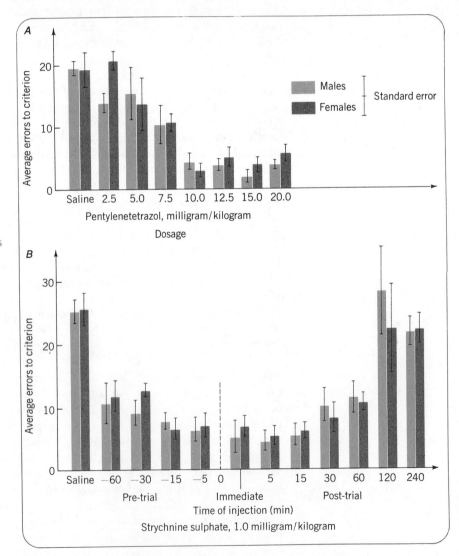

LEARNING DURING SLEEP

Even if alertness favors learning and memory storage, can some learning occur during sleep? You may have seen ads for a tape recorder device with a small speaker that fits under your pillow to teach you a foreign language while you sleep. Psychologists have tested whether "sleep learning" actually occurs. Part of the problem turns out to be defining whether the subject is actually asleep. Retention is good for material learned just before going to sleep, perhaps because there is relatively little to interfere with learning at that time. So the recording will be helpful if you turn it on as soon as you go to bed, especially if the sound keeps you awake long enough to accomplish some learning. Once you fall asleep, you may be awakened by a change in stimulation, as when the recorder goes on or off. If learning occurs at these times, again, it is not truly sleep learning. To obtain a definitive answer, investigators have used EEG recordings to monitor the state of sleep, as we described in the last chapter, p. 558. If verbal material (short sentences) is presented only when the person is in deep slow-wave sleep, and if he remains deeply asleep, the material is not remembered at later tests. But if presentation of the sentences causes the person to awaken for thirty seconds or more, as shown by his EEG, then he can later remember the material (Koukkou & Lehmann, 1968). The conclusion of several such studies has been that although you may learn from the recorder, it is not truly sleep learning.

But if you are a person who remembers dreams, you may properly ask if dreams are not material learned during sleep and retained afterward. Yes, they certainly are, but people usually remember only a small proportion of the total. It is rather unusual to remember more than one dream from a night, although the average young adult has each night about five fairly long periods of REM dream sleep. If awakened several times during the night in successive REM periods, a person will usually report a different dream on each occasion. But if a person is awakened only a few minutes after the end of an REM period, usually he or she cannot report any dream. It is likely that the only dreams that are remembered are those that cause a person to awaken briefly or those that are followed by a period of light sleep. Just as with material presented experimentally to a sleeper, if deep, slow-wave sleep follows a dream, then the dream is unlikely to be retained in long-term memory. Thus sleep may be somewhat like the state of light general anesthesia in which thought processes are carried out and short-term memories are formed, but in which there is no consolidation of long-term memories.

SLEEP AND MEMORY FORMATION

Although learning does not occur during sleep, sleep may be a favorable period for the further processing of recently acquired information and for forming memory traces. Experiments have been done, for example, in which some students learn certain material during the daytime, while others learn the same things just before going to bed. Both groups are tested for recall eight hours after learning. The usual result has been that retention is better overnight than during the day. The usual interpretation has been that memory is better overnight because fewer competing events cause interference than during the day. But recent animal experiments suggest that fast-wave sleep may be important in forming memories (Bloch, 1975). For one thing, when rats are given training, their subsequent period of sleep shows a higher percentage of

A great deal of publicity has been given since 1965 to reports of memory by injection. In such research, animals are trained in a habit—for example, in an apparatus with lighted and dark compartments, to go to the lighted part to avoid shock. Chemical extracts are then made from their brains and these are injected into other animals who have had no experience with the task. When tested in the apparatus, the naive recipients then appear—according to some reports—to show the effects of the training given to the donor animals, as if the naive animals had acquired the memories of the donor animals by injection.

Memory injection would be a wonderful tool for working on the chemistry of memory. Neurochemists could analyze the brain extracts and, using behavioral tests, could determine which chemical components were ef-fective in producing the same results as training. The next step would be to synthesize the active compounds—to manufacture memory molecules! If this could be done, then animals—and perhaps eventually students—could acquire knowledge by the spoonful or the syringeful.

So far, however, the reports of the basic phenomena remain controversial; many investigators have been unable to produce the alleged effects in their own laboratories. I took part in a large-scale unsuccessful effort to find such effects (Byrne et al., 1966). However, a few laboratories have reported consistent successes (see chapters in Byrne, 1970; and Ungar, 1975). Unless and until an effect can be produced reliably, it is not under control, and little can be done with it. For the present, at least, the only route to memory is through learning.

---

fast-wave sleep than does that of control rats not given training. Furthermore, if rats are prevented from having fast-wave sleep after a training session, then their memory of the training is very poor when they are tested the next day. These intriguing findings will no doubt soon lead to similar experiments with human subjects.

SUMMARY ON
CONSOLIDATION

Evidence is abundant that long-term memories are much more stable and re-sistant to disruption than short-term memories, but we no longer suppose that one process accounts for the transformation from short-term to long-term storage. Rather, it appears that a sequence of events takes place; some occur very promptly after training while others occur much later. This multistage formulation is supported by the observation that some drugs must be given immediately to alter subsequent memory, whereas others can be given with considerable delay. Also, the initial processing of new information appears to require wakefulness; but a later stage of processing can occur during fast-wave sleep. Some evidence indicates that certain brain regions are particu-larly involved in consolidation, and we will consider regional involvement more specifically in the next section. What consolidation accomplishes in anatomical terms will be taken up in the last main section of this chapter.

Are specific brain regions chiefly responsible for learning and memory?

Is there a special part of your brain for learning? Many scientists have searched for evidence of specific localization of the processes of learning and memory in the brain, and they have proposed a wide variety of answers. Here are three such hypotheses: (1) The father of conditioning, Ivan Pavlov, claimed that the cerebral cortex is required for conditioning in mammals; he held that condi-tioning involves the creation of "temporary connections" within the cortex,

How are life-long memories
stored in the brain?

forming new "reflex arcs" from sensory to motor areas of the cortex. (2) On the other hand, the distinguished neurologist Wilder Penfield proposed in the late 1940s that the fundamental connections in learning are formed in the basal center of the brain (the diencephalon) and that the cortex only elaborates the sensory and motor detail. (3) More recently, investigators have singled out the hippocampus as necessary for forming long-term memories; this hypothesis was based on observation of cases of brain damage such as those reported at the start of this chapter. We now have strong reasons to reject each of these three hypotheses; the experimental tests that have invalidated these hypotheses have also revealed much new information about the neural bases of learning and memory. Furthermore, new techniques continue to indicate that some regions of the brain are more importantly involved in learning and memory than are other regions.

**THE CEREBRAL CORTEX
AND LEARNING**

Pavlov thought that the cortex was the only site of new neural connections in learning. His evidence was that members of his laboratory were not able to condition dogs from whom the cortex had been surgically removed. But later, in Pavlov's laboratory and elsewhere, investigators found that they could obtain conditioning in mammals even after all the cerebral cortex had been removed. For example, a dog with its cortex removed can learn to lift its paw whenever a light flash occurs to avoid shock. Such conditioning occurs slowly and irregularly, however, because such animals tend to be distractible and irritable and they do not have keen sensory discrimination. But the evidence is clearly antagonistic to Pavlov's claim that the cortex is necessary. Furthermore, when the cortex is present, it is employed in conditioning, but the learned connections do not run horizontally through the cortex from sensory to motor areas as Pavlov supposed. Crosshatching the cortex with knife cuts, thus severing connections between cortical areas, has little effect on retention or on sensory or motor performance. Instead, the connections employed in the learned behavior appear to loop under the cortex or they go up and down between thalamus and cortex.

Even within the spinal cord, conditioning can take place. In one experiment with cats, the spinal cord was disconnected from the brain, thus ensuring that only spinal tissue was involved. The unconditioned stimulus was a shock to the skin that elicited flexion of the hind leg. When this stimulus was preceded regularly by a touch to the skin, the touch came to elicit the response—it became a conditioned stimulus (Patterson, Cegavske, & Thompson, 1973). Even though little learning probably occurs normally in the spinal cord of a mammal, such research shows that much of the nervous system is probably capable of learning and memory.

MEMORIES CONFINED TO A SINGLE HEMISPHERE

Penfield's hypothesis that learning occurs in the diencephalon came from his observations as a neurosurgeon. He found that removing areas of cortex did not prevent learning from occurring. On the other hand, damage to the diencephalon could interrupt consciousness and prevent learning. But interesting later experiments have shown that memory for a task can be confined to a single cerebral hemisphere. Because the diencephalon has abundant connections with both hemispheres, learning that occurred in the diencephalon should be available to either hemisphere.

Learning can be restricted to a single cerebral hemisphere in experimental animals by putting the cortex of the other hemisphere temporarily out of function. The cortex of one hemisphere is treated with potassium chloride or with a strong localized electrical shock that temporarily depresses its function. When a rat is placed in a maze or other learning situation with one hemisphere depressed (such as the right), it can learn with the other hemisphere. If it is later put back in the apparatus with the left (trained) hemisphere depressed, it shows no memory for the problem. Tested later with the right hemisphere depressed but the left functioning, it again shows that it had learned. In brief, memory for this learning seems to be confined to one hemisphere. If, however, the rat is once tested with both hemispheres functioning normally, the memory then spreads rapidly to the right hemisphere and thereafter either one shows the memory (Bureš & Burešová, 1970).

Split-Brain Research

The cortex of the two hemispheres can be permanently disconnected by transecting the **corpus callosum.** This surgery is occasionally done in patients suffering from severe epilepsy to prevent seizure activity from spreading from one side to the other and incapacitating the person. Results of hemisphere disconnection were first studied extensively in animals. For example, cats

Figure 21-4
Learning by Separated Hemispheres in the Same Head
The brains of cats were split—both the corpus callosum and the optic chiasm were transected. After the operation, when one eye was covered, only the opposite hemisphere received visual input. The two hemispheres of a cat could thus be trained separately, and the graphs demonstrate that the two hemispheres of each cat had similar learning curves. (Modified from Sperry, Stamm, & Miner, 1956)

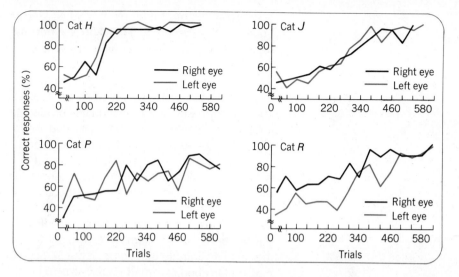

have had both the callosum and the **optic chiasm** sectioned so that each eye is connected only with the hemisphere on its own side. Such a cat can learn with the left eye that ∨ stands for reward but that ∧ does not, while with the right eye it can learn the opposite habit—∧ is rewarded rather than ∨ (*see* Figure 21-4). Each hemisphere is ignorant of what the other has learned (Sperry, Stamm, & Miner, 1956). This again refutes the hypothesis of learning in the diencephalon, because in the **split-brain** preparation, the diencephalon and its connections to both hemispheres remain intact. Incidentally, the independent learning curves of the two hemispheres in the cat are as similar as if the two hemispheres were identical twins.

In human split-brain patients, the hemispheres not only function separately but they also function somewhat differently—unlike the cat (Gazzaniga, 1970). Certain tasks can be carried out by either side. A person with a split brain can understand even fairly complex instructions with either hemisphere. For example, a split-brain woman could touch a few objects without seeing them and then signal with her raised fingers how many were there. This could be done accurately with either hand, so long as the same hand did both parts of the task. (The sensory and motor connections of each hand is associated with only one hemisphere.) But if she was asked to touch with one hand and to signal with the other, she could not perform the task. With the corpus callosum transected, neither hemisphere has access to the memories in the other. A similar disability was shown by the split-brain man in Preview Figure 5. For some tasks, as we note in the case of dichotic hearing (p. 681) and perception of form and space (p. 611), one hemisphere is superior to the other. For most people, the left hemisphere is superior in perception of speech, whereas the right hemisphere is superior in perception of music, form, and space.

LOCALIZED BRAIN DAMAGE

People with impaired memory caused by brain damage provide a major incentive to understand what parts of the brain are involved and how the damage may be remedied or prevented. These cases continue to provide a great deal of information about the neural processes underlying learning and memory.

Probably the most thoroughly studied kind of memory deficit resulting from brain damage occurs in **Korsakoff's syndrome,** a disease that may occur in severe alcoholism. Patients with this syndrome appear alert and cooperative; they speak correctly and can calculate with normal speed and accuracy, and they solve many sorts of problems well. But they seem to have lost many memories that had been formed before the onset of the disease. When asked about their past, they confabulate—producing rather garbled and incorrect information that seems to be fabricated to cover the gaps in their memory. The patients also appear to be unable to form long-term memories.

The disease has been found to be caused by extreme deficiency of thiamine (vitamin B) rather than by ingesting alcohol as such. Because severe alcoholics often neglect to eat enough they become vitamin-deficient. If Korsakoff's syndrome is recognized early enough, it can be cured by giving massive doses of B vitamins. The lack of vitamin B, while it has widespread effects throughout the body, causes damage especially in the brain structures that surround the medial ventricle (see color Figure 5). Severe damage is usually seen in the mammillary bodies, small paired structures at the base of the hypothalamus just behind the stalk of the pituitary gland (see Figure 19-6B). Because of this and because the patients seem to have lost past memories as well as being unable to form new ones, some neurologists believe that memories are localized in the mammillary bodies. But others claim that impairment of memory is more closely correlated with a different nearby structure—the medial dorsal nucleus of the thalamus (Adams, 1969). Closer examination of the behavior of Korsakoff patients indicates that memory cannot be located in either structure, because old memories survive even when these structures are severely damaged. But one or both structures are undoubtedly involved in the orderly recall of stored memories.

Patients with destruction of the hippocampus (like the case described at the beginning of this chapter) seem to be unable to form new long-term memories. This was one reason for renewed scrutiny of Korsakoff's syndrome. Because the hippocampus has strong connections to the mammillary bodies, are the behavioral symptoms in Korsakoff's syndrome essentially the same as those of hippocampal destruction, or are there important differences? Researchers at a major neurological institute in Paris tested both kinds of patients; they found that certain tests revealed clear differences between the hippocampal and Korsakoff's patients (Signoret & Lhermitte, 1976). Let us consider two of these tests:

1) *Memory for picture arrangement.* Nine pictures of common objects (such as a bathtub, postage stamp, and knife) are placed on a 3×3 grid; the subject is asked to observe the place into which each picture is put. A short while later, after other tests, the subject is given the pictures and asked to put them where they were on the grid. Normal subjects perform this task easily and accurately, but both hippocampal and Korsakoff's patients deny that they ever saw these pictures before. Nevertheless, when the examiner urges the patients to try, the Korsakoff patients perform the task accurately! Clearly they have formed and retained memories, even though their verbal report did not show it. But the hippocampal patients perform only at a chance level, showing no memory for the information presented only a few minutes earlier.

2) *Solving a serial code.* The examiner tells the patient that a red or a blue button will be placed on the table; the patient is to guess each time in the series what color the button will be (such as blue-blue-red-blue-blue-red). After a few presentations, hippocampal patients solve the code; they can hold enough information in short-term memory to do this. But Korsakoff's patients fail to solve the code; they say "red" or "blue" apparently at random. Even within the short-term period, they do not seem to be able to order their memories correctly. (This inability to retrieve the appropriate memory may also account for the apparent fabrication that occurs in confabulation: many of the apparently incorrect memories have been found to be true incidents from the patient's past, but they are not placed in the correct time or order.)

So the different sites of disease in the brain seem to produce different symptoms. Korsakoff's patients form memories but have trouble retrieving them. Hippocampal patients appear to form only short-term memories and to lose them whenever they are distracted or turn to a new task. Patients can learn and recall some tasks with sufficient practice, even though they never become familiar with the task. For example, one hippocampal patient was trained over several days to trace an outline that he saw in a mirror. Each day his mirror-tracing improved, but each day when presented with the test he would say that he had never seen it before; nevertheless his performance showed that he retained much of the proficiency that he had gained the previous day. Thus the verbal response indicated lack of memory, but the performance test revealed memory. Another patient, hospitalized for memory impairment after encephalitis, played in a hospital orchestra. One day a member of the staff taught him a new piece. The next day when the patient was asked to play the new piece, he appeared not to remember it at all. But when the staff member hummed a few bars, the patient said, "Oh, that piece," and played it perfectly. Rozin (1976) suggests that the failure in these patients is restricted to *episodic memories*—memories of specific incidents of personal relevance rather than more general *semantic memories* (the distinction between these two types of memory is discussed in the section on learning and memory, p. 420). In this case, the musician could not remember the episode of learning the music the previous day, but he had stored the meaningful (semantic) memory of the piece.

EFFECTS OF BRAIN LESIONS ON LEARNING AND MEMORY

In 1902 the American psychologist S. I. Franz combined the new method of animal training pioneered by Thorndike (see p. 370) with the placement of localized lesions in the brain. Although Franz had hoped to find precise brain locations for learning and memory, he found that no localized lesions could abolish these abilities. His younger collaborator Karl Lashley, after much further work on this question, also concluded that much of the brain participates cooperatively in learning and remembering. Lashley forcefully advocated the concept of "mass action" of the brain in learning and memory: because brain tissue tends to act as a whole, the greater the mass of brain that is destroyed, regardless of location, the worse will be the animal's performance.

The idea of regional specificity has continued to lure researchers, however, and large numbers of animal studies combining training and brain lesions have been conducted. Many relatively specific effects have been reported, but many critics remain unconvinced. Isaacson (1976), for example, claims that no lesion study has clearly demonstrated a pure impairment of learning or memory. Rather, he asserts, each deficit of performance caused by a brain lesion can be interpreted as being caused by altered sensory acuity or altered motivation—rather than by reduced capacity for learning and memory. For example, after lesions of the primary visual cortex, animals show reduced ability to recognize forms they had learned preoperatively; but tests showed that their visual acuity had been impaired by the brain operation. In other animals a similar reduction in acuity caused by scarring the lens also impaired form recognition—without touching the nervous system. As an example of motivational effects, it has been reported that animals with lesions in the amygdala are reluctant to undertake new responses and are quick to give them up. Learning or memory seem to be poor unless adequate controls for motivation are employed.

Because destruction of the hippocampus or of the mammillary bodies has produced dramatic disturbances of memory in human patients, similar lesions have been made in animal subjects. Tests have not shown gross impairments of memory formation in animals. Recall that, in some cases at least, the human patients were able to show memory by their performance although they claimed not to recognize the test materials. This finding has led to the suggestion that it is especially episodic memory that is deficient in these patients. When animals are tested, obviously only performance can be observed. Because most tests of patients and of animal subjects are not strictly comparable, it is not surprising that they do not always yield similar results.

Recently, a problem with the lesion technique has been emphasized. The damage is hard to specify and may involve brain regions remote from the site that the experimenter destroys. The living tissue of the brain can react in a variety of ways to even a localized injury. This reaction may result, for example, in a chemical imbalance in quite a different region. Furthermore, interrupting a tract may cause the neurons to grow abnormal connections to another region of the brain (Lynch, 1976).

MICROELECTRODE RECORDING—THE SEARCH FOR REGIONAL CHANGES

Recording activity of single neurons during training is a recent technique in trying to localize brain processes of learning and memory. This method permits study of the intact brain, whereas the lesion technique necessarily involves damaged brains in which functions may be organized somewhat differently than in normal brains.

In one set of experiments (Olds, 1973), each rat had microelectrodes implanted in several brain areas. In the experimental chamber where the rat was placed, a loud sound would occur from time to time, followed by delivery of a food pellet into a small box (see Figure 21-5). As this procedure continued the rat would learn to look toward the food dispenser whenever the sound (the conditioned stimulus) came on. The activity of most neurons was not affected by the training, but about 7 percent of the neurons showed increased rates of response whenever the conditioned stimulus occurred. Some cells in the hypothalamus showed conditioning even before the behavioral responses did. Among the many brain regions examined in this way, those where neurons were most apt to show conditioning were one nucleus of the thalamus (the

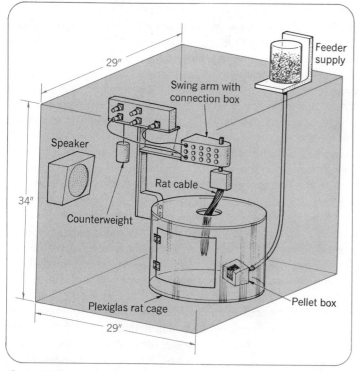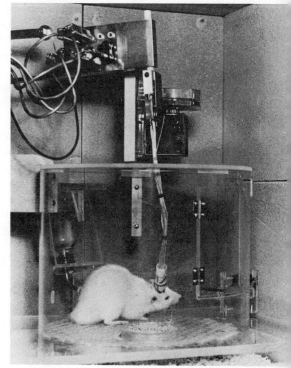

Figure 21-5
Recording Activity of Single Neurons in the Search for Regional Changes in the Brain During Training
The photograph and diagram show some main parts of the apparatus; *see* preceding page for the experimental procedures and results. (Olds, 1973)

posterior nucleus), the brainstem reticular formation, one part of the hippocampus, and one part of the hypothalamus. In other regions, such as sensory cortex, occasional neurons could be conditioned. Some regions contained few or none of these plastic units. Overall, this technique also indicates that widespread units in the brain participate in conditioning.

In what forms are memories stored in the brain?

CHANGES IN EXISTING SYNAPSES

Some theorists have proposed that memories can be stored by changes in existing synapses, others have proposed that memory storage requires formation of new synapses (or elimination of certain old ones). Since we saw in Chapter 20 that there are multiple parallel mechanisms for many kinds of motivated behavior, it may not surprise you to learn that there is some evidence that learning involves both changes at existing synapses and also changes in numbers of synapses.

It isn't easy to test whether individual synapses change during training. In fact, at present there isn't any way to do this directly in the complex brains of mammals. Therefore some investigators have looked for changes with training in the much simpler nervous systems of certain invertebrates or in isolated portions of the vertebrate spinal cord. Unfortunately, such systems do not seem to be capable of complex learning, although it is rather easy to demonstrate simple kinds of learning in them.

A kind of simple learning occurs when a stimulus is repeated over and over again with no special consequence; it is called **habituation.** Habituation means the decrease in size of a response as the stimulus is repeated. Although the first presentations of the stimulus evoke responses, as the series of stimuli continues the responses diminish in size. Eventually no response at all may occur. You usually habituate to the sound of a radio in the next room (unless it is quite loud), or to the pressure of clothing on your skin. (On the contrary, sometimes a repeated stimulus seems to become more and more insistent, at least for a while; in this case the phenomenon is called **sensitization.**)

Studies of the neural processes underlying habituation and sensitization have been made by recording the activity of single neurons in the spinal cord of the cat (Groves & Thompson, 1970). The spinal cord had been transected above the level of recording so that brain processes were excluded and only spinal processes were considered. Recording from sensory fibers showed that habituation or sensitization did not occur in the receptors or in the sensory fibers; the input message came through clearly at each stimulation. Nor did the motor fibers show any impairment; when they were stimulated repeatedly, they continued to conduct impulses to the muscles each time. The changes during repetitive stimulation were found at the **interneurons**—neurons interposed in functional circuits between sensory and motor cells. Some interneurons showed habituation, reducing their responses as stimulation continued, whereas others showed sensitization, at least for a while.

An even simpler circuit is a reflex arc in the spinal cord, where incoming sensory fibers make contact with motor neurons. There are no interneurons, so only a single synapse is present. Such a monosynaptic reflex arc in the frog spinal cord shows habituation (Farel, Glanzman, & Thompson, 1973), probably because a lessened amount of synaptic transmitter is released in response to the later stimuli of a series. The important role of chemical synapses in this modification of behavior is shown by experiments done on habituation in the crayfish, an invertebrate (Krasne, 1976). Here circuits have been studied where the same sensory fibers make electrical synapses to some cells and chemical synapses to others. (In electrical synapses, described on p. 526, the impulse in the presynaptic fiber stimulates the postsynaptic cell directly. In chemical synapses the arriving impulse causes the release of a chemical transmitter into the synaptic gap; it stimulates or inhibits the postsynaptic cell.) Recordings done with electrodes on both sides of these synapses showed that the electrical synapses do not habituate; their output keeps on reproducing their input. But the chemical synapses do habituate; perhaps this plasticity is a reason for the evolution of this kind of synapse.

Quite a different consideration shows that rapid learning must involve changes at existing synapses, in human beings as well as mammals. For example, you look up a number in a telephone book and a few seconds later you call the number. The formation of synaptic contacts requires hours to days. Obviously, then, when you show a response learned only seconds or minutes ago, it cannot be based on the formation of new synapses; it must involve the facilitation of some existing synapses and the inhibition of others. Whether this mechanism can store memory for long periods is not clear; perhaps anatomical changes are needed to store long-term memories.

For an analogy to these two ways of modifying neural circuits, we can think of a complex electrical circuit with many switches. We can modify the performance of the circuit rapidly by opening and closing various switches. But if none of these combinations provides what we want, then we can wire in some new connections or remove some old ones. Rewiring the circuit takes time, of course, and so does the analogous operation of forming new synaptic connections.

TRAINING CAUSES ANATOMICAL CHANGES IN THE NERVOUS SYSTEM

During most of this century, it was thought that the structure of the brain is determined by heredity and could not be altered by experience—certainly not in adults. Then experiments showed that placing rats—young or adult—in environments either more enriched or more impoverished than the standard colony condition led to measurable changes in the brain (Bennett, Diamond, Krech, & Rosenzweig, 1964). The differential environments are illustrated on page 596. In the enriched condition, the animals have a variety of stimulus objects to explore and to interact with. The presence of other animals is not required to produce these cerebral effects, provided some other means is found to keep the single subject interacting with its complex environment (Rosenzweig & Bennett, 1976b).

A variety of cerebral changes results from such differential experience. Compared with standard colony rats or rats from the impoverished condition, rats that have experienced a more complex environment show the following effects, among others: (1) a greater weight of cerebral cortex; (2) larger neuron cell bodies with a higher rate of chemical synthesis; (3) more branches of the dendrites of neurons, and more dendritic spines per unit of length of dendrite. (See Color Figure 7 for an illustration of dendrites and dendritic spines.) The increased number of dendritic branches and dendritic spines indicates greater numbers of synaptic contacts as a consequence of enriched experience (Bennett, 1976; Greenough, 1976).

Can these effects be attributed to learning rather than to some other aspect of the differential environments? Two kinds of evidence indicate that learning is in fact responsible. First, none of the other treatments that has been tested has yielded such effects—neither differential locomotion, nor stress, nor handling. Nor can the effects be interpreted as being due to precocious maturation (Rosenzweig & Bennett, 1976). Furthermore, formal training has produced some of these brain effects when compared to control conditions (Greenough, 1976; Rutledge, 1976).

Within the present decade, evidence of the anatomical plasticity of neurons has increased, which makes it more likely that learning can result in anatomical changes in the brain. Many neurons seem to be actively trying to secure their allotment of connections with other cells (Moore, 1976). Thus, in neurons that make connections at two places along their course, removing their endings at one place leads to proliferation at the other. Adjacent layers of the hippocampus receive inputs from different fiber tracts; if one tract is destroyed, fibers from other tracts now branch out and take over the abandoned synaptic sites. This growth of neuron endings happens more quickly and more completely in younger than in adult animals, but even in adults neural connections show substantial plasticity.

We have seen that informal experience and formal training lead to measurable changes in the nervous system and that neurons seem to compete to make synaptic connections. Because of this evidence for neural plasticity, the concept that some storage of long-term memories involves formation of new synapses seems much more probable than it did a decade ago.

SUMMARY

Research into neural processes in learning and memory currently involves investigators from many disciplines. A wide variety of experimental techniques is being used, and many different kinds of experimental subjects and preparations are being studied. Investigation is being carried out simultaneously at quite different levels of analysis, ranging from general neural processes (such as consolidation), through the involvement of particular regions of the brain, to identification of specific events at the synaptic level.

Much research has attempted to find a general process of **consolidation of memory** — that is, the transformation of unstable short-term memories into stable long-term ones. Abundant evidence for consolidation has been obtained, because a variety of treatments given after the initial acquisition of information can either impair or improve subsequent memory. Posttraining treatments that impair the establishment of long-term memory include head injuries, electrical shock to the brain, and chemical depressants. Posttraining conditions that improve the establishment of long-term memory include chemical excitants, weak stimulation of the reticular activating system, and fast-wave sleep.

As research into consolidation has continued, it appears that it is not a single general process but rather that a succession of processes is spread out in time and may take place at somewhat different locations in the brain. No single time course could be found for consolidation; rather, with different learning situations and with different posttrial treatments, the effective period for intervention has been found to be as short as seconds in some cases or as long as several hours in others. Electrical shock that interferes with consolidation is especially effective when delivered to specific brain sites (such as the **hippocampus** or the amygdaloid nuclei). Thus research concerning general brain processes influences, and is influenced by, research that looks for involvement of specific brain regions in learning and memory.

Special involvement of particular regions of the brain in learning and memory has been investigated by several techniques. Study of people with brain damage caused by disease or accident has revealed different kinds of impairment of memory with different locations of brain damage. Experimental lesions in specific sites of animal brains have produced a variety of behavioral effects, but it is not clear that any of these demonstrate pure impairment of learning or memory. Rather, it appears to be possible to interpret most, and perhaps all, of these cases in terms of alteration of sensory capacity or of motivation. A recent method for localizing brain processes in learning involves recording the electrical activity of neurons in different brain sites during training. This method permits study of the intact brain, whereas study of effects of lesions necessarily involves damaged brains. Some cells showed increased spike rates as soon as the behavioral indications of learning were observed. Such units were found in several regions of the brain, but most were in the thalamus, hypothalamus, reticular formation, and hippocampus. No single brain region appears to be responsible for learning or memory.

At the synaptic level, memory storage involves both chemical changes at already existing **synapses** and formation of new synapses. Short-term memory must involve changes at existing synapses because new associations can be acquired in seconds, whereas it requires considerable time (hours to days) to grow new synaptic connections. Changes at existing synapses have been demonstrated during **habituation** in the relatively simple nervous systems of various invertebrates. Electrical indications of habituation have also been recorded from single neurons in the isolated spinal cords of vertebrates. Whether long-term memories can also be stored as changes at existing synapses has not yet received much investigation. Changes in numbers of synapses have been found as consequences of differential experience. Several lines of evidence indicate that long-term memories can be stored in terms of changes in neural circuits, but this is not yet proved conclusively.

Figure 21-6
Effects of Experience on Brains of Rats

In most laboratories, rats live in colony cages (upper left). Relatively enriched environments (lower photo) lead to enhanced development of brain chemistry and anatomy. A restricted environment with each rat housed singly (upper right) depresses brain development. (Courtesy M. R. Rosenzweig)

22 Biological Processes in Perception

How does our visual system process forms, space, and color?
How does our auditory system process patterns of sound?

No machine yet devised comes close to matching the human ability to recognize faces, to identify spoken words, or to successfully travel over rugged terrain. This is true even though there are artificial sense organs that are more sensitive than our eyes or ears or touch receptors. We do not sense and perceive only with our sense organs but also with our nervous systems. The perceptual processes occur very swiftly, so that perceivers can adjust to a rapidly changing world. Skiers must adjust in a fraction of a second to changed angles and surface characteristics that they see ahead or that they feel through receptors in their joints and tendons. Listeners can identify 200 words a minute (and most of these have several distinctive phonemes or sound segments). It used to be thought that these complex decisions involve elaborate judgments or interferences too fast to follow introspectively, but it now appears that information is extracted from the sensory flux by many automatic neural processes.

A great deal of progress has been made in recent years in understanding the brain processes of perception. Some of this progress has come from new or improved ways of recording the electrical activity of individual cells in the nervous system. Some has come from increased precision in making surgical interventions in the nervous system. And much has come from combining ingenious and careful behavioral tests with electrophysiological and surgical procedures.

This chapter will take up some of the main processes that allow us to see and hear. It will increase your understanding of some of the aspects of perception—chiefly the perception of form and space and the discrimination of quality (hue and pitch)—treated in Chapters 16–18.

In many fundamental ways all the senses work similarly, once the initial processes of capturing the stimuli have occurred. For each type of stimulus energy—light, sound vibrations, mechanical energy on the skin, odors—a special receptor is needed. Each type of receptor converts stimulus energy into electrical energy, and this energy stimulates sensory neurons. Different aspects of the stimulus—spatial distribution, quality, and intensity—are coded into patterns of neural impulses. These are then decoded in specific parts of the nervous system. We will spend the most time on vision to develop the basic principles of neural processes in perception; many of these principles apply to other senses as well.

How does our visual system process forms, space, and color?

When you look at an object, light rays coming from different points on its surface are focused in an orderly array of points on the **retina** at the back of your eyeball (see Figure 22-1A). The pattern of light stimulation contains a great deal of information. To help you to extract some of it, the retina processes a great deal of information before transmitting nerve impulses to the brain, where further processing occurs. To accomplish its tasks, the paper-thin retina contains six main types of cells; furthermore these cells are precisely arranged in several layers and are intricately interconnected, as Figure 22-1B indicates. We will describe some of the stages of analysis performed at the retina and then follow the neural signals into the brain.

The first neural activity triggered off by the incoming light occurs at the receptor cell layer, even though this layer is located farthest from the stimulus. The receptor cells are of two sorts, rods and cones. The **rods** are more sensitive—they respond to weaker light than the cones. The **cones** differ from each other in responding more or less strongly to different parts of the visual spectrum, and they are necessary for discrimination of different hues. The human eye contains about 7 million cone cells (located most thickly toward the center of the retina) and about 120 million rod cells. The rods and cones contain special photopigments; when these chemicals capture **photons** (packets of light energy) they are altered and cause the cell to produce an electrical

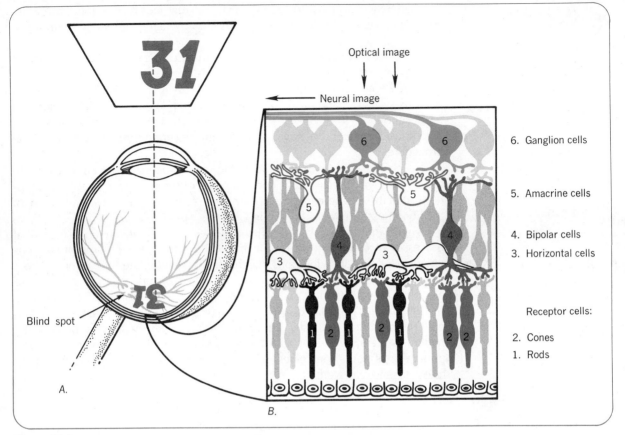

Figure 22-1
Main Types of Retinal Cells
A. The eyeball is opened to show an optical image formed on the retina. B. A small
section of the retina is enlarged about 500 times to show the main types of retinal
cells and their interconnections. For clarity, only a few cells of each type are
emphasized, but the retina is packed with hundreds of millions of cells.

potential. This electrical signal is conducted to the synapses where the receptor cell makes contact with the horizontal and bipolar cells.

Most receptor cells are connected synaptically to several horizontal and bipolar cells. For this reason, a message that starts at one receptor cell travels along many diverging paths and reaches many cells at higher levels of the visual system. Also, at any given cell at a higher level, messages converge from many receptors. This divergence and convergence of information permits a great deal of interaction among cells stimulated by parts of a figure. It enables the retina to form a sharp, high-contrast neural image over a wide range of external illumination.

Because of the convergence of messages upon it, each cell beyond the receptor layer has a moderately large **receptive field.** (The receptive field of a cell is that part of the visual field where stimulation alters the cell's activity —

either excites or inhibits it.) To map the receptive field, researchers first insert a fine-tipped electrode into a cell; then they record whether the cell's spontaneous electrical activity is increased or decreased when light or dark stimuli are presented in different parts of the visual field. Figure 22-2 illustrates this process. For any given cell, the investigators start by presenting stimuli and seeing whether the cell responds. Retinal ganglion cells (number 6 in Figure 22-1) produce impulses spontaneously; without any stimulations they fire off impulses at a rate of about ten per second. Inhibition is evidenced by a decrease in this rate and excitation by an increase. If the researchers do not obtain either type of response in one location, they are probably working outside of the receptive field of that cell; so they shift the position of the stimulus and try again. Retinal ganglion cells show concentric receptive fields. That is, stimuli in the center of their fields cause an opposite effect from stimuli at the outer ring of the field. Many of the ganglion cells respond as shown in

Figure 22-2
Retinal Ganglion Cells' Responses to Specific Stimuli

When a microelectrode is inserted into a ganglion cell in the retina, a slow rate of spontaneous nerve impulses (spike potentials) is recorded. If a stimulus is presented within the receptive field of the cell, it will either excite the cell (raise the rate of spikes) or inhibit the cell (lower the spontaneous rate). Retinal ganglion cells have concentric fields, with stimulations of the center and the periphery of the field yielding opposite effects, as the figure illustrates.

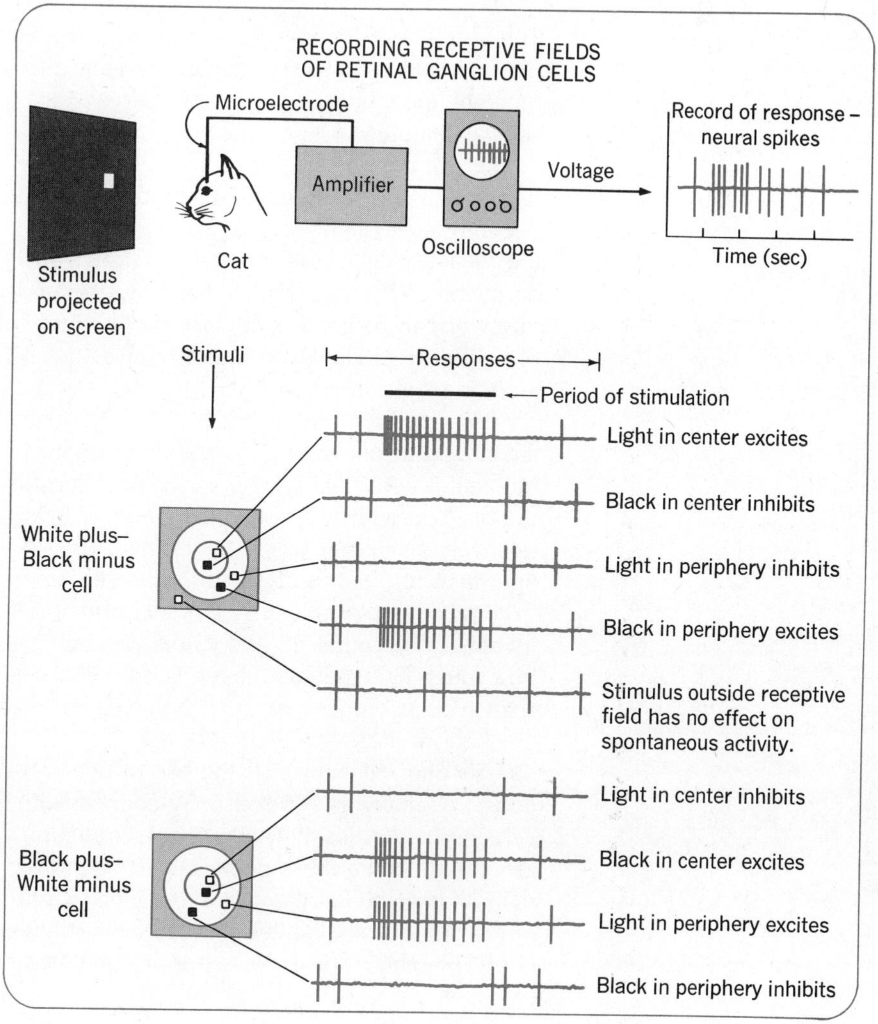

RECORDING RECEPTIVE FIELDS
OF RETINAL GANGLION CELLS

Microelectrode

Amplifier

Oscilloscope

Voltage

Record of response – neural spikes

Time (sec)

Cat

Stimulus projected on screen

Stimuli

Responses

Period of stimulation

White plus– Black minus cell

Light in center excites

Black in center inhibits

Light in periphery inhibits

Black in periphery excites

Stimulus outside receptive field has no effect on spontaneous activity.

Black plus– White minus cell

Light in center inhibits

Black in center excites

Light in periphery excites

Black in periphery inhibits

the upper part of Figure 22-2: light in the center of the cell's field evokes responses, but light in the periphery suppresses responses; conversely black in the center inhibits and black in the periphery excites. Such cells are sometimes called "on" center cells and sometimes "white plus–black minus" cells. Other ganglion cells show the reverse organization, with light in the center of the cell's field inhibiting and light in the periphery exciting; these can be called "black plus–white minus" cells. Which kind of organization a ganglion cell shows depends on whether input from the center makes excitatory or inhibitory synaptic connections; connections from the periphery of the cell's field are made with the opposite sign. (Later we will see that some ganglion cells respond specifically to colors.)

Visual forms are patterns of different intensities of light, whether we consider simple outline figures of black on white or figures with many intermediate intensities. So when we ask how forms are processed by the visual system, we must consider how intensities are discriminated.

DISCRIMINATION OF INTENSITY

The visual system codes for brightness of the stimulus in terms of frequency of **neural impulses** or **spikes;** that is, for white plus–black minus cells, the brighter the light, the more spikes the optic nerve axons carry per unit of time. But some special features of this relation require more detailed examination. For example, we are sensitive to very small differences in intensity, yet we can function over a very wide range of stimulus intensities.

The brightest light you can stand is over ten billion times more intense than the weakest light you can see (as shown in Figure 18-9). Your eyes could hardly be any more sensitive than they are; under optimal conditions a human observer can detect a light flash of only a few photons—the minimal packets of light energy. However, at these lowest levels, below bright moonlight, it is a colorless visual world.

Although your total capacity for discriminating brightness gives a ratio of ten billion to one (brightest to darkest), your operating capacity at any given moment is considerably less, giving a brightest-darkest ratio of about a hundred to one. Your entire ability to discriminate light intensities is thus devoted to a relatively small part of the total range, and your discrimination can be much finer than if it had to be spread across the entire range.

How does the visual system perform this feat? Several mechanisms are involved. The pupil adjusts to the prevailing intensity of light and regulates how much light reaches the retina. In very weak light the pupil becomes about sixteen times larger than it is in very bright light. Cameras employ a similar mechanism in the diaphragm or f stop.

A second mechanism is the use of two sets of receptors, the rods and the cones. As many as 100 rods may connect with a single bipolar cell. This convergence aids sensitivity, because stimulation of any of the rods within the group will excite the bipolar cell. Though their convergence promotes sensitivity, it is gained at the cost of reduced spatial acuity. Responding to any one of a group of rods, the bipolar cell cannot tell exactly where the stimulus occurred. Night vision then is not as spatially acute as day vision, where less convergence occurs. There is much convergence in the rod system but less in the cone system. The cones function above the level of moonlight, and when the cone system is active it inhibits the rod system. A photographic analogue to the two types of receptors is the use of more or less sensitive films.

A third mechanism is the receptive field organization that we described above for the white–black cells. It enhances relative differences between parts of the field, to whatever level of illumination the eye is adapted. This spatial interaction of excitatory and inhibitory effects has no analogue in photography, but the receiving elements in television have inhibitory connections to each other. You may have noticed that where a television camera picks up a very bright light—such as a flashbulb at a press conference or the flame of a satellite booster at blast-off—there appears to be a dark cloud around it.

Finally, adaptation has two mechanisms, chemical and neural. Bright light tends to bleach the photopigments so that the retina is less sensitive; in dim light the regeneration of the photopigments keeps up with the bleaching so that a maximum of stimulation can occur. Neural feedback is inhibitory so that activity tends to reduce sensitivity. Adaptation in vision is very effective: when you look at something for a minute or so, the chemical and neural adaptation would so deplete or inhibit the receptors that the object would disappear—if it were not for the fact that your eyes always tremble slightly. This normal tremor changes which receptors are stimulated and thus counteracts adaptation. If the object we see is *in* the eye, however, and "trembles" just as the receptors do, then the object does fade. For example, there are numerous blood vessels between the retina and the pupil, although we usually do not see them because of adaptation.

Cells in the optic nerve can fire no more frequently than about 100 spikes per second, but this is enough to account for the range of brightness that we can see at any given time. Sometimes this range is in the bright part of the total, sometimes the range includes only lower intensities; wherever it is, it is interpreted by essentially the same cells. In other words, to know how fast a cell is firing tells you how much stimulation it is receiving *relative* to other cells, but tells you nothing about the *absolute* brightness. In terms of what you experience, inputs above the operating range are seen as "white" and those below as "black" (*see* Figure 22-3).

This fact helps to explain some of the effects pointed out in Chapter 17 on perception. Black objects usually remain black, and white remain white despite major changes in illumination. But interesting illusions can be created if we conceal the relation between the illumination of the object and the illumination of its field (*see* Spotlight 17-2, p. 480).

Within the operating range, your impression of brightness does not increase in direct linear proportion to the amount of light energy of the source. As shown in Chapter 20, your perception of brightness follows approximately the logarithm or power law function of the stimulus intensity—the exact form of the function is still a matter of dispute. This nonlinear relation between stimulus and response is determined by the rods and cones. The receptor cells produce a generator potential that is approximately logarithmically related to the stimulus intensity.

Figure 22-3
Perception of Black and White

The level of illumination to which the eyes are adapted at any given time can change over a broad range. Any surface looks white if it reflects back about one logarithmic unit more light than the current adaptation level; any surface looks black if it reflects back about one log unit less light than the current adaptation level.

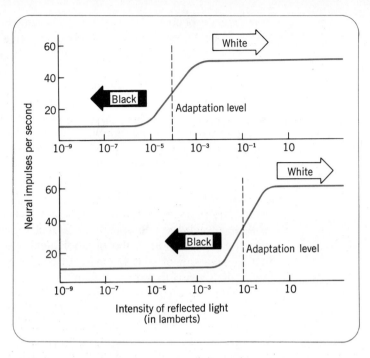

CONTRAST AND
ENHANCEMENT OF
CONTOURS

How bright one part of the visual field looks depends on the brightness of neighboring parts of the field. A gray patch looks darker where it touches a white patch and lighter where it contacts a black patch (demonstrated in Figure 5 in the preview to Perception). Such contrast sharpens borders or contours — lines between two "things." The outer shape or contour of something communicates a great amount of information; line drawings and cartoons, for example, make their point with little else.

The contrast and sharpening effects in vision are known to depend on complex interrelations among retinal cells as well as among cells higher in the visual system. Understanding of these mechanisms has been aided by the study of a simpler system where the units are readily accessible and where only one type of interaction among units occurs. The compound eye of the horseshoe crab, *Limulus,* has about a thousand separate units or *ommatidia* (from the Greek for "little eye"). (*See* Figure 22-4.) Each ommatidium is innervated by a single neuron. Soon after leaving the ommatidia, the neurons are interconnected by side branches that form a network. Through this network, any neuron that is activated inhibits its neighbors, and the closer they are, the stronger the inhibition. It is relatively easy to record the activity of one or more individual neurons from this compound eye.

If a narrow beam of light is focused on one ommatidium, then the neuron from that unit fires impulses. The stronger the light, the faster the rate of firing; the rate is roughly proportional to the logarithm of light intensity. If the light is maintained on unit *A* and a second light is focused on unit *B*, the rate of firing in *A* promptly falls, just as if the light on *A* had been dimmed. If the light on *A* is then extinguished, the rate of firing in *B* rises. Thus each unit inhibits its neighbor.

To study contrast, investigators illuminated half of the compound eye and prevented light from reaching the other half; this is diagrammed in Figure 22-4. Recording from units at various locations then revealed that the *greatest* rate of neural firing is found just to the lighted side of the light-dark boundary, while the *lowest* rate of firing is found just to the dark side of the boundary. Farther from the boundary, the rates of firing are intermediate. Because the rate of firing is more or less proportional to the logarithm of intensity of light,

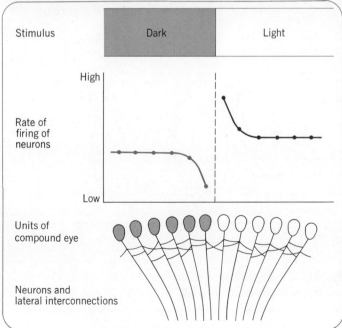

Figure 22-4
Study of Contrast in a Compound Eye
Each unit or ommatidium in the compound eyes (location shown above) of the horseshoe crab can be recorded separately. The graph shows the rate of firing of neural impulses depending upon the position of the ommatidium with respect to the light-dark boundary. The greatest difference in firing rates occurs at the boundary. This contrast effect is caused by the mutual inhibition among units. (Adapted from Ratliff & Hartline, 1959)

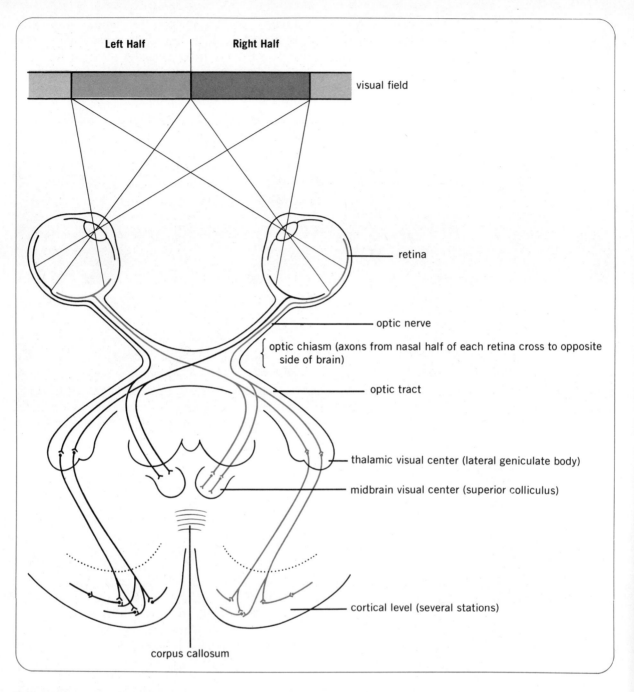

Figure 22-5
Map of the Human Visual System
This diagram shows some of the main pathways in the visual system. Note that the left half of the visual field (in color) stimulates the right half of each retina and sends neural impulses to the right half of the brain.

what does the observed pattern mean? The eye responds as if the light were brightest just inside its boundary and as if the surrounding area were darkest just outside the boundary. Differences in rates of firing are enhanced at the boundary between the light and dark areas.

DISCRIMINATION
OF FORM

Now we are ready to follow visual signals up the optic nerve and into the brain where further processing occurs. A map of the human visual system is given in Figure 22-5 (Figure 22-7 is a more realistic diagram). The **optic nerve** fibers are the axons of the ganglion cells in the retina. These fibers run to the thalamus before they form synapses with other cells. At the thalamus, **receptive fields** are simple and concentric, just as they are in the retina. Also, at the thalamus there are no connections between the fibers from the two eyes. But at the cerebral cortex the receptive fields become more varied and interesting — the receptive fields now become elongated rather than circular, and most cortical cells respond to stimulation of either eye.

For a particular cortical cell the best stimulus to evoke activity may be a bar at a certain angle and at a certain location in the visual field; such a cell is illustrated at *B* in Figure 22-6. Another cortical cell may best be stimulated by a line a little to the left of center in the visual field and at a 45° angle; a third cell will respond only to a horizontal line at a particular position in the lower right quadrant, and so on. Such cortical cells receive inputs from several neurons located closer to the receptor. In Chapter 21 we noted that many neurons will fire only when several converging inputs are active simultaneously, and these lower cells probably show a physical arrangement (in combination) that resembles the form of the effective stimulus. For example, the cells that feed into the unit shown in *B* in Figure 22-6 probably have their receptive fields aligned vertically. Illuminating a broad area will not stimulate such a cortical cell, because this will inhibit the cell just as much as it excites it. For this reason, many cells in the visual cortex do not respond when the lights in the room are turned on. This lack of response to general illumination puzzled many early researchers. They thought that the cells in the visual cortex ought to respond to *any* visual stimulus, but now we know that most cortical cells are much more demanding.

Cells that are close together in the primary visual cortex respond to stimulation in the same area of the visual field, but often also respond to quite different stimuli. This means that the primary cortex does "map" the visual field, each region of cortex receiving information from a specific part of the field. Within the map different cells represent different sorts of visual input—hues, brightness or darkness, angles, and so on. Two neighboring cells may then respond very differently, so detailed electrical recording does not support the commensense (or scientific) notions that what you see is accurately represented in the large-scale distribution of activity across the surface of the brain. Even the gross mapping may, however, prove useful in providing some vision to the blind by electrical stimulation of the brain (*see* Spotlight 22-1).

Some cortical cells act as if they could be fired only through other cortical cells. For example, some respond only to two lines joined at an angle (a corner), as if two "line detectors" fed into the "corner detector." Some cortical cells respond only to lines of a specific "tilt" or orientation but respond to such lines placed anywhere in a relatively large area of the visual field. They seem to be "abstracting" a common feature of several different and specific inputs. It appears that these generalized "orientation detectors" can be fired by the more specific cortical cells, each of which requires not only the angle but also a fixed position. In general, cortical cells that are both complex and yet highly specialized have been found with increasing frequency in recent years. One researcher discovered cortical cells in the monkey's temporal lobe that fired best to a precise stimulus, such as the shape of a hand or a forceps; the cell responded to that stimulus regardless of its orientation or its location within a wide extent of the visual field (Gross, Bender, & Rocha-Miranda, 1969).

The way that functions are distributed among brain regions is not necessarily the same for all species. Rather complex processes that occur in the

Figure 22-6
Brain Cells' Reactions to Specific Stimuli
Microelectrode recording reveals that cells in the brain vary greatly in their receptive fields. Visual cells in the thalamus have concentric receptive fields like those of retinal ganglion cells (see Figure 22-2). But cortical cells may show orientation specificity (B) or respond only to motion in a particular direction (C) or even be sensitive to only a particular shape.

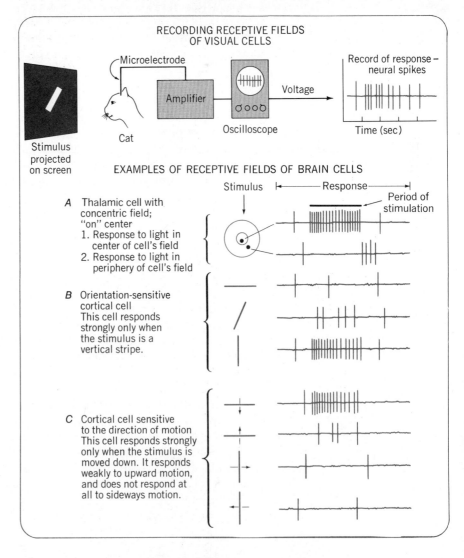

We have artificial limbs; why not artificial eyes?

Recent experiments show some success in giving vision to a totally blind person by delivering electrical stimulation directly to the primary visual cortex. When a point on the cortex is stimulated, the person reports "seeing" a glowing spot in a particular part of the visual field. If two points are stimulated in succession, the person can report their relative positions in the visual field. If several points are stimulated, the person sees a pattern of luminous spots, somewhat like a sign made up of light bulbs.

Following developmental work on monkeys, an array of electrodes was implanted through the skull in a volunteer subject blind for seven years (Dobelle, Mladejovsky, & Girven, 1974). When patterns of stimulation were fed into the electrode array, the subject could identify several of them by "sight"; for example, the subject could recognize and draw patterns such as a square or a backward *L*. The device did not work as well as was hoped, but plans have been developed to improve the system. It should be noted that the electrodes were rather large and each probably activated hundreds of cortical cells. Therefore a system of this sort cannot utilize the highly differentiated receptive fields of single cells but depends on the grosser spatial map of the visual cortex.

Popular Mechanics (Berger, 1974) foresees mounting a miniature television camera in an artificial eye and using a tiny computer to turn the television image into stimuli to be fed to brain electrodes. A workable system is probably far in the future, but even the crude and partial success of these studies is adding useful scientific knowledge, not only for the blind but also for an understanding of the normal visual system as well.

brains of mammals may occur peripherally in sensory systems of somewhat simpler animals. For example, in the frog, which does not have a cerebral cortex, shape discrimination occurs in the ganglion cells of the retina. Thus one type of cell in the frog retina will react only to small roundish moving stimuli such as the insects the frog eats; these retinal cells have been called "bug detectors." It is not that the frog sees and ignores stationary bugs; its visual system simply does not respond to such stimuli.

Effects of Brain Lesions on Form Vision

Electrical recording or stimulation is not the only means of studying the functions of biological tracts and centers related to vision. Another method is to study the behavioral effects of localized cuts or destruction of the brain — brain lesions. We will consider successively the effects of lesions in the three cortical regions most concerned with form vision (*see* Figure 22-7): (1) The *primary visual cortex* is where the signals from the eyes first reach the cortical level; it is often called the "striate area" because one layer of this cortex is a light-colored strip running parallel to the surface. (2) From the primary visual cortex, axons run to the surrounding area called the *secondary visual* (or circumstriate) *cortex*. (3) The last region lies at the base of the temporal lobe and is therefore called the **inferotemporal cortex;** some of the most complex visual integrations seem to occur here.

Localized lesions in the primary visual cortex produce both localized and more general effects. The visual field is mapped rather precisely on the primary visual cortex, and a partial destruction of this area results in blindness for the corresponding part of the field. This blindness (a "scotoma") is not a black patch, for blackness is just as much a result of an active process as is whiteness. Instead the scotoma is simply an area in which nothing is seen.

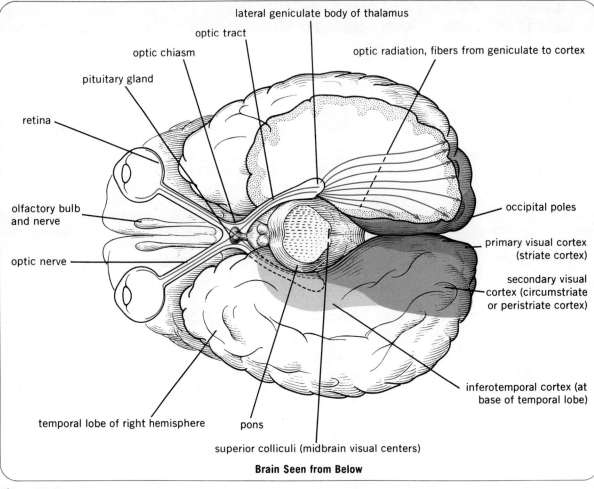

lateral geniculate body of thalamus

optic tract

optic chiasm

optic radiation, fibers from geniculate to cortex

pituitary gland

retina

olfactory bulb and nerve

optic nerve

occipital poles

primary visual cortex (striate cortex)

secondary visual cortex (circumstriate or peristriate cortex)

inferotemporal cortex (at base of temporal lobe)

temporal lobe of right hemisphere

pons

superior colliculi (midbrain visual centers)

Brain Seen from Below

Figure 22-7
Visual Pathways and Centers in the Human Brain

The visual pathways and centers are shown in color. Parts of the brain have been removed to reveal visual structures: the left temporal lobe (in the upper half of the diagram) has been largely cut away to reveal the thalamic visual center and axons running from it to the cortex. The cerebellum has been removed to show regions of the visual cortex. The brain stem has been cut across at the level of the midbrain visual centers.

The patient is not aware of a blind spot—until a visual object vanishes into it—just as you are not aware of your blind spot unless you look at a stimulus like Preview Figure 12 in the perception section (p. 441). To this extent, destruction of part of the primary visual cortex results in a sensory defect; there is simply no vision in that part of the field, although vision elsewhere is relatively normal.

Localizing function in the visual cortex is not quite so simple, however, because even the localized "sensory" lesion has other effects. For example, the ability to distinguish a flickering light from a steady light is somewhat impaired thoughout the visual field whenever any part of the primary visual cortex is injured.

The effects of a lesion in the secondary visual cortex (the circumstriate area) are still disputed. Although there is no hole in the visual field, the accuracy of discriminating shapes or sizes of objects decreases. Therefore, some investigators speak about *perceptual* damage here, in contrast to the *sensory* damage resulting from lesions in the primary visual cortex.

VISUAL PERCEPTION OF SPACE AND MOTION

How does the skier see the position of the slalom gates? How do you see the location of a book to pick it up? How can you tell in which direction a bird is flying? It might seem that solving the problems of visual form (what is it?) would also solve the problems of visual space (where is it?). Because forms are extended in space and we perceive and discriminate form, don't we also perceive and discriminate space? Research has demonstrated that the two abilities are rather different, as William James suspected when he wrote his *Principles of Psychology* in 1890.

The accuracy of discrimination of direction is quite good in the periphery of the visual field even though acuity for form is poor. If you detect a small movement out toward one edge of your field, you move your gaze in that direction very quickly and accurately; then you examine what is there. But if you try keeping your eyes directed straight ahead, you realize that you cannot discriminate shapes very well out to the side. For example, look at the center of this page while you wiggle a fingertip around the middle of the opposite page. You can see very well where the moving fingertip is, but can you read the words around it? Form discrimination is accurate in the center of the field and falls off rapidly as the target is moved to either side or above or below; you have to move your eyes to identify objects and to read. Because space discrimination does not deteriorate nearly so rapidly away from the central region, you can tell *where* objects are before you know *what* they are. Your spatial perception allows you to duck a rapidly approaching object before you can identify it as a stone or a bird or a snowball.

In at least some mammals, the visual midbrain is involved in discrimination of space but not of form. (The visual part of the midbrain consists of the paired **superior colliculi,** shown in Figure 22-7.) Schneider (1969) tested three groups of hamsters—normal animals, animals with the primary visual cortex removed, and animals with the superior colliculi removed. The hamsters were tested both for orientation to a moving stimulus (where is it?) and for recognition of such visual patterns as a triangle and a circle (what is it?). The moving stimulus was a sunflower seed—a favorite food for hamsters—waved back and forth in the experimenter's hand. Normal hamsters soon learned to come and get the seed, and hamsters with the visual cortex removed also oriented to the motion and learned to take the seed. But hamsters with the superior colliculi removed were first judged to be blind by this test because they found the food only by smell or touch. However, hamsters with the superior colliculi removed could learn to discriminate different test patterns, whereas those with visual cortex removed could not. So, at least in the hamster, form perception requires the visual cortex and does not need the superior colliculi, whereas discrimination of direction requires the colliculi but not the cortex. Monkeys without striate cortex also can localize visual targets although they cannot recognize forms (Weiskrantz, 1974).

Fine discrimination of *distance* is another matter; it depends largely on the slightly different views that the two eyes get of an object (see the discussion of *binocular disparity,* pp. 472–73). We noted that at the cortex most cells have

Recent research suggests a new answer to the long-disputed question of whether form perception is inborn (the nativist position) or acquired through experience (the empiricist position). Previously, much attention had been paid to people who were born with cataracts and who were able to see for the first time as adults when the cataracts were removed. Most of these case studies indicated that these people very quickly saw differences in color and could sense where an object was, but they could not immediately identify objects or discriminate distances. Only gradually, over weeks and months, did some people learn to identify faces and objects and to see them in depth; others gave up the attempt and never acquired useful form vision. These findings suggest that learning plays a more significant role in form perception than do inborn capacities. But another possibility is that some visual proficiency is inborn but can be lost during the period when cataracts cover the eyes. Some recent research supports this third possibility.

Hubel (1967) reported that newborn kittens had cortical visual receptive fields rather similar to those of adult cats. (Some other investigators stress the immature features of these early responses—broader tuning and easy fatiguability.) If the eyes were covered for the first two months, then many cortical cells did not respond to visual stimulation, and some cells gave abnormal responses. The longer the eyes were occluded, the less well did the cats regain useful vision. In an older cat, the eyes can be occluded for months, and vision returns very rapidly when the eyes are uncovered.

If only one of a kitten's eyes is covered for several weeks, later testing shows that the kitten can no longer discriminate forms *with that eye*. Similarly, a child can lose the use of an eye for form vision if she or he relies on the other eye. This often occurs if the two eyes do not converge—if they do not aim at exactly the same place. In such cases there would be double vision if the input from one eye was not suppressed. But even with normal convergence, a child may begin to use only one eye, and acuity then declines in the other. If a "lazy eye" is detected, the treatment is to put a patch over the favored eye for a period each day to force the use of the neglected eye. Without treatment, the neglected eye will lose form vision. Astigmatism—a condition in which lines in certain directions appear blurred—can also result in a permanent defect unless it is corrected early (Freeman & Thibos, 1973).

It appears that immature but rather normal organization of visual connections is present at birth. This is the nativist position. But the normal organization of visual connections also seems to *require experience* to confirm it and perhaps to strengthen it. This is another example of heredity-environment interaction, and it provides a further demonstration that the extreme empiricist and nativist positions have become outmoded.

© 1965 United Features Syndicate

binocular input. Furthermore, some cortical cells respond particularly strongly when the stimuli to the two eyes are slightly disparate (Pettigrew, 1972). Some cortical cells "prefer" slight disparity, some "prefer" moderate amounts, and some will not respond if any disparity is present. Thus the relative activity of such cortical cells provides an analysis for the feature of binocular disparity; this binocular network discriminates spatial depth.

Discrimination of direction of motion may be accomplished by simple networks at the retinal level (Michael, 1969). Figure 22-8 indicates such a network. Here a stimulus moving to the right excites the bipolar cells that stimulate the ganglion cell. But a stimulus moving to the left causes each bipolar cell to be inhibited by a horizontal cell, so the bipolar cell does not respond when the stimulus reaches it. Just as this circuit responds only to movement to the right, a mirror-image circuit would respond only to movement to the left. Presumably many circuits of both sorts extract information about directions of motion.

DISCRIMINATION OF COLOR

Color is another important feature of human vision for which a good deal of processing is accomplished at the retina. Recent research has shown how to combine and update two theories of color vision that used to be considered as competitors. One theory posited three types of cone, each sensitive to a different part of the spectrum—red, green, and blue. (This hypothesis is some-

Figure 22-8
A Retinal Circuit to Discriminate Direction of Motion
A stimulus moving in either direction excites the receptors, but the ganglion cell in this case is activated only by movement to the right. In the case of movement to the left, each bipolar cell receives inhibitory input (–) from the adjacent horizontal cell before excitatory input reaches it, so no excitation is passed on to the ganglion cell. But when the stimulus moves to the right, each bipolar cell is excited before inhibition reaches it, so the ganglion cell is activated. With circuits based on this principle, different ganglion cells detect motion in different directions. (Modified from Michael, 1969)

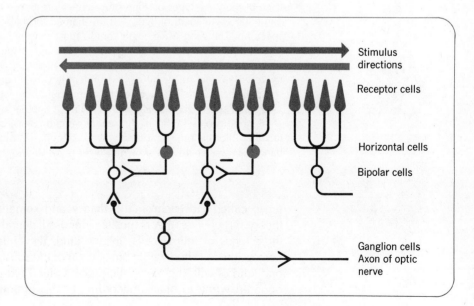

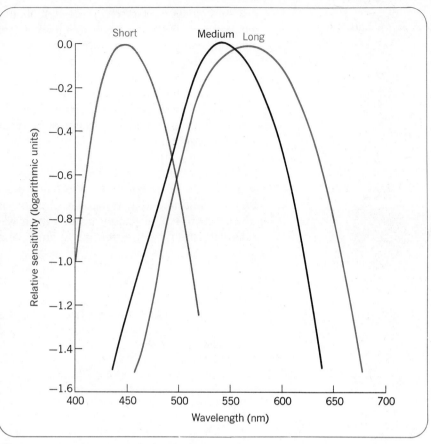

Figure 22-9
Broad Response Curves of Cone Receptors
Each of the three types of cone shows a peak response at a particular wavelength of light, and it is named for that part of the spectrum. The short wavelength cone is most sensitive around 435 nm, but it responds over a broad portion of the spectrum. The medium and long wavelength cones also have broad response curves. Therefore no single cone can identify wavelength: the stimulus that excites it at a given moment could be a weak light at its peak of sensitivity or a stronger stimulus at another wavelength —the cone can't tell which. But retinal ganglion cells, by putting together information from different types of cones, can discriminate bands of wavelengths, as shown in Figures 22-10 and 22-11.

times called the **trichromatic theory** and sometimes the Young-Helmholtz theory.) The other theory posited opposed neural or metabolic processes in three kinds of retinal cells: in one kind, the buildup of a substance caused perception of yellow while breakdown of the substance caused blue; in a second kind of cell, the metabolic process pitted red against green, and the third opposed white to black. According to this **opponent-process theory** (sometimes called the Hering theory) there are thus four primary hues—yellow, blue, red, and green. We now know that both of these theories had part of the truth, because cone receptors are trichromatic and the ganglion cells show opponent processes. Much progress has been made in this area recently, and both the older theories have had to be modified somewhat (De Valois & De Valois, 1975; Jacobs, 1976).

The human retina does possess three kinds of cones, but each responds to light from most of the spectrum, and they cannot be properly called red, green, and blue cones. Curves of cone responses at different wavelengths are shown in Figure 22-9. The type that is relatively most responsive to short wavelengths has its peak sensitivity around 435 nm; it is in the blue region of the spectrum (see Perception Color Figure 3). But the type of cone that is most sensitive to long wavelengths has a very broadly tuned curve with a peak sensitivity around 570 nm, which is in the yellow part of the spectrum rather than in the red zone.

We cannot record the activity of single human ganglion cells, but Old World monkeys show color discrimination just like that of human beings with normal color vision. What is found when we record from single ganglion cells of these monkeys and stimulate their eyes with various colors? Most of the ganglion cells can be classified into six types according to their responses. Two types ignore color—these are the white plus–black minus and black plus–white minus cells that we considered earlier (p. 602 and Figure 22-2). But four kinds are acutely sensitive to wavelength; each type is excited by light from one part of the spectrum and is inhibited by light from another part. The four kinds of color cell are red plus–green minus, green plus–red minus, yellow plus–blue minus, and blue plus–yellow minus (see Figure 22-10). Because these cells are excited by only a limited part of the spectrum, they can more properly be called color cells than the cones which respond to all the visible spectrum.

Figure 22-10
Color Discrimination by
Retinal Ganglion Cells
Because of their neural inputs, each ganglion cell is "turned on" by certain wavelengths and is "turned off" by other wavelengths. The upper graph shows the response of a yellow plus–blue minus ganglion cell; it is just the opposite of the lower graph, which is for a blue plus–yellow minus ganglion cell. Unlike the cone receptors (Figure 22-9), the ganglion cells actually discriminate color because they respond differently according to the wavelengths of light.

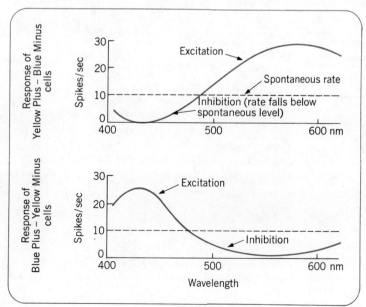

Figure 22-11
Retinal Systems for Detecting Hue and Brightness
The human retina contains three types of cone receptors. Each can be stimulated by any wavelength of visible light but is most sensitive to one of the three wavelengths shown at the top of the diagram. The receptor cells make contact with neurons, the bipolar cells. Each neural bipolar cell is excited by only one type of cone. The bipolar cells, in turn, synapse on the next set of neurons, the ganglion cells. The axons of the ganglion cells run out of the eye and form the optic nerve. The ganglion cells fire impulses spontaneously and can be excited to a higher rate of activity by certain bipolar cells and inhibited by other bipolar cells.

There are six main populations of ganglion cells: four kinds detect color, and the other two detect brightness or darkness. The color-detecting ganglion cells, unlike the bipolar cells, cannot be excited by all wavelengths of light; they are inhibited by part of the spectrum. For example, a yellow plus–blue minus cell (like the ganglion cell at the left of the diagram) fires faster than its spontaneous rate if the stimulus energy is mainly in the long wavelengths, but it stops firing if the light energy is concentrated in the short wavelengths.

The two types of ganglion cells that detect brightness differences have concentric receptive fields. For a black plus–white minus cell (like the ganglion cell at the right of the diagram), a light in the center of its field inhibits, while an off-center light excites. (Modified from De Valois, 1969)

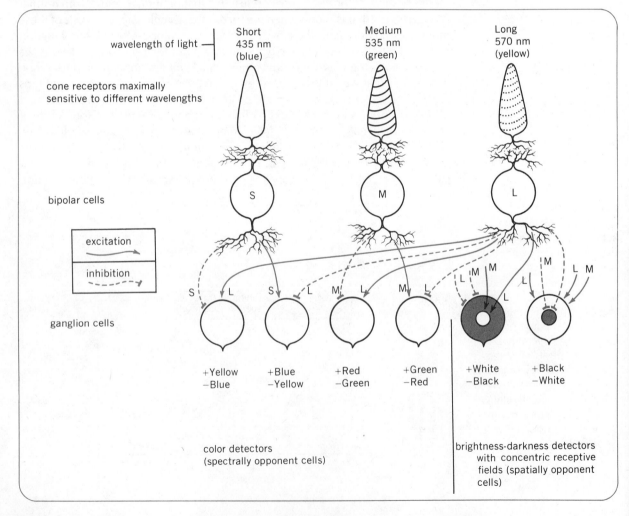

Unlike the broad tuning of the receptors, the sharper selectivity of the neural response is achieved by specific connections among the retinal cells. The retinal "wiring diagram" for analysis of wavelength is shown in Figure 22-11. The neural sharpening is brought about by the interplay of excitatory and inhibitory synaptic connections. For example, the yellow plus–blue minus ganglion cell (at the left in Figure 22-11) receives excitatory inputs from cones with greatest sensitivity for long wavelengths; it receives inhibitory inputs from cones with best sensitivity in the short wavelengths. Therefore, as Figure 22-10 shows, the yellow plus–blue minus cell is excited by long-wavelength light and is inhibited by short-wavelength light. The blue plus–yellow minus cell has the opposite wiring pattern (excitatory from short-wavelength cones and inhibitory from long), and it shows an opposite response pattern to the yellow plus–blue minus cells. In other senses too there are neural circuits to sharpen discrimination; for example, some cells in the auditory tracts discriminate among frequencies of sound even more precisely than do the receptor cells in the inner ear.

How does our auditory system process patterns of sound?

As you listen to words, you extract information in much the same way as you do when you see objects. Auditory sensations have both tonal qualities (which are analogous to hues in vision) and loudness (analogous to brightness). Spoken words are auditory patterns (just as written words are visual forms), and you can localize sounds in space just as you can localize visual objects. The auditory stimulus is a different kind of energy from the visual stimulus, so a different kind of receptor organ is needed to capture it and to transform it into neural impulses. From that point on, however, many processes in the auditory tracts and centers are similar to those in the visual system.

THE AUDITORY RECEPTOR   The inner ear is like a specialized strip of skin that is sensitive to mechanical vibration just as your fingertips can detect the vibration of an object that they touch. But the ear is far more sensitive to both frequency and intensity of vibration than the skin. As was pointed out in the perception section (p. 508), both the frequency and the intensity of vibration of a sound determine the pitch—whether it is low (a bass) or high (a soprano)—and both the intensity and the frequency also determine loudness.

The sensitivity of the auditory receptors is really quite amazing. Most young people can hear sounds as low in frequency as 20 Hz and as high as 20,000 Hz. (Hz stands for **hertz,** a unit of frequency equal to 1 cycle per second; see Figure 18-8.) We can hear such incredibly weak sounds that if our ears were any more sensitive, we would be bothered by hearing air molecules colliding! But we can also listen briefly to intense sounds without damaging the ear. The receptor accomplishes the first steps in capturing and discriminating sounds.

Sound is transmitted from the eardrum through a series of three little bones (or ossicles) that span the middle ear and that contact the inner ear (or **cochlea**) (see Figure 22-12). The cochlea is a fluid-filled coiled tube. (Anatomists derived its name from the Greek word for snail.) Running down the length of the

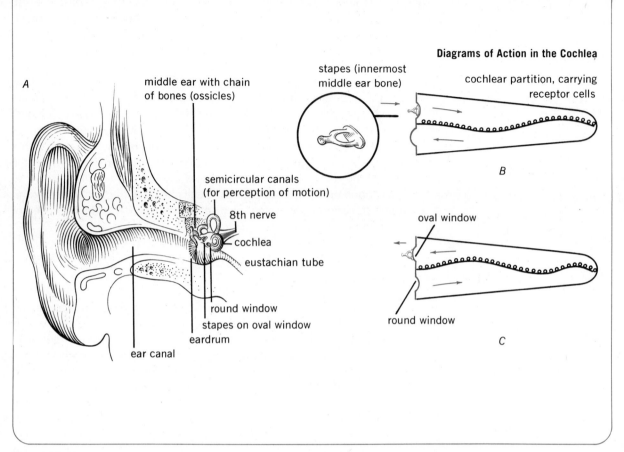

Diagrams of Action in the Cochlea

A

middle ear with chain of bones (ossicles)

stapes (innermost middle ear bone)

cochlear partition, carrying receptor cells

B

semicircular canals (for perception of motion)

8th nerve

oval window

cochlea

eustachian tube

round window

stapes on oval window

eardrum

round window

ear canal

C

Figure 22-12
Anatomy and Function of the Ear

cochlea is a partition that divides it into upper and lower chambers, as shown in Figure 22-12 *B* and *C*. During one half of a cycle of sound vibration, when the last of the ossicles presses in on the membranous oval window in the upper chamber, the fluid in the cochlea is displaced and the round window in the lower chamber bulges out (as shown in *B*). In the next half of the cycle, the ossicle pulls out and the round window bulges in (as shown in C). These movements of the windows and the fluid cause the partition to ripple up and down; a traveling wave moves along it. Something like this happens when you hold a cord that is secured at the other end and you snap your end up and down; you see a wave travel from your end to the far end. The greatest amplitude of up-and-down motion of the partition occurs near the windows when the frequency of vibration is high; the greatest amplitude occurs near the far end when the frequency is low; so the place of maximum movement is related to frequency of the stimulus. Also, the more intense the vibration, the greater the overall amplitude of movement of the cochlear partition.

The auditory receptor cells, the "hair cells," sit on the partition. They are stimulated by the traveling waves of motion that sweep along the partition. When stimulated, the hair cells develop an electrical potential that excites or inhibits the primary auditory neurons. This generator potential is such an accurate transformation of acoustic energy into electrical energy that it is called the cochlear microphonic, because it acts just like a microphone. In fact, when an electrode is put on the cochlea of an animal, and the electrical signal is amplified and fed into a loudspeaker in another room, listeners there hear clearly what is said into the animal's ear.

AUDITORY
DISCRIMINATION
Loudness Discrimination

In hearing as in sight, perceived intensity (loudness) is approximately a logarithmic function of stimulus intensity. Ten singers are needed to sound twice as loud as one singer. That is why the intensity of the auditory stimulus is usually given in logarithmic units, **decibels.** The rate of impulses in the auditory nerve shows that the logarithmic transformation between stimulus intensity and bodily response has already occurred by this level. Just how the transformation occurs between the linear cochlear microphonic and the logarithmic rate of impulses is not yet known.

Pitch Discrimination

How can you discriminate low pitches from high ones? In other words, how does the auditory system encode information on the frequency of vibration caused by the incoming stimulus? For many years two major possibilities were debated. The "telephone hypothesis" suggested that the system worked simply as a direct and exact transmission—if 100 Hz came in, 100 nerve impulses per second were sent to the brain. Analysis of the complexities was presumed to occur only in the higher brain centers. The second hypothesis was based on mechanical analysis of frequency in the cochlea. Because different incoming frequencies produce their greatest effect (the most up-and-down stimulation) at different places along the cochlear membrane, this "place hypothesis" asserted that different cells fired for different frequencies.

Both hypotheses are correct, but in different parts of the total range of frequencies. For low frequencies, the neurons follow the rate of vibration, transmitting this information rather directly to the higher auditory centers, like a telephone. Furthermore, the place of maximal activity in the cochlea does not differentiate well among low frequencies, so analysis of low frequencies must be accomplished in the brain, rather than peripherally in the cochlea. For higher frequencies this method would not be possible because auditory neurons can fire up to only about 1,000 impulses per second, whereas we can hear tones up to about 20,000 Hz. Even if several fibers took turns firing, this would permit following the stimulus up to only a few thousand cycles per second. Here is where the traveling waves in the cochlea play their role.

How precise is the mechanical analysis of frequency in terms of site of maximal amplitude of the traveling waves in the cochlea? There is not yet a sure answer, despite persistent and ingenious work by physicists using a variety of sophisticated techniques (Møller, 1973). The trouble is that the movements of the basilar membrane when we hear are tiny—it is estimated that they are smaller than the diameter of the hydrogen atom! Furthermore, the measurement techniques are either indirect and therefore subject to debate, or if they are direct they interfere with the delicate tissues in the cochlea.

According to the best current measures, the mechanical analysis of frequency in the cochlea is considerably less precise than are the responses of

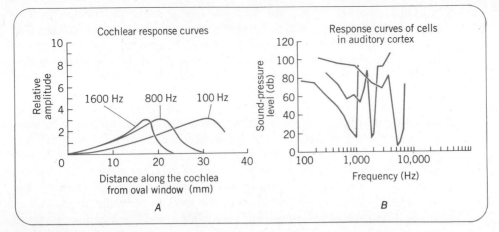

Figure 22-13
Frequency Discrimination
A. Within the cochlea, the traveling waves show different maxima, depending on
stimulus frequency, but this tuning is broad. The amplitude of movement in the
cochlea is shown for three different stimulus frequencies. These rounded curves for
the auditory receptor are somewhat like the broad response curves of retinal
receptors shown in Figure 22-10. (After Békésy, 1947)
B. Some neural cells in the auditory system show sharp tuning, responding strongly
at one frequency and weakly or not at all to nearby frequencies. Shown are
response curves for three different cells in the auditory cortex of the cat.

Other types of specificity are also shown in auditory receptive fields, for example,
responding only to a given pair of frequencies, or responding only to a tone that
rises in frequency, or responding only to a tone that comes from a particular
direction with regard to the head. (Redrawn from Hind et al., 1961)

nerve cells in the auditory system (Evans & Wilson, 1973). Individual auditory neurons can be studied using microelectrodes, and their "receptive fields" can be determined (*see* Figure 22-13). In many cases a cell is stimulated by only a narrow band of frequencies, and other frequencies inhibit its spontaneous activity. Such cells discriminate sound frequencies. Furthermore, in the part of the total frequency range where frequency discrimination is best, there are more cells tuned to these frequencies and their tuning is sharper than elsewhere in the scale.

**Neural Coding for
Sound Patterns**

Most sounds that we listen to include many frequencies arranged in definite patterns. When different musical instruments play the same note, each instrument can be recognized because it gives not just the fundamental frequency but also a characteristic pattern of overtones or harmonics. Bird songs, animal cries, and words are also patterns of frequencies. Each pattern can be described according to the frequencies, their relative intensities, and the changes in time of frequencies and intensities.

Just as investigators have found complex receptive fields in the visual system that suggest coding for elements or patterns of form, so some cells in the auditory system also have complex requirements. Some can be stimulated only by a combination of two frequencies (and finding such cells obviously requires

BIOLOGICAL PSYCHOLOGY

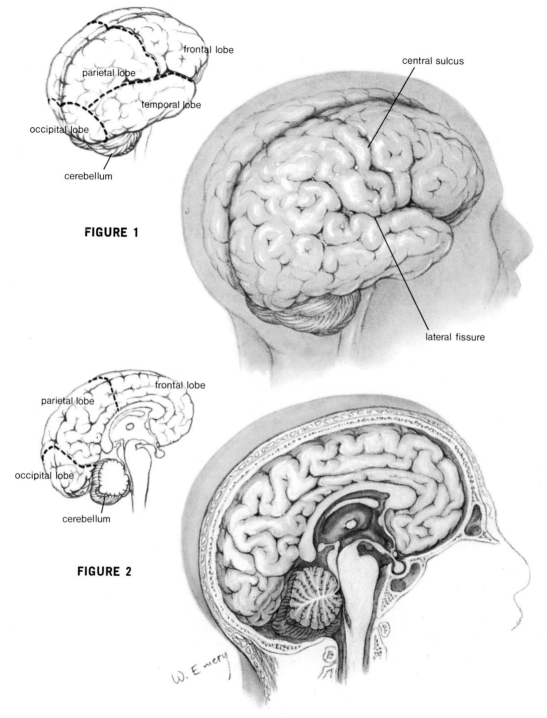

FIGURE 1

FIGURE 2

The adult human brain is seen from the right side and slightly from the rear in Figure 1. In Figure 2, the right half of the brain has been removed, and the left half of the brain is seen from the midline. The small drawings identify the lobes of the brain.

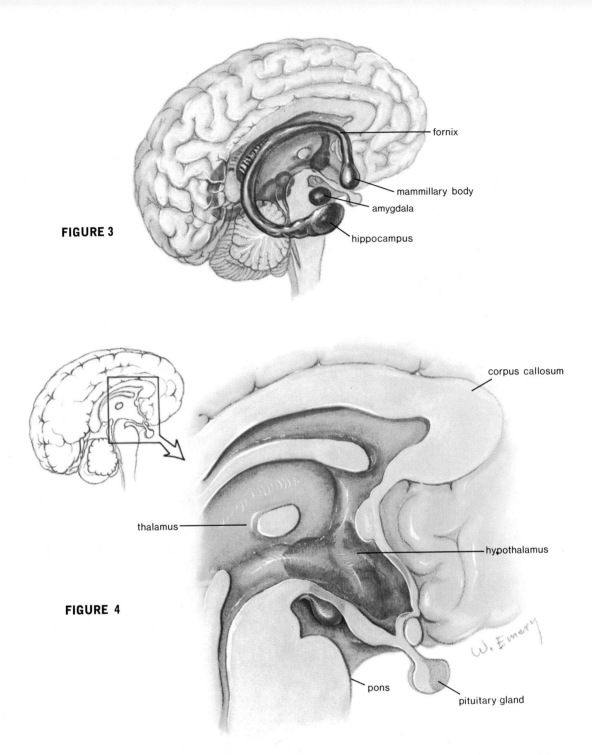

FIGURE 3

fornix

mammillary body

amygdala

hippocampus

FIGURE 4

corpus callosum

thalamus

hypothalamus

pons

pituitary gland

W. Emery

These drawings show parts of the limbic system. In Figure 3, most of the right hemisphere has been removed, leaving only the right hippocampus, fornix, mammillary body, and amygdala. In the intact left hemisphere, these structures are shaded. Figure 4 shows the hypothalamus and nearby structures. The roles of nuclei or subdivisions of the hypothalamus in control of motivated behavior are discussed in Chapter 25.

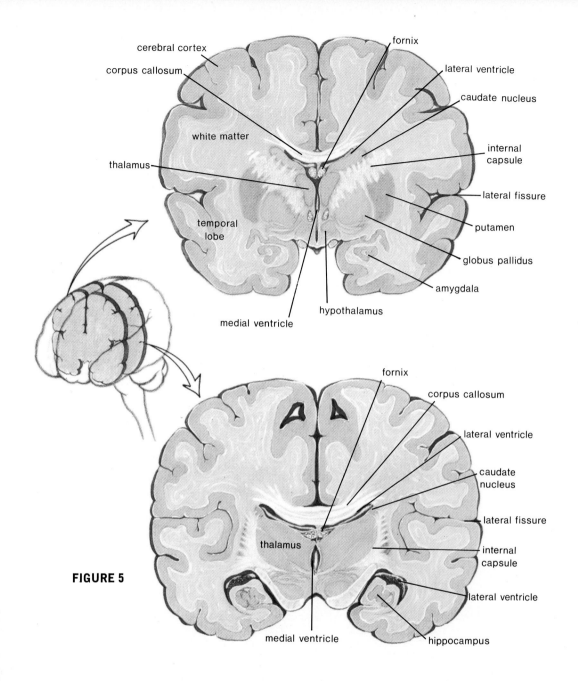

cerebral cortex

corpus callosum

fornix

lateral ventricle

caudate nucleus

white matter

internal capsule

thalamus

lateral fissure

temporal lobe

putamen

globus pallidus

amygdala

medial ventricle

hypothalamus

fornix

corpus callosum

lateral ventricle

caudate nucleus

lateral fissure

thalamus

internal capsule

lateral ventricle

FIGURE 5

medial ventricle

hippocampus

The upper transverse section through the human brain is somewhat farther forward than the section below. The sections show that much of the cortex lies in fissures and is not visible at the surface of the brain. A number of prominent structures are identified.

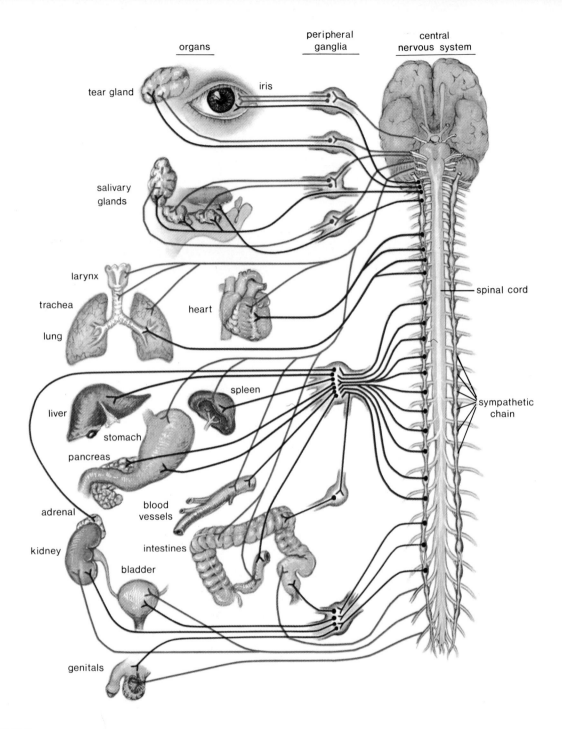

organs

peripheral
ganglia

central
nervous system

tear gland

iris

salivary
glands

larynx

trachea

heart

lung

spinal cord

spleen

liver

stomach

pancreas

blood
vessels

adrenal

intestines

kidney

sympathetic
chain

bladder

genitals

FIGURE 6

The autonomic nervous system controls the activities of many internal organs. Autonomic activities have recently been found to be modifiable by learning, as discussed at several points in the text.

Fibers of the sympathetic division of the autonomic system are shown in red; they arise from the chains of spinal ganglia on either side of the spinal cord. Above and below the sympathetic fibers, fibers of the parasympathetic division branch off from cranial or spinal nerves. The parasympathetic division is shown in green.

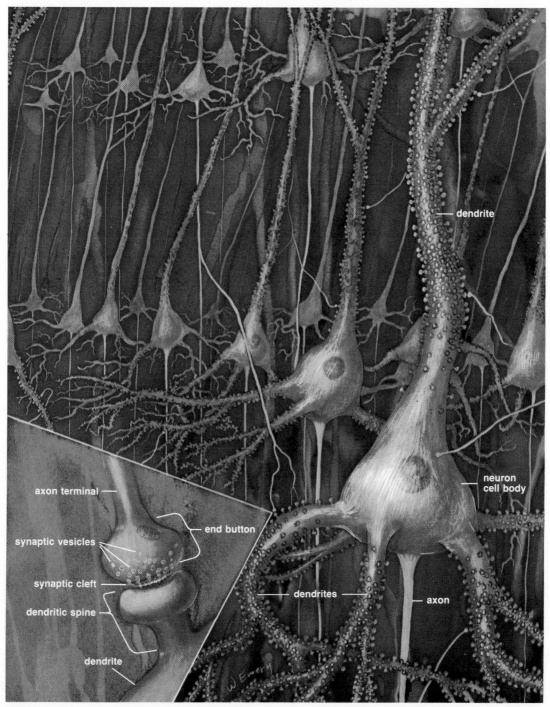

Labels on image:
dendrite
axon terminal — end button
synaptic vesicles
synaptic cleft
dendritic spine
dendrite
neuron cell body
dendrites
axon

W. Emery

FIGURE 7

Some of the complexity of structure of the cerebral cortex with its columns of neurons is suggested here. Each neuron has a single axon to send out impulses and many branching dendrites to receive inputs from other cells. Only a few synaptic junctions are shown here, although a cortical pyramidal cell (like those shown) may receive thousands of contacts. The nearby neuron is enlarged about 500 times. The synaptic junction at the lower left is enlarged about 10,000 times.

COMPARATIVE PSYCHOLOGY

(From Science Year, The World Book Science Annual. © 1970 Field Enterprises Educational Corporation.)

■ Infant ■ Juvenile ■ Adult female ■ Subadult male ■ Young adult male ■ Dominant male

FIGURE 1

When a troop of African savannah baboons travels in dangerous territory (above), juvenile baboons and females with infants stay close to the dominant males at the center of the group. The bolder juvenile males and young adult males walk in the vanguard and at the sides of the troop. When a leopard threatens (below), dominant males lead a mass attack and the rest of the troop flees. Chapter 28 contrasts this troop organization with that of other baboon species who live in one-male groups.

FIGURE 2

(Phyllis Dolinhow)

The antelope watch alertly from a distance, but do not
flee from the two female lions and cub.

FIGURE 3

(Phyllis Dolinhow, taken at Gombe Stream Reserve)

In this chimpanzee group there is close physical contact. Adults sit quietly, juveniles wrestle, and an infant
manipulates a small branch.

FIGURE 4

This is part of a troop of forest-dwelling baboons. An adult male (center) gives an open-mouth threat to an off-camera intruder. A female (upper right) grooms a juvenile while infants play in the grass.

FIGURE 5

A dead-leaf praying mantis has successfully captured a fly. The mantis uses mimicry to camouflage itself from potential prey.

FIGURE 6

A stick insect sits in relative safety while feeding on a guava leaf. This "walkingstick" uses mimicry to conceal itself from predators.

a great deal of searching by the experimenters). Some cells respond only to a stimulus that is rising in frequency; others to a falling tone. Much research is being done along this line, recording from the brains of experimental animals. Investigators hope that it will reveal how auditory patterns are analyzed and recognized. Meanwhile, unexpected evidence of specialization of cells in hearing has come from the study of auditory discrimination in human beings.

Conflict Between the Ears

If your hearing is reasonably normal, you can hold a telephone to either ear and understand your caller. But what if you wore a headset with a different conversation in each ear? You could attend to either ear, following that conversation accurately and with scarcely no interference from the other ear. Such **dichotic hearing** is discussed in Chapter 16 (p. 423) in relation to perception and personality. Recordings of receptive fields of cells in the auditory cortex show that some cells respond chiefly or exclusively to stimulation of the right ear and some to stimulation of the left ear. Most auditory cells respond more strongly to the contralateral ear (the one on the other side of the head), because the majority of the fibers from an ear cross to the other side in the brain stem. Apparently in attending to one ear or the other, you can select those circuits that respond to the desired ear and can partially inhibit the other channel.

What happens if you try to listen to two different words delivered simultaneously, one to your left ear and the other to your right? When the ears are put in conflict in this way, most people report a larger percentage of right-ear words correctly than of left-ear words. The right-ear channel goes more directly to the left hemisphere speech area; words put into the left ear stimulate the auditory cells in the right hemisphere, and impulses must then be relayed over the corpus callosum to the left hemisphere for verbal analysis. The slight delay of the more roundabout route (only a few milliseconds) is enough so that the left-ear signals find the word-analysis mechanisms already occupied by the right-ear words. This problem does not arise in normal hearing but only when different words are very accurately synchronized to arrive simultaneously at the two ears. (It also does not occur when you *select* which of two ears to listen to, since then the other channel is apparently inhibited lower down in the system.)

Recent anatomical evidence also indicates a predominance of verbal auditory function in the left hemisphere of human beings. The secondary auditory area (so-called association cortex) is larger in the left than in the right hemisphere for most people (*see* Figure 22-14). We saw earlier that the motor control of speech is also vested in the left hemisphere of most people. On the other hand, perception of music and of other nonspeech sounds depends more on the right than on the left hemisphere.

Spatial Hearing

We saw in Chapter 17 that an ability to hear the direction from which a sound comes depends on slight differences of stimulation of the two ears. Now we can describe how such stimuli are analyzed neurally. Auditory receptive fields of some cells are very sensitive to small time differences. Such cells respond best when the two ears are stimulated with a particular small time difference between them. Thus small dichotic time differences can be detected and used in the auditory system. Auditory discrimination of direction appears

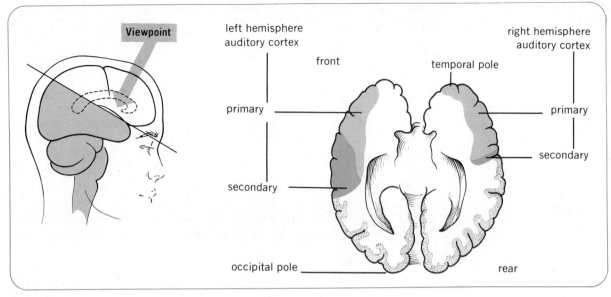

Figure 22-14
Size of Auditory Cortex in Each Hemisphere
The auditory cortex is situated on the upper surface of the temporal lobe. The primary auditory cortex is shown in light color, and the secondary auditory cortex is in dark color.

Investigators measured the size of the secondary auditory cortex in 100 adult human brains. They cut through the brains as shown in the left diagram to expose the upper surface of both temporal lobes. The diagram on the right shows this section in a typical brain. The secondary auditory area is seen to be considerably larger in the left than in the right hemisphere, and the majority of brains showed such a difference. (From Geschwind & Levitsky, 1968)

to be already "wired in" to the neural circuits at birth, in human babies. Snapping the fingers to one side or the other of the newborn baby will often cause it to move its head or eyes to the side of the stimulus—an orienting reflex that would be impossible without inborn localization abilities.

SUMMARY

Many similarities exist among different senses. Each has sensitive receptors to capture a special kind of stimulus energy. When it is stimulated, each type of receptor cell generates an electrical potential that can excite the neurons, so all stimuli are converted into the common currency of nerve impulses.

From each receptor, **neural impulses** are distributed rather widely in the nervous system, over successive relays of neurons. And impulses from a number of different receptors converge on any particular central cell. The **receptive field** of a neuron is that part of the sensory field where stimulation either excites or inhibits the cell. The divergence and convergence of sensory input permits different central cells to extract different combinations of information. Thus some visual cells extract information about shape, others about position, others about motion, and still others about hue. Some auditory cells extract information about frequency of sound, some about intensity, and some about difference in time of arrival of sound at the two ears. Both excitatory and inhibitory influences combine in most of these processes.

Different aspects of the stimulus world are analyzed by neural circuits at different levels of the sensory systems. For example, in the primate visual system, hue is analyzed at the level of the ganglion cells in the **retina;** discrimination of direction requires the midbrain visual centers (the **superior colliculi**); and perception of form and of binocular depth requires the visual cortex.

Many complex functions are built into the nervous system so that responses can be made automatically. Thus, perceiving the direction of a light or a noise does not, as was long supposed, require complex unconscious judgments, assembling and comparing the different information reaching the eyes or the ears. Rather, a particular combination of information may be extracted by certain specific cells whose input connections provide just that combination of stimuli. For example, certain cells in the visual cortex respond *only* when the stimulus is a horizontal line; and certain cells in the auditory system respond *only* when the stimulus arrives at the left ear a particular fraction of a millisecond before it reaches the right ear. Some of these connections are available at birth, but they may require early use and experience if they are to persist. Other specific connections are undoubtedly formed later as a result of individual experience.

RECOMMENDED READING

CALDER, N. *The Mind of Man.* New York: Viking Press, 1970.

A fascinating account of research on brain and behavior by a science journalist who visited laboratories around the world in 1970; many illustrations.

KIMBLE, D. P. *Psychology as a Biological Science.* Pacific Palisades, Calif.: Goodyear Publishing. 2nd ed., 1976.

An informative, readable and enthusiastic survey of biological psychology in about 200 pages.

KUFFLER, S. W. & NICHOLLS, J. G. *From Neuron to Brain: A Cellular Approach to the Function of the Nervous System.* Sunderland, Mass.: Sinauer Associates, 1976. Paperback.

A detailed account of how neurons transmit signals, how the signals are put together, and how sensory and perceptual systems work. Many excellent diagrams. Requires basic knowledge of physics and chemistry.

NOBACK, C. R. & DEMAREST, R. J. *The Nervous System: Introduction and Review.* New York: McGraw-Hill, 1972. Paperback.

A concise introduction to neuroanatomy. The second author is a medical illustrator, and the drawings are clear and numerous.

STEVENS, L. *Explorers of the Brain.* New York: Knopf, 1971.

The dramatic history of attempts to understand the brain, starting with eighteenth-century pioneers but emphasizing investigators of the present century.

THOMPSON, R. F. *Introduction to Physiological Psychology.* New York: Harper & Row, 1975.

A fairly detailed and comprehensive textbook of about 600 pages; rather difficult. Many references.

THOMPSON, R. F. *Progress in Psychobiology.* San Francisco, Calif.: W. B. Freeman & Co., 1975.

Thirty-seven articles reprinted from the *Scientific American* are grouped into ten sections with a brief introduction to each section. This collection provides a lively survey of the field.

VALENSTEIN, E. S. *Brain Control.* New York: J. Wiley & Sons, 1973.

An informative and thoughtful discussion about concerns that the behavior of individuals could be controlled by brain surgery or implanted electrodes. The author reviews much research with both human and animal subjects and allays the fears that have been fostered by science-fiction accounts and by overly enthusiastic accounts of some researchers.

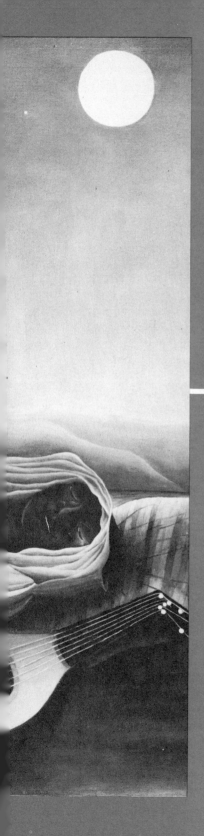

PART NINE

Comparative Psychology

By Stephen E. Glickman

We live on a planet with 3,200 species of mammals, 8,600 species of birds, 20,000 species of fish, and several hundred thousand species of insects. By comparing these species—examining their similarities and differences—much knowledge can be gained. The ways in which human beings, for example, are like all animals, the ways in which they are like some other animals, and the ways in which they are unique—this is information to be gained from a comparative psychology. Each individual species with its abilities and social interactions is of interest in its own right, and the need to know something of the interdependencies among species is reflected in the current concern about ecology. To provide knowledge on these issues is the goal of comparative psychologists.

The study of human and animal behavior was markedly affected by the publication in 1859 of Darwin's theory of evolution through natural selection. Darwin maintained that the variety and changes in animal form and function came about because, in any generation, some individuals possessed selective advantages that increased the chances of their survival in their environment. For example, stronger, swifter individuals are more likely to survive and reproduce, passing on those characteristics to their offspring. So natural selection operates, generation by generation, to bring about more adaptive bodily structure and behavior. The interaction between the demands of the environment and the responses of organisms can be seen as an ongoing feedback process. Although Darwin's original theory was concerned mostly with the evolution of anatomical structures, interest in the evolution of behavior came soon after. If human arms evolved from the same ancestral line as the limbs of mammals or the wings of birds, why should not our brain—and thus our thought processes and behavior patterns—be a product of evolution?

In its earliest stages, comparative psychology was heavily influenced by the implications and assumptions of evolutionary theory. One approach, which flourished in the United States, involved a search for humanlike characteristics in animals. Because great plasticity of behavior is most characteristic of human beings, scientists began studying the learning abilities of animals. These studies were conducted primarily in the laboratory, where careful experimental manipulations were feasible. General principles of learning, thought to apply to many species, were formulated. The popular book by B. F. Skinner, *Beyond Freedom and Dignity*, is a recent addition to the tradition that stresses generality of principles and of continuity of behavior among species.

A second line of investigation was directed at clarifying the ways in which the unique behavior patterns of different species adapted them for survival in particular ecological slots. Toward this end, a group of European and American zoologists began investigating the behavior of animals in their natural habitats; this approach is called ethology. Recently, some ethologists have begun to look for such behaviors in man. Popular books by Lorenz (such as *On Aggression*), Tiger and Fox (*The Imperial Animal*), and Brown (*The Descent of Woman*) reflect this tradition.

Thus, we had, for many years, one group—chiefly in Europe—investigating differences among various species and another—chiefly in America—concerned with continuity and similarity. The first group worked primarily in the field; the second, primarily in the laboratory. Today we are witnessing a synthesis of these two traditions, a true comparative psychology interested in both similarities and differences. Laboratory studies are valued for their potential for answering questions about the effects of a particular variable on behavior—effects that would be difficult if not impossible to isolate in field observations, where many factors vary all at once. But the comparative psychologist also knows that the artificial laboratory setting can lead to distortions and misinterpretations. Both laboratory and field studies are necessary; they can supplement each other.

The findings of comparative psychology are relevant to many topics. The *nativism-empiricism issue* has been discussed in several chapters, and the relative contributions of genetic predispositions and of learning (*heredity-environment interactions*) is an important question in this part as well. Results from comparative studies also shed light on many ecological issues. Without empirical knowledge, the best of intentions can sometimes lead to a cure worse than the disease. For example, as an alternative to the chemical control of pests, "biological controls" have been suggested: rather than try to poison a pest, we can introduce a natural predator. This natural control prevents pollution and saves other, innocent animals. Such a noble purpose was behind the importation of the mongoose to the West Indies in the nineteenth century. It was brought in to prey on the rats that were causing great crop damage. Indeed, it did the job; the mongoose drove the rats from the fields and, to some extent, into houses! The mongoose then turned its predatory talent toward the poultry of the farmers and became a significant pest in its own right. If you have never seen a mongoose in the zoo, it is partly because the West Indian story is well-known and most countries that do not have mongooses have placed strict bans on importing them.

In this part of the text, we will focus first on individual behavior. Chapter 23 deals mainly with studies of learning in various species—their similarities and their differences. Most of the studies were done in the laboratory. In Chapter 24 the social life of animals is the primary concern, and *cohesion* and *dispersion* are the central concepts. They encompass cooperation and competition, mating and aggression—we might even say love and hate—in the animal world.

Adaptation and Learning in Evolutionary Perspective

How did the primates evolve?
What is the significance of species-characteristic behavior patterns?
How has the evolutionary perspective influenced the study of learning?
What factors limit the learning of different species?

Under the influence of Darwin's theory of evolution, two broad traditions of animal research have developed. Darwin emphasized (1) the essential continuity between humans and other animals, in an evolutionary perspective, and (2) the importance of adapting to an environment, if a species is to survive. The first tradition—**comparative psychology**—is the study of the evolution of higher mental processes. Scientists began by using the hypothetical phylogenetic scale to classify the various species from simple to complex. Then evidence of emerging mental capacities was sought at different points on the

To permit identification and categorization of the millions of living and extinct forms of life, biologists have devised a taxonomic system in which any organism can be classified by a two-word sequence; the first word designates the general category or *genus* and the second, the specific group or *species*. For example, the domestic cat and dog are known as *Felis catus* and *Canis familiaris* respectively, as shown on the bottom line of the table. Each, in addition, belongs to broader *family* groups—the Felidae and the Canidae—as shown on the third line from the bottom. The family of the Canidae include the wolves, foxes, and coyotes, as well as the domestic and wild dogs.

The wolf and the dog both belong to the genus Canis and differ only in their species, the wolf being *Canis lupus* and the dog being *Canis familiaris*. Both the Canidae and the Felidae are members of the *order* Carnivora, which are marked by a certain tooth structure common to this group of meat-eating mammals. Relationships among the carnivores are shown on the next page. The order Carnivora is, in turn, one of twenty-one orders containing living members of the *class* Mammalia **(mammals).** The class Mammalia is part of the *phylum* Chordata, which in turn is included in the broad *kingdom* Animalia (animals).

This classification system is not based on superficial similarities; it is an attempt to categorize on the basis of descent from a common ancestral group. Thus, in external appearance, sharks are more similar to dolphins than dolphins are to dogs. However, the dolphins and dogs are properly placed together in the class Mammalia, while sharks are in the class of the cartilaginous fish, Chondrichthyes. (*See* the table below.) An ancestral group common to both dolphins and dogs made the crucial adaptations for maintaining a constant internal temperature (warm-bloodedness), nursing of the young by the mother, and breathing through the lungs; the ancestors of the shark and other cartilaginous fish did not make these adaptations. The similar shapes of the shark and dolphin are now seen as the result of adaptation to a common environment, the sea, which favors fishlike body shapes, even in mammals like the dolphin whose ancestry and internal structures are quite different from those of the shark.

As members of the order Carnivora, the Felidae and Canidae also are viewed as developing from a common ancestral group, the Miacidae. The Miacidae were an assemblage of small mammalian carnivores who lived tens of millions of years ago, and all the species that once comprised this family are now extinct. Although possessing certain traits in common by virtue of common ancestry, the Felidae and Canidae are classified as separate families because they show major differences both in structure (such as true cats have retractable claws) and in behavior. For the most part the cats evolved as solitary hunters, leading a generally asocial existence (although there are exceptions such as the lion). In contrast, virtually all the Canidae are highly social animals, frequently including communal hunting techniques as part of their behavioral repertoire.

Classification system showing similarities and differences

Common Names	Human Beings	Timber Wolf	Domestic Dog	Domestic Cat	Bottle-nose Dolphin	Bull Shark
Kingdom	Animalia	Animalia	Animalia	Animalia	Animalia	Animalia
Phylum	Chordata	Chordata	Chordata	Chordata	Chordata	Chordata
Class	Mammalia	Mammalia	Mammalia	Mammalia	Mammalia	Chondrichthyes
Order	Primatis	Carnivora	Carnivora	Carnivora	Cetacea	Squaliformes
Family	Hominidae	Canidae	Canidae	Felidae	Delphinidae	Carcharinidae
Genus	Homo	Canis	Canis	Felis	Tursiops	Carcharhinus
Species	Homo sapiens	Canis lupus	Canis familiaris	Felis catus	Tursiops truncatus	Carcharhinus leucas

At each level of classification, vertical lines separate animals that differ. Thus, the wolf and dog differ only in their species, while the shark differs from the other four animals in not being a mammal.

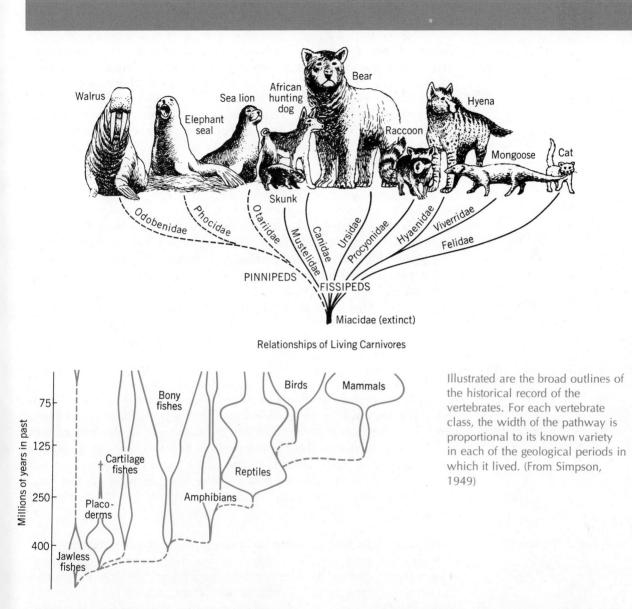

Relationships of Living Carnivores

Illustrated are the broad outlines of the historical record of the vertebrates. For each vertebrate class, the width of the pathway is proportional to its known variety in each of the geological periods in which it lived. (From Simpson, 1949)

The species designation is the basic unit of modern taxonomy. Although at one time any given species was viewed as being typified by a single ideal specimen, modern concepts emphasize the variability found within an interbreeding population of animals. Thus, the domestic dogs are categorized as a single species despite the wide variations in appearance of different breeds. As Lerner (1968) has indicated, one would probably not normally mate a Saint Bernard with a Chihuahua, but they could theoretically produce fertile offspring, and they share many common recent ancestors.

Within a species, we may find subgroups with varying degrees of distinctive genetic characters that can be used to define them as subspecies. With sufficiently long time spans, appropriate geographical isolation of subspecific populations, and with different selective pressures operating on those populations, new species may eventually emerge.

scale; in essence, scientists were testing the intelligence of the different animals. At first these "intelligence tests" consisted of little more than observations of domesticated animals, and reports of clever dogs were the empirical basis for claims that animals lower on the phylogenetic scale than human beings were also intelligent. Eventually, the search for similarities among animals gained in sophistication and concentrated on laboratory studies of learning in different species. This brand of animal psychology, which flourished in the United States, assumed a continuity of mental processes among species and attempted to discover the basic, general laws of learning. Some species might be more adept than others at particular tasks, but the general principles of learning were assumed to apply to all animals and all tasks.

The second research tradition—**ethology**—was sparked by the theory of **natural selection,** which implies that each species develops a distinctive repertoire of behaviors uniquely suited for survival. Within this tradition, scientists observe animals in their natural habitat and try to discern behavior patterns characteristic of all members of the species—patterns presumably with survival value. This kind of animal psychology, strongly influenced by European zoology, emphasizes differences among species, in contrast to the focus on continuity and similarities by American psychologists. (*See* Spotlight 23-1 for a brief review of the principles of classification and naming used in the animal world.)

How did the primates evolve?

Before we begin to examine the modes of behavioral adaptation in different animal species, it will be worthwhile to consider the evolution of the **primates,** which includes human beings. We will illustrate some of the principles of evolution and then show how both generality and specificity of adaptation arise. This section will summarize some of the main developments in the "family history" of the primates and will treat selection pressures that have led to specifically human traits and capacities (Washburn, 1968; Colbert, 1961).

BASIC ADAPTATIONS

The primate order had its origins in a group of insect-eating mammals (insectivores) that lived some 70 million years ago. The basic primate adaptations were in the structure of the front and hindlimbs, which permitted locomotion and existence in the trees. This arboreal life in turn permitted an escape from ground-dwelling predators and gave access to new food supplies of fruits and leaves. The earliest primates were members of the infraorder prosimians, and some of the existing members of this group (such as the lemurs) display the same characteristics found in their long-extinct ancestors, including a relatively small brain with a proportionately large representation of sense of smell, an elongated skull, and eyes spaced rather widely apart.

Life in the trees exerted new selective pressures and led to changes from the prosimian characteristics. Development of vision rather than smell was favored, particularly stereoscopic vision, which is crucial for good depth perception (see Chapter 17, p. 472). Stereoscopic vision requires an overlap of the two visual fields; natural selection therefore operated to bring the eyes closer together at the front of the head. There was also selection for specialization of the limbs for better arboreal locomotion and grasping. Over a span of many millions of years, these evolutionary pressures produced the forms that we classify as monkeys (*see* Figure 23-1). Prosimian ancestral groups independently gave rise to the ''Old World'' monkeys of Asia and Africa and the ''New World'' monkeys of the Americas. The development of monkeylike characters from geographically disparate prosimian ancestors is a striking example of ''parallel'' evolution: in two different places, common selective pressures, operating on a common ancestral stock, ultimately produced similar characteristics in species evolving independently. Of course, one would not

Figure 23-1
Evolution of the Primates
This reconstruction of the primate ''family tree'' contains the major taxonomic groups referred to in the text.

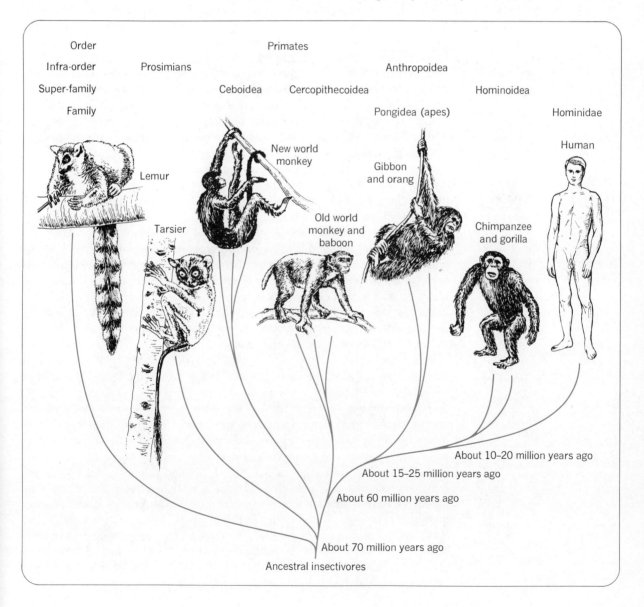

Order — Primates
Infra-order — Prosimians — Anthropoidea
Super-family — Ceboidea — Cercopithecoidea — Hominoidea
Family — Pongidea (apes) — Hominidae

Lemur
Tarsier
New world monkey
Old world monkey and baboon
Gibbon and orang
Chimpanzee and gorilla
Human

About 10–20 million years ago
About 15–25 million years ago
About 60 million years ago
About 70 million years ago
Ancestral insectivores

expect the results of such parallel evolution to be identical. The New and Old World monkeys are distinguished by several anatomical differences—for example, the presence of prehensile tails in New World monkeys.

It is one of the ironies of the evolutionary process that the development of these newer forms tended to eliminate the groups that gave rise to them. There are no longer any prosimians in the Americas (outside of zoological parks), and Old World prosimians, such as the lemurs of Madagascar, are restricted to islands or other isolated habitats where geography has protected them from direct competition with the more highly evolved monkeys.

BRANCHING OF THE PRIMATE FAMILY TREE

The branch of the evolutionary tree giving rise to human beings and their relatives, the apes, split from the main stem of the Old World monkeys some 60 million years ago. The time scale now grows more controversial, but it appears that 5 to 20 million years after the development of our apelike ancestors, several other branchings occurred. The first of these gave rise to the line that resulted in the gibbon and the orangutan. At a somewhat later date, a critical divergence produced two separate groups; one resulting in the chimpanzee and gorilla, the other in the emergence of man. Recent chemical analyses of blood proteins suggest a very close linkage between man, chimpanzee, and gorilla (Sarich & Wilson, 1967), and some researchers now place the point of this divergence as recently as 10 million years ago.

The initial primate adaptation involved an ascent into the trees; later adaptations were required to permit the more recent descent to the ground. Among the contemporary primates there is great variation in the extent to which daily life is distributed among arboreal and terrestrial modes. Some monkeys (like the langurs) spend virtually all of their days in the trees, while others (the baboons) forage for food entirely on the ground but ascend to tree limbs or cliffs for the night. Among the apes, the orangutan and gibbon are almost entirely arboreal. The chimpanzee and gorilla are basically terrestrial and have specially adapted knuckles for locomotion on the ground. The ground-dwelling patterns of life probably also entailed selection for characteristics that enabled defense against potential predators, including greater size and strength, weaponry (teeth), and social organization.

Both human beings (*Homo sapiens*) and our extinct relatives (such as *Australopithecus africanus*) are classified in the taxonomic family Hominidae. (*Australopithecus* comes from *Australo* = "southern," and *pithecus* = "ape.") The most striking characteristics of the early hominids were the structural changes that permitted upright posture and bipedal locomotion; these developments freed the hands for carrying and manipulating objects. About 2 million years ago, members of the genus *Australopithecus* lived in the African savannah. The fossil record suggests that they fashioned primitive stone tools and hunted small game. However, their brains were relatively small and their hands not so well adapted for delicate manipulation as those of modern human beings. The unique characteristics of the genus *Homo*, including the dextrous hand, the large brain, and, finally, truly human language, appear to be very recent events on the scale of evolutionary time. Fossil records do not allow precise estimates of the beginnings of language, but the dextrous hand and large brain have changed dramatically in the last million years. As Washburn

Early primate evolution favored good grasp and depth perception.

(1972) has emphasized, these changes must have occurred as the result of a complex feedback process, involving life as a social hunter. For example, pressure must have favored the survival of those individuals who could produce better tools for hunting. These individuals had brains capable of producing new tools and the hands to fashion them. Then, as tool-making became increasingly more complex, there would be selection for individuals who could best communicate tool-making to the next generation; this meant selection for those individuals with the most effective language.

Perhaps the most important conclusions to be observed in this short discourse on evolution are those dealing with similarities and differences: Human beings have certain behavioral characteristics that they share with all mammals (such as a postnatal period involving close mother-infant relations), others that mark them distinctively as primates (a highly visual and socially oriented life), and still others that are uniquely human (including complex grammatical language).

What is the significance of species-characteristic behavior patterns?

In tracing aspects of primate evolution, we briefly mentioned both structural characteristics and their behavioral correlates. As we pointed out previously, one of the fundamental assumptions of any evolutionary reconstruction is that characteristics found in all the members of the species must have been subjected to powerful selective pressures that shaped the uniformity. In his book on *The Expression of the Emotions in Man and Animals* Darwin showed that particular emotions are linked to particular facial and postural expressions for each species. He argued that these behavioral changes had survival value for the individual animal, preparing it for flight or fight or communicating its emotional state to other animals.

The study of behaviors that promote the survival of the species in its natural habitat is the province of modern **ethology.** Although the discipline dates back to Darwin, its emergence as a coherent area of research with established terminology, attitudes, and theory must be credited to the German zoologist Konrad Lorenz (1950). At the heart of the theory is a basic division of behavior into two broad categories: a variable, relatively unpredictable *appetitive* phase and a stereotyped, highly predictable *consummatory* phase. For example, in a hungry animal the search for food is appetitive behavior, and eating is the consummatory behavior. Ethologists claim that the consummatory phase is marked by the appearance of a set of invariant responses known as **fixed action patterns** (FAP's). Examples include feeding patterns, mating patterns, retrieval of the young, and grooming patterns, as illustrated in Figure 23-2. According to the ethologists, the FAP is the basic behavioral unit with functional adaptive significance. An FAP, like a body structure, exists because it confers on the animal a selective advantage in survival and reproduction. Thus, a particular FAP will generally be found in all members of the species, although it might vary between sexes; it is assumed to be genetically determined, and it will generally appear when the stimulus configuration is present in

Figure 23-2
Fixed Action Patterns in Mice
These drawings depict species-characteristic behavior patterns. (A) Rearing: an investigatory posture; (B) eating; (C) and (D), two forms of grooming; (E) social investigation; (F) wrestling; (G) copulation; and (H) "submissive" upright posture. (Adapted from Van Abeelen, 1963)

the environment. Recently, high-speed film analyses have revealed considerable variation in the timing and form of these species-characteristic sequences both between two animals and between the same animal at different times. For this reason, Barlow (1965) has suggested that the term *modal action pattern* (*MAP*) is preferable to FAP; MAP implies that a typical pattern is being described, but allows for individual variation in performance.

The environmental stimulus releasing a fixed action pattern was called a **sign stimulus** or a **releaser.** In the classic example cited by Lorenz, a graylag goose is sitting on its nest with a clutch of eggs. An egg is removed and placed several inches away. The goose then extends its neck and rolls the egg back into the nest with the underside of the bill. The egg in this case constitutes the sign stimulus, and the retrieval response (extension and retraction of the neck) is the FAP. If one removes the egg while the retrieval response is under way, the goose will still continue the FAP all the way back to its nest, as if it still had an egg to push. For reasons not entirely clear, the definition of an FAP came to include this triggered quality—the response pattern released by a sign stimulus and, once begun, inexorable. If one looks closely at animal behavior, it is surely difficult to defend the notion that each FAP, when triggered, goes automatically and uniformly to completion, and it is not intuitively obvious why selective advantage would be conferred on animals unresponsive to environmental shifts such as the disappearance of the sign stimulus.

Behind the FAP and the sign stimulus—behind the theory of consummatory responses—were Lorenz's views of appetitive or motivational states. Lorenz had to account for the fact that a given sign stimulus would not always evoke an FAP of equal intensity; the response was sometimes vigorous, sometimes weak, and sometimes it did not occur at all. These variations were explained by hypothesizing varying internal states—appetites and motives. In human terms, a hamburger might elicit vigorous eating in a starving person, indifferent eating in a reasonably well-fed citizen, and no eating at all in someone who has just finished a large plate of spaghetti.

Lorenz saw several behaviors—feeding, sex, aggression—as biologically necessary for the survival of the animal or its species. As a motivational explanation of such behaviors, he adopted a hydraulic model, illustrated in Figure 23-3. Lorenz saw the effects of motivation as analogous to the effects of fluids under pressure. As appetite grows, like the water level rising in a vat, pressure to respond builds up; a sign stimulus is considered to open a valve; this *releases* the pressure and triggers an FAP. Repeated FAP's result in lowered "fluid" pressure, thus accounting for decreasing intensity of response in such cases.

The hydraulic model can also account for **vacuum activities.** These FAP's are emitted in the *absence* of obvious triggering stimuli, as when a kitten might stalk or attack nonexistent objects in the environment. To explain such anomalous behaviors, it is assumed that the energy reservoirs have become so full that the valve mechanism can no longer function; the energy bursts through the checking mechanism and triggers the patterns despite the absence of an appropriate sign stimulus.

If you operate on the assumptions inherent in a hydraulic theory of motivation, you are likely to see certain behaviors as inevitable. If aggression, for

Figure 23-3
Hydraulic Model of Motivation
In this system, the valve mechanism (IRM) is operated by a sign stimulus. The vigor of the resulting fixed action pattern is dependent upon the fluid level in the vat—that is, on the accumulation of action-specific energy.

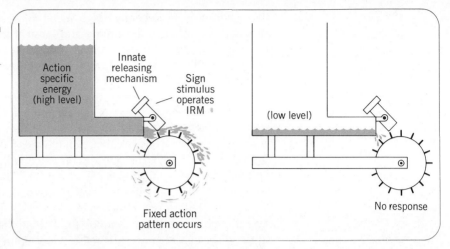

example, is not released by a sign stimulus, the pressure to aggress builds and eventually the behaviors will occur spontaneously (vacuum activity). However, these possibilities are not the only ones; motive energies can also be *redirected* or *displaced.* A rooster is confronted by another rooster; instead of pecking his rival, he pecks at the ground. This behavior is labeled **redirection**—the aggressive energy comes out, but the motor act has been channeled toward a new object. Two cats face each other in a hostile encounter; one suddenly begins to groom himself. This is labeled **displacement**—two drive systems, aggression and fear, are in conflict; they cancel each other out, and an irrelevant activity occurs. The concepts of redirection and displacement in ethology and many concepts in Freudian personality theory are strikingly similar (p. 164). Freud, who also used a hydraulic model of drives, saw the pressure of psychic energy finding an outlet, if not in direct behavior, in redirections or compromises as exhibited in defense mechanisms or neurotic symptoms.

The motivational theory of Lorenz (and of Freud, for that matter) has often been criticized. For example, if you allow for direct and indirect manifestations of a drive and also for compromises and displacements, there is very little possibility of testing the theory; you can maintain your belief in an underlying sex or aggression drive no matter what behaviors are exhibited. Many psychologists prefer to concentrate their energies on clarifying the actual neural and hormonal mechanisms rather than to rely on an imprecise hypothetical theory based on an analogy with plumbing systems. A second criticism—with important societal implications—is that these largely unverifiable theories assume that "outlets" for such drives as aggression must be found because these behaviors are inevitable. Accepting hostile and destructive behavior as inevitable in human beings leads one to propose quite different social policies from those that would be suggested by a theorist who views aggressive behaviors as learned or capable of significant modification through experience.

Nevertheless, classical ethology has been extremely valuable in identifying the relatively stereotyped action patterns in various species and the stimuli that are functionally related to these behaviors. The concepts of fixed action patterns and sign stimuli have done much to organize the observations of animal psychologists and to encourage the accumulation of systematic data in a specialty once characterized by anecdotal evidence of little scientific value.

How has the evolutionary perspective influenced the study of learning?

While ethology was developing in Europe as a science that stressed the unique inherited behavioral adaptations of each species, psychologists in America were pressing forward with studies of intellectual function in animals. After all, a second route to survival is through being sufficiently "flexible" to adapt to different situations—that is through learning. Research in American laboratories until the early 1960s focused on two issues: (1) the development of tests of learning capacity that would arrange species on some reasonable scale of intelligence; and (2) the search for general principles of learning that would apply to all species. The search for common principles, carried out in the laboratory using a limited range of species (such as rats and pigeons), has resulted in the specifications of classical and operant conditioning (see Chapter 14). We will now consider the historical roots of comparative studies of learning, including a survey of attempts to scale animal intelligence. Following a brief review of the general-principles view of the learning process, we will examine recent comparative and evolutionary studies that challenge the generality of some of these principles.

THORNDIKE'S PUZZLE BOXES

The American psychologist Edward Thorndike invented an experimental tool with which to investigate animal intelligence—a set of puzzle boxes (Figure 23-4). He placed an animal in a box with food visible but out of reach outside the box. To obtain the food, the animal had to emit an appropriate response such as pulling a string to release it from the box. Thorndike recorded escape time on successive trials and thus generated the first learning curves ever obtained for animals. In his doctoral dissertation, published in 1898, he included performance data for chicks, cats, and dogs; the general form of the learning curves was the same in each species tested.

Figure 23-4
Thorndike Puzzle Box
Pulling the loop releases the door, allowing the animal inside to emerge and obtain food. Other puzzle boxes require different solutions.

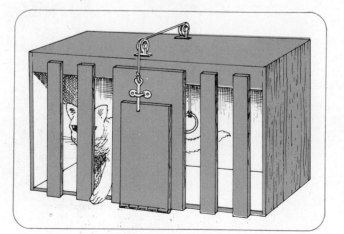

Thorndike's pioneering research seemed to support the notion of general principles of learning. On the basis of his data, Thorndike suggested that learning is a slow process of trial and error; responses that lead to rewards are gradually strengthened, according to what Thorndike called the **law of effect.** These general principles applied to all the species he studied, which was taken to mean that these species had similar "mental processes" and, more broadly, that "mental evolution" had proceeded in the same orderly manner as physical evolution.

INSIGHTFUL LEARNING

Köhler's Insightful Chimps

Thorndike's theories challenged students of mental evolution: Can all animal learning be explained by common trial-and-error principles? Wolfgang Köhler responded to the challenge. He asserted that complex animals like chimpanzees can reorganize their perceptual worlds and produce insightful solutions (*see* p. 324). For example, when food was placed outside their cage so they could not reach it by hand or by using a small stick, they quickly solved the problem. The chimpanzees used the small stick to pull in a long stick that they then used to reach the food. The ability to learn insightfully was viewed as a unique skill that *emerged* as a result of increased size and complexity of the brain—that is, it suddenly appeared among animals at a certain point on the phylogenetic scale.

Figure 23-5
Problem Solving by a Chimp
The chimp's method of getting the banana was not what Köhler expected. (Drawn from a photo in Köhler, 1925)

By describing a type of learning found only in some species, Köhler's work threatened the general-principles view of the learning process. In addition, his research suggested that attempts to scale animal intelligence were likely to meet with limited success. In some ways, this chimp work foreshadowed (not always intentionally) current research in which investigators are more careful to choose tasks and problems corresponding to those the animal faces in its natural habitat. An interesting illustration is the problem Köhler set for his chimps to get a banana. He hung a bunch of the tasty fruit high out of reach, but he left in the cage a long stick with which, Köhler expected, the chimp would knock down a reward or two. This is undoubtedly what a human being would have done. Chimps, being chimps, placed the stick vertically and climbed it quickly before it could fall. At the top they simply reached out and picked off a banana (see Figure 23-5).

THE DELAYED-RESPONSE
TEST

W. S. Hunter, in 1913, published a report comparing "ideational processes" in various species. The problem he set for his animals called for a **delayed response.** The animals were kept from responding directly to a stimulus and had to wait. This ingenious procedure was designed to see how various animals "bridged the gap" between stimulus and response, presumably by means of memory and cognition—that is, ideational processes.

Let us consider a concrete case. In one situation (see Figure 23-6), the animal faces three panels and with practice learns that the illuminated side contains food and the others do not. (Which side is lighted on a particular trial is, of course, determined randomly so that the animal cannot solve the problem by learning a spatial sequence.) When the animal has *demonstrably* learned that light means food, it is placed in a holding compartment where it can see the light but is not allowed to react promptly to it. The light in one of the three sides is turned on, then off. After a variable time interval—seconds, minutes, or

**Figure 23-6
A Delayed-Response
Apparatus**

The animal is retained in a box while a light is briefly turned on and then off. The door is then raised and the subject is allowed to attempt entry to one of the compartments. If it chooses the compartment just illuminated, it is rewarded; if not it is returned to the start compartment for another trial.

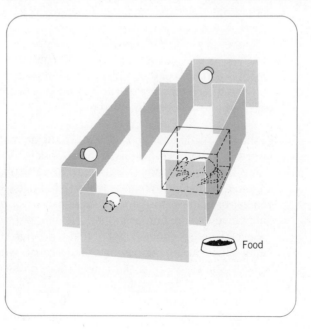

Food

hours—the subject is released from the compartment. Does it go to the correct side after this delay?

Various species were tested in similar situations, and raccoons, monkeys, and human children did well; they could tolerate fairly long delays. Other species, such as the rat, failed at delays of more than a few seconds unless they were allowed to maintain a postural set; rats (and some other species) could bridge longer delays by seeing the light, pointing their body in that direction, then running straight ahead (following their noses) when released. Raccoons, on the other hand, could move around or could be moved by the experimenter and still respond correctly after lengthy delays. Dogs showed still a different pattern of behavior; they often lost interest in the task altogether and tried to gain the reward by whining and otherwise eliciting sympathy from the experimenter!

In the succeeding twenty years or so, Hunter's delayed-response test proved an inspiration for many researchers interested in making a scale of animal mental abilities. By 1935, however, the attempt to make comparative ratings of intelligence based on this test was in serious difficulty. The results obtained, in terms of maximal possible delay, were found to vary more as a function of the particular conditions of testing than of the phylogenetic status of the species. In a comprehensive review of the available studies, Maier and Schneirla (1935) noted that, with appropriate test procedures, rats and cats seemed capable of delays similar to those obtained by Köhler with chimpanzees.

Attacks came from other sides, too, most notably from European investigators. Tinbergen (1951) pointed out that if delayed response was used as the measure of ideational or intellectual ability, the digger wasp would be considered among the most intelligent of animals. It can "remember" exactly how much food to bring to each of many larva nests (of varying population) even if delayed by as much as twenty-four hours; this delay is longer than most demonstrated by mammals in situations like Hunter's. This criticism, while telling, is not completely fair. The digger wasp can delay only in a very specific task, one on which the survival of its species depends. Animals who can delay in a *variety* of situations may be demonstrating a capacity for flexibility—which is certainly part of intellectual ability—that far exceeds that of the wasp. Still, the search for a scale of animal intelligence by means of delayed-response tests came to a not undeserved end.

ALTERNATIVE
EXPLANATIONS OF
INSIGHTFUL LEARNING

At the same time their approach to scaling animal intelligence was being questioned by other investigators, general-principles theorists were simultaneously doing some questioning themselves. In particular, Köhler's studies of insight-learning in higher animals, mentioned above, were a potential threat to the general-principles position; so American psychologists set out to provide an alternative explanation in proper scientific fashion—empirically.

Several studies showed that primates deprived of the opportunity of manipulating sticks during infancy and adolescence were unable to demonstrate insightful solutions to stick-manipulation problems as adults (Birch, 1945; Schiller, 1957). The implication was that apparent insight was a function of prior trial-and-error learning. Thorndike, too, had made this point, criticizing anecdotal reports of brilliant reasoning in animals by saying that those ob-

Figure 23-7
Learning-Set Formation in Species of Mammals
This family of curves depicts the improvement in performance demonstrated by various species when subjects were given hundreds of problems with a common principle underlying their solution. The curves for human beings, gorillas, and chimpanzees are based on individual subjects; the remaining curves represent "grouped" data. (From Hodos, 1970)

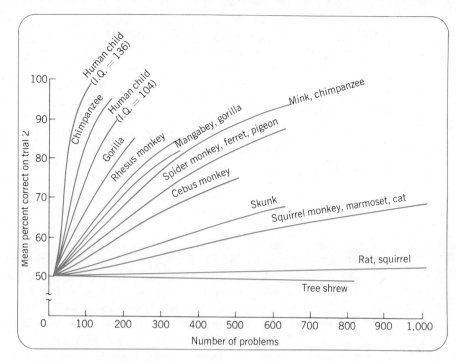

servers were seeing only the final product of a long and arduous chain of trial-and-error bumbling.

The study of **learning sets** (Harlow, 1949) provided another trial-and-error explanation of insight, and it was also another attempt to find a general-purpose intelligence test for animals. Essentially, learning sets are formed when an animal—a monkey, for example—is given as many as 300 problems, one after the other, all based on the same principle. For example, in a series of object-discrimination problems, the monkey is rewarded on the first problem if it chooses the one of a pair of objects (circle vs. triangle) that the experimenter has arbitrarily designated as correct. After a number of trials the monkey masters that problem, and then it is given another pair of objects and again has to learn which is correct. After hundreds of successive problems of this type, each with a different pair of objects, the monkey can solve a new problem very quickly. If its choice on the first trial is rewarded, it stays with that choice and makes no errors at all; if not rewarded, it switches to the other object and thereafter never errs. If one were to observe these monkeys after 300 prior problems, one might see their brilliance as insight; but *we* know that would be a mistake.

The degree to which different species improve in their performance from the first to the tenth, to the fiftieth, to the hundredth problem, and so on, has been used to scale the "intelligence" of species (Hodos, 1970). This learning-set measure (see Figure 23-7) has many of the difficulties of the other measures that have been tried, but it at least involves an ability—discrimination—that is common and useful in a wide variety of species.

The assumption that one can simply scale animal intelligence poses several difficulties. If one gives the same task to a number of species without regard to their sensory-motor capabilities or to their motivational characteristics, one might indeed generate a scale; but is it an intelligence scale? Certainly we would find that different species would perform differently on any given task; but is better performance an indication of higher intelligence? We have noted that on a delayed-response test, the digger wasp scores as one of the most intelligent of creatures. The ability of rats to learn mazes (which are similar to their natural burrows) is probably equal to that of people. In a Ping-Pong test, blindness and ignorance would become equivalent. In testing human intelligence we have devised different tests for people who cannot read or write, for the blind and deaf, and for numerous other categories of people who vary in one capacity or another; we worry a lot about "culture-fair" tests (p. 304). But when comparing our intellectual abilities with those of subhuman animals, we have been rather inconsiderate of simple differences in capacity. Very often animals with sensory-motor and motivational systems quite different from ours are required to perform tasks best suited to human or primate abilities.

It is worth mentioning, too, that many psychologists act as if the sequence from rat to cat to monkey to human beings is an evolutionary sequence. This assumption is patently false (Hodos & Campbell, 1969). In no way are people descended from the monkeys of today; we may have common ancestors who lived millions of years ago, just as branches of a tree have a common trunk. But one branch—though it may be considered higher in some sense—does not grow from another. Thus we can recognize that even if it were possible to construct a scale of animal performance, that scale would not reflect an evolutionary sequence.

COMPARING WIDELY DIFFERENT SPECIES

The research of M. E. Bitterman and his associates (1960, 1965, 1975) probably provides the most interesting bridge between traditional attempts to scale animal intelligence and modern approaches to the study of animal learning that seriously question the principle of species- and task-generality. Bitterman's research strategy had several unique facets. First, in the belief that quantitative differences in the learning of different species would be difficult to interpret, he argued that the proper search is for the operation (or nonoperation) of laws that are well established in conventional laboratory species. Second, Bitterman believed that the chances of finding such differences in fundamental "laws" would be greater if the psychologist compared animals taken from widely divergent phyletic groups (such as rats, fish, and earthworms), rather than following the common practice of comparing closer species—a rat with a hamster or a rat with a cat, for example. Finally, Bitterman came to grips with one of the most persistent problems of direct species comparison: the difficulty in equating motivational states and sensory-motor capabilities across species. For example, a crab can go for months without food, but a rat cannot survive more than a few days. Therefore 24 hours without food results in quite different motivational states in a crab and in a rat. Bitterman recognized this difficulty and proposed to handle it by *systematic variation* rather than by fruitless attempts at *equation*.

For example, suppose one presents various species with the following **habit-reversal** problem. Two stimuli are presented: a response to one brings a reward; the other brings nothing. After solving this simple problem in a number of trials, the animal gets a new task, one that requires reversal of the habit. The same two stimuli are presented, but the one that was previously neutral now brings the reward and the one that was previously rewarded is now neutral. When the animal solves this second problem, the value of the two stimuli is again reversed. This procedure is continued through a series of reversals. Does the animal improve over problems? Does it learn successive reversals faster and faster? Rats do; fish don't. Now, maybe fish could improve if properly motivated. To test this possibility, you might present a set of problems to several groups of fish, systematically varying the level of motivation in each group. If within this wide range of fish motivational states, no group shows progressive improvement, the possibility that motivational differences accounted for the original observation is surely decreased. The burden of proof now lies on the critic who still wishes to explain the difference between rat and fish performance as "merely motivational."

LEARNING TASKS

Bitterman and others working with this approach have tested a number of animals in simple tasks like habit reversal and probability matching. In the probability-matching test, the choice between two stimuli is rewarded on the basis of a certain probability less than 1.00; for example, the right-side stimulus is rewarded on 70 percent of the trials and the left-side on 30 percent. In such situations, animals either make responses that correspond to these probabilities (the fish responds to the right-side stimulus about 70 percent of the time) or they attempt to maximize their rewards by some response pattern such as *always* responding to the stimulus that is more frequently associated with reward (the rat does this).

Neither the approach nor the data, however, have been free of controversy. Ethologists have criticized Bitterman for not knowing his animals, for asking them to learn behaviors that are not particularly useful in their natural habitat. He is also criticized for saying "fish" when he means one particular fish (the African mouthbreeder) and "rat" when he uses only one variety (the common docile Norwegian rat). Bitterman himself wholeheartedly accepts this second criticism as valid, and he calls for work on other classes and phyla. Other researchers (such as Mackintosh, 1969) have claimed Bitterman's data are misleading, that with appropriate manipulation of the stimulus situation, even fish can show improvement in habit reversals. Still, Bitterman can justly assert that he has started research on a rather wide range of species and that he has changed the issue of phylogenetic variation in general learning principles from a matter of speculative theorizing into a topic in empirical research. And that, certainly, is as it should be.

ASSUMING SIMILARITIES AMONG SPECIES

During the three decades from 1930 to 1960, theories of learning were heavily influenced by two Americans, Clark Hull and B. F. Skinner, who had, in turn, been influenced by Thorndike and his successors. Their theories assumed that various species learned by the same general principles. Skinner was fond of presenting three learning or response curves—one from a rat, one from a pigeon, and one from a monkey, for example—without telling his audience which was which. The three curves looked nearly identical, as you can see in

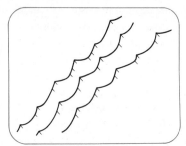

Figure 23-8
Learning Curves of Three Species

The curves show responses of a pigeon, rat, and monkey when taught to press a lever to gain a food reward. The "blips" represent reinforcements. (From Skinner, 1956)

Figure 23-8. After asking which curve belonged to which species, Skinner answered his rhetorical question: "It doesn't matter. Of course, these three species have behavioral repertoires that are as different as their anatomies. But once you have allowed for differences in the ways in which [these species] . . . make contact with the environment, and in the ways in which they act upon the environment, what remains of their behavior shows astonishingly similar properties. Mice, cats, dogs, and human children could have added other curves to this figure" (Skinner, 1956, p. 230).

These theorists assumed that the basic principles of learning (classical conditioning, operant conditioning, and so forth; see Chapter 14) *do not vary among species*. Animals may learn at different rates, but they all learn the same way. Thus, if you are interested in basic principles, you need not study all species. You can build a psychology on empirical data gathered from one species, and you can generalize the conclusions from research on the rat or the pigeon to all other species capable of learning, including human beings.

Hull wrote a book in 1943 titled *Principles of Behavior*. He described it—literally—as a general introduction to the theory of *all* social science, despite the fact that the principles were derived almost exclusively from data on rats. This book became one of the most frequently cited books in the history of psychology. In 1971, B. F. Skinner wrote a popular nonacademic book titled *Beyond Freedom and Dignity*. He extended his principles of learning, based mostly on rat and pigeon experiments, to a full-scale discussion of the notions of human freedom and responsibility. Such wide-ranging extrapolations are the natural by-products of the assumption that all species are pretty much alike. In the following discussion on factors limiting the learning of different species, we will find this assumption difficult to hold.

What factors limit the learning of different species?

Until recently, statements about animal learning often gave the impression that "stimulus," "response," and "reinforcement" are such general terms that any animal can be taught to make any response to any stimulus using any reinforcer an investigator desires. Today, however, psychologists in every country are becoming aware of constraints on learning imposed by an animal's nervous system; these constraints can often be viewed in terms of the animal's life in its natural habitat. These limitations to learning in any species involve several factors—the age at which certain kinds of learning can occur (critical periods), the types of stimulus-reinforcer linkages that can be learned readily, and the influence of the reinforcer on the responses that can be learned. We will discuss and give examples of each of these factors that make the learning of one species different from that of another.

Before reviewing some critical limitations on the general-principles view of learning, it is worth noting that certain kinds of species differences were always recognized by the general-principles theorist. Stimuli had to be within the sensory capacity of the organism, and responses within the motor repertoire of the organism. Thus, Thorndike, Hull, or Skinner would not have been distressed by the failure to train dogs to discriminate colors because dogs cannot detect color; nor would they have worried about the ineffectiveness of sweet substances as a reward for cats because cats lack receptors for sweetness on their tongues.

CRITICAL PERIODS
OF LEARNING

One important constraint has to do with the age at which certain types of learning can occur. Some kinds are limited to early life, as the following examples show. In 1873 an Englishman named Spalding published reports of learning in chickens and ducks. He noted some unexpected findings. First, newborn chicks separated from their mother for 8 to 10 days after birth would not later respond to the retrieval calls of the hen. Second, newborn ducklings kept from water for several days would refuse to enter the pond when brought to it. Spalding speculated that there was an "established course" of learning in these birds and that artificial rearrangement of this course might result in behavioral abnormalities persisting for life. In other words, he was suggesting that for some behaviors there are **critical periods** in life during which the responses are apparently easily learned, but if the behavior is *not* learned *then*, it may never be learned. (*See also* p. 231.)

Imprinting

This intriguing hypothesis received no research attention in animal psychology for over fifty years, as psychologists turned to puzzle boxes and mazes in their efforts to substantiate general principles of learning. In 1935 Konrad Lorenz

Konrad Lorenz leads the goslings that have been "imprinted" on the ethologist.

performed a simple experiment. He divided the eggs laid by a graylag goose into two groups, one group hatched by the mother and the other by him (in an incubator). The first thing the goslings in one group saw after hatching was their mother; they became very attached to her, following her around, running to her when frightened, and generally behaving like loyal and normal offspring. The first thing goslings in the incubated group saw upon hatching was Konrad Lorenz. They followed *him,* and when frightened, they ran to Lorenz for comfort, even if their real mother was also present (*see* photo). Lorenz called this phenomenon **imprinting.** He postulated that it was a result of learning during a critical period immediately after birth. At this time the bird learned which stimuli it "should" make its social responses to. These early effects are sometimes long-lasting, as Lorenz discovered when a female turtle dove that had imprinted on him came to him in mating season and fully expected him to do his duty as a male of her species!

Imprinting does not mean the same thing for all species nor is it governed by the same mechanisms in all animals. Often the obvious requirements of nature can be used to predict whether or not, or how, a bird will imprint. Some birds like the cuckoo lay their eggs in the nests of birds of other species (from which we get the word "cuckold"). If the newborn cuckoo was hatched in the nest of birds of another species and imprinted on the first adult it saw, it would not mate with one of its own species as an adult. Therefore it is not surprising to find that cuckoos do not demonstrate this type of imprinting.

Imprinting is found not only in birds. It has been observed in insects, fish, and mammals. A number of theories of human behavior (for example, Freud's

Figure 23-9
Imprinting in a Duckling
The duckling is imprinted by placing it in the runway behind a model of a male duck that is wired for sound. Near the duckling is a trap door through which it is removed. The duckling is tested for imprinting by placing it between the male model and the female model, which emits a different sound. If it follows the male, response is scored as positive. (From "Imprinting in Animals," by Eckhard H. Hess. Copyright © 1958 by Scientific American, Inc. All rights reserved.)

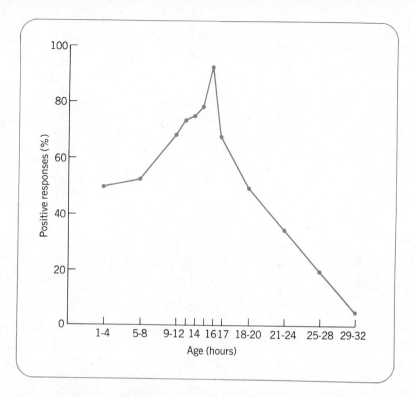

Figure 23-10
Critical Age for Imprinting in Mallard Ducklings
It can be seen that the probability of obtaining successful imprinting first increases following hatching and then declines. (Adapted from "Imprinting in Animals," by Eckhard H. Hess. Copyright © 1958 by Scientific American, Inc. All rights reserved.)

and Erikson's; see Chapter 7) also postulate critical periods for learning certain social behavior. In particular, Freud's theory of psychosexual stages in development postulates periods of changing sensitivity in various regions of the body—oral, anal, and phallic. As each of these body regions becomes relatively sensitive in turn, learning is more likely to occur in relation to this region. This line of reasoning is strikingly similar to that used in animal research.

In the laboratory, psychologists have investigated the exact timing of imprinting—when the critical period begins, when (and why) it ends, and when the strongest imprinting occurs. A typical study used mallard ducklings as subjects; after hatching, the ducklings were exposed to a model of a male mallard much like the duck decoys used by hunters, and later they were tested for imprinting by exposure to both male and female models. Response (usually "following") to the male model was considered imprinting (Hess, 1958). (See Figure 23-9.)

In some of the earliest studies (Hess, 1958), various groups of ducklings were first exposed to the male model at different times after birth. As you can see in Figure 23-10, some imprinting occurs within the first four hours after hatching, and imprinting normally terminates within 29–32 hours after hatching. Maximal imprinting was found between 13 and 16 hours.

Other research has focused on factors related to the end of the critical period. Why, for example, will ducklings, whose first exposure to a male model occurs after age 32 hours, show no evidence of imprinting? Many observers noted that simultaneously with the end of imprinting periods, the

Figure 23-11
Effect of Age and Prior Visual Experience on Imprinting
Domesticated mallard ducklings reared under normal conditions of illumination show an increase in avoidance (A) and a decrease in following (B) beginning 24 hours after hatching. Similar ducklings, reared with translucent hoods that restrict patterned visual stimulation, continue to follow vigorously for 48 hours after hatching. The appearance of avoidance responses is still further delayed. (Moltz & Stettner, 1961)

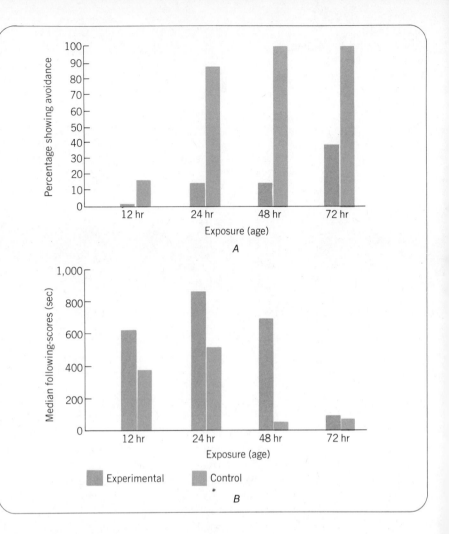

infants in many species also become fearful of new stimuli. Perhaps the development of the fear response, which is incompatible with approach and attachment behavior, is the primary factor in the decrease in imprinting; a duckling obviously cannot follow an object if he is fleeing from it in terror.

To test whether fear could be reduced and the critical period modified, Moltz and Stettner (1961) deprived newborn ducklings of patterned visual stimulation by attaching translucent hoods to their heads; the ducklings could see light but no patterns. This procedure markedly reduces emotionality and fear, especially in reaction to new stimuli (see Figure 23-11A). Deprived ducklings showed significantly more imprinting than the normally raised control subjects if their first exposure was delayed until 24 or 48 hours after hatching (see Figure 23-11B). These ages are beyond the normal critical period. The fact that imprinting could take place beyond the normal critical period when fear did not occur supports the hypothesis that fear is a conflicting drive. However, other results suggest that additional factors are also implicated in the termination of the critical period; perhaps some sort of neural and hormonal maturation is involved.

The beginning of critical periods has also been studied. Some research (Gottlieb, 1971) has shown that certain social responses in birds develop even before birth. The vocal response of unborn offspring to the calls of the mother, for example, can be detected from inside the egg, a few days before hatching. If eggs are artificially incubated away from the mother (and her vocalizations), the ducklings born from these eggs do not respond as quickly or as effectively to maternal calls. The vocal response to the mother's calls does not seem to be learned in the same sense that following behavior is. Even if they are innate stimulus-response connections, such abilities seem to lose effectiveness if not exercised during critical periods.

Other Critical Periods

Although we have been focusing on imprinting, the many behaviors other than infant-mother attachments are acquired during critical periods, and these periods are not necessarily restricted to a few days after birth. The development of normal sexual or aggressive behavior in the adult rhesus monkey, the appearance of normal adult patterns of social interactions between dogs, and the development of language ability in human beings are behaviors learned only during a circumscribed period early in the life of the organism (Scott, 1962). Similarly, formation of social bonds may come early in birds (shortly after birth) while in other animals they might come much later. The critical period for dogs appears to occur between six and eight weeks of age. If they are deprived of contact with human beings during this time, they will never form the strong social bonds to people that are characteristic of the species. Critical bonding periods also appear in many birds and some mammals around mating time. These periods probably depend on hormonal and neurological effects (like arousal) that occur at that time, and the result is a bond between mates that lasts for many years, even for life.

Critical periods for adult learning often occur around the time of giving birth. Just as infants of many species imprint on their mothers, it is also true in some cases that the mother imprints on her offspring. It has been shown that if a mother goat is not allowed to lick and smell her kid within an hour after birth, she will reject it (Klopfer, Adams, & Klopfer, 1964). This period is probably related to the smell and taste of the mother's afterbirth. These sensory cues decrease rapidly in the first hour. An orphan goat kid will be accepted by an adoptive mother if it has been rubbed with the afterbirth of that mother (Hersher, Richmond, & Moore, 1963).

Birdsong Learning

Adult male white-crowned sparrows normally sing a complete song during the spring breeding season, a behavior that is crucial to establishing a territory and mating with a female. Current evidence suggests that many aspects of the adult male song are learned in this species, although the details of such learning vary from the precepts of a general-principles theory of learning. A series of experiments with white-crowned sparrows reared in isolation (Marler, 1970) has demonstrated that adult song is learned during a critical age (between 10 and 50 days past hatching). Failure to hear an adult male sing during this period will result in an abnormal song when the deprived bird reaches the adult stage. This finding alone indicates an important age constraint on song learning. However, this learning process has other fascinating and unusual aspects. Although the bird is normally exposed to the song during the "critical period," it doesn't actually sing the song for two to six months following exposure. So we have a situation in which there is no obvious response at the time of original learning, no conventional reward, but efficient performance two to six months later. However, in the initial stages of adult singing, the bird must refine the elements of its song; it must be able to hear itself sing. Deafening the bird before it has had the opportunity to perfect its song will result in a permanently abnormal song. Deafening the bird after it has perfected its song will not interfere with production of a normal song. Therefore, the bird needs both to hear the species song during development and to hear its own singing during the early stages of adult song production, if the true species song is to be produced. It does not need auditory feedback to produce the song, however, once it is truly "learned." These features have led to the suggestion that the bird initially possesses a crude "template" in its brain—that is, a neural representation of the broad outlines of the species song. This template is first modified by listening to the adult song during the critical phase of development. Later, the modified template serves as a guide for the adult sparrow as it gradually matches its emitted sounds to the template and forms a true species song.

It should not be assumed from the preceding account that all birds have a critical period for acquiring species-typical songs. Some birds (for example, the chicken and the ringdove) produce essentially normal songs even if deafened immediately after hatching. Other birds (for example, blackbirds) may acquire the species-typical song at any age. And some birds are extraordinary mimics of songs produced by alien species: the mockingbird receives its name from this propensity. Thus some species show a critical period in their acquisition of song whereas other species do not.

The distinctively human ability of language learning may also have a critical period. If a child suffers injury to the left or "speech" hemisphere of the brain before the age of ten or so, recovery of language function is generally possible; the other hemisphere can still acquire language. However, similar injuries after puberty are followed by only minimal recovery (Lenneberg, 1967). This difference suggests that the plasticity of the brain necessary for basic language learning is at its maximum during the early years of life.

THE NATURE OF THE STIMULUS REINFORCER LINKAGE

There has been a growing awareness in recent years that different animals have evolved through natural selection to the point where they learn some stimulus-response relationships more quickly or better than they learn others. Imprinting may be one example, a very rapid association between a stimulus (sensory cues from the mother or Konrad Lorenz) and a response (following) that occurs with no obvious reinforcement. We will consider some examples that stress the role of the stimulus in learning, some examples that emphasize the role of the response, and some that consider the importance of the type of reinforcement.

One of the most interesting and most thoroughly studied phenomena of this type has been called by several names—the Garcia effect (after the psychologist who has done most of the research), the bait-shyness effect, or simply poison-avoidance learning (Garcia & Ervin, 1968). By any name, the effect is this: if a rat eats something and then gets sick, it will avoid that food in the future. The strange thing about **bait shyness** is not so much that learning occurs so rapidly—in one trial or in no more than two or three—but that learning occurs despite the fact that the negative reinforcement—feeling sick—comes *hours* after the response is made to the stimulus. General principles of learning typically include assumptions, based on much evidence, that a delay of even 1 second between response and reinforcement or between a conditioned stimulus (CS) and an unconditioned stimulus (US) results in significantly decreased learning.

Whatever the biological mechanisms that underlie this curious learning ability in the rat, it is clearly to its advantage in terms of survival, as anybody who has tried to exterminate rats with poison can tell you. The advantage is compounded by other features of rat behavior. When a rat encounters a novel food in its habitat, it will take only a small portion and then wait a long time before taking more. If the novel food is a poison, the rat is therefore unlikely to die from the small portion; it will become ill—and thereafter it will avoid the bait. Thus, it is possible to see this learning ability as one that evolved through processes of natural selection. Those rats capable of becoming bait-shy were more likely to survive and reproduce, while other rats without the ability died. (The survival of coyotes may also depend on bait shyness; *see* Spotlight 23-2.)

Additional features of bait shyness are equally curious. The sickness, for example, can be unrelated to the food; if the rat eats a pure food and later is injected with a chemical that makes it sick, the rat will still avoid that food. And what it avoids is the taste of the food; it will eat food with different tastes even if identical in appearance to the "poisoned" food. Similarly, it will not avoid food of like temperature or texture, nor will it avoid the dish from which the poisoned food was eaten (Rozin & Kalat, 1971). In short, the rat avoids only food that *tastes* like the food that made it sick.

Taste avoidance is not characteristic of all rat food avoidance, however. If, for example, a rat is shocked immediately after eating, it will reject food similar in appearance or food accompanied by the same distinctive sounds; it will not, in this case, avoid foods of similar taste.

Suppose a rat eats from several dishes, only one of which contains an unfamiliar food, and it then becomes ill. Under these conditions, it will subsequently reject only the new food among the many eaten before becoming ill. Again the advantage to rat survival is obvious. An atypical, significant effect (an annoying or a satisfying state of affairs) is likely to be related to a new and unusual stimulus, at least in most natural habitats.

Bait shyness is not unique to rats, although they have been the most thoroughly studied. It has also been demonstrated in bobwhite quail (Wilcoxon, Dragoin, & Kral, 1969). In this experiment, quail and rats were given a sour dark-blue liquid to drink; 30 minutes later they were injected with a sickness-inducing chemical. Both species were later tested with liquids that were sour or blue or both. Rats avoided the taste—they rejected sour drinks but not blue liquids. Quail, however, avoided both the sour and the blue solutions. Considering that birds are highly visual animals and that food selection for them is based more on visual cues than for rats, these results make sense. Because

In 1972, around 90,000 coyotes were shot, trapped, or poisoned in the United States, according to official records. Off the record, probably an equal or greater number were killed, many by sheep ranchers protecting their flocks. Conservationists are aghast at this wholesale slaughter. They claim that coyotes do not kill as many sheep as the ranchers suspect. In addition, the coyotes' natural prey include a number of pests—mice, rabbits, and grasshoppers—that, uncontrolled, could do much more harm to sheep herds (through competition for available grassland and diseases carried by the pests) than the coyote could possibly do. As the debate continues, both sheep and coyotes are being killed, and the price of lamb and wool goes up.

What psychologists have learned about bait shyness provides a possible solution to this problem (Gustavson & Garcia, 1974; Gustavson, Kelly, Sweeney, and Garcia, 1976). Perhaps if coyotes are fed lamb laced with lithium chloride, a chemical that induces nausea and vomiting, they will avoid sheep as food, just as rats avoid poisoned bait. To investigate this possibility, three coyotes were given tainted lamb and then observed in interaction with a live lamb, which they would normally kill and eat. Not one coyote attacked. They did kill and eat rabbits, however, showing that the avoidance response did not generalize to other animals.

The next step was to experiment on a real sheep ranch. Pieces of tainted lamb, wrapped in lambs' hide, were left in the areas frequented by sheep-killing coyotes. It's possible that the procedure won't always work in the wild. Coyotes may learn to distinguish between "live" and

(Courtesy Carl R. Gustavson)

"dead" sheep, eating only animals they have themselves killed; the coyote is not called "wily" for nothing. But the results so far indicate that the bait-shyness technique will be more effective than others now used, such as spraying lambs with chemicals that smell like skunks or mountain lions, tactics that often cause the mother sheep to reject her lambs. If the coyote can be taught to avoid the lamb, both animals can live in peace. And sheep ranchers and conservationists can stop battling, too!

---

of bait shyness, organisms that are toxic or have an unpleasant taste to other animals are thereby protected from predation. Certain other organisms gain protection by evolving to resemble those with an unpleasant taste; *see* Spotlight 23-3 on *mimicry*.

THE RESPONSE-REINFORCER RELATIONSHIP

The bait-shyness phenomenon describes a specific stimulus-response association that is rapidly instituted, given a certain kind of reinforcement. Now consider a case where the reinforcement appears to be related to the *response* in such a way that some responses are harder to learn than others. This research was done with stickleback fish. An investigator trained male sticklebacks to (1) bite a rod or (2) swim through a ring in an operant-conditioning procedure (Sevenster, 1973). The reinforcement was the opportunity to display to a sexually ripe female. The fish learned both responses, but his performance rate for rod-biting was considerably lower than for ring-swimming. Moreover, when reinforcement was discontinued (extinction), the rate of rod-biting actually *rose* for a time before the behavior was eventually extinguished.

How is one to understand these facts? A probable answer is that rod-biting, an *aggressive* response, is basically incompatible with the sexually motivating nature of the reward. Thus, during acquisition, the fish would often swim to the rod, but instead of biting it, he would perform the zigzag dance that is typical of courtship in the stickleback (shown in Figure 23-12). Performing this dance in front of the rod indicated conflict between sex and aggression. Finally, the fish would bite the rod. Apparently courtship behavior activated a sexual motivational system that was incompatible with the aggressive rod-biting. When the presence of the female as reinforcement was discontinued, the conflict disappeared, so the rate of rod-biting dramatically increased for a time.

Figure 23-12
Courtship and Mating in the Stickleback
In the first stage of courtship, the male (left) zigzags toward the female. She swims toward him with her head up; her abdomen bulges with 50–100 eggs. The second and third stages are both seen from above. The male swims toward the nest he has built and makes a series of thrusts into it with his snout. He turns on his side and raises his dorsal spines toward the female, who swims into the nest. The male then prods the base of her tail and causes her to lay her eggs. When the female leaves the nest, the male enters and fertilizes the eggs. In the fourth stage, the male "fans" water over the eggs to enrich their oxygen supply. (Redrawn from "The Curious Behavior of the Stickleback," by N. Tinbergen. Copyright © 1952 by Scientific American, Inc. All rights reserved.)

The monarch butterfly (*Danaus plexippus*) and the viceroy butterfly (*Limenitis archippus*) are beautiful familiar visitors to gardens in the eastern United States. Both are orange with black and white markings, and to the casual observer could easily be mistaken for one another. However, they are in fact from different families of butterflies, and close examination would reveal differences in the arrangement of wing veins, leg structure, and the like, which clearly show their disparate ancestry. In addition, the majority of the "relatives" of the viceroy within the genus *Limenitis* are blue-black in color, and it is commonly believed that the blue-black color is the ancestral form from which the orange-based species evolved. Why, then, do the two butterflies look so much alike?

The commonly accepted answer relies on the fact that the taste of the monarch butterfly is aversive to some species of birds (such as the Florida scrub jay) that are potential predators. We have mentioned (p. 653) that quail can learn to associate the appearance of a liquid with its aftereffects. No doubt, visually oriented birds can also learn to associate characteristic patterns of color and form with bad tastes. Thus, they learn to avoid preying upon the bad-tasting monarch butterflies. In the meantime, they do continue to prey upon the blue-black viceroys. However, in an area where both genera of butterflies and their common potential predators dwell,

some viceroys are born with an orange cast. These "new" variants are avoided by bird predators because of their resemblance to the bad-tasting monarchs. Selective pressures favoring the variants develop as a result of reduced predation and therefore greater chances of reproduction among the orange viceroys. The more closely the viceroy comes to resemble the monarch — that is, the more successful the mimicry — the greater is the likelihood of survival. These evolutionary pressures continue until differences in color and form between the monarch and viceroy are almost undetectable by predatory birds. There are many other examples of this kind of evolutionary mimicry.

Brower and Brower (1962) have carried out several experiments in the laboratory designed to investigate the mechanisms underlying the evolutionary advantages of mimicry. In one study they employed toads as predators and bumblebees, dragonflies, and robberflies as prey. After receiving several painful stings, all toads avoided eating bumblebees, but they continued to feed upon dragonflies, which do not look like bees. The robberfly has no capacity for stinging, but it is strikingly similar in appearance to the bumblebee, with a dark and light color pattern and a plump hairy body. Toads that had been stung by bumblebees would also avoid robberflies; control toads that had not been stung by bumblebees accepted robberflies as food 67 percent of the time. The

---

If this reasoning is accurate, then we should expect to find a very high rate of rod-biting if the reward is an opportunity to display aggressively to another male, and this is exactly what occurred.

It is often assumed that a reinforcer is a reinforcer is a reinforcer, and that rewards which increase the probability of one response will work with equal effectiveness on other behaviors. From evidence like that just reported, such assumptions do not seem tenable.

INSTINCTIVE DRIFT

As we have just seen, if you want to train an animal to perform a response at a consistently high rate, you have to take care in the choice of the response to be taught. The response should be compatible with the motivational state arranged by the experimenter, and frequently a "good" response for a particular animal is one that has meaning in its daily activities in its natural habitat. The maze was first chosen as a good test of rat learning because it involved the kind of behavior — running about and exploring — that is common to the wild rat (Small, 1900). Similarly, using the pecking response of pigeons in a Skinner box utilizes a behavior that is natural and has survival advantages

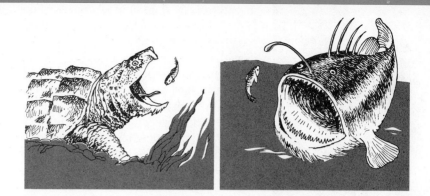

The alligator snapping turtle (left) uses its tongue as a lure to entrap unwary fish, while the angler fish (right) attracts its prey by wiggling a wormlike projection from its snout.

only toad that consistently rejected robberflies without having been stung by a bumblebee happened to get hit on the nose by the robberfly the first time he tried to eat one and apparently developed a selective avoidance response on this basis. It is therefore plausible that the robberfly evolved toward its present coloration and configuration because of its evolution in an area where both bumblebees and potential predators resided. In this kind of environment, its ability to mimic the appearance of the bumblebee would protect it from experienced (but not inexperienced) predators, and selective pressure would operate to produce an ever more realistic replica of the bee.

Predators, on the other hand, can also mimic to the detriment of prey. This mimicry often involves specialized body structures that lure the prey to capture. For example, the alligator snapping turtle has a special wormlike projection from its tongue. Lying in wait with its mouth agape, the turtle wiggles this projection enticingly until an unwary fish approaches too closely and becomes the victim instead of predator of the "worm." The angler fish has evolved a similar wormlike projection from the top of its head, again luring other fish to their demise.

(see p. 383). The pigeon peck is also remarkably suitable for a range of motivational situations—feeding, attacking, and others.

What can happen when the choice of response is not so wise or fortunate was told by two psychologists who were engaged in training animals for zoo shows, television commercials, and the like (Breland & Breland, 1961, 1966). Using operant-conditioning techniques, they trained over 5,000 animals from a wide range of species. Generally they were quite successful, but there were failures, and they began to notice a pattern in their unsuccessful training attempts. For example, the psychologists wanted to teach a raccoon to put coins into a metal container. After some difficulty, they got the raccoon to put a single coin into the container, but when they tried to train it to deposit two coins at once, they were totally unsuccessful. The raccoon picked up the two coins and brought them to the container, but it would not let go. Instead it stood by the container and rubbed (and rubbed and rubbed) the coins together, occasionally dipping (but not dropping) them into the container. Despite nonreinforcement, the rubbing behavior came more and more to dominate the performance, and this trick had to be abandoned.

The species-characteristic behavior of food-washing interfered with attempts to train raccoons to pick up and release coinlike objects.

Another "piggy bank" trick was planned for—appropriately enough—a pig. The "coins" were large wooden disks that the pig was required to carry several feet and deposit in a large container to obtain a food reward. A number of pigs were successfully trained to do this, but in every case, their performance soon began to deteriorate. Instead of trotting rapidly from the coin pile to the piggy bank, the pigs began to drop the coin on their way to the container—repeatedly, deliberately. Then they would root it along for a while—push it along with their snout—and then pick it up and toss it in the air. All this fancy behavior was hardly to their advantage; the wasted time increased so that the pigs were not receiving enough nourishment to survive.

Both examples demonstrate a failure of the general procedures of conditioning. In the case of the pigs, the response is learned and then deteriorates. The "interfering behaviors" in both cases are those the animal typically displays when hungry in a food-gathering situation: "washing" in the raccoon (see photo) and rooting in the pig. The authors of this report call this interference **instinctive drift,** meaning that the response wanted was often replaced by behaviors that the animals instinctively perform in the wild.

Another example of a species-characteristic response that is emitted even when it is counterproductive is that of a pigeon pecking in an operant-learning situation. As described in Spotlight 14-6 on autoshaping, the pigeon will peck on most trials even if pecking results in food being withheld.

EFFECTIVE REWARDS

The view that all rewards have the same effect on all responses should by now be thoroughly discredited. Still, there remains the problem of specifying the biological or theoretical nature of reinforcement, an issue that has a long history in psychology. Thorndike's position (p. 640) was one of the earliest. He claimed that the bond between a stimulus and a response will be strengthened—that is, learning will occur—if the response leads to a "satisfying state of affairs." There was not much discussion of why an effective reward was satisfying.

After Thorndike, views on reinforcement developed in two nearly opposite directions. On one hand, Skinner defined a reinforcer as any stimulus event contingent upon a response that increases the probability of occurrence of that response. This approach is purely empirical: *what* is reinforcing is determined by observing changes in frequency of behaviors that are followed by various events. In this tradition, there is a very active avoidance of questions concerning the underlying biological or functional nature of the reward; for example, *why* is food reinforcing for a hungry animal?

The second approach was led by Hull (1943), who was influenced by the biological concept of **homeostasis**—the tendency of many biological systems to achieve a relatively stable state with component elements in equilibrium. The model for this view was probably the biological feeding system. If the body lacks food, it somehow sets up a state of tension **(drive)** that leads to behaviors designed to reduce the tension **(drive reduction)** and restore the original equilibrium. Events that are *drive-reducing,* therefore, are reinforcing. For a hungry rat, food is reinforcement because food reduces the hunger drive.

(For current views of the biological nature of such systems, *see* Chapter 20.)

For hunger, thirst, and the avoidance of pain, the drive-reduction hypothesis functioned reasonably well. Some intractable phenomena, however, soon began appearing in scientific reports. Most of these involved sensory stimulation that was "satisfying" and increased the probability of a response without obviously reducing biological tension. A hungry rat will work to obtain saccharin solutions, which are sweet but have no nutritive value and therefore do not reduce the biological need for food. A male rat will work for the privilege of copulating with a female, even if no ejaculation (tension reduction) is permitted. A wide range of species will work for nothing more than the opportunity to explore the environment. For example, a monkey will quickly solve a discrimination problem for the privilege of being able to look out of its cage at the goings-on in the laboratory (Butler, 1954). In fact, the monkey will solve complex puzzles for no external reward (Harlow, 1953). *See* Spotlight 23-4 on curiosity in animals.

A number of animals will work very hard to get electrical stimulation to certain areas of their brain (the pleasure centers; *see* p. 571), and it is difficult to see how this stimulation relates to any kind of tension reduction. Finally, many studies indicate that a change of stimulation may be rewarding in itself. For example, if a monkey is in darkness it will work to have the light turned on. If it is in the light, the monkey will work to have the light turned off.

Advocates of tension-reduction theories of reinforcement came up with an ingenious set of explanations for sensory rewards and other anomalies. For example, to explain exploratory behavior, they cited studies showing that unfamiliar stimuli arouse fear and suggested that exploration reduces anxiety tension. There is probably some truth in these patchwork explanations, but with all the loopholes and qualifications, the drive-reduction theories were becoming simply too cumbersome to be useful. Many psychologists, perhaps most, turned to other approaches, and learning psychologists have more or less abandoned the issue of reinforcement altogether.

In comparative psychology, however, the reinforcement issue remains vital. The questions of *why* an organism does something, or why it does this and not that, or why it does this at age *X* and that at age *Y* are all being investigated. Within comparative psychology, two approaches to the question of reinforcement have received particular attention; they can be characterized as the American view and the European ethological view.

An American View

One of the most influential American comparative psychologists in this century is T. C. Schneirla. Schneirla (1959) proposed that the only objective descriptions of motivated behavior applicable to all species were in terms of *approach* and *withdrawal*. Therefore, he suggested, rewards are best characterized as the introduction of events that typically induce approach or as the removal of events that typically induce withdrawal. This view is similar to that of Thorndike in some ways. Events that are "satisfying" and hence reinforcing were defined by Thorndike as those which the animal will approach and not withdraw from.

Schneirla also proposed that approach behavior is instituted by mild stimulation and withdrawal by intense stimulation. This theory explained the

One of the major adaptations of many species is their plasticity, their flexibility in learning about the world in which they live. Psychologists have frequently acted as if laboratory animals would work only if rewarded with food, water, or avoidance of pain. However, it is apparent that many species will emit responses and learn about their environment without such externally supplied rewards; as is evident in the case of latent learning (p. 384). The motivational basis of such learning is generally considered to be curiosity, and the behavior patterns are commonly classified as investigatory or exploratory behavior. Learning about new sources of food, locating potential mates, and forming the "map" of one's territory that permits security of movement and rapid escape to burrows or other places of safety, are all potential benefits to the curious animal. However, curiosity is not without its dangers. While engaged in inspection of some novel feature of the environment, an animal may be particularly vulnerable to predation.

Some years ago, we examined the responses of several hundred mammals and a smaller group of reptiles to novel objects introduced to their cages at various zoological parks (Glickman & Sroges, 1966). As can be seen in the graph, all the mammalian orders that we studied reacted to the novel objects and displayed habituation.

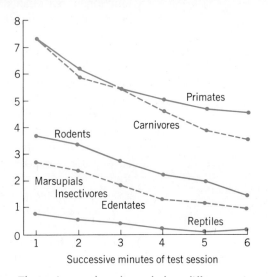

The various orders showed clear differences in reactivity to novel stimulus objects. Note the decline in response during the course of the test session. (From Glickman & Sroges, 1966)

That is, as they grew familiar with the objects during a single 6-minute test session they showed a decline in

rewarding effects of sensory stimulation without requiring the concept of homeostasis, but it elicited other criticisms. In particular, the theory defined a reinforcement as an event producing mild arousal. What is "mild arousal"? How is it to be measured? Sexual arousal may be sought although it is very intense, while even mildly bitter drinks will be avoided; how can the theory account for these qualitative differences?

A European View

In contrast to Schneirla's stimulus-intensity theory of reinforcement, the European ethologists (notably Niko Tinbergen) have seen the consummatory response as the basis for reinforcement. In broad terms, this view holds that animals will learn responses that result in the activation of species-characteristic behavior patterns necessary for the preservation of the species. In more common terminology, food is not the reinforcement; eating is!

Ethologists have a traditional interest in the description of fixed action patterns in lower animals like birds and fish; thus, it comes as no surprise to find them very conscious of the role of responses in reinforcement. However, several psychologists working in the American behaviorist tradition have also noted the response as the critical element in what is normally called reward or reinforcement. Premack (1965) has proposed that if one of two different responses is preferred at a given time, the preferred one can be used to rein-

response to the simple wooden, metal, and rubber objects that were supplied for their investigation. The orders of mammals differed in terms of the average time spent investigating the objects. The primates and carnivores in our sample exhibited considerably more total reactivity than rodents, insectivores, edentates, and marsupials (although there were wide individual and species differences, with some marsupials being more reactive than some primates). Equally striking was the range of investigatory patterns that each species showed. These patterns were obviously limited by the sensory-motor equipment of the animal and tended to approximate the kinds of responses observed during food-gathering behavior. Confronted by a novel object, most rodents would smell it and possibly bite it; most primates would emphasize visual inspection and would use their dextrous manipulatory capacity to examine it. The greatest variety and amount of investigatory activity was observed in those animals possessing (1) a relatively large, well-developed brain, (2) good manipulatory ability, (3) a varied diet under natural habitat conditions, and (4) relative security from predators in the natural habitat. These conditions are met by various primates including baboons, chimpanzees, and, most notably, human beings.

In the laboratory, a variety of different tasks and measures have been employed to assess curiosity, including (1) the orientation of the sense receptors to a novel source of stimulation (Pavlov's "what is it?" reflex); (2) the reactions of caged animals to a novel object placed in their environment (as we did at the zoo); (3) the locomotor responses of animals placed in an unfamiliar environment; and (4) the emission of some arbitrary behavior such as lever-pressing or running a maze to gain access to a new source of stimulation.

Some additional generalizations emerge from the myriad studies carried out in this area. Stimuli likely to evoke the most direct investigation are those which are

This chimpanzee is using a stick to "fish" termites from a mound. The development of such tool-using behavior requires a very high level of manipulatory curiosity.

moderately novel, but not so unusual as to evoke fear, or so familiar as to be dismissed without further concern. In addition, there is apparently an optimal age for each species during which curiosity is at its maximum. Most research places this somewhere between childhood and early adult stages, with both young infants and mature experienced members of the species showing relatively less direct investigatory behavior. This almost surely correlates with the importance of early life as an optimal time for learning within the mammalian orders.

force the less preferred one. He formulated this hypothesis after observing his wife induce eating behavior in his children by offering permission to play when the dinner was finished. This reverses the typical sequence of events in a psychological laboratory, where the experimenter usually "rewards" other behavior by giving the animal the opportunity to eat or drink. In subsequent laboratory research, Premack did indeed show that if a rat was not thirsty, nevertheless it would lick at the tube of a water bottle when it learned that licking behavior led to the privilege of running in an activity wheel.

The consummatory-response view of reinforcement has been strengthened by several recent studies on various species, all suggesting that the opportunity to engage in a species-specific behavior can be used to increase the probability of a preceding response. For example, a deer mouse will press a lever if it is then allowed to burrow in sand (King & Weisman, 1964). In several bird and fish species that exhibit species-characteristic aggressive or sexual displays (for example, the peacock spreads his beautiful tail feathers in sexual display), it has been shown that they can be trained to perform a different response for the opportunity to display (p. 654).

It would be nice to end our review of ideas about the nature of reinforcement by pointing to one view as correct. Alas, such certitude is rare in science. All the views we have described have some merits and some demerits, and each has a particular body of research to which it is best suited. Certainly history is replete with examples of the dangers of taking one extreme view in exclusion of others. Perhaps the answer lies in some synthesis of all the valid important points from the various approaches. If you care to try your hand, I can assure you that success would bring great rewards—even if we do not fully understand the nature of those rewards!

If this chapter has led you to the conclusions that each stimulus, each response, each reward—each instance of learning—must be evaluated for each species in each specific situation, then we have done our job successfully. It is perhaps unfortunate that nature is not simpler. It should not be assumed that generalizations are impossible—we have reached the generalization that the effectiveness of stimuli, responses, and rewards for any animal depends on survival requirements in its natural habitat. But generalizations based on limited information, obtained from observation of only a few species, were bound to come into conflict with facts. In science, this is healthy and productive. In comparative psychology, we are only now experiencing the excitement and the increased knowledge that result from the conflicts between hypotheses and observations.

SUMMARY

This chapter has examined the similarities and differences among various animal species in their ability to learn or to adapt to their environments. The search for similarities and general principles across species has been largely an American tradition. The emphasis has been on abilities that result in flexibility and modifiability in response—that is, learning abilities. In Europe, more attention has been paid to the species-characteristic behavior patterns through which insects, fish, and birds adapt to their environments.

Because of their fascination with problems of learning, American psychologists generally emphasize the use of **mammals** in laboratory settings and assume that general principles of learning would emerge, applicable even to human beings. A review of the evolution of homo sapiens indicates that we share some traits with all mammals (nursing of the young), other traits with just the primates (emphasis on vision), and possess still a third set of characteristics that are unique to the human species (language). We might therefore expect that both general principles and specific differences will emerge when learning is viewed in comparative perspective.

European ethologists have studied the **fixed action patterns (FAP's)** that promoted adaptation and survival in lower animals. These patterns of behavior, which are not dependent on specific learning, were viewed as released by **sign stimuli**—that is, particular stimulus configurations that trigger the FAP's. An example is the retrieval behaviors of birds to eggs placed outside the nest.

Thorndike's puzzle-box experiments were among the first comparative studies of animal learning in the United States. The puzzle boxes represent an early attempt to develop a kind of "general intelligence test" appropriate for all species; the **delayed-response** test was another example, and more recently, the **learning-set** procedures of Harlow have been used. It was expected that most animals would perform in similar fashion but at different levels of competence. Generally speaking, this expectation was not realized; unavoidable differences in perceptual and motor abilities and in motivation made differences in performance a poor measure of intellectual or learning ability. Bitterman has proposed that systematic variation of motivational states, rather than futile attempts to equate motivational levels across species, can resolve at least some of the classic issues.

Köhler presented evidence for a different type of learning called insight. General-principle theorists, however, countered with data suggesting that insight required prior trial-and-error learning. For example, for a chimpanzee to show insightful solutions to stick-manipulation problems, it must have had the opportunity to play with sticks during infancy and adolescence. Also, in learning-set studies, monkeys could "insightfully" solve simple discrimination problems in a trial or two only after performing a long series of tasks incorporating the same general rule.

In the learning theories of Hull and Skinner the hypothesis that all species learn the same way became almost an axiom, and researchers used rats and pigeons to examine *general* principles of learning. Recently ethologists and some American scientists like Bitterman have asserted that *differences* (even in general principles) should be considered along with the similarities. This view has led comparative psychologists interested in learning back to the study of animals across a wider phylogenetic range.

Each animal species is adapted for life in a particular habitat. Any given species might be expected to learn responses crucial to survival with great ease, while responses that are irrelevant or detrimental to survival would be less easily acquired or performed. These constraints on learning were first discussed in terms of critical periods, developmental stages in which certain learning proceeds quickly and outside of which the same learning seems difficult or impossible. Many animals, for example, learn to make social responses to their parents (or, in unusual circumstances, to ethologists) in a short, critical period after birth; this has been called **imprinting.**

The **bait-shyness** effect describes another constraint on learning. If a rat eats something (such as poison bait) and later becomes ill, it will avoid (shy away from) that food in the future. The stimulus avoided is often quite specific; in the rat, it is the taste of the food. Also, the rapid learning of bait shyness occurs even though the negative reinforcement comes hours after taking the bait; the effectiveness of this reinforcement despite its long delay poses problems for learning theories in general.

Just which response is reinforced also makes a difference in learning. Behaviors that are characteristic of the animal in its natural habitat seem easier to train, and if one reinforces a response different from the animal's "instinctive" response for a given motivational state, there may be **instinctive drift** back to the typical response. Thus a raccoon trained to drop a coin in a box to get food will often try to clean and wash the coin before dropping it.

What constitutes an effective reward? Some prominent notions include the "satisfying state of affairs" (Thorndike), "drive reduction" (Hull), and the "consummatory response" (Tinbergen). Skinnerian psychologists have defined reinforcement empirically, asserting that an event that follows a response and leads to the increased probability of occurrence of that response is a positive reinforcer. Recently it has been found that a preferred response will reinforce a less preferred response: a child will eat in order to play, and a rat may be trained to drink in order to get the opportunity to run in an activity wheel.

24

A Social Existence

What functions does social cohesion serve?
When does social dispersal occur?
What mechanisms contribute to cohesive behavior?
What mechanisms underlie dispersal behavior?
What can we learn about human social behavior from
comparative psychology?

Shortly after sunrise, the hamadryas baboons of the Ethiopian lowlands leave their sleeping rocks and ascend to the "waiting" areas that lie above. The more than one hundred animals that comprise a troop of *Papio hamadrayas* baboons have spent the night lodged against the face of a cliff, secure from predators. But now it is time to forage for food; the troop members leave their sanctuary and venture into the surrounding savannah or plain in search of food and water. The troop leaves en masse, but as the march proceeds, parties of animals depart from the main group and begin to feed. This process continues until the members of the troop are scattered across an area of one mile or more.

An experienced observer can see that the parties that break off from the main group are all similar in composition; in fact, these subgroups represent the fundamental social unit of the hamadryas society, the **one-male group,** usually composed of one adult male, one to five females, and their offspring. Shortly after midday, the first of these units will begin the return journey, and by midafternoon the majority of the troop members will once again be in place in the waiting areas atop their cliffside retreat. Each day begins and ends with a prolonged period of social interaction among all members of the troop. The most common adult interaction involves one baboon carefully grooming the fur of another, although sex, aggression, and the vigorous play of the young are also in evidence. Finally, as dusk approaches, the animals return to their sleeping rocks on the cliff face, each one-male group remaining closely clustered together (*see* Figure 24-1).

In the savannah and fields to the south and west some closely related baboons (*Papio anubis*) live a rather different existence. Their nights are generally spent in trees and the troops move as a group in their feeding activities throughout the day. The one-male unit is not to be found. In its place, we have a complex system of troop organization that is better described in terms of roles, with key positions occupied by one or more adult males who control much of the troop's activities, interpose themselves when danger threatens the troop, and engage in the majority of the mating activity. In these *Papio anubis* baboons, the dominant males occupy a position near the center of the troop, surrounded by females in estrus and females with infants. The peripheral positions are taken by other adult males (where they can act as "sentries"), and the remaining females and juveniles are located between the core and the periphery (Hall & DeVore, 1965). Finally, in the Ethiopian highlands, a third species of baboon (*Theropithecus gelada*) exhibits either the troop or the one-male group form of social organization, depending on various ecological factors (Crook, 1967).

Within the contrasting life-styles just described are contained virtually all the puzzles about social behavior. How are these contrasting social systems adaptive for survival in different habitats? What are the ties that bind members of these groups to one another, and what factors ultimately promote their dispersal?

Figure 24-1
One-Male Baboon Group
A one-male unit of hamadryas baboons sleeps on the ledge of a cliff.

The analysis of social behavior takes place at several levels. In the sections that follow, we shall first consider the presumed evolutionary-adaptive advantages of social grouping and dispersal. Grouping is advantageous for some purposes, but dispersal is advantageous for others, as we shall see. Then we will turn to the mechanisms that produce such behavior patterns.

What functions does social cohesion serve?

PROTECTION

A primary advantage of a cohesive social group is the protection it affords the individual member against harm and injury. In the case of the savannah baboons, the females and young are protected by the adult males who are physically powerful, possess impressive canine teeth (*see* Figure 24–2), and can band together to defeat powerful foes. In the one-male groups of the hamadryas baboon, the male must, of course, face the predator alone, but even so the females and young are considerably better off than if they were unprotected.

At a superficial level, the patas monkeys (*Erythrocebus patas*) are also organized into groups consisting of a single male associated with a number of females, infants, and juveniles (Hall, 1965). However, the single adult patas male is not a leader but a follower. It is his role to remain on the periphery of the main group as it moves through the savannah and to act as a sentry. Should a predator appear, the patas male informs his party, and they all take rapid flight across the plains in which they live. The male does not confront the

The females, juveniles, and infants of a group of patas monkeys cluster around the edge of a waterhole. Note the slender build of this species compared with the baboon in Figure 24-2.

In mobbing behavior, birds that would be powerless alone band together for defense. Here two terns divebomb a herring gull, probably to drive it away from their nesting area.

Figure 24-2
An Adult Male Hamadryas Baboon
The canine teeth are formidable weapons against potential predators.

predator, and the females determine the direction of movement—behavior that is the opposite of the one-male groups of baboons in the Ethiopian lowlands, even though in other respects the social organization is strikingly similar.

The hamadryas baboon is a powerful animal, whereas the patas monkey is a tall, slender, and exceptionally fast-moving animal. Each seems to have achieved a means of predator evasion that accentuates its particular talents, which are largely determined by bodily structure. Although both species live in environments that promote a social organization we call one-male groups, the means of group protection is quite different. We can begin to see the complex interrelations among heredity, habitat, and social organization.

Cohesion for protection in other species is organized in quite different ways. The grouping-together or schooling of fish, for example, has been viewed as a protective maneuver in two senses (Shaw, 1960). First, schooling tends to confuse the predator by presenting a welter of attractive stimuli. Second, if the predator does strike a peripheral fish, the remainder are "warned" and have time to swim away. Presumably if the school members were widely dispersed, the predator could actually consume more, picking them off one at a time. Human duck hunters (predators) will tell you that they would much prefer to shoot at a lone duck and that it is difficult to bag even one of a large flock. Perhaps similar principles are operating here.

Among small birds who are potential victims of larger hawks and owls, the bonding-together or mobbing technique of defense is common (Hinde, 1954). The smaller birds literally mob the potential predator; they use their greater speed and agility and fly at it in great numbers, harassing it relentlessly until it leaves the vicinity.

Why don't these fast birds simply flee from the slower predator, as the patas monkeys do? They must protect their nests, the eggs, and their young who cannot yet fly. Their response, of course, is not born of a conscious decision to be a good parent, but it does promote the survival of the species; the behavior pattern has evolutionary advantages. Many fish show a similar pattern of fighting ferociously in their own territory, even against great odds. But these same fish will flee an opponent when they are *away* from their home grounds. In some species, this pattern of fighting at home and fleeing when away from home is so precise that an experienced observer can predict almost to the inch (away from home territory) which of two fish will "win" the confrontation.

In some social groups members will display apparent **altruism** or *self-sacrificial behavior* to protect others. Perhaps the best-known example is the "broken-wing" display of some bird species such as ducks or partridges. Threatened by a predator, the female bird protects its young (or its nest) by feigning injury and suggesting easy capture. It flutters helplessly an attractive (but safe) distance away to draw the predator from the nest. It stumbles and flutters again and again, always farther from the nest. Finally, when the predator is safely distant from the nest, the female bird flies away with two obviously healthy wings.

Many altruistic animals are not so fortunate. Often one animal of a group fights the predator and is killed; its actions, however, allow the others to escape and live. For many years such altruistic behavior was viewed as a major evolutionary puzzle. How could such self-sacrificial behavior result in superior transmission of genes from the "martyred" animal? The most widely accepted contemporary explanation relies on the concept of *kin selection*. If by its sacrificial act the altruistic animal enhances the survival of close relatives who share its genes, altruism can be explained by natural selection (survival) of gene-sharing relatives. A related issue is posed by alarm calls. It might appear that a bird or mammal sounding the alarm at the approach of a predator is attracting attention to itself and raising the probability of its own capture. Presumably, if the behavior is in fact sacrificial, it could only be selected for by increasing the survival of close relatives. However, it has been noted that alarm calls are usually of high frequency (pitch) and short duration, making them very difficult to localize in space. Thus the danger to the caller may be much less than would be expected on casual observation. (For a more complete discussion of altruistic behavior, *see* Hamilton, 1964; Campbell, 1972; and Wilson, 1975.)

PREDATION AND FOOD-GATHERING

Just as social structure can benefit the **prey,** so can it benefit the **predator.** Among the mammals, this behavior is most easily seen in wolves and wild dogs. Through cooperative hunting, these animals can capture much larger prey (like deer) than would be possible for any one individual (Allen & Mech, 1963). Predation in the natural habitat is a food-gathering behavior, not a hostile act.

Among species that are not predators, most social groups also use their cohesion in some way to increase their "take" over what it would be if all functioned as individuals. Bees, for example, have an elaborate social system that includes widely dispersed scouts. If a scout detects a good food source,

Figure 24-3
Honeybee "Dances"
Information about the richness of the food source and its location is conveyed by the dancing patterns given by "scout" bees. (After M. Lindauer, 1961)

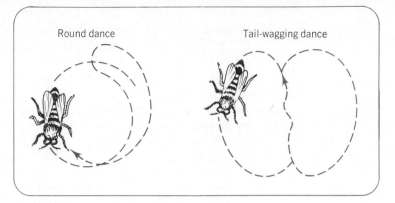

Round dance

Tail-wagging dance

it flies back to the hive and "communicates" the location to other members of the hive. The food source is then visited by large numbers of bees.

How does the scout transmit this information on direction and distance of the food source? Karl von Frisch, an Austrian zoologist, spent most of his life investigating the intriguing communication system of bees. To study the process, von Frisch (1950) constructed special hives with glass plates so that he could observe the social interaction. One of his earliest observations was that scouts, when returning to the hive, do a kind of dance and that the other bees are obviously excited by the dance. The other bees then fly from the hive, usually directly to the food source from which the scout has come. So the dance must communicate something. Von Frisch began translating.

Bee dances can be classified into two main types: circling and wagging (*see* Figure 24-3). Von Frisch surmised at first that the circling dance meant "nectar" and the wagging dance meant "pollen," but later observations showed this translation to be inaccurate. The communication patterns were much more complex than he supposed, and cues other than the dance were in-volved. The type of food tends to be communicated by odors on the scout, and the vigor of the dance seems to be related to the quantity of the food source. When the nectar starts running low, the dance is slower.

But what of the two different kinds of dances? What do they indicate? By setting up food sources at various distances, von Frisch discovered that with sources more than 100 meters away, bees did only the wagging dance, and with sources less than 50 meters away bees did only the circling dance. He also concluded that the vertical direction of the dance is related to the direction (in relation to the sun) of the food source.

The language of bees is even more complex than this. The number of turns per second conveys information about distance, and the number of waggles per second is probably also important. Some bees do not perform the short-distance round dance at all; instead they dance in a kind of semicircle called the "sickle dance" (Lindauer, 1961). Although recent research (Wenner, 1967) has raised questions as to whether bees always use the information contained in their dances, the intricate communication patterns represent a remarkable aspect of food-gathering behavior in a social insect.

In complex mammals such as the baboons, past experience and learning play a role in determining food-gathering patterns. Certain older males often decide the direction of troop travel in search of food. Before these adults assume leadership they have probably spent a decade or so as followers. No doubt they learn much about terrain and safety in this early period. In some chimpanzee troops, dominant males sometimes defer to old (wise?) males for leadership in gathering food.

In predatory animals, the period of infancy is a time to learn appropriate hunting techniques. Learning may occur in play with peers and inanimate objects or in specific maternal tutelage. It has been demonstrated that polecats need this early training period if they are to exhibit the intricate killing behavior of adults. Polecats raised in isolation have all the proper actions but the sequence is often incorrect; for example, these cats "worry" their prey (shake it back and forth to break its neck) before making the proper bite. Often individual acts such as biting are directed to an improper target area (Eibl-Eibesfeldt, 1961). It is still not clear in the social situation whether the young animal learns by itself or whether the parent guides this learning.

A clearer example of maternal tutelage may be seen in Indian tigers (Schaller, 1967). The cubs remain with the mother for a year or more, sharing the fruits of her predation and sometimes joining in the kill itself. It is difficult, however, in field studies to distinguish observational learning on the part of the cubs from learning by direct experience, when the mother slows down the prey and allows the young to make the kill. Probably both types of learning take place.

In species where past experience is a factor in adult food-gathering, the period of infancy and adolescence is obviously important. But the young of a species sometimes make their own original contributions. In the Japanese macaque monkeys, juveniles frequently try food sources neglected by the adults, and if the food source is a good one, the adults proceed to try it themselves (Itani, 1959).

MATING

Sex, of course, is one of the most important reasons why members of a species have to meet now and then, even if they are dispersed for most of each year. The simultaneous physical presence of two partners is not required in all species—for example, in salmon the female lays eggs and the male swims by some time later and fertilizes them. Nevertheless, the evolutionary trend seems to be in the direction of both partners coming together for mating. Similar evolutionary trends are toward internal fertilization, live birth, and the prolonged presence of one or both parents after birth. These trends enhance the chances of any particular infant for survival; large numbers of offspring, necessary in species where only a minute percentage will survive, give way in higher species to small brood sizes. Fewer offspring generally result in a more elaborate and flexible social structure.

For the vast majority of mammals, sex is a periodic activity dependent on hormonal cycles in the male and female. In the hamadryas baboon one-male group, each adult male builds his "harem" slowly, apparently by literally kidnapping juvenile females and retaining them through maturity. Mating occurs when the female goes into **estrus** (her period of sexual receptivity) and only during those times of the day when the animals are not searching for

A pair of baboons at the Gombe Stream Reserve in Tanzania display a typical copulatory posture.

food. Either the male or the female can initiate the mounting. Males are either gentle—lightly touching the female's genital swelling—or rough—grabbing her by the hair on her head, jerking her into position. Females initiate copulation by presenting their rear end to the male, and copulation is from the rear, as shown in the photograph.

The hamadryas baboon male is completely loyal to the females of his group, and the females are reasonably loyal to the male. Generally only the youngest females, those in estrus for the first time, will mate with males outside the group. This promiscuity is facilitated by the fact that the dominant male is apt to be occupied with the older, experienced females whom he prefers as sexual partners. If females are caught in infidelity, however, they can expect a painful neck bite from the leader, even if their lover is a juvenile male from their own group.

In the elk of the western United States, a social organization similar to the one-male groups of the baboon can be observed (Altmann, 1956), but only during the mating (or "rutting") season. In the late summer, the antlers of the adult males develop, and they are used in aggressive encounters with other adult males. Victory in these encounters ensures exclusive mating rights with a larger harem of cows. Once the mating season is over, however, the males and females go their separate ways, the female as part of a herd composed exclusively of females and juveniles. Next fall, the process will repeat itself, and males must fight again for mates. So in this case the annual hormonal cycles affect not only the cohesion of the species, but also the nature of the social organization at various seasons of the year.

In the troop-organized savannah baboon, dominant males do not have the monopoly that exists in one-male groups. A number of adult and subadult males may be witnessed mounting a sexually receptive female. However, during the peak of estrus when the chances of successful impregnation are highest, the dominant males do most of the copulating.

In all these social systems, despite variations in organization, the net effect is to promote the genetic transmission of traits desirable from the standpoint of survival; the biggest, strongest, and most aggressive males do most of the copulating, and hence account for most of the offspring. On the other hand, it should not be assumed that the male always determines whose genetic characteristics get transmitted. We know that female beagles are extremely selective in their acceptance of sexual partners (Beach & Le Boeuf, 1967). In wolves observed in a zoo setting (Ginsburg, 1965), the dominant female prevented the other females from mating with the resident males.

DIVISION OF RESPONSIBILITY

In many cases, membership in a social group involves a specific social role determined by sex. This fact binds the animals together in the sense that the survival of the group depends on several behaviors, some of which are provided by each sex; either sex alone would have a difficult time of it.

Sex roles tend to be different whenever there is sexual **dimorphism** in a species; that is, if the male and female exhibit prominent physical differences,

the likelihood is also great that the sexes provide different behavioral contributions to group survival. Among the baboons, the much larger males with their powerful canine teeth are well adapted to their roles as protectors. The smaller females are more involved in the nurturance of infants.

In certain monkeys, however, the two sexes both look and act much more alike. Many birds (such as the penguin) divide responsibility for incubation, nest defense, and feeding the young in an essentially equal fashion between sexes. One partner stays at home caring for the eggs or the young while the other searches for food; then they reverse these roles. Typically, in birds, the exchange between the roles of hunter and babysitter is accompanied by a ceremony of some type. The male (or the female) who is about to take over the incubation of the eggs bows and nods in an elaborate behavior sequence; the female (or male) then relinquishes its place atop the eggs.

In many species, hunting is a male activity. But again no universal generalizations can be made, for in some animal groups the female does most or all of the hunting. The female African lion does most of the hunting, to such an extent that several observers began wondering if the King of the Jungle had any social role beyond occasional copulation. Later studies (Schaller, 1972) indicate that the male lion's primary responsibility is protecting the territory from intruding lions.

When does social dispersal occur?

We have indicated some of the advantages of a social existence in animals, but there are also disadvantages. If the aggregation of an animal species leads to the starvation of some—because the food supply is limited—the effects on the species and on its chances for survival are complex. One might assume that in times of overpopulation or limited food resources, only the weaker would die, and the population would simply be reduced to some manageable size. But there are cases of overpopulation leading to virtual extinction of an entire species. Let us now look more closely at some of the problems of a social existence that may make **dispersal** an adaptive response.

FOOD SCARCITY

At the beginning of this chapter we described the lifestyles of three different baboon species. Modern animal behaviorists have tried to account for such variations in social structure in terms of the ecological realities faced by different species. In particular, the availability of food has been thought to play a major role in shaping the different social organizations. In the baboons, one typically finds either the one-male group or the troop organization. One-male units are more frequently found in places where food is scarce. A large and tightly organized baboon troop would have to cover enormous distances each

Both male and female Adelie penguins participate in building their nest of rocks. Subsequent incubation of the eggs is also a shared responsibility. When one parent leaves the eggs (right) and the other takes over the incubation there is often a ceremony of mutual display.

day to feed all members; troop organization requires a rather lush environment. Even among baboons organized into troops, it has been noted that the size of the troop is correlated with its food supply; smaller sizes are found in less favorable habitats (DeVore & Hall, 1965). In the coatimundi, a small carnivore with an elongated snout found in Mexico and Central America, females, juveniles, and infants form the basic social unit. During the portion of the year when food is scarce, the females will chase away males who approach their group. Only when food is abundant are males allowed to join the group and engage in mutual foraging and mating activities. Where food is most scarce we find an almost solitary existence, with social interaction limited to brief periods of sexual activity and infant care, as in the case of the kangaroo rats of the western American deserts (Kaufman, 1962).

Recent reviewers have examined the relationship between the social organization of grazing animals and the availability of food. A correlation was established in both the antelopes and their relatives (Geist, 1974) and in the many species of kangaroos found in Australia (Kaufmann, 1974). However, many exceptions were noted within these groups, where the social structure seemed unrelated to food resources. Ultimately it seems likely that a multifactored explanation which includes predator pressure and the intellectual capacity of each species will be required to account for social organization.

Predatory animals need prey to survive. Among the most social carnivores such as wolves, wild dogs, and hyenas, the maintenance of the group social structure requires a reasonable population of large prey (like deer) or an enormous population of smaller animals (like rodents). Many hunting cats, like the American cougar, live rather solitary lives to survive. The African lion, which is a relatively social hunting cat, is extraordinarily defensive of its group territory; it is one of the few animals that will literally kill an intruder of its own species (Schenkel, 1966; Schaller, 1972).

INCREASED POPULATION

When population of a species increases, the usual social interactions become more difficult and complex. The result is often social dispersal or social disorganization. Such effects probably occur because social interactions largely depend on the ability to recognize the members of one's social group, and the mechanisms of control are based on such recognition; in groups too large, recognition of individuals is more difficult, and the likelihood of social disorganization is thereby increased.

In the troop-organized savannah baboons, it has been suggested that new troops are formed whenever the size of an existing troop exceeds certain limits (DeVore & Hall, 1965). It seems unlikely that dispersal in this case is exclusively a function of food scarcity. More probably, the population density affects social organization, causing a decrease in social cohesion. One might speculate that only a certain degree of social disorganization can be tolerated by a troop in their collective efforts to eat, mate, rear their young, and evade predators; when those limits are exceeded, the troop splits into two.

Some investigators have carried such reasoning further and asked, What happens if the population density is artificially controlled, so that natural limits are exceeded? Several such studies have been done with animals in large outdoor plots (for example, Calhoun, 1962). If rat populations are allowed to exceed natural limits, social disorganization follows. Dominance

Many animal populations undergo drastic cyclic fluctuations in number and density. Probably the best-known example involves the small Arctic rodents popularly known as lemmings. According to a widely held belief, the density of their population swells to a point at which social disorganization occurs and a mass migration ensues. At the end of this wild march, hordes of lemmings supposedly hurl themselves into the water and drown in a kind of "ritual" suicide. Such behavior would obviously have the effect of drastically reducing population density and, presumably, a few survivors would be left to begin the population expansion anew.

Recent careful observations (reported in Brown, 1966) suggest that this account of lemming death through drowning is greatly exaggerated. Lemmings sometimes show seasonal migration in search of food, mates, or better dwelling areas. However, much of this migration is carried out by solitary animals. Even when in groups, lemmings carefully follow pathways with a protective cover from predators. Arriving at a body of water, they avoid entry unless land can be seen at the other side, and they normally swim for the far shore with heads held high and nostrils kept well out of the water. Some lemmings do miscalculate and drown during windy conditions when they cannot combat high waves, but that is surely not the major cause of large population decreases in the lemming.

Rapid growth of populations within an area must be associated with a high birth rate, good survival in the resident population, or low rates of migration or dispersal. Alternately, rapid decline in population density would be accompanied by high rates of mortality of animals residing in the affected area, extensive migration, or low rates of successful reproduction. Although many factors have been suggested as being responsible for population cycling, and much research has been done, we are still far from understanding this complex phenomenon. Scarcity of critical foods (Lack, 1954), predator pressure (Pearson, 1964), hormonal changes (Christian, 1956) and selective survival of high-aggressive, but poor-reproductive individuals (Chitty, 1957; Krebs, 1972) have all been suggested as mechanisms that could produce the rapid decline of very dense animal populations. These mechanisms are not mutually exclusive, and we might well find two or more factors interacting in a particular case of regulation of population cycling.

---

hierarchies collapse, aggressive behaviors increase, and maternal behaviors become inefficient. In mice, such extreme crowding has been found to affect physiology (Christian, 1956). The adrenal glands become enlarged, and the hormonal balance in females is upset, producing numerous miscarriages in pregnant mice.

We must be cautious in generalizing such artificial, laboratory-based conclusions to the effects of crowding in a natural environment. In some species like the lemming (see Spotlight 24-1), the proposed mechanisms might well operate to control population size, but in most species, adaptive corrections (like splitting into two groups) occur before the unusual densities observed in the laboratory are reached. In the most adaptable of species—human beings—it seems that crowding can be tolerated to a much greater extent than in less flexible animals, largely by making accommodations in the social structure (Freedman, 1971).

What mechanisms contribute to cohesive behavior?

In the social existence of an animal, a great number of activities have been classified as cohesive—they bring the animals together (sex), they make life more secure (evading predation, locating food), or they make specialized individual behaviors more effective (division of responsibility). Such activities

In many species, courtship displays serve to cement pair bonds. A pair of gannets, with necks extended, engages in a "billing" display. Above, a male king penguin extends his beak toward the sky in the beginning of an "ecstatic" display, while the female bends her head downward to preen the abdominal feathers.

have been described in general for various species; more detailed studies of the underlying mechanisms of such activities can increase our understanding of these behaviors. We will focus on courtship and mating and the bonds between parents and offspring, with briefer mention of other cohesive mechanisms.

COURTSHIP AND MATING

The courtship **displays** of animals are certainly among the most beautiful behaviors that can be observed in nature (see photographs). Bird displays are always striking: males strut and dance in colorful plumage, sing intricate and compelling songs, or demonstrate their attractiveness in sweeping and acrobatic flight, and these displays may go on for extended periods before a relatively brief instance of actual copulation. Fish and even lowly spiders engage in similar displays.

The function of such displays is not entirely clear. In hunting spiders, the male displays apparently to identify himself as a member of the species—a potential lover and not a potential meal. The female of such species is typically larger, with strong predatory instincts, so the display triggers innate mechanisms that allow the smaller male to approach and fertilize her eggs. The famous black widow is named in recognition of the fact that the male's identification behaviors are not always as successful as he would hope.

A second function of courtship display is simply to release stereotyped mating behavior (fixed action patterns) in the female. Some students of animal behavior (Armstrong, 1947) liken the function of courtship displays to that of traffic lights at an intersection. Motorists are rather finely tuned to colors in a vertical stand at the street corner. If the color is red, they uniformly stop; if green, they go. Similarly in many animal species, certain specific colors or odors or touches or other stimuli trigger mating behavior that would not otherwise occur. In some species, such as the graylag goose, these stimuli seem to be associated with identification of an individual animal that serves as a basis for pair-bonding that continues beyond mating, even for life.

Among fish, the courtship and mating behavior of the stickleback has been extensively studied (Tinbergen, 1952). (See Figure 23-12.) First the male sets up a territory in which he builds a nest; he defends his territory against intrusion by other males. If a female with a swollen belly (full of eggs) approaches his territory, his protective-hostile behavior is inhibited; his behavior changes radically. He approaches *as if* to attack, but at the last moment, he turns and retreats toward the nest. He repeats this pattern that has been termed a "zigzag dance" several times. With each zigzag the female moves closer and closer to the nest. When she is finally over the nest, the male swims above her and nudges her back with his nose, inducing her to release her eggs; the female then swims away. The male swims over the nest and fertilizes the eggs. He now has full responsibility for the eggs; he defends the nest from predators, and he will provide oxygen for the eggs by rapid fin movements, which keep the water circulating through the nest (Tinbergen, 1952).

The courtship display of the male peacock is legendary. The peacock in full display is a popular sight at zoos, but often only a single bird is in action. In their natural habitat, the peacocks' display is a kind of festive contest held in a large "arena"; several males show their colors at the same time to win the attentions of the peahens. If a peahen is aroused by one of the cocks, she indicates her choice by running to him and pecking the ground in front of him. With his colorful train raised, he turns his back to her. She runs around to his front. He rattles his plumes. After a few repetitions of this behavior sequence, the hen squats and copulation ensues (Armstrong, 1947).

<table>
<tr><td>Varieties of
Reproductive
Behavior</td><td>In primitive animals, asexual reproduction is common. There is no combination of male and female sex cells; a single organism, like an amoeba, simply splits in half, forming two organisms. But in the higher animals, sexual reproduction is more common, and the participation of two individuals has distinct evolutionary advantages for a species. Perhaps most important is the increase in genetic variability produced by combining two different sets of chromosomes; genetic variability in offspring is the basis on which natural selection operates. If it were not for genetic variability, many species would become extinct if their habitat or living conditions changed only slightly.</td></tr>
</table>

In some common land snails, each snail is a true hermaphrodite, because each possesses both male and female reproductive organs. Even though the capacity for self-fertilization exists, these snails reproduce by pairing. In fact, they engage in a stimulating though primitive courtship behavior; on approach, the partners stimulate each other by driving hard darts into the other's soft parts. Soon thereafter, the male part of each snail copulates with the female organs of the other.

One major development of the evolution of reproductive behavior has been the shift from external to internal fertilization. Many fish, like the salmon, rely on external fertilization. Salmon females migrate upstream and release their eggs; the males, following behind, discharge their sperm over the eggs. Such procedures are obviously inefficient. An egg becomes an adult salmon if and only if (1) the egg is alive when the sperm reaches it, (2) the sperm fertilizes the egg, (3) the fertilized egg hatches, and (4) the infant salmon survives such dangers as pollution and predators. Needless to say, millions of eggs produce only a relatively small number of adult salmon.

Even with external fertilization, some fish have developed more efficient means of protecting eggs from potential destruction. The stickleback male protects the eggs. In another kind of fish, the bitterling, the female deposits the eggs inside a live clam and the male fertilizes them there; the clam provides unknowing protection (see Figure 24-4). Fish called grunions reproduce outside the water, on beaches; the eggs hatch almost immediately when the next high tide hits and carries the infants out to sea. Their parents, in the meantime, might have become a meal for enterprising humans who respond to the call, "The grunions are running," and scoop the grunions off the beach before the next large wave can carry them to safety.

In the guppy (Lebistes reticulatus), a popular fish in home aquariums, internal fertilization is followed by live birth of the offspring. The male guppy, smaller and more brightly colored than the female, courts his mate when her belly is swollen with eggs. He swims in front of her while bending his body into an S-shape and "quivers" in this position, checking the females' forward motion. He then swims alongside the female and swings a specialized portion of his ventral fin away from his body and inserts it into the abdomen of the female. This ventral "fin" is known as the gonopodium, which has developed specialized appendage for the delivery of sperm.

Internal fertilization is necessary for live births, but many species that have internal fertilization do not have live births. The eggs of most birds are fertilized internally, but the eggs are laid—as eggs—and must be incubated before birth. The parents are the ones to incubate the eggs, of course, and they protect the eggs at the same time. The evolutionary trend we are describing is essentially toward greater protection of the eggs and the infants, and internal fertilization provides greater protection during a critical period, even if the births are not live. In some fish, a new twist is added; infants (or eggs) live in the mouth of the parent until able to survive independently (see Figure 24-5).

Among marsupials like the kangaroo and the opossum, there is similar protection of the infants after birth. The females of these mammals have pouches containing nipples. The young are born alive through the birth canal and must travel to the pouch to survive. If they reach the pouch in time, they are fed and protected until they are large enough to fend for themselves. A dramatic example of this life-or-death behavior sequence has been described in the American opossum (Hartmann, 1962). The young are born alive but, at birth, they measure no more than a quarter of an inch in length. Because more babies are born than there are nipples in the opossum pouch, the infant opossums race wildly from the birth canal, across the mother's abdomen, to the pouch. These tiny opossums are literally running for their lives, for the last-place finishers are doomed to starvation and death.

Figure 24-4
Bitterling Laying Eggs in Clam
The clam shell provides a secure repository for the developing eggs.

Figure 24-5
Parental Care in Fish
The male Siamese fighting fish (left) catches some eggs that have been displaced in order to return them to his bubble nest. Some species of African fish known as mouthbreeders (right) protect the developing young within the mouth. In the drawing, a mouthbreeder releases its young into the water.

In the primates, including human beings, the reproductive pattern includes internal fertilization, live births, and usually extended care of infants by the mother, at least, and often by the father and other adults as well. These evolutionary developments not only increase the probability that any given egg will develop into a mature adult but also provide a social environment in which learning can replace the less flexible instinctive behaviors of lower animals. The period of extended care for infants favors survival, and it provides the infant with experiences that shape adult behavior patterns in a highly adaptive fashion. Human beings are the most flexible of animals, capable of living in almost any habitat, and this extreme adaptability would not be possible if it were not for reproductive and child-care patterns characteristic of the more highly evolved animals.

Mating Patterns

In the laboratory rat the adult female has a period of sexual attractiveness and receptivity—estrus—that occurs about six hours after ovulation. Most mating occurs at this time, and it is an especially favorable time for fertilization to take place. When an adult male rat is placed with a female rat in estrus, he will approach her, sniffing at her genital region. The female locomotes in short darting movements as the male approaches. The male mounts the female, touching her flanks with his forepaws. At this point, the female stops and assumes a posture known as **lordosis**—her rump is elevated and her tail is moved to the side, permitting insertion of the penis **(intromission).** After intromission, the male dismounts quickly and vigorously, and proceeds to groom his genital region. The female now has several options: she may simply wait until the male's next approach, or she may go to the male and groom or sniff him. After perhaps thirty seconds, the intromission sequence is repeated; after a dozen or so of these intromissions, ejaculation occurs. The period of contact between the animals during ejaculation is perhaps 1.5 seconds and, if this is the first ejaculation, there will be a quiet postejaculatory period lasting approximately 5 minutes before the mating sequence is resumed.

The reasons for this multiple intromission pattern—which occurs in many but not all rodents—are not completely understood. Repeated intromissions are necessary to stimulate the flow of progesterone in the female; and this hormone is necessary for successful implantation of the fertilized egg in the uterine wall (Adler, 1969). Female rats who receive an ejaculation after few intromissions are less likely to become pregnant (Wilson, Adler, & Le Boeuf, 1965). But why some rodent species exhibit this repeated intromission pattern, while others (like the guinea pig) do not, remains a puzzle.

In contrast to the multiple intromission pattern, there is the single intromission pattern, characterized by a prolonged period of repetitive thrusting by the male, usually leading to ejaculation. This pattern can be observed in dogs, monkeys, and, of course, human beings. In all three species the females take an active role in the coital process; they frequently solicit the attention of a male by grooming or by assuming a provocative posture. Often the female of these species will not allow an "unacceptable" male to mate with her—a fact that owners of a prize-winning male dog have often discovered, to their dismay, when trying to breed him with an attractive bitch.

Role of Social Experience

Several studies (for example, Harlow, 1962) lead one to conclude that if some mammals like rats and monkeys are deprived of social contact with their peers during infancy, there is some impairment of their adult sexual behavior. This finding suggests that experience is important in these species. Males who lack the usual early social experience fail to make the normal sequence of properly oriented sexual responses to a sexually receptive female; in the rhesus monkey, the lack of early social contact seems to prevent successful adult performance.

Sexual responses generally depend less on experience in mammals with limited cortical development (the rat, as compared to the monkey); thus sexual performance is generally impaired less in socially deprived rats than in similarly deprived monkeys. Also, the passive sexual responses required of the female of most species are governed more by innate neurological and hormonal systems than the more active "initiating" responses required of the male. Thus, in both rats and monkeys the lack of early social contacts affects male performance more than female sexual behavior. However, these latter conclusions are based primarily on the data gathered by psychologists studying the passive components of the female sex role (for example, lordosis in the rat). Some more recent work stresses the important role that the female mammal plays in initiating copulatory activity (Doty, 1974; Beach, 1976). Further study of these more active components of sex behavior of the female mammal may show that social experience is more important for female mating behavior than had been previously thought.

Sensory Cues in Mating Behavior

In a sexually experienced mammal, information about the receptivity of a partner can arrive through a variety of sense organs such as touch or smell, and the loss of any single sense is not apt to eliminate the behavior. However, recent evidence tends to place particular weight on olfactory stimulation as a prime determinant of the attractiveness of females in the rat, dog, and monkey. In all these species, experienced males have been shown to approach selectively the odors emitted in the urine or the vaginal secretions of females in estrus. If the vaginal secretions of a female rhesus monkey in estrus are smeared on an out-of-estrus female, the male will attempt copulation. The male will persist in his copulatory behavior despite discouragement by the nonreceptive female (Michael, 1971).

Other senses are involved in mating behavior, despite the relative importance of odors for many species. The degree of participation of any sense depends on the species and the stage of the mating process. Auditory cues are often important in early stages; we are all familiar with the yowls of courting domestic cats. The synchronization of auditory and tactile cues can be seen in frogs who aggregate in the spring amid a chorus of vigorous vocalization. The male frogs have grown expanded "thumbs" during the preceding months, and these "nuptial pads" are used to clasp the female's sides, stimulating her to release a group of eggs, which will then be externally fertilized by the male. However, male frogs make mistakes during this process and frequently mount and clasp other males. Under these conditions, the clasped male emits a "release call," which signals the offending male, now informed of his error, to move on.

Because vision is an important sense in primates, visual cues are significant in primate mating behaviors. In many primate species, estrous females develop prominent reddish swellings of the skin in the vaginal region. Such swellings can be used by potential mates (and by human primatologists) as indices of sexual receptivity. These swellings are, however, not characteristic of all primates; in some forest-dwelling African monkeys of the genus *Myopithecus*, the sexual skin is much reduced in size. It has been suggested that in the dense forests where their lines of sight are limited, the adaptive advantages of visual signaling of sexual state may be somewhat reduced (Rowell, 1971).

Hormonal Mechanisms

It is clear that the development of normal sexuality in the vertebrates depends on the presence of appropriate hormones. Hormones affect almost every aspect of anatomy and physiology underlying sexual differences of a species, and they play a significant role in the specific mating behaviors. Estrus, for example, depends on hormonal cycles in the female. (*See* pp. 564ff. for a more complete discussion of the biology of sexual behavior.)

Sex hormones are produced mostly in the testes of the male and in the ovaries of the female. If the gonads (testes or ovaries) are removed from a vertebrate, effects on sexual behavior can usually be observed, although the extent of the effect varies greatly among species, between the sexes within species, and among animals of different ages. Early removal of the gonads generally has more profound effects on adult structure and behavior than adult gonadectomies. Among species, the effects of surgery in adult mammals are greater in species with proportionately smaller and simpler cerebral cortexes; rats are affected much more than humans. Indeed, in humans, it is often difficult to observe any effect on reproductive behavior whatsoever if the testes or ovaries of an experienced adult are removed. Such findings have led many investigators (for example, Beach, 1948) to hypothesize an evolutionary trend toward decreasing hormonal control of mating, with a correlated increase in the importance of experience.

Some theorists carry this speculation even farther, suggesting that the relatively permanent pair-bonding found in human beings is an indirect result of freedom from the hormonal control of sex. In rats and other infraprimate mammals, mating activity in females is tightly bound to hormonal cycles. However, the human female is physiologically capable of attracting and accepting a male at any time in the hormonal cycle. Thus, sexual behavior can act as a reinforcement and help to maintain the pair bond at all times (Eibl-Eibesfeldt, 1975). This theory of the roots of human socialization is certainly an interesting variant on the theme that sex serves a purely reproductive function, but it is difficult to imagine how one could actually test the theory.

Homo sapiens is not the only primate species whose mating is not strictly bound to the ovulatory cycle of the female. Young and Orbison (1944) found that mating in chimpanzees was frequently more dependent on the details of the general social relationship between the male and the female than the specific stage of the female's ovulatory cycle. Such freedom from the hormonal bond has also been observed in many African monkeys (Rowell, 1971), but most copulatory activity clearly tends to take place during a particular phase of the ovulatory cycle.

PARENT-OFFSPRING BONDS

In some fish the care of the fertilized eggs is the sole responsibility of the male. We have discussed one such pattern in the stickleback. In the beautiful Siamese fighting fish, the male builds a bubble nest at the water surface with mucus-like secretions from his mouth. Once the nest is constructed, he induces the female to lay her eggs in the nest. After she does so, he drives her away and will not tolerate her presence in the vicinity of the nest (see Figure 24-5).

It is interesting to note a difference in nest-building behavior between the stickleback and the Siamese fighting fish. The stickleback builds the nest at the bottom of the stream, whereas the Siamese bubble nest is constructed at the surface. To get oxygen to the eggs, the stickleback must "fan" them with its fins. This would not be possible for the Siamese fighting fish, for it lives in streams that do not have adequate oxygen; it must surface at regular intervals to gulp air. If it built its nest at the bottom, even assuming the eggs could survive, it would have to leave them unguarded during its trips to the surface. Thus its surface nest is a necessary adaptation to the environment, providing oxygen for both father and eggs and permitting continued protection for the eggs.

Males and females in many birds share the responsibility of caring for the eggs and the young. We have discussed this in the case of the penguin (p. 673). However, in mammals, where there are live births and extended periods of infant care, the primary responsibility for the offspring almost always falls to the female. The general relation between mother and infant can be seen as going through three stages (Schneirla & Rosenblatt, 1961): in the first, contact is initiated primarily by the mother; in the second, there is mutual approach behavior; in the third, the infant approaches but the mother "rejects," leading to eventual independence of the offspring. The timing of this process in the cat is shown in Figure 24-6.

In primates, unrelated adults often exhibit an interest in infants. If the unrelated adult is a female, this is called **aunt behavior.** The aunt is typically a childless female in the mother's group. At first her interest in the infant is resented by the mother, but gradually the two cooperate in child care—interactions that have obvious survival value for the infant. Should the mother die, for example, the aunt usually "adopts" the infant as her own. It has also been observed that the presence of an aunt affects the interaction of mother and infant; with aunts present, mothers are less likely to reject their infants, probably because the infants depend less on the mother for all their needs (Hinde & Spencer-Booth, 1967).

Figure 24-6
Stages of Mother-Infant Interaction in Cats
The initiation of feeding is first characterized by maternal approach, then by mutual approach, and finally reaches a stage where the kitten's attempts to initiate feeding are as frequent as mutual approaches. (From Schneirla & Rosenblatt, 1961)

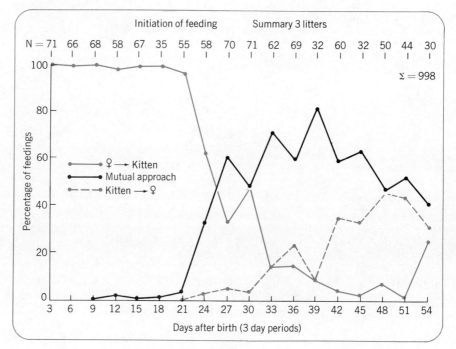

Parent-young interactions are shown in several species. Under appropriate conditions, adult male rhesus monkeys protect infants, as seen below. The lioness (right) keeps her infant separate from the pride for a few months after its birth; during this period there is intensive mother-infant interaction. The infant langur (below, right) must grasp the mother's fur actively and strongly in order to travel with her.

Uncle behavior has been observed in Japanese macaques (Itani, 1959). Adult males become interested in infants who are more than a year old; the adult male will hug the infant, sit with it, and protect it from danger. The females at this time have entered a new birth season and cease protecting last year's baby, so the infant with no uncle would probably not survive. But, as is typical in primate interactions, uncle behavior has other functions as well. Just to name one, an uncle who protects an infant of parents in a higher caste — these primates have a strict caste system — is tolerated by the leaders of the higher caste; he may therefore rise in social status. Another interesting fact is that uncle behavior is observed in only some macaque troops; it was common in only 3 of the 18 troops studied, and not observed at all in 8. It therefore appears to be a local cultural tradition, learned and passed on generation to generation, although this conclusion remains highly speculative. It does seem clear, however, is that monkey troops with uncles have an adaptive advantage; their "protected" infants have a much greater chance of survival.

NEST-BUILDING

Thus far we have been discussing mother-infant and adult-infant bonds in broad terms. It is now appropriate to consider some of the more important specific response patterns involved. For example, constructing nests for sleeping is a year-round activity for many mammals, but in the hours preceding the delivery of young, this activity is frequently intensified.

In the interaction of inherited and learned components of nest-building in the female rat we see another demonstration of the fact that strict nativist or empiricist positions are inadequate to deal with observed behavior (*see* pp. 458–65, 612). Some years ago a psychologist reported that although female rats typically build nests for their young on their very first exposure to a nest-building situation, their behavior is strongly influenced by prior experience (Riess, 1950). In rats deprived of the opportunity to manipulate objects (such as food, other rats) before giving birth, nest-building in a test cage was severely impaired. This study, however, was criticized on several counts (Eibl-Eibesfeldt, 1961). First, by moving the mother rat to a test cage for observation of nest-building, the investigator introduced the possibility that strong competing responses, such as exploration, would interfere with building. Moreover, rats would be unlikely to build nests in an open wire-mesh cage under any circumstances; in natural settings, they build nests only in enclosed protected areas.

When the experiment was replicated in a more naturalistic nesting environment, rats that had been deprived of manipulative experience built nests on their first opportunity. Still, some obvious deficits remained in the nest-building behavior. The inexperienced mothers made many more trips than necessary to get building materials; they performed acts out of sequence, and they would sometimes carry strips of paper to the nest, yet fail to release them from their mouths. So again, we have a demonstration, in a rather primitive mammal engaged in a complex activity, that instinctive *and* learned components interact to produce the response pattern observed in the usual situation. Neither a strict nativist nor a strict empiricist position can explain the behavior.

RETRIEVAL BEHAVIOR

If an infant mammal strays from the mother or nest area, generally it is quickly retrieved to more secure grounds. The cues eliciting retrieval behavior have been most closely analyzed in common laboratory rodents: mice, rats, and hamsters. Originally the attempts at analysis involved surgical interference with one sense or another; the animals were blinded or deafened or they were prevented from tasting or smelling. A systematic set of such studies led to the conclusion that deficits in retrieval behavior were proportional to the number of sensory systems eliminated (Beach & Jaynes, 1956). All senses seem to play some role.

More recently, investigators have begun exploring the role of sensory cues that previous work had completely overlooked. It has been shown that a primary cue eliciting retrieval in many rodents is an ultrasonic cry emitted by the errant pup (Noirot, 1966). These cries went unnoticed for many years for a very good reason: human experimenters could not hear them. The frequency range was far above the upper threshold for human hearing, and electronic instruments were necessary for people to detect these sounds.

Retrieval of infant rats and mice by the mother is most frequently observed in the first two weeks or so after birth, after which it decreases rapidly. This behavior change is highly (but not perfectly) correlated with the decrease in ultrasonic signaling from the pup. The decrease in responsiveness in the mother to her litter is caused by a change in the stimuli coming to her from the pups. This interpretation fits not only retrieval but can be applied to other behaviors — licking, nursing, and nest-building — as well.

OTHER COHESIVE RELATIONS

Infant-Infant

Cohesion in complex social groups involves many relations besides those in mating or parental behavior. Among the most important are the interactions of infants and juveniles that we call "play." In primates the young spend much of their day in play groups, play-fighting, jumping, running, threatening, chasing, exploring strange objects, and "practicing" sex (see Figure 24-7). No doubt these interactions lead to certain cohesive bonds between playmates, but the biological significance of play remains somewhat of a mystery. A nineteenth-century investigator (Groos, 1898) hypothesized that the function of play in mammals was to prepare the infant for adult behavior; play was seen as practice for activities that would eventually occur in a more serious context. This argument is appealing — it *sounds* so obviously correct — but there is not a lot of empirical evidence to support it. For some unknown reason, we have very little systematic data on play in mammals (including human beings), so speculation proceeds without the benefit of limitation by facts.

Assuming that the play-as-practice hypothesis is at least partly accurate, one can cite several observations that fit. We have already mentioned evidence that an infant mammal deprived of the opportunity to play will likely become an adult deficient in sexual behavior (p. 680) or predatory behavior (p. 670). These data fit, but social isolation during infancy is a rather complex and severe intervention; one cannot be sure that the lack of play is the only, or even the most important, factor. Another fact compatible with the play-as-practice hypothesis is the difference between the play of the two sexes, which often foreshadows differences in the behavior of male and female adults. The play of young males, for example, is often more rough-and-tumble and aggressive, at least in primates, and this is in keeping with their more aggressive role as adults.

Figure 24-7
Play in Young Gorillas

Some gorilla play takes place while the juveniles are alone and in the trees. Other play patterns are of a more social nature, as in the bottom drawing, which Schaller (1967) describes as a "snake dance."

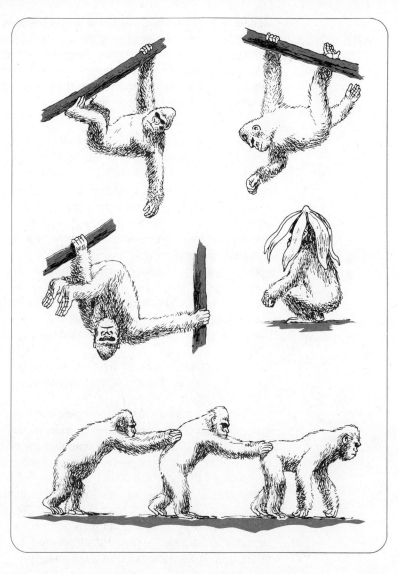

Play is also, very simply, good exercise, and the absence of playful behavior is often a sign of illness or retardation. Another function of play is exploration. Many primate juveniles choose to play with moderately unfamiliar objects, animate and inanimate; their experience with a variety of environmental events results in learning that is useful in later life. (It should be noted, however, that extremely novel objects will typically elicit fear and withdrawal rather than interest and approach. But this too can be seen in terms of survival advantage.)

Finally, many investigators have noted that by playing, the young receive practice in the communication patterns they will have to know as adults (Mason, 1960). Juveniles in play groups often have occasion to try out or respond to alarm calls, sexual invitations, threat gestures, and all the other myriad signals that do so much to bond group members together. They can do this in relative safety; while at play they are not usually allowed to stray into real danger, and their calls are often false alarms. The alarm call of a juvenile produces only mild interest in adults, who are content merely to satisfy themselves that no real danger exists and that the cry has been elicited, as is typical, by an unexpected but harmless object.

Adult-Adult

If play is the major interaction of infants with infants, **grooming** is probably the most time-consuming activity observed in relations between adult primates (*see* photographs). This behavior has an immediately apparent goal — cleanliness; the various bugs, parasites, burrs, and clots of dirt picked up in a day's march with a primate group are cleared away. An animal with a wound presents itself more often for grooming, and many observers have noted a relationship between the seriousness of the wound and the amount of grooming received (Simonds, 1965).

But grooming is also clearly much more than a cleaning behavior; it is a friendly social interaction, and both the opportunity to be groomed *and* to groom can be used as an effective reinforcer for laboratory chimpanzees. One psychologist was able to train a chimp to press a lever for nothing more than the privilege of grooming *the psychologist's arm* (Falk, 1958). Grooming is also related to sexual relations. One male baboon with a large secure harem was never observed grooming the females, but when he grew older and lost most of his females, he conscientiously groomed the two he was able to retain (Kummer & Kurt, 1965).

In the wild hamadryas baboon described at the beginning of this chapter, grooming accounts for a major portion of the social interactions (Kummer, 1968). About 20 percent of the time that these animals were observed above the sleeping rock, they were either grooming or being groomed, far larger percentages than for all sexual and aggressive behaviors combined (around 1 percent). Grooming was also prominent in the wild chimpanzees studied by Jane Goodall (1965). Other kinds of tactile contacts observed in chimpanzees ranged from simply putting an arm on another chimp to those that could be called "kissing." The contact seemed to indicate interest and friendly intent, and it also appeared to allay anxiety.

In mammals like cats and rodents, licking and grooming with the teeth are common. Such behaviors are seen in maternal behavior toward babies after birth, before copulation, and even preceding aggression. It appears that one class of behavior can serve many different functions.

Sensory Cues

Auditory signals and olfactory cues must also play a significant role in group cohesion, although the precise function of these cues has been studied little. Several species of monkeys participate in regular periods of very loud calling that occur every day. Howler monkeys, who of course get their name from such behavior, have a specially developed vocal apparatus, and they use their howls for aggressive encounters, for indicating troop movement, and apparently to show clan identity. When two groups of males meet in the jungle, they have what some have described as a "shouting contest"; the losers shut up

Grooming is a fundamental cohesion-promoting behavior in primates. These photos show grooming in three different social contexts. The female langur (above, left) carefully grooms the back of her partner. A male baboon (above) grooms a female carrying an infant, and, in a family group of bonnet macaques (left), the female grooms the adult male.

and move on (Carpenter, 1965). They also have a regular morning howling period, in which one member starts to howl and others join—almost as if the urge were **contagious**—until the hills are alive with the sound of raucous barks and shrieks. The periodic howling probably serves to maintain a kind of auditory territory for the clan, trumpeting security for the clan member and warning potential intruders.

Calling also serves similar functions in some wild rodents. Prairie dog social organizations consist of small groups that combine to form "towns" of several thousand animals (King, 1955). (*See* photograph.) A great deal of calling occurs within the smaller familial units and also between groups in the town. These cohesion calls are replaced by alarm calls if an airborne predator appears, and the "news" is spread rapidly on the prairie dog "grapevine." When the predator disappears, an "all-clear" call communicates this fact, and social calling resumes.

In mammals like the rodents where olfaction is a dominant sense, it is to be expected that olfactory cues could be used to promote cohesion. Many rodents have specialized glands for **scent-marking;** the rabbit has one on the underside of his chin, hamsters on their flanks, and gerbils on the abdominal surface. When these body areas are rubbed against objects in the environment, an oily substance is deposited on the objects. In many mammals, urine and feces are also used to mark a territory, as anyone who regularly walks a dog can attest.

If you consider the amount of potential information in scents, you can understand why most psychologists attribute multiple functions to scent-marking. The sex of the animal, the age, the health, and, in females, the stage of the estrous cycle can be determined from the smell. One theorist proposes that scents serve to describe a population; a male can determine the number of estrous females and the number (and health) of rivals in the vicinity (Wynne-Edwards, 1962). Another suggests that, in wolves at least, scents define territory and "legitimize" the leader; in many species, dominant males do most of the marking (Schenkel, 1947).

Sexual communication through scent-marking is observed in many species. A female dog in estrus increases her urination rate markedly and thus leaves small advertisements for herself throughout her home range. All of us with male cats are aware of their "spraying" behavior; it seems to serve a dual function, to warn other males and to attract females in estrus.

Finally, scent deposits possibly function as landmarks or "memory devices." Rats will follow an odor trail, for example, in a maze. Urination and defecation in a strange place make it more familiar upon return. Fear-induced urination and defecation, of course, are responses to extremely novel environments, and many psychologists have suggested that these involuntary responses were the original source of scent-marking. The evolution of the behavior toward

King (1955) identifies the "coterie" as the basic social unit of prairie-dog society. Both the cohesion of this kind of group and the upright, attentive posture so characteristic of this species are evident here.

more deliberate and voluntary control allows for more diversified use in social organization. Nevertheless, novel stimuli remain one of the primary releasers to deliberate scent-marking in many species (Kleiman, 1966).

Aggression and Dominance

We usually think of aggression and threats as behaviors that lead to dispersion, but within groups these behaviors are often used to promote cohesion. The male leader of a hamadryas baboon group enforces close following in his females by means of a graduated series of aggressive signals ranging from a discouraging stare to a vicious neck bite for recalcitrant offenders (Kummer, 1968).

Dominance hierarchies, found in many species, promote cohesion and efficiency by providing established answers to several questions. Who eats first? Who leads? Who copulates? Military ranks have a somewhat similar function in the armed forces.

Some of the first work on social hierarchies was done on domestic chickens who set up a rather clear "pecking order" (Schjelderup-Ebbe, 1935). On first acquaintance, chickens fight frequently, but soon the winners are recognized, and a simple threat is enough to chase a bird of lower status away. A dominant animal can even peck another without being pecked in return. The chicken hierarchy is linear, that is, if A is dominant over B, and B is dominant over C, A is dominant over C. This is not always the case in other species.

Discovering a dominance hierarchy in wild animals is not so easy to observe, because the existence of the hierarchy tends to prevent the appearance of precisely those behaviors, such as aggression, that provide the clearest measures of dominance. Because dominance is difficult to determine under natural conditions, many studies of dominance hierarchies have been carried out with animals in captivity, where small enclosures, moderately high population densities, and manipulation of the food supply can promote the frequent social interactions from which we can infer the dominance hierarchy. However, even in situations where dominance hierarchies exist, different measures of "dominance" may yield a variable picture of social interactions within the group. In a caged group of baboons, there was a significant difference between dominance orders determined on the basis of "who threatened whom" and dominance orders characterized by "who was friendly with whom" (Rowell, 1971). So, even under conditions where close observation is possible, what behavior one observes influences his or her estimate of the dominance hierarchy.

In wild animals whose social organization includes dominance hierarchies, these status arrangements probably have several functions. The dominance hierarchy of elephant seals reduces intragroup aggression—after the hierarchy is established—and it promotes the survival of the species by the fact that dominant males—the strongest, healthiest, and most courageous—do most of the copulating when the cows arrive. In the savannah baboon described at the beginning of this chapter, nondominant males are not allowed to copulate frequently. They nevertheless play a vital social role as food-gatherers and sentries from their positions at the periphery of the troop and may get opportunities to mate when they are older.

What mechanisms underlie dispersal behavior?

Within a species, the degree of dispersion or spacing often depends on food resources. This is one explanation of why some baboons are found in large troops and others forage in smaller, one-male groups. Many animals will also defend territory against other members of the species; lions will literally kill intruders, whereas howler monkeys take the more civilized approach of just out-shouting their rivals.

In considering dispersion more broadly, relations between species must also be considered. Two concepts are paramount: avoidance and aggression. The nature of aggression will be our central concern here, but it should be recognized that avoidance behaviors are crucial too—especially for animals that are the natural prey. Many animals will allow the approach of a predator or a strange object (such as the ethologist's truck) up to a rather closely defined distance; then they flee. These flight distances have been studied extensively by the Swiss zoologist H. Hediger (1955). In general, smaller species of animals have shorter flight distances than larger species. A small wall lizard will tolerate closer approach by man than a large crocodile. In addition, where animals have been protected from predation by man, as in national parks, their flight distance is gradually reduced. Flight distances may also be correlated with the relative speeds of the two animals; thus the antelope will let a tiger approach only to a certain distance—slightly farther than the distance the tiger can leap—for in open chase, the antelope has a great advantage (Schaller, 1967).

TYPES OF AGGRESSION

Aggression is one of the most diversely defined words in all of psychology, including everything from ambition to "cold-blooded murder." At the least, we must describe three classifications: competitive, protective, and predatory aggression. These are the most common types of aggressive behaviors in the world of animals.

Competitive Aggression

One can commonly observe aggression, usually within a given species, that results from competition for food resources, mates, or land. In the classic case, the fight is over all three simultaneously. The male robin establishes a territory within which he will mate and rear his offspring. He will attack any intruding object with a red breast, which in nature is usually another male robin—although in the yard of a comparative psychologist may be an inanimate object designed to study the sign stimuli eliciting aggression in the robin.

The concept of **territory** in which the animal feeds and breeds has an interesting history. That animals seem to "carve out" home grounds and defend them against intruders has been noticed for centuries, even idealized in poems, plays, and novels. Over 2,000 years ago Aristotle made mention of the phenomenon. The scientific concept is usually credited to Howard (1920), who discussed its evolutionary advantages, especially those to newborn birds. Since then territorial defense has been observed in ants, bees, fish, lizards, seals, deer, monkeys, and apes, just to name a few (Armstrong, 1947). Some writers have extended the concept to human beings, suggesting that phrases like

A pair of male elephant seals are fighting to claim breeding dominance.

"home turf" (as used by juvenile gangs) and "a man's home is his castle" reflect human territoriality. Some have even suggested the need for territorial possession as the root of all aggression, including human aggression (Ardrey, 1966).

The problem with the concept in its more extravagant forms is that it has become so broad as to be virtually incapable of disproof. There is, first of all, a trend toward defining territory even in cases where the territory *moves*. The anemone fish is so named because it adopts a living sea-anemone as its territory; immune to the poisonous darts of the anemone, it lives, breeds, and feeds in the tangle of anemone tentacles; it vigorously defends its home turf against intruders. But its territory, being alive, floats and swims around, so its home is here one day, there the next (Eibl-Eibesfeldt, 1975).

Though the behavior of the anemone fish may reasonably be described by extending the concept of territoriality, the concept has been invoked to explain quite unterritoriallike behaviors. An interesting example of nonterritorial competitive aggression is found in the northern elephant seal. In one study, these animals were observed from the time of their arrival at an island near Santa Cruz, California. Soon after they arrive on the island early in December each year, the elephant seal bulls begin fighting and threatening one another. Unlike fur seals, who fight only to defend their "territory," the elephant seal bulls fight to determine dominance. The most dominant bulls do most of the copulating after the elephant seal cows arrive late in December and thus father most of the pups born the following year (Le Boeuf, 1971).

From an evolutionary point of view, there is a significant advantage to the species if the strongest and healthiest bulls are those who reproduce, for this helps assure the survival and adaptation of the species. Establishing the dominance hierarchy by threat and fighting reduces the need for active battle once the cows arrive; once the hierarchy is established a threatening gesture from a dominant bull is usually sufficient to drive away a competitor, leaving the dominant seal to copulate with the cow. The elephant seal does not have a home turf; it fights only to establish a dominance hierarchy. This is true of many other animals, too, for example, the elk (p. 671). The true believer in the territory-and-aggression hypothesis, when faced with such facts, resorts to the "mobile territory" explanations supported by studies like those of the anemone fish; "personal space"—apparently the air surrounding the animal's body—is its territory. In these extreme formulations, territorial defense does not differ from individual defense.

Protective Aggression

If a predator enters the vicinity of an animal or his group, the prey will often resort to aggression for protection. It might flee, if possible, fight if not—the "cornered rat" phenomenon. I have discussed some cases of protective aggression already—for example, the mobbing reactions of smaller birds. As I write this, two male bluejays are dive-bombing an intruding cat outside my window; jays are well known for their **sympathetic reactions** to the scolding shrieks of other jays (Armstrong, 1947). They fly over to help and then quickly leave, for the resident jay might well turn on them after the predator is banished.

Competitive and protective aggression often take different forms in the same species. The male American elk uses its antlers in combat with other males during the mating season, but to attack a predator it will most likely rely on his sharp hooves. The odoriferous defense of the skunk (*see* photograph) and the prickly defense of the porcupine are common examples of specialized protec-

The Eastern striped skunk has a highly stereotyped set of threat responses, which are generally evident prior to expulsion of its infamous odor. In this photo, all three animals show the tail erection and "fluffing" of the hair that characterizes the basic pattern. In addition, the animal on the left is "thumping" forward with its forepaws, while the skunk in the middle has pulled back from this position, drawing some straw under its body.

tive defense mechanisms. In primates, protective aggression often takes the form of throwing or dropping branches or even feces at the intruder, something rarely witnessed in competitive aggression.

Predatory Aggression

Predatory aggression is more properly classified as feeding behavior, but because many insist on viewing predation as aggressive we will briefly mention this category of behaviors. Again, the behaviors in this class are generally quite different from those in other categories of aggression. Cats provide a good example. The predatory pattern of most cats includes crouching, stalking, and pouncing, with an absolute minimum of sounds. In contrast, when fighting another cat or when facing a belligerent member of another species, we see the classic "Halloween" cat: spitting and hissing, with arched back, and clawing with extended claws at the opponent.

RESEARCH ON AGGRESSION

There are two primary approaches to understanding animal aggression. The first approach is that of Lorenz, whose hydraulic model of motivation was discussed in Chapter 23, p. 637. From this vantage point, aggression is seen as resulting from an innate drive; its manifestation is therefore inevitable and will occur either directly or will find expression in some apparently nonaggressive activity. At the other extreme, there is the perspective that aggressive behaviors are like any others, learned on the basis of rewards and extinguished by non-reinforcement. Within this latter view, animals (or people) will only be aggressive when such behavior enables them to gain access to some desired reward (such as food or a mate), or removes a source of discomfort. These two "theories" of aggression lead to very different conclusions about how to control violence in human society. Adherents of the instinctive "energy-reservoir" view would argue that because the behavior is inevitable, the best tactic is to redirect the energy into some socially acceptable activity—such as competitive sports. Alternatively, the learning model suggests that aggressive behavior patterns will not be acquired or performed if we (1) minimize the competitive, frustrating circumstances that produce it, and (2) arrange for aggression not to be rewarded. In actual fact, very few psychologists today hold strictly to one extreme view over the other, but understanding the two approaches can sometimes help us to understand the behavior of human researchers in studying aggression.

Effects of Isolation

If you assume that aggression is an innate drive that must be periodically satisfied, then you would expect social isolation to result in increased aggression when two animals are put together after weeks without opportunity to aggress. This is indeed what happens. In fact, investigators with no interest in the hydraulic theories of aggression commonly use isolation to produce aggressive interactions so they can study, for example, the effect of various tranquilizing drugs.

However, it is by no means clear that isolation-induced aggression supports the hydraulic theories of motivation. Isolation is a severe treatment and involves much more than the lack of opportunity to aggress. For example, if isolation starts early in life, it also means the animal has not had opportunity to learn the complex interpersonal communications that in many species are designed to avoid overt aggression, and it has not learned its place in a dominance hierarchy. An even simpler explanation is based on skin sensitivity. Animals in isolation, because of the lack of normal contacts with the animate and inanimate environment, might become quite sensitive to even affectionate grooming when later paired with another animal. If the grooming is now painful, the previously isolated animal would thus respond with pain-induced protective aggression. Many humans have noted that skin deprived of normal contact with the environment—after wearing a cast some weeks, for example—becomes unusually sensitive, and a normally pleasant experience like a massage may be painful for a time following the removal of the cast.

Hormonal Control

In the vast majority of animals that have been studied, the male hormone testosterone has been linked to aggressiveness. Animals deprived of this hormone, especially early in life, tend to place low in adult dominance hierarchies. But the overall picture is quite a bit more complicated. Most females become aggressive if their young are threatened, and these behaviors seem to result from a complex mix of changes in hormonal balance—in particular an increase in the female hormones, estrogen and progesterone—coupled with environmental stimuli such as the presence of the young.

To complicate matters further, in some species the female is typically the more aggressive; in mammals, hamsters are an example. The female hamster will ordinarily drive the male from her presence. She is the larger of the pair and quite capable of imposing her wishes in the interaction. During estrus, however, she becomes relatively docile and receptive. After estrus, she drives the male away again.

Sensory Cues

Adult aggression is very often triggered by specific sensory cues. In rodents, olfactory cues play an important role, and the elimination of the ability to detect odors may also eliminate aggressive behavior. In birds, visual cues are frequently sign stimuli releasing attack patterns, as we mentioned in the case of the robin and the "red breast" stimulus.

Male red-winged blackbirds use the red bars on their wings to threaten and hopefully intimidate other males (*see* Figure 24-8). If they are deprived of their red bars of courage (by some dispassionate human experimenter with a

Figure 24-8
Structural Correlates of "Threat"
The red breast feathers of the robin (left) and the red wing markings of the blackbird serve a communicatory function, warning potential rivals to avoid the resident's territory.

can of black paint), they cannot hold their territory against intruders. Thus, in this case, the sensory cue is not so much an elicitor of aggression in other birds as it is a component of the total picture that enables the resident bird to maintain his territory—often without requiring actual combat.

Monkeys have a complex set of visual and auditory cues related to aggression. These cues range from facial expressions that can communicate anything from "be careful" to "be ready for immediate attack" and even "I submit," to a series of auditory calls of similar flexibility.

How do adult animals come to "understand" and utilize these cues? Are reactions to specific stimuli inborn, or do animals have to learn the language during early experiences? Certainly the answers vary among species, but rarely do they support exclusively the nativist or empiricist position; typically some components of the complex behavior patterns are instinctive and some are dependent on experience, and interactions are everywhere. Monkeys raised in isolation get into more fights than do normally raised monkeys. The isolation-raised animals recognize aggression situations, but they fail to respond properly to the signals that normal monkeys use to reduce the incidence of overt aggressive behaviors (Mason, 1960). (See Figure 24-9.)

Figure 24-9
Communication in Primates
Primates can communicate through facial expression and posture. *A, B,* and *C* portray facial expressions and posture characteristic of "fear" or "submission"; *D, E,* and *F* show expressions and posture indicative of threat or high dominance status in rhesus monkeys.

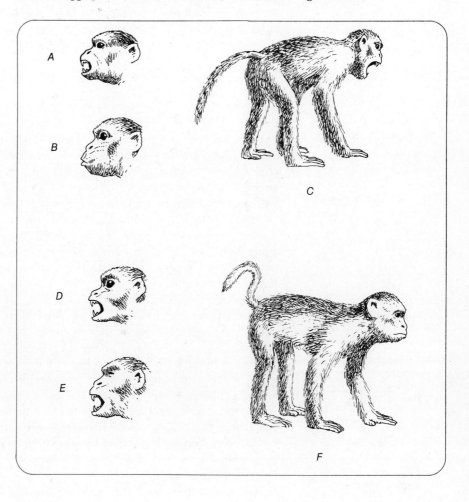

Aggression as Reward

The opportunity to aggress can often be used as a reinforcement. The Siamese fighting fish, which is characterized by its general aggressiveness and fighting displays, can be trained to do tricks if his response is followed by exposure to an intruding male. (The "intruding male" can even be himself. Siamese fighting fish have been trained using the reward of a mirror placed against the tank, in which the fish sees himself and displays in a threatening fashion; his "opponent," of course, does so simultaneously.) Similarly, roosters can be trained to peck at a target if that pecking is followed by the sight of another rooster toward whom the training rooster can perform his aggressive display (Thompson, 1964).

What should we make of these findings? Those theorists who claim that aggression is an innate drive see these results as support for their hypothesis, and the facts do fit with such assumptions. Opponents of such views, however, point out that aggressive interactions will retain their reinforcing effect only if the animal does not *lose* in the encounter. Some have suggested that aggressive behaviors are only secondarily reinforcing; they may be associated with primary rewards at a very early age. For example, in mammals with multiple births—like rats and dogs—the young compete for access to the nipples. Aggression often allows a newborn to pursue such truly innate goals as sucking at its mother's nipple from which it has just banished an infant rival.

What can we learn about human social behavior from comparative psychology?

Can the findings and concepts derived from animal social behavior be applied directly to the analysis of human social interactions? A number of ethologists and comparative psychologists think so, and works by Lorenz (*On Aggression*), Ardrey (*The Territorial Imperative*), Morris (*The Naked Ape*), Tiger and Fox (*The Imperial Animal*) and Morgan (*The Descent of Women*) are speculative attempts to discern animal behavior patterns in humans. In most of these books, we can recognize the traditional conceptual tools of the animal behaviorist. Investigators seek to find fixed action patterns and attempt to identify more or less innate releasers or sign stimuli; social organization is seen in terms of adaptation to a particular habitat and its evolutionary advantages. Whether or not these concepts contribute much to the understanding of human behavior is an issue of controversy.

FIXED ACTION PATTERNS

Are there fixed action patterns in humans? Agreement is almost universal on certain responses. No matter whether one calls them simple reflexes or instinctive behavior, the human baby is known to respond, without learning, to the nipple by sucking and to touches of the palm by clasping. Serious controversy begins at the level of more complex behaviors; smiling is a good example. Children, even blind children, smile when satisfied, and this behavior appears to please mothers and tighten the mother-child bond. According to Eibl-Eibesfeldt (1975), even when the smile comes under partial voluntary control, it is used as an effective signal of appeasement in every known human culture. In the context of a threat, it is supposed to "turn off" aggressive behavior from another human.

The opponents of such a view, however, note studies showing that smiling behavior not only varies between countries but also that, within the United States, the smiles in one subculture are apt to be misinterpreted by people residing in different cultural habitats (Birdwhistell, 1963, 1966). One can hold a compromise position by saying that smiling may be a universal signal of appeasement—*within* a culture or subculture—but also that the behavior in its specific form adapts to the particular social environment in which it must be integrated, so that the signal from one culture could be misinterpreted in another. In other words, both instinct and the effects of experience in a culture affect the precise form of the response.

Eibl-Eibesfeldt also claims that rapid raising and lowering of the eyebrows is a human fixed action pattern, characterizing friendly greetings between people. There are other patterns of social interaction that Eibl-Eibesfeldt believes to be species-characteristic, but which may not actually appear in all human cultures. "Flirting" would be one of these behavior sequences. The absence of such behavior may be attributed to **cultural overlay,** when learning overcomes instinctive reactions. This ploy makes the original hypothesis virtually incapable of empirical test, because both the presence and the absence of the FAP are readily explained.

AGGRESSIVE BEHAVIOR

Many popular books have focused on the roots of human aggression, most specifically those of Ardrey (1966), Lorenz (1966), and Tiger and Fox (1971). They assume a powerful division of sex roles in people as a part of our evolutionary heritage. Human males, who evolved for group hunting, are supposed to establish a "home ground" and defend it aggressively against potential intruders; they fight for castle, water, and sources of food. These propositions are not unreasonable in the light of human history, but they are not based on systematic data gathered in observations of human interactions. In fact, one can produce a feminist theory of human evolution by drawing upon a different set of anecdotes or facts. Elaine Morgan has outlined just such a system in her book, *The Descent of Woman* (1972).

Lorenz argues for the inevitability of aggression, as encompassed in his hydraulic theory of motivation. According to Lorenz, to live in peace, men must have outlets for aggression—sport hunting or ritualized contests like football games. And they must broaden their view of "clan" and territory to include more people. Most important, they must learn to recognize the sign stimuli that release aggression, in order to more consciously control them. These stimuli include a threatened in-group, a hated out-group, an inspirational leader, and a number of people acting aggressively in concert (contagion).

Lorenz also speculates about why human males are almost unique among animals in killing members of their own species. He declares that weapons—tools that make people capable of swift and efficient elimination—produce the killing. If all wars were fought without weapons, few would die, mainly because we lack the sharp claws and powerful teeth of other predators; it is quite difficult to kill someone with your bare hands. Mammals with claws and teeth, Lorenz points out, have evolved strong inhibitions against killing a member of their own species. When a wolf loses in combat, it will exhibit a submissive gesture such as exposing its neck, and the victorious wolf—who could kill with a single bite—turns away. In people, no such inhibitions developed, for, with their puny natural weapons, they were unnecessary. But with artificial weapons, we have the power without the usual controls—and this is a deadly combination. Lorenz likens the human predicament to that of a hypothetical dove who, by some cruel and unnatural trick of nature, suddenly acquires the powerful beak of a raven.

According to this view, the human male is an aggressive animal with powerful weapons and few inhibitions. Even so, Lorenz is optimistic about the chances of reducing or eliminating war. Recognition of the nature of the beast, he argues, will permit us to establish artificial controls to go with our artificial weapons. Space flight may be helpful because it promotes the view of the whole earth as one's territory. He also commends the advantages of humor and satire in subtly identifying the unreasoning biological nature of human aggression. What Lorenz says might be true or it might not; there does not seem to be any objective way of testing his statements.

Criticisms of Lorenz and Ardrey are many-faceted; without an empirical base, it is as easy to criticize as it is to state. Lorenz has often been accused of begging the question in that he starts with a controversial position on the nature of aggression: that it is innate and will inevitably be exhibited. This propostion is unproved or unprovable. In other cases, some of Lorenz's generalizations are seriously overstated. For example, it is claimed that animals with powerful natural weapons develop displays that inhibit an animal from killing another animal of its own species. However, lions have such "weaponry" but have not developed a display that prevents them from killing one another.

Many criticisms, especially from Americans, are based on a fear of the social implications of Lorenz's position. Acceptance of his theory, critics suggest, would blind investigators to elements in the social structure that have the effect of teaching aggression and rewarding it. They also point out, from numerous human studies, that the response to particular sign stimuli, such as frustrating situations, is extremely varied in humans. If the Lorenzian counters with the "cultural overlay argument," we are again faced with the virtual impossibility of testing the assertions.

Many students of human behavior are not convinced of Lorenz's argument that outlets for aggression must be provided. Some maintain, in fact, that providing outlets may actually increase aggression by providing situations in which aggression can be practiced and learned. The controversy over the effects of television violence (see p. 144) is caught up in this debate over catharsis versus modeling.

The discussion could be carried much farther, for it is easy to make statements, criticisms, and counterarguments. We can agree with Eibl-Eibesfeldt that there is a great need for more data from ethological observation of Homo sapiens. But perhaps a fit conclusion is a word of caution about generalizing conclusions from animal observations. We hope this chapter has shown that individual behaviors and social organizations are remarkably varied in both structure and function among the many animal species. One cannot even generalize safely from observations of one baboon group to another neighboring group. There are often similarities, but equally often the differences are striking. The research that we have cited on the social existence of various species indicates that each species must be studied on its own terms, without preconceptions. And this includes Homo sapiens.

The social existence of animals may be viewed in terms of the selective advantages and the mechanisms of social **cohesion** and **dispersal.** One of the primary advantages of cohesion is protection against potential **predators.** Many predators, on the other hand, band together to hunt and kill **prey** that would be too large and swift for an individual, as African hunting dogs subdue the antelope on which they feed. Food-gathering is a social activity in many insect species (such as bees). In primates, the social interactions and communication necessary for food-gathering appear to require a period of learning. Learning promotes flexibility of response to the environment, and in some macaque monkeys, juveniles have been known to introduce their elders to new sources of food.

Mating in most vertebrate species requires cohesion for at least a brief period of time. In some species, dominant males typically do most of the copulating, which provides for the selective genetic transmission of such traits as strength and size.

The division of responsibility for various tasks between the sexes varies considerably among animal species; very few universal generalizations can be made. One can find groups in which the female does the hunting (lions), the male tends the nest (many fish, including the Siamese fighting fish and the stickleback), and the female exercises considerable control in choice of a sexual partner (beagles). The sexes tend to look alike in species that have no clear division of responsibility.

Social dispersion also has advantages. If food is in short supply, dispersal of the species over a wider area is desirable and sometimes necessary. Even without food scarcity, dispersal often occurs when the group population exceeds a certain size; such dispersal may result from a breakdown of the social organization caused by the large number of animals. Communication is more difficult, for example, and **dominance hierarchies** are less easily instituted and maintained in large groups.

Reproductive behavior, in an evolutionary sense, shows a trend from asexual reproduction (for example, the splitting of an amoeba) to sexual interactions that result in greater genetic variability. Similar trends include those toward internal rather than external fertilization of the eggs, toward live births, and toward greater periods of maternal care after birth. Because of these trends, the number of fertilized eggs per female varies from millions in lower species to one in many primate species; the chances of survival of a single fertilized egg in the latter species are relatively high. Learning (experience) is also more important in the sexual behavior of higher animals.

The sensory cues most closely related to sexual behavior are typically those important for the species in general, although olfaction seems to be particularly important for both rodents and some presumably vision-dominated primates. Appropriate gonadal hormones are crucial for the appearance of mating behavior. However, removing the hormone-producing glands has varying effects, depending on the species, sex, age, and individual experience of the animal before it loses hormonal support. The male is often the nest builder and protector of the eggs and young in lower species, but in mammals the female inevitably carries certain responsibilities by virtue of relatively prolonged periods of pregnancy and nursing. After birth, adults other than the mother can take an interest in the infant; fathers, "aunts," and "uncles" often do so.

Nest-building behavior in rats is a good example of the interaction of innate and learned factors; experience-deprived rats do build nests, but relatively slowly and inefficiently. Retrieval of the young and sensory cues (such as ultrasonic cries from rat pups) have been a major focus of recent research.

Cohesive relationships other than parent-infant include infant-infant and adult-adult. The most prominent interaction between infants is play. We have often assumed that the function of play is to practice adult behaviors, but there is surprisingly little relevant data. **Grooming** is a widely observed adult-adult interaction and appears to have many functions (such as maintaining a social bond or dominance relation) beyond the obvious hygienic one.

Sensory cues play a significant role in group cohesion, as demonstrated by the calling of howler monkeys and prairie dogs. Scent-marking can function as a means of defining territory, indicating sexual readiness, or tracing a path.

The mechanisms underlying dispersal have been studied most extensively in terms of aggression (although within a group aggression is often a cohesion-promoting behavior as well). Interspecies or intergroup aggression may be divided into three categories: competitive, protective, and predatory—although comparative psychologists usually consider predatory aggression as feeding behavior. In competitive aggression, defense of **territory** is a prominent concept. Within a species, the behavior patterns exhibited during protective aggression may be different from those in competitive aggression (for example, the elk uses antlers in the latter, hooves in the former).

Research on aggression centers around several factors. For example, a period of isolation appears to make many animals more aggressive. Hormonal factors, such as the amount of the male hormone testosterone, are clearly related to aggressive behaviors within the vertebrates. The sensory stimuli eliciting aggression have been studied in many species (such as the red bars on the "shoulders" of an intruding male red-winged blackbird), although the particular cues that are effective vary from one species to the next. Finally, the opportunity to aggress (or to display aggressively) is, for some species, a reward for which they will emit a learned response.

The chapter concludes with a discussion of the social psychology of human beings, the topic with which this book began. From a comparative perspective, we are indeed animals, but the generalizations contained in recent popular books, although very thought-provoking, must be recognized as highly speculative and sometimes inaccurate. Nevertheless, the understanding of people will benefit greatly by the consideration of our similarities with and differences from the other species with which we share this planet.

RECOMMENDED READINGS

DETHIER, V. *To Know a Fly*. San Francisco: Holden-Day, Inc., 1962.
A light and witty description of how one can learn about the behavior of flies, using simple techniques and creative common sense. As they say in the ads: recommended for ages 8 to 80.

EIBL-EIBESFELDT, I. *Ethology: The Biology of Behavior*. New York: Holt, Rinehart and Winston, 1975.
A textbook that presents a traditional ethological viewpoint with great vigor and fine illustrations.

HINDE, R. *Animal Behavior*. New York: McGraw-Hill, 1970.
The most thorough contemporary attempt to synthesize current knowledge and concepts in ethology with those of modern comparative psychology. A very thoughtful, if somewhat difficult book.

KUMMER. H. *Primate Societies*. Chicago: Aldine-Atherton, Inc., 1971.
A description of the varieties of social organization to be found among primate species; coordinated with an attempt to relate social organization to ecological factors.

LORENZ, K. *King Solomon's Ring*. New York: Thomas Y. Crowell Co., 1952.
An entertaining description of some animals that Lorenz has known, what he learned about them, and how he studied their habits. Along with the Tinbergen books listed below, this must be considered one of the best popular accounts of animal behavior study by a major scientist.

MORGAN, E. *The Descent of Woman*. New York: Stein & Day, 1972.
A feminist reconstruction of human evolution that responds to many of the Lorenz/Ardrey assertions regarding human nature.

MARLER, P., & HAMILTON, W., III. *Mechanisms of Animal Behavior*. New York: John Wiley & Sons, Inc., 1967.

A comprehensive textbook of animal behavior that is particularly useful for the student wishing to obtain an introduction to a particular research area, e.g., migration.

SCHALLER, G. *The Year of the Gorilla*. Chicago: The University of Chicago Press, 1964.

A detailed account of the ecology and living habits of the mountain gorilla, as observed by Dr. Schaller in its natural habitat in the eastern Congo and western Uganda.

TINBERGEN, N. *Curious Naturalists*. Garden City, N.Y.: Anchor Books (Doubleday & Company), 1968.

An account of ethologists engaged in problem-solving behavior—learning about the habits of a varied assortment of insects and birds. Written in a delightful style that conveys both the beauty of nature-watching and the excitement of scientific discovery.

———. *The Herring Gull's World*. New York: Basic Books, 1961.

A description of the lifestyle of a predatory bird, based primarily on field and laboratory studies carried out by Tinbergen and his colleagues.

VAN LAWICK-GOODALL, J. *In the Shadow of Man*. Boston: Houghton Mifflin, 1971.

The classic account of behavior of chimpanzees in their wild habitat; many excellent photographs.

WILSON, E. O. *Sociobiology: The New Synthesis*. Cambridge, Mass.: Harvard University Press, 1975.

An encyclopedic and creative attempt to analyze social organization in animals from an ecological-evolutionary vantage point. The student should be warned, however, that Wilson's concluding remarks on the nature of human societies contain a genetic bias that has aroused a great deal of controversy.

PART TEN

Epilogue

By Mark R. Rosenzweig
James Geiwitz
Paul Mussen

Song learning by the white-crowned sparrow provides a clear example of interaction between environmental influence and hereditary constraints.

Summing Up and Looking Ahead

Summing Up: Key Concepts

In the first chapter we introduced six key concepts in psychology: heredity-environment interactions, learning, reinforcement, motivation, feedback, and information processing. We now return to these concepts to review how they have been used throughout the text. For each concept, we will give a few examples from different sections of the book. Later in this concluding chapter, we will undertake the risky business of making some predictions about the future of scientific psychology.

You have read of many areas of psychological inquiry that raised the question: Which is more important, heredity or environment? Typically it has been left unanswered. Instead, as researchers discovered more about the complex *interplay* between genetic and environmental factors, a new question has emerged: How do **heredity and environment interact** to produce a given behavior pattern?

One answer to this question is that heredity can *predispose* an individual to certain behaviors—schizophrenia, for example. In such cases, however, the environment becomes the critical factor in determining whether the person leads a normal or an abnormal life. Similarly, heredity can *set limits* to what an individual can accomplish. We know that even a favorable environment cannot make a genius of someone with little intellectual capacity, although we are far from understanding the complex interactions of intelligence and learning opportunities.

In the area of perception too, attempts to reconcile the nativist and the empiricist positions give some indication of the important role environment plays in the development of largely innate abilities such as depth perception. Without the opportunity to move about and explore actively, young kittens do not display the typical avoidance of what appears to be a sharp drop-off. Apparently experience is necessary for the normal development of this behavior, even though the behavior itself does not seem to be learned. In an even more complex interaction, male white-crowned sparrows must be exposed to an adult song at a critical or sensitive period during their development or they will never sing their species-characteristic melody (p. 651). Moreover, because heredity sets limits, the white-crowned sparrow cannot learn the song of other species. According to many linguists, human language is also a species-characteristic communication system. According to this view, language is mostly built-in, and only specific features need to be learned. There are sensitive periods in childhood in which language learning is especially easy.

LEARNING

The "environment" in heredity-environment interactions usually refers to aspects of a behavior pattern that are learned. (Other environmental factors include nutrition, injury, and so on.) **Learning,** the most pervasive of the key concepts, has been discussed at length in almost every chapter of this text. In Chapter 14, we described the general principles of classical and operant conditioning. In Chapter 23, we considered some constraints on these general principles developed through the study of learning and adaptation in an evolutionary perspective. One such constraint is hereditary potential, which sets limits on learning. There are also time limits that create the critical or sensitive periods mentioned above.

Applications of general principles of learning in other areas of psychology reflect the particular concerns of these specialties. In developmental psychology, learning often involves a stimulus, a response, and a reward or punishment; but the child may not be an *active* participant in the event. He or she may simply observe and later demonstrate learning through imitation. Learning in the young of any species must be distinguished from maturation. A chick improves its pecking accuracy as it grows older; but it does so because of maturing sensory and motor capabilities, not because of learning. Biological experiments support the notion of a distinction between a short-term memory and a long-term memory (*see* Chapters 15 and 21).

REINFORCEMENT

Biological studies have greatly amplified our understanding of **reinforcement,** that mysterious process that somehow increases the probability of occurrence of responses that are followed by rewards. It seems that activation of parts of brain circuits related to pleasurable behaviors such as eating or sex is itself reinforcing. This conclusion fits well with the results of studies of reinforcement in comparative psychology in which the consummatory act (for example, eating)—not simply the stimuli associated with the act (for example, food)—is shown to be reinforcing.

Whatever the underlying basis for effective rewards, they play a significant role in the explanation of human and animal behavior. Modern therapies for people with behavior disorders stress positive reinforcement; a therapist, for example, will try to draw a child out of isolation with approval and praise for group activities. However, a simple "reward theory" is often inadequate to explain human social behavior. It has been shown that people tend to like people who make errors now and then and those who deliver an increasing rather than a constant level of reward. In some cases, the least possible reward is the *most* effective, for a large reward enables people to attribute their actions to the reward and not to their own personal preferences.

MOTIVATION

Concepts of **motivation** are closely related to the concept of reinforcement. What is reinforcing often depends on the motivational state (food is reinforcing only if one is hungry), and rewards are often called "incentives"—which reflects the ability of reinforcements to produce a motivational state. In the part on biological psychology, you read about hunger, thirst, sex, and aggression, and in the part on personality psychology, you read about self-actualization, self-esteem, and aggression. The fact that aggression was considered in these two parts and also in Chapter 24 on social behavior in animals shows the interplay between social and biological research on questions of *why* individuals behave the way they do.

Many human motives are not directly related to the primary drives of hunger, thirst, sex, and pain-avoidance. Instead, they are motives that emerge as the organization of the individual personality develops; they represent the need to *defend* and *improve* that organization. In this respect, the human personality is like a business or political organization that is slow to admit fault and tends to become bigger—whether or not increased size is desirable! Similarly, the organization we call the human personality—which is created to satisfy basic needs—defends itself and strives for further growth and self-actualization. Cognitive dissonance and other threats upset the internal harmony of personality.

FEEDBACK

Reinforcement is a kind of feedback, a consequence of behavior, but feedback is a more general term. **Feedback** is any information gained through a response. The child gains experience as he or she acts and notes the feedback (consequences) of these actions, be they good, bad, or indifferent. Feedback also occurs in an evolutionary sequence. If a behavior leads to an increased probability of survival, that behavior is likely to be promoted in the genes of succeeding generations.

Biofeedback is a recent and intriguing application of feedback techniques to the voluntary regulation of internal responses. Previously, people had difficulty controlling blood pressure, heart rate, and other physiological responses because they had no information on how well they were doing. Anxious patients were constantly told to relax, but how could they know if they were successful? By amplifying the signals produced by the body and presenting them to the person, scientists have provided the necessary feedback. Some people who were troubled by anxiety, high blood pressure, or allergies aggravated by tension are now living happier, healthier, and more productive lives. It should be noted, however, that caution has replaced unbridled enthusiasm in reports of biofeedback applications. Like all therapeutic techniques, biofeedback has its limits, and further research is clearly needed.

INFORMATION PROCESSING

Feedback processes typically focus on the changes in information that result from an action. **Information processing** is a major concept in psychology, as psychologists learn how to investigate unseen and theoretical "mental" structures and processes without discarding the invaluable methodologies of behaviorism. Interests in concept formation, problem solving, and creativity are being revived, and new approaches to old questions are adding significantly to our knowledge. The information-processing approach is not limited to higher thought processes, however. In perception, psychologists are trying to discover how the organism uses the information in the stimulus to form basic percepts of such qualities as brightness, color, and form. Biological psychologists search for the neural and chemical transformations that reflect such perception. It has been discovered, for example, that retinal cones respond selectively to different wavelengths of light and that further analysis is provided by special color-coding cells.

The information-processing approach was first used extensively in the study of human memory, and in this field we see some of the analogies to computers that provide much of the structure of the approach. The division of memory into a sensory storage system, a short-term store, and a long-term store, which each handle information in a different way, has given order and organization to a great amount of data and impetus to much additional research. Partly because the approach has been so useful in memory investigations, similar approaches are being tried in other areas of psychology. In developmental psychology, the cognitive emphasis has increased enormously, and the theory of Jean Piaget and his associates has become prominent. The child's differing abilities to process information at various stages of intellectual development also help to explain the growth of other abilities, such as moral judgments.

Looking Ahead

Psychology has become a well established discipline, but it continues to expand vigorously and to change in new and exciting ways. In this final section of the book we will speculate on where psychology will go from here. How is

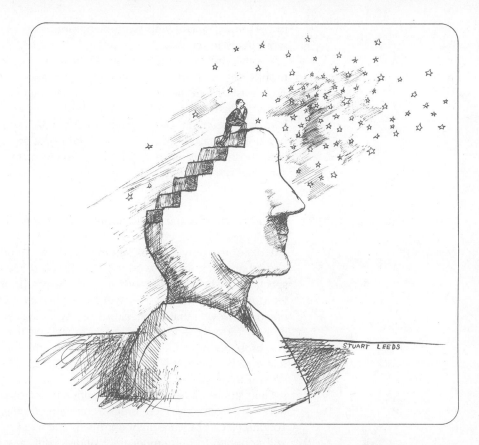

research in psychology likely to develop over the next few decades? In what new ways will psychology affect our lives and those of the next generation?

PREDICTING THE FUTURE OF PSYCHOLOGY

When Wilhelm Wundt founded the first formal laboratory in psychology in 1879, Gustav Fechner offered his congratulations and predicted that with these excellent facilities, Wundt would solve all the problems of psychology in ten years, and the laboratory would then close! In fact, Wundt did come up with at least tentative answers to many of the questions that were being asked at the time. But research usually uncovers new questions as it solves old problems, and psychology has continued to grow.

To predict the future of psychology, we need to know something of the impetus to growth in the past. One source of the impetus, as the Wundt anecdote illustrates, is research. Scientific investigation has a kind of momentum of its own, as the results of one study raise new questions that can be answered only by more research. For example, observations of hospital patients with brain damage show that nearly complete recovery is possible in many cases. Researchers noticed, however, that the degree of injury was not always the critical factor in recovery. Two patients might have essentially the same amount and type of brain damage, yet one would recover nicely while the other showed little or no improvement. This prompted further investigations into the nature of these individual differences. Patients' personal motivations seemed to be critical; those who were highly motivated to function effectively were more likely to recover.

Another major source of change in the field of psychology is pressing social problems that inevitably challenge psychologists to do new research. These problems include aspects of international relations, conflict between groups within a nation, education, crime, mental disorders, medical problems that involve perception and behavioral abnormalities, and ecology. Changes in psychology that are responses to social needs are somewhat easier to predict than those arising from research, for many of the social problems that will stimulate research tomorrow are with us today.

TRENDS AND DIRECTIONS IN PSYCHOLOGICAL RESEARCH

So, undaunted by the perils of prediction, we will present a few of the areas and approaches we believe will be stressed over the next few decades. These are, of course, only examples from a much longer potential list we could make, and other psychologists would probably select somewhat differently. We will speculate first on some trends in basic research; and in the next section, we will turn to psychology as it will be applied to social problems. It should be noted, however, that applications of psychology depend on firm knowledge derived from research in the basic areas. On the basis of your knowledge, you probably have ideas of your own about the future of psychology, and you might enjoy recording them; Spotlight 25-2 (p. 719) provides an opportunity for you to do so.

Field studies, in which people or animals are observed under natural conditions, will become increasingly common. In the laboratory, experimental conditions can be carefully controlled, and therefore laboratory investigations will continue to outnumber field studies. But new techniques of observation and new statistical methods for analyzing complex relationships will allow greater precision in interpreting data gathered in real-life situations. The findings will provide us with a richer picture of many phenomena such as learning *in the school,* parent-child interactions *in the home,* and the range and variation of behavior of different species *in their own habitat.* These data will provide a firmer basis for both theory and applications.

In the past, observational studies have often been used descriptively—to show "This is how it is"—while laboratory research has delved into the underlying mechanisms. It seems probable to us that investigations both in the field and in the laboratory will be increasingly focused on the mechanisms involved in various behaviors. For example, Piaget has described many facets of a child's intellectual development (pp. 245–51); now psychologists are asking more basic questions about *how* the transition from one stage to the next is achieved. The behavior of learning and remembering has also been described in considerable detail, and now many investigators are studying the processes involved—both in terms of formal models (p. 422) and in terms of biological mechanisms (Chapter 21).

There are numerous other trends and directions in psychology that are apparent in its recent past and probable in its immediate future. In several areas, as research data accumulate, mathematical models have proven valuable. In areas where behavior can be measured with precision—learning, memory, and perception, for example—psychologists will find formal models to be extremely useful for both describing and predicting behavior.

Computers promise to influence psychology in many ways. They provide a means of testing and expanding the formal, mathematical models we have just mentioned. They have already made feasible more complex statistical analyses of data. Computers are also being used as "research assistants" to present stimuli to subjects and record their responses during very complex experiments. Attempts to match the performance of human subjects in intellectual tasks (such as problem solving) with the output of a computer programed according to a theory of intelligence have led to more sophisticated views of this important human ability. All of these uses are in the beginning stages and will undoubtedly be developed further. We can hardly imagine all of the future applications of the computer, but they are certain to come; a new methodological tool frequently brings with it a surge of scientific activity.

More aspects of behavior will be explained in biological terms. In many theories of schizophrenia, for example, very early parent-child interactions are seen as crucial. But many children who experience severe parental rejection do not develop this mental disorder. This has led to the investigation, and discovery, of a number of genetic and physiological factors that are involved in a kind of susceptibility to schizophrenia.

Multidisciplinary approaches to various basic issues will probably increase. Investigators from many disciplines—neuroanatomists, neurochemists, neurophysiologists, neuropsychologists—are already collaborating in the attempt to understand how memories are laid down, stored, and retrieved in neural tissue (Rosenzweig & Bennett, 1976a).

Cross-cultural investigations of one topic in different countries are also likely to become more numerous. Such research is invaluable for testing the generality of conclusions that come from studies in only one culture. Are males always more aggressive than females? Are certain forms of emotional expression universal? Do children reared in Asia go through the same stages of moral development that North American and European children do? Often cultural differences point to important underlying mechanisms in the particular behavior under study. For example, people in certain cultures have little experience with rectangular shapes and are less affected by the famous Müller-Lyer illusion (p. 458).

Evolutionary interpretations of behavior and behavioral mechanisms will become more powerful and more widespread. They will help us to understand, for example, the enormous capacities for learning in certain species and their weakness or narrowness in others. Furthermore they will aid our investigations into the specificities and constraints on learning that exist in each species (see p. 646). The study of behavior from an evolutionary viewpoint may even become a separate field, which some are already calling "sociobiology" (p. 703). Through this new approach, ethological methods and approaches to *human* behavior will achieve increasing recognition and prominence.

APPLICATIONS OF PSYCHOLOGY

Each of the eight principal areas of psychology has practical applications to personal and social problems. In the future, the applications will draw on the special knowledge of each area, although the particular problems may change.

Since 1956 the American Psychological Association has presented annual awards for distinguished scientific contributions—advances in basic research and conceptualization. In 1973 the Association inaugurated a similar annual award for distinguished contributions to applications in psychology. The first three awards were presented to these psychologists.

1973   Conrad L. Kraft. Kraft is a psychologist and Chief Scientist for the Personnel Subsystem of Boeing's Commercial Aircraft Division. After a series of mysterious nighttime crashes of the Boeing 727 jets, Kraft was able to determine the cause with the aid of a model of a lighted city set against a dark background. Showing that the lack of a perceptual frame of reference made it nearly impossible to judge distance and rate and angle of descent, Kraft convinced the Civil Aeronautics Board that instruments should be required for all night landings, no matter how clear the pilot's view of the landing strip.

1974   Gerald S. Lesser and **Edward L. Palmer.** The joint award was given for their work on the television programs "Sesame Street" and "The Electric Company." Lesser is chairman of the Board of Advisors of the Children's Television Workshop and Professor of Education and Developmental Psychology at Harvard University. Palmer is Vice-President for Research at the Children's Television Workshop, creators and producers of "Sesame Street" and "The Electric Company."

1975   Nathan H. Azrin. "For diligence and imagination in applying learning principles to ameliorate a variety of human problems . . . he has demonstrated the efficacy of multifaceted treatment programs for enuretics, stutterers, alcoholics, and individuals with marital problems and nervous habits. . . . Most important, his efforts provide a model for psychologists indicating that both spe-

"Sesame Street."

cific skills and general well-being of individuals now can be markedly improved with innovative applications of established principles and procedures" (*American Psychologist* 1976, *31, 72*).

Principles of social psychology will be applied to reduce international conflicts (*see*, for example, Doob, 1970) and tensions between groups—such as those that sometimes exist between blacks and whites in integrated schools. Understanding the factors involved in interpersonal attraction will help psychologists plan more "friendly" living arrangements in dormitories or cooperative communes. In some cases, social psychologists will work with architects to design buildings that promote satisfying human interactions as well as provide efficiently for the ordinary amenities of living and working. Findings from research on communication and persuasion will be used to combat prejudice and to encourage conservation.

Clinical psychology is an application of personality psychology. As more biological and social causes of mental disorders are understood, clinical treatments will improve. Discoveries of effective ways of reducing tension and feelings of hostility and dependency will benefit us all. It seems likely that the use of behavior-modification techniques will increase, and biofeedback will permit control of processes previously considered involuntary. At the same time, however, humanistic therapies stressing self-actualization will probably also be more widely used. We may well see a combination of behavioral techniques to combat fears and other "negative" motivations with humanistic support for programs of self-improvement. As devices for personality assessment improve, clinical and counseling psychologists will be able to plan such programs more effectively. Matching clients with therapists is one possibility, but it seems more likely that particular problems will be matched with particular therapies.

In addition to developing more effective treatments for individuals, clinical psychologists will become increasingly involved with institutions and the key social agents that affect the mental health of many people. There will be extensive programs for parents, designed to improve parent-child relations and to promote maximum personal growth. More psychologists will be involved in organizing local communities and neighborhoods to cope with people with emotional problems, helping these people in the community rather than sending them away to a hospital.

In the area of developmental psychology, we will learn more of the social and intellectual changes that occur from birth through adolescence—and we will begin to understand how social and intellectual development interact. These findings can be applied in child guidance and therapy, in counseling parents about childrearing, and in training workers in day-care centers and schools. The methods of developmental psychology will be increasingly applied to the study of early and middle adulthood and old age. The result will be practical knowledge about good adjustment during the most productive years of our lives and during retirement.

Cognitive psychologists will continue to find applications for their research findings in education. The concept of intelligence will probably be clarified and expanded in the next few decades, and I.Q. tests will be used more effectively and in ways that are less subject to bias. There can be no question about the need of our society for creative solutions to many problems. In-depth studies of creative people and the creative process—in the arts, science, politics, and economics—will yield information that can be used to facilitate innovative thinking in all citizens.

The findings from research on learning and memory have been applied in settings as diverse as the television program *Sesame Street* and the college language laboratory (*see* Spotlight 25-1). Personalized systems of instruction, in which each student works at his or her own pace and masters each unit of course material before going on to the next, are becoming more common at many levels of education. The computer, with its vast memory and infinite patience, will be an invaluable aid in many of these systems. Computer-assisted programs are also helping mental patients and criminals to learn new skills and develop their abilities to relate effectively to other people.

The growing emphasis on information processing will result in more precise estimates of deficits due to brain injury or drugs. Damage to certain areas of the brain, for example, seems to affect the transfer of information from short-term stores to more permanent memory systems. Similarly, marijuana does not seem to affect retrieval of previously learned material but, rather, appears to impair storage of new information (Darley, Tinklenberg, Roth, Hollister, & Atkinson, 1973).

Research on perception will be applied increasingly both to prevent development of deficiencies and to make up for impairments of sensory-perceptual systems. Routine testing of infants' sensory capacities is likely in the future, and corrective devices will be prescribed early to insure normal perceptual development. New prosthetic devices will undoubtedly be able to restore at least partial sight or hearing in cases where the sense organ has been damaged by accident or disease. Promising experimental results have already been obtained with artificial sense organs that convey electrical signals to the visual cortex or the auditory nerve.

The growing scope and power of biological-behavioral research will undoubtedly bring many useful applications. We have already mentioned the potential use of biofeedback in clinical psychology and the development of prosthetic devices. Biobehavioral methods will also find increasing use in aiding recovery from brain damage. Although new neurons cannot be created to replace those destroyed by injury or disease, existing cells can form new connections and participate in new circuits to take over at least some of the lost functions. A combination of behavioral therapy and treatment with drugs that encourage the growth of synaptic connections may prove to be most effective means of promoting recovery.

Chemotherapy will become more and more *potentially* useful in the treatment of problems ranging from psychotic behavior to pathological violence. Chemotherapy brings with it a host of ethical questions, however, and its abuse would represent a serious threat to civil liberties. Consider, for example, the problem of violence. Brain pathology is not a factor in most violence, and thus the use of chemotherapy to inhibit it would constitute a form of social/political control, not therapy. Chemotherapy is only appropriate when the individual, acting freely, seeks help and clearly understands the nature of the therapy. On the other hand, chemotherapy should not be denied to someone simply because it *can* be abused. Already thousands of people who are prone to epileptic seizures successfully avoid attacks with drugs that prevent over-excitability of brain cells, and manic-depressive swings of mood can be alleviated with lithium compounds. Chemotherapy is often more effective, less risky, and less objectionable than methods such as brain surgery. In many instances, it may represent an individual's only hope of leading a normal life.

Comparative psychologists will continue their efforts to understand the behavior of our animal relatives, to interpret some aspects of human behavior with insights derived from animal research, and to make our interactions with animals more harmonious. Certain laboratory methods devised to study animals have proved fruitful in research on people: for example, the study of perception in infants (see p. 240 and p. 459). Undoubtedly, other methods invented for the study of animal behavior, including ethological methods, will find increasing use in research on human behavior. Principles derived from animal research will also continue to provide a fertile source of hypotheses about human behavior in such areas as mother-infant relations, causes of aggression, and factors underlying abnormal behavior.

Because the variety of life forms is of keen interest to many lay people as well as being a basic resource for many scientists, there is increasing concern about saving species from extinction. Students of animal behavior are aiding this effort by increasing our understanding of crucial feeding habits, mating behaviors, and migratory patterns. Even predators living in the wild may be conditioned to avoid attacking domestic animals and thus *be spared from extermination* (see Spotlight 23-2, p. 654). As natural habitats are increasingly replaced by "civilization," zoos and game preserves may become the only places where certain species can be saved. The whole question of zoos is being debated at present, and comparative psychology will aid in the resolution of this and related issues, to the benefit of the species involved.

CHANGES IN PSYCHOLOGY
Even as the application of basic psychological research is changing many aspects of our lives, the applied areas will, in turn, modify the structure and content of psychology as a discipline. The specialities of psychology that can be applied to social needs will attract interest from large numbers of concerned psychologists and promote government support for research. Certain areas will undoubtedly expand more quickly than others. For example, in the period just after World War II, clinical psychology received great impetus from the need for psychotherapeutic aid for veterans, and clinical specialists soon constituted a much larger proportion of the total number of psychologists than they had before the war.

Wholly new specialties will emerge in the future—often by splitting off from established areas (fission) or by combining with others (fusion). One new area that is presently emerging from social psychology is environmental psychology, which reflects increased social concern about pollution, over-population, and other ecological problems. Within experimental psychology, psychologists who follow B. F. Skinner's approach to behavior have formed their own, separate division of the American Psychological Association—the Division for the Experimental Analysis of Behavior. At the same time, a fusion of the general interests of many different specialists has resulted in an area called behavior modification, which reflects a predominantly Skinnerian approach to learning, personality, development, and other areas. Information processing, as a specialty in psychology, combines findings from research on perception, memory, and other cognitive processes.

Over the longer run, it is possible that psychology may break up into separate parts, just as "natural philosophy" split off from the parent philosophy, fissioned again into physics and chemistry, and finally formed the many scientific fields we know today. Perhaps someday there will be "the psychological sciences" instead of one unified science. On the other hand, it is possible that psychology will be absorbed into other disciplines such as biology and sociology, although this seems less likely.

AND FINALLY . . .

We hope that this book, as an introductory survey, has helped you to gain basic concepts and information about the active, growing field of psychology. Even if you do not take any further courses in psychology, advances in this field are bound to affect your life. The time and thought you have spent with this book should prepare you to understand more about yourself and others and to meet some of the changes and challenges that the coming years will bring.

It will help you to understand what psychologists have accomplished so far and what psychology is likely to achieve during the next few decades if you write down some of your own thoughts and predictions. We will be happy to receive copies of your ideas on these questions, and the replies we receive will be reflected in later editions of this book.

We would also appreciate your evaluations and suggestions to help us to improve the next edition. Please send them to Mussen/Rosenzweig, D. C. Heath & Co., 125 Spring St., Lexington, Massachusetts, 02173. Thank you.

Problems I would like to see psychologists try to solve:

Ways in which I expect to see the field of psychology change by the end of this century:

Which chapters did you like best? Which chapters were the worst? Use a scale of 1 to 5: 1 = poor, 2 = fair, 3 = average, 4 = good, and 5 = excellent. How would you rate each chapter, taking into account both the information conveyed and your personal interest? Do not rate chapters you did not read.

Rating   Chapter

Part One: Psychology: The Study of Behavior
_____   1. The Science of Psychology

Part Two: Social Psychology
_____   2. Social Influence: Communication, Persuasion, and Conformity
_____   3. Attitude Change by Self-Persuasion
_____   4. Prejudice
_____   5. Attraction: Who Likes Whom and Why

Part Three: Personality
_____   6. Personality and Assessment
_____   7. Theories of Personality
_____   8. Psychopathology and Therapy

Part Four: Developmental Psychology
_____   9. What Is Developmental Psychology?
_____   10. Growth and Cognitive Development
_____   11. The Development of Personality and Social Behavior

(Continued on p. 720.)

Topics I would like to see discussed in future editions:

General comments and/or specific suggestions:

I used this text in the following course: _____

at the following institution: _____

Appendix: Statistics

Making observations or conducting experiments usually produces quantitative data—for example, the *numbers* of aggressive acts in a specified situation, or *scores* on a test of reasoning, or *ratings* of conformity, or *measures* of parental permissiveness. Psychologists regularly use statistical methods to put their raw data into manageable form, to measure relations within the data, and to interpret the results.

Almost all of the findings and conclusions in this book depend upon the use of statistical concepts and methods, although we have not usually presented the results in statistical form. In some cases we wanted to present results rather precisely and therefore we employed such terms as "mean," "median," "standard deviation," "coefficient of correlation," or "statistical significance." Because the use of statistics is so pervasive and so basic, we will briefly consider some of the most important concepts here. Our purpose at this point is only to give you some comprehension of these concepts, not to teach computational skills. Brief presentations of statistical formulas and computational methods are also included for those who are curious about them; this material is printed in smaller type and follows the discussion of each main topic.

DESCRIBING DATA

Suppose that you want to describe the performance of a group of people on some test or experiment or to determine where a particular individual stands in relation to the rest of the group. The measure in question could be the number of aggressive responses children made in an experimental situation, estimates of intelligence, or scores on a test of creativity. Each person in the group is observed or tested and gets a score. But it is hard to tell much about the group or about any person just by examining the list of scores. For example, consider the intelligence test scores for 100 people given in Table 1.

TABLE 1	Scores of 100 subjects on an intelligence test								
72	91	139	78	99	79	100	84	100	124
128	88	92	85	109	96	90	93	75	98
84	95	81	119	102	123	100	92	82	69
81	106	95	97	88	89	110	132	⃝111	116
101	101	96	102	97	127	108	112	107	107
113	137	104	120	61	105	98	80	121	100
103	93	83	94	87	99	109	100	120	106
94	105	87	114	103	87	115	110	98	113
101	108	104	80	95	107	97	102	112	118
86	91	76	117	99	104	92	102	77	99

If you are interested in a particular individual—for example the one whose score is circled—and want to know where he or she stands in the group, you need to have a way of describing the whole set of data, or the **distribution** of scores.

DETERMINING THE
DISTRIBUTION

DETERMINING THE DISTRIBUTION

The first step in describing the distribution is to arrange the scores in order from the lowest to highest and to see how many people made each score. This has been done in Figure 1, which shows the number of people making each score (the **frequency**). Each dot stands for one person. Now you can easily see that the lowest score in the group is 61, the highest is 139, and that most of the scores cluster around 100. Five people scored 100; 4 received the score of 99, 3 scored 101, and 4 are at 102. In order to describe the distribution of scores more adequately, we need some measure of the average of the group or central tendency. We also need a measure of how much the scores vary around the center, that is, a measure of variability. This kind of measure tells us whether the scores are closely clustered around the average or are dispersed and spread out over a wide range.

Two frequently used measures of central tendency are the median and the arithmetic mean, both of which can be called an "average." The **median** is the point that divides the group into equal halves—the upper and lower halves of the distribution. To get the median, you arrange the scores in order from the lowest to the highest, then you find the middle score. Thus, if there are 5 scores, the third is the median; if there are 100 cases, you take a value halfway between the 50th and 51st. To get the arithmetic average or **mean,** you find the sum of all the scores and then divide by the number of cases. In the example of Table 1, the median and the mean are both 100. This is the mean I.Q. of a representative sample of the general population; the mean I.Q. of a group of college students would, of course, be higher. Using the mean as a reference point, we can now say that the circled score is 11 points above the mean.

The mean and median tend to be similar when the scores are distributed symmetrically around the center, but they may differ widely in other types of distributions. For example, take the following set of numbers: 1, 1, 2, 2, 3, 4, 50. The median is 2 while the mean is 9. A few extreme scores in a distribution affect the mean but not the median. In this example, the median would still be 2 if the largest number had been 50, 5, or 5,000, but the mean would be changed considerably. The mean family income in the United States is much higher than the median because the mean is influenced by a few very high incomes. But the median more accurately reflects the fact that most people have low or moderate incomes. The mean is the more frequently used measure of central tendency because it is based on more information, that is, each and every score plays an equal role in its determination.

FINDING THE STANDARD DEVIATION

We cannot adequately describe a distribution just by giving the average; we also need a measure of **variability.** For example, we need to know whether a score 11 points above the mean puts the individual who makes that score very high, or only moderately high, within the total distribution. The range from the lowest to the highest score gives a rough measure of variability. A better measure is the average deviation of all scores from the mean; to get

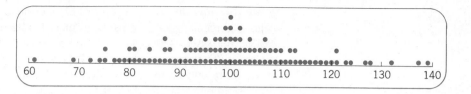

this, you find the difference between each score and the mean, and then you find the arithmetic average of these differences. The most commonly used measure of variability of scores is the **standard deviation,** a statistic based on squaring the deviations from the mean.

The primary advantage of the standard deviation is that it describes with great precision the distribution of scores in a normal curve. The frequency distribution of Figure 1 was somewhat irregular because it was based on a relatively small number of cases drawn randomly from a large population. If a large number of people—say, thousands—were sampled, the overall distribution of I.Q. scores would become more regular and would approach the bell-shaped curve shown in Figure 2. This is called a **normal curve.**

As is clear from Figure 2, in a normal distribution the score with the highest frequency is the mean; that is, more people get the mean score than any other. The farther a score is from the mean, the lower the frequency of that score. In a normal distribution, 68 percent of all scores are within one standard deviation (S.D.) of the mean, 34 percent above, and 34 percent below the mean. And 95 percent are within two S.D. of the mean. Figure 2 represents the distribution of intelligence (I.Q.) scores in the general population; the mean is 100 and the standard deviation is 15 points. An I.Q. score of 130, therefore, is two S.D. above the mean; a score above 130 occurs only about 25 times in 1,000 people drawn from the general population.

Figure 2
The Normal Curve
Distribution of I.Q.
Scores

The distribution of I.Q. scores in a large sample approximates closely the bell shape of a normal curve. Here the mean is 100 and the standard deviation (S.D.) is 15.

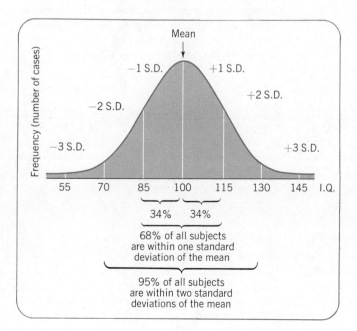

We can now describe the set of I.Q. scores of Table 1 with only two numbers—the mean (99.8 in this case) and the standard deviation (14.9 in this case). These two statistics also help us to locate the individual's standing in the group. For example, the circled score of 111 is now seen to be 11 points, or not quite one standard deviation, above the mean. It is higher than 77 percent of the others and falls in the top quarter of the distribution.

Calculating the Mean, Standard Deviation, and Standard Score

Now let us note some of the main symbols, formulas, and calculations used with regard to the sort of example we have just considered. Table 2 lists some of the basic terms and concepts. Look through it now, and refer back to it later whenever you find the need.

We have just seen that a distribution of scores or measures can be described in terms of its mean and standard deviation.[1] The mean can be found by adding all the scores and dividing by the number of scores:

$$\bar{X} = \frac{\Sigma X}{N}$$

For the standard deviation, there are two equivalent formulas: one in terms of raw scores (X) and the other in terms of deviation scores (x). The deviation-score formula looks simpler, but it requires first finding the deviation value for each item.

$$\sigma = \sqrt{\frac{\Sigma x^2}{N}}$$

That is, find the deviation (x) of each score from the mean, square these and sum them (Σx^2), divide by N, and take the square root.

The raw score formula for the standard deviation is more frequently used, especially when a calculating machine is available:

$$\sigma = \sqrt{\frac{\Sigma X^2}{N} - \bar{X}^2}$$

Once you know the mean and standard deviation of a distribution, then you can express any score by taking its deviation from the mean and dividing this by the standard deviation. This is called a z-score. Thus, if $\bar{X} = 20$ and $\sigma = 10$, then a raw score of 25 can be expressed as a z-score of

$$\frac{25 - 20}{10} = 0.5$$

a raw score of 12 can be expressed as a z-score of

$$\frac{12 - 20}{10} = -0.8$$

So

$$z = \frac{X - \bar{X}}{\sigma}$$

[1] In this appendix we are assuming that the data are distributed approximately according to the normal curve (see Figure 2) and that all samples are at least moderately large (consisting of 30 or more cases). Special statistics are needed for non-normal distributions and small samples.

TABLE 2 Some basic statistical terms and symbols

X	An individual item or measure.
N	The number of cases or items in a sample.
$\overline{X}$ or M	The mean of a distribution.
Σ	The sum of a number of items. (Σ is the capitalized form of the Greek letter sigma.) ΣX means the sum of all items or scores in the distribution.
σ or $S.D.$	The standard deviation of a distribution. (σ is the lowercase form of the Greek letter sigma.)
x	The deviation of an item or measure from the mean; $x = X - \overline{X}$. For a measure smaller than the mean, x is negative.
z	A way of expressing a score or measure in which its deviation from the mean is divided by the standard deviation; thus the deviation score is given in units of the standard deviation.
$\sigma_{\overline{x}}$ or SE_M	The sampling error of a mean.
r	Coefficient of correlation. Also written $r_{X,Y}$ to show that it is the correlation of two sets of measures, the X distribution and the Y distribution.
p	Probability of occurrence. If $p < .05$, the result is likely to occur less than 5 times in 100.

Many scales commonly used in psychological and educational measurement are based on z-scores. In such scales the z-score is typically multiplied by a constant (such as 100) to eliminate decimals; to the product, a constant (such as 500) is added to eliminate negative values. Such transformed z-scores are called standard scores. Table 3 gives two such scales. The Stanford-Binet intelligence test is arranged to have the mean of a representative sample fall at about 100, while the standard deviation is about 15 points. The Graduate Record Examination scores are set to have the mean at 500 and each standard deviation equal 100.

TABLE 3 Two scales derived from standard scores

Standard Score	I.Q. Score	Graduate Record Examination
$+3\sigma$	145	800
$+2\sigma$	130	700
$+1\sigma$	115	600
0σ	100	500
-1σ	85	400
-2σ	70	300
-3σ	55	200
$\overline{X}$ 0	100	500
σ 1.0	15	100

When we test a hypothesis, we usually work with a limited number of subjects but hope to generalize the results to a much larger group. For example, we might use twenty or thirty nursery-school children in an experiment and phrase our conclusion in terms of what nursery-school children in general are likely to do. The small group used in the experiment is called a **sample,** hopefully a representative sample from the total population—in this case, all nursery-school children.

Adequate sampling requires the application of precise and mathematical rules, as you know if you follow public-opinion polls. The opinions of a thousand individuals, chosen in such a way that they are representative of the larger population, give us a fairly accurate estimate of an entire nation's television preferences or political beliefs. But results based on biased sampling can be very misleading. If you asked only your friends what they thought of marijuana, you might incorrectly assume that your sample was representative of the thoughts of a nation. But your friends are probably a restricted group in several ways—they may come from a certain geographical area and be above average in education and intelligence. In principle, nonbiased samples from the population you hope to understand must be selected *randomly*, that is, so that any member of the total population has an equal chance of being selected.

Even if a sample is not biased, it may give misleading conclusions if the number of subjects is too small. Imagine asking three people what their favorite television shows are and basing next year's schedule on their answers. Even if they were randomly selected, their answers would not be likely to reflect the judgments of millions of television watchers.

Let us return to the sample of 100 I.Q. scores in Table 1. We discovered that the mean and standard deviation of the "total population" were 99.8 and 14.9 respectively. Suppose we randomly sample 10 scores from that group; since there are 100 scores, we can form 10 such "subsets" of 10 scores each. The means and standard deviations of 10 subsets drawn this way are given in Table 4; most of them are fairly close to the total population values, but none hits them "right on the nose." This demonstrates that sampling provides "estimates," and that these estimates are subject to error.

The larger the sample in relation to the total population, the less the sampling error, of course. While we have been using the terms "estimates" and "error" in a rather casual fashion, statisticians can give precise measures of the probable error in any estimate based on a small sample, if they know the size of the sample.

Now we can state these relations quantitatively. If we know the standard deviation of a sample and its N, then we can estimate the standard deviation of a population of means (that is, means of samples of the same size drawn from the same population).

TABLE 4	I.Q. scores in ten random samples of ten subjects each								
Sample	A	B	C	D	E	F	G	H	I	J
Mean	96.3	101.5	95.7	100.6	94.0	101.6	101.9	100.7	100.3	105.0
S.D.	16.5	14.3	17.8	16.3	13.3	15.2	8.2	15.1	17.1	15.4

This sampling distribution of the mean is often called the standard error of the mean ($\sigma_{\bar{x}}$ or SE_M). Here is the formula:

$$\sigma_{\bar{x}} = \frac{\sigma}{\sqrt{N-1}} \quad \text{or} \quad SE_M = \frac{\text{S.D.}}{\sqrt{N-1}}$$

The size of $\sigma_{\bar{x}}$ varies inversely, not with N, but with the square root of N (actually of $N-1$). This means that to cut the standard error of the mean in half, you must increase your sample size fourfold

$$\left(\frac{1}{\sqrt{4}} = \frac{1}{2}\right)$$

DECIDING WHEN A DIFFERENCE MAKES A DIFFERENCE

In Table 4, we have ten independent estimates of the mean of the total group, most of which are close to, but do not match exactly the true value (99.8). Suppose we performed an experiment using two groups, X and Y. We injected subjects in Group X with a chemical we felt might "increase intelligence," but we gave the subjects in Group Y no special treatment. After the experiment, we test the intelligence of subjects in both groups and find that the mean for Group X is 101.9 while the mean for the untreated Group Y is 97.3, a difference of 4.6 points. Can we confidently assume that the chemical was effective? Or is this difference one that could have occurred even if the treatment had had no real effect? That is, could it be caused by sampling errors resulting from the use of relatively small samples?

These questions can be given a probable answer by statistics that determine the **significance** of a difference. As used statistically, significant means trustworthy, or likely to be replicated. That is, if the same experiment were repeated with two new groups, the results would be similar: the two groups would probably differ in the same way, although not necessarily in the same exact amount. In short, a statistically significant difference is one that is likely to be reproducible or replicable.

There are very few experiments in psychology that yield *no* measured differences between groups, so we almost always use statistics to tell us if our obtained difference is significant or not. In the case above, the statistics would, of course, show that the differences between Group X and Group Y were *not* significant. If we took two new samples, say Groups K and L, and repeated the experiment, we might find that the treated group (K) scored 100.5 and the untreated subjects (L) averaged 103.1. Our grand hopes for an "intelligence-enhancing" chemical would be dashed.

In general, statistical tests of significance compare the obtained difference to differences that might occur due to sampling errors. If a very large number of subjects is used and the measuring techniques are very precise, these variations will be relatively small; in such cases a quite small difference can be significant. On the other hand, if the sample is small and the measures crude and imprecise, a very large difference can be nonsignificant. The degree of "trustworthiness" in a difference is typically assigned a **probability** (p) that indicates the likelihood that one would get a difference of this magnitude *if the treatment had no real effect*, given the sampling error in the particular situation. A probability of less than .05 ($p < .05$) indicates that a difference this large would have occurred by chance fewer than five times in a hundred; such a difference is considered significant. A probability of "less than once in 100 cases" ($p < .01$) indicates an even more trustworthy result.

TABLE 5 I.Q. scores of 63 real parent-child pairs

Parent	Child	Parent	Child	Parent	Child	Parent	Child
136	131	117	113	112	96	114	105
98	125	92	107	116	95	112	109
114	126	94	106	118	99	124	106
113	129	93	100	120	98	121	108
102	122	96	108	83	91	83	100
111	121	103	104	94	90	87	104
115	123	105	100	95	92	89	101
127	124	108	103	104	94	121	91
93	116	107	111	107	93	83	85
97	119	114	102	118	94	88	89
118	117	132	118	107	78	86	86
126	118	80	95	76	82	120	88
127	119	84	99	99	84	124	87
125	117	79	99	87	80	107	81
129	115	76	97	63	67	102	79
112	111	104	98	107	107		

Just as we can calculate the standard error of a mean, so we can calculate the sampling distribution of the differences between means of the X distribution and the Y distribution $(\bar{X} - \bar{Y})$. If we know the standard deviation of this distribution, we can compute a z-score for our obtained difference:

$$z_{\bar{X}-\bar{Y}} = \frac{\bar{X} - \bar{Y}}{\sigma_{\bar{X}-\bar{Y}}}$$

where $\sigma_{\bar{X}-\bar{Y}}$ is computed from the formula

$$\sigma_{\bar{X}-\bar{Y}} = \sqrt{(\sigma_{\bar{X}})^2 + (\sigma_{\bar{Y}})^2}$$

Just as a z-score for other data (for example, exam scores) is considered very high or very low if it exceeds ± 2.0, a z-score for a difference between two means is considered to be large if it exceeds 2.0. If the means of the two groups represent nothing more than two estimates of the same "true" mean—if the difference, that is, represents merely random, chance fluctuations and there is no "real" difference between groups—then a z-score of 2.0 would occur less than 5 times in 100. With a z-score of 2.0 or more, we would feel fairly confident that the difference is *not* due to chance but rather indicates a true difference between the two groups. We express this confidence by saying the obtained difference is "significant at the .05 level" ($p < .05$).

A z-score for a difference between means (sometimes called a "critical ratio") as large as 2.6 would occur only once in 100 if there were no real difference, so we can feel even more confident about these results ($p < .01$).

If an experimental group has these statistics: $\bar{X} = 25$, $\sigma = 4$; and the control group has these: $\bar{X} = 19$, $\sigma = 3$; would you conclude that the difference is statistically significant?

$$\frac{25 - 19}{\sqrt{4^2 + 3^2}} = \frac{6}{5} = 1.2$$

The result is less than 2.0, so we conclude that the difference is *not* statistically significant.

What if the means were 25 and 19 but the standard deviations were 1 and 2?

$$\frac{25 - 19}{\sqrt{1^2 + 2^2}} = \frac{6}{2.3} = 2.6$$

In this case, since the z-score of the difference is 2.6, there is only one chance in 100 that the difference is *not* real.

RELATING MEASURES TO EACH OTHER

Often we want to know how closely two sets of measures are related to each other. For example, in Chapter 1 we looked at the question of how closely the I.Q. scores of children are related to those of their parents. Table 5 presents the same data for 63 families, with one parent and one child taken from each family. Looking over the figures, we saw that if the parent had a relatively high score, so did the child; low parental scores tended to be associated with low children's scores. But the relationship is not perfect; some parents with relatively high scores have children with relatively low scores. We then plotted the scores on a **scatterplot,** Figure 3. Here each parent-child pair is represented by one point on the graph. The first pair in the table—parent, 136, child, 131—is represented by a black point. The **coefficient of correlation**— generally referred to simply as the correlation—is the statistic used to quantify the relationship between any two variables—whether between parents' and children's I.Q. scores, measures of frustration and measures of aggression, or intelligence and creativity. The correlation shows the extent to which paired measures vary together. Correlation values range from 0 (no relationship) to 1.00 (perfect relationship); the higher the coefficient, the stronger the relationship.

Figure 3
Scatterplot Showing Relationship Between Children's and Parents' I.Q.'s
This scatterplot is constructed from the data given in Table 5 to show the relationship between the I.Q. scores of parents and their children. The point for parent 136– child 131 is shown in black to illustrate how points are plotted on the graph. The coefficient of correlation in this sample is 0.52.

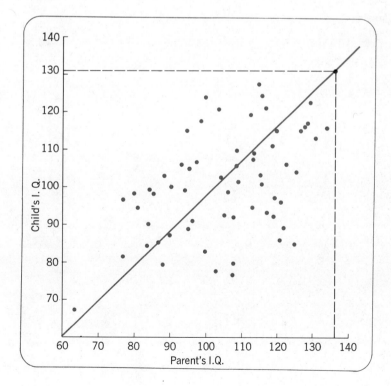

The correlation (abbreviated *r* in statistical work) in Figure 3 is 0.52 (*r* = .52). In psychological research, a correlation of .50 or more is considered relatively strong; correlations between .30 and .50 are moderate; those below .30 are considered low. Correlations can be positive (+, or often no sign is shown) or negative (always indicated by −). A positive correlation indicates that if the score on one variable is high, the other is also likely to be high.

A perfect correlation (+1.00 or −1.00) would have all the points in the scatterplot falling on a straight diagonal line and there would be perfect correspondence in relative standing in the two measures. If a subject scores third (or thirteenth) from the top in one variable, she or he would also stand third (or thirteenth) from the top in the other. A scatterplot for +1.00 is shown in Figure 4. The more the points deviate from such a straight line, the lower is the correlation.

Figure 5 shows two scatterplots for I.Q. data. Figure 5A is based on scores of parents and their adopted children; one can barely detect a relationship, and the correlation is only .18. The closest possible hereditary relationship occurs between identical twins; these are twins formed from a single egg cell. Even if they are raised apart from infancy, such twins usually resemble each other closely in intelligence and many other characteristics. A scatterplot for I.Q. scores of identical twins raised apart is given in Figure 5B; the correlation is .82. The size of this correlation, which is very high, and the fact that I.Q. correlations are higher the closer the hereditary relationship, suggest that there is a strong genetic factor in intelligence.

Figure 4
Scatterplot Showing
1.00 Correlation

With a correlation of +1.00 there is perfect predictability of the relationship of scores on one measure to scores on the other.

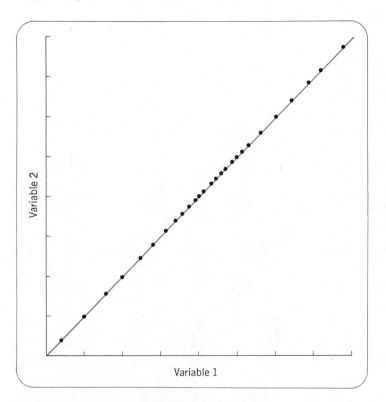

Variable 2

Variable 1

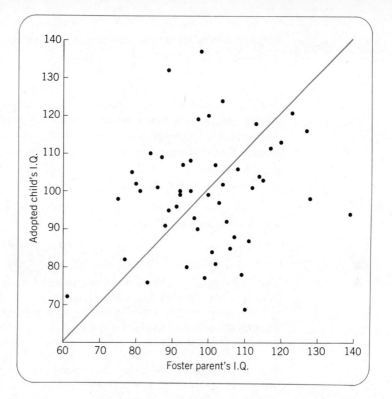

Figure 5A
Scatterplot Showing Relationships Between I.Q.'s of Foster Parents and Their Adopted Children
The coefficient of correlation in this study is 0.18.

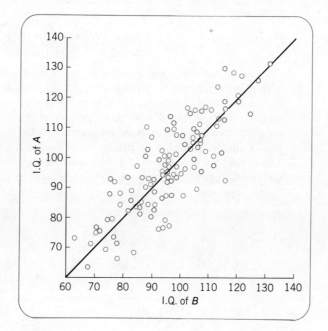

Figure 5B
Scatterplot Showing Correlation Between I.Q.'s of 122 Sets of Co-Twins (A and B, assigned at random)
The coefficient of correlation in this study is 0.82.

One of the primary uses of a correlation is to predict the standing on one variable if you know the standing on the other. For example, if you know a person's I.Q. score, you can predict the I.Q. of his or her identical twin with high accuracy; you can also predict the I.Q. of that person's biological child with reasonable accuracy. On the other hand, you can do little more than guess at the I.Q. of an adopted child. College admission boards use high-school grades as a major factor in selecting applicants because it has been demonstrated that there is a clear correlation between high-school and college grades; those who earn relatively high grades in school are likely to get good grades in college. A prediction based on such a correlation is not infallible, but it is much better than a guess.

The formula for the product-moment coefficient of correlation can be written in several different ways. This is one way:

$$r_{X,Y} = \frac{\Sigma z_X z_Y}{N} = \frac{\Sigma xy}{\sqrt{\Sigma x^2 y^2}}$$

That is, for each individual, find the product of his or her z-scores in the two distributions, sum these products, and divide by N.

This way of expressing the formula shows that the correlation can be thought of as the average of the products of z-scores. If the two measures are positively related, then an individual who has a score above the mean in one distribution will tend to have a score above the mean in the other; so the product of his z-scores will be positive. A person below the mean in both distributions will also have a positive product (since two minus terms have a positive product). If the two measures are unrelated, then some individuals will have positive products, some will have negative, and the mean product will be zero. If the relation between the two is negative (being high on one distribution means that you are likely to be low on the other), then the mean of the products will be negative.

For computation with a calculating machine, this formula using raw scores is practical:

$$r_{X,Y} = \frac{N\Sigma XY - (\Sigma X)(\Sigma Y)}{\sqrt{[N\Sigma X^2 - (\Sigma X)^2][N\Sigma Y^2 - (\Sigma Y)^2]}}$$

In interpreting correlation coefficients, be careful not to think of them as percentages, even though correlations vary from 0 to ± 1.00. Actually, the *square* of the coefficient (r^2), multiplied by 100, indicates how much of the variation in predicting Y you can account for if you know X. If the correlation is .80, then knowledge of the X scores would allow you to account for 64 percent ($.80^2 \times 100$) of the variation in Y scores. This is a high correlation, as psychological measurements go, but it still leaves quite a bit of variance unaccounted for. As another way of picturing how tight (or how loose) such a relationship is, look back at Figure 5B, and look again at the other scatterplots in this Appendix.

Glossary

Abnormality (1) Quantitatively, a deviation from the norm or from a statistical average. (2) Any mental or emotional disorder characterized by a disabling degree of social maladjustment, inability to cope with the environment, inappropriate and uncontrolled behavior or emotional expression, or high levels of anxiety and distress.

Absolute threshold The minimum physical intensity required for a stimulus to be detected.

Accessibility Characteristic of memory: stored information can be retrieved at time of test. *See* **Availability.**

Acetylcholine A chemical that acts as a transmitter agent at many synapses and at neuromuscular junctions. *See* Figure 19-3.

Acoustic similarity Similarity of sound among items in a test of short-term memory.

Acquisition A process resulting in the formation of an association—as in classical conditioning or verbal learning.

Action potential *See* **Neural impulse.**

Actualization theories Humanistic approaches to personality study that place great stress on the role of a person's aims and aspirations in determining behavior. *See also* **Self-actualization.**

Acuity The resolving power of the eye for spatial detail.

Additive color mixture Adding lights of various wavelengths to mix colors. *See* Color Figure 3.

Adrenal cortex The outer layer of the adrenal gland; it secretes a large number of hormones including androgens, estrogens and hormones that influence food and fluid balances and responses to stress. *See* Figure 19-8.

Adrenal medulla The inner part of the adrenal gland that secretes the hormone epinephrine (adrenalin). *See* Figure 19-8.

Adrenogenital system (AGS) Aberrations in genital and other structures caused by excessive secretion of adrenal androgen hormones during fetal development.

Affective disorder A group of psychoses characterized by severe and persistent mood disturbances, especially extreme depression and/or irrational euphoria.

Afterimage Visual sensation that persists after the stimulus producing it has stopped.

Agents of socialization Individuals and institutions that participate in socialization. Parents, teachers, neighbors, ministers, friends, characters in stories, movies, and television are all agents of socialization.

Alpha rhythm A 10 Hz rhythm in electrical activity of the brain; it is most likely to occur during relaxed wakefulness. *See* Figure 20-6.

Altruism Self-sacrificial behavior that benefits others, not the actor.

Amnesia Loss of memory caused by injury or by interference with the establishment of long-term memory.

Amplitude *See* **Intensity.**

Amygdala Nuclei in the temporal lobes that modulate aggression and other motivated behaviors. *See* Color Figure 3.

Analysis-by-synthesis Theory of pattern recognition that maintains that the perceiver actively synthesizes his or her percept from a portion of the available sensory information.

Androgens So-called male hormones, actually secreted by both sexes, although in greater amounts by males.

Angiotensin A substance produced by the kidneys that stimulates the brain to facilitate drinking fluids and to release antidiuretic hormone.

Antidiuretic hormone A hormone released by the posterior pituitary gland that helps govern fluid balance in the body.

Antisocial (sociopathic) personality Character disorder showing pervasive moral deviation.

Association A relationship that links a stimulus to a response or two items to one another.

Association value Number of associations given to an item by a group of subjects.

Attitude A judgment about a person, group, or thing. It consists of a cognitive component (opinion), an emotional component, and a disposition toward action.

Attribution theory Deals with (1) the rules people use in attempting to bring meaning and predictability to events by attempting to infer the causes of the behavior they observe, and (2) the different situations that produce different kinds of attributions.

Aunt behavior Maternal behavior toward an infant manifested by an adult female animal other than the mother.

Authoritative A style of childrearing that is supportive and affectionate at the same time as it maintains clearly defined and consistently enforced standards of behavior.

Autokinesis Apparent motion of a stationary pinpoint of light in a completely dark room.

Autonomic nervous system The part of the nervous system that controls the heart, smooth muscles, and several glands. *See* Table 19-1 for its divisions and functions; *see also* Color Figure 6.

Autoshaping In laboratory studies of learning, regular stereotyped responses that have no effect on obtaining a reward and that are not shaped by the experimenter; also known as "superstitious behavior."

Availability A characteristic of memory; information exists whether or not it can be retrieved. Compare **Accessibility.**

Axon The conducting zone in many neurons over which nerve impulses are conveyed to synapses. *See* Figure 19-1 and Color Figure 7.

Bait shyness Avoiding poisoned food. For example, a laboratory rat learns to avoid food if the food has made it ill an hour or so after eating. This learning is (1) very rapid—one "trial" is often enough; and (2) the negative reinforcement is relatively delayed from the stimulus and the response.

Basal age The mental age level at which a child passes all intelligence-test items.

Behavioral samples Part of an objective approach to personality assessment. An observer notes and records actual behaviors rather than judgments or inferences, as is the case with rating scales.

Behavior modification Psychotherapeutic technique that applies the principles of learning in order to modify disturbed behavior, generally focusing on specific behavioral disturbances.

Behaviors Responses of an individual, including thought, language, and speech as well as motor acts.

Behavior therapy *See* **Behavior modification.**

Binaural cues Cues to the location of a sound source that depend on the use of two ears. Because the ears are slightly separated, they receive different stimuli from the same source.

Binocular disparity The difference in the images cast on the two retinas by an object.

Biofeedback A method that provides subjects with information about their significant biological processes, enabling them to monitor and modify such normally involuntary responses as heart rate, blood pressure, and stomach contractions.

Brightness Psychological dimension referring to the perceived intensity of a light.

Brightness constancy The perception that the brightness of an object remains the same despite changes in illumination.

Buffer model Atkinson and Shiffrin's theory of memory that emphasizes the role of the short-term store in processing information.

Castration anxiety According to Freud, the young boy's fear that his father will retaliate for the boy's attraction to his mother and resentment of the father by castrating him. *See also* **Oedipal complex.**

Cephalocaudal direction The progressive development of the parts of the body and motor abilities in a direction from head to tail.

Cerebellum Part of the hind brain; it participates in control of body movements. *See* Figure 19-6.

Cerebral cortex The outer layers of the cerebral hemispheres, consisting of neurons and their connections; also called gray matter. It is deeply folded in human beings and higher mammals but is smooth in rodents and lower mammals. *See* Figure 19-7 and Color Figure 5.

Cerebral hemispheres The largest part of the brain of mammals, including everything above the brain stem. It includes the cerebral cortex, white matter, and such deep structures as the thalamus and basal ganglia. *See* Figures 19-5, 19-6, and 19-7.

Chunks In memory, the organization of familiar material for storage as a unit.

Circadian rhythm The 24-hour cycle of activity showed by almost all mammals.

Classical conditioning The procedure originally developed by Pavlov to establish an association between a stimulus and a response. By repeatedly pairing a conditioned stimulus (*CS*) with an unconditioned response (*UR*), *CS* eventually elicits *UR* or a similar response, which is then called a conditioned response (*CR*).

Client-centered therapy Psychotherapeutic technique introduced by Rogers in which therapists follow the lead of the clients, encouraging them to explore and accept their feelings and thoughts. The therapist attempts to convey unconditional acceptance and understanding of the client.

Closure A principle of perceptual organization: parts of the stimulus field that produce a closed or almost closed unit are perceived as belonging to the same unit.

Cochlea The inner ear. *See* Figure 22-12.

Coefficient of correlation Coefficient of correlation is a numerical value that indicates the degree of correspondence between two sets of paired measures; it ranges from +1.00 to −1.00. (*See* Appendix on statistics.)

Cognition The knowledge, interpretations, understandings, thoughts, and/or ideas that people have about themselves and the environment.

Cognitive dissonance A state of tension generated when

a person holds two cognitions that are inconsistent with one another. In dissonance theory this inconsistency refers to cognitions that carry contradictory implications for behavior.

Cognitive styles   Stable, characteristic ways of approaching and handling cognitive tasks (*see* e.g., **Reflectivity-impulsivity, Leveling-sharpening**).

Cohesion   The condition of social organization in which groups stay together to increase their chances of survival. *See also* **Dispersal.**

Collective unconscious   What Jung termed "archetypes," the attitudes and feelings that are the residue of the ancestral past of humanity.

Color circle   Two-dimensional diagram summarizing various phenomena of color sensation and color mixture. *See* Color Figure 3.

Common fate   A principle of perceptual organization: parts of the stimulus field that act together tend to be perceived as belonging to the same unit. *See* Figure 17-40.

Comparative psychology   The branch of psychology that studies and compares the behaviors of animals, including human beings.

Complementary colors   Colors that when mixed in appropriate proportions form an achromatic (gray) mixture.

Compliance   The least permanent level of social influence; a person complies (carries out an action) in order to obtain a reward or to avoid punishment.

Concept   The symbol—usually a word or label—for a class of objects that share a common property.

Concept formation   Learning and applying the rules for grouping diverse objects or events.

Concrete operations   Period of the third stage in Piaget's theory of intellectual development, in which the child reasons in a systematic and logical way. He or she is able to use rules based on concrete instances, but not those dealing with abstract qualities; the period lasts from approximately 7 to 11 years of age.

Conditioned response (CR)   The learned or acquired response to a conditioned stimulus. *See* **Classical conditioning.**

Conditioned stimulus (CS)   A stimulus that through classical conditioning evokes a conditioned response.

Cone   Type of retinal receptor used in daylight vision. Three types of cone cells respond to different parts of the visual spectrum. *See* Figure 22-1.

Conformity   A change in a person's opinions or behavior as a result of social influence. This influence usually takes the form of real or imagined pressure from another person or a group.

Conjunctive concept   A concept defined by the joint presence of two or more attributes—for instance, "large blue squares."

Consistency, theories of   The idea that people strive to keep their attitudes, behavior, and cognitions consistent. If they find them inconsistent, they attempt to reduce discrepancies by altering beliefs, changing behavior, or both.

Consolidation of memory   Transforming the neural basis of memory from a temporary form into a stable long-term form.

Construct validity   Relationship of a measure of a personality dimension to a particular theoretical formulation of that dimension.

Contagious behavior   A response that spreads from one animal to the whole group. For example, if one howler monkey starts calling, the entire troop soon joins in.

Continuity   The theoretical position that learning is a gradual (continuous) strengthening of associations.

Control group   A group of subjects sharing all characteristics with the experimental group but *not* given the treatment whose effect is under study.

Convergent thinking   Thinking that moves in the direction of conventional and socially accepted paths—for example, a dictionary definition.

Corpus callosum   Large band of axons uniting the cerebral hemispheres across the midline of the brain. *See* Figure 19-6C and Color Figure 5.

Cortex   Outer layer or bark. *See* **Cerebral cortex, Adrenal cortex.**

Creativity   Ability to find a new, original, and imaginative solution to a problem that may be cognitive, philosophical, or aesthetic.

Criterion validity   Degree to which scores on a test are related to an agreed-upon reference point for the behavior being assessed.

Critical (sensitive) periods   Periods of time that are particularly important in the development of body organs, physical attributes, cognitive functions, acquisition of new responses, and personality and social characteristics. Interruption of normal development during these periods may lead to deficiencies or malfunctions in the organism.

Cross-sectional study   A study in which groups of individuals of different ages are observed and tested at a single point in time. Data are collected only once.

Culture-fair test   An intelligence test constructed to minimize bias caused by different cultural experiences and environments—that is, biases related to social and ethnic group membership.

Culture overlay   The veneer of social organization; learning based on cultural traditions and needs often overlies or hides more instinctive behaviors.

Decibel (db) A ratio measurement of physical sound intensity: the number of decibels is one-tenth the logarithm of the ratio of a particular intensity to a reference intensity. *See* Figure 18-17 for the decibels for some common sounds.

Deep structure The underlying or meaning level of language.

Defense mechanisms Modes of coping with anxiety-arousing situations and of resolving conflicts. Examples are **repression, denial, projection, hysteria** (reaction formation), **rationalization,** and **sublimation.**

Deindividuation The loss or submersion of one's identity as a responsible, accountable individual resulting in the weakening of inhibitions against the performance of impulsive or antisocial behavior. Deindividuation may be brought about by anonymity—either physical (the wearing of masks, uniforms), social events (submersion in a mob), or chemical events (the use of drugs).

Delayed-response test Measure of memory and mental ability that imposes a delay between the presentation of a stimulus and the opportunity to respond. *See* Figure 23-6.

Demand characteristics Responses to a situation based on the individual's perception of what is expected of him or her, rather than on actual observation.

Dendrite A specialized part of a neuron. Many kinds of neurons have dendrites branching from the cell body to increase their receptive surface. *See* Figure 19-1 and Color Figure 7.

Denial A defense mechanism that permits awareness of unacceptable impulses and associated ideas but frees them of their threatening implications.

Dependent variable The observed variable, which, according to the hypothesis, will change as a result of changes in the independent variable.

Deprivation motives In the personality theory of Abraham Maslow, motivation oriented toward the simple maintenance of life—food, safety, belongingness—rather than toward its enhancement. *See also* **Growth motives.**

Depth perception The ability to perceive relative distances of various objects.

Dichotic hearing. *See* **Dichotic stimulation.**

Dichotic stimulation Stimulation that differs at the two ears. From the Greek roots *dich,* meaning "two" and *otic,* meaning "ear."

Diencephalon One of the five fetal divisions of the brain. In adults, it includes the thalamus and the hypothalamus. *See* Figures 19-5, 19-6.

Difference thresholds The minimum detectable change in a physical stimulus.

Dimorphism Differences in body structure. *Sexual dimorphism* means that the male and female of a species have different body structures.

Discriminative stimulus Signal that indicates whether reinforcement is available if a response is made.

Disjunctive concept Concept derived by combining concepts that do not overlap—for example, children, derived from *boys* and *girls.*

Dispersal A splitting apart or separating of a group, as opposed to cohesion.

Displacement (1) In Freudian personality theory, a defense mechanism indicated by behaviors toward a person or object other than the "true" person. For example, a person may be angry at the boss, but yell at his or her spouse. (2) In animal behavior an irrelevant activity that occurs in the midst of directed behavior, e.g., grooming in the middle of a fight. These behaviors are believed to represent a conflict, such as between fear and aggression.

Display Species-specific behavior that evokes a response from members of the same or other species. For example, in sexual displays, the peacock signals its readiness to mate by spreading its tail plumes. In aggressive displays, some animals may bare their teeth or hiss; grooming behavior is a display in some social organizations in animals.

Distractor technique A method to study forgetting over brief periods of time by diverting the subject's attention from the to-be-remembered material.

Distribution All the data from the entire sample of a measurement, arranged along a range of lowest to highest and giving the frequency of occurrence for each score.

Distribution of practice Spacing of study time during learning. Whether distributed practice or massed practice is more effective depends on the task. *See also* **Total-time hypothesis.**

Divergent thinking Thinking that moves away from the conventional and socially acceptable. *See also* **Creativity.**

Dominance hierarchy The organization of social relationships that regulates who dominates whom in such activities as sex, aggression, and feeding. For example, a dominant male eats first, copulates most, and "wins" threat contests with nondominant males.

Down's Syndrome The technical term for mongolism, a form of mental retardation associated with a genetic abnormality. Such physical problems as thick tongue, extra eyelid folds, and heart deformities—as well as mental deficits—are manifested.

Dreams Vivid experiences that occur during paradoxical or rapid-eye-movement phases of sleep.

Drive A motive force for behavior, often seen as resulting from a biological need. A state of tension that leads to behaviors to reduce the tension and restore the original equilibrium. *See also* **Homeostasis.**

Drive reduction The reduction of tensions, usually of biological drives such as hunger. Drive-reduction theories of reinforcement suggest that substances that reduce drives can be used to increase habit strength, e.g., food can be used in teaching a hungry animal.

Ego Freud's term for that part of the personality that coordinates and directs behavior; the ego mediates between the impulsive demands of the **id** and the constraints of the **superego** and reality.

Ego diffusion The inability of an individual to integrate his or her various roles or identities into a coherent sense of self.

Electroconvulsive shock (ECS) therapy A treatment used for severely depressed or schizophrenic patients.

Electroencephalogram (EEG) A record of the electrical activity of the brain measured by electrodes placed on the outside of the head. *See* Figure 20-6.

Empiricism The philosophical position that behavior results almost entirely from training, learning, and past experience. *See also* **Nativism.**

Encoding The representation of one thing by another; the registration of information in memory via sensory receptors and the afferent nervous system.

Endocrine gland Gland that secretes hormones directly into the bloodstream. *See* Figure 19-8.

Episodic memory Memory for recent items and events that can be dated.

Estrogens So-called female hormones, actually secreted by both sexes, although in greater amounts by females.

Estrus The sexually receptive state in female mammals. (The related adjective is estrous.)

Ethology The study of animal behaviors—usually in the animal's natural habitat—that promote the survival of the species.

Evolution through natural selection Darwin's theory (1859) that variety and changes in animal form and function occurred because, in any generation, selective advantages increased some individuals' chances of survival.

Experience Learning or practice; one of the two complex and interacting processes involved in all the changes that take place as an organism grows to maturity. *See also* **Maturation.**

Experimental group The group of subjects for whom the experimenter changes the independent variables whose effects are under study.

Extinction Procedure or process that, by failing to reinforce an established association, weakens and eventually eliminates it. *See also* **Classical conditioning.**

Extroversion Jung's term for the tendency to focus on the outside world.

Fast-wave sleep *See* **Rapid-eye-movement sleep.**

Feature analysis Theory of pattern recognition that implies the extraction of parts of patterns—such as vertical or horizontal lines and arcs of circles—to discover which combination of features characterizes a particular pattern.

Fechner's Law Psychophysical law stating that perceptual magnitude increases in proportion to the logarithm of the physical intensity of the stimulus: $\psi = k \log \phi$.

Feedback Return of part of the output of a system back to the input, especially that which corrects and controls an activity. Feedback occurs in both the endocrine and nervous systems. *See also* **Biofeedback.**

Field independence/dependence Individual differences in cognitive styles, in which one relies on either external or internal clues for spatial and physical orientation.

Figural aftereffect Distorted perception of such dimensions of a figure as size, shape, or distance caused by prior visual stimulation with another figure.

Filter theory Broadbent's information-processing theory of memory. It stresses that the capacity for processing information is limited.

Fitts' law A principle of skill learning stating that skills continue to improve with practice, but the rate of progress becomes continually slower (a power function).

Fixed action patterns (FAP's) A species-characteristic response pattern that is presumed to have survival value for the organism.

Forebrain The part of the brain that develops from the forward end of the embryonic neural tube. It includes the telencephalon and the dicephalon. *See* Figures 19-5, 19-6.

Formal operations Period of the fourth stage of Piaget's theory of intellectual development, in which the child becomes able to use abstract rules; the stage of adult logic, it begins around 11 years of age and continues through adulthood.

Fovea The central portion of the retina, in which vision is most acute.

Free association A psychoanalytic technique in which the patient focuses on a past event and says whatever comes to mind. Such associations are believed to be manifestations of unconscious wishes or fears.

Free recall A learning or short-term memory procedure in which a subject recalls items from a list in any order.

Frequency (1) In describing the distribution of data from research, the number of subjects that make each score or measurement. (2) In sound, the physical attribute that specifies the number of cycles per second of vibration. The unit of measure is the hertz (Hz).

Frustration Emotional state resulting from interference with goal attainment.

Functional fixedness A mental set in which it is difficult to see potential functions of an object beyond its customary use.

Gain-loss theory of attraction The idea that increases in the amount of reward one person gives to another, rather than the amount of reward, determine how much one individual is attracted to another. Increases in reward have more impact than constant or invariant rewards; a person whose esteem for another person increases over time will be better liked than one who has always liked the other person.

Ganglion A cluster of neural cell bodies and synapses. See Figure 19-11.

Gender role The outward appearance and behavior of being male or female, determined by both heredity and environment.

Generalization (1) Broad principles of behavior, the ways in which all people (or animals) are alike. (2) In stimulus generalization, any of similar stimuli that evoke a particular response; in response generalization, a specific stimulus evokes a variety of similar responses, as in conditioning.

Gestalt A German word meaning "configuration." The Gestalt approach to psychology stresses organization in perception.

G factor (general intelligence) Said by some psychologists to be the most general factor common to all measures of mental ability, present to some extent on all tests of intelligence.

Goal gradient Increase in the motivation to attain a goal as one draws nearer to it.

Goodness A Gestalt measure of the perceptual organization or salience of a stimulus pattern.

Gray matter Collections of cell bodies in the nervous system such as the cerebral cortex and basal ganglia; they appear darker than the white fiber tracts. See Figure 19-6 and Color Figure 5.

Grooming Many animals wash themselves or others, picking off bugs and dirt. Apart from hygiene, grooming helps maintain social cohesiveness between members of a species, males and females, and parents and children.

Group therapy A form of psychotherapy in which a number of patients, under the guidance of a qualified therapist, help each other to gain new insights and perspectives into problems or conflicts.

Growth motives In the personality theory of Abraham Maslow, the category of human motives characterized by a push toward the realization of inherent potentialities (self-actualization). See also **Deprivation motives.**

Habit reversal Learning the opposite of what has just been learned. For example, if a white door has previously been associated with food, the animal must learn that the black door now leads to food.

Habituation The decrease in the size of a response as the stimulus is repeated.

Heredity-environment interactions The amount or extent to which a particular trait or skill can be attributed to the relative influence of inborn factors (heredity) and learning and experience (environment). See also **Empiricism, Nativism.**

Hertz (Hz) Measurement of frequency of sound waves in cycles per second.

Hindbrain The third part of the embryonic neural tube. In adults it subdivides into the metencephalon and the myelencephalon. See Figures 19-5, 19-6.

Homeostasis The tendency of the body's systems to return to one particular state or level of functioning. For example, the human body maintains a relatively stable body temperature; internal mechanisms work to increase temperature if it falls below 98.6° and decrease if it goes above 98.6°.

Hormone The secretion of an endocrine gland. See Figure 19-8.

Hue The dimension of visual perception determined by the wavelength of the stimulus. Red, yellow, green, and blue are hues. See Color Figure 4.

Hypothalamus A part of the diencephalon containing specialized centers related to motivation and drives. See Figures 19-5, 19-7, and Color Figure 4.

Hypothesis Tentative explanatory statement or "best guess" about the relationship between two variables. Hypotheses are tested by experimental or observational studies.

Hypothesis testing Gathering information and testing possible alternative solutions to a problem.

Hysteria The impairment of a bodily function for psychological, as contrasted to organic, reasons; also known as a "conversion reaction."

Iconic memory Literal representation of a stimulus in memory for about 1 second after a stimulus affect.

Id Freud's term for that part of the personality that consists of unconscious sexual and aggressive impulses seeking immediate expression and gratification.

Identificand The person or group with whom the child identifies.

Identification The process by which people (especially children) internalize the characteristics of another person or group; modeling one's behavior after that of another.

Identity crisis The struggle that takes place within individuals when they seek to answer questions such as, Who am I? and arrive at a definition of identity.

Illumination The stage in creative thinking when the solution to a problem unexpectedly becomes clear—a form of insight.

Illusion Lack of correspondence between a percept and a physical stimulus object that evokes it.

Imprinting A species-specific learning that typically occurs within a limited critical period shortly after birth. Such behaviors are usually limited to social responses (like following or identifying a parent or child).

Inaccessibility *See* **Accessibility.**

Incidental learning Inadvertent learning that occurs without deliberate intent to learn.

Incubation stage The stage in creative thinking when the thinker stops working actively on the problem and during which information is absorbed and assimilated, perhaps unconsciously.

Independent variable The variable selected or manipulated by the investigator to determine its effects on the dependent variable(s).

Induced motion The perception of motion of stationary objects caused by contextual changes. *See* Figure 17-20.

Inferotemporal cortex Cerebral cortex at the base of the temporal lobe that is involved in visual form perception. *See* Figure 22-7.

Information processing An approach to learning, perception, and other topics in psychology that seeks to determine how information is transformed (elaborated, stored, retrieved) between stimulus and response.

Inoculation effect Achievement of attitudes resistant to change by "infecting" a person first with a weakened form of an attitude or argument to be encountered later. When these arguments are eventually encountered, the person is able to resist them.

Insight The sudden recognition of the nature of a problem and its correct solution.

Instinctive drift The tendency of an animal to drift toward species-characteristic behavior despite learned behavior.

Intellectualization The use of intellectual sophistication to avoid arousing angry, painful, or anxious feelings when discussing potentially threatening content.

Intelligence The ability to think and act in adaptive ways; also encompassing such complex mental abilities as thinking, reasoning, and problem solving.

Intelligence quotient (I.Q.) The ratio of mental age to chronological age: I.Q. = M.A./C.A. × 100.

I.Q. stability The constancy of I.Q. over time as measured by test scores. Only major environmental change and increasing age are thought to cause significant changes after the age of four.

Intensity In sound, the physical strength of an auditory stimulus.

Interaction When the effect of one variable differs depending on the level of another variable(s); e.g., when the same situation affects different people in different ways.

Interference In learning and memory the negative transfer effects of other learning. *See* **Proactive interference, Retroactive interference.**

Internalization Process by which individual accepts influence because the induced behavior fits in with a personal value system or with what he or she thinks is "right." Once established, an internalized belief is very difficult to change.

Interneurons Neurons interposed between sensory and motor cells that affect habituation and sensitization to repeated stimuli.

Intromission Insertion of the penis into the vagina.

Introversion Jungian term for a person's tendency to focus on the inner world of subjective experience. *See also* **Extroversion.**

Just noticeable difference (jnd) Minimum change in the physical stimulus required to yield the perception that the stimulus has changed.

Korsakoff's syndrome A disease that may occur in severe alcoholism. The patient's memory is distorted because of brain lesions caused by a lack of vitamin B.

Language The primary symbolic system created to codify meaning and enable communication to occur.

Latent learning Learning that occurs unobserved; it becomes evident only with motivation and reinforcement.

Lateral hypothalamic nucleus Part of the brain that participates in control of food intake. *See* Figure 20.5.

Law of effect Thorndike's theory that learning is a trial-and-error process in which responses that lead to rewards are gradually strengthened.

Learning The relatively permanent modification of behavior through experience.

Learning curve Curve that shows the functional relationship between some amount of practice (independent variable) and some measure of performance (dependent variable).

Learning set Conditioning that prepares an organism to learn in a specified way. For example, animals that have solved several problems of the same general type seem to have acquired the general principle underlying such problems; they can learn new solutions to such problems more readily.

Leveling-sharpening Dimension of cognitive style determining whether an individual sees and remembers differences or similarities between objects or events observed.

Libido A Freudian concept referring to a basic pleasure-seeking drive of erotic nature.

Linear perspective A consequence of geometry and objects that induces visual depth perception; for example, parallel railroad tracks extending into three-dimensional space.

Longitudinal study A study in which the same individuals are observed and tested repeatedly over an extended period of time, often a decade or longer.

Lordosis The elevation of the hind quarters by some female mammals during breeding periods in response to tactile stimulation of the back or flanks.

Loudness The perceived strength of a sound, usually measured in decibels.

Mach effect Perception of distinct lines or bands at places in a stimulus array with abrupt changes in the intensity.

Mammals A member of the subphylum of vertebrates characterized by maternal suckling, internal regulation of body temperature, and hair-covered skin.

Mands According to B. F. Skinner, verbal responses of a kind that have been positively reinforced in past experiences.

Manic-depressive psychosis A mental illness characterized by abrupt changes in mood from extreme excitement and euphoria to deep depression, and vice versa.

Maturation The physical, neural, physiological, and biochemical changes that take place within the organism over a period of time.

Mean A measure of central tendency of scores in a distribution. The arithmetic mean is the sum of all scores divided by the number of scores.

Mechanoreceptors Receptors that detect mechanical stimuli such as touch to the skin, limb position at a joint, and blood flow in blood vessels.

Median A measure of central tendency of scores in a distribution. The median divides the scores exactly in half when the scores have been arranged from largest to smallest.

Mediating processes Internal processes that enable children to reason and solve problems by thinking.

Mediator Additional information added to help relate two items; e.g., ring-rung-ladder.

Mel A measurement of pitch (from "melody").

Memory span The number of items that can be reproduced in order after a single presentation, typically 7 ± 2.

Memory storage The persistence of information over time.

Mental age (M.A.) A person's score on an intelligence test, expressed in years and months; based on age at which average children make a specific score.

Mental operations Jean Piaget's term for **Mediating processes.**

Mental retardation Endogenous retardation is genetically determined retardation; it includes low intelligence, poor coordination, and other sensory deficits. Exogenous retardation is environmentally determined retardation caused by any of a variety of externally caused traumas (or deprivations).

Midbrain (mesencephalon) The middle part of the embryonic neural tube. In adults, it includes the visual and auditory colliculi. *See* Figures 19-5, 19-6.

Milieu therapy A means of treating hospitalized mental patients in which they are encouraged to establish relationships with other patients and with staff and to assume some responsibility for themselves.

Mnemonic devices Aids and associations for remembering specific items—such as the rhyme "i before e except after c."

Modal action patterns (MAP's) *See* **Fixed action patterns.**

Modelling In social learning theory, the mechanism that enables the child to learn complex social and cognitive behaviors by observation and imitation of others.

Modulation sensitivity function A measure of visual acuity using the threshold contrast required for detecting gratings of different widths.

Monism The theory that there is only one kind of learning and that all examples of learning follow the same basic principles.

Motion parallax Differential change of retinal images of different parts of the visual field as the observer moves.

Motivation Theoretical term referring to activating states of the individual that direct behavior toward the fulfillment of specific needs and desires.

Multifactor theories Theories that propose intelligence test performance is a product of at least several different abilities, instead of one general factor.

Nanometer (nm) A billionth of a meter (10^{-9} meters). Wavelengths of light are measured in nanometers.

Nativism Position that various skills or processes are

independent of learning; that is, that they are built into the basic functions of the nervous system.

Naturalistic observation   Observation of events in real-life settings, such as nursery schools, playgrounds, or at home, without experimental manipulation of the variables involved.

Negative afterimage   An afterimage with colors complementary to those in the inducing stimulus. *See* Color Figure 3.

Nerve cells   The cells that, along with supporting cells, make up the brain and other parts of the nervous system. *See* Figure 19-1.

Nervous system   The brain, spinal cord, autonomic system, and peripheral nerves running to all parts of the body. *See* Figure 19–4.

Neural impulse (also called **action potential**)   A wave of electrochemical activity that can be propagated along a neuron. Most neurons are specialized to conduct such activity.

Neurons   Single nerve cells. *See* Figure 19-1.

Neurosis   Diagnostic term referring to emotional and behavioral disturbances that disrupt adequate adjustment but are not intense or comprehensive enough to severely diminish contact with reality. Examples are irrational fears, anxiety reactions, compulsions, and sexual impotence and frigidity.

Nightmares   Apparent disorders of arousal that occur at the deepest level of nondreaming sleep or during sudden arousal from such sleep. *See* Spotlight 20-5.

Normal curve   The bell-shaped frequency distribution that describes the graph of many measures in psychology and other sciences. Its properties are used in making statistical inferences from measures based on samples. *See* Appendix.

Object permanence   Term used by Piaget to refer to people's realization that objects continue to exist even though they are not visible to them.

Obsessive-compulsive neurosis   Recurrent words, thoughts, or impulses a person cannot control (obsessions); repetitive motors acts that the individual feels impelled to carry out (compulsion).

Oedipal complex   Freud's term for the boy's sexual attraction to his mother and consequent fear and resentment of his father.

One-male group   A social organization in which the basic group consists of one male, several females, and a number of infants and adolescents.

Operant conditioning   A type of conditioning in which the response is controlled by the reinforcement following it.

Operant-conditioning techniques   Procedures for producing behavior change based on Skinner's applica-

tions of principles of reinforcement. These techniques have recently gained wide application in therapy of behavior disorders.

Operant procedure   A method of training in which a desired behavior is reinforced by giving a reward.

Operational definition   Defining each of the terms used in the statement of an experimental hypothesis objectively, that is, as observable responses or measurements.

Opponent-process theory   The color vision theory proposing that opposing processes (excitation and inhibition) in ganglion cells underlie perception of contrasting primary hues—yellow versus blue and red versus green. *See* Figures 22-10 and 22-11.

Optic chiasm   The crossing of the optic nerve fibers. *See* Figure 21-4.

Optic nerve   Nerve formed by axons of the ganglion cells in the retina. It leaves the eye at the blind spot and runs to the optic chiasm. From the chiasm to the thalamus, the fibers are called the optic tract. *See* Figure 22-5.

Paired associates   A learning procedure in which a subject learns to relate or associate pairs of items.

Paradoxical sleep   *See* **Rapid-eye-movement sleep.**

Parasympathetic system   Part of the autonomic nervous system that predominates in restoring body energy. *See* Table 19-1 and Color Figure 6.

Partial reinforcement   Schedule of reinforcement in which only some fraction of the total responses is reinforced.

Peak experience   According to Abraham Maslow, a moment of pure happiness, ecstasy, or sense of oneness with the world. Such moments are experienced occasionally by everyone but more frequently by the healthy, self-actualized person.

Peers   Agemates.

Penis envy   In Freud's psychoanalytic theory, the girl child's sense of being "incomplete," weak, and inferior is symbolized by her desire for a male sexual organ.

Percept   That which is perceived; the result of the process of perception.

Perception   Awareness by the organism of its environment through various senses.

Perceptual constancy   The ability to recognize different stimulus patterns as representing the same object.

Perceptual contrast   Perceived enhancement of physical differences between stimuli, such as size and brightness.

Perceptual defense   A response characteristic referring to an observer's refusal to see unwanted stimuli.

Personality disorder   Deeply ingrained, generalized,

and usually lifelong maladaptive behavior style and character structure. Often people suffering from personality disorders do not perceive themselves as disturbed.

Personality dynamics   Functions of behavior; explaining the why, where, and when of the workings of personality.

Peterson paradox   The fact that memory for a repeated item improves when presentations are separated.

Phobia   Neurosis characterized by irrational intense anxiety reactions to specific objects and situations.

Photons   Packets of light energy. These can be captured by photopigments in the rod and cone cells of the eye. *See also* **Quanta.**

Photopic vision   The perceptual experience of color at daylight levels of light energy.

Pitch   The psychological perception of how high or low a tone sounds.

Pituitary gland   A major endocrine gland. Its hormones govern growth and influence other endocrine gland secretions. *See* Figure 19-8.

Pluralism   The theoretical position in learning that there are many kinds of learning. *See also* **Monism.**

Pons   Part of brain stem lying above the medulla and below the midbrain containing specialized centers; it is composed in part of fibrous tracts that form a bridge from one side of the cerebellum to the other. *See* Figure 19-6A.

Power law   Psychophysical law stating that perceptual magnitude increases in proportion to the physical intensity of the stimulus raised to a given power $(n): \psi = k\phi^N$; also known as Stevens' Law.

Prägnanz, law of   Gestalt law stating that the organization of any whole will be as good as prevailing conditions allow.

Predator   The attacking animal in a food-gathering situation; e.g., a herring gull attacking and eating baby terns.

Prejudice   A set of hostile attitudes based on and supported by generalizations derived from faulty or incomplete information.

Preoperational period   Second stage in Piaget's theory of intellectual development, in which representational thought begins; the first time that the child's reactions are based on the meaning of the object rather than on its physical nature; the period from approximately 2 to 7 years.

Preparation stage   The first stage in the creative process, in which a person is immersed in all the information available about a problem or project.

Prey   The animal being pursued by others that are gathering food. For example, the deer is the prey for hungry wolves.

Primacy effect   Better memory and stronger influence of early information over later information in word lists, cognitions, impressions, and attitudes.

Primary drives   Motivational states that govern behavior with regard to such basic biological systems as control of eating, fluid balance, and sex.

Primary mental abilities (PMA)   The many independent abilities (such as verbal comprehension and memory) that underlie performance on mental tests, discovered by factor analysis.

Primary motor cortex   The part of the cerebral cortex that sends impulses to the muscles. *See* Figure 19-10.

Primary somatosensory cortex   The part of the cerebral cortex that receives neural impulses from the skin. *See* Figure 19-10.

Proactive interference   Interference with learning or remembering new associations caused by previously learned associations.

Probabilistic inference   The tendency to reason on the basis of probability rather than on formal rules of logic.

Probability (p)   In statistics, assessment of the degree of trustworthiness to be accorded differences obtained in research, expressed in terms of the likelihood that the difference would occur a given number of times out of a hundred by chance alone. For example, in a large, precise sample, $p > .01$ (less than once in 100 cases) would indicate that the difference obtained is due to manipulation of the variable and not sampling error.

Probe technique   In studying short-term memory, a method of using a probe or cue to test memory for an item on a long list.

Problem solving   Seeking to attain a desired goal by overcoming a barrier.

Projection   A defensive reaction that attributes to others one's own unacceptable repressed feelings and ideas.

Projective tests   Tests using ambiguous stimuli, such as inkblots and pictures, for the purpose of revealing aspects of the personality of which the subject is usually unaware.

Prototype comparison   The process of comparing incoming information with ideal representations stored in memory—for example, various forms of the letter *A*.

Proximity   A principle of perceptual organization: parts of the stimulus field near each other tend to be seen as belonging to the same unit.

Proximodistal direction   The characteristic direction of progressive physical and motor development from the central part out to peripheral or terminal segments.

Pseudoretardation   Low intelligence-test scores caused by severe emotional or social deprivation when potential for achievement is significantly higher.

Psychedelic The hallucinogenic effect of LSD and other drugs that alter experience and perception. The subject may experience extreme mood changes, heightened and inappropriate emotional reactions, tactile and visual distortions, and vivid hallucinations.

Psychoanalysis Psychotherapeutic procedures developed by Freud to uncover and resolve unconscious emotional conflicts that underlie neurotic symptoms; examples of procedures are **free association** and dream interpretation.

Psychoanalytic theory A theory of personality and psychotherapy developed by Freud, emphasizing unconscious motivation and the importance of the early psychosexual development of the child in subsequent adult behavior.

Psychodrama A spontaneous role-playing technique used in psychotherapy.

Psychopathology The study, assessment, and treatment of individuals whose behavior is irrational, bizarre, or uncontrolled.

Psychophysics The study of the relation between physical dimensions of a stimulus and the psychological dimensions of the corresponding sensation.

Psychosexual stages According to psychoanalytic theory, the oral, anal, phallic, and latency stages through which human development progresses. Each stage is characterized by a specific locus and mode of gratification of sexual impulses.

Psychosis A diagnostic term referring to a group of important mental disorders in which the patient has lost contact with reality; examples are **schizophrenia** and **manic-depressive psychosis.**

Psychosocial stages Erik Erikson's analysis of personality and social development, emphasizing eight life crises or stages that span the period from infancy to old age.

Psychosomatic reaction A physical disorder caused by emotional difficulties; examples are neurodermatitis and asthma.

Punishment A negative reinforcement.

Purkinje shift The change in the relative brightness of colors caused by a shift from photopic to scotopic vision.

Quanta Very small packets of electromagnetic radiation energy. Each quantum can be measured by its wavelength.

Random assignment Assignment of individuals to groups solely by chance—without regard to their characteristics—so that all groups are essentially equal in all respects.

Rapid-eye-movement (REM) sleep Phase of sleep during which the closed eyes show rapid movements and EEG patterns resemble the high-frequency low-voltage waves of the waking pattern. Dreams usually occur during this "paradoxical sleep." *See* Figure 20-6.

Rating scale A continuum ranging from low to high used to quantify interview impressions of personality characteristics or observations of behavior in natural settings.

Rationalization Defense mechanism using the rules of reason to provide acceptable explanations of otherwise unacceptable and painful ideas and actions.

Reaction formation Defense mechanism that produces behavior directly opposite to unconscious feelings and attitudes.

Reasoning Solving a problem by assessing it and drawing logical conclusions.

Recall Method of testing memory in which the subject generates the response. *See also* **Recognition.**

Recency effect The stronger influence of later information over the earlier information in word lists, cognitions, impressions, and attitudes.

Receptive field The part of the sensory surface or the part of the visual range that excites or inhibits a receptor cell or central cell. *See* Figure 22-2, 22-13.

Recognition Method of testing memory in which the subject identifies the correct response when it occurs among alternative possibilities. *See also* **Recall.**

Redirection Behavior directed toward a different object or animal than usual—for example, a bird pecks at the ground instead of its foe.

Reflectivity-impulsivity Dimension of cognitive style determining the extent of hesitation (reflection) before the subject takes action.

Regression to the mean The statistical finding that, on the average, parents at either extreme of a distribution (such as intelligence) tend to have children who are closer to the mean.

Reinforcement Stimulation following occurrence of a response that affects the probability that the response will be made again in a similar situation. Giving a reward for a response is **positive reinforcement;** punishment for an act is **negative reinforcement.** (For reinforcement in operant conditioning, *see* Chapter 14; for biological processes in reinforcement, *see* Chapter 21.)

Reinforcement schedules Reinforcement contingencies; patterns of partial reinforcement in operant conditioning.

Releaser Stimulus that triggers a **Fixed action pattern.**

Reliability Extent to which a test yields similar results each time it is used.

Repression Unconscious exclusion from awareness of unacceptable impulses and ideas; considered by Freud to be the primary defense mechanism.

Response criterion In perception, the separation of responses to signals, measured by β.

Retina Paper-thin layer at the back of the eye that transmits nerve impulses to the brain. *See* Figure 22-2.

Retinal disparity The difference in the image cast on one retina from that cast on the other.

Retrieval In **recall** or in **recognition,** utilization of stored information to generate an answer.

Retroactive interference Interference with remembering previously learned associations caused by learning intervening (newer) associations.

Retrograde amnesia Amnesia for events preceding an accident (such as a head injury) or an experimental treatment (such as electroconvulsive shock).

Reversal shift Experimental procedure in which a subject must—to receive a reward—make a response opposite to that previously learned. For example, in discrimination warning, the subject must pick a white stimulus on an occasion for which he or she previously would have chosen a black one.

Reward theory of attraction The theory that we like people whose behavior is rewarding and dislike those whose behavior is punishing.

Rod Type of retinal receptor cell that responds to weak as well as strong light. *See* Figure 22-1.

Sample A set of scores or individuals selected from a population. If the sampling is done randomly (without regard to characteristics of the individuals chosen) and is large enough the sample may be considered an unbiased representation of the population.

Saturation Richness or intensity of **hue;** it ranges from a full hue to a gray of the same brightness. Pink is a weakly saturated red.

Scapegoat theory Prejudiced behavior that is the result of the displacement of aggression from a vague or dangerous source onto a safe, easily identifiable target.

Scatterplot A graph showing scores made by individuals, or by defined pairs of individuals, on two different variables. (Figure 1-2, for example, is a scatterplot showing I.Q. scores of parents and children.)

Scent-marking Marking an object or area with a characteristic smell—with urine, feces, or specialized chemicals (such as the "spray" of a male domestic cat). Scent-marking may serve to establish a territory, reduce fear, or mark a trail.

Schema A theory of concept-formation that proposes that information is stored in memory as a general representation or composite, rather than as an individual instance.

Schizophrenia Severe and complex psychosis characterized primarily by withdrawal from reality and social relationships, perception and thought disturbances (hallucinations, delusions), and emotional and behavioral peculiarities.

Scotopic vision Visual perception of gray color evoked at night when the number of quanta per second are low.

Secondary (or conditioned) drives Motivating states acquired mainly through a conditioning process through which they become associated with primary drives; examples are fear, hostility, and the need for affiliation and approval.

Secondary reinforcement Reinforcement by a stimulus that has gained reinforcing value by consistent association with a primary reinforcement.

Selective advantages Those physical or behavioral qualities of a species that increase its chances of survival; survival enables reproduction to occur and thus these advantages are passed on genetically to future generations.

Self A person's internalized sense of identity, the fundamental source of human motivation. In the personality theory of Carl Rogers the self consists of one's perceptions of oneself and the values attached to those perceptions.

Self-actualization The fundamental human tendency toward maximal realization of one's potentialities. It is a basic concept of humanistic theories of personality such as those developed by Rogers and Maslow.

Self-esteem The individual's evaluation of his or her own competence, ability, and personality.

Self-fulfilling prophecy A prediction that leads to changes in behavior that are likely to produce the predicted outcome.

Semantic memory Long-term memory; the representation of knowledge.

Semantic similarity Similarity of meaning among items on a test of memory.

Sensitization Increased response to a series of stimuli.

Sensorimotor period First stage in Piaget's theory of intellectual development, in which the child learns to deal with objects; the period from birth to 2 years of age.

Separation anxiety Fear in infancy of losing one's mother. The mother is viewed as so important that infants become upset when she is absent.

Serial ordering Learning a list of items in order—such as the alphabet.

Serial-position effect Functional relationship, represented by a curve, between the position of an item in a list and performance—either the probability of errors in serial-ordering learning or of **recall** in short-term memory. *See* **Primacy effect, Recency effect.**

Set An inhibiting effect from past experience on present orientation.

Sex hormones Hormones secreted chiefly by the gonads and the adrenal cortex that help to organize such secondary sex characteristics as facial hair and breast development, as well as reproductive behavior. *See* **Androgens, Estrogens.**

Sex-linked behaviors Behaviors that differ for the sexes but are not involved in reproduction; for example, different taste thresholds for same substances in men and women.

Sex typing Adoption of personality traits, beliefs, attitudes, and behaviors that the culture defines as appropriate for an individual's sex.

Shaping Method of successive approximations in which responses must become more and more similar to the desired response to be rewarded.

Shared coping Working together to solve a problem of mutual concern.

Signal detection Theory of sensory and decision processes involved in perceptual judgments. Sensitivity of the observer is measured by d' (d prime), and the criterion the observer uses is measured by β. *See* Figure 18-2.

Significance In statistics, the trustworthiness of a conclusion about whether an obtained result is likely to be found upon repetition of the same set of observations.

Similarity, principle of A principle of perceptual organization in which similar elements tend to be perceived as belonging to the same unit.

Sinewave A simple pressure wave containing only one frequency of one amplitude.

Size constancy The ability to know that the physical size of an object does not change even though the retinal image of the object changes.

Social learning theory Several related approaches to personality study that emphasize the individual's expectancy that certain behaviors will be rewarded by parents and society and are thus repeated.

Socialization Process by which an individual learns to behave in a manner approved by the culture and society; the result of all the individual's social experiences that affect his or her personality, motives, values, attitudes, and behavior.

Somatopsychic illness A mental conflict or disturbance brought about by a physical illness or injury.

Spacing effect *See* **Peterson paradox.**

Spikes *See* **Neural impulse.**

Split brain A brain in which the corpus callosum has been cut, thus removing most of the connections between the two cerebral hemispheres.

Spontaneous recovery Process in which a response that had been extinguished regains some of its original strength.

Standard deviation A measure of the variability of scores around the central tendency of a distribution. Specifically it is the square root of the mean of the squared deviations of each score from the mean.

Stereopsis The visual mechanism converting binocular disparity into perceived depth.

Stereotypes The attribution of identical characteristics to all members of a particular group, regardless of the actual degree of variation within the group. Familiar stereotypes are sets of characteristics attributed to ethnic and racial groups.

Stevens' Law *See* **Power law.**

Stimulation-bound behavior Behavior that is elicited by direct electrical stimulation of the brain and that resembles normally motivated behavior.

Stimulus control The ability to discriminate between cues to increase the probability of a response in one situation and decrease it in another.

Storage *See* **Memory storage.**

Stroboscopic motion Apparent motion caused by the presentation of slightly different stimuli, such as the frames in a film.

Sublimation A form of displacement in which an unacceptable or unsatisfied impulse is expressed in socially acceptable form.

Subtractive color mixture Mixing colors by subtracting various wavelengths (as in mixing watercolors).

Superego Freud's term for that part of the personality that contains internalized prohibitions and imposes on the individual the restraints and moral edicts of society.

Superior colluculi Visual centers of the midbrain. *See* Figure 22-7.

Surface structure The overt or expressive level of language.

Symbolic function According to Piaget, a child's ability at about age two to create symbols and to defer imitation; necessary for the development of true language.

Sympathetic reactions Behavior that "supports" the behavior of another animal; for example, other jays come to the aid of one defending its territory against a predator.

Sympathetic system Part of the autonomic nervous system which facilitates expenditure of bodily energy and is usually active at the same time as the skeletal musculature. *See* Table 19-1 and Color Figure 6.

Synapse A functional junction from one neuron to another. *See* Figure 19-2 and Color Figure 7.

Synaptic vesicle A small globule inside an axon terminal; it contains a synaptic transmitter chemical. *See* Figure 19-2.

Systematic desensitization Behavior therapy technique developed by Wolpe and based on principles of classical conditioning. It is most successful in the treatment of specific nonadaptive anxieties.

Tabula rasa A blank wax tablet, used to symbolize the mind at birth in an analogy, by extreme empiricists, who hold that perception is completely unorganized at birth and that the mind is originally like a blank wax tablet upon which experience writes.

Tacts According to B. F. Skinner, verbal responses to nonhuman stimuli in the environment.

Telencephalon Part of the forebrain; it includes the cerebral hemispheres and the corpus callosum. *See* Figures 19-5, 19-6.

Template-matching Theory of pattern recognition that implies comparison of a stimulus with a standard form (the template).

Temporal lobe The part of the cerebral hemisphere lying at the side of the head below the lateral fissure. It contains the primary auditory cortex, the visual inferotemporal region, and the amygdala. *See* Color Figures 1 and 5.

Territory The "home turf," usually the land on which an animal mates and raises its young and which it defends against the intrusion of competitors.

Test profile Patterns of performance on test items—for example, in the Wechsler-Bellevue intelligence scale.

Thalamus A part of the diencephalon. It mainly relays sensory impulses to the cerebral cortex and integrates cortical activity. *See* Color Figure 5.

Theory An integrated set of principles or hypotheses that explains a wide array of phenomena and findings and that predicts new events and experimental outcomes.

Timbre Distinctive sound quality determined by the relative intensities of various overtone frequencies.

Total-time hypothesis In rote learning, the time required to learn a list depends on the total-time spent studying, regardless of how time is distributed.

Trait Any relatively stable characteristic of a person; its measurement is useful in describing and quantifying individual differences.

Transfer of training The effect of previously learned associations on the formation of new associations. In positive transfer the past associations help, and in negative transfer they hinder forming new associations. *See also* **Proactive interference, Retroactive interference.**

Transmitter agent The chemical substance released at a neuronal terminal that diffuses across the synaptic gap. It combines with a receptor chemical to either excite or inhibit the receiving (postsynaptic) cell.

Trichromatic theory A vision theory positing that perception of three primary hues corresponds to sensitivity of three types of retinal cones to different parts of the spectrum—red, green, or blue.

Unavailability *See* **Availability.**

Uncle behavior In primates, care and attention given to infants by male adults other than their fathers.

Unconditional positive regard According to Rogers, the experience of personal acceptance needed by the individual in order to develop and maintain a healthful psychological adjustment.

Unconditioned response (UR) The original response to an **Unconditioned stimulus (US)** that is similar to the **Conditioned response (CR)** acquired during **Classical conditioning.**

Unconditioned stimulus (US) Stimulus that evokes the **Unconditioned response** without any prior training. *See* **Classical conditioning.**

Unconscious An aspect of psychoanalytic theory asserting that a significant part of human behavior is governed by forces of which we are unaware and which are inaccessible to the conscious mind.

Underachievement Academic performance falling below the potential level indicated by intelligence-test scores.

Vacuum activities Instinctive behavior that occurs without its usual trigger or releaser.

Validity Extent to which a test measures what it is supposed to measure.

Variability The spread of scores around the central tendency in a frequency distribution; the **Standard deviation** is a measure of variability.

Ventricle A cavity in the brain filled with fluid. *See* Color Figure 5.

Ventromedial nucleus of hypothalamus A brain region that participates in control of food intake. *See* Figure 20-5.

Verification The last stage in creative thinking in which a hypothesis is tested and confirmed (or not confirmed).

Visual cliff Device for studying space perception in babies and animals. The subject is placed on a piece of glass. Half the surface under the glass is several feet down; in the other half it is just under the surface. *See* Figure 16-11.

Wavelength The distance between two adjacent crests of a vibratory activity. *See also* **Quanta.**

Weber's Law Psychophysical law stating that the smallest detectable increment in the intensity of a stimulus is a constant (k) proportion of the intensity of the stimulus already present: $\frac{\Delta I}{I} = k$.

White matter Fiber tracts in the nervous system with a white fatty coating of axons. *See* Figure 19-6 and Color Figure 5.

References

Adams, R. D. "The Anatomy of Memory Mechanisms in the Human Brain." In G. A. Talland and N. C. Waugh (Eds.), *The Pathology of Memory*. New York: Academic Press, 1969. **590**

Adler, A. "Individual Psychology." In C. Murchison (Ed.), *Psychologies of 1930*. Worcester, Mass.: Clark University Press, 1930. **166**

Adler, N. T. "Effects of the Male's Copulatory Behavior on Successful Pregnancy of the Female Rat." *Journal of Comparative and Physiological Psychology*, 1969, *69*, 613–22. **680**

Adorno, T. W., Frankel-Brunswick, E., Levinson, D. J., & Sanford, R. N. *The Authoritarian Personality*. New York: Harper, 1950. **88**

Ahlskog, J. E., Randall, P. K., & Hoebel, B. G. "Hypothalic Hyperphagia: Dissociation from Hyperphagic following Destruction of Noradrenergic Neurons." *Science*, 1975, *190*, 399–401. **553**

Ainsworth, M. D. S. *Infancy in Uganda*. Baltimore: Johns Hopkins Press, 1967. **265**

Ainsworth, M. D. S. "The Development of Infant-Mother Attachment." In B. M. Caldwell & H. N. Ricciuti (Eds.), *Review of Child Development Research*. Vol. 3. Chicago: University of Chicago Press, 1973. **265, 270, 271, 272**

Ainsworth, M. D. S., Bell, S. M. J., & Stayton, D. "Individual Differences in Strange Situation Behavior of One-Year-Olds." In H. R. Schaffer (Ed.), *The Origins of Human Social Relations*. London: Academic Press, 1971. **266**

Ainsworth, M. D. S., Bell, S. M. J., & Stayton, D. J. "Individual Differences in the Development of Some Attachment Behaviors." *Merrill-Palmer Quarterly*, 1972, *18*, 123–43. **266, 267**

Albert, R. "The Role of Mass Media and the Effect of Aggressive Film Content upon Children's Aggressive Responses and Identification Choices." *Genetic Psychology Monographs*, 1957, *55*, 221–85. **145**

Allen, D. L., & Mech, L. D. "Wolves versus Moose on Isle Royale." *National Geographic Magazine*, 1963, 200–19. **668**

Allport, G. W. *The Nature of Prejudice*. Cambridge, Mass.: Addison-Wesley, 1954. **91**

Allport, G. W. *Patterns and Growth in Personality*. New York: Holt, Rinehart and Winston, 1961. **127**

Allport, G. W., & Vernon, P. E. *Studies in Expressive Movement*. New York: Macmillan, 1933. **127**

Altmann, M. "Patterns of Herd Behavior in Free Ranging Elk of Wyoming, *Cervus canadensis nelsoni*." *Zoologica*, 1956, *41*, 65–71. **671**

Anderson, J. R., & Bower, G. H. *Human Associative Memory*. Washington, D.C.: Winston, 1973. **431**

Ardrey, R. *The Territorial Imperative: A Personal Inquiry into the Animal Origins of Property and Nations*. New York: Atheneum, 1966. **693, 699**

Argyle, M. *The Psychology of Interpersonal Behavior*. Baltimore: Penguin, 1967. **103**

Armstrong, E. A. *Bird Display and Behavior* (2nd ed.). London: Lindsay & Drummond, Ltd., 1947. **676, 677, 692, 694**

Aronson, E. "Dissonance Theory: Progress and Problems." In R. P. Abelson, E. Aronson, W. J. McGuire, T. Newcomb, M. J. Rosenberg, and P. Tannenbaum, *Theories of Cognitive Consistency: A Sourcebook*. Chicago: Rand McNally, 1968. **78**

Aronson, E. "Some Antecedents of Interpersonal Attraction." In W. J. Arnold & D. Levine (Eds.), *Nebraska Symposium on Motivation 1969*. Lincoln: University of Nebraska Press, 1969. **78, 114**

Aronson, E., Blaney, N., Sikes, J., Stephan, C., & Snapp, M. "Busing and Racial Tension: The Jig-Saw Route to Learning and Liking." *Psychology Today*, February 1975, 43–50. **93**

Aronson, E., & Carlsmith, J. M. "Effect of the Severity of Threat on the Devaluation of Forbidden Behavior." *Journal of Abnormal and Social Psychology*, 1963, *66*, 584–88. **76**

Aronson, E., & Carlsmith, J. M. "Experimentation in Social Psychology." In G. Lindzey & E. Aronson (Eds.), *Handbook of Social Psychology* (2nd ed.), Vol. 2. Reading, Mass.: Addison-Wesley, 1969. **59**

Aronson, E., & Cope, V. "My Enemy's Enemy Is My Friend." *Journal of Personality and Social Psychology*, 1968, *8*, 8–12. **102**

Aronson, E., & Linder, D. "Gain and Loss of Esteem as Determinants of Interpersonal Attractiveness." *Journal of Experimental Psychology*, 1965, *1*, 156–71. **115, 116**

Aronson, E., Turner, J., & Carlsmith, J. M. "Communicator Credibility and Communication Discrepancy and Determinants of Opinion Change." *Journal of Abnormal and Social Psychology*, 1963, *67*, 31–36. **50, 51**

Aronson, E., Willerman, B., & Floyd, J. "The Effect of a Pratfall on Increasing Interpersonal Attractiveness." *Psychonomic Science*, 1966, *4*, 227–28. **110, 111**

Aronson, E., & Worchel, P. "Similarity versus Liking as Determinants of Interpersonal Attractiveness." *Psychonomic Science*, 1966, *5*, 157–58. **106**

Asch, S. "Effects of Group Pressure upon the Modification and Distortion of Judgment." In H. Guetzkow (Ed.), *Groups, Leadership, and Men*. Pittsburgh: Carnegie Press, 1951. **57, 58, 61, 62, 90**

Atkinson, R. C. "A Stochastic Model for Rote Serial Learning." *Psychometrika*, 1957, *22*, 87–95. **386**

Atkinson, R. C. "Mnemotechnics in Second-Language Learning." *American Psychologist*, 1975, *30*, 821–28. **390**

Atkinson, R. C., Bower, G. H., & Crothers, E. J. *An Introduction to Mathematical Learning Theory*. New York: Wiley, 1965. **405**

Atkinson, R. C., & Schiffrin, R. M. "Human Memory: A Proposed System and Its Control Processes." In K. W. Spence &

J. T. Spence (Eds.), *The Psychology of Learning and Motivation: Advances in Research and Theory.* (Vol. 2) New York: Academic Press, 1968. **426**

Atkinson, R. C., & Schiffrin, R. M. "The Control of Short-Term Memory." *Scientific American,* 1971, *224,* 82–90. **426**

Attneave, F., & Frost, R. "The Determination of Perceived Tridimensional Orientation by Minimum Criteria." *Perception and Psychophysics,* 1969, *6,* 391–96. **471**

Ayllon, T., & Azrin, N. H. "The Measurement and Reinforcement of Behavior of Psychotics." *Journal of Experimental Analysis of Behavior,* 1965, *8,* 357–83. **195**

Ayllon, T., & Azrin, N. H. *The Token Economy: A Motivational System for Therapy and Rehabilitation.* New York: Appleton-Century-Crofts, 1968. **185**

Backman, C. W., & Secord, P. F. "The Effect of Perceived Liking on Interpersonal Attraction." *Human Relations,* 1959, *12,* 379–84. **105**

Bakan, P. "Hypnotizability, Laterality of Eye Movement and Functional Brain Asymmetry." *Perceptual and Motor Skills,* 1969, *28,* 927–32. **138**

Baldwin, A. L. "The Effect of Home Environment on Nursery School Behavior." *Child Development,* 1949, *20,* 49–62. **229, 275**

Baldwin, A. L., Kalhorn, J., & Breese, F. H. "Patterns of Parent Behavior." *Psychological Monographs,* 1945, *58* (3). **275**

Bales, A. "A Theoretical Framework for Interaction Process Analysis." In C. Cartwright & A. Zander (Eds.), *Group Dynamics: Research and Theory.* New York: Harper, 1953. **110**

Bandura, A., Grusec, J. E., & Menlove, F. L. "Vicarious Extinction of Avoidance Behavior." *Journal of Personality and Social Psychology,* 1967, *5,* 16–23. **178, 281**

Bandura, A., Ross, D., & Ross, S. A. "Imitation of Film-Mediated Aggressive Models." *Journal of Abnormal and Social Psychology,* 1963, *66,* 3–11; *67,* 527–34. **13, 145**

Bandura, A., & Walters, R. H. *Social Learning and Personality Development.* New York: Holt, Rinehart & Winston, 1963. **178**

Banta, T. J., & Hetherington, M. "Relations Between Needs of Friends and Fiancées." *Journal of Abnormal and Social Psychology,* 1963, *66,* 401–04. **108**

Barlow, G. W. "Ethological Units of Behavior." In D. Ingle (Ed.), *Central Nervous System and Fish Behavior.* Chicago: University of Chicago Press, 1968. **637**

Barnes, J. M., & Underwood, B. J. "Fate of First List Associations in Transfer Theory." *Journal of Experimental Psychology,* 1959, *58,* 97–105. **395**

Barron, F. "Originality in Relation to Personality and to Intellect." *Journal of Personality,* 1957, *25,* 730–42. **344, 345**

Bartlett, Sir F. H. *Remembering.* Cambridge: Cambridge University Press, 1932. **339, 341**

Baumrind, D. "Child Care Practices Anteceding Three Patterns of Preschool Behavior." *Genetic Psychology Monographs,* 1967, *75,* 43–88. **276**

Bayley, N. *Bayley Scales of Infant Development.* New York: The Psychological Corporation, 1969. **238, 301**

Bayley, N. "Development of Mental Abilities." In P. H. Mussen (Ed.), *Carmichael's Manual of Child Psychology,* Vol. I. (3rd ed.) New York: Wiley, 1970, pp. 1163–1209. **301**

Beach, F. A. *Hormones and Behavior.* New York: Harper, 1948. **682**

Beach, F. A. "Sexual Attractivity and Receptivity in Female Mammals." *Hormones & Behavior,* 1976, in press. **681, 682**

Beach, F. A., & Jaynes, J. "Studies of Maternal Retrieving in Rats: III. Sensory Cues Involved in the Lactating Female's Response to Her Young." *Behavior,* 1956, *10,* 104–25. **686**

Beach, F. A., & Le Boeuf, B. J. "Coital Behavior of Dogs. I. Preferential Mating in the Bitch." *Animal Behavior,* 1967, *15,* 546–58. **672**

Beach, L. R., & Wertheimer, M. "A Free Response Approach to the Study of Person Cognition." *Journal of Abnormal and Social Psychology,* 1961, *62,* 367–74. **456**

Beers, Clifford. *A Mind That Found Itself.* New York: 1908. **184**

Békésy, G. von. "Variation of Phase along the Basilar Membrane with Sinusoidal Vibrations." *Journal of the Acoustical Society of America,* 1947, *19,* 452–60. **620**

Bem, D. J., & Allen, A. "On Predicting Some of the People Some of the Time: The Search for Cross-Situational Consistencies in Behavior." *Psychological Review,* 1974, *81* (6), 506–20. **23, 127, 128**

Bem, S. L. "Sex-Role Adaptability: One Consequence of Psychological Androgyny." *Journal of Personality and Social Psychology,* 1975, *31,* 634–53. **96, 150**

Benary, W. "Beobachtungen zu einem Experiment über Helligkeitskontrast." *Psychologische Forschung,* 1924, *5,* 131–42. **481**

Bennett, E. L. "Cerebral Effects of Differential Experience and Training." In M. R. Rosenzweig & E. L. Bennett (Eds.), *Neural Mechanisms of Learning and Memory.* Cambridge, Mass.: MIT Press, 1976. **595**

Bennett, E. L., Diamond, M. C., Krech, D., & Rosenzweig, M. R. "Chemical and Anatomical Plasticity of Brain." *Science,* 1964, *146,* 610–19. **595**

Bennett, E. L., Flood, J. F., Orme, A. E., Rosenzweig, M. R., & Jarvik, M. E. "Minimum Duration of Protein Synthesis Needed to Establish Long-term Memory." Fifth International Meeting of the International Society for Neurochemistry, September 1975, Barcelona, Spain. Abstract, p. 476. **583**

Benson, H. *The Relaxation Response.* New York: William Morrow, 1975. **561**

Berger, I. "TV Implants May Help the Blind See." *Popular Mechanics,* July 1974, 94–95. **609**

Berkowitz, L., & Alioto, J. T. "The Meaning of an Observed Event as a Determinant of Its Aggressive Consequences." *Journal of Personality and Social Psychology,* 1973, *28,* 206–17. **145**

Bernstein, B. A. "A Sociolinguistic Approach to Socialization with Some Reference to Educability." In F. Williams (Ed.), *Language and Poverty.* Chicago: Markham, 1970, 25–61. **358**

Binet, A., & Simon, T. "Le Développement de l'Intelligence des Enfants." *L'Année Psychologique,* 1908, *14,* 1–94. **223, 296**

Birch, H. G. "The Relation of Previous Experience to Insightful Problem-Solving." *Journal of Comparative and Physiological Psychology,* 1945, *307.* **642**

Birdwhistell, R. L. "The Kinesis Level in the Investigation of the Emotions." In P. H. Knapp (Ed.), *Expressions of the Emotions in Man.* New York: International University Press, 1963. **699**

Birdwhistell, R. L. "Communication Without Words." In P. Alexandre (Ed.), *L'aventure humaine.* Paris, 1966. **699**

Bishop, M. P., Elder, S. T., & Heath, R. G. "Intracranial Self-Stimulation in Man." *Science, 1963, 140,* 394–96. **572**

Bishop, P. O., & Henry, C. H. "Spatial Vision." *Annual Review of Psychology,* 1971, *22.* **473**

Bitterman, M. E. "Toward a Comparative Psychology of Learning." *The American Psychologist,* 1960, *15,* 704-12. **644**

Bitterman, M. E. "Phyletic Differences in Learning." *The American Psychologist,* 1965, *20,* 396–410. **644**

Bitterman, M. E. "The Comparative Analysis of Learning." *Science,* 1975, *188,* 690–709. **644**

Bloch, V. "Brain Activation and Memory Consolidation." In M. R. Rosenzweig & E. L. Bennett (Eds.), *Neural Mechanisms of Learning and Memory.* Cambridge, Mass.: MIT Press, 1976. **585**

Block, J. *The Q-sort Method in Personality Assessment and Psychiatric Research.* Springfield, Ill.: Charles C Thomas, 1961. **148**

Block, J. *The Challenge of Response Sets.* New York: Appleton Century-Crofts, 1965. **150**

Block, J., in collaboration with Haan, N. *Lives Through Time.* Berkeley, Cal.: Bancroft, 1971. **286**

Bloom, K., & Esposito, A. "Social Conditioning and Its Proper Control Procedures." *Journal of Experimental Child Psychology,* 1975, *19,* 209–22. **243**

Bloom, L. "Language Development." In D. G. Horowitz (Ed.), *Review of Child Development Research.* (Vol. 4.) Chicago: University of Chicago Press, 1975. **353**

Bodis-Wollner, I. "Visual Acuity and Contrast Sensitivity in Patients with Cerebral Lesions." *Science,* 1972, *178,* 769–71. **504**

Boe, E. E., and Church, R. N. "Permanent Effects of Punishment during Extinction." *Journal of Comparative and Physiological Psychology,* 1967, *63,* 486–92. **381**

Bogardus, E. S. "Measuring Social Distance." *Journal of Applied Sociology,* 1925, *9,* 299–308. **42**

Boneau, C. A., and Cuca, J. M. "An Overview of Psychology's Human Resources," *American Psychologist,* 1974, *29,* 821–40. **13**

Boring, E. G. "A New Ambiguous Figure." *American Journal of Psychology,* 1930, *42,* 444–45. **315**

Bower, G. H. "A Descriptive Theory of Memory." In D. P. Kimble (Ed.), *Learning, Remembering and Forgetting.* (Vol. 2.) New York: New York Academy of Science, 1966. **478**

Bower, G. H. "Imagery as a Relational Organizer in Associative Learning." *Journal of Verbal Learning and Verbal Behavior,* 1970, *9,* 529–33. **389**

Bower, G. H. "Memory Freaks I Have Known." *Psychology Today,* 1973, *7*(5), 64–65. **421**

Bower, G. H., & Trabasso, T. "Concept Identification." In R. Atkinson (Ed.), *Studies in Mathematical Psychology.* Stanford, Cal.: Stanford University Press, 1964. **337**

Bower, T. G. R. *Development in Infancy.* San Francisco: W. H. Freeman, 1974. **240**

Brackbill, Y. "Extinction of the Smiling Response in Infants as a Function of Reinforcement Schedule." *Child Development,* 1958, *29,* 114–24. **244**

Bransford, J. D., & Franks, J. J. "Abstraction of Linguistic Ideas." *Cognitive Psychology,* 1971, *2,* 331–350. **339, 340**

Braun, B. "Awareness of EEG-Subjective Activity Relationships Directed Within a Closed Feedback System." *Psychophysiology,* 1971, *7,* 451–64. **209**

Brehm, J. W., & Cohen, A. R. *Explorations in Cognitive Dissonance.* New York: Wiley, 1962. **78**

Brehm, J. W., & Cole, A. H. "Effect of a Favor Which Reduces Freedom." *Journal of Personality and Social Psychology,* 1966, *3,* 420–426. **112**

Breland, K., & Breland, M. "The Misbehavior of Organisms." *The American Psychologist,* 1961, *16,* 681–84. **657**

Breland, K., & Breland, M. *Animal Behavior.* New York: Macmillan, 1966. **657**

Broadbent, D. E. *Perception and Communication.* New York: Pergamon, 1958. **422, 426**

Bronson, W. C. "Stable Patterns of Behavior: The Significance of Enduring Orientations for Personality Development." In J. P. Hill (Ed.), *Minnesota Symposia on Child Psychology,* vol 2. Minneapolis: University of Minnesota Press, 1968, pp. 3–27. **286**

Bronson, W. C. "The Role of Enduring Orientations to the Environment in Personality Development." *Genetic Psychology Monographs,* 1972, *86,* 3–80. **286**

Broughton, R. J. "Sleep Disorders. Disorders of Arousal?" *Science,* 1968, *159,* 1070–78. **563**

Brower, L. P., & Brower, J. V. Z. "Investigations into Mimicry." *Natural History,* 1962, *71,* 8–19. **656**

Brown, J. F. "Uber gesehene Geschwindigkeiten." *Psychologische Forschung,* 1928, *10,* 84–101. **485**

Brown, L. E. "Home Range and Movement of Small Mammals." *Symposia of the Zoological Society of London,* 1966, *18,* 111–142. **675**

Brown, P. L., & Jenkins, H. M. "Auto-Shaping of the Pigeon's Key-Peck." *Journal of Experimental Analytical Behavior,* 1968, *11,* 1–8. **401**

Brown, R. *Social Psychology.* New York: Free Press of Glencoe, 1965. **258**

Brown, R. *A First Language.* Cambridge, Mass.: Harvard University Press, 1973. **258**

Brown, R., and McNeill, D. "The 'Tip of the Tongue' Phenomenon." *Journal of Verbal Learning and Verbal Behavior,* 1966, *5,* 325–37. **418**

Bruner, J. S. "On Perceptual Readiness." *Psychological Review,* 1957, *64,* 123–52. **339**

Bruner, J. S. "The Course of Cognitive Growth." *American Psychologist,* 1964, 1–15. **339**

Bruner, J. S., & Goodman, C. C. "Value and Need as Organizing Factors in Perception." *Journal of Abnormal and Social Psychology,* 1947, *42,* 33–44. **454, 455**

Bruner, J. S., Goodnow, J. J., & Austin, G. A. *A Study of Thinking.* New York: Wiley, 1956. **336**

Bryan, J. H. "Children's Reactions to Helpers." In J. R. Macaulay & L. Berkowitz (Eds.), *Altruism and Helping Behavior.* New York: Academic Press, 1970. **226**

Bureš, J., & Burešová, O. "The Reunified Split Brain." In R. E. Whalen, R. F. Thompson, M. Verzeano, & N. J. Weinberger (Eds.), *The Neural Control of Behavior.* New York: Academic Press, 1970. **588**

Burt, C. "The Structure of the Mind: A Review of the Results of Analyses." *British Journal of Educational Psychology,* 1949, *19,* 110–111, 176–99. **317**

Buskirk, E. R. "Energy Balance of Obese Patients During Weight Reduction: Influence of Diet Restriction and Exercise." *Annals of the New York Academy of Science,* 1963, *110,* 918–40. **553**

Buss, A. H. "Physical Aggression in Relation to Different Frustrations." *Journal of Abnormal and Social Psychology,* 1963, *67,* 1–7. **141**

Buss, A. H. "Instrumentality of Aggression, Feedback, and Frustration of Determinants of Physical Aggression." *Journal of Personality and Social Psychology,* 1966, *3,* 153–62. **141**

Buss, A. H., & Plomin, R. *A Temperamental Theory of Personality Development.* New York: Wiley, 1975. **138**

Butler, R. A. "Curiosity in Monkeys." *Scientific American,* 1954, *190,* 70–75. **659**

Byrne, D. "Repression-Sensitization as a Dimension of Personality." In B. A. Maker (Ed.), *Progress in Experimental Personality Research.* (Vol. 1.) New York: Academic Press, 1964. **165**

Byrne, D. "Attitudes and Attraction." In L. Berkowitz (Ed.), *Advances in Experimental Social Psychology.* (Vol. 4.) New York: Academic Press, 1969. **103**

Byrne, W. L. (Ed.) *Molecular Approaches to Learning and Memory.* New York: Academic Press, 1970. **586**

Byrne, W. L., Samuel, D., Bennett, E. L., Rosenzweig, M. R., Wasserman, E., Wagner, A. R., Gardner, F., Galambos, R., Berger, B. D., Margules, D. G., Fenichel, R. L., Stein, L., Corson, J. A., Enesco, H. E., Chorover, S. L., Holt, C. E., III, Schiller, P. H., Chiappetta, L., Jarvik, M. E., Leaf, R. C., Dutcher, J. D., Horovitz, Z. P., & Carlton, P. L. "Memory Transfer." *Science,* 1966, *153,* 658–59. **586**

Cahalan, D. *Problem Drinkers.* San Francisco: Jossey-Bass, 1970. **200**

Calhoun, J. B. "Induced Mass Movements of Small Mammals." *Public Health Monographs,* 1962, *59,* 1–33. **674**

Campbell, D. T. "On the Genetics of Altruism and the Counterhedonic Components in Human Culture." *Journal of Social Issues,* 1972, *28,* 21–37. **668**

Canadian Commission of Inquiry into the Nonmedical Use of Drugs. Ottawa: Inform. Can., 1972. **202**

Carew, T. J. "Do Passive-Avoidance Tasks Permit Assessment of Retrograde Amnesia in Rats?" *Journal of Comparative and Physiological Psychology,* 1970, *72,* 267–71. **582**

Carey, J. J. *The College Drug Scene.* Englewood Cliffs, N.J.: Prentice-Hall, 1968. **202**

Carlsmith, J. M., Collins, B. E., & Helmreich, R. L. "Studies in Forced Compliance: I. The Effect of Pressure for Compliance on Attitude Change Produced by Face-to-Face Roleplaying and Anonymous Essay Writing." *Journal of Personality and Social Psychology,* 1966, *4,* 1–13. **75**

Carmichael, L., Hogan, H. P., & Walter, A. A. "An Experimental Study of the Effect of Language on the Reproduction of Visually Perceived Form." *Journal of Experimental Psychology,* 1932, *15,* 73–86. **454**

Carnegie, D. *How to Win Friends and Influence People.* New York: Simon and Schuster, 1937. **105, 118**

Carpenter, C. R. "The Howlers of Barro Colorado Island." In I. De Vore (Ed.), *Primate Behavior: Field Studies of Monkeys and Apes.* New York: Holt, Rinehart & Winston, 1965. **689**

Carroll, J. B., & Casagrande, J. B. In E. E. Maccoby et al. (Eds.), *Readings in Social Psychology.* (3rd ed.) New York: Holt, Rinehart & Winston, 1958. **357**

Cattell, R. B. *Description and Measurement of Personality.* New York: Harcourt, Brace and World, 1946. **150**

Cattell, R. B. *The Scientific Analysis of Personality.* Baltimore: Penguin Books, 1965. **127, 129**

Chapanis, A., Garner, W. R., & Morgan, C. T. *Applied Experimental Psychology.* New York: Wiley, 1949. **499**

Chapman, L. J., & Chapman, J. P. "Atmosphere Effect Re-Examined." *Journal of Experimental Psychology,* 1959, *58,* 220–26. **331**

Cherry, E. C. "Some Experiments on the Recognition of Speech, with One and with Two Ears." *Journal of the Acoustical Society of America,* 1953, *25,* 975–79. **452**

Chitty, D. "Self-Regulation of Members through Changes in Viability." *Cold Springs Harbor Symposia on Quantitative Biology,* 1957, *22,* 277–80. **675**

Chomsky, N. *Syntactic Structures.* The Hague: Mouton, 1957. **354**

Chomsky, N. *Aspects of a Theory of Syntax.* Cambridge, Mass.: MIT Press, 1965. **354**

Chomsky, N. "The Formal Nature of Language." In E. Lenneberg (Ed.), *Biological Foundations of Language.* New York: Wiley, 1967. **258**

Chorover, S. L. "The Pacification of the Brain." *Psychology Today,* 1974, *7*(12), 59–69. **571**

Chorover, S. L., & Schiller, P. H. "Reexamination of Prolonged Retrograde Amnesia in One-Trial Learning." *Journal of Comparative and Physiological Psychology,* 1966, *61,* 34–41. **582**

Christian, J. J. "Adrenal and Reproductive Response to Population Sizes in Mice from Freely Growing Populations." *Ecology,* 1956, *37,* 258–73. **675**

Cialdini, R. B., Vincent, J. E., Lewis, S. K., Catalan, J., Wheeler, D., & Darby, B. L. "Reciprocal Concessions Procedure for Inducing Compliance: The Door-in-the-Face Technique." *Journal of Personality and Social Psychology,* 1975, *31,* 206–15. **54**

Cleary, T. A. "Test Bias: Prediction of Grades of Negro and White Students in Integrated Colleges." *Journal of Educational Measurement,* 1968, *5,* 115–24. **306**

Cofer, C. N., & Appley, M. A. *Motivation: Theory and Research.* New York: Wiley, 1964. **389**

Cohen, A. R. "Social Norms, Arbitrariness of Frustration, and Status of the Agent of Frustration in the Frustration-Aggression Hypothesis." *Journal of Abnormal and Social Psychology,* 1955, *51,* 222–26. **142**

Colbert, E. H. *Evolution of the Vertebrates: A History of the Backboned Animals through Time.* New York: Science Editions, 1961. **632**

Condry, J. C., Jr., Simon, M. L., & Bronfenbrenner, U. "Characteristics of Peer- and Adult-Oriented Children." Department of Child Development, Cornell University, 1968. (Unpublished manuscript.) **283**

Conger, J. J. *Adolescence and Youth: Psychological Development in a Changing World.* (2nd ed.) New York: Harper & Row, 1974. **283**

Cooper, D., & Dinerman, H. "Analysis of the Film 'Don't Be a Sucker.' A Study in Communication." *Public Opinion Quarterly,* 1951, *15,* 243–64. **91**

Coopersmith, S. *The Antecedents of Self-Esteem.* San Francisco: W. H. Freeman, 1967. **276**

Cornsweet, T. N. "Information Processing in Visual Systems." *Stanford Research Institute Journal, Feature Issue* 1969 *5,* 16–27. **441**

Couch, A. S., and Kenniston, K. "Yeasayers and Naysayers: Agreeing Response Set as a Personality Variable." *Journal of Abnormal and Social Psychology,* 1960, *60,* 151–74. **146**

Craik, F. I. M. "A Levels of Analysis View of Memory." In P. Pliner, L. Frames, & T. M. Allowy (Eds.), *Communication and Affect: Language and Thought.* New York: Academic Press, 1973. **429**

Craik, F. I. M., & Lockhart, R. S. "Levels of Processing: A Framework for Memory Research." *Journal of Verbal Learning and Verbal Behavior,* 1972, *11.* **429**

Craik, F. I. M., & Watkins, M. J. "The Role of Rehearsal in Short-term Memory." *Journal of Verbal Learning and Verbal Behavior,* 1973, *12,* 599–607. **430**

Cronbach, L. J. "Beyond the Two Disciplines of Scientific Psychology." *American Psychologist,* 1975, *30,* 116–27. **23**

Crook, J. H. "Evolutionary Change in Primate Societies." *Science Journal,* 1967, 1–7. **665**

Crandall, V., Preston, A., & Rabson, A. "Maternal Reactions and the Development of Independence and Achievement Behavior in Young Children." *Child Development,* 1960, *31,* 243–251. **274**

Darley, J. M., & Berscheid, E. "Increased Liking as a Result of the Anticipation of Personal Contact." *Human Relations,* 1967, *20,* 29–40. **93**

Darley, G. F., Tinklenberg, J. R., Rosh, W. T., Hollister, L. W., & Atkinson, R. C. "Influence of Marihuana on Storage and Retrieval Processes in Memory." *Memory and Cognition,* 1973, *1,* 196–200. **716**

Darwin, Charles R. *The Expression of the Emotions in Man and Animals* (1873). Westport, Conn.: Greenwood Press, 1955. **635**

Davis, K. E., & Jones, E. E. "Changes in Interpersonal Perception as a Means of Reducing Cognitive Dissonance." *Journal of Abnormal and Social Psychology,* 1960, *61,* 402–10. **78**

Davitz, J. "The Effects of Previous Training on Postfrustration Behavior." *Journal of Abnormal and Social Psychology,* 1952, *47,* 309–15. **143**

Day, M. E. "An Eye-Movement Indicator of Individual Differences in the Physiological Organization of Attentional Processes and Anxiety." *Journal of Psychiatry,* 1967, *66,* 51–62. **138**

Deaux, Kay. "To Err Is Humanizing: But Sex Makes a Difference." *Representative Research in Social Psychology,* 1972, *3,* 20–28. **111**

Delgado, J. M. R., Roberts, W. W., & Miller, N. E. "Learning Motivated by Electrical Stimulation of the Brain." *American Journal of Physiology,* 1954, *179,* 587–93. **571**

Dement, W. "The Effect of Dream Deprivation." *Science,* 1960, *131,* 1705–07. **155**

Dement, W., & Kleitman, N. "Cyclic Variations in EEG During Sleep and Their Relation to Eye Movements, Body Motility, and Dreaming." *Electroencephalography and Clinical Neurophysiology,* 1957, *9,* 673–90. **560**

Denti, A., McGaugh, J. L., Landfield, P. W., & Shinkman, P. "Effects of Posttrial Electrical Stimulation of the Mesencephalic Reticular Formation on Avoidance Learning in Rats." *Physiology and Behavior,* 1970, *5,* 659–662. **584**

DeSoto, C., London, M., & Handel, S. "Social Reasoning and Apatial Para Logic." *Journal of Personality and Social Psychology,* 1965, *2,* 513–521. **330**

Deutsch, M., & Collins, M. E. *Interracial Housing: A Psychological Evaluation of a Social Experiment.* Minneapolis: University of Minnesota Press, 1951. **95**

Deutsch, M., & Gerard, H. B. "A Study of Normative and Informational Social Influence upon Individual Judgment." *Journal of Abnormal and Social Psychology,* 1955, *51,* 629–36. **62**

Deutsch, M., & Solomon, L. "Reactions to Evaluations by Others as Influenced by Self-Evaluation." *Sociometry,* 1959, *22,* 93–112. **112**

De Valois, R. L., & De Valois, K. K. "Neural Coding of Color." In *Handbook of Perception: Seeing.* (Vol. 5). New York: Academic Press, 1975. **615**

Devor, M. G., Wise, R. A., Milgram, N. W., & Hoebel, B. G. "Physiological Control of Hypothalamically Elicited Feeding and Drinking." *Journal of Comparative and Physiological Psychology,* 1970, *73,* 226–232. **573**

DeVore, I., & Hall, K. R. L. "Baboon Ecology." In I. De Vore (Ed.), *Primate Behavior: Field Studies of Monkeys and Apes.* New York: Holt, Rinehart & Winston, 1965. **674**

Dicara, L. V. "Learning in the Autonomic Nervous System." *Scientific American,* 1970, *222,* 30–39. **209**

Dickhoff, H. "Reactions to Evaluations by Another Person As a Function of Self-Evaluation and the Interaction Context." Doctoral dissertation, Duke University, 1961. **112**

Dix, D. L. *Memorial in Behalf of the Pauper Insane and Idiots in Jails and Poorhouses Throughout the Commonwealth.* Boston: Monroe and Francis, 1843. **184**

Dobelle, W. H., Mladejovsky, M. G., & Girven, J. P. "Artificial Vision for the Blind: Electrical Stimulation of Visual Cortex Offers Hope for a Functional Prosthesis." *Science,* 1974, *183,* 440–44. **609**

Dodd, D. H., & Bourne, L. E., Jr. "Test of Some Assumptions of a Hypothesis Testing Model of Concept Identification." *Journal of Experimental Psychology,* 1969, *80,* 69–72. **338**

Dohrenwend, B. P., & Dohrenwend, B. S. "Field Studies of Social Factors in Relation to Three Types of Psychological Disorders." *Journal of Abnormal Psychology,* 1967, *72,* 369–378. **183**

Dollard, J., Doob, J. W., Miller, N. E., Lowrer, G. H., & Sears, R. R. *Frustrational Aggression.* New Haven: Yale University Press, 1939. **140**

Dollard, J., & Miller, N. E. *Personality and Psychotherapy.* New York: McGraw-Hill, 1950. **29, 177**

Donaldson, M. A. *A Study of Children's Thinking.* London: Tavistock, 1963. **334, 335**

Doob, L. W., *Resolving Conflict in Africa: The Fermeda Workshop.* New Haven: Yale University Press, 1970. **714**

Doty, R. W. "A Cry for the Liberation of the Female Rodent: Courtship and Copulation in *Rodentia*." *Psychological Bulletin,* 1974, *81,* 159–172. **681**

Dove, A. "Taking the Chitling Test." In *Newsweek,* July 15, 1968. **305**

Duncker, K. "Über Induzierte Bewegung." *Psychologische Forschung,* 1929, *12,* 180–259. **487**

Duncker, K. "On Problem Solving." *Psychological Monographs,* 1945, No. 270. **328**

Dunham, H. W. "Epidemiology of Psychiatric Disorders as a Contribution to Medical Ecology." *Archives of General Psychiatry,* 1966, *14,* 1–19. **183**

Dunn, L. W. *Peabody Picture Vocabulary Test.* (Rev. ed.) Circle Pines, Minn.: American Guidance Service, Inc., 1965. **305**

Ehrhardt, A. A., & Baker, S. W. "Fetal Androgens, Human Central Nervous System Differentiation, and Behavior Sex Differences." In R. C. Friedman, R. M. Rochart, & R. L. Vande Wiele (Eds.), *Sex Differences in Behavior.* New York: Wiley, 1974. **567**

Ehrlich, D., Guttman, J., Schonbach, P., & Mills, J. "Postdecision Exposure to Relevant Information." *Journal of Abnormal and Social Psychology,* 1957, *54,* 98–102. **70**

Eibl-Eibesfeldt, I. "The Interactions of Unlearned Behavior Patterns and Learning in Mammals." In J. F. Delafresnaye (Ed.), *Brain Mechanisms and Learning.* Oxford: Blackwell, 1961. **670, 685**

Eibl-Eibesfeldt, I. *Ethology: The Biology of Behavior.* (2nd ed.) New York: Holt, Rinehart, & Winston, 1975. **682, 693, 698**

Erlenmeyer-Kimling, L., & Jarvik, L. F. "Genetics and Intelligence: A Review." *Science,* 1963, *142,* 1477–79. **311**

Elton, C. F., & Shevel, L. R. "Who Is Tolerated? An Analysis of Achievement." (Research Report No. 31). Iowa City: American College Testing Program, 1969. **304**

Emery, F. E. "Psychological Effects of the Western Film: A Study in Television Viewing: II. The Experimental Study." *Human Relations,* 1959, *12,* 215–32. **145**

Engel, B. T., & Chism, L. A. "Operant Conditioning of Heart Rate Speeding." *Psychophysiology,* 1967, *3,* 418–26. **209**

Epstein, A. N., Kissileff, H. R., & Stellar, E. (Eds.). *The Neuropsychology of Thirst: New Findings and Advances in Concepts.* Washington, D.C.: Winston, 1973. **548**

Erdelyi, M. H. "A New Look at the New Look: Perceptual Defense and Vigilance." *Psychological Review,* 1974, *81,* 1–25. **456**

Erikson, E. H. *Childhood and Society.* New York: Norton, 1950. **165, 231**

Erikson, E. H. "A Healthy Personality for Every Child: A Fact-Finding Report: A Digest." Midcentury White House Conference on Children and Youth. In J. Seidman (Ed.), *The Adolescent: A Book of Readings.* New York: Dryden (Holt, Rinehart & Winston), 1953, 203–21. **267, 272, 273, 283**

Erikson, E. H. "Identity and the Life Cycle." *Psychological Issues,* 1959, *1,* 1–65. **283**

Erikson, E. H. *Identity: Youth and Crisis.* New York: Norton, 1968. **284**

Evans, E. F., & Wilson, J. P. "The Frequency Selectivity of the Cochlea." In A. R. Moller (Ed.), *Basic Mechanisms in Hearing.* New York: Academic Press, 1973. **620**

Fairweather, G. W., Sanders, B. H., Maynard, H., & Cressler, D. L. *Community Life for the Mentally Ill: An Alternative to Institutional Care.* Chicago: Aldine, 1969. **185**

Falk, J. L. "The Grooming Behavior of the Chimpanzee as a Reinforcer." *Journal of the Experimental Analysis of Behavior,* 1958, *1,* 83–85. **688**

Fantz, R. L. "Pattern Vision in Newborn Infants." *Science,* 1963, *140,* 296–297. **463**

Farel, P. B., Glanzman, D. L., & Thompson, R. F. "Habituation of a Monosynaptic Response in the Vertebrate Central Nervous System: Lateral Column-Motoneuron Pathway in Isolated Frog Spinal Cord." *Journal of Neurophysiology,* 1973, *26,* 1117–30. **594**

Fast, J. *Body Language.* New York: M. Evans and Lippincott, 1970. **147**

Fechner, G. T. *Elemente der Psychophysik.* Leipzig: Breitkopf und Hartel, 1860. **495**

Feshbach, N. "Sex Differences in Children's Modes of Aggressive Responses toward Outsiders." *Merrill Palmer Quarterly,* 1969, *15,* 249–58. **136**

Feshbach, S. "Aggression." In P. H. Mussen (Ed.), *Carmichael's Manual of Child Psychology,* Vol. II. (Rev. ed.) New York: Wiley, 1970. **135, 141, 154**

Feshbach, S., & Feshbach, N. "The Influence of the Stimulus Object upon the Complementary and Supplementary Projection of Fear." *Journal of Abnormal and Social Psychology,* 1963, *66,* 498–502. [Reprinted in G. Lindzey, C. Hall, & M. Manosevitz (Eds.) *Theories of Personality: Primary Sources and Research.* New York: Wiley, 1973, 120–27.] **133, 164**

Feshbach, S., & Singer, R. *Television and Aggression.* San Francisco: Jossey-Bass, 1971. **145**

Feshbach, S., & Sones, G. "Sex Differences in Adolescent Reactions Towards Newcomers." *Developmental Psychology,* 1971, *4,* 481–86. **136**

Feshbach, S., Stiles, W. B., & Bitter, E. "The Reinforcing Effect of Witnessing Aggression." *Journal of Experimental Personality,* 1967, *2,* 133–39. **177**

Festinger, L. *A Theory of Cognitive Dissonance.* Evanston, Ill.: Row, Peterson, 1957. **69**

Festinger, L., & Carlsmith, J. M. "Cognitive Consequences of Forced Compliance." *Journal of Abnormal and Social Psychology,* 1959, *58,* 203–11. **74**

Fisher, G. H. "Measuring Ambiguity." *American Journal of Psychology,* 1967, *80,* 541–57. **453, 454**

Fitts, P. M. "Perceptual-Motor Skill Learning." In A. W. Melton (Ed.), *Categories of Human Learning.* New York: Academic Press, 1964, pp. 243–85. **398**

Flavell, J. H. *The Developmental Psychology of Jean Piaget.* New York: Van Nostrand, 1963. **251, 353**

Flavell, J. H., Cooper, A., & Joiselle, R. H. "Effect of the Number of Preutilization Functions on Functional Fixedness in Problem Solving." *Psychological Reports,* 1958, *4,* 343–50. **330**

Flood, J. F., Bennett, E. L., Rosenzweig, M. R., & Orme, A. E. "Comparison of the Effects of Anisomycin on Memory across Six Strains of Mice." *Behavioral Biology*, 1974, *10*, 147–60. **583**

Floyd, J. M. K. "Effects of Amount of Reward and Friendship Status of the Other on the Frequency of Sharing in Children." Doctoral Dissertation, University of Minnesota, 1964. **116**

Flynn, J. P. "The Neural Basis of Aggression in Cats." In D. C. Glass (Ed.), *Neurophysiology and Emotion*. New York: Rockefeller University Press, 1967. **569**

Flynn, J. P., Edwards, S. B., & Bandler, R. J. "Changes in Sensory and Motor Systems during Centrally Elicited Attack." *Behavioral Science*, 1971, *16*, 1–19. **569**

Frank, C. M. "Behavior Modification and the Treatment of the Alcoholic." In R. Fox (Ed.), *Alcoholism: Behavioral Research*. New York: Springs, 1967. **201**

Franks, J. J., & Bransford, J. D. "Abstraction of Visual Patterns." *Journal of Experimental Psychology*, 1971, *90*, 65–74. **339**

Freedman, J. L. "Long-term Behavioral Effects of Cognitive Dissonance." *Journal of Experimental and Social Psychology*, 1965, *1*, 145–55. **77**

Freedman, J. "The Crowd May Be Not So Madding After All." *Psychology Today*, 1971, *5*, 58–61. **675**

Freedman, J. L., & Fraser, S. C. "Compliance Without Pressure: The Foot-in-the-Door Technique." *Journal of Personality and Social Psychology*, 1966, *4*, 195–202. **54**

Freeman, R. D., & Thibos, L. H. "Electrophysiological Evidence That Abnormal Early Visual Experience Can Modify the Human Brain." *Science*, 1973, *180*, 876–78. **612**

Freud, A. *The Ego and Mechanisms of Defense*. New York: International Universities Press, 1946. **163**

Freud S. *Group Psychology and the Analysis of the Ego*. London: Hogarth, 1921. **278**

Frisch, K. von. *Bees, Their Vision, Chemical Senses and Language*. Ithaca, N.Y.: Cornell University Press, 1950. **669**

Fromm, E. *Escape From Freedom*. New York: Holt, Rinehart & Winston, 1941. **166**

Gagné, R. M. *The Condition of Learning*. New York: Holt, Rinehart & Winston, 1965. **399**

Gaibraith, G. G. "Effects of Sexual Arousal and Guilt upon Free Associative Sexual Responses." *Journal of Consulting and Clinical Psychology*, 1968, *32*, 707–11. **133**

Galanter, E. "Contemporary Psychophysics." In R. Brown, E. Galanter, E. H. Hess, & G. Mandler (Eds.), *New Directions in Psychology*. New York: Holt, Rinehart & Winston, 1962. **490**

Gall, M. D. "The Relationship between Masculinity, Femininity, and Manifest Anxiety." *Journal of Clinical Psychology*, 1969, *25*, 294–95. **96**

Garcia, J., & Ervin, F. R. "Gustatory-Visual and Telereceptor-Cutaneous Conditioning—Adaptation in Internal and External Milieus." *Communications in Behavioral Biology*, 1968, *1*, 389–415. **653**

Gardner, R. A., & Gardner, B. T. "Teaching Sign Language to a Chimpanzee." *Science*, 1969, *165*, 664–72. **350**

Garner, W. R. "Good Patterns Have Few Alternatives." *American Scientist*, 1970, *58*, 34–42. **471**

Garrett, M., Bever, T., & Fodor, J. "The Active Use of Grammar in Speech Perception." *Perception and Psychophysics*, 1966, *1*, 30–32. **449**

Gazzaniga, M. *The Bisected Brain*. New York: Appleton-Century-Crofts, 1970. **589**

Gazzaniga, M. S. "One Brain—Two Minds?" *American Scientist*, 1972, *60*, 311–317. **352**

Geist, V. "On the Relationship of Social Evolution and Ecology in Ungulants." *American Zoologist*, 1974, *14*, 205–220. **674**

Gelb, A. "Die Farbenkonstanz der Sehdinge." In H. von Bethe (Ed.), *Handbuch der Normalen und Pathologischen Physiologie*, 1929, *12*, 594–678. **480**

Geschwind, N., & Levitsky, W. "Human Brain Left-Right Asymmetries in Temporal Speech Region." *Science*, 1968, *161*, 186–87. **622**

Ghiselli, E. *The Validity of Occupational Aptitude Tests*. New York: Wiley, 1966. **304**

Gibson, J. J. *The Perception of the Visual World*. Boston: Houghton Mifflin, 1950. **479**

Gibson, J. J. *The Senses Considered as Perceptual Systems*. Boston: Houghton Mifflin, 1966. **479**

Gibson, J. J., & Walk, R. D. "The 'Visual Cliff.'" *Scientific American*, 1960, *202*, 64–71. **241, 440, 459**

Ginsburg, B. E. "Coaction of Genetical and Nongenetical Factors Influencing Sexual Behavior." In F. A. Beach (Ed.), *Sex and Behavior*. New York: Wiley, 1965. **672**

Ginsburg, H., & Koslowski, B. "Cognitive Development." In M. R. Rosenzweig & L. W. Porter (Eds.), *Annual Review of Psychology*, Vol. 27, 1976. **253**

Glanzer, M. "Storage Mechanisms in Recall." In G. H. Bower (Ed.), *The Psychology of Learning and Motivation: Advances in Research and Theory*. (Vol. 5.) New York: Academic Press, 1972. **428**

Glass, D. C. "Change in Liking as a Means of Reducing Cognitive Discrepancies between Self-Esteem and Aggression." *Journal of Personality*, 1964, *32*, 531–49. **79**

Glickman, S. E., & Sroges, R. W. "Curiosity in Zoo Animals." *Behavior*, 1966, *26*, 151–88. **660**

Goldberg, L. R. "Objective Diagnostic Tests and Measures." In M. R. Rosenzweig & L. W. Porter (Eds.), *Annual Review of Psychology*, 25, 1974. **150**

Goldberg, P. "Are Women Prejudiced Against Women?" *Trans-Action*, April 1968, 28–30. **97**

Goldfarb, W. "The Effects of Early Institutional Care on Adolescent Personality." *Journal of Experimental Education*, 1943, *12*, 107–129. **269**

Goldhamer, H., & Marshall, A. *Psychoses and Civilizations*. Glencoe, Ill.: Free Press, 1949. **183**

Goldiamond, I. "Indicators of Perception: I. Subliminal Perception, Subception, Unconscious Perception: An Analysis in Terms of Psychophysical Indicator Methodology." *Psychological Bulletin*, 1958, *55*, 373–411. **455**

Goldstein, K. *The Organism*. New York: American Book Co., 1939. **171**

Goldstein, M. J., Judd, L. I., Rodnick, E. H., & LaPolla, A. "Psychophysiological and Behavioral Effects of Phenothiazine Administration in Acute Schizophrenics as a Function of Premorbid Status." *Journal of Psychiatric Research*, 1969, *6*, 271–87. **193**

Goodall, J. "Chimpanzees of the Gombe Stream Reserve." In I. De Vore (Ed.), *Primate Behavior.* New York: Holt, Rinehart & Winston, 1965. **688**

Goor, A., & Sommerfeld, R. E. "A Comparison of Problem-Solving Processes of Creative Students and Noncreative Students." *Journal of Educational Psychology,* 1975, *67,* 495–505. **345**

Gore, P. M., & Rotter, J. B. "A Personality Correlate of Social Action." *Journal of Personality,* 1963, *31,* 58–64. **131**

Gottesman, I. I., & Shields, J. "Contributions of Twin Studies of Perspectives on Schizophrenia." In B. A. Maher (Ed.), *Progress in Experimental Personality Research.* (Vol. 3.) New York: Academic Press, 1966. **138, 193**

Gottlieb, G. *Development of Species Identification in Birds: An Inquiry into the Prenatal Determinants of Perception.* Chicago: University of Chicago Press, 1971. **651**

Gough, H. "The Adjective Check List as a Personality Assessment Research Technique." *Psychological Reports,* 1960, 6, 107–22. **148**

Gray, P. H. "Irrelevant Cue Learning in the Chick." *Psychological Reports,* 1957, *3,* 345–52. **96**

Greene, W. A. "Operant Conditioning of the GSR using Partial Reinforcement." *Psychological Reports,* 1966, *19,* 571–78. **209**

Greenough, W. T. "Enduring Brain Effects of Differential Experience and Training." In M. R. Rosenzweig & E. L. Bennett (Eds.), *Neural Mechanisms of Learning and Memory.* Cambridge, Mass.: MIT Press, 1976. **595**

Greenspoon, J. "The Reinforcing Effects of Two Spoken Sounds on the Frequency of Two Responses." *American Journal of Psychology,* 1955, *68,* 409–16. **162**

Gregory, R. L. *Eye and Brain: The Psychology of Seeing.* (2nd ed.) New York: McGraw-Hill, 1972. **444**

Gregory, R. L., & Wallace, J. G. "Recovery from Early Blindness: A Case Study." *Experimental Psychology Society Monograph,* No. 2 (Cambridge, Mass.), 1963. **458**

Groos, K. *The Play of Animals* (tr. by Elizabeth L. Baldwin). New York: Appleton, 1898. **687**

Gross, C. G., Bender, D. B., & Rocha-Miranda, C. E. "Visual Receptive Fields of Neurons in Inferotemporal Cortex of the Monkey." *Science,* 1969, *166,* 1303–06. **608**

Groves, R. M., & Thompson, R. F. "Habituation: A Dual-Process Theory." *Psychological Review,* 1970, *77,* 419–50. **594**

Guilford, J. P. "Progress in the Discovery of Intellectual Factors." In C. W. Taylor (Ed.), *Widening Horizons in Creativity.* New York: McGraw-Hill, 1964. **344**

Guilford, J. P. *The Nature of Human Intelligence.* New York: McGraw-Hill, 1967. **317**

Gustavson, C. R., & Garcia, J. "Aversive Conditioning: Pulling a Gag on Wily Coyote." *Psychology Today,* 1974, *8*(3), 68–72. **654**

Gustavson, C. R., Kelly, D. J., Sweeney, M., & Garcia, J. "Prey-Lithium Aversions. 1. Coyotes and Wolves." *Behavioral Biology,* 1976, *17,* 61–72. **654**

Guttman, L. "A Basis for Scaling Qualitative Data." *American Sociological Review,* 1944, *9,* 139–50. **42**

Haber, R. N. (Ed.) *Current Research in Motivation.* New York: Holt, Rinehart & Winston, 1966. **389**

Hailman, J. P. *The Ontogeny of an Instinct: The Pecking Response in Chicks of the Laughing Gull (Larus atricilla L.) and Related Species. Behavioral Supplement 15.* Leiden, Netherlands: E. J. Brill, 1967. **461**

Hall, K. R. L. "Behavior and Ecology of the Wild Patas Monkey. *Erythrocebus patas,* in Uganda." *Journal of Zoology,* 1965, *148,* 15–87. **666**

Hall, K. R. L., & De Vore, I. "Baboon Social Behavior." In I. De Vore (Ed.), *Primate Behavior.* New York: Holt, Rinehart & Winston, 1965. **665**

Halloran, J. D., Brown, R. L., & Chaney, D. C. *Television and Delinquency.* Leicester, Eng.: Leicester University Press (Television Research Committee Working Paper No. 3), 1970. **145**

Hamilton, W. D. "The Genetical Theory of Social Behavior." *Journal of Theoretical Biology,* 1964, *7,* 1–52. **668**

Hampson, J. L. "Determinants of Psychosexual Orientation." In F. A. Beach (Ed.), *Sex and Behavior.* New York: Wiley, 1965. **565**

Harlow, H. F. "The Formation of Learning Sets." *Psychological Review,* 1949, *56,* 51–65. **327, 392, 643**

Harlow, H. F. "Mice, Monkeys, Men and Motives." *Psychological Review,* 1953, *60,* 23–32. **659**

Harlow, H. F. "The Heterosexual Affectional System in Monkeys." *American Psychologist,* 1962, 1–9. **680**

Harlow, H. F., & Harlow, M. H. "Learning to Love." *American Scientist,* 1966, *54*(3), 244–72. **264**

Harlow, H. F., Harlow, M. H., & Suomi, S. J. "From Thought to Therapy: Lessons from a Primate Laboratory." *American Scientist,* 1971, *59,* 538–49. **265**

Harlow, H., and Suomi, S. J. "Social Recovery by Isolation-Reared Monkeys." *Proceedings National Academy of Sciences,* 1971, *68,* 1534–38. **265**

Harlow, H. F., & Zimmermann, R. R. "Affectional Responses in the Infant Monkey." *Science,* 1959, *130* (3373), 421–32. **264**

Harris, C. S. "Perceptual Adaptation to Inverted, Reversed and Displaced Vision." *Psychological Review,* 1965, *72,* 419–44. **459**

Harter, S. "Discrimination of Learning Set in Children as a Function of I.Q. and M.A." *Journal of Experimental Child Psychology,* 1965, *2*(1), 31–43. **302**

Hartman, D. P. "Influence of Symbolically Modelled Instrumented Aggression and Pain Cues on Aggressive Behavior." *Journal of Personality and Social Psychology,* 1969, *11,* 380–88. **145**

Hartmann, C. G. *Possums.* Austin: University of Texas Press, 1962. **678**

Hartmann, H. *Ego Psychology and the Problem of Adaptation* (tr. by David Rapaport). New York: International Universities Press, 1958 (1939). **163**

Hartup, W. W. "Peer Interactions in Childhood." In P. Mussen (Ed.), *Carmichael's Manual of Child Psychology.* (Vol. 2.) New York: Wiley, 1970. **280**

Hastorf, A., & Cantril, H. "They Saw a Game: A Case Study." *Journal of Abnormal and Social Psychology,* 1954, *49,* 129–34. **68**

Hathaway, S. R., & McKinley, J. C. *The Minnesota Multiphasic Personality Inventory.* (Rev. ed.) Minneapolis: University of Minnesota Press, 1943. **149**

Hayes, K. J., & Hayes, C. "Imitation in a Home Raised Chimpanzee." *Journal of Comparative and Physiological Psychology*, 1952, *45*, 450–59. **350**

Hebb, D. O. *The Organization of Behavior*. New York: Wiley, 1949. **580**

Hebb, D. O. *A Textbook of Psychology*. (2nd ed.) Philadelphia: Saunders, 1966. **314**

Hediger, H. *Studies of the Psychology and Behavior of Captive Animals in Zoos and Circuses*. London: Butterworth, 1955. **692**

Heidbreder, E. "The Attainment of Concepts: Terminology and Methodology." *Journal of General Psychology*, 1946, *35*, 173–89. **336**

Hein, A., Held, R., & Gower, E. C. "Development and Segmentation of Visually Controlled Movement by Selective Exposure during Rearing." *Journal of Comparative and Physiological Psychology*, 1970, *73*, 181–87. **460**

Held, R. "Two Modes of Processing Spatially Distributed Visual Stimulation." In F. O. Schmitt (Ed.), *The Neurosciences: Second Study Program*. New York: Rockefeller University Press, 1970. **459**

Held, R., & Hein, A. "Movement-Produced Stimulation in the Development of Visually Guided Behavior." *Journal of Comparative and Physiological Psychology*, 1963, *56*, 872–76. **459, 460**

Henle, M. "On the Relation Between Logic and Thinking." *Psychological Review*, 1962, *69*, 366–78. **332**

Henle, M. "A Comparison between Gestalt Therapy and Gestalt Psychology." Unpublished Presidential Address to Division 24, Division of Philosophical Psychology, American Psychological Association, Chicago, Illinois, September 1, 1975. **466**

Hersher, L., Richmond, J. B., & Moore, A. U. "Modifiability of the Critical Period for the Development of Maternal Behavior in Sheep and Goats." *Behavior*, 1963, *20*, 311–20. **651**

Hess, C., & Pretori, H. "Messende Untersuchungen über die Gesetzmässigkeit des Simultanen Helligkeitskontrastes." *Albrecht von Graefes Archiv für Klinische und Experimentelle Ophthalmologie*, 1894, *40*, 1–24. **479**

Hess, E. H. "Space Perception in the Chick." *Scientific American*, 1956, *195*, 71–80. **460**

Hess, E. H. "Imprinting in Animals." *Scientific American*, 1958, *198*, 81–90. **649**

Hess, R. D., & Shipman, V. C. "Early Experience and the Socialization of Cognitive Modes in Children." *Child Development*, 1965, *36*(4), 869–86. **244, 358**

Hind, J. E., Rose, J. E., Davies, P. W., Woolsey, C. N., Benjamin, R. M., Welker, W. S., & Thompson, R. F. "Unit Activity in the Auditory Cortex." In G. L. Rasmussen & W. F. Windle (Eds.), *Neural Mechanisms of the Auditory and Vestibular Systems*. Springfield, Ill.: Charles C Thomas, 1961. **620**

Hinde, R. A. "Factors Governing the Changes in Strength of a Partially Inborn Response, as Shown by the Mobbing Behavior of the Chaffinch (Fringilla coelebs), I. The Nature of the Response, and an Examination of Its Course. *Proceedings Royal Society, London, Serial B*, 1954, *142*, 306–31. **667**

Hinde, R. A., & Spencer-Booth, Y. "The Behavior of Socially Living Rhesus Monkeys in Their First Two and a Half Years." *Animal Behaviour*, 1967, *15*, 169–96. **683**

Hochberg, J. E., & McAlister, E. A. "A Quantitative Approach to Figural Goodness." *Journal of Experimental Psychology*, 1953, *46*, 361–64. **471**

Hodos, W. "Evolutionary Interpretation of Neural and Behavioral Studies of Living Vertebrates." In F. O. Schmitt (Ed.), *The Neurosciences: Second Study Program*. New York: Rockefeller University Press, 1970. **643**

Hodos, W., & Campbell, C. B. G. "Scala Naturae: Why There Is No Theory in Comparative Psychology." *Psychological Review*, 1969, *76*, 337–50. **644**

Holland, J. L., & Richards, J. M., Jr. "Academic and Nonacademic Accomplishment: Correlated or Uncorrelated." *Journal of Educational Psychology*, 1965, *45*, 165–74. **304**

Hollander, E. P., & Webb, W. B. "Leadership, Followship, and Friendship: An Analysis of Peer Nominations." *Journal of Abnormal and Social Psychology*, 1960, *61*, 176–80. **110**

Holzman, P. S., & Gardner, R. W. "Leveling, Sharpening and Memory Organization." *Journal of Abnormal and Social Psychology*, 1960, *61*, 176–180. **342**

Holzman, P. S., & Klein, G. S. "Cognitive System Principles of Leveling and Sharpening: Individual Differences in Assimilation Effects in Visual Time Error." *Journal of Psychology*, 1954, *37*, 105–22. **342**

Homans, G. C. *Social Behavior: Its Elementary Forms*. New York: Harcourt, Brace & World, 1961. **101**

Honzik, M. P., Macfarlane, J. W., & Allen, L. "The Stability of Mental Test Performance between 2 and 18 Years." *Journal of Experimental Education*, 1948, *17*, 309–24. **306, 307**

Horney, K. *Neurotic Personality of Our Times*. New York: Norton, 1937. **166**

Houston, S. "A Reexamination of Some Assumptions about the Language of the Disadvantaged Child." *Child Development*, 1970, *41*, 947–64. **360**

Hovland, C. I., Harvey, O. J., & Sherif, M. "Assimilation and Contrast Effects in Reaction to Communication and Attitude Change." *Journal of Abnormal and Social Psychology*, 1957, *55*, 244–52. **50**

Hovland, C. I., & Pritzker, H. A. "Extent of Opinion Change as a Function of Amount of Change Advocated." *Journal of Abnormal and Social Psychology*, 1957, 257–61. **50**

Hovland, C. I., & Weiss, W. "The Influence of Source Credibility on Communication Effectiveness." *Public Opinion Quarterly*, 1951, *15*, 635–50. **43, 44**

Howard, H. E. *Territory in Bird Life*. London: Murray, 1920. **692**

Hubel, D. H. "Effects of Distortion of Sensory Input on the Visual System of Kittens." *The Physiologist*, 1967, *10*, 17–45. **612**

Hull, C. L. "Quantitative Aspects of the Evolution of Concepts." *Psychological Monographs*, 1920, No. 123. **335**

Hull, C. L. *Principles of Behavior*. New York: Appleton-Century-Crofts, 1943. **365, 646, 658**

Hulse, S. H., Deese, J., & Egeth, H. *The Psychology of Learning*. (4th ed.) New York: McGraw-Hill, 1975. **382**

Hunt, G. H., & Odoroff, M. E. *Follow-up Study of Narcotic Drug Addicts after Hospitalization*. (U.S. Public Health Service Report No. 77.) Washington, D.C.: U.S. Government Printing Office, 1963. **205**

Hunter, W. S. "The Delayed Reaction in Animals and Children." *Behavior Monographs*, 1913, *2*. **641**

Inhelder, B., & Piaget, J. *The Growth of Logical Thinking from*

Childhood through Adolescence. New York: Basic Books, 1958. **248, 249, 251**

Inhelder, B., & Piaget, J. *The Early Growth of Logic in the Child.* New York: Harper, 1959. **249**

Isaacson, R. L. "Experimental Brain Lesions and Memory." In M. R. Rosenzweig & E. L. Bennett (Eds.), *Neural Mechanisms of Learning and Memory.* Cambridge, Mass.: MIT Press, 1976. **592**

Iscoe, I., and Williams, Martha S. "Experimental Variables Affecting the Conformity Behavior of Children." *Journal of Personality,* 1963, *31*(2), 234–46. **58**

Itani, J. "Paternal Care in the Wild Japanese Monkey, *Macaca fuscata.*" *Journal of Primates,* 1959, *2,* 61–93. **670, 685**

Jackson, D. W., & Messick, S. "Content and Style in Personality Assessment." *Psychological Bulletin,* 1958, *55,* 243–52. **146**

Jacobs, G. H. "Color Vision." *Annual Review,* 1976, 27. **615**

James, W. *The Principles of Psychology.* New York: Holt, 1890, 1893. Reprinted by Dover Publications, 1950. **407, 418, 611**

James, W. H., Woodruff, A. B., & Werner, W. "Effect of Internal and External Control upon Smoking Behavior." *Journal of Consulting Psychology,* 1965, *29,* 184–86. **131**

Janis, I. L., & Field, P. B. "Sex Differences and Personality Factors Related to Persuasibility." In C. I. Hovland & I. L. Janis (Eds.), *Personality and Persuasibility.* New Haven: Yale University Press, 1959. **52**

Jecker, J., & Landy, D. "Liking a Person as a Function of Doing Him a Favor." *Human Relations,* 1969, *22,* 371–78. **114**

Jencks, C., et al. *Inequality: A Reassessment of the Effect of Family and Schooling in America.* New York: Basic Books, 1972. **304**

Jensen, A. R. "How Much Can We Boost IQ and Scholastic Achievement?" In *Environment, Heredity, and Intelligence.* Cambridge, Mass.: *Harvard Educational Review,* Reprint Series No. 2, 1969. **313**

Jones, E. *The Life and Work of Sigmund Freud.* 3 vols. New York: 1953–57. **158**

Jones, E. E. "Flattery Will Get You Somewhere." *Trans/Action,* May/June 1965, 20–23. **112**

Jones, E. E., Bell, L., & Aronson, E. "The Reciprocation of Attraction from Similar and Dissimilar Others: A Study in Person Perception and Evaluation." In C. G. McClintock (Ed.), *Experimental Social Psychology.* New York: Holt, Rinehart & Winston, 1971. **108**

Jones, E. E., & Kohler, R. "The Effects of Plausibility on the Learning of Controversial Statements." *Journal of Abnormal and Social Psychology,* 1958, *57,* 315–320. **72**

Jones, E. E., & Nisbett, R. E. *The Actor and Observer: Divergent Perceptions of the Causes of Behavior.* New York: General Learning Press, 1971. **85**

Julesz, B. "Binocular Depth Perception without Familiarity Cues." *Science,* 1964, *145,* 356–62. **474**

Jung, C. G. *The Basic Writings of C. G. Jung* (ed. by V. de Laszlo). New York: Random House, 1959. **166, 169**

Kagan, J. "Reflection-Impulsivity: The Generality and Dynamics of Conceptual Tempo." *Journal of Abnormal Psychology,* 1966, *71,* 17–24. **341**

Kagan, J. "Attention and Psychological Change in the Young Child." *Science,* 1970, *170,* 826–32. **240**

Kagan, J., & Moss, H. A. *Birth to Maturity.* New York: Wiley, 1969. **286**

Kaplan, I. T., & Schoenfeld, W. N. "Oculomotor Patterns During the Solution of Visually Displayed Anagrams." *Journal of Experimental Psychology,* 1966, *72,* 447–51. **328**

Kaufman, J. H. "Ecology and Social Behavior of the Coati, *Nasua narica,* on Barro Colorado Island, Panama." *University of California Publication Zoology,* 1962. **674**

Kaufman, J. H. "The Ecology and Evolution of Social Organization in the Kangaroo Family (Macropodidae)." *American Zoologist,* 1974, *14,* 51–62. **674**

Kellogg, W. N., & Kellogg, L. A. *The Ape and the Child.* New York: McGraw-Hill, 1933. **350**

Kelly, G. A. *The Psychology of Personal Constructs.* New York: Norton, 1955. **132**

Kendler, H. H., & Kendler, T. S. "From Discrimination Learning to Cognitive Development: A Neobehaviorist Odyssey." In W. K. Estes (Ed.), *Handbook of Learning and Cognitive Processes.* New York: Lawrence Erlbaum, 1975. **338**

Kendler, T. S., & Kendler, H. H. "Inferential Behavior in Children as a Function of Age and Subgoal Constancy." *Journal of Experimental Psychology,* 1962, *64,* 460–66. **333**

Kendler, T. S., & Kendler, H. H. "Experimental Analysis of Inferential Behavior in Children." In L. P. Lipsett & C. C. Spiker (Eds.), *Advances in Child Development and Behavior.* (Vol. 3) New York: Academic Press, 1967. **338**

Kety, S. S., Rosenthal, D., Wender, P. H., & Schulsinger, F. "The Types and Prevalence of Mental Illness in the Biological and Adoptive Families of Adopted Schizophrenics." In D. Rosenthal & S. S. Kety (Eds.), *The Transmission of Schizophrenia.* London: Pergamon, 1968, 345–62. **193**

Kiesler, S. B., & Baral, R. L. "The Search for a Romantic Partner: The Effects of Self-Esteem and Physical Attractiveness on Romantic Behavior." In *Personality and Social Behavior,* Kenneth J. Gergen and David Marlowe (Eds). Reading, Mass.: Addison-Wesley, 1970. **109**

King, J. A. "Social Behavior, Social Organization, and Population Dynamics in a Blacktailed Prairie Dog Town in the Black Hills of South Dakota." *Contributions from the Laboratory of Vertebrate Biology,* 1955, No. 67. **689**

King, J. A., & Weisman, R. G. "Sand Digging Contingent upon Bar Pressing in Deer Mice (*Peromyscus*)." *Animal Behaviour,* 1964, *12,* 446–50. **661**

Kinsey, A. C., & Gelhard, P. H. *Sexual Behavior in the Human Female.* Philadelphia: Saunders, 1953. **21**

Kinsey, A. C., Pomeroy, W. B., & Martin, C. E. *Sexual Behavior in the Human Male.* Philadelphia: Saunders, 1948. **21**

Kintsch, W. *The Representation of Meaning in Memory.* Hillsdale, N.J.: Lawrence Erlbaum, 1974. **432**

Kleck, R. E., & Rubinstein, C. "Physical Attractiveness, Perceived Attitude Similarity, and Interpersonal Attraction in an Opposite Sex Encounter." *Journal of Personality and Social Psychology,* 1975, *31,* 107–14. **108**

Kleiman, D. "Scent Marking in the Canidae." In P. A. Jewell & C. Loizos (Eds.), *Play, Exploration and Territory in Mammals.* London: Academic Press, 1966. **691**

Klein, W., Plomp, R., & Pols, L. C. W. "Vowel Spectra, Vowel Spaces and Vowel Identification." *Journal of the Acoustical*

Society in America, 1970, *48,* 999–1009. **450**

Kling, A., Lancaster, J., & Benitone, J. "Amygdalectomy in the Free-Ranging Vervet (*Cercopithecus Althiops*)." *Journal of Psychiatric Research,* 1970, *7,* 191–99. **571**

Klopfer, B. (Ed.) *Developments in the Rorschach Technique.* Yonkers-on-Hudson, N.Y.: World Book Co., 1954–70. **152**

Klopfer, P. H., Adams, D. K., & Klopfer, M. S. "Maternal Imprinting in Goats." *Proceedings, National Academy of Sciences,* 1964, *52,* 911–14. **651**

Koffka, K. *Principles of Gestalt Psychology.* New York: Harcourt, Brace & World, 1935. **466**

Kohlberg, L. "The Development of Children's Orientations Toward a Moral Order: 1. Sequence in the Development of Moral Thought." *Vita Humana,* 1963, *6,* 11–33. **252**

Kohlberg, L. "Stage and Sequence: The Cognitive-Developmental Approach to Socialization." In D. A. Goslin (Ed.), *Handbook of Socialization Theory and Research.* Chicago: Rand McNally, 1969, 347–480. **256**

Kohler, J. "Experiments with Goggles." *Scientific American,* 1962, *206,* 62–72. **459, 485**

Köhler, W. *The Mentality of Apes.* New York: Harcourt, 1925. **324, 640**

Kopp, R., Bohdanecky, Z., & Jarvik, M. E. "Long Temporal Gradient of Retrograde Amnesia for a Well-Discriminated Stimulus." *Science,* 1966, *153,* 1547–1549. **581, 582**

Koukkou, M., & Lehmann, D. "EEG and Memory Storage in Sleep Experiments with Humans." *Electroencephalography and Clinical Neurophysiology,* 1968, *25,* 455–62. **585**

Kramer, B. M. "Dimensions of Prejudice." *Journal of Psychology,* 1949, *27,* 389–451. **95**

Krasne, F. B. "The Use of Invertebrate Systems to Gain Insight into the Nature of Learning and Memory." In M. R. Rosenzweig & E. L. Bennett (Eds.), *Neural Mechanisms of Learning and Memory.* Cambridge, Mass.: MIT Press, 1976. **594**

Krasner, L. "Studies of the Conditioning of Verbal Behavior." *Psychological Bulletin,* 1958, *55,* 148–70. **162**

Krebs, C. J. *Ecology: The Experimental Analysis of Distribution and Abundance.* New York: Harper & Row, 1972. **675**

Kummer, H. *Social Organization of Hamadryas Baboons.* Chicago: University of Chicago Press, 1968. **688, 698**

Kummer, H., & Kurt, F. "A Comparison of Social Behavior in Captive and Wild Hamadryas Baboons." In H. Vagtborg (Ed.), *The Baboon in Medical Research.* Houston: University of Texas Press, 1965. **688**

Lack, D. *The Natural Selection of Animal Numbers.* London: Oxford University Press, 1954. **675**

Ladefoged, P. "The Perception of Speech." In *The Mechanization of Thought Processes.* London: H. M. Stationery Office, 1959. **448**

Ladefoged, P., & Broadbent, D. E. "Perception of Sequence in Auditory Events." *Quarterly Journal of Experimental Psychology,* 1960, *12,* 162–70. **448**

Laing, R. D. *The Politics of Experience.* New York: Ballantine, 1967. **194**

Lambert, W. E., Hodgson, R. C., Gardner, R. C., & Fillenbaum, S. "Evaluation Reactions to Spoken Languages." *Journal of Abnormal and Social Psychology,* 1960, *60,* 44–51. **456**

Lasky, R. E. "The Ability of Six-Year-Olds, Eight-Year-Olds and Adults to Abstract Visual Patterns." *Child Development,*

1974, *45,* 626–32. **339**

Lazarfeld, P. F. (Ed.) *Radio and the Printed Page.* New York: Duell, Sloan, Pearce, 1944. **90**

Lazarus, A. A. "The Elimination of Children's Phobias by Deconditioning." In H. J. Eysenck (Ed.), *Behavior Therapy and the Neuroses.* New York: Macmillan, 1960. **209**

Lea, H. C. *Materials toward a History of Witchcraft* (Ed. by A. C. Howland, 3 vols.) Philadelphia: University of Pennsylvania Press, 1939. **183**

Le Boeuf, B. J. "Social Status and Mating Activity in Elephant Seals." *Science,* 1969, *163,* 91–93. **693**

Le Bon, G. *The Crowd.* New York: Viking, 1960 (original 1895). **64**

Leeper, R. "A Study of a Neglected Portion of the Field of Learning—The Development of Sensory Organization." *Journal of Genetic Psychology,* 1935, *46,* 41–75. **453**

Lefkowitz, M., Blake, R. R., & Mouton, J. S. "Status Factors in Pedestrian Violation of Traffic Signals." *Journal of Abnormal and Social Psychology,* 1955, *51,* 706–08. **61**

Lefkowitz, M. M., Eron, L. D., Walder, L. O., & Huesmann, L. R. "Television Violence and Child Aggression, A Follow-up Study." In G. A. Comstock & E. A. Rubinstein (Eds.), *Television and Social Behavior.* Vol. 3, *Television and Adolescent Aggressiveness.* Washington, D.C.: Government Printing Office, 1972, 35–135. **145**

Leibowitz, H. W., Pollard, S. W., & Dickson, D. "Monocular and Binocular Size-Matching as a Function of Distance at Various Age Levels." *American Journal of Psychology,* 1967, *80,* 263–68. **478**

Leiter, R. G. "Manual for the 1948 Revision of the Leiter International Performance Scale." *Psychological Service Center Journal,* 1950, *2,* 259–343. **305**

Lenneberg, E. H. *Biological Foundations of Language.* New York: Wiley, 1967. **652**

Lerner, I. M. *Heredity, Evolution and Society.* San Francisco: W. H. Freeman, 1968. **631**

Levant, W. P. "Grammar in the Story Reproductions of Levelers and Sharpeners." *Bulletin of the Menninger Clinic,* 1962, *26,* 283–87. **342**

Levine, S. "Sex Differences in the Brain." *Scientific American,* 1966, *214,* 84–90. **565**

Levitas, M. *America in Crisis.* New York: Holt, Rinehart, 1969. **83**

Levy, D. M. *Maternal Overprotection.* New York: Columbia University Press, 1943. **273**

Lewin, K. *A Dynamic Theory of Personality.* New York: McGraw-Hill, 1935. **170**

Lhermitte, F., & Signoret, J.-L. "Amnesia Syndromes and the Hippocampal-Mammillary System." In M. R. Rosenzweig & E. L. Bennett (Eds.), *Neural Mechanisms of Learning and Memory.* Cambridge, Mass.: MIT Press, 1976. **577, 590**

Liberman, A. M., Cooper, F. S., Shankweiler, D. P., & Studdert-Kennedy, M. "Perception of the Speech Code." *Psychological Review,* 1967, *74,* 431–61. **450**

Lidz, T. "The Influence of Family Studies on the Treatment of Schizophrenia." *Psychiatry,* 1967, *32,* 235–51. **193**

Likert, R. "A Technique for the Measurement of Attitudes." *Archives of Psychology,* 1932, *140,* 44–53. **42**

Lindauer, M. "Communication by Dancing in Swarm Bees."

In M. Lindauer (Ed.), *Communication Among Social Bees.* Cambridge: Harvard University Press, 1961. **669**

Linton, H. B. "Dependence on External Influence: Correlates in Perception, Attitudes and Judgment." *Journal of Abnormal and Social Psychology,* 1955, *51,* 502–07. **130**

Loehlin, J. C., Lindzey, G., and Spuhler, J. N. *Race Differences in Intelligence.* 1975. **314**

Lorenz, K. "Der Kumpan in der Unwelt des Vogels." *Journal für Ornithologie,* 1935, *83,* 137–213, 289–413. **647**

Lorenz, K. "The Comparative Method of Studying Innate Behavior Patterns." *Society for Experimental Biology, Symposia,* 1950, *4,* 221–68. **636**

Lorenz, K. *On Aggression.* New York: Harcourt, Brace and World, 1966. **699**

Lott, B. E., & Lott, A. J. "The Formation of Positive Attitudes toward Group Members." *Journal of Abnormal and Social Psychology,* 1960, *61,* 297–300. **101**

Lovaas, O. I. "Effect of Exposure to Symbolic Aggression on Aggressive Behavior." *Child Development,* 1961, *32,* 37–44. **145**

Lovaas, O. I., Freitag, G., Gold, V. J., & Kassorla, I. C. "Experimental Studies in Childhood Schizophrenia: 1. Analysis of Self-Destructive Behavior." *Journal of Experimental Child Psychology,* 1965, *2,* 67–84. **154**

Lynch, C. "Some Difficulties Associated with the Use of Lesion Techniques in the Study of Memory." In M. R. Rosenzweig & E. L. Bennett (Eds.), *Neural Mechanisms of Learning and Memory.* Cambridge, Mass.: MIT Press, 1976. **592**

Maas, H., & Kuypers, J. *From Thirty to Seventy: A Forty-Year Longitudinal Study of Adult Life Styles and Personality.* San Francisco: Jossey-Bass, 1974. **287**

McBrearty, J. F., Garfield, Z., Dichten, M., & Heath, G. "A Behaviorally Oriented Treatment Program for Alcoholism." *Psychological Reports,* 1968, *22,* 287–98. **201**

McClelland, D. C. "Testing for Competence rather than for Intelligence." *American Psychologist,* 1973, *28,* 1–14. **304**

McClelland, D. C., & Apicella, F. S. "A Functional Classification of Verbal Reactions to Experimentally Induced Failure." *Journal of Abnormal and Social Psychology,* 1945, *40,* 376–90. **142**

McClelland, D. C., Atkinson, J. W., Clark, R. A., & Lowell, E. L. *The Achievement Motive.* New York: Appleton-Century-Crofts, 1953. **153**

Maccoby, E. E., & Jacklin, C. H. *The Psychology of Sex Differences.* Stanford: Stanford University Press, 1974. **135, 136, 279, 566**

MacCrone, I. D. *Race Attitudes in South Africa.* London: Oxford University Press, 1957. **90, 96**

McDonough, J. H., & Kesner, R. P. "Amnesia Produced by Brief Electrical Stimulation of the Amygdala or Dorsal Hippocampus in Cats." *Journal of Comparative and Physiological Psychology,* 1971, *77,* 171–78. **582**

McGaugh, J. L. "Time-Dependent Processes in Memory Storage." *Science,* 1966, *153,* 1357–58. **582**

McGaugh, J. L., & Gold, P. "Modulation of Memory by Electrical Stimulation of the Brain." In M. R. Rosenzweig & E. L. Bennett (Eds.), *Neural Mechanisms of Learning and Memory.* Cambridge, Mass.: MIT Press, 1976. **582**

McGaugh, J. L., & Krivanek, J. "Strychnine Effects on Discrimination Learning in Mice: Effects of Dose and Time Administration." *Physiology and Behavior,* 1970, *5,* 1437–42. **584**

McGinnies, E. "Emotionality and Perceptual Defense." *Psychological Review,* 1949, *56,* 244–51. **455**

McGuire, W. J., & Papageorgis, D. "The Relative Efficacy of Various Types of Prior Belief-Defense in Producing Immunity Against Persuasion." *Journal of Abnormal and Social Psychology,* 1961, *62,* 327–37. **52**

Mach, E. *The Analysis of Sensations.* New York: Dover, 1959. **483**

Mackintosh, N. J. "Comparative Studies of Reversal and Probability Learning: Rats, Birds and Fish." In R. M. Gilbert & N. S. Sutherland (Eds.), *Animal Discrimination Learning.* London: Academic Press, 1969. **645**

Maier, N. R. F. "Reasoning in Humans: II. The Solution of a Problem and Its Appearance in Consciousness." *Journal of Comparative Psychology,* 1931, *12,* 181–94. **323**

Maier, N. R. F., & Schneirla, T. C. *Principles of Animal Psychology.* New York: McGraw-Hill, 1935. **642**

Main, M. "Exploration, Play and Level of Cognitive Functioning as Related to Child-Mother Attachment." Doctoral Dissertation, The Johns Hopkins University, 1973. **270**

Main, M. "Mother-Avoiding Babies." Paper presented at the biennial meeting of the Society for Research in Child Development, Denver, April 1975. **267**

Mark, V. H., "A Psychosurgeon's Case for Psychosurgery." *Psychology Today,* 1973, *8*(2), 84–94. **571**

Mark, V. H., & Ervin, F. R. *Violence and the Brain.* New York: Harper, 1970. **569, 570**

Marks, L. E. "On Scales of Sensation: Prolegomena to Any Future Psychophysics that Will Be Able To Come Forth as Science." *Perception and Psychophysics,* 1974, *16,* 358–76. **497**

Marks, L. E. *Sensory Processes: The New Psychophysics.* New York: Academic Press, 1974. **497**

Marler, P. "A Comparative Approach to Vocal Learning: Song Development in White-Crowned Sparrows." *Journal of Comparative and Physiological Psychology Monograph,* 1970, *71* (1), 1–25. **651**

Maslow, A. H. "Deprivation, Threat and Frustration." *Psychological Review,* 1941, *48,* 364–466. **141**

Maslow, A. H. *Motivation and Personality.* New York: Harper, 1954. **173**

Maslow, A. H. "Lessons from the Peak-Experience." *Journal of Humanistic Psychology,* 1962, *2*(1), 9–18. **174**

Maslow, A. H. "Self-Actualizing People." In G. B. Levitas (Ed.), *The World of Psychology.* (Vol. 2.) New York: George Braziller, 1963. **174**

Mason, W. A. "The Effects of Social Restriction on the Behavior of Rhesus Monkeys: I. Free Social Behavior." *Journal of Comparative and Physiological Psychology,* 1960, *53,* 582–89. **688, 697**

Mayer, J., Roy, P., & Mitra, K. P. "Relation between Caloric Intake, Body Weight, and Physical Work: Studies in an Industrial Male Population in West Bengal." *American Journal of Clinical Nutrition,* 1956, *4,* 169–75. **552**

Mead, M. *Sex and Temperament in Three Primitive Societies.*

New York: Morrow, 1935. **136**

Mednick, S. A. "A Learning Theory Approach to Research in Schizophrenia." *Psychological Bulletin*, 1958, *55*, 316–27. **192**

Meehl, P. E. "Schizotaxia, Schizotypy, and Schizophrenia." *American Psychologist*, 1962, *17*, 827–38. **193**

Mehrabian, A. "Significance of Posture and Position in the Communication of Attitude and Status Relationships. *Psychological Bulletin*, 1969, *71*, 359–72. **147**

Melton, A. W. "Implications of Short Term Memory for a General Theory of Memory." *Journal of Verbal Learning and Verbal Behavior*, 1970, *9*, 596–606. **418**

Meltzoff, J., & Kornreich, M. *Research in Psychotherapy*. New York: Atherton Press, 1970. **213**

Mendelson, J. "Role of Hunger in T-maze Learning for Food by Rats." *Journal of Comparative and Physiological Psychology*, 1966, *62*, 341–49. **574**

Mettee, D. R. "Changes in Liking as a Function of the Magnitude and Affect of Sequential Evaluations." *Journal of Experimental Social Psychology*, 1971, *7*, 157–72. **116**

Mettee, D. R., Taylor, S. E., Friedman, H. "Affect Conversion and the Gain-Loss Like Effect." *Sociometry*, 1973, *36* (Dec.), 505–19. **116**

Michael, C. R. "Retinal Processing of Visual Images." *Scientific American*, 1969, *220*(5), 104–14. **613**

Michael, R. P. "Neuroendocrine Factors Regulating Primate Behavior." In L. Martini & W. F. Ganong (Eds.), *Frontiers in Neuroendocrinology, 1971*. New York: Oxford University Press, 1971. **681**

Michener, J. *Kent State: What Happened and Why*. New York: Random House, 1971. **91**

Miller, N., & Campbell, D. T. "Recency and Primacy in Persuasion as a Function of the Timing of Speeches and Measurements." *Journal of Abnormal and Social Psychology*, 1959, *59*, 1–9. **49**

Miller, N. E. "Learning of Visceral and Glandular Responses." *Science*, 1969, *163*, 434–45. **209**

Miller, N. E., & Banuazizi, A. "Instrumental Learning by Curarized Rats of a Specific Visceral Response, Intestinal or Cardiac." *Journal of Comparative and Physiological Psychology*, 1960, *65*, 1–7. **402**

Miller, N. E., & Dollard, J. *Social Learning and Imitation*. New Haven: Yale University Press, 1941. **176**

Miller, R. J. "Cross-Cultural Research in the Perception of Pictorial Materials." *Psychological Bulletin*, 1973, *80*, 135–50. **402, 457, 458**

Mills, J., & Aronson, E. "Opinion Change as a Function of the Communicator's Attractiveness and Desire to Influence." *Journal of Personality and Social Psychology*, 1965, *1*, 173–77. **46**

Milner, B. "Amnesia Following Operation on the Temporal Lobes." In C. W. M. Whitty & O. L. Zangwill (Eds.), *Amnesia*. London: Butterworth, 1966. **577**

Mischel, W. *Personality and Assessment*. New York: Wiley, 1968. **127**

Møller, A. R. (Ed.) *Basic Mechanisms in Hearing. Proceedings of the First Royal Swedish Academy of Sciences Symposium, Stockholm, 1972*. New York: Academic Press, 1973. **619**

Moltz, H., & Stettner, L. J. "The Influence of Patterned-Light Deprivation on the Critical Period for Imprinting." *Journal of Comparative and Physiological Psychology*, 1961, *54*, 279–83. **650**

Money, J., & Ehrhardt, A. A. *Man & Woman, Boy & Girl*. Baltimore: Johns Hopkins University Press, 1972. **565**

Moore, B. R. "The Role of Directed Pavlovian Reactions in Simple Instrumental Learning in the Pigeon." In R. A. Hinde & J. S. Hinde (Eds.), *Constraints on Learning*. London: Academic Press, 1973. **401**

Moore, R. Y. "Synaptogenesis and the Morphology of Learning and Memory." In M. R. Rosenzweig & E. L. Bennett (Eds.), *Neural Mechanisms of Learning and Memory*. Cambridge, Mass.: MIT Press, 1976. **595**

Moray, N. "Attention in Dichotic Listening: Affective Cues and the Influence of Instructions." *Quarterly Journal of Experimental Psychology*, 1959, *11*, 56–60. **452**

Moreno, J. L. *Psychodrama*. Beacon, N.Y.: Beacon House, 1946. **211**

Morgan, Clifford T., & Deese, J. *How To Study*. (2nd ed.) New York: McGraw-Hill, 1969. **431**

Morgan, E. *The Descent of Woman*. New York: Stein & Day, 1972. **699**

Müller, G. E., & Pilzecker, A. "Experimentelle Beiträge zur Lehre von Gedächtnis." *Zeitschrift für Psychologie*, 1900, *1*, 1–288. **580**

Murdock, B. B., Jr. "The Serial Position Effect of Free Recall." *Journal of Experimental Psychology*, 1962, *64*, 482–88. **415**

Murphy, G., & Murphy, L. B. *Asian Psychology*. New York: Basic Books, 1968. **180**

Murray, H. A. "The Effect of Fear upon Estimates of the Maliciousness of Other Personalities." *Journal of Social Psychology*, 1933, *4*, 310–29. **164**

Murray, H. A. *Thematic Apperception Test*. Cambridge, Mass.: Harvard University Press, 1943. **152**

Murray, H. A., et al. *Assessment of Men*. New York: Rinehart, 1948. **154**

Murstein, B. I. *Theory and Research in Projective Techniques*. New York: Wiley, 1963. **154**

Mussen, P. "Early Socialization, Learning and Identification." In G. Mandler (Ed.), *New Directions in Psychology III*. New York: Holt, Rinehart & Winston, 1967. **277**

Mussen, P., & Distler, L. "Masculinity, Identification, and Father-Son Relationships." *Journal of Abnormal and Social Psychology*, 1959, *59*, 350–56. **279**

Mussen, P., & Distler, L. "Child Rearing Antecedents of Masculine Identification in Kindergarten Boys." *Child Development*, 1960, *31*, 89–100. **279**

Mussen, P., & Parker, A. "Mother Nurturance and Girls' Incidental Imitative Learning." *Journal of Personality and Social Psychology*, 1965, *2*, 94–97. **278**

Mussen, P., and Rutherford, E. "Effects of Aggressive Cartoons in Children's Aggressive Play." *Journal of Abnormal and Social Psychology*, 1961, *62*, 461–64. **145**

Neimark, E. D. "Effect of Differential Reinforcement upon Information-Gathering Strategies in Diagnostic Problem-Solving." *Journal of Experimental Psychology*, 1967, *74*, 406–13. **326**

Neimark, E. D., & Lewis, N. "The Development of Logical Problem-Solving Strategies." *Child Development,* 1967, *38,* 107–18. **325**

Neisser, U. *Cognitive Psychology.* New York: Appleton-Century-Crofts, 1967. **403, 444, 448**

Neisser, U., & Weene, P. "Hierarchies in Concept Attainment." *Journal of Experimental Psychology,* 1962, *64,* 640–45. **337, 338**

Neumann, P. G. "An Attribute Frequency Model for the Abstraction of Prototypes." *Memory and Cognition,* 1974, *2,* 241–48. **340**

Nickel, T. W. "The Attribution of Intention as a Critical Factor in the Relation between Frustration and Aggression." *Journal of Personality,* 1974, *42,* 482–92. **142**

Nizer, L. *My Life in Court.* New York: Pyramid, 1961. **48**

Noirot, E. "Ultra-Sounds in Young Rodents. I. Changes with Age in Albino Mice." *Animal Behaviour,* 1966, *14,* 459–62. **686**

Norman, W. T. "Psychometric Considerations for a Revision of the MMPI." In J. N. Butcher (Ed.), *Objective Personality Assessment.* New York: Academic Press, 1972. **150**

Olds, J. "Self-Stimulation Experiments and Differentiated Reward Systems." In H. H. Jasper, L. D. Proctor, R. S. Knighton, W. C. Noshay, & R. T. Costello (Eds.), *Reticular Formation of the Brain.* Boston: Little, Brown, 1958. **572**

Olds, J. "Multiple Unit Recordings from Behaving Rats." In R. F. Thompson and M. M. Patterson (Eds.), *Bioelectric Recording Techniques, IA.* New York: Academic Press, 1973. **592, 593**

Olds, J., & Milner, P. "Positive Reinforcement Produced by Electrical Stimulation of Septal Area and Other Regions of Rat Brain." *Journal of Comparative and Physiological Psychology,* 1954, *47,* 419–27. **571**

Oltmans, G. A., & Harvey, J. A. "LH Syndrome and Brain Catecholamine Levels and Lesions of the Nigrostriatal Bundle." *Physiology and Behavior,* 1972, *8,* 69–78. **554**

Orne, M. T. "On the Social Psychology of the Psychological Experiment: With Particular Reference to Demand Characteristics and Their Implications." *American Psychologist,* 1962, *17,* 776–83. **455**

Orne, M. T. "Hypnosis, Motivation and the Ecological Validity of the Psychological Experiment." In W. J. Arnold & M. M. Page (Eds.), *Nebraska Symposium on Motivation 1970.* Lincoln: University of Nebraska Press, 1970. **455**

Osborn, A. G., Bunker, J. P., Cooper, L. M., Frank, G. S., & Hilgard, E. F. "Effects of Thiopental Sedation on Learning and Memory." *Science,* 1967, *157,* 574–76. **583**

Oswald, I., Taylor, A. M., & Treisman, A. M. "Discrimination Responses to Stimulation during Human Sleep." *Brain,* 1960, *83,* 440–53. **452**

Papousek, H. "Experimental Studies of Appetitional Behavior in Human Newborns and Infants." In H. W. Stevenson, E. H. Hess, & H. L. Rheingold (Eds.), *Early Behavior.* New York: Wiley, 1967. **241**

Pastore, N. "The Role of Arbitrariness in the Frustration-Aggression Hypothesis." *Journal of Abnormal and Social Psychology,* 1952, *47,* 728–31. **142**

Patterson, G. R., Littman, R. A., & Bricker, W. "Assertive Behavior in Children: A Step Toward a Theory of Aggression."

Monographs of the Society for Research in Child Development, 1967, *32*(5), 1–43. **281**

Patterson, M. M., Cegavske, C. F., & Thompson, R. F. "Effective of a Classical Conditioning Paradigm on Hind-Limb Flexor Nerve Response in Immobilized Spinal Cats." *Journal of Comparative and Physiological Psychology,* 1973, *84,* 88–97. **588**

Pearson, O. P. "Carnivore-Mouse Predation: An Example of Its Intensity and Bioenergetics." *Journal of Mammalogy,* 1964, *45,* 177–88. **675**

Penfield, W., & Jasper, H. *Epilepsy and the Functional Anatomy of the Human Brain.* Boston: Little, Brown, 1954. **540**

Peterson, L. R., Hillner, K., & Saltzman, D. "Time Between Pairings and Short-Term Retention." *Journal of Experimental Psychology,* 1962, *64,* 550–51. **417**

Pettigrew, J. D. "The Importance of Early Visual Experience for Neurons of the Developing Geniculostriate System." *Investigative Ophthalmology,* 1972, *11,* 386–94. **612**

Pettigrew, T. F. "Personality and Socio-Cultural Factors in Intergroup Attitudes. A Cross-National Comparison." *Journal of Conflict Resolution,* 1958, *2,* 29–42. **89**

Pettigrew, T. F. "Social Psychology and Desegregation Research." *American Psychologist,* 1961, *16,* 105–12. **90**

Pfaff, D. W. "Morphological Changes in the Brain of Adult Male Cats after Neonatal Castration." *Journal of Endocrinology,* 1966, *36,* 415–16. **565**

Phoenix, C. H., Goy, R. W., & Resko, J. A. "Psychosexual Differentiation as a Function of Androgenic Stimulation." In M. Diamond (Ed.), *Perspectives in Reproduction and Sexual Behavior.* Bloomington: Indiana University Press, 1968. **566**

Piaget, J. *The Language and Thought of the Child.* New York: Harcourt, Brace, 1926. **244**

Piaget, J. *Play, Dreams and Imitation in Childhood.* New York: Norton, 1951. **246**

Piaget, J. *The Origins of Intelligence in Children.* New York: International Universities Press, 1952; Norton, 1963. **224, 236, 244**

Pitts, W., & McCulloch, W. S. "How We Know Universals: The Perception of Auditory and Visual Forms." *Bulletin of Mathematical Biophysics,* 1947, *9,* 127–47. **446**

Pols, L. C. W., van der Kamp, L. J. Th., & Plomp, R. "Perceptual and Physical Space of Vowel Sounds." *Journal of the Acoustical Society of America,* 1969, *46,* 458–67. **450**

Posner, M. I. *Cognition: An Introduction.* Glenview, Ill.: Scott, Foresman, 1973. **322, 325, 356**

Premack, D. "Reinforcement Theory." In D. Levine (Ed.), *Nebraska Symposium on Motivation.* Lincoln: University of Nebraska Press, 1965. **661**

Premack, D. "A Functional Analysis of Language." *Journal of the Experimental Analysis of Behavior,* 1970, *14,* 107–25. **351**

Pylyshyn, Z. W. "What the Mind's Eye Tells the Mind's Brain: A Critique of Mental Imagery." *Psychological Bulletin,* 1973, 1–24. **444**

Ramey, C. T., & Watson, J. S. "Nonsocial Reinforcement of Infants' Vocalizations." *Developmental Psychology,* 1972, *6,* 538. **242**

Rank, O., *The Trauma of Birth.* New York: Harcourt Brace, 1929. **166**

Rank, O. *Will Therapy and Truth and Reality.* New York: Knopf, 1945. **166**

Ratliff, F., & Hartline, H. K. "The Responses of Limulus Optic Fibers to Patterns of Illumination on the Receptor Mosaic." *Journal of General Physiology,* 1959, *42,* 1241–55. **605**

Reeves, A. G., & Plum, F. "Hyperphagia, Rage and Dementia Accompanying a Ventromedial Hypothalamic Neoplasm." *Archives of Neurology,* 1969, *20,* 616–24. **554**

Rheingold, H., Gewirtz, J. L., & Ross, H. "Social Conditioning of Vocalizations in the Infant." *Journal of Comparative and Physiological Psychology,* 1959, *52,* 68–73. **243**

Riess, B. F. "The Isolation of Factors of Learning and Native Behavior in Field and Laboratory Studies." *Annals of the New York Academy of Science,* 1950, *51,* 1093–1102. **685**

Roberts, A. H., Kewman, D. G., and MacDonald, H. "Voluntary Control of Skin Temperature: Unilateral Changes Using Hypnosis and Feedback." *Journal of Abnormal Psychology,* 1973, *82,* 163–68. **402**

Robinson, W. P. "The Elaborated Code in Working Class Language." *Language and Speech,* 1965, *8,* 243–52. **354**

Rock, I. "The Role of Repetition in Associative Learning." *American Journal of Psychology,* 1957, *70,* 186–93. **405**

Rock, I., & Harris, C. S. "Vision and Touch." *Scientific American,* 1967, *216,* 96–104. **459**

Rodnick, E. H., & Garmezy, N. "An Experimental Approach to the Study of Motivation in Schizophrenia." In M. R. Jones (Ed.), *Nebraska Symposium on Motivation.* Lincoln: University of Nebraska Press, 1957. **192**

Rogers, C. R. *Counseling and Psychotherapy: Newer Concepts in Practice.* Boston: Houghton Mifflin, 1942. **207**

Rogers, C. R. *Client-Centered Therapy: Its Current Practice, Implications and Theory.* Boston: Houghton Mifflin, 1951. **206**

Rogers, C. R. "A Theory of Therapy, Personality and Interpersonal Relationships as Developed in the Client-Centered Framework." In S. Koch (Ed.), *Psychology: A Study of a Science.* (Vol. 3.) New York: McGraw-Hill, 1959. **171**

Rogers, C. R. *Freedom To Learn, A View of What Education Might Become.* Columbus, Ohio: Merrill, 1969. **173**

Rorschach, H. *Psychodiagnostics.* Berne: Hans Huber, 1942. **151**

Rosenberg, M. J. "When Dissonance Fails: On Eliminating Evaluation Apprehension from Attitude Measurement." *Journal of Personality and Social Psychology,* 1965, *1,* 28–42. **75**

Rosenhan, D., & White, G. M. "Observation and Rehearsal as Determinants of Prosocial Behavior." *Journal of Personality and Social Psychology,* 1967, *5,* 424–31. **225, 280**

Rosenthal, D. *Genetic Theory and Abnormal Behavior.* New York: McGraw-Hill, 1970. **196**

Rosenzweig, M. R. "Salivary Conditioning Before Pavlov." *American Journal of Psychology,* 1959, *72,* 628–33. **372**

Rosenzweig, M. R. & Bennett, E. L. (Eds.), *Neural Mechanisms of Learning and Memory.* Cambridge: M.I.T. Press, 1976a. **713**

Rosenzweig, M. R., & Bennett, E. L. "Enriched Environments: Facts, Factors, and Fantasies." In J. L. McGaugh & L. Petrinovich (Eds.), *Knowing, Thinking, and Believing.* New York: Plenum Press, 1976b. **595**

Rotter, J. B. *Social Learning and Clinical Psychology.* Englewood Cliffs, N.J.: Prentice-Hall, 1954, **177**

Rotter, J. B. "Generalized Expectancies for Internal versus External Control of Reinforcement." *Psychological Monographs,* 1966, *80* (Whole No. 609). **130, 178**

Rotter, J. B., *Applications of a Social Learning Theory of Personality.* New York: Holt, Rinehart, 1972. **177**

Rowell, T. E. "Hierarchy in the Organization of a Captive Baboon Group." *Animal Behaviour,* 1971, *19,* 625–45. **681, 682, 691**

Rozin, P. "The Psychobiological Approach to Human Memory." In M. R. Rosenzweig & E. L. Bennett (Eds.), *Neural Mechanisms of Learning and Memory.* Cambridge: MIT Press, 1976. **591**

Rozin, P., & Kalat, J. W. "Specific Hungers and Poisoning as Adaptive Specializations of Learning." *Psychological Review,* 1971, *78,* 459–86. **653**

Rubin, E. *Synsoplevede Figurer: Studier i Psykologisk Analyse.* København: Kristiania, 1915. **467**

Rumbaugh, D. M., von Glaserfeld, E., Warner, H., Pisani, P., Gill, T., Brown, J., & Bell, C. "A Computer-Controlled Language Training System for Investigating the Language Skills of Young Apes." *Behavioral Research Methods and Instrumentation,* 1973, *5,* 382–92. **351**

Rusak, B., & Zucker, I. "Biological Rhythms and Animal Behavior." *Annual Review,* 1975, *26,* 137–71. **561**

Russell, W. A., & Storms, L. H. "Implicit Verbal Chaining in Paired Associative Learning." *Journal of Experimental Psychology,* 1955, *49,* 287–92. **393**

Russell, W. R., & Nathan, P. W. "Traumatic Amnesia." *Brain,* 1946, *69,* 280–300. **580**

Rutherford, E., & Mussen, P. "Generosity in Nursery School Boys." *Child Development,* 1968, *39,* 755–65. **280**

Rutledge, L. T., "Synaptogenesis: Effects of Synaptic Use." In M. R. Rosenzweig & E. L. Bennett (Eds.), *Neural Mechanisms of Learning and Memory.* Cambridge: MIT Press, 1976. **595**

Salzinger, K. "The Immediacy Hypothesis and Schizophrenia." In H. M. Yaker, H. Osmond, & F. Cheek (Eds.), *The Future of Time.* New York: Doubleday Doran, 1973. **192**

Sanders, M., Smith, R. S., & Weinmon, B. S. *Chronic Psychosis and Recovery.* San Francisco: Jossey-Bass, 1967. **185**

Sangstad, P., & Roaheim, K. "Problem-Solving, Past Experience and Availability of Functions." *British Journal of Psychology,* 1960, *51,* 97–104. **329**

Sarich, V. M., & Wilson, A. C. "Immunological Time Scale for Hominid Evolution." *Science,* 1967, *158,* 1200–03. **634**

Scarr-Salapatek, S. "Race, Social Class, and IQ." *Science,* 1971, *174,* 1285–95. **313**

Scarr-Salapatek, S. "Genetics and the Development of Intelligence." In D. G. Horowitz (Ed.), *Review of Child Development Research.* (Vol. 4.) Chicago: University of Chicago Press, 1975. **314**

Schachter, S. "Deviation, Rejection, and Communication." *Journal of Abnormal and Social Psychology,* 1951, *46,* 190–207. **103**

Schachter, S. and Rodin, J. *Obese Humans and Rats.* Potomac, Md.: L. Erlbaum Associates; distributed by Halsted Press, N.Y., 1974. **23, 557**

Schachter, S. S., & Singer, J. E. "Cognitive Social and Physiological Determinants of Emotional States." *Psychological Review,* 1962, *69,* 379–99. **144**

Schaefer, H. H., & Martin, P. L. "Behavioral Therapy for 'Apathy' of Hospitalized Schizophrenics." *Psychological Reports,* 1966, *19,* 1147–58. **195**

Schaeffer, J. H. "Cannabis Sativa and Agricultural Work in a

Jamaican Hill Community." In V. Rubin & L. Comitas (Eds.), *Effects of Chronic Smoking of Cannabis in Jamaica.* New York: Research Institute Study of Man, 1973. **202**

Schaffer, H. R., & Emerson, P. E. "Patterns of Response to Physical Contact in Early Human Development." *Journal of Child Psychology and Psychiatry,* 1964, *5,* 1–13. **265, 266**

Schaller, G. B. *The Deer and the Tiger: A Study of Wildlife in India.* Chicago: University of Chicago Press, 1967. **670, 692**

Schaller, G. B. "Predators of the Serengeti: Part I. The Social Carnivore." *Natural History,* 1972, *21,* 38–49. **673, 674**

Schenkel, R. "Ausdruck-studien an Wolfen." *Behavior,* 1947, *1,* 81–109. **690**

Schenkel, R. "Play, Exploration and Territoriality in the Wild Lion." In P. A. Jewell & C. Loizos (Eds.), *Play, Exploration and Territory in Mammals.* London: Academic Press, 1966. **674**

Schiller, P. "Innate Motor Action as a Basis of Learning Manipulative Patterns in the Chimpanzee." In C. H. Schiller (Ed.), *Instinctive Behavior.* New York: International Universities Press, 1957. **642**

Schjelderup-Ebbe, T. "Social Behavior in Birds." In C. Murchison (Ed.), *A Handbook of Social Psychology,* Worcester, Mass.: Clark University Press, 1935. **691**

Schmidt, F. L., & Hunter, J. E. "Racial and Ethnic Bias in Psychological Tests: Divergent Implications of Two Definitions of Test Bias." *American Psychologist,* 1974, *29,* 1–8. **306**

Schneider, G. E. "Two Visual Systems: Brain Mechanisms for Localization and Discrimination Are Dissociated by Tectal and Cortical Lesions." *Science,* 1969, *163,* 895–902. **611**

Schneidman, E. S., & Farberow, N. L. "A Socio-Psychological Investigation of Suicide." In H. P. David & J. C. Brengelmann (Eds.), *Perspectives in Personality Research.* New York: Springer, 1960. **196**

Schneirla, T. C. "An Evolutionary and Developmental Theory of Biphasic Processes Underlying Approach and Withdrawal." In M. R. Jones (Ed.), *Nebraska Symposium on Motivation.* Lincoln: University of Nebraska Press, 1959. **659**

Schneirla, T. C., & Rosenblatt, J. S. "Behavioral Organization and Genesis of the Social Bond in Insects and Mammals." *American Journal of Orthopsychiatry,* 1961, *31,* 223–53. **683**

Schreiner, L., & Kling, A. "Rhinencephalon and Behavior." *American Journal of Physiology,* 1956, 486–90. **570**

Schultz, T. R., & Horibe, F. "Development of the Appreciation of Verbal Jokes." *Developmental Psychology,* 1974, *10,* 13–20. **253**

Schwartz, G. E. "Biofeedback, Self-Regulation and the Patterning of Physiological Processes." *American Scientist,* 1975, *63,* 314–24. **402, 561**

Scott, J. P. "Critical Periods in Behavioral Development." *Science,* 1962, *138,* 949–58. **651**

Scoville, W. B., & Milner, B. "Loss of Recent Memory After Bilateral Hippocampal Lesions." *Journal of Neurology, Neurosurgery and Psychiatry,* 1957, *20,* 11–21. **577**

Sears, R. R., Maccoby, E. E., & Levin, H. *Patterns of Child Rearing.* New York: Harper & Row. 1957. **280**

Sears, R. R., Whiting, J., Nowlis, V., & Sears, P. "Some Child Rearing Antecedents of Aggression and Dependency in Young Children." *Genetic Psychology Monographs,* 1953, *47,* 135. **77**

Segall, M. H., Campbell, D. T., & Herskovits, M. J. "Cultural Differences in the Perception of Geometric Illusions." *Science,* 1963, *139,* 769–71. **457**

Segall, M. H., Campbell, D. T., & Herskovits, M. J. *The Influence of Culture on Visual Perception.* Indianapolis: Bobbs-Merrill, 1966. **457**

Sekuler, R. "Spatial Vision." *Annual Review of Psychology,* 1974, *25,* 195–232. **447**

Sem-Jacobsen, C. W., & Torkildsen, A. "Depth Recording and Electrical Stimulation in the Human Brain." In E. R. Ramey & D. S. O'Doherty (Eds.), *Electrical Studies on the Unanesthetized Brain.* New York: Hoeber, 1960. **572**

Senden, M. von. *Space and Sight.* Methuen, Mass.: Free Press, 1960. **458**

Sevenster, P. "Incompatability of Response and Reward." In R. A. Hinde & J. Stevenson-Hinde (Eds.), *Constraint on Learning: Limitations and Predispositions.* New York: Academic Press, 1973. **654**

Shapiro, D., Tursky, B., & Schwartz, G. E. "Control of Blood Pressure in Man by Operant Conditioning." *Circulation Research,* Supplement 1, 1970, *26,* 1–27, *27,* 1–32. **209**

Shapiro, K. J., & Alexander, I. E. "Extroversion-Introversion, Affiliation, and Anxiety." *Journal of Personality,* 1969, *37,* 387–406. **130**

Shaw, E. "The Development of Schooling Behavior in Fishes." *Physiological Zoology,* 1960, *33,* 79–86. **667**

Sheldon, W. H. *The Varieties of Temperament.* New York: Harper, 1942. **136**

Sherif, M., Harvey, O. J., White, B. J., Hood, W. R., & Sherif, C. W. *Intergroup Conflict and Cooperation: The Robbers Cave Experiment.* Norman: University of Oklahoma Book Exchange, 1961. **86**

Sherman, S. J. "Internal-External Control and Its Relationship to Attitude Change under Different Social Influence Techniques." *Journal of Personality and Social Psychology,* 1973, *26,* 23–29. **131**

Sigall, H. "The Effect of Competence and Consensual Validation on a Communicator's Liking for the Audience." *Journal of Personality and Social Psychology,* 1970, *16,* 251–58. **109, 116**

Signoret, J.-L., & Lhermitte, F. "The Amnesic Syndromes and the Encoding Process." In M. R. Rosenzweig and E. L. Bennett (Eds.), *Neural Mechanisms of Learning and Memory.* Cambridge, Mass.: MIT Press, 1976. **390, 590**

Simonds, P. E. "The Bonnet Macaque in South India." In I. De Vore (Ed.), *Primate Behavior.* New York: Holt, Rinehart & Winston, 1965. **688**

Sinclair-deZwart, H. "Developmental Psycholinguistics." In D. Elkind & J. H. Flavell (Eds.), *Studies of Cognitive Development: Essays in Honor of Jean Piaget.* New York: Oxford University Press, 1969. **355**

Sistrunk, F., & McDavid, J. W. "Sex Variable in Conforming Behavior," *Journal of Personality and Social Psychology,* 1971, *2,* 200–07. **59**

Skeels, H. M. "Adult Status of Children with Contrasting Early Life Experiences." *Monographs of the Society for Research in Child Development,* 1966, *31*(3). **309, 314**

Skinner, B. F. "How to Teach Animals." *Scientific American,*

December 1951. **378**

Skinner, B. F. *Science and Human Behavior*. New York: Macmillan, 1953. **174**

Skinner, B. F. "A Case History in Scientific Method." *The American Psychologist*, 1956, *11*, 221–33. **646**

Skinner, B. F. *Verbal Behavior*. New York: Appleton-Century-Crofts, 1957. **349, 352**

Skinner, B. F. *Beyond Freedom and Dignity*. New York: Knopf, 1971. **176, 646**

Skodak, M., & Skeels, H. M. "A Final Follow-up of 100 Adopted Children." *Journal of Genetic Psychology*, 1949, *75*, 85–125. **314**

Slater, E. A. "A Review of Earlier Evidence on Genetic Factors in Schizophrenia." In D. Rosenthal & S. S. Katz (Eds.), *The Transmission of Schizophrenia*. New York: Pergamon Press, 1968. **190**

Slobin, D. *Psycholinguistics*. Glenview, Ill.: Scott, Foresman, 1971. **353, 354**

Slobin, D. I. "Seven Questions about Language Development." In P. C. Dodwell (Ed.), *New Horizons in Psychology, No. 2*. Baltimore: Penguin, 1972. **259**

Small, W. S. "An Experimental Study of Mental Processes of the Rat." *American Journal of Psychology*, 1900, *11*, 133–65. **656**

Snyder, F. "The Physiology of Dreaming." *Behavioral Science*, 1971, *16*, 31–44. **559**

Snyder, S. H., Banerjee, S. P., Yamamura, H. I., & Greenberg, D. "Drugs, Neurotransmitters, and Schizophrenia." *Science*, 1974, *184* (4143), 1243–53. **193**

Society for Neuroscience. *Bulletin*, 1974. **571**

Solley, C. M., & Murphy, G. *The Development of the Perceptual World*. New York: Basic Books, 1960. **444**

Sontag, L., Baker, C., & Nelson, V. "Mental Growth and Personality Development: A Longitudinal Study." *Monographs of the Society for Research in Child Development*, 1958, *23*(2). **308**

Spearman, C. *The Abilities of Man*. New York: Macmillan, 1927. **316**

Sperling, G. "The Information Available in Brief Visual Presentations." *Psychological Monographs*, 1960, *74* (Whole No. 498). **425**

Sperry, R. W. "Hemispheric Deconnection and Unity in Conscious Awareness." *American Psychologist*, 1968, *23*, 723–33. **136**

Sperry, R. W., Gazzaniga, M. S., & Bogen, J. E. "Function of Neocortical Commissura: Syndrome of Hemispheric Deconnection." In P. J. Vinken & G. W. Bewyn (Eds.), *Handbook of Clinical Neurology*. Amsterdam: North Holland, 1968. **136**

Sperry, R. W., Stamm, J. S., & Milner, N. "Relearning Tests for Interocular Transfer Following Division of Optic Chiasms and Corpus Callosum in Cats." *Journal of Comparative and Physiological Psychology*, 1956, *49*, 529–33. **589**

Staddon, J. E. R., & Simmelhag, V. L. "The 'Superstition' Experiment: A Reexamination of Its Implications for the Principles of Adaptive Behavior." *Psychological Review*, 1971, *78*, 3–43. **401**

Stephenson, W. *The Study of Behavior*. Chicago: University of Chicago Press, 1953. **148**

Sternberg, S. "Memory-Scouring. Mental Processes Revealed by Reaction-Time Experiments." *American Scientist*, 1969, *57*, 421–57. **410**

Stevens, S. S. *Psychophysics: Introduction to Its Perceptual, Neural, and Social Prospects*. New York: Wiley, 1975. **497**

Stevens, S. S., Volkman, J., & Newman, E. B. "A Scale for the Measurement of the Psychological Magnitude of Pitch." *Journal of the Acoustical Society of America*, 1937, *8*, 185–90. **509**

Straits, B. C., & Sechrest, L. "Further Support of Some Findings about the Characteristics of Smokers and Nonsmokers." *Journal of Consulting Psychology*, 1963, *27*, 282. **131**

Stunkard, A. "New Therapies for the Eating Disorders. Behavior Modification of Obesity and Anorexia Nervosa." *Archives of General Psychiatry*, 1972, *26*, 391–98. **556**

Sullivan, H. S. *The Interpersonal Theory of Psychiatry*. New York: Norton, 1953. **166**

Suppes, P. "On the Behavioral Foundations of Mathematical Concepts." In *Cognitive Development in Children*. Chicago: University of Chicago Press, 1970. **335**

Suppes, P., & Hull, S. "Set Theory in the Primary Grades." *New York State Math Teachers Journal*, 1963, 46. **335**

Swets, J. A. "The Relative Operating Characteristic in Psychology." *Science*, 1973, *182*, 990–1000. **492**

Taft, R. "Extraversion, Neuroticism and Expressive Behavior: An Application of Wallack's Moderator Effect to Handwriting Analysis." *Journal of Personality*, 1967, *35*, 570–84. **133**

Tapp, J. L. "Psychology and the Law." In M. R. Rosenzweig & L. W. Porter (Eds.), *Annual Review of Psychology*, Vol. 27, 1976. **254**

Tapp, J. L., & Kohlberg, L. "Developing Senses of Law and Legal Justice." *Journal of Social Issues*, 1971, *27*(2), 65–91. **254, 256**

Taylor, S. P., & Epstein, S. "Aggression as a Function of the Interaction of the Sex of the Aggressor and the Sex of the Victim." *Journal of Personality*, 1967, *35*, 474–85. **136**

Tedeschi, J. T., Schlenker, B. R., & Bonoma, T. V. "Cognitive Dissonance: Private Ratiocination or Public Spectacle?" *American Psychologist*, 1971, *26*, 685–95. **79, 113**

Teghtsoonian, R. "On the Exponents in Stevens' Law and the Constant in Ekman's Law." *Psychological Review*, 1971, *78*, 71–80. **494, 498**

Terman, L. M., & Merrill, M. *Measuring Intelligence: A Guide to the Administration of the New Revised Stanford-Binet Tests of Intelligence*. (Rev. ed.) Boston: Houghton Mifflin, 1960. **296, 298**

Thigpen, C. H., & Cleckly, H. M. *The Three Faces of Eve*. New York: McGraw-Hill, 1957. **198**

Thomas, A., Birch, H. G., Chess, S., Hertzig, M. E., & Korn, S. *Behavioral Individuality in Early Childhood*. New York: New York University Press, 1963. **262**

Thompson, C. M. *Interpersonal Psychoanalysis*. New York: Basic Books, 1964. **161**

Thompson, T. I. "Visual Reinforcement in Fighting Cocks." *Journal of the Experimental Analysis of Behavior*, 1964, *7*, 45–49. **698**

Thorndike, E. L. "Animal Intelligence: An Experimental Study of the Associative Processes in Animals." *Psychological Review Monograph Supplement*, 1898, *2*, 8. **370, 639**

Thurstone, L. L. "Primary Mental Abilities." *Psychometric Monographs,* 1938, No. 1. **316**

Tiger, L., & Fox, R. *The Imperial Animal.* New York: Holt, Rinehart & Winston, 1971. **699**

Tinbergen, N. *The Study of Instinct.* Oxford, Clarendon Press, 1951. **642**

Tinbergen, N. "The Curious Behavior of the Stickleback." *Scientific American,* 1952, *187,* 22–26. **677**

Tolman, E. C., & Honzik, C. M. "Introduction and Removal of Reward and Maze Performance in Rats." *University of California Publications in Psychology,* 1930, *4,* 257–75. **384**

Treisman, A. M. "Contextual Cues in Selective Listening." *Quarterly Journal of Experimental Psychology,* 1960, *12,* 242–48. **452**

Treisman, A. M. "Strategies and Models of Selective Attention." *Psychological Review,* 1969, *76,* 282–99. **453**

Turiel, E. "An Experimental Test of the Sequentiality of Developmental Stages in the Child's Moral Judgments." *Journal of Personal and Social Psychology,* 1966, *3,* 611–18. **252**

Turiel, E. "Conflict and Transition in Adolescent Moral Development." *Child Development,* 1974, *45,* 14–29. **252, 256**

Tulving, E. "Episodic and Semantic Memory." In E. Tulving & W. Donaldson (Eds.), *Organization of Memory.* New York: Academic Press, 1972. **431**

Tyler, L. "A Factorial Analysis of Fifteen MMPI Scales. *Journal of Consulting Psychology,* 1951, *15,* 541–46. **150**

Tyler, L. *Tests and Measurements.* (2nd ed.) Englewood Cliffs, N.J.: Prentice-Hall, 1971. **306**

Ungar, G. "Peptides and Behavior." In C. C. Pfeiffer & J. R. Smythies (eds.), *International Review of Neurobiology,* 1975, *18,* 37–60. **586**

Ungerstedt, U. "Adipsia and Aphagia after 6-Hydroxydopamine Induced Degeneration of the Nigro-Striatal Dopamine System." *Acta Physiologica Scandinavica,* 1971, Supplement 367, 95–122. **554**

Valenstein, E. S. *Brain Control.* New York: Wiley, 1973. **571**

Valenstein, E. S., Cox, V. C., & Kakolewski, J. W. "Reexamination of the Role of the Hypothalamus in Motivation." *Psychological Review,* 1970, *77,* 16–31. **573, 574**

Venables, P. "Psychophysiological Aspects of Schizophrenia." *British Journal of Medical Psychology,* 1966, *39,* 289–97. **192**

Vernon, P. E. *The Structure of Human Abilities.* New York: Wiley, 1950. **317**

Voeks, V. *On Becoming an Educated Person.* (3rd ed.) Philadelphia: Saunders, 1970. **431**

Vygotsky, L. S. *Thought and Language.* Cambridge, Mass.: MIT Press, 1962. **353**

Wallace, R. K., & Benson, H. "The Physiology of Meditation." *Scientific American,* 1972, *226*(2), 84–90. **561**

Wallach, H. "Über Visuell Wahrgenommene Bewegungsrichtung." *Psychologische Forschung,* 1935, *20,* 325–80. **486**

Wallach, H., & O'Connell, D. N. "The Kinetic Depth Effect." *Journal of Experimental Psychology,* 1953, *45,* 205–17. **486**

Wallach, M. A., & Kogan, N. *Modes of Thinking in Young Children: A Study of the Creativity-Intelligence Distinction.* New York: Holt, Rinehart & Winston, 1965. **346, 348**

Wallach, M. A., & Wing, C. W. *The Talented Student: A Validation of the Creativity-Intelligence Distinction.* New York: Holt, Rinehart & Winston, 1969. **344**

Walster, E. "The Effect of Self-Esteem on Romantic Liking." *Journal of Experimental Social Psychology,* 1965, *1,* 184–97. **106**

Walster, E., Aronson, E., & Abrahams, D. "On Increasing the Persuasiveness of a Low-Prestige Communicator." *Journal of Experimental Social Psychology,* 1966, *2,* 325–42. **44**

Walters, R. H., & Thomas, E. "Enhancement of Punitiveness by Visual and Audio-Visual Displays." *Canadian Journal of Psychology,* 1963, *17,* 244–55. **145**

Washburn, S. L. "Behavior and the Origin of Man." *Rockefeller University Review,* 1968, 10–19. **632**

Washburn, S. L. "Primate Studies and Human Evolution." In G. Bourne (Ed.), *Non-Human Primates and Medical Research.* New York: Academic Press, 1972. **634**

Watson, J. "Some Social and Psychological Situations Related to Change in Attitude." *Human Relations,* 1950, *3,* 15–56. **90**

Watson, J. B. *Behavior: An Introduction to Comparative Psychology.* New York: Holt, 1914. **349**

Watson, J. D. *The Double Helix.* New York: Atheneum, 1968. **347**

Watson, J. S., & Ramey, C. T. "Reactions to Response-Contingent Stimulation in Early Infancy." *Merrill-Palmer Quarterly,* 1972, *18,* 219–27. **242**

Weatherly, D. "Anti-Semitism and the Expression of Fantasy Aggression." *Journal of Abnormal and Social Psychology,* 1961, *62,* 454–57. **89**

Webb, W. B. "Sleep Behavior as a Biorhythm." In P. Coloquohon (Ed.), *Biological Rhythms and Human Performance.* London: Academic Press, 1971. **562**

Wechsler, D. *The Measurement of Adult Intelligence.* Baltimore: Williams & Wilkins, 1939. (Revised in 1949, 1960.) **298, 300**

Wechsler, D. *The Wechsler Intelligence Scale for Children.* (Rev. ed.) New York: The Psychological Corporation, 1958. **300**

Weil, A. T., et al. "Clinical and Psychological Effects of Marijuana in Man." *Science,* 1968, *162,* 1235–38. **202**

Weiner, B., & Kukla, A. "An Attributional Analysis of Achievement Motivation." *Journal of Personality and Social Psychology,* 1970, *15,* 1–20. **132**

Weiner, B., & Sierad, J. "Misattributions for Failure and Enhancement of Achievement Strivings." *Journal of Personality and Social Psychology,* 1975, *31,* 415–21. **133**

Weisberg, P. "Social and Nonsocial Conditioning of Infant Vocalizations." *Child Development,* 1963, *34,* 377–88. **243**

Weiskrantz, L. "The Interaction between Occipital and Temporal Cortex in Vision: An Overview." In F. O. Schmitt & F. G. Worden (Eds.), *The Neurosciences, Third Study Program.* Cambridge, Mass.: MIT Press, 1974. **611**

Weiten, W., & Etaugh, C. F. "Lateral Eye Movement as Related to Verbal and Perceptual-Motor Skills and Values." *Perceptual and Motor Skills,* 1973, 423–28. **138**

Welsh, G. S. "Factor Dimensions A and R." In G. S. Welsh & W. G. Dahlstrom (Eds.), *Basic Readings on the MMPI in Psychology and Medicine.* Minneapolis: University of Minnesota Press, 1956. **150**

Wenner, A. M. "Honey Bees: Do They Use the Distance Information Contained in Their Dance Maneuver?" *Science,* 1967, *155,* 847–49. **669**

Wertheimer, M. "Experimentelle Untersuchungen über das

Sehen von Bewegung." *Zeitschrift für Psychologie,* 1912, *61,* 161–265. **463, 487**

Wertheimer, M. "Untersuchungen zur Lehre von der Gestalt, II." *Psychologische Forschung,* 1923, *4,* 301–50. **466**

Wertheimer, M. "Der Einfluss der Mikrostrukturwahrnehmung auf das Gelbphänomen." *Psychologische Beiträge,* 1960, *5,* 273–82. **502**

Wertheimer, M. "Psychomotor Coordination of Auditory and Visual Space at Birth." *Science,* 1961, *134,* 1692. **463**

White, R. K., & Lippitt, R. *Autocracy and Democracy: An Experimental Inquiry.* New York: Harper, 1960. **141**

Whorf, B. L. *Language, Thought and Reality.* Cambridge, Mass.: MIT Press, 1956. **322, 356**

Wilcoxon, H. C., Dragoin, W. B., & Kral, P. A. "Differential Conditioning to Visual and Gustatory Cues in Quail and Rat; Illness-Induced Aversions." Paper presented at meetings of the Psychomonic Society, St. Louis, 1969. **653**

Williams, D. R., & Williams, H. "Auto-Maintenance in the Pigeon: Sustained Pecking Despite Contingent Non-Reinforcement." *Journal of Exceptional Analytical Behavior,* 1969, *12,* 511–20. **401**

Williams, H. L., Holloway, F. A., & Griffiths, W. J. "Physiological Psychology: Sleep." *Annual Review of Psychology,* 1973, *24,* 279–316. **561**

Wilkins, M. C. "The Effect of Changed Material on Ability To Do Formal Syllogistic Reasoning." *Archives of Psychology,* 1928, No. 102. **330**

Wilson, E. O. *Sociobiology: The New Synthesis.* Cambridge, Mass.: Harvard University Press, 1975. **668**

Wilson, J. R., Adler, N., & Le Boeuf, B. "The Effects of Intromission Frequency on Successful Pregnancy in the Female Rat." *Proceedings National Academy of Sciences,* 1965, *53,* 1392–95. **680**

Wilson, W. C. "Development of Ethnic Attitudes in Adolescence." *Child Development,* 1963, *34,* 247–56. **89**

Winch, R. F. *Mate-Selection: A Study of Complementary Needs.* New York: Harper, 1958. **108**

Winterbottom, M. R. "The Relation of Need for Achievement to Learning Experiences in Independence and Mastery." In J. W. Atkinson (Ed.), *Motives in Fantasy, Action and Society.* Princeton, N.J.: Van Nostrand, 1958. **274**

Witkin, H. A., Dyk, R. B., Faterson, H. F., Goodenough, D. R., & Karp, S. A. *Psychological Differentiation.* New York: Wiley, 1962. **130, 343**

Woodworth, R. S. *Personal Data Sheet (Psychoneurotic Inventory).* Chicago: C. H. Stoelting La., 1919. **149**

Worchel, P. "Hostility Theory and Experimental Investigation." In D. Willner (Ed.), *Decisions, Values, and Groups.* (Vol. 1.) New York: Pergamon Press, 1960. **141**

Wynne-Edwards, V. C. *Animal Dispersion in Relation to Social Behavior.* Edinburgh: Oliver & Boyd, 1962. **690**

Yerkeś, R. M. (Ed.) "Psychological Examining in the U.S. Army." *Memoirs National Academy of Science,* 1921, *15,* 890. **300**

Young, W. C., & Orbison, W. D. "Changes in Selected Features of Behavior in Pairs of Oppositely Sexed Chimpanzees during the Sexual Cycle and After Ovariectomy." *Journal of Comparative Psychology,* 1944, *37,* 107–43. **682**

Zajonc, R. B., "Attitudinal Effects of Mere Exposure." *Journal of Personality and Social Psychology,* Mono. Suppl., 9, 1968, 1–27. **52, 91**

Zajonc, R. "Family Configuration and Intelligence." *Science,* 1976, *192,* 227–36. **312**

Zimbardo, P. G. "The Human Choice: Individuation, Reason, and Order versus Deindividuation, Impulse, and Chaos." In W. J. Arnold and D. Levine (Eds.), *Nebraska Symposium on Motivation, 1969.* Lincoln: University of Nebraska Press, 1969. **65**

Zubin, J., Eron, L. D., & Schumer, F. *An Experimental Approach to Projective Techniques.* New York: Wiley, 1965. **152, 154**

Acknowledgments and Credits

Spotlight 1-1, p. 7, © 1975 by The New York Times Company. Reprinted by permission.

Figure 1-3, p. 23, modified from *Obese Humans and Rats* by S. Schachter and J. Rodin. New York: Halsted Press, 1975. Reprinted with the permission of the authors and Lawrence Erlbaum Associates, Inc.

Items from the Minnesota Multiphasic Personality Inventory, in **Chapter 6,** p. 149, reproduced by permission. Copyright © 1943 by the Psychological Corporation, New York, N.Y. All rights reserved. Verses 17-19 from Chapter III of *The Bhagavad Gita*, Franklin Edgerton, translator, reprinted in **Chapter 7,** p. 180, by permission of Harvard University Press, Cambridge, Mass. Copyright 1944 by the President and Fellows of Harvard College; 1972 by Eleanor Hill Edgerton.

Items from the Bayley Scales of Infant Development in **Table 10-1,** p. 238, and **Table 12-2,** p. 301, reproduced by permission. Copyright © 1969 by the Psychological Corporation, New York, N.Y. All rights reserved. Quotation in **Spotlight 10-4,** p. 259, from D. I. Slobin, "Seven Questions About Language Development," in D. C. Dodwell, ed., *New Horizons in Psychology, No. 2,* 1972, reprinted by permission of Penguin Books Ltd. **Spotlight 11-1,** pp. 271–72, from Mary Ainsworth, "The Development of Infant-Mother Attachment," in B. M. Caldwell and H. N. Ricciuti, *Review of Child Development Research,* 1973, *3,* 77–82. © 1973 by the University of Chicago.

Figure 13-2, p. 326, modified from Figure 1 in "The Development of Logical Problem-Solving Strategies," by E. D. Neimark and N. Lewis, *Child Development,* 1967, *38.* Copyright © 1967 by the Society for Research in Child Development, Inc. Excerpt in **Chapter 13,** p. 340, "Prototype Sentences and Three Ideas," from J. D. Bransford and J. J. Franks, "Abstraction of Linguistic Ideas," *Cognitive Psychology,* 1971, *2,* 331–50, reproduced by permission of Academic Press. Quotation in **Chapter 13,** p. 358, from "Early Experience and the Socialization of Cognitive Modes in Children," by R. D. Hess and V. C. Shipman. Reproduced by permission of the Society for Research in Child Development.

Drawing in Part Seven, **Preview Figure 8,** p. 440, and **Figure 16-11,** p. 464, reproduced through the courtesy of David Linton. © *Scientific American,* May 1961. **Table 18-1,** p. 490, from *New Directions in Psychology, 1* by Roger Brown, Eugene Galanter, Eckhard H. Hess, and George Mandler. Copyright © 1962 by Holt, Rinehart, and Winston, Inc. Reprinted by permission of Holt, Rinehart, and Winston. **Figure 18-6,** p. 498, from S. S. Stevens, *Psychophysics: Introduction to Its Perceptual, Neural, and Social Prospects.* New York: John Wiley & Sons, 1975. Reprinted by permission. Figure 18-9, p. 500, based on figure in L. A. Riggs, "Visual Acuity," in C. H. Graham, ed., *Vision and Visual Perception.* New York: John Wiley & Sons, 1975. Reprinted by permission.

Figure 21-5, p. 593, based on figure in J. Olds, "Multiple Unit Recording from Behaving Rats," in R. F. Thompson and M. M. Patterson, eds., *Bioelectric Recording Techniques,* IA, 1973. Used by permission of the author and Academic Press, Inc.

AMERICAN PSYCHOLOGICAL ASSOCIATION

The following figures and tables are reproduced by permission of the American Psychological Association:

Figure 2-1, p. 51, from E. Aronson, J. Turner, and J. M. Carlsmith, "Communicator Credibility and Extent of Credibility and Communication Discrepancy as Determinants of Opinion Change," *Journal of Abnormal and Social Psychology,* 1963, *67,* 31–36. **Table 3-1,** p. 74, adapted from L. Festinger and J. M. Carlsmith, "Cognitive Consequences of Forced Compliance," *Journal of Abnormal and Social Psychiatry,* 1959, *58,* 203–11. **Table 3-2,** p. 77, adapted from E. Aronson and J. M. Carlsmith, "Effect of the Severity of Threat on the Devaluation of Forbidden Behavior," *Journal of Abnormal and Social Psychology,* 1963, *66,* 584–88.

Figures 13-3 and **13-4,** p. 329, from I. T. Kaplan and W. N. Schoenfeld, "Occulomotor Patterns During the Solution of Visually Displayed Diagrams," *Journal of Experimental Psychology,* 1966, *72,* 147–51. **Figure 13-7,** p. 339, from T. S. Kendler and H. H. Kendler, "Vertical and Horizontal Processes in Problem Solving," *Psychological Review,* 1962, *69,* 1–16.

Figure 14-8, p. 395, modified from Figure 1 in J. M. Barnes and B. J. Underwood, "'Fate' of First-List Associations in Transfer Theory," *Journal of Experimental Psychology,* 1959, *58,* 97–105. Figures in **Spotlight 15-4,** p. 425, from G. Sperling, "The Information Available in Brief Visual Presentations," *Psychological Monographs,* 1960, *74* (whole no. 498). Copyright 1960 by the American Psychological Association.

Figure 16-5, p. 450, modified from Figure 2 in A. M. Liberman et al., "Perception of the Speech Code," *Psychological Review,* 1967, *74,* 436. **Figure 16-8,** p. 455, from Figure 2 in J. S. Bruner and C. C. Goodman, "Value and Need as Organizing Factors in Perception," *Journal of Abnormal and Social Psychology,* 1947, *42,* 40.

Figure 21-4, p. 589, modified from Figure 2, R. W. Sperry, J. S. Stamm, and N. Miner, "Relearning Tests for Interocular Transfer Following Division . . ." *Journal of Comparative and Physiological Psychology,* 1956, *49,* 531.

Figure 23-8, p. 646, from Figure 14 in B. F. Skinner, "A Case History in Scientific Methods," *American Psychologist,* 1956, *11,* 230. **Figure 23-11,** p. 650, after Figure 1, H. Moltz and L. J. Stettner, "The Influence of Patterned-Light Deprivation on the Critical Period for Imprinting," *Journal of Comparative and Physiological Psychology,* 1961, *54,* 281.

Photo Credits

Page 5 Van Bucher, Photo Researchers. **8** (left) Gaston Le Page, National Audubon Society; (right) Nick Passmore, Stock, Boston. **10** Clemens Kalischer. **12** Owen Franken, Stock, Boston. **15** (left) Courtesy A. Bandura; (center & right) Mimi Forsyth, Monkmeyer Press Photo Service. **20** (left) Mimi Forsyth, Monkmeyer Press Photo Service; (right) Charles Gatewood; cartoon by Sidney J. Harris. **24** Patricia Hollander Gross, Stock, Boston. **29** Courtesy Pfizer, Inc. **30** (left) Ted Polumbaum; (right) courtesy U.S. Navy. **32** Virginia Hamilton.

Page 37 Wide World. **39** Donald Dietz, Stock, Boston. **41** George Roos, Peter Arnold Photo Archives. **45** (left) Peter Southwick, Stock, Boston; (right) Lee Lockwood, Black Star. **46** Donald Dietz. **47** Robert Phillips, Black Star. **50** Alex Webb, Magnum Photos. **53** Cartoon by Stuart Leeds. **57** William Vandivert © 1955 by *Scientific American.* **60** (left) Elliott Erwitt, Magnum Photos; (right) Frank Siteman, Stock, Boston. **64** Richard Stack, Black Star. **67** Ted Polumbaum. **68** Peter Southwick, Stock, Boston. **71** Virginia Hamilton. **76** Erika Stone, Photo Researchers. **78** Cartoon by Stuart Leeds. **80** Drawing by Buck Brown, reproduced by special permission of *Playboy* magazine; copyright © 1971 by Playboy. **82** Monkmeyer Press Photo Service. **84** War Relocation Authority, National Archives. **85** Cartoon by Stuart Leeds. **86** The Bettmann Archive. **87** (top) Bob Adelman, Magnum Photos; (lower) Arnold Hinton, Monkmeyer Press Photo Service. **92** Charles Gatewood. **94** Ted Cowell, Black Star. **97** *Ms.* magazine (April 1976) from *Insurance Salesman.* **99** Bob Adelman, Magnum Photos. **100** (left) Clemens Kalischer; (right) Elizabeth Hamlin.

Index